The Trade in the Living

FERNAND BRAUDEL CENTER
STUDIES IN HISTORICAL SOCIAL SCIENCE

Series Editor: Richard E. Lee

The Fernand Braudel Center Studies in Historical Social Science will publish works that address theoretical and empirical questions produced by scholars in or through the Fernand Braudel Center or who share its approach and concerns. It specifically seeks to promote works that contribute to the development of the world-systems perspective engaging a holistic and relational vision of the world—the modern world-system—implicit in historical social science, which at once takes into consideration structures (long-term regularities) and change (history). With the intellectual boundaries within the sciences/ social sciences/humanities structure collapsing in the work scholars actually do, this series will offer a venue for a wide range of research that confronts the dilemmas of producing relevant accounts of historical processes in the context of the rapidly changing structures of both the social and academic world. The series will include monographs, colloquia, and collections of essays organized around specific themes.

VOLUMES IN THIS SERIES:

Questioning Nineteenth-Century Assumptions about Knowledge, I: Determinism
Richard E. Lee, editor

Questioning Nineteenth-Century Assumptions about Knowledge, II: Reductionism
Richard E. Lee, editor

Questioning Nineteenth-Century Assumptions about Knowledge, III: Dualism
Richard E. Lee, editor

The *Longue Durée* and World-Systems Analysis
Richard E. Lee, editor

New Frontiers of Slavery
Dale W. Tomich, editor

Slavery in the Circuit of Sugar: Martinique and the World-Economy, 1830–1848
Dale W. Tomich

The Politics of the Second Slavery
Dale W. Tomich, editor

Race and Rurality in the Global Economy
Michaeline A. Crichlow, Patricia Northover, and Juan Giusti-Cordero, editors

The Trade in the Living
Luiz Felipe de Alencastro

The Trade in the Living

The Formation of Brazil in the South Atlantic,
Sixteenth to Seventeenth Centuries

Luiz Felipe de Alencastro

Translated by
Gavin Adams and Luiz Felipe de Alencastro

Revised by
Michael Wolfers and Dale Tomich

FERNAND BRAUDEL CENTER
STUDIES IN HISTORICAL SOCIAL SCIENCE

Published by State University of New York Press, Albany

© 2018 State University of New York

All rights reserved

No part of this book may be used or reproduced in any manner whatsoever without written permission. No part of this book may be stored in a retrieval system or transmitted in any form or by any means including electronic, electrostatic, magnetic tape, mechanical, photocopying, recording, or otherwise without the prior permission in writing of the publisher.

For information, contact State University of New York Press, Albany, NY
www.sunypress.edu

Library of Congress Cataloging-in-Publication Data

Names: Alencastro, Luiz Felipe de, author.
Title: The trade in the living : the formation of Brazil in the South Atlantic, sixteenth to seventeenth centuries / Luiz Felipe de Alencastro ; translated by Gavin Adams and Luiz Felipe de Alencastro ; revised by Michael Wolfers and Dale Tomich.
Other titles: Trato dos viventes. English
Description: Albany : State University of New York Press, 2018. | Series: SUNY series, Fernand Braudel Center Studies in Historical Social Science | Includes bibliographical references and index.
Identifiers: LCCN 2017023406 (print) | LCCN 2017024046 (ebook) | ISBN 9781438469317 (ebook) | ISBN 9781438469294 (hardcover   ) | ISBN 9781438469300 (pbk.)
Subjects: LCSH: Slavery—Brazil—History—16th century. | Slavery—Brazil—History—17th century. | Slavery—Angola—History—16th century. | Slavery—Angola—History—17th century. | Brazil—Foreign relations—Angola. | Angola—Foreign relations—Brazil. | Brazil—History—16th century. | Brazil—History—17th century.
Classification: LCC HT1126 (ebook) | LCC HT1126 .A7313 2018 (print) | DDC 306.3/62098109031—dc23
LC record available at https://lccn.loc.gov/2017023406

10 9 8 7 6 5 4 3 2 1

CONTENTS

List of Illustrations — vii

Presentation of the English Edition — ix
Patrick Manning

Author's Preface to the American Edition — xvii

1 The Apprenticeship of Colonization — 1

2 Africans, "The Slaves from Guinea" — 39

3 Lisbon, Slave-Trade Capital of the Western World — 71

4 Amerindians, the "Slaves of the Land" — 117

5 Evangelization in One Colony — 153

6 The War over the Slave Markets — 185

photo gallery follows page 252

7 Brasílica Angola — 253

Conclusion: Brazil's Singularity — 317

Appendix 1 Luís Mendes de Vasconcellos and His Offspring — 343

Appendix 2 The Supply of Northern Captaincies by Southern Captaincies during the Dutch War 1630–1654 — 345

Appendix 3 The Salvador Correa de Sá e Benevides Family — 349

Appendix 4	Notes on Some Portuguese and Brasilico Expeditionaries of 1648 Task Force that Recaptured Angola	351
Appendix 5	1600s Portuguese Atlantic Hand Firearms	353
Notes		357
Bibliography		515
Index		587

ILLUSTRATIONS

Table

Table 1.1	African Captives Carried on Vessels Leaving the Main Ports Where Slave-Trading Voyages Were Organized, 1514–1867	22

Maps

Map 2.1	Main Trade Routes in the Ethiopic Ocean	53
Map 3.1	Main Trade Routes in West Central Africa in the Seventeenth Century	103
Map 6.1	Probable Itinerary of the Raposo Tavares' *Bandeira* in 1648–1651	239
Map 6.2	Portuguese and Brazilian Slave-Trade 1550–1850	242
Map 7.1	Portuguese and Brasílico Offensive in Seventeenth Century West Central Africa	296

Figures

Figure 1.1	Slaves Arriving in the Main Americas Regions 1576–1850	37
Figure 3.1	Estimated Number of Slaves from West Central Africa Landed in Ibero-America during the Portuguese *Asientos* and Beyond, 1581–1715	104

Figure 7.1 Major Regions from which the Enslaved left Africa for Brazil, 1576–1850   315

Figure C.1 *Botocudos Attack in the Goyatacá Land* (c. 1700)   326

Figure C.2 Economic Growth, Geopolitical Crisis, and Enslaved Disembarked in the Americas, 1550–1850 (in thousands)   339

PRESENTATION OF THE
ENGLISH-LANGUAGE EDITION

Patrick Manning

English-speaking readers now have direct access to this important volume by Luiz Felipe de Alencastro, in which he displays vividly the complex struggles of the South Atlantic in the sixteenth and seventeenth centuries. As the Atlantic underwent exploration and then conquest by European mariners, Portuguese vessels traced the whole Atlantic coast of Africa and half that of the Americas. With time, as the Portuguese came to focus their efforts on Angola and Brazil, two great struggles overlapped in this newly opened circuit of ocean and littoral. The first was that of building a Portuguese-led empire. In this long campaign for wealth and control, slave production of sugar arose on both sides of the Atlantic, captaincies in Brazil expanded through exploitation of Amerindian labor, and Portuguese seizure of land and labor in Angola and Kongo fed New World exploitation. Then came three decades of war with Dutch invaders, who seized parts of Brazil and Angola until Brazilians finally drove them out, re-established Luso-Brazilian dominion, and heightened their system of exploitation.

Alencastro demonstrates the importance of this great maritime region and its struggles for power in the early modern world. For instance, he emphasizes that the South Atlantic encompassed "the South American and Angolan fronts of the Thirty Years' War." He also labels the regions and the protagonists as they were called in documents of the time: the "Ethiopic Ocean" linked Portugal to the north with Brazil in the west and the African coast on the east. The key groups' characters were the Portuguese from the metropole, the "Brasílicos" or Portuguese-descended settlers in Brazil, the Amerindians of Brazil, the "Angolistas" or Portuguese-descended settlers in Angola, the Africans, and the mixed descendants of these groups, the "mulattos." The "Brazilians" were then the subjects of imperial Brazil after independence in 1822.

Alencastro argues consistently that the history of Brazil has extended far beyond the limits of the South American mainland. From the earliest Portuguese visit in 1500 to the conclusive abolition of slavery in 1888, Brazil relied heavily on slave production to build its economy. Further, the slave production of Brazil could only go ahead with the reproduction of slaves, especially in Angola. This pattern of Brazil's dependence on the exploitation of Angola's human capital not only persisted through the long colonial period, but expanded again during the "second slavery" of the nineteenth century—the sixty years of independence under the empire of Brazil. Rather than a "triangular trade" in slaves such as that linking England, West Africa, and the Caribbean, Brazil carried on a largely "bilateral trade" in slaves with Angola and a smaller bilateral trade in slaves to the Bight of Benin, sending tobacco, manioc, and alcoholic beverages (often slave-produced) to Africa in return for more slaves.

The original Portuguese version of this book, *O Trato dos Viventes* (2000), appeared in an elegant and thoroughly illustrated edition. This translation has been revised in two major ways: it adds reference to numerous works that have appeared since 2000, and especially, it draws on the updated results of the transatlantic slave-trade data set. These quantitative results confirm the argument of the text, showing the density of slave-trade shipping based in Portugal and especially in Brazil. That is, for the Slave Voyages data set (www.slavevoyages.org), prepared under the leadership of David Eltis, the initial 1999 version documented 27,000 slave voyages across the Atlantic, but by 2010 the number of documented voyages had risen to 35,000. More important for present purposes is that the majority of the voyages added during the intervening decade carried captives from Angola to Brazil. Thus, while the recorded total disembarkations of captives in the New World were 4.4 million in 1999 and 5.6 million in 2010 (an increase of 27 percent), the recorded disembarkations of captives in Brazil were 0.77 million in 1999 and 1.99 million in 2010 (an increase of 157 percent). Surviving documentation of the Angola-Brazil slave trade is not as dense as that for English, Dutch, and French slave trades, but the 2010 results are much closer than the 1999 results to showing the quantitative prominence of slave trade to Brazil. Meanwhile, the interpretations of Atlantic history published between 1999 and 2010, in relying on the earlier summaries, may have substantially underestimated the size and significance of the slave trade to Brazil. The present volume is perhaps of the first to use the updated figures in thinking about the place of Brazil in the overall Atlantic slave trade.

This is Atlantic history, but it is different from the Atlantic history of the North Atlantic, which is written especially in terms of British North America in the hands of Bernard Bailyn or in terms of North Atlantic maritime slave trade, piracy, and rebellion in the hands of Marcus Rediker, or even in terms of slavery and revolution in Haiti in the hands of C. L. R. James and Michel-Rolph Trouillot. The full history of the Atlantic world must therefore expand to encompass fully the great South Atlantic wars of the seventeenth century as well as the North Atlantic wars of the eighteenth century.

Translation of this book into English, in addition, brings it closer into contact with the other major work on the slave trade as a link in the history of Brazil and Angola. Joseph C. Miller's *Way of Death: The Angolan Slave Trade, 1730–1830* (1988) focused on a later period, the eighteenth and nineteenth centuries, and gave primary attention to Angola rather than Brazil. Miller, too, traced an Atlantic narrative, linking Angola, Brazil, and Portugal. Miller's book, while gaining wide praise as it appeared, did not succeed in provoking a shift in the Atlantic literature to establish an appropriate balance between the North Atlantic and the South Atlantic. It may be that a closer interaction of the Miller and Alencastro books, now both in English, will expand thinking about the parallels and interactions of North Atlantic and South Atlantic history. In addition, we must anticipate the sequel that Luiz Felipe de Alencastro is preparing, in which he will extend the analysis presented in this volume to the eighteenth and nineteenth centuries.

This book is written with explicit attention to the construction and reconsideration of Brazilian nationhood. Today, although Brazilian nationalism is growing because of economic success, Brazil's schools and public discourse also give attention to the historic close relationship with Angola. While commerce linking Brazil and Africa came almost to a halt from 1850 to 1950, the rise of the Brazilian economy at the end of the twentieth century began to include Africa in an expanded Atlantic commerce, modifying the overall Atlantic system yet again. For readers of English, the same attention to the complexity of Brazil's colonial history is now readily available.

Overall, the interpretation by Luiz Felipe de Alencastro emphasizes, first, the system of war and exploitation that sustained the slave trade and production by slave labor, and second, the imperial wars for control of the South Atlantic system of trade and production. The individuals and groups participating in this complex story include those of Portuguese descent in Portugal, Brazil, and Angola; those of African descent in Angola, in other parts of Africa, and in Brazil; Amerindians in Brazil and sometimes in Angola; and those with mixed ancestry resulting from interactions among these groups. The first half of the book centers on the Portuguese-led effort to expand economic exploitation of the Ethiopian Ocean in the sixteenth and early seventeenth centuries; the second half of the book centers on the long seventeenth-century struggle for dominance between Dutch and Portuguese and on the renewed Portuguese exploitation of Brazil and Angola.

The details of this book skillfully reveal the workings of empire. The complex structure of empire was part monarchy, part war machine, part greedy merchants, part bureaucracy, part church to rationalize the system, many people recruited (often forcibly) to carry out the work of empire, and part opportunists at every level who were ready to steal and oppress in hopes of advancing their wealth or power. Throughout, enslavement stood out as the principal way of obtaining scarce labor at a cheap price. This is Atlantic history, but it is a fundamentally interactive history, linking the various elements of Brazil, Angola, Portugal, the Amerindians, the Africans, the Dutch, and other European powers. It is especially a history of the tight connection between Brazil and Angola in the sixteenth and seventeenth centuries.

The pages of this volume convey the colonial system through many types of stories. Included are tales of the fates of commoditized humans; of the careers of soldiers, administrators, priests, and merchants; of commerce in an interacting set of commodities; and of social movements in Angola and Brazil. As the author reminds us periodically, all of these processes unfolded in just a part of the world during the early modern era, a time when every region underwent such great struggles for exploitation, wealth, and identity.

The eight chapters of the book may be divided into two major sections. The first five chapters address Portuguese Atlantic colonialism and slave trade from the fifteenth century to the early seventeenth century. In this era sugar production grew steadily. Along with it grew the African slave trade, the *Asiento*, the enslavement of Amerindians, the development of bilateral trade between Brazil and Angola, the political and social role of the Catholic Church, and endless Portuguese desire to obtain Spanish silver. The concluding three chapters of the book describe three chaotic decades of Dutch-Portuguese war in the South Atlantic, followed by expansion of the Portuguese colonial system in the late seventeenth and eighteenth centuries. These chapters show the links between the Dutch-Portuguese wars and the wars of both powers against Angolans, Amerindians, and the *quilombos*, or maroon colonies, of Brazil; the distinction and antagonism between the Brasílicos of São Paulo and those of Rio de Janeiro in the accumulation of Brazilian wealth; and the Portuguese-Spanish contention in the competing colonial economies of sugar and silver.

The early chapters trace the era of the fifteenth and sixteenth centuries when the Portuguese became the leading power in oceanic commerce, with networks focusing especially on African and Asian trade. Enslavement was part of the system from the earliest mapping of the African coast, but it expanded significantly with the rise of sugar production in São Tomé and later with the transfer of sugar production to Brazil. From Da Gama's 1498 voyage to India, Portuguese expansion focused primarily on Asian commerce and war. But the rise of competitors in Asia—Arabian, Indian, and European—eventually caused the Portuguese to develop greater interest in the South Atlantic, where they faced little competition. Sixteenth-century captives delivered by Portuguese merchants to Spanish America came mostly from Senegambia and Guinea in western Africa. But the development of sugar plantations in São Tomé brought enslavement in Congo and neighboring Angola. Brazilian interests then grew, and trade began to link Brazil and Angola.

Portuguese seizure of Luanda in 1575 confirmed the link between Angola and Brazil. A bilateral system of trade soon grew up in which Brazil provided manioc flour (produced by Amerindians under forced labor), other food crops, alcoholic beverages, and later tobacco to Angola in return for captives. Soon Angola was providing captives to Brazil, to the Spanish colonial ports of Cartagena and Veracruz, to Buenos Aires in exchange for silver, and to a declining degree to São Tomé. Even horses and building materials were shipped from Brazil to Angola to support the effort for war and colonization.

This expansion of Portugal's colonial system took place even though Portugal fell under Spanish rule. In 1578, Portugal lost its king and its monarchy on the Moroccan battlefield of al-Qsar al-Kabir. Spanish kings controlled the throne of Portugal for sixty years, and during that time confirmed the coalescence of Spain's American empire. Yet Portuguese society and even its state maintained substantial autonomy. The Angolan regime spread its power inland, pressing on the *sovas* or regional chieftains to open their lands to slave trade. The Catholic priesthood debated but reaffirmed the legality and morality of enslavement. Trade between Rio and Luanda grew steadily; Brazilian slave populations grew especially in the hinterlands of Rio, Bahia, and Pernambuco. In another aspect of the colonial dynamic, escapees from plantations formed *quilombos*, the most substantial of which was the community of Palmares, which developed at the start of the seventeenth century inland from Pernambuco. In yet another aspect of the colonial dynamic, the enslavement of Amerindians expanded, especially from a Brasílico base in São Paulo. Amerindian captives were divided into those already imprisoned, those captured in a "just war," and those whose settlements were forced to move to São Paulo and other inland centers of Brasílico control.

The expanding commercial system of the Ethiopic Ocean, under Portuguese rule, became attractive to the expanding Dutch. The Netherlands, a region of flourishing commercial and military strength that had fallen under Spanish control in the 1520s, rebelled against Spain in 1580. Dutch vessels challenged Portugal in the Indian Ocean from 1600 and in the Atlantic from 1620. The result was a great struggle between Portuguese and Dutch empires from roughly 1620 to 1650: basically, the Dutch were victorious in the Indian Ocean, while the Portuguese were victorious in the Atlantic. The Dutch settlement at the Cape of Good Hope in 1652 at once acknowledged their defeat in Angola and sustained their victory at Malacca and in Indonesia.

Alencastro divides the Atlantic struggle between the Dutch and Portuguese into five periods. The opening of European war in 1618 brought a decade of privateering and eventual invasion to the Americas. Second, the 1630 Dutch seize of Recife and expansion into Pernambuco brought establishment of a new colonial power but also continued resistance from Brasílico planters. Third, in 1637 the Dutch West Indies Company (WIC) addressed its difficulty in ruling Pernambuco by appointing a skilled governor, Johan Maurits van Nassau-Siegen. He conciliated the Brasílicos and launched African conquests to bring in more slaves. In 1637 his forces seized the Portuguese fort at Elmina in West Africa. Meanwhile, Portugal rose up in rebellion against Spanish rule. Then, in the Portuguese metropole, the 1640 rebellion brought João IV and the Braganza dynasty to power in Lisbon, with Dutch support. At the same time, in 1641 the Dutch seized Luanda, the main center for supply of African captives, and Malacca, the key to the trade of the eastern Indian Ocean. Angola was harder to hold, as Angolistas retreated inland, remaining a threat to the Dutch.

As the wars continued, the number of African captives coming to Brazil declined, encouraging expanded seizure of Amerindian captives. Enslavement was reinforced by smallpox, yellow fever, and chickenpox, the latter a children's disease. As Amerindian populations declined, the lands they had farmed became choked with forest. Portuguese relations with Spain remained broken until 1668, so that the Portuguese supply of captives under the *Asiento* declined sharply. Under these circumstances, Dutch military advantage was not enough to sustain their conquests. Dutch regulations managed slavery badly, squeezed plantations, and imposed and collected debts. Van Nassau-Siegen, in disagreement with tight WIC policy, resigned his position as governor in 1644, while Brasílico rebels again challenged Dutch rule.

In Alencastro's fourth period, a Luso-Brazilian counterattack expelled the Dutch from Angola and eventually from Pernambuco. Salvador de Sá, a wealthy planter and merchant based in Rio de Janeiro, led the political and military campaign for expulsion of the Dutch from Angola and Brazil. As early as 1645 he was consulting with the Portuguese king, proposing a comprehensive plan for expulsion of the Dutch. Two 1645 attacks by the Brazilians failed to dislodge the Dutch from Angola. But by 1648 Salvador de Sá had recruited enough ships, soldiers, supplies, and political will from Rio, and led an expedition that forced Dutch withdrawal from Angola. In addition, Salvador de Sá gained appointment by the king as governor of Angola, and remained in office for three years. As governor he imposed policies to maximize the volume of captives collected and exported—for instance, expanding the territory of the Angolan colony and executing numerous *sovas* in the interior, forcing the opening of slave markets to Portuguese merchants.

In the long period from the 1650s, Alencastro shows how the forceful policies of de Sá were extended throughout Angola and in Brazil. The Dutch withdrew from Pernambuco and Maranhão in 1654, under the pressure of the first Anglo-Dutch war as well as local rebellion. In this era of assertive exploitation, the long period of minor conflicts between Palmares and Pernambuco (under Dutch and Portuguese rule) gave way to an increasingly aggressive Portuguese war, which destroyed Palmares by 1700. Similar policies continued in Angola and Brazil into the eighteenth century, for instance with the expansion of slave trade from Benguela, in the south of Angola, in response to the Brazilian gold rush. The prices of slaves rose so much in that era so that some of the gold went to the Gold Coast, where gold served as currency, to buy more slaves.

In sum, by 1575 the link between Angola and Brazil became the key element in the economy and politics of the Ethiopic Ocean, up to the mid-nineteenth century. That relationship was reinforced in different ways in the seventeenth, eighteenth, and nineteenth centuries. The largest numbers of people in this story were Africans on their home continent and African-descended people of Brazil, both slave and free. Next in numbers were Amerindians, in independent communities, in subjugated communities, and in slavery. Third in number were the Portuguese-descended Brasílicos and the less numerous Angolistas. Fourth were a growing number of persons descended from the combinations of these groups, who played roles at all levels of this colonial society. Alencastro's narrative weaves the careers of mobile individuals, traveling throughout the world of Portuguese colonialism, into a fabric derived from their interactions and enmities. He is especially skillful in conveying the outlook of central personalities, but he also provides colorful stories of commodities (animal, vegetable, and manufactures) as they moved through marketplaces to consumers. With these tales he portrays the shifting experiences of communities—whether defined by ethnicity, class, religion, or economic interest—in Brazil and Angola.

The life of the author fits logically into the interactive pattern of Brazilian life described in the text. Luiz Felipe de Alencastro grew up in Brazil, then carried out his doctoral studies in France under Frédéric Mauro, a noted historian of Portuguese empire who was himself an associate of Fernand Braudel, I remember Luiz Felipe's stories of the Brazilians in France—in exile during the time of Brazil's military dictatorship (1964–1985)—as they started up a Brazilian-style celebration of Carnival in Paris. Then he moved back to Brazil to teach for years at the University of Campinas in São Paulo state, and participated as well in the influential research group, CEBRAP—where I visited him in 1991. The opening of a position in Brazilian history at the Sorbonne took him again to Paris, and it was there that this book was written, published, and later translated. As this translation is published he has again returned to Brazil. The author has thus seen the Brazilian nation from within and from the outside.

I consider Alencastro to be brilliant in finding Brazilian angles on issues almost anywhere in the history of the modern era. It is an angle of view and an approach that should be much more broadly considered in the present era, when the significance of Brazil has become unmistakable in economic, political, and cultural life at continental and global levels. This book provides background to today's prominence of Brazil. More than that, it is more than background and goes well beyond simple celebration of the nation within its borders. It emphasizes that the development of Brazil came not simply from within and not simply from Portuguese colonialism, but through Amerindian, Atlantic, and African connections, especially those with Angola. Further, it emphasizes that the expansion of the Brazilian economy and society was achieved through the most severe exploitation, with wars of subjugation and generations of enslavement and painful hierarchy. The Brazilian connections in world history are manifold; the Brazil of these connections is itself a complex unit. This is a welcome and valuable addition to the English-language literatures on Latin American, Atlantic, and global history.

AUTHOR'S PREFACE TO THE AMERICAN EDITION

Since this book appeared, numerous studies have offered innovative approaches to the history of West Central Africa and of the Iberian and Dutch South Atlantic. At the same time, access to archived and digitized documents has made available additional primary sources. However, merging this new research and documentation into the chapters would lead to a wholly different book. Instead, I chose an alternate solution. While the statistical data and analysis on the Atlantic slave trade were updated and chapters, notes, and appendices were modified, the structure of the original edition remained unchanged. The complementary book I am writing on the eighteen and nineteenth centuries, the period on which most recent research focuses, analyzes the new studies on the history of the South Atlantic.

In 2000, when this book was first published, Brazil commemorated the fifth centennial of its discovery by the Europeans. Then, as in 2008 at the bicentennial of the transfer of the Portuguese Court to Rio de Janeiro, the celebrations favored narratives that interpreted the Brazilian past through the prism of its current national territory. Brazil, the only American colonial aggregate that did not fragment at independence and the only Portuguese-speaking country in the Americas, has been studied in its territorial continuity. Still, the history of colonial Brazil is not confined to the history of Portuguese America.

Hence, the idea expounded in this book is different and relatively simple: Portuguese colonial and mercantile activities in the South Atlantic, grounded on the slave trade, have given way to a bipolar social and economic space, encompassing both a slave production zone sited on the South American shores and a zone of slave reproduction centered chiefly in Angola, from which seventeenth-century Brazil emerged.

We shall not engage in the comparative study of the Portuguese colonies throughout the Atlantic. What I intend, on the contrary, is to show that these two parts united by the ocean completed one another in a colonial network.

Does this mean that Brazil's history is better understood through the prism of Atlantic history, which has experienced a remarkable development? Not quite, since this scholarly field has been generally centered on the North Atlantic. Moreover, its periodization does not envision the transformations of the first half of the nineteenth century and the Second Slavery, decisive to Brazil's independence, when South Atlantic slave traffic peaked.

As a matter of fact, it was below the equator that the longest and most intense forced migration of the modern era took place. Indeed, Brazil accounts for the greatest number of introductions of enslaved Africans in the Americas.

Aside from the density and the persistence over time of the trafficking activities, the bilateral exchanges between African and Brazilian ports stand as another key difference between the South and North Atlantic. More than any other community from the European settlements in the Americas, the Portuguese, Luso-Amerindians, and Luso-Africans from Brazil had an extended knowledge of the process of commoditization of the African peoples. From the seventeenth century to the beginning of the nineteenth century, several bishops and prelates as well as twelve governors occupied similar posts in Portuguese America before or after holding their posts in Luanda. Research on the royal officers, magistrates, clergy, seamen, troops, militias, merchants, middlemen, and freedmen unveil networks of social agents moving between Brazil, the Río de la Plata, Angola, the Gulf of Guinea, Upper Guinea, and Mozambique. In other words, several thousand persons from Portuguese America and early post-independence Brazil were directly involved with the cultures and peoples they deported from Africa and exploited in Brazilian territory.

Ultimately, nautical and trade conditions enabled Luso-Brazilian vessels and interests to prevail over European competitors in West Central Africa. Bilateral routes followed the currents generated by the South Atlantic gyre. Combining the westerlies and the southeast trade winds, the northeastern limits of this maritime system situated between 5° and 10° N, overreaching the mathematical equator. Up to the last quarter of the nineteenth century, sailing guides and maps embrace the sub-Saharan coast south of Senegambia within the South Atlantic Ocean. Alongside "South Atlantic" the name "Ethiopic Ocean" was employed until the end of the Sailing Age to depict this basin as a whole distinct system, as an ocean of its own, rather different from the North Atlantic, which was considered to be the "Atlantic proper."[1]

Accordingly, the term "Ethiopic Ocean" is used in the following chapters to characterize this geohistorical aggregate. This denotation provides a more appropriate definition of the context, the boundaries, and the 1500–1850 period discussed in this book and my next book. Conversely, it also helps to emphasize the specificity of South Atlantic history in the face of the concepts and contours that have generally focused on North Atlantic history.

Several colleagues, friends, and students helped me in the writing of this book and I thank them all for their critical comments. I am also grateful to Norman Fiering, who received me twice for research stays at the John Carter Brown Library.

Translating and editing these chapters has been a long process, during which I had the inestimable help of the late Michael Wolfers. Dale Tomich's generous and attentive interventions have now made possible its publication.

The book is dedicated to the ever-present memory of Heleny Guariba, Paulo de Tarso Celestino, and Honestino Guimarães, murdered by the Brazilian dictatorship (1964–1985).

Chapter 1

The Apprenticeship of Colonization[1]

In August 1499, King Manuel wrote to the Holy See from Lisbon to announce Vasco da Gama's return from the first maritime voyage to India. The king bestowed on himself a new royal title: "King of Portugal and the Algarve, afore and beyond the Sea in Africa, Lord of Guinea, of the Conquest of Navigation and Commerce of Ethiopia, Arabia, Persia and (. . .) India."[2] Supported by pontifical bulls and caravels, the king was able to attribute to himself the lordship of the trades in distant territories. Matters would become more complicated when the metropolis tried to enforce its policy overseas.

Anchored in four continents and dealing with distant communities, the Iberian powers tried different ways to establish control over indigenous peoples and to exploit the conquered territories. These undertakings did not always converge with the Iberian trading and institutional structure. Before the Age of Discovery came to an end, the Iberian Crowns resumed the overseas expansion in order to colonize their own colonists.

"Among remote people they built the new kingdom they so much exalted," Camões wrote in the opening lines of *The Lusiads*. But how did the overseas "new kingdom" relate to the European "old kingdom?" How did Lusitanians master the "remote people" and make them work for the king?

Even in the places where power relations favored the European invaders, it was not enough to realize their twin goals of domination and exploitation. Although slavery and other forms of coerced labor allowed the domination of conquered populations, they did not always lead to successful colonial exploitation. Colonial surplus might be consumed by settlers or traded outside areas under the control of metropolitan powers. The control of indigenous communities did not guarantee that coerced labor could be transformed into merchandise that could be integrated into metropolitan commodity flows, or guarantee the emergence of dependent tributary economies in overseas territories.

A second factor developed on the political plane. Even though the economic surplus of the possessions was incorporated into the Iberian networks, mercantile expansion did not necessarily lead to the reinforcement of monarchic authority. New power relations emerged inside metropolitan states and conquered territories as mercantile zones expanded and merchants increased their influence. Overseas dominion did not always flow into colonial exploitation, nor did it immediately determine the colonists' and merchants' submission to metropolitan authority.

Three distinct problems trod the stage of the discoveries: the consolidation of royal authority over the colonists; the inclusion of production from conquered areas in Atlantic trade; and the confrontations among authorities, colonists, and clergy over the control of natives. In Peru, Angola, Goa, Mozambique, Brazil, and other places, colonization went astray from the very start.

The Colonists' and the Missionaries' Paths

In Peru and most of Spanish America, conflicts pitting colonists against clergy and Crown derived from the fight to control the natives. In light of Hispanic political and doctrinal influence in Portuguese America, the Peruvian case merits consideration. Between 1542 and 1543, Charles V proclaimed the "New Laws" (*Leyes nuevas*) acknowledging a certain sovereignty over the Amerindians. These laws abolished concessions of Indians (*encomiendas*) granted to the conquerors, and gradually converted all natives to dependence on the Crown, to whom they would pay tribute. The contradiction immanent in the Spanish imperial project burst out straightaway.

As one of the inspirers of the *Leyes nuevas*, the Dominican Bartolomé de Las Casas, expressed it, Charles V, in order to assert himself as "emperor over many kings," had to recognize the sovereignty of the Amerindians, a condition for establishing a bond of vassalage, the quintessence of imperial being. Las Casas, confirming this new legislation, stated in 1545 that the Superior Court of Guatemala should consider the Amerindians as the "free vassals" of His Majesty.[3] Consequently, Spanish colonists and officials were urged to endorse the authority of the native "natural lords."[4]

However, this innovative indirect government policy—put into practice three centuries later in Africa and India by Victorian England—invalidated former concessions that had allowed the colonists to construct the first stages of the overseas edifice with the Amerindian labor granted by the Crown. Insurrections then broke out in Peru.

The attorney of the High Court in Lima, searching for reasons for the mutiny led by Hernandéz Girón in 1553, summarized the rebels' point of view: "They started saying that they realized your Majesty's wish was to have the whole of Peru to himself, and that being so, Peru could not forbear becoming sovereign and governing itself freely, as Venice did."[5] Yet troops loyal to the Crown, mobilized and led by the clergy, triumphed over reluctant colonists. A compromise was reached by the two sides. The conquistadores kept the vanquished Indians, but resigned themselves to the taxation imposed on the *encomiendas*. The Crown prevented the emergence of hereditary fiefs and succeeded in establishing its authority over the conquered lands and peoples, as well as over future possessions.[6]

But the essential development occurred in rather different circumstances. By the mid-1540s, the Potosí silver mine was both reorienting trade networks and opening Peru up to commercial access from the metropolis.[7] Subsequently, in the context of the Iberian Crown's Union (1580–1640), Peruvian silver exports to the four corners of the world would become one of the basic aspects of the "universal kingdom" ruled by Spain's Catholic Crown.[8]

The situation in Angola bore some resemblance to the preceding case, except that there the Crown also fought against colonists and the Jesuits. In 1571, the colony was given to Paulo Dias Novais, grandson of Bartolomeu Dias, in the form of a hereditary possession, according to the method already tried in the African island of São Tomé and in Brazil. Novais was troubled by high expenses and was abandoned by the Crown after the military and political disaster of the Battle of Ksar El Kebir (1578). Therefore, he granted to the conquerors—some of his captains and to the missionary Jesuits—concessions of natives and lands, in a system similar to the Hispanic-American *encomiendas*.[9]

These new feudatories, called *amos*, controlled Angolan native chiefs (*sobas*) and collected taxes from the Mbumdu population. Most of the time these taxes were paid in the form of slaves, whom the *amos*—Jesuits and captains—soon began to export to America.[10] Luanda's Jesuits relied greatly on their fellow missionaries of Brazil, especially on Colégio da Bahia. Thus, in 1586, when José de Anchieta was the provincial father of Portuguese America, Father Balthazar Barreira, Luanda's Jesuit Superior, made a request to Rome for the transfer of the Congo and Angola missions, subordinate to the province of Portugal, to the Jesuit province of Brazil, created in 1553. Rome did not accede to this demand. Still, the proposal illustrates the Jesuits' precocious perception of the South Atlantic as a unified colonial space.[11]

The Crown, finding that Angola had no silver mines and that the slave trade had turned out to be an important activity in the area, resumed control over the colony. Hereditary possession was abolished, and a governor general—an immediate entrustee of royal authority—received orders to halt the institution of the *amos*.[12] Indignant, captains and Jesuits revolted against Governor Francisco de Almeida (1592–93), who was following the new royal instructions. In discussion with the Jesuit Superior in Angola, the governor declared he was "much astonished" to see a challenge to the royal order halting the concession of *sobas*.[13] The *amos* faction temporarily gained the upper hand. Francisco de Almeida, excommunicated by the missionaries and jailed by the rebel colonists, was expelled from Angola a mere ten months after his arrival.[14] His brother Jerônimo, a pawn of the Jesuits, assumed the governance of Angola and restored the authority of the *amos*.[15]

King Felipe II, when informed of the revolt, decided to ban the Society of Jesus (hereafter S.J.) from Angola and to entrust the colony's missions to another religious order. An ally of the Jesuits who was one of the most powerful men in the Iberian Peninsula, the Cardinal-Archduke Albert of Austria, viceroy and grand inquisitor for Portugal, dissuaded him. Notwithstanding, Felipe II ordered the expulsion and the immediate return to Lisbon of the Jesuit Superior in Angola, Balthazar Barreira, whose singular endeavors in Africa will be considered below.[16]

A few years later, a Jesuit chronicler justified the missionaries' attitudes in Angola: "There will be no better way of attracting and keeping them [the Mbundu] than by making them the [Jesuit] priest's *sobas*; for in doing so, they do not diminish one jot of His Majesty's jurisdiction and authority." The king, however, was of another opinion.[17] In 1607, the institution of *amos* was abolished, and vassal native chiefs were placed under the control of the Crown. Though quarrels still went on between governors and captains who intended to restore the *amos*' privileges, the action of the Crown and of metropolitan merchants dragged Angola into the Atlantic trading system.[18]

From 1595 to 1640, Madrid's *Asiento* granted to the Portuguese the monopoly of supplying Spanish America with African slaves.[19] The Portuguese merchants who owned the *Asiento* were sometimes also Contractors (*Contratadores*) for collecting royal taxes from Cape Verde and from Angola, enjoying privileged access to operations in the slave-trade ports. For now, it is worth recalling that the growth in maritime exchanges—induced by the slave traders—both rendered the African possessions viable and clipped the colonists' wings.

Unlike events in Africa and America, Portuguese activities had a more muted impact in Asia but caused immediate repercussions in Europe. Impelled by the monarchical and missionary apparatus on overseas expeditions of trade and conquest, the Iberian states threatened the Venetian mercantile oligarchies. João de Barros, in the first *Década* (c. 1545) of his *Ásia*, vividly describes the turnaround produced in the West by the opening of the Cape route. Knowing that King Manuel was negotiating the spice trade with the Kannur (Cananore) and Kochi (Cochin) ambassadors, Venice's diplomats in Lisbon maneuvered to sabotage the business. Presenting themselves as merchants without ambitions for dominance in the Indian Ocean, they argued that the Portuguese Crown ventures had a military and ideological bias. "The Venetians filled the ears of the ambassadors," claiming that Venice was peaceful and that the Portuguese would wage war against the "Moors" in the Indic shores, spoiling the time-honored Venetian spice trade from India to the Mediterranean.[20] In truth, the Portuguese tried to appropriate areas that were the reserve of Omani Arab merchants and of the Muslim Indians from Gujarat, a major textile producer.[21] Around 1550, they opened to European markets the Goa-Malacca-Macao-Nagasaki trading route, interrupted since the end of the Cheng-Ho expeditions in the 1430.[22] For decades, the Crown sought to divert these exchanges into waters controlled by Lisbon through the Cape route.[23] This policy led to conflicts between the metropolis and the Portuguese in India, who sometimes sailed "against the wind, against the monsoon, against the tide and against reason," as the celebrated author of *Peregrinação* (1614) wrote.[24]

In Goa, the colonists called *casados* (married men)—as opposed to the Portuguese soldiers and itinerant traders called *solteiros* (bachelors)—were wholesalers who carried out most of the important commercial business at seaports along trade routes to China and Japan.[25] The *casados*, represented by Goa's House Senate and directly subordinated to the State Council in Lisbon, imposed the rule that no New Christians (Iberian Jews and their descendents forced to embrace Christianity) or Indians converted to Catholicism were to be allowed to associate with Portuguese officials trading at Asian seaports.[26]

The *casados* then secured from Portugal's Crown limitations on the activity of Lisbon's agents who had business with India. To counter alleged collusion between Goa's New Christians and the ancient Jewish community of Cochin, a center for the diversion of pepper, Jesuits and Portuguese authorities succeed in establishing the Goa Inquisition Tribunal (1560), the single such instance in a Portuguese overseas settlement.[27] To be labeled New Christian in India was "very dangerous" as Diogo do Couto warned around 1600, "since bought testimony would not be lacking, if one should wish to accuse another of such a defect."[28]

Also up against the *fidalgos* (the Portuguese military aristocracy holding royal authority in India), the *casados* tried to control the whole brokerage of European trade in Asia. Apparently, the Crown drew no advantage from this situation, for in 1587, it gave the indigo trade monopoly—the main economic activity in Goa—to a group of Lisbon merchants.[29] Revolts then broke out among the *casados*. Indeed, Goa was shaken by the colonists' mutinies every time the Crown tried to increase tributes or sought to capture the Persian Gulf and Asian exchanges, which were lucrative for the Portuguese and Indian merchants but disadvantageous to metropolitan traders and the Royal Treasury.[30] Michael Pearson, who has studied such revolts, concludes that the *casados* placed their interests above their loyalty to the Crown.[31]

A broad range of interests linked Portuguese merchants and crown officials to local communities in India and the Persian Gulf.[32] They exchanged items that were easy to smuggle and circulate outside the control of local rulers and European authorities—coral from the Mediterranean and diamonds from the Golkonda Sultanate in southern India—in an extensive network involving the Fuggers from Augsburg, Hindus from Goa, and Sephardi from Leghorn and Lisbon.[33] In this transfrontier, intercultural environment, profitable transactions outside the Crown's control undermined Lisbon's administration of the Estado da Índia, which embraced Portuguese territories east of the Cape of Good Hope.[34]

It was in Goa that Diogo do Couto wrote, in 1593, his masterpiece *O Soldado Prático*, a key book of Lusitanian historical skepticism, pointing out the frauds practiced by colonial officials. According to Diogo do Couto "Nowhere else is the King [of Portugal] less obeyed than in India."[35] But as Magalhães Godinho explains: "Whatever were the military and naval means assembled, and however righteous the official's honesty, the Portuguese could not afford replacing all Moors and Gentiles in interregional circuits of trade." Between the beginning and the middle of the sixteenth century, a crack opened in the Eastern enclaves: "From that time the Luso-oriental economic complex was opposed to the interests of Lisbon and of the Cape route."[36] As shown by Artur Teodoro de Matos, regional exchanges with the Indian ports, East Africa, the Persian Gulf and the Far East sustained Goa and other marketplaces of the Estado da Índia. Yet, those exchanges were not integrated with the Cape route and the Lisbon networks.[37] This picture illustrates one of the colonial impasses mentioned earlier. The colonial surplus was achieved and transformed into mercantile production, but evaded the metropolitan networks.

In Mozambique, the fragility of Lusitanian colonial intervention in the Indian Ocean was even more transparent. In its first stage, the Monomotapa (*Mwenemutapa*) pre-European empire was permeated by Portuguese conquerors who took over the powers of native feudatories (*amambo*) in the domains (*prazos*) of the Zambezi valley. In recognition of the local ruler's authority, the first Portuguese *prazo* holders, the *arrendatários*, were confirmed in their posts by the Monomotapa emperor himself.[38] The *prazo* holders paid the Portuguese Crown a tax in powdered gold and received from their vassals, natives from the Tonga people, a rent in ivory or maize, or a labor rent (*mussoco*). Where there was no Portuguese sovereignty, the colonists paid a tribute in textiles (*fatiota*) only to the native authority.[39]

Every year the Monomotapa would send emissaries to the tributary chieftaincies to seal the bond of vassalage. In case of refusal, the refractories suffered military retaliation from the Monomatapa's army, which in 1576 numbered 30,000 soldiers.[40]

Despite the attacks on natives—legitimated by the "Just War" declared in 1569 against the Monomotapa and the "other kings and kaffir [*cafre*] lords," Portuguese sovereignty only skirted Mozambique, in contrast with the conquest triggered in Angola.[41] Friar João dos Santos, in his *Ethiopia Oriental* (1609), commented that the Portuguese captain of the Massapa Fair, in a gold-bearing area, was empowered by the Monomotapa and by the Portuguese crown as a representative of both powers.[42] While he acted as a judge for the viceroy of Portuguese India, he also on the Monomotapa's behalf collected duties for the Zambezia ruler from the settlers and Moors trading in the area.[43]

Gradually absorbed by native society and institutions, the colonists tended to Africanize, or to "kafffirize," as Alexandre Lobato, Portuguese historian of Mozambique, has pointed out.[44] A seventeenth-century narrative sketched the difficulties of populating Mozambique by colonials: "These lands are divided between several [colonist] lordships, and each [lord] took control of whatever he wished, and of the income from it."[45] Leaving untouched native conditions of production, the Portuguese were unable to change the regional trade. External exchanges remained directed toward the North and the East, with Omani Arabs controlling the slave trade to the Persian Gulf, the main market in the area.[46]

In 1752 Mozambique was separated from the Estado da India, on which it was dependent, and became an autonomous colony, directly administered by Lisbon. The slave trade then took a new step in the Indian Ocean. In fact, the first

Portuguese tariff schedule to collect taxes on slaves was set in 1756, two-and-a-half centuries after similar tariffs had come into operation in Portuguese Guinea, and two hundred years after those set in Luanda and Benguela.[47] In this period, Omani Arab, Indian, Swahili, Dutch, and French regional demand fostered the growth of the slave trade in the southwest Indian Ocean.[48]

Except for some sporadic deliveries, Brazil regularly received East African slaves only from the first decade of the nineteenth century on: 94.7 percent of Africans deported from Mozambique to Brazilian ports, mostly to Rio de Janeiro, disembarked in the period 1801–1850.[49] The emerging intercolonial division of labor had already designated the other side of Africa, mainly Angola, as the preferred market for the Luso-Brazilians slave ships.[50] In addition to exports of ivory to Europe and Asia, and of gold to Goa, Gujarat, and Kannara, Mozambique gained strategic importance as a port of call on the India route. Portuguese fleets remained for several months at the Mozambican harbors waiting for the maritime monsoons to cease.[51] Failing to achieve economic control over the area, Lisbon modified the alliance and inheritance rules to be observed by the *prazo* holders, redefining metropolitan policy in this part of the overseas territory.

After 1625, the domains of Zambezia were no longer hereditary possessions. Changed into "*prazos* of the Crown," they were issued—under an emphyteusis contract—to petitioners for a period of three generations, after which the Crown resumed ownership. The concession could either be renewed for the same family or granted to other petitioners. Concentration of *prazos* in the hands of one grantee alone was, however, very common, as the Crown preferred to let the law lapse rather than leaving *prazos* uninhabited—"Not to break off the continuity of its control over the natives," as Fritz Hoppe explains.[52]

In his *Tratado dos Rios de Cuama*, written in 1696, the missionary Antonio da Conceição describes the dual significance of the bond between the leaseholders and the Crown: "Those who have Crown lands receive considerable benefit from them, but no one can maintain the State [the Crown's dominion]. . . . Even so, one should not think that the State is superfluous, but rather that it is essential in order to make us respected in this Kaffir Land [*Cafraria*]." In other words, the leaseholders did not pay much tax to the Royal Treasury, but their relation with the Crown, set by the *prazo* concession, helped to prop up Lisbon's sovereignty in the Zambezi valley (*Rios de Cuama*).[53]

The emphyteusis contract, linking the Crown with the *prazo* holder, marked the originality of Portuguese policy in the region. Contrary to Lusitanian legislation in its entirety—which excluded women from inheriting concessions as well as property bestowed by the Crown—this contract determined that *prazos* were inherited in the female lineage, when the heiress married a colonist born in Portugal, that is, a *reinol*, or a *reinol*'s son.⁵⁴ The *prazo* holder was therefore subjected to metropolitan sovereignty by a double temporary contract: the contract of three generations (the emphyteusis) established by the Crown with his wife's father, and the contract of one generation, which he took over by marrying the holder of the *prazo*.⁵⁵ By constraining each heiress to marry a *reinol*, the Crown hoped to restrain the colony's self-sufficiency and the overwhelming ascension of mulattos who took possession of the *prazos*.⁵⁶

Relying on the Makua's matrilineal kinship as much as on colonial support, this system brought about unusual marriages.⁵⁷ Many of these ladies became widows and soon remarried pretenders eager to become proprietors. Such was the case of Dona Catarina de Leitão, the great holder of the Quelimane *prazo*, who contracted marriage for the fourth time around 1770, when she was over 80 years of age.⁵⁸ Or else Dona Francisca Josefa de Moura Meneses (died in 1825), nicknamed *Chiponda*, or "the Lady who steps on all," which managed several advantageous marriages to her and her nieces.⁵⁹

Despite this singular juridical arrangement, the powers of the *prazo* holders rested more on compromise with natives than on the legal status acknowledged by Lisbon. Among fifty-five *prazos* found in 1750 in the province of Tete, five had a title of concession and twenty-five had no title at all. The other twenty-five *prazos* were either merely confirmed by local authorities or had doubtful property warrants, while the further twenty-five lacked deeds or justification.⁶⁰ In 1763, when the Marquis de Pombal tried to centralize the Mozambique administration, a revolt broke out among the *prazo* holders, driving the Crown to temporize with the rebels.⁶¹ Lisbon thus shared power with the *arrendatários*, who in turn depended on pacts celebrated with African chieftains.

Following a practice previously adopted by Arab merchants, Portuguese governors bestowed a gift on the Monomotapa and the king of Kiteve—as a symbolical bond of vassalage—at the moment they took their posts in Mozambique. When this tribute—called *curva* and generally consisting of a certain amount of cloth—was not paid, trouble developed in the colony and subverted the relations with the natives.⁶² Friar João dos Santos records that the payment of the *curva* to the Monomotapa was more coercive than that to the king of Kiteve, who relied more on the alliance with the Portuguese.⁶³

At the turn of the eighteenth century, the monetary value of the *curva* seemed insignificant. The São Paulo–born cartographer Lacerda e Almeida, governor of Rio de Sena in Zambezia, called the Monomotapa emperor a "drunkard," and the longevity of the Portuguese presence would lead one to suppose that this obligation to pay tribute was lost. However, when the Portuguese governor of one of Zambezia's provinces decided not to pay the *curva*, in 1806 a revolt broke out 1806 that ended only in 1826, when the Portuguese finally offered the tribute to the Monomotapa.[64] Portuguese America, involved in the Atlantic market and repopulated by African deportees, did not come close to incidents of this kind. No South American native community ever held sufficient power to sustain an enduring sovereignty and to collect regular tributes in the Luso-Brazilian settlements.

The fragility of the links of the Mozambique domains with the metropolitan networks caused continuous rebellions among the *arrendatários*.[65] The *prazos* were disconnected from the pre-Portuguese social system in the first quarter of the nineteenth century when the Brazilian slave traders effected the "Atlanticization" of Mozambique, attaching the territory's maritime exchanges into the Rio de Janeiro network—and later still, when foreign concessionary companies transformed the region.[66]

The facts show more plainly the impasses considered at the outset of this chapter. The overseas surplus did not reach the metropolis when it fell into circuits unrelated to the Lisbon networks (as in Goa), or was stranded within the supposedly conquered territory (as in Mozambique), where the product of labor extorted from the native communities was directly consumed by colonists or drained away by regional trade. Three centuries after the Century of Discoveries, Mozambique was still entangled in the misunderstanding pursued in Peru in the mid-sixteenth century. Hernandez Girón's companions intended to found republics, "like Venice." Were it not for the epidemics that devastated the Inca empire and for the silver mines that turned local society upside down, the Peruvian rebels would have created "republics" of the Zambezia type, where they would live more in the "*cafrealized*" manner of the Mozambican *prazo* holders than in the luxurious style of Venetian aristocrats. It is again noteworthy that the presence of European colonists in a territory did not necessarily occasion colonial exploitation of that territory.

In Brazil, measures were taken in 1534 to consolidate the occupation and valorization of the colony in response to both the French invasion of the territory and the decline of Portuguese trade in Asia. The colony was divided into fifteen hereditary captaincies awarded to twelve grantees. The Crown offered several privileges to attract candidates. Nevertheless, six of the first twelve donataries either never went to Brazil or came back at once to Portugal. Two were killed by Tupinambás Indians, two others gave up their rights, and only two thrived: Duarte Coelho in Pernambuco and, up to 1546, Pero do Campo Tourinho in Porto Seguro. The captaincy (*capitania*) of São Vicente prospered for a certain time, though its donee had never visited it. In 1549 a general-government was established, impelling a movement of centralization designed to reduce donees' privileges.[67]

Circumstances peculiar to Pernambuco allowed Duarte Coelho and his descendants to resist Bahia's governor general's attempts to assume their prerogatives until the mid-seventeenth century.[68] In all other places, however, a central government authority was set up. The difficulties involved in this change will be noted below. It is worth remembering that the economy based on Indian labor and exploitation of brazilwood started to change into an economy based on sugar plantations and African slave labor. The colony's linkage with the Atlantic trade was deliberately emphasized by royal legislation restricting employment of Amerindian slave labor and stimulating the use of African slaves, as well as by measures restraining internal trade among Brazilian captaincies.

This geographic and economic context shapes an aterritorial space, more South Atlantic than South American, which reveals the flagrant anachronism of transposing contemporary national boundaries onto colonial maps, in order to draw conclusions about Portugal's enclaves of Terra de Santa Cruz (later Brazil)—a land that was not a unified entity. Because of the prevailing winds, the currents, and the trade predominating in the South Atlantic until the end of the seventeenth century and even after this date, the Brazilian East-West coast (the Amazon region proper, plus Maranhão, Pará, Piauí, Ceará, and part of present Rio Grande do Norte), embraced by the Estado do Maranhão, remained dissociated from Brazil's African slaving core, while Angola became attached to it.

Far from being an arbitrary act of Iberian bureaucracy, the establishment of the Estado do Maranhão, created in 1624 with a government distinct from the Estado do Brasil, whose capital was Bahia, perfectly dovetails with maritime trade and winds.[69] "Maranhão . . . it is closer to Portugal than any other port of that State (of Brazil), with easier navigation and route . . . because this Land is so, Her Majesty has established it as a government separate from Brazil," stated Captain Sylveira, a representative of Maranhão council, in his 1624 history of Amazonia.[70]

Maritime guides of the British Admiralty and of others nations signaled such a partition of the South American coast up to the end of the Transatlantic Sailing

Age.[71] As we will see below, the Papacy followed those same geographic determinants in the management of its dioceses. Created in 1676, the archbishopric of Bahia gained jurisdiction over the Brazilian dioceses of Rio de Janeiro and Olinda, plus the African bishoprics of Congo and Angola and São Tomé. In contrast, because of the difficult navigation to Bahia, the new bishopric of Maranhão (1677) was made suffragan of the Lisbon's archbishopric.[72]

Portuguese America and the genesis of modern Brazil assumed their full dimensions in the South Atlantic. Consequently, the continuity of colonial history cannot be bracketed within the continuity of the colony's territory.[73] In fact, conditioning by the Ethiopic Ocean, complementary but distinct from the North Atlantic linkages, only disappeared from the country's horizon after 1850, following the end of the transatlantic slave trade and the split of the colonial spatial matrix. Such conditions mark the originality of Brazilian historical development.

This summary illustrates the antagonisms that arose on the colonial horizon when the Crown no longer confined itself to mere exercise of domination (*dominium*) but also asserted its right over lands to be conquered and its guardianship of conquered peoples (*imperium*). The conflict between Iberian powers and their subjects had different effects on overseas territory. In Peru, the rise of the mining economy put an end to the colonists' move toward autonomy and stimulated integration of Spanish American markets into European trade. In Angola, maritime exchanges—triggered by the slave trade—gave Portugal additional means of control over the colonial enclaves. In Mozambique, where Portuguese trade took its place in a pre-European mercantile network, colonists became kaffirized and fulfilled roles in the traditional trade network of native society. Finally, in Goa, where exchanges with Arab and Indian merchants as well as with the Far East provided profitable choices, trade with the Portuguese gave way to more attractive opportunities outside metropolitan control.

The Metropolis's Options

The nineteenth-century historian Francisco Varnhagen noted an apparent incoherence in Portuguese overseas policy. Regarding the prerogatives granted to the donataries in sixteenth-century Brazil, he stated that these were "much wider than expected at a time when Europeans kings tried to concentrate authority, enforcing imperial royal authority over ancient lords or over certain privileged corporations."[74] It is well known that private investment in the first stage of Lusitanian colonization was not exclusively Portuguese. Except for some royal monopolies, Catholic foreigners, settled or not in Portugal, could get privileges similar to those of national Catholics for trade with Portuguese colonies. Moreover, if they employed a Portuguese crew, those foreigners were also allowed to use their own ships in this commerce. Such traders were obliged to pay certain taxes, but were exempt from specific duties that nationals had to meet. Legally or illegally, half and perhaps two-thirds of the sugar produced in Brazil had been transported by the Dutch into Amsterdam until the beginning of the seventeenth century.[75]

Even after the anti-Spanish Flanders insurrection, Lisbon kept cordial relations with the United Provinces, to whom King Sebastião provided pecuniary and political support, despite protests from his uncle Felipe II.[76] The so-called "colonial exclusive," that is, the metropolitan trade monopoly over colonies, was imposed only after 1580. Through association with the Spanish monarchy, the Portuguese Crown became so involved in European conflicts that it ended by ruining its overseas domains.[77] Therefore Lisbon started to restrain the activities of traders from other countries. Foreigners were forbidden to go to overseas territories after 1591 in order to avoid heresies—but also because it was "against all reason and good sense" that foreign merchants should be allowed to damage "the trade of the kingdom." In 1605 all foreign transactions in Portuguese domains were prohibited.[78] Non-Portuguese aliens settled in Brazil had to go back to the kingdom within a year.[79]

Hence, a sharp shift occurred in Portuguese colonial policy on the eve of the Century of Discoveries. Initially, the Crown granted powers both to its subjects possessing capital and to Catholic foreigners trading with its overseas markets. Some decades later, the monarchy stepped back and initiated a movement of "metropolitan restoration" abroad, restricting the autonomy of the main actors of overseas possessions. On the one hand, a national monopoly (the *exclusivo*) was established over colonial trade. On the other hand, new laws subjected settlers to governors general entrusted with ample powers and charged with reinforcing the "purpose of colonization."[80] The Crown had to learn how to make all colonial rivers flow toward the metropolitan sea. The colonists had to understand that the apprenticeship of colonization was mainly the apprenticeship of the market, which was, first and foremost, the metropolitan market. Only then could colonial domination and colonial exploitation coincide and correlate with each other.

Imperial power, having taken the role of the only bestower of lands and the only controller of natives to be conquered, appeared also as the organizer of productive labor, the conveyor of social privileges, and the gendarme of religious orthodoxy. The latter acquired its full strength in the sixteenth and seventeenth centuries, considering the influence of the Counter-Reformation and, above all, the weight of the most powerful ideological apparatus of the Iberian Peninsula: the Inquisition.

Like the Spanish monarchy, the Portuguese Crown exercised direct control over secular clergy thanks to the *jus patronatus* (the Padroado), a set of privileges that popes granted to Iberian kings between 1452 and 1514. According to these texts, the Iberian religious hierarchy could undertake its functions only after royal approval. The Crown supported the secular clergy financially, and could forbid the proclamation of pontifical edicts and briefs.[81]

Framed by the Padroado, the secular clergy and episcopate became chains of metropolitan power, especially in Brazil and Africa. In the context of migrations and cultural transfers, where accusations of heresy spread easily, exclusion from the ecclesiastic community brought harsh consequences. At the same time, religious repression transposed its doctrinaire framework overseas in order to intervene as a disciplining instrument for metropolitan policy.

Truly the founding text of Portuguese colonial law, the *Romanus Pontifex* bull of 1455 excommunicated those who breached the overseas monopoly bestowed by Pope Nicholas V on King Afonso V and Infant Dom Henrique.[82] This repressive resource was occasionally activated on request. In 1613, at the behest of Cape Verde's governor, the diocese bishop excommunicated on a large scale "all those who have stolen from His Majesty's property or who have evaded His taxes."[83]

Instruments to intimidate freelancers who interfered with the metropolitan trade circuit sprang from the post-Tridentine movement, which maintained the sacraments' compulsory nature. European middlemen settled in the Jagas's *kilombo* at Kasanje,[84] away from the Luanda's authorities' control, received "tight orders" to shelter in the Angolan capital, because they "lived amongst barbarians" and were thus unavailable to receive the holy sacraments.[85] It is clear that the religious orthodoxy played an active role in the colonization of the colonists.

The perspective of Jesuits, Franciscans, Carmelites, and Benedictines, the regular clergy present in Portuguese America, was quite another matter. In their strategy for the evangelization of local Amerindians, the Jesuits conflicted with the colonists, with the bishops, and with the Crown. However, it is also necessary to highlight the role of the missions as occupation units in overseas territories. As Charles Boxer recalls, in the absence of substantial military contingents overseas before the second half of the eighteenth century, it was mainly the Catholic priesthood that kept the colonists and the natives alike loyal to the Iberian Crowns.[86] In this context, the role of missionaries is key, especially with regard to the Society of Jesus, which exerted in Portugal a greater influence than in any other European country.

Even if we confine ourselves only to the history of the South Atlantic, there are several examples of this process. Accordingly, the Jesuits of the Guanabara Bay mission helped organize the Rio de Janeiro expedition that expelled the Dutch from Angola in 1648. Following that, the Jesuits opposed the proselytism of Spanish and Roman Capuchins, whose mission in the Congo hindered Portuguese policy in West Central Africa. Still on the periphery of Portuguese America, Jesuits of the Estado do Maranhão neutralized French influence on the Amapá tribes, enlisting Amerindians for the recapture of the Macapá and Parú forts (1697), occupied by French troops from Cayenne during the War of the League of Augsburg (1689–1697).[87] Inside Portuguese America, the Jesuits helped suppress the São Paulo rebellion in the 1650s and favored the restoration of royal authority in Maranhão after the Beckman mutiny (1683–1684).[88] The activity by Jesuits in favor of the Braganza dynasty gained stronger inflection in the 1640–1668 period, when the overseas dioceses lay vacant by virtue of the contention between Rome and Lisbon.[89]

The role played by the Inquisition was more complex and diversified. Missionaries and Goa's colonial authorities pestered Hindus who crouched to urinate, a practice considered deviant.[90] Franciscans and Jesuits quarreled in the Amazon missions, arguing over whether the river turtle (*tracajá*) was a fish or a beast, so as to determine if the Tapuya Amerindians who ate it during Lent incurred in mortal sin or not.[91]

However, greater damage would be inflicted by inquisitorial agents in the kingdom and overseas. In the metropolis, the Holy Office often appeared as a weapon of the aristocracy against the mercantile bourgeoisie.[92] Also, when metropolitan merchants or the Crown faced foreign competition, denunciations of Judaism abounded. In Upper Guinea, gold was the main object of the European trade until the middle of the seventeenth century, when the slave trade prevailed.[93] Flemish, French, and English vessels carrying trade goods such as fabrics and iron bars—valuable merchandise in the area—easily gained access to the coastal ports of Senegambia.[94] Adding to European competition, the existence of two New Christian communities south of the Cape Verde peninsula, on the Senegal coast, appeared as a critical threat to the alleged royal Portuguese monopoly.[95] In response, denunciations against New Christians in the Rios de Guiné—the Senegambia coast—were constant from the beginning of the sixteenth century. The captain of

Santiago (Cape Verde) informed the court in 1544 that "Guinea [was] lost" to Portugal, since the land was already "crowded" with New Christians engaged in smuggling.[96] In 1611 the bishop of Cape Verde received orders to find out if there were people living "Jewishly" in Upper Guinea, so as to have them incarcerated and sent to the Inquisitorial Tribunal in Lisbon.[97] Later, the rising price of slaves, driven by European slave-traders' demand, led a committee formed by the bishop and the governor of Cape Verde to propose the nomination of a Commissioner of the Inquisition for Cacheu to extract (*tirar*) "Judaism" from Upper Guinea.[98] After the coronation of King João IV, the outbreak of the Portuguese-Spanish war, and the conquest of Elmina (1637), São Tomé, and Angola (1641) by the Dutch, the Overseas Council was also concerned with foreign assaults on Upper Guinea ports, "because without Angola, there is no other another remedy, but these ports, to populate Brazil with Blacks."[99] In this context, Cacheu's New Christians were also suspected of being pro-Castillian.[100] At the same time, as we shall see below, the Spanish Inquisition accused Portuguese New Christians in Peru of "Judaism" and betrayal in favor of the Crown of Braganza.

The practice of the Portuguese Inquisition presents several distinguishing features. First, the Portuguese Inquisition almost always appeared as an instrument of the aristocracy that was deployed against a mercantile bourgeoisie that was intertwined with Judaism.[101] Next, the repressive activity of the inquisitors against Judaism assumed a more constant pace in Portugal than in Angola and Brazil, where blasphemies and superstitions were the main origin of the denunciations at the turn of the sixteenth century.[102] Further, condemned New Christians were more likely to be executed than condemned Old Christians. Deaths were also more frequent among jailed New Christians. Finally, physicians and merchants, often New Christians, were more likely to be subjected to capital punishment than those of other occupations who had been condemned by the Inquisition.[103]

Notwithstanding the absence of inquisitorial tribunals in Portuguese America, the reduced presence of Inquisition's lay officials (*familiares*) and the low number of settlers convicted in Lisbon's autos-da-fé, from the early seventeenth century on, the Holy Office established a control network grounded in local clergy and royal officials in Brazil.[104] Subsequently, merchants and sugar mill owners were denounced and taken in chains to the Inquisition of Lisbon.[105]

Unlike in Brazil and Portuguese Africa, in Spanish America permanent Inquisition tribunals were set up in Lima (1570), in Mexico (1571) and in Cartagena

(1610). The latter court was created in response to the influential Portuguese New Christian merchants in that key *Asiento* port.[106] Often held by Portuguese New Christians, the *Asiento de Negros* was, as Jonathan Israel has noted, "the most important loophole" in Seville's transatlantic monopoly convoy system during the Iberian Union.[107] Spanish merchants in Peru manipulated the inquisitors to ruin the Portuguese merchant community in the years of the 1630s.[108] In the post-1640 period, there was a new development when the Portuguese Inquisition operated alongside Madrid, thrashing the economic agents that supported Portuguese independence.[109]

The "unfaithful," whether real or alleged, lived in constant insecurity as the Crown vacillated between repressive fury, direct extortion, and the desire to take advantage of the New Christians' economic activities. The laws of the period registered such hesitation. The royal decree of 1587 prohibited New Christians from leaving the kingdom. In 1601, the Crown backtracked as the Jewish community paid a donation of a 100,000 *cruzados* to the Royal Treasury. Three years later a general pardon was conceded in exchange for a fresh donation, ten times larger that the previous one. Another decree, in 1610, reinstated the 1587 interdict. New franchises were cancelled by new bans.[110] In the ensuing back and forth, repression became more insidious. Although only around two dozen individuals from Brazil seem to have punished by the Inquisition and the number of people brought before it on charges was not more than 500, the fear instilled by the Inquisition effected a much greater number of people.[111]

Because of coastal winds and the Benguela current, Angola remained more protected from competition by foreign vessels than Upper Guinea, affording some shelter to the trade and government of Luanda and Benguela.[112] New Christians were allowed residence if they restricted themselves to the role of merchants.[113] Yet disputes among colonists often led to denunciations against "Hebrew" merchants in Congo and Angola.[114] Indeed, missionaries' correspondence record several examples of the indirect action of the inquisitorial hand.[115] In 1631, an old Angolan hand, Jesuit Pero Tavares, undertook an evangelizing journey into the backlands of Golungo, in the modern province of Cuanza Norte. Along the way, Father Pero Tavares found an indigenous idol enthroned in a village and tried to destroy it. Seeking to recover the image, considered by the local community as their "physician" and "medicine," the *soba* sought help from a colonist, his ally. Tavares, entangled in a quarrel with the colonist amid dangerous agitation in the hamlet, acted quickly:

I feared there would be some disturbance and, thus, brought the matter to an end in a few words. I clearly told the man—for I knew that he belonged to "the nation" [was a New Christian] but was of good character: "that he should no longer discuss such an affair with me, as I would have to tell the governor and the bishop of everything, since these matters were the jurisdiction of the Holy Office." These were my last words because with them the poor Hebrew was almost struck dumb. Then, regaining his composure, he said to me: "Father of my soul, the one who spoke is no longer here. Your Reverence may thus then burn the idol." With that, we parted with much friendship and the natives were gone, some crying and others bursting with rage against me.[116]

This apparently banal incident shows the force of intimidation exerted by priests in Brazil and Angola, even though the fires of the Inquisition did not burn in those territories. Yet this incident is not that banal. Following his Order's instructions, Father Pero Tavares sent his reports to the colleges of the Society of Jesus in Lisbon. Collected alongside similar texts under the title *Sumária relação* (1635), it was read in Jesuit seminars throughout Europe. Such narratives served the purposes of case-based doctrinal reasoning and of evangelization, as well as a "lesson on how to proceed in such bushland."[117] In this regard, the much advertised antipathy of the Jesuits to the Holy Office did not stop them from making use of the inquisitorial threat.[118] A historical trait of Portuguese authoritarianism stands out here. Without thoroughly banishing Muslim and Jewish populations from its territory as Spain had done, Portugal persecuted and plundered its Jewish and allegedly Jewish mercantile bourgeoisie.[119] In a report addressed to King João IV in 1643, Father Antonio Vieira underlined the paradox of the kingdom's policy: "Truly, it is very difficult to understand Portugal's reason of state because being a kingdom entirely dependent on commerce this kingdom expelled its merchants [Jewish or allegedly so] to alien kingdoms."[120] Thus, the contingency of the civil rights of a socioeconomic community invested with a key role in modernization was established. This revenge of the aristocracy on the merchant bourgeoisie marked the evolution of Portuguese and Luso-Brazilian societies. Through the oblique power of the Inquisition or the political zeal of the clergy, the Iberian Church played a double role. It helped to consolidate *dominium* by securing in place the colonial population of the overseas regions, and it strengthened *imperium* to the degree that it promoted the vassalage of overseas peoples to Lisbon.

Referring to "international relations" at a time when the nations did not yet exist (but instead to the notion of the aterritorial or transfrontier space employed here), the literature on Iberian overseas expansion also transposes to the past concepts of the Berlin Conference (1884–85) correlating empire and continuity of the imperial territory. In contrast, Robert Ricard calls attention to the military and geopolitical role of the "restricted occupation" zones around the Portuguese, Spanish, and English North African strongholds before the Second European Colonial Expansion.[121] Other authors underline the role of the trading posts, trading diasporas, and transcommunitarian merchant networks in African and Asian areas where European sovereignty was feeble, symbolic, or nonexistent from the sixteenth century until the end of the nineteenth century.[122]

Macao, whose capitalistic statute was respected, protected—and above all contained—for four centuries by the Ming, the Qing, the Warlords, Mao Zedong, the Gang of Four, and Deng Ziaoping, constitutes a paradigmatic instance of a great trading post.[123] Consequently, it is important to recall the contrasting evolution of European presence overseas. Most of the historiography on the Latin American countries skips over the crucial transition that converted coastal factories and enclaves into a colonial, protonational territory. Why was Iberian America much more extensively occupied since the seventeenth century than Africa and Asia? How did the small seaport of Rio de Janeiro, founded by the Portuguese in 1565, turn out to be the head of the largest unified European colony in the Americas and then capital of a nation-state, whereas the factory of Macao, established in 1557, remained a trading post until 1999, when it was retaken by China?[124]

At the beginning, the colonies' links with the Iberian metropoles depended more on knots tied by royal officials and clergy than on links provided by world market exchanges. Only after the mining production in Spanish America and the connection of slave trade with Brazil would the dynamics of the Atlantic system come to involve Iberian possessions in Africa and America.

Spanish metropolitan authority exercised relatively weak control over the colonial process of production, but strongly regulated the commercialization of colonial goods. Spanish colonial goods—precious metals—were stocked and carried by a fleet system channeled through three American seaports and Seville, the only communication points allowed between Spain and America. Given the fact that the slave trade did not fit in with such restrictions, Madrid was compelled to establish *Asientos*, subcontracting to the Genoese and Portuguese the slave trade to Spanish America.

In Portuguese America, the colonial process was rather different. Rigid centralization and long waits in buying, storing, and carrying goods, which characterized Spanish trade, were inadequate arrangements for the perishable nature and price fluctuations of Brazilian agricultural products, as well as the growing activity of Portugal's secondary ports.[125] In fact, the introduction of Africans and the prohibition of Indian enslavement allowed Portugal to take control both upstream and downstream from Brazilian colonial production. Colonists depended on the metropolis, too: they had to export their merchandise, but also had to import their factors of production, that is, the African slaves. This situation fundamentally framed Portuguese colonization and the South Atlantic.

Intermetropolitan wars in the second half of the seventeenth century led Lisbon to organize trade fleets between Brazil and Portugal—a system that would be kept during the first half of the eighteenth century—to carry Brazilian gold to Lisbon. But that system was less severe than the one in Spanish America. Brazil's organized fleets, discredited by colonists and merchants, were abolished in 1765.[126]

The slave trade, which formed the basis of colonial production, was a decisive instrument in the achievement of the Portuguese colonial system in the Atlantic. Gradually this trade transcended the economic field and became integrated into the metropolitan political apparatus. The two issues presented in the preceding pages thus assume their full meaning. The exercise of imperial power in overseas territories and the set of exchanges between metropolis and colonies converged in the sphere of slave traffic.

Nevertheless, by allowing the colonization of the colonists, that is, their inclusion in the metropolitan network, the slave trade's dynamics transformed the colonial system in contradictory ways. By the seventeenth and eighteenth centuries, this colonial pattern was breached as Luso-Brazilians—or, to use a better term, the Brasílicos, that was adopted at the time to designate Portuguese America colonists—established themselves in the South American slaving areas and in Luanda.[127] In a counterpoint to the direct exchanges of Portuguese America with Lisbon, they created direct trade links between Brazil and Africa.

Hence, two major transformations occurred in the Atlantic during the second half of the seventeenth century. In the North Atlantic, new organizational centers of the slave trade arose in Liverpool, London, Bristol, and Nantes, alongside those already existing in Lisbon and Seville.[128] In the South Atlantic, a bilateral trade emerged between Rio de Janeiro, Bahia, Pernambuco, and to a lesser extent, Buenos Aires, and the Angolan and the Gulf of Guinea ports.

Underestimated and sometimes ignored by many historians, the bilateral trade across the South Atlantic was recorded by well-known seventeenth century authors such as the French traveler François Pyrard, the Portuguese Fray Vicente de Salvador, and the merchant and planter Ambrósio Fernandes Brandão, as well as the eighteenth-century Luso-Bahian historian, Rocha Pitta.[129] A cartographer, the Luso-Bahian José Antonio Caldas, described in 1759 the round trip between Bahia and the Gulf of Guinea, which lasted four months.[130] This network was designated the "Mina Coast circuit" (*giro da Costa da Mina*) by an 1800 royal order.[131] Postwar historians of Brazil also highlighted or studied the South Atlantic networks.[132] More recently, improved figures collected in the Transatlantic Slave Trade Database provide definitive evidence of the bilateral trade between Brazil and Africa: 95 percent of the voyages carrying African slaves to Brazil were organized and began in Brazilian ports. Of the top ten largest American and European ports where slave-trading voyages were organized between 1514 and 1867, Brazil stands out: Rio de Janeiro has first place, Salvador de Bahia second, and Recife seventh. Lisbon only appears at the ninth place. Taken together, Brazilian ports organized voyages carrying 63 percent of the enslaved Africans transported by the ten leading slave-trade ports in the world.[133]

Only one slaving-trade voyage in ten was completed by a vessel raising anchor in Lisbon bound for an African port. There it took on enslaved Africans to carry them to a Brazilian port. In Brazil it loaded a cargo of tropical goods for its voyage back to Lisbon, thus tracing the contours of the so-called "triangular trade."[134]

Much of the investment in such ventures originated in Portugal. As Pyrard first noted in 1610, vessels leaving Lisbon used to make a long loop that included ports of call of the bilateral trade: Lisbon, Brazilian port, African port, Brazilian port, Lisbon.[135] In the eighteenth century, the metropolitan share of the slave trade was still significant, although the overwhelming majority of slaving-trade voyages were organized in Brazilian ports.[136] In the nineteenth century, Ethiopic Ocean geopolitics changed significantly. The withdrawal of American and English slave-trade competition in African ports (1807), combined with the opening of direct trade between Brazil and England (1808), gave Brazilian ports the ascendency portrayed in table 1.1 on page 22.

Over all, the role of the Brazilian slave ports remained decisive in the South Atlantic network. Shipping equipment, selection of barter goods, navigation practices, the agency on both shores of the ocean, the regional deals and services that generated the 14,161 round-trip voyages from Brazil to Africa and Africa to Brazil,

Table 1.1. African Captives Carried on Vessels Leaving the Main Ports Where Slave-Trading Voyages Were Organized, 1514–1867

Ports	Numbers of Captives
Rio de Janeiro	1,507,000
Salvador da Bahia	1,362,000
Liverpool	1,338,000
London	829,000
Bristol	565,000
Nantes	542,000
Recife	437,000
Lisbon	333,000
Havana	250,000

Source: D. Eltis and D. Richardson, *Atlas*, table 3, p. 39.

depended on the trading expertise and social capital accumulated over the course of three centuries in Rio de Janeiro, Bahia, and Recife. Far from being circumstantial, the bilateral slave trade in the Ethiopic Ocean stands as one of the constituent elements of the whole Atlantic system. As will be discussed below, Brazilian ports shipped cassava flour and cowry to Angola and Congo from the end of the sixteenth century.[137] Through Bahia, Rio de Janeiro, Luanda or directly from Buenos Aires, Potosí silver arrived in the hands of slave merchants in Lisbon or Seville. In the second half of the seventeenth century, sugar-cane rum (called *jeribita* in Angola and *cachaça* in Brazil) started to be dispatched to West Central Africa and occasionally to the Slave Coast.[138] In practice, exports of Pernambuco and Bahia tobacco predominated in exchanges with the Gulf of Guinea, and specifically, with the Bight of Benin, from the 1670s onward.[139] No other region in the Americas recorded such extensive bilateral exchanges with Africa. Favorable nautical and commercial conditions enabled Portuguese and Luso-Brazilian ships to overcome European competitors in West Central Africa. Adverse winds and longer routes to the Angolan coast made slave-trading vessels of other European ports sail generally to ports north of Ambriz, toward the Congo estuary and beyond.[140] Further, the combined consequences of the end of the British and American slave trade and of the opening of direct commercial relations between Brazil and England fostered the Brazilian slave trade.

Thus, the Brazilian external trade evolved along two complementary routes. One entailed the direct exchanges with Portugal, and after 1808, with Portugal and England. The other involved the direct relations with Africa that stood until 1850, coupled with the growing British trade to Brazil. Consequently, the economic and maritime South Atlantic network does not correspond to the system characteristic of the North Atlantic system.[141] Neither does it correspond to the current periodization of Atlantic history, since most of the historiography on the slave trade emphasizes the 1807 British and American Abolition Acts, disregarding the rapid growth of the deportation of Africans during the first half of the nineteenth century, directed chiefly to Brazil.[142] Shaping the whole of Brazilian economy, demography, society, and politics, the slave trade involved many more complex aspects than those derived from the single operation of purchase, transport, and sale of Africans.

The Aims of the Portuguese Slave Trade

In the political and military field, the treaty of Alcáçovas, signed by Portugal and Spain in 1479, put an end to the War of Succession in Castile and transferred the Canary Islands to Castilian sovereignty, but also recognized the Portuguese king as the only lord of Madeira, the Azores, the Fez Kingdom (Morocco), and the Cape Verde islands, as well as of the lands "discovered and . . . the ones to be discovered" in Guinea, that is, in black Africa.

In the doctrinal sphere, papal decrees issued beginning in 1455 suppressed the excommunication imposed on the Portuguese who had purchased slaves and gold from Muslims. The 1481 papal bull justified the license to trade with Muslims with the argument that the aim of such trade was to "diminish the strength of the infidel and not to augment it."[143] Portugal thus became a global trader between Europe and the merchant zones aggregated by the caravels. Recognized by Madrid and Rome as the legitimate lord of the trades and the conquered territories in Africa, Portugal swept up the spatial and economic trumps that allowed her to play a pivotal role in the slave trade. Ultimately, it allowed her to stay on both sides of the South Atlantic for over three centuries.

Exploiting the cosmopolitan and aterritorial character of the merchant capital accumulated in Europe, Portugal precociously laid the foundation of an imperial market area.[144] Nonetheless, the Crown had neither the means nor the necessary strength to maintain this transcontinental space. Defeated by better-equipped overseas powers, Lisbon lost markets and territories, especially in the East. However, the Portuguese Crown did manage to advance the European colonial system by implanting an economy of production in the Atlantic that was better exploited than the economy of circulation of its Asian enclaves.

In the absence of a regular surplus that could be incorporated into maritime exchanges, the Crown—seconded by national and foreign capital—stimulated the production of goods for the world market by improving colonial exploitation.[145] It soon became patent that the Atlantic system, grounded as it was on the pillaging of African peoples and on slavery in Americas, offered new advantages to the Crown and to the settlers. Benefiting from the Lusitanian example, other European maritime powers set up similar systems between Africa and the Caribbean in the seventeenth and eighteenth centuries. From this perspective, what was the dimension taken up by the slave trade?

In the first place, the African slave trade constituted a segment of the networks linking Portugal to the Middle and Far East. In its relations with Asia, Lisbon paid for its exchanges by sending out shipments of gold (to the Ottoman empire), silver (to the Far East), and copper (to India). In fact, Portugal had access to only small amounts of these metals at its disposal.[146] The first expeditions to Africa sought ore and local markets where precious metals could be traded.

Portugal fulfilled one of the aims of the expansion begun with the conquest of Ceuta (1415) when she subsequently established maritime contact with the Akan peoples, who controlled the gold-bearing area between the Komoé and Volta Rivers.[147]

The castle of São Jorge da Mina was built in 1482 to the West of Cape Three Points, a promontory at the entry of the Gulf of Guinea. Erected with stones and construction materials precast in Portugal, the castle, later called Elmina, was the first European building erected south of the Sahara "after the creation of the world had been given," as Renaissance geographer Duarte Pacheco Pereira wrote.[148] Pope Sixtus IV lent power and legitimacy to the Crown by conceding in 1481 full indulgence to any Christian who died in the castle, a naval base planted in the center of the Gold Coast (present-day Ghana). For Catholics steeped in religious practices and bound to the traditional life, death, and funeral rituals of Iberian villages, papal grace was certainly much appreciated.

Much of the importance of Elmina derived from the gold obtained in its trading post. Elmina gold was worth three times its local price when it reached Lisbon.[149] Other Europeans, however, intervened in the area. At the same time, the Elmina castle royal factor (*feitor*) complained in 1510 of the "turbulence" caused to the port of trade by the dealings of the Mandinka in the hinterland. Traveling from Timbuktu, the main trade center of Western Sudan, a ten-month march away from Elmina, the Mandinka traders purchased gold and sold Senegambia fabrics valued by the Akan.[150] In response, Lisbon set up combined transactions, trading European, Asian, and African goods all along the coast.

The Akan often bought slaves from the Portuguese in Elmina, using them as prospectors, bearers of trade goods, and in other activities.[151] From 1482, the date of the castle's construction, to the mid-1500s, when the trade with Spanish America and Brazil took off, around 30,000 individuals from the Slave Coast and the Congo were sold by the Portuguese slave traders at the Elmina castle.[152]

At the same time, exports of sub-Saharan captives to the Iberian Peninsula set the black and mulatto enslavement and commodification as a modern habitus. Lisbon and Seville included a significant number of black slaves by the middle of the sixteenth century.[153] As recompense for their services to the Crown, seamen and royal officials could import slaves without paying taxes on their return to Portugal.[154] Since 1509, a Regimento (statute) prescribed the surveying of slave ships, the procedure to assess and tax the value of the enslaved, as well as the care of the sick by Lisbon's port authorities.[155] In the same way, a 1518 royal edict, concerning the Senegambia's slave trade to Elmina and Lisbon through São Tomé, regulated for the first time in Europe the management of slave-ship decks, the use of the branding iron, and the feeding, selecting, and care of the enslaved before, during, and after transportation.[156] Such rules and practices and exchange networks shaped the early stages of the Atlantic slave trade.

For at that point, slave trafficking was a source of income for the Royal Treasury. Hence, fiscal benefits accrued on top of the economic gains from the slave system. Despite the Coimbra and Évora Courts' protests and Portuguese slave-owners' complaints concerning the increase in the domestic price of enslaved Africans, King Afonso V (1477–1481) refused to ban the re-export of slaves introduced into Portugal. In fact, the Casa dos Escravos was founded in 1486, as a royal department integrated into the Casa da Mina e Tratos de Guiné that managed the Portuguese West African trade.[157]

Notwithstanding the surge in prices for Africans recorded in Portugal from 1560 to 1570, the Crown did not give priority to metropolitan demands and encouraged the sale of slaves to Spanish America.[158] In the great Atlantic slaving business, the Portuguese demand for slaves—either metropolitan or colonial—was far from enjoying exclusivity. Up until 1600, the Portuguese had introduced 122,000 enslaved Africans into the Americas. Yet Brazilian ports received only a quarter of this total.[159] Slaves from the African Portuguese ports continued to be exported abroad, with the aim of increasing the Treasury's income, a strategy clearly achieved in the Luso-Spanish *Asientos* between 1594 and 1640.

After the Braganza Restoration (1640), despite repeated edicts by King Felipe IV prohibiting his vassals from trading with the "Portuguese rebels," King João IV of Braganza was quick to authorize the sale of Africans to Spaniards in America, provided they reserved a third of the slaves for the Brazilian market.[160] The lesson learned from the Iberian royal monopoly's failure in the East influenced the decision to make this commercial opening. Indeed, the continental blockade imposed on the English and Dutch by Felipe II led to disastrous consequences in the Pacific and in the Portuguese Atlantic. Banned from purchasing Asian goods in Lisbon warehouses, the two new Protestant sea powers seized the Estado da Índia's enclaves and trading posts, and invaded parts of Portuguese America and Africa. For this reason, it was better for Lisbon to open the Angolan market to Spain than to have her armada and slavers sailing into Luanda bay. In 1647, the free sale of African slaves to Spanish America was confirmed and the reservation of one-third of the slaves for Brazil was eliminated.[161]

Four years later Lisbon's Conselho Ultramarino (the advisory council to the king in Lisbon on overseas matters) established a new policy: ships sailing to Angola directly from Spanish America would enjoy preference, for they purchased slaves with silver coins (*patacas*) and paid high duties to the Crown as well. However, ships originating in mainland Spain could not dock at Luanda's port, for they carried fabrics instead of hard currency and thus competed with Portuguese goods. A certain priority was recognized too for the Brazilian demand: "Furthermore, if one type of ship or the other is admitted, there will be a lack of slaves required for the sugar mills in Brazil."[162] However, only in 1751, at the peak of gold mining in Minas Gerais, was there a royal interdiction of the export of Africans to non-Portuguese colonies, thus establishing the exclusivity of Brazilian demand over the supply of African slaves.[163]

The initial dissociation between overseas trade and overseas colonial policy was a reflection of merchant capital's aterritoriality, and it took place both in the slave trade and in slave-based production. Genoese, Florentines, Germans, Dutch, Catalans, Castilians, and Portuguese associated with one another in sugar producing, shipping, and slaving enterprises throughout the eighteenth century, both within and outside of Lusitanian imperial space.[164]

Around 1550, about thirty sugar mills were operated by more than 200 Portuguese craftsmen in Hispaniola, the name that Columbus gave to the island later divided between Haiti and Dominican Republic. Hailing from the Canary Islands, Madeira, or mainland Portugal, sugar masters, planters, bricklayers, carpenters, ironsmiths, and other Portuguese artisans brought their crafts over to Hispaniola. At the height of sugar-cane production, from 1560 to 1570, there were between 12,000 and 20,000 African slaves on the island, mostly brought over by the Portuguese. Thanks to the Genoese bankers and the Portuguese slave traders, "sugar masters," and artisans, Hispaniola produced more sugar and relied on more enslaved Africans than Brazil itself. Later, the reorientation of the fleets and of Spanish America's markets due to the rise of the continent's silver mines caused the decline of this first Caribbean plantation economy.[165] In fact, a 1606 census indicates that by that time Hispaniola had only twelve sugar mills remaining, where around 800 slaves worked.[166]

Increasingly, the slave trade emerged as the productive vector of the economy of the Atlantic islands. Even where activities revolved around wheat cultivation and free labor—as in the island of Madeira—African slavery, in the end, became significant.[167] The African slave trade and slavery had grown in the archipelago since the first decades of the sixteenth century.[168] A key text concerning Madeira provides a means for understanding the shift in which slavery (the legal apparatus allowing the transformation of the direct producer into private property) converted into a slave system (a form of colonial production based on slave labor and integrated into the world-system). Further, this text also shows the comparative advantages of the slave system over free labor in Atlantic sugar plantations. This text was the 1562 royal law sent by Lisbon to the Madeira Island planters: "Concerning the great expenses faced by owners on their plantations and sugar mills in Madeira, with laborers and men paid in wages and by the day; and how some of said owners, afraid they might not meet such expenses, often give up cultivating the soil and end up not getting as much sugar as they would *if they had their own slaves* continually working on the plantations and tending the crop; . . . since such a fact leads the owners of those properties to incur heavy losses, and my taxes suffer (too) . . . it is my wish to give them place and permission to fit a (yearly) ship in the said Island of Madeira . . . to go barter [*resgatar*] for slaves in the rivers of Guinea . . . according to each of the said owners' need for slaves"[169] (italics added).

The meaning of this document is clear. Given the experience accumulated by the Crown, it was understood that both royal income and the plantations' productivity would increase as soon as the Upper Guinea's slaves substituted the Madeira free laborers. By proceeding to make this possible, the king of Portugal offered "place and permission" for the spreading of the slave system, deeply transforming the Atlantic economy and society.[170]

In the course of the evolution that began in the mid-1400s, the Portuguese slave traffic developed on the periphery of the metropolitan economy and of African exchanges. The trade then became a source of income for the Crown and responded to the demand for slaves from other European regions. Finally, Africans were used to consolidate overseas commodity production.

In the last quarter of the sixteenth century, Portuguese America appeared as an attractive market for slave traders. Until then, only 2,400 enslaved Africans had been disembarked in Brazil, while Spanish America—where their entry had been regular since 1510—received around 85,000.[171] In the same time, the Atlantic Islands (Canary Islands, Madeira, Cape Verde) and São Tomé, connected to the slaving trade since the end of the fifteenth century, had imported 124,000 enslaved.[172]

After 1580, Brazilian sugar was the first-place product among Lisbon's overseas territories. At this time, Portuguese American sugar mills produced around 9,831 metric tons per year, while those in São Tomé and Madeira, declining for different reasons, as we shall see below, produced 3,000 tons and 588 tons of sugar per year, respectively.[173]

Initially based on Amerindian slavery and coerced labor, the development of the Brazilian sugar became a tributary of African forced migrations. This change occurred in response to a series of circumstances that will be examined.

The Slave Trade as an Instrument of Colonial Policy

The Crown's action is sketched out in the origin of the productive process established in Portuguese America. Stimulated by tax exemptions published in the 1554 royal warrant (*alvará*), the building of sugar mills was given further support by the 1559 warrant, which allowed each sugar mill owner to import 120 Africans at the rate of only a third of the usual taxes.[174] Such measures attracted to Brazilian plantations a segment of the forced migrations formerly directed toward the Caribbean.

Gradually, in successive stages that were mostly regular and generally predictable, the slave trade with Brazil tied Portugal's African enclaves to the Atlantic exchanges. Far from being contradictory, the events that took place on the American and African coasts clarify one another through a series of reciprocal effects. The deportation of Africans to American plantations progressively synchronized various stages of the colonial system. This consolidation was activated on different levels.

The metropolis was invested with preeminent power, to the degree that control of the slave trade gave it control over the reproduction of the slave system. For three centuries, economic complementarities tied Africa to Brazil, making remote the possibility of diverging, let alone competing, developments between Portuguese tropical enclaves on both sides of the South Atlantic. However, the relevance of the Angola's trade to the South American plantations was clearly evaluated by Lisbon in mid-seventeenth century, when the Dutch invasions exposed the strategic unity of the two colonial spaces. Up until then, it was sometimes thought that Portuguese Africa could become another Brazil.

André Álvares de Almada, the first Luso-African author from Cape Verde, concluded his *Tratado Breve* (1594) by emphasizing Upper Guinea's riches: "The populating (of Guinea) would make it a bigger market than Brazil, because in Brazil there is no more than sugar, brazilwood and cotton; whereas this land has the cotton and the wood that one finds in Brazil, plus ivory, beeswax, gold, amber, maleguetta pepper, and many sugar mills can be built; and there is iron, abundant firewood for the (furnaces of) sugar mills and slaves to work at them."[175] In the same period, a settler from Sierra Leone compared its products advantageously with Brazil's, recalling that the local ports were much closer to Lisbon.[176] Further, settlers in Angola had enslaved Africans in rural properties similar to the *fazendas* of Portuguese America.[177] Accordingly, the Crown regularly sent instructions stating that sugar cane was to be cultivated there, "as it is done in Brazil." To do so, the *Angolistas* (the Portuguese settlers in Angola and their descendants) were conceded the same tax exemptions, plus "privileges and favors" granted to the sugar mill owners in Portuguese America.[178] Governor Fernão de Sousa's royal directives, signed in 1624, included new incentives, offering to Angola's settlers who would build sugar mills along the shores of the Bengo and Cuanza Rivers "broader privileges and favors than those given to (settlers) of Brazil."[179] Through bureaucratic routine, the topic came to be included in other Angola governors' directives.

Yet in 1655, the Luanda municipal council made clear that the enterprise ran up against local obstacles (lack of firewood and the bad quality of African sugar cane) and, above all, it sailed against the South Atlantic network. Given Luanda's trade routes, with little direct transportation to Lisbon and a continuous slave trade to Portuguese America, the cotton and sugar eventually produced in Angola had to call at Brazilian ports before sailing on to Portugal. Burdened with freight coasts, the Angolan commodities could not compete with their Brazilian analogue, rendering the whole scheme unviable.[180]

Drawing the consequences of the problems that the Luanda municipal counselors made explicit to the Crown for the new division of labor in the South Atlantic, the Angolan governors' royal directives ceased to include the clause recommending the cultivation of cotton and sugar cane, as well as the establishment of sugar mills.[181] For three centuries, the colonial and native farms of West Central Africa skated across the regional economy, selling maize, manioc flour, and beans to the local communities and the slave traders. The cards to be played in the South Atlantic game had been dealt: Angola would not export sugar and São Tomé's furnaces were to cool down.[182] Colonization was to be complementary, not competitive: Brazil would produce sugar, tobacco, cotton, coffee; Portuguese Africa would provide slaves. The project of creating "another Brazil" in Angola gained an outline only in the nineteenth century, when the Brazilian slave trade was extinguished and the "second colonial period" began.[183]

The Crown and royal administration found new income sources in the slave trade. Such incomes were provided by export duties in African ports, from entrance fees in Brazilian ports, from "donations," "subsidies," "preferences," and sales taxes (*alcavalas*), as well as other duties successively levied on the owners and traders of enslaved Africans. The royal administration was not the only beneficiary of such income. There was also a tax paid to the clergy for the compulsory baptism of each deported African in the ports of origin, in addition to slave export franchises conceded to the Jesuits and to the Missions Board (*Junta das Missões*).[184]

In his economic treatise *Suma de tratos y contratos* (1571), Thomas de Mercado, the Spanish Dominican friar and jurist, had already dubbed the Portuguese tributary legislation on slaves a "labyrinth." "A pandemonium," stated Mauricio Goulart four centuries later, unknowingly sharing the frustration of his illustrious predecessor.[185] Despite such difficulties, it is possible to calculate that, around 1630, an enslaved African entered Brazil burdened with tributes equivalent to 20 percent of his price at the port of origin, and to Spanish America with taxes corresponding to 66 percent of his price in Angola. In the second half of the seventeenth century, taxes on exports to Brazil reached up to 28 percent, leading Angola's chief justice (*ouvidor-geral*) to consider a slave the most taxed commercial item of the overseas territory.[186] Fresh taxes were established in 1710 on enslaved blacks and mulattos sold from Pernambuco, Bahia, and Rio de Janeiro to inland Minas Gerais. From

1809 on, a 5 percent tax was levied on the purchase and sale of slaves throughout Brazilian territory.[187]

Up to the first half of the seventeenth century, Portugal derived other advantages from its quasimonopoly over the slave trade. Thanks to its dominance in this sector, the Portuguese penetrated the Castilian Indies, defeated the Spanish monopoly on silver, acquired gold, and speculated on regional produce such as Venezuelan cocoa exported to Mexico.[188]

The triangular confrontation between the royal administration, settlers, and the Jesuits was provisionally avoided. The introduction of enslaved Africans rendered the evangelization of Amerindians easier, relieving indigenous communities from the slavery and coerced labor imposed by settlers and colonial authorities. As we shall see below, it also contributed to the reduction of the autonomy that settlers enjoyed when they kept control over Amerindian labor.[189]

The first serious clash between a donatary captain and the metropolitan bureaucracy took place in the captaincy of Porto Seguro, and concerned, among other issues, Amerindian labor. Donatary Pero do Campo Tourinho had an argument with the local vicar. He was then accused of heresy, imprisoned, put in chains, and taken to the Inquisition Tribunal in Lisbon. The interrogation, made in 1550, when Tourinho had already been jailed for four years, detailed the accusations:

> Asked whether he had said that no day of Our Lady, nor the Apostles or Saints holiday was to be kept in his captaincy . . . so much so that he had ordered his (Amerindian) servants to work in such days, he denied doing so; but, instead, he did order them to keep such days and to celebrate; he only sometimes told the vicar off (. . .) since the priest had ordered the keeping of the days of Saint William, Saint Martin and Saint George and other saints that the Holy Mother Church did not order to be kept, nor did the prelates observe such days in their own constitutions, because the land (Porto Seguro) was new and it was necessary to work in order to populate it.[190]

Ultimately, Tourinho was found innocent. Having had enough, he decided to remain in Portugal and did not return to Brazil. Enduring attacks of the Aymoré Indians, most of the settlers abandoned his captaincy.[191]

The conflict between the colonists' mercantile productivity and the evangelization (or, perhaps more accurately, "compassionate exploitation," to use Claude

Meillassoux's expression) of the Amerindians carried out by the clergy would be eased by the African's enslavement. Two of the most resolute protectors of the Amerindians, Spanish Dominican Las Casas in the sixteenth century and Portuguese Jesuit Antônio Vieira in the seventeenth century, suggested to their respective Crowns recourse to the African slave trade to free Amerindians from the servitude imposed on them by the settlers.[192]

The Jesuits would quarrel with settlers in areas where the slave trade had not penetrated and where Amerindian coerced labor prevailed. Insofar as their temporal power increased, based on credit control, landed property, and, mainly in Amazonia, forest exploitation and management of Amerindian villages, the Jesuits made new enemies. Contention dragged on into the 1750s, when the Society of Jesus was expelled from Portugal and its overseas possessions. In a certain sense, this conflict demonstrated the political unavailability of the American enclaves based on Amerindian coerced labor and located outside metropolitan control.

Portuguese merchants combined the advantages of a position of oligopsony (in the purchase of sugar) with the advantages inherent to an oligopoly (in the sale of slaves). Sustained by brokers and royal officials of Angola, the Mina Coast and Senegambia, these merchants facilitated the sale of enslaved Africans by providing credit to the planters in order to control the commercialization of plantation products.[193] The lack of currency in Portuguese colonies in the sixteenth and seventeenth centuries and the intensification of Atlantic exchanges shaped direct credit. In Brazil, sugar was exchanged for enslaved Africans.[194] In Luanda and other West Central African ports, standard units of barter goods (called *banzos*) were furnished to local middlemen on the condition that they were to be exchanged for slaves.[195] Slaves and *panos*, a piece of cloth measuring one by two meters, were the standard measure of value in Upper Guinea. Reflecting the rising prices triggered by the *asentistas*' purchases, one slave was worth 120 *panos* in 1613–1614 and 150 *panos* in 1616–1618.[196]

Of course, South American planters kept on exporting brazilwood during the sugar low season.[197] Likewise, on the other side of the ocean, slave exports did not exclude trade in several African products. Portugal imported ivory and Brazil carried beeswax (valued for making fine candles and for waterproofing sails) from Angola and fabrics from the Senegambia and the Niger Delta until the mid-nineteenth century. Yet all such exchanges took place because of the slave trade, and did not survive its end.[198]

Exchanges between Portugal and Brazil widened. In the macroeconomic sphere, the Atlantic slave trade enlarged demand and increased the porousness of Brazilian colonial economy: the slave trade became a privileged instrument for showing the way forward to colonial complementarities. Its consequences were also relevant on the microeconomic level. Given that the potential profits of plantations and sugar mills served as a guarantee for the purchase of new factors of production (slaves), the surplus was invested productively: slaves represented one-fifth of a sugar mill's investment and half the amount invested by sugar-cane growers (*lavradores de cana*).[199] At the same time, the transfer of the productive sector's income to the mercantile sector, a crucial factor for the realization of colonial exploitation, was thereby assured.

With regard to imports from Europe, aside from the purchase of equipment for the sugar mills, several authors emphasize the weight of luxury products bought by the planters and sugar mill owners.[200] Research carried out by Stuart Schwartz has shown, however, that such assets—jewelry, table silver, furniture, clothing, religious objects, and books—were a minor item in foreign purchases of the colony's seigneurial class.[201] In any case, ostentatiously employed in households or in the landlords' social presentation, the slave also became a luxury item. One of the most ingrained traces of Brazilian traditional society is the habit of counting the number of domestic servants as a sign of wealth. Obviously, the captive's eventual "qualification" did not change the essence of his or her economic and legal character. Whatever his or her function, aptitude, or color, the slave remained a factor of production and a tradable good. Therefore, the slave could also be "downgraded"—reintegrated into fieldwork or sold—at the master's convenience. It is also clear that the ostentatious behavior of the ruling class contributed to increased demand for Africans. As royal officials arrived from the kingdom, they adopted the ostentatious habits of the locals, surrounding themselves with captives in their homes. Whence the warning addressed in 1687 by the Crown to the Pernambuco military officers, who used royal funds to buy their domestic slaves: "I do not give, nor find it necessary to give, (slave) servants to any military officer, for they must be purchased with the regular pay I provide."[202]

Much later, in the mid-nineteenth century, when the free population of Rio de Janeiro was already permeated by the culture diffused by bourgeois Europe, playwright Martins Pena cast a young wealthy Rio de Janeiro man on his way to pay his fiancée a visit. He carried a gift to his sweetheart in a large basket. What was the gift so carefully bundled up? A slave child, "seven or eight years old, wearing a blue loincloth and red cap," meant to become the girl's pageboy.[203]

Over the long term, access to credit and the anticipated purchase of slaves favored colonial planters as well. Considering the magnitude of the investment in the slave trade during the Portuguese monopoly over the *Asiento* and the ease of the South Atlantic routes, the supply of enslaved Africans became more regular and flexible than that of enslaved Amerindians. In addition, the circumstances of enslavement—the long marches toward the ports, the successive barters of the enslaved before embarkment, as well as the crossing of the Atlantic, the selling in America, and the violence suffered on arrival in the plantations—submitted the slaves to intense desocialization.[204] In his *Tratado da Terra do Brasil* (1570), Gandavo observed the social and economic advantages of the initial desocialization of the Africans in America: "One of the reasons that keeps Brazil from growing even more are the [Amerindian] slaves' rebellions and daily escapes to their land . . . there are also [in Brazil] many slaves from Guinea, who are more constant than Indians and who don't escape [because] they have no place to go."[205]

Unlike the Amerindians, whose high mortality was due to their vulnerability to the "viral and microbial shock" caused by the Discoveries, many Africans had been partially immunized against the predominant Mediterranean and tropical African epidemics.[206] At the turn of the 1500s, Brandão noticed that Amerindians from Brazil, when brought over to Portugal, "died hurriedly," for they came from "such a healthy land," whereas Asians or Africans, originating from a "sick land," were able to survive in Europe.[207] Besides Old World and Asian diseases, yellow fever, the most lethal species of malaria (*Plasmodium falciparum*), and ancylostomiasis (*amarelão*), maladies originating from Western Africa, contaminated the American tropical enclaves, generating an epidemiological environment particularly hostile to whites and Amerindians.[208] Hence, the Atlantic slave trade increased the morbidity and mortality of free and captive Amerindians alike, leading settlers to increase the demand for enslaved Africans. All these factors converged into a process of colonial repopulation based on the implantation of European colonists and African slaves.

The Iberian powers in the Canary Islands and the Caribbean had experimented with such a mode of colonial exploitation, leading to the annihilation of both indigenous populations, the Guanches in the Canaries and the Taínos in the Caribbean. Later, it also condemned the Amerindian communities surrounded by the expansion of ranches and plantations in Portuguese America.[209]

Completing his *Brevísima relación de la destrucción de las Indias* in the 1550s, Las Casas discusses the Iberian invasion of the Canary Islands in the previous century. In doing so, he interprets the extermination of the Guanches, mainly in Tenerife, in parallel with the African slave trade to the islands as a process transposed on a large scale to Iberian America, where the natives were decimated along with the introduction of the enslaved Africans.[210]

Of course, Amerindian coerced labor continued to be used extensively in the Amazon basin and the colonial enclaves far from Atlantic networks. Nonetheless, following the reconquest of Angola by the Luso-Brasílico task force in 1648 and the incorporation of the slave-trade circuits, until then serving the *Asiento* in Spanish America, and the decline of the coastal Amerindians, the royal authorities considered the slave system as the dominant factor of South Atlantic's colonial exploitation.

Two mid-seventeenth century reports, elaborated in Lisbon by palatine councils, recorded the lessons learned from the changes that occurred after the Portuguese Restoration. For the Revenue Council of the Exchequer (*Conselho da Fazenda*), there was no doubt about the system set up in three parts of the Atlantic: Angola was the "nerve of Brazil's sugar mills," whose income represented the "chief substance of this Crown."[211] The Overseas Council (*Conselho Ultramarino*), in its turn, examined the potential for precious-metal mines in the Portuguese territories. At that time, the war against Felipe IV had closed Portuguese access to the Spanish empire's ores. Pressed by the scarcity of gold and silver in foreign markets, the Braganza monarchy increased the fiscal pressure on the kingdom, coming into conflict with the opposition to the taxation "malady" that had already fueled the revolt against Spain's Crown.[212]

To avoid troubles in the metropolis, it was necessary to expand colonial exploitation. Recalling the difficulties surrounding Angolan and Mozambican mines, the Council pointed to a more favorable situation in Brazil. To the councilors, the proximity to Peru gave Brazil a better chance of containing precious metals. Actually, small silver and gold mines were being exploited in Paranaguá (modern state of Paraná).[213] How could mining activities in the American colony be widened? The councilors took for granted that "a great number of Indians are today destroyed." For them, there was no more Indian labor available for the mines to be exploited in Brazilian latitudes near to Potosí. Under such circumstances, the Council understood that only the Angolan slave trade could "sustain" Brazil.

It was not just demographic concerns about colonial Indians—natives under Portuguese control—that guided the Overseas Council's statement.[214] Among the four councilors signing the report, three had direct connections with the Atlantic slave trade. One of them had gained a high profile in the court and in overseas politics: Salvador de Sá e Benevides, a member of the Rio de Janeiro oligarchy, reconqueror and ex-governor of Angola, mentor of the expeditions launched beyond the Mantiqueira sierra in search of silver, gold and emeralds.[215]

A few decades later, with the discovery of gold in Minas Gerais, the search for precious metals met with success. However, since mid-1600s, a fundamental factor in the evolution of Portuguese America and independent Brazil had been defined: the "xenophagy" of the Brazilian economy, that is, its proclivity to aggregate the human labor reproduced outside its productive space. This historical feature is the convergent result of the planters' demand and of the African slave-traders' pressure on the supply side.

After the ending of the Atlantic Slave Trade (1850), the demand for foreign labor also resulted from power relations in Brazil. To avoid interregional dissensions, the Parliament and Rio de Janeiro's central government preferred to sustain the deterritorialization of the Brazilian labor market. Insofar as São Paulo's coffee planters drew mostly on the immigrants, Northeast sugar mills' owners accordingly held their labor reserve.[216]

Demand and Supply of African Slaves: What Is the "Primum Mobile?"

A sketch of the social forces driving the colonial system can be drawn from the demands and memorials written by the settlers.

It is surely correct that the colonists had been complaining about the "lack of hands," that is, coerced labor, since the seventeenth century. It is also true that they protested, around the same time—more surprisingly—the "lack of land."[217] Actually, the plantation and mining economy was under constant pressure from European demand. In such a context, land and labor were not independent factors but, rather, variables resulting from the motive forces ruling merchant capitalism. Whether intentional or not, the effects induced by the slave trade ensured an accumulation peculiar to merchant capitalism and to the *Pax Lusitana* in the Atlantic.

More than any other, the slave trade was an administered trade. As has been suggested, metropolitan control over the reproduction of American slavery—the political instance of the colonial system—played a decisive role in the Atlantic system. It is also evident that the trade in African slaves reached a significant volume, and above all, a high degree of integration with the Atlantic market, even before being connected to plantations of Portuguese America.

Under submission to the European power controlling the largest portion of the market for enslaved Africans for three centuries, and by his own decision after his independence (1822), Brazil became America's biggest slave importer, as sharply demonstrated in figure 1.1. In parallel, Angola became the area from which most of the Africans were deported. In practice, profiting from the winds and currents of the South Atlantic gyre, voyages to Brazil from West Africa were 40 percent shorter than those to the Caribbean.[218]

Truly, the new data estimates are impressive and rather somber to today's Brazilian, Portuguese, and Angolan citizens. Portuguese or Brazilian flagged vessels carried the majority (46.7 percent) of the deportees crossing the entire Atlantic during three-and-a-half centuries. Rio de Janeiro and Salvador da Bahia were the two most important American slave-trade ports. On the other shore of the Atlantic, Luanda came to be the largest port of embarkation of enslaved Africans.[219]

A sometimes overlooked connection in Portuguese America's history, such an overwhelming system of human commodification documents that the slave trade was not a secondary effect of slavery. This characteristic distinguishes Luso-Brazilian slavery from its American counterparts and imposes an aterritorial interpretation for the formation of contemporary Brazil.

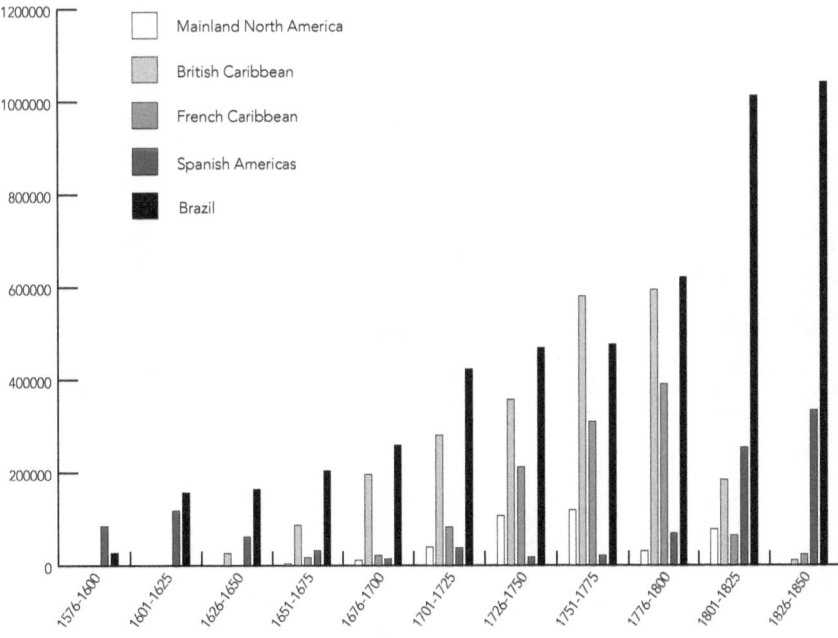

Figure 1.1. Slaves Arriving in the Main Americas Regions 1576–1850. *Source:* TSTD.

Chapter 2

Africans, "the Slaves from Guinea"[1]

The emergence of the transatlantic slave trade intensified the accumulation of capital goods and the exchange of merchandise in sub-Saharan societies. Long-distance trade, spread throughout the sub-Sahelian regions, favored forced migration in 1500s Africa.[2] To a lesser extent, long-distance exchanges had also occurred in West Central Africa.[3] Located between the Cuanza and Longa Rivers, south of Luanda, the Demba rock-salt mines of Kisama, an important source of salt-money, drove a significant pre-European network trade that lasted until the early nineteenth century.[4]

Atlantic routes redirected the continental networks, dragging hinterland exchanges into the world-economy. The role played by modern slavery and African products in the formation of the world market has always been emphasized. Other studies have provided evidence of the importance of the African intracontinental exchanges and the variety of European, American, and Asian goods imported into African states or decentralized societies.[5] Ultimately, the sixteenth century sub-Saharan market resembled Asian markets much more than American, in view of the grand totals yielded by foreign trade, the reach of its exchange networks, and the density of its domestic economy.

Incidentally, the phrase "China's trade" (*negócio da China*), possibly coined in Portugal at the beginning of the exchanges with the Far East and defining a very lucrative transaction, corresponds to an 1800s Brazilianism deriving from the slave trade: "Mina Coast trade" (*negócio da Costa da Mina*).[6] Accordingly, Asia and Africa, Macao and the Mina Coast, the two rings at the extreme points of the Portuguese circulation economy, were imprinted on the imaginary of the lusophone merchants as synonyms for a safe and profitable trade. This notwithstanding, the overseas trade in Africa and Asia involved operations of great complexity.

Initially, the traffic in slaves took place along certain sections of the coast, since the continental trade was taking place along the north-south axis or toward

Eastern Sudan markets. Camel caravans trooped "against the sea" and "still have no knowledge" of the caravels anchored off the coast, wrote Zurara in the middle of the fifteenth century.[7] His *Crônica de Guiné* (1453–1460) offers a glimpse of the slave trade's precarious nature, still based on "roping" raids, akin to the way captives were caught in the skirmishes of the Iberian Reconquest.[8]

With regard to the flotilla that arrived in 1455 at the delta of the Senegal River, Zurara narrates the tribulations of novice Portuguese slaver Estevão Afonso. Anchored offshore, a group of Algarve corsairs advanced upriver on foot, ambushing persons along the banks.[9] Suddenly, Estevão hears a sound and soon sees a Guinean chopping wood. "Estevão went on his way, and, with the good cover he gave his unhurried steps and the intent that the Guinean had on his work, he never saw the other (Estevão) coming, only when he was jumped on. I say jumped because Estevão Afonso was thin and lightly built, and the Guinean much the opposite. And he firmly grabbed the Guinean's hair, who, on straightening his back, caused Estevão Afonso to lift off the ground, feet dangling." Months later, in the Canary Islands, in a similar throw, Estevão Afonso tackled a Guanche he intended to enslave—but it ended badly for the Portuguese man, as Estevão was killed by his would-be prey.[10]

It is easy to understand that the pillage (from the Latin *piliare*, "grab by the hair") of African villages by European corsairs and pirates alone would not meet the mounting demand for slaves in the Iberian Peninsula, in the Canary Islands, in the Madeira Islands and Cape Verde, even before the discovery of America. Indeed, the Portuguese in Upper Guinea did not remain with their feet dangling for long.[11]

The last paragraphs of Zurara's *Crônica* point to the changes in the operation of African ports. "The affairs that followed were not dealt with so much labor and force as in the past; from this year (1460) onwards, the deeds in those parts were done more by accord and trade agreements than by force or by the labor of arms."[12] Although looting was not abandoned, exchanges set to dates previously agreed on, at fixed locations, were more often the case in the harbors and dealers' meeting havens.

As recorded by Leo Africanus, Cá Da Mosto, and other Renaissance travelers, the negotiating and trading posts (*postos de tratos e avenças*) embedded in the Age of Discovery's cartography correspond to the institutions defined by Polanyi as "ports of trade." Here, trade remained circumscribed, leaving no room for a market.[13] Exchanges took place inside enclaves made neutral by mutual agreement, in which prices were arranged between foreign dealers and indigenous authorities and merchants.[14]

Fairs and ports of trade contributed to the widening of the sub-Saharan African slave market.[15] But they find no equivalent in lowland South America, where there has never been a social basis apt to generate an indigenous slave trade. The Campos de Piratininga—future São Paulo—"stopover for many Indian nations," as the Jesuit Luís da Grã noted—constituted a trading post where João Ramalho and his men were intermediates in the selling of Indians captured in the São Paulo plateau down the sierra, with their destination Santos. However, Indian slave demand in seaside Santos and São Vicente declined as the maritime routes were redirected toward the north of Brazil. Some local settlers then moved into the plateau and transformed Piratininga into a community of Portuguese and Luso-Indians raiders and sharecroppers employing slave and coerced Indian labor in local farms and households.[16]

Pre-European commercial geography favored Portuguese merchants' access to Upper Guinea trade. Rivers navigated by the Upper Guinea traders, and in particular the Senegal, the Cacheu, and the Gambia, brought exchange goods down to the seashore. A network of exchanges with the Niger basin radiated from the Senegal River, connecting a mercantile system of rivers, lagoons, and land routes to the Gulf of Guinea.[17] In Senegambia, slaves and ivory were exchanged for European goods, and particularly for iron bars. Barely produced locally, iron bars were used by coastal communities as currency, and to forge weapons. Its imports involved regional chieftaincies and stateless societies with slave traders.[18]

In the places where such preconditions were not in place, assembling the slave traffic proved to be problematic. Almada observed in 1594 that two groups of Jola, the "Arriatas" and the "Falupes" (Felup), from the south margin of the Gambia and Casamance Rivers, "do not have a slave trade because they do not trade with ours [traffickers]."[19] Makhroufi Traoré scrutinized the factors that substantiated the Soninke of the Galam's refusal to engage in the Atlantic slave trafficking. Isolation from the Senegal fluvial network, economic and fiscal practices formed by the control of Galam's and Bambuck's gold mines, and lastly, the political divide between the princely families of the Bacili dynasty and the Juula marabout merchants, engendered the enduring resistance of the Galam to the Atlantic slave trade.[20]

Farther south, in Benguela, a Portuguese report on certain cattle-raising communities, probably the Mukuando, explicitly recorded in 1618: "In this kingdom, there is no slave trade because it is not their practice to sell one another." Later, the deadlock remained: "They never wanted to pay tribute [*baculamentos*] nor sell slaves because they don't usually do so, and only tend to their seedbeds and the cattle they raise." Such activities, the document concluded, present "no interest to H.M. Treasury."[21]

Raids by the Portuguese and the Jaga in the second half of the seventeenth century destabilized the area's communities, dragging them into the Portuguese, Brasílico, and then, after 1822, Brazilian slave trades. Up to 1850, Benguela would deport around 500,000 individuals from South Angola to slavery in Brazil, mainly to Rio de Janeiro and Recife.[22] In the 1820s, seeking to continue the slave trade, the Benguela colonists organized a sedition movement intent on joining independent Brazil.[23]

Ultimately, the Wolof, horse importers and first sub-Saharan people to sell slaves to the Europeans, along with the Berber, the Serer, the Fulani, the Hausa, and the Mandinka (Mandinga), circulated between the Mediterranean and Sudan among deserts and savannahs, shepherds and farmers, blacks and Moors. In 1625, Donelha considered the Mandinka as "the greatest traders there are in Guinea."[24] Estimates indicate that the trans-Saharan trade of black slaves and Sudanese gold sustained a steady flux during the Middle Ages. In the sixteenth century, around 5,500 individuals were deported annually from West Africa through the Sahara, while 2,766 left their land yearly, pushed into the European maritime slave trade.[25] Indeed, since the Discoveries, Portuguese and Cape Verde Luso-African boats pierced Moorish terrestrial exchange networks, draining the trans-sahelian trade through Atlantic navigation.[26] By resorting to Portuguese coastal factories, "the land of Guinea was bled of the gold it contained within . . . which did not reach Moorish hands, who came for it over so many deserts in camel trains," argued João de Barros (c. 1545).[27]

Besides gold, the enslaved Africans—*peças da Índia*—stood out as a profitable investment.[28] Attentive to price fluctuations in the oceanic trade, the directors of the Casa da Mina e Tratos da Guiné (the royal agency entrusted with overseeing and collecting duties on the trade with the sub-Saharan region) instructed their agents to acquire less ivory and more Africans in the year 1523, a high-price season for slaves in the Atlantic.[29]

To avoid the long and deadly transshipments in European ports, the Crown authorized the direct embarkation of Caribbean-bound slaves from Cape Verde and São Tomé. From then on, the African deportations increased, chiefly after the

Manco Capac Inca revolt in 1535. Little inclined to flight that would expose them to hostile Indians, enslaved Africans became valuable in Peru.[30] At the same time, the shipping of captives to the metropolis and to the Atlantic islands declined.[31]

Celebrated verses by Garcia de Rezende portray the profit of the slave trade to Seville, Lisbon, Setúbal, Cape Verde, Madeira and the Canary Islands, São Tomé, and into the Caribbean.

> Great sum arrives in Portugal,
> Every year and also in the Islands,
> An affair of riches prodigal, /
> Which trebles the capital /
> In Castile and Antilles. (*Miscellanea*, 1554)[32]

Whites and mulattos, called *lançados* (castoffs)[33] or *tangomaos* by the Portuguese, crisscrossed the rivers of Upper Guinea trading foreign and local wares.[34] Adventurers, deportees, banished New Christians, the castoffs, operating along the outer lanes of metropolitan monopoly, relayed the European impact inland away from the coast. Dressing in indigenous ways, scarring their faces with the marks of local ethnic groups, the castoffs were the first Portuguese—and the first Europeans—to adapt to the tropics. "They walk naked for comfort, and . . . taking up the uses of the gentiles [natives] of the land they deal in, they scratch the whole body with an iron . . . (so that) they form many figures, such as lobsters, serpents . . . and . . . they tread all over Guinea dealing and buying slaves," wrote a Jesuit chronicler.[35] Since the last quarter of the fifteenth century, the *lançados* did business in the delta of the Senegal River.

In the 1570s, the New Christian *lançado* João Ferreira, nicknamed by the Fulani Gana-Goga ("the man who speaks all languages"), went 300 km up the Gambia River, entered the Fulani kingdom court, and married a local princess. With his relatives and agents, he snatched any sizeable business in Senegambia.[36] The castoff Gana-Goga played in Guinea a much more important role than the shipwrecked Portuguese nicknamed Caramuru did in the Brazilian shore of Bahia.[37] Embodying alliances between local traders, Gana-Goga and other *lançados* expanded Portuguese and European penetration in Upper Guinea. One small slave dealer in West Central Africa summarized in 1539 his expatriation from Portugal's penury into the African pillage in the world-economy. "For fourteen years and over I have been in this kingdom of Congo, where I came to flee the miserable poverty (of Portugal)."[38]

Alongside slaves and gold, Upper Guinea's export agenda included ivory, amber, wax, musk, hides, Arabic gum, kola nut, ivory, copper, and malagueta peppers.³⁹ Breton, Flemish, Portuguese, and North African goods arrived for exchange, as well as iron from the Nordic countries and Biscay; Iberian wine and spirits; horses from Spain, Morocco, and Cape Verde; and beads from India (*miçangas*).⁴⁰ Regarding the horse trade, the Portuguese employed a special type of ship, the *taforeias*, that they used also in the Indian Ocean to import mounts from Ormuz to Goa during the first decades of the sixteenth century.⁴¹

Linda Newson's analysis on the accounts of Antonio Nunes da Costa, associate of Manuel Batista Peres, one of the most important slave traders of the vice kingdom of Peru, offers more indications on their business in Senegambia. Like several merchants established at the Asian enclaves, Manuel Batista Peres and Antonio Nunes da Costa were affiliated with the networks of Portuguese New Christians that drove oceanic exchanges during the Iberian Union.

A dweller in Cacheu, Nunes da Costa registered accounts covering the years 1616–1620, showing the mix of goods and merchant networks connected to the Atlantic exchanges. Slaves represented 24 percent of his purchases, followed by locally obtained provisions (mainly millet) for the captives' maintenance before shipment and on the Middle Passage (18 percent), and beeswax (14 percent). Half of the slaves were acquired directly from African dealers and the other half from the Portuguese dealers and the *lançados*.⁴² As we will see below, the expenses for food for the captives before their deportation underline the significance of this item in the Atlantic slave-trade operations.

Moreover, exploiting breaks opened by coastal shipping, the Portuguese did triangular transactions. As we mention above, at the turn of the sixteenth century, Portuguese vessels inaugurated the maritime slave trade in West Africa seas, carrying captives from the Bight of Benin and Congo to Elmina. On the right bank of the Senegal River they purchased cattle from the Fulani to exchange for "gold, horses, slaves and other merchandise" in other ports of the area. From the Great Scarcies River (Caces) and the Little Scarcies River (Mitombi), in Sierra Leone, the Portuguese shipped kola nuts to the Geba River (next to Bissau), "the larger marketplace" of the Mandinka traders. There, slaves, ivory, beeswax, and local cloths were exchanged for the kola. Some of those textiles being traded again in other ports.⁴³ The Jesuit Manuel Alvarez, very knowledgeable about the area, writes in his *Ethiopia Menor* (c. 1615) that Mandinka sold Sierra Leone's kola even as far as Mecca.⁴⁴

The combination of such regional and intercontinental exchanges pulled the Upper Guinea trade into the Atlantic networks. French, English, and Flemish vessels traded alongside the Portuguese along the coast from Senegambia to the Mina Coast, from Cap Blanc (modern Mauritania) up to the Cape of Three Points (Ghana). But Portuguese vessels carried more of Senegambia's enslaved from 1600 on, increasing the voyages to Brazil and the Río de la Plata, Vera Cruz, and Cartagena de Índias.[45] Father Manuel Alvarez confirmed in 1615 that the slave trade was the best and most important business of Cacheu, the economic capital of Upper Guinea.[46]

Among the imported goods, three had direct impact on the mercantile creation of slaves: horses, iron bars, and firearms. The Fulani raised the zebu cattle and also *dumbes*, ponies native to Guinea, small animals of little military use.[47] Agile horses, stirrups, saddles, and bridles, brought by the Arabs from the fourteenth century onward, made possible the emergence of a war cavalry south of the Sahara. Cá Da Mosto referred in 1456 to the exchange of African slaves for imported mounts—each horse fetched ten to twenty slaves—involving several slave-trade circuits to the north of the Senegal River.[48] Some of these were trans-Saharan circuits, connected to the Mediterranean. Others, freshly opened, flowed out to the African Atlantic coast, pulled by the Portuguese in the Arguin factory (an island off the coast of present-day Mauritania) or by Genoese merchants.[49] Fifty years later the horse/slave ratio seemed to have decreased a little, but the exchange continued to be profitable: a fitted horse could fetch from nine to fourteen slaves.[50]

Lances, swords, shields, and padded costumes secured the superiority of horsemen in the face of archers and assegai lancers fighting on foot.[51] In the open savannah, the cavalries of the Wolof were viewed as "good horsemen, good warring people" by Almada; the Serer and the Fulani were called "dexterous horsemen and good warriors" by Donelha. In the same way, the Songhay, the Oyo, and the Mossi cavalries facilitated the capture of enemies, that is, the capture of goods suitable for exchange for more horses. The exchange of captives for imported horses must have been constant, since the sleeping sickness carried by the tsetse fly hindered horse breeding in the area. In fact, below Cape Verga (present-day Conakry), no one bought horses, a sign that, yesterday as today, the epidemiological barrier erected by the trypanosomiasis had been reached.[52] Although horse-raising zones emerged in the area, equine imports continued to promote the slave trade in Senegambia.[53]

Hence, the horses that the Fulani purchased from the Berbers to sell to the Wolof, as well as the saddles and the horses brought in by the Europeans, must be considered means of producing slaves.[54] In the beginning of the sixteenth century, several Senegambia rulers were able line up 10,000 horsemen, some sources state.[55] As in medieval Europe, horses were reserved as ostentation goods and for military use.[56] In the wake of conflicts, the demand for mounts increased, as confrontations entangled the Wolof, Mandinka, and Fulani in the conflicts following the decline of the Mali empire.[57]

Based on the animist nucleus of Gao (in mid-Niger), the Songhay empire, ex-vassal to Mali, began an expansionist move, a drive that would be only halted by Moroccans at the battle of Tondibi (1591).[58] The battle heralds the high point of Moroccan Saadi's expansionism, which reactivated the trans-Saharan caravans and dragged part of the Guinean gold back into the Mediterranean, to the detriment of the Portuguese ports of trade in the Mina Coast.[59] Evicted from traditional exchange networks by their African and European rivals, the Portuguese focused on the new market: maritime slave trafficking and the *Asiento de Negros*, held from 1595 by Portuguese merchants, as we shall see in the next chapter.

Tondibi also demonstrated the supremacy of musketeers in the face of horsemen, archers, and assegai lancers, increasing the arms race drive in Sudan.[60] Imports of iron bars grew in proportion to the regional production of arms. Donelha mentions the activities of the "Sozo" (Susu) blacksmiths, a Mande subgroup who crafted arms and agricultural tools from imported and locally produced iron, noting that they "forge iron in quantity from which they made spears, assegais, knives, and tools to cultivate the fields."[61] Likewise, portable firearms and gunpowder constituted important items in European shipments to the sub-Saharan region from the mid-1600s onwards.[62] In practice, no firearms were regularly made in sub-Saharan Africa.[63] As was the case with horses, foreign arms in Guinea were exchanged for slaves and regional goods.

Let us make a quick turn to the other side of the ocean to underline the difference: none of the European goods exchanged for Amerindian slaves of Brazil provided Amerindian or Mestizo traffickers with returns equivalent to those of the guns and horses secured by African slaving groups. There were native peoples who fought bearing foreign weapons in the last decades of the seventeenth century, such as the Jandui marksman, who lived in today's Rio Grande do Norte territory, and the eighteenth-century Guaicuru of Mato Grosso turned into good horsemen.[64] Nevertheless, the possession of firearms or horses did not convert those ethnic groups into Amerindian slave traders.

It is also true that cavalry or guns did not always decide the battle in Upper Guinea.[65] Indeed, the Mane people managed to defeat the Wolof horsemen fighting on foot with poisoned arrows.⁶⁶ There is a well-known debate among historians regarding the efficacy of muskets and the advantage of cavalry in the battles of the West Africa peoples.⁶⁷ However, there is no doubt that the importation of horses and other weapons—swords, muskets, and other guns,—increased African enslavement and forced migration on a scale never reached in the Amerindian slave trade in Portuguese America.

"Salvation's Way"

As a consequence of ethnic and religious conflicts that shook the Sahel and the Sudan, Moorish traders offered kaffir (pagan) black slaves in exchange for Muslims taken captive by the Portuguese.⁶⁸ The exchange of Muslims ("infidels") for animists ("idolaters") continued: in 1543 a denunciation reached the court that the Canary Castilians took "captives" (Muslims) to exchange them for "pieces" (animists Black Africans) with the "Moors" (Mandinka) in the Mina Coast.⁶⁹ Note the distinction between the "captives," prisoners of war and of direct looting, and the "pieces," the slaves of the Atlantic trade mercantile circuit. In chapter 4 this point is discussed further.

Such exchanges provided evangelizing principles for the slave trade. Zurara stated, with regard to the animist captives, "These Negroes do not hail from the lineage of the Moors, but from that of the gentiles [pagans], therefore [they are] best to be brought over to Salvation's Way."⁷⁰

Publicized by King Afonso V of Portugal, such edifying arguments became a religious doctrine and a norm of *Jus gentium*, international law endorsed by the bull *Romanus Pontifex* (1455). Fr. Antonio Brásio, an eminent twentieth-century missiologist and Africanist, considered the document as the "Magna Charta" of the Portuguese overseas.⁷¹ In this bull, Pope Nicholas V lent support to the king's fight against the Muslims and formulated the first evangelical justification for the African forced migrations. The trade and possession of black Africans was considered just, since many of them, deported to Portugal, became Christians. "Many Guineans and other Negroes taken by force, and also some exchanged for nonbanned goods, or bought by any other legitimate purchase contract, were taken to the said kingdoms [Portugal and Algarve], where many have converted to the Catholic Faith, in the hope that, with the assistance of Divine mercy, if affairs do take that turn, that those peoples convert to the Faith, or at least that many Souls are saved in Christ."⁷²

Well before the discovery of America, one century previous to the Valladolid debate (1550–1551) and the controversies of the Iberian theologians on the Amerindians' nature, the Pope Nicholas V. set the fate of sub-Saharan Africans.[73] The Church decided that animist Africans possessed a soul whose salvation should be promoted by the slave trade and perpetual and hereditary enslavement.

Narratives about the strangeness of African fauna and the harshness of its climate widened the unhuman aberrations attributed to the African continent. Pacheco Pereira, in his celebrated *Esmeraldo do Situ Orbis* (1506), stated that Africans sporting dog tails and one-mile-long snakes ran about freely in Guinea.[74] Meanwhile, Jesuit Alonso de Sandoval suggested that geographic determinism was at work, asserting that Africa's heat and deserts brought all species and races together to mix within the vicinity of water wells, creating an ecosystem apt to engender monstrous hybridizations. Such circumstance rendered Africa as the continent of all bestiality, the devil's elected territory.[75]

Widely publicized in Europe by the Pigafetta and Duarte Lopes chronicle (1591), the cannibalism and the alleged selling of human meat in African shops—"they sell [there] human meat in butcheries as much as we (sell) here the cow's meat," makes the Atlantic slave trade appear like an act of generosity.[76] In the very first lines of his *História Geral das Guerras Angolanas* (1681), Cadornega, the father of Angolista historiography, enunciates the redemptive virtues of the slave trade. "The ransom of *peças* [slaves] is useful in commerce, and with such ransoms one avoids having so many butcheries of human flesh, hence [slaves] instructed in the Faith of Our Lord Jesus Christ, are duly baptized and evangelized as they are sent to Brazil or shipped to other regions holding Catholic beliefs."[77]

Spared from ending up quartered and hung in pieces in the "butcheries"—a reiterative allegation used to justify the slaving wars on both sides of the South Atlantic—the African prisoners could be hoisted onto the slave ships to be saved, body and soul, in overseas Catholic slavery. As we shall see further in this text, Jesuit missionary and statesman Fr. Antonio Vieira interpreted African slavery as a "great miracle" by Our Lady of the Rosary: extracted from pagan Africa, Africans could be saved for Christ in Catholic Brazil.[78]

As the Dutch took up the slave trade during the second quarter of the seventeenth century, they adopted a similar doctrine: the ruling Calvinism in their American colonies would redeem the souls of the deported Africans.[79] In its turn, Lisbon considered that the Africans enslaved by such "heretic" dealers incurred great spiritual danger. Since the beginning of the sixteenth century, the priests of

Cape Verde's Cathedral excommunicated all Portuguese who sold slaves to "heretic" foreigners.[80] By the same token, when in 1690 João de Lencastre, governor of Angola, slave trader and later Brazil's governor-general, imposed a treaty on the Count of Soyo (the territory south of the Congo River delta)—a zone crisscrossed by the Portuguese, the English, and the Dutch—he included a clause in which the Count committed to sell slaves exclusively to those "who profess the law of O. L. Jesus Christ so that they [the slaves] are instructed."[81] At the same time, the *Code Noir* prohibited the Protestants from disturbing the Catholic practices of the slaves in the French Caribbean.[82]

The categorical change in the legitimation of African slave trafficking is noteworthy. Stirred up by the fall of Constantinople and the appeal for a new Crusade by Pope Nicholas V, the bull *Romanus Pontifex* conceived of the slave trade as a consequence of the global war against Islam, a side effect that "at least" allowed that "many Souls are saved in Christ." Two centuries later, the evangelizing task came to impose the Portuguese monopoly in African ports to undertake the "miraculous" forced migration, according to the interpretation of Fr. Antonio Vieira. In the eighteenth century, the lay and the Enlightenment's concept of "civilization" complemented the benefits supposedly enjoyed by the enslaved Africans in America.[83]

Even so, in the first binomial, paganism/evangelization, as in the second, barbarity/civilization, the ideological argument bears the same figure: the slave trade is represented as a pathway carrying the individual from the worst to the least bad, from African nature purportedly surrounded by darkness and death to the overseas community open to alleged spiritual and cultural redemption.[84]

Despite their precedence in the region, the Portuguese dominion in Upper Guinea always seemed fortuitous.[85] Ultimately, Lisbon tried to set up an administered economic system that backfired. Cape Verde, and more precisely the city of Ribeira, on the island of Santiago (a supposed safe port for the defense of royal monopoly), brought together the administrative, missionary, and military centers of Africa's West Coast. Africans from Cacheu and surrounding areas had to be taken to Ribeira, have the proper taxes and duties collected, and only then could the slaves be shipped on to Portugal or on to foreign lands.[86]

Similar to the circuit that Venice built in the Mediterranean, around Rhodes, Crete, and Cyprus, such initiatives sought to obtain a maximum of economic exploitation with minimal territorial occupation. Such a system worked fitfully in the Eastern Portuguese empire, but reached its zenith in the Caribbean in the second half of the seventeenth century as it was put into practice by the Dutch.[87]

However, in Upper Guinea, as in the Lisbon–São Tomé–Mina Coast triangle, the "Venetian" model rehearsed by the Portuguese did not take root due to reasons that are worth highlighting.

Foreigners in those parts were afflicted with fevers called "first disease." Travelers often died on the overseas routes, both on the crossing to Brazil and on the eastbound trip. One out of three missionaries sent over to China in the seventeenth century died before getting there.[88] However, such deaths escalated in the course of long journeys, subject to shipwrecks and adverse monsoons. Notwithstanding its relative proximity to Europe, West Africa represented a much greater danger because of the epidemiological scenario. Notorious cases are recorded in the missionary chronicles. Thirteen of the fifteen priests who arrived in Cacheu at the turn of the sixteenth century soon perished to the "first disease." In another instance, of a mission composed of twelve priests, seven breathed their last while the ship that carried them still lay at anchor in the port.[89] The area, above all the Mina Coast—"the most disease-ridden of all lands sailed by the Portuguese" wrote a missionary in 1554—had widespread yellow fever and types of malaria lethal to Europeans as well to Africans from other parts of the continent.[90]

From his islands, the Cape Verde governor warned the court about the losses that local diseases inflicted on mainland troops. "For two hundred Mainland soldiers to survive, the climate of the land makes it necessary to send over . . . eight hundred."[91] Jesuit chronicler Fernam Guerreiro expressed the pity and the price of the deaths that the African diseases caused in the ranks of missionaries so laboriously prepared in European seminaries. "Although for them it is of great gain to die obediently in the course of their work and towards the saving of souls, for the Company [of Jesus] it is a great loss, as it costs to prepare them, and for the lack they create when they are lost."[92] Superior Claudio Acquaviva, the head of the Society of Jesus, warned more crudely that he would not allow Upper Guinea to become the "slaughterhouse" of Jesuit missionaries.[93] Accordingly, Acquaviva redirected his efforts in Africa to more intensely undertake the two great projects of his mandate (1581–1615): the apostolate in China and the Guarani missions in South America.[94]

Even the building of Portuguese factories on the shore seemed doomed. Pierced by rivers, the Upper Guinea coast allowed free access to "thieves," that is, other European traders. French, English, and Dutch goods were in great demand there, particularly northern European iron.[95]

Significantly, the dilemma of the choices between two Portuguese strategies in sixteenth century India was reproduced in Upper Guinea: trade or conquest? To dominate the land or to secure the sea? As a supporter of the latter stance, the Cape Verde governor criticized the building of the inland Cacheu fortress, belittling the "novel and very costly manner of possession" that the kingdom was adopting.[96]

Above all, intermetropolitan rivalries made the island of Santiago of Cape Verde—sitting astride the South Seas route—a punching bag for Lisbon's enemies. The island's sergeant-major apologized for the small amount collected for the royal taxes because of "the many thieves [European corsairs] that come to the coast."[97] In the absence of an income of its own, the São Tomé diocese came to be directed and supported, from 1687 until 1844, by the Salvador de Bahia archbishopric.[98]

A rosary of complaints bemoans the decadence of Upper Guinea. In fact, Cacheu's Christian population felt from 1,500 in the 1620s to 700 in 1694.[99] Yet leaving aside the ambitions of converting the ocean between Cape Verde, Sierra Leone, and São Tomé into a Portuguese *mare nostrum*, gains were considerable up to the Braganza Restoration. Thanks to the market secured by the *Asiento*, to the protection provided by the Spanish royal fleet, to Iberian barter goods (Biscay iron in particular), both Portuguese slavers and royal Customs garnered handsome profits from those parts. In the space of forty-five years (1595–1640), it was estimated that an average of 1,329 slaves per year were brought into Cartagena (present-day Colombia) alone, carried from Upper Guinea by Portuguese *asentistas*.[100] Thus, despite the failures of evangelization and of colonial dominion, overseas exploitation was nevertheless carried on in Upper Guinea.

Execrated by administrators and missionaries, target of corsairs, the Cape Verde archipelago was increasingly left aside in the first decades of the seventeenth century, to the gain of zones more protected against attacks due to adverse winds and currents, such as the Angolan coast.[101] Winds and tides helped to make the difference between the trade in Amerindians and the trade in Africans, at the moment when the Iberian *Asiento* capitalists embraced the African ports.

The Slaving Trade Winds

It is worth recalling some of the everyday nautical knowledge from our ancestors who lived in the Age of Sail. To carry out regular journeys between Portugal and South America, a maritime calendar had to be followed. A vessel would leave Lisbon between October 15 and 25, reaching Recife about two months later.[102] On the journey's return leg, it was necessary to set sail from Pernambuco or Bahia no later than the end of April to reach Lisbon in July. These were the ideal parameters for such a voyage. In any case, the ships had to depart Lisbon in spring at latest, "because when the summer starts in our Europe, the winter began from the equinoctial line to the South, and the winds blow on the bow," writes in 1656 Francisco Brito Freyre, one of the most experienced Portuguese admirals.[103] Outside these deadlines, known as "ordinary monsoons," the time for each leg at least doubled, with an exponential increase in risk for the crew, exposed to seasonal storms and to thirst and illnesses in the doldrums.[104]

Royal cosmographers such as Manoel Figueiredo, Antonio Mariz de Carneiro, and Manuel Pimentel, mapped out Ethiopic Ocean navigation.[105] On leaving Rio de Janeiro or Bahia toward Maranhão or the Caribbean, captains had to avoid the São Roque sandbanks (on the modern Rio Grande do Norte coast). There, one had to reach the high seas before swerving back toward the coast. The September monsoon, resulting from the northeasterly trade winds, generated such an adverse atmosphere in the area that "it makes us lose the estimate of the way," warned Manuel Pimentel in his *Arte de Navegar* (1699).[106]

By Cape Santo Agostinho's latitude (in modern Pernambuco State), the subequatorial current forks out, yielding to the Guiana current, which drifts up the coast toward the Caribbean, and to the Brazil current, flowing down southward. This phenomenon explains the Dutch concern with gaining control of Fernando de Noronha during their South American offensive. The archipelago was the bridgehead for two strategic attack routes against the Iberian Union: that leading toward the Caribbean and the one that went down along the Brazilian coast. Therefore, Cape Santo Agostinho was a key landmark of the Western shore of the Ethiopic Ocean. If a vessel approached the Brazilian Coast north of the Cape, she would be pushed north by northeast by the Guiana current.[107]

The North Brazil current, which feeds the Guiana current, can extend as far as 300 nautical miles, reaching speeds of 2.5 knots on the coastline starting at the Cape São Roque and drifting up to Cape Orange (the modern state of Amapá). Such is the strength of the currents in this area that, even with lowered sails, tall vessels could cover the 790 nautical miles separating Cape São Roque from the port of São Luís do Maranhão in few days.[108] Conversely, the current represented an almost insurmountable obstacle to sailing on the return leg, from the Estado do Maranhão to the Estado do Brasil. Until the advent of steamboats in the second half of the nineteenth century, only the brigantines (*sumacas*) managed to sail round-trip between Bahia, Pernambuco, or further south, and Pará and Maranhão. Even so, it all depended on luck.

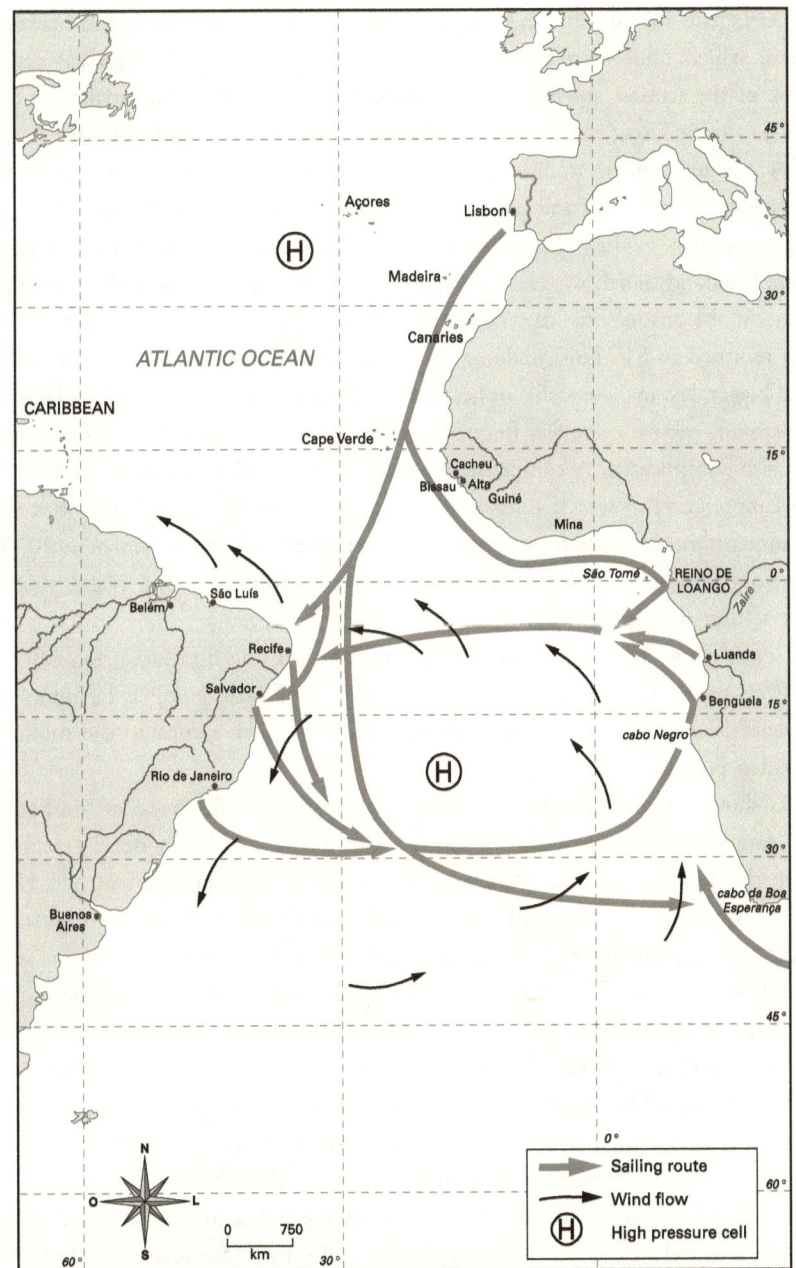

Map 2.1. Main Trade Routes in the Ethiopic Ocean. *Source:* Joseph C. Miller, Way of Death—Merchant Capitalism and the Angolan Slave Trade 1730–1830, Madison, Wis., 1988, Map 10.1, p. 319.

During his mission in the Amazon region, Fr. Vieira wrote about this maritime hazard, which, on its own, impeded a unified economic space in Portuguese America. "One of the hardest and most troublesome navigations of all the Atlantic is that which is done along the coast from Maranhão up to Ceará, not only due to the numerous and hidden sandbars that dot the entire area, but even more due to the pertinacity of the winds and perpetual current of the waters." In 1655, a brigantine carrying soldiers and missionaries from São Luís (Maranhão) to Camocim, the Ibiapaba Sierra headland, north of Ceará captaincy, did not manage to cross the Maranhão coast. At the end of fifty days of continuous struggle against winds and tides, the ship returned to São Luís, undoing in twelve hours almost two months of toil.[109]

If bigger, less maneuverable or heavier vessels persisted, they got stuck—"bagged" (*ensacados*)—above Cape São Roque.[110] To sail back reaching out for higher waters was also complicated. A compensation current begins at the equator, the equatorial countercurrent, which turns strongly east.[111] From March to September, this countercurrent flows far from the coast, beyond Fernando de Noronha, at 20° W. But from September to March, it moves westward, close to Marajó Island, driving waters from the equator line toward the Gulf of Guinea.

Considering such scenarios, on returning from São Luís do Maranhão or Belém do Pará, sailing ships had to seek winds well to the North, going as far up as the Madeira Islands, Canary Islands, or Cape Verde, to then return to the southern Brazilian ports.[112]

As shown below, such nautical systems led to the establishment of the Estado do Maranhão with a government separated from the Estado do Brasil (1624).[113] From this perspective, one of the criticisms made of the establishment of a High Court in Bahia (1609) resulted from the difficulty in submitting pleas originating in the other captaincies to this tribunal. Arrangements involving the institution were thus dependent on monsoons favorable to coastal navigation, "which much delays the dispatching of the cases," Fernandes Brandão noted in 1618. Hence, it was better to send out petitions from other captaincies directly to Lisbon's tribunals.[114]

Exasperated with his Amazonian isolation, in which a single vessel from Lisbon would call once a year, Father Antonio Vieira wrote from São Luís: "one more easily sails from India to Portugal than from this mission [Maranhão] to [the Estado do] Brazil,"[115] Missionaries and civil authorities leaving Bahia to São Luís and Belém must first travel to Lisbon, and only then to sail on to Maranhão and Pará.[116]

There are well-known examples of the difficulties of south-north (and vice-versa) navigation along the Brazilian coast. After crossing Brazil's center-west and Amazon region in the years 1648–1651, in the largest and most extraordinary terrestrial expedition of the seventeenth century, Raposo Tavares and his Paulista companions made an even longer return journey home to São Paulo. Having arrived in Belém do Pará via savannahs, forests, trails, and rivers, they followed the only possible route to regain the way home: they went up to Lisbon and from there back to Santos.[117]

Later on, during Brazil's struggle for Independence (1822), when Admiral Cochrane set sail to force the governments of the Maranhão and Pará captaincies to adhere to Rio de Janeiro, a revealing incident took place. There were so many high-sea twists of the British mercenary's meandering trip to Maranhão that Lisbon sent out a warning to Luanda, concluding that the slave-trade port was the true target of the Brazilian imperial navy's foray.[118]

In his *Chronicles* on Maranhão and Pará, the Jesuit missionary Bettendorf narrates a surprising event of 1696: the arrival in Belém of "men from Brazil," Bahia's ranchers who had come on horseback, riding through the backlands to ask the governor of Pará for grazing land for their cattle. On their return "into Brazil," the ranchers were accompanied by the Pará Superior Crown Magistrate (Ouvidor Geral) already appointed as High Court Magistrate of Bahia, Manuel Nunes Collares.[119] Collares preferred to ride 2,000 km on horseback through wild hinterland, dotted with hostile Amerindians, rather than wait for a hypothetical sea transport from Belém to Bahia. In fact, the Pará backlands route initiated the first link between the Amazonian north and the rest of Portuguese America.

There was a shorter terrestrial route along the coast, but sandpits and dunes denied the horses passage. This was the path taken by André Vidal de Negreiros in 1656, when he left the post of General-Captain of Maranhão to take office as governor of Pernambuco. Due to winds and the north-coast currents, he traveled on foot from São Luís up to the Ceará shores, whence he set off to Recife.[120]

Farther down the South American coast, an area of dense instability moves alongside Sergipe and the São Francisco River delta. "Many boats have been lost there, thence it is convenient to skirt round it well into the sea," stated Pimentel. A recent nautical guide of the American National Geospatial-Intelligence Agency confirms Pimentel's observations: "Sailing craft should use caution along this part of [the Brazilian] coast because of the strong prevailing winds and currents, which tend to set them on shore."[121]

In the September monsoon, also called the northeastern monsoon, northeast and east-northeast winds blow as late as March, forming a north-south current along the coast. The inverse movement takes place during the March monsoon or the southeast monsoon. Southeast, east-southeast, and south-southeast winds drive the currents northward from April to August. Such is the dominant regime from Cape São Roque (present-day Rio Grande do Norte) to the Abrolhos archipelago (17° 40' S off Bahia). From then on begins the area of the "below wind"—the southeast trades—blowing from the south.

Unlike the seventeenth-century royal cosmographers, who described only the oceanic routes to and from Lisbon, José Antonio Caldas, the Bahian engineer and cartographer, detailed the south-south voyages between Bahia, São Tomé, and the Gulf of Guinea. Carrying out bilateral trade, this itinerary was the second-most-important slave-trade route after the Luanda-Rio de Janeiro thoroughfare, equally based on bilateral exchanges. Born and active in Bahia, Caldas collected information from local merchants and captains, sailing to the Mina Coast around 1750.

Following his teachings, during the September monsoon, Bahian vessels would sail east-southeast up to the Trindade archipelago (20° 5' S–29° 3' W). There, catching the winds of the St. Helena high, the captains would sail southward before turning north at the West Central African coast, at the latitude of Angola. If unable to do so, captains should sail farther south to 25° or 26° S (south of the Tropic of Capricorn) to take advantage of the northward winds close to the South African coast. Ships from Bahia that missed such winds "made five- [or] six-month long voyages, and others drifted up to the Maranhão Coast whence they never returned," warned Caldas.[122]

Cabo Frio (Cold Cape), as the name indicates, signals the northerly reaches of the cold front borne by the Falklands current during the austral winter and spring, brushing against the hot winds carried from the north and southeast by the Brazil current. A further zone of turbulence makes difficult sailing from Cape São Tomé (Rio de Janeiro) down to Santa Catarina, above all during the March monsoon, dubbed the "southwest monsoon" in southern Brazil. The São Tomé sandbar, hard by the cape of same name, again forces the traveler to take to the high sea between Rio de Janeiro and Espírito Santo.[123]

For this reason, the Rio de Janeiro–Lisbon voyage demanded six or seven months if the direct route was taken. But the duration doubled if there was a stopover in Bahia, argued Salvador de Sá in 1646, as he tried to make his Rio de Janeiro captaincy independent from the Bahia general government.[124] Years later, Rio de Janeiro colonists also underlined the trouble generated by the difficult navigation along the Brazilian coast. They begged for and obtained a royal provision for those local residents accused of minor crimes to serve preventive arrest in their own captaincies, instead of being transferred to Bahia.[125]

Much later in time, in the beginning of the Balaiada Revolt (1839–42), the *Beranger*, a Brazilian war navy brig, sailing from Rio de Janeiro to Maranhão laden with troops, met contrary winds forcing it to lay anchor in . . . Montevideo.[126]

In the 1840s, the losses caused in the transportation of Rio de Janeiro sugar production by the São Tomé sandbanks and the Paraiba River delta winds led to the building of the first large-scale civil engineering work in Brazil: the fluvial canal linking Campos to Macaé.[127]

Today, Rio de Janeiro's seasonal oblique winds and tides concern only two communities, who ignore each other: the poor Macaé fishermen and the Velux 5 Oceans, the world's longest solo sailing race, whose rich sportsmen sail by in April, during their crossing at this part of South America's coast. In the past, however, these turbulences entangled travels at the center of Portuguese America, and eventually hindered the Amerindian slave trade alongside the South Atlantic coast.

To be sure, Gê slaves from Maranhão were exported to Pernambuco in the 1620s. But part of their trip was probably made over land so as to reach the more accessible southward ports.[128] At the end of the eighteenth century, Alexandre Rodrigues Ferreira considered the transfer of Amazonian Indians to enlarge the supply of coerced labor into the more southern captaincies.[129] At this point, it is worth underlining the forgotten reality of the geohistory of that time. Even if all of the Amazon's indigenous communities were to turn up in fetters on the shores of Pará and Maranhão to give themselves up, the obstacle of the winds would continue to hinder the would-be Amerindian slave traders along the Pernambucano, Bahian, and São Paulo maritime routes. In contrast, the Brazil-Angola crossings were "nearly always accompanied by good weather or by very little annoyance from the sea and winds," wrote an Angolan governor in 1799.[130] Accordingly, Joseph Miller concludes, "Highly stable winds and currents promoted the Brazilian's prominence in the slave trade of the Southern Atlantic."[131]

The axis of the slaving poles linking Africa to Portuguese America revolves around the route generated between the two margins of the ocean by complementary currents and winds, around the continuity of the Brazil current, of the South Atlantic drift, of the Benguela current, and of the south equatorial current.[132] The drive of the circular movement of the winds and currents is the consequence of a giant high-pressure pulley—the St. Helena high—moving on the ocean between 6° and 28° S.[133]

Although longer than the direct route sailed from England or Netherlands ports to the Congo or North Angola, the westbound itinerary generally taken by the slave vessels leaving Lisbon circumvented most of the doldrums and provided a safe stopover in Brazilians ports. Thus, as a result of the ease with which the ships sailed from Pernambuco, Bahia, and Rio de Janeiro bound for Luanda or the Mina Coast, and vice-versa, the Luso-Brasílico navigation was to be transatlantic and connected to the African slave trade, instead of taking place on the north-south coastal routes in discontinuity with the Indian slave trade, against the Southern Trade Winds.

Commenting on the atmospheric and maritime regularity of east-west navigation, Jesuit Antonio Vieira interpreted the phenomenon in his "Sermon XXVII" as a divine omen: the "transmigration," the continuous transport of Angolans across the South Atlantic seas, by special mercy of Our Lady of the Rosary, allowed their being brought over to Portuguese America to be saved from African paganism: "Some great mystery is verily enclosed in this transmigration, and more so if we note that it is so singularly favored and assisted by God, since there is no navigation in the whole of the ocean that is free of danger and of the contrariety of the winds, except that which removes these peoples from their motherlands and brings them over to the exercise of captivity, and it is always on the wind, and without change of sail."[134]

São Tomé—Laboratory of Tropical Slavery

All maritime lanes crossing the area reached São Tomé, occupied in 1484 to support the route to India and the Guinea ports of trade. Several points linked the island and the continent: Elmina (São Jorge da Mina), the Benin River (Rio Formoso), the Bonny River (Rio Real), the Niger delta (Rio Forcados), on the Nigerian coast, and the port of Mpinda, later Santo Antonio do Zaire, in the Congo River delta.[135] Transplanted from the Mediterranean and the Algarve to the islands of Madeira, the Canary Islands, and Cape Verde, sugar-cane slavery took a decisive step toward overseas adaptation in São Tomé. The fields of São Tomé also served as a distribution area for plants and seeds from other continents to the peoples of the Gulf of Guinea and West Central Africa.[136]

Before 1500, when Brazil was not yet even on the map, plants, cultures, agricultural techniques, livestock, poultry, and white and mulatto settlers from

Europe and Cape Verde had all acclimatized to the tropical environment of those areas.[137] At the beginning of the sixteenth century, enthusiastic about the advance of sugar-cane plantations in the Madeira Islands, Valentim Fernandes considered that São Tomé would become what Madeira had been in the fifteenth century. In fact, the Madeira and São Tomé complex configured a vector of its own in the widening of Portuguese presence in America and their adaptation to the tropics.

King Manuel's regiment to the São Tomé factor in 1519 established methods of slavery management.[138] Problems with the supply of the factories, of the riggers, and of the crew were solved by food substitution. Yam, banana, palm oil, coconut, and malagueta pepper, cultivated in those areas and long integrated into the Guinean diet, replaced wheat biscuits, cheese, European olive oil, and garlic in the sailors' victuals and in the slave-trade diet.[139] In the beginning of the sixteenth century, American tropical plants such as manioc, peanuts, maize, and pineapple entered in the African economic circuits, generally through São Tomé and Angola, as we shall see in the next chapter.

Changes nurtured in São Tomé Island influenced overseas policy, most importantly in the plantation enclaves of Brazil, which were connected to the Santomese archipelago from the beginning until the end of the colonial period. Based on the report by the Santomese captaincy's donatary, King Manuel widened the settlers' franchises in 1500, authorizing them to trade from the Gulf of Guinea up to the Congo. "Being the said island so distant from our kingdoms, people do not wish to go live there but with very great liberties and franchises."[140] The lesson would be incorporated into the royal directives to the donataries of Portuguese America's captaincies. Wide-ranging powers and assorted privileges were granted to them to facilitate their investments in remote Brazil.

Based in a plantation colony and a revolving platform for the slave traders, São Tomé merchants transported Benin slaves and Nigerian cowries to be sold to African dealers in exchange for gold at Elmina and Axim.[141] In 1524, the Crown allowed São Tomé's slave traders to deal from the Bonny River up to the Congo's ports.[142] They then grafted the Congo markets into the Atlantic system, redirecting their slave traffic to the Caribbean and Brazil.[143] Some of those deportees, already acclimated in the island's plantations, happened to be more resistant to European diseases, and were versed in the Afro-Portuguese pidgin first observed by Fr. Alonso de Sandoval, the "language of São Tomé"—the slaving idiom. They were also sometimes skilled in sugar production.[144] The trafficking of Africans became more interesting to São Tomé colonists than the planting of sugar cane. At the beginning of the sixteenth century, the island held 2,000 settled slaves, in addition to some 5,000 to 6,000 itinerant individuals awaiting transportation to other markets.[145]

Mpinda emerged as West Central Africa's first outlet. Africans, ivory, and copper became objects of exchange on the coast.[146] Political struggles and the progress of Western military technology conferred strategic value to copper. Bronze cannons emerged as a decisive weapon in bringing down feudal walls in the Western Europe monarchic centralization.[147] New bronze foundries pushed European copper prices up and induced the search for the red metal in foreign lands, and, in particular, in the Congo estuary.

To evade the obstacles imposed by the Congo's king, the Portuguese carracks sailed around the port of Mpinda and went farther South, opening the Angolan market.[148] In the 1530s, Santomese slave traders were loading around 4,000 individuals per year in Mpinda and Angola. It was then the biggest slave-trading operation carried out in a specific area of the African continent.[149] Half a dozen vessels laid anchor monthly in São Tomé harbor, where 650 settlers and their families resided.[150] Granted the title of "city" by the Crown in 1535, São Tomé became the seat of the first Christian diocese established in the Tropics. Such honors foreshadowed the promising outlook that the Crown and the Roman Curia envisioned for the island, the first real plantation Atlantic economy.[151] However, the racial "tumults" (*alvoroços*) that spelled doom to São Tomé flared up.[152]

The Santomese Mocambos and the Bahia's Indians

In the 1520s, São Tomé's sugar-mill owners clashed with mulatto planters, who had experienced a process of social ascension.[153] Then, from 1545 on, slave revolts erupted on a scale never seen before in the Atlantic.[154] The island's hills sheltered the rebels.[155]

Mukambo, a Kimbundo language word meaning "summit," and more precisely, the fork fitting a house's roof (characterizing the family's or community's fixed abode) came to denote the rebel's refuge in São Tomé. In Brazil, the word became a synonym for an insurrectionary black village.[156] Later, it would be substituted by *kilombo*, the original name of the Jaga warriors' camp in the kingdoms of Matamba and Kasanje.[157] Once Brazilian slavery was abolished, *mucambo* or *mocambo* indicated places inhabited by blacks or popular dwellings, and the term was generalized as the synonym for the northeastern favelas.[158]

The first overseas large-scale slave revolt, the São Tomé mutinies sparked a panic among the colonists similar to that generated two centuries later by the Saint-Domingue Revolution. Both islands contained the ingredients bolstering slavery's dangers: geographic isolation, factional fighting among the masters, conflicts opposing religious and civil authorities, and a large proportion of slaves and freed men among its inhabitants.

Raimundo da Cunha Matos, who spent nineteen years at São Tomé, which he governed in 1814–1815 and who knew the island's archives and oral traditions, underlined the violent infighting between authorities and settlers that generated the Santomese slave revolt, a worrisome issue to him in his time as Crown officer during Brazilian independence struggles.[159] According to him, the governor's excommunication pronounced by the São Tomé's bishop in 1594, "caused the forever unfortunate Black Amador's uprising and rebellion" in 1595.[160]

A slave named Amador, resorting to a tactic later employed in slave insurrections in Brazil, started a general rebellion while the settlers attended the Sunday mass of 9 July 1595. A parochial church was invaded and the white and mulatto men were slaughtered. Four or five thousand blacks, some with guns, joined the rebel ranks commanded by "King" Amador, as his followers called the rebel leader. Many settlers were killed and more than seventy sugar mills were burned down; only twenty-five remained on the whole island. Once captured, Amador was hanged and the revolt was drowned in blood.[161] Still, maroons' villages never entirely disappeared from the Santomese hills.[162]

As in the Saint-Domingue Revolution in 1791 and in the Bahia slave uprising of 1835, the objective was not to run away or to create free and distant communities—as in Palmares and hundreds of other Americans places—but rather to take power, to destroy slavery. Such was the historical novelty that reverberated on the two sides of the Atlantic in 1595.

At the same time, black slave insurrections broke out on the other side of the equator, where African disembarkments intensified. At that stage, the Brazilian enclaves already showed differences with the European settlements based on the vassalizing of natives such as Angola, Mozambique, Mexico, and Peru. More specifically, they resembled the slaving nuclei of Cape Verde and São Tomé, founded on the import of instruments of labor (the Africans), of technology (the sugar mill), and of the plant whose product was to be exported (sugar cane). The launching of Angolan's deportations to Bahia, Recife, and Rio de Janeiro, and the disembarkment of 61,000 Africans between 1591 and 1610, formed the social matrix of the next three centuries: facing the Amerindians, Brazil had more African descendants than Luso descendants.[163] In this context, Portugal's Amerindian policy would change dramatically. Henceforth, missionaries and authorities sought to ally with Indians communities to protect themselves from black uprisings in the heart of colonial enclaves.

In a report sent from Bahia to the Crown in around 1580, the bishop of Bahia, the Brazil's Chief Justice and the rector of Jesuit's College, Gregorio Serrão, an experienced man who knew also Rio de Janeiro and lived in São Paulo and Rome, were unanimous: "Brazil cannot be supported without [the help of] the gentiles [Indians] of the land . . . especially now with the great number of Guinea people that everyday rebel, kill and steal."[164]

Some years later, the Crown gathered a board (Junta) of experts in Lisbon to discuss instructions, resulting in the 1596 royal ordinance on the Amerindians.[165] Four councilors, all of them old Brazil hands, composed the Junta: Fr. Marçal Beliarte, former Jesuit Provincial in Bahia (1587–1594) and three former Crown judges of Portuguese America. Supported by his colleagues, one of the judges emphasized the need to preserve the Amerindian populations so as to use them in resisting the black revolts in the northern captaincies. In a peculiar estimate, which reveals the alarm provoked by the growth of the disembarkment of Africans, he guaranteed that there were 200 Africans to each white person on that section of the coast.[166]

Later, announcing to the S.J.'s superiors in Rome the 1596 royal ordinance declaring "free all the gentiles [Indians] of Brazil," the Jesuit Pero Rodrigues insisted again on the alliance with the Indians to protect the colonial enclaves. His report is very precise: "[our] main enemies [in Brazil] are the insurrected Guinea Blacks, who hole up in some sierras, whence they come down to raid, and cause much trouble. And there can be the time when they dare assault and destroy the plantations as their relatives do in the island of São Tomé."[167]

A few decades after the founding of the Atlantic slave system the specter of a systemic antislavery revolt alarmed the settlers and the high-ranking royal officers. Although it is known to historians, this quote has been insufficiently contextualized.

The author of this recommendation to the Crown was not an opinionated low-level cleric. Pero Rodrigues was the Jesuit Provincial of Brazil (1594–1603). He participated in the critical 1592 Jesuit congregation in Bahia to discuss, in a complementary way, the issue of the captivity of natives in Brazil and Angola. Nominated *visitador* (itinerant general inspector) of the Jesuits in Angola, he had made inquiries in the missions of Luanda and Massangano in 1593, during the conflict between the governor and missionaries concerning the *soba* chiefs.[168] By that time, the black revolts that led to the King Amador uprising were growing in nearby São Tomé Island, where missionaries and traders from Angola often traveled.[169]

As Jesuit Provincial, he earned great authority in matters of the South Atlantic. He was known as one of the rare experts who had traveled the whole extent of the Angolan-Brazilian system—from the trading fairs of the West Central African hinterland up to the Bahia sugar mills—crossing aboard slave ships, and judging issues about the legality of the captivity of Africans and Amerindians.[170] Based on such experience, Fr. Pero formulated a commentary that synthesized the slaver societies' paranoia. For him, slavery was based on violence and racial oppression. Therefore, in São Tomé and Bahia, slaves shared an insurrectional parenthood, transforming conflict between blacks and whites in a war spilling over both sides of the ocean.

Two decades later, writing about the pro-Indian policy introduced by general governor Diogo Botelho (1602–1607), friar Vicente do Salvador restated the necessary alliance with the settled Indians, "mainly against the Guinea Blacks . . . that every day rebel and steal . . . and if they don't do worse things it is because they are frightened by such Indians who, with a Portuguese captain, search and take them under arrest to their masters."[171]

Gradually, the Portuguese Indian policy featured a new directive. "Meek" (*manso*), that is, friendly or subjugated Amerindians,[172] flocked together into settlements (*aldeamentos*),[173] began to be located inside colonial zones to stop enslaved blacks from escaping, to halt the flourishing of *mocambos* and to defend against "wild" (*bravos*) Indians.

Polemics on the origins of the July 1595 troubles in São Tomé and its significance appeared in the colonialist historiography and continued until our days.[174] Influencing transformations in the Indians policy in Brazil and, most probably, as we shall see in the next chapter, in the *Asiento*'s regulations, the Santomese insurrection is best understood as the first Atlantic Revolution.[175]

It is worth noting that from that time until the end of the Brazilian slave trade in 1850, the statute for Amerindians has always been habitually defined as a counterpoint to the statute for black slaves. This relation renders inoperative historiographical analysis that regards Indians' legislation as an autonomous variable in Brazil's colonial and national past.

The role played by this first overseas colonial society, which Philip Curtin calls the "first Atlantic system"—formed by the Ibero-African enclaves of the Canaries,

Cape Verde, Madeira, the Azores, and São Tomé—became evident with the adaptation to the Tropics and to slavery of the Luso-African culture developed on a large scale in Brazil.[176]

Current in the Atlantic islands, many cultural practices were all the more easily introduced in Brazil,[177] including plants (sugar cane, banana, yam, and coconut), cultivation methods, large livestock (cattle, horses, and mules), smaller livestock (swine, goats, and sheep), acclimatized chickens and ducks, types of sugar mills, free men and slaves immune to tropical diseases and skilled in colonial work, slave-trade methods, and curative and feeding methods. Even indirect control institutions of the slaves—such as the brotherhood of the Rosary of São Tomé's Negroes, established by the royal decree of 1526, took place before the foundation of a similar establishment in Bahia (1581) and Rio de Janeiro (1631).

With the decline in the demand for slaves in Portugal, Cape Verde, and São Tomé, the slave trade assumed the transatlantic profile characteristic of the coming centuries. We shall see in the next chapter that Portuguese slavers seemed to be more active in foreign slave markets than in those of Cape Verdes, Madeira, São Tomé, and Brazil. In fact, the trade to Brazilian ports reached a new level in the first decades of the seventeenth century, when the alliance between the Portuguese and Jagas triggered the massive pillage of Mbundu villages.[178]

Invasion and Evangelization in West Central Africa

Diogo Cão intended to find Prester John and the way to India as he crossed the Congo River mouth in 1483, in the first European fleet to reach this extremity of the world. He bumped into the kingdom of Congo and opened one of the most dramatic chapters of Western presence in Africa. For the next two centuries, the Congo would be the stage for the sleights-of-hand and contradictions of the kings of Spain and Portugal, popes, the Dutch, the French, Jesuits, Capuchins, Portuguese, Angolistas, and Brasílicos—that is, for the string of historical agents that made the South Atlantic revolve—up to the last quarter of the seventeenth century, when the African kingdom collapsed after the war waged by the Brasílico governor of Angola, André Vidal de Negreiros.

Part of the Congo aristocracy embraced Christianity to use the new creed to contend against rival animist lineages. "Having attended mass and the other divine cults, the [king of Congo], noblemen and other people all left content, and soon he . . . and other notables had themselves baptized and turned Christian, but wished that no one else did so, stating that such a good and holy thing should not be granted to just any villain," narrated Pacheco Pereira in the *Esmeraldo*.[179] Indeed, the "Mani" (lord) Nzinga Nkuwu, the Manicongo, turned Catholic and took the name of King João I. Part of the kingdom's nobility followed him in conversion and in changing names.[180] As a nonhereditary and elective monarchy, Congo experienced factional fighting during the interregnum years. When King João I died, the throne nevertheless passed to his first-born, Afonso I, Nzinga Muemba (1506–1543), after a battle where the Christianized lineages defeated the animists. Consonant with the Iberian imaginary, which attributed victories to divine will, King Afonso stated that he had seen "Christ's cross in heaven and the apostle Saint James" in the battlefield.[181] Traditional hierarchic titles, represented by the word *mani*, were replaced by Portuguese medieval titles of king, duke, marquis, count, baron, "dom," and "dona." Gradually, Portuguese evolved into the standard language employed by the Congo court in its relations with the Europeans.[182]

Hesitating about the meaning of the colonization—about the need of coupling missions to territorial domination—Rome, Madrid, and Lisbon avoided the establishment of dioceses in territories that submitted to native sovereigns. So, the Board of Conscience (Mesa de Consciência), a royal tribunal for issues concerning the Church, questioned the convenience of establishing bishoprics among Eastern peoples, as in Cochin (India), Malacca (present-day Malacca City), Macao and, above all, in Funai (present-day Oita), created in 1588 in Japan. However, the tribunal explicitly recognized the legitimacy of the Congo bishopric because it was a kingdom "very ancient in Christianity."[183] Following that, the capital Mbanza Congo was renamed São Salvador and was graced in 1596 with the status of seat of the Congo and Angola dioceses.[184] This followed the founding of Bahia's bishopric (1550), but was earlier than the creation of the Rio de Janeiro and Olinda dioceses (1676).[185]

Grounding political power through the intermediation of religious creed is a constitutive element of monarchies.[186] The kings of São Salvador do Congo also made use of the religious hierarchy as an external power lever, attracting the support of popes and, later, of Italian Capuchins, so as to serve as a counterweight to the hostility of Lisbon and local settlers. For this reason, the history of the Congo kingdom extrapolates the region into the wider picture of Atlantic conflicts.

Troubled with the slave traders' greed and seeking to keep the monopoly of trade with Europeans for himself, king Afonso I, born Mvemba a Nzinga, announced in 1526 to the king of Portugal, João III, his desire to end the slave trade. "We ask Your Highness to help and assist us in this matter, commanding your factors that they should not send either merchants or wares. Because it is our will that in this kingdom there should be neither a trade in slaves nor a demand for them."[187] King Afonso had, of his own accord or else induced by Portuguese traders more interested in their own gains than in their Crown's monopoly, solicited a license to buy a ship in Portugal to evade the middlemen and practice direct exchange with Europe.[188] After procrastinating for twelve years, the Portuguese king responded to Afonso I. The document deserves a place in economic history manuals.

"You say in your letters that you do not wish enslavements by barter [*resgates de escravos*] in your kingdom, for they depopulate your land . . . but it does not seem to me that this honors you or your kingdom, because the highest honor for you is to buy each year from Congo 10,000 slaves and 10,000 bracelets (of copper) and so many ivory teeth, more than saying that in Congo there are no more *resgates.*"[189] With regard to the purchase of a ship, the king of Portugal stated: "You ask, in addition, for a ship, which much surprises me, for my ships are yours . . . for whatever end you may wish, you have my ships as if they were yours."

Concluding, King João III expounded on the advantages of the free trade. Of Portugal's trade: "Your desire not allow the entry of wares into Congo is against the condition of every land, because into Portugal there come (goods) from all parts of the world and whoever wishes may buy and sell."[190] However, King Afonso I recovered the control over the Congolese commercial exchanges and in 1540 wrote to the king of Portugal to promote the Congo trade, including the slave trade.[191]

Having closed the maritime gate that could allow some commercial autonomy to King Afonso in the Atlantic, Portugal tried to block the diplomatic privileges of the Congo kingdom in Europe: its special relations with the Holy See. King Manuel had already held up in Lisbon a Congo embassy on its way to Rome, where it would meet the Pope. Nevertheless, the diplomatic negotiations between the Congo and the Holy See continued, and in 1518, Pope Leo X consecrated Henrique, son of D. Afonso I Nzinga Muemba, bishop of Utica *in partibus infidelium*.[192]

As Charles Boxer wrote, regardless of their dispute over the control of the Catholic missions, the Portuguese Crown and the Pope intended to play a "Constantinian" strategy in the Congo: to promote Westernization and European domination via the baptism of the dominant lineages and the ensuing cascade effect that should encourage the Bakongo hierarchy to follow suit. Five years later, King Afonso I nominated Congolese ambassadors to the court of Pope Clement VII. This act was confirmed in 1547 by D. Diogo Nkumbi a Nzinga, who dispatched other envoys to Pope Paul III.[193]

At this stage, Portugal's overseas policy fitted into two systems. The first, the enclaves or "Atlantic system"—characterized by territorial domain, by populating or repopulating the conquered lands with enslaved Africans, and by a slave-based economy of sugar production—encompassed the Canaries, Madeira, Cape Verde, São Tomé, and the Portuguese America enclaves. The second, the trading post or "Asian system"—featuring indirect dominion, circulation economy and mercantile involvement—included enclaves in the zones connected to the Atlantic and also to indigenous networks in Senegambia, the Gulf of Guinea, Congo, Mozambique, India, Ceylon, China, and, partially, in the Amazon basin.

In Congo the strategy of indirect domination, by way of trade and religious influence, lasted for a century and a half.

The instructions given by King Manuel to his ambassador to the Congo kingdom formulate precise and sharp questions regarding the potential of the new market and the country's economic scenario. To begin with, the king charged his envoy not to allow hostility between Portuguese settlers and traders against the Bakongo. The goal was trade, and not territorial conquest. "You shall labor to know about the trade that there may be." Did copper, ivory, slaves "and other wares that in this land may be" constitute the Manicongo`s royal monopoly? Or was there a native merchant caste? What volume and what exchange arrangements were taking place between the indigenous communities? "What sums of the said things there are and may be taken each year and in exchange for what goods?" Was the king of the Congo willing to pay regular tribute to the Portuguese Crown?[194]

Motivated by the same concerns, eighteenth- and nineteenth-century British officers in India wrote reports on similar matters, whose substance would be analyzed by Marx and Henry Maine.[195] Both in the 1800s India and in 1500s Congo, it was necessary to understand the language, the circulation of tradable goods, the forms of property and labor, the kinship categories, the political systems, and the native economy so that colonial administrators would properly exploit and tax them.[196] In Congo as in India, metropolitan domination was for a long time exerted by means of an indirect government in which native authority was left standing.

A century and a half of contention between the Congo kingdom and Portugal—settled with bullets by André Vidal de Negreiros' musketeers in the battle of Mbwila (1665)—was born in a territorial dispute about silver mines belonging to the Bakongo kingdom. This was unlikely to happen on the other side of the sea, where no settler or royal officer would think that Amerindian chieftains could hold sovereignty over any portion of the Portuguese American territory.

Indeed, Portugal's presence in Asia and most of Africa was much more restricted than in America. What was intently sought was to make accessible, to "discover"—in the meaning proper to the Renaissance—a hidden market, a trade zone sometimes guessed at (Congo), sometimes well known (India), but up to then closed to Europeans. In these regions, access was gained by means of alliances with indigenous authorities.

Whence the ostentatious goods offered to the Congo kings, such as horses, asses, hares, greyhounds, falcons, "some of those Venetian golden mirrors," "a full silk frizzled sewn open cape," and "a trimmed hood dotted with sewn silk ornaments." Also offered were "two pairs of trousers, one purple, the other black"; "a length of fringed frizzled velvet and one more waistcoat of the same fabric . . . and the sleeves lined with taffeta"; and "satin kerchiefs, hats, [and] china."[197] Further presents, at first sight uncanny, included cushioned chairs or the so-called "piss pans" (*bacias de mijar*) donated to the king of the Assin, living close to the Elmina castle.[198]

Symbols of royal apparatus, offerings of these ostentatious goods led the way to the initial contract, the opening of the trading port or fair.[199] Beyond their monetary value, such offerings represented the political tribute that the European paid to indigenous sovereigns.

According to the steps observed in fifteenth-century Upper Guinea and in sixteenth-century Asia, the fortress succeeded the factory. First, native barters were tied to a coastal outlet; then walls were built to keep safe the regal monopoly in the area.[200] Decisive steps for the insertion of Portuguese and European mercantile activity took place in Asian sites in which the equivalence of weights and measures by different cultures was carried out. Such was the case of Cochin, on the Kerala (Malabar) coast, where the Viceroy Francisco de Almeida succeeded in harmonizing Indian and European scales by the creation of the "new weight."[201] In other places maritime exchanges would grind to a halt and the ports had to be incorporated by force into the world-economy. Indeed, looting—"the labor of weapons," in the revealing expression by Zurara—would never be discarded. Studies of the early Portuguese overseas enclaves underline the opposition between looting and trade.[202] The reality is that plunder and trade replaced one another and had complementary effects in economic exploitation.

King João III stated the place and function of pillage in 1532 as he donated the Bijagos Islands (off Guiné-Bissau) to Infant Luís, his brother: "If the Blacks who now live or who will live there and are in the said islands did not wish to trade in slaves on their own accord . . . [the Infant] may wage war on them and hold them captive and as such have them sold in my kingdom or outside it, wherever you may wish, paying me, for those taken by war in this manner, the rights collected on my behalf for traded slaves."[203] In circumstances where European goods were devalued or when the exchanges seemed blocked by the indigenous communities, looting intervened as a mechanism of mercantile regulation.

In the beginning of the 1540s, incidents in Sofala, south of Mombasa, reveal that the opening of a factory in a promising area could well come to nothing.[204] Hoping to capture the gold exported to the Indian Ocean by the Monomotapa emperor, the Portuguese seized this East Africa warehouse from the Kilwa sultanate.[205] Praising the conquest, João de Barros compared the Portuguese Sofala's fortress, the first European military building in the Indian Ocean, with the castle of São Jorge da Mina (Elmina).[206] Still, the Sofala fortress-factory blocked in the wake of a losing game in which no Swahili community would let its neighbors grow stronger with European trade. "The war [the Swahili wage among themselves] is about forbidding one another to make deals or take goods from the factory, because whoever acquires them will be more powerful than the others," informed a former Sofala Portuguese factor.[207] To break the coastal natives' blockade and to reactivate inland trade, the Portuguese had to unleash forays into the Zambezi region.[208]

The general purpose of the plundering was defined in the warning dispatched in 1658 to the Lisbon War Council by the sugar-mill owner, commander of the anti-Dutch guerrillas in Pernambuco, and then governor of Angola, João Fernandes Vieira. "It is convenient to take war to the field in order . . . to avoid the obstruction of the Gospel's preaching, enslavement by barter [*resgates*] or exchanges . . . which they [the Angolan *sobas*] will not do so easily, if fear does not compel them to."[209]

The network of inland fortresses and trading posts—which unlocked and drained the hinterland trade to Luanda and Benguela—would be a decisive triumph for Portugal's multisecular Ethiopic Ocean domination. As we shall see in the next chapters, it would be in Angolan lands that the complementarity of direct pillage and overseas trade reached unparalleled intensity.

Part of the historiography has been permeated by the interpretation that envisions Angola's conquest as a sequence of struggles aiming to dominate lands rich in minerals and suitable for colonization. This is a properly distorted approach that hides the essential: the region was the scene of the devastating hunting of men in the constitutive movement of the modern era's world market.

In the first decade of the 1660s, Angola had already been incorporated into the imaginary of the Amerindian seaside communities as one of the components of the colonial web involving the Atlantic world. By that time, Caraibebê-guaçu, the "Great Angel," a prominent South Brazil Carijó shaman, stated that the paths leading to Heaven followed only three routes: the first crossed the Patos, the Brazilian lakes where he lived, the second crossed Portugal, and the last crossed Angola.[210]

Chapter 3

Lisbon, Slave-Trade Capital of the Western World

Settled on the largest European estuary, Lisbon stood out as the biggest Iberian city of the 1600s and served as Europe's platform for exchanges overseas, especially with Africa, where Portuguese sails prevailed.[1] The Treaty of Tordesilla's clauses, reiterated by the Agreement of Tomar (1581), sealed the Iberian dynastic unification and secured Portuguese sovereignty over the African coast and trade. Habsburg Spain observed her part in the agreement, as she chased Lisbon's competitors away from the trade ports of Africa and the Atlantic islands.[2]

Gradually, Portuguese slave traders won control of the Hispanic American markets, displacing Andalusian and Genoese rivals in the last quarter of the sixteenth century.[3] Next, the Portuguese managed to secure African ports, also obtaining almost all of the *licencias*, export forms issued by Madrid for the provision of Spanish America with *piezas de Indias*.[4] Signed in 1583, the first wholesale agreement between Felipe II and the Portuguese Cape Verdes *Contratadores* (royal tax-collectors), concerning the trade of 3,000 slaves from Upper Guinea to Spanish America, set the stage for the *Asiento de Negros*.[5]

While the Atlantic islands (the Canaries, Madeira, the Azores, and Cape Verde), São Tomé, and the Iberian Peninsula (mainly Lisbon and Seville) formed the largest consumer market for enslaved Africans, two zones of Africa attracted European merchants, the Senegambia and the Congo-Angola area. In the last decades of the 1500s, as the American market reaffirmed its preeminence, most of the trade shifted to the Congo basin, and to Angola, which was plundered by Paulo Dias Novais and his men.[6]

According to the testimony of a missionary, an "infinity" of natives was enslaved in Angola in the 1580s. At the head of 10,000 native archers (the Chombari), Novais further relied on 150 European harquebusiers and some cavalry. Supplied partially with mounts brought over from Pernambuco and Bahia, his troops also boasted fifty mastiff dogs, feared "as death itself" by the Mbundu.[7] From that time on, the number of Africans deported into the Americas superseded the volume of both the trans-Saharan slave trade into the Maghreb and Egypt and the forced migration into European ports and the Atlantic Islands.[8] The slave trade thus became the main pillar of the Portuguese Atlantic.

The Ibero-American Slave Market

Within the scope of the new Iberian Union, Domingos de Abreu e Brito, Jerônimo Castanho, who was Paulo Dias Novais's legal representative (*procurador*) in Madrid, Diogo Ferreira (or Herrera), and Duarte Lopes, formed the Portuguese lobby who acted to convince the Habsburg Crown to expand the European occupation and the slave trade in Angola.[9] Paulo Dias Novais had businesses in Brazil. Represented by his agent in Rio de Janeiro, he rented a sugar mill and land on the large Jesuit properties on Guanabara Bay in 1579. On the Jesuit's side, it was Fr. Anchieta who signed the lease.[10] As a correspondent of Balthazar Barreira, Jesuit superior in Luanda, Anchieta followed the battles waged in Angola by Dias Novais and his captains.[11]

Another man of the Luanda lobby and Ethiopic Ocean expert, Abreu e Brito, in his 1591 report on the South Atlantic commissioned by the Crown, cast over the Mbundu the objective gaze of a lumberman who sees a tropical forest for the first time. "Seeking in the aforesaid kingdom [Angola] all the ways leading towards the growth of Your [Royal] treasury, I thought that the slaving matter [*a coisa dos escravos*] was of the greatest scale known to date, which would not wear out until the end of the world, because the land is so populated."[12] Novais's associate in Luanda, Jerônimo Castanho, also knowledgeable about Brazil and about Luanda, where he lived with his family, outlined the advantages of Angola amid the European rivalry in Portugal's overseas. "São Tomé is lost . . . and the same [happens] in the Elmina and Pepper [Malagueta] Coast and Sanaga (Senegal), only Brazil remains, as [the] India (situation) worsens every day." In three memorials to the Crown, he detailed the number of soldiers, horses, mules, guns, and powder barrels needed for the Angola invasion.[13] Ultimately, the Duarte Lopes report to the Crown, critical to the establishment of the *Asientos de Negros*, envisioned the Mbundu peoples as a vast bondage reservoir and conceived of the slave trade as the instrument for the Iberian conquest of Angola.[14]

In this context, Felipe II sent Governor Francisco de Almeida with a strong military corps to Luanda in 1592 and created the *Asiento de Negros* system. European investments, multiannual Crown-guaranteed contracts, and broad business perspectives in the America's colonial markets, especially in the precious-metal-mining markets, led to large-scale commoditization of enslaved Africans.

Madrid had its own motives to put the *Asiento* contracts out for auction. Taken into the Flanders War quagmire, involved in maritime and continental battles, lacking sufficient capital, with no ports of trade in Africa, holding a fleet system unfit for the transportation of slaves, Spain was in want of alternatives. Consequently, the Habsburg only practiced fiscal monopoly as they instituted the *Asientos de Negros*: a unified system of concessions for the provision of enslaved Africans to Spanish America, auctioned by the Crown for a specified length of time, according to certain modalities. Portuguese slave traders, ship owners, and prominent Iberian merchants controlled the Spanish-American market by purchasing all the *Asientos* auctioned from 1595 to 1640, during the Iberian Union. As a result of the high mortality among the Amerindians exploited in mining labor, the enslaved Africans imported through the *Asiento* became a determinant factor in the Spanish America's economy.

Asiento shipments, concentrated in Vera Cruz, Cartagena, and sometimes Buenos Aires, improved terrestrial and coastal routes as well as Spanish American markets. A significant number of Africans shipped to Vera Cruz or Cartagena landed illegally or with the agreement of local authorities in other Caribbean ports.[15] The contraband in the Río de la Plata is discussed below. Transcontinental transport of Africans operated through Cartagena de Índias into Venezuela or the Caribbean toward Lima (via Portobello and the Panama isthmus), then into Alto Peru by land. Such overland and coastal transfers took their toll on the Africans' lives.[16] Cartagena, first *Asiento* port and the main American slave-trade port at that time, was the headquarters of two of the most prominent Portuguese factors in Spanish America: Jorge Fernandes Gramaxo, the factor for *asentistas* Reynel and the Coutinho brothers, from 1595 to 1610, and Jorge Fernandes de Elvas, which was the *asentista* Antonio Fernandes de Elvas' son and factor from 1619 to 1622.[17] Later in this chapter we shall examine the extent of their influence.

The enlargement of the *asentista* markets explains the steep growth of the forced migration to Spanish America in the period 1595 to 1625 (see Figure 3.1, p. 104). The figures may have been even higher. As a matter of fact, illegal deals practiced by the *asentistas* and their agents were substantial. Lisbon taxed since 1575 the enslaved sent from Senegambia and Angola to Spanish America at a substantially higher rate than those exported to Brazil, as mentioned in chapter 1.[18] The difference between the two taxes widened during the Portuguese *Asientos*. Likewise, the import taxes were higher in Spanish America ports than in Portuguese America ports.[19] Such taxes disparities prompted illicit embarkments to Spanish American ports. Portugal's authorities in Upper Guinea and Angola denounced the "abuse" of merchants and ship captains who, to pay lower taxes on their embarked slaves, declared Brazilian ports as their destination, and then sailed directly to Spanish America.[20] The practice persisted after the end of the Portuguese *Asientos*. In the 1650s, Luanda authorities denounced overcrowded vessels that sailed to Buenos Aires illegally carrying more than 1,000 "heads."[21] Others reports, dated 1675 and 1676, inform Lisbon of the presence of Spanish slave ships on Angola's coast.[22]

As shown below, there was also a contraband slave trade carry on directly from Brazil's ports, particularly towards the Río de la Plata. Therefore, the figures of the TSTD related to the Africans imported in the Rio de la Plata are underestimated, as those deported into Brazil during the Portuguese *Asientos* and beyond are possibly overestimated.

The Portuguese *Asientos* and Angola

Pedro Gomes Reynel, of Lisbon, placed the winning bid at the first slaving *Asiento* auction in 1595.[23] Renewing prohibitions on the transatlantic transport of Moriscos and Turkish slaves, the *Asiento* regulation, probably in reaction to the São Tomé rebellions, also included "Mulatto and Mestizo" slaves in the ban, and characterized "very black Negros" (*Negros atezados*) as the single human commodity allowed to be sold in Spanish America. Far from its Mediterranean stages, the slave traffic enlarged Atlantic exchanges through the plundering of the sub-Saharan communities designed as its primary resource.[24]

Well positioned in the Habsburg court, Reynel also held the Angola Contract (regarding the collection of royal taxes). Such circumstances helped him to win the *Asiento*. Reynel thus secured the two ends of the business. Royal tax collector and chief buyer of enslaved Africans in Angola, he was also nearly the sole supplier of Africans to Spanish America.[25] As Magalhães Godinho and Vila Vilar observed, the Reynel *Asiento* displayed a scheme typical of the first *Asientos* purchased by the Portuguese: at least until 1624, the *asentistas* also held the Angola Contract or figured as partners in it.[26]

The second *asentista*, João Rodrigues, also kept the position of contract-holder. Moreover, he was appointed head the Angolan government (1602–1603). A Knight of the Order of Christ, former member of the Council of Portugal, former governor of the Elmina fortress (as his father, Lopo Sousa Coutinho, had been), João Rodrigues drew up ambitious plans.[27] Significantly, his Angola governorship was conceded for the same length of time as covered by his *Asiento* (nine years), constituting the longest overseas government term ever granted. Before leaving Europe, Coutinho ordered vessels and equipment in Hamburg for his Luanda sojourn, as he intended to erect new fortresses in Angola. He also sought to bring 2,500 horses over from the Río de la Plata and Panama, where he had lived while dealing in slaves and cattle, so as to form cavalry companies, an important European military advantage in the Angolan wars.[28]

In doing so, Coutinho did not seek partnerships with the capitalists usually interested in such enterprises. Instead, he associated with small Spanish shareholders, probable proxies for Iberian New Christian merchants, and put forward his own property as a guarantee for bonds and investments necessary for the *Asiento* lease.[29] As additional support, he also obtained a royal decree granting West Central African officials with privileges akin to those conceded to royal agents in North Africa and Indian fortresses, as well in the imperial armadas.[30]

At the head of Iberian soldiers, some of them veteran of the Moroccan wars, the governor disembarked in Luanda and soon attacked the Kisama chiefdoms. Kisama was a stronghold of the *sobas* holding the Demba rock-salt mines, the source of one long-distance trade network, as mentioned in the previous chapter.[31] From early on, the invaders were aware the strategic role of the salt trade. The salt mines were as valuable "as those of precious metal," stated the missionaries of the Luanda's College.[32] At the end of the sixteenth century, another Jesuit report, one of the many texts about the African economy and politics written by missionaries to support the European conquest, related: "One could conquer a considerable part of the kingdom (of Ndongo) without war, just by preventing the sacks of (Kisama) salt from reaching other parts."[33] Having lent his ear to the captains seasoned in the African campaigns, Coutinho made Kisama his "chief aim." He did not, however, march as far as he intended, for he came down with tropical fevers.[34]

After the death of João Rodrigues Coutinho, his brother and partner, Gonçalo Vaz Coutinho (the elder), who held a degree in literature at Coimbra University and was son-in-law of the kingdom's chief treasurer, took up the post of *asentista* until 1609.[35] Fearful of the Angolan fevers, the "calamity of the land," which had already consumed his son, Luís de Sousa, as well as his brother João, Gonçalo declined the governorship of Angola. He preferred to later take command of the Portuguese citadel of Mazagan (now El Jadida), in Atlantic Morocco.[36] With the cavalry and soldiers brought over by João Rodrigues Coutinho, Manuel Cerveira (1603–1607), his lieutenant and successor at the head of the Angolan government, also raided the Kisama, Ilamba, Libolo, and Cambembe villages.[37] Striking the first blows, to be resumed half a century later by the Luso-Brasílico[38] offensive and the battle of Mbwila (1665), the new governor harassed the local *sobados*, at the meeting point of the paths forking out to the North Angolan and Congo coast and into the hinterland.[39] At the end of his term as governor, 10,000 slaves were deported annually from Angola.[40]

Several reasons explain the steady growth of the slave trade in West Central Africa, mainly in Angola. For now, it is worth drawing attention to the activities of some key *Asiento* entrepreneurs in the Habsburg Iberian Peninsula.

During the Coutinho brothers' *Asiento* (1602–1609), one of their brothers, Manuel de Sousa Coutinho, former military officer, lived and traded in Cartagena de Índias, in the Río de La Plata and in Rio de Janeiro.[41] Active in the lucrative Rio de Janeiro–Buenos Aires–Luanda circuit, he dealt in silver, horses, and slaves.[42] Writing from Rio de Janeiro to Madrid in 1606, Manuel de Sousa asked the Court if he could succeed his brother Gonçalo in Angola's government. Meanwhile, Gonçalo was himself on the list of applicants to the Government-General of Brazil. The two brothers' requests, granting to the Coutinho family the control of the Iberian South Atlantic, were rejected by the Crown.[43] When he later retired to a Dominican monastery in Lisbon, Manuel de Sousa took orders and assumed the name of his nephew, who had died in Angola. Then, known as Friar Luis de Sousa, he wrote his remarkable literary and historical oeuvre. Commenting later on works by Friar Luís, father Antonio Vieira referred to the author's troubled life, stating that he had studied history "in the University of the World" and not "in the Science Academies."[44] At his death in 1632, Friar Luís de Sousa left most of his estate to another nephew, Francisco de Sousa Coutinho, also a son of Gonçalo Vaz Coutinho.[45]

That same year, Francisco de Sousa Coutinho accomplished an important task as the Braganza's envoy in Madrid. On behalf of the Duke of Braganza, he signed the marriage contract between the duke and Luisa de Guzman, later the king and the queen of Portugal. Portugal's most influential diplomat of his time, Francisco de Sousa Coutinho lived in Madrid from 1623 as the Braganza House's envoy. Acquainted with merchants and royal officers, he became quite aware of the connections of his family and his country with the *Asiento de Negros*.⁴⁶ In chapter 6, we shall see that the great slaving business and Angola, from which the Francisco de Sousa Coutinho family had extracted their wealth and prestige, where his brother and uncle perished in the effort to implement their interests, played a significant role in his diplomatic strategy to settle the Braganza's dynasty in the Lisbon throne.

Another son of the *asentista* Gonçalo Vaz Coutinho, Lopo de Sousa Coutinho, married Joana, daughter of Manuel Pereira Coutinho, governor of Angola (1630–1635). Their son, named Gonçalo Vaz Coutinho (the younger), wedded Barbara da Veiga, daughter of Diogo da Veiga, an important slave trader in the Río de La Plata, as we shall see later in this chapter.⁴⁷ One of Lopo's and Joana's granddaughters, Joana de Castro (the younger), married Heitor Mendes de Brito, grandson of the *asentista* Antônio Fernandes de Elvas.⁴⁸

At the end of the Coutinho brothers *Asiento*, the Angola Contract (1607–1611) belonged to Duarte Dias Henriques, linked to Diogo da Veiga and partner of Angola governor Manuel Forjaz (1607–1611). The broker between Duarte Dias Henriques and the governor was Manuel Drago, Henriques's factor in Angola, and an agent of the Lisbon–Rio de Janeiro–Luanda–Buenos Aires slave-trade network.⁴⁹

In fact, Duarte Dias Henriques (1570–1631) was a grandson of the Portuguese Jewish patriarch Duarte Dias (also known as Abraão Aboab), and started his career in Pernambuco, where he invested in sugar mills and in the slave trade. His family had relatives and representatives in the main markets of Europe and America. At the end of the 1620s, Duarte Dias Henriques became a Spanish Crown banker as well.⁵⁰

Generation by generation, through marriages, wills, and cartels, prominent Iberian families got involved in Angolan affairs, evincing the globalizing dimension of the slaving business at the time of the *Asientos*.

Captives and Slaves in the Ethiopic Ocean

The well-funded, large-scale organized *Asiento* voyages improved knowledge of the Middle Passage through the South Atlantic and the Caribbean. Navigation hazards became more predictable to the Portuguese authorities, merchants, and missionaries. From January to April, heavy rains in West Central Africa delayed the march of the inland *libambo*—a string of tied-up captives—to the fairs and ports. (In a revealing variant of Brazilian social hardship, in the twentieth century, *libombo* designated the waves of the inhabitants from the *Nordeste* migrating to São Paulo in search for work).[51] May, June, and July were not convenient for departures from the Gulf of Guinea and Angola, due to the recurrent storms of the east-west routes at the beginning of the boreal summer.[52]

Seasonality therefore concentrated voyages and departures in African ports, increasing the despair of deportation. In the meantime, thousands left their kin, their village, and their land, pushed into ships, as many others waited, penned in the areas near ports, being chosen, fed, and, often, buried. Physical exhaustion, ill treatment in the overland itinerary, malnutrition, and Luanda port's diseases reaped a portion of the outsider slaves' lives, torn from the Ovimbundo plateau and further, as the inland trade networks expanded.[53] By the last quarter of the seventeenth century, most of the enslaved individuals endured a 500- or 750-mile march before their arrival in Luanda.[54]

The coastal preeminence of the Luanda port, its high integration with the mercantile capital following the *Asientos*, the extension of its inland networks, and its time-concentrated and massive embarkments could explain the paradox analyzed in the crossings of the first decades of the eighteenth century by Joseph Miller and, with more comprehensive data, by Eltis and Richardson.[55] During the years 1638 to 1775, for which the available information is more inclusive than for earlier decades, Africans crossing from Angola to Brazil died in greater numbers (12.1 percent) than those from Senegambia (8.2 percent) or the Bight of Benin and the Gold Coast (7.2 percent), even though the Luanda route to Brazilian ports was shorter than that of the West African ports. As Eltis and Richardson observe, this pattern is the opposite of that for the Caribbean traffic, where longer voyages correlate with higher mortality at sea.[56]

For nearly three centuries, multitudes of panicking individuals were taken in fetters from their inland homes to be crammed into ships that left Luanda, the biggest slaving port in history. At that time, Angola's capital was also the most populated European enclave of sub-Saharan Africa. Although numerous European witnesses were active in the place, they did not record such facts. There are additional significant gaps in the documentation. Bernard Bailyn underlined the "vastness of our ignorance" with regard to the European migrations that populated colonial America.[57] But the ignorance involving the African forced migration is of a distinct nature. It concerns here a wider movement of about 14,907 voyages made to deport 4.864 million individuals into Brazil in the course of three centuries.[58]

In addition to the crew, other free people traveled aboard the slave ships, the only means of transportation from Africa to South America. There were few cabins.

At night and in adverse weather, one could not risk staying on the upper deck. Many royal officers, members of the military, tradesmen, colonists, clergy, and missionaries traveled from Luanda and Benguela to Brazil, either as a final destination or to seek further transportation bound for Europe. All those individuals heard and saw the suffering of the deported for six weeks or more. And yet there are exceedingly few direct references to the Middle Passage.

One of the rare direct testimonies of the 1600s, offered by the Italian Capuchin friar Sorrento, allows a peek into the tragedy of 900 slaves shipped from Luanda to Bahia in December 1649: "That boat [. . .] by force of its unbearable stench, of its lack of room, of the continuing screams and the infinite misery of so many unhappy souls, seemed like hell."[59] Another report, made a few years later, also by an Italian Capuchin, Friar Piacenza, provides details about the distribution of slaves on board. It must be noted that, since the middle of the sixteenth century, some slave ships bound to Brazil and Spanish America were insured to cover losses caused by enslaved revolts at sea.[60] To prevent mutinies, the men were usually chained on the lower deck, the women stayed on the middle deck, pregnant women on the quarterdeck, and children on the upper deck. "This navigation is the most painful there is in the whole world," wrote Friar Piacenza.[61]

There are a few more eighteenth-century narratives, and a greater number from the first half of the nineteenth century, sometimes compulsorily recorded in the course of judicial or parliamentary inquiries. To my knowledge, the testimonials regarding the Portuguese, Brasílico, and Brazilian (in the first half of the nineteenth century) slave ships number fewer than thirty. Many are written by foreigners, but none by the missionaries who traveled most along that route, the Portuguese Jesuits. Why? Probably because their superiors issued instructions to avoid such narratives. This is the only reason I can find for the sources' impressive silence on the issue. Italian Capuchin friars Sorrento and Piacenza, like many individuals of their generation, knew about the massacres and suffering endured by European peoples throughout the Thirty Years War. And yet, they understood that the Middle Passage stood out among the most impressive miseries of their time. Other missionaries, other Europeans, the Portuguese clergy, royal officers, merchants, and colonists traveling in the South Atlantic knew it. They knew it, but they ignored it or hid it away.

Renewed over and over in the course of almost three centuries on the same Luso-Angolan shores, along the same route toward the same Brazilian ports, the deportation of Africans contrasts with the fragmented scenario of the Amerindian slave trade in Portuguese America. Such contrast deserves analysis.

The Agreement of Tomar (1581), in which the Portuguese Courts recognized Felipe II of Spain as king of Portugal, also secured Lusitanian administrative autonomy in Portugal and her colonies. However, the Hispanic doctrinal influence has also weighed down the politics imposed on the South Atlantic Amerindians in the beginning of the seventeenth century. Hardly to be suspected of condescending toward Madrid, Father Antonio Vieira assessed later that the relevance of the laws protecting Amerindians in Portuguese America had been greater during the Habsburg period than under the Braganza.[62]

In West Central Africa, the Habsburg intent of submitting the *sobados* to royal authority led the Crown to confront the Jesuits and the captains who extorted "pieces" from the Mbundu. The result was the 1592 mutiny, when the conquistadors and the Ignatians expelled the governor of Angola, Francisco de Almeida. A different set of alliances was knitted in Brazil. Here, the Crown joined the Jesuits to break the alliance between local authorities and colonists who enslaved Amerindians. There, the Crown faced the missionaries, reduced the Jesuit's tutelage over the Mbundu villages, and stimulated the African forced migration to the Americas. What could account for such difference?

Unlike in Portuguese America, there were in Angola communities involved in precolonial long-distance trade, which allowed for the extraction, by the missionaries, of tributes paid in the form of slaves and other merchandise.[63]

Seeking to control the *sobas*, the Jesuits clashed with royal agents who accused them of appropriating natives' income due to the Crown. In Brazil, colonial exchanges based on regular Indian enslavement did not take root. Generally considered illegal, the seizure of captives was denounced by the missionaries and to a lesser extent by royal authorities. Clearly, the Luso-Brasílico predatory expeditions (*bandeiras*), based on regional domination and exploitation, did not fit the Crown's South Atlantic political strategy or that of the Company of Jesus. However, keen on the advantages of coerced labor for their service and for the settlers, local authorities sought to control the Indian villages.

At first, Madrid extended to Portuguese America the liberating precept installed in Spanish America by the *Leyes Nuevas* of 1542. Accordingly, all the Amerindians, both those living in their native villages and those who had flocked into the colonial settlements, were supposed to be born free and thus remained free. "I declare all the gentiles of that part of Brazil to be free, according to Law and their natural birth," proclaimed Felipe III in the 1609 decree.[64] Moreover, the law widened the Jesuits' powers over the settled Indians. When proclaimed in Bahia, the news sparked a mutiny against the authorities and, above all, against the Ignatians.[65]

Diogo de Menezes, governor-general of Brazil (1608–1612), endorsed the colonists' complaints and declared his hostility to missionary control over the Amerindians. He then connected the political conjunctures on both sides of the Ethiopic Ocean, relating the troubles in Bahia to the Angolan 1592 mutiny. "Such misadventures arise from clergy meddling in government. Because the chief cause of the Angola uprising was the Company's (of Jesus) priests," wrote the governor to the Crown.[66] The plea seems to have been heard, for the king backtracked and authorized certain forms of Amerindian enslavement, in the context of the 1611 Laws.[67]

In parallel, the settlement system (*aldeamentos*), consisting of the forced transfer, mingling, and sedentarization of indigenous communities, was consolidated. In this system the mechanical arts and trade were to be taught to the settled Indians.[68] Barely recognized for Africans, the Habsburg juridical precept of "natural freedom" was fully introduced into the Portuguese doctrine regarding the Amerindians. In practice, the Habsburg and the Braganza Crown generally referred to the enslaved Amerindians in royal edicts as "captives," contrasting with the decrees issued to Africa and Africans, in which the fiscal and mercantile terms "pieces" and "slaves" cropped up.

More significant developments relate to these definitions. In the Indo-European vocabulary in general, and in the Latin vocabulary in particular, the word "captive" defined the individual who was a prisoner (*captivus* = prisoner), still held by his captor or the dealer. Through the sixteenth and seventeenth centuries, when Arabs and Berber Muslims (the "Moors") sailed the Mediterranean, raiding the coasts kidnapping Christians and taking them to the Maghreb fairs, "captive" denoted a transitory, accidental status of privation of freedom. The constant relationship between Muslims and Christians, captors and captives, helped to bring together the Mediterranean economic, social, and political space.[69]

Many Europeans became captives (*cativos*) in the hands of the Maghribis, until their relatives, the order of the Trinitarian priests, the Mamposteiro, or the Alfaqueque managed to pay their ransom in Algiers, Tunis, Tripoli, or Malta.[70] Even Amerindians from Brazil aboard Portuguese ships sailing to Lisbon were held up and ended up captive in Algiers. The most impressive case would be the captivity and later ransom by the Trinitarians of 2,000 Portuguese military, among them many aristocrats, made prisoner in the battle of Ksar El Kebir (1578).[71] Recalling the ancestral fear on the Iberian shores in the face of Maghrebian raids, the phrase "there are Moors on the shore" is still used to scare children in the Iberian Peninsula, Spanish America, and the Brazilian northeast.[72]

A different meaning is borne, therefore, by the word "slave" (*escravo*), characteristic of a juridical status of permanent reification of the individual acquired as property to be used or to be sold.[73] Some royal edicts clearly refer to the two nouns in their distinct juridical meaning. Thus, the 1519 Royal Regulations to the São Tomé Islands call for the confiscation of the properties, implicitly including the *escravos*, of Santomese merchants who breached the law and donation of half of the goods for the rescue of North Africa's Christian captives (*cativos*).[74] Chokwe, Mbundu, Kimbundu, Kikongo, Yoruba (Nagot), Makua, the idioms of the West and East African peoples deported to Brazil, have distinct terms for "slave" and "captive" or "slave born in the master's house."[75] Bluteau, as he codified the Portuguese vocabulary at the beginning of the eighteenth century, likewise reiterated the social and juridical lines separating the two concepts: a captive (*cativo*) is a "prisoner of war, or imprisoned by pirates," and slave (*escravo*) is "one who was born a captive, or was sold, and is under the power of the master."[76]

The Crown confirmed the slave trade's primacy in Angola at the same time as it recognized the freedom of the Amerindians, "according to law and their natural birth." Hence, in 1604, royal orders halted the search for silver mines in the Angolan territory and stimulated the slaving business, "the land's ancient trade and enslavement by barter (*resgate*)."[77] Taking advantage of the growth in the slave trade and ignoring royal orders, the Jesuits kept control over some *sobados*, extorting tribute in the form of slaves. Before, "they [the governors] would eat our guts, but now, filled with fear or shame, they do what we want," as a Luanda Jesuit complacently informed Rome.[78] Challenged, the Crown included in Governor Forjaz's statute (1607) the order to invalidate for once and for all the "*amos*" institution, that is, the concessions of *sobados* to captains and priests. From then on, the Crown would collect due tribute directly from the subjugated *sobas*.[79]

At that time, already in Angola for one generation, the Portuguese became more acclimatized, more *baqueanos*,[80] as the seasoned settlers used to be called. For the first time, one of the settlers, Bento Banha, was made governor between 1611 and 1615. Aiming to widen the conquered territory and to enslave more natives, Banha allied with the Jaga, the most feared warriors in West Central Africa.[81] Originating from the Imbangala people, the Jaga incorporated into their ranks the most apt prisoners, following an initiatory rite, swelling their army after each campaign.

They sparked great panic in other native ranks when they charged shouting their *"Pouteh! Pouteh!"* war cry. As the bishop of Congo witnessed in 1619: "they fear the Jaga so much that, on hearing about them, they break off and run."[82] The Jaga were also feared by the Portuguese, due among other reasons to their military skill as they charged ranked in the *songo*, the attacking squad, and due to their use of iron in the manufacture of the assegai (short spear), arrow tips, and above all, battle axes.[83]

Although missionaries, captains and old Angolan hands that knew the Jaga stated that they were roving multiethnic warriors, and not an ethnic group per se, historical controversy has surrounded their origins.[84] As previously defined, I call Jaga the marauding warriors designated under such name in the seventeenth and eighteenth centuries by Portuguese sources.[85] Some of such warriors joined the Portuguese side. With them, Banha launched offensives into the Ndongo kingdom, preying on many people and vassalizing dozens of *sobados*. An official registry was set up to fix the yearly number of slaves that each *sobado* should pay to the Crown.[86]

Portuguese slave traders and the Jaga remained in alliance during Manuel Cerveira's second government (1615–1617) in Benguela. Cerveira then tried to open an export route out of the Bié plateau to Benguela, meeting staunch resistance from interests established in Luanda.[87] Such conflict was usual in the overseas economic geography, in Africa as well as Asia and America. The opening of a new port of trade drained the inland exchange circuits and shifted sea thoroughfares, to the loss of merchants settled in more distant, older trading ports.[88]

Vessels leaving Benguela to Brazil included enslaved Jaga who fought the Portuguese. As with all the Jaga, these individuals carried the distinctive hallmark of the Jaga warrior initiation: the two upper front teeth pulled out.[89] This is probably the source of the name in Brazilian Portuguese for a toothless person: *benguela* or *banguela*.[90] The Jaga's role in the Portuguese warlike activities in Angola clearly appeared during Luís Mendes de Vasconcelos's governorship (1617–1621). A refined political and military writer in Europe, Luís Mendes de Vasconcelos turned into a brutal predator in Africa.

Predators, Governors, and Bankers

Luís Mendes de Vasconcelos joined the 1583 Spanish expedition against the Prior of Crato's partisans on Terceira Island (Azores), fought in the Flanders war, and navigated as captain-major the Eastern Armada in the 1610s. While in the Indian Ocean, he followed the feats of the *grão-capitão* André Furtado de Mendonça, who died in 1611, a chaste warrior, staunch Catholic, and slaughterer of Muslims.[91] Author of the *Diálogos do Sítio de Lisboa* (1608), a key book for seventeenth-century Iberism, and of other political, military, and literary books, Vasconcelos was one of those Iberian commanders skilled in verse, prose, and decapitation.

Yet his family's influence in Madrid, his military and strategic reflections, registered in his *Arte Militar* (1612), his experience in the Flanders battlefields, and in the Asian markets, as well as his considerations on the overseas dominium, stated in his *Dialogos*, led him to sketch a global view of Angola's role in the Iberian world.[92]

Initially, Vasconcelos planned to cut across Austral Africa to access the precious-metal mines of the Monomotapa. In his view, the overland route from Luanda to Mozambique would avoid the currents and corsair threats of the Cape route to India. Therefore, he hoped, in vain, to obtain from the Crown the title of "viceroy of Ethiopia, with everything there is from the Congo and the Cape of Good Hope up to the Red Sea." Aware of European wars and rivalry overseas, he wrote from Luanda to the Court, stressing Angola's geopolitical significance. In a 1616 report to Madrid, Vasconcelos clearly emphasized the need for "strong vigilance over all the conquests and territories of Her Majesty's dominions, and much more over Angola, a very rich place on which all of the Indies' [Spanish America] and Brazil's management depends."[93] On his arrival in Luanda, he repudiated the alliance with the Jaga, who, in his words, were used by the governors and colonists "as hunting dogs in order to unfairly have them deliver slaves."[94] Later, he changed his mind. As reported by denunciations from the bishop of São Salvador do Congo, the new governor "instead of getting rid of the Jaga, embraced them" and mobilized the warriors in his raids.[95] Shielded by the Jaga, Vasconcelos systematized the *bacula-mento* (tribute) extortions imposed on the *sobados*.[96] His excesses were denounced in Lisbon. Stating that only "defensive war" was allowed in Angola, the Crown decided in 1620 to launch a probe of him and his two sons for the war waged against the "sobas."[97]

His shift regarding the Jaga alliance is significant. Before arriving in Angola, Vasconcelos wrote optimistic lines about overseas wars in his learned military treaty, *Arte Militar*. "Despite the fact that the enemy may have an excessive number of soldiers, if they are not bellicose, just a small army need be raised against them, as the conquests in the Eastern and Western Indies clearly show."[98] Like other

European chroniclers, Vasconcelos depicts overseas battles where a few conquerors and settlers, heroically on their own, destroy huge native armies. Paradoxically, this bias, typical of a more boastful colonial historiography, is comforting for the militant interpretation by politically correct authors, who imagine that the Africans or the Amerindians have always kept a united front against the European invaders. Yet the Jaga constituted a significant component in the Portuguese military supremacy in the South Atlantic, together with the Paulo Dias Novais's Chombari or the Temininó and the Potiguar Indians allied respectively to the São Paulo and Bahia colonists.[99] Thus, Vasconcelos formed an alliance with the Jaga to hunt for "*piezas de Indias*." "If there are Jaga [with the Portuguese], the [governor's] wars present no danger," wrote the bishop of Congo at that time. Some years later, in a memorial about Dutch-occupied Angola requested by the Crown in 1643, Salvador de Sá considered that the alliance with the Jaga constituted one of the chief strengths of the Portuguese in West Central Africa.[100]

Like João Rodrigues Coutinho in his time and several Angola governors later, Vasconcelos considered that European power would be better secured with the help of a cavalry force. Prior to his travel to Luanda, he had already traded Angolan slaves into the Río de La Plata in exchange for horses. He suggested, further, a measure carried out in the second half of the seventeenth century, giving preference in Luanda to slave ships importing horses from Brazil or Spanish America.[101] Claiming different reasons, he ravished Angola with his two sons, Francisco and Joane Mendes de Vasconcelos, plundering even allied villages and extorting slaves exchanged at the inland fairs, to the loss of the Luanda merchants.[102]

Enemy of the bishop of São Salvador do Congo (*M'banza Congo*) and hostile to the Jesuit missionaries, Vasconcelos kept an eye on political maneuvering in Europe. As Loyola and Francisco Xavier were beatified in 1620 to be soon canonized, he concluded that the Society of Jesus, fostered by a founder saint and a missionary saint to boot, had increased its prestige in Madrid.[103] He then made peace with the Jesuits, offering a feast and even a poetry contest in Luanda, in homage of Saint Francis Xavier. The first prize to the winning poem was a "*Pieza de Indias*," that is, a male adult slave, of good aspect, worth 22,000 réis. Being Angola, the "land where one only dealt in merchandise," where it seemed natural to reward poets with readily marketable slaves, a slave trader won the contest. In his poem, he venerated the saint by means of verses imbued with the highest merchant inspiration.[104]

> With enacted commodity of Grace and Life
> The divine Xavier, on this contract
> Says and warns you to sell cheap
> Or else you'll be held accountable in Heaven for any fraud.

Sealing his alliance with the S.J., the governor nominated as royal factor a nephew of father Jerônimo Vogado, the Ignatians' superior in Angola. Uncle and nephew would later be accused of participating in a scheme to smuggle Africans into Spanish America.[105] By the way, father Vogado made progress in his career, as the Angola's Inquisition commissar in 1620–1623 and, later, as the Jesuits' Superior in Portugal.[106]

On the Ethiopic Ocean scene, Vasconcelos' governorship (1617–1621) and Antonio Fernandes de Elvas's activities as *asentista* and *Contratador* (royal tax-collector) of Angola (1615–1622) corresponded to a new peak in the docking of ships and the loading of slaves in Luanda.[107] Cartagena, Vera Cruz, and Santo Domingo, the main *Asiento* ports in Spanish America, witnessed a surge in arrivals from Angola from 1617 to 1625. This period corresponds to the most intense flux from a single African region crossing over to an American port since the beginning of the Atlantic slave trade: fifty-six ships arrived from Angola and Congo and landed 11,328 Africans in Cartagena de Indias between 1619 an 1624.[108] It is noteworthy that Madrid conceded to Elvas a privilege refused to the previous *asentistas*, the *derecho de internación*, authorizing him to deposit his slaves in the American ports pending the arrival of buyers from inland colonial enclaves. Through inland agents called "*encomenderos de negros*," Elvas was then able to expand the slave trade and contraband in Spanish America during his *Asiento*.[109]

Slave departures from Angola between 1616 and 1625 reached a number surpassed only in the 1730s. By then, the Ethiopic Ocean had much wider economic networks, with Brazilian gold production and the large-scale deportation of the Ovimbundu from the Bié Plateau to Rio de Janeiro (and the gold mines) through Benguela, which, after Luanda and Whydah, became the third-largest slaving port in Africa.[110] The evidence of so many voyages carried out via Luanda in the years 1616–1625 deserves a few remarks.

Asiento voyages involved long and risky transactions. It was not easy to mobilize capital, fit bought or hired ships, have them registered in Seville, purchase and stock barter merchandise accepted in specific African markets, recruit sailors and arrange for equipment for the trips from Sanlúcar de Barrameda, Seville, and Lisbon all the way to Cacheu, Elmina, or Luanda, then sail on toward Cartagena, Vera Cruz, Santo Domingo, or Buenos Aires, where local factors and agents had to receive, house, feed, heal, and sell the enslaved.[111] Seasonal storms in the Caribbean and sparse winds along the West Central Africa coast resulted in navigational hazards. Not counting the onshore setup delays at the Iberian ports, a round *Asiento* voyage lasted eighteen to thirty-six months.[112] The most delicate phase was the stage in African ports. A mismatch between inland and maritime trades, gaps in food and water stocks, and overloaded ships increased mortality during the wait and the Middle Passage.[113]

Under such circumstances, it seems clear that the strong flux of vessels arriving and loading up in Luanda resulted from a previous agreement between the *asentista* Elvas and Angola's governors and authorities. A capitalist of wide transit in the Iberian businesses, Elvas enjoyed influential support at King Felipe II's court.[114] As we shall see below, Elvas played a defining role in the expansion of the Angolan slave trade.

As is well known to African historians, such pillaging cycles succeed one another in a conjuncture in which the *asentistas* accumulated, in person or via their associates and proxies, the position of Angola contractors. Thanks to the legal and illegal shipments to the Caribbean or Buenos Aires, silver passed on into the hands of the Angola slave traders. Stuart Schwartz estimates that two-thirds of the African enslaved purchased in Spanish America during the Portuguese *Asientos* (1595–1640) were paid for in silver.[115]

Explaining the increase in the Angolan forced migrations, important historians have perhaps overlooked the *asentistas*' partnership with governors. Thus, they emphasized endogenous factors at the expense of the Atlantic demand. Perhaps impressed by missionaries' accusations circulated in the seventeenth century by Severim de Faria, Father José Mathias Delgado, Cardonega's commentator and himself a missionary in Angola in the first half of the twentieth century, attributed the intensification of enslavement expeditions to the bellicose frenzy of Luís Mendes Vasconcelos. Beatrix Heintze partially follows such an interpretation. By contrast, Phillip Curtin and Joseph Miller wrote that the phenomenon derives from the alliance established between the Jaga and the Portuguese slave traders. John Thornton restates the same argument with more emphasis.[116]

Nevertheless, contemporary documents reveal that the enslaving escalation, the "time of war," had begun in 1602–1603, before Vasconcelo's arrival—that is, when João Rodrigues Coutinho, for the first time in Iberian history, accumulated the posts of Angola's governor, *asentista*, and royal contractor.[117] In addition, estimates of the embarkation regions demonstrate that the shift from Senegambia to Congo and Angola had been taking place since 1580.[118] More precise data on Vera Cruz and Cartagena shows that ships from Angola had been more numerous than those from Upper Guinea since the years 1593 to 1601.[119]

In other words, the great enslavement cycle predated the alliance of the Portuguese and the Jaga (c. 1610), and extended beyond Vasconcelos's government. New figures analyzed by David Wheat indicate that the peak in arrivals of individuals from West Central Africa in Cartagena, the "Angolan wave," lasted from 1626 to 1640.[120]

Years later, in 1680, when the *sobados* had been generally vassalized and the inland fairs had been opened, Cadornega assessed the expeditions of the first quarter of the seventeenth century. By cross-referencing family memory (his father lived in Buenos Aires as a factor for the *asentista* Elvas), his own experience, documents from the municipal chambers in Luanda and Massangano, plus the oral tradition of both seasoned settlers and native "knowledgeable negros," he explained the motives for the Portuguese expeditions. "The first enterprise that (governor Bento Banha, in 1611) turned his attention to was to go against the *sobas* of the Lumbo province," who did not allow the slave fair there, "which was a thing of great importance to [slave] trade at that time."[121]

Rather than being provoked by the Vasconcelos belligerency or the ferocity of the Jaga, the enslavement raids resulted from the demands by the *asentista* slave-trading cartel. Hence, governors struggled to "allow bartering of slaves" (*abrir resgates*), to break the *sobas* resistance, to relocate hinterland fairs and fortresses to drain the hinterland trade to Luanda. This was the impetus for the establishment of a trading port in Benguela (1617) and the assaults on Embaca (1618–1619) by Vasconcelos's son, Joane Mendes de Vasconcelos. Praised later as Portugal's "greatest soldier" of his century, due to his skillful command in the Portuguese Restoration War (1640–1668), Joane was feared by the Mbundu. It was then known that in just one expedition against allegedly rebel villages, he decapitated twenty-eight *sobas*, causing a great slaughter.[122]

Favoring some degree of *soba* sovereignty, so as to have them play the role of a transmission belt under Lisbon's control, the bishop of Congo and Angola denounced Luis Mendes de Vasconcelos's expeditions: "A very great carnage has been going on for more than two years and many dead bodies have infected the waters of voluminous rivers," something "unheard of," occasioning the enslavement of "a great multitude of innocent people."[123]

Responding to the consortium between the Angola governors and the *asentistas*, the increase in overseas demand amplified the volume of deportations. Complementarily, the coalition of Portuguese and Jaga troops played its role in the growth of the slave trade at this juncture. In brief, the 1610–1620 Jaga episode or the "Imbangala period" (Thornton) was, in fact, fostered by *Asiento* demand. In the same way, the eighteenth-century gold rush demands in Brazil generated the major event we mentioned above: the growth in the Benguela slave trade.

At the same time, a decisive turn overseas emerged in the Habsburg empire. Behind the sequences of consortia, merchant clans, and blood ties, whose web is hard to pick apart due to the frequent homonymy of agents and proxies, there was a recycling of capitals, coming from the Portuguese empire of the East into the empire of the West.

Antonio Fernandes de Elvas's family, as well as the relatives of his wife, Elena Rodrigues Solís, owned capital invested in the Pepper Tax-Farm (Estanco da Pimenta) and other Asian spice trades.[124] Indeed, Elena's father was Jorge Rodrigues Solís, a prominent Marrano personality in Madrid who partnered in the Asian pepper business with Manuel Caldeira, also an experienced slave trader and Luís Mendes de Vasconcelos's father-in-law.[125] Activities in trading pepper to Europe and slaves to America were also carried out at that time in Lisbon and Seville by Italian merchants.[126]

Connections between the Asian merchants and the *Asiento* business were pursued through marriages and cut across generations. Antonio Fernandes de Elvas had himself traded in spices in previous years. His and Elena's son, Jorge Fernandes de Elvas, married the daughter of Duarte Gomes Solís, the economics writer.[127] Councilor to Felipe IV, merchant-capitalist and an expert on Asia, Solís was influential in Madrid.[128] As mentioned before, Jorge Fernandes de Elvas became his father's *Asiento* factor in Cartagena de las Indias (1619–1622).[129] Later, he returned to Spain and squandered his family's money on parties at Madrid.[130] One of Antonio Fernandes de Elvas's brothers-in-law, Jerônimo, became his agent in Cape Verde and Angola. Another brother-in-law, Francisco Gomes Solís, enjoyed considerable influence in Cartagena, where he had been a factor of Portugal's Contract.[131]

Marriages and kinship of the same sort would connect Elvas's descendants with Marrano, as well with Old Christian elites, as indicated elsewhere (see appendix 1). Through his widow, Elena Rodrigues Solís, the Elva's consortia remained in the slaving business after his death in 1622. Although Elena failed to get the *Asiento* auction in 1623, she was still trading in slaves in 1629, through her brother and Cartagena's agent Francisco Gomes Solís.[132]

Within this context, the acquisition of the Angolan and the Cape Verde Contract as well as the *Asiento* in both areas, an unheard-of operation carried out by Antonio Fernandes de Elvas, configured a movement of Portuguese capital flowing back from the Indic into the Atlantic Ocean, after the Anglo-Dutch offensive in the East and the decline of the pepper cycle and of the Estado da India.[133] In fact, Portuguese merchants and bankers lent money to the Crown in Madrid as well to slave traders into the South Atlantic.

From Asian Spice to the Atlantic Slave Trade

As is well known, from 1627 on, following King Felipe IV's default, the Genoese ceased to be the sole bankers to the Madrid Court. Portuguese New Christian capitalists entered the stage, many of whom had become wealthy through India contracts, taking over also as bankers to the Spanish Crown.[134] All three *asentistas* of the period 1615–1640, Elvas (1615–1622), Manuel Rodrigues Lamego (1623–1631), and Melchior Gomes Angel (1632–1638), affiliated themselves to families whose fortunes and influence derived from the Asian pepper trade or from lending money to the Crown.[135]

Other groups of New Christians had investments shuttling between the Asian trade, banking activities with the Spanish Crown, and the slave trade.[136]

The migration of capitals from the East to the West is also suggested in a book well known to Brazil's colonial history readers: *Diálogos das grandezas do Brasil* (1618). Its author was a Marrano merchant and colonist living in the Paraíba captaincy, Ambrósio Fernandes Brandão. His associate was the Pernambuco and Bahia Royal tax collector (*dizimeiro*), Bento Dias de Santiago, uncle of Duarte Dias Henriques, the Pernambucan Marrano who took up the Angola Contract between 1607 and 1611.[137] Landlord of sugar mills in Paraíba, Ambrósio was also affiliated to the Brandão consortium formed by Marrano merchants in the Asian trade.[138]

Knowledgeable in European dealings on both oceans, Ambrósio Fernandes Brandão appears as a genuine representative of mercantile capitalism: a merchant-entrepreneur seeking worldwide business-generating investments.[139] Aptly, his book exposes the advantages of Luso-Brazilian slave-based production economy over Luso-Asian circulation economy. As Gonsalves de Mello observed, the *Diálogos* spells out the specific process in Portuguese America. To Ambrósio, the proof of Brazil's economic advantage would reside in the fact that the capital invested in the sugar industry remained in the colonial enclaves as fixed capital, as real estate (*bens de raíz*). In contrast, in Portuguese India the colonists removed their capital as they returned to Portugal.[140]

In his famed treatise dedicated to Olivares, "Alegación en fauor de la Compañia de la India Oriental" (1628), Duarte Gomes Solís states that the Portuguese from "the Hebrew caste," better than the Old Christian settlers and merchants, understood the "usefulness" of Brazil, as they did in India, where they exercised "trade and not arms," improving Portugal's "peopling and the wealth" in Asia.[141] Such considerations led Nathan Wachtel to define Solís as the theorizer of the "Marrano mercantilism."[142] In this sense, Ambrosio Fernandes Brandão's businesses and life illustrate Solís's ideas as well as Wachtel's analysis.

Successful Conversos careers indebted to the South Atlantic and Asia business are also worthy of attention. Summed up by Boyajian, the extraordinary life of Manuel da Paz (1580–1642), born in Olinda (Pernambuco) and a relative of Ambrósio Fernandes Brandão, clarifies the dynamics of merchant capital. In fact, Manuel belonged to the Converso communities of Olinda and Camaragibe, today a Recife neighborhood, from whence the first globalized Brasílicos gained the world. Enriched by sugar mills and the slave trade in Pernambuco, Manuel's family returned to Europe at the end of the sixteenth century. Inheriting his fathers' property in Brazil, Manuel da Paz invested in the Asian trade and left Portugal to reside in Goa (1607–1616).[143]

On returning to Lisbon, he married a cousin, establishing blood ties with Asian trade merchants such as Duarte Gomes Solís and, more closely, with the Lamego clan, holders of the *Asiento de Negros* between 1623 and 1631. Granted a Portuguese title of nobility (*fidalgo*), Manuel da Paz moved to Madrid (1626). Maintaining his Asian and American (brazilwood) business, he associated with Gonçalo Nunes de Sepúlveda, an emerging Seville personality, as we shall see below. Manuel da Paz also became a royal financier, being given the status of banker to Felipe IV. His palazzo in *carrera* San Jeronimo, opposite the Buen Retiro Palace, impressed all by the luxury it displayed. The Luso-Pernambucan Manuel da Paz died in Madrid rich and famous in 1642.[144]

On his side, born in Lisbon from a merchant trading in Asian goods, Gonçalo Nunes de Sepúlveda (1585–1655) preferred to engage in the slaving *Asiento* business. In 1604, at the time of the Coutinho brothers' *Asientos*, he moved to Luanda and there lived for more than twenty years.[145] A factor of the *asentista* Antonio Fernandes de Elvas, Sepúlveda became the representative of the *asentista*'s widow and heir, Elena Rodrigues Solís, in 1622.[146] Two years later he represented also the royal Contractor of "Angola, Congo and Loango," Henrique Gomes da Costa, an Oporto resident.[147] As mentioned above, during the period in which Sepúlveda lived in Luanda, the enclave developed as a major slave-trade port in Africa.

In the second half of the 1620s Sepúlveda moved from Luanda to Seville.[148] There he joined the Portuguese New Christian bankers' cartel directed by Manuel da Paz, previously known to him through his Angola businesses.[149] At that time, helped by the count-duke of Olivares, the Portuguese Marrano bankers started to finance Felipe IV after the Crown defaulted on its debt to the Genoese bankers in 1627.[150] From Seville, he kept up his businesses with the Portuguese slave traders in Spanish America, as a partner of the Cartagena-based merchant Antonio Nunes Gramaxo, heir of Jorge Fernandes Gramaxo, the powerful *asentistas*' factor, as mentioned above.[151] In this context, thanks to his participation in the loan contract to the Crown managed by Manuel da Paz in 1630, Sepúlveda was granted Spanish citizenship,[152] at which time his dazzling social ascension started. The following year, he married Mencía de Andrade, from an old Christian and influential Sevillan family. Appointed as *Caballero Veintecuatro* (municipal councilor), he entered the elite ranks of the main Iberian mercantile city. With the support of the Olivares' in-law, the count of Monterrey, known for accepting bribes, Sepúlveda was given the status of Knight of Santiago by a 1639 royal decree.[153] Since Sepúlveda was of Portuguese origin and, much more serious, a New Christian, the royal religious tribunal hesitated to implement the order. But the Crown raised its voice and Sepúlveda obtained the knighthood.[154]

Thus, desiring "to achieve some worthy Christian act"—following the expression of a contemporaneous chronicler—Sepúlveda bequeathed his estate to Seville's cathedral,[155] so obtaining the privilege of being buried with his wife in the Capela de la Conception, one of the main chapels of the cathedral. Lavishly refurbished and decorated by Sepúlveda and his agents with artistic ornaments, among others by the painting *El nacimiento de la Virgen*, a Murillo masterpiece now in the Louvre, the Capela de la Conception turned into an outstanding baroque monument inside the gothic cathedral.[156] To make room for the Sepúlveda sepulcher, the remains of the Christian commanders who conquered the town from the Muslims in 1248, among them the famed knight Lorenzo Suárez Gallinato, were removed from the chapel, reburied in a corner, and later lost. Writing in the middle of the nineteenth century, a Spanish chronicler considered the removal of the knights' remains as disrespectful to the tradition and as a priests' sycophantic act to the nouveaux riches of the seventeenth-century mercantile bourgeoisie.[157] So: the Reconquista warrior's tomb was soon forgotten, and the slave trader's mausoleum, much admired even today, took its place. Besides the Capela de la Conception, the street Gonzalo Nuñez de Sepúlveda, next to the cathedral, immortalizes the name of the knight of Santiago and pious Christian. Few people knew then—and even fewer know today—that the influential ruler of the Iberian mercantile metropolis owed his wealth and power to the massive slaving plunder performed during his twenty years' businesses in Luanda.

As a matter of fact, from 1640 onward, the rupture between the two Iberian capitals gradually undid some of the banking networks and the Asian, African, and American trades, causing the decline of the New Christian consortia that operated in the mainland and overseas marketplaces.[158] Nevertheless, in the corridors connecting overseas businesses to core capitalism, the Braganza coronation closed a few doors but opened others. The reshuffling of the Portuguese monarchy's cards generated by the flight of some nobility and high administration officials to Madrid opened the way for new actors from the overseas elites to step in.

The Colonial Men and the Overseas Men

At this point, a distinction can be established between two significant imperial actors: the "overseas man" and the "colonial man." The former led his overseas career seeking profit, rewards, and titles to be enjoyed at the Iberian mainland courts. The latter, a "colonial man," circulated over many overseas regions, but played all his cards, his accumulated social, economic, and cultural capital, in one particular place, in a colonial enclave that sometimes was not his birthplace but where he owned property, housed his heirs, and had a sepulcher set aside for his final rest and that of his descendants.

Portugal's longstanding Catholic rural tradition honors burials close to the remains of one's ancestors, an act that was, and still is, a mark of kinship and communitarian identity. And yet, throughout the seventeenth century, certain Iberian overseas communities achieved a higher level of social complexity as they retained in their cemeteries generations of merchants and settlers who could have otherwise returned to die in Europe. Local Catholic brotherhoods and mortuary administrations became habilitated, in the settlers' judgment, to manage the passage into the Beyond as conveniently as similar institutions in the Iberian Peninsula.

The decision to be buried overseas is particularly significant for prosperous settlers who would be otherwise have been able to transfer their money and their family to their European hometown. Truly, the intent to maintain their own and their descendants' remains in an overseas community cemetery until Judgment Day reveals a belief in the historic continuity of that community.

Hence, the European merchant or colonist redefined himself as a "colonial man" as he decided to build tombs for himself and his descendants in a specific overseas cemetery, and as he instituted Church donations and rents to generate perpetual income for the purchase of masses to be said after his death for the rescue of his suffering soul in the Purgatory.[159]

To stick to the characters that made an appearance in this book, it is interesting to distinguish the fates of Salvador Correia de Sá e Benevides, Joane Mendes de Vasconcelos, and Alexandre de Moura e Albuquerque. All of them turned into "overseas men" who made careers in the Ethiopic Ocean to enjoy their wealth and privileges in Lisbon.[160] Instead, some prestigious commanders of the Atlantic wars, who accumulated gains in other parts of the overseas world, notably in Brazil and Angola, preferred to improve their status in Brazil. Such is the case with "colonial men" such as João Fernandes Vieira, André Vidal de Negreiros, Salvador Correia Vasqueanes, and other notable seventeenth-century military men and civilians. Having transferred to Angola, they could have remained there or moved to Portugal, where some of them possessed rents and titles of honor granted by the Crown. Yet they decided, as will be seen at the end of this book, to make the Angolan episode a step in their social ascension in Brazil.[161]

The spatial and social features of the overseas world changed the outcomes of the merchant and military conflict involving Portugal, Spain, Britain, and the Netherlands. In the Estado da India, the Portuguese had opened the way to the European market, but lost their dominant position with the entry of the Dutch and the British. In the following phase, in the South Atlantic, the game changed its nature, as the Brazilian-Angolan network resisted to the West-Indische Compagnie (WIC) offensive. Thus, like Britain and other European entities, the Dutch opted to open a competing sugar-producing area in the Caribbean. Ultimately, the control of the African slave trade, and particularly of Angola, helped Lisbon to regain and protect its independence from Madrid.

During the Antonio Fernandes de Elvas *Asiento*, two significant changes took place in the Portuguese slaving geography. First, instead of leaving Sanlúcar de Barrameda or Seville, most of the *asentistas*' ships left from the Tagus, loading local equipment and crew, imprinting a markedly Lisbon character to the *Asiento* from the beginning of the 1620s,[162] to the point that Elvas allowed himself to continue to reside in Lisbon, instead of moving to Seville, which was the *Asiento* headquarters and official residence of his predecessors.[163] Second, leaving aside the Guinea ports, exposed to corsairs and European rivals, Elvas concentrated the loading of his ships in Luanda, consolidating the West Central Africa slaving thoroughfare.[164]

Plunder and Trade in Angola

João Correia de Sousa, former captain of Ceuta and Angola governor (1621–1623), was the son of a Cape Verde donatary.[165] Like other Upper Guinea royal officers and merchants, he migrated to West Central Africa in search of better opportunities in the slave trade. Experienced in the slave business his family had long practiced in Cape Verde and Upper Guinea, João Correia was also interested in the Congo's copper mines.[166] Despite royal orders forbidding military raids and prescribing conciliatory means in dealing with the *sobas*, João Correia continued pillaging.[167] He was then accused of illegally selling enslaved Angolans in Cartagena de Indias.[168] In his next step, Sousa prepared to invade São Salvador, Congo's capital. Beatrix Heintze observes that João Correia's attacks, marked by the Mbumbi battle (November 1621), aimed to seize control of the copper mines of Bembe, which are still exploited today.[169]

As Mendonça Furtado, the new general governor of Brazil (1621–1624), arrived in Bahia, he informed Madrid about the copper exploitation noticed by João Correia, and the issue was discussed by the Crown's councilors. The move illustrates the concern of Portuguese America's authorities about Angolan affairs and the global activities achieved in West Central Africa.[170] Valued in Europe, copper was also traded in West Africa to be bartered for slaves or gold and in Indian Ocean, where it appeared as the main commodity sold by Europeans.[171] Nevertheless, João Correia's inland raids ended up exposing Luanda to the attacks of the Jaga of Kasanje.[172] The Jesuits intervened, succeeding in obtaining the surrender of a few restive Kasanje *sobas*. Yet the governor preyed on many natives under the missionaries' wing, deporting the Africans to Pernambuco in five crowded ships. Following those inland wars, João Correia was deposed, excommunicated, and expelled from Luanda by the Jesuits and the colonists.

Thirty years after the "amos" rebellion led by the Jesuits, another mutiny shook Angola. But the political odds had changed. *Angolistas* traders, who relied on exchanges with the backlands fairs and on native porters, wanted to avoid the war against the Congo kingdom, since it would cause losses to their barter merchandise and the interruption of terrestrial trade. According to a 1623 report, over a thousand Portuguese traded slaves, ivory, and copper up the Congo basin. These settlers' goods and life were put in danger by the governor's raids against the inland *sobados* and the Congo kingdom.

Besides, having again settled in São Salvador do Congo in 1618, the Jesuits also felt threatened by the governor's attacks against some *sobados* under their protection. Thus, they demanded the release of the enslaved Congolese, who were "vassals of the King of Congo, His Majesty's brother in arms, who keeps the episcopal See and the (Catholic) bishop in his court." Further, the Jesuits refused the confession sacrament to colonists who sold or owned natives illicitly enslaved by the governor.[173] The newly found rigor of the Jesuits' examination of Angola's slavery may have a material reason, however. It was perhaps caused by João Correia's attempt to revoke the testament in which wealthy slave-dealer Gaspar Álvares benefited the S.J. For decades this inheritance remained the source of contention between the Jesuits and local authorities. Ultimately, excommunicated by the missionaries and chased from Luanda by the Crown's orders, the governor fled to Havana, taking with him "numerous" slaves to trade.[174] However, he returned to Lisbon, where he was arrested, and he died in prison.[175]

The pathetic closing of João Correia's career demonstrates that the Crown and the missionaries could rein in the pillage when it was convenient for them. At that time, the authorities tried to limit inland expeditions. As the Dutch launched their offensive in the South Atlantic, seizing Bahia and attacking Luanda, Governor Fernão de Sousa (1624–1630) sought to strengthen alliances with the *sobas* to secure Portuguese endeavors in West Central Africa. Also, he reestablished the sovereignty of the king of Ndongo. In an unusual move, he brought back to Angola, as free men, the Kasanje *sobas* deported to Pernambuco by the previous governor. What is the meaning of such Portuguese political shifts in West Central Africa?

After participating in the plunder, missionaries, municipal councilors, settlers, and Luanda's established merchants (*mercadores de portada*)—a group shaping the Angolistas' interests—began to oppose the predatory expeditions launched by the governors. The Crown also shared this approach. Fearful of the blows thrown by European rivals in the Angolan littoral, the Crown and the Luanda municipal council sought to reduce confrontations with the indigenous communities. Similar moves were made by colonial authorities in Brazil, where conflicts along the Amerindians' borders were slowed down to protect the seafront against corsairs. Yet there was another reason for limiting plunder in Angola. In fact, the hinterland wars had scrambled the relay trade, cut into the Luanda merchants' monopoly, and disturbed the *sobados*. Squeezed by merchants and the captains of the inland forts (*presidios*) demanding porters, and by the governors who requested food and men to form predatory troops, many *sobados* collapsed in the course of the seventeenth century.[176] "I am harassed by people who each day ask to take private party's loads to the *pumbo* [inland fairs]," the king of Ndongo, Felipe Hari A Ngola, wrote to the Portuguese Crown in 1653.[177]

For one, the Angolistas colonists also suffered pressure from governors to form troops, take up arms, and provide rations and slaves for the official slave-hunting expeditions. To avoid such abuses, a war-regulating instance was incorporated by the Crown into Governor Fernão de Sousa's (1624–1630) statute. The bishop, the Jesuit's superior, a Crown judge (*ouvidor-geral*), and the Luanda municipal councilors should compose a special tribunal. This court would decide whether the governor's expeditions constituted defensive and legal operations or mere plundering raids.[178] However, to understand the effects of the conflicts between the Angolistas and the governors, between trade and pillage, it is necessary to take a longer perspective on the facts. Sure enough, governors and captains sacked villages and extorted *sobas* and fair traders, seeking to accumulate booty during their three years in unpaid office[179]—hence the military expeditions that put at risk the safety of colonial enclaves and the Luanda businesses and threatened inland markets with collapse. Yet it is also true that the slave-trade cartel and the Luanda municipal council did not always restrict themselves to peaceful policies in dealing with the Angolan hinterland.

Enjoying little access to the slaving networks flowing into the Congo delta, where European competition was stronger, Luanda merchants and the *asentistas*' agents exploited the monopoly they enjoyed in the inland fairs. Still, when there was a strong supply of foreign commodities in the fairs, the Luanda merchants turned belligerent to reinforce their domination in the backlands markets. Early on, sack and violence were imposed on the *sobados* who were refractory to Luanda's exchanges, or committed to European competitors. Captain Silva Correa aptly described the peculiar movements of the war-trade-war-trade cycle of the Portuguese in Angola in 1782.[180]

Some data on the expedition that sacked Pungo-Andongo (1671), the last independent capital of the Ndongo kingdom, allow us to evaluate the costs of one of such plundering war; such wars were denominated "hinterland wars" (*guerras do sertão*). In the end, the Mbundu enslaved by that expedition and sold in Brazil netted a grand total of 3,351 réis to the Royal Treasury—a sum sufficient to cover only five months of the 500-strong militia's pay, part of which was from Bahia and Pernambuco. In fact, those men spent a year and a half enduring tough marches and combats.[181] Accordingly, the operation made a loss in the short term. This is what the anonymous author of the expedition's narrative suggested, as he wrote that the victory "was more for boasting than for interest."[182]

Nevertheless, the plunder's outcome must be evaluated within the wider South Atlantic framework. A Portuguese fair and a fortress were erected at Pungo-Andongo, on the margins of the Kwango River and at the crossing of the trails leading to Luanda and Benguela, thus opening fresh hinterland markets (*pumbos*) to the Angolistas' agents (*pombeiros*) and widening the radius of slaving activity in West Central Africa.[183] Clearly, the anonymous author also recognized that the aim of the war had been to allow "the freedom of [slave] trade, which the king of Ndongo had nearly fully blocked."[184]

Contrary to the practice in the late seventeenth and the eighteenth centuries, when indirect forms of enslaving became more frequent in Angola, the deportations of the first half of the seventeenth century seem to derive predominantly from war. A 1618 protest against governor Vasconcellos's raids stated that the Luanda merchants, after such expeditions, only managed to buy in the inland fairs the "leftovers, which are the elderly and the kids."[185] The complaint has an indirect meaning: the merchant's words show that the availability of freight channeled into Luanda by the *Asiento* contractors made it advantageous to extend the slave trade, making it profitable to capture or exchange, feed, watch over, and bring over from the hinterland fairs the elderly and children who would not, in other circumstances, find a buyer in the port of trade. More to the point, figures of the period 1637–1645 regarding the Dutch slave trade, which was mainly furnished by the inland Portuguese networks in Angola, indicate an unusually high number of children being deported through Luanda, as compared to the deportations from the Gulf of Guinea.[186]

Another significant consequence of the Portuguese *Asiento* period was the connection that was woven between Rio de Janeiro and Buenos Aires.

Luanda, Rio de Janeiro, and the Río de La Plata

The Spanish Crown accepted the coastal South-American exchanges activated by the African slave trade, although Madrid did repress raids by Paulista Amerindian hunters in Paraguay. Similar to the connections between the Macao Luso-Chinese and the Manila Hispanic-Filipinos, the tolerated exchanges between Rio de Janeiro and the Río de La Plata took shape in the first two decades of the 1600s.[187]

Buenos Aires customs data note that 18,100 Africans were officially imported into the port between 1597 and 1645. But this number should be multiplied at least by two and a half to include figures yielded by smuggling.[188] For a few years, the area was open to the *Asiento*, with slave ships sailing directly from Luanda into Buenos Aires, whose population had a considerable number of Portuguese.[189] In turn, smuggling took place via Bahia and Rio de Janeiro, during the prohibition years. Caravelões, ships smaller than the caravels, linked Rio de Janeiro to Buenos Aires in ten to fifteen days of navigation.

On returning, the *caravelões* brought to Rio de Janeiro, but also to Bahia and Recife, silver coins (*patacas*), minted and unminted silver, and gold. "All silver that exists in Brazil and Angola comes from there [la Plata]," wrote Pyrard, the much-traveled Frenchman who spent two months in Bahia in 1610. At the same time, Ambrósio Fernandes Brandão praised the merchants from Rio de Janeiro and Bahia who sailed with local products to trade coins and raw and crafted silver and gold in the Rio de La Plata.[190] Thus, in his navigation guide written during the Iberian Union, royal cosmographer Antonio Mariz de Carneiro, as well as Manoel de Figueiredo in his *Hidrografia* (1625), described the sailing between Rio de Janeiro and Río de La Plata as a standard voyage. Entitling his 1630s rutter (a mariner's handbook) *Roteiro de Portugal para o Brazil, Rio da Prata, Angola e S. Thomé*, Mariz de Carneiro understands the Rio de Janeiro–Río de La Plata itinerary as a segment of the Portuguese network encompassing European goods, Brazilian sugar, Peruvian silver, and Angola and São Tomé slaves.[191]

Buenos Aires held a significant Portuguese population, often from *converso* families. Among them was Diogo da Veiga (1575–1640). As mentioned above, Veiga played a central role in the Río de La Plata illegal trade. Named Diego da Vega in Spanish, he belonged to a family connected with the Madrid New Christian bankers' consortia.[192] Since the 1590s, slaves from Angola had arrived in Upper Peru and Chili through Buenos Aires.[193]

Like others Portuguese merchants, Diogo da Veiga played a key role in Spanish America. Living mainly in Buenos Aires, Veiga traveled and in North and South Atlantic.[194] Hernandarías, the well-known governor of Buenos Aires, denounced him in 1616 for tax evasion and illegal introduction of Africans. Depicting Veiga as "a powerful man with many relationships in Brazil, Angola, the (Atlantic) Islands and Flanders," Hernandarías noted his wide influence as creditor of many settlers of Buenos Aires, Tucuman, Chile, and Peru, to whom he sold slaves and other merchandise.[195] Around 1615, Veiga was the main merchant in Buenos Aires.[196] One of his associates in Lisbon was João de Argomedo, who had direct connections with the Angolan governor, Manuel Forjaz, whose administration intensified the slave trafficking.[197] An Old Christian of Basque origin, Argomedo held an influential position as a member of the Portuguese Inquisition. As such, he made use of his position to pressure New Christian merchants in Seville and in the overseas factories. A 1611 report from an appellate judge accused the Argomedo-Forjaz association of transgressing the *Asiento* regulations and Sevillian interests.[198]

In Rio de Janeiro, the interests of Iberian salesmen active in the La Plata region (*peruleiros*), represented by the Sá oligarchy and their Buenos Aires allies, crystallized around the exchange of Angolans for Potosí silver.[199] This group would help to set up one of the most revealing enterprises in the history of the Ethiopic Ocean: the Luso-Brasílico expedition for the retaking of Angola (1648) from the Dutch. As a matter of fact, the transatlantic expedition was more motivated by avidity to reopen the slave trade between Luanda and Buenos Aires, in order to access Peruvian silver, than by the need to provide enslaved Africans to the second-rate Rio de Janeiro sugar industry. I shall deal with this subject further in the final chapters of this book.

This episode left behind a well-known feature in Brazil's landscape. During the Iberian Union, Rio de Janeiro's *peruleiros* brought down from Potosí the cult of Our Lady of Copacabana.[200] A chapel dedicated to the saint was built in 1637 on the beach that took the Copacabana name in southern Rio de Janeiro, on the extreme southeast stretch of the route linking the Guanabara Bay to Río de la Plata and Potosí.[201]

The Río de La Plata trade outlined the scope of the operation carried out under the cover of the *Asiento*. The Portuguese made use of such contracts to penetrate the Spanish American ports and thus broke the Madrid monopoly over the mining economy. Such were the conclusions of the inquiry carried out by Seville businessmen and the Spanish authorities. In their words, three kinds of loss resulted from the Portuguese *asentistas*' activities: the increase in smuggling into Spanish American territories; the leakage of gold, silver, and other merchandise subject to regal monopoly; and the free access to the colonies gained by heretics, unbelievers, and Judaizing individuals.[202]

Suspected as New Christians, many of the *asentistas*, merchants and rentiers could be blackmailed by their Old Christian rivals. Madrid saw the *Asientos* as a minor evil, set up to avoid smuggling and to provide activities that the Spanish Crown could not afford. However, suspicion of leaks and bypassing prevailed. From 1605 onward, the *Asiento* contractors lost the right to navigate into Buenos Aires, whose port was then closed to the slave trade. Trying to directly run these exchanges, the Crown suspended the *Asientos* between 1609 and 1615. In the meantime, Antonio Fernandes de Elvas maneuvered in Madrid, and finally obtained the *Asiento* in 1615.[203]

In another development, the Inquisition's fist fell on the Portuguese traders' heads as the political decline of Olivares, protector of the New Christians bankers, became evident.[204] The Vera Cruz, Cartagena, and Buenos Aires *converso* communities became the target of confiscations, purges, and imprisonment. Groups of Portuguese *conversos* still remained in those cities, as demonstrated by the later confiscations carried out in Cartagena after the Braganza Restoration.[205] Yet their transcontinental mercantile network began to collapse in the 1630s. Alarmed, *asentistas* Melchior Angel and Cristóvão Sousa had been warning Madrid since 1638, that they could not fulfill their contract. Under the pretext of "religious cleansing," the Holy Office had incarcerated most of their agents in Spanish America.[206]

With the ascension of the Braganzas to Lisbon's throne and the war with Spain, Portuguese traders returned to Portugal, causing bankruptcies in Spanish American ports and Seville. Although he possessed a special license by Felipe IV to continue residing in Spain, Melchior Angel preferred to leave for Portugal.

Nevertheless, Lisbon sought to continue with the Portuguese-Spanish trade, especially the overseas trade. Only two months after the 1640 Restoration and the beginning of the war between the Iberian capitals, King João IV issued a decree authorizing continuation of the loading of Africans into Spanish America, also determining that a third of the shipments should be set aside for Brazilian ports.[207] A 1642 report by the marquis of Montalvão, viceroy of Brazil, proposed the creation of a royal agency committed to prompt exchanges of Angolan slaves, Brazilian sugar, and Asian spices for Peruvian silver. Other Portuguese authorities were consulted, and their arbitration also favored the continuation of the Angolan trade into the Castilian Indies. Military considerations also weighed in favor of free trade. Portugal needed the Potosí silver, and knew that blocking the Angolan trade into Spanish America could lead Madrid to take over Luanda. To curtail this danger, Father Antonio Vieira proposed that Pernambuco and Maranhão be converted into free-trade ports for the Spanish trade with Angola.[208]

On Madrid's initiative, the legal trade of slaves into Spanish America remained suspended for ten years after the Restoration. Substituted in the *Asiento* by the Genoese, Dutch, French, and English, the Portuguese redirected their trade of Africans into the growing Brazilian market.

It is noteworthy to consider the long-lasting effects of the events on both margins of the Atlantic. Within the context of decreasing royal incomes and soaring European and overseas military expenses, the Iberians *asentistas*' investments helped to broaden the Portuguese dominion in West Central Africa.[209] The forts of Benguela, Luanda, Muxima, Massangano, and Cambambe, were built or reinforced in the period of the *Asiento* contracts taken by the Portuguese (see map 3.1).[210]

Those military positions secured Lisbon's presence in Angola ports and inland markets, helping to restrict the Dutch and later the French trade to the mouth of the Congo. Following the West-Indische Compagnie (WIC) conquest of Luanda and Benguela in 1641, the retreat of the Portuguese and their locals' allies into the inland forts of Muxima, Massangano, and Cambambe undercut Dutch control of Angola's coast. Throughout the seventeenth and eighteenth centuries, those enclaves allowed the enlargement of the Portuguese markets and territories in West Central Africa.

With the war breaking between Madrid and Lisbon (1640–1668) and the closing of Spanish American markets to the Portuguese flag, sections of the networks and equipment generated by the *Asiento*'s management fitted into the slave trade encompassing Brazil. Set up in the course of a century and a half to provide the Castilian Indies, the Portuguese slave-trade apparatus had lost access to Buenos Aires, Cartagena, and Vera Cruz—hence the increase in the provision of enslaved Africans to Brazilian ports as the *asentistas*' agents abandoned Luanda.[211]

Altogether, these circumstances fostered the connections between the colonial enclaves in Angola and Brazil. Such a process undertook transformations in both sides of the Ethiopic Ocean. In fact, the overall data on the three-and-a-half centuries of African forced migration shows Luanda as the main slave-trade port of Africa, and Rio de Janeiro as leading importer of slaves in the Americas.[212]

A related question, referring to Amerindian slavery, must also be considered. Even if thousands of Native Americans had been pressed into coerced labor in the

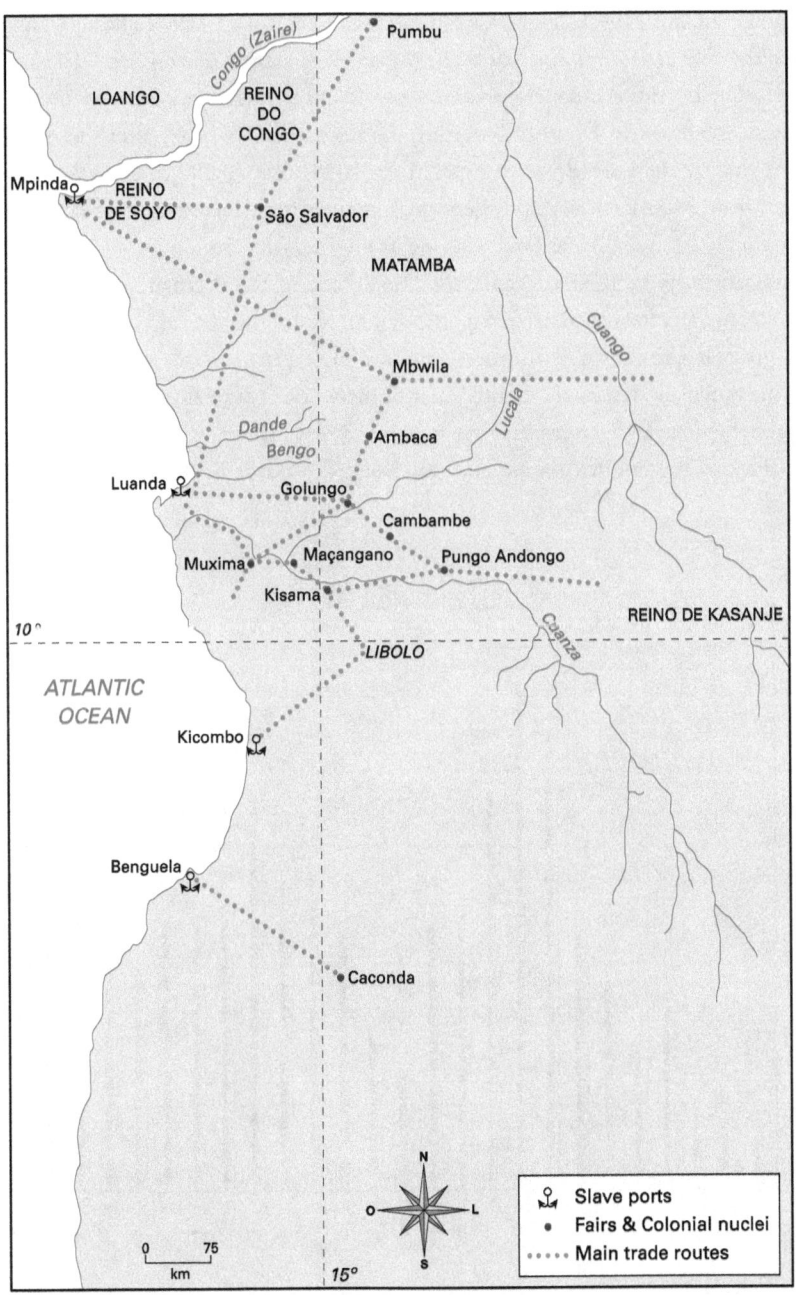

Map 3.1. Main Trade Routes in West Central Africa in the Seventeenth Century. *Source:* CEBRAP, São Paulo.

colonial enclaves, the Ethiopic Ocean labor market would have radically changed after the Restoration. Sooner or later, the massive supply of enslaved Africans set in motion by the Portuguese *asentistas* would meet increasing demand in Brazil. Indeed, as shown in Figure 3.1, during the decade 1651–1660, after the retaking of Angola by the Luso-Brasílico expedition (1648), the 70,000 disembarkments in Brazil from West Central Africa deportees, mainly from Luanda, under Portuguese flag equal the 69,500 enslaved arriving from the same region in all the Iberian American ports in 1631 to 1640, the last decade of the Portuguese *Asientos*.[213]

Not as paradoxical as it seems, the fallout from the Iberian Union that had the greatest impact on Portuguese America took place outside the New World, on the Angolan side of the South Atlantic network.[214] Therefore, the story of the displacement of indigenous captives by African slave labor in Brazil was written in the tides of the South Atlantic and not along the tracks of the Brazilian forests.

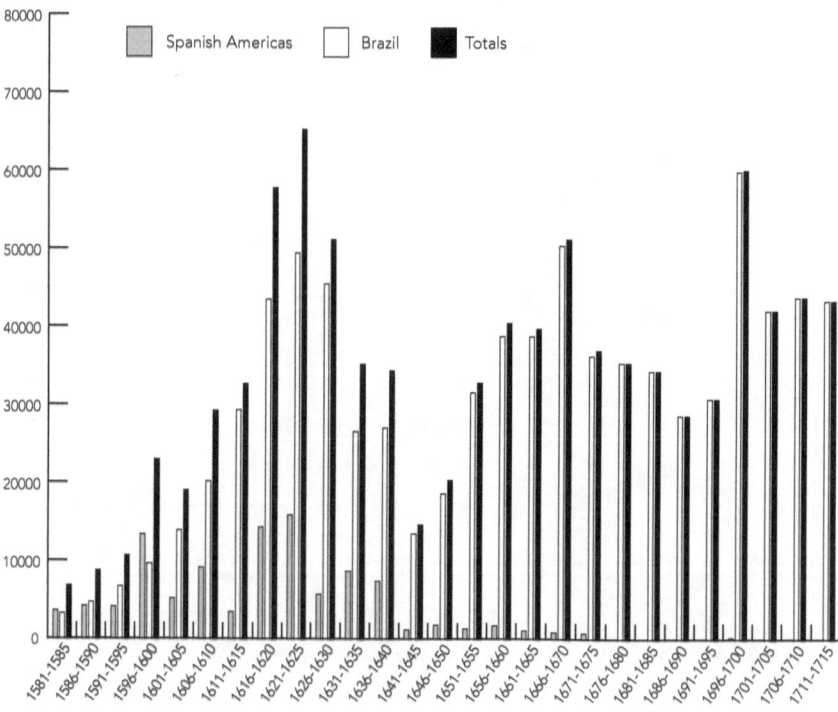

Figure 3.1. Estimated Number of Slaves from West Central Africa Landed in Ibero-America during the Portuguese *Asientos* and Beyond, 1581–1715. *Source:* TSTD.

After 1668, when Madrid and Lisbon reestablished diplomatic relations, Portuguese slave traders again bid for *Asientos*, offering enslaved Africans, particularly Angolans, to the Spanish Crown. Despite the appeal of profits, of American silver, and of fiscal gains for the Portuguese Crown, the opposition from the Brasílico and Angolista representatives in Lisbon, as we shall see below, halted the initiative. They, and some Crown counselors, believed that the economic complementarities between the Portuguese American slave-based production pole and the Angolan slave reproduction pole should prevail. The tables turned again in Southern Atlantic.

Former calculations underestimated the number of Africans deported into Spanish America. New data demonstrate that the number of slaves shipped by the Portuguese *Asiento* contractors was much more important. Above all, the rooting up of West Central Africa communities seems to have been deeper than has been admitted up to now. The captives deported from the area represent 61.8 percent of the total of shipments between the years 1550 and 1600, and reached 92 percent from 1601 to 1650.[215]

Portraying the expanding plunder of African peoples, such figures underline the role played by the Angolan trade in Portuguese attempts to break into Spanish American markets.[216] Even though direct profits secured by the Portuguese *asentistas* appeared to be meager, Lisbon won significant gains with her continued presence in the Atlantic. Staying on the Senegambia coast, strengthening territorial dominion, connecting inland markets to the sea trade in West Central Africa, accessing American silver markets, and fomenting a large slave-ship fleet proved decisive to Lisbon, especially in the context of the early seventeenth century Portuguese decline in Asia.

At that time, bullion became the main Portuguese export in the area. Thus, in the first decades of the seventeenth century, when the *Asiento* slaves were sold in greater number in Cartagena, Vera Cruz, and Buenos Aires, the Spanish silver reals of eight (*el real de a ocho*) appeared as the most lucrative Portuguese export product in Asian markets.[217] Accordingly, the overall data on money and silver shipped to Asia on behalf of the Portuguese royal administration indicate an abrupt fall from 1630 on.[218] In practice, the Chinese demand for American silver engaged exchanges that enlarged the African slave trade during the Iberian Union.[219]

After the rupture caused by the Braganza's assuming the throne, Lisbon tried to resume her business with Spanish American ports. In a session held in 1646, the Overseas Council highlighted the pivotal role played by the Portuguese *Asiento*, from the Atlantic to the Pacific, from Potosí silver to Macao silk. Meeting at a time when the Dutch overseas and the Spanish all along her continental frontiers attacked Portugal, the Council reflected on the kingdom's fate. Deciding to look for "all means" to reestablish the kingdom's wealth, the councilors advised the Crown to allow again the Portuguese slave trade into Spanish America.[220]

By doing so, wrote the councilors, the external trade would increase, "making the kingdom plentiful, enriching the vassals, improving customs' revenues and letting the overseas possessions breath." Exports of Africans into Spanish America would provide new taxes for the Crown, reopening Indian textile trafficking to Angola and Upper Guinea. The growth of royal revenues would enforce the king's officers and clergy's authority in the African enclaves, strengthening Portuguese rule overseas. As they returned from the American ports, stated the Council, the Portuguese ships would carry cochineal, indigo, and leathers that should pay taxes at Lisbon's customs. More importantly, wrote the councilors, those ships would also "perforce" (*de força*) bring American silver and gold, endowing the vassals and the Crown with more wealth.

In the Council's opinion, strangled by Madrid's military threat and the European competition overseas, the Crown had only one card to play: the resumption of the slave trade into Spanish America. Triggered by the trade in the living, a worldwide chain of exchanges would be set again in motion to the benefit of the king's treasury, its overseas dominion, and the mainland merchants. "And the *reales* [Spanish silver coins] will be so abundant (in Lisbon) that they will suffice to be sent to India and China, to purchase goods that will increase the income of the Casa da India (the Royal administration of overseas trade)."[221] From that time on, the South Atlantic slave trade emerged as a critical component of the world system.

Highlighting the significance of Portuguese control over the slave-trade regions in Africa, the Crown had by that time already sent rescue ships from Brazil, in an attempt to recover Angola, occupied since 1641 by the Dutch. As we shall see in chapter 6, the recovery of Angola seemed somehow more significant to Lisbon than the reconquest of the Pernambuco's sugar plantations, equally occupied by the Dutch.

French jurist Georges Scelle, one of the founders of international legal studies, published his pioneering book about the *Asientos* in 1906. Scelle conceived of his work as an "economic interpretation of history." Analyzing for the first time numerous documents from the Seville archives, he unpacked the mechanisms through which the foreigners snatched the *Asientos* and converted the contracts into "a commercial weapon" to rip Spain off her colonial incomes.[222] Since then, research on the slave trade has undergone great developments. Yet the focus on the trade of Africans as a commercial weapon in intermetropolitan rivalry, or, as was the case in Brazil, as a factor of economic antagonism between the colonists and the Crown, has not received its due attention.

Such questions emerge in the history of the Ethiopic Ocean. Similar to the Portuguese, Dutch, Genoese, French, and English *asentistas* and contractors who used the *Asientos* to break the Castilian monopoly in America, the merchants and settlers from Rio de Janeiro, Pernambuco, and Bahia also appropriated part of the Lisbon incomes by means of the same slave trade.

Started in Upper Guinea in response to the demand of the Iberian Peninsula and Atlantic islands, the flux of the oceanic trade moved to West Central Africa in the mid-sixteenth century, when the shipping of Africans into the New World prevailed. In this context, the deportation of Angola's peoples followed two successive drives. First, it responded to the growth of São Tomé's sugar-cane plantations. Secondly, it resulted from the trade into Spanish America within the framework of the *Asientos* taken up by Lisbon.

The slave trade into South America was achieved in the context of such mercantile flows. At the turn of the sixteenth century, Brazil emerged as America's most powerful magnet of African forced migrations, a place it would maintain for most of the duration of the slave trade to the Americas.

Intertropical Experiments

Adding to the navigation between African and American coasts, the route Lisbon-Goa-Macao, with vessels calling in Bahia, linked the South Atlantic to Asia beginning at the turn of the sixteenth century. The tropical agriculture of three continents, and particularly of the richest biomes of the planet, the Amazon basin and the Atlantic forest, the Congo basin, and the Malay Archipelago—were thus related. In this context, colonial experiments crisscrossed the South Atlantic. Amerindians had long cultivated the cassava (or manioc), sweet potato, and maize that composed almost all of the settlers' meals.[223] Crown's warehouses in Portuguese America included, since the 1550s, cassava flour and maize, called *abati* by the Tupi, among the provisions provided to royal officers and clergymen.[224] Jesuit Manuel da Nóbrega recorded in 1549 that cassava flour "is eaten by all."[225] Faced with the few European foodstuffs apt to be preserved unspoiled in the tropics, the colonizers drew attention to the advantages of cooking and conserving some native crops.[226] Even more so as Amerindians under coerced labor supplied these foodstuffs, a system then prevalent in Brazil.

Except in the São Paulo plateau, where maize predominated, cassava flour was the staple food in all of Portuguese America. "It is the chief provender," declared the Rio de Janeiro municipal council in an ordinance of 1646, forcing small planters to exclusively cultivate cassava.[227] A quarter of the troops' pay was made in the form of cassava flour.[228] Later, a royal edict stated that all the Pernambuco merchants who sent slave ships to the Costa da Mina (the area from the Cape Palmas to the Niger delta) should have fields with cassava crops.[229] An administered cassava flour market thereby emerged, based on Amerindian coerced labor and on African slavery, which diffused the foodstuff all over South Atlantic.

Together with an African crop, the banana, cassava gained such prominence in the South American settlements that missionaries and colonists reinvented its origin. Indeed, they attributed the introduction of cassava crops to the benefactions of apostle Saint Thomas, assimilated by them to the Amerindian divinity "Sumeh" during his supposed journey through pre-Columbian America.[230] The cultural mix proposed by the missionaries did not prosper, and the Sumeh legend withered away. The episode illustrates the reluctance of Europeans to admit that agriculture had been developed in pre-Columbian America.[231]

Bahian Jesuits exported cassava flour to the Angola missionaries in exchange for slaves. During the 1592 famine, the Luanda Jesuits helped out the Portuguese troops, providing 150 soldiers a day with cassava flour imported from Brazil.[232] Further, the maintenance of military men and clergy, and the transport and month-long keeping of hundreds of enslaved individuals in transit, led to the storage of foodstuffs next to African fairs and ports of trade. A lot of wheat and manioc flour was accounted for in the Angolan governor and slave trader Forjaz's estate (he died in Luanda in 1611): "many flours from Portugal and Brazil."[233]

Very soon, the Tupi cassava "war flour" (*wee-antam*) caught the attention of a notable Portuguese author and military writer. In his pioneering treatise on modern naval strategy, *A Arte da Guerra no Mar* (1555), Father Fernão de Oliveira, a well traveled man, suggested the use of rice in India and cassava flour in Brazil in the absence of European cereals.[234] Another military expert, Luís Mendes de Vasconcelos, future governor of Angola, in his celebrated *Arte Militar* (1612), also wrote that manioc flour could provide high-quality rations for troops and sailors. Captain Sylveira, quoting Vasconcelos a few years later, went a step further, advising captains and ship owners to include cassava flour in the feeding of Africans during the middle passage.[235]

In Central and Southern Iberian America, cassava flour, maize, and araucaria nut (*curi* in Tupi and *pinhão* in Portuguese) constituted the provisions of the São Paulo's *bandeirantes* and their Amerindian militias in the course of their enslaving raids. Highlighted by these three military writers and by royal officers and missionaries, cassava flour earned a prominent status not only in the feeding of colonial troops but also in the slaves' ration on the Ethiopic Ocean and Caribbean. David Wheat shows that since 1579, overseers employed by planters in Matanzas (Cuba) were paid with several local products, among them cassava and maize cultivated by "blacks and servants." Moreover, two-thirds of Hispaniola Island's slaves were employed in the cultivation of ginger, cassava, and maize, in 1606.[236] Taking in account those slavery alimentary practices in the Caribbean and Portuguese America, Colbert's *Code Noir* (1685) established that French planters should provide, weekly, cassava flour or, "three cassava weighing three and half pounds each at least," to their slaves.[237]

Maize soon spread in West Central Africa. Duarte Lopes mentioned its cultivation in the kingdom of Congo around 1578.[238] The crop was also introduced in the Gulf of Guinea from São Tomé.[239] Following a report from the mid-eighteenth century, maize yields in the fields stretching from Accra to the Niger delta seemed to be higher than in Portuguese America.[240]

In contrast to maize, cassava preparation demanded skill, and so it took longer to be transplanted to the new territory. As it is well known, several centuries before the Europeans arrived, the Amerindians had learned how to remove cassava toxins, the cyanogenic glucosides, rendering its flour edible. This agricultural practice was transferred to Africa. An account collected by Capuchin missionaries relates that the cultivation of cassava would have first spread to São Tomé Island and then to the African mainland.[241] A 1625 document says "it has been a few years now that cassava is planted as in Brazil by the Portuguese who live in Mpinda."[242] São Tomé's ships frequented Mpinda, south of the mouth of the Congo River, the main seaport in the Congo basin.[243] The port concentrated enslaved Africans prior to embarkation, who, as in Luanda, worked the cassava fields until transportation was due.[244] In fact, São Tomé appears as the main diffusion point of tropical crops to both shores of the Atlantic. As we have see above, sugar-cane techniques and the banana cultivation came from São Tomé to Brazil. Prescribed since 1519 by the Portuguese Crown as appropriate food for the slave ships leaving São Tomé, the banana arrived in Brazil as a component of the South Atlantic diet.²⁴⁵ On the way back, peanuts, manioc, and, later, cacao came from tropical America to São Tomé and then to tropical African fields.

Mpinda must have also been another diffusion point for the farming of Brazil's peanut, since "Mpinda" is one of the names for this crop in West Central Africa. However, the local production of foodstuffs was in the hands of exporting slave traders, little being left for the arriving missionaries. "Regarding subsistence, it is the highest misery that one usually goes through," claimed Friar José de Pernambuco on disembarking in Mpinda. A Luso-African from Olinda (Pernambuco), with a university degree from Salamanca, Father José de Pernambuco was a pioneer Capuchin missionary in the Congo who became an expert in the Kicongo language.²⁴⁶

In Luanda, the food supply was greater. Seeking to compensate for the losses caused by the Dutch strikes along the maritime thoroughfares, Governor Fernão de Sousa (1624–1630) stimulated the cultivation of some imported foodstuffs around the town. Missionaries took along their cassava pouch (*matula*) on their journeys around the African hinterlands. Ports in the Congo delta sought the product from Luanda. Brazil's method of producing cassava flour prevailed in colonial enclaves in Angola and Congo. Fifty to sixty slaves cultivated the fields and extracted and cut the tuber. In the grating operations, the Angolistas employed elderly and child slaves, of little worth in the field or in the slave market.²⁴⁷

As we shall see in chapter 6, as the Dutch got involved in the South Atlantic slave trade, they made use of maize and cassava flour in their shipments.²⁴⁸ Cassava flour served as nourishment for captives and the soldiers, as well as for the terrestrial, fluvial, and sea slave traders in Angola and Congo.

Alongside sweet potato and the maize named *masa Mputo* in Kicongo, "spike from Portugal," to set it apart from the native sorghum, called *masa Mbela*, "spike of the village," the two crops spread in Angola.²⁴⁹ Hence, colonial officers compelled the *sobas* to pay 10 percent (the *dízimo*) of their maize crops to the Crown.²⁵⁰ Manioc flour also became part of the pay for troops, royal officers, and clergy in Angola, spreading its alimentary use.²⁵¹

In fact, the cassava culture generated an alimentary revolution in the South Atlantic.²⁵² Cassava had no natural pests or herbivores in Africa. It was one of the most drought-tolerant crops, able to grow in marginal soils. Cassava is actually cultivated in all sub-Sahara areas, and it features today as Africans' most significant primary caloric source.²⁵³ Since it takes at least ten months to grow to harvesting size, its cultivation presupposed a certain sedentary condition. Contrariwise, maize, easily transported, was harvested three to six months after sowing. Hence, it was chosen as the stock food by São Paulo dwellers and their native allies as they crossed inland during the *entradas*.[254]

Another sort of slave hunters, the Jaga hordes, also adopted maize, incorporating it into their chief-making rituals.[255] Englishman Andrew Battel recounts that maize was widely used by the Jaga.

Battel had the unfortunate idea of going ashore on a beach of Ilhabela (an island in São Paulo coast) as he and his fellow corsairs ambushed Spanish galleons along the South American coast. The local Tupinambá captured him and handed him to the Portuguese. Deported to Luanda in 1589, Battel fell into the hands of the Jaga. Forced to fight alongside them, Battel, the Hans Staden of Angola, recorded that the Jaga took on their maize provisions in their raids.[256] With this *matula* of food, Angolan slave hunters were able to increase their mobility and preying efficacy. By the 1610s, maize was already available in local markets around the Congo and Angola.

In short, the advance of the South American plants and agricultural products in African tropical zones unfolded in three phases. First, America exported manioc via the Bay of Guanabara and São Vicente ports. In the second phase, manioc, maize, sweet potato, and South American fruits were cultivated in African soil. In the third phase, such cultivation spread out into the African hinterlands. At this stage, the components of the Southern Atlantic alimentary system were in place. In Brazil, and in the vessels leaving her ports, manioc flour replaced the European wheat biscuit and the São Tomé yam in the sailors' and slave traders' victuals, at the same time as it furnished freight for the African market. Then, the American cultures were transplanted to Africa, strengthening regional crops and widening the reach of African slave traders. In his compilation of missionary narratives published in 1776, the Abbot Pryoart wrote that manioc flour was "the people's bread," in Loango and Kacongo.[257] Portuguese who traveled from the Mozambican coast through to the Kazembe kingdom at the turn of the eighteenth century recorded the cultivation and the dietary use of cassava flour and dry potato among local villagers.[258]

Having helped to transplant Asian spices into Brazil, the Jesuits also created, in their seventeenth century Angola farmyards, diffusion points for European, Asian, and American plants in West Central Africa. The cultivation of alien plants in the areas surrounding the Angolan ports and inland fairs contributed to the extension of terrestrial networks, consolidating the Atlantic slaving business. Some plants were brought from East Asia (lime, orange, Asian yams), Central Asia (eggplants and chick peas), and from other African regions (banana). From South America came such crops as cassava, maize, sweet potato, pumpkins, beans, peanuts, tomatoes, pineapple, papaya, guava, Brazilian cherry (*pitanga*), and Pará guava (*araçá*); the last-mentioned was qualified in Angola by the Tupi suffix as *mirim* (small) or *açu* (great).[259]

In the Bengo valley, fifty km outside Luanda, a Jesuit's farm cultivated by slaves produced, in the 1630s, bananas, pineapples, maize, sorghum, *ncanza* beans, mustard, oranges, limes, citrons, and "a lot of war flour" (cassava flour).[260] Three decades later, the Capuchin Cavazzi wrote that maize was the "best and most common" grain in Africa. Like Cavazzi, another Capuchin missionary, Friar Merolla, wrote that the *ncanza* bean was introduced from Brazil by the Portuguese and was called in Angola and Congo "Brazil's beans."[261] Cadornega mentions a Luanda dish, the *moamba*, very similar to the Brazilian *feijoada* much appreciated by Angolistas and Portuguese.[262]

In the opposite direction of food, germs, peoples, and colonial practices from South America, the African watermelon, okra, banana, sorghum and palm oil also crossed the ocean. In the first decades of the eighteenth century, the *Paulistas* who penetrated the Mato Grosso hinterlands introduced the banana in those parts. Alongside native wild rice (*abatiapé*), the banana would make up the staple food many indigenous peoples of Brazil.[263] In Bahia and Pernambuco, sorghum kept its Kicongo name: *maçambará*, which derives from *masa Mbela*.[264]

Employed by the early-seventeenth-century Angolistas, the Portuguese Brazilian word *moquém* (from the Tupi *moka'em*) refers to game, cow, whale, or fish meat lightly roasted on a grill in the Amerindian way and exported from Brazil to Angola.[265]

Potatoes were as yet little known in Portugal and Italy, so the Capuchin missionary Cavazzi, born in Modena, did not quite fathom what he was staring at, as he described the tuber's cultivation in Angola.[266] The pineapple, "the royal fruit of the *ananas*" (Cadornega), which originated in the Caribbean and South America, had been cultivated in the Guinea Coast since the end of the sixteenth century.[267] Next, it spread to West Central Africa, to the point that the fruit appears in the frontispiece of Cadornega's *História Geral (*1681) as one of Angola's symbols. In his Abomey Palace, in the capital city of the Dahomey, King Kpengla's (1774–1789) mural bears a pineapple illustrating a local proverb about the virtues of modesty: "lightning strikes the palm tree, but never touches the pineapple, which is close to the ground." Interestingly enough, this Amazonian fruit was grown in Western and

West Central Africa before it was cultivated, in the beginning of the nineteenth century, in Pernambuco and further south in Brazil.[268]

Brazilian and African vocabularies both contribute to the names of South Atlantic dishes, a result of the transfer of edible plants and the forced migration of Africans. In Congo and Angola, the Tupi word *beiju* refers, as in Brazil, to the cassava bolus. However, tapioca meal, in Brazil known as *quiçamã*, derives its name from the Angolan province of Kisama. In the same way, the Brazilian Portuguese word *fubá*, maize flour, comes from the Kimbundo *fuba*. *Mungunzá* is from the Kimbundo, or *canjica*, derived from the Kikongo, suggesting that the meal, which mixes grated maize with cow's milk, was common among the Angolan peoples, traditional cattle-raisers, before entering the Brasílico diet. All those dishes were mixed in porridges, broths, and flours,[269] as an easily kept foodstuff, quickly prepared, divided into bowls, kneaded with the hands, and swallowed in hinterland stopovers, on the slave ship's lower deck, in the Brazilian *senzalas*, and in the cane fields.[270]

"Cotton armor," commonly known as *gibão*, doublets light in weight and resistant to Amerindian arrows, made and worn by the Paulistas in their enslaving raids *bandeiras*, was imported from São Paulo by the Angola governors from 1612 onward.[271] The doublets were quite practical. Narrating one of the attacks perpetrated in 1628 by the Paulistas' slave raiders against the missions of Guayrá, Fr. Montoya underlined its efficiency: "Even if they (Paulistas) were hit by arrows they were not injured, because the arrows did not cross that outfit."[272] Luís Mendes de Vasconcelos, the respected military writer and belligerent Angola governor (1617–1621), went so far as to state to the Crown that the use of "cotton armor" by the American Portuguese rendered the conquest of Brazil easier than that of Angola. Used in West Central Africa since the seventeenth century to carry colonists, officers, and missionaries, the hammock (from the Arawak *hamaka*) is known as *tipoye*, from the Tupi *ti'poya*, suggesting, as indicated by Câmara Cascudo, its Luso-Brazilian origins.[273]

Conversely, the enslaving practices of the indigenous networks of trade in Angola and São Paulo led to the borrowing of the luso-kimbundu word *pombeiro* by Luso-Americans.[274] Thus, Martin de Sá, who had exported horses from São Paulo to Angola, denounced in 1624 a murder by the Paulistas' proxy Indian slave traders who he referred to as the "Whites' *pombeiros*" (*pombeiros dos brancos*).[275]

In the beginning of the seventeenth century, many mainland Portuguese and Luso-Africans hailing from Upper Guinea and São Tomé acclimatized to Angola.

Such skilled tropical soldiers, "seasoned by the air of those provinces," integrated the Benguela invasion expedition (1615).[276] Later in the century, the Overseas Council took an interest in recruiting seasoned Brasílico soldiers and officers to defend Angola. Likewise, Italian Capuchins heading to São Tomé Island sought to open a house in Bahia for fresh European missionaries to build some sort of acclimatization, a way to "take" protective Bahian airs to ward off African illnesses. In the same way, if missionaries became ill in Angola or Congo, they traveled back to Bahia to recover their health.[277]

Agglutinating Good and Ancillary Good

It is well known that the slave trade linked up the supply of a series of other African products. Even with the use of camels in the Sahel, of canoes in the Upper Guinea, of the Mina Coast fluvial networks and of the Angolan river ferryboats, the captive slave still featured as a commodity able to carry other commodities. Thus, the slave-trade terrestrial routes shaped up many other commodity transportation paths between the hinterland and the African coast. Particularly active, the Angolan fairs were designated in Kimbundo by the name that came to mean any small business at all in Brazil: *kitanda*.[278] Shipments of ivory, beeswax (much appreciated in Brazil for the manufacture of candles and waterproofing sails), hides, textiles, musk, copper, gold, gum, and palm oil flowed into the slaving ports, allowing for rounding off the profits obtained in the loading of slaves.

Business was set up in the overseas markets along the axis of an agglutinating commodity, defined in 1618 by Ambrósio Fernandes Brandão as the "nerve of the trade," whose value oriented other regional exchanges. In the wake of the main circuit there flowed ancillary commodities.[279] An experienced overseas merchant, Brandão makes a distinction between the two types of products, referring to India, where the agglutinating commodity was pepper.

Hence, the Portuguese settlement in Africa was favored by the ability to drain into the Atlantic the interregional exchanges previously channeled into other markets. At the end of the 1620s, Netherlands ships bartered copper and ivory in Mpinda. But they incurred in the disfavor of the count of Soyo, lord of Mpinda, as they refused products usually purchased by the Portuguese: the *infulas* and the *quimbes* (straw or *raffia* fabrics, used in Angola as currency), the *xinga* (elephant tails), the *ensalas* (parrot feathers), ostentation or tradable goods, imported from

Luanda to be sold into the inland fairs.²⁸⁰ Unable to mobilize a naval force to expel the Dutch, Governor Fernão de Sousa retaliated against the sovereign of Soyo by prohibiting Portuguese ships from leaving Luanda bound to Mpinda in search of such merchandise. Soon, the count of Soyo yielded and forced the Dutch to leave the Congo. Only later, when they entered the slave trade once and for all, were the Dutch able to set foot in that port.²⁸¹

Meeting the variety of African supply, there was a widespread and diversified demand for American goods in Africa. Alongside Asian and European manufactured goods, Brazilian products were also exported to the colonists and to Africans: the *zimbos* (cowries), cassava flour, *"jeribita"* (seventeenth-century name for *cachaça*, the well-known Brazilian sugar cane rum), tobacco, horses, timbers, furs, maize flour, marmalade, dry and salted fish and beef, cheeses, earthenware, and gold (in the eighteenth century).²⁸² Some of these goods were used in religious rituals and political ceremonies. Other products were indispensable in the composition of the *banzo*, the purchase unit of a slave formed by an assortment of goods used to buy captives in the hinterland fairs.²⁸³ Different trade networks converged on the fairs and inland slaving kingdoms. Such exchanges led the long-distance continental trade and the maritime routes to couple up with the domestic economy of the coastal villages in Western and West Central Africa.

The permanence of hundreds of merchants, colonists, military men, and clergy, as well as settlement infrastructure and institutions in Angolan enclaves, yielded a demand for specific materials. Building timber, roof tiles, bricks, and tools made in Brazil were usually exported to Luanda and Benguela.²⁸⁴ In the exchange with Africa, Portuguese America put forward, in different stages, several merchandises: cassava flour, *zimbo*, *jeribita*, and tobacco.

Brazilian commodity exchanges with Africa have not received their due attention, with the exception of *jeribita* and tobacco, whose importance came to a head in the eighteenth century. However, cassava flour and *zimbo* have also had a significant impact on the slave trade and the connection between the two poles of the Portuguese Atlantic. Their role is described in chapter 7. Cassava flour became the base for the slaves' ration in the Ethiopic Ocean. The Bahian *zimbos*, money cowries circulating in Congo and Angola, helped the Luso-Brasílicos break into West Central Africa inland markets. Finally, the *cachaça* sold in Angola places Brazil among the first world exporters of distilled alcoholic beverages.

The slave trade between America and Portuguese Africa overflowed the usual parameters defining colonial commerce. The bipolarity of relations between Brazilian and African markets features a dynamic that bent Portuguese policy in the Atlantic, yielding a series of consequences. Such fluxes helped attract capital and shipping equipment to this sector, lowering transportation costs within the South Atlantic. This factor led Immanuel Wallerstein to suggest that the transportation costs of enslaved Africans could have been lower than the expenses caused by the flight of enslaved Amerindians in American plantations.[285] In line with Braudel, Wallerstein considers the slave trade as a leg of the triangular trade.[286] However, this is a reductive idea with regard to a phenomenon with vast implications.

In any case, this argument does not clarify the set of problems of Amerindian slavery in Brazil. That subject should be approached from the perspective of the Atlantic market, as we will see in the following chapter.

Chapter 4

Amerindians, the "Slaves of the Land"

Let us hypothesize that the pro-Amerindian policy of the Jesuits had been neutralized since the sixteenth century in Portuguese America; let us conjecture that the totality of the Portuguese slave trade could have been captured by the *asentistas* and redirected to Spanish America; let us suppose, finally, that the Crown, confronted with such encumbrances, decided to promote Amerindian captivity, even though the market for indigenous slaves would have remained small compared to the Africans traded into the enclaves of Portuguese America. Contrary to what has been sometimes written, such a presumption does not follow from the fortuitous demographic limits of the South American lowlands' Amerindian peoples. In practice, the conditions that could have yielded a regular trade in native slaves were not given from the start. Despite attempts carried out by the Portuguese, Brasílicos, and Curibocas or Mamelucos (mestizos), the social organization of the Tupi, Gê (or Tapuya) Arawak, and Karib speakers remained refractory to the extensive exchange of slaves. Moreover, as observed by Santos-Granero in a systematic analysis of the issue, Indian captives were not a commodity in native tropical America.[1]

When a dominant Amerindian community, potentially interested in outside goods, pressed its dominated groups with the view of transforming them into exchange goods, dissension and village fissioning caused the community's fragmentation.[2] From the beginning, the availability of land and game, the gathering of food in the jungle, and slash-and-burn agriculture—the *coivara*—featured as alternatives for survival to dissidents.[3] This set of factors seems to lie at the root of the constant segmentation of pre-European societies. The role of native chiefdom represented too unstable a power to allow the extraction of captives from its own community or to transform his own group in a regular preying community, for such power rested on the constitution of complex systems of exchange and accumulation of goods.[4]

A knowledgeable expert in 1600s Amazonia, Jesuit João Daniel, drew arguments from the chiefdom's weakness to justify the government of Amerindians by missionaries. According to him, without the priests' direction in the native villages, colonial authorities could not enforce the royal orders pertinent to Amerindians.[5] Devoid of effective power, the Tupi and Gê chiefs could not manage to transmit such orders or have them implemented. "Ordinarily such principals, or *caciques* as the Spanish call them, are principals but in name, not in practice. It is an honorary dignity, without application or recognition."[6]

Consequently, chiefs did not succeed in selling consistently to the colonial market the groups subjugated or enslaved by their communities. Besides, slave-trade networks—a decisive component in sub-Saharan regions—did not emerge to wrest the contingent supply of Amerindian captives into Portuguese coastal enclaves. One of the only traces of long-distance trade extant in precolonial Brazil seems to have been left by the Tupinambá and the Kaingang of the center-south. The object of exchange was an article of restricted demand—feathers of the *ema* (*Rhea americana*), the South American bird resembling an ostrich, used by the Rio de Janeiro coast Murubixaba (chieftains) in their headpieces.[7] In a letter addressed to the governor general of Portuguese America in 1559, Father Nobrega, the Jesuits' superior in Bahia, judged that it was the Portuguese who introduced the "infernal root" of the Amerindian slave trade.[8]

Although many Indians joined the Portuguese and mestizos' slaving raids, no Amerindian community appeared on the horizon of Portuguese America as a regular supplier of slaves to the settlers. The authors of an incisive study of the Tupinambá wars state that such conflicts were founded essentially on revenge (on the death of the enemy), but did not fit into a wider social reproduction process.[9]

The historical process took a different turn in sub-Saharan Africa. There were, as pointed out in the case of the Soninke of Galam and the Benguela Ovimbundu, communities that repelled the slave trade. However, in Western and West Central Africa, at the turn of the 1500s, there emerged native formations structured around the trade between inland areas and the coast. In neighboring Luanda, the Ndongo kingdom collapsed under predatory European raids. Nevertheless, in the Angolan hinterland, sufficiently close to carry out exchange with the ports of trade but far enough to avoid Portuguese forays, the kingdoms of Matamba and Kasanje gained strength with the Atlantic slave trade in the course of the seventeenth century.[10] In the following century, on the Mina Coast, the Dahomey kingdom took advantage of the European intermetropolitan competition on its coast to protect its independence and to secure better deals in the slave trade with the Europeans.[11]

Nothing of the sort took place on the other side of the Ethiopic Ocean, where the Amerindian communities did not expand this form of social transformation on a wide scale. Yet as we shall see, the Indians' coerced labor remained decisive in seventeenth-century São Paulo, in the Amazon basin, and on the fringes of the plantation and mining zones. In this regard, it is worth recapitulating the circumstances in which slavery and other forms of indigenous compulsory work were authorized in Portuguese America.

Amerindian Coerced Labor

Seeking to determine the contrasts between the trade in Africans and the trade in Amerindians, I examine the context linked to the commutative practices by means of which the slave was obtained by previously agreed methods and preestablished transactions. A succession of laws shaped three modes of appropriation of Amerindian individuals: *resgate*, captivity, and the *descimentos*.

Resgates ("enslavements by barter") consisted of the exchange of goods for Amerindians taken prisoner by other Amerindians. In the terms of the royal decree of 1574, only the "roped" natives, that is, those already arrested and tied up to be killed, could be the objects of a ransom by a settler. Individuals obtained by this expedient had, according to the law, a captivity time limited to ten years.[12]

Captivities (*cativeiros*) constituted the second mode of possessing native individuals. This category covered those Amerindians taken prisoner in a "just war," consented to and determined by the authorities against certain communities for limited periods of time. Amerindians captured in this context became slaves for life.[13] In the second half of the seventeenth century, the Amazon-region Jesuits interpreted both *resgates* and *cativeiros* as a single practice by authorities and settlers that opened the path to perpetual enslavement.[14]

The *descimento* ("bringing down") referred to the coerced displacement of Amerindian communities into the vicinity of European enclaves. This is why the Instituto Histórico's nineteenth-century scholars used to follow a distinction inopportunely abandoned by many contemporary authors. I refer to the difference, fundamental to Portuguese American ethnohistory, between the Indian *aldeia* (village), or better still (for the Tupi speaking peoples), *taba*, and *aldeamento* (forced settlement). The *aldeia* or *taba* defines a habitat chosen by a given Amerindian community, before and after the European contact, consonant with the ecological and social determinants of their culture. In contrast, the *aldeamento* was a dwelling site for individuals from one or more Indian communities, who were compulsorily displaced, mixed, settled, and confined by Portuguese missionaries and royal authorities.[15] Once freed, the labor of such settlement Amerindians could only be used in exchange for wages, in the terms laid down by the law.[16]

At first sight of secondary importance, the *descimento* turns out to have been the initiative yielding the most devastating consequences for Amerindians, because of the dimensions such practices took within the scope of Portuguese America. Harassed by *entrada* raids against villages and the pressure exerted by civil and religious authorities, the hinterland communities were "brought down" and settled in the vicinity of colonial ports, villages, and cities. Badly fed, exposed to coerced labor in an epidemiological environment that was particularly hostile to settled Amerindians, they perished in great numbers. The *descimento* was a practice inscribed in royal legislation as the less violent way of intervening in indigenous societies, but it probably caused more extensive death than the *resgates* and *cativeiros*.

Moreover, it is worth keeping in mind that most of the texts prohibiting the captivity of Amerindians were ineffective. John Monteiro quotes a will by a São Paulo couple, dated from 1684, as he analyzed the captaincy's fraudulent and widespread process of Amerindian enslavement. Ten Amerindians, whose possession was transferred by means of inheritance, were declared as being "free by the laws of kingdom and are of compulsory service only according to custom."[17] Indeed, Alcântara Machado relates the string of terms used in 1600s São Paulo inventories to dissimulate the indigenous person's captive statute: "service *pieces*," "freed people," "people from Brazil," "obligation people," "freed pieces," "servants," "compulsory services," "administration souls," "administered ones."[18] John French examined the wills of sixty-eight Paulistas who died before 1625, showing that by far most of the captive labor was composed of formally free Indians. Thus, this group of Paulista owners possessed nine African slaves (1 percent), 124 Amerindian slaves (14.5 percent), and 723 so-called "freed" Amerindians (84.5 percent). Such percentages illustrate merchant capital's shallow penetration and the endogenized mode of exploitation then predominant in the São Paulo plateau.[19]

The contrast between the ways in which legal texts on slavery, stemming from the common juridical ground of Roman law and from Iberian Reconquista practices, evolved in Portuguese America and Africa becomes patent.[20] Twists and turns notwithstanding, a sequence of royal directives issued in the course of three centuries—constituting the densest Portuguese normative body regarding a single colonial issue—sought to restrict practices of Amerindian slavery. In Africa, in contrast, doubts about the legitimacy of slave possession decreased as the Iberian Crowns stimulated and levied the slave trade alongside the growth of merchant capital investments in the Portuguese-Spanish *Asientos*.

The structural variables imposing the slave trade on the Portuguese American markets were settled in the course of the second half of the seventeenth century. São Paulo underwent a production cycle of wheat and food crops based on Amerindian slavery. This was, however, a conjunctural phenomenon, generated by the disturbances reverberating from the Thirty Years War (1610–1648) into the southern Atlantic, which is examined in more detail in chapter 6. The case of the Estado do Grão-Pará e Maranhão, that is, of the whole of the Amazon region, where Amerindian captivity was the main, if not the sole, form of labor enforced up to the mid-eighteenth century, is described later in this text.

Even when bonded to local logistics in Brasil, settled Amerindians seem to have constituted a problematic resource in comparison with the African slaves supplied by maritime networks. From this point of view, consider the pace of building works at the Fonte da Carioca and the "Arcos Velhos," an aqueduct in Rio de Janeiro that was later replaced by the Lapa Arches. The building works, employing both Amerindian wage and coerced labor, dragged on for half a century after starting in 1671, delayed by the scarcity of such laborers, and by Jesuit demands regarding the hired natives' wages. In the end, Governor Silveira e Albuquerque (1702–1704) decided to buy Africans and also to employ black slaves hired from Rio de Janeiro masters to finish the job. At that time, the gold economy—the first colonial sellers' market—attracted once and for all the trade in Africans into the continent.[21]

An anonymous report written at the beginning of the eighteenth century explains the usefulness of gold in the transformation of the slave market and in the widening of the African slave trade:

> At the end of the last [seventeenth] century, Paulistas who were out to conquer the gentiles [Indians] who peopled those hinterlands, who were the slaves they helped themselves to, had camped on the margins of a brook in Minas Gerais territory (when they) heard a din that is heard in the places where there is gold . . . , on the following day they took to prospecting and found the first gold, which was present in the Guaripiranga [sic] Sierra in such abundance that it was more profitable to buy Blacks with what they extracted, than to undertake the capture of Indians.[22]

The magic nocturnal sound announced the enrichment of the Paulistas. They were thus able to cease their pillaging of Amerindian communities and they began to buy Africans.

The Trade in Amerindian Slaves

Generally, during the 1500s European occupation spread over the coastal zone previously invaded by the Tupi around the sixteenth century of the Christian era.[23] After enslaving and decimating some of the seaside communities, the settlers faced other Tupi, much more hostile, as well as the Gê peoples.[24] From 1500 onward, the Potiguar attacked the European enclaves in Paraíba and in Pernambuco, while the Aymoré hit dwellers in Bahia, Ilhéus, and Espírito Santo, and the Tamoyo acted against Rio de Janeiro.[25] The colonists' panic can be gauged in a contemporary letter from Bahia: "this land is peerless on Earth as a land for the cultivation of all things in this world, but the gentile [Indian] is the demon."[26] The collapse of the Indian network on which the settlers rested is referred to in a letter sent to the Crown by the rector of the Bahia College: "Each day sugar mills are lost and depopulated due to the deaths of many settlers and to the slaves who are continually killed and eaten by other Indians who never had any exchange or peace with the Portuguese. Nor were they seen when the coastal fringe was peopled with Indians with whom the settlers had peace and where they have built their farms. And because they [the settlers] have emptied it, those [Gê Indians] who destroy the land have now come." Therefore, concluded the rector, "there is no remedy but to bring over other Indians contrary to those and friendly towards the settlers."[27]

At that time, when predatory expeditions sparked lively resistance among the hinterland Indian villages, Portuguese America faced maritime assaults by other Europeans.[28] On the one hand, authorities sought alliances with the seaside Indian communities from the beginning to hold off the offensive by hostile inland Amerindians, and on the other, they endeavored to protect the ports against Europeans corsairs. The method of settling allied "meek" Indians between colonial dwellers and enemy Amerindians gave way to the *descimento* policy, that is, the transportation of hinterland villages into settlements founded in the vicinity of colonial enclaves. In this sense, these concentrated nuclei of coerced Amerindians can be seen as a distant prefiguration of the much later settlements created in Africa in the 1960s and 1970s by the Portuguese colonial army seeking to isolate the pro-independence guerrillas.[29]

The aims of the subjugation of the Indian frontier were made explicit in a document sent to Lisbon by the Jesuit superiors in Brazil, who attended the congregation that took place in Bahia (1592). Refuting Gabriel Soares de Souza's memorial, which defended the lawfulness of Amerindian captivity, the Jesuits explained, "The only remedy in this State [of Brazil] is to have many peaceful gentiles [natives] in villages around the sugar mills and farms, because in this way there will be people who are of service, who will resist the enemy, French as well as English, or the Aymore [Indians] who have done so much harm and still do, and who can restrain the Guinea Negroes who are many and who fear the Indians alone."[30] Missionaries with long experience in the modes of captivity in Brazil and Africa took part in the congregation. There were several influential Jesuits, among them Fathers Fernão Cardim, José de Anchieta, and Luís da Grã, but also Fr. Pero Rodrigues, supervisor of the S.J. in Angola and Brazil, whose remarks about the Santomese slave revolt and the Indian policy in Brazil were quoted in chapter 2. Fr. Pero's presence in the conclave underlined the transatlantic strategy—adapted to the social relations in Africa and in Portuguese America—that guided the S.J. policy.

Aware of its tenuous military presence in America, and having become wise with the setbacks in Asia, the Crown tried to preserve peace with the Amerindians. In this regard, the 1548 statute granted to the first governor-general of Brazil, Tomé de Souza, a man who experienced the frailty of the Portuguese establishments in Africa and Asia, is telling.[31] In a context where Indian resistance was a central issue, it was stated that the governor-general should ban the selling of weapons to the natives, halt both the expeditions to capture Amerindians and the colonists' journeys into the hinterland.[32] Laws imposing bans on enslaving expeditions and the traffic of Amerindians were not observed by the locals, being issued again in 1595, 1605 and 1609.

Royal orders given to Martim de Sá, as he left Lisbon in 1617 to take up Rio de Janeiro's governorship, emphasized the grafting of settlements to hinder Dutch and English trade in Cabo Frio, north of the Guanabara bay.[33] According the testimony of Fr. Antonio Vieira, when the Dutch invaded Bahia (1624–1625), the allied Amerindians came to constitute "the main part of our army, and the one that inspired the most horror in our enemies."[34] In line with other documents of the kind, a Rio de Janeiro land grant (*sesmaria*) given to the Jesuits in 1630—a vast territory covering the land stretching from the banks of the river Macaé and surrounding hinterland up to the Paraíba River valley—indicates the motive for the concession. The aim was to settle Amerindians able to fight the Dutch and other Europeans who carried brazilwood away and were intent on erecting fortresses in the area.[35] In a striking document, revealing of the alliance policy toward the Amerindians, but illustrative of the lack of knowledge about the Portuguese enclaves in Africa and America, the Habsburg Crown suggests a symbolic militant union of the Gulf of Guinea's Akan and the Tupinamba on Rio de Janeiro's shores. Indeed, a royal letter to the governor of Rio de Janeiro recalled the victory at Elmina (1625), in the Gulf of Guinea, by the Portuguese and some Akan communities united against the Dutch. Celebrating the military feat, the Crown ordered the publication of the news in Rio de Janeiro, so that it could feature as a resistance model for the local Indians to adopt against the Dutch.[36]

Later, when some of the Indians went over to the invaders' side, Franciscan priest Manuel Calado wrote that the Dutch held ground in Portuguese America only because of their Amerindian allies, "because in the Indians alone they have their Samson's hair."[37]

Another factor that limited hostilities against Amerindians was the internal threat posed by African and black slaves. As related in the second chapter, the fear generated in Brazil by the "troubles" involving the São Tomé slaves led to the employment of Amerindians in the capture of *quilombolas* and in the destruction of the *quilombos*.[38] Underlining the need of Indian military support in the repression of runaway slaves, the Bahia's Jesuit superior justified the authority of his fellow missionaries over the *aldeamentos*: "if we retired to our colleges, they [the Amerindians] [will retire] to their jungle or to wherever they wished, and the Guinea slaves—who are their muzzle and bridle—would be masters of the jungle, and, as a result, their [the Amerindians'] masters too."[39] There is a measure of the usual Jesuits exaggeration in the statement, since they often gave much relevance to their own role as guardians of colonial order. But it also notes the fear generated by the first sizable *quilombos* in the region.

The Rio Grande and Bahia Potiguars, commanded by Zorobabé, distinguished themselves as the masters' henchmen. Fifteen hundred Potiguar bowmen, transported from Rio Grande by seven caravels, crushed the Aymoré revolt in Bahia. Still on the authorities' orders, they attacked a *quilombo* composed of former African and black slaves on the margins of the Itapicuru River, in the Bahian north, next to Sergipe. But Zorobabé was ill-served by his collaboration with the Portuguese. Returning to his Potiguar homeland, he faced the hostility of Franciscan missionaries and authorities, who increasingly feared his leadership over the Indian villages. He ended up being deported to Evora (1609), where he was poisoned. Brazil's governor-general justified Zorobabé's deportation and his poisoning in Portugal thus: "Y.M. keeps him, and the gentiles [Potiguar] do not see him being killed."[40] Like the Temimino in the center-south, used by the Paulistas, the Potiguar furnished auxiliary troops to the northern settlers and authorities.[41] Also, the 200 Amerindians who left Pernambuco to invade Luanda as part of the 1641 Dutch expedition were recruited from Potiguar ranks. Luso-Brasílico expeditions to Angola integrated allied and captive Indians in its ranks.[42] At that time, a significant report of Gaspar Brito Freire, a sugar-mill owner in Bahia and influential in Portugal, pointed out problems caused by the shortage of coerced labor in Brazil following the fall of Luanda into West-Indische Compagnie (WIC)hands. Brito Freire thought the Crown should allow the *descimentos* and the enslavement of backlands Indians "to supplement the need of blacks from Angola" in the plantations and households. But also to help the colonists "bring back from the bush . . . thousands of runaway blacks."[43] Later, in the second half of the century, Potiguar warriors joined Luso-Brasílico troops to attack the Palmares *quilombos*.

Always perspicacious, Fr. Vicente do Salvador stated that "the good governance of Brazil" demanded that governors cultivate good relations with the Amerindians to be able to muster troops against European enemies. In addition, "and chiefly, against the Guinea Blacks, slaves of the Portuguese, who every day rebel and go around robbing along the roads, and if they don't do worse it is for fear of the Indians I have mentioned, who, with a Portuguese captain, seek them out and bring them in fetters to their masters." Even when he endorsed the purchase of Indians made prisoner by other natives (those "roped"), the Franciscan recognized that the preying on Amerindians "damned" the whole missionary enterprise in Brazil.[44] Furthermore, some the documents quoted sought to avoid Amerindian captivity and to keep good peace with the Indians near colonial enclaves. However, these texts do not explain the motives limiting the long-distance trade in Amerindian slaves.

Hindrances to the Trade in Amerindians

Obviously, the vast territory of Portuguese America could incorporate regular exchanges of Amerindian slaves between one and another captaincy. It is a circumstance that would have reduced the risk of escape, forcing greater desocialization of captives. Attentive to this fact, the missionaries sought to operate long-distance *descimentos*, regrouping Amerindians in settlements situated at least fifteen days away from their original villages[45]; this effort was often in vain, for Amerindians continued to flee. Luso-Brazilian naturalist Alexandre Rodrigues Ferreira thought that desertions were unavoidable "so long as [Brazilian] captaincies do not exchange *descimentos*." "Let us establish," he wrote in 1785, "that if the [enslaved] blacks do not flee to Africa whence they come, it is not for lack of will, but for the lack of the means to cross so many and so distant seas."[46] This was an illusory solution for three reasons.

First, there was the irregularity of maritime transport: north-south sailing along the Brazilian coast was a lot more burdensome than the east-west route, bound to African ports of trade. Second, from the beginning, the Crown introduced the "insulation" (*ilhamento*, the expression is Varnhagen's, in another context) of Portuguese America's enclaves in order to enhance their dependency on metropolitan trade. Direct exchange between the captaincies was forbidden from 1549, and coastal navigation was only freely permitted in 1766, a time when the African slave trade was at full throttle in Portuguese America.[47] And, above all, there was no mercantile network capable of carrying on, regularly and on a large scale, the sale of Amerindians from one captaincy to another.

I shall further discuss this issue in chapter six. For now, it is interesting to recall a Braudel postulate: when it is impossible to close the commercial circuit, it is also impossible to close the deal ("*bouclage impossible, affaire impossible*"). In other words, "if in certain circumstances a trade circuit could not be closed at all, it was clearly doomed to disappear."[48] Even if it was not impossible, the accumulation propitiated by trading Amerindian slaves was incompatible with the colonial system. It was hindered by the more dynamic sphere of merchant capital (invested in the African slave trade), by the Crown's fiscal network (coupled to the African Atlantic trade), and by Church doctrine (which privileged the evangelization of Amerindians and deterred their enslavement). Such circumstances rendered unviable a regular exchange system similar to the African slave trade's. Ultimately, the deadlock also explains the structural factor blocking the development of the São Paulo's *bandeirante* community based on Amerindian coerced labor. Indeed, reference to an African or "Guinea" slave only appeared in 1607 in São Paulo, where the settlers relied on Amerindian slavery for much of the seventeenth century.[49] We shall return to this issue in chapter 6.

Besides these structural elements, tropical epidemiology also contributed to the atrophy of the Amerindian slave market.

The Microbial Unification of the World[50]

Indeed, Amerindian vulnerability to the epidemiological shock—resulting from the microbial unification of the world brought to a conclusion by Columbus—

constituted a factor restricting the extension of Amerindian captivity, and thereby encouraged the growth of African slavery in Portuguese America. New research, mainly on Spanish America, questions the extent of Amerindian population decline and the epidemiological impact of Europeans' arrival.[51] Other authors observe that ethno-genesis and changes in ethnic identities could also influence the European perception of Amerindian population decline.[52] Therefore, it is worthwhile to recall the stages of contact between Europeans, Africans, and Indians in Portuguese America. By virtue of demographic fractioning, of territorial dispersion, and the absence of domesticated animals (susceptible to the spread of zoonosis), the pre-European peoples remained insulated from the pandemics that scourged the Old World. Comparative analyses of blood groups taken from diverse peoples from several continents reveal that Amerindians—like Australian aboriginals—do not feature blood type B. Moreover, South American indigenous peoples do not have blood type A either; they only have type O, a sure sign of a prolonged isolation from other human communities.[53] The reduced genetic diversity of South American indigenous peoples, proved by protein polymorphisms and by DNA study, may have diminished the capacity to resist the invasion of pathogenic cells.[54]

Other factors also contributed to widening the microbial shock in Portuguese America. Vessels setting sail from Europe, Africa, and Asia arrived in Portuguese America in the sixteenth century. Calculations made by Warren Dean regarding Cabo Frio, a brazilwood trading area, show that 300 Portuguese, Spanish, and French vessels had cast anchor in those waters by around 1550. By then, the region's Tupiniquim, Tupinambá, and Macro-Gê-speaking (Goitacá, Aymoré-Botocudos) peoples had been exposed to contact with around 10,000 Europeans.[55] In parallel, the compulsory settlements (*aldeamentos*) relocated Indians from previously isolated communities, regrouping them in the vicinity of ports and of the new pathogenic field formed by Europeans, Africans, and Asians.[56] As mentioned in the previous chapter, Salvador de Bahia had become a port of call for the vessels of the Lisbon-Goa route since the turning of the sixteenth century. In the initial months, before the preparation of the fields and the first maize and manioc harvests, poor food increased the settled natives' morbidity and mortality.[57] In the colonial enclaves, the clearing of jungle areas and the advance of sugar-cane plantations stimulated the proliferation of mosquitoes and fevers. Such circumstances led the natives of the South American Atlantic coast to suffer the full impact of the world's microbial unification.

Goiter, parasites, dermatosis, and perhaps mild types of malaria (*terçãs simples* and *quartãs*) constituted the most frequently occurring diseases among the Amerindians before the Discovery.[58] Europeans carried smallpox, rubella, scarlet fever, tuberculosis, leprosy, venereal diseases, and dermatoses such as *sarna* (scabies). On their side, Africans brought over, directly from the sub-Saharan regions or via the Caribbean, another host of diseases: trachoma; dracunculiasis (filariasis of the circulatory system and the conjunctive and serosal cavities), causing elephantiasis—significantly, in Brazil this was called "worm of the coast," that is, "of the African coast"[59]; ancylostomiasis, caused by the hookworm, an intestinal parasite whose scientific name is *Necator americanus* (American killer), despite its African origin[60]; the most lethal malaria (*terçãs dobres*), caused by a protozoan parasite, *Plasmodium falciparum;* yellow fever; and, probably, a subtype of dengue.[61] Gene sequence analysis of the yellow fever virus confirmed the West African origin of South America's strain and its spread around 300–400 years ago, in the context of the slave trade.[62]

In his *Tratado de las Siete Enfermedades* (1623), considered by Francisco Guerra to be the first book on tropical medicine, Aleixo de Abreu discusses diseases of Luanda, where he stayed for nine years (1594–1603), and Bahia, where he also lived (1604–1606).[63] Abreu was the first physician to practice in Lisbon and on both sides of the South Atlantic. His work contains the first explanation of the scurvy studied in Angola (*mal de Luanda*) and observations on the chigoe flea, cause of Brazilian tungiasis; yellow fever (*enfermedad del gusano*); and dracunculosis. All were registered during his stay in Bahia.[64]

Conversely, a few new diseases in Europe came from the New World. Evidence suggests that syphilis spread out to the world from Central America, in the wake of the genetic mutation of the *Treponema pallidum* bacteria.[65] A similar phenomenon took place with *bouba* or *piã* (yaws), an illness carried by the *Treponema pertenue* with symptoms similar to syphilis and often confused with it.[66] In addition, even under less acute forms, the sexually transmitted diseases that spread throughout the South American coast could cause sterility in women, which also contributed to the demographic decline of the Amerindian peoples.[67] In the first half of the eighteenth century, the migrations, the insalubrities of the camps, and the sudden drops in temperature seem to have made tuberculosis a chronic disease in all social classes in Minas Gerais. In his *Erário Mineral* (1732), Gomes Ferreira, boasting of twenty years of paramedic activity in the mining villages, noted that "pleural sharp pain" (*pontada*) (tuberculosis, very likely) was the main cause of mortality in the region.[68] Twenty years later, the enlightened physician António Ribeiro Sanches also mentions the "pestilential fevers" prevailing in the gold-mining regions of inland Brazil.[69]

Studies on colonial nosography and contemporary witnesses sketch out the main epidemic waves.[70] From the beginning, missionaries narrated the damage done to natives by the new diseases. For five years, from 1549 and 1554, the São Vicente Amerindians suffered a "terrible plague of pleurisy," possibly a strong flu that developed into lung complications.[71] The introduction of oxen, horses, pigs, chickens, ducks, and dogs stimulated the incubation and contagion of diseases carried by the settlers, such as measles, flu, chigoe flea (*bicho do pé*), brucellosis, and bovine smallpox.[72] Fr. Cardim related that the Indians much appreciated chicken, and by 1585 they were rearing them well into the hinterland. Precious helpers in hunting, dogs were breast-fed by the Amerindian women, according to the ritual already practiced involving collared peccaries. Amazonian Amerindians considered dogs—like captives and *muiraquitãs* (jade or wood amulets)—to be prestige goods to be exchanged for future wives.[73] At the turn of the sixteenth century, an outbreak of *mordexim*—a Luso-Asian name for cholera—took place in the northern captaincies.[74]

However, the most lethal diseases—here as in all post-Columbian America—were the "poxes" (*bexigas*)—chicken pox, rubella, and, mainly, smallpox. Chicken pox is trivial today, but it manifested itself with great virulence then, especially among Amerindian children, leading the Tupi to dub it *catapora*, a terror-inducing name whose meaning is now lost in the memory lapses of the Brazilian language: "the leaping fire." In the Reritiba village, in present-day Anchieta, in the state of Espírito Santo, Fr. Anchieta staged a play he had written in the Tupi language, as homage to Our Lady of Assumption. One of the verses, to be said by an Amerindian boy dressed up as an angel, reveals the panic caused by the diseases: "Come Virgin Mary Mother of God, /and visit this village (. . .) / Drive away the diseases, fevers, dysenteries and coughs / So that its inhabitants / Believe in God, your son."[75]

In fact, the missionaries themselves carried diseases and involuntarily infected the Amerindians, particularly with tuberculosis. Some communities refused the establishment of missions in their vicinity, arguing that the priests carried the contagious evil (*Caruguara*).[76]

Carried by vessels sailing from Lisbon, smallpox (*Variola major*, the only one of the disease's three types to be active at the time)[77] infected Bahia in 1562, when a "pestilent corruption" killed three-quarters of the settled Amerindians. The illness then spread northward to Pernambuco and southward to Piratininga.[78] Outbreaks flared in many quarters of the Portuguese world, including from Japan where Fr. Luís Fróis noted that a "universal pox disease" had invaded the archipelago.[79]

Brazilian ports felt the backlash of smallpox waves originating in Portugal between 1597 and 1616. The same relationship between morbidity and mortality noted at the time must have taken place in native communities on the other side of the Andes: 30 to 50 percent of the Amerindians exposed to the illness perished within the first few days.[80]

A fresh smallpox epidemic hit Maranhão between 1621 and 1623. Two larger outbreaks occurred in the area the 1660s and the 1690s.[81] Referring to the 1660s epidemics, Crown judge Mauricio de Heriarte recorded that fifteen of the eighteen big Indian settlements established there had been decimated during that period by the pox diseases, "which are a plague in these parts."[82] At the end of the 1620s, Angola was also infested by "quality poxes," that is, smallpox, to the point where a certain area of West Central Africa came to be called the Vulture Quilombo, due to the great number of vultures and other birds that fed on dead bodies that had gathered there after the epidemics.[83] From West Central Africa, the pestilence leaped into Dutch Brazil in the early 1640s, including Pernambuco, Paraiba, Ceará, and Maranhão.[84] Then it advanced to Bahia in 1641, and shortly after to Rio de Janeiro, where there was an additional outbreak of the *tabardilho* (eruptive fever).[85] At the beginning of the 1660s, Grão-Pará and Maranhão were once again hit by the malaise, "with such harm to Indians that most of them were finished off, also having died a few of the sons of the Land with some mixed blood," wrote a missionary.[86] From then on began the long 1662–1685 smallpox cycle that spread throughout Portuguese America. News of the damage crossed the ocean: in 1666, the British ambassador in Lisbon informed the Court in London that the disease had already exterminated 16,000 slaves in Brazil, not specifying whether they were Indians or Africans.[87]

Because of such outbreaks, the Franciscans built in 1665 the first cemetery in Rio de Janeiro for the burial of Amerindian and African slaves, whose dead bodies were usually left out in the streets in what is today Largo da Carioca. Besides uncertain Christian charity, the measure, imitated by the Luanda municipal council, was guided by the prophylactic practice that attributed the smallpox epidemics to emanations from the rotting bodies.[88] Until recently, Rio de Janeiro's ground retained the memory of the numerous deaths, as bones still surfaced in the 1950s, when municipal authorities carried out building works in the Largo da Carioca.[89]

The smallpox waves crossing the ocean at the turn of the sixteenth century originated above all in Africa. This disease is exclusive to humans, has no nonhuman reserves or vectors, and is therefore solely carried by human migrations originating from different European, African, and Asian ports. Thus, South American territory did not experience the epidemiological pause that took place in Europe in mid-seventeenth century.[90] According to the data analyzed by James Sweet, mortality rates for African and black slaves remained high in Pernambuco and Bahia during the seventeenth century.[91]

In the meantime, microbial shock decreased Amerindian armed resistance against European contact. Enemy Indians were decimated and vassalized by the colonizers. It is known that smallpox played the role of an ally to the Spanish in the fight for the Aztec and Inca empires.[92] In one of the Dutch enclaves in North America, later known as New York, an outbreak of smallpox devastated hostile Hudson River indigenous villages from 1656 on, providing security to local colonizers, who had been immunized in their areas of origin, already subject to the disease spread by the Thirty Years War.[93] The same phenomenon took place north of Rio de Janeiro and Espírito Santo, where the Goitacá factions, who had been waging a no-quarter war against the settlers, ended up being beaten by the "deadly pox disease."[94] Traces of the trauma generated by post-Columbus pestilences may have been crystallized in Tupi mythology. There were four malevolent entities in their religion at the end of the 1500s: Taguaíba (evil ghoul), Macacheira (the one who makes us lose our way), Anhangá (the one who bags us), and the Curupira (the one covered with pustules).[95] In the course of the centuries, the Curupira figure has been subject to metamorphoses, being invested with other representations. However, it seems reasonable to suppose that the Curupira emerged in the first decades of the Discovery, as a symbolic representation of the panic caused by the poxes and by other pustular contagions. The Yanomami hold a generic term, Xawara, to designate diseases, of white origin that decimate villages and defy the knowledge of the shamans.

Many a Xawara was brought over by Africans. All of the Mediterranean was a smallpox zone. Arabian caravans dispersed the contagion throughout the sub-Saharan regions from the eighth century onward. In the mid-1500s, when the Portuguese reached Upper Guinea, smallpox was raging in the kingdom of Mali.[96] Obaluaê, the smallpox *orisha* worshiped in Afro-Brazilian religions of Jejé and Yoruba origin, testifies to the endemic character of the disease in the Gulf of Guinea. Thus, certain African ethnic groups had already been contaminated—and partially immunized—by smallpox. Brandão, a witness to the 1616–1617 outbreaks in Bahia and Pernambuco, records: "Many rich men . . . became poor, due to the numerous deaths among their slaves." Deadly among Amerindians, Mestizos,

Africans, and settlers, smallpox spared the recently arrived Europeans, who were presumably immune to the illness. Brandão further reveals that the pestilence had been circulated by persons from Congo (northern Angola and Congo) and *Ardra* (Allada, actual Benin), suggesting that the disease was common in those lands.[97]

At least eight months passed between an individual's capture in Africa—his or her entry into the slave trade's mercantile selection circuit—and arrival on Brazilian shores.[98] It is possible that there were, among them, individuals already rendered resistant to the virus. It has been noted that the slave-trade flux into the northeast increased after the mortality inflicted on the Amerindian captives by the smallpox and rubella epidemics in the years 1559–1663. Likewise, the opening and reopening of Buenos Aires to slave-trade initiatives (in 1590, 1605, and 1606), as well as requests by the Rio de Janeiro municipal councilors for the intensification of the Angolan slave trade (1670), were motivated by smallpox outbreaks that had decimated Río de la Plata and Rio de Janeiro indigenous communities in previous years.[99]

Eventually immune to smallpox, many Africans developed resistance to three diseases unknown in Europe and in pre-Columbian America but endemic in West Africa: ancylostomiasis, yellow fever, and the *falciparum* malaria. The combined effect of the three diseases over the indigenous Amerindian and European populations led to the extension of African slavery in Brazil.

Later, when those diseases spread all over Portuguese America, they became an obstacle to colonial occupation as well as to the European immigration to nineteenth-century Brazilian ports.[100]

Also known in Portuguese America as *opilação* or *mal-da-terra* (illness of the land), the verminosis responsible for the ancylostomiasis produces different complications, according to the ethnic group of the affected individual. Some studies seem to demonstrate that individuals from West Africa and their descendants are more tolerant to ancylostomiasis than Europeans and whites in general, who were chronically weakened by the disease.[101] In Luso-Brasílico 1600s medicine, *opilação* was the term for the general anemia and oligemia (diminution in blood levels) as well as the hepatic diseases resulting from the verminosis.[102] Presumably, Amerindians must also have been more susceptible to the illness.

Likewise, studies demonstrate that yellow fever caused less mortality among individuals of African ancestry, a circumstance noted by Brazilian sanitarians during the epidemics of nineteenth-century Brazil.[103] Obviously, the perception of a disease varied a great deal from one culture to another. In general, Portuguese physicians of the 1600s assimilated American tropical diseases into the European academic nosology, rejecting both indigenous and Luso-African popular medicine.

With regard to malaria, a revealing dispute raged between physicians certified in Europe and local "empiricists" in 1600s Pernambuco.

Doctors and Empiricists

At the beginning of the sixteenth century, the Latin edition of the complete works by Hippocrates and Galen introduced the canons of Greek classic medicine into Renaissance medical culture.[104] In this context, Simão Pinheiro Morão, a New Christian physician deported from the metropolis by Inquisition torturers, supported the "rational medicine" of the classics, which he had learned at the Salamanca and Coimbra universities, against Brazil's "empiricists."[105] Living in Recife during the 1670s, he attacked the "empiricists" who claimed to be physicians just because they read Portuguese translations of medicine books usually written in Latin and—worse—because they learned their art from the "gentile [Indians] of the land" and from "Black witchdoctors."[106] Besides the episodic presence of physicians aboard ships stopping over in South American ports, European medicine was little if at all practiced in the colony. There is no sign of resident physicians in Portuguese America until 1635, when a former ship's surgeon established his practice in Rio de Janeiro.[107]

A list of Amerindian phytotherapeutic drugs was compiled by Fernão Cardim in the last quarter of the sixteenth century. *Caapiá* (against snake venom), *copaíba* (a skin healer), *jeticuçu* (an antipyretic), *ipecacuanha* (an emetic), *manjerioba* (an antidysenteric), *guembé-guaçu* (an antihemorrhagic), *caraxixu* (an antivermin), as well as other herbs and barks extracted from American flora found good use among missionaries and settlers.[108] Since the seventeenth century, most of them were sold in Lisbon and shipped to Portuguese territories in Africa and Asia.[109] Many of these medicines are displayed today in the stands of herbalists in the vicinity of Brazilian public hospitals for the benefit of those who lack the resources or the trust to purchase expensive and sometimes fake pharmaceutical products.

Piso and Marcgrave, the Dutch physician and his German assistant who came over to Brazil with the Nassau-Siegen expedition, analyzed the Amerindian use of plants and nosology. Piso introduced into European pharmacology herbs such as the *ipecacuanha* and the *jaborandi* (an analgesic); against verminoses, he recommended the ingestion of tobacco—which was extensively used among the Amerindians, and was dubbed "holy herb."[110] In fact, until recently, rural Brazilians, following an Indian practice, used tobacco leaves in wound healing.

Piso and Marcgrave's teachings, which included the need for Europeans to adapt to the tropical lifestyle, gained recognition in Portuguese America, as proved by references to their works years after by Dr. Mourão and by Fr. Simão de Vasconcelos.[111] However, European physicians in general took a hostile stance toward Amerindian or Afro-Brazilian therapies. Followers of the naturalist etiology system, in tune with Hippocrates's and Galen's principles, believed that disease resulted from an imbalance in the body's constitutive elements: the cold, heat, dryness, moisture, and fluidity of its liquids.[112]

As Fr. Cardim's writings demonstrate, the missionaries' behavior seems to have been different. Sérgio Buarque states that the Jesuits chose, among Amerindian drugs, those that proved to be more suitable, more in tune with the science and superstition of the time.[113] But the Jesuits' practice appears to be more ambivalent than that. When confronted with pestilences, the missionaries, just like the remainder of European clergy and Catholic settlers, taught providentialism, attributing epidemics to divine will—to punishment. "God's scourge" is how the Iberian peoples, from the humblest Algarve sailor up to Felipe II, named the bubonic plague that decimated Lisbon dwellers in 1580.[114] On the other hand, around that same date, Iberian Jesuits in South America inquired into the nature and uses of the Amerindian pharmacology.[115] By around 1580 they had already compiled a volume of indigenous remedies used in Paraguay, Chile, and Brazil. As stated by Timothy Walker, the volume describes the healthful effects of 200 native medicinal plants, whose names are listed in Spanish and the Tupi and Guarany languages.[116]

As a matter of fact, the interpretation of pestilences could combine arguments from different sources. In his *História* (1730), Rocha Pitta described the 1686 yellow fever outbreak in Pernambuco and Bahia, referring to a sequence of heterogeneous factors. It had all started with a warning from heaven: "a tremendous eclipse of the Moon" that took place in 1685. It preceded a solar eclipse, in which a strange fog had appeared, that Jesuit mathematician and "celebrated astrologer" Valentim Stancel denominated "the Sun's spider."[117] From there on, grounded on the "mathematical judgment" of the two eclipses, Father Stancel foretold the diseases that would afflict Brazil for a long time to come. Ten years later, Fr. Stancel forecast new epidemics as he observed the December 16, 1694, solar eclipse, a little before the Pernambuco yellow fever outbreak. Two Recife physicians, Drs. João Francisco da Rosa and Domingos Pereira da Gama, both holding medical degrees from Coimbra, provided scientific warrant to the mathematician priest's prognostic.[118]

Rocha Pitta sustained the view that the "cause" of the 1686 outbreak had been the colonists' sins, who were "corrupt with vices and serious guilt." But the malady's "origin" could have been the emanations from the São Tomé Island meat barrels unloaded in Recife. The author lines up, within the same explicative frame, the providentialist theory (divine punishment of the colonists' sins), the science of the time (the "mathematical judgment" on the eclipses), and empiricism (reference to the outbreak's African origin—São Tomé).[119]

However, when it came to the individual cure of the sick and the topic of treating the more common diseases and wounds, the Jesuits, unlike European doctors, opted for the efficacy of Native medicine, not only in Brazil, but in the African, Canadian, and Far Eastern missions.[120] And that despite Urban VII's directive (*brevis*) of 1637, where the pope, heeding the chemists' pressures, banned priests from selling drugs; despite other papal decrees forbidding clerics from entering the chemists' trade, both overseas missionaries and metropolitan clergy continued to practice medical and pharmacological activities.[121]

A strong point of contention of the "rationals" against the "empiricists" regarded the fever treatment. Seeking to have his work read by laymen, Morão avoided the use of Latin, the usual practice in medicine books, and disputed in Portuguese.[122] Following his example, Dr. Ferreira da Rosa, in his book about yellow fever, also criticized the empiricists as people devoid of science and, in addition, as "romancists," that is, readers of medical literature written only in "romance," that is, in Portuguese, the common tongue.[123]

Furious, Morão denigrated all Pernambucans, "the whole people including the noblest and the most knowledgeable ones," who gave the title of *maleita* to *terçã dobres* fevers, claiming them to be incurable.[124] However, Dr. Morão was wrong, and the anonymous Pernambuco empiricists were right. *Terçãs simples* and *quartãs* fevers denominated benign malarias (of the *Plasmodium vivax* type), known in the Mediterranean and, perhaps, in pre-Columbian America by the name of *tariri*.[125] Described since the times of Homer, this kind of malaria appeared in Greek, Roman, and Arab vulgates consulted by 1600s doctors.[126] But the *terçãs dobres* were radically distinct from them. Originating in a primary center in West Africa, they derive from the *Plasmodium falciparum* protozoan, which causes the comatose or delirious encephalopathy, as well as the fevers that destroy red blood cells and leads to renal obstruction. Less violent in previously immunized Africans, the parasite had a much more lethal impact in Europeans and Amerindians.[127] It thus made complete sense to classify such *terçãs dobres* under the name of *maleita* (a contraction of the Latin *febris maledicta*), as practiced by the Pernambucanos. Different from what Morão alleged, imbued with academic good faith that laxatives and bleedings healed any illness in any part of the world, none of the malaria-type fevers disappeared if the diseased dwelt in infected palustrine zones—as was already the case in the northeastern coast—where he or she would continue to be a victim of interactive contagions. The Pernambucano empiricists had, therefore, successfully detected the risk and the specificity of the *falciparum*-type malaria brought over from Africa.[128] They were not the only ones not to trust physicians and to take advantage of empiricism.

Slave traders and plantation masters realized that many Africans developed immune reaction not only to diseases common among Europeans, such as smallpox, but also to contagions of African origin afflicting both whites and Amerindians, such as the *falciparum* malaria, hookworm, and yellow fever.[129]

A similar phenomenon took place in other parts of the Americas. Possessing a survival edge in tropical environments, the African slaves appeared more resistant, and thus more profitable, to the Caribbean colonists than European indentured servants. In Barbados, where the environment did not seem particularly unhealthy to Europeans until 1640, the transition from European servants to African slaves in the local sugar-cane plantations coincided with the advance of yellow fever. Deadly above all for whites, the disease became known as the "Barbados fever" as the island became a platform for the distribution of slaves and goods for the British West Indies in the seventeenth century.[130] Mutatis mutandis, the masters who made use of captive Indians in Portuguese America's plantations and mills probably made the same calculation.

Although settlers did not always fully understand the fact, authoritative voices within the Atlantic colonial universe made explicit the comparative costs driving the spread of the slave trade and African slavery. Cheaper than Africans, the Amerindian slaves ended up being more expensive because they died in greater numbers.[131] This was the analysis formulated by historian and sugar mill owner Rocha Pita, in the wake of the yellow fever outbreak that afflicted Pernambuco and Bahia in the years 1686–1687, intermittently returning until 1695, which also took brave Dr. Morão away.[132] In Amazonia, where Indian coerced labor was extensively employed by the settlers, the devastation caused among the natives by a smallpox epidemic that occurred in 1697 led local authorities to ask the Court for the very urgent (*urgentíssima*) introduction of African slaves in the region.[133]

The epidemiological and social encumbrances to the use of the enslaved Amerindians, and the advantages of the use of Africans, were described in a response by Fr. Antonio Vieira, then superior of the missions settled in the Portuguese Amazon, to the Belém do Pará municipal council in 1661. "No matter how many [Indian] slaves are made, always more numerous are those who die, as is shown by the everyday experience in this *Estado* [of Maranhão], as was also shown in [the *Estado do*] Brazil, where settlers had never been able remedy [this situation] before they helped themselves to slaves from Angola; for the Indians of the land are less capable of work and are less resistant to diseases, and who, being closer to their homeland, more easily either escape or die for want of it."[134]

From the perspective of this book, the Amazonian case referred to by Fr. Vieira, missionary and statesman, deserves reflection. It demonstrates how the Metropolis made use the African slave trade to pry out the regional economy and integrate it into the Atlantic system.

African Slavery and the Plunder of Amazonia

As discussed in chapter 1, the Crown adopted the *prazos* regime in Mozambique, conceding land and direct administration of native villages to the colonists. It is also known that the *encomienda* system—through which Spanish American indigenous compulsory labor was organized—was repeatedly requested by the settlers and by certain colonial Amazonian authorities despite the Overseas Council having explicitly condemned in 1645 the system as "strange to Christian mercy and charity, and contrary to Divine and human laws."[135]

Besides metropolitan legal prohibition, other obstacles rendered the introduction of either *encomiendas* or *prazos* impractical in the Estado do Grão-Pará and in the Estado do Brasil. Unlike the Peruvian *encomenderos* or the Mozambique *prazo* holders, Portuguese America settlers had to deal with the native populations' nomadic ways. From early on, royal authorities and missionaries noted the problems thus produced. In correspondence sent from São Paulo to Ignatius of Loyola in Rome, Father Luis da Grã considers the "continuous movement" of Amerindians and their villages to be the "biggest difficulty" of evangelization. In the Amazon and others regions of Portuguese America, the missionaries complained of the same problem.[136]

To extract income in the form of labor or products from indigenous communities, Luso-Brasílico dwellers would have to inherit from pre-European empires what the Hispanic Americans and the Luso-Mozambican *prazos* owners had: settled indigenous groups in a determined territory and the constitution of village-type communities cultivating regular crops. However, even in favorable circumstances, this mode of exploitation would end up encouraging the colonists to economic isolation and to political rebellion, as took place in Peru and in the Luso-Mozambican *prazos*—and as more experienced authorities feared would happen in Brazil.

As we shall see below in the text, João de Lencastre, governor-general of Brazil (1694–1702), after having been governor of Angola, fought Paulista autonomy, which was based on Amerindian captivity. From the same perspective, he informed Lisbon that the intent of Garcia d'Ávila Pereira, heir to the Casa da Torre's very large estate, should be confronted.[137] Garcia d'Ávila planned to control the direct administration of Indian settlements within his lands in the Bahian interior. According to the governor-general, the Crown should deny the request to avoid Garcia d'Ávila, boasting control over 20,000 indigenous archers, becoming a hinterland kinglet and defying metropolitan authorities.[138]

In the first chapter I pointed out that the advance of precious-metal mining considerably reduced the inconvenient aspects of the *encomienda* system in Mexico and Peru. The new level of Spanish exploitation eliminated the colonial enclaves' autarky, strengthening interregional and oceanic trade. Thus, the political and economic control exerted by Madrid over its American territories increased. Still, the Amazonian hunter-gatherer economy was far different from that of the Andean mining areas.

Ultimately, it seems more reasonable to compare Portuguese Amazonia to French and British Canada in the seventeenth and eighteenth centuries, and even with the Missouri River valley and the Rocky Mountains in the first decades of the nineteenth century, after the cession of Louisiana to the United States. In such vast areas, economic activity was unstable, grounded on the trade of furs exchanged with Amerindians or directly obtained from the Canadian *coureurs de bois* and the American free trappers.[139]

In fact, in the seventeenth century, Grão-Pará and Maranhão exported cloves (*cravos*) brought in by the *cravistas* (entrepreneurs who employed coerced Indians in the gathering of the product), as well as some cocoa and cultivated tobacco. Later, trade in parsley, indigo, and other plants products was developed, such as that of the *copaíba*, which was used as a dye and in the treatment of certain diseases. In the last quarter of the eighteenth century, Rodrigues Ferreira described the disarray of the "hinterland drugs" (*drogas do sertão*) trade, due to overharvesting and excess supply. "In this Estado [do Grão-Pará] the wealth or poverty of the villages depends on the wealth or poverty of the jungle (. . . ;). According to him, if there was word that cloves had been sold at a high price, "this was enough for all canoes (. . .) to be employed in that business; as, however, the [amount of the] product increases, it naturally follows that the price goes down; lo and behold, if the poor village was bankrupt, it then found itself even further ruined."[140] In addition, there was pests that attacked the farms and plantations. As a consequence, gatherers and the planters lived in chronic debt to the traders who sold them goods on credit. "Everyone is steep in debt," wrote Fr. Bettendorf in the last quarter of the seventeenth century about Pará settlers.[141]

A basic difference between the exploitation of Canada and the Amazon region is grounded in the systematic use of compulsory Amerindian labor in Brazil. Amerindians were employed in gathering drugs and eventually in their cultivation, as well as rowers in canoes, an essential means of transportation. Badly fed, coerced to work relentlessly, afflicted by diseases in the ports and in the villages, Amerindian rowers died in great numbers.[142] According to Fr. Bettendorf, an old Amazonian hand, of the twenty-five Amerindians in an average canoe crew, six to ten always died, and sometimes all of them died, forcing the traveler to leave the empty vessel in Belém "because there was no one left to row back to the village or mission." Whole settlements were consumed in the coerced labor of the traders', missionaries', or authorities' canoes. Fr. João Daniel used to say that in the Amazon region, someone without a canoe was like a bird without wings. As a matter of fact, gathering activities, fluvial canoeing, and the coerced labor of the Amerindian rowers—dispersion factors in the colonial population drive—all figure as one of the yet-to-be-written chapters in the historiography of Brazil.[143]

The dispersion of the *coureurs de bois* in French Canada worried Vauban, economist and military organizer of France and its overseas territories in the reign of Louis XIV. To remedy the problem, Vauban proposed a kind of colonization similar to that practiced by Rome in antiquity: regiments of carefully chosen soldiers, accompanied by their wives and transformed into peasant landlords, would colonize the Canadian territory, producing wheat for the metropolis.[144]

In the Amazon region, the increase in export agriculture was coupled with African slaves. To link the Amazonian economy to the metropolis, the authorities had to first tie it to the African market. Since 1620, Diego de Cárcamo, first Iberian governor of the Maranhão, explained to Madrid that the import of Angolan slaves was the fundamental condition for the establishment of sugar-cane plantations in the area. Other regional initiatives, stimulated by the example of the slave trade with the Estado do Brasil, flowed in this direction.[145] Indeed, the São Luís municipal councilors requested slaves "from Angola and Guinea for the cultivation of their farms and mills" in 1665.[146] A royal provision of 1672 granted the settlers a two-thirds discount off the entry duties on Angolan slaves imported in Maranhão. The motive alleged for the fiscal concession: "the ambition of those settlers for the captivity of Indians will decrease."[147] Shortly after, to start the cultivation of indigo—more expensive in Lisbon due to the loss of Asian trade zones that specialized in the product—the governor of Maranhão brought in an "indigo engineer" from Lisbon and fifty slaves from Angola.[148]

These initiatives found a place within the recentering drive of the overseas economy in the Atlantic. In the second quarter of the seventeenth century, as shown in chapter 3, there was a transfer to the Atlantic of the Portuguese capital invested in the East. At the end of the century, Asian spice plants and African slaves were introduced in the Amazon to capitalize and increase the regional economy's productivity.[149]

The Crown associated with the Jesuits, who sought to restrict the exploitation of Indian labor, established a company to control the two ends of the market. On the one hand, the company snatched the monopoly in Maranhão exports; on the other, it was in charge of regularly furnishing Africans to the region.

Such are the statutes of the Companhia do Estanco do Maranhão, organized by Lisbon in 1679. The company started off badly, in a scenario where the Portuguese Atlantic trade was diving into the recession vortex of European economy.[150] As a result, the company did secure the monopoly in exports, but was unable to fulfill the commitment to deliver 10,000 Africans to the settlers.[151] Conceived by Fr. António Vieira, the enterprise was meant to have a second phase as important as the first: the royal decrees of 1680 limited the captivity of Amerindians and the coerced use of their labor by the colonials. The royal letter communicating the delivery contract for the first lot of slaves was explicit: "in order to avoid the state of fright and scandal in which the Estado do Maranhão Indians have found themselves, I saw fit to arrange, at the expense of my own Treasury (. . .), 600 slaves from Angola to be introduced into that possession."[152] Whence the metropolitan intervention, operating in two complementary phases: the market for African slaves was opened in the region, and the access of colonists to the American slave market was denied. The second part of the project was set in motion, but the first part was not executed. Thus, the *estanque*, that is, the Company's monopoly, proved unbearable to the settlers.

The deadlock sparked the Maranhão revolt of 1684, led by Manoel Beckman, whose program was based on the promise to concede "numerous slaves [Amerindians]" to the settlers. The mutiny led the Crown to further lean on the Jesuits. Thus, the Missions' Statute (Regimento das Missões) of 1686 entrusted the Company of Jesus with the totality of the Amerindian population's administration.[153]

Following the reawakening of colonial and global trade in the first half of the eighteenth century, the Jesuit Amazonian missions grew both economically and demographically.[154] But the prosperity and the influence of the Jesuits ended up titillating the cupidity of the Crown and the colonists, resulting in their downfall: in 1759 the Crown expelled the S.J. from the kingdom and overseas, and expropriated the totality of its property.[155]

Simultaneously, the Crown set up, this time successfully, a large-scale operation intent on changing the region's economic and social variables to best fit it into the Atlantic system and into metropolitan control. Royal laws definitely prohibited Amerindian captivity, at the same time as commercial agriculture was stimulated. Fiscal subsidies were conceded to the two northern captaincies, and a new monopolistic company, the Companhia Geral do Grão-Pará e do Maranhão. The company's monopoly encompassed the export of products, and snapped up the trade in slaves, free from royal taxes, from Angola and Guinea into the Amazonian coast between 1755 and 1778. As a measure of the synchrony of the diverse measures and the macroeconomic picture that they intended to transform, note that the three royal decrees elaborated by the marquis of Pombal—declaring the Amerindians to be free, transferring the administration of the settlements run by the Jesuits to the hands of civilian authorities, and the founding of the company—were signed by King José I on June 6 and 7, 1755—a single stroke of the pen.[156]

A century later, in the middle of the nineteenth century, when the slave trade came to a close, the Amazonian planters recycled their activities: they sold slaves off to the coffee growers in the south, and sought, as before, the exploitation of Amerindian or Caboclo gathering activities in the forest.[157]

There is a certain parallel between the macroeconomic process, of Atlantic scale, that I have just described, and the reproduction of production on a microeconomic level in West African domestic societies studied by Claude Meillassoux.

In such African societies, the rule of exogamy—engendered by the transformation of endogamy into incest—created the conditions for social control by the eldest son over his younger brothers. Younger brothers must remain subject to the eldest to have access to the women of other groups, for the women could only be gotten in exchanges organized by the first-borns of the different communities. By controlling matrimonial power—that is to say, the conditions for reproduction—the eldest sons dominated their own groups.[158] Mutatis mutandi, as the royal authorities and Jesuits banned access to Amerindian coerced labor, they stifled the endogenous (territorial) reproduction of colonial productive units. Portuguese American planters and sugar-mill owners were now dependent on the slave trade and on metropolitan traders to obtain African slaves. In this way, the foundations of the metropolitan domination in the colony were established.

A few of the great authors of Brazilian and Portuguese historiography have already noted the complementarity between the African slave trade, royal laws, and papal bulls issued in favor of Amerindian freedom in the sixteenth and seventeenth centuries. Varnhagen attributed the introduction of African slavery into Portuguese America to the "measures of ill-understood philanthropy" in favor of the Amerindians, decreed by the kings and supported by the Jesuits.[159] Realizing that the publication in Brazil of Pope Urban VIII's veto banning Amerindians' captivity (1639) increased profits yielded by the Crown's dealing in enslaved Africans, Mauricio Goulart wrote, "Rigged game or mere coincidence, the effects are the same either way; it is evident that once more the point of view of a Pope marvelously harmonizes with the interests of the Portuguese Treasury."[160] Finally, Magalhães Godinho emphasized, "The (royal) protective measures for certain (Portuguese American) indigenous groups play too much into the hands of the slave traders for us to be perplexed at the social forces that have really imposed them."[161] Such are the considerations that should be kept in mind.

The Uprooting of Captives in Africa and America

Dissocialization was a crucial element in the slavery system, a process in which an individual was captured and separated from his or her native community. This process was completed in depersonalization, in which the captive was converted into a commodity in the wake of the reification carried out by slaving societies. Both processes transform the slave into a versatile production factor, and feature as one of the constants in the slavery systems studied by historians and anthropologists.[162]

To become recurring, institutionalized, commoditized, and taxable, captivity must befall individuals foreign to the slave-owning community. In ancient Greece, as in 1500s Congo, the community is destabilized when some of its members reduced another part of its members to slavery to sell them to third parties.

In line with other pan-Hellenic thinkers, Plato asserts that Grecian cities should not own slaves of Hellenic origin, so as to avoid the internal hatred that would stop all Greeks from uniting and fighting together against the barbarians.[163] Moses Finley insists that the slave is an outsider: it is only because of this that he or she can be uprooted and reduced from person to thing, transformed into property.[164]

The grafting of slaves into a community that has not previously known this kind of exploitation reordered its social structure, leading to the coinage of new concepts. Benveniste observes that, in the Greek language, the employment of a foreign term (*dûlos*) to designate a slave is not surprising, "because—and this is a frequent condition of this denomination in Indo-European languages—the slave is necessarily a foreigner." Likewise, the word *servus* (slave), current in Rome, is not of Latin origin, but Etruscan.[165] When the status of the *servi* evolves, and the word loses its meaning in the midst of the social transformations of the Middle Ages, the term *sclavu* emerges in medieval Latin. As with analogous names in various languages, the word comes from *slavus*, the ethnic name for the Slavs.[166] At that moment, *sclavu* defines the state of radical subjection to which the Slavs were submitted in the Balkans, deported to places throughout the Mediterranean, in the condition of victims of a multisecular tragedy that periodically tears them apart, with the enthusiastic blessing of the monotheistic religions. Dissocialized by the violence of capture, depersonalized by the Mediterranean slave traders, such *sclavi*, usually women and children—Catholic, Orthodox, or Muslim, depending on who imprisoned whom—were usually employed in domestic work or in the urban textile sector of other European countries.[167]

In the Portuguese language, the individual who became somebody else's property was named *cativo* and, later, during the Reconquista, *mouro* (Moor). From the second half of the fifteenth century on, at the exact time when the Atlantic slave trade is set up in Portugal, the word *escravo* was disseminated, a word derived from the Catalan language, which, in its turn, extracted it from the French. In the 1550s a distinction was created, mentioned in the second chapter, between captive (*cativo*) and slave (*escravo*), a difference distinguishing royal texts pertaining to Amerindians or to Africans.[168] In New England, the word *servant* referred both to white British indentured servants and to the first African slaves introduced since 1619. As the statutes regarding these forms of compulsory labor increasingly separated them, *slave* appears in 1650s Virginia texts as a technical term in the trade and legislation regarding African slaves.[169] The slaving grammar has also left its mark in the Nhêengatú or "Brasílico language," the general language grounded on Tupi-Guarani languages codified by the Jesuits. Besides the traditional pre-Cabralian and 1500s terms *miaçuba, miasua tapuigya*, and *tapyi*, which correspond to "prisoner" or "captive," a neologism emerged after the African slave trade: *tapanhuno*, derived from *tapya* (man) *uno* (black) and referring to a "black slave."[170]

The increase in the exploitation of dissocialized individuals' labor led also to the employment of foreigners as slaves. The farther and more isolated the slave was from his or her native community, the more complete was his or her conversion into a production factor, and the more profitable the individual's labor became. In the African continent, a captive's degree of dissocialization constituted an important variable in price calculations. The farther captives were from their country, the less prone they were to escape, and therefore, the higher their value.[171] In a limited transaction, but revealing of the mercantile value embedded in the dissocialization of the captive, Fr. Antonio Vieira proposed a clever deal to the Bahia provincial, with whom he traveled out of Pará: "Father Gonçalves told me he had asked Your Rev. to send us a few *tapanhunos* and *tapanhunas* on the first possible occasion, and I again beg you, for they are so necessary to us. Admitting that the *tapanhunos* here [in Pará] have nowhere to escape to, it would be convenient if there were a few who could be [sold] more cheaply because of this wrongdoing [*manha*]."[172]

Black slaves, already familiar with the American tropics, who had fled but then been recaptured fetched lower prices in the local markets, as they came to be considered fomenters of *quilombos* and revolt. In judicial sales, the law incorporated the observance of the dissocialization criterion for reasons of public safety. The slaves named *filhos do mato* (children of the bush), the free-born infants over twelve years of age living in Palmares and captured by the gang of Domingos Jorge Velho, could not be sold back into the captaincies where they had roots. They were to be traded down to Rio de Janeiro or to Buenos Aires.[173] However, the Rio de Janeiro masters usually refused rebel slaves brought down from the north. Local municipal chamber minutes recorded the 1637 protest against settlers who had acquired "risen blacks from the Bahian *mocambo*." The city's attorney alleged that such slaves, used to fleeing into the jungle, would incite their Rio de Janeiro region peers into rebellion. As a consequence, the chamber ordered that they should be removed from the captaincy.[174] Two hundred years later, this would constitute one of the factors encumbering the interregional slave trade between the north and the mid-south after 1850. This was a time when the oceanic slave trade had ceased: reputed to be rebels, the *ladino* slaves sold in the northern provinces were ill-accepted by the center-south coffee growers, accelerating the movement in favor of foreign immigration.

Dragged by the Atlantic circuit, the African individual was introduced into a mercantile spiral that underlined, from transaction to transaction, his or her depersonalization and dissocialization. In the sixteenth and seventeenth centuries, the captive could be subject to five transactions, at least, between departure from the African village to arrival in Portuguese American farms.[175] Such exchanges were interspersed by more or less long periods. Until the end of the seventeenth century, most Angolans had to march from their place of origin for two months before reaching the port of trade.[176] By adding the time spent waiting for embarkation, which could be as along as five months, plus the two months necessary for the Atlantic crossing, it follows that these slaves may have already been enslaved for a whole year or longer when they were unloaded in Brazil.[177]

Although the King Manuel ordinances allowed only a single month for a buyer to return a slave with "*manqueira* [physical handicap] or disease," the slave traders widened this period to four months at the end of the sixteenth century. In practice, this allowed for the supplementary selection of "pieces" in the mills and plantations.[178] In the last quarter of the eighteenth century, when the market favored the buyer, the African slave's "rehearsal" period in the hands of the master is reduced to eight days, at least in Angola.[179] At that time the slave-trade routes reached very deep into the African continent, with captives originating from regions situated over a six-month march from the Angolan ports.[180]

The following quote from the Capuchin Cavazzi, one of the few missionaries to record observations on the drama of Angola's slavery, can be used to measure the depth of dissocialization thus induced and its effects on slave control.

> In the kingdom of Congo, the number of slaves is nearly the same as of free people. There is, however, a great difference between the slaves owned by the Portuguese and those owned by Blacks. The former obey not only the word, but even gestures, for they fear above all to be taken to Brazil or to New Spain, for they are persuaded that, on arriving in those lands, they would be killed by the buyers, who, they think, would extract gunpowder from their bones, and from their brains and flesh the oil that arrives in Ethiopia [Africa] [. . . ;] therefore, just the terror of being sent to America makes them frenetically restless and, if possible, they flee into the jungle. Others, at the moment of boarding the ship, defy the beatings and kill themselves, jumping into the water.

Some years later, another Capuchin missionary, Friar Caltanisetta, noted that "the most rigorous punishment" that Luanda's masters inflicted to their slaves was to export them to Brazil.[181]

At the end of the eighteenth century, a Luanda physician confirmed that slaves continued to think that they would be devoured by whites on the other side of the sea. For the Angolan indigenous communities, the true cannibals were the Portuguese and the Brasílicos.[182] Accordingly, the Luanda doctor considered "their fright and melancholia" as the first cause of mortality among Africans before embarkation, caused by the trauma of slavery and the expectation of deportation.[183] In addition, consider the mix of idioms and ethnic groups aboard the slaver. The deportees almost always hailed from distinct areas, due much more to the segmentation of the hinterland networks than to the slave traders' desire for security.[184] Jesuit Alonso de Sandoval, in his enquiries on vessels at anchor in Cartagena at the beginning of the seventeenth century, recorded over seventy languages and dialects spoken among the deportees.[185]

Unloaded in Portuguese American ports, once more submitted to sale, the African captive was usually beaten on arrival at the plantations. "The first act of hospitality that they [the masters] performs, once the purchased individuals appear in their presence, is to have them rigorously flogged, with no reason other than their will to do so, and they boast about it [. . .] as if inculcating [into the slave] that only they [the masters] have been born to competently dominate slaves, and to be feared and respected." Such is the testimonial by priest and jurist Ribeiro Rocha, dwelling in Bahia, in his treatise on Brazilian slavery published in the middle of the eighteenth century.[186] A hundred years later, French traveler Adolphe d'Assier confirmed the practice of beating slaves on arrival, to resocialize them into the context of oppression in Brazil's houses, ranches, and plantations.[187] This method of Luso-Brasílico terror, later authentically national, Brazilian, the arbitrary shock of the master aiming to demonstrate to the new arrival his or her new subhuman statute, was once again practiced during the 1964–1985 dictatorship. Instructed by the long-standing slaving experience, the government torturers also made use of sudden beatings on arrival in the police stations or military barracks, to dehumanize and terrorize those suspected of "subversion."

The Social Reproduction of Slaves

The dynamics of the Atlantic slave trade rendered the mercantile reproduction of slaves more effective and faster than the demographic reproduction eventually generated within the captive families of the Luso-Brazilian sugar mills and plantations. With the retaking of Angola by Salvador de Sá's expedition (1648), the Brazilian economy appropriated—for two whole centuries—the largest reserve of African labor in the Atlantic. In the wake of military invasion, an exchange product carried over in the Brasílico militiamen's knapsacks took over the Central African slave fairs: *cachaça*. At the turn of the seventeenth century, another Brazilian product, tobacco, led to the Bahian slave traders' domination over a good slice of the Mina Coast trade.

Relying on a compulsory labor market set up in African villages, Portuguese American colonists complied with the slave-system's macroeconomic practices. It was more convenient to make sugar for sale in European markets, thus obtaining the means to buy more slaves, or to cultivate tobacco and make *cachaça* to exchange for adult Africans, than to invest in the production of food, to stimulate unions between captives, to preserve pregnant women and children in the sugar mills and plantations, in the expectation of producing, in the medium run, new locally born and bred slaves. With the trade in Africans, the burden of the reproduction of direct producers was transferred to the African families and villages.[188]

Consequently, Portuguese America concentrated on the production of exchange values aimed at overseas, at the world-economy. In the metropolis, part of such merchandise allowed for the purchase of goods and services for the masters. The other part, the barter products—*cachaça* and tobacco—were exported to the trade ports of Africa in exchange for human energy, for slaves. Goods manufactured in Europe or brought over from Asia to the African fairs could also be bought in the metropolis in exchange for Portuguese American products, from which derived two consequences of decisive impact in the *longue durée* of Brazilian colonial and national history. The first, proper to the generality of slaving systems, has been noted by scholars: the hindrance of the increase in labor's productivity, since production can increase, independently from productivity, by means of the simple multiplication of the slave producers. The second consequence, the effects of which have marked the evolution of the Brazilian economy and society, refers to the atrophy of alimentary agriculture.

As the slave trade regularly introduced fresh instruments of labor, it went beyond the simple demographic reproduction of slaves by replacing deceased individuals, by also securing the replacement of those who legally or illegally had left the system: the freed men or women and the *quilombolas* rebels.[189] As a consequence, a part of the *social reproduction* of the slave contingent was guaranteed.

This notwithstanding, it was only when the Africans were incorporated into the sugar mills and plantations, and were made to conform to the statute imposed by

Luso-Brazilian society, that the process of social reproduction was concluded. The African died as a person on capture in Africa, becoming a commodity, a "piece," branded and taxed by the Crown in the trade port, to be reborn as a production factor in Portuguese America. In the wake of the social death suffered in Africa, the slave was introduced in the New World by means of an existential relationship mediated by the labor controlled by the master. In this way, for the colonial productive process not to be interrupted as it incorporated new production factors, the African individual was to be resocialized into the new status of Luso-Brazilian slave. Masters, overseers, and local slaves had to strike an understanding with the newly arrived captives to promote their integration into the cooperative activities of commercial agriculture in the shortest possible time. For this reason, the slaving culture preexisting in the community conditioned the search for fresh slaves.

In classical antiquity, Greek and Roman agriculturists described the most favorable characteristics of the slaves according to their ethnic groups and cultures. New World colonists and authorities left observations of a similar kind about African ethnic groups.[190] It would be interesting to systematize past and present opinions, comparing the masters' preference for such and such ethnic groups to the slave-trade flows predominant in such society and at such conjunctures. In South America, there is evidence that the culture of the *ladinos* (seasoned slaves) predetermined the choice of *boçais* (newcomers) hailing from Africa.

Expounding on the characteristics of African cultures in a report to the WIC's board in Amsterdam, an agent of the Dutch in Pernambuco attributed the greater productivity of Luso-Brazilian sugar mills to *ladino* slaves. According to the document, the slaves hailing from Angola were better workers, while those from the Mina Coast (Benin and Calabar) seemed "obstinate, bad, lazy and of hard adaptation to work." Thus, the author recommended the revaluation of the WIC's trade with the Mina Coast, for the Africans obtained there were not in much demand in Dutch Brazil.[191] Such analysis resulted from Luso-Brazilian slaving culture, molded by the slave trade's previous networks, mostly linked to the Angolan coast. Decades later, in Suriname and other Caribbean sugar-plantation areas, the same Dutch colonists would lose interest in Angolans, who were from then on considered inept. Following the general movement of the slave trade into their areas, they came to prefer slaves from the Gold Coast and the Slave Coast, in the Mina Coast area.[192]

An example of the need of the cultural relationship between the slave and the master—in other words, the operation of a common speech between slaves and slavers—can be observed in Raposo Tavares's *bandeira* to the Amazon region

(1648–1651). According to Fr. Antonio Vieira, the expedition failed because the Paulista marauders gave up on capturing center-west Amerindians whose language they did not understand. "The languages are completely diverse, and it was the languages that have provided defense from the São Paulo men, for no resistance, arms or multitude [of Amerindians] would have been enough."[193]

Other people who saved their skins thanks to the "defense" of language were certain southern Africans. One Angolista sent to seek both the Cunene River's delta and a way into Mozambique brought back to Luanda captives who were "savage-like people." Cadornega, who saw them in 1664, wrote that "nothing they said could be understood," for they "spoke in clicks." Most probably, they spoke a Khoisan language, featuring the dental click. Anyway, no slave trader wanted to buy such strange captives.[194]

An even more radical evidence of the necessity for cultural mediation of the captives seized by the slave trade emerges in a story current in 1600s Angola. It was said that in the kingdom of Congo there was a race of big apes. They were so "cheeky and insolent" that they raped women. Cardonega claims to have seen one such ape in chains, who "on seeing a woman, made much effort reach her, but not so much men; and if the chains broke due to repeated pulling, it went after them [women] very quickly, seeking their lower parts." According to our author, some of the rapes perpetrated by the apes "begot against nature's order (. . .) and monsters [begotten] from such mating were seen." But such monsters, the Angolans said, pretended to be apes, avoiding the use of speech in order not to end in captivity. "They did not speak in order not to work."[195]

A century later, Fr. João Daniel related a similar story in the Amazon region and compared it to the tale of Angolan origin, proving that the story told by Cardonega has circulated on both sides of the Portuguese Atlantic. The Amerindians said that there were humanlike Amazonian apes, who did not speak in order not to work, to escape the specific form of coerced labor prevailing in Amazonia, rowing the colonist's canoes. "They say the apes are people, and they disguise themselves, not willing to speak so that the White men will not be able to force them, as [they do] with the Indians, to row their canoes."[196] Beyond such stories, one glimpses the sinister violence that the peoples of Amazonia and West Central Africa were subjected to by colonial exploitation. On both shores of the Atlantic, the sweeping movement of slavery only spared the natives who cut all communication with humankind. Willingly mute and disguised as apes, such individuals, taking advantage of their hybrid origin, entered the world of savage animals, erecting over themselves the species barrier to flee captivity at the hands of the white men.

Alongside the endless wars of the Aymoré-Botocudo, of the other Indians revolts, of the *quilombos* resistance, of the Angolan Jaga combats, the tale on the anthropomorphism of the Angolan and Amazonian apes stands as a dramatic representation of the refusal of enslavement and colonial labor by indigenous communities on both sides of the South Atlantic. Made subhuman by slavery, the native imagined that the only way to safe keep his freedom would be to cease belonging to humanity.[197]

Slavery, the practical denial of other men's human essence, has grappled with such contradictions since antiquity. There was a need to break the presumed humanity that leveled warriors at the beginning of the whole affair, at the initial combat, before the victory of one party resulted in promotion to mastery and the defeat of the other, yielding reduction to enslavement. A classic work on ancient Greek economy portrays the deadlock. Xenophon, made into a landlord after the epic *Anabasis*, wrote in around 380 BC the *Oeconomicus*, a Socratic treatise on economic management and agriculture. In the text, later translated by Cicero and much quoted in antiquity and during the Renaissance, Xenophon writes well of benevolent warriors and conquerors, benefactors who, instead of executing their war prisoners, reduce them to slavery, "forcing them to become better, and thus leading them to have, from then on, an easier life." In other words, slavery is defined as an act of generosity, underlining the prisoner's human nature, as it redeems him or her from certain death, integrating them into a possibly more advanced society. The argument would be again mobilized by highly literate as well as mediocre writers over the course of the centuries, to the point of constituting the ideological foundation for the name that designates the acquisition of the African or Amerindian slave: the *resgate* (barter for enslavement).[198]

However, the slave's subjection to discipline implied the employment of specific methods that denied their affiliation to humankind. As he approaches the framing of rural activities, Xenophon asserts, "regarding slaves, a good way to teach them obedience, is the educational method that seems so convenient with beasts," referring to the domestic animals employed in rural life, and, in particular, to horses and dogs.[199]

Hegel explains that the unfolding of the labor process rehumanizes the slave. According to Kojève's celebrated lesson in the *Phenomenology of the Spirit*, the slave's labor does not destroy the object but shapes it and modifies it, transforming the natural universe into a historical world. Through labor, the slave acquires consciousness of his freedom. Xenophon referred to historical slavery, while the Hegelian master and slave dialectics refers to humanity's original drama, the human struggle with nature.²⁰⁰ This is why it makes more sense to recuperate, in Marx's analysis, the element of Hegel's reflection on the point that interests us. After recalling that antiquity's authors distinguished slaves from inert tools and animals solely by the fact that the former featured voices, Marx observes that the slaves ill-treat animals and work tools precisely to establish a difference between them, affirming themselves as humans. The rehumanization of the slaves leads them to sabotage the productive process. Whence, Marx concludes, southern United States masters let their slaves handle only the heavier and harder-to-deteriorate work tools, as well as mules, instead of horses, which were more fragile animals.²⁰¹

Another paradox, however, emerges. The awareness of humanity dawning on the slave in the work process can be used by the master—by means of negative incentives (punishment) or positive incentives (rewards)—to render exploitation more acute. René Martin notes that the slaves' demand for dignity, ignored by Greek agronomists, was well noted by Roman authors. Adept at paternalistic methods, the Romans relied on collaboration and the self-esteem of the slaves to have them participate in their own exploitation and thus render the system profitable.²⁰²

In the nineteenth-century southern United States, paternalism worked as a structural element of slavery. As Eugene Genovese explains, the slavery reformers of the South convinced the masters that the humanization of the slave's life strengthened the system instead of weakening it.²⁰³ While paternalism had operated in other systems, and particularly in Brazil, the North American case is singular. The end of the slave trade from Africa into North America (1807) territorialized the reproduction of production, completely embedding the Southern slavery system into American economy and law. The system was transparent (the slaves were born in American soil) and irrefutable (the slaves were born of enslaved mothers legally owned by their proprietors), closing a sphere in which demographic reproduction and social reproduction fused. There resulted a cohesive slavery system that could only be broken from the outside. Such is the sequence of the facts leading to the Civil War.

The situation in Portuguese America, and later, in postindependence Brazil, would be very different. Forced to handle the vast trade in human beings between two territories within the same metropolis's overseas territories, between two provinces, the civilian authorities and the missionaries had to continually deal with the founding violence of the system: pillaging, purchase, oceanic transport, unloading, and the incorporation of inhabitants from another continent commoditized as a goods. The demographic reproduction of the system was exteriorized. Thus, when the African slave trade ended, Brazilian slavery would collapse into a crisis.

With regard to social reproduction, evangelization contributed to the smooth running of the South Atlantic slavery, in its doctrinaire and institutional aspects as well as in the forms closer to popular religiosity, placed as it was between nature and culture, labor and spirit, Africa and Brazil.

Chapter 5

Evangelization in One Colony[1]

Behind the caravels, merchandise, and harquebuses, missionaries faced problems alien to the teachings meted out in European seminars.

The Company of Jesus's goals in Asia were increasingly displaced. In the wake of Francisco Xavier's evangelizing of India, the Jesuits traveled farther away from Islam. They went to Japan, where Xavier had set foot in 1549, and where Christianity made some progress.[2] However, the order's itinerant inspector (Visitador), Alessandro Valignano, warned in 1580: "Japan is a country of much change and little stability."[3] Eight years later, the land-holding military lord, Toyotomi Hideyoshi, expelled the Jesuits on the grounds that they "destroyed the root of the Japanese kingdom."[4] The Jesuits managed to remain in the area for some more time, promising in 1592 to Kyoto authorities that they would keep a low profile, "with no preaching and without making a bang [*estrondo*] in Japan."[5] But the radical expulsion measure was renewed by the Shogun Hidetada in 1612 and completed with a 1614 edict decreeing the expulsion of the missionaries.[6] Some years later, new decrees restricted foreign trade. Japan entered the Sakoku era, the age of the "locked country." Not so locked, however, since the Dutch, sheltered from 1641 on in their Deshima post, an outstanding example of Polanyi's "port of trade" in the Far East, were able to preserve some of their commercial activities.[7]

Persecutions and martyrdoms caused the Jesuits to swerve away from Japan toward China. Fascinated with the administration of the Celestial Empire, whose stability contrasted with the upheavals of European countries and Japanese feudalism, they gained influence over the Ming emperors.[8] The estrangement with Japan and the empathy with China were later translated into the legend of Xavier's trouble learning Japanese, contrasted with the ease with which he assimilated Mandarin. "God has rewarded Xavier's huge pains suffered with the Japanese language by miraculously infusing him with the Chinese language," wrote Jesuit Francisco de Souza, the celebrated author of *Oriente conquistado* (1697).[9]

San Pablo de Lima, São Paulo de Piratininga, São Paulo de Luanda, São Paulo de Goa, São Paulo de Diu, São Paulo de Malacca, São Paulo de Macao. Embedded in the European merchants' expansion, the Jesuits erected over the world churches in honor of the polyglot saint, the "apostle to the gentiles," who preached across the Mediterranean. Moreover, an interpretation of verses 18 to 23 of Saint Paul's first *Epistle to the Romans* would lead theologians to claim that overseas gentiles had a knowledge of God even before the Age of Discovery and evangelization.[10] Nevertheless, indigenous communities took different aspects from one longitude to the other. Early on, the missionaries realized, and vindicated, the specificity of missionary work overseas.

From India, Fr. Luís Fróis, with refined objectivity, showed cultural limits of sacred rhetoric: "As to the course of our studies [at the college of São Paulo in Goa] and the order therein, I very much believe that they should not expect the reputation of Coimbra's public ceremonies nor the large number of classes and scholars extant there; for there [Coimbra] is the proper place to acquire the sciences, and here [Goa] to practice them, there to dispute and raise questions, here to have them solved for those living in the valley of the shadow of death."[11]

Certainly, the duty to catechize imposed on missionaries a process of social reflection so as to allow understanding of overseas cultures. However, just as important was the proslavery doctrinal adjustment that the Jesuits carried out in Angola and Brazil.

As David Brion Davis points out, since antiquity the process of transforming human beings into slaves has generated a dualism in religious and philosophical thought. However, the peak of this dualism, continues Davis, took place in the sixteenth and seventeenth centuries, as the chasm between the rising cult of freedom in Europe and the expansion of colonial slavery in America increased.[12] In the Iberian Peninsula, this contradiction took shape within the framework of the Counter-Reformation. In fact, the sixteenth century Catholic Reformation revived the practice and dimension of the seven sacraments, against Protestant doctrine, which recognized only two (Eucharist and Baptism), and questioned their mandatory character.[13] In this context, missionary practice overcame the impasses resulting from the effects of the sacraments of marriage, baptism, and confession on the status of the rights of slaves and masters.

Free from rhetoric, without celebrated debates, the missionaries crisscrossed the Atlantic tackling problems concerning the purpose of colonization in the regions and shadows of death.

Early on, the Jesuits experienced problems in West Central Africa. At King João III's request, a Jesuit mission departed to Mbanza Congo in 1548.[14] Setting out even before the first Jesuits came to Brazil, the expedition brought fervent hope to the Society of Jesus's colleges.[15] *Doutrina christã na língoa do Congo* (1556), written by Fr. Cornélio Gomes, a Portuguese Jesuit born in Mbanza Congo, features as the first book printed in a Bantu (Kikongo) language.[16] It was published a little later than the *Arte da língoa malabar em português* (1549), by the Jesuit Henrique Henriques, and the *Cartilha em tamul e português* (1554), written by three Hindus converted by the Jesuits, but forty years before the *Arte da grammatica da língua mais usada na costa do Brasil* (1595) by Fr. Anchieta, on the Tupi language, and fifty years earlier than the *Arte da língoa de Japam* (1604–1608) by the Jesuit João Rodrigues.

The decline of Latin as the universal language of Europe and the contact with new cultures resulting from the Age of Discovery had transformed the world into a new Babel. Methodically, scholars of the Society of Jesus would try to translate overseas tongues, preliterate in most cases, into sixteenth- and seventeenth-century Spanish and Portuguese. Guided by the linguistic model provided by Latin grammar, the S.J. linguists tried to decode all languages.[17]

In this respect, the *Arte da língua de Angola* (1696) by the Jesuit Pedro Dias establishes a double innovation.[18] In the first place, there is a linguistic shift, since the author does not take into account the paradigms of Latin grammar used by his predecessors.[19] Instead, Pedro Dias describes essentials traits of the Bantu languages whose analysis would only be resumed in the second half of the nineteenth century, as noted by Emílio Bonvini. Second, Fr. Dias, helped by Fr. Miguel Cardoso, an Angola-born Jesuit, wrote his grammar at Salvador da Bahia's College to help to catechize Mbundu and their descendants in Brazil, dedicating the book to Our Lady of the Rosary, "mother of these blacks."[20] Therefore, the *Arte da língua de Angola* is not just the foremost systemic grammar of the Kimbundu. It is also the first book on an African language spoken outside Africa destined to communicate with an African-American community.

The fact that the Jesuits took a pioneering role in the study of overseas languages derived from their privileged position in the Iberian expansion movement. As will be seen, it also has to do with the importance Jesuit doctrine attached to the sacraments of Eucharist and Confession. In the post-Tridentine conception observed by the Society of Jesus, confession presupposed a direct and reserved contact between confessor and penitent, requiring a knowledge of native tongues from the outset.[21] By unifying the exotic speeches around the words of Christ, the Ignatians also opened the way to the messages from the European market and the world-economy.[22]

The early efforts to create a grammar of the Kikongo demonstrate the keen interest in the Congo kingdom. On setting foot in Bahia after crossing the Atlantic in the first Jesuit mission to Brazil, Fr. Manuel da Nóbrega impatiently asked in one of his first letters to the metropolitan superior, "Is there news from the Congo mission?"[23] There was news, but not good news. One of the missionaries sent to Congo had returned to Portugal. The other two, converted to the slave trade, ended up expelled from the Society of Jesus.[24]

Except for some visits, they resettled in the region in 1618, though only for a short time, since the Society of Jesus closed the college of São Salvador do Congo (formerly Mbanza Congo) once and for all in 1669.[25] In the mid-seventeenth century, an Ignatian chronicler summed up the lack of results following the Congo apostolate, a veritable disaster, where the sole merit seemed to have been the advertising of the missionaries' infinite patience before the eyes of divine mercy. "Despite many times having lost the work we always secure the [spiritual] prize."[26]

In the year of 1559, the first group of Jesuit missionaries traveled to Angola.[27] Wary after the Congo fiasco, the mission's superior opted for military conquest. "Without subjugation, neither this nor any other barbarian people, no matter how well inclined, will be able to remain steadfast in faith, as can be clearly seen in Congo, where Christianity has been so badly secured."[28] Angola—the Ndongo kingdom—suffered the impact of the affronts to the Jesuits in Congo. Together with the villages, the *sobas* were removed from the sovereignty of the king of Ndongo and handed over to the Jesuits.[29]

In addition to some experience occasionally acquired in Upper Guinea, many Iberian missionaries already maintained close contact with black and Moorish slaves. Three generations of slave traders had spread African slavery in the Iberian Peninsula. Around 1550, Portugal held some 32,000 captive Moors and blacks. As mentioned in chapter 2, in Lisbon, Évora, and the Algarve, black and Mulatto slaves reached the highest percentages to be found in Europe.[30]

Consequently, the clergy in Brazil professed the doctrine disseminated by the papal bull *Romanus pontifex* (1455). Slavery was tolerated, because it made catechesis easier. Pulled out of the woods of paganism, the blacks' souls would be saved in the Christian environment of the mainland and American Catholic enclaves. Still, it was also necessary to adapt the pontifical doctrine to the South American scene, where slavery, unlike that which prevailed in Iberian cities such as Seville and Lisbon, progressively assumed a systemic character.

It is worth noting that the involvement of the Portuguese in the slave trade during the sixteenth century was severely condemned by the Dominican friar Fernão Oliveira in his *Arte da Guerra do Mar* (1555).[31] Meanwhile, Lisbon already appeared as the main center of the trans-Atlantic slave trade. As observed in chapter 1, at around the same date, criticizing a business he previously accepted, another Dominican, Bartolome de Las Casas, denounced Portugal's kings Manuel I and João III, who stimulated the slave trade, "filling the world with Black slaves" and causing them to "spill over" the Spanish Indies.[32]

In Brazil, the Jesuit Manoel da Nóbrega was shocked at what he saw and heard in Bahia. Referring mainly to the Amerindian slaves, he wrote "All, or almost all" residents bore a guilty conscience over illicitly owning slaves. In 1550 he asked the Crown to send, without delay, Holy Office inquisitors to free the natives who had been "illicitly enslaved" (*mal cativados*) and kept in paganism by unjust masters, a clear uncompromising attitude that he subsequently abandoned.[33] In fact, the Jesuit superior was busy with a fresh dilemma a year later: settlers prevented slaves from marrying, fearful they should soon be compelled to manumit both spouses.

However, the sacrament of marriage was changing. Feudal customs of Roman origin, which characterized marriage as a *connubium legitimum*—the union of free individuals decided between persons of the same social status—had fallen into disuse.[34] As a source of divine grace and remedy for concupiscence, marriage had to be facilitated by the Church. For this reason, the spouses' mutual consent was enough to sanction their union before a parish priest.[35]

Favorable to morganatic, socially unequal marriages, this practice threatened lineages and social hierarchies. Hence, French ambassadors in the Council of Trent (1545–1563), formalizing complaints by the nobility, requested a stricter canon law on marriage. At the end of the conciliar work, the bishops decided on the presence of witnesses and of the parish priest of one of the betrothed during the ceremony, but maintained the prevalence of mutual consent. For the prelates, parental or family consent was not a necessary condition to validate the sacrament. Discontented, the French monarchy rejected the Council's disciplinary decrees, considering them offensive to the rights of secular power.[36] A royal ordinance by Henry III established a norm to guarantee patrimonial interests that would last until the French Revolution: marriage without parental consent amounts to abduction and punished with death.[37]

A different sort of conflict concerning marriage thrived in slave-holding colonies. What was the social autonomy granted to an enslaved family under the sacrament of marriage? Did the captive married by the Church take up the status of pater familias, thus being given freedom and control over his wife and children?[38]

Following pre-Tridentine Thomist doctrine, Fr. Nóbrega and the Society of Jesus in Brazil did not believe so. Wishing to reconcile the duty of catechizing and the requests of slave owners, the Jesuit superior suggested a new charter to King João III: it should be clear that marriage between slaves did not exempt spouses from bondage or force their masters to manumit them. Envisioning the Ethiopic Ocean, Nóbrega wrote to the Crown in 1551 recommending the enforcement of this law in Brazil, São Tomé, and other slave-holding regions.[39] Such would be the Crown's will. In parallel, Nóbrega requested "Guinea's slaves" for the College of Bahia.[40]

Later, at the turn of the seventeenth century, the Jesuit Jorge Benci recorded in his breviary on Luso-Brasílico slavery that masters used to prohibit slaves from marrying. If they were already married, such masters cared little about separating slaves couples when it came to sales.[41] Cowritten in Bahia by several Church authorities, under the direction of the Bahia archbishop and the Rio de Janeiro and the Luanda bishops, the *Constituiçoens Primeyras do Arcebispado da Bahia* (1707) codified, among other matters, the binding canonical norms on slavery until its abolition in Brazil (1888). Furthermore, the *Constituiçoens* appears as the only code written by bishops sitting in the two main American slave ports and the main African slave port. This Code mentions several times the slaves from Brazil and two times those from Angola and Mina Coast without questioning their status.[42] Yet the enslavement of Indians, baptized or heathen, is considered a grave sin whose absolution was not within the power of common priest but was "reserved" to the bishops.[43]

Referring implicitly to enslaved blacks and Africans, the Code says that slaves could marry each other or free persons according to divine and human law.[44] Equally, masters should not prevent slaves from marrying and the couples should not be separated. However, the *Constituiçoens* did not mention the condition of the couple's children or the pater familias's status.[45] In other words, the children could be separated from their parents to be sold elsewhere. The right to marry was designed solely as a remedy for sensuality or illicit unions and not as the right to establish a family.[46] Likewise, the *Constituiçoens* do not recognize the legitimacy of customary marriages contracted by the slaves "in their motherland."[47] Thus, Catholic matrimony subjected the enslaved to an imperfect contract, which untied the family links they had woven in their indigenous communities and prevented them from lawfully holding their offspring. It is at this point that the statement of the *Constituiçoens*' Canon 303 becomes all the more clear: slaves who get married "remain slaves, as they were before."[48]

In the middle of the nineteenth century, jurist Perdigão Malheiro summarized the legal doctrine prevailing in Brazil with regard to slave marriages: "The Civil Law [. . .] as a rule has almost no effect on them."[49]

Thus, Fr. Nóbrega's 1550s judgments illustrate the tortuous process of adjusting religious doctrine to the new overseas order. On the one hand, his 1550 letter firmly stated the justification for evangelization: bondage would be legitimate only if followed by catechesis. On the other hand, he established a year later the primacy of the right of property—of the full right to enslave—over the contractual norms implicit in sixteenth-century religious practice. From this perspective, it is worth recalling Orlando Patterson's analysis: the slave was a slave not because he was property, but because he could not own it; not because the slave was an object of property, but because he was prevented from becoming the subject of property, since he did not hold the rights in the acts in which he appeared as a contracting party.[50] On restricting the social and legal effects of religious marriage between slaves, Fr. Nóbrega and the Jesuits stimulated an institutional adjustment to slavery by modern Christianity.

From the same perspective, the royal letter of 1557 to the Portuguese governor of India determined that converted Moorish slaves and gentiles could only be resold to Christian masters to prevent them from returning to heresy and paganism. But baptism did not change slaves' status in any way. They would not become "free Christians for that reason."[51]

Incorporated into the practices of slave trade, baptism opened a one-way path to slavery. As a captive, the native was invested with the status of a Christian, which rendered him unable to return to natural freedom, a den of idolatry. A captain in Angola reported in 1618 that Mbundu dealers sold slaves in lots, good ones mixed with bad ones. But slave traders would reject the "bad pieces" (*peças ruins*)—the sick, the old, and children—compelling merchants to resell them to free Mbundu, who employed these slaves in their fields. For the captain, those "bad pieces" should be exported to Rio de Janeiro and pay the royal tribute, thus preventing these individuals from returning to paganism in the Angolan hinterlands.[52]

Friar Vitoriano, bishop of Cape Verde in the beginning of the eighteenth century, would be driven to sleeplessness by merely thinking of the fornication taking place among his island's residents. Spurred by his wish to halt intercourse, he used to get up and "go out during the night to remove, personally, the concubines not only out of priests' houses but also from secular homes, even in distant and out-of-town places." Free concubines were banished to other islands of the African archipelago, whereas enslaved concubines were sent for sale in Rio de Janeiro.[53] It was necessary to stop concubinage, but no one had to lose any money over the affair.

Concerning the Lusitanian attachment to the commodity slave, treatise authors stressed the discrepancy of Iberian legislation on the status of slaves belonging to defendants before the Holy Office. In Spain, the tribunals would eventually manumit them. In Portugal, in contrast, they were confiscated and later sold by royal foremen to the benefit of inquisitors.[54] Freeing the "refuse" composed of old slaves, children, concubines, and heretics' captives was unthinkable.

The Antislavery of the Holy Sacraments

More concerned with securing the material bases of overseas residences, the second generation of Jesuit missionaries directly managed slaves. In Europe and Asia, the Society of Jesus succeeded in obtaining privileges that provided missionaries with revenues, as was the case with the Contrato de Japão (sale of Chinese silk from Macao to Japan) and land revenues in Portugal and in India,[55] such as the revenues from *namoxin* lands confiscated from Hindu temples in Goa.[56] The maintenance of missions justified the Order sidestepping Tridentine guidelines and even the restrictions declared by Superior General Francisco de Borja, who banned Ignatians from commercial activity.[57]

In West Central Africa and, on a lesser scale, in Portuguese America, the Jesuits' resources came from the compulsory labor of natives and, even more problematically, from the Angolan slave trade.[58]

Property received or acquired by the missionaries included a growing number of slaves. In the higher spheres of Society of Jesus, the missionaries' involvement in Atlantic slaving transactions was so embarrassing that Superior General Francisco de Borja (1565–1572) protested against slave ownership by the S.J. In that context, antislavery reactions burst at the Bahia's Jesuit College, especially the incidents triggered by Fathers Miguel Garcia and Gonçalo Leite. Deciding to impose strict obedience to the sacrament of confession, these two Jesuits understood that absolution suited only those masters able to prove they owned slaves legally.[59] It was not only the general status of slavery in the Renaissance that was under discussion. More precisely, they debated the problems caused by the daily witnessing of violence by masters against slaves.

Outraged by the missionaries who gathered black and Indian slaves, Fr. Miguel Garcia warned Rome in 1583: "The abundance of slaves the Society [of Jesus] owns in this Province, particularly in this college [of Bahia] is something I cannot swallow by any means." In his opinion, all Indians, blacks and Africans employed in Bahia had been illicitly enslaved. From the outset, he refused to hear the confession of any slave owner, including his own fellow Jesuits.[60]

He was not the only Jesuit to think in this way. From Lisbon, the representative of the missions, Fr. Jerônimo Cardoso, wrote to the superior general to criticize the fact that the Society of Jesus owned slaves in Brazil and Angola. "We ask the Crown to order that all [the natives] be freed, and we have many captives and make use of those from the villages, more than all other Whites." In Angola, he concluded, all say that "we traffic and practice commerce *sub praetextu conversionis* [under the pretense of conversion]: and I would say that, if we cannot maintain many [priests] without them owning [slaves] then we should maintain fewer without [slaves], for thus did the ancients."[61]

Sent from Lisbon to Bahia to settle the conflict, the Jesuit's itinerant inspector (Visitador) Fr. Cristovão de Gouveia, bearing opinions formulated by the Society of Jesus's treatise writers, met the most important missionaries of Portuguese America.[62] Again, the Visitador decided that slavery was a "safe contract," as the Board of Conscience had determined. Thus, Fr. Garcia's opinions seemed "quite contrary to common use, dangerous and scandalous in these parts." Consequently, the superiors of the order decided to send Garcia back to Spain, where he had been born.[63]

Fr. Gonçalo Leite's antislavery discourse generated a more serious incident. Master of the novices, professor in the Bahia college, superior of the Porto Seguro and Ilhéus Jesuits' residences, he exerted great influence on his fellows. Other priests, close to Miguel Garcia and Gonçalo Leite, also decided to deny the sacrament of confession to slave masters. The Visitador disqualified them, determining that they would hear confessions only at the college entrance hall, prohibiting them from exercising their ministry inside the church.

At that point, the sacrament of confession, as in the case of marriage, was undergoing transformations. Tridentine reforms established individual confession within closed cubicles inside the church (confessionals date back to that time), abandoning the collective or private acts in parish residences.[64] Penitents should submit to contrition, to confession proper, and to compunction for the sins committed. Influenced by Baius (1513–1589), theologian at the University of Louvain and precursor of Jansenism, a current of clerical thought understood that, in the absence of the penitent's repentance, devoid of real contrition, confessors should refuse or postpone the sacrament. *Contrito caritate perfecta*, the rule of the Council distinguished perfect *contrition*, characterized by sincere and disinterested hostility to sin, from *attrition*, regrets motivated only by fear of divine punishment.[65] Tolerated in the baptism of natives, mere attrition seemed to some Ignatians insufficient to render confession effective.[66]

The Jesuits stood out for their action in favor of assiduous communion and confession.[67] In 1556, under the influence of the Society of Jesus, Cardinal Infant Dom Henrique, regent of the kingdom and inquisitor-general, issued a royal provision on the matter, in which he summoned Catholics to confess and partake of the Holy Communion regularly, "finding very odd the contrary abuse."[68] However, there were priests in Bahia who insisted on refusing the sacrament to the many slave-owning faithful. It was urgent to resolve the impasse: Gonçalo Leite ended up being banished to Lisbon by decision of the Visitador.

Witness to the facts, Fr. Fernão Cardim, who had arrived from Lisbon with the Visitador to conduct interrogatories in Bahia, is elusive about this serious dissent: "the Father Visitador has sometimes, together with some prelates and scholars, dealt with cases of great importance regarding bondage, baptism, and marriage of Indians and Guinea slaves, yielding great fruit from their resolutions and improved Christianity after we arrived in Brazil."[69] In fact, the Visitador's "resolutions" did not convince Fr Gonçalo Leite at all. From Lisbon, he continued to protest to the head of the Society of Jesus in Rome, demanding confessions based on contrition: "I see our priests giving confession to homicides and robbers of other people's freedom, property and sweat, devoid of either restitution of the past or remedy for future evils, which are committed every day." As he observed in Bahia, slaveholders refused to demonstrate the necessary regret and did not "restitute" past sins, maintaining their property of illicitly enslaved individuals. Therefore, they should be prevented from confessing.[70]

The refusal to confess, an extreme measure, does not seem to have been applied collectively again, as it had happened in Bahia. A quarter of a century later, Fr. Antônio Vieira himself defended the agreement between missionaries and Indian slave owners. According to him, the Jesuits, gathered in São Luís do Maranhão, had made explicit the most pressing question of Amazonia, the empire of Indian slavery: "what obligation had we, the confessors, concerning the sin, as usual, in which all these [settlers] lived, with the bondage of Indians, which for the most part is presumed to be unjust?" Putting the Jesuit probabilism (at that very moment the target of Pascal's severe criticism, as will be seen) into practice, Vieira answers: "It was decided that, to those who did not confess this sin [of enslaving Indians], we did not have the duty to ask them about it."[71]

Antislavery and Proslavery Thought in Times of *Asientos*

Miguel Garcia, Gonçalo Leite, and their religious community of Bahia saw in slavery an obstacle to the teaching of the gospel overseas. Amador Arrais and Pedro Brandão, Carmelite bishops, expressed their criticism based on a different ideological basis. Grounded in the conservative, seigniorial, antimercantilist field, the Carmelites attacked slavery. For them, what mattered were the evils engendered by it at the heart of Portugal's traditional society. Even so, on attributing a redeeming legal effect to the baptism of slaves, the two bishops also expressed the antagonistic character that existed between catechesis and modern slavery.

Friar Pedro Brandão had witnessed slave-trading practices in the Cape Verde and Upper Guinea diocese, where he performed Episcopal functions (1589–1594).[72] Based on his direct knowledge, he concluded that it was "humanly impossible" to deter the unlawfulness of the slave trade. Brandão was a disciple of Friar Amador Arrais, bishop of Portalegre (Portugal). Affiliated with the sixteenth-century antihumanist camp, Friar Amador Arrais judged in his *Diálogos* (1589) that slavery should be condemned for jeopardizing seigniorial order. The introduction of enslaved Africans in Portugal took away jobs and social status from the poor white men in the country. "In earlier times, before this rabble [the slaves] came to the kingdom, there were as many Portuguese people as now, nobody begged [. . . ,] the poor lived with the rich, and the rich maintained them and all had remedy for life." Next, evangelical reasons proper intervened: the traffic had brought illicitly enslaved people, offending Christian morals: "Even giving as an excuse of bringing them [the Africans] to become Christians, since Christianity cannot be exchanged for bondage."[73]

In the same vein, Bishop Brandão coupled his reactionary convictions with antislavery arguments. Slavery seemed reprehensible to him, because it increased the disorder of seigniorial and traditional society, enhancing the evils caused in

Portugal by the prevalence of the commodity and new forms of enrichment generated by the Discoveries. Thus, Brandão listed the troubles the African traffic caused Portugal: economic unbalance; food shortages; the wheat trade monopoly in the hands of foreigners; unemployment for poor whites, since the rich would only employ slaves: "hence so many lost [poor] without the means of living"; degradation of manual crafts performed by slaves; "mixing of blood"; a mixed race that "uglified" (*enfeava*) the kingdom; concubinage; public immorality; and disgrace of the kingdom before Europe. "We do not know of a republic other than the Portuguese who trades slaves as commodities."

In practice, Brandão's memorial was a petition for the Court to determine the manumission of converted slaves. As stated previously with regard to marriage and confession, baptism was declared mandatory by the Council of Trent.[74]

An anonymous petition, maybe authored by Brandão himself, written in the late sixteenth century takes up the arguments of Brandão and Amador Arrais, the underlying social disorder generated in Portugal by the introduction of overseas slaves. "Indians and Blacks [slaves] carried to Portugal gather, become thieves and ordinarily live in concubinage, because their master prevents them from marrying."[75]

Yet what were the direct and indirect consequences of divine remission infused in colonial peoples by the sacrament of baptism? Understanding that baptism had a general and intrinsic redeeming effect, as taught by the theologian Jesuit Fernão Rebelo at the University of Évora, Brandão formulated his forceful antislavery argument: "Among Turks and Moors freedom is given to captive Christians if they adopt their damned sect, and there is more reason to give it to the gentiles of the overseas territories (*conquista*), which the popes granted to this kingdom, to make them Christians."[76]

Evoking divine providence, Bishop Brandão asserted that Portuguese guilt in the spreading of slavery had caused the misfortune (the Portuguese royal army defeat in Ksar-el-Kebir and the tragic death of King Sebastião, new threats of war) that had befallen the kingdom as God's punishment.[77] Facing the hostility of the colonists and slave traders of his Cape Verdean diocese and of the Catholic hierarchy, Friar Brandão resigned the bishopric.[78] Ultimately, Brandão's and Amador Arrais's reflections foreshadow the racist and reactionary antislavery thought that constituted a distinct and influential element of the nineteenth-century abolitionism.

In contrast with the denunciations of Indian and African enslavement voiced by Las Casas, Domingo de Soto, and Thomas Mercado in the mid-sixteenth century, in the early stages of America's settlements, Brandão's and Arrais's criticism occurred when the transatlantic slave trade underwent a sharp change, raising many more controversies in Spain and Portugal.

Indeed, the unification of the Iberian Crowns under Felipe II (1580), who ruled henceforth over most of the African and American regions involved in the Atlantic exchanges, opened debates in the Madrid Court about the replacement of the royal *licencias* by the *Asiento* contracts (1595), as well as the intensification of the Atlantic slave trade to an unprecedented volume and extension, and it raised new religious and political concerns over the matter. Truly, the *Asiento* provided the highest and steadiest certifications of the legitimacy and lawfulness of the African's enslavement. Through such royal contracts, the African slave trade turned into a central instrument of the Spanish Crown's fiscal policy and of the Iberian transatlantic design, a stage certainly not reached by Amerindian slavery. Iberian theologians' and jurists' essays on slavery written by the generation after Las Casas, Domingo de Soto, and Thomas Mercado should be read in light of these changes.

At the University of Coimbra, the Dominican theologian Antônio de São Domingos, a former disciple of Francisco de Vitoria at the University of Salamanca, taught that the African slave trade, properly submitted to the royal contracts and taxes, should enjoy full ipso facto legal and legitimate sanction.[79]

Such is the context of the Jesuit Luís de Molina's (died in 1600) essays. As noted by Hespanha, Molina is the first theologian to systematically scrutinize the African slave trade.[80] After twenty-six years as a student and teacher at Coimbra and Évora universities with sojourns in Lisbon, where he learned details about the Upper Guinea slave trade, Molina wrote his book *De justitia et jure* (1593–1597), which includes eight *disputatio* related to the enslavement of Africans.[81] Although condemning the slave trade and even wishing for the end of the slave system, Molina conclusively accepted the legality of the African's enslavement.[82] Indeed, he believes that the purchaser in good faith may own slaves: *in dubio melior sit conditio possidentis, quando possessio bona fide incepit* ("in doubt, the right of the owner must prevail if the ownership is in good faith").[83] As we shall see bellow, this juridical axiom and its variants are often quoted on matters related to slaves as property.

However, the theologian's thought, the Crown's policies, particularly during Portugal's union with Spain (1580–1640) and the institution of the Portuguese *Asientos*, were not the only forces driving the early transatlantic slave trade. Despite the objections from priests such as Oliveira, Brandão, and García, many of the field missionaries, particularly the Jesuits in Africa and Portuguese America, played a crucial role in legitimating African bondage.

The Jesuit Theory of the Slave Trade

I am the mantle of the world
whose sins I covered

—"Auto de la Visitación de Santa Isabel" (1597), José de Anchieta S.J.

In 1592, Fr. Pero Rodrigues embarked in Lisbon for a long sea journey that would take him to two continents to carry out two challenging tasks. Appointed Visitador of the S.J. in Angola, he would prepare a report to the superior general in Rome on the missions among the Mbundu. Then he would cross the Atlantic again to take over his position as provincial of the Society of Jesus in Brazil (1594–1603). On leaving the Tagus, he already knew of the trouble brewing on the South Atlantic horizon. The governor of Angola, Francisco de Almeida, in whose fleet Pero Rodrigues was traveling, carried categorical royal orders: the system of *amos* had to be extinguished. Jesuits and Portuguese captains who controlled the Angolan *sobados* should hand over villages, revenues, and natives to the Crown's representative.

However, instead of sailing to Luanda with the fleet, Fr. Pero's vessel touched land in Bahia first. Thus, the Visitador could hear from the missionaries of Brazil about the dispute of the *amos* in Angola.[84] At that point, the Society of Jesus was striving to consolidate its missions in Portuguese America, following a system that subjugated to the missionaries and the authorities the indigenous communities coercively transferred from the hinterlands. As stated in the previous chapter, the Brazilian Jesuits conceived the Indian's coerced labor within the Ethiopic Ocean framework: subject natives had to protect the colonists and Crown from the attacks of the French, the English, the hostile Indians, and rebel black slaves.

In this context, was Father's Pero Rodrigues's stopover in Bahia a coincidence, caused by a ship in poor condition, as stated in a document? Or was it purposeful, in collusion with Brazil's leading Jesuits, assembled in Bahia to hold a congregation of the order? In any case, the Visitador took the providential stop to debate with the missionaries gathered in Bahia on the issues regarding Angolan troubles.[85]

Although the social context of Portuguese America, exporter of inert goods, was different from that of Angola—where the trade in the living thrived—Indian settlements in Brazil resembled the system of Angolan *sobados*, managed by Jesuit *amos*. Consequently, José de Anchieta, Luís da Grã, Fernão Cardim, the provincial Marçal Beliarte, and other Ignatians of Portuguese America would support their fellows in Angola. Contrary to the royal order of 1592, they decided that the Jesuits should continue controlling the *sobados*.[86]

Armed with this decision, Fr. Pero resumed his journey to Luanda, where events had come to a head. Thus, on the high seas, the Visitador's ship could have crossed two vessels from Luanda, which would alight in Pernambuco before proceeding to Lisbon. Each vessel was carrying a central figure of the conflict that took place in Angola. The first carried Governor Francisco de Almeida, expelled by the Jesuits and captains involved in the *amos*'s rebellion, and the second, the Jesuits' superior Balthazar Barreira, banished from Angola by the Crown for having headed the rebellion.[87]

"Apostle of Africa" (as stated in the Ignatian chronicle), evangelizer of Angola, Cape Verde, and Guinea, Balthazar Barreira entered the Society of Jesus in 1556.[88] After studying at Coimbra's novitiate, he preached in the Alentejo and helped the victims of the "great plague," the bubonic plague that hit Lisbon in 1569. Amid the agonies of the illness that afflicted 10,000 dwellers and killed 200 people every day, the dedication of Barreira and other Jesuits impressed Lisbon's inhabitants and authorities.[89] Maybe this was the first great impact made by the Company of Jesus, which was still then characterized as an aristocratic institution by the Portuguese.[90]

Ten years later, Barreira landed in Angola as superior of the mission, together with Paulo Dias Novais.[91] Barreira erected the church of São Paulo de Luanda, which lent its name to the town, and fought beside the conquerors, exhorting them in the battles.[92] In spite of having baptized the first converted Ndongo nobleman as Constantino, Barreira remained skeptical regarding the possibility of "Constantinism," already attempted in parts of Asia, thriving in Angola. In fact, he did not think that Christianity could be inculcated from above, cascading through the traditional native hierarchy after the conversion of the Mbundu aristocracy.[93] On the contrary, the failure of the policy of indirect government in neighboring Congo made the Jesuits' fight to defeat Ndongo through a total war of economic, territorial, and ideological conquest. For providing captains with moral and material help, being attentive to Mbundu war tactics, and bringing soldiers and gunpowder to form troops, Father Barreira must be considered a real military chief who shared with Paulo Dias Novais the command of the offensive launched in West Central Africa beginning in 1580. Underlining the complementary role played by the chief Jesuit missionary and the governor of Angola, an eighteenth century author wrote that in one key victory against the Ndongo warriors, Father Barreira led as Moses and Paulo Dias Novais commanded as Joshua. [94]

Summoned by Felipe II to appear before the Court after the *amos*'s rebellion, Barreira was in Madrid and proceeded to Évora, where he took over the position of novice master. He was about sixty-six years old when he resumed his African apostolate in Upper Guinea, Cape Verde, and Sierra Leone. Revered by the Jesuits and the faithful, he died in Cape Verde in 1612, after having served the Crown and the Society for more than half a century.[95]

An old hand in West African affairs, surviving Upper Guinea's harshness, which took the lives of most of his fellow missionaries, Barreira was tireless on journeys and influential among allied native chiefs. He might be, in the Jesuit African saga, as distinguished as Francis Xavier and José de Anchieta for their apostolates in Asia and America.[96] This was the feeling Fr. Balthazar Telles expressed in his *Chronica* (1645), the first history of the Portuguese Jesuits. Years later, passing through Cape Verde, Fr. Antônio Vieira paid homage to the memory of the "Old Saint."[97] It remains true, however, that the whole beatification process of Balthazar Barreira must come to terms with the Old Saint's voluntary, meditated, and compelling activity in favor of the Atlantic slave trade.

To Loyola, Laínez, Borja, Mercurian,—superior generals of the Society of Jesus in the sixteenth century—the Jesuits ownership of slaves was disturbing. "It is been many days now that I have resolved that it does not suit the Society [of Jesus] to make use of slaves. To Your Most Rev. I recommend trying to gently get rid of those you have in Portugal," insisted Superior General Francisco Borja, later made a saint, to the provincial of Portugal in 1569.[98] Some years later, Superior General Claudio Acquaviva determined that the Jesuits should neither own nor trade in "suspicious enslavements." Besides, missionaries should not follow those who said that it was better to maintain these individuals in bondage than confirm them in paganism. Nevertheless, later, Acquaviva went back on his word and authorized missionaries to own slaves.[99]

Amid these uncertainties, Barreira sent in 1583 a memorial from Luanda to the scholars of Salamanca, Évora, and Coimbra, who were debating the lawfulness of the slave trade. For Barreira, there were no doubts about the legality of African enslavements. Counting as money everywhere, a slave—pondered Barreira—was the currency of the conquered territory. To him, prisoners of war, delinquents, and descendants of other captives composed the African hinterland traffic. Pulled from villages and sold and resold to fairs, all these people were mixed, making it impossible "to clearly establish" the legitimacy of their bondage. Finally, Barreira alleged, the Mbundu asked for missionaries to convert them and later abjured the Christian faith, therefore incurring apostasy. Thus, the war that was waged on them should be understood as a "Just War." "And the conclusion will be that the further we get into the land and we have knowledge of the Blacks, the more we experience [the fact] that from nowhere else in Guinea come out slave commodities [*peças*] that can be more safely bought than those from Angola."[100] In a related text, Barreira explained that, among the peoples of Angola, there was no "legitimate marriage in the law of nature." For him, the slave trade did not obliterate any authentic Angolan native family.

Significantly, the Jesuits had the very opposite judgment concerning the conjugality of the Amerindians. In his *Catecismo na Lingoa Brasilica* (1618), a vocabulary and canonical treatise designed for the Amazon's Jesuits missionaries, Fr. Antonio de Araújo judged that the Amerindians' customary union was equivalent to a true matrimony.[101] Debating in 1655 on juridical issues aroused by the same Maranhão's Indians, Fr. Antonio Vieira reaffirmed that Indians' marriages, performed in their communities as a "natural contract," constituted "a true matrimony."[102]

The argument stating that the Angolan traffic seemed more licit than in any other part of Africa is summed up by the provincial of Portugal, Francisco de Gouveia, who was influential with the Curia, and conveyed to the leadership of the S.J. in Rome.[103]

Therefore, the legal basis for the "Just War" that legitimized the enslavement of prisoners in West Central Africa became a nonissue. Already enslaved by other natives, the captives were acquired through purchase and barter in hinterland fairs, and not through direct capture by the Portuguese, as was usual with indigenous bondage in Brazil.

Due to the safety of the maritime routes to West Central Africa and the Lusitanian monopoly in the region, the *asentistas* invested in Angola. Thus, Barreira's ideology for justifying the Angolan traffic spread as slave traders flowed into Luanda in greater numbers.

A gifted epistolarian, a resourceful thinker knowledgeable about the sugar mills of Pernambuco, São Tomé, and Cape Verde, considered to be the greatest Jesuit expert and, certainly, the most experienced missionary of sub-Saharan Africa, Barreira efficiently rebutted the moral and religious restrictions raised against the Atlantic slave trade.

According to the Society of Jesus's procedures, his letters, like those by missionaries in the East and in America, were often reputed to be "edifying." As such, they were to be read in college and seminary refectories to motivate preachers, novices, and the faithful, causing them to reflect.[104] Recopied and deposited in libraries, part of this correspondence would serve as a reference on the arts of the devil among overseas pagans. For this reason, Barreira's thoughts on slavery reached opinion makers living far beyond the nominal addressees of his letters. His point of view was repeatedly imposed on the Superiors of Portugal's Jesuits whose weight over the Order's direction in Rome was considerable, as demonstrated by the incident involving Fr. João Polanco, Loyola's old mate.

In 1572, Portuguese Jesuits vetoed the candidacy of the Order's general vicar, Juan Polanco, to the succession of general Laínez at the head of the S.J. The motive? Polanco, a Spaniard, had a "blood defect": he had New Christian ascendancy.[105] The same missionaries obtained the privilege, exclusive to Portuguese Ignatians, of participating as consultants in the Holy Office tribunals. Then they became inquisitorial commissars in Angola, using official attributions to intimidate governors, colonists, and also the Capuchin missionaries, their rivals.

On commenting on the correspondence between Loyola and Jesuits from the four parts of the world, Pierre Chaunu points out the beginnings of the modern bureaucratic information system that the S.J. established, a system centralized on the choice of ends and wisely decentralized in the choice of means.[106] In this respect, the pro–Atlantic slavery realpolitik of the province of Portugal—chiefly inspired by Father Barreira—has its share of responsibility for the decisive reversal made by the Jesuit hierarchy in 1599. That year, an instruction arrived at overseas missions from the order's directory in Rome: "we can make use of slaves."[107]

Barreira was convinced that it was necessary to destroy the Ndongo kingdom to save it for Christ. Arguing before the insider audience of the S.J., since his *Angolistas* parishioners needed no persuasion with regards to the licit nature of the slave trade, Barreira was a powerful aide to Paulo Dias Novais.[108]

His battle accounts omit the presence of thousands of allied native archers, in order to highlight the valor of the Portuguese. Divine signs in favor of the invaders were promptly recorded: crosses in the sky, visions of the Virgin in battles, swords of fire, and suchlike miracles. Sometimes, celestial signs formed a rhetorical tool, since the 1625 papal bull, which forbade ascribing miraculousness to a nonauthenticated event and calling a saint one who had not yet canonized, had not yet been issued.[109] Equally unrestricted was his praise of pillage and of the invaders' bravery—or truculence.

In a letter addressed to Fr. José de Anchieta, then S.J. provincial of Brazil, he narrated the battle of Ilamba (1585), in which almost all warriors of three Ndongo squads had been killed or enslaved. Together with hundreds of severed noses, the chiefs' heads were placed in bags and sent to Luanda on the backs of twenty bearers. Sixty years later, the chronicler Balthazar Telles was startled by these mutilations, and considered them a "cruel curiosity."[110]

Patterson observes that all stratified societies are born from violent appropriation of individuals by other individuals. In most cases, this act of "original accumulation" is restricted to the prehistory of societies and gets lost in it. However, in the slave-holding system, the act of reifying the vanquished is continuously renewed,[111] especially in Brazil I would add, where the slave-holding system—connected to the Atlantic slave trade circuit from 1550 to 1850—remained based on the pillaging of African villages. Hence the importance of following the theological and legal arguments that, over those three centuries, legitimated the initial, African stage of the slave trade, a decisive moment for the legal foundation of slavery in Brazil.

Within the framework of continuous violence that involved the enslavement of Africans, epistolary documents sometimes reveal the ambiguous feelings raised by raids. Fr. Balthazar Afonso, Barreira's fellow, described one of Paulo Dias Novais's raids in bright colors:

> At that time [1580] the governor already had with him 300 Portuguese and some 200 slaves of Portuguese owners, and as there was a shortage of food they started to seek it at gunpoint, conducting some four or five assaults in which they caused great destruction, burning and devastating everything, and bringing plenty of food that satiated all. Here it happened that a father with his son were running away from our people, and seeing that he would not be able to save his son, he turned to our people and discharged as many arrows as he had, until he was killed, standing fast where he was, so that his son could hide. Then the father died and went to Hell.[112]

Straightforward language, realist narrative, explicit rapine, and an extreme gesture of fatherly heroism. The emotion flowing until the end of the text in the desperate fight of the Mbundu father is nevertheless stanched by a judgment without remission: "The father died and went to Hell." Not to our impoverished Hell, which furnaces have been put out by the contemporary Church, and that the Neo-Pentecostals try to rekindle. But the 1500s Hell, imagined by the Iberian rural world, by the Inquisition's flames, shroud of the so-called infidels, heretics, idolaters, and cannibals fought by captains and missionaries the world over.[113]

Adhering to Barreiras's theses, the S.J. annual letter of 1588 from the province of Portugal emphasized the preeminence of colonial war over catechesis in Angola: "The whole kingdom should submit in order to mold these gentiles more safely and uproot idolatry."[114] *Molding* (*enformar*) is shaping natives for the colonial society. By the same token, Visitador Pero Rodrigues's report, whose draft Barreira examined closely, ordered missionaries not to baptize any nobleman of the Ndongo kingdom until the whole land was subjected to vassalage.[115]

Nonetheless, the replacement of Angolan *sobas* with captains and missionaries in the tutelage of the *sobados* had been interrupted by the royal ordinance of 1592, which extinguished the *amos* system. King Felipe II himself, and not only rival missionaries or envious settlers, refused the Jesuits' property and trade in slave "pieces." The Jesuit response was given on a double register. On the one hand, the missionaries challenged royal authority and fomented the *amos*'s mutiny. On the other hand, the Jesuits' proslavery arguments adjusted to coeval mercantile thought, as shown in an emblematic text written in 1593 by the Jesuits of Angola after a discussion with their coreligionists in Brazil.

> There is no scandal when the priests [Jesuits] of Angola pay their debts with slaves, because, just as in Europe currency is coined gold and silver, and in Brazil it is sugar cane, in Angola and neighboring kingdoms it is slaves. For this reason, when the priests [Jesuits] of Brazil send us over what we have asked them for, like [manioc] flour and lumber for doors and windows, and when the owners of goods who come to this land sell us biscuits, wine and other things, they do not want to receive from us payment on any other currency than the one valid in the land, which is slaves, carried by them each year to Brazil and the [Castilian] Indies.

Further on, the document reiterates the mercantile character of enslaved and deported Africans: "in the custom houses of Brazil, where we have sent our slaves until now, we do not pay taxes because of the privilege bestowed by His Majesty. By the same privilege, [Jesuit] priests do not pay taxes for the sugar cane they sell in Brazil or for other things in Portugal." Finally, the text underlines the missionaries' dependence on the mode of exploitation in each possession: in Spanish America there were the *encomiendas*; in India, the Society of Jesus boasted revenues from the lands of Salsette (Sashti); in Portugal, the missionaries had revenues from land and some country estates in Alentejo, "and the *sobas* are [like] the country estates of Alentejo," property meant to generate commodity slaves for the Society of Jesus in Angola.[116]

Already appointed provincial of Brazil, Fr. Pero Rodrigues figures as the main signatory of this synthesis of the purpose of colonization written for the Crown. Nonetheless, it is clear that the Jesuits gathered in Bahia had previously endorsed the document. Barreira had not signed the memorial quoted above. Besides being disliked at the Court, he was not in Luanda anymore. Still, he should be considered its intellectual author, since the text sums up, almost literally, the arguments he had formulated ten years before.[117]

A concise history of the Jesuits in Angola, written in 1594 to be sent to the Superior General Claudio Acquaviva, emphasized Barreira's ideas. Only a military offensive could guarantee catechesis. Individuals made captive in war were few, most of the slaves would come from the "extremely old and always used" trade practiced by natives in hinterland markets. Submitting *sobas* directly to the Crown would cost much and produce little. The artifices and apostasies of Angola's sovereign—of the Ndongo—had provided the "Just War" justification to enslave all those people. At the end of the document there is an unsuccessful blow against the governor Francisco de Almeida, the Crown's counselors, and eventually, King Felipe II himself, who had vetoed the system of *amos*: the missionaries were watching over Angola very well, "until those who had the obligation to protect this work have obstructed it." Guerreiro endorsed the same arguments in the *Relação Anual* (1603–1611), in which he publicized the epic mission of the Society of Jesus.[118]

Back to Africa in 1604, now in mainland Sierra Leone, Barreira sent to his superiors a report on Africans deported via Cape Verde. Most likely, the document was a reply to the antislavery libel by Bishop Pedro Brandão.

Barreira openly admitted the stark reality: "What one can say in general about Blacks bought and sold in this Guinea called Cape Verde is that no examination is made as of the title of their bondage, and nobody inquires about it." After narrating the different ways by which Africans could lose their freedom, the memorial closes as plainly as it had begun: "And as to slaves taken from these parts thus far, since the fairness of the title under which they were enslaved is doubtful, and that *in dubio melior est conditio possidentis* [in doubt, the right of the owner prevails], it seems that nothing has to be changed."[119]

Still, most of the theologians and jurists admitted that the owner's right to possession could prevail over the captives' right to freedom in a single situation: when the owner was totally unaware of the controversy over the Atlantic slave trade and there were no doubts in favor of the slave.[120] Based on the same legal principle, Fr. Antônio Vieira developed in 1655 an interpretation diametrically opposed to Barreira's, in favor of the Indians enslaved by Maranhão's settlers. For Vieira, the postulate *in dubio melior est conditio possidentis* guaranteed the possession of freedom to the captive: "in this case one does not question whether the Indians belong to Peter or Paul, but one doubts whether the Indians are free or captive, and in this doubt is the possession of freedom."[121]

Barreira swept such scruples aside and preached the legitimacy of the Atlantic slave traffic, although he recognized that the matter was "beset with doubts." Such is the meaning of a letter he sent to the Roman leadership of the Society of Jesus.

> Concerning the bondage of these Blacks, a matter so beset with doubts *pro utraque parte* [from both sides], it is not possible to do other than either allowing it to be carried on or to forbid this trade completely. I say this because it is usual to sell Blacks for the misdeeds that they themselves or their relatives and children carry out. This is like law among them. Sometimes it happens that they are sold in spite of being guiltless or for a misdeed that did not merit bondage. But it is impossible to verify it.[122]

From the same vessel that left Sierra Leone, he sent an account to the provincial of Portugal, reinforcing the same thesis.[123] The S.J. could either adjust to the facts or face the Crown, the merchants, and the settlers. Under the overwhelming influence galvanized by the mercantile and production complex of the Atlantic world—from lobbyists of the Madrilenian *Asientos* to the merchants and masters in Rio de Janeiro and Río de la Plata—there could only be one response: the Jesuits should let the slave traffic carry on. It should be noted that such letters contained meditated reflections, elaborated by Barreira during the preceding years, since his times in Luanda during the first steps of the Portuguese invasion.

Four years later, on answering the inquiry about African slavery prepared in Cartagena by the Jesuit jurist Alonso de Sandoval, the superior of the S.J. in Angola, Fr. Luís Brandão, reiterated with conviction Barreiras's theory on the lawfulness of the Angolan traffic.

> Your Reverence would like to know whether the Blacks sent [from here] are licitly enslaved. To which I answer that it seems to me that Y. R. should not have scruples about it. For this is something the Board of Conscience

members in Lisbon have never condemned, and they are learned men of good consciences. Furthermore, the bishops who have been in São Tomé, Cape Verde and Luanda, being learned and virtuous men, have never condemned it. Also, we have been here for 40 years and very learned priests [Jesuits] have been here, and in the province of Brazil, where there always have been priests of our religion eminent in letters, who never considered this trade illicit: and thus we, and the priests of Brazil, bought these slaves for our service, with no scruples at all. And I say more: if someone could have no scruples, these are the residents of this region, because as the merchants who get these Blacks get them in good faith, they can well buy from such merchants with no scruples at all, and they can sell them: for it is common opinion that the owner of the thing in good faith can sell it, and it can be bought [. . .] And losing so many souls that leave from here, of which many are saved, [just] because some are illicitly enslaved, without knowing who they are, does not seem to be so much the service of God, for they are few [illicitly enslaved], and those saved are many.[124]

Sandoval included this pro-slave-trade manifesto in his influential book. Certainly, he condemned the tortures inflicted on the deported. But Fr. Sandoval also thought that the slave traffic was a lesser evil, since it allowed taking Africans from the heart of paganism.[125]

Devoid of rhetoric, Barreira took the part that fell to him—by no means small—in the enunciation of the purpose of colonization.

In the world of the triumphant commodity, the most definitive argument in favor of the traffic emerged from "the valley of the shadow of death," as Luis Fróis called the overseas missions: the Atlantic slave trade was a fundamental link in the insertion of Africa into the world market. Suppressing it would mean endangering Portuguese overseas control and breaking the chain of commerce set up in the Atlantic. Moreover, the souls of Africans who could be redeemed by slavery in America would be lost to paganism in Africa's hinterlands.

Enunciated in the papal bull *Romanus pontifex*, the fifteenth-century justification for evangelization in favor of the slave trade had a univocal character. It basically convinced the followers of Christian proselytism, those who worried about rescuing the souls of the gentiles. In turn, the sixteenth-century proslavery argument based on the existence of cannibalism—denaturalized to the point of presenting anthropophagy as the "ordinary food" of warlike ethnicities and the reason for

Africa's depopulation—covered a broader scope.[126] It justified the Atlantic slave traffic for both believers and unbelievers also aware of the salvation of bodies, in the rescuing of prisoners from African indigenous wars.

Even so, this argument, as the enunciation in the papal bull, had an ideologically circumscribed character. It presupposed the view that it was necessary to save the natives from themselves, from their supposed barbarism. Affirmed since Xenophon, as shown in the previous chapter, this postulate was reasserted in the sixteenth century by the Dominican Domingos de Soto, at the University of Salamanca.[127] Accordingly, the Jesuit João Baptista Fragoso, a theologian at the University of Évora, conceived slavery as a process that "blossomed out of a sentiment as delicate as mercy, introduced into the Law of Nations to mitigate the fury and rigors of war."[128]

In a much more efficient and universal way, Barreira was based on a secular supposition that was significant in the age of commercial capital: the exchange of the commodity legitimates the business.

Yet like some treatise writers of the Company of Jesus, Fr. Fernão Rebelo, knowing about the antislavery manifesto written by the bishop of Cape Verde, stated that, in case of suspicious bondage, it was necessary to decide *pro favore libertatis* (in favor of freedom).[129]

Living in sub-Saharan slave-trade ports, crucial places for qualifying Africans for colonial slavery, Barreira championed the opposing thesis: in suspicious cases, the right was on the side of the owner, the slave master, the slave trader. *In dubio melior est conditio possidentis*. His presupposition underlies a general justification for slave traders and slaveholders from all quadrants.

Liber theologia moralis (1644), by the Spanish Jesuit Antonio de Escobar, was published forty years later.[130] In the same vein as Barreira, Escobar claimed that the property of a purchased chattel would exempt the owner from inquiring into the legitimacy of its entry in the mercantile circuit. In his well-known essay, Pascal flayed Escobar's theses. In his *Huitième provinciale* (1656), he criticized the idea that chattel obtained by criminal methods could be legitimate and insisted on the "rules of conscience" to compel the restitution of such chattels.[131] However, some historians of the Society of Jesus and commentators on Pascal's work maintain that the philosopher decontextualized Escobar's ideas. Referring to this dispute, João Lúcio de Azevedo (died in 1933), the Portuguese biographer of Fr. Antonio Vieira S.J., wrote that the critics of the Jesuits had not proved the evils of the probabilistic doctrine: "they failed to demonstrate concrete evidence of the harm caused."[132]

More recently, P. H. E. Hair wrote that the Jesuits' casuistries about the Atlantic slave trade and other affairs were "somewhat unfairly savaged" by Pascal.[133] Jean Delumeau, also appears understanding toward the Jesuit's doctrine. For him, probabilism implied that moral science was made for action and conditioned by life's changing circumstances. In a bold displacement of the debate, he argued that General de Gaulle, in June 1940, disobeyed the government of France, deciding for the "most probable" opinion from his point of view and certainly the "least probable" for most French moralists of the time. "And history proved he was right," concludes Delumeau.

For the historian of Brazil, compelled to follow the complete arc of South Atlantic historical events, the conclusion is rather different. Inside the gears of commercial capitalism, within the scope of slavery, the devastating effects of the justifications provided by Balthazar Barreira and Antônio Vieira's probabilism reveal the pertinence of Pascal's criticism.[134]

Those who knew the transatlantic network and the concreteness of the slave commodity could perceive the reach of Barreira's and the Jesuits' reflection in favor of Trade in the Living. Many people understood those words, including the rudest sugar-mill owner in São Tomé or Rio de Janeiro; the bishop of Congo and Angola, whose annual fee of 600,000 *réis*, was paid by slave export rights;[135] the *Asiento* bankers; or the Luanda officer who branded the deportee with a hot iron, earning forty *réis* per arm or chest burned, up to 10,000 times a year.[136]

"Brand," in Kimbundu, is *karimu*.[137] *Karimbo* was the official red-hot branding tool made of silver or iron to brand Africans at the moment of shipping and collecting export taxes.[138] Hence the words *carimbo* (the stamp) e *carimbar* (to stamp). Thus, the noun and the verb—used only in the Portuguese language of Brazil—that define administrative hierarchies, scope of property, validity of documents, and public authority exerted by the Brazilian governments derive from the gesture and from the tool that imprinted legal approval on the human commerce. The noun and the verb that identify the precise moment of the reification of the African.

Contrasting with the life of antislavery Bishop Pedro Brandão, who died rich in his Lisbon country estate, the proslavery missionary Balthazar Barreira suffered the rigors of the African hinterland and died poor in a shack in Cape Verde. In fact, the "Old Saint" seemed realistic and disillusioned at the same time. He was disillusioned about the future of missions in Africa, since he had lived long enough to evaluate how little they had progressed in one century of catechesis. Yet he was a realist about the course of the commercial revolution that he had observed around him. Barreira knew that colonial dynamics would tie the future of Africa to that of the New World. Nothing decided in Rome, Madrid, or Lisbon could, at that point, counter the slaving bustle in the Atlantic.

The *Descimento* of Indians and the Atlantic Traffic in Africans

The process of commodification of the Africans radiated throughout the ocean to reach an unheard-of level in the last quarter of the sixteenth century.

Coupled with the slave trade, the invasion of Angola brought about, for the first time in modern history, a European dominion fully based on organized pillaging with no production sector. Taking into consideration these circumstances, Jan Vansina states that at the end of the seventeenth century, Angola turned out to be "the first substantial" European colony in Africa.[139]

At that time, regularly undone by the looting and the extension of the slave trade, the missions' failure in Angola was already evident. "All over this Angola there is not one *soba* of whom one can say that he is truly rooted in the Faith, therefore, if missions are so many, why is there so meager and ruined a fruit?" asked the governor of Angola in the heat of a controversy with the Jesuits in 1678. Completing his criticism, the governor considered the Jesuits' conduct in abandoning missions close to the gentiles in the hinterlands to settle in Luanda to assist the residents to be a "manifest mistake." In their own defense, the Jesuits attributed their retreat into the college of Luanda to the "malignity of the climate" reigning in the Angolan hinterland, acknowledging the failing of their missions in the native villages.[140]

The saga of the Jesuits of Japan and China—where the situation became unfavorable to them under internal political reversals (in Japan) or changes of the Roman missionary strategy (in China)—can be regarded as "glorious failures." But the record of their missions' setbacks in Angola and Congo, at the core of the slave-trade network, appears as "shameful failures." Studies on Jesuits missions often neglect their involvement in the West Central Africa slave trade.[141] In fact, Portuguese Jesuits carried out a complementary missionary system in the Ethiopic Ocean that justified the commerce in slaves while favoring pro-indigenous policy in Brazil.

As is well known, the Jesuits of Portuguese America joined the authorities in carrying out the *descimentos* ("bringing down") of indigenous communities. This system had a threefold aim: first, the establishment of settlements (*aldeamentos*) for "meek" Amerindians to protect the settlers from the "wild" Indians; second, the settlements surrounded colonial enclaves, preventing black slaves from escaping from plantations into the tropical forest[142]; finally, authorities and residents encouraged the *descimentos* of Amerindians to keep contingents of coerced labor in the neighborhood of enclaves and ports. However, *descimentos* played an important role in another area: halting the tribes' migratory flow, the major inconveniency for the missions in Portuguese America, as Luís da Grã wrote to Ignatius of Loyola.[143] Indeed, the *descimentos* increased the Amerindians' desocialization, rendering them susceptible to catechesis.

Paratiý, *Rerytýba* and *Tupinambá*, three short theater plays by José de Anchieta, written around 1580 in the Tupi language to be staged by the natives from Espírito Santo, depict the Indians' removal from the original village and their transfer to a colonial settlement. In *Tupinambá*, an Indian sings:

> My people, in old times,
> Followed primitive customs.
> The missionaries, later, looked for them,
> To reveal God
> [. . .]
> Crossing the great river
> I came; I wished to see you [Saint Mary]
> Come, our protector!
> Provided that he can meet you
> My father Tupinambá![144]

"Crossing the great river" was the reason why the Jesuits helped the authorities to transport Amerindians downstream from the hinterlands into the colonists' enclaves. That was also why the slave trade became acceptable in the eyes of the Church. In fact, what is the traffic in Africans if not another great crossing, a lengthy maritime, transatlantic *descimento*? Removed from the sub-Saharan backlands, where resistance by native communities, epidemiological conditions, and slaving pillage obstructed missionary activity, the African, uprooted in America, became permeable to the teachings of the Church.

In this sense, it is necessary to realize the specificity of the Luso-Brasílico slave trade and the status of Portuguese Jesuits on both sides of the Ethiopic Ocean. In Angola, constantly turned over by pillaging, the Jesuits established a missionary province analogous to that of Brazil, reinforcing the ideological foundation of the Age of Discovery: the evangelization task in pagan lands justified the royal monopoly over the conquests and profits obtained from overseas commerce.

Those ideas had been elaborated ever since the first Portuguese travels to sub-Saharan Africa. A cosmopolitan humanist and a Portuguese "commercial agent of the highest-order" (Bataillon), Damião de Gois refuted criticism against the Portuguese overseas monopoly during his stay in Louvain in 1544. Unlike the French, Spanish, and Italians, he asserted, Lisbon's Crown undertook costly overseas expeditions, often without economic interest, for the exclusive benefit of the Faith. Among other significant examples of such doctrinaire endeavor, Gois quotes the conversion of the Congo's kingdom to Christianity.[145]

Later, the Portuguese friar Serafim de Freitas systemized the complementarity between overseas trade and the propagation of the Christianity. A professor at the University of Valladolid, Freitas stated his thesis in his *De justo Imperio lusitanorum asiatico* (1625). The treatise, a Portuguese reply to the *Mare Liberum* (1608), restructured ideas previously proposed by royal and missionary Portuguese authorities.

The imperative of evangelization, asserted Serafim de Freitas, "the right and duty of the kings of Portugal," justified royal monopoly over Asian and overseas commerce in general, "since this mission can be neither performed nor advanced, amidst so many most powerful nations, unconquered and far distant from each other, except under the appearance of commerce."[146]

The proposition emphasized the arguments formulated almost two centuries before by the papal bull *Romanus pontifex* (1455), a text postulating that *dominium* and overseas monopoly were granted to the Portuguese Crown "to compensate for the great perils, efforts and expenses [. . .] for the protection and growth [. . .] of the Catholic Faith." It was this same papal bull that advanced the first evangelical justification for the slave traffic.

Two centuries later, such doctrine would be clearly developed in "Sermon XIV," one of the Rosary Sermons Fr. Antônio Vieira preached in Bahia to the blacks, free and slave, of the Brotherhood of the Rosary. Latent in religious and social practice, the justifications for trading in slaves became more robust with prayer and sacred rhetoric in order to legitimate seventeenth-century everyday reality.

Vieira set a cultural limit for the remission of the Africans' souls: only Christian blacks would enjoy eternal redemption in Heaven. The others, who lived in paganism in Africa, were condemned to Hell. Vieira taught that, after the discovery of Upper Guinea by the Portuguese in the sixteenth century, the prophecies for the salvation of the Africans' souls, inscribed in Psalms 71 and 77 of the Old Testament, began to be fulfilled. "And they are being fulfilled today, more and better than in any other part of the world, in this America," where Africans were being brought in "innumerable numbers." Next, addressing his black audience, Vieira enunciated one of the boldest ideological justifications for the Atlantic traffic in Africans:"Thus the Mother of God, foreseeing your faith, your piety, your devotion, has chosen you among so many others from so many and so different nations, and has brought you to the brotherhood of the Church, so that you did not lose yourselves there [in Africa], like your parents, and you save yourselves here [in Brazil], as Her children. This is the greatest and most universal miracle of all those Our Lady of the Rosary works every day, and has worked for her devotees." Further on, he reiterates: "Oh, if the Black people taken from the dense woods of their Ethiopia, and brought to Brazil, knew how much they owe to God and to His Most Holy Mother for this which can seem like exile, captivity and disgrace, but is nothing but a miracle, and a great miracle!"[147]

In the spheres of the Atlantic marketplace, God's invisible hand guided the African to eternal redemption in Brazil. A miracle, "and a great miracle," resulted from the massive deportation of men, women, and children on slave vessels across the ocean. Thanks to Our Lady of the Rosary, the Africans were being saved from Africa and brought to redeeming labor in Brazilian lands.

Such slave-trade epiphany has been little noticed by Vieira's present-day commentators.[148] But it has not escaped the lay humanism of the historian of Maranhão and author João Francisco Lisboa, who commented on Vieira's reflections in the late 1840s, when enslaved Africans arrived in massive numbers in Brazilian ports: "Thus, this eternal exile from their native land, and all the horrors of the crossing, to which from then until now the wretched Africans have been condemned, were an attenuation of evil, and a true advantage, in the conception of the Jesuit missionary!"[149]

Frequently quoted by scholars and missiologists, "Sermon XIV" is studied above all for its second part, where the slave's sufferings in the sugar mills are compared to the martyrdom of Christ on the cross. Yet the decisive moment of Vieira's doctrine is expressed in the first part of the text, in the argument that assimilated the slave trade into the evangelization movement overseas. Bought in African markets (and drawn away from paganism), branded with the royal seal upon embarkation (and baptized on the slave ship), resold in Brazil (and placed out of harm's way in a Christian land), the African was already halfway toward Heaven as he or she landed in Portuguese America. Therefore, the problem of the legitimacy of black slavery in the New World becomes a subsidiary if not invisible element. Enslaved by other Africans and carried to Brazil through mercantile operations authorized and taxed by the Crown, the African and his or her offspring became slaves in fact and in law. The work and grace of Our Lady of the Rosary solved the main issue—hotly discussed by theologians and jurists—about the conditions in which the African had been tried, captured, enslaved, and sold in African factories.

In "Sermon XXVII," Vieira brings his contemporaries' attention to the historically unprecedented character of slave trade in seventeenth-century Bahia: "One of the extraordinary things observed in the world today, and about which, due to everyday habit, we do not wonder at, is the immense transmigration of Ethiopian [black] peoples and nations who are continuously passing from Africa to this America [. . . .] A vessel from Angola enters and unloads, on a single day, 500, 600 or perhaps 1,000 slaves." Next, he explains the transcendental meaning of the phenomenon: "the captivity of the first transmigration is ordained by her [Our Lady of the Rosary's] mercy for freedom in the second."[150] Thus, the "first transmigration," that is, selling and deporting the African to the lands of Brazil, appeared as a necessary stage of the second journey, transmigration to Heaven.

In the seminary, Vieira had as his master and protector Fr. Fernão Cardim, one of the repressors of the antislavery dissidence that emerged at the end of the sixteenth century among the Jesuits of Bahia. Later, the slave trade's legitimacy too ceased to be questioned and partook of the colonial order in its own right. His "Sermon XIV," built with Latin citations, would have been preached in a sugar mill in Bahia to the Brotherhood of the Blacks of the Rosary on the patron saint's feast day in 1633. "Sermon XXVII" referred to a sermon allegedly also delivered in Bahia on the same feast day in 1680. Revised and sometimes written especially for publication in the years 1670–1690, the *Sermons* must be interpreted as doctrinal metatexts. Years after the fact, Vieira asserted that he preached for such believers, in those places, on those dates.[151] Determinedly normative, his texts are imbued with the doctrine's propagandistic character that the author bequeathed to Christians of the kingdom and overseas.

Indeed, at the time of the *Sermons*' publication, Portugal and the Portuguese Jesuits were the only European powers settled in the century-old Angolan and Brazilian enclaves connected by the transatlantic slave trade. The Jesuits were missionaries and slave owners on both shores of the South Atlantic. It was up to them to morally validate the African's enslavement and deportation. As we shall see in the next chapter, Portuguese Jesuits were instrumental in upholding Lisbon's control over the Ethiopic Ocean. Such is the geopolitical and cultural framework that underpins Vieira's writings.

Illustrating the scope of dissemination of Fr. Vieira's pro-slave-trade arguments, the *Peregrino da América* (1728), a manual of Christian principles with five editions in the eighteenth century, and as such considered a bestseller in Portuguese America, quoted almost literally the arguments of "Sermon XIV" in a parable intended for masters and slaves in Brazil.[152]

Balthazar Barreira legitimated the slave business with arguments drawn from commercial practice: guaranteed by the act of purchase, the owner was not bound to inquire into the origin of the slave owned. Antonio Vieira thought that the slave traffic made sense because it allowed the spiritual salvation of Africans condemned to paganism in their native land. Both agreed, however, on the imperative of slave trafficking in the Portuguese Atlantic.

Antonio Vieira had emerged as a brilliant novice among the Jesuits of Bahia, at eighteen, when he wrote the Brazil's Jesuits annual report (*Carta ânua*) of 1626, in which he made clear, among other thoughts, the need for the Angolan slave trade. Seventy-two years later, on the eve of his death, paralyzed, blind, almost deaf, but always the owner of the brightest strategic mind in the Lusitanian Empire, he still dictated letters reiterating the same imperative. In his last text, five days before dying at the College of Terreiro de Jesus, in Salvador, Vieira took upon himself for the last time the defense of Bahian slave owners. Writing to the duke of Cadaval, he considered "a manifest injustice" the attitude of Bahian merchants, who forced a reduction in the price of sugar in conjunction with an increase in price "of things from Angola," that is, Angolan slaves.[153]

Indeed, throughout his long life in Bahia, Olinda, Lisbon, Paris, The Hague, London, Rome, Maranhão, Pará, Oporto, and Coimbra, Fr. Antônio Vieira always saw the Atlantic slavery as the unsurpassable horizon of his time.

Once the doctrinal foundation of the trade in the living was defined, it was time to make clear the evangelical duties of the slave master, who was responsible for the social reinsertion of the African in overseas Christian territory.[154] In the same *Sermons of the Rosary* (XIV, XX, and XXVII), Vieira strongly condemned the mistreatment and contempt suffered by the slaves. For his part, in 1707, Fr. Jorge Benci insisted on the "Christian Doctrine masters are obliged to teach their servants": the right to own slaves "ignorant of the Commandments of the Law of God" had as a corollary the duty to supply bread for the captives' body and soul, teaching them the Catholic faith, according to the broad sense taught by Saint Augustine: *panis, ne succumbat*.[155]

A law graduate from Coimbra established in Bahia, Fr. Ribeiro Rocha dedicated part of his "theological-juridical" treatise *Ethiope resgatado* (1758), which sold out in Brazil, to doctrinal edicts on the evangelizing role reserved for slave owners, especially when their slaves came directly from the African hinterlands: "Everything theologians say about the Christian Doctrine, that parents should teach their children, they declare that it is also true for masters regarding their slaves and, specifically speaking, those who came from infidelity [in Africa]." Refuting the belief that slaves seemed wanting in understanding and, for this reason, unable to assimilate Christianity, Fr. Ribeiro Rocha returned to pre-Tridentine doctrine to affirm the magical character of prayer: a parrot taught to pray "miraculously saved its own life by repeating the Hail Mary when a hawk carried it in its claws."[156] If even American birds "miraculously" received the protection of the divine mantle when parroting prayers, then Africans too could develop this skill, all it would take was the diligence and perseverance of their masters. Thus, Jesuit theory of slavery helped to give shape to Luso-Brazilian seignorial patriarchalism.

Confronted with the obstacles to catechesis that the resurgence of native cults, the climate, and the slave trade created in Africa, the Jesuits choose Portuguese America as the main target for their activity in the Atlantic. Later, after the forced retreat from Japan and China and the isolation of missionaries in India and Insulindia, Brazil became the center of the Portuguese Jesuits' enterprise. Evangelization in just one colony, Brazil, explains the complementary, and only apparently conflicting, character of Jesuit policy regarding the bondage of natives on both sides of the South Atlantic. This background defined a second complementary system, which brought together slave production zones in Brazil and slave reproduction zones in Africa.

The Bipolarity of Luso-Brasilic Slavery

Within the unstable Portuguese overseas territory, a mode of exploitation was defined, a mode that yielded close complementarity between the zones of slave production in Brazil, and the zones for the reproduction of slaves in Africa. The following chapter, which diachronically studies the Luso-Dutch conflict, will attenuate doubts that may have persisted from the preceding pages. As they decided to take possession of the Brazilian sugar-producing zones, the Dutch verified and empirically confirmed the bipolarity of the Luso-Brasílico slavery system.

Chapter 6

The War over the Slave Markets

The Thirty Years War gave birth to the upheavals that changed the modern world in Europe and overseas. As Charles Boxer stated, it was the "First World War."[1] Diplomatic volte-faces complicated the conflict's stage after 1640, when Portugal established a truce with the Dutch States-General in order to resist Spain, sought alliances with Richelieu's France, and distanced herself from Cromwell's Britain.[2]

Two counterweights softened the contenders' impetus. On one side, Portugal found herself next door to the enemy, rattled swords with Spain, and was in danger up to 1668, when both Madrid and the Pope finally recognized the Braganza monarchy. Dependent on the stream of trade ships and merchandise hailing from the Netherlands, Lisbon faced an even bigger obstacle: the United Provinces' superiority was crushing, and always had been.[3] On the other side, the Netherlands' mercantile oligarchy, grouped around the territory of the United Provinces and represented in the federative republic governed by the States-General, dealt with contradictory interests. To wage war on Portugal meant to once again lose access to Setubal salt (nearly completely blocked from 1621 to 1641), to the detriment of the Dutch fishing industry, which was active in the Baltic and North Seas.[4] Dried and salted fish was in strong demand, consumed in homes, barracks, and ships. It is worth recalling that in Catholic countries liturgy banned the consumption of red meat, poultry, and eggs on 166 days of the year.[5] The mobility of the religious calendar and the multiplicity of prescriptions interfered with everyday cooking. In his moral essay *Carta de guia de casados* (1651), Francisco Manuel de Mello expresses the doubts of a *fidalgo* who told his servant, before ordering his meals, "Go to the vicar's house and ask him [. . .] if today is a fish or a meat eating day."[6] In this context, salted herring, product of a dynamic industrial transformation, was geared to the international exchanges that made of the United Provinces a leader in per capita commercial activity at the time.[7]

Overseas, however, the picture was different. The States-General gave no quarter, as they set up two trading companies to snatch Portuguese possessions. Peace in

Europe, war overseas.[8] The economic factor prevalent in the conflicts of the time weighed in outside of the Old World. In tune with mercantilist thought, conceiving world riches as limited and territorialized resources, one country could only grow at the expense of another, grabbing productive zones and trade ports from their rivals. "To put oneself in place of the other"—this is the title that Braudel gave to his analysis of the Luso-Dutch conflict.[9] The contention shaped up as a close-quarters dispute the world over. The Dutch appeared as the main and most dangerous enemy to Lisbon because "they are effective in what they undertake, and they endure to overcome difficulties," stated Feliciano Dourado at the Overseas Council. A native of Paraíba, in Brazil's northeast, ex-hostage of the WIC in the United Provinces, ex-diplomat in The Hague, where he lived a long time, Dourado well knew the Netherlanders' determination and will.[10] The Estado da India was declining under the blows delivered by European rivals.[11] The discussions around the Luso-Dutch armistice carried out in 1641 in The Hague began under the impact of Lisbon's disastrous defeat. The Dutch forces had taken Malacca in January 1641, cutting the main artery of Portugal's eastern empire.[12] Two years later, the Braganza Crown took a radical stance. If it came down to choosing between its various possessions to obtain a lasting peace with the Dutch States-General, the diplomats should let Asia go and hold on to Brazil.[13] Seemingly lost in the Indic and Pacific, the war would come to a very different end in the Atlantic.

The Luso-Dutch war in Portuguese America is usually divided in three phases: resistance to the occupation (1630–1637), collaboration with the occupier (1637–1645), and restoration of Portuguese sovereignty (1645–1654). Framed in the transcontinental context of the Ethiopic Ocean, where the conflict found its theater of operations, the study of the war should include two more phases, bracketing the three preceding ones: in the beginning, the Atlantic privateering war (1621–1630) and, at the end, the Portuguese and Brasílico counterattack in Angola (1648–1665). The struggle for the Brazilian slave-based production zones and for the African slave reproduction zones revealed the two poles of the sugar economy.

The African Slave-Trade Crisis and the Amerindian Slave-Trade Cycle

The privateering war, first blow in the Luso-Dutch conflict, began in 1621 with the establishment of the West-Indische Compagnie (WIC) and flowed into the taking of Olinda and Recife in 1630. From the years 1624 and 1625, Portuguese navigation was in disarray with the fall of Bahia, attacks on other ports of the Brazilian coast, and across the ocean, on the African section of the slaving system: Elmina, Benguela, Luanda, Fernando Pó, São Tomé, and Cape Verde.[14]

Portuguese slave ships were attacked on the high seas. Some of the 3,000 slaves sold by the Dutch in the New World between 1619 and 1637, including the first Africans to set foot in Virginia, were prizes looted not from African shores, but from Portuguese ships captured in the Atlantic.[15] Corsairs and pirates repeatedly plundered ships hailing from Africa in the 1640s and 1650s.[16] When Dutch pressure eased, Portuguese and Brasílico slave traders overloaded their vessels in Luanda, causing the death of many Africans on the return voyage.[17] Fresh difficulties cropped up in African ports. Seeking the gold extracted in the Volta River by the Akan peoples, the WIC prowled the Gold Coast from Fort Nassau in Moure.[18] Poorly supplied, the Portuguese fort of Elmina was unable to carry out any *resgates* (enslavements by barter) in the 1630s.[19] São Tomé, base for the re-embarkation of slaves from the whole area, fell into disarray and its contract to collect royal taxes found no bidders after 1627.[20]

Angola faced the Queen Njinga uprising from 1626. Five years later, many hinterland trade fairs were dispersed.[21] Out in the ocean, Cape Verde seemed of little import to Portuguese America, since most of the individuals deported from the archipelago continued to be reserved for the *Asiento*, that is, for the Castilian Indies.[22]

Enemy sea raids, lack of transportation, and the preference for Spanish America enjoyed by the *asentistas* in African ports had generated a demand for captive labor in Brazil beginning in the 1620s. This was the source of the voracity with which the commanders of the Brasílico war stole black slaves from the WIC at the time.[23] In the first forays against the Dutch in Recife, in October 1645, the Portuguese and Brasílicos advanced all the way up to the enemy's fortress walls, driven "by the interest in taking Blacks and in a little pillaging," friar Manuel Calado explained.[24]

Data on the Atlantic slave trade show that the number of Africans introduced into Brazil fell after the WIC occupation of Bahia (1624–1625) and in the first stage of the Dutch war (the privateering war of 1621–1630 and the resistance to the occupation of 1630–1637), increased under Portuguese and Dutch flags in the third phase (collaboration with the occupier—1637–1645), only to decrease shortly thereafter.[25] Yet, as observed previously, illegal voyages from Bahia and Rio de Janeiro introduced Africans into the Río de la Plata, especially in the first three decades of the seventeenth century. Additionally, to avoid higher taxes, vessels leaving Cacheu and Luanda for Spanish America declared Brazilian ports as their destination.[26] Hence, the enslaved disembarkments in Portuguese America were, perhaps, less significant than the estimations of the Trans-Atlantic Slave Trade Database during that period.

The Atlantic disruptions reinvigorated the trade in Amerindian captives. In 1625, Mathias de Albuquerque, governor-general of Brazil, proclaimed a "Just War" against the Potiguar, who dwelled in the Raiz Sierra (in the Paraíba captaincy). With a keen eye on the news, Friar Vicente Salvador wrote, "The just war allowed the taking of slaves [Amerindians], which in Brazil are the soldiers' spoil, as well as their [the troops'] pay."[27] Bahia then tried to widen its access to the continental slave market. In 1626 its municipal council related the damage wrought by the anti-Dutch wars. Shaken by the crisis, the councilors requested São Paulo Indians from the Crown "in order to make up two villages and to have them fetched in two ships."[28]

Wasting no time, Bahian authorities launched their militias against the Gê people on the Paraguaçu River. Thus, the *bandeira* led by Afonso Rodrigues Adorno, Caramuru's great-grandson and relative of Indian hunters, returned in 1628 from Bahia loaded with many tradable Indian slaves, "backland pieces" (*peças do sertão*), thanks to the support of Diogo Luís de Oliveira, the new governor-general who had come to a deal with the slave-hunters.[29]

In this context, the great *bandeira* led by Raposo Tavares was organized in São Paulo. The São Paulo municipal council supported the enterprise, involved as it was in predations on Indian villages. One-third of its members were active in the slave-hunting *bandeiras* launched between 1585 and 1625. Almost every able man, among them relatives of captaincy magistrate Amador Bueno, joined Raposo Tavares.[30] The captaincy's columns, its three wings, plus allied Indians and other Paulista bands, captured thousands of Guarani from the pueblos and *reducciones* of the Jesuitic province of Guayrá in the heart of the present-day state of Paraná in the 1620s.[31] Guayrá and Tapes (in the present state of Rio Grande do Sul), then Spanish territory, had already been raided by *bandeiras* led by brothers Manuel (1606 and 1619) and Sebastião Preto (1612), by Fernão Dias Paes (1623), by Paulo do Amaral, and by Raposo Tavares himself (1627).[32]

At the head of one of the bands, Manuel Preto raided the Guayrá again in 1629. Other *bandeirante* raids, associated to Guayrá Castilians, devastated the province in 1631.[33] Jesuits and the remaining Guarani flew in terror, in a dramatic episode

Paraná historiography dubbed "the great exodus." Some 12,000 Amerindians retreated via the Paranapanema and Paraná Rivers into the Paraná-Uruguay region.[34]

The next target was found in the far west, aimed at the Itatim missions (in the present day state of Mato Grosso do Sul), sacked in 1632–1633.[35] Ten of the twelve Guayrá missions were destroyed.[36] Seeking prey, the Paulistas assaulted Tape *reducciones* and settlements in the southern pampas.[37] Six years later the Tape were also decimated.[38] A notice written twenty years after the events recorded that the Cananéia coast, up until the Patos (stretching over 720 nautical miles of South Brazil littoral), was deserted "because of the São Vicente (Paulista) settlers having gone over to take the Indians who populated it."[39]

Warren Dean observed that the extinction of the indigenous communities who practiced slash-and-burn agriculture (*coivara*), which had been responsible for preserving a sparse jungle configuration for centuries, engendered a reflourishing of the rainforest in some colonial enclaves at the turn of the sixteenth century. Established in the middle of an open savanna, São Paulo village found itself surrounded by bush. The same thing happened in Rio de Janeiro, where settlers received orders to cut down the advancing trees.[40] In the pampas, the disappearance of Amerindian villages caused another ecological phenomenon, with more enduring consequences. Dispersed after the destruction of the Tape, cattle from the Jesuit *reducciones* on the margins of the Ijuí, Ibicuí, and Taquari Rivers (in the present state of Rio Grande do Sul) scattered freely in the region stretching from Laguna (in present-day Santa Catarina) to Montevideo. A huge cattle reserve "that will never be extinguished," as stated by the governor of Colônia do Sacramento in 1694, would be thus constituted in this region, later incorporated into the Atlantic leather market and the meat-consuming markets of Minas Gerais's gold-mining areas.[41]

Paraguayan Jesuits recalled the violence perpetrated in the south a century after the destruction of the Guayrá-Tape, as they were informed of the new configuration of the South American borders on the eve of the Treaty of Madrid (1750). Foreshadowing the anti-Portuguese guerrilla war carried out by the Guarani that shortly followed, the Jesuits warned Madrid of the unfaltering resentment against the Paulistas nurtured by three generations of natives: "The Guarani or Tape Indians hold greater opposition and hatred for the Portuguese than the Spanish hold for the Moors."[42] From then on, the word still used today in Paraguay as a synonym for bandit gained currency—*bandeirante*.

As for the terrestrial slave trade in Africa, figures on the number of enslaved Amerindians are uncertain. Nevertheless, the *bandeirante* raids in the period between

1627 and 1640, concentrated in the Guayrá-Tape zone, are most probably one of the biggest slaving operations of modern history. Where did this multitude of Indians go?

Twentieth-century historians of the Paulistas give two answers to this question. The main thesis sustains the idea that this Amerindian "slaving cycle" responded to a rupture in the Atlantic African slave trade. The second thesis, supported by Taunay—who goes wrong here—states that the majority of the Amerindians captured by the *bandeirantes* were sold to the northern sugar plantations. The late American Brazilian historian John Monteiro questioned Taunay's statement, demonstrating that most of the captives hailing from the south and southwest ended up employed in São Paulo wheat fields, homesteads, and transport. Only an undetermined, but necessarily smaller, number of Amerindians would have been sent to Rio de Janeiro and northeastern sugar mills to fill the voids left by the Atlantic slave trade.[43]

There is no doubt that the establishment of an Amerindian slave trade would have faced the uncertainties of coastal navigation as well as the political hindrances pointed out above: São Paulo Jesuits would not accept the task of seeking Indians in the hinterland to have them deported up north, as requested by the Salvador municipal council. Taunay and other Paulistas authors who have relied on him overestimate the practical consequences of the Bahians' request asking for São Paulo's Indians. Certainly, the Indian presence and workforce in Pernambuco's colonial enclaves was significant, as shown by the documents and also in Franz Post's paintings (1637–1644).[44] Nevertheless, John Monteiro is right: there is no documentary evidence to prove the regular transfer of southern Amerindians into the northeastern sugar mills. Still, I think that the Paulista historiography's main thesis is pertinent. In other words, there is a causal relationship between the disarray of the flow of African slave trade and the *bandeiras* against the Guayrá-Tape.

In fact, the Atlantic thoroughfares' wars reduced both products imported from the mainland and products imported from Africa, that is, workforces for the cultivation of sugar cane and tropical foodstuffs, just at the time when the arrival of Iberian troops increased the demand for rations and victuals in northern markets.[45] From the second quarter of the 1600s, the Bahian government-general became dependent on provisions originating in the south (appendix 2).

São Paulo, a marginal zone in the Atlantic system, developed as a food provider for many colonial settlements, anticipating the analogous process that would drive the reconversion of the Minas Gerais mining economy in the production of food products to Rio de Janeiro and São Paulo at the turn of the eighteenth century. In the second quarter of the seventeenth century, the northeastern and Angolan markets imported from São Paulo products such as lime, manioc, wheat flour, maize, beans, salted meats, lard, sausages, quince preserve, rustic fabrics, and arrow-proof cotton doublets. Except for the lime excavated from the coastal shell mounds (*sambaquis*), the goods were carried down the mountains on Amerindian backs. Inversely, imported goods were carried uphill—always with Amerindian sweat: salt, fabrics, spices, wine, tools, and gunpowder.[46] Such a quantity of goods, such loads, intensified the use of captives in São Paulo, where the average number of Amerindian slaves per owner reached historical highs: 36.6 in the 1640s and 37.9 in the 1650s. These were high rates, even when compared to the areas fed by the African slave trade.[47]

The nexus between the halt in the supply of African slaves and the increase in the demand for aboriginal captives was also sketched out within Dutch Brazil, where the price for Africans doubled during the period. However, the virtual non-existence of indigenous slave trade and the impossibility of wage labor generated a deadlock there: "As the Blacks are now few in this country, the Indians are more sought after for work than before, which is very clear to them; they do not labor if not paid for in advance, and, on having the occasion, they flee and the master loses his payment," wrote Van der Dussen, a WIC councilor.[48] Other clues suggest the emergence of the "Amerindian slaving cycle," according to the term coined by Jaime Cortesão, in the crevices of the European and African trades.

As a matter of fact, both the Mesa de Consciência (the royal tribunal for issues concerning the Church) and the Jesuits recognized the legitimacy of the compulsory employment of Amerindians in royal service—a privilege, by the way, enacted in the Estado do Maranhão 1655 Law on Amerindians, nearly wholly written by Fr. Antônio Vieira.[49] To avoid confrontation with slave owners, the authorities preferred not to request private captives, resorting instead to settled Indians or "colonial Indians," as demonstrated by John Monteiro.[50]

Yet the private demand for slaves voiced by the settlers, and the Crown's demand requested by the authorities, joined together to put pressure on the Indian settlements. Thus, the Rio de Janeiro legislation increased the repression of fleeing Indians captives and forced the Jesuits to lower the wages charged on the hired labor of settlement Indians working for colonists.[51]

The natives did not only work in the settlers' fields.[52] Hinterland transportation; crewing river and coastal canoes; fishing and hunting for the troop's ration;

cattle-raising on Jesuit ranches; felling and preparing wood; services in brick and tile works and on weaving machines; work in the fortresses, palisades, and houses; the opening and maintenance of roads; canoe- and ship-building; stevedore chores; and work aboard ships—all of these and a little more were usually assigned to "public" Amerindians, people enslaved or gathered in the settlements. In São Vicente captaincy, 2,800 Amerindian families—from 11,000 to 14,000 individuals—were employed in the São Paulo, São Miguel, Guarulhos, Pinheiros, and Barueri settlements during the 1640s. A Spanish mineralogist who lived for decades in São Paulo reported in 1636 that the captaincy's settlers possessed around 40,000 Indians slaves.[53] Ten years later, Salvador de Sá endorsed this evaluation, adding that were many carpenters among those Indians.[54] São Paulo, Santana de Parnaíba, and surrounding areas held public and private Amerindians who could be hired to transport cargo and people up or down the mountains.[55] Sérgio Buarque suggests that interests linked to this trade of Amerindians porters could be the origin of the paradoxical disappearance of horse-raising in the Paulista region in the middle of the 1600s.[56]

There is a lack of systematic studies of such different activities, especially shipbuilding. In a time of pirates, corsairs, and sea battles, Amerindian labor helped to replenish the fleet. Aside from the canoe industry, there was a sizeable activity furnishing vessels for the Atlantic trade. Of the nineteen Portuguese vessels captured by the WIC in Luanda Bay (1641), at least seven had been built in the Rio de Janeiro or São Vicente shipyards.[57] Furthermore, *Padre Eterno* was fully built in Rio de Janeiro. A 2,000-ton galleon, prepared to fit 144 cannons and featuring a mainmast made out of a single tree trunk 2.97 meters circumference at the base, she was one of the biggest vessels in the world, and certainly the largest vessel of the Portuguese empire to enter the Tagus.[58] Her fame echoed in Portugal before she left Guanabara. In March that year, Antônio de Sousa de Macedo, state secretary of the Crown, wrote a short notice in his Lisbon monthly gazette *Mercúrio Portuguez* announcing the voyage of the *Padre Eterno*, "the most famous war vessel that the seas have ever seen." When she reached the Lisbon piers on October 20, 1655, the *Padre Eterno* was object of another enthusiastic notice: "In this fleet [from Brazil] came that famous galleon [. . .] the biggest there is today." This prodigy of 1600s naval building, which attracted the admiration and envy of European chanceries, belonged to Salvador de Sá and was made by him on the Guanabara Bay island called since then Galeão (Galleon), site of today's Rio de Janeiro's international airport.

Ultimately, the *Padre Eterno* represented a new conception of the ocean, expressing the Rio de Janeiro oligarchy's ambition. Salvador de Sá intended to face corsairs and storms regardless of the royal fleet's schedule. The seas were converted into a single territory, a single market, dominated by the all-powerful Rio de Janeiro galleon. Such projects may well explain Salvador de Sá's disagreement, expressed since 1655, with the claim of the Companhia Geral do Comércio to seize the vessels sailing between Brazil and Portugal outside of the fleet.[59] Certain pieces of the *Padre Eterno*'s equipment had been made in Britain, from which Salvador de Sá also brought over shipbuilding techniques. But colonial artisans manufactured the largest part of the vessel, and, in particular, the inlaid woodwork and the "golden chapel" that two visiting Italian Capuchins so marveled at.[60] The *Titanic* of the Ethiopic Ocean, the *Padre Eterno* was also defeated by the sea, sinking in the Indian Ocean years later.

From the Rio de Janeiro coast's Ilha Grande shipyard, another famous vessel of the time took the seas, the war frigate *Madre de Deus* (c. 1666).[61] A repair stopover for ships in Bahia Bay along the route between Lisbon and the Indian Ocean represented an important manufacturing activity. The carrack *Nossa Senhora da Conceição* (1686), the first vessel of a series made for the Indian Ocean thoroughfare, was entirely built by the Bahian shipyard.[62] As elsewhere in Brazil, enslaved and coerced Indians were extensively employed as carpenters and lumberjacks and in logging and wood transportation.

Regarding the comparison between Amerindian and African coerced labor at that time, it is worth recalling the price curves for African and black slaves in Bahia elaborated by Stuart Schwartz. Such indices feature two surges in the seventeenth century, the first between 1625 and 1650, in the war context I have just described, and the second at the end of the seventeenth century, when the colonial economy changed from top to bottom. Then, export agriculture increased at the same time as the Minas Gerais gold vortex consumed Africans.[63] Moreover, the series collected by Joseph Miller demonstrates that between the years 1640 and 1650 the differences in the price of slaves in Angola and in Brazil reached the highest level recorded in the century,[64] a trend confirmed by documents from the Overseas Council and the Luanda municipal council.[65] The slave prices registered at the famous Sergipe do Conde sugar mill, situated in Bahia, indicate the impact of each phase of the Dutch War. There is a first high in 1623–1624, as a consequence of the naval offensive that resulted in the taking of Salvador de Bahia; a second high between 1629 and 1631, during the conquest of Pernambuco; a peak in 1633–1634, when the Dutch naval blockade intensified; and a sharp surge from 1646 with the opening of direct hostilities against the WIC forces in Brazil.[66] A 1643 report from the council of finance stated that the invasion of Angola by the WIC caused a sharp rise in slave prices, "while a Black was worth before [the loss of Angola] from 20,000 to 30,000 *réis* in Brazil, there is information they now [are] worth more than 80,000 *réis*."[67] Another index confirming the disruptions of Atlantic exchanges is the rise of sugar freight rates from Brazil to Portugal in the period 1628–1640.[68]

In short, the great Paulista Amerindian overland slave-hunting drive took place when the sequels to the Thirty Years War in the South Atlantic trade doubled the price for Africans in Brazil. Other overseas peoples also ended up being hunted as a result of the interruption in the slave trade.

The labor constraints in Brazil were summarized in the report submitted in 1644 to the Overseas Council by Gaspar de Brito Freire. Knowledgeable about the South Atlantic and a sugar-mill owner in Bahia, he was also influential in Lisbon. To him, Brazil was close to its "total ruin" without Angola's slaves. "The remedy" to the colonists would be the enslavement of the hinterland Amerindians. He recognized, however, that this measure could displease the missionaries and their allies. He therefore recommended that the Crown favor the slave trade in "Mozambique and others regions where this traffic could be made."[69] The two known slaving operations between Mozambique and Brazil during the first half of the seventeenth century took place precisely in 1643 and 1644. Considering the lack of slaves generated by the loss of Luanda, the council of finance consented to the two enterprises.[70] These successful operations were set up by Francisco Fernandes Furnas and Gaspar Pacheco, solid Lisbon merchants whose names figured among the founders and directors of the Companhia Geral do Comércio do Brasil in 1649.[71]

As a matter of fact, the *bandeiras* to enslave the Guarani of the Guayrá-Tape missions appeared as a consequence of the rupture of Brazil's exchanges with Africa and Europe. But they did not constitute a direct response to the fall in the import of Africans into the northeast. Southern Amerindians did not supply the lack of Africans in the north. Instead, they remained captive in São Paulo and Rio de Janeiro, cultivating foodstuffs to replace European, North Brazilian, and Río de la Plata products now lacking in the northeast barracks and colonial enclaves. During the second half of the 1600s, when the Dutch were expelled from Pernambuco and Angola, São Paulo foodstuffs and wheat cultivation stagnated after the demobilization of the Luso-Brazilian troops and the regularization of trade with Lisbon and Luanda.

Ultimately, the Paulistas' historiography is wrong regarding the secondary proposition (the *bandeiras* hunted Amerindians to sell them in the north), but got it right regarding the main thesis (the *bandeiras* were initiated by the rupture in the Atlantic slave trade). Guarani and Kaingang peoples in the south, Tupy and Temimino in the central region, and Aymore, Potiguar, Kariri, and Aruan in the north were enslaved due to the decline in the import of African slaves and European foodstuffs into Brazil. The rupture in regular relations with Lisbon opened the way for the 1600s Brasílicos to take part in the Atlantic market, hunting Amerindians in Paraguay and Africans in West Central Africa at their own initiative. The expression "at their own expense" (*à sua custa*) was often inscribed in the requests that the Brasílicos and the Angolistas sent to Lisbon at that period.

Peruleiros and Bandeirantes

In the first half of the seventeenth century, a new South Atlantic geography emerged, exposing the differences between São Paulo's Amerindian hunters (the *bandeirantes*) and the Bahia and the Rio de Janeiro African slave traders and *peruleiros* (the Portuguese American traders who did business with the Río de La Plata and imported silver from the mines of Potosí). Subequatorial routes dragged Rio de Janeiro closer to sea exchanges and away from the continental economy. The Guanabara Indian-hunting expeditions, still practiced in the second and third decades of the 1600s, were abandoned for shipbuilding, African trading, and exchanges with the Río de la Plata. This reshuffling of southern South America led the Rio de Janeiro maritime, African slave-trading, manioc-food culture, transatlantic network to grow apart from the continental, Amerindian enslavement, maize-food culture, anti-Jesuitical, and antimetropolitan enterprises of the Paulistas. In practice, Rio de Janeiro's Atlantic turn yielded political consequences, as it helped to isolate the autonomism breeding in São Paulo plateau around an economy based on enslaved and coerced Amerindian labor.

Active from the last decades of the sixteenth century, the exchanges between the Río de la Plata and the Guanabara Bay were consolidated by three marriages between the two regions' oligarchies.

Salvador Correia de Sá e Benevides (the younger, 1602–1686), born of a Spanish mother who was the daughter of the governor of Cadiz, was the son and grandson of Rio de Janeiro governors.[72] His grandfather, Salvador Correia de Sá (the elder), governed Rio de Janeiro between 1567 and 1572. In 1586, he was praised by the Crown for opening the exchanges between South Brazil and the Alto Peru and Potosí through the Río de la Plata. Yet in 1595, the elder Salvador was accused of illegally trading slaves "from Angola and other parts" in Buenos Aires.[73] The younger Salvador's father, Martim de Sá, first Rio de Janeiro–born governor, was twice at the head of the captaincy (1602–1608 and 1623–1632). Aware of the Rio de Janeiro–Rio de la Plata business connections, he also sailed from Brazil or Buenos Aires to Angola carrying horses and, most probably, returned with enslaved Africans.[74] He still was governor when his son was elevated to an important position in the Río de la Plata region. By choice of the general-captain Luis Cespedes Xeri'a, his cousin's husband, Salvador Correia de Sá e Benevides took command of the troops pitched against the Paiaguas and Guaicuru communities on the west bank of the Paraguay River, the present-day Chaco of central Argentina. Made colonel of the forces of Upper Paraguay, he attacked the Calchaqui villages and made an alliance with the *encomenderos* pillaging the Christian Indians pueblos.[75] Then Salvador de Sá married Catalina de Velasco, widow of a rich Plate-region Spanish landowner. She was a relative of Juan de Velasco, ex-governor of Paraguay and of Tucuman, nephew of Luis de Velasco, viceroy of Peru. At the same time that Salvador started his political climb, the Benevides (or Benavides) family, his maternal cousins, took prestigious positions in Buenos Aires (see appendix 3).

Juan de Avalos y Benavides, Salvador de Sá's Spanish-Platense cousin, married one of Sá's cousins on his father's side. A captain in the cavalry, Avalos joined Salvador de Sá to crush the 1640 Rio de Janeiro's settler rebellion against the Jesuits and the encyclical in favor of the Indians' freedom.[76] After the proclamation of the Portuguese Restoration (December 1640) and the beginning of the Luso-Spanish war, Avalos remained in Rio. However, after Salvador de Sá's departure to Lisbon in 1643, he fled to Buenos Aires and his Rio de Janeiro properties were confiscated.[77] In that same year, all unmarried Portuguese were expelled from the Río de la Plata to Cordoba and Chile. Illustrating the two communities' ties, the Buenos Aires authorities and population opposed the governor's orders for the expulsion of the married Portuguese and their families established in the area.[78] A harder conflict prevailed in Rio de Janeiro, as witnessed by Juan de Avalos. In a petition to Madrid's Court presented in 1652, his argument was based on his past services in Rio de Janeiro, where he had served the Habsburg Crown for "more than ten years." He pretended to have tried to maintain Rio de Janeiro under Spanish control after 1640, regretting that the Spaniards in the town were few in number. Rio de

Janeiro governor Duarte Correa Vasqueanes (Salvador de Sa's uncle) covered up the flight to Buenos Aires of Avalos and his family aboard a "foreign ship" in 1643. According to him, this was the reason the Braganza Crown dismissed Vasqueanes from his governorship.[79] In parallel with the expulsion of unmarried Portuguese from Buenos Aires, also decided in 1643, the episode indicates a deepening of the rift opened between the two South Americans ports by the Braganza Restoration.[80]

The third significant Iberian marriage relates to Luís Céspedes Xeri'a, nominated captain-general of Paraguay. On his arrival in Rio de Janeiro, he married (1628) Victoria de Sá, niece of Governor Martim de Sá and cousin of Salvador (see appendix 3). In association with his powerful relatives, Xeri'a purchased Rio de Janeiro sugar mills and profited from the captive Guarani brought in by Raposo Tavares and his Paulistas after the pillage of the Guayrá.[81] Xeri'a was associated with both Peruleiros and Paulistas. His properties must have been considerable. The donation made by his widow Victoria de Sá to the São Bento monastery, still towering on the shore of Guanabara Bay, included houses in Rio de Janeiro and three large plantations in Jacarepaguá, which stretched along the coast, reaching as far as Sepetiba, southwest of Guanabara Bay.[82]

Salvador de Sá amassed much property in the Río de la Plata region, adding war booty to his wife's estate. Nominated governor of Rio de Janeiro, he still declared himself to be a Tucuman settler and *encomendero* (landlord and owner of Amerindians).[83] A six-year stay in the Río de la Plata region, a trip to the Potosí mines, and the imbrication of Spanish businesses with his family's Portuguese, Angolan, Brazilian, and Platense businesses lit up in Salvador de Sá a fascination with Peruvian silver, the *peruleiro* spirit that animated greedy Portuguese America colonists.[84]

From Rio de Janeiro, Luanda, or Lisbon, he made many transactions to get hold of Potosí silver. On taking office as governor of Rio de Janeiro (1637), Salvador also held command of the other southern captaincies. On becoming governor, he secured one of the most lucrative public concessions in Brazilian history. Thanks to a perpetual authorization by the municipal council, he obtained for himself and his heirs the monopoly on the weighing and stocking of sugar exported from Rio de Janeiro. Only 200 years later, in 1850, was the Brazilian government able to revoke, in exchange for a rich compensation, the Sás' rights on the shipments of goods in the Guanabara port.[85]

Salvador took office again as governor of Rio de Janeiro in 1647–1648 and from 1658 to 1661. His granduncle, Duarte Correia Vasqueanes, closely associated with his grandnephew's maneuvers in Portugal and the South Atlantic, was

Rio de Janeiro governor many times (1632–1633, 1642, 1644, 1645–1648).[86] It was Duarte who promptly arranged help in the preparations for the 1648 Angola expedition. One of Salvador's sons, João Correia de Sá, would become field-master of the Rio de Janeiro regiment and provisional governor in 1661. Salvador Correia Vasqueannes, son of Duarte, commanded an infantry company in Rio until 1640, and, later, a cavalry company on the Alentejo front in the war against Spain. He was given the post of flagship captain of the 1648 force task against the Dutch in Luanda, and was made sergeant-major in retaken Angola.[87] His son, Martim Correia Vasqueannes, was a Rio de Janeiro sergeant-major for a long time. Likewise a relative of the Sás, Tomé Correia de Alvarenga twice obtained the interim government of Rio de Janeiro (1657–1659 and 1660). Another cousin of Salvador de Sá, Pero de Souza Pereira, held the post of superintendant of finance in the city. In the so-called "Cachaça riot" (1660) that shook Guanabara Bay, as we will see below, the rebels had harsh words for the Sás and their allied families, "who are as closely blood-related as they are alike in tyranny, as close relatives as united in the violence with which they govern."[88]

Vast properties in Rio de Janeiro city and captaincy belonged to the Sás. It is their name that appears at the foot of the old ligations on land properties in Campos de Goitacazes and Barra da Tijuca, whose appeals are still crawling through the maze of today's Carioca tribunals.[89]

The whole of this oligarchic power was coupled to the Rio–Luanda–Buenos Aires triangle, the base of a mercantile network whose activity both interested and concerned Lisbon, Seville, and Iberian merchants in Asia. Although it also sought to reopen access to Peruvian silver after the Braganza Restoration, the Crown feared that Salvador de Sá—attracted by honors, profits, and family links—would defect to the Spanish camp. A report on the situation of the Braganza power overseas suggested that trusted Jesuits should secretly contact Salvador, promising honors in exchange for loyalty to King João IV.[90] Two days after news of the Braganza restoration reached Guanabara's shores, Salvador de Sá secretly dispatched a ship loaded with twenty soldiers to Buenos Aires, presumably to feel out the political situation in the Río de la Plata region and to take away his belongings, before news of the rupture between the two Iberian powers reached the city.[91] Named Rio de Janeiro governor, Francisco Souto Maior (1644–1645) came from Bahia aware of the insurrectional ambiance created in Rio by the cessation of the trade with Luanda and the Río de la Plata.[92] Writing to the Crown a memorial contrary to the Angola expedition and to the reengagement of the Luso-Dutch hostilities in the South Atlantic, Souto Maior warned the Crown of possible pro-Spanish maneuvers by Salvador de Sá, "covetous of property and a great merchant." After the task force left Guanabara to attack Luanda (May 1648), the governor–general count of Villa Pouca did not hesitate to proclaim Duarte Vasqueanes, who had replaced his nephew Salvador de Sá at the head of the Rio de Janeiro government, an "arisen" rebel.[93] Nevertheless, the Sás' power remained intact until the Rio de Janeiro uprising of December 1660, now called "the Cachaça Riot" and studied in the next chapter. In the official correspondence of the end of the 1650s, governor-general Francisco Barreto still sounded very deferential to the members of the Sá oligarchy.[94]

Gradually, the hegemony of the Guanabara port took form. Signaling the intensification of the movement of passengers bustling through the port, in 1645 the municipal council set the transportation tariffs for whites ("for each White passenger with his/her box, basket and bed") and of enslaved blacks traveling north (Espírito Santo, Bahia, and Pernambuco), south (Ilha Grande and São Vicente), and overseas (Azores, Madeira, and the mainland).[95] Cut off by the Serra do Mar cliffs, Rio de Janeiro consolidated its oceanic vocation, reaffirmed in the eighteenth century by its position as a node in the Minas Gerais trade circuit and as capital city of the vice-kingdom (1763). Such a circumstance would ease the territorial consolidation of Brazil's central government after the 1822 Independence: two-thirds of Brazil's foreign trade passed through Rio de Janeiro in the nineteenth century. Well into the twenty century, when Santos took the lead, Guanabara Bay still held its position as the main Brazilian port.

In the second half of the 1600s, the Lisbon and Rio de Janeiro's strategy of aggregating Africans with silver—from its Angola and Río de la Plata tributary zones—unfolded in several steps: the Luso-Fluminense expedition to reconquer Angola (1648); the foundation of Laguna in the south of present-day state of Santa Catarina (1674); the creation of the Rio de Janeiro bishopric, with its jurisdiction reaching as far as the Río de la Plata (1676); the royal donation to Salvador de Sá and his sons, granting coastal leagues reaching as far as the Río de la Plata (1676); and finally, the foundation of the Sacramento Colony at the mouth of the Río de la Plata as a base for the smuggling of the silver from Potosí (1680).

Parallel to Rio de Janeiro's Atlantic drive, Lisbon took action to halt Paulista autonomism. Santos and the southern coast were subjected to the Rio de Janeiro government (1698), the captaincy of São Paulo and Minas de Ouro was created (1709), the Paulistas were defeated in the War of the Emboabas (1709–1711), the

Crown purchased the captaincies of Santos and São Vicente from their donatories (1712), Minas Gerais formed a captaincy of its own (1720), the Paratí gold-trail terminus was removed from São Paulo and annexed to the Rio de Janeiro captaincy (1726), Goiás and Mato Grosso also gained autonomy (1648), and eventually, the very government of São Paulo became, for a while, an administrative dependency of Rio de Janeiro (1748–1765).[96] The demand for slaves generated in Minas Gerais supplied precious metal and led to the gradual abandonment of the Sacramento Colony. However, as the Minas Gerais magnet was deactivated in the last quarter of the eighteenth century, the Guanabara slave traders reestablished the Luanda–Rio de Janeiro–Buenos Aires trade triangle.[97]

Another link with the Río de la Plata region and Alto Peru was consolidated in São Paulo. Contrary to the Rio de Janeiro–Buenos Aires "peruleiro" axis, linked to sea routes and to the African slave trade, the Paulista-Platense link was grounded on terrestrial exchanges and on the trade of Amerindians employed in regional production.[98]

Amerindian Captivity and Paulista Autonomism

In the 1620s and 1630s, Spanish Castilian and Paraguayan families, some of whom were linked to the Paulistas, converged on São Paulo and mingled with locals.[99] Associated to Paraguay by kinship and by trade, the Paulistas—to the amazement of the Crown and the Castilian missionaries—also joined with Spaniards when launching assaults on the *reducciones*.[100] Inquisitorial agents launched accusations of Judaism against the Paulistas from 1620 on, illustrating the instrumental character of the Inquisition in the exercise of the Crown's power.[101] The episode is part of the wider framework of the anti-Jewish persecution launched in Asia and America as a reprisal against the growing influence of the Portuguese New Christian bankers in Madrid.[102]

At the end of the following decade, Jesuits and royal authorities came down hard on the subversive connection between man-hunters and slave-based planters in the Iberian colonies. Subsequent to Father Montoya's journey to Madrid, in 1638, where he complained against the "pirates" who came from São Paulo to enslave the Paraguayan converted Indians, King Felipe IV called for the arrest of Raposo Tavares and his fellow *bandeirantes*, who attacked the Guayrá.[103] Determined to instill "more terror, more authority and respect, and efficiency" in the laws against Amerindian captivity, the Spanish Crown sought to open a tribunal of the Inquisition in Rio de Janeiro, even though the enslavement of Amerindians did not constitute a crime fit to be judged by inquisitorial tribunals.[104] In parallel, the Complicidad Grande proceeding (1635–1639), culminating in a great auto-da-fé, was taking place in Lima. Among the accused, 57 Portuguese, mostly merchants, were condemned for the crime of Judaism.[105] The Spanish grip on São Paulo tightened. The authorities demonized the *bandeirantes*, accusing them of Judaism, while the Holy Office intended to set up a tribunal in the region.

The Paulistas soon responded. In July 1640, the Jesuit maneuver to enforce the encyclical against Amerindian enslavement, secured by the Jesuits from Pope Urban VIII, sparked mutinies in Rio, São Vicente, and São Paulo. Settlers in the latter two cities reached a compromise with the priests and with Salvador de Sá, protector of the Company of Jesus.[106] The understanding was that the Jesuits would supervise only the settlements, would return to their proprietors the Amerindians who had fled, and would not meddle with captive Amerindians in private houses and private farms.[107] But the Paulistas rejected any compromise, even when threatened by Salvador de Sá's militia, which arrived by sea in Santos.[108]

This was the state of affairs were when news of the ascension to the throne of duke of Braganza reached São Paulo. The alleged "Acclamation" of Amador Bueno as "King of São Paulo" was have then taken place. Setting aside the nationalist fictions later elaborated around this pseudo-event, the antimetropolitan movement in the captaincy deserves closer examination. Contrary to royal orders issued in 1643 and 1647, the Paulista municipal council remained in an insurrectional state up to 1654, maintaining the banishment of the Jesuits, the confiscation of their property, and control over the settlements. The seriousness of the Paulista effrontery can be gauged by the discussions at the Lisbon Court about a project involving the immigration of Irish nationals to Brazil.

Following the defeat of their rebellion against the earl of Carlisle, lord proprietor of the island, 400 Catholic Irish in Saint Christopher (Saint Kitts) Island, in the Lesser Antilles,[109] requested in 1643 a license from the Lisbon Crown to move down to Maranhão. The project was turned down, but six years later the same group presented a new petition. Now the Irish intended to move to São Paulo, which was met with a fresh refusal by the Overseas Council. Indeed, the councilors claimed that the São Paulo captaincy settlers—"strong and impregnable"—had expelled the Jesuits and were still rebellious against the Crown, despite a royal amnesty. In such circumstance, the Irish immigration would spark a "continuous civil war" in the area, creating serious complications.[110]

With regard to another immigration flux, that of the Paraguay Spaniards, who arrived in São Paulo in the 1620s and 1630s and were eventually involved in the legendary April 1641 Paulista independence movement, Taques states that it was suspected that these families were "involved in *lèse-majesté* crimes that have forced them to such transmigration."[111] Would they be New Christian families and similar persons exposed to the Asunción Inquisitorial commissariat after the Paulistas offensive against the Guayrá? I think so[112]—certainly so: Amador Bueno, one of the main Paulista citizens and leader of the 1641 São Paulo autonomist movement, belonged to an old Sephardic family. Such persons were in a delicate position when the news of the Portuguese Restoration broke in São Paulo. Threatened by Castilian authoritarianism, they also had reason to fear the new Braganza dynasty. As subjects of the Spanish Crown, their property in São Paulo would be confiscated as a consequence of the war between the two Iberian capitals.[113] Thus, it was in their interest to escape both Portuguese and Spanish sovereignty. This gives the Paulista uprising of the 1640s a wider, anti-Iberian significance.

Reliant on Amerindian captives, the captaincy's colonists thought they had enough reason to rebel. In the wake of the anti-Jesuit uprising, the memorial that Amador Bueno took to the Court curtly states that the Jesuits "surreptitiously have impetrated a *brevis* [a directive] by His Holiness, . . . to deprive and exploit the settlers of their immemorial and most ancient possession [of Amerindians], which they have held from the foundation of this Estado [do Brasil] to the present day; without which they cannot and will not sustain and preserve [themselves], and from which results big increases to the aforementioned Estado, and to Your Majesty's royal Treasury." Much said in a few words. The captaincy depended on the captivity that could not be questioned because it was "immemorial and most ancient." Moreover, the natives' freedom would ruin the colonists, the colonial settlement, and the very Royal Treasury.[114] Supporting the Jesuits' removal, the Paulista municipal council underlined the "great subsidies in flour, vegetables, and meats" sent to Bahia for the sustenance of the troops fighting the Dutch, thus expecting both due recognition from the Crown and orders for the governors of Brazil not to ill-treat those who aided them.[115]

The use of settled Indians alone allowed for the production of wheat, meats, and food for the succor of Brazil and even Angola, reasoned another São Paulo municipal council memorandum.[116] On their side, the Jesuits protested to the Crown in 1646 against their expulsion and the confiscation of their churches and property "by men known to be criminals," who "captivate and sell free men against the divine and human laws."[117] That same year the São Paulo revolt spread to Santos, where the Paulistas also attacked and expelled the Jesuits. In a report about the São Paulo situation commissioned by the Crown in 1647, Salvador de Sá, who was close to the Society of Jesus, listed the Paulista excesses. To preserve the captive Amerindians, they had expelled the Jesuits, "operating in everything as if they were a free Republic, independent" from the government-general. Despite the seriousness of these felonies, Salvador recommended the concession of an amnesty to avoid the worst. Fearful of punishment, the Paulistas could betray King João IV and defect to the Spanish side.[118]

Lasting until 1654, the Paulista rebellion unveiled the anger created by the embargo on Amerindian captivity. The defense of Amerindians' freedom was not the only spark of the troubles. Resentment against the Jesuits grew as they appropriated the property of heirless deceased colonials and the lands of villages abandoned by the Native Americans. The Paulista memorial of 1642 stated that the Jesuits had acted with prepotency after enriching themselves at the settlers' expense.

Even in the areas where the S.J. willingly accepted slavery, and even had a stake in the slave trade, as in Upper Guinea, Angola, and Mozambique, the Jesuits were usually charged with cupidity. "Because of these and other reasons," warned an Angola governor in 1678, "the priests of the Company are abominable and odious; and for that reason are not admitted in various parts of our kingdom."[119] And it was not only the laity who complained. Franciscans, Benedictines, and Carmelites in Brazil; Paraguayan bishops; Congo Capuchins; Dominicans in China; Franciscans in Japan; and the priests of India also lashed out at Jesuit greed.[120]

Muted in Africa and the northeast, loud in Maranhão and in Asia, anti-Jesuit resentment assumed an insurrectional bias in south Brazil due to the strong demand for Amerindian coerced labor in the São Paulo plateau. A report written by the Franciscans reported that the 1640 Paulista uprising resulted from a disagreement about the tutelage of Amerindians, from the growing power of the Company of Jesus, and from the prosecution of Raposo Tavares and Paulo do Amaral, commanders of the Guayrá pillage, by the S.J. Altogether, the 1640 anti-Jesuit mutiny, the 1641 Amador Bueno antimetropolitan movement, and the fourteen-year-old rebellion against pro-Jesuit Crown orders revealed the autonomism empowered in São Paulo by the concentricity of the exploitation (through local farms) of Amerindian slaves and the reproduction of Amerindian slaves (through local *bandeiras*). As examined in chapter 1, another episode of the colonial deadlock thus took form regarding similar situations in the Amazon region, in Peru, in Angola, and in Mozambique.

The southern Indian hunters were made safe against Felipe IV's henchmen with the crowning of King João IV in December 1640. In need of *bandeirantes* and their bowmen to protect Portuguese sovereignty in south Brazil, Lisbon granted amnesty to the Paulistas guilty of the crime of capturing Amerindians, or, according to the formula coined by Salvador de Sá, Paulistas involved in "crimes committed in the backland raids [*nas entradas dos sertões*]."[121] In the meantime, the *bandeirantes*' Spanish accomplices were punished by Felipe IV. Río de la Plata officers were incarcerated, and Luís Céspedes Xeri'a lost his positions in Paraguay and ended up being sentenced by the Charcas Tribunal (present-day Sucre, in Bolivia).[122]

The biggest hindrance to Paulista activity was posed by the resistance of the *reducciones*. Better informed, the Spanish Jesuits organized their fighting force in the middle 1630s, this time forewarned and wielding firearms.[123] Nicknamed "the Tiger," Fernando Camargo commanded a *bandeira* that was routed in Caaguá in 1635, in the Laguna hinterland. Other *bandeiras* led by André Fernandes (1637), by Pedro Leite Pais (1638), by Domingos Cordeiro (1639), and by Jerônimo Pedroso de Barros (1641) each met defeat when they clashed with Jesuit-led Guarani warriors.[124]

The biggest of these debacles hit Paulistas hard. A fierce battle raged for a whole week in March 1641 on the banks of the Mbororé River, tributary of the Uruguay River. There, 300 Paulistas and 600 allied Tupi archers and *zagaia* lancers led by Jerônimo Pedroso were defeated by 4,000 Guarani fighters commanded by Spanish Jesuit Domingos de Torres, a former military man. In addition to this skilled commander, the Guarani relied on 300 firearms, among them small campaign cannons dubbed *tacuaras*. Made of bamboo tightly wrapped in leather straps, such weapons discharged rounds of shot that wrought great damage among the attackers.[125] Actually, the *tacuaras* appear as a Jesuit and Guarany version of the "leather cannons" celebrated for their use as mobile artillery in Gustav Adolph's Swedish army in the Polish campaign (1628–1629).[126] Against the Paulistas, who faced cannonades for the first time, the *tacuaras* seem to have been very effective.

Bandeirante bands still roamed the south after the Mbororé disaster. Nonetheless, most switched from seeking southern Guarani captives to hunting the midcountry Tupi and the midwest Temininos. They left the Guayrá zone for the then so-called "Sertão do Parapuava" (Araguaia and Tocantins Valleys) and the western banks of the São Francisco River.[127] There were also changes in the preparation of the post-Mbororé *bandeiras*. Big expeditions, such as those launched against the Guayrá and the Tape, were abandoned in favor of smaller groups, better equipped with firearms, and more concerned with capturing Amerindians for use in their own fields than for the slave trade.[128] In the second half of the seventeenth century, when the African trade into Brazil was reactivated, the *bandeirantes* left the south to become Indian killers in the north. As we shall see below, employed by planters, ranchers, and authorities in Bahia, Pernambuco, Ceará, and Piauí, they launched extermination raids against Amerindian communities who halted the advance of cattle-raising and against maroon villages (*quilombos*) threatening plantations.

The Amerindian hunters' setbacks in the south coincided with the opening of hostilities between the two Iberian capitals in the 1640s. Portugal had to avoid an intensification of the Luso-Spanish conflict in the Plata region, as it was attacked in Asia and Africa, in addition to having the mainland invaded by Castilian troops. When, in 1644, the Overseas Council examined Salvador de Sá's plan to seize Buenos Aires, the councilors disapproved of the initiative. In their judgment, "It seems that is not convenient, in such difficult times, to resort to fresh conquests."[129] Times were indeed difficult. Beside troubles in Europe and in the East, the picture grew darker in the Atlantic.

Several setbacks hit the Portuguese overseas territories during 1641. After the fall of Malacca (January), in August, when at the same time that Jerônimo Pedroso's *bandeirantes*, routed in Mbororé, beat a retreat from the colonists' Southern America slave reserve, Angola's governor, Pedro César de Menezes, abandoned Luanda under the fire of the WIC's invading fleet. The other Atlantic slave reserve again came to the fore: West Central Africa. The control of the Mina Coast, of the Congo watershed, and Angola came to polarize Luso-Dutch hostilities in the West.

The War for Africans

Some authors, influenced by a Weberian interpretation of history, have elaborated a comparison between the Dutch colonial enterprise and Portuguese America. On the one hand, there was Dutch semiprivate, capitalistic, and allegedly "rational" colonization, and on the other, the "bureaucratic and aristocratic" colonization, said to be economically irrational, practiced by the Portuguese. In fact, Max Weber himself defined the Iberian empires as related to the "feudal type," while their Dutch and English counterparts were otherwise "capitalistic."[130] On closer examination, however, the distinctions between the two approaches were less sharply defined.

The end of the Twelve Years' Truce (1609–1621) rekindled Spanish-Dutch hostilities and denied access of the States-General to Iberian colonial merchandise.

Like its older sister, the East India United Company (Vereenidge Oost-Indische Compagnie [VOC]), established in 1602 to exploit Asian markets, the West-Indische Compagnie (WIC) was founded in 1621 also with the double intent of making war and engaging in trade.[131] Nonetheless, the WIC never enjoyed the scope and resources at the disposal of the VOC.[132] Deemed dubious, the WIC attracted few important investors, and its capital had to be completed with public funds.[133] Soon, the conquest of sugar zones in Brazil pushed the WIC into a series of impasses.

In light of Dutch strategy, the Portuguese Atlantic trade ports in Brazil and West Central Africa were featured as joint objectives. Such was the battle plan of 1624–1625, leading to the seizure of Bahia and the naval blockade of Benguela and Luanda. In the same year of 1625, on the shores of Elmina, 50 Portuguese and 900 Akans beheaded 450 of the WIC's sun-stricken soldiers. The defeat would tone down the Dutch impetus in Africa.[134] The second campaign hit the target in 1630 with the capture of Olinda and Recife. In 1635 the Pernambucan coastal area (Zona da Mata) fell into WIC hands. In the wake of the combat, the Dutch discussed the alternatives that opened up with their victory.

Often, the Compagnie hesitated between monopoly and freedom of trade, between pillaging of the Caribbean seas and the establishment of a colonial enclave in Pernambuco. The dilemma was recurrent. Favorable to a colony of Dutch free burghers in the east, Jan Coen, Dutch governor of Insulindia, clashed with VOC directors, who sought to skim quick profits off their conquests.[135] Economic policy and colonial strategy mixed with one another. Nominated in 1636 for the recently created position of governor (Statthalter) of the Dutch territory in Brazil (named New Holland), Johan Maurits von Nassau-Siegen saw free trade as a necessary condition for luring northern European colonists so as to secure lasting possession of the territories snatched from Portuguese America.[136]

In 1638, an intermediate compromise was reached. The WIC held the monopoly in navigation, the slave trade, brazilwood, and the sale of ammunition, leaving the remainder of the export-import trade open to the inhabitants of the United Provinces.[137] The sugar mills started grinding cane afresh, leading the WIC to set its eyes on the African slave trade.

Nassau-Siegen: "Humanist Prince" and Slave Trader[138]

Intent on consolidating productive areas, Nassau-Siegen sold to Dutch and Portuguese settlers in Pernambuco the sugar mills and slaves previously confiscated from Portuguese proprietors who had fled to Bahia and Rio de Janeiro.[139] His first report to the WIC's directors' board in Amsterdam, issued in 1638, compiled the rules of the "Great Game" between the Portuguese and the Dutch for supremacy in the Ethiopic Ocean.

Nassau-Siegen listed the 150 sugar mills under his control. He emphasized the main obstacle: the lack of colonists, and, particularly, of Low Countries colonists. Further, it was not any old *gueux*, any ragged Flanders pauper, who was fit to be a colonist in New Holland. Candidates should above all have at their disposal capital and the means to invest in tropical production. "In order to make the factory they need, for it cannot be brought over from Holland as it is needed here, and to buy some Negroes, without whom nothing of value can be made in Brazil," the governor emphasized, "There necessarily must be [African] slaves in Brazil, and in no way they can be done without. If someone is offended by this, it will prove a useless scruple [. . .] It is much needed that all the appropriate means are employed in the related trade of the African Coast."[140]

Another report, written in 1640 by Van der Dussen, the WIC's councilor in Brazil and former VOC agent in the Moluccan Islands, a practical man in the tropics and influential politician in Rotterdam, reiterated that the Dutch colonists should set capital aside for the purchase of Africans. His original and innovative proslavery argument deserves attention: "Without Negroes nothing can be cultivated here, and no White—no matter how well disposed to work he may have been in the homeland—can dedicate himself in Brazil to such labors, nor can he bear them; it seems that the body, as a consequence of such an extreme climate change, loses much of its stamina; this takes place not only with the man, but also with everything that comes from Europe to Brazil, including iron, steel, copper etc., and I do not refer to those things more subject to deterioration."[141] Van der Dussen puts forward one of the first allegedly scientific justifications, if not the first, for the deportation of Africans into tropical America. Ideological, economic, and cultural statements legitimated the trade in Africans. Still, Van der Dussen went further as he referred to the normative framework that has informed Western knowledge in the centuries of the bourgeois revolution. His defense of African slavery and the slave trade follows from a supposed general principle, the desubstantiation of matter and of white European men transported to tropical Brazil.

European settlers and capital plus tropical soil and agricultural techniques ("for it cannot be brought over from the Netherlands as it is needed here") plus African labor—the WIC agents recapitulated the full equation elaborated by Iberians in the 1500s with the intent of exploiting the Atlantic Islands, the Caribbean, and

South America. Whence Nassau-Siegen's tirade: "The Portuguese say, in the form of an adage: 'he who wishes to take Brazil away from Brazil, must bring Brazil into Brazil,' that is, whoever hopes to make fortune and amass good capital in Brazil must bring over a considerable capital to Brazil."[142]

Johan Maurits von Nassau-Siegen (1604–1679), northern European, director of a powerful semiprivate company, born into Protestant ethics and the spirit of capitalism, radically enlightened, did not hesitate to endorse the postulate elaborated a century previously by the Catholic and bureaucratic merchants of inquisitorial Portugal. Actually, to bring Brazil over to Brazil was, to a good measure, to bring Angola over, to bring Angolans to Brazil's sugar planters.[143] In the free air of Dutch urban society, Spinoza conceived the thesis of atheistic humanism that would be crushed at birth by the Inquisition in Portugal, land of his parents. On leaving the Netherlands, Nassau-Siegen, the humanist prince, governed a Portuguese colonial enclave (1637–1644); his methods of exploitation induced him to sweep away the "useless scruple" of his fellow-countrymen to incorporate slavery into the economic calculations of the Amsterdam burghers. Primitive accumulation carved its niche in the social regression imposed on the center of advanced capitalism by the Portuguese overseas periphery.[144] In a book published for the tercentennial of Nassau-Siegen's death (1979), the authors did not mention his African slave-trading militancy, an essential component of Dutch modernity. The matter was addressed in a later book in honor of Nassau-Siegen, which restates the control of Brazil and Angola as the main objective of the WIC offensive in the South Atlantic.[145]

Once the need for the slave trade was admitted, there was still the transatlantic network of purchase, feeding, transport, and sale of Africans to be built up. Dutch vessels had bartered African goods to be sold in Europe (gold, copper, ivory, musk, ebony, melegueta pepper) in ports of Senegambia, the Gulf of Guinea, and in the Congo delta since the end of the 1500s. All this exchange with Africa, an average of twenty ships per year, was incorporated into the WIC's monopoly. Compagnie directors and the States-General discussed the legitimacy of slavery and slave trade. The possession of captives was banned in Dutch European territory at the end of the sixteenth century (it is worth remembering that Portugal would only do the same in the second half of the eighteenth century). Since 1623, in one of the first board meetings of the WIC, there were concerns over the moral legitimacy of the trade in enslaved Africans.[146] Doubts about the matter persisted within the States-General and even in Johan Maurit's circle in The Hague, such as the philosophical remorse of his biographer and friend, former pastor Caspar Barlaeus.[147]

Did such scruples embarrass the Compagnie's regular exchange with African ports of trade? It does not seem so. In no instance after 1623, except for a single exception, did the WIC's commanders cease to take advantage of the "pieces" captured aboard Portuguese and Brasílico slavers, selling them off to the Virginia and Caribbean English, or else making use of such captives themselves in Pernambuco. In practice, the Compagnie's slaving activities were delayed for a more trivial reason: the Dutch did not yet know how to deal in slaves in Africa.

The African slave trade demanded specific and appropriate vessels, African ports, food, and merchandise. It also depended on contact with African agents and even some knowledge of Portuguese, a lingua franca operating in Africa's trading ports. This is why, in the first slaving voyages, the WIC resorted to Brasílico and Luso-African agents on both sides of the Atlantic.[148] With the agreement of the Compagnie and the support of her trading post in Moure (Gold Coast), Nassau-Siegen launched a fleet from Recife in 1637 to capture Elmina, take the regional gold trade, and solve the problem of the lack of slaves in New Holland.

This time the Dutch did better than in 1625 and managed to secure a lasting foothold on the Mina Coast, where they remained until 1872. A few months later the Compagnie set up trading ports in Mpinda, in the Soyo kingdom, below the Congo delta, and in Loango, farther north. In contrast with the other Dutch brokers operating in the area, whose task was restricted to the exchange of ivory and Congo copper, the director sent to Loango had precise orders to engage in the slave trade. He took two Portuguese translators with him.[149] As noted above, mixed with Kimbundo and Kikongo, the Portuguese language was the region's trade language. The same process took place in India and in Insulindia, where Portuguese incorporated Tamil, Malay, and Arabic terms. In the following year the WIC shipped out its first load of slaves bought from African middlemen. From Alladah (Benin), Warri (the Niger delta), Calabar, and Cameroon, 2,400 Africans were deported to Pernambuco. The ivory and gold traded at Elmina, after a stopover in Recife, was carried to the States-General Amsterdam storehouses.[150] The WIC's African activities found greater stability after the nomination in Benin of a factor commissioned to stimulate the deportation of Africans.[151] With the trade of the living set up, the Dutch took the lead offered by the Luso-Brasílicos. It would be so successful that the WIC soon abandoned control over inert merchandise and Atlantic thoroughfares, but kept the monopoly on the slave trade until 1730—nearly the date of its demise. The WIC episode in Brazil and Angola taught the Dutch about Atlantic African traffic and slave plantations, experience that was useful in the Caribbean and in the nutmeg slave plantations in the Banda Islands, under VOC control.[152]

The confusion embedded in the Dutch-Portuguese Truce signed in 1641 opened an opportunity for the WIC to continue its assault on the Portuguese Atlantic. King João IV would only enforce the armistice signed in the document after ratification of the Treaty. As the Crown waited for months before he finally did so, Nassau-Siegen was encouraged by his bosses to consolidate his position in the Ethiopic Ocean.

A revealing disagreement between the Statthalter and the Amsterdam WIC board emerged from the Portuguese hesitation. Uneasy about the vulnerability of the Dutch settlement in Recife, the Heeren XIX estimated that the offensive's target should be Bahia, the main anti-WIC citadel. Nassau-Siegen was of a different opinion. Realizing that Mpinda and Elmina could not manage to properly supply Pernambuco with slaves, the Statthalter left Bahia aside and launched his vessels on the economic pole complementary to New Holland, that is, on the biggest Atlantic slave-trade port—Luanda.[153] Not waiting for metropolitan endorsement, Nassau-Siegen submitted his justifications after the task force of nineteen vessels and 1,950 soldiers left Recife to seize Angola. Like Salvador de Sá and other Iberian authorities and merchants, Nassau-Siegen had a global view of Angola's role in the world-economy. His justifications were clear. Luanda was the chosen target because it constituted Africa's main slave market. Without it, the cultivation of sugar cane in Brazil seemed impossible. Besides, Spain would also be hit, as the Peruvian mines would devalue if Felipe IV was unable to buy slaves from Angola to exploit the Peruvian silver.[154]

Luanda, Benguela, and the satellite ports of São Tomé and Ano Bom fell into Dutch hands between August and November, 1641. In the same offensive, Maranhão was invaded.[155] After setting foot in West Central Africa—placing a fait accompli before the WIC—Nassau-Siegen tried to institutionalize the complementarity between Brazil and Angola. Indeed, he maneuvered so that Angola, as well as São Tomé and Ano Bom, would be "annexed to and subject to" his Recife government.[156] He reasoned that if the trade was carried out with Brazil, it fell on the Pernambuco Dutch, already acclimatized to the tropics, to administer and defend Angola. But the Compagnie directors refused the proposal and decided that the Heeren XIX delegates commissioned by the States-General would direct Angola.[157] Barlaeus suggests that Amsterdam's merchants, opposed to bilateral exchanges between the Dutch merchants in Pernambuco and Luanda, vetoed Nassau-Siegen's proposal.¹⁵⁸ Two administrative districts were created. The first covered the Gulf of Guinea trading posts and was submitted to the Dutch Elmina fortress's director. The other, based in Luanda, encompassed the Congo and Angola.¹⁵⁹

The capture of the two poles of the plantation economy—the South American slave-based production zones and the African slave reproduction zones—was indispensable for setting up the sugar industry.¹⁶⁰ Nassau-Siegen was emphatic: without the slave trade and Angolan ports, Dutch Brazil would be "useless and bear no fruits to the Compagnie."¹⁶¹ Other Dutch texts repeated the same idea. "There is a strong inter-relationship between the slave trade, New Holland and the advance of the WIC in Africa," concludes Johannes M. Postma, author of an authoritative book on the Dutch slave trade.¹⁶² The regional distribution of WIC personnel in Brazil and West Africa between 1642 and 1645 underlines the Luso-Dutch confrontation over the plantation–slave trade axis. Brazil (4,000) and Angola (650) had many more of the Compagnie's servants than São Tomé (300) and Gold Coast (220).¹⁶³

Once the enclaves on both sides of the Atlantic had been conquered, it remained for the Compagnie to adapt to the management of the slave trade. However, this was hardly successful. Indeed, rejection of the WIC in Brazil resulted, in a large measure, from inadequate coordination of the binary slave-based production and slave trade. Simplifying the phases of the conflict, one can say that the Portuguese were dogmatic in religious affairs, but unorthodox in economic matters. The Dutch were the opposite—relatively tolerant in religious affairs, they were tough with the debt-ridden sugar planters.¹⁶⁴ Half a century later, Fr. Antonio Vieira wrote to the count of Ericeira: "They [the Dutch] had never had skills to deal in Blacks, nor plantations, or sugar mills, and without the Portuguese planters they were unable extract profit from that land [Pernambuco]."¹⁶⁵

Colonial Planters versus European Shareholders

Because of the slow turnover of invested capital, the hazards of weather and sugar-cane fields, as well as the fluctuation in slave and sugar prices, the sugar-mill owners' indebtedness was one of plantation economy's constants. Further, the sale of Africans on credit—preferably in exchange for the sugar to be produced—constituted the usual Portuguese pattern. The practice evolved into a restriction on the creditors' right over the property pawned by the sugar planter. Hypothecary executions of sugar mills had not been allowed since the general-government of Telles Barreto (1538–1587), because the merchants "came over to destroy the land, taking away as much as they could in three or four years," explained Friar Vicente Salvador. The establishment of the High Court of Bahia (1609) and the Law of 1612 consolidated this concession, known as the "sugar mill owner's privilege," which, under different guises, is still in force today for the benefit the modern-day sugar-mill owners.[166]

Nonetheless, the WIC directors were not inclined to grant credit or patrimonial status to the planters.[167] Ultimately, as a stock exchange company, the WIC's strategy was entrepreneurial, not colonial,[168] a fact made evident in the management of the slave business, a crucial point in tropical colonialism. When the Breton merchant Auguste de Quelen returned from Pernambuco in 1640, he warned Amsterdam directors of the WIC's agents "abuse" as they bet on monopolistic profit. Instead of selling many slaves at a low price, WIC agents preferred to sell few Africans at high prices.[169] The problem spilled over from the prices into the credit arena. From 1636 to 1642, nearly all slaves had been sold by the WIC on credit, according to Portuguese custom.[170] However, the tightness of both United Provinces' shareholders and the New Holland board, composed by directors who only wanted to "stuff their purses," as denounced by Dutch pamphlets, led the Compagnie to get tough.[171] Credit was increasingly cut: 41 percent of the Africans were sold for cash in hand in 1643, 78 percent in 1644, and 100 percent in 1645.[172] The WIC's tightening smoothed the way for maneuvers by middlemen, who bought cash in hand and sold on credit at high interest rates, aggravating the sugar-planters' debt.[173] Then, all went astray in Pernambuco—the sale of enslaved Africans declined, there were judicial disputes, and debt-ridden Portuguese proprietors fled. From Amsterdam, the Heeren XIX tried to backtrack in 1645, dividing the payment for Africans into three installments. Yet the planters' purchases fell, and to prevent loss, the WIC reexported its Africans to the Caribbean plantation areas.[174] Meanwhile, the confrontation between debtors and creditors was already in place.

Within the same enterprise, the profits skimmed off by the Dutch bourgeois shareholders produced a lack of capital for the slave-based producer in New Holland. This contradiction, engendered by the misperception of Dutch capitalists and merchants of the role played by the slave trade—of the exterritorial reproduction of the plantation system—was perfectly analyzed by Joan Nieuhof. After staying with the WIC in Pernambuco from 1640 to 1649, Nieuhof served also the VOC in India, Ceylon, Java, and China. Experienced therefore in both South American plantations and Asian trading posts—in production economy and circulation economy—he concluded his critical report on the WIC in Brazil in 1670. Reviewed by Nassau-Siegen, his book presents a significant appraisal of the WIC's troubles.[175] "The Compagnie and commerce, both creditors of the mill owners, joined efforts to force those proprietors to meet their obligations through foreclosures. Such state of affairs [. . .] generated such disarray that everything pointed to the imminent annihilation of the sugar mills, and, consequently, of the trade and of the Compagnie [WIC] itself."[176] Here was the spark of the armed struggle, of the "War of Divine Freedom" declared by the Portuguese and Brasílico mill owners and sugar planters' debtors.

The tribulations of the WIC in Brazil were certainly not caused only by the derailment of credit. The Compagnie's directors realized early on that the recolonization of the Catholic Portuguese colonists by northern European Calvinist merchants—an unprecedented event overseas—would be hard work. In the midst of the "Nassau's peace," at the end of 1642, the Dutch High Council in Brazil warned: "the Portuguese settlers, due to the differences in religion, language, custom, and other reasons, regard our government with aversion and it is only by violence that they can be kept under our dominion."[177] Yet the awareness of the problems did not stop the WIC from getting it all wrong in the management of the slave system.

Absorbing the great expenses incurred in the conquests, the WIC became vulnerable to the fluctuations of the sugar market. Beside the anti-Dutch hostilities in Pernambuco and Angola the Compagnie endured other troubles in the Americas. Nieuw Nederland, on the North American coast, with their Nieuw Amsterdam and Fort Orange enclaves, was waging a war against Algonquin communities allied to the Nouvelle-France French.[178] Reeling with troubles, the enterprise made investors jittery. From 1640 onward, a more serious shock shattered the Compagnie, when the fall in sugar prices in Amsterdam caused a reflux of the capital invested in Pernambuco.[179] Unable to neutralize the speculative maneuvers by capitalists in Amsterdam, the WIC board was also unable handle the management of the two slaving poles in Brazil and Angola. This key episode of the Ethiopic Ocean history deserves to be examined more closely.

From the start, the Heeren XIX deemed the payment deadlines granted by Nassau-Siegen to those purchasing confiscated sugar mills and slaves to be too generous. Then it did not realize the scope of the Angola invasion. The military to-and-fro increased both expenses in West Central Africa and the shareholders' wariness.[180] The WIC's shares plummeted after news of the Dutch victory at Bengo camp (May 1643), the Portuguese provisional capital in Angola. At first sight favorable, the news indicated that to hold Luanda far from guaranteed control over Angola's markets. The subsequent fall in the WIC's shares revealed to the Portuguese ambassador in The Hague the volatility of the capital invested in the Compagnie.[181] In addition, the Compagnie's board refused credit for the reinforcement of troops in Angola.[182] Rumors in Amsterdam about the fitting of vessels in Lisbon to relieve the Angolan Portuguese further depressed WIC's shares (April 1644). The lack of resources to help out the Dutch in Brazil and West Central Africa was notorious.[183]

In the meantime, tension mounted in Pernambuco, where creditors acting "with cat claws" pressed the sugar planters, as Friar Manuel Calado protested. The sugar planters' debt had two origins—the installments owed by those who bought confiscated property, and the debts taken on from the middlemen who resold slaves purchased from the WIC.[184] With the increase in Angolan expenses, the WIC pressed its debtors in Brazil. Suddenly, Brasílico planters felt their patriotic vein pulse and resisted the occupiers. Extortive creditors, the Dutch also began to be seen as heretics and treacherous enemies of the Portuguese Crown.[185]

There had always been skirmishes in Pernambuco. However, military activity followed its own logic. Attacks by one side generated reprisals on the other, leading to a losing game that could ruin all of the sugar plantations. Thus, there emerged a limit to the destruction of sugar mills, and therefore to the war. This limit consisted of the Dutch expectation that they would take the Luso-Brasílico property unspoiled. This expectation seemed justified at the end of 1640, when Nassau-Siegen explained to the Heeren XIX the motives that had led him to accept a regional armistice: "it is to be expected that the region still held by the enemy (Bahia), will come, today or tomorrow, to be under your (the WIC's) dominion, and this is why, if we ruined it, we would be causing ourselves a loss."[186] Confirming Naussau-Siegen's analysis in their own way, Portuguese ambassadors in The Hague threatened to burn down the sugar plantations in the occupied zone, as the *ultima ratio*—the "last resort," in Ambassador Sousa Coutinho's words—if diplomatic negotiations failed.[187]

The picture changed completely when the front stabilized. Subsequently, to the Portuguese the sequestration of Luso-Brasílico sugar mills by Dutch creditors seemed more likely than harm from war. The guerrilla's means and ends came to enjoy more support from colonists and Portuguese authorities. Hostilities reached a higher level. The covert war unveiled its true colors. In December 1644, Captain Antônio Dias Cardoso and his men left Bahia, crossing the hinterlands and Dutch lines to join João Fernandes Vieira in Pernambuco in order to take part in the full-blown war started in June 1645.[188] From this point of view, the anti-Dutch northeastern revolt figures as a mutiny prompted by a group of debtors in arrears. An anonymous denunciation sent to the Crown in 1647 said that João Fernandes Vieira, the main commander of the anti-Dutch rebellion, "launched the war more motivated by the great debts he had with the Hollanders and Jews settled in Recife . . . than by [the willingness] to serve Your Majesty." Trying to defend João Fernandes Vieira in the Overseas Council, Salvador de Sá noted the irony of the anonymity of the accusations against him: "one person is enough to write an anonymous pamphlet, and if he has a relative who is a Friar, he will write a lot."[189] Nevertheless, a year later the authoritative pen of Fr. Antonio Vieira wrote almost the same judgment in a report commissioned by the Crown: "the main (settlers) who have moved (to wage war against the WIC in Pernambuco) did so because they had taken a lot of money from the Dutch, and could not or would not pay back."[190]

The Luso-Brasilico Counterattack in Angola

Well before the Dutch attacked below the Equator, Angola's slave traders had learned to link their fate to that of Brazil's colonists. Jerônimo Castanho, Paulo Dias Novais's representative in Madrid and one who was knowledgeable in the ways of the South Atlantic Ocean, warned the Crown in 1591 that the lack of support for the Portuguese of Angola would bring losses to the kingdom. Besides, Brazil would be ruined in no time. "[All] will be lost, the *Estado do Brasil*, [and] its tithes, because slaves from Angola have been lacking for a year, there is no sugar cultivation, and if the lack continues for a second year the mills will begin to close down, and if the third year comes round all mills will shut down, and there will be no people left to cut the sugar-cane."[191]

Taken by surprise by news of the fall of Bahia in 1624, the Crown warned the governor of Pernambuco about the imminence of a fresh WIC attack, this time in order to control the Angolan trading ports. Luanda was on the lookout.[192] The raid on Angola was effectively forecast even before the American forays. The above-mentioned governor of Angola, Luís Mendes de Vasconcelos, a prominent military and economic writer experienced in Portuguese India, then under attack from the VOC, alerted the Madrid Court in 1616. It was necessary to sustain the colonies, especially Angola, "because it is the market [*praça*] on which the whole of the management of Brazil and West Indies depends."[193]

Despite Bahia having been recovered in 1625 and the attacks in Angola repelled, this dress rehearsal for the invasion had drawn the transatlantic arc of the Dutch offensive. Friar Vicente Salvador reflects that "the aim and intent that led them [to Angola] was that of taking it and from there be able to bring Blacks over to the sugar mills."[194] In the same tenor, in his first known text, Fr. Antonio Vieira stated that the WIC's raid in Luanda was explained by its importance "to the trade in Brazil, whose head [Bahia] had already been taken."[195] In his 1628 book on Iberian overseas geopolitics, Duarte Gomes Solís writes that the Spanish and the Portuguese should unite to repel the Dutch incursions in the "*mar de el Sur*," the South Atlantic. In his view, the strengthening of Angola's defenses was critical to protect Bahia and Pernambuco, because without Angola the Dutch could not cultivate sugar-cane fields in Brazil.[196] Two years later, when Olinda and Recife fell into the hands of the Dutch, other men versed in Atlantic affairs soon realized that Angola was next in line. Fernão de Sousa, who had repelled the WIC's raids during his Angolan government (1625–1630), warned in 1631 about the urgency of building walls around Luanda. With direct maritime access from Pernambuco, the port was vulnerable.[197] Nothing was done. Thus, the exasperated tone with which the Council of Portugal—an organ with headquarters established in Madrid as a tutelary instance for Portuguese policy under the Habsburg's—pleaded for help in 1636.

"Since Pernambuco was lost, it has always been represented before Your Majesty by this Council the danger that the kingdom of Angola was in and that it was pressing to help them and to fortify it because it was unavoidable that they [the Dutch] would desire it, in order to take slaves to the mills of the captaincies they occupy in Brazil." As a consequence, Felipe IV should order, "without further ado" that men and arms be sent to Angola.[198] The unhurried manner in which Madrid reacted to overseas hostilities seemed to the Portuguese a plot carried out by Spain and the European powers to deprive Lisbon of its colonies.[199] After the Braganza Restoration (1640), the Dutch invaded Angola. Another imbroglio emerged in the Atlantic.[200]

As mentioned above, the Dutch-Portuguese Treaty of Truce, signed in 1641 for ten years, froze the battle fronts. Additionally, it brought in arms from the Low Countries to support the Braganza struggle against Spain on Portugal's frontiers. Soon a Dutch fleet reached the Tagus to assist the Portuguese. Around 20,000 firearms, mostly pistols, calivers (a lighter version of the musket), and muskets—many of which ended up in the hands of Pernambucano warriors fighting against the WIC soldiers—and two regiments of Dutch cavalry reinforced the Portuguese defenses in Alentejo.[201]

If Lisbon opened hostilities against the WIC in Brazil, it would place itself in the crossfire between Spain and the United Provinces, also exposing the Portuguese India ports of trade to the VOC's reprisals. France, an ally of the Dutch and in war against Spain since 1635, would oppose Portuguese hostilities against the WIC. By supporting the Portuguese, Paris hoped to avoid war with the Dutch, in order to concentrate all fire on Spain, France's direct enemy.[202] In a message to the French Court, King João IV explained the difficulty of his frail kingdom "to wage offensive war on two so powerful enemies, as is the king of Castile, declared, and the Dutch, covert, with the hand and cloak of the Companies [the WIC and the VOC], the more prejudicial and dangerous."[203]

On par with the strategic contradictions, institutional complexities made it even more difficult to manage the Dutch-Portuguese truce. A federative republic, the United Provinces' government reflected the power relations between the corporations and the political units composing the States-General.[204] Moreover, the VOC and the WIC were semiprivate companies, whence the double talk so often resorted to by the Dutch. When a clause in the truce was violated in their favor in the Indic or the Atlantic, the States hid behind the pretext of an isolated action by agents of one or the other company.[205] Following the same alibi, the WIC's commanders claimed to obey orders from the Compagnie's board and not from the States-General.[206] Typically, the States-General's stratagem consisted of reflecting that the rules of the WIC and VOC—their policy, their overseas aims—would be reviewed in 1645, the deadline for their contract. When the statutes were renewed, the States-General would restrain the two enterprises' impetus overseas in exchange for a peace treaty with Lisbon. Such was the hope that the Dutch negotiators instilled in King João IV's diplomats up to mid-1644.[207]

In contrast with Dutch republicanism, the Portuguese monarchy seemed better equipped to define a coherent overseas policy. It seemed so, but it was not, if one considers the diversity of interests operating in the palatine councils and tribunals.[208] For, three times—in 1641, 1645–1646, and 1653–1654—King João IV, albeit "with a great reluctance" according to the words of on his councilors, had to convoke the Cortes (the assembly of the Estates of the Realm) to legitimate his power, to set royal taxes, and to resolve military matters.[209] Assessing the different corporations and bureaucratic circles surrounding the new Braganza Crown in Lisbon, Hespanha arrives at this conclusion: "The policy of the royal government was not the policy of the king. . . . What existed with certainty was the sheaf of policies of the diverse tribunals and councils."[210] Regarding Brazil, the Crown and its diplomats used a double-talk similar to that of the Dutch. On the occasions when The Hague protested against guerrilla action in Pernambuco or in Maranhão, they blamed Brasílico criminality: "the arisen thieves." This ascription of blame was somewhat true in both cases. The WIC and VOC did not always accommodate the States-General's designs, and Pernambucano rebels did not always yield to Lisbon's commands.

Military and diplomatic misunderstandings confused the Portuguese Crown's action. Remarking on the delay in the relief of Luanda from the Dutch occupation, the count of Ericeira stated, "The remedy was not as prompt as so considerable a loss demanded."[211] A considerable loss, but who lost? Who was who in West Central Africa at that time?

Luanda 1648: The Battle of the Ethiopic Ocean

At that stage, when other European nations began to set foot in Africa, evolving from "onboard trade" (carried out between the ships and native canoes along the coast) to "inland trade" (established in trading ports and outposts), Portugal already boasted two whole centuries of exchange with sub-Saharan maritime regions. In shaping Portuguese African policy, the first such policy to appear in Europe since the end of the Roman Empire, slave traders, merchants, clergy, and colonial agents constituted powerful interest groups in Lisbon.

Influential at the Braganza court, the slave traders hitherto associated with the *Asiento* obtained in February 1641 a royal decree authorizing the continuation of the Luanda trade with the Castilian Indies. Despite the open war with Madrid, the Portuguese Council of Finance studied measures to stimulate this trade, a privileged means for the capture of Spanish Peru's silver.[212] A second pro-Angola Lisbon group, whose efforts seemed politically and economically more circumscribed, involved missionaries, other merchants, and royal agents close to Angolista colonists. Among them, Fernão de Mattos de Carvalhosa, High Court magistrate and later Crown attorney and member of the Council of Finance, featured prominently.[213] At the request of the Crown, Carvalhosa made criminal investigations and resided in Luanda between 1630 and 1632.[214] A few days after the news of the fall of Luanda into the hands of the WIC, he wrote a report proposing the prompt reconquest of the Angolan capital.[215]

Meanwhile, the Crown had opted for an agreement with the Dutch. The Portuguese established their capital in the Bengo camp, near Luanda, and trade between the two rival centers was authorized. Months later, in the beginning of 1643, responding to attacks in Maranhão, the Dutch attacked Bengo.[216] Two hundred Angolista refugees soon arrived in Bahia. From there, the Angola factor, Diogo Lopes de Faria, boasting sixteen years of service in Angola, informed Lisbon that no profit would be obtained in West Central Africa while the WIC stayed.[217] In the middle of 1643, Telles da Silva, governor-general of Brazil (1642–1647), warned the king: "Angola, Milord, is completely lost, and without it Your Majesty does not have Brazil, because settlers will lose heart without slaves for the sugar mills, [and] will dismantle them and Your Majesty's Customs will lose the rights on their sugars."[218] Such was the point of view informing a third and decisive pro-Angola groups, the wing formed by those who had bet on Brazilian export agriculture: without Luanda's trade the American colony was doomed.

Reports were sent to the Council of Finance, where Mattos de Carvalhosa, newly promoted to the Council, took up the charge again.[219] To him, the loss of Angola enriched the United Provinces and impoverished Portugal. "Without extracting Angolan Blacks, the Dutch cannot sustain and preserve Pernambuco and the other places they occupy in Brazil." Supported by the other Councilors, Mattos de Carvalhosa presented the slave trade as an enterprise cosubstantial to the Portuguese presence in West Central Africa: "the kingdom of Angola [. . .] with maritime trade, and with exports of Blacks, is a kingdom and one of great consideration. Without the trade and this export it is not a kingdom, and we cannot keep our people in it."

Lisbon's merchants claimed that the Angolan trade was indispensable for the capture of Peruvian silver. The governor-general of Brazil explained that the loss of Angola would destroy the sugar plantations and Portuguese American economy. Mattos de Carvalhosa stated that Angola's mode of exploitation (the practices to extract its economic surplus) and the mode of dominion (the policy for the conservation of the indigenous people and the enclaves under Lisbon's sovereignty) rested on the slave trade. Well-argued, grounded on the postulate of overseas evangelization and on the imperatives of Atlantic policy, Mattos de Carvalhosa's theses were endorsed by the supporters of the retaking of Angola. The Finance

Council members annexed a revealing addendum. Troops, vessels, and ammunition in sufficient amount for the relief of West Central Africa could not set sail from Portugal. The task of furnishing people and equipment was up to Rio de Janeiro and adjacent Brazilian captaincies—interested parties in the reestablishment of the slave trade—"because the whole of Brazil needs slaves for its preservation." Ultimately, the Angolan war effort was delegated to Portuguese America, and particularly to the Rio de Janeiro captaincy.[220] By the force of circumstances of European war that inhibited Lisbon's action, room for Luso-Brasílico comanagement opened up in the Ethiopic Ocean. Thus began the drift that would change the framework of Portuguese activity overseas.

At the same time, in October 1643, Salvador de Sá entered the Tagus from Rio de Janeiro. He did not spend the night in Lisbon, but promptly rode up to Evora, the Court's provisional headquarters. He was updated on news of the aggravation of the Atlantic fronts since his departure from Brazil. Bahia was in a bad state, in fear of a WIC attack, and Angola was in danger.

"Having the Dutch remove their mask," the War Council urged the relief of Luanda: "Because without Angola one cannot support Brazil, and even less can Portugal do without that Estado (of Brazil)." Battles on both sides of the Southern Atlantic fused into a single war. This is why the councilors asked the king to order Salvador de Sá, who had great understanding of the "affairs of one and the other part," to prepare three complementary reports—one on the conflict in Brazil, another regarding the Río de la Plata region, and the third on Angola. The Council's document bears the date of October 17, 1643, a Saturday. The king issued the order and, four days later, on a Wednesday, Salvador de Sá submitted the three reports.

The celerity with which the process was concluded should be noted. Évora was—and is—a very small town. News traveled fast among the nobility and high-ranking agents residing there. Salvador called on the king on his arrival. Most probably, the War Council's request, purposefully prepared, formalized the proposals presented orally by Salvador. This explains the short lapse of time in which the three reports were written and submitted. It was Salvador himself, or people close to him, who started the protocol initiatives included in the reports. They are well written, well thought out, and possibly sketched during the trip from Rio de Janeiro. The transcontinental outlines of the Southern Atlantic Luso-Dutch conflict are drawn out from the War Council's questions and the answers written by Salvador.

Regarding the Río de la Plata region, the intention was to reestablish the links between Rio de Janeiro and Buenos Aires, with the aim of bringing Peruvian silver back into Portuguese trade. Like Angola, Buenos Aires appeared as an appendix to Portuguese America. Both competitors knew that much and both of them, at different junctures, planned to seize the Río de la Plata.[221] During the Iberian Union, the authorities from Luanda and Rio de Janeiro, more closely linked to Buenos Aires, raised the alarm against the WIC's threats on the Río de la Plata. Indeed, in 1638, Buenos Aires's governor, Mendo de la Cueba y Benavides, was alerted by the Rio de Janeiro and Angola governors that the Dutch command in Recife, changing its strategic objectives, would lift the siege of Bahia and send a sixty-vessel fleet to attack the Río de la Plata.[222] In the middle of 1642, when the WIC had already seized Angola, the Dutch organized a fleet in Recife to attack Buenos Aires. The operation was eventually halted because of the anti-Dutch revolt in Maranhão and by fear of an uprising in Pernambuco.[223] From this perspective, the Spanish authorities, well aware of Portuguese involvement in the Río de la Plata, and mainly, in the African and silver contraband, sounded the alarm when the news of João IV assuming the throne arrived in Buenos Aires. Writing from Lima, the marquis de Mancera, viceroy of Peru, alerted Madrid that the Portuguese settlers, already very active in the Río de la Plata, had opened a new path toward Peru through the Amazon River, by which "many" of them arrived in Quito.[224] In fact, following the Braganza Restoration, Lisbon and Brazil's authorities emphasized the need to maintain the trade with Buenos Aires and, eventually, to take the port from the Spanish. In a report on Portugal's geopolitics, a long-winded text dated 1643, Father Vieira pointed out, in tune with Telles da Silva, Salvador de Sá, and other Ethiopic Ocean experts, Brazil's vulnerability due to the loss of the trade with its two satellites: Luanda and Buenos Aires. "Brazil—which is what sustains trade and customs and what attracts to our [metropolitan] ports such few foreign ships as we have in them—with the separation of the Río de la Plata, is devoid of money, and with the loss of Angola, will soon have no sugar, because this year it gathered no more than half a harvest and in the following year it will necessarily be less."[225] Notwithstanding the war between Lisbon and Madrid, the Overseas Council in 1646, with the vote of Salvador de Sá, advised the Crown to extend to Angola the permission already granted to Cape Verde and Guinea ports to export enslaved Africans toward Spanish America.[226]

By stepping out from the Habsburg Empire, Portugal lost access to Spanish American precious metals. "It is notorious that Your Majesty's Crown suffers from the lack of mines," declared the Overseas Council at that time,[227] whence the search for indirect means—the trade and smuggling of Africans—to tap into the Peruvian silver carried through the Río de la Plata.[228] This situation explains the obsessive search for precious metals in Brazil, later carried out by João Correa de Sá under command of his father, Salvador de Sá.[229] As noted by the authors of a new biography of King João IV, Salvador de Sá's appointment to the Overseas Council in 1644 put the South Atlantic in the agenda of the palatine councils in Lisbon.[230]

The Luso-Brasilico Enslavers' Task Force

In his answer to the War Council's request, Salvador underlined the basic problem of trade in the Río de la Plata region. "Negroes"—such was the merchandise that the Castilians came over to Guanabara to fetch. Without Angola it was difficult to relaunch the Rio de Janeiro–Buenos Aires thoroughfare. There was one way out: invade Buenos Aires. A fleet bearing 600 soldiers and Amerindians would leave Rio de Janeiro and São Vicente. In parallel, marching through the fields, the Paulistas would send a *bandeira* expedition into Paraguay to block the way of any relief eventually sent by the Spanish to relieve Buenos Aires. As a reward for the help, the Paulistas would be allowed to capture the area's Amerindians.

Two radical options also emerged on the Brazilian front. First, the hard alternative: "With dissimulation" the governor-general would encourage sackings in Pernambuco. When the Dutch complained, he would allege that these were acts perpetrated by "arisen thieves." One must not underestimate the guile of those involved. The "furtive war" (*guerra dissimulada*) was not a cheap expedient to fool an unknowing opponent. Much more than just hiding the guerrilla's principals, the stratagem aimed at fielding the full weight of support, both formal (clergy, allied Indians, colonists, and their slaves) and informal (acclimatization, knowledge of the terrain and of tropical war), that a century of struggle against American natives, *quilombos*, and nature had taught the Portuguese. From this point of view, the covert war is on a par with the war of attrition waged in the European theater of the Thirty Years War. In both cases the tactics consisted of exhausting the invader with skirmishes, and forcing retreat from the positions taken in frontal battles. After proposing a covert war, Salvador presented the moderate option: to strike a deal with the Dutch to have them let go of Portuguese America and Africa—even if a lot of money were to be paid to the States-General. In the end, the Brazilian and Angolan incomes would cover the costs of the compensation paid to the WIC.²³¹

Regarding Angola, Salvador counseled sending soldiers from Bahia and the Paulistas with their Indian warriors. The expeditions' commander would carry two royal orders. One would instruct that the Dutch should not be harassed and that the commander should only be concerned with trade and with aiding the settlers. The other order, secret, would give him powers to expel the Dutch. Concluding, Salvador stated, "The [Angolista] settlers are not very trustful and delay can cause much loss, . . . because without it the Brazil's plantations are affected and the increase in your Majesty's Treasury will be annihilated, in Brazil as in this kingdom."²³²

Salvador hesitated with regard to the opportunity to confront the Dutch in Pernambuco—hesitated to the point of causing the tactical shambles resulting in the Tamandaré naval disaster (Pernambuco, September 1645) two years later, when Admiral Lichthardt sank Serrão de Paiva's fleet. Salvador deemed Angola to be the central target of the counteroffensive in the Atlantic empire since 1643. He aimed not only at the continuation of the slave trade, but at securing the occupation's political bases: the vassalage of both Angolista settlers and allied *sobas*—the *imperium*.²³³

From the War Council, the reports went to the recently created Overseas Council.²³⁴ The councilors agreed with the Angola expedition, stated a preference for diplomatic agreements in the case of Brazil, and disapproved the attack on Buenos Aires, as mentioned above.²³⁵ In short, the solution for the problems in the Río de la Plata region, in Brazil, and in Africa—in the whole of the Ethiopic Ocean economic space—involved Angola. The income to buy a settlement from the Dutch would be provided by Angola. The human merchandise bringing silver *patacas* and Peruvian silver ingots back to Rio de Janeiro would be provided by Angola. The human energy employed in the sugar-cane plantations and in the mills to place sugar once again in the Portuguese mercantile and fiscal circuit would be provided by Angola. At once, retaking Angola came to the fore of the military targets.

Pursuing the enquiries, the Overseas Council examined in 1646 a memorial by Jesuit Brother Gonçalo João, author of other reports on the issue, on which his expertise was notorious thanks to his thirty-five-year stay in Angola.²³⁶ "Above all it is necessary that Your Majesty should promptly send succor to that city [Luanda], for it is of great importance, because without Angola there is no Brazil."²³⁷ Interpreted as a true syllogism, apodictic, Gonçalo João's phrase will serve as an epigraph for and proof of the two interconnected poles of Luso-Brasílico and Angolista slave trade and slavery. A memorandum submitted to the Crown at that time defined the status of the offensive. Unlike the tactical battles fought in Pernambuco, the West Central African war carried strategic value—it aimed to expel the Dutch from Angola in order to have them out of Brazil. Otherwise, the Dutch States-General would strike an alliance with the Spanish to secure Angola, and Portugal would have no means to defend itself, either in Africa or in Brazil.[238]

Reactions by the United Provinces confirm the identity of opposites uniting the two colonies. Since 1642 the Dutch Council of Brazil recorded that the Portuguese had great interest in Angola, where the Dutch would try to foment revolt.[239] Barlaeus, Nassau-Siegen's spokesman, foresaw that Portugal would go to extremes to recapture Angola.[240] From The Hague, Sousa Coutinho summed up the conversations held to convert the Truces into a peace treaty in 1644. With regard to the places invaded after the Restoration, he believed that the Dutch would return São Tomé and Maranhão, from which they extracted no profit. However, with Angola, "without which they shall not be able to keep Brazil," the picture was different. They wanted the slave trade. But if they held the Angolans, they would not let Pernambuco go, nor would they want a treaty with Portugal. What should be done? How to act without compromising Luso-Dutch discussions? By stealth, plotting in the same way as their opponent did, answered the ambassador. After a surprise assault on Luanda, the commander should write up a false report aimed at fooling European capitals and the States-General.[241] The idea coincided with the project conceived the previous year by Salvador and endorsed by the Overseas Council.

The proposal was carried out four years later. Under the pretext of relieving the colonists besieged in Massangano by the Jaga headed by Queen Njinga, Salvador attacked Luanda and expelled the Dutch. He promptly sent a false report to Lisbon—to be presented before the European courts—in which he protested his good faith, attributing the attacks on WIC's soldiers to a misunderstanding.[242] To lend credence to the pretence, Portuguese agents in Holland spread the rumor that King João IV was incensed with the attack on Luanda and had sequestered Salvador de Sá's property.[243] Jerônimo Nunes da Costa, also known as Moseh Curiel, Portuguese representative in Amsterdam, and, notwithstanding, a WIC shareholder, greatly helped Portuguese diplomacy on the occasion.[244]

However, there was much uncertainty between the suggestions put forth in 1643 and the surrender of the WIC in 1648. The two European capitals reacted differently to the tribulations of the West Central African war, revealing as it were the distinct concepts guiding their overseas policies. Amsterdam shareholders rejected the WIC's shares, fearing increased costs of the war in Angola. Lisbon, on the other hand, was disquieted by the shrinking of her imperial and economic territory in the South Atlantic.

In the beginning of 1644 a rescue expedition was prepared in Lisbon with the view of liberating São Tomé, Angola, and, "as a consequence," Brazil, Sousa Coutinho guaranteed.[245] Meanwhile, the battle of Montijo (in May 1644, at the Spanish-Portuguese frontier) forced the redeployment of the troops meant to be shipped to West Central Africa. Thus the first serious plan to retake Angola petered out. Underlining the ambiguities of the truce north and south of the equator, soldiers who were meant to go fight the WIC's men in Angola sided with two Dutch cavalry regiments in Montijo.[246] In the battle, the most celebrated Portuguese field master was Joane Mendes de Vasconcellos, Angola veteran, fierce enemy of the Dutch in Brazil and in Flanders (appendix 1).

Despite the scarcity of resources, two small fleets left Brazil to relieve Angola in 1645. First, three vessels left Bahia carrying 200 soldiers—among them a company of 32 musketeers of Henrique Dias's Afro-Brasílico Pernambucan regiment—to cast anchor at Quicombo bight, north of Benguela.[247] The aim was to reach Massangano by land. At the head of one of the columns marched sergeant-major Domingos Lopes Sequeira. Despite being an Angolista and "very dexterous and intelligent in the negro wars," as highlighted in a report on the expedition, Sequeira was ambushed and killed by the Jaga. His column was then destroyed. Out of the 107 soldiers only 4 survived.[248] Among those who escaped was the Afro-Brasílico Paulo Pereira, later a sergeant major, whom I discuss later in the book.[249]

Another fleet left Rio de Janeiro. Commissioned by Salvador de Sá, Francisco de Souto Maior (or Soto Maior), who had fought in the Brasílico wars since 1633 and had been nominated Rio de Janeiro's interim governor (1644), left Guanabara to take office as governor of Angola with five ships lent by local slave traders, 300 soldiers, and a few dozen Amerindians.[250] From his office in The Hague, Sousa Coutinho was pleased with the move. "If the governor who is now on his way to Angola carries out business conveniently, we shall have Angola and we shall have Brazil."[251] The governor did not carry out business conveniently, and the expeditionary force ended in disaster. But they took advantage of the voyage to load slaves. Two thousand "pieces" were carried off to Rio with the chief aim of reestablishing the Atlantic slave trade: "with which merchants of Brazil and of this kingdom will take heart to renew the ancient trade."[252] Soldiers in other relief efforts dispatched from Rio de Janeiro and Bahia ended up being captured by the Dutch. Souto Maior died in the African outback, in conflict with settlers who were partners in trade with the Dutch, possibly poisoned by Angolista opponents.[253]

Logistical obstacles and the hostility of the environment and natives rendered an anti-Dutch guerrilla analogous to that waged in Pernambuco unviable in Angola.[254] The massacre of Sequeira's column by the Jaga just as it set foot on dry land, Queen Njinga's offensive, and the death of Souto Maior all showed once again, the Portuguese and Angolistas did not enjoy a safe rearguard. On the other side of the ocean, the partial failure of the anti-Dutch uprising in Pernambuco had created a deadlock. The rebels had only been able to take inland territory, thus exposing the Portuguese Crown to diplomatic and military reprisals by the Dutch. As Cabral de Mello wrote, "not taking all had been worse than retaking nothing at all."[255]

So, contrary to the various battle outcomes in Brazil, the Luso-Dutch struggles turned into an all-or-nothing situation. However, "all" in the battles south of the equator, could mean "too much" in the fronts north of the equator.

Negotiations carried out in Münster and Osnabrück from 1643 onward signaled the end of hostilities in Europe. One hundred and sixty ambassadors, acting in the name of 194 great and small European governments, placed all of the planet's troubles on the table. Protected by French and Swedish diplomats, the envoys of the Braganza Crown, albeit not officially present, were also on hand in Westphalia.[256] The first arrangement, of high risk to King João IV, was drawn up at the end of 1646 between the Dutch States-General and Spain. After obtaining the endorsement from the great powers to exclude Portugal from ratification of the general treaty, Felipe IV agreed to recognize Dutch sovereignty over the Portuguese territories invaded by the WIC or by the VOC. In other words, Luanda, Pernambuco, Ceylon, India, and Insulindia were handed to the Dutch on a platter. In exchange, the States-General vowed to preserve the New World Spanish domains. A provisional treaty between the two countries was arranged at the beginning of 1647.[257]

Lisbon expected little from Britain, as the island was mired in civil war (August 1642). In his turn, Louis XIII unveiled his overseas ambitions as he occupied Madagascar (called "Ilha de São Lourenço" by the Portuguese), threatening the Cape Route trade.[258] Paris turned out to be even less trustworthy after the battle of Rocroi (March 1643), when French forces routed the Spanish army, dismissing the military alliance with Lisbon.[259] A confident Mazarin advanced his intentions regarding the Portuguese overseas territories in 1647. In exchange for more substantive help to King João IV, France asked for a commercial port in Brazil or Portuguese India, and another one in Portuguese Africa.[260] In the Atlantic, the Luso-Brasílico insurrection in Pernambuco (June 1645) came to aggravate the tensions between the Dutch States-General and Portugal. The heavy hand imposed on João IV was defined: it was crucial to keep an alliance with France, but also to avoid a separate peace between Paris and Madrid, which would follow from the Dutch-Spanish agreement, thus setting Felipe IV free to pounce on Portugal. It became clear that King João IV should reformulate his diplomatic alliances and recompose the military balance, otherwise Portugal would be won overseas by Holland and on the continent by Spain.[261]

As the picture sketched by the 1648 peace treaties emerged, two camps were formed in the Court. On the one side stood the "diplomats" and on the other the "bellicists." Among the former figured Fr. Antonio Vieira, Sousa Coutinho, ambassador in The Hague, and a few individuals of high nobility, all of whom favored a defensive frontier war against Spain and negotiated peace with the Netherlands, even though the price to pay was the loss of Pernambuco and Angola to the WIC. Merchants operating in Asia had also joined this side, fearful that the Atlantic battles would result in retaliation by the VOC against Portuguese trading ports in the Estado da Índia.[262] In the opposite camp stood the "bellicists," persuaded that Portugal could manage, single-handed, to get rid of its two powerful rivals. The start of the first Anglo-Dutch War (1652–1654) weakened the States-General and precipitated the Dutch retreat from Brazil, supporting the "bellicist" claims. But the WIC retreat was envisioned before the Anglo-Dutch war.

As pointed out by Cabral Mello, none of the military successes achieved in Brazil—the victory at Mount Tabocas (August 1645), the rout of the Dutch in Itaparica (December 1647), or the first Guararapes Battle (April 1648)—had shaken the resolve of the "diplomats," who were influential at Court.[263] Such was the force of the link between the Angolan trade and Brazilian slavery that Fr. Antonio Vieira reinterpreted Gonçalo João's syllogism ("without Angola there is no Brazil") to reach conclusions diametrically opposite those of his fellow Jesuit. "The whole of the debate now is about Angola, and it is an issue in which they shall not yield, because without negroes there is no Pernambuco, and without Angola there are no negroes, and as we hold the hinterland trade, even if they hold the city of Luanda, they fear [that, as] we hold other ports, we [could] divert all [trade] through them," warned Vieira, at the same time that Salvador de Sá attacked Luanda.[264] A doctrinaire of the "diplomat" side, Vieira judged that the victories already obtained in Pernambuco lacked military significance, for the WIC continued to hold Luanda and Benguela.

Word of Dutch surrender in Angola reached Europe during this state of affairs. News was received in Lisbon on November 2, in Recife on the November 19, and ten days later in The Hague.[265] Supporting a peace treaty with the Dutch States-General until then, most of the royal councilors changed sides and now considered that Portugal could, indeed, defeat both the Dutch and Spanish. With some resentment, Father Vieira noted that the change in opinion originated in a "miraculous success, which one should never rely on," for Luanda remained vulnerable to a counterattack.[266] In the same way, Sousa Coutinho did an about-face. Not in favor of the attack on Luanda, the ambassador changed his opinion as he realized the strong impact of Angola's recapture on The Hague diplomats and on Amsterdam merchants unhappy with WIC's monopoly.[267] A good politician, Sousa Coutinho endorsed the triumph and embraced the victory he had doubted. With this success, he informed the king, "Your Majesty has gained a kingdom [Angola], the soldiers [of the expeditionary force] a great reputation, and myself a notable [standing], not only among other princes' ministers, but also among the best of the States-General, so that some canonize me as a talented ambassador."[268]

In fact, the Portuguese victory achieved in West Central Africa destabilized the opponent. Military setbacks in Pernambuco and the rising cost of the Anglo-Dutch war forced the Netherlands to retreat in all South Atlantic fronts in 1654. Yet, Luanda figured as the weakest link in the Dutch network built between Brazil and Africa, becoming a prime target for the 1648 counterattack. Years later, Father Antonio Vieira summed it all up: "What was recovered in Angola were two cities [Luanda and Massangano], two kingdoms [Angola and Benguela], seven fortresses, three conquests [Angola, Congo, and Matamba], the vassalage of many kings, and the very rich trades of Africa and America."[269] To Fr. Antonio Vieira, who was also a fine statesman, the battle of Luanda defined the stakes in the Ethiopic Ocean: the restoration of Portuguese control over West Central Africa and Brazil. This point of view was shared by Boxer, as historian and military expert, who concluded in his seminal book that "the final victory in Brazil was, to a good measure, the consequence of the retaking of Angola, thanks to Salvador [de Sá]."[270] Truly, the battle of Luanda yielded immediate gains to Portugal, both on the military and diplomatic fronts, in contrast to Pernambuco, in which a lapse of five years separated the victories in Guararapes (1648 and 1649) from final surrender in Recife (1654).[271]

Who Retook Angola?

Salvador de Sá had not been the only one to propose the reconquest of Angola, as other informed opinions had also supported this strategic imperative. Three reports by Overseas Council councilors and Crown's attorneys spelled out the situation in 1643. The expedition for retaking Angola should originate in Brazil, and, more precisely, in Rio de Janeiro,[272] a port with great interest in Angolan slaves because of its connections with the Río de la Plata silver trade. It is also beyond doubt that King João IV supported this semiclandestine operation. Reengaging a debate that divided Brazilian and Portuguese historians at the Restoration Tercentennial Congress (1940), it is worth asking: ultimately, who decided the affair?[273]

In his *History of the Future*, a millenarist book written from 1649 on, Fr. Antonio Vieira put forward his opinion on the matter. Vieira defined the empirical principles for retaking Luanda: Brazil and Angola formed one organism. Brazil "lives and supports itself" off Angola; "one can rightly say that Brazil has its body in America and its soul in Africa." With regard to the operational part of the expedition, Vieira distinguished two phases. In the beginning, King João's will prevailed. However, all went wrong on the of Rio de Janeiro side of things. Harassment by the Dutch fleet rendered the whole enterprise "totally impossible, judged by all as untimely." From then on, Vieira attributed a sacred character to the expedition, likening it to a modern-era crusade. For him, the change in strategic aims resulted from the mystic revelations received by Jesuit Joam de Almeida while saying mass in the Rio de Janeiro College.

Pleased to attribute to divine will a success that his previous memorials to the Crown had regarded as impossible, Vieira elaborated on the greatness of the wondrous event. "In such marvelous manner, against the King's orders, against the general's [Salvador de Sa's] intent, against the kingdom's opinion, against even the will of Brazil and against the very hope of Angola, in short, against all the rules of war, of navigation, of the winds, of the seas and of nature herself, the Lord accomplished the word of Fr. Joam de Almeida, proving His Will."[274]

Against Salvador de Sa's intent? Fr. Vieira exaggerated here. Besides divine designs and royal orders, Salvador de Sá—and he alone—had the resources in Rio de Janeiro to fund and organize the expedition and make it happen. Only he, his relatives, his allies, and his henchmen could provide the needed help to the task force—the necessary foodstuffs, men, weapons, and ships. Indeed, the Court formally recognized that fact, granting to him in one go the double government of Rio de Janeiro and Angola. In the royal letter nominating Salvador as governor of the African colony, the king spelled it out: "In view of the state in which that kingdom [of Angola] was, your help was the most important that could have been sent."[275]

The preparations in Lisbon of both the fleet of the count of Villa Pouca, the new governor-general (1647–1650) who was to take reinforcements to Bahia, and Salvador's fleet, fitted for the counterattack in Angola, divided the available equipment and soldiers. Salvador stated that "everything is necessary, and everything is too little" for the Angola foray. Yet, asserting his determination, Salvador wrote to King João IV in an irreverent tone, as he received orders to leave under the command of Villa Pouca and to tag along with the rest of the fleet to Bahia, before sailing on to Rio de Janeiro: "Sir, I wish to serve, and have done so for 32 years, crossing the [Equator] line 18 times; and no one in Portugal has been more successful than myself in sailing the seas. I have always performed well . . . and I can handle what is assigned to me."[276]

Illustrating the complexity of Angola's affairs and the control Palatine councils sought to exert over the Crown, the Overseas Councilors expressed their concern about the discussions secretly held by the king and Salvador de Sá. Writing in February 1648 to the Crown about the "news" "that some orders are given to Salvador de Sá," the councilors asked for copies of it "to avoid a mismatch between the orders" on the subject.[277] Three months later, when Salvador de Sá and his vessels had already left Rio de Janeiro to attack Luanda, the councilors restated their concerns. According to them, "there is no notice at all to this Council" about the king's orders that were provided to the fleet that sailed to Bahia and to ships sent to Rio de Janeiro with Salvador de Sá. A later note on the document from the marquis of Montalvão, Council's chairman, suggests that an additional report on Salvador de Sá's endeavors was given verbally and discretely to the councilors,[278] probably to prevent such information from being leaked to Holland.

Once in Rio de Janeiro, Salvador with his numerous relatives and his granduncle, interim governor Duarte Vasqueanes, mobilized resources, requesting money, property, and help from the city's colonists and missionaries. By doing so, he rendered viable an expeditionary force, until then a problematic affair due to the lack of metropolitan resources.[279] Cattle were slaughtered in the Sá's and Jesuit corrals for the expedition's provisions.[280] Besides the more-or-less voluntary help from local settlers and merchants, Salvador expropriated the Rio de Janeiro estate of New Christian banker Duarte Silva and his associates, recently arrested in Lisbon by the Inquisition. The city's councilors justified this measure saying that the failure of the "Angolan journey" would result in "unbearable losses, both to Your Majesty and to the whole of this Estado do Brasil."[281] In the same drive, according to the count of Ericeira and Cadornega, Salvador de Sá gathered the most important Rio de Janeiro citizens to explain that the "destruction" of Angola by the Dutch penalized all parts of Brazil subject to Portugal, and, particularly, the "inhabitants of Rio de Janeiro to whom greatest damage resulted."[282]

Associated with the Guanabara-based planters and merchants, Salvador de Sá preached well-understood patriotism. The retaking of Angola served the imperatives of Portuguese geopolitics, of the illegal trade to Buenos Aires and Potosí, and of the Rio de Janeiro economy's profit. Merchants and rural landowners were convinced, and they gathered funds and equipment for the journey. Mathias de Albuquerque Maranhão, ex-commander against the French in Maranhão and against the Dutch in Pernambuco, future captain-major of Paraíba, and at that time (1643–1657) a sugar-mill owner in Rio de Janeiro, donated material and money. Cristóvão Vaz, planter and future Rio de Janeiro municipal councilor, came accompanied by musicians playing the flute, bringing "sacks of money" to help in the enterprise.[283]

Nonetheless, other colonists found this apparent strategic incongruence strange. Indeed, the immediate consequences of the "new Pernambuco war"—the name that the Rio de Janeiro municipal council gave to the Brasílico war started in 1645—caused much commotion in the city.[284] Beginning that year, Salvador de Sá already had trouble in Rio de Janeiro providing Francisco Souto Maior's expedition with troops to Angola. Two important Rio de Janeiro captains refused to join the expeditionary troops. Salvador Sá insisted that they should sail to Angola, "where the danger [to the Portuguese Crown] was greater." Facing a new refusal and other desertions, he arrested both captains.[285] Later, in May 1647, the Overseas Council expressed concerns about the safety of Bahia and especially Rio de Janeiro "with far fewer defenses . . . and few persons experienced in war" against a probable Dutch naval attack.[286]

It was said that a Dutch task force was about to reach Brazilian ports.[287] In fact, the WIC's fleet, boasting twelve warships and 3,500 men under the command of experienced admiral Witte de With, had arrived in Recife three months previously.[288] It was rightly feared that this armada could attack Bahia and Rio de Janeiro. On the verge of leaving with his ships to Luanda, Salvador himself warned the king, "The people in Rio de Janeiro are despondent as they see that they lack the means to defend themselves."[289] One of the expeditionaries, the Luso-Mbundu

Jesuit Antônio do Couto, recorded the Rio de Janeiro inhabitants perplexity: "There was much delay [in Rio de Janeiro] and there seemed to have been no resolution for the armada to leave for Angola, it seeming to many to be more reasonable to defend the city of Rio de Janeiro, which was ours, than to leave it unprotected to restore Angola, which was then subject to the Dutch."[290]

Salvador de Sá had to convince Rio de Janeiro's inhabitants of the viability and necessity of the Angola expedition. Here, as elsewhere, as a Jesuit brother and powerful ally, he counted greatly on the missionaries' help.

The Jesuits and Control of the Ethiopic Ocean

In the patriotic context that emerged with the Restoration, amid the hindrances caused by war on land and sea, Catholic faith helped to undertake difficult enterprises. Phyllis M. Martin, in her book on the Loango kingdom, commented on the Luso-Dutch rivalry and war in West Central Africa that "in the long run, the Portuguese won because of their tenacity." Would that be the tenacity flared by colonial conquest's religious scope, as observed by Charles Boxer, an author hardly accepting of Portuguese colonialist ideology?[291]

Closer to concrete facts, it is interesting to follow the Jesuit intervention on the South Atlantic's military fronts. Along with other Jesuits, Fr. André Gouvea took part in the Luso-Spanish fleet that reconquered Salvador de Bahia from the Dutch in 1625. Commissioned by his superiors, he wrote a perceptive report on the sugar mills owned by the S.J. in Bahia. Among others issues, he expressed concerns about the increase of slave runaways in those properties following the disruptions caused by the conflict in Bahia.[292] All along the period, the missionaries showed concern about slavery, the slave trade, and Angola's situation. They were part of the expeditions that rescued Angola after the Dutch invasion of Luanda, Benguela, and São Tomé in 1641. Fr. Matheus Dias, treasurer of the Rio de Janeiro Jesuit College, traveled in Souto Maior's fleet, which set sail from Guanabara bound for Angola in 1645, while brother Antonio Pires, nicknamed the "Wise Priest" (Nganga-Anjaire*)* by the Mbundu and an avowed expert on West Central Africa, was the pilot of the governor's ship. On arrival, both priests mobilized slaves, natives, and *sobas* dependent on the Society of Jesus to aid Souto Maior and his officers.[293]

The Jesuits' intervention in the 1648 task force was even more decisive. The military threat on Rio de Janeiro increased in the first months of 1648, when admiral Witte de With bypassed Bahia with his combat fleet. In April, Salvador de Sá's vessels were still anchored in Guanabara Bay. The end of the Angola-bound monsoon got closer as mid-May approached. As is well known to navigators past and present, the turn of the weather in that part of the ocean is the result of the stretching of the Saint Helena High, also known as South Atlantic High, toward the equator during the Austral winter. Turbulences generated in the Antarctic pole move up to the Tropic of Capricorn, complicating departure from Brazilian ports from mid-May to mid-June. Typically, that sort of storm could be crossed or skirted by a slave ship sailing alone to the West African coast. But this was not the case for fleets, particularly war fleets, which should navigate together.[294]

In the beginning of April, Salvador de Sá put pressure on the Rio de Janeiro municipal council to obtain more resources and expressed his "great hurry" to set sail immediately and "not miss the occasion" offered by favorable meteorology. Restless, the governor-general sent from Bahia "very strict" orders that the fleet would not miss the Angola monsoon.[295] As stated above, fearing a naval raid by the Dutch, the people of Rio de Janeiro opposed the fleet's departure. Facing such unfavorable circumstances, Salvador de Sá along with the Jesuits executed a miraculous maneuver to have the expedition leave.

It so happened that Jesuit Joam de Almeida, Salvador de Sá's private confessor and "a priest deemed holy all over Brazil," launched a manifesto calling the expeditionary force to leave for Luanda "on Tuesday, 12th of May, day of the Angels, taking as patron saint Michael and all of the Angels because they would be successful." Received as "a prophecy and as something revealed by God," the manifesto sparked an enthusiastic movement in Rio de Janeiro. Taking advantage this situation, Salvador embarked with his officers, weapons and equipment. Stirred into action, the rest of the troop followed suit and the expedition set sail toward Angola.[296] As a good prophet, Fr. Almeida left room for maneuver in his augury. Indeed, the "day of the Angels" did not feature in the Christian calendar, and the true feast day of Saint Michael—observed as a holy day—took place months later, on September 29. Little did it matter. A warrior saint, celestial champion in battle, patron of generals and swordsmen, represented donning his shining armor against the enemies of the Church, Saint Michael should, in one way or another, emblazon the flags of the slaving Catholic crusade to expel the heretic slave traders from Angola.[297] However, the expedition had to leave before the end of May, when bad weather started in the Ethiopic Ocean.

Further, Father Simão de Vasconcellos, at that time rector of the Rio de Janeiro Jesuit College, offered a slightly different version of the prophecy. According to him, father Joam Almeida foretold the retaking of Luanda precisely on September

29, feast of Saint Michael, "God's little ensign." As part of his interpretation of the saint's calendar, Joam de Almeida also predicted that the good news of the victory would reach Rio de Janeiro on the day of Saint Ursula and the 11,000 Virgins (October 21). By the way, the date marked the usual period for the return of slave vessels sailing the Rio de Janeiro–Luanda route.[298] But the forecast failed. Fr. Almeida then retorted to the expeditionaries' relatives that the news would be announced in Rio de Janeiro not on the "day" of Saint Ursula, but on her "feast."[299]

As the college's priests had conveniently changed the feast for the following month (November 8–10), it all fit in. The news of the victory in Angola arrived in Rio de Janeiro at that date, for the greater glory of Fr. Almeida, promptly proclaimed "God's oracle."[300] Writing some years later, after his stay in Angola, the Italian Capuchin Cavazzi offered yet another version of the story. According to him, it had been Jesuit João Paiva, ex-missionary in West Central Africa then sheltering in Rio de Janeiro, who had advised Salvador to move up the fleet's departure from the 15th to the 12th of May. Despite the fact that the announcement recorded in the heat of the hour by Jesuit-expeditionary Antônio do Couto was the more widespread, Friar Cavazzi's variant also emphasized the Jesuit's actions and set the (meteorological) deadline of the 12th of May, without any reference to the climate turn in the South Atlantic.[301]

For his part, as a witness to the expedition's preparations, Fr. Simão de Vasconcellos had no doubts. The invasion of Angola had not been decided in Rio de Janeiro or in Lisbon, but in Heaven. Divine Will had ordered the recapture of Angola. God, by means of the miraculous voice of Jesuit Joam de Almeida, had ordered the transformation of the expedition in aid of the Angolistas into a frontal attack against the "enemies of the Faith" settled in Luanda.[302] Another witness to facts, the military expeditionary Luis Felix Cruz, who left Rio de Janeiro with Salvador's fleet, recorded a additional aspect of divine intervention. According to him, João IV had sent last-minute orders for Salvador de Sá to remain in Rio de Janeiro to defend the city against a likely Dutch attack. Allegedly dispatched from Lisbon in three different ships, the royal order got stranded, although all three vessels did reach Rio de Janeiro. For Luis Felix Cruz, divine providence, because it hid the royal order with such prodigious effects, meant that it did not mean to "hamper" the expedition for the retaking of Angola.[303]

From his Lisbon prison cell, Francisco Manuel de Melo, a Catholic rationalist, expressed still his belief in divine intervention and in the crusadelike character of the expedition: "the restoration of Angola was miraculous, God has made use of Salvador de Sá as an instrument of his revenge for the injuries that had been inflicted upon Him by His and our opponents."[304] Finally, in a fragment of his *História do Futuro*, Fr. Antonio Vieira emphasized the again-miraculous character of the expedition, highlighting the blessings poured out by Our Lady of the Assumption on the Portuguese and Brasílico soldiers, as well as the military marvel that took place on August 15, day of their entry in Luanda and date of the Solemnity of the Assumption.[305]

Salvador de Sá undertook the ritualization of the prophecy, changing the name of the city of Luanda to São Paulo of the Assumption and building a chapel dedicated to the "ensign saint" in the Luanda fort called "do Morro," which came to be named Fort of Saint Michael (Forte de São Miguel). Salvador placed the image of the saint he had brought over from Rio de Janeiro in the Fort's chapel.[306] At the end of his government, he returned to Guanabara and continued to promote the cult of Saint Michael.

A carrack of the Companhia Geral do Comércio's fleet, with which Salvador de Sá was closely associated, was called *São Miguel de Angola*.[307] He also installed the image of the saint in the church of his Campos dos Goitacazes estate and rebuilt the Jesuit College in the city of Santos, granting the institution incomes and naming it Saint Michael Archangel. The refoundation of the Santos College was revenge for the Jesuits and Rio de Janeiro against the Paulista Amerindian hunters, who, despite Salvador de Sá's opposition, had seized the college in 1640.[308] Thirty years later, Cadornega was able to include Fr. Almeida's Guanabara ecstasies in the plethora of miraculous visions that had underscored the great victories of the Christian West: Saint Barnard of Clairvaux visualizing from France the victories by Afonso Henriques in Portugal, Pius V watching from Rome the defeat of the Turkish fleet in Lepanto, among others.[309]

Yet the Jesuits' aid was not restricted to prophecies. Three missionaries with extensive experience in Angola and Congo ranked among the 1648 expeditionaries: the Luso-Bakongo Fr. Antônio do Couto, born of a Bakongo mother in São Salvador of Congo, where he would be nominated Portuguese representative and would work against the Italian Capuchins; brother Gonçalo João, mentioned above, missionary in West Central Africa for about thirty-five years, considered by the Overseas Council as the greatest specialist in the region and author of the celebrated memorial about the need for the recapture of Angola ("without Angola there is no Brazil"); and, finally, Fr. Felipe Franco. Fr. Franco had taken refuge in Rio de Janeiro after being rector of the Luanda College, which had earned him authority over the sobas able to mobilize men and aid in the Angolan hinterland. On returning to Brazil, he established himself as superior in the Ilhéus's Society of Jesus residence and as manager of the great Santana sugar mill. Like the celebrated Sergipe do Conde sugar mill, founded by Mem de Sá, the Santana sugar mill also belonged to the Jesuit College of Santo Antão, a Lisbon institution that had been bequeathed to the estate of the Linhares countess, Felipa de Sá, Salvador de Sá's aunt.[310] The strong ties uniting the Company of Jesus and the Sá oligarchy are thus made clear.

In the preface of his hagiography *Vida do padre Joam d'Almeida* (1658), on the "God's oracle" life, Fr. Simão de Vasconcellos dedicated his work to Salvador de Sá and added: "as God Our Lord has taken Europe's great princes as a means to found and increase the Company (of Jesus), He has likewise willed that the most illustrious Sás were to be the first and greatest benefactors [of the S.J.] in America."[311]

Therefore, with the help of the Heaven and the earth of Rio de Janeiro, Salvador de Sá, builder of the "Pax Lusitana" in the Ethiopic Ocean, led the third Luso-Brasílico fleet for the retaking of Angola. Composed of eleven carracks and four brigs (*patachos*), carrying around 2,000 men, the expedition had been funded to the tune of 70 percent by funds collected among Guanabara's merchants and planters.[312] Boasting a staff experienced in the South Atlantic and "good people and infantry experienced in the Portuguese frontier wars and in the Pernambuco campaign," the expeditionary force disembarked under fire, linked up with allied *sobas*, and after fighting in Luanda, defeated the Dutch in August 1648. Two ships were sent down south to accept the surrender of the WIC's Benguela detachment. São Tomé island also had fallen again be in Portuguese hands.[313]

Equipped mostly by planters and slave traders, the first New World colonists' task force sailed from Rio de Janeiro to Luanda in 1648, 260 years before General Pershing's army crossed the Atlantic to fight in the trenches of World War I (1918).[314] In a memorial sent to the Court shortly after the attack, the Luanda municipal council explicitly recognized that the successes of the retaking of Angola "would hardly have been achieved if the settlers of that illustrious city [of Rio de Janeiro] had not donated a very large sum of money with which the fleet was furnished and achieved the desired end."[315] Five years later, in a petition against the privileges granted to the Companhia Geral do Comércio, the Rio de Janeiro chamber proudly boasted of the expedition's merit: "Who can deny this city the glory of the reconquest of Angola?"[316] Nevertheless, Salvador de Sá never forgot his own central role, played not only in the preparation of the expeditionary force, but in the choice of Luanda as the strategic target for the Ethiopic Ocean reconquest. Two decades later, in a special session of the Lisbon's Overseas Council, he noted his past political and military actions with forceful words.

Times had been difficult for Salvador de Sá, who escaped a political imbroglio that nearly ended with his banishment to Africa in 1671.[317] He was a man, therefore, who needed to make himself useful to the Crown. This is what he did during the Overseas Council's discussions about the opening of a pathway between Angola and Mozambique, which I will examine further below. From the start, he insisted on taking for himself the command of the projected expedition in southern Africa. To stamp his intention more forcefully, Salvador de Sá recalled the retaking of Angola in the session of August 21, 1672, on precisely the day of the twenty-fourth anniversary of his feat of arms. According to him, the king's endorsement in the preparation of the task force of 1648 had been obtained with hard work. It happened thanks to his insistence alone, against the will of royal ministers and councilors. It had been him, Salvador de Sá, who had been fighting for it since 1643. "First spending five years chasing [royal] ministers, until King João IV . . . , almost of his own accord, ordered me to restore it [the sovereignty on Angola], granting me . . . in the same day . . . one government in Brazil [Rio de Janeiro's captaincy] and another in Angola."[318] Salvador de Sá gave to himself almost exclusive credit for the operation that resulted in the retaking of Angola. In the delicate context of his political rehabilitation, before the council members, some of them witnesses of the 1648 events, he gave his version of the Luanda victory and no councilor contradicted him.

The exploitation of slave-based agriculture demanded command of the two poles of the system: the Africans ports of trade and the South American slave zones. From the start, Dutch and Portuguese combatants considered Brazil and Angola to be a unified strategic field. Spanish, Portuguese, and Dutch witnesses and the geographical sequence of the battles attest that the shots fired in Africa did not represent just a ricochet of the war waged in Brazil. Mainland and Luso-Brasílico forces obtained a strategic victory in West Central Africa.

Given the Portuguese seventeenth-century monopoly on ports of trade, the African zones open to the slave trade still seemed relatively restricted. To explore their colonies in America, the European powers found the Portuguese already in place in the African ports of trade. It is worth insisting that the opening of a combat front in Africa, dragging naval forces and infantry from the mainland and Brazil into Angola—when most of the northeast had been taken and Dutch raids threatened Bahia and Rio de Janeiro—plainly illustrates the key role played by the control of African slave ports. Rio de Janeiro planters, slave traders, *peruleiros*, and merchants, helped by Brasílicos from Bahia and Pernambuco, got involved in the expedition. This stood in sharp contrast to the Paulista refusal, who were equally encouraged to participate in the enterprise.[319]

Indeed, there is no trace of the most skilled combatants of the Portuguese tropics, the Paulistas, among the expeditionaries. To be sure, São Paulo had been in a semi-insurrectional state since the 1640s, rising up against the Jesuits. Salvador de Sá had brought with him the amnesty granted to the São Paulo colonists. But he also had instructions to act prudently to reintroduce the Jesuits in that captaincy— by "gentle means"—and to reestablish Lisbon's sovereignty in the area. To do so, the Crown determined that 300 of Rio de Janeiro's soldiers were to be transferred to the São Paulo plateau.[320] Ironically, in his 1643 plans, Salvador de Sá intended to recruit Paulista militias for the Angolan expedition.[321] The opposite took place. Instead of furnishing men for the task force, insurgent São Paulo forced Lisbon to reassign resources and settle additional troops around their villages. Truly, the Paulistas showed little or no interest in the two businesses that led the Guanabara settlers and merchants to engage in the Angolan expedition, sugar plantations and the African slave trade with the Río de la Plata.

Illustrating the divergent paths taken by Portuguese American colonists, Raposo Tavares launched in March-April 1648 the oddest slave-hunting expedition of the modern era, the inland raid later denominated by Paulista authors the "Borders' *bandeira*" (1648–1651).[322] It aimed to hunt Indians from other communities after defeats endured in the South Guarani missions. Two columns of 200 *bandeirantes* and over 1,000 Indian warriors roamed through the west and the Amazon basin for three years, marching and canoeing up the Mamoré, the Madeira, and the Amazon Rivers up to Belém do Pará, in a 12,000-kilometer journey.[323] The *bandeira* amazed contemporaries. Father Antonio Vieira, who met Raposo Tavares and the surviving Paulistas in Belém, wrote the Paulistas performed "like the Argonauts, . . . a veritable great example of constancy and valor, if the cause [enslaving Indians] did not remove its luster."[324] Such an expedition, a peerless feat in the history of the Americas, resulted in a fiasco. It revealed to the Paulistas that the center-western and Amazon territory of South America did not shelter Amerindian concentrations similar to those pillaged by the *bandeirantes* in Guayrá and Tapes. In this sense, the long and fruitless journey by Raposo Tavares signals a historical limit to the great *bandeirante* expeditions. Not enough attention has been given to the simultaneity and the contrast between the two longest New World slaving expeditions—the failed Paulista autonomist Amerindian-hunting expedition and the Rio de Janeiro African-enslaving successful expedition, launched to reinsert Portuguese America in West Central Africa.

Who were, in fact, the expeditionaries who fought in Luanda? Dozens of promotion patents granted by Salvador de Sá to civilians and military men in the course of his government draw a profile of the combatants on both sides of the ocean (see appendix 4). There were militiamen and soldiers of various origins—troops from

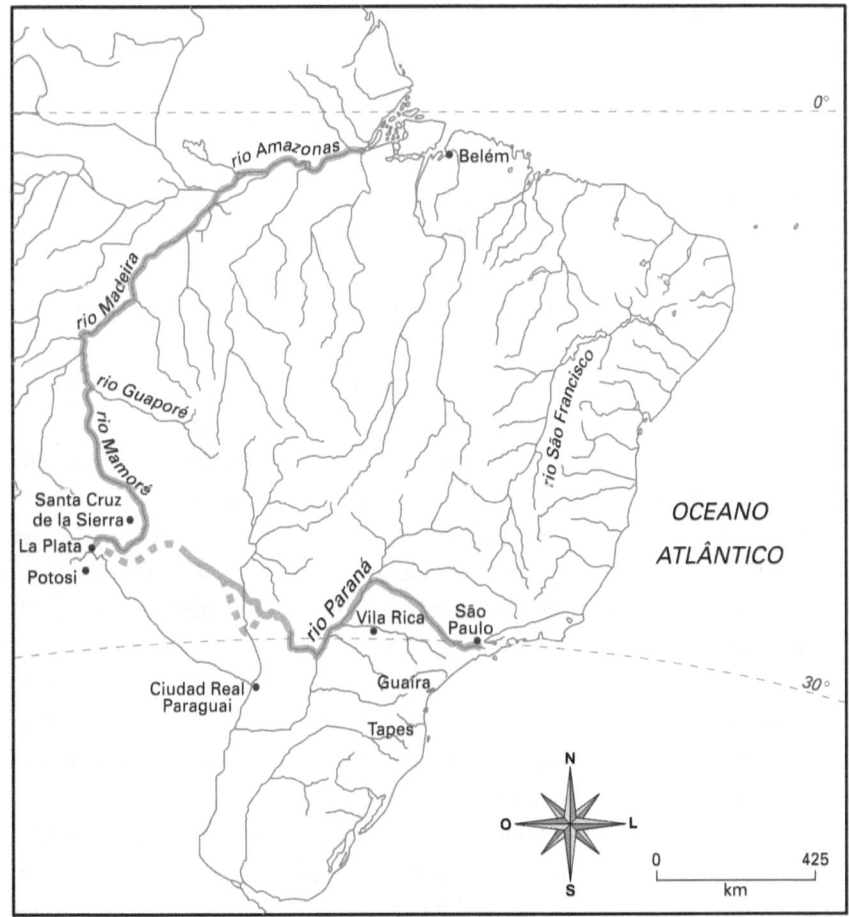

Map 6.1. Probable itinerary of the Raposo Tavares' *Bandeira* in 1648–1651. *Source:* Adapted from a map draw by Max Justo Guedes.

Portugal, Angolistas who had taken refuge in Brazil or in Europe after the WIC's attack, soldiers who had battled in Pernambuco and who had returned to Lisbon, other Brasílicos recruited in Rio de Janeiro and on the fronts of Pernambuco, Paraíba, and Bahia. Some of the soldiers embarked in Lisbon, "the scum of the armada and of the Limoeiro [Lisbon's jail]," complained Salvador, had deserted, others fallen ill in Rio before departing to Luanda. There seem to have been serious rivalries between officers hailing from the kingdom and those from Guanabara, Sá's captains.[325] It is reasonable to believe that most of the task force was composed—as was Souto Maior's fleet in 1645—by men from the northeastern Brasílico war and from the Rio de Janeiro's infantry regiment (*terço*).[326]

Rio De Janeiro–Buenos Aires, and Bahia–Benin

Another military expedition from Brazil, this time to recapture Elmina from the Dutch, was planned in 1657, when the Luso-Dutch war resumed. Admiral Brito Freyre, the author of the plan of attack, was a skilled Naval commander, and also a member of an important family of sugar-mill owners in Bahia. According to his strategy, Recife would be the base for an expedition composed of ships and experienced soldiers from Rio de Janeiro and Bahia. He also hoped to embark Luso-African militiamen from the Brasílico war, the "Blacks of the Henrique Dias' regiment," for the transatlantic offensive.[327] Despite the historical appeal (Elmina was "the first patrimony of this Crown," stated a royal letter of 1633), the expedition would not be carried out. Besides the strain that the attack would cause in Luso-Dutch relations (the capture of Elmina Castle in 1637 by the WIC had been less controversial than that of Luanda in 1641, as the latter broke the 1640 Truce Treaty between Portugal and the Netherlands), the economic gains were uncertain. The Mina Coast's littoral was subject to increasing European competition and some Europeans powers possessed fortresses in the area. Thus, in 1671, São Tomé's governor, intending to break the maritime and economic isolation of his captaincy, again proposed Brito Freyre's plan to the Crown.

Pretending that some Akan communities and local mulattoes, "Portuguese descendants . . . anxious to be Catholics," would help Portugal's task force attack the Dutch, he detailed the vulnerability of the WIC forces at Elmina.[328] Yet the proposal was not followed. One year later, in a letter to the Portuguese envoy in Madrid, Fr. Antonio Vieira regretted that Elmina had not yet been "recovered" by Lisbon.[329] Ultimately, the Mina Coast trade was recovered for Portuguese businesses some years later, thanks to the export of Bahia's tobacco. Disfavored in Luanda by the Pernambuco and Guanabara slave-trading competition, Bahian merchants took the Mina Coast route with tobacco and, later, with smuggled gold from Minas Gerais.[330] In the wake of the emergence of the slaving kingdoms of Asante and Daomey, the Bahians consolidated their hegemony in the area up to the end of the Atlantic slave trade.

By and large, the Brasílicos' designs redrew the Ethiopic Ocean's map after the Portuguese Restoration and the Thirty Years War. Plans for expeditions to recapture of Elmina fizzled out, mostly because they did not enjoy an economic and social drive comparable to that which Angola had generated in Rio de Janeiro.

To Salvador de Sá and his allies in Rio de Janeiro and Lisbon, the control of Angola, besides meeting the sugar planters' demand, was the key to penetrate the Río de la Plata. Critical for the Portuguese exchanges in Asia in the first decades of the seventeenth century, the slave trade to Buenos Aires and access to the Potosí silver fostered the 1648 expedition to Angola. In practice, compared with the axis Bahia–Mina Coast, the axis Buenos Aires–Rio de Janeiro-Luanda was much more integrated into the world-economy.

Two centuries after the WIC's attacks in Pernambuco and Bahia, in 1825, when Brazil's independence shook Portugal, a memorial of Lisbon's merchants and manufacturers pointed out the long-term negative consequences of the seventeenth-century Luso-Dutch war in the Atlantic. Recalling the "lucrative and advantageous" trade between Portugal and Africa's coast that created the "splendor" of Luanda, and the times when Lisbon had "more than thirty vessels bound to Angola," they stated: "the war with the Dutch . . . being fatal to the direct navigation we had from here [Lisbon to Africa's Coast]," diverted the Portuguese trade to the direct exchanges that Bahia and Rio de Janeiro undertook with Africa.[331]

The Dutch wars also reshaped Portuguese America. After the invasion of Pernambuco, sugar-mill owners from the region migrated to Bahia and to Rio de Janeiro.[332] Managing an important booty of slaves from Angola disembarked in 1652, Salvador de Sá developed the five sugar mills and forty cattle ranches he owned in the Guanabara Bay.[333] Once again governor of Rio de Janeiro (1660–1661), he expanded his lands in Campos, from which he expelled the Waitaká (Goitacá) Indian communities devastated by smallpox.[334] Easily accessible fertile land was thus opened up to the Rio de Janeiro planters, prompting the expansion of commercial agriculture and the increased entry of Africans in the Brazilian center-south.

In north Brazil, among others consequences, the Dutch wars spurred slave revolts and runaways, strengthening the Quilombos of Palmares in the Pernambuco's backlands.

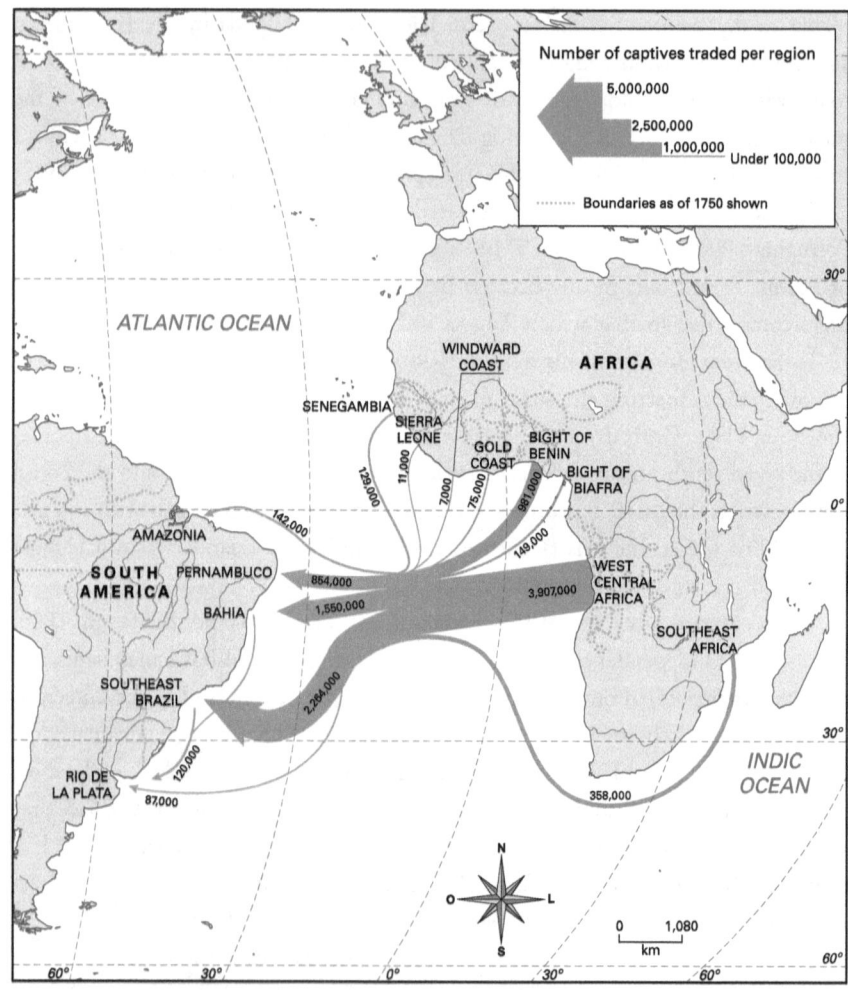

Map 6.2. Portuguese and Brazilian Slave-Trade 1550–1850. *Source:* Adapted from D. Eltis and D. Richardson, *Atlas of the Transatlantic Slave Trade*, 2010, map 170, p 257.

Consequences of the Palmares Wars

Once the Dutch War was concluded, Palmares stood out as one of the central concerns of the neighboring northeastern captaincies. Taking office in Recife to govern Pernambuco (1661–1664), Francisco de Brito Freyre wrote to the king, "Y.M. has just finished the war with the Dutch and has already started [that war] with the blacks of Palmares."³³⁵ After launching ill-fated attacks against the Palmares *quilombos*, Brito Freyre decided to support an appeasement policy. "After frightening the Blacks of Palmares . . . I tried by all ways to persuade them . . . to live quietly in obedience to my government."³³⁶ Therefore, he proposed a deal in which he granted, by royal authority, recognition of freedom for all Palmaristas and their descendants, as well as ownership of the land where they lived. In exchange, the *quilombolas* would not take in any runaway slaves, returning to their masters those who sought refuge in Palmares. Negotiations broke down and hostilities resumed. Shortly after taking office, governor of Pernambuco Miranda Henriques (1667–1670), former captain of a company in Angola, launched a troop of 1,400 men against Palmares. In all, twenty-five colonial expeditions were sent against Palmares in the years between 1654 and 1678.³³⁷

Nonetheless, Brito Freyre, an admiral and an old hand in Portuguese overseas affairs, persisted in the defense of a peaceful solution. He thought that the Palmaristas could be employed as an auxiliary territorial force, if "favor and freedom" were granted to them, so as to persuade them to "live free in the way their relatives had enlisted in Henrique Dias's *terço*, who the king had ordered to be freed."³³⁸

Years later, Oratorian missionaries went over to the Serra da Barriga in the attempt to build peaceful relations between the Palmaristas and colonial authorities. Their efforts also came to nothing. A proposal by Jesuit Antonio Maria Bonucci now took the stage. Convinced of the possibility of solving the conflict peacefully, Bonucci intended to settle a permanent mission among the Palmares inhabitants. Thus, "it will be possible to reduce them to a life subject to the Church and to Your Majesty's and this government's laws . . . If it pleases Your Majesty, they should be promised the safety of their lives and freedom."³³⁹ Fr. Antônio Vieira, consulted by the Crown in his role as Visitador (Jesuit inspector) in Brazil, wrote from Bahia against this petition in which he firmly exposed the political imperative of the anti-Palmarist war. Addressed in August 1691 to Roque Monteiro Paim, high court magistrate and president of the Board of Missions (Junta das Missões), the document begins by disqualifying the Italian missionary, "of little or no experience in such matters." Another more experienced missionary had conceived of the same project, deemed impossible by the experts who had been consulted. To Fr. Vieira, the only "efficacious and effective" way to solve the conflict would be the concession of freedom to the black rebels, granted by the Crown and by their masters, so that they could live in the region "like the other Indians and free gentiles [non-Christians]," indoctrinated by missionaries and vicars. Displaying his admirable dialectics, Vieira expounded the particular solution to the conflict to vigorously refute it in the name of the systemic coherence of slavery. "However, this same freedom thus considered would mean the total destruction of Brazil, because, as the other negroes become aware that by such means they could manage to achieve freedom, each city, each village, each place, each sugar mill, would soon become so many other Palmares, [as slaves would] flee and enter the jungle with all their capital, which is none but their own body."[340]

Vieira did not seal Palmares's fate. The petition by the Italian Jesuit had been examined at the beginning of January 1691 by the marquis of Montebelo, governor of Pernambuco. At that time, Domingos Jorge Velho's Paulistas, called on six years before by another governor, had already laid siege to Palmares.[341] There were no longer conditions for missionary work in the area: Fr. Bonucci's initiative was destined to fail independently of Fr. Antonio Vieira's opinion. Nevertheless, it is Fr. Vieira who once more enunciated the implacable law of Brasílico slavery. No mercy, no amnesty should be granted to the Palmaristas. Otherwise, so many more *quilombos* would erupt, in the whole of colonial society, in every city, in every village, in every sugar mill. If Palmares remained, Brazil would come to an end.

Three years later, in a report on São Paulo Amerindians, Fr. Antonio Vieira would perform the exact opposite reasoning. Against the vote of his S.J. superiors in Brazil and in Portugal, he recognized the right to escape of the Indians enslaved by the Paulistas. His argument cut sharp in a period of Moorish corsair activity in the Mediterranean: to force such Amerindians to stay in São Paulo under the pretext that the economic survival of the captaincy depended on them "would be the same as to say that the [Christian] captives of Algiers were forced not to escape or to seek their freedom by other means, in order to preserve Algiers."[342] The inviolable right to escape of the Amerindians captured by the Paulistas was equated to that of European Christians captured by the Moors in Algiers. But the *quilombolas* were inexorably condemned to persecution, to captivity, and to death. Such was the price of the continuity of Luso-Brazilian slavery. As seen above, the contradiction between the two stances is only apparent. To the Jesuits, the enslavement of the black people was a necessary condition to secure the freedom of the Indians.

The Paulistas' Paradox

The demand for coerced labor led the Paulistas to enslave Amerindians in the hinterlands. What were the motives of their sedentarization? From the 1650s on,

Paulista militias had been called to Bahia to attack Indian communities around the expanding farms of the Recôncavo, the area surrounding Bahia's bay. In 1672 and 1673, "they destroyed the nations of the Tapuya, Tupi . . . , freeing those lands and tranquilizing the settlers," stated an Overseas Council report in 1674. The captains of those militias, Bayão Parente and Braz Arzão, together with their men and their families, "more than 400 White persons, aside from Mestizos [Mamelucos] and Indians," settled in the area and started to raise new villages.³⁴³ Further documents contained in the proceedings generated by the contention between Domingos Jorge Velho and authorities after the destruction of Palmares, also help us to understand the *bandeirantes*' metamorphosis.

Sotto-Mayor, governor of Pernambuco (1685–1688), related the circumstances that gave rise to the *bandeirantes*' fight against Palmares: "I have received a letter from some Paulistas who roam the hinterlands, [. . .] in which they asked for the patents of Captain-Major and Captain to conquer those gentiles [Indians]. As that went against Your Majesty's orders, I did not have them sent. And, because those men are true hinterlanders [*sertanejos*], and because they number 400 men-in-arms, I have requested [the patents] for this conquest of Palmares, granting them patents of *conquistadores* [. . .] the time for those arisen [blacks] to see their own ruin has arrived." The Paulistas, banned from hunting Amerindians, accepted the offer. With other *bandeirantes*, relatives, partners, and war servants, Domingos Jorge Velho laid siege to the *quilombolas*. "War servants" were Indian slaves, usually Temiminos, trained for the slave-hunting expeditions.³⁴⁴ According to the tactics of the long Paulista wars, as opposed to the short Amerindian wars, Jorge Velho avoided frontal battles, blockaded rebel villages, captured isolated individuals, blocked the pathways, spoiled the fields, set fire to crops, poisoned wells, and set up prolonged sieges in Palmares's surroundings. After several years of fighting, skirmishes, and terrorism the *bandeirantes* routed the organized resistance of the Africans and Afro-Brasílico fighters in 1694.³⁴⁵ But the victors would not be able to enjoy the fruits of their victory.

Very quickly, the former planters repossessed their land abandoned due to the Palmarista guerrilla fighting and until then promised to the *bandeirantes*.³⁴⁶ The dispute reached the Courts in Lisbon, in a wave of protests, requests, and memorials sent to the mainland by the Paulistas. Helped by his agent, Bento Sorrel Camiglio, Domingos Jorge Velho was clever in the defense of his interests.

The manifestoes in which they underline the sacrifices incurred in the effort to serve the Crown are well written, perspicacious, and ironic. In a lively text, an exemplary document of the dialogue between Brasílicos and the mainland regarding the purpose of colonization, they compiled a "brief digression" to the king about the nature and aims of the *bandeirantismo*. In fact, the Paulistas' commander developed an audacious defense of the Amerindian enslavement, a practice once again banned by the Jesuits' provisional victory in 1693.[347]

> Our troops, with which we set out to conquer the gentile [Indians] in this vastest of hinterlands, are not people in Your Majesty's books, neither are they obliged in exchange for pay or supplies. They are gatherings carried out by some of us, each one with his armed servants [*servos de armas*]; and together we set out [. . .] not to capture, as some hypochondriacs are intent of leading Y.M. to believe, but instead [. . .] to acquire the savage and human flesh-eating Tapuia [Gê] gentile [Indians] in order to reduce him to the knowledge of urbane humanity and human community, to association and rational customs, so as to have them reached by the Laws of God and by the mysteries of the Catholic faith, sufficiently for them to achieve their own salvation.

The *bandeiras* constituted private enterprises. They owed nothing to metropolitan initiatives or to the Royal Treasury and helped to save the Indians' souls. The document continues as follows:

> For those who wish to turn them [the Indians] into angels before making them men toil in vain; and with those [Indians] so acquired and reduced, we strengthen our troops and we wage war on the others, obstinate and stubborn, to reduce them. And if, later, we help them in order to work our crops, no injustice is done unto them, because it is so both for their own maintenance and that of their offspring as much as it is for ours and our kin's. And this is far from enslaving them, but, instead, they are rendered an invaluable service as they are taught to plough, to seed, to harvest and to work for their own maintenance. Things that, before being taught by the Whites, they could not do. Is this understood, Sir?

The Indians' enslavement incorporated them into "human society," inculcating the practice of useful labor or commercial agriculture. Only the Amerindians forced to "rational custom" would become sensitive to religion. By correlating Amerindian social and religious promotion to work useful in colonial terms, such arguments inverted the doctrinal postulates of the Discoveries: Jorge Velho suggested that evangelization should follow, not precede, the compulsory socialization of the Amerindians.

In their allegations, the *bandeirantes* took pleasure in stating their merit and bravery. But the true target of their attack on Palmares shows in a turn of phrase. The concrete, material reason that launched the southerners to endeavor, in the middle of the "toughest, most rustic and famished hinterland in the world," to kill and die in a troublesome march, "the most unaided [march] that there has been to date in the said hinterland, and perhaps ever will be." As Jorge Velho listed the documents in which he was promised the possession of the lands taken from the *quilombolas*, he underlined that without the guarantee that they will have those lands, "what reason would there be for the supplicants [the Paulistas] to come over to conquer other lands, leaving behind [their] bigger, better and peerless land, lest the distance from maritime markets [*praças*], and which unencumbered possession they have enjoyed without opposition?"

In the midst of legal argument and patriotic oaths, the detail revealing the greed of the Paulistas rooted in the Pernambuco's bushland stands out. Elsewhere in the South, the Paulistas owned "bigger and better land" compared to that around Palmares, as well as numerous Indian "servants." But this property had a big disadvantage—its distance from the maritime marketplaces. The key factor for the use of soil in Brazil is thus revealed. The availability of land, a variable much used in Brazilian economic history, loses all meaning if studied outside this context. If this were not the case, what reason would there have been for the Paulistas to migrate north?

Portuguese America's territory encompassed sparse economic sprawls connected to trading ports. The colonists who lived around such areas were captured by the Atlantic exchange network. However, those who remained isolated in the backlands were disconnected from the Atlantic. Thus, the surprising argument by Domingos Jorge Velho: "The supplicants have many of their kin in the São Paulo captaincy, in which there is no more land for them to spread out, and they wish to come over and join the supplicants." Another document confirms that "the intention of the said *Paulistas* is to call other colonists, their fellow countrymen, who desire to swarm in; because in São Paulo there is nowhere for them to plough and seed: and this transmigration will be a very useful thing to these [northern] captaincies."[348]

Here is the paradox. If we are to believe his and other *bandeirante* testimonials, those of the most able experts in the backlands, at the end of the 1600s there was a serious "lack of land" in São Paulo. Evidently this is not a reference to the land's physical limits, or to the scarcity of land along the coast. After all, when Jorge Velho pointed out the inconveniences of the farms kept by his men and by himself in São Paulo and in the Bahian backlands, he referred not to the distance from maritime ports—geographical location—but to the distance separating such lands from maritime marketplaces (*praças*), their economic location. To realize the value of the goods produced by their Amerindians, the *bandeirantes* needed to transact with merchants at seaside marketplaces. Indeed, it was the presence of such brokers that transformed, throughout the Lusitanian empire, a maritime port into a specific trade marketplace. The problem, the whole of the problem, is that the very merchants who were buying regional products for export were also sellers of imported products—more specifically, sellers of Africans.

Having followed diverse paths, we find again the Braudelian postulate previously elaborated: when it is impossible to close the trade circuit, it is also impossible to close the deal—"*bouclage impossible, affaire impossible*": ownership of land and enslaved Indians did not secure regular access to the Atlantic market. To transform the surplus extorted from the Amerindians into merchandise, colonists must find a way to insert their products into the exchange circuit. From the start, he faced the commercial—and not only demographic (the eventual inexistence of Indian labor force)—imposition of buying Africans and becoming even more linked to the Atlantic networks. "Lack of lands" and "lack of hands," therefore, have little to do with aboriginal geography and demography of Portuguese America. These are connected variables that are explained by and compensate one another in the wider scope of the Southern Atlantic slave-based system.

Thus the incoherence that the slave trade imprinted on land ownership laws and on Amerindian status is made clear. The two issues bear distinct meanings, but are imbricated with one another. The laws on colonial property were essentially determined by the possession of captives. This first economic subordination is defined, in its turn, by the social subordination studied in the previous pages: African slavery was the determinant mode, while captivity and Amerindian compulsory work figured as a secondary mode of colonial exploitation. In other words, the dynamics of Atlantic slavery overdetermined the laws on land and on Portuguese America's Indians. Such conclusions apply, mutatis mutandis, to Angola, where the slave trade undermined Lisbon's attempts to organize fixed colonial settlements.

Spatial Capacity and Social Control of Colonization

If it is true that the Overseas Council understood the scope of the Paulista raids, it is also certain that authorities in Brazil damned the *bandeirantes* as "hinterland corsairs," half-Indians unable to speak the Portuguese language.[349] Armed, of mixed blood, undisciplined, unbeatable in bush war, advancing on the trail of Amerindians and Africans, the Paulistas frightened authorities and northern sugar planters as much as the *quilombolas* did. Porto Seguro (Bahia) was the stage for an uprising in 1691 and found itself occupied by dozens of *bandeirantes* from the Palmares expedition sheltering there, headed by four Paulistas who bossed around the village "as if it was theirs." Five Paulistas were shot and another forty banished to Angola in the ensuing repression carried out by the governor-general.[350]

As the hostilities against Zumbi came to a close, Caetano de Melo e Castro, governor of Pernambuco (1693–1699), aware of the troubles caused by the Luso-African kinglets of the Mozambican "*prazos*," where he had been governor (1682–1685), sent the Court a warning. The Paulistas, he reflected, "as a savage people, indomitable and who live off what they steal," should not be authorized to fix residence in the Palmares region. "Because the neighboring captaincies will experience greater damage to their cattle and farms than the [damage] done by the same arisen negroes [from Palmares]." The Council retorted that this was an exaggeration, because, if the Paulistas so desired, "as knowledgeable in the whole of the Brazilian hinterland, they would have chosen impregnable sites from which they could harass your Majesty's vassals." The councilors presumed that the *bandeirantes*' camps would be useful "in the defense of Your Majesty's posts and in the offensive against the maroon's villages and the savage gentiles [Indians]." The situation demanded prudence, however: the plots eventually granted to the Paulistas should be divided and interspersed between "those granted to Pernambucano settlers, thus [the Paulistas] will be divided and free from the objection of fear."[351]

The mainland's "objection of fear" regarding the bandeirantes turned up again in the 1700 dispatch sent by the King to the governor-general of Brazil and ex-governor of Angola, João de Lencastre. Lencastre was disturbed by the absence of military defenses around São Paulo and the gold-mine territory, at a troubled period. Indeed, there was the War of the League of Augsburg [1689–1697], featuring the French strategic naval turn, favoring the corsair raids leading to the sack of Cartagena (1697), and the already-announced War of Succession in Spain (1702–1713). Pirates roamed the coast between Paraty and Cabo Frio, precisely at a time when the shipments of inland gold to Lisbon increased. At once, the governor-general made explicit the political ambiguity of the Paulistas. They

> have shown a suspicious degree of fidelity in many occasions, in the little obedience with which they observe Your Majesty's laws, and are, for the most part, criminals, . . . and above all very freedom-loving, in which they have been living for the many years since the creation of their village. And, on seeing the opulence and wealth that fortune has bestowed on them in the discovery of the said [gold] mines, [. . .] they could well choose to subject themselves to any foreign nation that would preserve the freedom and insolence in which they live, and also to whoever they believe can let them have the conveniences that ambition usually facilitates to such people, the chief one, the one they crave for, being the enslavement of the Indians.[352]

The political consequences of the economic hindrances resulting from the enslavement of Amerindians are evidenced here. Conversely, the advantages of the appropriation of enslaved African slaves through the Atlantic networks are confirmed. Evolving outside the established mercantile networks, the Indian-hunting expeditions escaped metropolitan social control. Their existence seemed potentially dangerous to colonial domination.

In the same order of ideas, it is interesting to observe that the French example of La Rochelle ("Rochelas" in Portuguese), citadel of regional and Huguenot resistance to the centralizing policies of Richelieu, would be recalled in very precise political-military incidents in 1600s Portuguese America. There were four enclaves in Portuguese America where allegedly "Rochelas"—understood as poles of resistance to monarchic and metropolitan power—were denounced as such to the Crown: São Paulo, in the year 1654, in the context of the anti-Jesuit and anti-mainland Paulista movement in favor of Amerindian captivity (as denounced by Brito Freyre); Pará and Maranhão, in 1654, in the conflict of the settlers against Jesuits and royal authorities regarding the management of Indian labor (letter by Fr. Antonio Vieira); the Ibiapaba Sierra (Ceará), pointed out as the den of various kinds of apostates and unbelieving Amerindians left after the Dutch occupation (memorial by Father Vieira); and finally, for the above analyzed reasons, Palmares in 1694 (a letter by Governor Caetano de Mello e Castro).[353] In other words, there were four La Rochelle–like places ("Rochelas") in 1600s Brazil: two in Brasílico regions based on Indian coerced labor and two in non-European enclaves engaged in an open war against colonial and European authority. To my knowledge, no La Rochelle-like places were then denounced within zones by the African slave trade.

The turbulence that resulted in the nonintegration of the man-hunters into the Atlantic exchanges disappeared in the beginning of the 1700s, when the gold rush generated an internal market in the colony. The *bandeirantes* had used their Amerindians in mining since the discovery of gold in the area later called Minas Gerais. Thanks to the Indians owned by his family, Garcia Rodrigues Pais, Fernão Dias Pais's eldest son, obtained a royal contract (1699) to open the New Road (Caminho Novo) between Rio de Janeiro and Minas Gerais, becoming the first great road contractor in Brazil.[354] Before that, the Paulistas and their Amerindians had already been employed to open another strategic pathway in the Ceará hinterland: the terrestrial path between Maranhão and the Estado do Brasil, isolated from one another by the winds and currents halting navigation between the two regions.[355] More Paulistas then migrated to the São Francisco River Valley, where they established cattle ranches. Important Paulista people such as Mathias Cardoso de Almeida and Antônio Gonçalves Figueira followed the same itinerary. Others, such as Francisco Pedroso de Almeida, built farms and ranches for food production along the trails leading into the Minas Gerais region.

A new market opened in the colony, a market where gold merchants predominated. This market would connect to Atlantic circuits, and in particular to the African slave trade. Opening fresh possibilities for cattle raising and the cultivation of foodstuffs in the São Francisco Valley, this economic scenario ruined the productive areas and trade networks based on Indian coerced labor in the mid-south. The Portuguese administration soon perceived the *bandeirantes'* metamorphosis. The Overseas Council considered in 1705 sending a column of *bandeirantes* to help the Colonia do Sacramento, in the mouth of the Río de La Plata, surrounded by Amerindians emboldened by the Spanish. However, arguments put forward by Freitas Serrão, former magistrate of the Bahia High Court and a man of high military acumen, led to the plan being dropped. His vote summed up in a few lines one century of *bandeirante* enterprise.

> Admitting that years ago they [the Paulistas] successfully attacked the Indians in Castilian villages, they [the Castilian villages] had not at that time, however, the slightest fear of such invasion, and there is no force able to resist an unexpected assault; and the Paulistas usually penetrated the hinterland, supporting themselves from its fruits, guided and defended by the many

Indians they had domesticated; however now, lacking such [Indian] people and experience, and given to the greed for gold and [enjoying] sustenance from the foodstuffs that the gold mines attracted from all parts of Brazil, they will not accept such enterprise easily.[356]

The defeat in the *Emboabas* War (1707–1709) was *bandeirante* autonomism's death knell.[357] But the arrogance that Indian enslavement imprinted on São Paulo colonists left a lasting impression on colonial and mainland writers. In the melancholic pages dedicated in his 1880 book to the independence of Brazil, Oliveira Martins meditates on the tough confrontation that would have shaken Portuguese America if the 1822 independence process had been headed not by "statesman" José Bonifácio, but "some genuine representative of the Paulista spirit."[358]

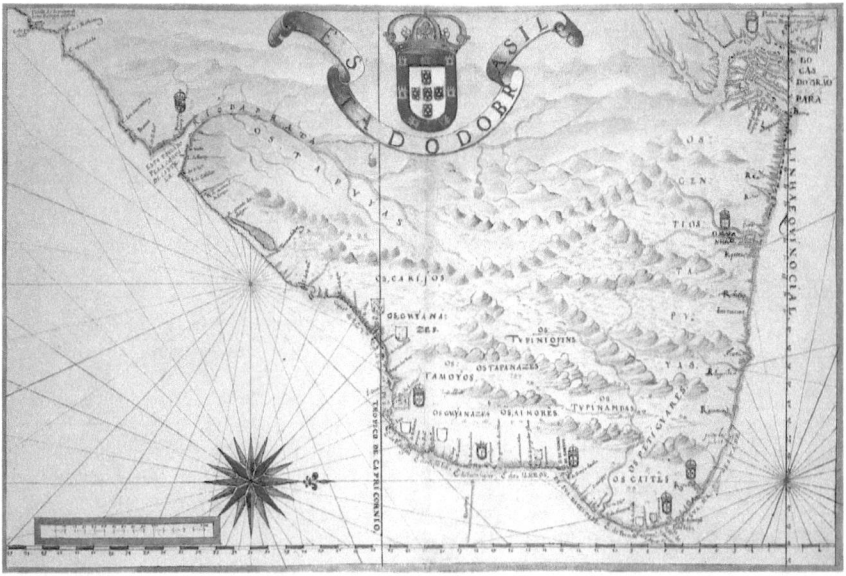

1. João Teixeira Albernas, *Mapa do Estado do Brasil* (1631). The royal cosmographer Albernas depicted the geography of South America through the prism of the sixteenth century shipmasters. The Abrolhos Archipelago appears as a long strand of reefs, but pilots didn't know its full extent. Almost perpendicular in the map, the Estado de Grão Pará Maranhão is located in the counter way of the Estado do Brasil, pointing out the distinctive sailing routes of North and Center-South of Portuguese America. *Source:* Itamaraty Map Collection, Rio de Janeiro.

2. Unknown author, *Chafariz d'El-Rey em Lisboa* (c. 1570–1580). A painting recently discovered by art historians offers an uncommon perspective on sixteenth-century Lisbon. By an anonymous Dutch painter, it portrays the astonishment of northern Europeans over the significant presence of blacks in Portugal's capital. *Source:* The Berardo Collection, Lisbon.

3. Georg Marggraf and Johanes Blaeus, *Brasilia Qua Parte Paret Belgis* (1647). The full extent of Dutch Brazil. Its instability is evident in the battle scenes and troop movements. Also visible are sugar mills. The São Francisco valley, where ranches and cattle fields were expanding, stands out in the image. *Source:* Beatriz and Mario Pimenta Camargo Collection, São Paulo.

4. Jan van Kessel, the Elder, *Americque* (1666). It is one of Jan van Kessel's four paintings of the four continents, a series completed between 1664 and 1666. In the allegory entitled *Europe*, the central image shows Rome. The painting entitled *Asia* has Jerusalem at its center, and the *Africa* painting has a "Temple of the Idols." In the painting *Americque*, the central plate represents Paraíba, a province of the former Dutch Brazil. It is depicted as the region at the heart of the New World. Behind the portray of couple formed of a South American black and an Indian with their children, an overseas landscape includes artifacts, animals and images from America and Asia. *Source:* Alte Pinakothek, Munich. Copyright © Blauel/Gnamm–Artothek (Public domain, https://commons.wikimedia.org/wiki/File:The_Continent_of_America_1666_Jan_van_Kessel_the_Elder.jpg).

5. *Rei de Manicongo* (c. 1530). At the turn of the fifteenth century, King Nzinga Nkuwu, the Manicongo, ruler of Congo, converted to Christianity and was baptized João I by the Portuguese missionaries. An independent kingdom with a bishopric in its capital Sao Salvador, today Mbanza Congo, the Congo boasted diplomatic ties with Lisbon, Madrid and Rome, and sent embassies to other European capitals. The image displays the Coat of Arms of the Manicongo in an royal illuminated manuscript with 134 others coat of arms of European monarchs and Portuguese aristocratic families, ordered by the Portuguese king João III. *Source:* Antônio Godinho, *Livro da nobreza e perfeição das armas* (1521–1541), Lisbon, Instituto dos Arquivos Nacionais, Torre do Tombo

6. Unknown author, *Salvador Correa de Sa* (c. 1660). Son and grandson of two Rio de Janeiro governors, Salvador de Sá (1602–1686) and his family also governed that captaincy. Victor over the Dutch in Angola, member of the Overseas Council, he was, alongside the Jesuit Antonio Vieira, the European statesmen who best knew the South Atlantic. *Source:* Florence © Galeria degli Uffizi.

7. *Cortege of Njinga, queen of Matamba* (c. 1660). An enemy of the Portuguese, of Salvador de Sá, and of the Brasílicos in Angola, Queen Njinga (1582–1663), the great African warrior, in a procession with her followers, musicians, favorites, and officials, carrying an arch and the Jagas' hatchet. *Source:* Cavazzi manuscript, Modena, Carlo Araldi Collection.

8. *Queen Njinga punishing her vassals* (c. 1660). The narratives on the Matamba kingdom, governed by a tyrant and warmonger queen, attracted the attention of later European writers and thinkers. Among others, Hegel and the Marquis de Sade wrote their reflections about Queen Njinga. *Source:* Cavazzi manuscript, Modena, Carlo Araldi Collection.

9. Unknown author, Frontispiece of *Historia Geral das Guerras Angolanas*, Luanda (1681). An essential work for understanding the South Atlantic, Antonio de Oliveira de Cadornega's book, written from the perspective of the colons in Angola, the Angolista, is a history of Portuguese West Central Africa. *Source:* Antonio de Oliveira de Cadornega, *Historia Geral das Guerras Angolanas*, Luanda, 1681, Lisbon, Academia de Ciências.

10. *Jagas beheading prisoners* (c. 1660). Feared warriors, the Jagas sometimes allied with the Portuguese in slaving raids for the transatlantic slave trade. *Source:* Cavazzi manuscript, Modena, Carlo Araldi Collection.

11. *Jaga warrior* (c. 1660). The war hatchet was the main weapon of the Jagas. In hand-to-hand combat, it was equal to European weapons. The *lunga* or *malunga*, a double clapperless metal bell, known in Brasil by its Yoruba name, the *agogo*, was a sacred object to the Jagas. *Source:* Cavazzi manuscript, Modena, Carlo Araldi Collection.

12. *Angolan woman with hoe* (c. 1660). The iron hoe was common in sub-Saharan Africa. Field work was generally the province of women, and many performed the same activity in Brazil. *Source:* Cavazzi manuscript, Modena, Carlo Araldi Collection.

13. Zacharias Wagener, *Slaves Market in Recife* (c. 1640). Despite reservations and moral objections expressed in the Netherlands, the Dutch of Brazil, at the instigation of Maurits van Nassau-Siegen, became actively involved in the Atlantic slave trade. *Source:* Zacharias Wagener, *Their Buch*, f. 106, Berlin, Kupferstich Kabinett.

14. Unknown author, *Slaves uprising in a ship* (1776). One of the rare representations of a tragic event. The 1776 ex-voto of the captain of a slave ship, in gratitude for the "miracle of Our Lady of the Rosary of the Castle" that allowed him to escape alive from an on-board rebellion near the port of Ilheus. The ship had Africans who had disembarked in Recife and were being sent south to Rio de Janeiro. *Source:* Museu de Etnologia do Porto, Portugal.

15. Zacharias Wagener, *Woman in a Palanquin* (c. 1640). In the seventeenth century, the Dutch painter Zacharias Wagner did the first painting of a scene that would become a classic in the drawings by foreign artists who visited Brazil in the nineteenth century. Known in West Central Africa as *tipoye*, from the Tupi word *ti'poya*, the hammock probably has colonial Luso-Brazilian origins. *Source:* Zacharias Wagener, *Their Buch*, f. 104, Berlin, Kupferstich Kabinett.

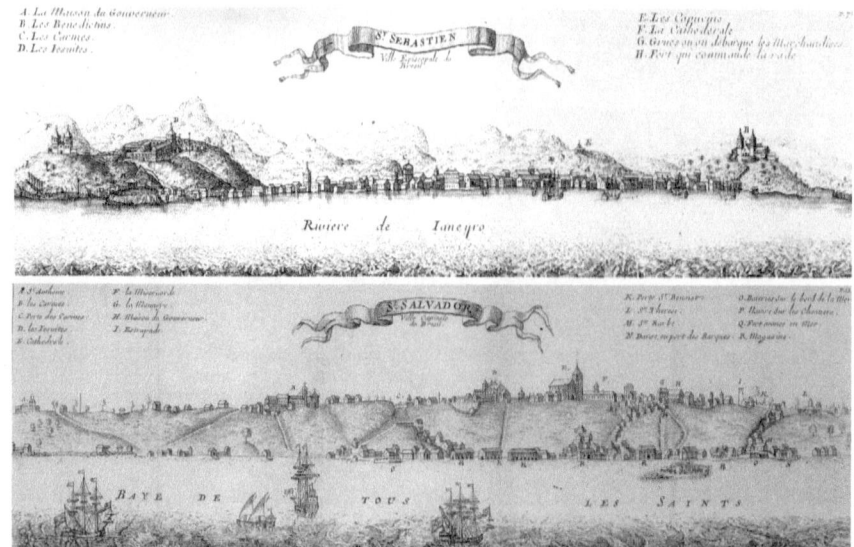

16. *Rivière de Janeiro et Saint Salvador, ville capitale du Brésil* (1698). Salvador de Bahia was the capital of the government and the main city of Portuguese America. But Rio de Janeiro also played a fundamental role in developing a Brazilian economic space in the South Atlantic. *Source:* François Froger, *Rélation d'un Voyage fait en 1695, 1696 & 1697*, Paris, 1698, Biblioteca Brasiliana Guita e José Mindlin, Universidade de São Paulo.

Chapter 7

Brasílica Angola

The Dutch invasion unified the strategic field formed of the South American and West Central African fronts of the Thirty Years War. From then on, slavery's two complementary poles became part and parcel of the canons of overseas politics. Impaired in Asia, Lisbon's policy refocused on the Atlantic. Brazil influenced the 1500s Portuguese imaginary only slightly (*The Lusiads* only makes two brief references to Portuguese America), but it emerged in the Braganza Restoration as the mainstay of the kingdom. Indeed, in 1655, in a meeting with the Chevalier de Jant, Mazarin's envoy to the Lisbon Court, King João IV complained about the "very great (*grandíssimas*) expenses" he had in India and praised the high yields he had in Brazil, that he reckoned as Portugal's "milch cow."[1] The outstanding new position of the South American colony figures in a revealing passage in Father Balthazar Telles's *Chronica* (1645–1647), the first global history of the Portuguese Jesuits. As he narrated the missions to the Amerindians, Telles presented a summary of the geography and history of Portuguese America since the Discovery. But he concedes that his countrymen were already familiar with all that, stating that his summary was meant for foreign readers only, because in Lisbon "much known [are] the affairs of Brazil, since they are today as natural as those of Portugal."[2]

There was more. It had been likewise made evident in Lisbon that Brazil represented continuity beyond American frontiers, in Angola. Royal letters, provisions, Crown contracts, palatine council minutes, all such documents disseminated the postulate stated in the anti-Dutch war: Angola supported Brazil, which in turn supported Portugal.[3] Designated at around that time as "Chronicler of Brazil," the Brazilian born Diogo Gomes Carneiro was assigned the task of writing a *História do Brasil*.[4] This *History*, bringing together years of documentary research, has been lost, leaving behind an absence that has been felt by generations of historians up to today. Still, the only surviving reference to it is significant for the study of the formation of Brazil in the Ethiopic Ocean. Indeed, by a royal order of 1661, the yearly wage of 200,000 *réis* allotted to the chronicler for the execution of the work would be paid in equal parts by four municipal councils: Bahia, Recife, Rio de Janeiro, and Luanda.[5] Angola's colonists, incorporated into the fate of Brazil—of Atlantic slave-trading Brazil, to the exclusion of the São Paulo and Maranhão Amerindian-hunting municipal councils—were to contribute to the funding of this now-missing *History of Brazil*.[6]

Up to here, we have focused on the deportation of the Angolan peoples into American lands. Now we must examine the movement that rendered Brazil's history so singular: the transport of its settlers, priest, militiamen, traders, and merchandise into Africa. Various types of exchanges united both sides of the ocean. The thoroughfares ran along five itineraries, according to the economic junctures and the maritime currents' seasonal movements: Portugal-Angola-Brazil-Portugal, Portugal-Brazil-Angola-Portugal, Portugal-Brazil-Angola-Buenos Aires-Portugal, Portugal-Brazil-Angola-Brazil-Portugal, and, at last, Brazil-Angola-Brazil.[7]

The first route, from Lisbon straight down to Luanda (corresponding to the first step of the so-called triangular trade) was determined by a monsoon: favorable winds blowing between mid-September and mid-January. Outside of the favorable period, the trip could take up to seven months, instead of the habitual two. Delays due to the doldrums off the Congo estuary, the so-called "Palmar," feared by the Portuguese sailors since the sixteenth century, caused deaths among the crew.[8]

"A few vessels set sail on May 5 from this city [of Lisbon] and others on October 20, and all arrived together in Angola on January 1," warned an anonymous pilot at the end of the 1500s.[9] Later, the *Roteiro de Portugal para Angola* (1712) alerted sailors that voyages along the African coast should be taken in small boats able to pierce through the calms. Such was traveling "by the North," coasting north and west Africa. There was another itinerary, discovered by Duarte Lopes on his voyage to the Congo (1578), the "wide voyage" (*viagem larga*), which became the almost exclusive route for the Lisbon-Luanda leg.[10] The captain could wait up to March when leaving Lisbon aboard large vessels (*naus grossas*) (above 300 tons capacity). But it was convenient to sail southwest, toward Brazil, following the wide voyage. As taught by the royal cosmographer Antonio Mariz de Carneiro (1631–1642), "if you wish to sail [from Portugal] to Angola, you should follow the path of the vessels bound to India in March [. . .] and the more windward you follow the Brazil's coast the better sailing you achieve," a statement repeated by the royal cosmographer Pimentel in his 1712 *Roteiro*. At 30° S one tacked NNE, toward the Cape of Good Hope, and then turned north, sailing up to Benguela or Luanda (8° 50, S). May, June, and July, months of interseasonal storms, should be avoided in this last step.[11]

As a safety measure, due to the corsairs stalking the Upper Guinea coast, and, above all, to benefit from the southwest trade winds, Lisbon's vessels sailed the wide voyage, coasted South America and often called on Brazilian ports before taking the southern westerlies to follow on to Luanda.[12] Adding to the ban on calling in Angola, imposed on ships sailing from India, such factors made of Brazil's ports almost an obligatory stopover for Lisbon's voyages to West Central Africa. Conversely, the communications between Angola and Portugal depended on the Brazilian ports of call. "The ships from Angola cannot come here, if they do not first stop over in Brazil" noted the pope's representative in Lisbon in 1624.[13] When the Dutch invaded Brazil, they had to bow to the same geographic and maritime determinants. Soon the WIC's board of directors in Amsterdam ordered that vessels leaving the United Provinces bound to Angola should stop over in Recife on both legs of the voyage.[14]

Later, on the other direct and shorter route between Europe and the Congo—crossing Cape Palmas—that used to be sailed by Liverpool slavers, Lisbon pilots continued to sail the "wide voyage," crossing well down SSW before turning to Luanda. This added up to 50 percent more mileage beyond the new, short direct route, "Perhaps because [the pilots] are too fond of old theories," protested a governor of Angola at the end of the eighteenth century.[15] Such theories were grounded on the practice of the bilateral trade between the Brazilian and the African ports. Only after Brazil's independence (1822), when Portuguese-flagged vessels sometimes faced hostility in Brazilian ports, did the Lisbon-Luanda route come to be used more frequently.[16]

The African trade involving Brazil, Angola, and the Mina Coast has been incorrectly assimilated to the triangular trade of the North Atlantic. Except for the eighteenth-century network between Guinea-Bissau and the Amazon ports of São Luís and Belém, the slave trade into Portuguese America resulted, for ninety-five percent of the total voyages, from a bilateral commerce whose consequences radically transformed colonial and Brazilian national history.[17] How did this trade develop?

Manioc in Slave-Ships and in African Fairs

In the first quarter of the seventeenth century, when slavers crossed the ocean from Angola to Brazil, the ports of disembarkation were Recife (thirty-five days away from Luanda), Bahia (forty days), or Rio (fifty days). The royal decree of March 18, 1684, took into consideration these average travel times to calculate the food and water required for the captives and the crew during the crossing. An additional ten-day time was taken into account for unspecified ports of embarkation located outside of the Angolan coast. The voyages for which there are data during the years 1600–1800 in the Trans-Atlantic Slave Trade Database show a longer time for the Luanda-Recife crossing (forty-four days), but approximately the same duration as the Luanda-Bahia itinerary (thirty-eight-and-a-half days) and Luanda–Rio de Janeiro crossing (fifty-one days).[18]

At the turn of the sixteenth century, the goods exported from Brazil to Luanda were almost always manioc flour and smuggled Peruvian silver. Pyrard, Ambrosio Fernandes Brandão, Friar Vicente Salvador, and other seventeenth-century authors highlight what could be called the "manioc cycle," overlooked by many historians, that reached its peak between 1590 and 1630 and continued until the beginning the nineteenth century.

Vessels sailing from Lisbon loaded manioc flour in Brazil, ordinarily in Rio de Janeiro, before leaving for African ports. Such supplies initially provided food on board for the return voyage. According to Aleixo de Abreu, the physician who lived in Luanda between 1594 and 1603, the manioc flour from Brazil and the *ncanza* bean were the main dishes furnished to the enslaved before their embarkment at the Luanda island.[19] Brazilian manioc-flour exports increased rapidly in the beginning of the sixteenth century. In around 1610, Rio de Janeiro exported the production of neighboring captaincies, sending away around 680 tons of manioc flour every year to Angola.[20] As it was unloaded on the other side of the ocean—where the *asentistas'* agents deported a growing number of slaves, enlarging the food consumption in Luanda—manioc flour increased its worth fourfold.[21]

Spurred by the growing *asentista* demand in Angola, manioc-flour exports contributed to Rio de Janeiro's economic lift-off at the turn of the sixteenth century.[22] Benefitting from the sale of the produce essentially extorted from Indian coerced labor, more Rio de Janeiro sugar planters raised themselves to the status of mill owners, in the wake of the introduction, probably from Asia, of the vertical three-roller mill,[23] a change "which demands less labor," as noted by Fernandes Brandão at the time.[24] In fact, as pointed out by Barros de Castro, the three-roller mill was cheaper and more productive than the old horizontal one.[25] The cost of a productive unit was thus decreased, allowing more investments in another sector: the purchase of Africans. At the end of the 1620s, Pernambuco, with 150 mills, and Bahia, with 80, featured more production units than Rio de Janeiro, where 60 mills crushed the sugar cane. But the Rio de Janeiro captaincy recorded a greater increment in the creation of new units in the course of the three preceding decades.[26] One deduces that a portion of the sugar mills, mainly the smaller mills (*engenhocas*), specialized in making *cachaça*, the new and promising regional export product, as will be seen below.

Aboard the slavers, manioc flour constituted an important component of the sailors' and Africans' food. In the 1600s crossings, each slave got a daily ration of 1.8 liters of manioc flour, a fifth of a liter of beans or maize, flour made out of *emba* (the *dendê* palm-tree nut), dried and salted fish, as well as ox, whale, hippopotamus, or elephant meat.[27] Part of the bovine meat, dried and salted, came from Benguela; whale meat and some of the fish came from Brazil; a bigger proportion of Brazilian dried and salted meat entered African thoroughfares in the course of the eighteenth century.[28] The 1.8 liters of manioc per person/day was also observed in the composition of the ration for Amerindian rowers in 1600s Amazonia.[29] It probably corresponded to an alimentary standard in the Portuguese Atlantic coerced labor space. The predominance of American products in the African slave's ration, in particular manioc flour, cheapened the freight between Brazil and the African ports, contributing to consolidation of the commerce between the two colonies and easing the adaptation of Africans to Brasílico slavery.

As stated above, Rio de Janeiro and São Paulo flour was included in the victuals of the Iberian and Brasílico troops engaged in the war against the Dutch. In the face of such a tactical disadvantage, the Amsterdam Herren XIX became exasperated with the Recife WIC agents who neglected the cultivation of tropical goods. The council then ordered the substitution of wheat for manioc in the provisions loaded in Recife for the Compagnie's militiamen in Luanda.[30]

After the recapture of Angola, the Dutch attacked at sea and the scarcity of ships increased the losses caused by the slavers' overloaded cargoes.[31] Epidemics and delays contributed to the multiplication of deaths. Slave traders and captains sought to reduce mortality during the crossing, because they not only paid for the value of the slaves, but also export taxes and freight.[32]

Aiming to regulate the Atlantic trade, the royal order of 1664 prescribed the care to be taken in transportation, as well as a daily measure corresponding to 2.5 or 3 liters of water per slave.[33] Despite this, dehydration must have caused most of the deaths on the high seas due to high temperatures on the decks, leading to excessive sweating, as well as the lack of drinking water for the voyage, a chronic problem in Luanda, an area poorly served by wells and infiltrated by seawater.[34] Bacillary and amoebic dysentery, frequent among the deportees, as well as deadly types of anorexia and apathy (a form of *banzo*), which the English slave traders called *mortal melancholy*, derived from the continued dehydration of the human body.[35]

Current research concurs that, in the long run, shipboard mortality of all the nations declined from the end of the seventeenth century on. Meanwhile, better-adapted vessels, equipped with capacious reservoirs able to collect rain water and capable of crossing the Atlantic in shorter time, were deployed. As Herbert Klein observed, the downward tendency in mortality means that, after calamitous experiences, the slave traders only embarked individuals fit to cross the Atlantic.[36] As shown in the TSTD mortality data analyzed by Eltis and Richardson, besides the health status of the enslaved, the shipboard losses were generally correlated with the voyage length.[37] In the same order of ideas, the systematic analysis of thousands of vessels from diverse countries reveals to be statistically groundless the argument attributing to this or that slaving nation the dubious primacy of having given "better treatment" to the deported Africans.[38]

Active since the fifteenth century in the Atlantic trade and controlling the main embarkation zones, the Portuguese accumulated more experience than other European slave traders up to the last quarter of the seventeenth century. As mentioned in chapter 4, scurvy was diagnosed in Angola in around 1600 and branded as the "Luanda's disease" (*mal de Luanda*).[39] Scurvy strikes individuals who lack sufficient food or vitamin C for more than five months. Scurvy outbreaks on board indicate, therefore, that Africans were undernourished before being forced into the slave ships.[40] Yet the reports of Pieter Moortamer, the WIC director in Luanda in the beginning of the 1640s, later published by Dapper, related the hygienic and feeding practices of the Portuguese slave traders designed to decrease mortality during the crossing at the beginning of the 1640s.[41] There are no statistics on mortality before embarkation, and most probably none will ever be found.[42] A rare indication appears in the initial period of the invasion: in the year of 1576, 14,000 Africans left Luanda, while another 4,000 (28.5 percent) died on dry land in the course of an unspecified period of time. Another later piece of information regards the activities of the Grão-Pará and Maranhão General Company in Cacheu and Bissau. In the years 1756–1777, that company recorded the embarkation of 20,338 Africans and the loss of 1,920 captives (9.4 percent) in the sheds in both ports, as a consequence of escapes and of deaths resulting from uprisings and disease. Eventually, the company had an improved organization that imported dried meat and other foods from Brazil to stock them in African embarkation ports. Such mortality is linked to individuals already held in the ports and does not include previous deaths on the itinerary from the hinterland to the African coast.⁴³

As stated in chapter 3, the diffusion of Asian and American plants contributed to improved food supply in the terrestrial networks and ports, consolidating the slave trade. In the mid-1600s, besides maize, beans, sorghum, and bananas, Luanda consumed from 35,000 to 40,000 sacks of manioc flour per year, extracted from the fields around the stopover ports. The volume represented a daily average of 1.5 tons of manioc flour consumed in the slaving port, including the food for the sailors and slaves, both embarked and those waiting on land.⁴⁴ At the same time, manioc and maize fields were established in the stopover and resting areas of the *libambos*, easing the terrestrial transportation of a greater number of hinterland captives.⁴⁵

Such circumstances increased the creation of commercial slaving in West Central Africa. Luanda became a large slaving port because it produced, imported, and stocked food to support the stream of people dragged from the inland villages to be exported overseas. Obviously, Luandan traders would not purchase enslaved individuals who could not be fed up until embarkation.⁴⁶ It is plausible to state that most of the colonial farms existing in Angola in the second quarter of the seventeenth century—some with over 300 captives—cultivated manioc, maize, and sorghum.⁴⁷ In the 1630s the annual value of Angolan production of food was equal to the price of 4,000 "pieces," a value close to a third of the amount obtained with the export of slaves.⁴⁸

In southern Brazil, the increase in the consumption of food generated by the anti-Dutch mobilization generated a shortage of the product. Indeed, there is a strong indication of a rise in the prices for manioc in Rio de Janeiro at the end of the 1620s.⁴⁹ At that time, the manioc cultivation was transplanted to São Tomé and West Central Africa and the exports from Rio de Janeiro declined. However, African manioc fields remained vulnerable to dry spells, to slaving raids, and to grasshopper invasions, a recurrent plague in that part of the globe. By and large, Luanda and Benguela could never have done without flour coming from Brazil if they were to cope with slave-trade demand.⁵⁰ In the beginning of the nineteenth century, Angola's governor reiterated royal orders demanding that ship captains' bring over manioc from Brazilian ports in the return voyage, due to the insufficiency of local production.⁵¹

When Braudel studied American alimentary plants, he sang long eulogies to maize and potato, but shunned manioc. Manioc, he argued, served only as the basis for "primitive and regularly mediocre cultures."⁵² Contrary to what the master wrote, manioc constituted one of the pieces that fit the Ethiopic Ocean into the world-economy.

Nzimbu, Zimbo, Jimbo

Of more lasting economic consequence, cowry export also contributed to the support of Brasílico trade in West Central Africa. A small univalve cowry that served as currency and ornament in the kingdoms of Congo, Ndongo, and Matamba, the *zimbo* was (and still is) collected on Luanda Island beaches. Trade of the shell-money was a monopoly of the king of Congo, and it spurred mercantile exchanges in the whole of West and Central Africa.⁵³ This cowry was called by the Mbundu *nzimbu*, whence *zimbo*, or *jimbo*, a word incorporated into the Brazilian language as a synonym for money, alongside correlated terms such as *jibungo* and *jibongo*. In fact, cowries could be collected in several points of the northeast Brazilian coast, and especially in the mouth of the Caravelas River and other Bahian beaches. While Río de la Plata colonists made use of Potosí silver to purchase Angolans, Brazil resorted to the *zimbo* from the Caravelas River beaches "mine" for the same reason. Although it is well known that foreign shell-money was introduced in Africa, playing an important role in European exchanges, the case of the Brazilian *zimbo* has not received enough attention. Originating in the Maldives Islands, Asian shell-monies were usually purchased in India by Dutch, French, and British traders, later being re-exported from European ports into western Africa. However, shipments of Brazilian shell-money to Africa resulted from bilateral trade, imprinting a different significance to these exchanges.⁵⁴

Exported via Salvador or Rio de Janeiro, the Bahian *zimbo* left the country untaxed—which is why one cannot evaluate the amounts exported—evading Portuguese metropolitan control.⁵⁵ "In Brazil, quantities of the same seashell [*zimbo*] that is traded are fished and taken to Angola to sell, and they make a lot of money but nothing is paid in [Brazil] or in Angola," a royal agent in 1612 complained. Thus, the shipping of Bahian *zimbo* came to be considered an operation typical of the Brasílico trade in West Central Africa: "those from Brazil bring over much [*zimbo*], which is sold to the kingdom of Congo and Pinda," warned another report at that time.⁵⁶ Friar Vicente Salvador confirmed that in the Caravelas River "a lot of zimbo, Angola's money, which are very small cowries, are carried away in full barrels and through them vessels loaded with blacks return."[57] In the *Atlas do Estado do Brasil* (1631) by royal cosmographer Albernas, the summary including the map of the Ilhéus captaincy points out the *zimbo* as one of the region's chief riches. Fr. Antonio Vieira, in his *Papel Forte* report, which depicts the Portuguese Crown's overseas strengths, points the Bahia's *zimbo*'s role in the African Slave trade.[58]

At the same time, disseminated in the backland markets, the Bahian cowries changed the West Central African trade. Albeit to a lesser extent, the *zimbo* also favored Brazil's trade in the Bight of Benin, as we will see below.[59] Calculated in *réis*, the *cofo*—the Angolan *zimbo* standard measure basket—suffered a devaluation of four-fifths in the second half of the 1600s.[60] Undermining the parity between means of payment, the Bahian *zimbo*s facilitated the slave-trade's penetration and broke the monopoly of the Congolese monarchy on the shell-money.

Consequently, Mbiki-a-Mpanzu, dom Álvaro III (1615–1622), king of Congo, imposed an anti-inflation policy, banning the import of *zimbo*. The Portuguese and Angolista sectors, inclined toward the exercise of indirect government in which colonial control was grounded on the collaboration of native aristocracies, approved the new Congolese economic measure. The bishop of the Congo and Angola dioceses, Franciscan Manuel Baptista Soares, resident of São Salvador do Congo or Mbanza Congo, related to the Court: "The King of Congo has forbidden on pain of harsh punishment that Y.M.'s vassals should not take *zimbo* from Brazil and other parts into his kingdoms, because, as this is their currency, due to the great amounts coming in from outside his [*zimbo*] is so devaluated that he loses in it two parts of his revenue." As he and the deans assisting the São Salvador do Congo Cathedral and the twelve churches of his diocese had their income paid with such devalued *zimbos*, Bishop Soares helped to implement Mbiki-a-Mpanzu's anti-inflation measures, fulminating damnation on the smugglers hailing from Brazil. Without success. "I have forbidden, on pains of excommunication, but to no avail. Even with the punishments that the king [of Congo] has imposed, does [Brazilian zimbo] not cease to come in, and in such amounts that it is laying the kingdom to waste."[61]

Bishop Soares's anti-inflation zeal can be explained. As in the case of the São Tomé prelates, the Congo-Angola bishops and deans exchanged the *zimbos* they received as ecclesiastic pension for slaves, who were quickly exported to the New World. With the same slaving goals, the Santa Casa de Misericórdia of Angola received an annual tribute of 2,000 *zimbos* from each native couple living in Luanda Island, a cowrie collection zone.[62] Bishop Soares, influential in Court because he was the brother of two royal councilors, Lope and Cristóvão Soares, made a good business slaving with the *zimbo* trade. Three years after his death, the Roman Curia, the Royal Treasury, and his brother Cristóvão still disputed the possession of his estate. Cristóvão Soares took the effort to come all the way to Brazil to recuperate the part of the slaving business that was his due in this "ghastly inheritance," as defined by Fathers Cuvelier and Jadin, two eminent Belgian missionaries and Africanists of the last century.[63]

By snatching the two poles of the South Atlantic economy, the Dutch engaged in the slave trade in the Luso-Brasílico mode. The WIC's slave traders from Pernambuco promptly realized the importance of the *zimbo* and requested that a shipload of such cowries be sent to Angola,[64] in vain, since the *zimbo* was collected in Bahia, outside the territory controlled by the WIC.[65] After the expulsion of the Dutch from Angola, one of the demands that the king of Congo included in the peace treaty with Portugal regarded, precisely, the embargo on the import of Bahian *zimbos*.[66] Around that time, the village of Caravelas had forty families engaged in gathering the *zimbo* exported into West Central Africa.[67]

Silva Corrêa, Luso-Brasílico captain who had served many years in West Central Africa in the second half of the eighteenth century, revealed in his *Historia de Angola* (1787–1799) the significance of Bahian *zimbo* at that time: "without the *zimbo* money there is no business with the blacks." Top-quality *zimbo*, gathered on the island of Luanda, yielded a 600 percent profit for the slave traders, while the Bahian *zimbo*, reputed to be inferior by the natives, netted 200 percent per *arroba*.[68] According to Manolo Florentino, in the last decades of the eighteenth century, 94 percent of cowries imported in Luanda came from Brazilian beaches.[69] Other studies emphasize the high costs involved in the import of shell-money to Africa. Indeed, slaves and other merchandise financing its purchase rendered such cowries more expensive than the currency produced in Africa (pieces of fabric, salt rocks, metal bars).[70] In the Gulf of Guinea, where Europeans regularly introduced Asian cowries that were more appreciated by the natives, the Bahian *zimbo* seems to have enjoyed limited acceptance. Thus, in the course of the eighteenth century, the Tobacco Board chose to operate in the region with the shell-money imported from the Indian Ocean. Such currency also sparked "anti-inflation" reactions. More fragile than the Indic cowries, the Bahian *zimbos* were refused in the Gulf of Guinea markets in the first half of the nineteenth century.[71]

Crossing the seas, missionaries, military personnel, merchants, and royal agents exchanged information about the fortunes of the South Atlantic colonial enterprise.

The demand of the sugar mills, bilateral navigation, and the supply of manioc flour and *zimbos* offered a relative edge to Portuguese and Brasílico slave traders active in the African markets. From the second decade of the 1600s, "the ones from Brazil" started to form their own personality, separate from the Portuguese traders and the Angolista settlers in West Central Africa. However, it was in the Portuguese-Dutch war that the differentiation process of the agents engaged in the Ethiopic Ocean exploitation gained its significance.

Portuguese, Angolista, and Brasílico in West Central Africa

From the lookout posts along the African routes, observing the to-and-fro of the WIC's vessels, Brasílico war commanders accumulated experience and authority over the two sides of the ocean. As mentioned above, both Bahia and Rio de Janeiro dispatched two flotillas in aid of Angola in 1645. They included, besides mainland and Angolista soldiers, a company of mulattos and black men from Henrique Dias's *terço*, as well as dozens of Rio de Janeiro Amerindians. In the following year, Martim Soares Moreno, André Vidal de Negreiros, and João Fernandes Vieira—at that moment commanders of the Pernambuco uprising—sent reports to Lisbon on the situation of Congo and Angola.[72] After the taking of Luanda (August 1648), the Pernambucan commanders followed the events in Angola with the same care that they reserved for the events in Rio de Janeiro, Bahia, and Maranhão. Thus, João Fernandes Vieira promptly warned the Court against maneuvers by Salvador de Sá—guided by the Rio de Janeiro and Lisbon *peruleiros*—seeking to reopen the slave trade between Luanda and the Río de la Plata, in order to gain access to Potosí silver. According to Fernandes Vieira, the silver-oriented plan to attack Buenos Aires prepared by Salvador de Sá could prompt a Spanish raid against Luanda, precisely at the moment when the war started again in Pernambuco.[73] This incident illustrates the regional, plantation-based interests that guided the Pernambucan's policy in Angola, in contrast to the silver and global scheme of the Rio de Janeiro's oligarchies. The battles of Fernandes Vieira commanded against the Dutch in Pernambuco did not cancel his interests on West Central Africa affairs. Indeed, in 1653, he wrote to Lisbon to denounce the smuggling of Canarian wines into Angola by three Spanish ships.[74] A year later, Vidal de Negreiros arrived in Lisbon to present to King João IV the Dutch act of surrender in Recife.[75] Yet conflicts still threatened the Portuguese Atlantic.

Portugal continued its overseas war with the Netherlands and the frontier battles with Spain when her European alliances collapsed. Cromwell's warships pursued English monarchist vessels to Lisbon and blockaded the Tagus River in 1650. Sensing danger, the Overseas Council warned King João IV: "it is convenient not to give the [English] Parliament a reason to be displeased with Y.M."[76] There was a general alarm in the Portuguese Atlantic in 1655, when an English fleet set sail to conquer Jamaica. It was feared in Portugal and Brazil that Bahia was the true target of the expedition.[77] At the same time, the Overseas Council received another disturbing spy report that the Dutch United Provinces' "general of the sea" (admiral) had criticized his government's strategic options, forsaking the South Atlantic in favor of Dutch military reinforcement in the Baltic Sea. It was the admiral's opinion that it would be more profitable to attack Portuguese enclaves in Africa and America, where the "profit would be greater." The councilors recapitulated the warnings previously given by the Overseas Council regarding the urgency of defending Luanda, with the view of exempting themselves from the responsibility for underestimating the WIC's offensive.[78] In face of the slave-trading demand from the diverse American possessions and the narrowness of the existing African trade areas, the Portuguese Crown suspected all the Europeans powers. More precisely, Lisbon had great concern about the new Dutch slaving business. Where would the Compagnie seek the Africans it sold, in increasing numbers, to the new Caribbean plantations? Forecasting fresh raids by the WIC after the end of the first Anglo-Dutch war (1654), the Court prompted Brazil and especially Angola, to be aware of Dutch desire to obtain Africans to sell in the Caribbean.[79] Note that the British and Dutch sugar production in the Caribbean had not yet emerged in European markets. In the decade of 1650, Brazilian sugar-export levels and prices were high, and the inversion of the conjuncture, signaling the impact of the secular economic crisis in Portuguese Atlantic, intervened only twenty years later.[80] In the mid-1600s, Lisbon preserved its conviction that it held the most desired overseas territories for sugar production. Brazilian sugar plantations should be defended "not only against the Dutch, but also against nations who know how profitable they are, because the San Domingo and Barbados islands, which the English seek, are not so good," explained the Overseas Council in 1656.[81]

Dangers also mounted on the Castilian side. Lacking African slaves since the interruption of the Portuguese *Asiento*, Hispanic-American colonists protested against the shortage of enslaved blacks. Consequently, Madrid abandoned reforms aimed at restricting compulsory Amerindian labor—the *mita*—and sought to relaunch the slave trade into America's vice-kingdoms.[82] In this context, the arrival in the Congo in 1645, with the support of King Felipe IV, of the first Italian and Spanish Capuchin mission, appeared to the Portuguese as a prelude to a Spanish invasion,[83] even more so as the Capuchin mission was headed by Friar Francisco de Pamplona, previously known in secular life as dom Tiburcio de Redin. Former Spanish general and aristocrat, as well as a close friend of King Felipe IV, Redin was highly influential in Madrid. Braganza spies closely followed Spanish movements toward West Central Africa. Thus, João IV's warning to the Overseas Council regarding Redin is dated the same day that the Capuchins left the Spanish port of San Lúcar to the Congo.[84]

From then on, rumors spread in Lisbon. Friar Pamplona, or worse—dom Tiburcio de Redin, reputed to be a false friar—would command the avant garde of an army of 11,000 Spanish troops intent on expelling the Portuguese from Angola and Congo.[85] Evidence for a Spanish assault on the ports of trade mounted. Following an alarming report debated in Lisbon's Overseas Council, Redin had orders from Madrid to make an alliance with the king of Congo in order to buy "22,000 blacks" and send them to Spanish America, otherwise the silver mines would stop their production "in two years."[86] No such things happened. Still, twenty years later, the Congo Capuchins were presented by the *Mercúrio Portuguez* as base agents of Castile.[87] In 1681, thirteen years after the peace treaty between the Iberian capitals, the Overseas councilors restated that part of the Italian Capuchins, known as subjects of the Spanish Crown, could not enter Angola.[88]

Meanwhile, Lisbon remained afraid of a maritime attack in Angola. Luanda—the largest port of slave trade—seemed threatened by the new European slaving powers.[89] It urged defense of Angola "against the desire that the Castilians, English and Dutch have of taking the Blacks away from us and shipping them to the [West] Indies, to Barbados, and to other parts," warned the Overseas Council.[90]

Actually, the recapture of Angola in 1648 featured a victory as surprising as it was fragile. "The ease with which the Dutch took this city [of Luanda] from us and us from them clearly shows how little defensible it is" wrote Fr. Vieira at the beginning of 1649.[91] It all depended on the control of inland Angola, and, more precisely, on the markets and inland networks leading to Luanda.

In fact, the expeditionary force that left Rio de Janeiro to attack Luanda introduced the Brasílico stakes in the game up to then played by the European and West Central African peoples. Thus began the period that Fr. Silva Rego—a staunch partisan of the colonialist orthodoxy in twentieth-century Portugal—entitled "the

Brazilian period of the history of Angola."⁹² Stretching from 1648 to 1665, this period encompasses the governments of Salvador de Sá, João Fernandes Vieira, and André Vidal de Negreiros, all of them having a strong interest in Brazil's slaving economy. Supporting this focus, contemporary Western Africa historians delineate the profile of the new agents intervening in the pillage of the Africa from the beginning of the seventeenth century: the Luso-Brazilians, whom I have called Brasílicos for the motive explained in the first chapter.⁹³ Different from the Angolistas' trading networks and from Lisbon's minimalist control based on ports of trade, the plundering raids launched by the Brasílicos in Angola changed the balance of power in West Central Africa.

The Brasilico Offensive in Angola and Congo

Tangled in the European theater of war, vulnerable at sea, and under attack in Africa and Asia, Lisbon became increasingly dependent on Brasílico military support in the Ethiopic Ocean territories. Accepting the impossibility of closely monitoring its Angolan territory, the Crown delegated full powers to Salvador de Sá. "[I] cannot give you precise orders from here, and, in the face of the zeal you have shown in my service . . . , I will rely on your judgment for you to do your best," wrote King João IV in 1649 to the new governor of Angola.⁹⁴ Called Nfumu-Etú-Lálânâ—Our Savior Lord—by the vassalized Mbundu, the governor shook Angola from end to end for three years (1648–1651).⁹⁵

The Portuguese and Brasílico task force, the largest European-led military contingent launched in Africa since the battle of Ksar el-Kebir, drove the Dutch to the sea and then turned against the insurgent Angolan *sobados*, Matamba, and the kingdom of Congo.⁹⁶ To reopen terrestrial trade, Salvador de Sá reported having "fielded an army that, as it beheaded a great number of powerful *sobas*, smoothed the path and cowered the gentile [natives]."⁹⁷ Italian Capuchin missionaries in a denunciation written to Rome recorded the scope of the bloodbath and the amount of booty. "They [Salvador de Sa's troops] have destroyed many villages, killed many people and made over 7,000 slaves."⁹⁸ Hard pressed, Garcia II Afonso (1641–1661), king of Congo, derogatorily called Kimpako (sorcerer) by the Angolistas, gave away part of his territory to the Portuguese Crown. Likewise, the governor imposed truces on Njinga, the queen of the Matamba. Seasoned by three decades of war against all kinds of European predators, Njinga accused Salvador de Sá of having been one of the Angola's most voracious governors. Salvador received many slaves from her, but he did not keep his promises and did not release her sister, Princess Bárbara (or *Kámbu*), who was kept as a hostage, nor had he ceased hostilities against the Matamba kingdom.[99]

In the same drive, Salvador de Sá's captains destroyed the Mbundu resistance within a 150-kilometer radius of Luanda, etching the Portuguese eastern borders in West Central Africa. Part of the expedition's expenses were met by the "new rights" created by the governor, which translated into a 75 percent increase in taxes on the export of slaves.[100] Always in search of Potosí silver, Salvador de Sá dispatched vessels to the Río de la Plata "due to the interest that Y.M. may have in the results of the blacks being carried out from this port [of Luanda] and the silver that would come in from that one [Buenos Aires]," and leased for his own benefit a contract for furnishing slaves to the Buenos Aires region.[101] Tomas Filgueira Bultão, Salvador de Sá's trusted lieutenant and surely a front man, held the Angola Contract (regarding the collection of royal taxes) between 1649 and 1654.[102]

However, the vicissitudes of the war between Spain and Portugal led the Spanish Río de la Plata authorities to confiscate slavers from Luanda and ended up halting the reopening of that trading route.[103] A large part of the economic benefit that Salvador de Sá expected to extract from the Luanda venture—the reactivation of the slave trade into Buenos Aires in exchange for Potosí silver—thus ceased to materialize. Aside from his complaints about the harshness of life in Luanda, such mercantile frustration explains his petition to the Crown requesting to leave Angola's government (1651). It also explains the expeditions in search of precious metals and emeralds he launched years later, beyond the Sierra de Mantiqueira mountains in São Paulo.[104]

We must now draw the profile of the forces present in West Central Africa. Two sectors supported a minimalist policy, voicing restricted domination in Angola. The port of trade strategy defined in the 1620s guided the first sector, which was well represented in the Court. Indeed, for the king's advisers, the miseries of the climate, the sparse colonial presence, and native resistance rendered the conquest of the Angola's territory a risky, if not useless, enterprise. Besides, harassment by European rivals on the maritime waters forced Portugal to concentrate her forces on the coastal garrisons. Consequently, the Overseas Council vetoed the expeditionaries' raids and forbade Salvador to disperse troops inland.[105] The second sector, which nearly always opposed the predatory raids, was composed by Luanda's main merchants (*comerciantes de portada*). Forming a cartel, dependent on native porters and the *pombeiros*, middlemen who went inland seeking for slaves and ivory, such merchants sought to preserve the terrestrial trade and backland market activity, where the enslaved were bought and sold.[106] For commercial reasons, this sector sided with the ports of trade policy defended by the Crown for strategic reasons.

Such motives explain the rivalry opposing Luanda's merchants to those of Benguela, who siphoned off Luanda's trade, as well as the dispute between them regarding the creation of the Misericórdia (Holy House of Mercy Catholic brotherhood) in Massangano. For the Luandans and some governors, the privileges granted to Massangano, at the margin of the Cuanza River, would attract settlers from the coast and inland, opening new trade paths to the detriment of Luanda.[107] Reaffirming its interests, the Angolista merchant group at the Luanda municipal council dared to send to Lisbon, in 1650, at the height of the Luso-Brasílico enslaving raids, a protest against governor Salvador de Sá's policy. Addressing the Crown, they warned that the backland war (*guerra do sertão*) led by Salvador's troops caused "irreparable damage [. . .] because it destroys the vassalized allies wherever it goes [. . .] with no respect for the fact that [the *sobas*] are [our] friends." The terrestrial trade network was broken in a single stroke, the backland fairs were dispersed, "everything being closed to trade, there being no certain or safe place."[108] Prudently, the municipal council unloaded onto the shoulders of the "black people"—native troops—the responsibility for the raids organized by the governor and by his captains, white people, eager to extract from African villages the reward for fighting the battles in defense of the Crown in the South Atlantic.

Salvador de Sá's Successors in Luanda

Rodrigo de Miranda Henriques, the new governor of Angola (1652–1653), was close to his predecessor, Salvador de Sá. Along with the governor came his two nephews, Henrique Henriques de Miranda, experienced in the Brasílico war and a future slave trader of considerable import, and Bernardo de Miranda Henriques, made captain of an Angolan company and future governor of Pernambuco (1667–1670).[109] As happened with Salvador de Sá, Rodrigo Miranda Henriques went to Luanda to find the way to Potosí. He knew the Peruvian silver routes and the Southern Atlantic trade well, for he had been governor of the Rio de Janeiro captaincy (1633–1637), associated to the Sás' administration. In Lisbon, Miranda Henriques had obtained a royal license to try to reopen the Luanda-Rio-Buenos Aires thoroughfare.[110] Once more, the significance of Angola was evident for carrying out Lisbon and Rio de Janeiro commercial ambitions in the Río de la Plata region.

Succeeding Miranda Henriques in the government of Angola, Luís Martins de Sousa Chichorro (1654–1658) bore the mark of a notorious misfortune. As Malacca's captain-major, he surrendered in 1641 to the Dutch, leaving to them the key city of the Straits of Malacca, taken 130 years earlier by the Portuguese in the most decisive feat of arms by Afonso de Albuquerque.[111] Nonetheless, Chichorro later felt the taste of revenge, as he was in Bahia when the Dutch surrendered to the Portuguese in Recife (1654). From Bahia, he resumed the Angola business, ordering the construction of a galleon slaver in the Bight of Bahia shipyard, on which he sailed to Luanda. The vessel was named *Nossa Senhora do Populo*, a popular saint at that time, and some years later, patron saint of the first church founded in Benguela.[112]

During the government of the eastern empire's defeated captain, the winners of the western empire were granted important rewards and widened Brasílico influence in Africa. Since 1650, João Fernandes Vieira had been requesting as a reward for his Pernambucan war, the government of Pernambuco for life, of Maranhão for nine years, or of Angola for six years, among other benefits. This was a very excessive request, since no overseas government was granted for life. As he forced the limits of royal administration, João Fernandes made explicit his own interests. Nouveau riche, a new sugar-mill owner, he included among his priority goals the control of the market of Angola slaves.

Five months after the Dutch surrender in Recife (January 1654), João Fernandes obtained the succession to Chichorro as the head of Angola. Months later, André Vidal de Negreiros, who had carried to the Court the news of the Dutch capitulation in Pernambuco, was granted the patent to succeed João Fernandes as the head of the Angolan government (1661), and on the same day, he was given the government of Maranhão (1655–1656). On the following day, aside from the honors and incomes granted to his person and his relatives, Negreiros was nominated governor of Pernambuco (1657–1660), so as to complete the time left before taking his post in Angola. Joao Fernandes was also given in February 1655 the government of Paraiba (1655–1657), as he waited for the equivalent post in Angola.[113] Within seven months, João Fernandes and Negreiros were granted, together, aside from various honors, five governments. Considering that Chichorro was sworn governor of Angola only in October 1654, there were three individuals chosen at one stroke for a single post in Luanda—a rare event in colonial annals.[114] Again, it is worthwhile to note the different perspectives of the new governors of Angola. The governors from Rio de Janeiro—Salvador de Sá and Rodrigo de Miranda Rodrigues—sought to make use of their governorship to reopen the slave trade with Buenos Aires to attain the Potosí silver production. On the other hand, the governors from Pernambuco—João Fernandes Vieira and his fellow commandant André Vidal de Negreiro—sought to furnish their own plantations and sugar mills in Brazil with the enslaved carried from Luanda.

Another participant in the Brasílico war rewarded at the same time with a post in Africa was Friar Mateus de São Francisco, to whom the king conceded the bishopric of São Tomé.[115] Former minister of the Luanda convent, known as a turbulent and thieving Franciscan, Friar Francisco gained notoriety as chaplain-major of the Pernambucan troops. Also significant were the nominations of former captain of the Pernambuco war, Cristóvão de Barros Rego (1656–1661) for the government of São Tomé, and of his relative Roque de Barros Rego (1648–1650) for the Cape Verde government, ("in attention to his many services rendered in the war of Brazil"), where one of the commanders of the second Guararapes battle, Francisco de Figueroa (1658–1663), would also be governor. Nearly all of these posts were granted between 1654 and 1655.[116]

What was the motive that led João IV to decree all such nominations at one stroke?

Canon José Mathias Delgado, a twenty-century Angolista historian, noted the "great anxiety" with which the king had nominated João Fernandes and Negreiros for the governorship of Angola.[117] Such concern surely originated in the dissatisfaction brewing among the Brasílico troops in the northern captaincies. Since the relaunching of the war against the Dutch (1645), the self-rule of local command had caused Brasílico sentiment to erupt. In a deliberately ambiguous message dating from 1646, Martins Soares Moreno and Vidal de Negreiros warned the Bahian governor-general, who was hesitant about the course of the hostilities, that the Pernambucan settlers should be "very fine and very loyal vassals to the prince"—by which they meant any European prince—ready to send them arms to free them from invading heretics.[118] Dutch sources in Recife confirmed the rebels' warning, adding that they threatened to seek help from the Spanish and even from the Turks.[119] Three years later, when Francisco Barreto, sent from Lisbon by the Crown, took charge of the Brasílico forces, a mutiny shook the João Fernandes' regiment.[120]

Increasing the rivalry between Brasílico and the mainland troops, the "sugar mills dispute" raged in Pernambuco, as examined by Cabral de Mello. The sugar-mill owners who had evacuated the captaincy by order of royal authority saw their properties confiscated by the Dutch invader and sold to figures such as João Fernandes, who bought everything and then were in arrears with the WIC.

Exiled in other captaincies, the original sugar-mill owners sought the return of their property once the Dutch surrendered, creating a dispute with the new proprietors. Called on to arbitrate, the Crown preferred to let the dispute run its course. Another source of tension originated in the ambitions that Pernambucan officers and combatants nurtured with regard to the houses and improvements left behind by the Dutch in Recife, as well as to the lands and honors apportioned by the Crown.[121]

The commanders of the Brasílico and Angolan wars had secured for Portugal decisive trumps. Unlike other European princes, tangled up in dynastic, religious, and territorial disputes, King João IV de facto held most of the possessions that he claimed de jure at the end of the Thirty Years War. The Braganza achievement was recognized in most European capitals, and it served as an argument for France to strengthen its alliance with Spain. Indeed, in the midst of diplomatic bargaining with King Felipe IV of Spain, Mazarin affirmed in 1656 that the king of Portugal was "almost serenely the lord" over the kingdom and its dependencies, "both in Europe as in Asia, Africa and America." In this context, a military rebellion in Pernambuco would have had very adverse consequences for Lisbon's prestige in Europe.[122]

João Fernandes Vieira in Angola

While still governor of the Paraíba captaincy (1655–1657), João Fernandes Vieira requested Angola's documents in Lisbon and studied the colony's situation, asking the Crown for authorization to transfer part of the artillery taken from the Dutch to his new seat on the other side of the sea.[123] He further requested royal license to take along 400 soldiers, 3,000 muskets, and other weapons. Deemed excessive, the request was limited to 100 soldiers, artillery, 1,000 muskets, and six tons of gunpowder.[124]

Actually, João Fernandes had set up a triangular enterprise, in which two English vessels, the *Brazil Frigate* and the *Hopewell*, hired in Lisbon to sail to Pernambuco and carry him over to Angola with his men, were to return to Brazil laden with 1,200 slaves and ivory. The vessels would then follow on to Lisbon, taking sugar from his mills together with the ivory. The very high number of enslaved—thrice the average volume of a slaver—demonstrates that João Fernandes already had agents in Luanda in charge of purchasing, maintaining, and sheltering all these Africans at his disposal. The ivory, a commodity of guaranteed demand in Europe but monopolized by the royal contractor of Angola, must have been the result of a special favor given to the new governor.

There were those in the Overseas Council who suspected the transaction proposed by João Fernandes, an enterprise involving "much capital" and founded on a motive reputed to be fallacious (the lack of great vessels in Pernambuco). Favoring Brasílico commanders during his presidency of the Council (1651–1659), the count of Odemira nonetheless authorized the English vessel to take João Fernandes, "because of the risk to his person from the Dutch."[125] A direct witness in Angola, Cadornega stated that João Fernandes set foot in Luanda with 200 trusted soldiers, 100 over the limit set by the Crown.[126] Besides the *Brazil Frigate* and the *Hopewell*, two other vessels were part of the governor's flotilla. One of them, built to order at the Bahian shipyards by João Fernandes, carried forty artillery pieces.[127] After a quarrel with one of the English captains, João Fernandes confiscated the *Hopewell* for his own enterprises in Angola. The incident caused a diplomatic protest to be sent from London to Lisbon.[128]

In a way, João Fernandes' costly preparations reproduced, on a smaller scale, the more complex businesses (grounded on bills of exchange, previous contracts, hired vessels, and orders and freights in various ports) of the *asentista* governors of the first quarter of the 1600s. By chance or by design, in view of the value of the load and the name of the owner, a Dutch corsair attacked and looted the *Brazil Frigate* in the Paraíba coast, on her return leg from Africa. But João Fernandes would send many other lucrative shipments from Angola to the Brazilian north.

Alongside his soldiers, the governor brought his relatives and captains for posts of command—Manuel Berenguer de Andrade, his wife's nephew and son of his legal representative in Lisbon; Agostinho César de Andrade, his brother-in-law and protégé; Sebastião Muniz da Câmara, also his relative. Veterans of the Brasílico war, they were all provided with companies of soldiers in Angola.[129] At least two captains of the 1648 expedition were active in the region, Álvaro de Aguilar Osório and Francisco Vaz Aranha, called "the Storm" (o Tormenta).[130] João Fernandes nominated Antonio de Buíça as secretary of the Angolan government. Buíça had already taken an analogous post in the government of Rodrigo de Miranda Henriques, who, as pointed out above, had links with the Sá oligarchy and with combatants of the Brasílico war in Pernambuco.[131]

Sergeant-major Francisco Ferreira de Vasconcellos and Antônio Jorge de Góes, a veteran of the two Guararapes battles, were also part of the contingent. Regarded by the Overseas Council as the most experienced person to command Angola in the event of a Dutch attack and strongly supported by Salvador de Sá, Góes would be nominated captain-major of Benguela (1661–1664).[132] Likewise, João Fernandes made the point that his men, used to African-type climates and experienced in tropical warfare, would be of great use in West Central Africa. The Benedictine priest João da Ressurreição, called Friar Dust (Frei Poeira), took the post of chaplain-major, a post analogous to the one he had held in Pernambuco in João Fernandes's regiment.[133] Additional men at arms, as well as horses sufficient to form two mounted companies, arrived from Pernambuco and Bahia.[134] Angolista twentieth-century historian Ralph Delgado regarded João Fernandes as the right man in the right place, "since Angola was dependent on Brazil."[135] But there were protests from Angolan colonists against the Brasílico governors' numerous nominations. These officials, claimed the Angolistas in a petition to the Crown, nominated their own servants for military and civil posts, to the detriment of the local settlers.[136]

The Dutch invasion jumbled up the conquered territories and the alliances with the native communities.[137] Other power relations, other partitions in areas of influence, were imposed on missionaries, on the Angolistas and authorities. In addition to the new Brasílico influence, the post-1648 period witnessed the entrance of the Italian Capuchins in the West Central African stage.

The Marvelous Conversion of Queen Njinga

João Fernandes promptly quarreled with the Ignatians of Luanda and was excommunicated by them. The alleged motive of the conflict seems to have been more a pretext than a justification. The governor's soldiers had arrested slaves belonging to the missionaries during a wrangle about some pigs that were loose in the streets.[138] Fernandes was not the first Angola's governor to quarrel with the Jesuits. Some years before, Sousa Chichorro wrote from Luanda to the Crown, complaining against the missionaries' endeavors in Angola and asking for a Jesuit itinerant inspector (Visitador) to be sent to discipline them.[139] Yet João Fernandes's attack against the Jesuits revealed another power struggle in West Central Africa. In a report to Propaganda Fide cardinals, João Fernandes accused the Jesuits of being ambitious and careless, relapsing in the evangelization of their own slaves. Written in Italian and sent directly to Rome—an administrative practice as irregular as it was unusual—the letter demonstrates that João Fernandes was probably being advised by Italian Capuchins. Indeed, prolonging a missionary quarrel started 350 years before, Fr. Antonio Brasio sided with the Jesuits, and saw a wily maneuver by the Capuchins behind João Fernandes's criticisms.[140]

It is true that the Society of Jesus faced the missionary competition of the Discalced Carmelites, and, chiefly, of the Capuchins. The latter recruited some of its members among the Italian and Spanish nobility; they were supported by Rome and deeply engaged in the evangelization of West Central Africa. Opposed to the slave trade, they refused to own slaves, unlike the Jesuits.[141] In a letter to the Propaganda Fide—an instrument of Roman policy in the overseas dioceses—a Capuchin missionary attributed the difficulties faced in the Congo to the Jesuits' slaving business.[142] "The motive driving those Jesuits is the great interest they have [in the Congo], because the number of slaves they own, it is said, is more than 2,000, and that demands continuous commercial transactions. This is why they cannot bear the presence of other clergy who are intent on having slaves only for Heaven."[143] Another Angola Capuchin denounced Jesuit involvement in the Brazil-bound slave trade and asked for papal intervention to "remove such abuse."[144] Operating an audacious infiltration policy in the African kingdoms, different from the prudent backyard preaching of the Luanda and Massangano Jesuits, the Capuchins stood apart from the Company of Jesus's machinations. This policy was crowned by an event presented as one of the greatest missionary (and colonial) trumps of 1600s Africa: the definitive conversion of Queen Njinga (1582–1663), undefeated enemy of the Europeans, achieved by a Neapolitan—thus a Spanish subject—Antonio de Gaeta, or Emilio Laudati, duke of Marzano in secular life.[145]

This success was much propagated by the Roman Curia and by the Capuchins, notably by Friar Gioia di Napoli's book *La maravigliosa conversione . . . della Regina Singa e del suo regno di Matamba* (1669), which revisited both a report by Friar Gaeta and Cavazzi's book (1687). The achievement contrasted with the stagnant side of the Jesuit missions in Africa. It mattered little that, at the time both books were published, the Catholic mission in Njinga's land had fallen apart after her death, and according to a report, only the Jaga's chickens attended her Santa Ana de Matamba church. Njinga had become the paradigm of African barbarity, the specter of chaos in which overseas pagans lived. And the Capuchins had brought her back into the Kingdom of God.

Truly, Njinga had been baptized in 1621 with the name of Ana de Sousa, but had relapsed into pagan practices, transforming Matamba into a kingdom of luxury and perversities. Such was the missionaries', colonists', and European travelers' view. "You find yourself in a condition much worse than beasts," said Friar Gaeta to Njinga, "rebellious to God and a tyrant of men." Inspired by the commentary by Friar Saccardo da Leguzzano on Cavazzi's work, John Thornton has traced Njinga's implacable progress. Having been denied her rights to the Ndongo throne, Njinga's first step was to join the Jaga community and found the Matamba kingdom. At the head of a warrior society up to then commanded by men, Njinga completely took up male roles, creating a seraglio composed of boys "transformed into women, even in dress [. . .], as if they were female, and her, the man," Cadornega relates.[146] Following the Jaga initiatory rites and customs, Njinga practiced anthropophagy and infanticide.

In a letter to the Portuguese Court, written by Njinga herself shortly after her conversion by the Capuchins, the queen announced her new Christian life: "We already have built a church, we have a Capuchin priest[147] [. . . .] You know that in the past I had 100 husbands, and that was the style of my ancestors, the other ones I had were just for boasting [*por grandeza*], but I did not beget life with them, now I will marry only one." Certainly inspired by a Capuchin adviser, Njinga recants polygamy and infanticide, but does not mention anthropophagy, a practice too infamous to be revealed, even to portray previous great sins in the act of conversion.[148]

To highlight the change in Njinga's personality—and to stress the contrast between barbarism and Western culture, between paganism and Christianism, Africa and Europe—Gaeta, Cavazzi, and other Catholic authors adopted a literary style that would merit analysis by a literary critic. Friar Gaeta proposed to narrate Njinga's "barbarous cruelty" so that "the world should know how she became different after her conversion." Dealing with delicate sexual issues, Gaeta created a significant suspense: "of the Jaga women I say nothing, because they are worse than the men, indeed more dishonest and lascivious, all immersed in the infamous vice of the flesh."[149] Cavazzi also developed a narrative of suggestive effect. Only insinuated, the details of Njinga's perversions and cruelty reach secret, disturbing dimensions. First, the Capuchin expresses his firm intent: "I do not wish to soil these pages with the tragic narration of the torrents of blood spilled by Njinga in the space of twenty-eight years, during which she has professed the most barbarous sects among as many as impiety personified could have imagined." The author narrates in the pages that follow the deliria imputed to Njinga, nonetheless interspersed with conclusions about the organic, complementary character of human perversions: "As the many vices are by nature connected like the links in a chain, it is very rare that cruelty is not accompanied by sensuality." Transsexualism, male harems, infanticide, anthropophagy, witchcraft, luxury, all were linked in the infernal rhythm that the Capuchin friar lends to Njinga's reign, until the queen's definitive conversion by Antonio Gaeta, and her Christian death, at the age of eighty-one, in the arms of missionary Cavazzi.[150]

Disseminated in Italian, translated or adapted by other writers, the Capuchin narrative of Njinga's story flared the imaginations of illustrious European authors.[151] An anonymous account published in 1749 in Lisbon emphasizes the descriptions of Njinga's cruelty and hypersexuality to underline her later conversion and her probable holiness: "She died a Catholic, with all the sacraments and many signs of predestination."

Some years later, with different styles and purposes, de Sade and Hegel would recall what they had read about the queen of Matamba to illustrate philosophical themes. Like Friar Cavazzi, the marquis de Sade believed in the correlation between cruelty and sensuality. In his theater play *La philosophie dans le boudoir* (1795), Sade puts forward the example of Njinga to expound on the difference between irrational cruelty, which he considered useless, and erotic cruelty—"known to extremely delicate beings" only; according to him, Njinga was an instance of the latter practice. De Sade lines Njinga up with other celebrities who formed his pantheon of tyrannical and libidinous women, such as a certain Zoé, "empress of China," Theodora, wife of emperor Justinian, and the inevitable Messalina.[152] In his lectures in *Reason in History* (1822–1823), based on Cavazzi or on one of his disseminators, Hegel mentioned Njinga's "horrific" reign and the "terrible laws" of that "feminine State" in order to reach conclusions about the customs of Africans and black people in general. Dominated by the energy of "natural will," black people did not seem to him as susceptible to human development, since the "moral moment" did not prevail among them.[153]

Around the same time, the Portuguese poet Bocage voiced another record about Njinga. Offended by the literary jealousies prevailing in the Academia dos Renascidos, with headquarters in Lisbon and presided over by Luso-Brazilian poet Domingos Caldas Barbosa, whose pen name was Lereno Selinuntino, Bocage wrote a sonnet in 1792 as an affront to the association and its president. Alluding to the fact that Caldas Barbosa was a mulatto whose mother was Angolan, Bocage added to his verses insults to Njinga, apes, and things from Brazil, a place where beasts became people who came over to the mainland to pester the Lusitanians. The vile, adulatory, insane scum / Is presided by Njinga's grandson.[154]

In Brazil, Njinga is still present, emerging in the *congadas* staged in the various regions of the country, in which the chorus celebrates the great African warrior: "Queen Njinga is a woman of battle / She has two chairs surrounded by swords."[155]

In such dramatic dances, the queen of Matamba always embodies the negative pole, the native warrior, opposed to the Christian and pacific positivity of the Christian king of Congo.[156] The constant element in all such records is that de Sade, Hegel, Bocage, and the *congadas* represent Njinga as an evil person, a character who disturbs the imagination and ritual order. Carried out and made public by the Capuchins, the queen of Matamba's "marvelous conversion to the Catholic faith" did not convince European writers and Brazilian popular artists. Still a national heroine in Angola, Njinga also became popular among Afro-Brazilians and Afro-Americans.[157] Many a girl was and is named Njinga. Reggae and rap songs as well as Internet sites in honor of Njinga have been created. She is also honored by American feminists and UNESCO.[158]

The persistence of the pagan Njinga, the warrior Njinga against the white man's world, is transfigured in the continuity of the pre-Christian African culture, in the failure of Jesuitical and Capuchin preaching in Angola, and, more deeply, in the failure of five centuries of Western missionary activity in black Africa.

Beyond the ulterior projections in African, European, North American, and Brazilian imaginaries, the story of Njinga must also be interpreted in light of the rivalry between the Jesuits and the Capuchins in West Central Africa. Aside from the alliance with the Capuchins, the antagonism between João Fernandes and the Society of Jesus had deeper roots. Salvador de Sá, since 1642 a Jesuit brother (he took vows but did not receive holy orders), had always maintained close relations with the Ignatians.[159] Yet during Chichorro's term in office, affairs became tangled. Noting the "many farms and slaves" owned by the Company in Angola, the governor also denounced to the Crown the order's poor administration of their own property in Goa, in Portuguese India, where the governor had maintained contacts since his ill-fated term as captain in Malacca. Salvador de Sá defended the Jesuits in the Overseas Council, and also referred to Chichorro's opinions on Goa, thinking it was strange that the Angola governor should extrapolate his functions, meddling in someone else's government.[160] The warning contrasted with the endorsement given to the continuing recommendations on Angolan and Congolese issues sent by the Brasílico governors of Rio de Janeiro, Pernambuco, and Bahia to the Overseas Council and other mainland authorities.

Regarding João Fernandes's excommunication, it is worth keeping in mind that two other governors of Angola had been punished by the Jesuits with similar condemnations: Francisco de Almeida (1592), opposed to the Society of Jesus's lordship over the *sobados*, and João Correia de Sousa (1623), looter of backland villages and objector to the estate left to the S.J. by former slave trader Gaspar Álvares. João Fernandes Vieira angered the Jesuits as he proposed the reduction of royal donations allocated to the order. Revisiting Chichorro's suggestion, he asked for a reduction in the annual amount of 2,000 *cruzados*—originating in rights on exported slaves—granted by the Crown to the Jesuits while they did not have their own income.[161] The Company of Jesus now enjoyed a great deal of income, protested João Fernandes: over fifty *arimos* (farms) located in the best sites, "over 10,000 blacks as their slaves," a lot of cattle, private *pombeiros* carrying out *resgates* (enslavements by barter) in the backland, and houses for rent in Luanda. The number of slaves owned by the Jesuits seems exaggerated, but it would be given an even higher number (12,000) years later by the Italian Capuchin Carli da Piacenza.[162]

Moreover, continued João Fernandes, the Jesuits evaded missionary tasks in the hinterland and remained in Luanda doing business. This was why the governor requested a royal order forbidding religious personnel to own "so many slaves." João Fernandes further accused the Jesuits of intending to "absolutely govern the royal jurisdiction," abusing, as they did in Macao and Maranhão, the fact that they were Inquisition commissars. He suggested dismissing them from such posts in favor of clergy less given to "excesses."[163]

Mentioning disputes in the Amazon region and in China, João Fernandes unveiled a wider imperial context and demonstrated once more the extension of anti-Jesuitism in the overseas territories.[164] As Magalhães Godinho recalls, the suspicion that the Jesuits intended to establish a "Secular Company of Jesus" encompassing the main trade of the West and East was current at the time.[165] Despite the Crown continuing to pay an allowance to the Company and to investigate the "excesses and robberies" that João Fernandes was accused of perpetrating, the Court provisionally rejected the governor's excommunication.[166] Jealous of the royal prerogatives delegated to his agents, King Afonso VI sternly warned the Jesuits: "If again in any part of this Kingdom, or of its conquests, similar excesses are committed, I will have them (the Jesuits) denied of everything they own in this Kingdom."[167]

Another conflict illustrative of the changes introduced in African politics by the Brasílico intervention was staged in the kingdom of Congo.

Schismatic Congo

At the height of the Portuguese and Brasílico counterattack in Angola, Salvador de Sá imposed a harsh treaty on the Congo. Reviewed by the Overseas Council, the treaty was lightened on the grounds that one needed to act "with all possible moderation, so that there is no scandal, no show of cupidity."[168]

Aside from the moderating influence of Luso-Mbundu Jesuit Antonio do Couto, informal Portuguese ambassador to the Congo, the predominant opinion in Lisbon was the thalassocratic doctrine favoring command of the sea over territorial conquest, and consequently the preference for the reinforcement of ports instead of backland wars. Nonetheless, Chichorro and João Fernandes revisited what Negreiros would take to its ultimate conclusion: the destruction of the Congo. Why was there such a warring impulse, such an expansionist movement? Is it be because of distrust of the kingdom that had allied itself with the "heretic" Dutch and had tried to obtain, through the Capuchins, exclusive sovereignty from Rome or Madrid, to the detriment of the king of Portugal? Certainly.[169] The post–Dutch war period is characterized by Luso-Brasílico military attacks, from Palmares, in Pernambuco, to the Congo, to regain control of the colonial networks on both sides of the Ethiopic Ocean. Nevertheless, the Brasilico offensive against Congo also involved competition between the governors and the Luandan slaving cartel. Indeed, the backland exchanges depended on native middlemen—the *pombeiros* and the *mubiris* (of the Vili people)—who, with the acquiescence of the *sobas*, circulated in the fairs and villages trading and transporting barter goods for Luandan merchants.[170] Unable to have such intermediaries, the governors obtained slaves by means of the backland wars, which secured for them a fifth of the enslaved prisoners ("the royal fifth"), as well as favorable terms in the purchase of slaves after the battles.

Thus, like the *asentista* governors of the first quarter of the century, the Brasílico governors launched predatory expeditions into the hinterlands. Such is the backdrop for the wars that flared in West Central Africa during the 1648–1665 period.

João Fernandes Vieira started military preparations for the invasion of the Congo as soon as he set foot in Luanda, having clearly stated that he had made his mind up while still in Pernambuco. The conversion of Queen Njinga (1656) had neutralized the Matamba Jaga, clearing the way for Luanda's raids against the neighboring kingdoms. The sights of the commanders from Brazil were then set on the Congo sovereigns, deemed apostates, and "traitors" plotting with the Dutch and Spanish. On principle and in practice, such Brasílico captains conceived of the West Central African kingdoms as covens of rebels and fleeing slaves, as if they were the *quilombos* of the Brazilian hinterland. Some of the troops brought over from Pernambuco had once fought against the Quilombos of Palmares, whose defensive forces were comparable to the forces of some African *sobados*.[171] The pretext put forward by João Fernandes for launching his military expedition is characteristic of the anti-Palmares doctrine prevailing in Brazil. To him, the Congo was so dangerous not because of its offensive capabilities, but because it constituted a pole of antislavery attraction, subtracting slaves from the Angolistas. Shortly after being sworn in, João Fernandes declared: "the greatest ruin suffered [by Angola] was the insolence with which the king of Congo sheltered the most part of the settlers' [fugitive] slaves in his land."[172] However, those settlers who owned Africans in Angola and Mozambique—like the owners of Amerindians in Pará and Maranhão—enjoyed a feeble domination over only slightly dissocialized and only formally enslaved natives. In this context, the flight of captives had always seemed inevitable, to the point of blocking the system of exploitation. In Angola, as in Mozambique and the Amazon region, the natives' coerced labor more closely resembled servitude than slavery.[173] By contrast, the Brasílico governors, aware of the threat represented by Palmares and other *quilombos* scattered in Portuguese America, took the issue much more seriously.

Manipulated by João Fernandes, the Luandan municipal council swerved away from its traditional policies favoring indirect trade when it came to backland commerce, and supported the Congo war. In a document whose boasting tone showed that its authors plotted with João Fernandes, the councilors also condemned the "insult" by Kimpako, king of Congo. According to them, the Congolose "persecution" of settlers would soon stop, because "there had never been a governor with such great fame and who inspired so much fear among the gentiles [natives] as Governor João Fernandes Vieira, which is all that we needed to tame the insolence of those blacks."[174] However, Kimpako was not so isolated. He relied on allies among the mestizo clergy of Congo and the Angolistas who carried out barters in his provinces. Differences regarding the Congo war sparked Angolista revolts against Luandan troops in Massangano—a city dependent on the backland trade and vulnerable to the natives' hostility—spoiling the invasion plans designed by

João Fernandes.[175] The governor then directed his troops south of Luanda to attack the Kisama communities, against whom he was successful. Half a century after the *asentista* governor João Coutinho set Kisama in his "main sights," João Fernandes's captains succeeded in conquering that province, enslaving a great number of families, opening the navigation of the Cuanza River, and gaining control over Kisama's mineral salt trade.[176] The campaign demanded considerable military organization. The Capuchin Cavazzi was nominated chaplain of the troops, and he recorded that João Fernandes had mobilized 500 whites, "men of proven valor and nearly all of them skilled," and over 2,000 black combatants for the expedition. During the offensive, João Fernandes's troops crossed the Cuvo River, the southernmost point of the Portuguese incursions in West Central Africa.[177] Seeking new slave reserves and terrestrial paths safe from the corsairs stalking the coast, João Fernandes dispatched seasoned Angolistas and Brasílicos to open a trail from Luanda to Benguela.[178]

Unlike the Estado da Índia governors and captain-majors, insulated in trading posts and enclaves where Asian native hegemony was unavoidable, the Brasílico governors brought over to Africa the experience of territorial conquest and the war-without-quarter waged on the Amerindians.[179] The practices of indigenous sovereignty and of indirect government applied to the Estado da India and most of Portuguese Africa seemed alien to the officials hailing from Portuguese America. João Fernandes had cut his teeth in the Brasílico war, where the strategy had been their own initiative, and there was an attitude of rebelliousness toward whatever European authority existed—Dutch, Spanish, or Portuguese. Like Vidal de Negreiros and then Salvador de Sá before him, João Fernandes was not predisposed to observe the royal orders securing the autonomy of the Angolan sobas or the sovereignty of the Congo. Shortly after his arrival in Luanda, on learning about the blockade of terrestrial trade set up by a few *sobas*, João Fernandes wrote to the War Council in Lisbon to dramatize the fact that "there is no doubt that Y.M.'s arms have lost their reputation among these gentiles [natives]."[180]

When the Portuguese-Dutch war resumed (1657–1661), the Crown warned João Fernandes of the danger of a Dutch attack, and provided aid from Pernambuco for the defense of Angola.[181] Shortly thereafter, news broke that the WIC had attacked São Tomé and was prepared to assault Luanda. Interpreting the events as a prolongation of the Brasílico war, João Fernandes, who used to begin his orders in Angola entitling himself "The First to Call for Revolt" against the WIC in Pernambuco, responded to the Court with his natural immodesty. If the Dutch enemies attacked the city, he "expected to achieve a great victory with the same success with which he had achieved others [against them in Pernambuco]."[182] João Fernandes left his post in 1661, staying behind a few months with his fellow sugar-mill owner and comrade-in-arms, the new governor Vidal de Negreiros. Nothing is known of the reasons holding him in Luanda. But it seems evident that the two Brasílico war commanders reached an understanding about the attack on the Congo, a subject that had been a priority in Luanda's policy since 1648. In any case, from his residence in Pernambuco, João Fernandes continued to intervene in Angolan affairs in the following years.

Vidal De Negreiros and the Routing of Congo

Here lies the Congo kingdom, great and strong,
Already led by us to Christian ways;
Where flows Zaïre, the river clear and long,
A stream unseen by men of olden days.[183]

—Camoens, *The Lusiads*, v, 13

Could Paraiba's field-master and sugar-mill owner André Vidal de Negreiros have read Camoens before taking office in Angola? If he did, it mattered little. The fact that the Congo had already been led "to Christian ways" did not stop the kingdom from being bled by his troops, just like the Guarani of Guayrá, who were not spared the *bandeirante* fist even though they were Christians living peacefully with their missionaries. The demand for slaves in Brazil's economy trampled the missionary enterprise, imposing its iron law in the Ethiopic Ocean.

Vidal de Negreiros continued to harass the Congo, but changed the pretext justifying the war up until then. While João Fernandes accused the king of Congo of being a traitor and poacher of Angolistas' slaves, Negreiros accused him of taking precious-metal mines belonging to the Portuguese Crown.

While still in Pernambuco, the new governor requested royal license to take along 200 soldiers "of the more seasoned and experienced in war, whom the climate of Angola should offend less with the illness that is certain to befall those who leave from this kingdom of Portugal [to Angola]." The Overseas Council, whose councilors once again brought to mind Brazil's dependence on Angolan slaves, endorsed the request.[184] The argument of Brasílico adaptation to African tropical climate was recurring. In 1703, the Overseas Council approved another request for the transfer of 300 infantry from Pernambuco to Angola: "the climate of Angola will be less noxious to those used to that climate."[185]

André Vidal Negreiros's term in office lasted double the usual time. Taking advantage of a turn in the external conjuncture, he set out to attack and destroy the kingdom of Congo, headed since 1660 by d. Antonio Afonso I, the Mani Mulaza, son and inheritor of Kimpako.[186]

Luanda constituted a strategic target for countries with which Portugal found herself in conflict: the Netherlands and Spain. Once the Dutch threat had waned, Lisbon feared an attack by Madrid after 1663.[187] Thus, in 1664, the Crown prohibited military campaigns in the backland and determined that colonists should garrison the Angolan costal ports while a Spanish military expedition was likely.[188] Spain's naval movements, which Lisbon deemed part of an invasion of Luanda, aimed at military goals on the Portuguese mainland coast. In fact, they were part of the operations marking Madrid's last great offensive against the Braganza, to be defeated by the Portuguese in the battle of Montes Claros (17 June 1665).[189] Nonetheless, reinforcements recruited in Lisbon, Pernambuco, and Bahia arrived in Luanda. Despite royal orders received shortly before the offensive, instructing him to keep a "rigorous peace" with the kingdom of Congo, Negreiros then made the most of the newly arrived troops and launched an attack against the Congo.[190]

Indeed, in the preceding years, a protest by settlers and an official investigation had convinced the Crown that the governors' wars were counterproductive. In their complaint, the colonists claimed that they have been wandering "around in the bush, constrained by the governors who [. . .] force them to go to the backland wars, and these are of such quality and arranged in such a way that it would be better never to attempt them because [. . .] they hamper the common trade in the whole of that kingdom [of Angola]." The petition was followed by a royal inquiry on "the damage to your vassals resulting from the war expeditions [*entradas*] that the governors carry out on the backland." In charge of the report, the royal adjudicator (Provedor) of Angola forcefully exposed Brasílico pillage in Angola. According to him, the governors attacked allied *sobas*, enslaving natives and having them sent to Brazil.[191] João Fernandes imprisoned a whole *sobado* in Libolo, dispatching these "vassals of Y.M." to Brazil, where "all these people [. . .] are in a sugar-mill owned by the aforesaid João Fernandes Vieira." On his side, Vidal de Negreiros attacked allied *sobas* in Dembo, capturing nearly 2,000 people, then divided them between himself (he kept 500 "heads") and his officials and soldiers.

Like the settlers in their petition, the royal adjudicator claimed that such "unjust wars" started with Governor Bartolomeu de Vasconcelos da Cunha (1653–1654). Actually, the predatory offensive started in the previous government (1648–1653), at the time of Salvador de Sá, who the royal adjudicator would not dare incriminate, given the former's influence in the Overseas Council and in Lisbon's Court.[192] In the same Council, Feliciano Dourado, close to his fellows countrymen of Brazil, rejected the accusations against João Fernandes and Vidal de Negreiros, "who serves Y.M. well and has always proceeded well satisfactorily both in war and in peace." In particular, councilor Feliciano recalled that the then-governor of Angola, "after spilling his blood in the service of Y.M. against the enemies of Faith and Crown and was one of the main subjects to whom the recovery of Pernambuco was due, carried on to govern Maranhão and then Pernambuco, during which terms there were no complaints against him."[193]

Backed by the prestige of his allies in Court, Vidal de Negreiros could thus organize the military expedition desired by all the predators who had occupied the government of Angola: the attack on Congo.

Mbwila: The Tri-Continental Battle

However, the Congo was an independent kingdom, recognized as such by Lisbon and Rome, and not a Dembo *sobado* or, still less, a kind of African *quilombo*, in the derogatory sense that the Brasilico captains gave to this term.

From the start, the deans and priests of São Salvador of Congo thought that the offensive ordered by Negreiros had a Christian kingdom for a target and therefore did not constitute a "Just War," in the terms both of canonical and royal laws. Of the nine ecclesiastics who signed the protest against the war that was sent to the governor of Angola, eight were mulattoes or Bakongo generally related to the Congolese royal family. Friar Giuseppe de Bassano, an Italian Capuchin, was the only non-African signatory.[194] Fully recognized by Pope Paul V in 1608 at the reception in Rome of the Congolese ambassador, Marquis of Funta, the status of Congo as a Christian kingdom had been reiterated by the Roman Curia in 1648.[195] Then, Pope Innocent X received two Capuchins who had been nominated as Congolese ambassadors and sent a regal crown to Kimpako. On the same occasion, the pope acknowledged the full political sovereignty of the kingdom of Congo.[196] Ironically, at that time the king of Congo had more legitimacy in Rome than the king of

Portugal, insofar as the papacy would recognize Braganza's sovereignty only in 1668. Furthermore, the Overseas Council itself had established Congo's statute in 1651: "The king of Congo is not a vassal of this [Portuguese] Crown, but a brother-in-arms [*irmão em armas*] of its kings."[197] Such circumstances represented a serious hindrance to the invasion planned by Negreiros. This is why the governor covered his back, obtaining a prior refutation of the Christian character attributed to the Congolese Court. Fr. Manoel Curado, who was the dean of Angola and Congo, wrote the certificate. Obliged to reside in the episcopal see of São Salvador by force of his post, he had nevertheless decided to live in Luanda.

According the Dean Curado, the Congolese deans allied with the Congo's Crown, Simão de Medeiros and Miguel de Crasto, were "schismatic and idolaters." Both were accused of spoiling King Antonio I, the Mani Mulaza, inculcating in him ideas of sovereignty, "Because it has been put in his head that he is brother of the king of Portugal, [despite] being a Negro in manners and in government, as is the case with all in those kingdoms." Taking advantage of the deadlock between Lisbon and Rome that blocked the provision of Portuguese bishoprics, the Bakongo dean Simão de Medeiros requested the support of Madrid in order to be nominated bishop of Congo and Angola.[198] Worse, the two deans allegedly advised the people of Congo and neighboring kingdoms that they should "cut the throat of all Whites on the arrival of the Castilian armada," which had been supposedly sent to invade Angola.[199]

Without pronouncing in favor of the punitive war, the Overseas Council sent the "schism" case records made by the two deans over to the Inquisition. But Dean Manuel Curado's diatribe had already opened the way for the looting of the Congo, whose king had just lost—from other motives—the support of the Capuchins.[200] There was now legal recognition that the Mani Mulaza was a "traitor," and the religion of his kingdom "schismatic." On the Congo's side, the declaration of war against Vidal de Negreiro's troops shows the degree of inculturation that operated in that kingdom at the end of a century and a half of continued contact with the Church and the Portuguese.[201] Associating biblical quotations with the Christian names attributed to Bakongo nobility, the declaration of war reveals important changes in the Congolese power system.

> Dom Antonio the first of such name, by Divine Grace, Augmenter of the Conversion of the Jesus Christ's Faith, Its Defender in those parts of Ethiopia, King of the Very Ancient Kingdom of Congo, Angola, Matamba, Veanga,

Sundi, Lula and Sonso, Lord of the Mbundu, and of the Matambulas, who interpret themselves as deceased and resurrected men, and of many other kingdoms, and landlord of neighboring vassals near and far . . . , and of the most awesome River Zaire, its banks and flowing waters, and of all the coast of the salty sea coast, and of its beaches etc.

As was his custom with all documents, King Antonio I kept his Christian name and did not write his name in Kikongo, Vita-a-Nkanga, nor his clan chief name, Mani Mulaza.[202] But he proclaimed his sovereignty over the ancient provinces of his kingdom, Angola and Matamba, then taken by the Portuguese. As a knight of the Order of Christ, he proclaimed his Christian titles. Still, in the same paragraph where he declared himself "Augmentor" and "Defender" of Christianism, Dom Antonio I incorporated, as observed by Anne Hilton, a new title linked to traditional religion: "Lord of the Matambula who interpret themselves as deceased and resurrected men." Exposed to the colonial offensive, the king of Congo mobilized the support of the Luso-African clergy of São Salvador. On the other side of the coin, he reestablished the alliance with the *nganga* Matambula, the sorcerers who resurrected the dead, and with the Kimpasi rite of the Bakongo religion, in order to widen his political and military base. A secret brotherhood, the Kimpasi founded the pact between generations, uniting the lineage around the cult of Nzambi Mpungu, the supreme ancestral being of the Bakongo community.[203] Then, the manifesto takes on a dramatic tone, justifying the war "to defend our lands, estates, sons and daughters, and our own lives and freedoms that the Portuguese nation wants to appropriate and lord over them."

A call to arms to save the Congolese subjects from death and enslavement, the document bore many signatures. Besides that of King Antonio I, the declaration of war was also signed by his ministers and of the "Secretary Major of Purity, Dom Calistro Sebastião Castelobranco Tears of Magdalena at the foot of the Cross on Mount Calvary's."[204] The titles read like characters from a play by Brazilian playwright Ariano Suassuna, but they refer directly to the Portuguese history of the time.[205] It should be noted that on being baptized, Bakongo nobles took a Christian name together with a passage from the Bible ("Magdalen's Tears at the foot of the Cross on Mount Calvary"), plus the names and honors of the officiating priest or of the godfather. More significant than the name is the title given to the minister. Indeed, the relevance attributed to the title of Secretário Maior da Puridade, which means "Crown's Private Councilor," fits into the political profile of the Portuguese monarchy in the reign of Afonso VI. During that period (1662–1667), the power granted to the count of Castelo Melhor effectively covered the functions of a prime minister, but his title, Escrivão da Puridade, had fallen into disuse and was then temporarily reintroduced.[206]

Advancing against the invaders, the king of Congo prepared for battle on the field of Mbwila. Mani Mulaza defended his position with 190 musketeers and tens of thousands of archers, *zagaia* lancers, and other warriors, "with 100,000 bows," boasted Vidal de Negreiros later. An unverifiable and unrealistic figure, for not all Congolese present in the battlefield actually fought. Both Cavazzi and his Capuchin colleague, Diogini da Piacenza (born Giuseppe Flaminio Carli), offer an even more extravagant figure: 900,000 Congolese fighting 400 Portuguese.[207] As usual, the warriors of the Congo, like those of the Ndongo, Matamba, and Kasanje, carried only their own weapons along. This is why so many other porters carrying the *matula* and equipment would accompany the troops. Easy targets after defeat, such individuals constituted the booty of the winners, who sold them as slaves. Alongside Mani Mulaza warriors marched a company of whites and mulattos, Portuguese as well as Angolistas and Congolese, commanded by the mulatto Pedro de Cabrada.[208] At his side, three priests also marched, one Capuchin and two secular. All of them were Bakongo people, born in São Salvador do Congo. The Capuchin was the chaplain major of the Congolese army, Friar Francisco de São Salvador, born Manuel Roboredo, son of a Portuguese and a woman from the Congolese royal family. Teaching the Bakongo language and customs to the missionaries, Friar Francisco secured Capuchin influence over the Congo's Court. Jealous, the Jesuits were hostile to the proselytism of such missionaries, who were usually from Italy and Spain. More threatening to Portuguese nationalism, Capuchins from some regions of Italy were subjects of the Habsburg Crown. Confirming the antagonism between the two religious orders, Friar Francisco signed the manifestos of São Salvador's clergy calling on the authorities, Jesuits, and Angolistas not to wage war on the Congolese. Because of his own bad luck or of someone's hatred, Friar Francisco ended up being killed by the Luso-Afro-Brasílico troops at the Mbwila battle.[209]

At the head of the tri-continental troop fielded by Governor André de Vidal de Negreiros was one of the heroes of the Angolistas, captain-major Luís Lopes Sequeira, a military man experienced in the West African wars, son of a Mbundu woman and of Domingos Lopes de Sequeira, another commander of the Angolan wars mentioned above.[210] Under his command marched 450 musketeers and thousands of native warriors, among whom the Jaga stood tall. With 3,000 archers and

100 African musketeers, the core of the Portuguese "black troops" (*Guerra preta*) marched under the command of the black captain Simão de Matos. In addition, there were two light artillery pieces, some cavalry, several Angolista companies, and the company formed by forty Afro-Brasílicos, Pernambucan militiamen from the Henrique Dias's regiment (*terço*) headed by the mulatto captain Manoel Soares.[211]

All this apparatus shaped an extraordinary battle in Mbwila. On one side were the Portuguese, Brasílicos, Angolistas, and Africans commanded by an Angolista officer and sent from Luanda by a governor coming from a major slaving region in Brazil. On the other side was a Bantu sovereign reigning over an independent kingdom that had traded with Europeans for one-and-a-half centuries. It was recognized as Christian by the pope, by The Hague, Lisbon, and Madrid, by the Capuchins, and by a large proportion of the Portuguese colonists. In a way, the battle represented the clash of the two alternatives available to Portuguese expansion: pillage and trade; military conquest and the policy of indirect government; Angola and Congo; Brazil and Portuguese India; Atlantic colonies and Pacific trading posts. The outcome of the battle would elucidate the prolongation of the Luso-Brasílico policy of pillage on the West Central African stage. As missionaries had warned since the sixteenth century, the main impetus of attacks carried out by the natives concentrated on the front lines. This is why Sequeira composed his avant garde with his most potent or most frightening units: the two cannon pieces, cavalry, the Jaga, the company of Captain Anjo's black musketeers, and the Afro-Pernambucan company of Manoel Soares.[212] This crowd of armed men balanced out in a military calculation that left no room for doubt. The Luso-Afro-Brasílico edge resulting from the Jaga combat expertise and the superiority of the firearms surpassed the Congolese numerical advantage (see appendix 5). The two artillery pieces, "cradle" cannons shooting two kilograms of grapeshot, caused more fear than damage to the warriors advancing in groups.

However, to understand the meaning of Mbwila, one must highlight a few points of 1600s military colonial history.

Brasílico Maneuvers in the African Wars

Most probably, the Brasílico war methods facilitated the victory of the Negreiro's captains in the Battle of Mbwila. The tactics deployed by the Portuguese-American had been brought over to Africa by the 1648 expeditionaries, and, before them, by transferred military men since 1635–1639, when Francisco Vasconcellos da Cunha's governed Angola. Among these were figures such as da Cunha's nephew, Bartolomeu, a mainland Portuguese who fought in Pernambuco and Bahia before becoming interim governor and a powerful Angola kinglet. Others included the Afro-Pernambucano Paulo Pereira and other militiamen of Henrique Dias's *terço*, as well as Brasílico officials of the two aid expeditions in 1645.[213] Resources deployed in South American skirmishes against Amerindians, *quilombolas*, Guarani *reducciones*, the French, and the Dutch appeared as novelties in the Angolan wars of the time, as was the case in the 1655–1656 campaign against the Kisama villages: the use of the Paulista doublet and pouches containing maize and manioc, quick barefoot marches, systematic destruction of native crops and water holes, and night raids. Such tactics must be considered to be contributions of the Brasílico lumpen-colonialism to the consolidation of the "Pax Lusitana" in West Central Africa.

As mentioned, Pernambucan militiamen preferred muskets or wheel-lock and flintlock guns, instead of matchlock.[214] In the tropics, besides failing when damp—especially if the fuse was made of *imbira* fiber, in the absence of European linen—the matchlock was not fit for irregular terrain and guerrilla warfare.[215] During the day, the Indians allied to the Dutch could smell the lit matches from far off, even when there was no smoke to be seen.[216] At night or in the shadows of the woods, the glow of the burning fuse exposed the ambush. Shortly after setting foot in Olinda (1630), the WIC troops panicked in the tropical night, when they confused a swarm of fireflies with the burning fuses of the enemy.[217]

Wheel-lock guns, on the other hand, seemed more adequate to irregular troops. They had a shorter range, but they were lighter and featured a bigger grip, not demanding a fork, which was an obligatory support when it came to muskets.[218] This is why they regarded as better adapted to the jungle, appropriate as they were to night ambushes and more trustworthy in tropical humidity. Such motives led the Brasílico troops to resort to the wheel-lock, and then the flintlock, instead of the matchlock, before regular Western troops did (appendix 5).

In the tropical wars, opting for matchlocks by European troops sometimes resulted in disaster. On the Olinda beaches, during a clash between ninety soldiers that escorted Admiral Pieter Ita and Captain Flores's men (May 1630), rain rendered the WIC's harquebuses and matchlocks useless, exposing the invaders to Brasílico arrows, lances, and swords.[219] Thirty Dutchmen were killed and their admiral narrowly escaped. A similar incident involved VOC personnel in the vicinity of the Cape, today's South Africa. A Khoi chief called Doman, a former Dutch captive, stirred up an uprising among the natives. Known as the first Khoi-Dutch War, the conflict entered military annals. Knowing that the Dutch matchlocks failed when damp, Doman always attacked in the rain. Only the interest of the Khoi in European maritime trade stopped the ruin of the Cape's trade port.[220] There is a record of another battle in 1660, between the Abrambu and Fetu armies, two Gold Coast city-states, in which the Abrambu armies were routed in a downpour that put out the fuses of their muskets. Incidents of this kind led the Africans to ask for wheel-locks and flintlocks, instead of matchlocks, when trading with Europeans.[221]

In the afternoon of the 29th of October 1665, in the Ulanga River valley northwest of Luanda, a downpour also made a difference in a decisive battle, in the most important colonial battle fought up to that date in sub-Saharan Africa. The eight-hour combat in the Mbwila plain ended when the Congolese launched a massive attack in the middle of a heavy rain. The *Mercúrio Portuguez* (August 1666) recorded, with regard to the battle, "because it started raining a lot, [the enemy] hoped to take advantage of the situation, which rendered our firearms useless." An excited anonymous Portuguese witness was more explicit: "the enemy insisted, greatly trusting the heavy rain that poured down, because it seemed to them that we would not be able to resort to our firearms, a mistake, for the Portuguese can make lightning out of water."[222] In other words, the Congolese offensive had been launched on the presumption that the enemy wielded matchlocks (usually employed by Europeans) that were rendered useless by the rain. Most probably, the fire from the wheel-locks and flintlocks, the Brasílico weapons, surprised the Congo forces. Wounded by one such weapon, Mani Mulaza fell and was beheaded by a Jaga. When his head rolled to the ground, his army collapsed. According to a report sent by André Vidal de Negreiros to the Court, over 5,000 Congolese were killed in combat, among whom were "400 titled [Congolese] nobles."[223]

Two mulatto captains, Pernambucano Manoel Soares and Angolista Simão de Matos, were among the officers that defeated the Congolese army and won the day. However, contrary to expectations, there was no mass capture of the vanquished "and a great prey was lost."[224] The 400-man contingent from the allied Mbwila *sobado* still managed to catch a few fleeing Congolese, but it was an autonomous force, not obliged to share its booty of enslaved with the governor's militiamen. Those who had come from Luanda and Massangano, and even further from Bahia and Pernambuco, on little or no pay in the expectation of enslaving Africans, were sorely disappointed, a loss that may have caused, as I point out below, a mutiny that took place shortly after in Luanda.

Mani Mulaza's head was brought to the capital of Angola, where it was received with full honors by the Portuguese authorities. It was taken in a procession to the church of Our Lady of Nazareth, where it was walled into a niche. Negreiros was a devotee of the saint, who was considered "the authoress of this miracle and victory." He had built the church of the saint in Luanda in 1664 "at his own expense" to fulfill a vow.[225] During the funeral ceremony, the governor placed the king of Congo's crown, sent years previously by the Pope to d. Garcia, the Kimpako, father and predecessor of Mani Mulaza, at the foot of the saint. Later, Negreiros had the crown sent to Brazil, trusting his nephew captain Antônio Curado Vidal, Recife infantry field-master, to take it to King d. Afonso VI. The crown was stolen in Pernambuco, through the arts of captain Curado Vidal—a troublesome individual—or of someone else.[226]

The thief would not have made much profit from the deed, as the crown was made of brass, as ordered by its maker, Pope Innocent X. Yet the piece had a great symbolic value, especially for the Congolese monarchy. Twenty years after Mbwila, Angolan black priest Manuel de Sá tried to recover the crown, or to get a new one, to reconsecrate the power of Congolese sovereigns and restore the political protection that the popes had given the African kingdom. Moved by the afflictions of the Africans, of the "Ethiopians from whom I descend," Father Manuel addressed the metropolitan hierarchy and the Propaganda Fide. Denouncing André Vidal de Negreiros's war on the "last peaceful king" of the Congo, he alleged that the lack of the crown consecrated by the Pope destabilized the new monarchs of São Salvador and drove the Congo into chaos.[227] Such disorders harmed the missionary tasks of the Capuchins who relied on the king of Congo. Later, writing in 1702 from Soyo, Friar Laurent de Lucques stated that Mbanza Congo, the kingdom's capital, had been deserted since the Battle of Mbwila and that all the Congo's kings had been murdered. Referring to the vain efforts of Friar Luc de Caltanissetta to overcome these troubles, he concluded, "We do not find a way to restore the [Congo] Kingdom's unity."[228]

Putsch in Luanda and Knives Drawn in Recife

In the aftermath of the Battle of Mbwila, Negreiros requested from Bahia, Pernambuco, and Rio de Janeiro more soldiers, "vagrants, and horses that can be saddled and bridled." All these set foot in Luanda shortly thereafter.[229] In a manifesto sent to the Crown, the Luanda municipal council sang the praises of Mbwila. To them, victory represented no less than the Portuguese comeback after the setback in Ksar el-Kebir. "We must recount to Y.M. the most felicitous success that the arms of Y.M. achieved over the opposition that the king of Congo intended to carry out[. . . .] The success was so felicitous that under Y.M. protection and God's promise we hope to see Portugal's monarchy so expanded that it serves not only as aid and defense of the Church, but also as the terror of the whole of Mauritania."[230] "Mauritania" referred to the Moors' Africa (distinct from "Ethiopia" or "Guinea," that is, black Africa), where Portugal had suffered a catastrophic defeat at Ksar el-Kebir, where king Sebastian I and many Portuguese were slaughtered, at the time when the invasion of Angola by Paulo Dias Novais was taking place.[231] Indeed, Novais gave himself the title of "captain and governor of these new kingdoms of Sebaste [Sebastian] in the conquest of Ethiopia." With similar enthusiasm, the anonymous author of the Mbwila report saluted Vidal de Negreiros's feat: "In fact, this is the true restoration of Angola, because the whole of its kingdoms were then weakened by the Congo [king], [who] had vowed the total ruin of the Portuguese nation."[232] For the Angolistas, Mbwila marked the climax of the Portuguese and Brasílico counteroffensive in West Central Africa. For Braganza's zealots, Mbwila's victory dealt also a blow in Madrid, then at war against Lisbon. In the account of the battle published July 1666 in the *Mercúrio Portuguez*, Portugal's first printed periodical of political propaganda, Antônio de Sousa de Macedo praises the "miraculous victory," interpreting the defeat of the king of Congo and his army as revenge against Spanish maneuvers to incite a Congolese uprising against the Portuguese.[233]

Transformed into the biggest possession that Portugal enjoyed in the Africa, Angola emerged as one of the high points of the reestablishment of the Lusitanian overseas empire, after the long "captivity" imposed by the Spanish Habsburgs.

From the Ethiopic Ocean perspective, Mbwila is imbued with a wider meaning and joins the *bandeirante* battles of Guayrá in shaping the primacy of Luso-Brasílico pillage that sought to enslave peoples from South America and West Central Africa.

The mutiny that flared during the government of Tristão da Cunha (1666–1667), who had succeeded Negreiros, unveiled the aims of the Battle of Mbwila and the scope of Brasílico involvement in West Central Africa. Grandson of a governor of India, commander of a regiment that gained a reputation in the victory at Montes Claros against the Spanish (1665), Tristão da Cunha was a prestigious figure in Lisbon. But he ended up being expelled by the rebellious soldiery only a few months after being sworn in. The uprising could have been caused by the incensed troops—in part composed of soldiers and militiamen hailing from Pernambuco and Bahia—left behind and unpaid by Negreiros. The *Catalogue of the Governors of Angola* (1825), an anonymous text written in Luanda based on municipal council documents and Angolista oral tradition, states that Tristão had been unseated due to "the little attention and contempt with which he treated his predecessor [Negreiros]."[234] A denunciation submitted by a Tristão da Cunha partisan, a Luanda lawyer called Pedro Ansures, provides details. Arrested by the mutinous troops, he was embarked in fetters in Luanda on a ship bound to Pernambuco, and suffered an attempt on his life as he set foot in Recife. A few of "André Vidal de Negreiros's [then governor in Pernambuco] mulattos" fell on him and stabbed him because he was "his enemy and with the complicity of mutinous officials of the Luanda municipal council, to whom André Vidal had sent word [from Recife] of the knife attack that he wished to perpetrate." Submitting a complaint to the Overseas Council, Dr. Ansures stated that he had been victim of an attempt on his life "because he had not joined the Luanda mutiny partisans."[235]

What was the link between the two incidents, between the Luanda's mutiny and the knives thrust into Tristão da Cunha's supporter by Negreiros' mulattos?

Apparently, Tristão da Cunha was attempting to make a change in direction, as he dismantled the plundering operation that Negreiros and his men had planned to perpetrate in the Congo. After Mbwila, Negreiros could have launched his troops on the kingdom, as it was an enslaved labor pool that the Portuguese, Angolista, Brasílico, and African predators always desired. As usual, the governor, the merchants providing equipment and victuals, the officers, and the troops—who remained without pay for the second year—would be paid with booty, that is, with prisoners transformed into slaves, into export goods.[236] Yet the Battle of Mbwila took place at the end of October, in the beginning of the Angolan "winter," the *massanza*, the rainy season extending until January, as was announced by the downpour during the battle.[237] Rivers overflowed and swamped the land, making the troop's marches dangerous and halting all activity for months amid seasonal fevers.[238]

In the meantime, Negreiros's term came to a close, and Tristão da Cunha replaced him. Unlike previous governors of Angola, who since Francisco Vasconcellos da Cunha (1635–1639) had served in positions in Brazil or had remained for a time in Brazil before taking up the Angolan post, the new governor came straight from Lisbon. Not sharing the goals or, better said, the desire for future booty in slaves nurtured by the army camped out in the hinterland, governor Tristão da Cunha ordered the return of the troop to Luanda. "I found the army in campaign out on the Congo border with arms in hand, biding whatever time war might allow to gain more strength for hostility before taking to the field." Due to bad weather and lack of food, the new governor decided to order the soldiers to come back. He sought to "give time" for the Congolese to peacefully reduce themselves to obedience to the Portuguese Crown. Other measures taken by him caused trouble. More dogmatic than the Brasílico governors with regard to African religious practices, Tristão da Cunha repressed religious cults native to Luanda. Troubled by the high number of musketeers that Mani Mulaza had recruited for Mbwila, he banned the profitable Angolista trade of gunpowder with natives. Appointing his own people, brought over from Lisbon or recruited in Angola, Tristão went against the Angolista and Brasílico interests established in the region since the arrival of the 1648 task force. Legal representatives and officials appointed by Negreiros were dismissed. Among them was Antônio de Andrade, captain of the Ambaca's fort and a veteran of the battles of Tabocas and Guararapes in Pernambuco, who had served for nineteen years in Pernambuco and Angola. Also dismissed was the very victor of the Mbwila battle, Angolista commander Luis Lopes Sequeira.[239] Such were the events that sparked the military uprising in Luanda. Shortly after, the local municipal council administered the colony.[240]

Brasílico Continuity in West Central Africa

Mbwila put an end to the Congo as a centralized kingdom, but it did not shake other Bakongo groups located in counties directed by chiefs who eventually submitted to the former sovereign of São Salvador. One of them, the count of Soyo, Estêvão da Silva, strengthened by trading with the Dutch at the port of Mpinda, inflicted a resounding defeat on colonial troops. Five hundred Portuguese and native soldiers, more interested in the capture of slaves than in wielding arms, were killed by the Soyo warriors in the Battle of Kitombo (1670).[241] In deep trouble, the new governor of Angola (1669–1676), Francisco de Távora (future count of Alvor), sought help from Brazil's governors. Not waiting for a royal permission, "the governor of Pernambuco, Fernão de Sousa Coutinho, and João Fernandes Vieira, the latter at great expense to his estate and usefulness to Your Highness, sent me 200 foot soldiers and some horses [. . .] with such zeal in service of Your Highness and with such diligence and readiness, that both seem to me deserving of Your

Highness honoring them with your gratitude," Francisco de Távora informed the Crown. The efforts by João Fernandes Vieira in aid of Angola must have helped him to obtain the post of the northern Brazil captaincies' fortifications supervisor, to which he was nominated by the Crown shortly after.[242]

In the Overseas Council, councilor Feliciano Dourado endorsed the measures taken by Távora. Angola was in danger, he said. "And with the damage and loss [resulting] from the lack of trade with Brazil, which is a great deal to consider, because it is certain that Brazil without Angola cannot be sustained, [because] the cultivation of sugar employs Angolan negroes [. . .] and this is why [Angola] should be aided." He thought that very strict orders should be sent to Brazil "for the governors of Bahia, Pernambuco, and Rio de Janeiro to continue with the aid," because it was from those places that aid could more readily be provided.[243]

Mobilizing the troops and horses sent from Brazil, Távora relaunched the inland offensive and conquered the last capital of the Ndongo kingdom, Pungo-Andongo (1671).[244] The garrison settled there, at the margins of the Cuango River, carved out the most inland Portuguese outpost in Africa, which would only be crossed in the middle of the nineteenth century.[245] The trade fair opened in the area—the crossroads for the paths leading to Luanda and Benguela—prompted the emergence of new *pumbos*, backland slave markets, and of *pumbeiros* servicing the Angolistas. A treaty imposed on Queen Njinga's successor in 1683 forced the kingdom of Matamba to trade exclusively with the Portuguese.

With the help of Brasílico soldiers, the military framing of continental exchanges was crucial for the Portuguese, since French, Dutch, and British competitors had established maritime posts in the kingdom of Loango, to the north of the Congo delta, draining circuits previously captured by Luanda.[246]

The New Pact between the Crown and the South Atlantic Captains

Portuguese vulnerability in Europe and overseas, Dutch intervention in the Southern Atlantic, and the displacement of officials around diverse operational theaters induced Brasílico slaver oligarchies to closely follow Lisbon's affairs in the South Atlantic. Yet second-grade officers, clergy, and royal officers also peered across the sea. Wars in defense of Braganza overseas sovereignty gave rise to pretensions of merit that did not always find space to materialize in Portuguese America. For

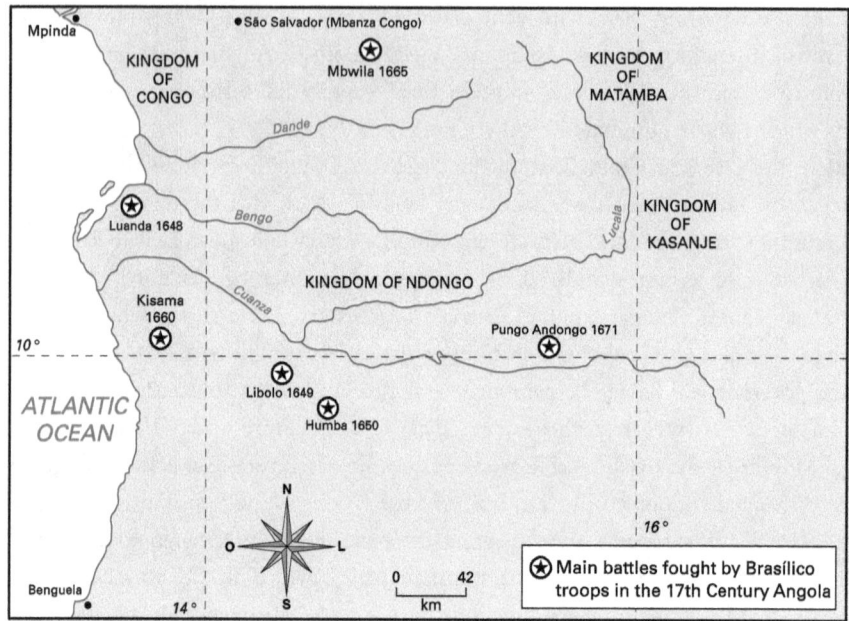

Map 7.1. Portuguese and Brasílico offensive in seventeenth century West Central Africa.
Source: CEBRAP, São Paulo, p. 301 of the Brazilian edition.

some time, before the eighteenth-century Minas Gerais gold rush opened new opportunities, the stagnant economy of Brazil in the last quarter of the seventeenth century was not robust enough for the officers and colonists' ambitions.[247] In this context, the Crown made a fresh political pact between the mainland and the periphery by means of the distribution of posts and the rearrangement of rewards gained in overseas combat.

Like Salvador de Sá, João Fernandes Vieira, and André Vidal de Negreiros, members of the Portuguese American clergy and the militias would claim the title of excombatant in the Dutch war, the first Luso-Brasílico action that was deemed a "live war" at the service of the Crown. Therefore, they applied for vacant posts in Portuguese Africa, mainly in Angola, where religious and civil offices—fortress captains, sergeant-majors, legal representatives, superintendents, magistrates, royal factors, vicars, deans, and parishioners—would all be periodically provided by the Crown. For military posts (captain, ensign, sergeant), the Frontiers Regulation (1659) requested that the candidates provide proof, certified by royal agents, of a certain number of years in service (between four and six years) in the "live war," that is, on the mainland anti-Spanish front or in one of the anti-Dutch conflicts overseas.[248] For each one of these posts, three candidates were to be indicated by the Overseas Council, from which the Crown would take its pick. As we shall see in the next section, the Brasílicos were attracted by such royal positions in West Central Africa, which were sometimes poorly paid, but rendered profitable by smuggling or by extortion of slaves and other "goods" from the Angolan *sobas*.

The hierarchy of preferences in force in the seventeenth century can be gauged from an analysis of candidacies, of the triple lists elaborated by the Overseas Council, and from the nominations ultimately decided on by the Crown. In a hypothetical dispute between candidates of equal social standing, the preference was for those who had made war on the mainland Europe against Spanish troops.[249] A candidate's merit would be greater if he had fought against the Dutch in Flanders during the Habsburg period, a war "[which was a school so famous] around the world that its hours were valued more than the years in other militias," as defined by Francisco Manuel de Melo, a writer and a military expert.[250] In any case, actions in the war against Spain were regarded more highly than service in Brazil. Thus, on writing in 1662 to Pedro de Mello, who took the post of governor of Rio de Janeiro, Governor-General Francisco Barreto recorded the "pity in the difference between beating Castilians and dealing with *mazombos* [Brazilian-born Portuguese]."[251]

Second in order of preference came royal servants of the Estado da India. It was the most prestigious overseas possession, where many nobles sent their illegitimate sons so that they could, by merit of service to the Crown, correct the demerit of their fathers.[252] It should be noted that, while issues related to Portuguese America had an increasing share in the Overseas Council sessions in the second half of the seventeenth century, those of its councilors experienced in overseas affairs had served mostly in Asia. This situation changed in the first decades of the eighteenth century, when the councilors who served in Brazil took a more prominent place in the Council.[253]

Third in line came those whose militancy was limited to the Brasílico war.[254] Participation in the Paulista *bandeiras* against mid-south Amerindians was usually unqualified and even considered detrimental to the candidates' application. Thus, restrictions were placed on an important candidacy in 1656. Antônio Pereira de Azevedo, commander of the second company of the so-called "Borders *Bandeira*," 1648–1651, mentioned in the previous chapter, headed by Raposo Tavares, submitted his candidacy for the post of treasury superintendent of the Espírito Santo captaincy. His record recalled engagement in a "live war" in Pernambuco and in Bahia, also highlighting his position of command in the 1648 *bandeira*, "during which a great amount of time was spent and [where] he saw the majority of his companions die of hunger and thirst." Azevedo did get the post. However, councilor Salvador de Sá annotated a significant reservation: he agreed with Azevedo's nomination because of his participation in the Brasílico war against the Dutch, but he did not recognize any "merit nor satisfaction" in the command of the *bandeira*, "in the service of backland expeditions." Through the voice of Salvador de Sá, the greatest authority on Brazilian affairs in the Overseas Council, the Court adjudged the "Borders *Bandeira*" to be null and useless.[255]

The value of the Angolan wars of pillage also seemed random to the Court. After the Battle of Mbwila, Vidal de Negreiros requested 400 *escudos* to reward his captains. But the Overseas Council considered the sum excessive for victories obtained in the Angolan wars. Such incidents motivated Cadornega's remarks in praise of "the war of the Angolan Portuguese, who some, in their contempt, call a negroes' war, and *coata-coata* [catch-catch], but this is because they do not see nor experience it [in person], it being, on the contrary, the most arduous and riskiest [war] there is in the world."[256]

At first, the palatine councils privileged rewards of combat against the European armies, and dismissed the colonists' action in the wars against African and American natives. Subsequently, there was a change in the decisions of the Overseas Council, reflecting a turn in the Ethiopic Ocean geopolitics in the last quarter of the seventeenth century. From then on, as will be seen in the conclusion of this book, colonial repopulating of Portuguese America, grounded on the Angolan slave trade, would provide the veneer of dignity to military actions against the Amerindians and *quilombolas*. In this way, the combats against the Amerindians of the north and northeast in the "Barbarians War" and the military actions against Palmares came to be seen as meritorious, favoring certain candidacies in the Overseas Council.

In parallel, dozens of officers and militiamen from Bahia, Pernambuco, and Rio de Janeiro were transferred to Angola in the second half of the 1600s, in the context of the military aid expeditions. In Pernambuco, such expeditionaries were remembered as legendary heroes. Loreto Couto, in his work *Desagravos do Brazil e Glórias de Pernambuco* (1757), highlights seven times that Pernambuco soldiers had been called to Angola, "where they obtained glorious victories," and where "at the cost of their own and others' blood, destroyed the power of the enemies [and] sustained in their arms that portion of the Portuguese empire."

It must also be considered that such transatlantic expeditions externalized Brasílico violence, thus contributing to the preservation of social order within the Portuguese America.

Actually, after the Dutch surrender, in the tribulations of the Palmares resistance war and in the "Barbarians War," Pernambuco and the surrounding captaincies went through a turbulent period. Used to looting during the Brasílico war, the toughs (*magnates*) at the head of armed gangs caused trouble. There were many recorded crimes committed in Pernambuco by individuals wielding guns between 1654 and 1660, a situation that led governor Brito Freyre (1661–1664) to punish on pain of death those accused of murder or wounding with the intent to kill. Another source of tension was the contingent of about 900 black men and mulatto soldiers who had either fled their Dutch masters or were given by their owners to the troops fighting the Dutch. Demobilized, such combatants grew restless, fearing being enslaved once again. Later, the Crown intervened, paying compensation to some owners and persuading others to grant definitive freedom to such former militiamen.[257] Other captaincies experienced similar problems. A good part of the troops sent to Angola hailed from such sectors, voluntarily or compulsorily mobilized for the war in West Central Africa. In a report about the situation in Angola, dated 1655 and commissioned by the Court, Salvador de Sá was explicit: "In the Estado do Brasil there are a great number of freed mulattos, criminals, rebellious characters, and low-life individuals who may serve in Angola to guard forts [. . . ;] it would seem convenient for Y.M. to ask the governors of Pernambuco and Rio de Janeiro to have as many as possible of these mulattos arrested and have them sent to Angola in the ships bound to such ports."[258]

In another social sphere, the imbrication of the careers of the ecclesiastical hierarchy and of the governors on both sides of the Atlantic must be noted. Besides the cases mentioned above, Angola was administered by more than ten governors who held equivalent posts in Brazil in the years between 1680 and 1810, before or after taking office in Luanda.[259]

Just as important as the movement of men was the movement of merchandise between the two shores of the Southern Atlantic. Indeed, the links between the two colonies were strengthened by a new kind of product from Brazil: the *cachaça*, the Brazilian rum.

The *zimbo*-money from Bahia, Rio de Janeiro manioc, later transplanted on the other side of the sea, or further, Bahian tobacco, exported in greater amounts in the 1700s, penetrated African markets without competition from similar metropolitan products. But Brazilian *cachaça* was another matter. Exported from Bahia, Pernambuco, and Rio de Janeiro, the *cachaça*—then called *jeribita*—competed with Iberian wine and spirits sold in Congo and Angola. Indeed, *cachaça* exports illustrate how intercolonial Southern Atlantic trade overlapped with the interests of metropolitan groups from the end of the seventeenth century.[260]

It is well known that the wholesale market for spirits was a relatively new phenomenon in the world market. Fabricated in Europe since the Middle Ages, alcohol used to be made in small amounts for use by chemists. Wine, beer, cider and other fermented drinks composed most of the beverage trade. In the seventeenth century, the aqua vitae—spirits made of cereal, grapes, and the fermented juice of other fruits—until then restricted to domestic or regional consumption, appeared on the export agendas of European countries.[261] Later, such drinks began to be distilled from selected wines, juices, and malts, kept in barrels to age, and transformed into brandies for refined consumption.

In a wider perspective, the alcoholic-beverage industry offered a way out of the seventeenth-century general crisis, which caused agriculture prices to tumble in the world-economy's center and periphery.[262] Studies on economic history demonstrate the effects of the century-long downturn: prices for wheat and rye fell in Germany, France, and England in the period between the decades of 1630–1640 and 1760–1770.[263] In this period of recession, Wallerstein asks, how could the lordly classes increase their sales to impoverished populations? The author himself provides the answer: by making alcoholic beverages, "the perpetual resource of the poor person who is in the process of becoming even poorer."[264]

Throughout the centuries and in all countries, alcoholic beverages, beside bacchic pleasure and intoxication, offer the cheapest calories the poor can afford.[265] In today's Brazil, the tendency to drink cheap alcoholic beverages by the poor is proven. Market studies reveal that the elasticity of national demand increases in inverse proportion to income: the lower the income, the greater the inclination to purchase *cachaça*, also known as "my consolation." Recent studies further point out a positive correlation between the consumption of *cachaça* and the increase in Brazilian unemployment rates.[266]

In a movement of anticyclic nature in relation to export agriculture, breweries multiplied and all sorts of spirits appeared in the world-economy market of the second half of the seventeenth century, from gin, introduced into the Low Countries by German soldiers and later spread to Britain, to Peru's grape distillate, *pisco*.[267] In Russia and Poland the link between making vodka and peasant exploitation was particularly sharp. In Russia, where the production of spirits became a state monopoly in 1478, the expansion of distilleries seems to have been started earlier than in other countries.[268] In Poland, the drink was made in increasing amounts from the second quarter of the seventeenth century, during the period of decline in Polish cereal exports. Crucial for the reestablishment of the rural lords' profit margins, vodka continued to be a profitable product in the course of the following decades. Usually consumed by serfs, vodka appeared as one of the factors in the brutalization and ruin of the exploited peasantry in the context of late Polish and Russian feudalism.[269]

In this way, the economic and social effects of spirits world trade differed according to the nature of the market they came to circulate in. Scottish whisky, English gin, French marc, Italian grappa, and German *branntwein* penetrated the vast market of Western Europe's urban and rural poor. On the American side it was different, since *pisco* (grape distillate), *pulque* (fermented agave), and the Mexican *chinguito* (sugar-cane distillate) remained confined to domestic consumption: production was limited and the regional market was too poor.[270]

Close to *cachaça* was the Caribbean rum, a byproduct of the sugar industry and, sometimes, an export product to Africa in 1700s. The rum produced by French colonists, besides being less important in the slave trade than *cachaça*, circulated in the mainland before being reexported to Africa. In New England, mainly in Massachusetts and Rhode Island, rum was made from molasses brought in from the West Indies. Exported via Boston and Newport, the beverage entered slaving exchanges with Africa, but it served above all for trading with other colonies (Pennsylvania, Maryland, and Virginia), where the foodstuffs imported by New England came from.[271] In any case, the rum trade into Africa also consolidated regional interests. When the British government wanted to tax the molasses imported from the Caribbean French, Spanish, and Dutch colonies in 1763, Massachusetts merchants protested, claiming that the measure would ruin the slave trade, make sailors redundant, and break the region's shipbuilders, distillers, and planters.[272]

Nearly ignored by Brazilian historiography, the growth in *cachaça* production represents an original case within the picture of the economic transformations induced by the seventeenth-century general crisis. Under the effects of the fall of consumption in European markets and the competition from the West Indies (sugar) and Virginia (tobacco), prices for Brazilian brazilwood, sugar, and tobacco tumbled in the second half of the seventeenth century.[273] In this scenario, *cachaça*, exported as a barter and trade good, lowered the South-Atlantic freight costs, strengthening the bilateral trade between Brazil and Africa, and transferred the cost of slave reproduction to African families. Conquering inland African fairs, *cachaça* yielded profits to sugar-mill owners, increased the supply of slaves, and secured Brazil's interests over the slave trade in West Central Africa. Given the scale of sugar-cane production and the ease with which it was possible to recycle part of the product, transforming it into molasses, and considering also that any free or enslaved artisan could make an alembic—which, lacking copper, was usually made out of soapstone or baked clay—the potential for the Brazilian production of *cachaça* was, and still is, considerable. The country retains today its status as a great world producer of spirits, a title held since the mid-seventeenth century, with an output of one billion liters of sugar-cane distillate made every year since the beginning of the 1990s.[274]

Based on accounts of Bahian sugar mills stretching over a century (1716–1816), Stuart Schwartz calculates that molasses and its byproduct *cachaça* represented between 7 percent and 17 percent of the sugar-mills' yearly income. Not shared with dependent cane farmers (*lavradores*), such byproducts increased the net profit of the mill owners up to around 25 percent[275]—a significant percentage, especially in the context of a low in sugar prices, as occurred between 1660 and 1690, at precisely the time of the takeover of the Angolan markets by Brazilian *cachaça*. By the way, contrary to what the graph elaborated by Stuart Schwartz suggests, the terms of trade with Africa very probably remained favorable to Brazil between 1680 and 1690.[276] An index incorporating the movement of *cachaça* prices, and not only those of white sugar, would show that the relative price of an African slave remained low for the Luso-Brasílico mill owners until the last years of the seventeenth century, when the gold rush provoked a steady increase in prices. In this way, the advantages of *cachaça* production should be carefully calculated on the macroeconomic level, within in the scope of the south-south trade.

Like the Amerindians, Africans of the pre-European period did not know about distillates, consuming only fermented beverages. At that time, the favorite beverage of the West Central African peoples was *malafo, melafo,* or *maluvo,* which the Portuguese dubbed "palm wine."[277] Thus, the grape wine was called in Kicongo *melafo manputo*, the "Portuguese wine."[278]

Extracted from several types of palm trees, among them the *dendê* palm tree, the *malafo* was greatly in demand for consumption, exchange, and a ceremonial good.[279] In the Lunda empire (1500–1850), thriving in northeast Angola, *malafo* was associated with masculinity and political power.[280] The wars waged by the Jaga and European predators had hampered the cultivation and trade of *malafo* since the beginning of the sixteenth century. Andrew Battel relates that the Mbundu and the sedentary peoples of Angola took care to extract the sap of the palm trees without cutting them down, preserving the grove, whereas the Jaga felled the trees to make *malafo*, destroying plantations as they advanced.[281] On their side, in reprisal against recalcitrant *sobas*, the Portuguese used to chop down the palm-tree groves of the attacked villages.[282] Besides *malafo*, the *dendê* palm tree—dubbed by Cadornega "the Queen of trees"—provided the natives of the Congo and Angola with nuts (with which they made *emba* flour), vinegar, cooking oil, medicinal unguents, soap, stilts for houses, and fibers for fabrics and ropes. The felling of palm-tree plantations constituted a disaster for the Mbundu, as it represented the *sobado*'s loss of social and economic power. An early report by Paulo Dias Novais relates the Portuguese attack against a *sobado*: "they destroyed it, burning the land and cutting down the palm tree groves, which is what [the natives] feel more deeply."[283] In the group of documents studied, a phrase stands out, one that emphasizes the nefarious consequences of the loss of the *dendê* palm tree beds and the capacity for *malafo* making: the Mbundu suffer more with the loss of the palm-tree grove "than the loss of their own sons."[284] That is not a figure of speech, as the alcoholic beverages imported as substitutes for *malafo* became one of the chief engines of the trade of Africans into the Americas.

A libertarian hypothesis immediately springs to mind. Could the *Quilombos* of Palmares (*palmares* = palm-tree grove), sited in the Sierra Barriga in Alagoas, have represented the re-foundation of the ancestral African community, prior to the cataclysm of the Atlantic slave trade, organized around the palm trees securing the beverage and the power and enjoyment of freedom? It is possible, but uncertain. In fact, I did not find any text with evidence for the use, among the rebel *quilombolas*, of the word *palmares* in Kimbundu (*máie*), in Kikongo (*máia*), or in any other West Central African language. But Captain Blaer, commander of the Dutch expedition launched against Palmares in 1645, recorded the systematic use of the palm tree known in the region as "catulé" (*Attalea barreirensis*) in the *quilombolas*' daily life. According to him, the *catulé* palm tree provided "a kind of wine," that is, a beverage analogous to the *malafo*, as well as beds, food, cooking oil, house roofing, and smoking pipes. A similar account is recorded in the report on the Palmares war written thirty years after the event, during the government of Pedro de Almeida, in Pernambuco (1675–1678).[285]

To return to West Central Africa, it is certain that European, American, and African human predators, when pillaging Angolan villages, deliberately destroyed palm-tree groves from which the *malafo* was extracted. On the other side, in the ports of trade, Iberian wines and spirits entered the country, sometimes replacing the *malafo*, which had become rare in the West Central African fairs.

The Victory of the *Cachaça*

In the first decades of the Angola invasion, after a number of failures in the sale of mainland wine, the Portuguese began to export more alcoholic wines from the Canary Islands, Madeira, and Malaga into West Central Africa.[286] The sales of the Spanish product increased during the *Asiento* period, when there was a true triangular trade involving Angola. The *asentista* vessels left Seville or Lisbon loaded with wines, spirits, and other products for African markets, sold or exchanged their load in the trade ports, and embarked slaves for the Spanish-American ports. Iberian wine was the main exchange merchandise in the society formed by Governor Manuel Forjaz, an enterprise aiming to export Angolan slaves into Spanish America.[287] A text of the first quarter of the seventeenth century records that Spanish wine yielded a 500 percent profit in Central Africa.[288]

Most of the imported amounts of wine and Portuguese grape spirit, today known as *bagaceira*, were sent to the lands of Kasanje and Matamba, from which most Africans were deported after 1648.[289] But the Spanish wine disseminated continued to enjoy preference in regional markets. Contrary to the royal orders banning Castilian trade in Angola after the Braganza Restoration (except if the Spanish slave traders brought in gold and silver coins for the purchase of slaves), four vessels from Spain arrived in Luanda laden with clay wine casks. Supported by metropolitan producers and exporters, the Crown again banned such commerce in 1655.[290] A few years later, mainland merchants and their Luandan agents realized that the Brazilian *cachaça* had also been taking a section of the Angolan market from them.[291]

Jeribita was the name by which the *cachaça* became known and traded in the West Central African hinterlands (but not in the Mina Coast, where the tobacco trade prevailed). Gregório de Matos used the word as if it were current in 1600s Bahia. Later, in the nineteenth century, Father Lopes Gama made the same remark regarding the Pernambuco's speech. According to dictionarist Bluteau, the word was of Brazilian origin.[292] It is very likely, *Jeribá* is the Tupi name of a common Brazilian-coast palm tree, and at the beginning of the 1600s a palm-tree wine similar to that made in the Africa was fabricated in Portuguese America.[293] Thus, the word *jeribita* could have been diffused in Africa in reference to the wine made from the Brazilian palm tree, the *jeribá*. In the inverse itinerary, *marafo* (from *malafo*), became, among Brazilians, and especially in Rio de Janeiro, a synonym for *cachaça*.²⁹⁴ Alongside the derivatives (*birita*, *piribita*, and *jurubita*), other Brazilian synonyms for *cachaça* are found that originate in African vocabularies or refer to that part of the globe: *angico*, *canjica*, *cumbe*, *geba*, *maçangana*, *malunga*, *mamãe-de-luanda*, and *otim* (Yoruba).²⁹⁵ Among such names, *malunga* deserves attention.

Malungo, *mulunga*, or *malongo* are Kimbundu synonyms designating the iron chains with which the captives were restrained. On this side of the slave trade, *malungo* came to mean the name given to those who came aboard the same slaver, and later, to the slaves belonging to a single master, or bound to the same plantation.²⁹⁶ Today, the word holds one meaning only: *cachaça*—precisely the merchandise that served in the exchange for thousands of captives torn from Africa by the Luso-Brasílico slave trade.

From a different perspective, another significant association was established between *cachaça* and Saint Benedict, the black saint. Born around 1525 in Messina, son of an African slave brought to Sicily by Iberian slave traders, then under Spanish domination, Benedetto Manasseri belonged to the Order of Friars Minor (Capuchin, of Franciscan rule) of the Santa-Maria-di-Gesù convent, near Palermo. There he lived, doing the humble chores of a cook, and died in 1589 with a reputation for sanctity. The process of his canonization began soon, in 1594. Although he was declared a saint only in 1807, Santo Benedetto il Nero's fame spread throughout the Mediterranean, especially Spain and Portugal, in the 1600s. The Saint Benedict Brotherhood was created in 1619 by converted Moors and blacks, at the same time Lope de Vega (1562–1635) wrote a play in homage to the black saint.²⁹⁷ Probably brought by the Franciscans, his cult (the first regarding a black person in the context of the Discoveries) took root in Angola. In the middle of the seventeenth century, the version stating that his mother, and even the saint himself, had been born in the Angolan province of Kisama, appeared in West Central Africa,²⁹⁸ from where the cult spread throughout the whole of Africa and Portuguese America.²⁹⁹ Well before Our Lady Aparecida emerged from the waters of the Paraíba River, in São Paulo, Saint Benedict was the protector of black people in the Portuguese American regions encompassed by the trade of Africans. The racial representation of the saint was so associated with the use of the *cachaça* that it was considered almost exclusive to black people in Brazil up to the beginning of the twentieth century. A popular verse collected in

Sergipe goes: "Saint Benedict / Is black by race, / Plays the tambourine / And drinks *cachaça*."[300]

The *Cachaça* Riot

Although limited, the Brazilian production of *cachaça* competed with the mainland beverages imported into Portuguese America. Prohibitions on its manufacture appeared in the mid-seventeenth century. Seen sometimes as curious adventures, the disputes generated by the *cachaça* gain fresh dimensions when seen in the scope of the Ethiopic Ocean history.

During the WIC occupation of Pernambuco and Angola, Lisbon wine merchants protested against producers of "honey wine" (the fermented sugar-cane crush) and of "a kind of aquavit drink" (sugar-cane rum, the *cachaça*) in Brazil. To them, competition from these beverages caused a drop in wine consumption in Brazil. This commercial shortfall also lowered the tax collected on imported wine and the resources of Bahia's general government. Therefore, the Overseas Council decided that Bahia's governor should "eliminate" the production of "such beverages" in Brazil.[301] Two years later, in the wake of the monopoly that the quasi-state-owned General Trade Company (Companhia Geral de Comércio [CGC]) secured over Brazilian trade and, in particular, over the sales of Portuguese wines, a royal order of 1649 forbade the sale of "honey wine" and *cachaça* in Brazil.[302] Two exceptions were included to the order. First, the measure did not apply to Pernambuco. Second, the consumption of *cachaça* in the rest of Brazil was to be restricted to slaves.[303] In other words, the exceptions referred to the anti-Dutch front zone, where nothing should oppose the pro-Lusitanian sugar-mill owners and the plantations' slave quarters, where few European spirits ever reached. Where, in any case, the consumption of domestic beverages predominated.

In Rio de Janeiro, a captaincy much involved in the fabrication and trade of *cachaça*, the measure caused trouble.[304] A long and well-founded memorial of Governor Luís de Almeida (1652–1655) sustained the colonists' complaints and defended Rio de Janeiro *cachaça*. In the text sent to the Overseas Council, Almeida reasoned that the sugar-cane spirit constituted the only way out of Guanabara's economic crisis. The interdiction would only "serve to extinguish many sugar mills." This is why he had decided to lift the 1649 ban. He further explained that the order for the discontinuation of *cachaça* production was effectively decreed in Bahia because the freight to the kingdom was cheaper and local sugar fetched better prices than Rio de Janeiro's, considered by Father Antonio Vieira to be Brazil's worst.[305]

Closely associated to CGC's business, Salvador de Sá supported the monopoly granted to Portugal's beverages.[306] When the Crown itself suspended the CGC's monopoly of wine, flour, olive oil, and imported cod, leaving the Company with the brazilwood contract only, Salvador de Sá insisted that the embargo on *cachaça* should again be enforced. Taking advantage of the fear generated by the *quilombos* rising in the Sierra de Órgãos, the mainland beverage importers claimed that the consumption of *cachaça* had caused the black *quilombolas* to revolt. As a consequence, the 1659 royal provision applied severe punishments to violators, ordering that all alembics in the Rio de Janeiro captaincy be brought to the capital to be "broken up and destroyed." Ironsmiths, boilermakers, potters, and others involved in the manufacture of pot stills would be fined, and on the third infraction, would be deported to Angola. Any vessel carrying *cachaça* would be burnt. The measure also opposed Brasílico coopers, since the fabrication of barrels and casks developed to the cadence of *cachaça* exports.[307]

Months later, when Salvador de Sá, again governor of Rio de Janeiro, tried to launch new duties to support the troops and the construction of his galleon, the *Padre Eterno*, the Rio de Janeiro municipal council proposed a bargain (1659). The city's councilors agreed not only to the new tax on *cachaça* to finance the troops, but also, and chiefly, to legalize its manufacture and allow its export to Angola. Salvador accepted the arrangement, but shortly after he claimed to have had "doubts" and backtracked, creating hindrances to the product's trade. Orders from Court arrived noting that the royal interdiction to the manufacture of *cachaça* was still in force. Seeking to widen the market for the wines traded by the CGC, Salvador de Sá extinguished the tax on the import of mainland wine ("the big subsidy") and, to compensate the loss of income, launched a fresh duty to support the maintenance of troops in the city.[308]

Suddenly, the December 1660 revolt that put an end to the Sá oligarchy's long domination in Rio de Janeiro flared up.[309] The uprising's focus was the São Gonçalo parish, a *cachaça*-producing zone, where Agostinho and Jerônimo Barbalho and other leaders of the revolt resided.[310] More or less authorized, the manufacture and sale of *cachaça* continued unabated in Rio de Janeiro.[311] However, Governor-General Francisco Barreto tried to obtain fresh royal orders banning sugar-cane spirits for reasons of public order, due to "deaths and disorders" allegedly caused by the beverage.[312]

Impossible to enforce, the embargo on *cachaça* seemed increasingly absurd to the municipal councils of the Estado do Brasil and the Estado do Maranhão. Indeed, in 1662 in Belém do Pará, Father Antonio Vieira decried that all *cachaça* (which was also used in the trade with the Amerindians) was already sold before it left the alembics.[313] Seeking to regulate the sugar aristocracy's activities, the municipal council also saw in the product's trade a source of income for the tottering municipal accounts. Such was the tone of the 1672 representation by the Bahian municipal council, seeking a contract for the "spirits of the land" analogous to that negotiated in Rio de Janeiro. The document suggests that Bahian *cachaça*, against the law, reached a considerable market, being exported to the villages located south of the Bay (Cairu, Camamu, and Ilhéus), Sergipe, the São Francisco River backlands, and to Angola.[314] Equally significant, the enlargement of Rio de Janeiro's sales led to the introduction in 1695 of a new tax on the *cachaça* exports[315] From a regional issue, linked to the dire economic straits of the Rio and Bahia mill and alembic owners, the dispute around *cachaça* reached another level as it penetrated greater Atlantic commerce by means of the African thoroughfares.

Although there had been previous shipments, it was during Vidal de Negreiros's term as governor (1661–1666) that the beverage came to regularly enter West Central Africa.[316] It was probably brought in for the provisions of the militiamen recruited in Rio, Pernambuco, and Bahia.[317] The import of *cachaça* for the benefit of Brasílico troops provided significant gains in Angola, since the royal treasury's factor, one of those incriminated for participating in the mutiny against Governor Tristão da Cunha (1667), was involved in the trade.[318]

In the Atlantic, as in other 1600s European theaters of war, spirits, less bulky than wine or beer casks, were incorporated into the ration of naval and land troops. In Africa, the Amazon region, and in the Estado do Brasil, *cachaça* became an essential product in the initial contacts by colonists and their agents with the natives.

Some mainland soldiers shipped to Angola died after drinking *jeribita*. A few African *sobas* also protested against the intoxication caused by the drink. Motivated by such incidents, a royal provision of 1679 banned the import of Brazilian *jeribitas* into Angola for ten years.[319] Poorly prepared, *cachaça* may contain ethanol and kill, especially when taken by those not used to spirits, such as African and Brazil's natives. But what was at play was the harm that *cachaça* did to the accounts of the European spirits salesmen, and not the health of Portuguese soldiers or of the Africans themselves.

The *jeribita* trade continued to prosper, despite the royal prohibition. One of the great smugglers was the governor of Angola, João da Silva e Sousa (1680–1684), former governor of Rio de Janeiro (1670–1675), where he probably associated with *cachaça* exporters. A later inquiry revealed that Silva e Sousa owned four vessels operating on the Brazilian passage, taking out slaves and in bringing *cachaça* to be sold in Luanda, despite the "notorious scandal" incurred in disobedience of the royal order.[320] Significantly, as the embargo deadline approached (1689), a coalition formed by former governors involved in the business, agents eager to increase royal incomes, municipal councilors, *cachaça* producers, and Brasílico and Angolista slave traders succeed in reopening the West Central African markets to *jeribita*.[321] The bulky Overseas Council dossier on the issue bears evidence of the plot by the economic interests consolidating the Pax Lusitana in the Ethiopic Ocean.[322]

First, the Luanda municipal council, supported by Governor João de Lencastre, realized the uselessness of the ban on the *jeribita* trade. One must not exclude the governor's possible direct gain in the business. Lencastre knew the interests at play in *jeribita* production in Pernambuco and Bahia: he was son-in-law of a former Pernambuco governor (Pedro de Almeida, 1674–1678) and cousin of Câmara Coutinho, governor of Pernambuco (1689–1690) and governor-general of Brasil (1690–1694). In addition, having been involved in the Angola slave trade, Lencastre already positioned himself as the future governor-general of Brazil, a post he took in 1694, succeeding his cousin.[323]

In any case, the embargo period had created many inconveniences. Ships from Brazil unloaded clandestinely on Angolan shores, selling *cachaça* to a group of Benguela salesmen. Practicing a monopoly that caused losses to Luandan traders and the royal treasury, these salesmen developed the trade that would make the port of Benguela exchanges dependent on Pernambuco and Rio de Janeiro, the main destination of its growing export of slaves. Indeed, the Luanda municipal council ceased to charge the duties on spirits (1,500 *réis* per cask) that it collected before the embargo.[324] Simultaneously, the Luanda councilors highlighted the reputation of *cachaça* as a barter good, "the spirits from Brazil being the main merchandise for which quantities of slaves are bartered in the confines of the Congo, in the Dembos and in other parts of the hinterland." The document confirmed that the *jeribita* was the product that "more slaves are bartered with than any other good."[325] The *jeribita* would soon be considered, in Angola and in Brazil, an invigorating drink. A 1700s medical treatise by a Luanda resident physician recommended that slave traders give "a few mouthfuls of *jeribita* to each slave in the morning and in the evening before retiring" to keep them in good health.[326]

Also opposed to the embargo, Angola's crown judge summed up the arguments in favor of the *cachaça* trade. "After the gentile [natives] of this kingdom got to know this class (of merchandise), it tasted so agreeable to him that it became impossible to persuade him not to ask for it." *Jeribita* was found to be sold several hundred kilometers into the hinterland, fetching good prices in all trade fairs. In addition, and here the judge came to the decisive point, Angola's settlers and merchants imported *cachaça* because of the "great loss they sustain in not having [their] vessels loaded on the return voyage from Brazil to this kingdom [of Angola], for as they sail away bearing a load of slaves, they cannot shorten the voyage back from Brazil if not loaded with the product."327 From the official voice of a crown judge came the evidence of the bilateral trade. Shipowners and importers and exporters of slaves had now a barter good that cheapened the freight and increased the profits in the exchange between the two margins of the Southern Atlantic.

The more properly Brasílico point of view was emphasized in a representation by the Bahian municipal council, dated 1690. "A good part of this city's colonists and nearly all of the Recôncavo [of Bahia]" lived off the *cachaça* industry, with which they paid for their slaves, stated the municipal council. Widening the argument to the rest of Brazil, the city's councilors reflected that the prohibition in the export of spirits into Angola "does total damage to this Estado [of Brazil]." Besides, low sugar prices rendered the embargo on the making of *cachaça* more harmful still to the sugar-mill owners. In short, the motive previously given by the Luanda municipal council to justify the prohibition of the import of Brazilian *cachaça* was a "pretense," because "a few businessmen who flog mainland wine in that market" were maneuvering that municipal council.328 In the same year, the marquis of Montebelo, governor of Pernambuco (1690–1693), expressed his doubts about the convenience, "for the benefit of these captaincies," of the ban on *cachaça* exports to Angola.329

Antônio Paes Sande was a member of the Overseas Council and a man of experience in the overseas commodities (he brought over from India the pepper and cinnamon seedlings that the Jesuits would acclimatize in Bahia). Nominated governor of Rio de Janeiro (1692–1695), Paes outlined the more general picture of the Atlantic conjuncture highlighted by the Bahian municipal council.330 Sande understood that the veto on the export of *jeribi*ta to Angola should be lifted because of the Brazilian sugar-market crisis in general, and the Rio de Janeiro sugar crisis in particular. "Y.M. has ordered the prohibition of the fabrication of crushed sugars that were made out of the syrups, the colonists of that Estado [of Brazil] not having another way of making use of them, if not in the [fabrication of] spirit of the land."331 The ban on the manufacture of crushed sugar played a part in the context of the anticrisis measures issued by the Crown, dated of a few months before. It applied to Rio de Janeiro, where the sugars, made dearer by the freight, found less demand than the sugars from Bahia and Pernambuco. White "crushed" or unrefined brown sugar was extracted from molasses, the syrup of the noncrystallized sugar from the first boiling. The measure was intended to improve colonial production, as there had been a strong drop in prices in the face of the growing competition from the Antilles during the period 1660–1690. However, as Sande noted, *cachaça* was also made out of molasses. If they were not able to sell the beverage or to make crushed sugar, the Rio de Janeiro mill owners would lose a considerable part of their sugar-cane production.[332]

All this paperwork was written, debated, and collected in the course of a few months between 1689 and 1690, a proof that the pleas of the various parts of it had been prepared previously and the interests had already been defined, only waiting for the end of the embargo. Revealing several motives, some appraisals sought to keep the prohibition. Nonetheless, in the various documents and in the final synthesis elaborated by the Overseas Council, I did not find an open defense of mainland spirits producers and traders. There are attacks on the Angolista and Brasílico cartel ("the four powerful" producers from Bahia, denounced the Treasury administrator) that controlled the *cachaça* trade, and extravagant attention was given to the health of the Africans. What was the motive for the absence of a vigorous reaction by the metropolitan beverage exporters into West Central Africa?

In fact, mainland alcoholic beverages had never dominated the Angolan market, always losing ground to Spanish wines and spirits. The Brazilian *jeribitas* managed to eliminate competing Spanish products. Conveniently taxed, they could provide fresh incomes for the municipal councils and for the royal treasury—this is the point of view that prevailed. The debate then took a markedly fiscal character. What would yield more, the contract of mainland spirits and wines in tandem with the embargo on *cachaça*, or the duly legalized contract of the latter? The higher-alcoholic-content Portuguese wines, particularly Madeira, were beginning to find favor among the British gentry and to enter, via Funchal British merchants, the British America possessions.[333] A redistribution of markets took place, reshaping the trade of alcoholic beverages in the Portuguese Atlantic. In the Northern Hemisphere, the sales of Portuguese wine to Britain reset the trade balance between the two countries at the end of the seventeenth century,[334] and in the Southern Hemisphere, *cachaça* rebalanced the exchanges between Angola and Brazil, leaving Spanish wine out of the picture. Secondarily, Luanda traders linked to the metropolis redirected their efforts to other profitable activities, such as the import of Asian fabrics ("a black man's cloth") and, at the margins of the slave trade, operating the transfer of several local letters of credit into markets in Brazil and in the kingdom.[335]

In 1695, the issue was settled. *Jeribita* exports would be allowed, taxed at 1,600 réis a cask on leaving Brazil, and at an equal sum as it entered Angola.

How much *cachaça* was exported to Africa? *Cachaça* formed "most of the load carried by the vessels navigating the Coast of Africa in search of slaves," wrote Rocha Pitta at the beginning of the eighteenth century, noting in addition that the number of ships sailing from Brazil bound to the African coast numbered close to one hundred, almost as much as the fleet of bigger vessels sailing to Portugal every year.[336]

There is no series allowing for the verification of Rocha Pitta's statement. But the Bahian historian—a sugar-mill owner and father-in-law of the daughter of Rodrigo da Costa de Almeida, a slave trader made rich in Luanda and later a potentate in Bahia—deserves credibility on this point. The smuggling of the product must have been considerable. During the prohibition period there was clandestine unloading on the coast close to Benguela and Luanda.[337] There was nothing to stop the continuation of such activity.

Nevertheless, some documents allow a glimpse of the total amount legally traded. According to José Curto, the total of *cachaça* legally imported into Luanda in 1699 amounted to 684 casks, that is, around 307,800 liters from Bahia (57.4 percent), 31.1 percent from Pernambuco, and 11.4 percent from Rio de Janeiro, shipped out on a total of fourteen vessels leaving these ports. In the meantime, Portuguese spirits, brought in from Lisbon on two ships, corresponded to only 7.4 percent of the total spirits introduced in to that African port.[338] A series regarding the years 1699–1703 shows that 3,447 casks of *cachaça*, 755.8 of wine, and 191 of Iberian spirits paid taxes in Luanda. With an average of 689.4 casks (310,230 liters), Brazilian *cachaça* corresponded to 78.4 percent of the total of alcoholic beverages legally imported into Luanda in the course of five years.[339]

From that time on, *cachaça* represented the key element in the Brazilian trade in Angola. "If *jeribita* is not part of the negotiation, the blacks refrain from closing their deals and it is felicitous to the trades of Brazil and of Africa to have their inclination in its favor," noted Silva Corrêa in 1782. According to him, a "multitude of uncouth people" hailing from Brazil transformed two-thirds of the Luandan houses into *cachaça* shops, widening the slave trade. "Profits return to

Brazil and the country [Angola] is left devoid of similar interests. If this class of merchants move, they take away with them the fruits of the business; if they persist, they don't stick to this way of life, [but] they soon begin to try their hand in the trade of captives."[340] In 1800, when other European slave traders drained the North Angolan and Congo trade into the Antilles, where the price for a slave reached twice the amount recorded in Brazil, the sales of gunpowder and of *jeribita*—"the most precious drink" for the natives—figured as the only way of continuing Portuguese trade in the region.[341] After Brazil's independence (1822), when the Portuguese government began the taxation of *cachaça* on the same level as cognac and other foreign spirits, the Overseas Council warned about the danger "of destroying the Angolan trade almost entirely, imposing such duties on the import of *cachaça* spirits from Brazil."[342]

From the last quarter of the 1600s, markets in the Mina Coast linked to Bahia imported chiefly tobacco. But *cachaça* represented the second item in the region's exchanges, constituting a prestige product that favored merchants from Brazil. Like tobacco and slaves, *cachaça* was part of the kingdom of Dahomey's royal monopoly. Only middlemen associated in Whydah with the Yovogan, Dahomey's foreign trade minister, could trade it. The most celebrated holder of post was, from 1815, Bahian mulatto Francisco Felix de Souza, known as Xaxá, "a man of exceptional qualities" as defined by Karl Polanyi. A prominent slave trader in Brazil's foreign trade, Xaxá made an appearance as a great merchant in the first half of the nineteenth century. He stands as a global entrepreneur whose role in Brazilian economy must be compared to that played by the baron of Mauá in the second half of the century.[343]

The Accounts of the Bilateral Trade between Brazil and Africa

As is known, the two main circuits of slave traffic to Brazil concern West Central Africa and the Gulf of Guinea. From 1680 to 1846, as mentioned above, there was a distinct slave-trade network, based on a triangular trade connecting Lisbon, the Senegambian ports of Cacheu or Bissau, and the Amazon ports of Belém and São Luís. However, the total enslaved disembarkments of this circuit represent 2.2 percent of the 4.864 millions disembarked in Brazilian ports between 1550 and 1850.[344] After 1830, a coastal slave trade drew part of the enslaved from the Amazonian regions to Rio de Janeiro.

José Curto estimates that the *jeribita* trade served to purchase 25 percent of the slaves exported from West Central Africa into Portuguese America between 1710 and 1830.[345] Just as *cachaça* helped the Brasílicos conquer West Central Africa's slave trade, Brazilian tobacco eased their penetration into the Gulf of Guinea and, more precisely, into the Slave Coast.[346] Cultivated chiefly in Bahia, but also in Pernambuco, in Maranhão and, on a smaller scale, in Rio de Janeiro and Minas Gerais, tobacco had been a Crown monopoly since 1634. In general, the metropolitan market absorbed one-fifth or one-fourth of the Brazilian exports into Europe in the seventeenth century. The rest was reexported to other European and Asian markets. In the eighteenth century, Portuguese re-exports of the product were more important. But the specific trait of such trade rested on exchange of tobacco for slaves, in the context of the bilateral trade that began in the last quarter of the seventeenth century between Bahia and the Slave Coast (present Togo, Benin, and western Nigeria). In the eighteenth century, 11,789 metric tons of tobacco was exported to the Slave Coast in voyages leaving from Bahia and Recife. Around 680,000 slaves from that region were introduced in Bahia and Pernambuco in the course of the same period.[347]

Consequently, the Brazilian *cachaça* and tobacco exports served to purchase 48 percent of the 2,330,000 slaves introduced in Portuguese America between 1701 and 1810.[348] Adding to this the export of horses, hides, manioc flour, maize, sugar, meats, and dried or salted fish, clayware as well as the smuggling of Minas Gerais gold and diamonds into slave trade ports, we may estimate that more than half of the Africans introduced by bilateral trade into Portuguese America in the course of the eighteenth century were purchased with Brazilian goods.

Such data should be considered in parallel with the Southern Atlantic dominant winds and currents system, which, as has been stated, favored bilateral navigation between Brazil and Angola. As mentioned in chapter 1, 95 percent of the voyages carrying African slaves to Brazil were organized and began in Brazilian ports.[349] It was also clear that the totality of Africans brought from the Slave Coast into Bahia were integrated into the bilateral trade. The case of Mozambique completes the picture.

Of the estimated total of 274,400 slaves introduced in Brazil from East Africa, mainly from Mozambique, 94.8 percent arrived between 1800 and 1850. The extent of Rio de Janeiro slave-trade networks, the presence of the Portuguese Court in the town from 1808 to 1821, and the coffee demand drew 83.8 percent of the East Africa Mozambican voyages to the Guanabara Bay.[350] Previously monopolized

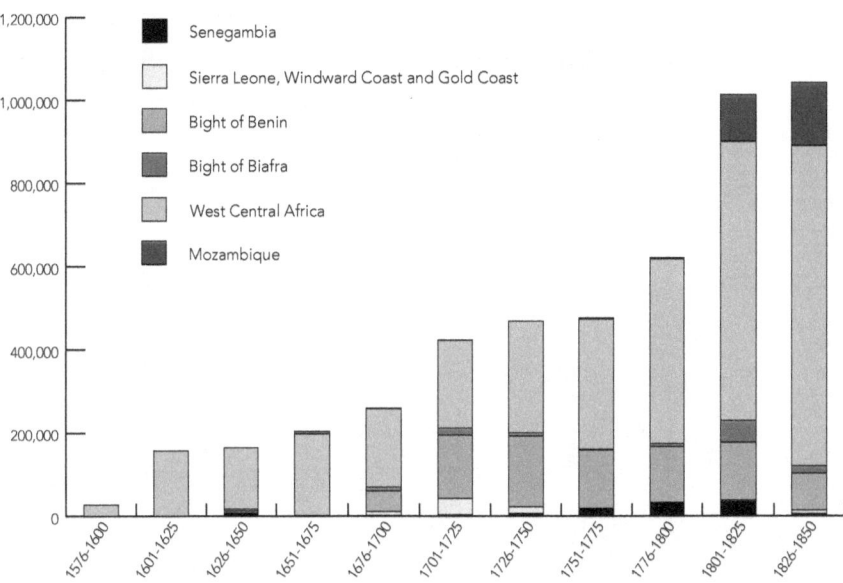

Figure 7.1. Majors regions from which Enslaved left Africa to Brazil 1576–1550.

by the Indian Ocean, the region's slave trade was integrated into the Brazilian network.[351] Although there is not much information on this issue, it is certain that some of the Portuguese vessels engaged in the trade between America and Portuguese Africa would have been built in Brazilian shipyards.

Two complementary exchange networks emerged (Brazil-Portugal and Brazil-Africa), distinct from the North Atlantic system and the triangular trade put into motion by other slaving nations of the Old World. In addition to the Rio de la Plata slave trade, such networks helped constitute the Ethiopic Ocean.

One should note the difference between the exchanges linking Bahia to the Slave Coast, on the one hand, and the trade of other Brazilian markets—particularly Pernambuco and Rio de Janeiro—directed to Angola, on the other hand. In the Gulf of Guinea, like the other European slaving nations, Portugal remained insulated in trading ports. By contrast, in Angola, Portugal traded in a wide territory drained by a network of backland fairs for the purchase and enslavement of hundreds of thousands of persons. With the help of the Brasílicos, Portugal was the only European country to engage in direct, official operations to undertake the hunting of Africans, thus obtaining in West Central Africa its largest African domain. In its biggest slave reservation, from which it helped itself in order to develop its domains on the other side of the Atlantic. The continued construction of Brazil generated the continued destruction of Angola.

Conclusion

Brazil's Singularity

In the last quarter of the 1600s the century's general crisis hit Portugal harshly.[1] Plunged into a recession marked by the lack of silver for the Asian trade and by the fall in royal incomes, Lisbon saw the new *Asiento* auctions as a great business. Effectively, the peace treaty between the two Iberian capitals (1668) reauthorized Portuguese participation in the royal contracts for the supply of enslaved Africans to Spanish America. But Madrid's game was not completely open. Visceral anti-Judaism and the persistence of anti-Lusitanism stigmatized the proposals traditionally put forward by Portuguese New Christian merchants. Therefore, front societies and front men emerged to cover some of the proposals. Even a heterodox Dominican, Friar Juan de Castro, mediated the sale of slaves to Madrid. Members of the Bravo family, Portuguese New Christians active in the Angolan trade in the first half of the century, also reappeared in the Spanish Court, now associated with Grillo and Lomelin, Genoese *Asiento* contractors (1663–1673).[2] Dutch investors from Curaçao put money in the Grillo and Lomelin's *Asiento* as well.[3] The favorable reception of the Genoese in Madrid can be explained: Catholic Genoa boasted a solid banking and shipping network and was neither Spain's enemy nor its imperial rival overseas, which was not the case with British, Dutch, French, or Portuguese slave traders. However, Genoese access to African ports was limited, forcing them into partnerships with British, Dutch, and Portuguese slave traders to fulfill the *Asiento* contract.[4]

In turn, Lisbon had also doubts with regard to Luso-Spanish economic agreements.

Duarte Ribeiro de Macedo, a wise counselor to the Crown, sought to protect mainland trade and industry, partisan as he was of the policy of stimulating national manufacture.[5] More precisely, Macedo opposed the access of Sevillian merchants to Cape Verde. From his post as ambassador in Madrid, Macedo warned the Crown that Spanish merchant ships and foreign goods introduced into Cape Verde would bring losses. The damage done to the Portuguese economy would be greater than the fiscal income and profits earned from the sale of enslaved Africans to Spain. In sum, Macedo sneered, "We will be fooled by a nation [Spain] that all nations in Europe fool."[6] Against the merchant and fiscalist groups close to the Crown, Macedo—a follower of Colbert's ideas—defended the subordination of slave-trading interests to mainland manufacturing industry. From the opposite side of the Portuguese world came another representation proposing the subordination of the slave trade to the colonial sugar industry.

This is what happened: at the end of the 1680s, Madrid quarreled with the Genoese and Dutch *asentistas* and sought business with the Portuguese slave traders. Bernardo Marin, a Spanish merchant and front man for the Portuguese, acquired the *Asiento* and associated himself with the Cacheu and Cape Verde Company (Companhia de Cacheu e do Cabo Verde, CCCV). With headquarters in Lisbon, the CCCV had already carried out shipments of Upper Guinea Africans into Brazil's ports.[7] The partnership was agreed on, and the contract between Marin and the CCCV was signed in Lisbon on February 6, 1693. Yet at the same time, a vehement protest against the Luso-Spanish consortium was submitted to the Portuguese Overseas Council.

The legal representatives (*procuradores*) of the Estado do Brazil and of Angola were fully aware that the CCCV had promised to supply 4,000 slaves a year to the Castilian Indies, and that it sought to take the Angola Contract to be able meet the demand. In a joint representation signed by the representatives of both Brazil and Angola, a cabal proof of the complementariness of their goals, the *procuradores* warned the Crown that the project would disturb the South Atlantic network. According to them, the agreement would result in the "perdition" of Angola and of Brazil and, "as a consequence," in the "ruin" of Portugal. Angola exported fewer than half the number of slaves that it did during the Habsburg period, while Brazilian demand had increased. Thus, the exports of enslaved Africans into Spanish America would form a chain of events with "very serious consequences," sparking an increase in prices for slaves in Brazil, the breaking of its plantation production, and the decline of Portugal's commerce and customs incomes. Furthermore, the Cacheu Company would impose a monopoly in West Central Africa to the detriment of the Brazil-Angola thoroughfare.

It should be observed that the *asentista* demand, shifted to Angola by the CCCV, would increase prices for slaves in Luanda, yielding profits and Peruvian silver to Angolista traders dealing with the Spanish American market. Nonetheless, the *procurador* of Angola associated himself with, or indeed submitted to, his Brasílico colleague demands, to protect Brazil's monopoly over Angolan ports. At a time when *cachaça* replaced Iberian alcoholic beverages in West Central African markets, the bipolar economy formed by Brazil's slave-based production and Angola's zones of reproduction of slaves was patent. That is precisely the point that the Crown attorney of the royal treasury insisted on, supporting the *procuradores*' request in the Overseas Council. "Angola was only valuable because [its] slaves populated and cultivated Brazil, so that Brazil was the cause for cherishing and conserving Angola." Thus, "it would be against the common axiom and all good reason" to favor the Angola trade "while impoverishing and losing" Brazil, which was the possession that gave full value to Angola.[8] The Overseas Council councilors followed the attorney's opinion and the CCCV's West Central African ambitions did not prosper.[9]

Common slave-trading interests led the Brazil (meaning Bahia, Pernambuco, and Rio de Janeiro) and Angola legal representatives in Lisbon to strike an alliance against the Crown's policy. Nothing similar occurred to the captaincies dependent on enslaved Indian labor, such as São Paulo, Espírito Santo, Ceará, and Maranhão. Equally resentful of the Crown and Jesuits' pro-Amerindian freedom policies, they did not sign any common protest in Lisbon. The reason for the joint approach of Rio de Janeiro, Bahia, Pernambuco, and Luanda lies, again, in the Ethiopic Ocean. The African slave trade and their full integration to the Atlantic market led them to unite their demands in Lisbon.

In fact, the South Atlantic complementariness was based on unequal exchanges. As the crown attorney stated, the only value of Angola consisted in the furnishing of slaves to Brazil. This asymmetry generated the conditioning of Lisbon's presence in Angola and the singularities of Portuguese America and of the forthcoming Brazilian nation.

Reaffirming the Portuguese Policy in West Central Africa

Surely, the extension of the Portuguese presence in Angola was not on Lisbon's agenda. The policy predominating until the nineteenth century corresponded to the Angolista practice of relay trade with hinterland fairs and to the trading post system followed in others parts of Africa and in Asia. The epidemiological environment and indigenous resistance restricted missionaries and colonists' endeavors in Africa. Yet other factors intervened in Lisbon's policy in Angola. Since the sixteenth century, Portuguese authorities had discussed intermittently the opening of a terrestrial route between Angola and Mozambique, called the "counter-coast journey" (*viagem à Contra-Costa*).[10] As we saw in chapter 3, Luis Mendes de Vasconcelos backed such a project during his governorship in Angola (1617–1621). The Overseas Council went further in 1656, with a plan that included cost calculations. To the councilors the enterprise figured as a simple "implementation" (*entabulamento*) rather than a true "discovery," as the paths were already more-or-less known.[11] Concerned with the enterprise from the time of his governorship in Luanda, Salvador de Sá supported the plan, nominating a seasoned Brasílico, a former captain in Pernambuco and Angola, for the command of the expedition. But the resumption of the Luso-Dutch war (1657–1661) and the aggravation of the Luso-Spanish war (1640–1668) prompted the veto of the Overseas Council's president, the count of Odemira. To him, the inland incursions would leave Luanda and Benguela vulnerable to European maritime attacks.[12] However, a few years later, Governor André Vidal de Negreiros sent from Luanda an experienced Angolista to open a path into Mozambique. Other attempts continued to be made.[13]

In the beginning of the 1670s European rivalries grew around the Cape route. As the Dutch Verenigde Oost-Indische Compagnie (VOC) enlarged its Cape activities, the Compagnie des Indes Orientales, founded by Colbert, approached Madagascar (called by the Portuguese Ilha de São Lourenço) and set foot on present-day Réunion Island, threatening the Portuguese India thoroughfare.[14] In Lisbon, the plans for the terrestrial route to Mozambique gained new momentum. Aside from strategic reasons for gaining a new path to the Indian Ocean, proponents of the *viagem à Contra-Costa* expected profits from the transportation of gold from Monomatapa (Mozambique) to Portugal, through Austral Africa and Angola.[15]

Not by chance, the two Overseas Council members formed by the Portuguese America experience, Feliciano Dourado and Salvador de Sá, defended the occupation of the African hinterland and the *viagem à Contra-Costa*.[16] For Feliciano Dourado, Councilor Salvador de Sá seemed the best commander for the Angola-Mozambique expedition, because he was "active in what he is ordered to do, resistant to those climes and respected in Angola" for his victory against the Dutch, and even for transcendental motives. Illustrating the admiration many in Lisbon had for Salvador de Sá, Dourado judged: "because God has given him a particular genius for such enterprises and experience shows that he is fortunate in them."[17] Besides divine design, luck was also held to intervene in politics. In Spain, at the same time, it was thought that the difference between Richelieu and Olivares, leading to the victory of the first over the second, rested on the luck of the French minister in contrast to the patent bad luck of the Spanish minister.[18]

Salvador talked several times in the Overseas Council about crossing Angola into Mozambique. Yes, the expedition should go ahead. Yes, he would be its best commander, for there was nobody else to match the practical experience he had acquired in the South Atlantic. In short, the control of inland Africa was necessary to consolidate the colonial enclaves in Angola. Ivory, tobacco, and iron, copper, and gold ores would allow for the development of mining and other activities in the area. In this way, Angola would be preserved "without violences," without the enslavement of Africans and the slave trade, "avoiding the captivities, which will result in service to God and to Your Majesty . . . and Angola will be populated, as was the Castile Indies." So confident was Salvador de Sá of the wealth of the region that he compared the indifference to his proposals to the mishandling of Columbus's plans before the discovery of America. According to him, the Portuguese Crown did not accept Columbus's propositions and therefore lost the American silver and gold mines snatched by Spain. Now the same would happen with Africa's precious mines, insofar as his plans were treated in Lisbon with the disdain once given to Columbus's project.[19] Aside from his immodest comparisons with Columbus, Salvador de Sá's statements are amazing. At the age of seventy, after a long life as a conqueror and predator on both margins of the Atlantic, he recognized the perniciousness of the African slave trade and formulated new ideas for the occupation of Angola. His plan aimed at reducing the devastation caused by Atlantic traffic to launch a production sector and populating policy in Angola.

The issue raged on after Salvador's and Dourado's deaths, until 1696, when a categorical judgment by the Overseas Council closed the debate.[20] The session's minutes underline the inconvenience of the Angola-Mozambique continental voyage. "Even if this affair was easy, it would not be useful," the councilors determined. The enterprise's uselessness rested on the fact that the Monomotapa gold and ivory were much more valuable in India, into which they were regularly exported, than in Portugal. The transport of such merchandise into Lisbon, through African hinterlands and Atlantic thoroughfares, would yield little profit for the Crown. Moreover, it would undermine Portuguese trade in the Indian Ocean. Besides, in view of African resistance, the opening of the pathway from Angola seemed impossible, for it would be necessary to erect "one million fortifications and to garrison them" along the way.

The irritated exaggeration of the final statement may have come from the president of the Council (1692–1701), Francisco de Távora, count of Alvor, ex-governor of Angola (1669–1676) and former viceroy of India (1681–1686), the only one of the signatories of the judgment with experience in the governments of Africa and India.[21] In his seven years in Angolan government, the longest recorded in this colony, Távora had previously resisted the pressure by Salvador de Sá and Dourado to engage in the Mozambique journey. Pretending to be more experienced in Angolan affairs, Salvador de Sá then criticized Távora harshly.[22] Nevertheless, Távora later gauged Portuguese frailty in India as he confronted the military offensive by the first Maratha sovereigns. In 1696, the count of Alvor had the latitude to impose his own view of overseas problems. The two modes of exploitation in the Ethiopic Ocean are thus clear. Discarding Salvador and Dourado's earlier proposals for a Luso-Brasílico shift based on expanding control over Austral African territory, the count of Alvor and the Council kept a Luso-Asian strategy grounded on factories, relay trade, and indirect government.

The Council's decision brought to a close the second expansionist cycle in Angola, sparked by Salvador de Sá's invasion in 1648. A second cycle—the first had been started by the pull of *asentista* big-merchant capital at the turn of the 1500s and concluded with the Restoration and the end of Portuguese *Asientos* in 1640. From this standpoint, the royal instructions about the *Contra-Costa* voyage should not be interpreted as a sequence of missed opportunities—from the sixteenth century until the 1890 British ultimatum—in bringing about the linkage of Angola to Mozambique. The nonimplementation of these measures was not caused by an incapacity to anticipate the moves by European rivals, as stated by Oliveira Martins, or by the insufficiency of settlers in the area, or by the negative impact of the slave trade, as Jaime Cortesão thought.[23]

For all practical purposes, the peopling of Austral Africa was not part of Ancien Regime overseas policy, which opted for trade and not for widening territorial occupation. Such is the content of a decision by the Overseas Council at the end of the 1680s. "In Angola, it was not convenient for us [to engage in] more conquest than was sufficient to secure trade, which is better achieved by fear of [our] war than with [its actual] execution, because, besides [its] successes being contingent, even in certainty of victory, experience has demonstrated that the battles were what most hindered trade."[24] The statement seems to prefigure a modern policy of military dissuasion at the service of economic exploitation and of indirect government that was similar to, for instance, that of the Lyautey government in French Morocco (1912–1925).

Actually, the Overseas Council's decision responded to the thalassocratic doctrine affirmed since the Age of Discoveries and reiterated in 1608 by Luís Mendes de Vasconcelos in a celebrated text: "No more than vain glory was achieved in the conquest of India, where, instead, we should prefer the usefulness; and so, we should not try (to control) more than just that which was necessary for a safe trade."[25] This is a text Karl Polanyi would have certainly appreciated had he come across it when formulating his ideas about the separation between trade and market in the European overseas.

Some of Brazil's historians and, in particular, the Paulista authors, make the same mistake, as they dismiss the conditioning of 1600s overseas policy, confusing the scope of the first with the second European expansion. As is known, the defeat of the Paulista constitutionalist movement in the confrontation with federal troops (1932) stimulated Paulista regionalism, which theorized the seventeenth-century *bandeirantes* as precursors of Brazilian territorial unity. Portuguese historian Jaime Cortesão joined this *bandeirantista* bias for other reasons. For him, the Paulista raids on the Spanish Guayrá and their advance toward the north-northwest should also be seen in the context of the Portuguese struggle against Habsburg Spain. He understands that the "Borders Bandeira" (1648–1652), led by Raposo Tavares, aimed to attack Spanish citadels in upper Peru.[26] The thesis does not find support in the Overseas Council documents, which, as stated in the previous chapter, disqualified the "Borders Bandeira." On his side, Father Antonio Vieira denied any trace of patriotism in *bandeirante* activity, which he was solidly hostile to. At the end of his life (1695), retaking a derogatory word used by Montoya to label the Indians hunters from São Paulo, he still considered them more threatening to the Portuguese Crown than Spain itself: "I do not fear Castile, I fear this [Paulista] scum [*canalha*]."[27]

Nevertheless, it remains to be seen why, well before that, Portuguese America, departing from the overseas policy enforced in both Portuguese Africa and Portuguese Asia, followed its own destiny.

The Repeopling of Portuguese America

The overseas scenario of the Thirty Years War (1618–1648) and its aftermath exposed Portuguese vulnerability in both oceans. Indeed, the maritime attacks—including the Dutch occupation of Pernambuco, Maranhão, and Angola, the loss of Elmina on the Gold Coast, as well as the fall of the trading fortresses at Malacca and Colombo (modern Sri Lanka)—left Lisbon's global strategy concentrated on the Ethiopic Ocean. From then on, it was necessary to prevent native communities in Brazil or Angola from making alliances with European rivals.

Referring to the Brazilian north coast within the reach of the European war vessels sailing to the Caribbean (a zone in full colonial "boom"), Jesuit Bettendorf, a seasoned missionary in the Amazon region, justified the general offensive against Amerindians during the open war between the United Provinces and Portugal (1657–1661): "Once the war with the Dutch was announced, it was intended to make peace with all these [Amerindian] nations, or to engage the State forces to destroy them, given the risk that any rival [European] nation join these barbarians to take possession of these captaincies."[28] As threats of a new WIC attack arose in Bahia in the 1660s, the Crown ordered a series of preventive expeditions against "the hostile Indians and Maroon villages" of Bahia Bay and its neighboring territories.[29] Alliance or extermination—such were the options imposed on native communities of West Central Africa and of Portuguese America by the Portuguese.

Truces were negotiated with native communities of Amazonia and Angola, as well with Queen Njinga of Matamba. In other Portuguese places, mestizo troops and their native allies waged war against real or allegedly rebellious communities. Examples include the "Barbarians War" (1651–1704) waged against northeast Indians; the resurgence of the raids on Palmares from 1660; the battle of Mbwila (1665), in which the Congo's king and his army were routed; the attack against the Soyo at Kitombo (1670); the assault of Pungo Andongo (1671) that ended the Ndongo independence; and the founding, with the support of Rio de Janeiro's merchants, of the trading post of Colonia do Sacramento facing Buenos Aires (1680). This unique cycle of military and commercial offensives, led by mainland and local overseas interests to achieve geopolitical dominance over the Ethiopic Ocean and its inland networks, was also associated with the growth of Rio de Janeiro's slave trade in Benguela and, as reaction, the shift of Bahian vessels from Angola to the Bight of Benin, where the first steps were made to build a Portuguese fort, partially funded by Bahian slave traders, at Whydah (1698–1721). Those offensives had the same aim: retaking control over communities evading Portuguese control and opening new trading areas during a period of increasing European competition overseas.[30] Having lost the "Spice Wars," in which control of Asian trading posts was at stake, the Portuguese, thanks to the support of the Brasílicos, won the "Sugar and Slaves Wars" fought in the South Atlantic.

Two motives contributed to the widening of the Portuguese presence in Brazil. First, in contrast to West Central Africa, the epidemiological environment and the balance of power were certainly unfavorable to the South American natives. Second, after 1650 the African slave-trade movement took over, reducing the economic importance of Amerindian captivity. From then on, and until the Marquis de Pombal in the middle of the eighteenth century, the issue of Indian labor was circumscribed to the regions of Portuguese America less integrated into the Atlantic market.

The Crown's and missionaries' action in favor of Amerindian freedom had been one of the factors stimulating the dissemination of African slave labor in America. At first, this policy protected the natives from the slaving pressure exerted by local authorities and settlers. Later, with the growing arrival of enslaved Africans, the Amerindians ceased to constitute a potential reserve of coerced labor. Their villages then become a hindrance to settlers' expansion, especially to the cattle raisers of the northeast. With the support of the Paulistas from the south and militiamen from the north recruited by the planters and ranchers, a war front against American natives was opened through the hinterland stretching from Bahia up to Maranhão, through the Borborema plateau in Paraíba and the Serra Grande on the border between Ceará and Piauí.

"The cattle against the men" taught Pierre Chaunu lessons on the expansion of the ranching frontier that destroyed Indian communities in the South American plains. Known as the "Barbarian Wars" (1651–1704), these campaigns in fact marked a rupture—for the first time, the colonial offensive aimed at exterminating rather than enslaving the Indians in a large area of Portuguese America.[31] Accordingly, an order from Matias da Cunha, governor general of Brazil (1687–1688), to Abreu Soares, captain-major of a troop of Pernambucanos who later joined the Paulista forces in Palmares, stated that all captured adult males of the Rio Grande Indians should be slaughtered. "You must not permit the adult barbarians to be spared from beheading just to enslave them, only women and children must be spared, as there is no danger of them escaping or rebelling," wrote the governor-general.[32] Denounced by the missionaries, those killings led the Crown to intervene to reign in *bandeirante* brutality. A royal letter of 1692 denounced the Paulistas, who were hired in Pará as "efficacious medicine for the extinction of the Tapuia [Gê] marauders," and also set upon Ceará, attacking the Amerindians of the Serra de Ibipiaba settlements, "long ago domesticated" by the Jesuits.[33] Another document condemns the attacks launched at that time against both the "settled . . . Indians and [against] the Tapuia [Gê]."[34]

The offensive in the hinterlands—a side-effect of the predominance of African slavery in the labor market—gave way to the transformation of unsettled Amerindians into beastlike individuals, as impressively portrayed in an ex-voto made in Campos dos Goitacases (Rio de Janeiro's captaincy) at the turn of the seventeenth century. This area was also the stage for raids against Goitacá or Waitaká and Botocudo communities who resisted ranchers and cane farmers associated with Salvador de Sá and his heirs. The painting shows a group of Indians returning to the forest after an ambush on a settler's convoy. Half-eaten corpses of white and black men are scattered on the ground. A few Amerindians are taking a black porter and human body parts along into the jungle. The representation by the anonymous artist reveals the imaginary of the time of the "Barbarians war": black slaves and white settlers, united as victims of the same drama, appear as the colonizing drive's agents hit by human flesh-eating aboriginals. No longer needed as slaves, given the regular flux of transatlantic traffic, the Indians were now equated to fierce beasts

Figure C.1. Unknown author, *Botocudos attack in the Goyatacá Land* (c. 1700). *Source:* Alberto Lamego, *A Terra Goytacá*, Paris, 1913, Biblioteca do Instituto de Estudos Brasileiros, Universidade São Paulo.

and could be put down like animals. There was no place for them in colonial labor. There was no room for them in colonial territory. They could be exterminated.

As I have stressed, the plundering of the African villages by the transatlantic slave trade diminished the role of enslaved Indians in the colonial enclaves. This process repopulated the São Francisco River valley and the backlands of Ceará with colonists, enslaved Africans, mestizos, and cattle.

Previously restricted to the sugar-cane plantation's borders, repopulation widened as the economic territory enlarged with the acclimatized cattle brought in from Cape Verde. For the first time, the Portuguese engaged in large-scale ranch activities within the overseas continental space. The consequences would be decisive.

Cattle Against the Amerindians

The cattle raised in Sergipe at the turn of the 1500s multiplied and, by midcentury, had already become a crucial addition to the sugar economy, to the point of constituting one of the important topics of the Luso-Dutch disputes in Portuguese America.[35] Scattered along the São Francisco River valley, the ranches took their herds up to Salvador de Bahia, to the Capoame cattle fair (present-day Camaçari) by means of three successive trails, Jeromoabo's (the oldest), Jacobina's, and Juazeiro's, at the tip of the cattle-raising vertex that pierced Piauí and Maranhão at the end of the seventeenth century. Antonil and Rocha Pitta stood in awe at the size of the territory tread by the oxen's hooves. Rocha Pitta speaks of a "very dilated circumference" thus peopled, whereas the Tuscan born Antonil, knowing that some of his readers were used to meager European herds, prudently concluded after describing the dimension of the Bahian cattle drive: "if I say so, I fear it may sound unbelievable."[36] In the Río de la Plata basin, another gateway for the cattle expansion in South America, the dimensions of the herds also impressed the Jesuit Sepp. In 1691, he sent his Yapeyu mission Guarani to bring in wild cattle on the left bank of the Uruguay River (in the present-day municipalities of Alegrete, Livramento, Quaraí, and Uruguaiana). Two months later, he witnessed the arrival of 50,000 head. "Had I ordered, they would have brought me 70, 80, or even 90,000," stated the much-impressed Tyrolese Jesuit.[37] In the following decades southern mules and cattle were dragged into Minas Gerais together with cattle from the northern and northeastern captaincies. The confluence of all these cattle in the gold-mining region during the eighteenth-century market established the amalgamation of the three main fluvial basins in South America—of the Uruguay, São Francisco, and Amazon Rivers–constituting the present-day dimensions of the Brazilian space.

At the same time as the colonial enclaves were enlarged, cattle-raising brought changes to Luso-Brazilian society. Hinterland meat production increased the food supply to coastal towns and plantations, allowing planters to concentrate enslaved labor on commodity production. But cattle ranches were also pulled into the Atlantic market by the increase in tobacco exports in the decade of 1680, since the tobacco shipped abroad was usually wrapped in leather, which represented 15 percent of the final price for a roll of the leaf.[38] At the same time, the export of leather products of all kinds surged.

Cattle-raising generated production relations that set it apart from slavery. The tenuous presence of mercantile capital, the nature of the productive process, and the absence of direct control by the owner all reduced the impact of the slave system in the large cattle pastures, even though the presence of black slaves may have been significant in cattle farms.[39] Ranchers paying cattle as income to landlords and waged cowboys employed in driving the herd—"whites, mulattos and blacks, also Indians who seek to get some profit from this work" (Antonil)—engendered a social stratum distinct from that of the coast. Enslaved or free, the cowboy (*curraleiro*) from the São Francisco valley had little in common with the plantation slave or with the free or freed sharecropper and small owners (*roceiro*), dependents of the sugar-mill owner. Relatively inappropriate for slave labor, cattle-raising extended the occupation and social framing of the territory.

The Militias of the Ethiopic Ocean

Aside from the military expeditions in Portuguese America, documents also reveal frequent movements of troops between the two sides of the Southern Atlantic. From the second quarter of the seventeenth century until the first decades of the eighteenth century, at least 4,000 soldiers crossed the ocean, bringing their skills in South America's wars to expand raiding for slaves in West Central Africa. Furthermore, the great majority of these military and militiamen returned to Brazil more experienced in attacking the Indians of the backlands and the *quilombos* of rebel slaves.[40] Hence, these troops were sometimes decisive in winning Angolan battles, such as the 1648 reconquest of Luanda from the Dutch, the 1665 defeat of Congo at Mbwila, and the overcoming of the Ngola a Kiluanuje resistance at Pungo Andongo in 1671. Commenting on this last battle, Salvador de Sá noted in the Overseas Council the destruction of all the sovereign kingdoms around Luanda, "There are no more [native] kings in Angola."[41] It is also noteworthy that imports of horses from Brazil expanded Luso-Brasílica slaving in Angola.[42] In the same way, tactics and strategies from colonial Brazil strengthened the Portuguese domination in Central Africa.

Along with the dispatch of troops from Brazil, some royal decrees reoriented the flows of *degredados* (convicts and others sentenced to penal banishment) to Angola, because of the "lack of people there."[43] As Ferreira observes, Portuguese inland raids in West Central Africa declined in the eighteenth century. At the same time, the absence of European threats in Angola diminished troop transfers from Brazil to Luanda and to Benguela.

Except for Henrique Dias's regiment—whose companies fought several times in Palmares, in Benguela in 1645, and at Mbwila in 1665—there are no indications of regular units operating on both sides of the South Atlantic. Typically, the troops were irregulars, who "volunteered" to fight in Angola to escape punishment elsewhere. Desertions certainly took place. In 1664, a whole vessel sailing from Recife to Angola with rescue troops defected on the Pernambuco coast.[44] However, many troops and officers were posted to Angola, as well as royal officials and even churchmen experienced in Brazil's colonial endeavors. A few Angolista militiamen fought also in Brazil.[45] As mentioned in the previous chapter, the Crown's councils had mixed feelings about the merit of the former colonial combatants who applied for career promotions. Still, these personnel were critical to the increase of the West Central Africa slave trade and to the enlargement of control in the South Atlantic. Consequently, the service records of the applicants for the positions listed the crossings and ambitions of the direct agents of colony-building.

A few examples among dozens of cases: Antonio Alemão, veteran of the Dutch war in Brazil, former captain of Sergipe, applied for and won the post of sergeant-major in Angola in 1685.[46] Antônio Simões, engaged in the military aid sent from Pernambuco to André Vidal de Negreiros, under whom he had fought in Brazil against the Dutch, served in Luanda's infantry and became captain of Massangano, near Luanda.[47] Pascoal Rodrigues, combatant of the two Guararapes' battles (1648 and 1649), was nominated lieutenant in Angola.[48] Jerônimo da Veiga Cabral, former captain of Itamaracá (Bahia), obtained the post of Angola Treasury superintendent in 1682.[49] Manoel Justo Santiago fought the São Francisco

River's Indians and the Palmares *quilombos*, obtaining later the post of captain of the Massangano.[50]

The itinerant transoceanic careers of four captains deserve more attention.

Paulo Pereira, an Afro-Brasílico who was captain of the musketeers in Henrique Dias's blacks regiment, fought against the Dutch in Pernambuco and later against the Palmares's *quilombolas*. He belonged to the contingent of 200 soldiers sent from Bahia to Angola in 1645. Eventually he escaped from the slaughter of the Portuguese troops by the Jagas, close to the Kikombo River.[51] In 1648, Salvador de Sá appointed Paulo Pereira as sergeant-major of the African auxiliaries of Benguela. Therefore, Pereira commanded Afro-Brasílicos and Africans in Pernambuco, and Afro-Brasílicos as well as Angolans in Benguela. A legendary character of the South Atlantic Wars, this Pernambucan died on the Angolan savanna fighting a lion.[52]

Bento Correa de Figueiredo served between 1656 and 1683 in various military capacities on three continents. Enlisted in Ceará, he was sent to Portugal and in 1658 participated in the siege of Badajoz against the Spanish. Returning to Recife, he then traveled to Luanda in 1661 with Governor Vidal de Negreiros. There he was promoted as captain of the governor's guards and fought at sea against a Dutch corsair. Later, he returned to Pernambuco, where he commanded a company in the attack on Palmares. In 1687, he became captain-major of Ceará, renowned for "destroying the Tapuia [Gê] [Indians] who disobeyed."[53]

Jorge de Barros Leite, a native of Portugal, participated in the battle of Ameixial (1663), a critical victory for Lisbon against the Spanish. In 1676, he was sent to Angola, where he became captain-major of Pungo Andongo. Later he went to Brazil to become captain in Bahia and captain-major in Sergipe. Then he became a lieutenant of the militia who battled the Indians and the maroon villages in the area. In 1699, he was promoted to captain-major on Ceará's anti-Indian front, replacing Fernão Carrilho, the anti-Palmares commander who was promoted lieutenant to the governor in Maranhão.[54]

Finally, there is Manoel de Inojosa (Hinojosa or Nojoza), descendant of a Galician family who arrived in Brazil during the Habsburg period. As a soldier, Inojosa embarked from Recife to Luanda in 1661. On his way back to Pernambuco in 1662, he stopped in Bahia and participated in the raids against the maroon villages. From 1671 to 1673, he joined the Paulista Baião Parente in an expedition that destroyed Indian villages in the Paraguaçú valley, in Bahia. In 1673, he was appointed "captain of the conquest of the barbaric heathens" of Santo Antônio da Conquista (Bahia).[55] With orders to settle those lands with colonists, he formed another company to expel the Gê Indians there. In 1676, he traveled to Lisbon to ask for renewal of his patent as captain.[56] An officer from Bahia endorsed this request, specifying that Inojosa's company was "very important in conquering the natives and the blacks of the maroon communities." The Overseas Council approved the captain's promotion, not only because of his valor in fighting the Indians of Bahia but also because "of his value and experience" that "will be necessary for Pernambuco's [maroons of] Palmares."[57]

Subsequently, Inojosa joined expeditions sent against Palmares in 1679, 1680, and 1681. In 1681, he mistakenly claimed to have killed Zumbí himself. In 1682, he brought assistance and provisions to the troops besieging the Palmaristas.[58] In 1683, he was back in Lisbon, where he applied for the position of captain-major of Ceará.[59] In fact, he was promoted to captain-major of Benguela, south of Luanda, from 1685 to 1687.[60] There is also a report of his presence in a later raid against Palmares, dated 1689.[61] Inojosa's replacement in Benguela was João Pereira Lago, who had also fought in Bahia and Palmares and probably had been his militia companion on both sides of the Atlantic.[62] After Lago, the position was awarded to Angelo da Cruz, who had been transferred to Angola in 1667 with the troops sent from Rio de Janeiro.[63]

Therefore, in this crucial period in West Central Africa, two or perhaps three of the Benguela's captains-major came from Rio de Janeiro and Pernambuco. Ultimately, the Benguela slave-trade route was dominated by slave merchants from Rio de Janeiro and Pernambuco: up to 1850, 500,000 enslaved were deported from Benguela to Brazil.[64]

In addition to Inojosa's involvement in the battles of Angola and Brazil, he made two trips to Lisbon, where he made reports about Palmares and shared information with many veterans of South Atlantic battles. In three decades, he met, fought beside, and traveled over land and sea with Vidal de Negreiros's officers experienced in the Dutch Wars; with the Paulistas familiar with raids against Indians in the South; and with the Africans, Angolistas, Brasílicos, and Portuguese captains of Angola. Inojosa did not hold a key command in Brazil, he had no official appointment in Lisbon, and we do not know much about his endeavors. His wide-ranging significance in the building of the Ethiopic Ocean can only be evaluated when the documents of Portuguese, Angolan, and Brazilian archives are read together.

Although not all combatants participated in these varied battles, they all contributed to disseminate strategies and tactics for war in the tropics. They also helped to spread the Indian-Brasílico ration, composed of manioc, maize, and *cachaça*, as well as slave trading and the cultural customs that became common practices in Brazil, in Angola, and later in the Bight of Benin. At this stage, the new colonial framework of the Southern Atlantic, already obvious in Amsterdam and Lisbon, also became evident in Rome.

The Papacy and the Ethiopic Ocean

In the wake of the reestablishment of relations between Rome and Lisbon (1669), the Portuguese bishoprics left vacant since 1640 were to be filled. It was then that Pope Innocent XI reorganized the overseas dioceses. With headquarters in São Luís, the Maranhão bishopric (1677) would be placed under the authority of the Lisbon archbishopric until Brazil's independence (1822), due to difficulties in maritime communication with Bahia. As mentioned before, the Guiana current flowing NNW hinders the northbound navigation from Ceará. In the same period the bishopric of Olinda was created (1676), encompassing the area stretching from the mouth of the São Francisco River up to Ceará. Varnhagen had already observed that "the prodigious population growth" induced by cattle in the Piauí and Maranhão hinterland had given birth to the Maranhão diocese.[65] The prelacy of Rio de Janeiro was promoted to a bishopric while Bahia now housed an archbishop (1676). The new Bahian archbishopric would have under its authority not only the dioceses of Olinda and Rio de Janeiro, but also the bishoprics of Congo and Angola, as well as the dioceses of São Tomé, including the Mina Coast. Sailed by Luso-Brasílico slave traders, those African coasts were also to be attended by Bahia's archbishop.[66] Practical with regard to the world of the living, the papacy redesigned the Ethiopic Ocean based on its geopolitical reality, that is, on the hierarchy of its regional powers and markets.

It is also worth noting that two other Portuguese bishoprics were founded in the second half of this century, those of Nanking and of Peking (1690). Still, both belong to an episode of Western history that would soon come to an end—the Portuguese and Christian penetration of modern China.

The Southern Atlantic scope of Brasílico expansion contrasted with the decline of the Estado da Índia. Aside from the loss of trading ports and factories, there was a decrease in Portuguese settlers. Sanjay Subrahmanyam calculates that around 1630, there were 800 Portuguese or foreign priests under Lisbon's Church Patronage regime, as well as 15,000 Portuguese or mestizos of Portuguese origin scattered across the breadth of Portuguese Asia. In the beginning of the 1600s, Goa, the capital of the Estado da Índia, held 1,500 settlers in the midst of a native population of 75,000 inhabitants. But both mainland and native populations of the Goan region dropped in the course of the century. Teotônio de Souza attributes the fall to Portuguese intolerance toward Hindu religious practices, as well as to the competition from British and Dutch ports of trade, which attracted wealthy Hindu merchants previously living in Goa into other Indian cities.[67] Significantly, D. Gregório dos Anjos, first bishop of Maranhão (1677–1689), was previously nominated bishop of Malacca, but was unable to take up his post: Malacca had fallen to the Dutch. The pages opened in the East by Afonso de Albuquerque, conqueror of Malacca (1511), were closed as the ongoing book of the Portuguese Atlantic increased in length.

To complete the analysis of the shaping of the Ethiopic Ocean there is an essential feature to be taken into account: the mulattos' social and demographic ascension in Brazil.

The Invention of the Mulatto

First, it should be noted that the Palmares wars led to an anti-maroon escalation.[68] Brazil's slaveocracy, sometimes acting against Lisbon's will, enforced repression. Indeed, in 1668, during a sharp juncture of the Palmares wars, the Crown decided to rein the masters' violence, in order to prevent slave rebellions. Writing to Brazil's governor-general, the regent Pedro ordered him "to prosecute summarily" the masters who "punished with cruelty" their slaves. Yet following colonists' complaints, the royal order was cancelled eleven months later, "to avoid troubles" between masters and slaves.[69] Again, the colonial slave system prevailed over metropolitan intents. Issued in the aftermath of Palmares's destruction, a royal order of 1699 exempted from punishment colonists who killed any maroon (or *quilombola*). What was more, a royal decree of 1741 prescribed that a group of five runaway slaves should be considered a *quilombo*. "Bush captains" (*capitães do mato*) in charge of capturing maroons, on duty since the first decades of the seventeenth century in Bahia and Pernambuco, had their general regulations (*regimento*) for Portuguese America published in 1724.[70] Free or freed blacks residing in the hinterland could, in the course of their lives or in the following generations, be falsely considered *quilombolas* and captured by *capitães-do-mato* in search of reward. Once reputed to be a *quilombola*, an isolated black family composed of a father, mother, and three children was at risk of being enslaved and eventually massacred. The criminalization of rebel and runway black slaves became a mortal threat to autonomous groups of African descent in the Brazilian territory.

Therefore, free and freed blacks were obliged to maintain links with former masters or colonial institutions, such as the Catholic brotherhoods and the parishes that could confirm they were not runaways.[71] Accordingly, those individuals would remain inside colonial enclaves, prompting the social stratification of mixed families and mulattos. Hence, besides miscegenation, the social reproduction of mulattos came about mainly from the racial constrictions of Luso-Brasílico slave society. Of course, we speak of radically hierarchized relations, as the pattern of the interracial is one-sided: the dominant white group always provided the male parent and more rarely the husband, while the black community always yielded the mother and more rarely the wife. From the start, miscegenation (the biological reproduction of mulattos) combined with acculturation to facilitate the social process of *mestizaje* (the social reproduction of mulattos).

Contrary to what took place in North America and in Angola, practices favoring mulattos had been in place since the first decades of Brazil's colonization. For what reason?

The extension of slavery in tropical America increased masters' insecurity and restricted the supply of qualified labor demanded by the sector developments of Portuguese America's economy. Such hindrances led the masters to concede better treatment to mestizos in general and to the mulattos in particular. Stuart Schwartz has calculated that mulattos received 45 percent of the letters of manumission granted in Bahia between 1648 and 1745, despite representing fewer than 10 percent of the total of captaincy's slaves. Likewise, mulattos constituted only 6 percent of the total of slaves in the sugar mills, but 20 percent of the more skilled roles of supervision, handicraft, and domestic service in the eighteenth century, whereas black people were confined to the hard labor of working the fields.[72] Vidal Luna and Klein found the same trends favoring mulattos in Minas Gerais and São Paulo in 1750–1850.[73] Results of their further research confirm the pattern, while also demonstrating the mulattos' social cohesion, inasmuch as their marriage rates were higher than those of free blacks.[74]

One of the most fascinating Portuguese characters of the 1600s, Francisco Manuel de Melo, during his deportation in Bahia, wrote a now-lost book on

Brazil with an elucidating title: *Paradise of Mulattos, Purgatory of Whites and Hell of Blacks*.[75] The quote is a variant of proverbs referring to social life in England and France, probably known to Francisco Manuel, a refined writer and a well-traveled man.[76] Fifty years later, the Jesuit Antonil, who also lived in Bahia, completed the thought: "Brazil is the hell of the blacks, the purgatory of the whites and paradise of the mulattos and mulatto women."[77] The addition of the mulatto women by Antonil quote may well be related to the cultural habitus that inspired the famous erotic poems, most debased, on mulatto women written by the Luso-Bahian poet Gregorio de Matos in previous years.[78]

The military use of mestizos in the context of colonial expansion also played a decisive role. As we have seen, during the second quarter of the seventeenth century, two major regional armed forces emerged in Portuguese America: the *bandeirantes*, or Paulistas, generally Amerindian mestizo militias from São Paulo, who launched slave-hunting expeditions against the southern Indians, and the Pernambuco and Paraiba volunteer forces, incorporating mestizo and mulatto militias, which fought the Dutch in northeast Brazil from 1630 to 1654, and later, the Angolan and Congolese kingdoms in West Central Africa. In this sense, the recruiting of mulattos and free blacks in the Henriques Dias's troop must be highlighted.[79] Formed to fight against the Dutch invader, such regiments attacked Palmares on various occasions. After the death of Zumbi and the destruction of Palmares, the Pernambucan regiment Terço dos Henriques, commanded by mulatto Domingos Rodrigues Carneiro, pursued and killed Camoanga (1700), Zumbi's brother, who continued to fight.[80] Transferred to the other side of the ocean, the Henriques's mulattos fought also for the slaving order in some key battles in Angola and, in particular, in the Battle of Mbwila (1665), as we saw above.

Privileges granted to them as a category contributed to individualize the mulattos. In the beginning of the nineteenth century, the Bahian chronicler Vilhena would notice the interest of the mulattos in their incorporation to the Henriques and to the military bodies that admitted them: "those who persist longer in the regiments are the freed mulattos."[81]

From the second half of the 1600s onward, stimulated by the example of Henrique Dias's *terços*, the Crown tried to organize regular regiments of mulatto and free blacks in Angola. Actually, the privileges granted to the Henriques of Angola generated tensions between mainland soldiers and displeased native troops allied to the Portuguese.

Authorities in Angola preferred to associate with groups of native gunmen and warriors—the *quilambas*, *quimbares*, and *empacasseiros*—who shared the booty in predatory expeditions, but had neither regular pay nor military statute.[82] At the end of the eighteenth century, Miguel Antônio de Mello, governor of Angola, recapitulated the legislation concerning the Henriques and taught the Court the differences between the two margins of the Atlantic. "As the political, military and economic system that this [Angola's] government follows is by necessity a path other than that taken by the captaincies in Brazil, it often so happens that laws that are useful to Brazil, are harmful in Angola, and, contrariwise, some that are indispensable here, can find no application to that Estado [do Brasil]."[83]

In the religious sphere the attempts to create a native clergy in Angola also failed. Either the African priest subverted the native social hierarchy, as when a Matamba priest was refused by Queen Njinga because he was the son of one of her slaves, or he was absorbed by it, like the Luso-Bakongo priests who had marched at the side of the king of Congo in the Battle of Mbwila. But the greatest distrust was reserved for Luso-Angolan mulattos whose ordination was explicitly vetoed by Rome, against the will of the Overseas Council.[84]

I think that this policy stemmed from the intimidation imposed on colonists and Church by a Mbundu culture that had been assaulted and sacked, but never quite truly dominated by Portugal or by the Church. Interestingly, Cardonega's *História Geral* described Mbundu and neighboring peoples transforming into lions and becoming Kifumbula vampires (one of which confronted by Cadornega, sword in hand); other Angolans were said to melt slaves' chains with secret herbs. According to Cadornega, during the WIC presence in Angola, the Portuguese sought the help of native sorcerers, particularly of the Pombolo, who could tame wild beasts, to launch lions and leopards against the Dutch settled in Luanda.

Such military tactics, deemed perfectly feasible by the Angolistas and colonial authorities, were taken seriously and debated in a 1642 assembly bringing together the bishop, town councilors, and other citizens in the Bengo provisional capital. It was not carried out only because the bishop considered it "dirty war, made by an inconvenient diabolical art." (It would be marvelous to read a Cadornega description of the Pombolo commanding a charge by lions and leopards against the Dutch troops.) I doubt that there is a document so fantastic, so strongly injecting native culture into a municipal council session, in any other part of the European overseas.[85]

The scope of the Angolistas' africanization and the limits of the local mestizaje are reflected in the sober beauty of the Luís Félix da Cruz poem.

> Here where my desire
> Does not meet its ending
> For I find me devoid of myself
> When I am myself searching
> Here where the son is Brown
> And almost Black the grandson
> And all Black the great-grandson
> And everything is dark[86]

Mirrored in these verses, the impediments to the growth of the mulatto population were fully analyzed some decades later in Luanda by Governor Sousa Coutinho (1764–1772). According to him, as in Brazil, local colonists had children with black women, but when the fathers died or moved away, the mother returned to her village with her mulatto offspring, bringing them back to the traditional community and to africanization.[87] In sum, there was miscegenation but no *mestizaje*. In point of fact, Sousa Coutinho described the kinship pattern of the Mbundu peoples. Once the ties with the colonist disappeared, the native mother and her sons moved to her family village and assumed their Mbundu status and culture. Belonging to matrilineal communities, the sons lived with their maternal family in the mother's brother's home.[88] Consequently, Sousa Coutinho tried, in vain, to obtain the freedom of the mulatto slaves, a measure that seemed to him the only way to promote their status and the colonial peopling of Angola.[89]

On the other side of the ocean, the social and economic significance of Brazil's mulattos was already patent. Their favorable situation was highlighted in a controversy arising from the enforcement of a sumptuary law of 1749, in which one clause denied free and freed mulattos the right to wear silk clothes or jewels. Criticizing this law, a statement by the Lisbon merchant guild (Mesa do Bem Comum) argued that "in [Portuguese] America mulattos constitute the largest group, and it seems that this inferior condition they are born with should not deprive them of the credit and the esteem they acquire."[90] Approving the merchants' arguments, the Crown lifted the prohibition some weeks later.[91]

In other words, while Sousa Coutinho tried to introduce the basic conditions for the emergence of a mulatto stratum in Angola, mulattos of Brazil formed a consumer market appreciated by Lisbon's merchants, who worked in favor of their social promotion. In practice, there was in Brazil a social process transforming miscegenation into mestizaje. The fact that this process was stratified, and eventually ideologized, or even sensualized, should not conceal its intrinsic violence, a consubstantial part of Brazilian society.

In view of the particularities and contingencies summarized above, the contrast between the two sides of the South Atlantic was clear in the eighteenth century. As shown by Linda Heywood and Roquinaldo Ferreira, an observable mulatto group and culture existed in Angola.[92] However, mulattos were effectively a more durable entity and a more stable historical subject in Brazil.

∽

At the end of the seventeenth century, Brazil was almost ready. But its body had one of its lungs in Africa, mainly in Angola—"Angola . . . whose sad blood, dark and unhappy souls, nourish, enliven, sustain and conserve Brazil," wrote the Jesuit Antônio Vieira.[93]

The Atlantic market had imposed the primacy of the slave trade, which was interpreted by the Church as a work of Christian charity and evangelization. Slavery dominated everything, the Amerindian resistance was no longer, the territory became repopulated within the South Atlantic framework, cattle expanded, and mestizos and mulattos found their way in colonial society. In the following decades, the gold rush in Minas Gerais instituted an interregional division of labor in Portuguese America, engendered an internal market and made it into a single whole colony. As a matter of fact, from 1550 onward, the so-called Brazilian economic "cycles" (sugar, gold, and coffee), derive from the multisecular cycle of slave labor resulting from the pillage of the African continent.

Thus, if we compare the slave trade to Brazil with the deportations to the rest of the Americas, there is one constant: every Brazilian cycle of commodity exports correlates positively with an increase of Africans imports. Such is the case between 1575 and 1625, the period of rising phase of sugar exports; in the years 1701–1720, the start of gold mining; and during the period 1780–1810, with a new plantation cycle pushed by the coffee expansion.

Conversely, the crisis years or shortage of colonial production correlates with a reflux of the slave trade. It happened in the seventeenth century following the Dutch invasion (1625–1650) and as a result of the combined effects of the general crisis and Caribbean competition (1675–1700). The same occurs in the eighteenth century, with the decline of the gold production (1761–1780). Few statistical curves summarize so closely the correlation of exports and imported enslaved labor in a given region in the *longue durée*.

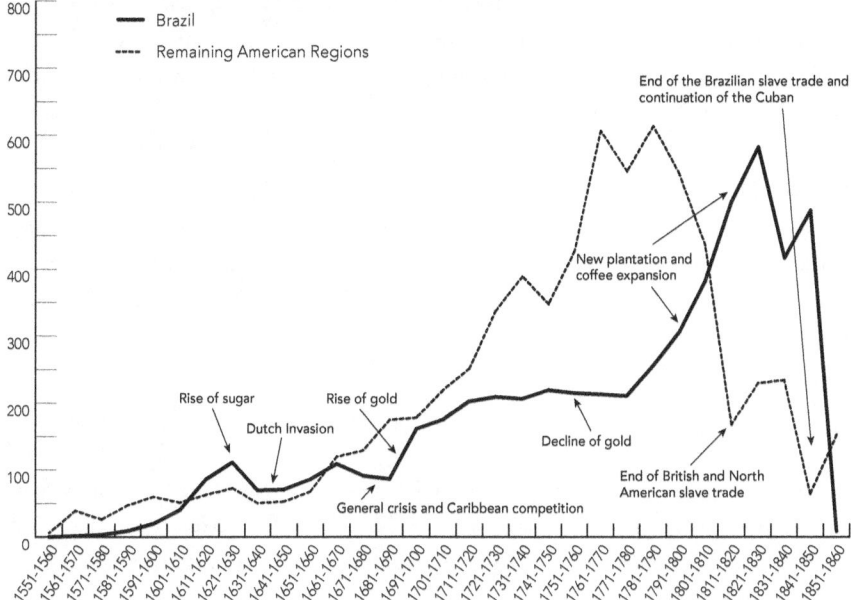

Figure C.2. Economic growth, geopolitical crisis, and Enslaved landed in the Americas 1550–1850. *Source:* TSTD.

As I stated in the first chapter, the continuity of colonial history does not coincide with the continuity of colonial territory. This geopolitical mismatch becomes clear when we note that Brazil's independence (1822) opens a long international crisis. Benguela, Luanda, Whydah, and Mozambique assert their proximity to the government of Rio de Janeiro, while British diplomacy and the Royal Navy tried to stop the illegal trade carrying 738,000 enslaved Africans to Brazilian ports between 1831 and 1850.[94]

The nineteenth-century resilience of the Atlantic slave trade showed that the colonial spatial matrix was larger than Brazilian national territory and sheds light on the building of the Ethiopic Ocean networks from the seventeenth century on.

We can therefore recall the questions concerning Portuguese overseas—and European expansion—that we asked in the first chapter. Why did Macao remain a more-or-less significant port of trade throughout the years 1557–1999, while Rio de Janeiro grew from a small seaport to the head of a colonial aggregate and to the capital of a large nineteenth-century nation-state? Such a comparison could also be done with Goa, center of a network of Portuguese enclaves that, unlike Macao, tripled its territory in the eighteenth century until it was absorbed by India in 1961. And it could also be done with Luanda, main port of a great area of deportations, then a Portuguese colonial enclave, and later capital of an independent country with a European official language and predominantly native, precolonial inhabitants.

In fact, Rio de Janeiro and Brazil differed across the centuries from colonial enclaves in Asia and Africa because of the connections they had with Angola. Because of the African slave trade, between 1550 and 1850, 86 of every out 100 individuals who disembarked in Brazil were enslaved Africans.

∽

I did not seek to abridge the history of Portuguese Africa for the benefit of the reader, nor have I sought in any way to "Brazilianize" overseas characters and feats. I have intended, instead, to sketch out the borders and historical stages that have constituted a transcontinental, Luso-Brazilian and Luso-African space, which resembled a Pacific Ocean atoll. Most of the time, the chain of mountains uniting the islands remains submerged, invisible. Only when the bottom of the sea quakes and storms rise does the big atoll ring pierce the horizon.

There were, indeed, two quakes that exposed the transcontinental arc of the economic and social zone formed by Brazil and Angola. The first took place during the Thirty Years War, when the Dutch assault on the Southern Atlantic joined Luanda and Recife into a single military front. The second period took place after Brazil's independence (1822), when the colonial spatial matrix was disrupted and the Royal Navy gunboats surged between independent Brazil and the African slaving ports.

It becomes patent that the colonial system was shaken by a deepening crisis in the 1600s: Portuguese and Brasílico comanagement of the Southern Atlantic economic space was established as the Dutch war flared. This is why the 1808 rupture would not be as radical as has been said and written: the Brazilianized arm of the colonial system, the slave trade, still moved across the ocean. Moreover, for three decades, it combined with the new order imposed by industrial England, leading Brazilian plantations to form an important component of the Second Slavery.

After 1850, the Brazilian labor market continued to be dependent on European, Levantine, and Asian immigrants. Only in the period 1930–1940 did economic activities rely predominantly on Brazilian-born workers. This is a defining characteristic of the formation of Brazil. From 1550 to 1930 the labor market was deterritorialized: the chief contingent of laborers was born and grew outside colonial and national territory.

The history of the Brazilian market, groomed by pillage and trade, is long, but the history of the Brazilian nation, founded on violence and on consent, is short.

Appendix 1

Luís Mendes de Vasconcellos and His Offspring

Luís Mendes de Vasconcellos was the second son of Joane Mendes de Vasconcellos (the elder) and Ana de Athayde, daughter of Antônio de Athayde, first count of Castanheira, and *privado* (chief advisor) of King João III. A commander of the Order of Christ, he served in the royal armada under Felipe II and Felipe III. Under the command of Álvaro de Barzan, marquis of Santa Cruz, he fought in 1583 against the prior of Crato's partisans at Terceira Island (in the Azores). He then followed the Iberian army in the Italian campaigns, whence he returned "very skilled and experienced" (Salgado de Araújo's words) in military affairs.

From these battlefields, he drew the lessons to write his celebrated *Arte Militar* (1610). In the same year, he sailed to India as captain-major of a royal fleet. Returning to Europe, his ship called at Luanda before arriving in Lisbon in 1611. Later, he was called to Madrid by King Felipe III to join a commission composed of the main royal councilors. Subsequently, Felipe III made him royal advisor and governor of Angola. He married Beatriz (or Brites) Caldeira, daughter of Manuel Caldeira, slave trader and later investor in the India thoroughfare. His older brother, Manuel de Vasconcellos, who had fought in Ksar El Kebir at the age of nineteen, was president of the Lisbon chamber and member of the state council of Portugal. Manuel died in Madrid in 1637. I did not find a record for the date of death of Luís Mendes de Vasconcellos, who was probably deceased in 1637, as related by the family's biographer João Salgado de Araújo, former deacon of Congo at the time of Vasconcellos' administration in Angola.

Francisco Mendes de Vasconcellos, Luís's eldest son, followed his father's literary vein. Although most of his oeuvre remained unpublished, specialists consider him a worthy writer. He wrote *Epítome da vida de d. Francisco de Portugal*, published as an introduction to the 1652 edition of the *Arte da galantaria* by Francisco de Portugal.[1] Francisco Mendes was also governor of the island of São Miguel in the Azores.

Joane Mendes de Vasconcellos (the younger), second son of Luís Mendes de Vasconcelos, was born in Évora in 1600. He became the chief captain in Angola at the age of nineteen, in the government of his father, Luís Mendes de Vasconcellos, where he was nicknamed Catunda (the "son of the Sun") by the Mbundu and was famed for beheading several *sobas* and for being "ill-inclined." He returned to Portugal and participated of the "Journey of the Vassals," the Iberian expedition that expelled the Dutch from Bahia (1625). In the same year, he returned to Luanda as sergeant-major, where he remained until 1629. On the return trip to Lisbon he was captured by the Dutch, remaining a prisoner in the Low Countries for two years. He served a further eight years in the Iberian armies of the Flanders War, as did his father. In 1635 he obtained the post of field-master in an expedition to secure Angola, but the mission did not materialize.[2] Then he was sent to Bahia (1640), where he replaced the count of Bagnuolo as general field-master (colonel). He was the first officer to acclaim the Duke of Braganza as king of Portugal when news of the restoration reached Bahia.[3] In 1642, he rejoined the mainland army, and later, he commanded all Portuguese troops in the Alentejo. After the failure of the attack on Badajoz (1658), he was replaced in the post. Seeking to rehabilitate him, King João IV nominated Joane as member of the War Council. He left many military writings.

Alão de Moraes wrote his obituary: "[Joane] died in this year of 1666 in his Castanheira estate, leaving perpetual longing among the Portuguese, because, besides being very keen and wise, he was the greatest soldier this century saw in Portugal." A twentieth-century Portuguese biographical notice, later widely distributed on the Internet and still serving as the basis for many contemporary notes, did not mention his assignments and his less reputable activities in Angola.[4]

Appendix 2

The Supply of Northern Captaincies by Southern Captaincies during the Dutch War 1630–1654

Since the end of the 1620s, Santos had been exporting to the north of the and to Angola products such as wheat, sugar, food supplies, cotton, and smelt iron.[1] There was, therefore, a supply of regional produce—lim volume but of varied merchandise—that flowed out from the São Paulo's Santos and São Vicente.

Once the invasion of Pernambuco had taken place in 1630, Martim governor of Rio de Janeiro and "superintendent in affairs of war" in the captaincies, mobilized personnel and supplies to strengthen the forts u command. Hundreds of Amerindians, gathered from the Rio de Janeiro se of São Lourenço, São Barnabé, Cabo Frio, and São Francisco Xavier, brought in from the south by the Jesuits, were concentrated around the and a liter of manioc flour were given to each settled Amerindian (aldea rations were usually purchased from the Rio de Janeiro and São Vicent With the beginning of the Dutch terrestrial war, the north experienced of food. Ill supplied, the 900 Iberian soldiers who had come along to the count of Bagnuolo (1631) were devoid of provisions.

This was the first regular European army to integrate manioc flou flour" of the Tupi-Guarani, into the troop's ration. In the following yea lingered on, as salted meats from the Río de La Plata region had cea Brazil after the loss of the Buenos Aires thoroughfare. Food also beca the kingdom, even for the troops fighting the Spanish in the Alen this problem, King João IV put pressure on the chambers situated the front, such as those of Viana do Castelo, of the Azores, and Ma supplies to Brazil.[3]

...disembarkation in Bahia (January 1639) of the count of Torre's ...ne ships, hundreds of sailors, and 5,000 soldiers, the Crown ...ration of supplies and the cultivation of manioc in Rio, São ...and Espírito Santo. Resources were mobilized to import wheat ...beef and pork, fish, and vegetables from the same areas. To ...yal letter of 1639 stated that ships, carts, mounts, and people ...ue to the "need of providing the Brazil's War with supplies." ...transported to Bahia, Pernambuco, or to wherever the king ...Pereira, cousin of Salvador de Sá, was placed in charge of ...rting such goods.⁴ A year later, the governor of Rio stated ...governor-general of Bahia with a lot of victuals and related ...troops and fleets, "people of the sea as well as people of ...lians." And he reiterated in 1642: militiamen, food, and ...north, at the cost of the government of Rio. On its ...er wrote to the Court to secure its important role as ...Dispatching every year "grandiose subsidies" of flour, ...e sustenance of Bahia, the chamber hoped to obtain ...authorities, as they asked for an end to demands ...governor-general regarding the indemnities claimed ...their expulsion from the São Paulo captaincy.⁵ ...despite knowing that Salvador de Sá was involved ...dition to Luanda, the governor-general, the count ...ore victuals for Bahia.⁶ Under pressure to furnish ...Janeiro captaincy mutinied after Salvador de Sá's ...y. Claiming to have already contributed funds, ...aration of the armada that sailed out to Angola ...e meant to go to Bahia," the townsmen of Rio ...d tore up the governor-general's orders regarding ...x carts. They further demanded that no inquest ...y, and refused to pay the twentieth tax (*imposto* ...1648. These demands were met. To remedy the ..., where an additional 400 men recruited in the ...São Vicente wheat flour and Cananéia manioc ...uthern captaincies. A ship sailing from Lisbon to ...e cargo requisitioned by the chamber of Rio de ...stopover port.⁷ Rio de Janeiro officials traveled to ...for the infantry.⁸

The food intake of the city and of the troops stationed in Bahia was considerable. A document of 1653 records that the yearly volume of codfish imported into Brazil amounted to 607 tons, of which 42 percent was unloaded in Salvador.[9] The Count of Atouguia, the new governor general, sent an order to São Vicente's captain-major requesting food in 1654. Two years later, concerned with the "general famine" in Bahia, the governor-general asked for a shipment of 6,000 *alqueires* (nearly 100 tons) of Rio de Janeiro manioc flour.[10] Given the lack of Indian and African coerced labor, the authorities tried to correct the structural imbalance between the production of foodstuffs and export agricultural production. Like the prescription introduced by the Dutch in Pernambuco, the chambers of Bahia and Rio de Janeiro forced the mill owners to cultivate a certain proportion of manioc and determined that small farmers should dedicated themselves exclusively to this kind of crop.[12]

Appendix 3

The Salvador Correa de Sá e Benevides Family

Gonçalo Correa da Costa married Filipa de Sá, daughter of Martim Lourenço de Sá; they begat Salvador Correa de Sá. Gonçalo was later widowed and married Maria Rodrigues, with whom he had already fathered Martim Correa Vasqueanes and Duarte Correa Vasqueanes. Salvador Correa de Sá (the elder) came to Brazil, where he served under his uncle, governor Mem de Sá, who made him a general. He married Victoria da Costa and fathered, perhaps with a common-law wife punished for judaizing, both Martim Correa de Sá and Gonçalo Correa de Sá. Martim Correa de Sá, like his father a knight of the Order of Christ, married Maria Mendonça e Benevides, daughter of Manuel Benevides, a Castilian noble governor of Cadiz, and begat Salvador Correa de Sá e Benevides (the younger), who married Catherina de Ugarte y Velasco and fathered Martim Correa de Sá, João Correa de Sá, Salvador Correa de Sá (who was at the Lisbon See and died young), Sebastião de Sá, a Jesuit, and Teresa de Velasco, wife of Luís da Silva Telles (later a Saint Albert nun). With a "black maiden," he further begat Joana Correa de Sá e Benevides.

Martim Correa de Sá was the first viscount of Asseca, field-master in the Moura and Setubal *terços*. João Correa de Sá, after being a Rio de Janeiro field-master and serving in southern Brazil, then took command in the Persian Gulf, from whence he was sent into the kingdom in chains for having killed his wife and father-in-law, besides other atrocities. On arrival in Lisbon, by means of his father's slight-of-hand, João escaped the ship, slipping out disguised as a friar, and then made his way into Spain.

Gonçalo Correa de Sá, uncle of Salvador (the younger), married Esperança da Costa in the São Vicente captaincy, where he was a governor (1617), and fathered Victória de Sá, wife of Luís de Céspedes Xeri'a, governor of Paraguay. He was captain of the Guanabara fort of Santa Cruz at the height of Salvador de Sá's (the younger) might; he further had an illegitimate son, Artur de Sá, who served in

India, who also fathered another illegitimate son, Artur de Sá, captain of a Rio de Janeiro fortress.

Martim Correa Vasqueanes, second son of Gonçalo Correa da Costa, lived in Rio serving with Salvador Correa de Sá's (the elder) half-brother. He married Maria de Alvarenga, daughter of Tomé de Alvarenga, and begat Salvador Correa Vasqueanes, Tomé de Alvarenga, Martim Correa Vasqueanes, and Maria Correa, wife of Juan de Avalos y Benevides. This Martim Correa Vasqueanes succeeded his father in the household and served as field-master in Rio de Janeiro, the post he held when he died in combat during the French invasion of 1710. He fathered Tomé Correa Vasques, Salvador Correa de Sá, Manoel Correa Vasques, and Martim Correa de Sá. Duarte Correa Vasqueanes, third son of Gonçalo Correa da Costa, begat Martim Correa Vasqueanes and Salvador Correa Vasqueanes.[1]

Vasques or *Vasqueanes*? Manso de Lima recorded *Vasques*, contemporary documents wrote *Vasqueannes*, and Court documents record a third variant, *Vasques Anes*.[17] In fact, the family had three branches: Correa de Sá, Correa Vasques, and Correa Vasqueanes. I was unable to completely extricate these branches, whose imbrications perplex even lineage experts. Thus, Friar Jaboatão confuses Salvador Correa Vasqueanes with Salvador Correa de Sá e Benevides.[2]

Alão de Morais wrote that Salvador Correa de Sá e Benevides's maternal grandmother was Jewish. According to him, governor of Rio de Janeiro Pedro de Mello (1662–1666) furnished that piece of information.[3] Alão did not hesitate to include this piece of gossip current in Rio de Janeiro in his *Pedatura* (1667), thus demonstrating the decline of the political influence of Salvador de Sá in Lisbon. Here we see the political role played by genealogy, genealogists and the Inquistion in favor of the aristocracy, against the emerging groups of the Restoration.

Appendix 4

Notes on Some Portuguese and Brasilico Expeditionaries of the 1648 Task Force that Recaptured Angola

Antônio Machado was a veteran of Angola, Pernambuco, and Paraíba and later sergeant-major of Benguela. Valentim da Rosa was an ex-combatant in Pernambuco and in the Alentejo. Tomé Dias da Costa claimed long experience in the "live war of Brazil." Antônio Moniz Barreto was a member of the Bahian oligarchy who had served in Rio de Janeiro between 1641 and 1647 under the Sás and was later made captain of Massangano, in Angola. Tomás Fernandes de Mesquita was a captain of infantry in Angola who raised a company of expeditionaries in Rio de Janeiro "in consideration of the lack of people" in the transatlantic assault. Diogo Coelho de Albuquerque was a veteran of Pernambuco and a former captain-major of Ceará who had been captured by the Dutch and taken to Barbados. He was returned to Lisbon, embarked with Salvador, and played a decisive role in the battle of Luanda.

Diogo Monteiro da Fonseca had marched with Luís Barbalho's troops in the famous retreat from Rio Grande do Norte to Bahia. Francisco Fernandes de Aguiar, from Rio de Janeiro, was a captain-major of Angola and later made procurador of the Rio de Janeiro chamber. Alonso Castelhano had fought in the 1630s in Brazil and on the mainland in the battle of Montijo (1644), where he was alleged to have suffered "five mortal wounds, many kicks and [was] trampled on by the cavalry." Bento Bandeira de Mello was a former ensign in Bahia. Paiva Severim was a captain in Luanda and a former combatant in Paraíba and in the kingdom's navy. Belchior da Silva had already fought in Angola against Queen Njinga. João Duque had been captured in Brazil in the 1630s by the Dutch and later freed, fought in the Alentejo, and was nominated procurador of the Luanda chamber.

Álvaro de Aguilar Osório, who served in Rio de Janeiro from 1634 to 1638 with Salvador de Sá, and who later fought in the Alentejo, was an "unpaid" expeditionary who counted on collecting his reward in Luanda, where he would serve for many years as captain. Antônio Lito, after taking various posts in the Portuguese Atlantic, was later commander of the Luanda fortress of Santo Amaro. Francisco Gonçalves Ferraz (from Bahia) was sent with ships by Salvador de Sá to seize Mpinda (in the mouth of the Congo) and Benguela after the Dutch surrender in Luanda, and later went to Lisbon, from whence he took governor Rodrigo de Miranda Henriques to Luanda (1652). He then sailed to Bahia "loaded with slaves."

Sergeant José Correia Ximenes was made a clerk in Luanda and later nominated notary in Rio de Janeiro. Tomas Filgueira Bultão, a former combatant in Pernambuco, was Salvador's trusted man in the Rio de Janeiro captaincy, treasurer of the expedition, and future Luandan potentate.[1] Antônio Castro de Sousa appeared as a royal clerk and later as magistrate and field-master in Angola; Francisco Fernandes Furnas was the entrepreneur of the two slave-trade operations between Brazil and Mozambique in the years 1643–1644 and future business partner of the Companhia Geral de Comércio. He was captain of a ship he had himself fitted to join the journey to Angola. Gaspar Lopes de Figueiredo was a Rio de Janeiro "resident and wealthy" man who had raised "at his own expense" an infantry company to fight in Angola. Manuel de Souza da Silva served in frontier posts in Brazil and was future captain-major of the captaincies of São Vicente and São Paulo. Gaspar Rubim fitted in Rio de Janeiro two ships "at his own expense" for the expedition to Angola. Manuel Corrêa de Sá, and Manuel and Álvaro Corrêa Vasqueannes, close relatives of the governor, were members of the Sá oligarchy. Salvador Corrêa Vasqueannes, the governor's nephew, was captain of a Rio de Janeiro cavalry company, official of the Alentejo, expeditionary, and sergeant-major of restored Angola.[2]

The physician-expeditionaries must not be forgotten. Bernardo Pinto was later nominated in Benguela, and João Pinto de Barros, experienced in war medicine in the Pernambuco war and in the care of Rio de Janeiro troops, was made surgeon-major of the expedition. As secretary-general of the government, Salvador chose João Antônio Correia, former holder of the same post in Rio de Janeiro.[3]

Appendix 5

1600s Portuguese Atlantic Hand Firearms

Different types of handguns were used in the Portuguese Atlantic in the 1600s. These included the wide-muzzled harquebus; the musket, a narrow-muzzled weapon of longer range, and more precise than the harquebus, but weighing around 11 kg and therefore requiring the support of a fork; the caliver (*espingarda* and *clavina*), narrow-muzzled like the musket, but with a shorter barrel and a lighter and shorter grip so it did not require a fork; the *escopeta*, with a short barrel, used to fire at close range; and the pistol. Alongside the matchlock, the wheel-lock or *roldete* began to be used in Europe between the second and the third decades of the sixteenth century, usually in cavalry pistols. Given its ease of handling, the wheel-lock pistols and *escopetas* began to be employed by the dragoons, a mounted infantry force that fought the cavalry's lancers. Like the pistol, the wheel-lock musket detonates the charge by means of a mechanism similar to a cigarette lighter—a striated little wheel driven by a wind-up mechanism turns as the trigger is pulled, striking a spark off the iron pyrite.[1] Expensive, well-worked wheel-lock muskets, generally used as hunting weapons, turned out to be ostentation goods. On his arrival at Yamaguchi, in 1551, the Jesuit missionary Francis Xavier offered to the *daimyo*, among others gifts, a "rich" triple barrel wheel-lock gun.[2] *Fusil*, an old French word used in the sixteenth century to define a type of lighter, came to designate this weapon throughout the Western world, except in Portugal and in the Lusitanian overseas, where it was named *espingarda* (from Provençal *espingala*), the name for an obsolete type of ballista.[3]

In the course of the seventeenth century, regular regiments of harquebusiers and musketeers continued to carry matchlocks, featuring a fuse and resting on forks. The musketeer and harquebusier were trained to light the fuse, place the musket on the fork, and shoot in a single sequence.[4] In the theater of the 1600s European wars, musketeers were always protected by a body of soldiers armed with pikes, responsible for stopping the enemy's cavalry charge.[5] At the end of the seventeenth century, the introduction of the bayonet solved the problem of the firearm/blade combination.[6] But until that time, seeking to keep the uniformity of the troop's firearms, European military chiefs opted for the matchlock musket, which was reputed to be safer in regular infantry combat. This was precisely the motive that led Louvois, Louis XIV's war minister, to impose matchlock muskets in the 1670s, ordering that the wheel-locks carried by French soldiers in war to be broken. Later, changing his mind, Louvois had his French soldiers wield the flintlock (1688).[7] In Portugal, the wheel-lock came to be used as a weapon for self-defense, and its possession was banned under the argument that it favored assassinations. In 1613, the Crown authorized the kingdom's magistrates (*oficiais de justiça*) alone to bear flintlocks.[8] But the governor of Algarve obtained a royal license for his subjects to bear flintlocks, for it was a zone often harassed by Maghreb corsairs.[9] Recognizing the difficulty of banning flintlock pistols and *espingardas*, as they were being used "by every malefactor," the Crown in 1626 extended permission to those already licensed to bear the matchlock harquebus.[10] Yet, the count of Sarzedas, vice-kingdom of the Estado do Índia, forbade in 1655 the use of flintlock arms both "short and long" due to the crimes committed with such guns.[11]

Around that time, percussion handguns were already in circulation. These featured a hammer holding a flint stone, which produced sparks as it hit the steel frizzen above the gunpowder pan. Cheaper than the previous models featuring the wheel-lock, this kind of gun was disseminated in the second half of the seventeenth century. Various museums, and in particular Geneva's Musée d'Art et d'Histoire, display firearms presented in a sequence that perfectly explains the technical evolution of Western handguns.

The adoption of the wheel-lock and percussion firearms seems to have been more prompt in Portuguese areas overseas, notwithstanding the fact that this shift was only generalized among European troops and in the North American colonies from the last quarter of the seventeenth century.[12] There were reports of *espingardas* in the hands of São Tomé colonists since 1554. In Angola, Jesuit Balthazar Afonso asked for a reinforcement of *espingardas* for the troops who were coming in aid of Paulo Dias Novais in 1585, and in 1592, he requested more than 1,000 *espingardas*, but those with a long barrel, "because if they are shorter one cannot hunt down the enemy."[13] The use of this weapon became more frequent around the Portuguese enclaves in Africa. In the second decade of the seventeenth century, Captain Diogo Simões Madeira, deep in the Zambezian outback, faced a native contingent wielding 150 flintlock muskets and *espingardas* bought from Portuguese traders.¹⁴ After the Braganza Restoration, mixed with numerous handguns bought in Europe or gathered from the military spoils in Pernambuco and the Alentejo (Portugal), a quantity of muskets, *espingardas, escopetas*, and flintlock pistols entered Portugal and Brazil.¹⁵ In the battle of Tabocas, in Pernambuco (August 1645), the Dutch were beaten by a Brasilic troop of 800, of whom 130 bore flintlock (*de fecho*) handguns, which Friar Manuel Calado distinguishes from the wheel-lock.¹⁶ Portuguese gunsmiths also made *espingardas*. A 1675 royal letter ordered the master-of-arms of Portalegre (Alentejo) to make 100 *espingardas* with long barrels, to be sent to Angola. The instruction met the request the governor of Angola, Aires de Saldanha, who considered the *espingarda* "of much better service than muskets."¹⁷

At the time, the Rio de Janeiro chamber, where residents and mill owners stated that they were often attacked by "runaway blacks," obtained in 1679 a royal license to bear flintlock firearms "because they are of quicker use in any situation."¹⁸ The particular context of the slaving colony was considered, since the prohibition remained in force in the kingdom. At the turn of the century, the possession of flintlock *espingardas* was authorized to the kingdom's auxiliary soldiers, "but for use in service alone."¹⁹ Improved, the flintlock *fusil* would be used in European armies up to the mid-eighteenth century. Modern flintlock hunting *espingardas* would be sold in Goiás (Brazil), in Quebec, and in other parts of the world up to the 1950s.²⁰

Based on statistics on an 1894 battle with French colonial troops in Burkina Faso, two historians of Africa observed that the number of casualties inflicted by lances and arrows was higher than the number wounded or killed by firearms, even when the natives were well stocked with *espingardas*.²¹ Sérgio Buarque had already noted the low impact of firearms in the wars against Amerindians, at least until the end of the seventeenth century. Geoffrey Parker also minimizes the effects of manual firearms in the African colonial wars before the introduction of the machine gun.²²

However, such arguments must be studied further. In a clearing or in an open field in America and in Africa, the *espingarda* volleys broke enemy attack lines, even if they caused relatively few casualties. In the battle of Bambi (1622), in which the duke of Bamba and the marquis of Pemba died, both tributaries of the king of Congo, the victory obtained by the Portuguese and allied Jaga was due to *espingardeiros* placed at the rear. In Mbwila (1665), it was also an *espingarda* shot that killed King Mani Mulaza, triggering the Congolese defeat. African and American natives made use of firearms against European, Angolista, and Brasílico predators.

The Jaga who destroyed Domingos Lopes Sequeira's column, arriving from Bahia in aid of Angola's settlers (1645), relied not only on their hatchets (their "chief weapon"), but also on firearms purchased from Portuguese arms dealers, shooting copper bullets smelted by native blacksmiths.[23] In 1600s Brazil, Amerindian tribes also wielded firearms. Since the 1670s, the Palmaristas employed firearms against the colonists' raids. In the Bahian hinterland, Domingos Jorge Velho's Indian *espingardeiros* and archers faced the Tapuia, who shot firearms exchanged with or stolen from settlers (1691); two years later, in the region of Açu, Apodi, and Mossoró, in Rio Grande do Norte, the Paulistas faced Jandui Amerindians armed with *espingardas*.[24]

During the whole of the modern era, the reestablishment of peace in Europe generated a cyclic increase in the supply of weapons in the overseas territories. Ultimately, the increasing import of firearms into sub-Saharan Africa demonstrates their importance in internal African conflicts and in the intensification of the slave trade. In Western Africa alone (Upper Guinea and Guinea Gulf), 200,000 muskets were imported every year in the eighteenth century.[25]

NOTES

Author's Preface to the American Edition

1. William Herbert, *A New Map, or Chart in Mercator's Projection of the Ethiopic Ocean with Part of Africa and South America*, London, 1763; A. G. Findlay, *A Sailing Directory for the Ethiopic or South Atlantic Ocean, Including the Coasts of South America and Africa* (London: 1867), 1–2; George Ripley and Charles A. Dana, *The American Cyclopaedia: A Popular Dictionary of General Knowledge*, vol. 2 (New York: 1873), 69; L. F. de Alencastro, "The Ethiopic Ocean—History and Historiography, 1600–1975," *Portuguese Literary & Cultural Studies* 27 (2015): 1–79.

Chapter 1

1. For an earlier version of this chapter, see Barbara L. Solow, ed., *Slavery and the Rise of the Atlantic System* (Cambridge, UK: Cambridge UP, 1993), 151–176; reprinted in P. Manning, ed., *Slave Trades, 1500–1800: Globalization of Forced Labor* (Aldershot, UK: Variorum, 1996).

2. Letter to the "Cardinal Protector" of Portugal, Jorge da Costa, Lisbon, August 25, 1499, A. da Silva Rego, *DHMPPO*, vol. 1 (Lisbon: 1947), 6–11. C. Boxer commented on King Manuel's letter in his magisterial *The Portuguese Seaborne Empire 1415–1825*, 37.

3. C. S. Assadourian, "Fray Bartolomé de Las Casas obispo: la naturaleza miserable de las naciones indianas y el derecho de la Iglesia. Un escrito de 1545," *Historia Mexicana* vol. 40, no. 3 (1991), 387–451, 414.

4. M. Bataillon, *Études sur Bartolomé de Las Casas* (Paris, 1965), 171–179.

5. A. Milhou, "Sufficientia. Les notions d'autosuffisance e de dépendance dans la pensée politique espagnole au xvie siècle: de la Castille des comuneros au Pérou colonial," *Mélanges de la Casa de Velazquez* vol. 17, 106–145; "Las Casas, Prophétisme et Millénarisme," *Etudes*, vol. 376, no. 3 (1992–1993), 393–404.

6. M. Bataillon, "La rébellion pizarriste, enfantement de l'Amérique espagnole," *Diogène* 43 (1963), 59.

7. It is known that around 1570 there was a "brutal and massive" entry of Peruvian silver from Potosí into the Spanish monetary circuit. See E. Le Roy Ladurie, J-N. Barrandon,

B. Collin, M. Guerra, and C. Morrisson, "Sur les traces de l'argent du Potosí," *Annales E.S.C.* 45, no. 2 (1990), 483–505. See also Huguette and Pierre Chaunu, *Séville et l'Atlantique, 1504–1650*, vol. 8, book 2, part 1, 255–352.

8. Serge Gruzinski, *Les quatre parties du monde—Histoire d'une mondialisation* (Paris: 2004), 24–25. In the same vein, the Elizabethan politics in the Americas was somehow inhibited by the absence of evangelizing projects or prospects for economic gains. David Armitage, "The Elizabethan Idea of Empire," *Transactions of the Royal Historical Society*, 14 (2004), 269–277.

9. C. Couto, "Documentos para a história da sucessão de Paulo Dias Novais na doação da capitania de Angola," *Estudos Históricos* 15 (1976), 133–185; Antônio Brásio, *Monumenta Missionária Africana*.Series 1 (West Central Africa), 15 vols. (Lisbon, 1952–1988), hereafter *MMA¹*; Series 2 (West Africa), 7 vols. (Lisbon, 1958–2004), hereafter *MMA²*. Act of Paulo Dias Novais donating the territory between the Lucala and the Zenza Rivers to the Jesuit Superior in Angola, Father Balthazar Barreira, Luanda, 26 August 26, 1581, *MMA¹*, vol. 15, 265–266.

10. *MMA¹*, vol. 3, 36–51; ibid., vol. 4, 276–277; R. Delgado, *História de Angola*, vol. 1, 258–262.

11. S. de Morales to C. Acquaviva, Lisbon, December 13, 1586, *MMA¹*, vol. 15, 304–305. For the establishment of the Jesuit's Province of Brazil, see A. Franco, "Vida do padre Manuel da Nóbrega," in M. da Nóbrega, *Cartas Jesuiticas 1: Cartas Do Brasil (1549–1560)*, 21–69, and 40.

12. B. Heintze, "Die portugiesische Besiedlungs-und Wirtschaftspolitik in Angola 1570–1607," *Aufsitze zur portugiesischen Kulturgeschichte* 17 (1979), 200–219; idem, "Luso-African Feudalism in Angola? The Vassal Treaties of the 16th to the 18th Century," *Revista Portuguesa de História* (*RPH*) 18 (1980), 111–131. The conflict between the Jesuits and the colonial authorities regarding the control of the *sobados* started at the end of Novais governorship, as stated in a letter to Acquaviva, the Jesuit's Superior General. "Carta do padre Sebastião de Morales ao Geral da Companhia," Lisbon, August 15, 1587, *MMA¹*, vol. 15, 314–315.

13. "Requerimento do padre Baltasar Barreira," Luanda, September 15, 1592, *MMA¹*, vol. 15, 323–327.

14. *MMA¹*, vol. 3, 476; vol. 4, 553–554; vol. 15, 384n1; S. Leite, *História da Companhia de Jesus no Brasil, 1549–1760* (hereafter *HCJB*), vol. 2, 496n1.

15. *MMA¹*, vol. 3, 466; "Parecer de Jerônimo de Almeida," Luanda, June 10, 1593, *MMA¹*, vol. 15, 339–340.

16. *MMA¹*, vol. 15, 328–330. Underplaying or hiding the seriousness of the rebellion, seventeenth-century Jesuit chronicler Balthazar Telles, followed by some twentieth-century authors, wrote that Felipe II had called Barreira because he admired the priest's knowledge on African matters. Thus, the Jesuit would have been received in Madrid as "an angel sent

from Heaven." See Balthazar Telles, *Chronica da Companhia de Jesu nos reinos de Portugal* (Lisbon: 1645–1647), vol. 2, 627–630.

17. F. Guerreiro, *Relação anual das coisas que fizeram os padres da Companhia de Jesus nas suas missões* (Coimbra: 1930–1932), book 1, 395; *MMA¹*, vol. 5, 50–57.

18. "*Regimento*" of governor Forjaz, March 26, 1607, *MMA¹*, vol. 5, 264–279.

19. In sixteenth- and seventeenth-century Spain, the *Asiento* configured a contract between the Crown and an individual or company, according to which the monarchy conceded to the contractor—the *asentista*—certain privileges, usually in the form of a semimonopoly. It also meant a contract between the king and a merchant-banker, where the latter forwarded to the former a certain sum in credit or currency to be delivered in a particular city, against the commitment of the monarch to pay the amount borrowed plus interest, etc. I use here the word *Asiento* exclusively to refer to the *Asiento de Negros*; that is, the royal contracts to the supply of enslaved Africans to Spanish America, "*Asientos.*" See G. Bleiberg, *Diccionario de historia de España*, vol. 1, 394–395; Andrea Weindl, "The Asiento de Negros and International Law," *Journal of the History of International Law* 10 (2008), 229–257. Overlooking the role of Lisbon's enclaves in West Africa and Angola, the latter author does not incorporate the full dimension of the Portuguese *Asientos*; see pp. 233–235.

20. J. de Barros, "Ásia, Primeira Década," in *Da Ásia de João de Barros e de Diogo do Couto*, Lisboa, [1552] 1777–1788, vol. 2, 25–27. Geographer, historian, and grammarian de Barros was also captain of the São Jorge da Mina (Elmina) fortress, would-be donatary of Brazilian captaincies, and the treasurer of the Casa da India e da Mina.

21. A. Ravichander, "Coastal Society of Gujarat in the Sixteenth Century," *Studia* 49 (1989), 161–180; S. Sanjay Subrahmanyam, *The Political Economy of Commerce: Southern India, 1500–1650*, 91–143.

22. O. Prakash, *European Commercial Enterprise in Pre-Colonial India* (London: 1998), 57–60; P. Malekandathil, *Maritime India: Trade, Religion, and Polity in the Indian Ocean* (Delhi: 2010), 62–76.

23. V. Magalhães Godinho, *Os descobrimentos e a economia mundial*, vol. 1 (Lisbon: 1981–1983), 183–208, and vol. 2, 183–223.

24. F. Mendes Pinto, *Peregrinação*, vol. 3 (Lisbon: [1614] 1967), 106.

25. The Asian trading conducted by "casados" was the most dynamic sector of the Portuguese *Estado da Índia*. See J. C. Boyajian, *Portuguese Trade in Asia Under the Habsburgs, 1580–1640* (Baltimore: Johns Hopkins UP, 1993), 52–85.

26. Royal decrees (Alvarás) of February 16, 1596, and November 20, 1596, banning New Christians from holding positions in the royal military, law, and treasure services of fortresses in India, *BNL*, cod. 2298, fs. 36 and 39; C. R. Boxer, *Portuguese Society in the Tropics: The Municipal Councils of Goa, Macao, Bahia, and Luanda, 1510–1800* (Madison: University of Wisconsin P, 1950), 12–41.

27. F. de Sousa, *Oriente conquistado a Jesus Cristo pelos padres da Companhia de Jesus da província de Goa* vol. 1 (Porto: [1710] 1978), 134–135; R. O. W. Goertz, "The Portuguese in Cochin in the Mid-Sixteenth Century," *Studia* 49 (1989), 5–38; inquisitorial activities and persecution of new Christians in Cochin had already started in 1553, see Pius Malekandathil, *Portuguese Cochin and the Maritime Trade of India, 1500–1663* (PhD thesis, Pondicherry University, 1998), 166–170, 189, 289.

28. D. do Couto, *O soldado prático* [1593–1610] (Lisbon: 1980), preface and notes by M. Rodrigues Lapa, 129.

29. Royal grant of the indigo monopoly in 1587; see S. Subrahmanyam, *The Portuguese Empire in Asia, 1500–1700, A Political and Economic History* (London: 1993), 224–248; C. R. Boxer, *A Índia portuguesa em meados do século XVII* (Lisbon: 1982), 26–31.

30. F. Guerreiro, *Relação anual*, 389–390; K. S. Mathew, "India Merchants and the Portuguese Trade on the Malabar Coast During the Sixteenth Century," in *Indo-Portuguese History—Old Issues, New Questions*, T. R. de Souza, ed. (New Delhi: 1985), 1–12.

31. M. N. Pearson, "The People and Politics of Portuguese India during the Sixteenth and Early Seventeenth Centuries," in *Essays Concerning the Socioeconomic History of Brazil and Portuguese India*, D. Alden and W. Dean, eds. (Gainesville: The University Presses of Florida, 1977), 1–25, 16–17, and 23.

32. D. Couto, "Algumas notas sobre a questão dos colaboradores dos Portugueses no Estado da Índia (séculos XVI e XVII)" in Nicolas Balutet, ed., *Contrabandista entre mundos fronterizos* (Paris: 2010), 265–284.

33. K. S. Mathew, *Indo-Portuguese Trade and the Fuggers of Germany* (New Delhi: Manohar, 1997), 10–14, and 167–168; F. Trivellato "Juifs de Livourne, Italiens de Lisbonne, hindous de Goa," *Annales: Histoire, Sciences, Sociales* 58, no. 3, 2003, 581–603.

34. E. van Veen, *Decay or Defeat? An Inquiry Into the Portuguese Decline in Asia, 1580–1645* (Leiden, 2000), 109–123; R. J. Barendse, *The Arabian Seas: The Indian Ocean World of the Seventeenth Century (Asia and the Pacific)* (London: 2002), 311–318.

35. F. de Carvalho, *Diogo do Couto, O soldado prático* (Lisbon: 1979), 30 and 54.

36. V. Magalhães Godinho, *Os descobrimentos e a economia mundial*, vol. 3, 81–134, chiefly 133–134; de Carvalho, *Diogo do Couto*, 95–103.

37. A. Teodoro de Matos, *O Orçamento do Estado da Índia, 1571* (Lisbon: 1999), 15–17.

38. T. D. Boston, "On the Transition to Feudalism in Mozambique," *Journal of African Studies* 8, no. 4 (1981), 182–187; A. Lobato, *Colonização senhorial da Zambézia e outros estudos* (Lisbon: 1962), 80–81.

39. F. Hoppe, *A África Oriental portuguesa no tempo do marquês de Pombal* (Lisbon: 1970), 40; A. Lobato, *Evolução administrativa e econômica de Moçambique 1752–1763*, 231; M. Newitt, *Portuguese Settlement on the Zambesi: Exploration, Land Tenure, and Colonial Rule in East Africa* (London and New York: 1973), 181–182.

40. J. A. Orta, "L'empire Monomotapa, Etat et Pouvoir dans une société étatique traditionnelle africaine," *Africana* 23 (2001), 32–63.

41. A. Guerreiro, "Inquérito em Moçambique no ano de 1573," *Studia* 6 (1960), 7–18; 6, 1960, 7–18; decree of 1569, *MMA¹*, vol. 2, 551–557.

42. On the Massapa's fair, see Innocent Pikirayi, "Palaces, Feiras, and Prazos: An Historical Archaeological Perspective of African-Portuguese Contact in Northern Zimbabwe," *The African Archaeological Review* 26, no. 3 (2009), 163–185.

43. João dos Santos, *Ethiopia Oriental*, 54–55. A Dominican missionary, João dos Santos, lived in Sofala, Tete, and others parts of today's Mozambique between 1586 and 1600. A more recent edition of the book, with an introduction by Manuel Lobato, was published in 1999 in Paris.

44. See Lobato, *Evolução administrativa e econômica de Moçambique 1752–1763* (Lisbon: 1957), 153; A. F. Isaacman and B. Isaacman, "The Prazero as a Transfrontiersman," *International Journal of African Historical Studies* 8, no. 1 (1975), 1–39; M. Newitt, "The Early History of the Marawi," *J. Afr. H.* 23 (1982), 145–162.

45. "Viagem que fez o Pe. Ant. Gomes, da Companhia de Jesus, ao império de Manomotapa [1648]," *Studia* 3 (1959), 155–242, and 239.

46. E. Alpers, *Ivory and Slaves in East Central Africa* (London: 1975); C. A. Hromnik, "Canarins in the Rios de Cuama, 1501–1576," *Journal of African Studies* 6, no. 1 (1979), 27–37; H. Gerbeau, "La traite esclavagiste dans l'Océan Indien," *La traite négrière du XVe au XIXe siècle* (Paris: 1979), 194–217; J. J. Sinclair, "Archeology in Eastern Africa: An Overview of Current Chronological Issues," *J. Afr. H.* 32, no. 2 (1991), 179–220; C. M. Kusimba, "Archaeology of Slavery in East Africa," *The African Archaeological Review* 21, no. 2 (2004), 59–88.

47. J. Capela, *O Tráfico de Escravos nos Portos de Moçambique, 1733–1904* (Lisbon: 2002), 138–141; L. F. Dias Antunes, "O comércio com o Brasil e a comunidade mercantil em Moçambique (séc. XVIII)," *Actas do Congresso Internacional Atlântico de Antigo Regime: poderes e sociedades* (Lisbon: Universidade Nova de Lisboa, 2005), 1–9.

48. M. Vink, "'The World's Oldest Trade': Dutch Slavery and Slave Trade in the Indian Ocean in the Seventeenth Century," *Journal of World History* 14, no. 2 (2003), 131–177, here 158–159; Abdul Sheriff, *Slaves, Spices, and Ivory in Zanzibar: Integration of an East African Commercial Empire into the World Economy, 1770–1873* (Athens, OH: Ohio UP, 1987), 33–76; F. Cooper, *Plantation Slavery on the East Coast of Africa* (New Haven, CT: 1977), 38–46.

49. R. Austen, "From the Atlantic to the Indian Ocean: European Abolition, the African Slave Trade, and Asian Economic Structures," in *The Abolition of the Atlantic Slave Trade: Origins and Effects in Europe, Africa, and the Americas*, D. Eltis and J. Walvin, eds. (Madison: University of Wisconsin P, 1981), 117–126. Of a total of 277,205 enslaved Africans

from Southeast Africa who disembarked into Brazilian ports from 1550 to 1850, 262,513 (94.7 percent) arrived between 1801 and 1850. Transatlantic Slave Trade Database (hereafter TSTD) online, accessed in December 2015.

50. From 1550 to 1850, 4,864,000 enslaved Africans disembarked in Brazil, of which around 3,396,000 (70 percent) came from West Central Africa, chiefly from Angola. TSTD, accessed in December 2015.

51. Godinho, *Os descobrimentos*, 183–209; W. G. L. Randles, *L'Empire du Muenemutapa du XVe au XIXe siècle* (Paris: La Haye, 1975), 41–48. After the loss of Muscat (1650) and Ceylon (1656), the Portuguese became more dependent on trade between Mozambique and India. See M. Lobato, "Relações comerciais entre a Índia e a Costa Africana nos séculos XVI and XVII: O papel do Guzerate no comércio de Moçambique," *Mare Liberum* 9 (1995), 157–73; C. R. Boxer, "Sailing Orders for the Portuguese East-Indiamen of 1640 and 1646," *Terrae Incognitae* 12 (1980), 37–48.

52. S. X. Botelho, *Memórias estatísticas sobre os domínios portuguezes na África Oriental* (Lisbon, 1835), 264–271; Hoppe, *A África*, 46; Malyn Newitt, "The Portuguese on the Zambezi: An Historical Interpretation of the Prazo System," *J. Afr. H.* 10 (1969), 67–85; M. Newitt, *A History of Mozambique* (Bloomington: Indiana UP, 1995) 225–228; A. F. Isaacman, *Mozambique: The Africanization of a European Institution: The Zambezi Prazos, 1750–1902* (Madison: University of Wisconsin P, 1972), 172.

53. A. da Conceição, "Tratado dos Rios de Cuama" *O Chronista de Tissuary* 2, no. 15 ([1696] 1867), 39–45, 43, 63–69, 84–92, and 105–111. For Portuguese text and an English translation, see Antonio da Conceição, *Treatise on the Rivers of Cuama* M. Newitt, ed. and trans. (Oxford, UK: Oxford UP/British Academy, 2009), 14–15.

54. The mandatory marriage between *donas de prazos* and Portuguese-born *reinóis* was established by a royal order of 1675. See M. Newitt, *Portuguese Settlement on the Zambezi: Exploration, Land Tenure, and Colonial Rule in East Africa* (New York: 1973), 65–69, 102; The Lei Mental of 1434 excluded the female line of succession in the inheritance of property or concessions granted by the Crown. See J. Serrão et al., *Dicionário de história de Portugal* (*DHP*), vol. 3 (Lisbon: 1975), 29–30. On the practice of this clause in Minho province, see M. Durães, "Herdeiros e não herdeiros: Nupcialidade e celibato no contexto da propriedade enfiteuta," *Revista de História Económica e Social* (*RHES*) 2 (1987), 47–56.

55. A. Lobato, *Evolução administrative e econômica de Moçambique, 1752–1763* (Lisbon: 1957), 216–218; M. Newitt, *Portuguese Settlement on the Zambezi*, 97–102; A. Lobato, G. Papagno, and Allen and Barbara Isaacman provide a different explanation for the "Crown *prazos*" feminine succession. For Lobato, it is assistance to widows and orphans of the court. See Lobato, *Colonização senhorial*, 103. Papagno considers it only as a decision meant to favor the populating of Mozambique. See G. Papagno, *Colonialismo e feudalesimo: La questione dei prazos da Coroa nel Mozambico alla fine del secolo XIX* (Torino: 1972), 39. Allen and Barbara Isaacman do not attach particular importance to the clause of female

succession. See A. F. Isaacman and B. Isaacman, "The Prazeros as Transfrontiersman: A Study in Social and Cultural Change," *The International Journal of African Historical Studies* 8, no. 1 (1975), 1–39.

56. In the middle of the twentieth century, when A. Lobato published his book, the Portuguese colonial writers distinguished *cafrealização*, the "social leakage" of whites into African families and communities, and *mestiçagem*, where individuals of mixed descent remained in the colonial network. See "Conclusion" below.

57. E. Rodrigues, "Chiponda, a 'senhora que tudo pisa com os pés': estratégias de poder das donas dos prazos do Zambeze no século XVIII," *Anais de História de Além-Mar* 1 (2000), 101–131.

58. Newitt, *Portuguese*, 87–88 and 145.

59. Rodrigues, "Chiponda," 114–131.

60. Lobato, *Evolução*, 228–233.

61. E. Rodrigues, "'Em Nome do Rei': O levantamento dos Rios de Sena de 1763," *Anais de História de Além-Mar* 4 (2003), 335–380.

62. Santos, *Ethiopia*, 54–55; D. Chanaiwa, "Politics and Long-Distance Trade in the Mwene Mutapa Empire During the Sixteenth Century," *International Journal of African Historical Studies* 5, no. 3 (1972), 424–435.

63. Santos, ibid.; M. Newitt, *A History of Mozambique* (Johannesburg: Wits UP, 1995), 95–97.

64. J. de Oliveira Boleo, "Vicissitudes históricas da política de exploração mineira no império de Muenemutapa," *Studia* 32 (1971), 167–209, 207; F. J. de Lacerda e Almeida, "Diário da viagem de Moçambique para os rios de Sena, 1797–1798," *Diários de viagem* (Rio de Janeiro: 1944), 127–174, 171. On Lacerda e Almeida, see Magnus Roberto de Mello Pereira, "Brasileiros a serviço do Império; a África vista por naturais do Brasil, no século XVIII," *Revista Portuguesa de História* 33 (1999), 153–190.

65. J. J. Lopes de Lima and F. Bordalo, *Ensaios sobre a statística das possessões portuguezas*, vol. 4 (Lisbon: 1844–1862), 245.

66. Papagno, *Colonialismo*, 141–174.

67. J. Capistrano de Abreu, *O descobrimento do Brasil* (Rio de Janeiro: 1976), 75–78; H. B. Johnson, "The Portuguese Settlement of Brazil, 1500–1580," in L. Bethell, ed., *The Cambridge History of Latin America* (*CHLA*), vol. 1 (Cambridge, UK: Cambridge UP, 1984), 263–267.

68. F. A. Dutra, "Centralization vs. Donatorial Privilege: Pernambuco, 1602–1630," in D. Alden, ed., *Colonial Roots of Modern Brazil: Papers of the Newberry Library Conference* (Berkeley: U of California P, 1973), 19–60.

69. The *Estado do Maranhão*, whose establishment was decided by the Crown in 1621 and made effective in 1624, was later called *Estado do Grão-Pará e Maranhão*. In 1652, Maranhão and Pará had separate governments, but were again united in 1655. In 1752,

the two captaincies were integrated to the *Estado do Brasil*. From 1811 on, Maranhão and Pará once again had a government distinct from the vice-kingdom of Brazil whose capital was Bahia, and from 1763 on, Rio de Janeiro. Yet in 1811, Maranhão again had a separate government from Rio de Janeiro.

70. S. E. da Sylveira, "Relação sumária das cousas do Maranhão dirigida aos pobres deste reyno de Portugal," *ABNRJ* 94 ([1624] 1974), 43.

71. J. Penn, *The South American Pilot*, Part 1, *The East Coast of South America from Cape St. Roque to Cape San Antonio, Rio de la Plata; and the North Coast from Cape St. Roque to the Rio Maroni in French Guyana* (London: 1864), 1–14. Disregarding the nautical analysis that led to the creation of the *Estado do Maranhão* in 1621, and Portuguese documents and historiography, many authors attribute to Isaac Vossius the discovery of the North Brazil or Guyana current in 1663; see R. G. Peterson, L. Stramma, and G. Kortum, "Early Concepts and Charts of Ocean Circulation," *Progress in Oceanography* 37, no. 1 (1996), 1–115, and Barbie Bischof, Elizabeth Rowe, Arthur J. Mariano, and Edward H. Ryan, "The Brazil Current," *Ocean Surface Currents* (2004). http://oceancurrents.rsmas.miami.edu/atlantic/brazil.html.

72. *MMA[1]*, vol. 13, 435–437.

73. Noting that the chroniclers of the sixteenth century write a segmented description of Brazil, Sérgio Buarque de Holanda, like Capistrano de Abreu before him, says that Friar Vicente do Salvador in his *História do Brasil* [1627] (São Paulo: 1982) displayed a fragmented view of Brazil: "[A]fter all his book [. . .] is more a kind of Histories of Brazil than a History of Brazil." The question of the two great historians should be reversed: Why would a seventeenth-century author, while the *Estado da Índia*—the constellation of trading posts and enclaves linking Mozambique to Macau—was the core of the Portuguese overseas, think about the unity of some coastal enclaves of South America that would become Brazil? How does one write a history of Brazil if Brazil is not yet Brazil? See S. Buarque de Holanda, *Visão do Paraíso*, 5th ed. (São Paulo: 1994), 315.

74. F. A. de Varnhagen, *História geral do Brasil* (*HGB*), vol. 1, book 1, 150; C. Verlinden, "Formes féodales et domainiales de la colonisation portugaise dans la Zone Atlantique aux XIVe et XVe siècles et spécialement sous Henri le Navigateur," *RPH* 9 (1960), 1–44; A. Wiznitzer, *Jews in Colonial Brazil* (New York: 1960), 6; C. Furtado, *L'Amérique Latine* (Paris: 1970), 10; H. B. Johnson, "The Donatary Captaincy in Historical Perspective: Portuguese Backgrounds to the Settlement of Brazil," *HAHR* 52 (1972), 203–214.

75. B. W. Diffie, "The Legal Privileges of the Foreigners in Portugal and Sixteenth-Century Brazil," in H. H. Keith and S. F. Edwards, eds., *Conflict and Continuity in Brazilian Society* (Columbia: U of South Carolina P, 1969), 1–19; Susan C. Schneider, "Commentary," in H. H. Keith and S. F. Edwards, eds., *Conflict and Continuity in Brazilian Society* (Colúmbia: n.d.), 20–23; J. Lang, *Portuguese Brazil: The King's Plantation* (Cambridge: Academic Press, 2013), 86–87.

76. E. Prestage, *A embaixada de Tristão de Mendonça Furtado à Holanda em 1641* (Coimbra: 1920), 11.

77. Stuart B. Schwartz, "Luso-Spanish Relations in Hapsburg Brazil, 1580–1640," *The A* 25, no. 1 (1968), 33–48, 45–48. On the contemporaneous debate on the political feud between the two countries, see Jean-Frédéric Schaub, *Le Portugal au temps du comte-duc d'Olivares, 1621–1640* (Madrid: 2001), 90–122. On the Spanish naval setbacks and the crisis of the Habsburg domination in Brazil, see Rafael Valladares Ramirez, "Las dos guerras de Pernambuco. La armada del conde da Torre y la crisis del Portugal hispánico, 1638–1641," in J. M. Santos Perez and G. F.Cabral de Souza, eds., *El desafío holandés al dominio ibérico en Brasil en el siglo XVII* (Salamanca: 2006), 33–66.

78. Royal letter of March 18, 1605, J. J. de Andrade e Silva, *Collecção chronologica da legislação portuguesa, 1603–1701*, vol. 1 (Lisbon, 1854–1859), hereafter CCLP, 108–109. Some Dutch merchants remained in Brazil and illegal trade to northwestern European ports continued after 1605; see Christopher Ebert, *Between Empires: Brazilian Sugar in the Early Atlantic Economy, 1550–1630* (Leiden: 2008), 47–52, 78–83, and 167–168.

79. *MMA¹*, vol. 1, 414, vol. 3, 192–196, and vol. 4, 62–66.

80. On the concept of the "purpose of colonization" ("sentido da colonização"), see C. Prado, Jr., *Formação do Brasil contemporâneo* (São Paulo: 1971), 19 and 31; F. A. Novais, "Caio Prado Jr. na historiografia brasileira," in R. Moraes et al., *Inteligência brasileira* (São Paulo: 1986), 68–69; ibid., *Portugal e Brasil na crise do antigo sistema colonial, 1777–1808* (São Paulo, 1979). On the European metropolitan restoration in the overseas in the wake of the colonies' independence in the Americas, see Gabriel Paquette, "After Brazil: Portuguese Debates on Empire, c. 1820–1850." *Journal of Colonialism and Colonial History* 11, no. 2 (2010) https://muse.jhu.edu/ (accessed December 2015); and Josep M. Fradera, *La nación imperial (1750–1918)*, 2 vols., Barcelona: 2015, passim.

81. Sixtus IV's Bull, "Clara devotionis," of August 21, 1472, and Alexandre VI's Brevis, "Cum sicut nobis," of August 23, 1499, *Descobrimentos portugueses, Documentos para a sua história* (hereafter *DP*), vol. 3 (Lisbon: 1971), 119–120, 549–550.

82. *MMA²*, vol. 1, 277–286; the bull revisits D. Afonso V's arguments, taken from the first version of Zurara's *Crónica da Guiné* (1453). As demonstrated by C. M. de Witte and confirmed by A. C. de C. M. Saunders, the papacy endorsed the justification of the slave trade formulated by the Portuguese Crown. See J. de Bragança, "Introduction to Zurara," *Crónica de Guiné* (Oporto: 1973), 79; C.-M. de Witte, "Les Bulles pontificales et l'expansion portugaise au XVe siècle," *Revue d'Histoire Ecclesiastique* 53 (1958), 5–46, and 443–471, 455; the preceding parts of the study in 48 (1953), 683–718; 49 (1954), 438–461; 51 (1956), 413–453, and 809–836; A. C. de C. M. Saunders, *A Social History of Black Slaves and Freedmen in Portugal, 1441–1555* (Cambridge, UK: Cambridge UP, 1982), 36–37.

83. *DP*, vol. 1, 510–503; *MMA¹*, vol. 4, 502. Pacheco Pereira states that the failure to pay the *vintena* (a five-percent royal duty on all goods, including slaves) on the Guinea's

trades implied "great mortal sin"; see Duarte Pacheco Pereira, *Esmeraldo de situ orbis* (1505–1508) (Lisbon: 1975), 70.

84. I use the noun *Jaga* to designate the Imbangala warriors, as well as combatants from other groups incorporated by them, so named in the seventeenth and eighteenth century's Portuguese sources. See below note 74 for chapter 3. Miller defines Kilombo as "a social institution with military and political functions."See Joseph C. Miller, "The Imbangala and the Chronology of Early Central African," *J. Afr. H.* 4 (1972), 549–574, and 560n41.

85. "Informação da Câmara de Luanda," August 3, 1703, *AHU*, Angola, box 17/50.

86. *HCJB*, vol. 6, 552; C. R. Boxer, *The Church Militant and Iberian Expansion, 1440–1770* (Baltimore: Johns Hopkins UP, 2001), 77.

87. Later, French Guyana's governor, marquis de Férolles, proposed retaking the Maranhão by France. See M. de Férolles, Correspondence, Cayenne, June 30, 1704. http://anom.archivesnationales.culture.gouv.fr/ark:/61561/zn401wrurtz, accessed September 2013. J. de la Mousse, *Les Indiens de la Sinnamary: Journal du père Jean de La Mousse en Guyane, 1684–1691*, G. Collomb, ed. (Paris: 2006), 10; Rafael Chambouleyron, Monique da Silva Bonifácio, and Vanice Siqueira de Melo, "Pelos sertões 'estão todas as utilidades.' Trocas e conflitos no sertão amazônico (século XVII)," *Revista de História* 162 (2010), 13–49.

88. J. F. Bettendorf, *Crônica dos padres da Companhia de Jesus no Estado do Maranhão* (Belém, Pará, [1698] 1990), 397, 623–627. On Bettendorf, see Karl-Heinz Arenz, *De l'Alzette à l'Amazonie: Jean-Philippe Bettendorf et les jésuites en Amérique portugaise, 1661–1693* (Luxemburg: 2008).

89. Rome recognized the Braganza Crown only in 1668, after the peace treaty between Lisbon and Madrid. In the meantime (1640–1668), no vacant Portuguese diocese was provided with bishops. Besides the five metropolitan dioceses, the vacant overseas ones included Angola and Congo for twenty-nine years, Cape Verde for twenty-eight years, São Tomé for thirty-four years, Cochin for forty-two years, Goa for nineteen years, Macau for forty-eight years, Malacca for thirty-four years, Mylapore (a neighborhood of modern Chennai, India) for fifty-four years, and Salvador da Bahia for twenty years. Father Brásio considers this period the "saddest and most ruinous of the whole religious history of Portugal"; see *MMA[1]*, vol. 9, 202; vol. 10, 12. José Pedro Paiva, *Os bispos de Portugal e do Império: 1495–1777* (Coimbra, Imprensa da Universidade de Coimbra, 2006), 57–66.

90. Carvalho, *Diogo do Couto*, 61.

91. J. L. de Azevedo, ed., *Cartas do Pe Antônio Vieira* (Lisbon: 1997), 357n2.

92. F. Mauro, "La bourgeoisie portugaise au XVIIe siècle," *Etudes economiques sur l'expansion portugaise* (Paris: 1970), 15–36; D. Grant Smith, "Old Christian merchants and the foundation of the Brazil Company, 1649," *HAHR* 54 (1974), 233–259; A. J. Saraiva, *Inquisição e cristãos-novos*, 5th ed. (Lisbon: 1985), 121–240. There is an English translation with an appendix containing the polemic between the author and I. Revah, A. J. Saraiva,

The Marrano Factory: The Portuguese Inquisition and Its New Christians, 1536–1765 (Boston: Brill, 2001).

93. R. A. Austen, *Trans-Saharan Africa in World History* (New York: Oxford UP, 2010) 44–45.

94. W. Hawthorne, "The Production of Slaves Where There Was No State: The Guinea Bissau Region, 1450–1815," *Slavery & Abolition* 20, no. 2 (1999), 97–124; L. A. Newson and S. Minchin, *From Capture to Sale: The Portuguese Slave Trade to Spanish South America in the Early Seventeenth Century* (Leiden, The Netherlands: Koninklijke Brill NV, 2007), 43–46.

95. P. Mark and J. da Silva Horta, "Two Early Seventeenth-Century Sephardic Communities on Senegal's Petite Côte," *History in Africa* 31, no. 1 (2004), 231–256; T. Green, "Further Considerations on the Sephardim of the Petite Côte," *History in Africa* 32, no. 1 (2005), 165–183.

96. *MMA¹*, vol. 2, 372.

97. Doc. of 1611, *MMA¹*, vol. 4, 473.

98. Doc. of June 27, 1623, doc. of December 3, 1641, *MMA²*, vol. 5, 3–7, and 355.

99. "Manuscritos, Consultas Mistas do Conselho Ultramarino," *BNRJ* cod. 25, fs. 50–50v, doc. of June 15, 1647.

100. Ibid., fs. 369–369v, doc. of September 13, 1646. A year later the Overseas Council discussed information on a Spanish fleet ready to leave Cadiz to take Portuguese ports in Upper Guinea, doc. of December 24, 1647, ibid., cod. 24, fl. 101.

101. James E. Wadsworth, "In the Name of the Inquisition: The Portuguese Inquisition and Delegated Authority in Colonial Pernambuco, Brazil," *The A* 61, no. 1 (2004), 19–54, and table 4, 50.

102. F. Bethencourt, *História das Inquisições, Portugal, Espanha e Itália* (Lisbon: 1994), 189–190.

103. R. Warren Anderson analyzes punishments of more than 8,000 individuals sentenced by the Portuguese Inquisition from 1636 to 1778. See R. Warren Anderson, "Inquisitorial Punishments in Lisbon and Évora," *E-Journal of Portuguese History* 10 (2012), 19–36.

104. Wadsworth, "In the Name," 31–32.

105. Wiznitzer, *Os judeus*, 29–35; ibid., "The Jews in the Sugar Industry of Colonial Brazil," *Jewish Social Studies* 18, no. 3 (1956), 189–198.

106. A. Domínguez Ortiz, *Los judeos conversos en España y América* (Madrid, 1971), 136–137.

107. J. I. Israel, *Diasporas within a Diaspora: Jews, Crypto-Jews, and the World of Maritime Empires (1540–1740)* (Leiden, The Netherlands: Brill, 2002), 102.

108. H. E. Cross, "Commerce and Orthodoxy: A Spanish Response to Portuguese Commercial Penetration in the Viceroyalty of Peru, 1580–1640," *The A* 35, no. 2 (1978), 151–167; Alfonso W. Quiroz Norris, "La Expropriacion Inquisitorial De Cristianos Nuevos

Portugueses en Los Reyes, Cartagena y Mexico, 1635–1649," *Historica* 10, no. 2 (1986), 237–303; P. T. Bradley, "The Portuguese Peril in Peru," *Bulletin of Spanish Studies: Hispanic Studies and Researches on Spain, Portugal and Latin America* 79, no. 5 (2002), 591–613.

109. V. Magalhães Godinho, "1580 e a Restauração," *Ensaios*, vol. 2: *Sobre historia de Portugal*, 2nd ed. (Lisbon: 1978), 407–409; J. Veiga Torres, "Uma longa guerra social: Os ritmos da repressão inquisitorial em Portugal," *RHES* 1 (1978), 55–68; M. C. Teixeira Pinto and L. M. L. Ferreira Runa, "Inquisição de Évora: Dez anos de funcionamento, 1541–1550," *RHES* 22 (1988), 51–76.

110. *MMA²*, vol. 4, 8–10, 15–17, and 477–479.

111. Wiznitzer, *Os judeus*, 29–35; Bethencourt, *História*, 279; Wadsworth, "In the Name," 40.

112. The Benguela current flows north along the African coast, from the vicinity of the Cape of Good Hope to the Gulf of Guinea. The current is stronger in December and January, when the southeast trade winds are well established. West of Cap Lopez (modern Gabon), a current's branch turns west and becomes part of the South Equatorial Current. See "Southwest Coast of Africa," *Sailing Directions (En Route)* (Springfield, VA: National Geospatial-Intelligence Agency, 2011), 71. Therefore, vessels from Brazilian ports or sailing the trade winds in the Northern Hemisphere, and then the westerlies and the Benguela current, arrived more easily at Luanda than ships sailing along the African coast from the north. See also chapter 2 for a more detailed discussion.

113. Delgado, *História*, 129–130.

114. Petition by Luis Brandão against Miguel da Orta, Luanda, September 15, 1617, *AHU*, Angola, box 1/77.

115. J. L. de Azevedo, *História dos cristãos novos portugueses* (Lisbon: 1975), 232; *MMA¹*, vol. 8, 68.

116. *MMA¹*, vol. 8, 78–79, passim; L. Jadin, "Pero Tavares, missionnaire jésuite, ses travaux apostoliques au Congo et en Angola, 1629–1635," *Bulletin de l'Institut Historique Belge de Rome* 38 (1967), 271–402.

117. Document of 1635, *MMA¹*, vol. 8, 39–40. On the instructions given by Loyola to the missionaries' correspondence, D. Bertrand, *La Politique de saint Ignace de Loyola* (Paris: 1985), 34–65.

118. Mercurian, the S.J. superior general, stated in 1557 about the relations with the Inquisition, that the Jesuits should not hinder the inquisitorial procedures, but they should avoid, as far as possible, serving as judges or tribunals' assistants. Yet in 1582, the Superior General Acquaviva authorized Portuguese Jesuits—and only them—to be consultants to the Holly Office. See J. Wicki, "Dois compêndios das ordens dos padres gerais e congregações da província dos jesuítas de Goa," *Studia* 43–44 (1980), 343–532 and 431; D. Alden, *The Making of an Enterprise: The Society of Jesus in Portugal, Its Empire, and Beyond, 1540–1750* (Palo Alto: Stanford UP, 1996), 670–673; J. E. Franco, "A Companhia de Jesus e a Inqui-

sição: afectos e desafectos entre duas instituições influentes (Séculos XVI–XVII)," *Actas do Congresso Internacional Atlântico de Antigo Regime: poderes e sociedades*.(Lisbon: 2005), 1–23.

119. C. Geffray, "Nobles, Bourgeois, Inquisition: Les Prémisses de L'expansion Coloniale Portugaise Au XVIe Siècle," *Cahiers d'études Africaines* 21, no. 84 (1981), 523–546; A. Blasco Martinez, "Razones y consecuencias de una decisión controvertida la expulsión de los judíos de España en 1492," *Kalakorikos* 10 (2005), 9–36. For an analysis of the expulsion of the "Moriscos" from Spain (1609–1614), in the framework of an antibourgeoisie, antiregionalist (against the Aragon and Valencia barons) move favoring the Castilian centralism, see F. Marquez Villanueva, "El problema historio-gráfico de los moriscos," *Bulletin Hispanique* 86, no. 1–2 (1984), 61–135. About the misnaming of the word "morisco" to designate the Muslims forcibly converted to Christianity in Spain, see L. Harvey, *Muslims in Spain, 1500 to 1614* (Chicago: U of Chicago P, 2005), 2–5, on their expulsion, 291–331.

120. A. Vieira, "Obras Várias," *Obras escolhidas*, vol. 4 (Lisbon: 1951), 20. Regarding the Inquisition and Portugal's economic decline, Peter Emmer asks more bluntly "Why did Portugal deliberately shoot itself in the foot by virtually expelling its commercial class?" See P. C. Emmer, "The First Global War: The Dutch versus Iberia in Asia, Africa, and the New World, 1590–1609," *E-Journal of Portuguese History* 1, no. 1 (2003). See https://www.brown.edu/Departments/Portuguese_Brazilian_Studies/ejph/html/issue1/html/emmer_main.html, accessed May 2015.

121. R. Ricard, "A propos de rebato. Note sur la tactique militaire dans les places portugaises du Maroc," *Bulletin Hispanique* 35, no. 4 (1933), 448–453; R. Ricard, "Le problème de l'occupation restreinte dans l'Afrique du Nord (XVe–XVIIIe siècles)," *Annales* 8, no. 41 (1936), 426–437. Writing in the 1930s, during the Second European Expansion, which propelled territorial conquest, Ricard unfavorably contrasts the Europeans' strongholds of the previous period to the full territorial domination then exerted in North Africa by France and Spain.

122. See, for instance, J. Devisse, "Routes de commerce et échanges en Afrique Occidentale en relation avec la Méditerranée: Un essai sur le commerce médiéval du XIe au XVIe siècle," *Revue d'Histoire Economique et Sociale* 50, no. 1 (1972), 43–73, and no. 3 (1972), 357–397. See S. Subrahmanyan, "Staying On: The Portuguese of Southern Coromandel in the Late Seventeenth Century," *Indian Economic and Social History Review* 22, no. 4 (1985), 445–463; R. da Cruz e Silva, "As feiras do Ndongo: a outra vertente do comercio no século XVII," *Actas do seminario: Encontro de povos e culturas em Angola* (Lisbon: 1997), 405–422; A. Molho and D. Ramada Curto, "Les réseaux marchands à l'époque moderne," *Annales* 58, no. 3 (2003), 569–579; I. Baghdiantz-McCabe, "Trading Diaspora, State Building, and the Idea of National Interest," in Neguin Yavari, L. G. Potter, and J.-M. Ran Oppenheim, *Views from the Edge: Essays in Honor of Richard W. Bulliet* (New York: Columbia UP, 2005), 3–18; A. C. Metcalf, *Go-Betweens and the Colonization of Brazil, 1500–1600* (Austin: U of Texas P, 2005); F. Bethencourt, "Political Configurations and Local Powers," in F. Bethencourt

and D. Ramada Curto, eds., *Portuguese Oceanic Expansion, 1400–1800* (Cambridge, UK: Cambridge UP, 2007), 197–254; idem, "Iberian Atlantic: Ties, Networks, and Boundaries," in Harald E. Braun and Lisa Vollendorf, eds., *Theorising the Iberian Atlantic* (Leiden: 2013), 15–36; C. Ebert, "European Competition and Cooperation in Pre-Modern Globalization: 'Portuguese' West and Central Africa, 1500–1600," *African Economic History* 36 (2008), 53–78; D. Ramada Curto "Early Modern European Empires and Networks," *International Journal of Maritime History*, 21 (2009), 318–325; R. J. Barendse, "Trade and State in the Arabian Seas: A Survey from the Fifteenth to the Eighteenth Century," *Journal of World History* 11, no 2 (2000), 173–225. L. Y. Andaya, "The 'Informal Portuguese Empire' and the Topasses in the Solor Archipelago and Timor in the Seventeenth and Eighteenth Centuries," *Journal of Southeast Asian Studies* 41, no. 3 (2010), 391–420.

123. S. J. Henders, "So What If It's Not a Gamble? Post-Westphalian Politics in Macau," *Pacific Affairs* 74, no. 3 (2001), 342–360. On the economic evolution of Macau, see Roderich Ptak, "Macao entre la Chine et l'Asie Maritime: cycles d'économie," in Francisco Bethencourt and L. F. de Alencastro, eds., *L'Empire portugais face aux autres empires XVIe–XIXe siècles* (Paris: Maisonneuve & Larose, 2007), 137–165.

124. The historical foundations of Portuguese sovereignty in Macau were recollected in 1845 by the Visconde de Santarém. J. F. Judice Biker, ed., *Memoria sobre o estabelecimento de Macau, pelo visconde de Santarem. Abreviada relação da embaixada que el-rei João v mandou ao imperador da China e Tartaria. Relatorio de Francisco de Assis Pacheco de Sampaio a el-rei José I dando conta dos successos da embaixada a que fôra mandado á côrte de Pekim, 1752* (Lisbon: 1879), 9–31. For the Peking's government point of view, see Huang Qichen, "O exercício da Soberania e da Administração por parte do governo chinês em Macau entre o século XVI e meados do século XIX," *Administração* 48, no. 10 (2000), 657–675.

125. Diffie, "The Legal Privileges," 21–22. After the change of overseas trade from the Indic to the Atlantic, the port of Lisbon continued to concentrate four-fifths of global movements during the seventeenth century. See J. Mattoso, ed., *História de Portugal*, vol. 4, ed. A. M. Hespanha (Porto: 1945), 101, table 2.

126. M. A. Soares de Azevedo, "Armadas do Brasil," *DHP*, vol. 1, 186–188; A. C. Ferreira Reis, "O comércio colonial e as companhias privilegiadas," in S. Buarque de Holanda (ed.) *História geral da civilização brasileira (HGCB)* book 5, vol. 2 (São Paulo: 1960), 316–318; V. Noya Pinto, *O ouro brasileiro e o comércio anglo-português* (São Paulo: 1979), 133–184.

127. Among other seventeenth-century authors, Brito Freyre mentions the "Brasílicos Portugueses," praising their struggle in the war against the Dutch. See F. de Brito Freyre, *Nova Lusitânia—História da Guerra Brasílica* ([1675] Recife: 1977), 399. Hence, I employ the seventeenth-century word *Brasílico* to designate the Lusophone individuals and communities of Portuguese America during the sixteenth, seventeenth, and the first half of the eighteenth centuries, when the noun *Brasiliense* referred primarily to the Indians, and *Brasileiro* mainly to the Brazilwood lumbermen and traders. By then, the settlers of the

Portuguese America enclaves expressed their own regional identity, but did not yet perceive themselves as a protonational society. The Brasílicos became Brasileiros in the modern sense of the name, throughout the eighteenth century, when the gold economy generated an internal market encompassing the whole colony. Thereupon emerged the idea of attachment to a supraregional community endowed with the same language and living in the same territory. Gregorio de Matos referred to the "Brazilian people" (*"povo brasileiro"*) in one of his verses. Nevertheless, authorship and dating of his poems are controversial. See J. Amado, ed., *Obras completas de Gregório de Matos*, vol. 1 (Rio de Janeiro: 1990), 224. According to the *Dicionário Houaiss da Língua Portuguesa*, the word *Brazilian* (*brasileiro*), in its modern-day meaning, appeared in 1706. But there is an early mention in 1696; see also chapter 7, note 4.

128. D. Eltis and D. Richardson, *Atlas of the Transatlantic Slave Trade* (New Haven, CT: Yale UP, 2015), map 26, 47.

129. F. Pyrard, *Voyage de François Pyrard, de Laval. Contenant sa navigation aux Indes orientales, Maldives, Moluques, Bresil . . .* (Paris: 1619), 231–232.

130. José Antônio Caldas, "Notícia Geral de Toda Esta Capitania da Bahia desde o Seu Descobrimento até o Presente Anno de 1759," *Revista do Instituto Geográphico e Histórico da Bahia* 57 (1931).

131. Royal order of December 1, 1800, L.Vianna Filho, *O Negro na Bahia* (Rio de Janeiro: 1946), 33.

132. Vianna Filho, *O Negro*, 23–104; C. Boxer, *Salvador de Sá and the Struggle for Brazil and Angola, 1602–1686* (London: 1952); J. F. de Almeida Prado, "Les relations de Bahia (Brésil) avec le Dahomey," *Revue d'Histoire des Colonies* 41, no. 143 (1954), 167–226; Pierre Verger, *Flux et reflux de la traite des nègres entre le Golfe de Bénin et Bahia de Todos os Santos, XVIe–XIXe siècles* (Paris: 1968), passim; Corcino Medeiros dos Santos, "Relações de Angola com o Rio de Janeiro 1736–1808," *Estudos Históricos* 12 (1973), 7–68; Katia de Queiros Mattoso, *Etre esclave au Brésil* (Paris: 1979), 32–33.

133. Estimated total voyages from Africa to Brazil, including ships that left Portugal's ports in the years 1550–1850, amount to 14,907. Thus, 14,161 (95 percent) would travel directly between Brazilian and African ports. A small proportion of those vessels illegally sailed to Buenos Aires during the first half of the seventeenth-century, as we shall see in chapter 3. In the eighteenth century there was an inverted flow: enslaved Africans were smuggled from neighboring European colonies into Brazil's gold-mining areas through the Amazon basin. TSTD, accessed in December 2015.

134. The TSTD has records of a slave vessel's departure for Africa from 188 harbors around the Atlantic, which embarked 9,024,000 individuals—that is, 72 percent of the estimated total (12,521,000) embarkments in Africa. See D. Eltis and D. Richardson, *Atlas of the Transatlantic Slave Trade* (New Haven and London: 2010), 39, 45, 46, 49, 52, 116, 120–122, 124, 141–143, 149, 151–153, and 156. TSTD, accessed in December 2015.

135. Pyrard, *Voyage*, 231–232.

136. Leonor Freire Costa, "Merchant Groups in the 17th-Century Brazilian Sugar Trade: Reappraising Old Topics with New Research Insights," *e-Journal of Portuguese History* 2, no. 1 (2004).

137. *HCJB*, vol. 8, 398. Here "Congo" refers to the river basin and the historical African kingdom whose capital was M'banza Congo or São Salvador do Congo. The modern kingdom of Congo covered territories of the north of present-day Angola and part of the Democratic Republic of Congo and of the Republic of the Congo. Historians of Africa, and many other authors, adopt the spelling *Kongo* to distinguish this ancient Bantu state from the colonies later created in the area by Belgium and France. I use Congo, as the Congolese rulers and the European agents and missionaries have spelled it in all documents quoted in this book. The capital of the kingdom was located in M'banza Congo, called São Salvador do Congo from 1596, and renamed with its original appellation in 1975, after Angolan independence. See A. de Albuquerque Felner, *Angola, Apontamentos sobre a ocupação e início do estabelecimento dos Portugueses no Congo, Angola e Benguela* (Coimbra: 1933), 70–71, 116–117.

138. Corcino Medeiros Dos Santos, "Relações de Angola com o Rio de Janeiro 1736–1808," *Estudos Históricos* 12 (1973), 7–68; José C. Curto, *Enslaving Spirits: The Portuguese-Brazilian Alcohol Trade at Luanda and Its Hinterland, c. 1550–1830* (Leiden: 2004), table 10.

139. Vianna Filho, *O Negro*, 23–104; J. F. de Almeida Prado, "Les relations de Bahia (Brésil) avec le Dahomey," *Revue d'Histoire des Colonies* 41, no. 143 (1954), 167–226; Verger, *Flux et reflux*, passim; Jean-Baptiste Nardi, *O fumo brasileiro no período colonial* (São Paulo, 1996); Gustavo Acioli Lopes, *Negócio da Costa da Mina e comércio atlântico: tabaco, açúcar, ouro e tráfico de escravos, Pernambuco (1654–1760)*, tese de doutorado em História (Universidade de São Paulo, 2008).

140. Carlo Toso, "Relazioni inedite di Cherubino Cassinis da Savona sul 'Regno del Congo e sue Missioni,'" *L'Italia Francescana* 45 (1974), 135–214, here 140–147.

141. Even for the North Atlantic routes, Herbert Klein questions "the myth of the so-called triangular trade," observing that most of the ships leaving Europe for African slave-trade ports and then for the Caribbean or the North American slaving areas did not return to Europe with American products. See H. S. Klein, *The Atlantic Slave Trade: New Approaches to the Americas* (Cambridge, UK: Cambridge UP, 1999), 96–102.

142. On this issue and on the Williams-Drescher debate, see I. Sundiata, "Capitalism and Slavery: 'The Commercial Part of the Nation,'" in *Capitalism and Slavery Fifty Years Later: Eric Eustace Williams—A Reassessment of the Man and His Work*, H. Cateau and S. H. H. Carrington, eds. (New York: Peter Land, 2010), 121–136; J. Walvin, "Why Did the British Abolish the Slave Trade? Econocide Revisited," *Slavery & Abolition* 32, no. 4 (2011), 583–588; D. Tomich, "Econocide? From Abolition to Emancipation in the British

and French Caribbean," in Stephan Palmié and Francisco Scarano, eds., *The Caribbean: An Illustrated History* (Chicago: 2011), 303–316.

143. Bull *Aeterni Regis Clementia DP*, vol. 3, 206, and 232, and also the bulls *Sedes Apostolica* and *Breve Desideras* (1505), *MMA¹*, vol. 2, 206, and 232.

144. A. Brásio, "Do último cruzado ao padroado régio," *Studia* (1959), 125–153; see analysis by A. J. Saraiva, "Le padre Antônio Vieira, S.J. et la question de l'esclavage des noirs au XVIIe siècle," *Annales E.C.S* 22 (1967), 1289–1309; Godinho, *Os descobrimentos*, 139–182.

145. Since the third decade of the sixteenth century, French smuggling of Brazilwood decreased the Crown's income and caused a fall in the wood's price in Antwerp. See H. B. Johnson, "*The Portuguese Settlement of Brazil, 1500–1580*," in L. Bethell, ed., *CHLA*, vol. 1 (Cambridge, UK: Cambridge UP, 1995), 258–259.

146. Godinho, "*Os Descobrimentos*," ii, 219–273, 36–49, and 134–341.

147. I. Wilks, "Wangara, Akan and Portuguese in the Fifteenth and Sixteenth Centuries: 1. The Matter of Bitu," *J. Afr. H.* 23, no. 3 (1982), 333–349; D. Curtin, "Africa and the Wider Monetary World, 1250–1850," in *Precious Metals in the Later Medieval and Early Modern Worlds*, J. F. Richards, ed. (Durham, NC: Carolina Academic P, 1983), 238–239.

148. Pereira, *Esmeraldo*, 114–115, 119; J. B. Ballong-Wen-Mewuda, *São Jorge da Mina, 1482–1637*, vol. 1 (Paris: 1993), 323–330.

149. Brief of 11.9.1481 by Sixtus IV to King João II, *MMA¹*, vol. 1, 7. São Jorge da Mina was then known as "Mina Velha" to distinguish it from the "Mina Nova," or Sofala, in *West Africa*, *MMA¹*, vol. 15, 35; Alberto Iria, "Da fundação e governo do Castelo ou Fortaleza de São Jorge da Mina pelos Portugueses e da sua acção missionária após o descobrimento desta costa," *Studia* 1 (1958), 25–69. On the Elmina's gold price in Lisbon, Pereira, *Esmeraldo*, 209, 211.

150. "There is so much Mandinka clothing among the Negros, that it hinders much of the *Casa* [da Mina]'s business," warned the Mina Portuguese factor in 1510, *MMA¹*, vol. 1, 210–214; *MMA¹*, vol. 1, 138; Colleen E. Kriger, "Mapping the History of Cotton Textile Production in Precolonial West Africa," *African Economic History* 33, no. 1 (2005), 87–116, 99.

151. The slave trade directed toward the Elmina may have increased due to the high mortality of the Akan as a consequence of malaria, which became an epidemic in the area with the development of agriculture by native communities who had previously been forest people. See A. Norman Klein, "Toward a New Understanding of Akan Origins," *Africa* 66, no. 2 (1996), 248–273.

152. Ballong-Wen-Mewuda, *São Jorge*, 323–330; "Slave Coast": a coastal area between the Volta River and the Lagos channel.

153. Around 1560, Seville held 8,000 enslaved Africans and blacks, plus an unknown number of Turkish and Moorish captives, in the midst of a population of 85,000. Lisbon

numbered at that time around 100,000 people, of which 10,000 were black and mulatto slaves. See A. Stella, "L'esclavage en Andalousie à l'époque moderne," *Annales E.S.C.* 47, no. 1 (1992), 35–64, here 50–51; Jorge Fonseca, *Escravos e senhores na Lisboa Quinhentista* (Lisbon: 2010), 94–104, here 99–100.

154. Royal order dated August 17, 1517, Damião Peres, *Regimento das Cazas das Índias e Mina* (Coimbra: [1509] 1947), 134–137.

155. Ibid., 28–29.

156. Ibid., 117–118; "Regimento do Trato de São Tomé," February 8, 1519, *MMA¹*, vol. 4, 124–33. For a detailed description of these practices, see Fonseca, *Escravos*, 139–153.

157. Saunders, *A Social History of Black slaves and Freedmen*, 8; R. de Almeida, *História do colonialismo português em África*, vol. 1 (Lisbon: 1979), 88. The Casa da Mina e Tratos da Guiné was the royal agency for the West African trade.

158. J. L. de Azevedo, *Épocas de Portugal econômico* (Porto: 1978), 74; Saunders, *A Social History*, 33–34.

159. TSTD, accessed in November 2015.

160. Spain's royal laws of February 21, 1644, May 20, 1645, January 31, 1650, and 1663, Visconde de Santarém, *Quadro elementar*, vol. 1, 55–56.

161. *MMA²*, vol. 5, 454–458, 488.

162. *MMA¹*, vol. 10, 28–29, and vol. 11, 67.

163. Royal decree of October 14, 1751, ordering that African and black slaves should not be exported into non-Portuguese ports. See Cf. F. C. Falcon and F. A. Novais, "A extinção da escravatura africana e Portugal no quadro da política econômica pombalina," *Anais do VI Simpósio Nacional dos Professores Universitários de História*, vol. 1 (São Paulo: 1973), 405–432.

164. M. Lobo Cabrera, *La Esclavitud En Las Canarias Orientales En El Siglo XVI: Negros, Moros Y Moriscos* (Santa Cruz de Tenerife: 1982), 108–109, 184–185.

165. A. Milhou, "Los intentos de repoblación de la isla Hispaniola por colonias de labradores (1518–1603): Razones de un fracaso," *Actas del Quinto Congreso Internacional de Hispanistas*, vol. 2 (Bordeaux: 1977), 643–654; Huguette and Pierre Chaunu, *Séville et l'Atlantique, 1504–1650*, 12 vols. (Paris: 1955–1960), 496–502.

166. D. Wheat, *The Afro-Portuguese Maritime World and the Foundations of Spanish Caribbean Society, 1570–1640* (PhD thesis, Vanderbilt University, 2009), 160.

167. From the beginning Madeira Island produced wheat, cultivated by free colonists. Then, between 1452 and 1475, sugar cane, black and *Guancho* (the Canary Islands' indigenous Berber inhabitants) slaves were introduced, leading to the demise of local wheat farms. See J. Serrão, "Le blé des îles atlantiques, Madère et Açores aux XVe et XVIe siècles," *Annales E.S.C.* 9, no. 3 (1954), 336–341. In 1552 the island numbered 3,000 slaves and a free population of 20,000. See F. Mauro, *Le Portugal et l'Atlantique au XVIIe siècle, 1570–1670* (Paris, 1960), 185; A. Vieira, *A Escravatura na Madeira nos séculos XVI a XVII: o ponto*

da situação (Funchal: 1996), 27–30, 40–45; ibid., *Escravos com ou sem açúcar: O caso da Madeira* (Funchal: 1997).

168. J. W. Moore, "Madeira, Sugar, and the Conquest of Nature in the 'First' Sixteenth Century: Part I: From 'Island of Timber' to Sugar Revolution, 1420–1506," *Review* 32, no. 4 (2009); ibid., "Madeira, Sugar, and the Conquest of Nature in the 'First' Sixteenth Century, Part II: From Regional Crisis to Commodity Frontier, 1506–1530," *Review* 33, no. 1 (2010), 1–24, 9–13, and table 1, 12.

169. Royal decrees of October 16, 1562, and October 30, 1562, *MMA²*, vol. 2, 491–498.

170. On the slave trade to Madeira, A. Vieira, *O Escravo no Arquipélago da Madeira, séculos XV a XVII* (Funchal: 1991), 45–62, 169–178.

171. TSTD, accessed in November 2015.

172. J. L. Vogt, "The Early São Tomé-Principe Slave Trade with Mina, 1500–1540," *The International Journal of African Historical Studies* 6, no. 3 (1973), 453–467; M. Lobo Cabrera, "El comercio entre Portugal y Canarias en el Quinientos," *RHES* 19 (1987), 1–16; T. Hall, *The Role of the Cape Verde Islanders in Organizing and Operating Maritime Trade between West Africa and Iberian Territories, 1441–1616* (PhD thesis, Johns Hopkins University, 1992), 215–303.

173. S. B. Schwartz, *Sugar Plantations in the Formation of Brazilian Society: Bahia, 1550–1835* (London: 1985), table 7–2, 168; Cristina Maria Seuanes Serafim, *As Ilhas de São Tomé no século XVII* (Lisbon: 2000), table 42, 257. See also Joaquim Romero Magalhaes, "O açúcar nas ilhas portuguesas do Atlântico séculos XV e XVI," *Varia História* 25, no. 41 (2009), 151–175.

174. *Documentos para a história do açúcar, Legislação 1534–1596*, vol. 1 (Rio de Janeiro: 1954), 111–113, 147–150.

175. A. A. de Almada, "Tratado breve dos rios de Guiné do Cabo Verde," *MMA¹*, vol. 3, 230–377, 376. Almada resorted to the experience of his family and his own, and to the Upper Guinea Luso-Africans' oral tradition.

176. Letter by Bartolomeu Velho to the Crown (1606), *MMA²*, vol. 4, 114–125.

177. *MMA¹*, vol. 9, 26; B. Heintze, "Traite de 'pièces' en Angola—ce que nos sources passent sous silence," in *Actes du Colloque International sur la Traite des Noirs (CITN)*, vol. 1, S. Daget, eds. (Paris: 1988), 147–172.

178. Following the observations of Mathias Delgado, I name "Angolistas" the Luso-African colonists rooted in Angola, to distinguish them from indigenous peoples and from the Portuguese newcomers (*reinóis*) and Brasílicos established in West Central Africa. I also consider "Angolistas Historians," the Portuguese authors identified with the Luso-Angolan tradition (Cadornega in the seventeenth century; Ralph Delgado, J. Mathias Delgado, Ruella Pombo, and Gastão de Sousa Dias in the twentieth century). See A. Cadornega, *História Geral das Guerras Angolanas* (hereafter *HGGA*), vol. 1 (Lisbon, [1681] 1972), 322–324n1.

179. B. Heintze, "Regimento do governador de Angola," *Fontes para a história de Angola do século XVII: Cartas e documentos oficiais da colectânea documental de Fernão de Sousa, 1624–1635*, vol. 1 (Lisbon: [1624] 1985–1988), 140–153, here 148–149.

180. Consultation to Conselho Ultramarino, June 21, 1655, *AHU*, Angola, box 6/18; *MMA¹*, vol. 11, 490–491.

181. The clause regarding the sugar plantations and the building of Angola sugar-cane mills, included in governor Forjaz's regiment (1607), appears for the last time in Governor Tristão da Cunha's *regimento* (1666). See *"Regimento"* of Governor Forjaz, March 26, 1607, *MMA¹*, vol. 5, 264–279, and doc. of April 10, 1666, *AHU*, Angola, box 9/25.

182. Mauro, *Le Portugal*, 190–192.

183. N. Valério and M. Paula Fontoura, "A evolução econômica de Angola durante o segundo período colonial: Uma tentativa de síntese," *Análise Social* 29, no. 129 (1994), 1193–1208.

184. Memorial of the Luanda's Jesuits, June 15, 1593, *MMA¹*, vol. 15, 333–339, here 337. The Company of Jesus superior in Luanda, Father Pero Rodrigues, and all Angola's Jesuits signed this document stating the Company of Jesus' mission rights on slave property and tax-free slave trade to Bahia.

185. T. de Mercado, *Suma de tratos y contratos*,[1571], vol. 1 (Madrid: 1977), 229; M. Goulart, *A escravidão africana no Brasil: Das origens à extinção do tráfico* (São Paulo: 1975), 126, 153, 194.

186. Around 1550, slaves' owners paid fifteen percent of their price (the 5 percent "vintena" plus the 10 percent "dizimo"), amounting to approximately 950 *réis* in taxes. See de Azevedo, *Épocas*, 71. Twenty-five years later, the rights had raised to 3,000 *réis* when a slave was sent to Brazil, and up to 6,000 *réis* when sent to Spanish America. See D. de Abreu e Brito, *Sumário e descripção do reino de Angola e do descobrimento da ilha de Loanda e da grãdeza das capitanias do Estado do Brasil*, Notas A. de Albuquerque Felner (Coimbra: [1592] 1931), 30. In the decade of 1630, royal customs took out 6,000 *réis* off each "piece" (slave) exported to Brazil and 19,800 *réis* off those sent over to Spanish America, including entry rights. See *MMA¹*, vol. 8, 243. At this date, the Angolan "pieces" priced at an average of 25,000 *réis* and at a maximum of 30,000 *réis*. See ibid., 394, and B. Heintze, "The Angolan Vassal Tributes of the 17th century," *RHES* 6 (1980), 57–78, note 14; *HGGA*, vol. 2, 199; Bartolomeu Paes Bulhão report, doc. of April 15, 1663, *AHU*, 7/87; Angelo Alves Carrara, *Receitas e despesas da Real Fazenda do Brasil, século XVII* (Juiz de Fora: 2009), 72.

187. J. J. Teixeira Coelho, "Instrucção para o governo de capitania de Minas Geraes" *Revista do Instituto Histórico e Geográphico do Brazil* (*RIHGB*), vol. 7 (Rio de Janeiro: Nacional, [1780] 1852), 255–481, here 324. In 1715, the collection of the tax was improved. See letter of the Marquez de Angeja to the Crown, Bahia, December 17, 1716, *Arquivo da Universidade de Coimbra* (hereafter *AUC*), Coleção Conde de Arcos, vol. 10, book 2, doc. 107, fl. 79. On the 1809 5 percent tax (*meia-siza*), see *Colleção das Leis do Brazil de*

1809, Typographia Nacional (Rio de Janeiro: 1891) 69–72; Guilherme Vilela Fernandes, *Tributação e escravidão: o imposto da meia siza sobre o comercio de escravos (1809–1850)* (monografia apresentado ao Curso de Ciências Econômicas, Universidade Estadual de Campinas [UNICAMP], 2006).

188. R. J. Ferry, "Encomienda, African Slavery and Agriculture in Seventeenth-Century Caracas," *HAHR* 61, no. 4 (1981), 609–636; A. Szaszdi and D. L. Borja Szaszdi, "El comercio de cacao de Guayaquil," *Revista de Historia de America* 57–58 (1964), 1–50.

189. The Jesuits were in conflict with civilian and religious hierarchies the moment they set foot in Brazil. In Bahia, Nóbrega antagonized Brazil's new bishop regarding evangelizing issues, royal agents regarding tributes due to the Crown, and colonists regarding the captivity of Indians. See M. da Nóbrega, "Cartas do Brasil," *Cartas jesuíticas*, vol. 1 (São Paulo: 1988), 137–143 and 150–155; S. Leite, *HCJB*, vol. 1 (Rio de Janeiro: 1938–1950), 38–41. In face of the crisis, Portugal's Jesuit Provincial sent Nóbrega to São Vicente in 1554. Only later the Jesuit's seat in Rome was informed about the incident. See *MMA¹*, vol. 15, 213–216.

190. J. Capistrano de Abreu, "Atribulações de um donatário," *Caminhos antigos e povoamento do Brasil* (Rio de Janeiro: 1930), 37–50.

191. On the Tourinho's inquisition trial, which concerned also blasphemy, heresy, and related inqueries, see Rossana G. Britto, *A saga de Pero do Campo Tourinho: o primeiro processo da Inquisição do Brasil* (Petrópolis: 2000).

192. Taking up the defense of Las Casas, Marcel Bataillon stated that when Las Casas proposed the introduction of African captives in Hispaniola (1516), the injustice of the African slave trade had not yet been discussed in Europe. See Bataillon, *Etudes*, 91–94. Although valid for Las Casas, the argument does not apply to Antônio Vieira (1608–1697). His famous letter to the Pará municipal council recommended the use of Angolan slaves instead of Indians; it was dated 1661, when the abuses of the slave trade were widely known and discussed by several authors and authorities. See de Azevedo, *Vieira*, 581. On this issue, see chapter 5.

193. *Costa da Mina*, the Mina Coast, might sometimes designate the whole Gulf of Guinea, but was generally understood by Luso-Brazilian officials and slave traders as the area from the Cape Palmas (at the present-day frontier between Liberia and the Ivory Coast) to the Cape Formoso (at the Niger Delta).

194. Brito, *Sumário*, 71–72.

195. A *banzo* is a bundle of trade goods in Angola. In 1612, the price of one slave was one hundred *banzos*. See doc. of January 26, 1612, *AHU*, box 1/17. *Banzo* derives from the Kimbundo verb *kubanza*, meaning both "to calculate" and "to think." In Brazil, the term became known only in the second meaning. See J. M. Delgado, *HGGA*, vol. 1, 143n1.

196. L. A. Newson, "Africans and Luso-Africans in the Portuguese Slave Trade on the Upper Guinea Coast in the Early Seventeenth Century," *J. Afr. H.* 53, no. 1 (2012), 1–24, here 7.

197. Mauro, *Le Portugal*, 118.

198. R. Law, "Trade and Politics Behind the Slave Coast: The Lagoon Traffic and the Rise of Lagos, 1500–1800," *J. Afr. H.* 24 (1983), 321–348; Kristin Mann, *Slavery and the Birth of an African City: Lagos, 1760–1900* (Bloomington: Indiana UP, 2008), 127–130.

199. F. Mauro and C. Furtado debated about the accounts of the famous Sergipe do Conde sugar mill, in Bahia. See Mauro, ""*Etudes Economiques*, 135–150, and ibid., *Le Brésil du XVe à la fin du XVIIIe s* (Paris: 1977), 68. Analyzing other sources, S. Schwartz concluded that expenses with slaves were greater than the amounts calculated by F. Mauro and C. Furtado. In a group of ten sugar mills, whose data stretches between 1716 and 1816, the costs with slaves represent, on average, more than 20 percent of the investment. In turn, sugar-cane growers (lavradores) expend 56 percent of their capital purchasing slaves. See Schwartz, *Sugar Plantations*, 212–218.

200. F. Cardim, *Tratado da terra e gente do Brasil* (São Paulo: [1585] 1978), 201–202.

201. In the sugar-mill accounts analyzed by S. Schwartz, only in a few instances did luxury goods require over 10 percent of capital. See Schwartz, *Sugar Plantations*, 212–218.

202. Royal letter of January 4, 1687, *Documentos Históricos* (*DH*), vol. 83 (Rio de Janeiro: Biblioteca Nacional do Rio de Janeiro, 1949), 29–30.

203. M. Penna, "Os dois ou o inglês maquinista" [1842], *Comédias*, scene 9 (Rio de Janeiro: n.d.), 130–131.

204. In his eighteenth-century treatise on slavery, the Bahia priest and jurist Ribeiro Rocha, knowledgeable in laws and in Luso-Brazilian social practices, wrote: "The first act of hospitality that they (the masters) perform, once the purchased individuals (black slaves) appear in his presence, is to have them rigorously flogged, with no reason other than their will to do so." Manoel Ribeiro Rocha, *Ethiope resgatado, empenhado, sustentado, corregido, instruído e libertado* . . . (Lisbon: 1758), 188–189. See also chapter 4.

205. Magalhães Gandavo, Pero de. *Tratado da Terra do Brasil* e *História da Província de Santa Cruz* (Rio de Janeiro: [1576] 1911), 38–39.

206. A. W. Crosby, Jr., *The Columbian Exchange: Biological and Cultural Consequences of 1492* (Westport, CT: Greenwood Publishing Group, 1972), 3–34; Pierre Chaunu, *Histoire, science sociale: la durée, l'espace et l'homme à l'époque moderne* (Paris, 1974), 141.

207. A. F. Brandão, *Diálogos das grandezas do Brasil* (Recife: [1618] 1962), 60–61.

208. On the impact of these epidemics over the indentured servants of British America and its consequences for the development of African slavery, see R. Coelho and R. A. McGuire, "African and European Bound Labor in the British New World: The Biological Consequences of Economic Choices," *The Journal of Economic History* 57, no. 1 (1997), 83–115. See chapter 4.

209. A. M. Stevens-Arroyo, "The Inter-Atlantic Paradigm: The Failure of Spanish Medieval Colonization of the Canary and Caribbean Islands," *Comparative Studies in Society and History* 35, no. 3 (1993), 515–543.

210. B. de Las Casas, *Brevísima relación de la destrucción de África: Preludio de la destrucción de Indias* (Salamanca: [1540–1554] 1989), 114–125; A. Esponera Cerdán, "Bartolomé de las Casas y la esclavización de los negros, según las aportaciones de I. Pérez Fernández O.," *Studium* 43 (2003), 87–100. I am grateful to Serge Gruzinski for his comments on that question.

211. "Representação do Conselho da Fazenda sobre as necessidades urgentes em que estava o Reino apontando os remédios," May 23, 1656, *ANTT*, Manuscritos da Livraria, Livro 1146, 63.

212. T. Rooney, "Habsburg Fiscal Policies in Portugal, 1580–1640," *The Journal of European Economic History* 23, no. 3 (1994), 545–562; Schaub, *Le Portugal*, 135–173; David Tengwall, "The Portuguese Revolution of 1 December 1640: A Reappraisal," *eHumanista: Journal of Iberian Studies* 17 (2011), 448–459.

213. See the documents edited by J. Cortesão, *Pauliceae lusitana Monumenta historica* (hereafter *PLMH*), vol. 2 (Lisbon: 1961), 108–310.

214. The late J. Monteiro designates "colonial Indians" as all the settled communities and natives that were in direct or indirect contact with the Europeans and their local allies. See John M. Monteiro, "500 Years of Native Brazilian History," *Diálogos Latinoamericanos* 2 (2000), 2–15; see chapter 4.

215. Two councilors, Francisco de Vasconcellos da Cunha (1635–1638) and Salvador de Sá (1648–1652), had been governors of Angola after having served in office in Brazil. Bartolomeu de Vasconcellos da Cunha, Francisco's nephew, fought the Dutch in Pernambuco before becoming deputy governor of Angola (1646 and 1648), where he lived like a potentate. José Pinto Pereira, the Overseas Council's third member who signed such conclusions, set up operations to extend the slave-trade web to Mozambique. See C. Ultramarino, February 12, 1656, *MMA¹*, vol. 12, 7–9.

216. L. F. de Alencastro, "Le versant brésilien de l'Atlantique Sud: 1550–1850," *Annales, Histoire, Sciences Sociales* 61, no. 2 (2006), 339–382.

217. See chapter 6, 248.

218. D. Eltis and D. Richardson, *Atlas of the Transatlantic Slave Trade*, tables 121 and 127 related to the years 1776–1830 (New Haven: 2010), 117 and 185.

219. The Rio de Janeiro area saw 2,263,914 enslaved Africans disembarked, Salvador da Bahia saw 1,550,355 disembarkments, and Luanda registered 2,826,000 enslaved embarked. See Eltis and Richardson, *Atlas*, 39 and 90.

Chapter 2

1. Jesuit chronicler F. Cardim reported at the end of the sixteenth century that most of the Bahian sugar mills had "one hundred and two hundred slaves from Guinea and from the Land (Brazil)." See F. Cardim, *Tratado*, 193.

2. E. Savage, "Berbers and Blacks: Ibādï Slave Traffic in Eighth-Century North Africa," *J. Afr. H.* 33, no. 3 (1992), 351–368; N. Levtzion, "Slavery and Islamization in Africa," *Slaves & Slavery in Muslim Africa*, vol. 1, J. R. Willis, ed. (London: 1985), 182–198; R. Austen, "The Trans-Saharan Slave Trade: A Tentative Census," in *The Uncommon Market*, H. A Gemery and J. S. Hogendorn, eds. (New York: 1979), 23–72; Roger Botte, "Les réseaux transsahariens de la traite de l'or et des esclaves au haut Moyen Âge: VIIIe–XIe siècle," *L'Année du Maghreb*, vol. 6 (2011), 27–59.

3. C. Meillassoux, "L'évolution du commerce en Afrique de l'Ouest," in *The Development of Indigenous Trade and Markets in West Africa*, Claude Meillassoux, ed. (London: 1971), 7–16, 519–530, and 543; J. Vansina, "Long Distance Trade Routes in Central Africa," *J. Afr. H.*, vol. 3, no. 3 (1962), 375–390; J. Vansina, *How Societies Are Born: Governance in West Central Africa Before 1600* (Charllottesville, VA: 2004), chapter 3; M. S. Bisson, "Trade and Tribute: Archeological Evidence for the Origin of States in South Central Africa," *CEA*, vol. 22, no. 3–4 (1982), 343–362n87–88; Peter Mitchell and Gavin Whitelaw, "The Archaeology of Southernmost Africa from c. 2000 BP to the Early 1800s: A Review of Recent Research," *J. Afr. H*, vol. 46, no. 2 (2005), 209–241.

4. "Informações do reino de Angola e das suas minas de prata e sal" (report written in Luanda in the final years of the sixteenth century by a Jesuit), *MMA[1]*, vol. 15, 368–373, here 370–371. By 1850, the salt-money trade declined and was "scarce" in 1876. See J. J. Monteiro, "On the Quissama Tribe of Angola," *The Journal of the Anthropological Institute of Great Britain and Ireland* 5 (1876), 198–201, here 201.

5. David Eltis, S. D. Behrendt, and D. Richardson, *The Volume of the Transatlantic Slave Trade: A Reassessment with Particular Reference to the Portuguese Contribution*, Unpublished paper, 1998; P. E. Lovejoy, *Transformations in Slavery* (New York: 1983), 103–107; R. Bean, "A Note on the Relative Importance of Slaves and Gold in West African Exports," *J. Afr. H.*, vol. 15 (1974), 351–366; D. Eltis and L. C. Jennings, "Trade between West Africa and the Atlantic World in the Pre-Colonial Era," *American Historical Review*, vol. 93 (1988), 936–959; D. Eltis, "Trade Between West Africa and the Atlantic World before 1870: Estimates of Trends in Value, Composition, and Direction," *Research in Economic History*, vol. 12 (1989), 197–239; ibid., "The Relative Importance of Slaves and Commodities in the Atlantic Trade of Seventeenth-Century Africa," *J. Afr. H.*, vol. 35, no. 2 (1994), 237–249. For the stateless societies, see M. A. Klein, "The Slave Trade and Decentralized Societies," *J. Afr. H.*, vol. 42, no. 1 (2001), 49–65. On the import of European, American, and Asian goods and their use in Angola in the eighteenth and beginning of the nineteenth centuries, see Joseph C. Miller, *Way of Death: Merchant Capitalism and the Angolan Slave Trade, 1730–1830* (Madison: U of Wisconsin P, 1988), 71–104.

6. On "negócio da Costa da Mina," see F. A. Pereira da Costa, "Vocabulário Pernambucano" (1916), *Revista do Instituto Arqueológico Histórico e Geográfico Pernambucano*, vol. 34, no. 159–162 ([1916] 1936), 517. On "negócio da China," see Rui Manuel Loureiro,

"Chinese Commodities on the India Route in the Late 16th–Early 17th Centuries," *Bulletin of Portuguese—Japanese Studies* no. 20 (2010), 81–94, here 83.

7. G. E. de Zurara, *Crónica de Guiné*, "Introduction" by J. de Bragança (1453–1460), 66; inspired by Zurara, V. Magalhães Godinho's "Caravels against Caravans," the third chapter of vol. 1 of his book *Os Descobrimentos*, 139–174. See also Dale Tomich, "Vitorino Magalhaes Godinho: Atlantic History, World History," *Review* 28, no. 4 (2005), 305–312. About Zurara's work, see J. Barradas de Carvalho, "As edições e as traduções da 'Crónica dos feitos da Guiné,'" *Revista de História* no. 61 (1965), 181–190; I. Wilks, "A Medieval Trade-Route from the Niger to the Gulf of Guinea," *J. Afr. H.* vol. 3, no. 2 (1962), 337–341; J. D. Fage, *An Atlas of African History* (London: 1975), 17, map 13.

8. A 1605 document clearly defines the verb "To rope" (*amarrar*) as the act to "raid and capture Blacks." See doc. of 1605, *MMA*[2], vol. 4, 53.

9. France and Portugal elaborated the first definition of piracy in international law in the 1484 treaty: "[A] private expedition with indiscriminate attack on ships and appropriation of booty without control." Hence, one deduces the legal framework of the corsair's activity: [a]n action carried out under official control, usually in the course of a war, in which friendly or allied ships are not attacked. See C. Darricau, "La course basque et bayonnaise au XVIIe siècle (1663–1698) d'après les registres de l'amirauté de Bayonne," *Revue Historique* vol. 588 (1993), no. 394, 401–419.

10. Zurara, *Crónica de Guiné*, 255–261.

11. F. de Medeiros, *L'Occident et l'Afrique XIIIe–XVIe s* (Paris: 1985), 23–33. Seventeenth-century pontifical documents use "Old Guinea" for Upper Guinea, and "New Guinea" for the gulf of Guinea, Congo, and Angola. See *MMA*[1], vol. 8, 311.

12. Zurara, *Crónica*, 406.

13. For a discussion on the Saharan and sub-Saharan commercial practices behind the so-called "silent trade," see P. F. de Moraes Farias, "Silent Trade: Myth and Historical Evidence," *History in Africa* 1 (1974), 9–24. And for a comment on this essay, see T. Green, "Silent Trade," *History in Africa* 1 (2013), 3–6.

14. Duby notes the *portus* of the eighth and ninth centuries, which correspond to the "ports of trade." See G. Duby, *Guerriers et Paysans* (Paris: 1978), 117–118. Polanyi underlines that Palmyra, Karakorum, and Kandahr caravan city-fairs of the ancient Middle East, between two distinct regions where the desert acts as the sea's "alter ego," constitute "quasi ports of trade." From that perspective, the sub-Saharan trade fairs can be similar to the "ports of trade." See K. Polanyi, "Ports of Trade in Early Societies," in *Primitive, Archaic, and Modern Economies—Essays of Karl Polanyi*, G. Dalton, ed. (New York: 1971), 238–260; G. Dupré and P. Rey, "Réflexions sur la pertinence d'une théorie de l'histoire des échanges," *Cahiers Internationaux de Sociologie* 46 (1969), 133–162; C. M. Good, "Markets in Africa: A Review of Research Themes and the Question of Market Origins," *CEA* 13, no. 4 (1972), 769–780n52. For a discussion on the Polanyi's concept, see L. Graslin and

J. Maucourant, "Le port de commerce: un concept en débat," *Topoi Orient—Occident* (2005), 216–257.

15. For the initial period of the Atlantic trade, see I. Elbl, "The Volume of the Early Atlantic Slave Trade, 1450–1521," *J. Afr. H.* 38 (1997), 31–75.

16. Letter by Luís da Grã to Inácio de Loyola, Piratininga, 8/6/1556, see Manuel da Nóbrega, *Diálogo sobre a conversão do gentio* (Lisbon: 1954), 113; C. Prado Jr., "O fator geográfico na formação e desenvolvimento da cidade de São Paulo," *Geografia* 1, no. 3 (1935), 239–262. See also Pasquale Petrone, *Aldeamentos Paulistas* (São Paulo: 1995), 35–41.

17. M. Tymowski, "Le Niger, voie de communication des grands Etats du Soudan Occidental jusqu'à la fin du XVIème siècle," *Africana Bulletin* 6 (1967), 73–98; Law, "Trade," 321–348.

18. Hawthorne, "The Production," 97–124; J. Boulègue, *Les royaumes wolof dans l'espace sénégambien (XIIIe–XVIIIe siècles)* (Paris: 2013), 99–115.

19. Almada, "Tratado" 230–377.

20. Makhroufi Ousmane Traoré, *Marge de manoeuvre, négociations et pouvoir de décision: les souverains de la Sénégambie dans le système des relations internationales transatlantiques et dans l'évolution du capitalisme moderne du XVe au XVIIIe siècle* (PhD thesis in history, Université de Paris Sorbonne, 2009), 507–648.

21. Doc. of 1618, *MMA¹*, vol. 6, 340, and doc. of 1633, *MMA¹*, vol. 8, 231; *Baculamento*: from the Kimbundu *bakula*; in Kicongo: *vakula* = "to pay tribute." Relating to the tribute that the *sobas* vassal to the Portuguese Crown had to pay, usually in the form of slaves. The tribute collector was called *baculador*. See Heintze, *Fontes*, I, 114. The *Mukuando* communities lived between Benguela and Namibe.

22. J. C. Curto, "Luso-Brazilian Alcohol and the Legal Slave Trade at Benguela and Its Hinterland, c. 1617–1830," in *Négoce Blanc en Afrique Noire: L'évolution du commerce à longue distance en Afrique noire du 18e au 20e siècles*, Hubert Bonin and Michel Cahen, eds. (Paris: 2001), 351–369; Roquinaldo Ferreira, *Transforming Atlantic Slaving: Trade, Warfare, and Territorial Control in Angola, 1650–1800* (PhD thesis, University of California, Los Angeles, 2003), 70–143; Mariana Candido, *Enslaving Frontiers: Slavery, Trade, and Identity in Benguela* (PhD thesis, York University, Toronto, 2006); ibid., "Merchants and the Business of the Slave Trade at Benguela, 1750–1850," *African Economic History* 35 (2007), 1–30.

23. Doc. of January 17, 1823, *AHU*, Angola, Papéis Avulsos, box 142, no. 5 (old cataloguing).

24. *Mandinga* in Brazil is a pejorative synonym for sorcery. The meaning would have been spread by the Luso-Africans living close to the Mandinka, who sold amulets with quotes from the Quran. See *MMA²*, vol. 4, 274. "There is no Black nation who has taken up Mohammed's law with more fervor than the Mandinga," who crossed the hinterland with "sorceries inside a ram's horn [. . .] and written papers that they sell as relics, and on

selling all this they spread Mohammed's sect throughout many a part." See "Memorial de André Donelha" (1625), *MMA²*, vol. 5, 90–146, 130 and 137. Indeed, the Mandinka or Malinke were traders "very knowledgeable about weights and, in addition, they bring along very subtle scales." See Almada, "Tratado," 229–378, 276.

25. In the period 1601–1700: 6,000/year via the trans-Saharan trade and 18,676/year via the Atlantic; in the years between 1701–1810, respectively, 6,000/year and 64,849/year; between 1811–1900, 7,000/year and 28,864/year. See K. Moseley, "Caravel and Caravan, West Africa and the World-Economies, ca. 900–1900 AD," *Review* 15, no. 3 (1992), 523–555; Ralph A. Austen, "The Mediterranean Islamic Slave Trade out of Africa: A Tentative Census," *Slavery and Abolition* 13, no. 1 (1992), 214–248. Numbers on the Atlantic slave trade have been reviewed via TSTD, accessed November 2015.

26. J. Devisse, "L'Apport de l'Archéologie à l'Histoire de l'Afrique occidentale entre le Ve et le XIIe siècle," *Académie des Inscriptions et Belles-Lettres—Comptes Rendus des séances de l'année* no. 3 (1982), 156–177; Fernand Braudel, *La Méditerranée et le monde méditerranéen à l'époque de Philippe II*, 9th ed., vol. 1 (Paris: 1990), 347–355; Andreas Massing, "Mapping the Malagueta Coast: A History of the Lower Guinea Coast, 1460–1510 through Portuguese Maps and Accounts," *History in Africa* 36 (2009), 331–365.

27. J. de Barros, *Ásia: Primeira Década* (Lisbon [1552] 1777–1778) 101; Godinho, *Os Descobrimentos*, 174; R. A. Austen, "Marginalization, Stagnation, and Growth: The Trans-Saharan Caravan Trade in the Era of European Expansion, 1500–1900," in *The Rise of Merchant Empires: Long Distance Trade in the Early Modern World, 1350–1750*, J. D. Tracy, ed. (Cambridge, UK: Cambridge UP, 1993), 311–350.

28. A *peça da Índia* in Portuguese, or *pieza de Indias* in Spanish, is usually understood as the fiscal unit equal to a potential measure of labor corresponding to a healthy African male, about 1.75 m. in height, aged around twenty. Hence, a *peça* could be worth two or three slaves of lesser build. See Azevedo, *Épocas*, 75; M. Goulart, *A escravidão*, 101–102. In the years 1524–1640, the *pieza de Indias* represented two things: the fiscal unit as defined above, or an adult African male slave, regardless of physical attributes. E. Vila Vilar wrote that the latter definition of *piezas* holds true to the Portuguese *Asientos*. To her, it was only in 1663, in the *Asientos* of the Genoeses Grillo and Lomelin, that the *pieza de Índia* came to mean only one unit of potential labor. See Enriqueta Vila Vilar, *Hispano-America y el Comercio de esclavos: Los Asientos Portugueses* (Sevilha: 1977), 186–193. Nevertheless, in 1649, the Luanda municipal council still distinguished the valuable *peças de Indias* from the cheaper *peças do Brasil*. See *AA*, vol. 2, no. 3 (1936), 484. At the end of the eighteenth century, following Degranpré, a slave five feet tall (around 1.6 m) was considered a *pièce d'Inde* in the West Central African ports. See L. Degranpré, *Voyage à la côte occidentale d'Afrique: fait dans les années 1786 et 1787, contenant la description des mœurs, usages, lois, gouvernement et commerce des états du Congo*, vol. 1 (Paris: 1800–1801), 44.

29. *MMA²*, vol. 2, 185.

30. F. Bowser, *The African slave in Colonial Peru, 1524–1650* (Palo Alto, CA: Stanford UP, 1974), 1–25.

31. TSTD, accessed in December 2015.

32. Around 1560 Seville held 10,000 enslaved Africans and blacks plus an undetermined number of Turkish and Moorish captives, in the midst of a population of 80,000. Lisbon numbered at that time around 100,000 people, of which 10,000 were African slaves. See Stella, "L'esclavage," 35–64, 50–51. In Garcia de Rezende's poem, the statement that the trade "trebles the capital" (*tresdobra o cabedal*) should be taken as a stylistic resource indicative of the handsome profits obtained in the activity.

33. *Lançado* is derived from the verb *lançar* meaning "to throw out," to banish, or exile, thus explaining the social statute of the "tangomaos" as deportees. See R. Bluteau, *Vocabulario portuguez e latino*, vol. 5 (Coimbra: 1712–1728), 33. The royal law of August 26, 1512, mentioned "[w]hite men thrown out '(*lançados*) in Guinea.'" See Maria da Graça Garcia Nolasco da Silva, "Subsídios para o estudo dos 'Lançados' na Guiné," *Boletim Cultural da Guiné Portuguesa* 25, no. 100 (1970), 513–560, here 524–525. In Asia, Lançado designed the Portuguese and their descendants who lived outside the Estado da India's enclaves.

34. Almada, "Tratado," 252. The first recorded *Lançado* was João Fernandes, esquire of the duke of Viseu, who lived among the Berber in Rio do Ouro (southern west Sahara) in 1444 so as to trade in slaves. In the discovery of Brazil, admiral Cabral left two banished "lançados" on Bahian shores. See Luís de Albuquerque, ed., *Dicionário de História dos Descobrimentos Portugueses*, vol. 2 (Lisbon: 1994), 582–584.

35. The royal provision of 15.7.1565 already took an interest in the *tangomaos*' bequests, confiscating their inheritance when registered in Lisbon. See J. Tavares de Macedo, "Do que eram os tangomãoes de que se fala na Ordenação do Reino," *Annaes do Conselho Ultramarino, parte não oficial* (Lisbon: [1854–1858] 1867), 313–315.

36. Besides selling hides, wax, and ivory to the French and English, the lançados took slaves to the Wolof and to the north Senegal Maures. See Almada, "Tratado," 253 and 301, and *MMA²*, vol. 4, 543–558. On the Lançados, J. Boulègue, *Les Luso-Africains de Sénégambie XVIe–XIXe siècles* (Lisbon: 1989); J. da Silva Horta, "Evidence for a Luso-African Identity in 'Portuguese' Accounts on 'Guinea of Cape Verde' (Sixteenth–Seventeenth Centuries)," *History in Africa* 27 (2000), 101–107; P. J. Havik, "A Dinâmica das relações de gênero e parentesco num contexto comercial: um balanço comparativo da produção histórica sobre a região da Guiné-Bissau, Séculos XVII e XIX," *Afro-Ásia* 27 (2002), 79–120, here 79–98; P. Mark, "The Evolution of 'Portuguese' Identity: Luso-Africans on the Upper Guinea Coast from the Sixteenth to the Early Nineteenth Century," *The Journal of African History* 40, no. 2 (1999), 173–191.

37. J. Amado and E. Jackson, "Mythic Origins: Caramuru and the Founding of Brazil," *HAHR* 80, no. 4 (2000), 783–811.

38. Doc. of 1539, *MMA¹*, vol. 2, 76.

39. Pereira, *Esmeraldo*, 64, 75–76, 79, and 81–91 passim; W. Rodney, *A History of the Upper Guinea Coast: 1545–1800* (New York: New York UP, 1970), 110.

40. Other overland networks were bypassed by the caravels. See Guerreiro, *Relação*, 212, and *MMA¹*, vol. 3, 106, and *MMA²*, vol. 4, 247; doc. of 1606, *MMA²*, vol. 4, 164. On the evolution of the Senegambia foreign trade from 1680 until 1830, see D. Curtin, *Economic Change in Precolonial Africa: Senegambia in the Era of Slave Trade*, vol. 1 (Madison: U of Wisconsin P, 1975), 334–341; B. Barry, *La Sénégambie du XVe au XIXe siècle: Traite Negrière, Islam et Conquête Coloniale* (Paris: 1988), 23–68.

41. A. Dias Farinha, *Os Portugueses em Marrocos* (Lisbon, 2002), 37; Rui Manuel Loureiro, "Portuguese Involvement in Sixteenth Century Horse Trade through the Arabian Sea," in *Pferde in Asien: Geschichte, Handel Und Kultur (Horses in Asia: History, Trade and Culture)*, Bert G. Franger, ed. (Wien: 2009), 139–145, 142.

42. Linda A. Newson and Susie Minchin, *From Capture to Sale: The Portuguese Slave Trade to Spanish South America in the Early Seventeenth Century* (Netherlands: Brill, 2007), 325–330, appendix F.

43. Doc. of 1606, *MMA²*, vol. 4, 164; Francisco Pires de Carvalho, "Roteiro da Costa da Guiné" (1635), *MMA²*, vol. 5, 287–293; F. de Lemos Coelho, *Duas Descrições Seiscentistas da Guiné* [1669 and 1684] (Lisbon: 1953). Kola: a caffeine-containing nut from the Sterculiaceae family tree, known in Bahia, Brazil as *órobo*, *ervilha-de-pombo* and *obi*. See George E. Brooks, *Kola Trade and State-Building: Upper Guinea Coast and Senegambia, 15th–17th Centuries* (Boston: 1980); Paul E. Lovejoy, "Kola in the History of West Africa [La Kola dans L'histoire de l'Afrique Occidentale," *Cahiers d'Études Africaines* 20, no. 77/78 (1980), 97–134.

44. Alvarez, *Ethiopia Menor e descripção geografica da Província da Serra Leoa* [c. 1615], 9.

45. Enslaved from Senegambia were mainly carried by the Spanish (88,223) and Portuguese (121,804) vessels, between 1551 and 1600. But in the period 1601–1625 the embarkments by the Portuguese (267,519) grew more than the Spanish (83,496); TSDT, accessed December 2014.

46. Alvarez, *Ethiopia*, 1–2. Almada, "Tratado," 242–243; "Memorial de André Donelha," 136. On native horses, H. J. Fisher, "He Swallowed the Ground with Fierceness and Rage: The Horse in the Central Sudan," *J. Afr. H.* 13, no. 3 (1972), 367–388; and Akinwumi Ogundiran, "Material Life and Domestic Economy in a Frontier of the Oyo Empire During the Mid-Atlantic Age," *The International Journal of African Historical Studies* 42, no. 3 (2009), 351–385, here 369–370. On the subject, Ivana Elbl, "The Horse in Fifteenth-Century Senegambia," *The International Journal of African Historical Studies* 24, no. 1 (1991), 85–110.

47. Doc. of 1456, Alvise Da Cà da Mosto, "Navigazione," *DP*, vol. 1, 182, 184–248; Alvise Cà da Mosto, Luís de Cadamosto, and Pedro de Sintra, *Viagens de Luís de Cadamosto e de Pedro de Sintra* [1455–1462] (notes of Damião Peres) (Academia Portuguesa de História, Lisbon: 1948); A. Mauro, "Il viaggio raccontato: Le quattro versioni del 'navigazione' di Alvise da Cà da Mosto," *Mare Liberum* no. 2 (1991), 161–176.

48. J. Heers, *Esclaves et doméstiques au Moyen-Age dans le monde méditerranéen* (Paris, 1981), 89–93; Robin Law, "A West African Cavalry State: The Kingdom of Oyo," *J. Afr. H.* 16, no. 1 (1975), 1–15; ibid., *The Horse in West African History: The Role of the Horse in the Societies of Pre-Colonial West Africa* (Ann Arbor: U of Michigan P, 1980), 46–64 and 89–149. António de Almeida Mendes, "Les réseaux de la traite ibérique dans l'Atlantique nord (1440–1640)," *Annales* 63, no. 4 (2008), 739–768.

49. V. Fernandes, *Códice Valentim Fernandes* (Academia Portuguesa da História: Lisbon, [1507] 1997), 190.

50. For a study on the preponderance of heavy cavalry (but also of archers and crossbowmen) in the Medieval West, see R. J. Bartlett, "Technique militaire et pouvoir politique 900–1300," *Annales* 41, no. 5 (1986), 1,135–1,159.

51. Pereira, *Esmeraldo*, 92; "Memorial de André Donelha," 113. Sleeping sickness is endemic in Africa between the fifteenth parallels to the north and to the south of the equator, where the tsetse flies host to the *Trypanosoma gambiense* and *Trypanosoma rhodesiense* proliferate. These are pathological agents distinct from the *Trypanosoma cruzi*, which causes Chagas disease in Brazil. See A. T. Grove, *The Changing Geography of Africa* (Oxford, UK: Oxford UP, 1969), 57–58.

52. When the Portuguese imports decreased, "Maures" horses continued to be brought over from the north. In the mid-seventeenth century, the Wolof offered thirty slaves for a good horse. See Almada, "Tratado," 239, 244. R. Law wrote that equine imports declined due to the increase in horse raising in the Senegal and Niger watersheds. See Law, *The Horse*, 47–61. Following Boubacar Barry, at the end of the 1600s, there was a predominance of the Atlantic over the continental trade of slaves exchanged for horses in the Maghreb. See Barry, *La Sénégambie*, 23–68. Notwithstanding, J. Webb demonstrates that horses continued to be imported from the Maghreb into Senegambia in the seventeenth and eighteenth centuries, causing ten times more slaves to be sent off to North Africa than to the port of Saint-Louis du Senegal, a French slave-trading port at the end of the seventeenth century. See J. L. A. Webb, "The Horse and Slave Trade between the Western Sahara and Senegambia," *J. Afr. H.* 34, no. 2 (1993), 221–246.

53. Hall, *The Role*, 109–122.

54. "The king of Wolof will field 10,000 (men) on horseback," while the "'king of Mandinka' relied on 20,000 horsemen." See Pereira, *Esmeraldo*, 81 and 86.

55. "Carta do padre Diego de Guadalcanal," Rio de Gambia, June 7, 1647, *MMA²*, vol. 5, 489–498, 496.

56. Almada, "Tratado," 234–243 and 281; A. W. Massing, "The Mane: The Decline of Mali and Mandinka Expansion towards the South Windward Coast," *CEA* 97, no. 25–26 (1985), 21–55; about the expansion of the Songhay, see M. A. Gomez, "Timbuktu under Imperial Songhay: A Reconsideration of Autonomy," *J. Afr. H.* 31, no. 1 (1990), 5–24.

57. R. Rainero, "La bataille de Tondibi (1591) et la conquête marocaine de l'Empire Songhay," *Genève-Afrique* 5, no. 2 (1966), 217–247. On the Moroccan expansion, see L. Kaba, "Les archers, les mousquetaires et les moustiques: une interprétation de l'invasion marrocaine du Soudan et la résistance Songhay, 1591–1612," *Bulletin de l'institut Fondamental d'Afrique Noire* 42 (1980), 1–36; ibid., "Background to the Change in West African Economic History: Songhay, 1492–1750," *Journal of African Studies* 4, no. 3 (1977), 344–356.

58. V. J. Cornell, "Socioeconomic Dimensions of Reconquista and Jihad in Morocco: Portuguese Dukkala and the Sadid Sus, 1450–1557," *International Journal of Middle East Studies* 22, no. 4 (1990), 379–418.

59. Handheld bombards were employed in the battles and there was "Mane Black, a very good bombardier." See Almada, "Tratado," 374; H. J. Fisher and V. Rowland, "Firearms in the Central Sudan," *J. Afr. H.* 12, no. 2 (1971), 215–239.

60. "Memorial de André Donelha" 103–104. See also Walter Hawthorne, "Nourishing a Stateless Society during the Slave Trade: The Rise of Balanta Paddy-Rice Production in Guinea-Bissau," *J. Afr. H.* 42, no. 1 (2001), 1–24.

61. In the eighteenth century, 200,000 muskets were imported annually in west Africa. See W. A. Richards, "The Import of Firearms into West Africa in the Eighteenth Century," *J. Afr. H.* 11 (1980), 43–59.

62. There were no large firearm factories in Africa, yet African blacksmiths fixed and adapted all kinds of weapons, increasing their working life. See J. K. Thornton, "The Art of War in Angola, 1575–1680," *Comparative Studies in Society and History* 30, no. 2 (1988), 360–378.

63. "Carta do Cap. Mor Domingos Jorge Velho sobre o levantamento do Tapuya q' estava em sua companhia," 7.8.1691. See Barão Studart, "Dezenove documentos sobre os Palmares pertencentes à Colleção Studart," *Revista Trimensal do Instituto do Ceará* (hereafter *RTIC*), 20 (1906), 254–289; doc. of 1693, E. Ennes, *Os Palmares—Subsídios para a sua História* (Lisbon: 1938), 115. With regards to Guaicuru horsemen, see S. Buarque de Holanda, *O Extremo Oeste* (São Paulo: 1968), 60–67.

64. J. Goody, *Technology, Tradition and the State in Africa* (New York: Cambridge UP, 1971), 42–56, J. Smaldone, "Firearms in the Central Sudan: A Revaluation," *J. Afr. H.* 13, no. 4 (1972), 591–607; Fox, *The Horse*, 184–196.

65. "Memorial de André Donelha," 113. On the Mane, John J. Grace, "Slavery and Emancipation among the Mende in Sierra Leone," in *Slavery in Africa: Historical and Anthropological Perspectives*, Suzanne Miers and Igor Kopytoff, eds. (Madison: U of Wisconsin P, 1979), 416–417.

66. Fisher and Rowland, "Firearms," 201; H. J. Fisher, "He swallowed," *J. Afr. H.* 13, no. 3 (1972), 367–388 and 14 (1973), 355–379. J. E. Inikori, "The Import of Firearms into West Africa, 1750 to 1807: A Quantitative Analysis," in J. E. Inikori, ed., *Forced*

Migration: The Impact of the Export Slave Trade on African Societies (New York, 1982), 45–51, and 126–153; J. Thornton, *Africa and Africans in the Making of the Atlantic World, 1400–1680* (New York, 1992), 98–116. For the horse versus slave cycle, see Webb, "The Horse," 221–246"

67. Zurara, *Crônica*, 86 and 392; *MMA²*, vol. 4, 271–216, 274.

68. *MMA¹*, vol. 3, 137–138; Robert Ricard, "Recherches sur les relations des Iles Canaries et de la Berbérie au XVIe siècle," *Hespéris* 21 (1935), 79–129. Lobo Cabrera considers that the exchange of Moor prisoners for non-Muslim black slaves with Moor slave traders, was "almost a routine" among the Spanish from the Canary Islands who raided the Barbary and the upper Guinea Coast during the sixteenth century. See M. Lobo Cabrera, *La Esclavitud*, 51–130, here 93.

69. Zurara, *Crônica*, 86; see da Silva Horta, "A representação," 209–327, 262.

70. Brásio, "Do último Cruzado ao Padroado Régio," *Studia* (1959), 125–153, 147.

71. *MMA²*, vol. 1, 277–286.

72. On the Valladolid debate, see Anthony Pagden, *The Fall of Natural Man: The American Indian and the Origins of Comparative Ethnology*, 2nd ed. (New York: Cambridge UP, 1986), 119–145 passim.

73. Pereira, *Esmeraldo*, 82 and 88.

74. J.-P. Tardieu, "Du bon usage de la monstruosite: la vision de l'Afrique chez Alonso de Sandoval (1627)," *Bulletin Hispanique* 86, no. 1–2 (1984), 164–178; Alonso de Sandoval, *Naturaleza, policía sagrada y profana, costumbres y ritos, disciplina y catecismo evangelico de todos los etíopes* (1627), reedited in 1647 in Latin under the title *De Instauranda Aethiopium salute*, which was again reedited in Spanish by E. Vila Vilar, *Un tratado sobre la esclavitud* (Madrid: 1987).

75. F. Pigafetta, *Relação do Reino do Congo e das terras circunvizinhas*, A.L. Alves Ferronha, ed. (Lisbon: [1591] 1989), 28. Published by Pigafetta, the report on the Congo and Angola by D. Lopes, "Relatione del Reame di Congo et delle circonvine Contrade," had thirty-four editions in Italian, Dutch, English, German, Latin, French, and Portuguese. See F. Leite de Faria, "A difusão extraordinária do relato de Duarte Lopes sobre o Congo," *Revista da Biblioteca Nacional* 7, no. 2 (1992), 103–128.

76. *HGGA*, vol. 1, 13–14. The son of a Río de la Plata factor of the *asentista* Antônio Fernandes de Elvas, Cadornega was born in Vila Viçosa (near Évora). He arrived in Luanda in 1639, and in 1641 he went on to Massangano, where he stayed until 1669 as a soldier, captain, and ordinary judge. He returned to Luanda where he became a member of the municipal council, finished his "História" in 1681, and died there in 1690; C. R. Boxer, "A 'História' de Cadornega no Museu Britânico," *Boletim Cultural* 1 (1960), 73–80; Beatrix Heintze, "Antônio de Oliveira de Cadornegas Geschichtswerk: Eine außergewöhnliche Quelle des 17 Jahrhunders," in *Studien Zur Geschichte Angolas im 16. und 17. Jahrhundert—Ein Lesebuch*, B. Heintze, ed. (Colônia: 1996), 48–58. Mathieu Mogo Demaret, "Portugueses

e Africanos em Angola no século XVII: Problemas de representação e de comunicação a partir da História Geral das Guerras Angolanas." In J. D. Rodrigues and Casimiro Rodrigues, eds., *Representações de África e dos Africanos na História e Cultura Séculos XV a XXI*, Linda-a-Velha: 2011, 107–130.

77. The fable of the "public human flesh butcheries," an efficient pretext for the slaving wars of the sixteenth and seventeenth centuries, was also current among the Portuguese in Amazonia, to the point that Spanish Jesuit Acuña, in his report on the Amazon River, emphasized: "[W]hat I desire is to attest that there are none of public butcheries all along this river . . . as alleged by those who, claiming to avoid such cruelty, practiced a greater one, turning into slaves those who were not." See Cristóbal de Acuña, *Novo Descobrimento do Grande Rio das Amazonas* (Rio de Janeiro: [1641] 1994), 120; Antônio Vieira, "Sermão XIV do Rosário," in *Sermões*, prefaced and reviewed by Gonçalo Alves, vol. 4 (Porto: 1993), 733–769.

78. "Rapport de F. Cappelle, março de 1642," in L. Jadin, "Rivalités luso-néerlandaises au Sohio, Congo 1600–1675," *Bulletin de l'Institut Historique Belge de Rome* 37 (1966), 137–360, 221–237, and 226.

79. Nolasco da Silva, "Subsídios," 397–420, here 403.

80. "Tratado de paz do Conde de Sonho e d. João de Lencastre," Luanda, October 18, 1690, article 8, *MMA*[1], vol. 14, 197–204, and 202. About the Soyo, or Sonho, and the Congo at that time, see J. K. Thornton, *The Kingdom of Congo: Civil War and Transition, 1641–1718* (Madison: U of Wisconsin P, 1983), 84–96.

81. L. Sala-Molins, *Le Code Noir ou le calvaire de Canaan* (Paris, 2012), 94–95.

82. E. Benveniste, "Civilisation: Contribution à l'histoire du mot," in *Problèmes de linguistique générale*, vol. 1, E. Benveniste et al., eds. (Paris, 1966), 336–345.

83. "The greatest service that one could render God is to redeem [the captives] from the hands of those barbarians [*sobas* chieftains] into our slavery, [because], even before mentioning spirituality, Your Majesty can rid yourself of the least scruples. The saddest Angolan slave abroad is not as miserable as he is under the treatment he gets under the *sobas* [. . .] who are barbarians, dispensing extremely cruel treatment [*vilíssimo trato*], faithless, lawless, merciless, selling and eating women, sons and relatives with great inhumanity," wrote Gonçalo da Costa e Meneses, governor of Angola, to the king Pedro II in 1692, *MMA*[1], vol. 14, 235–257.

84. Pereira, *Esmeraldo*, 79, 85, and 98.

85. Cape Verde's royal monopoly lasted until mid-seventeenth century. In 1614, the Crown upgraded the Cacheu status, appointing a captain-major for the factory. Yet on side-stepping the Ribeira port in his operations in Guinea at the end of the 1610s, *asentista* Antônio Fernandes de Elvas sealed the fate of the Cape Verde–based domination system. See *MMA*[2], vol. 5, 16, 19–20, and 289. The royal decree (*alvará*) of December 10, 1647, allowed the export duties for outgoing slaves to be paid at Guinea ports and not in

Ribeira any longer. See A. Carreira, "A Capitania das Ilhas de C. Verde," *RHES* 19 (1987), 33–76.

86. P. C. Emmer, "The Dutch and the Making of the Second Atlantic System," in *Slavery and the Rise of the Atlantic System*, B. L. Solow, ed. (New York: Cambridge UP, 1991), 75–96.

87. A. Disney, "Getting to the China Mission in the Early Seventeenth Century," in *As Relações entre a Índia Portuguesa, a Ásia do Sueste e o Extremo Oriente*, A. T. de Matos and L. F. F. Reis Thomaz, eds. (Macau-Lisbon, 1993), 95–109, and 95–96.

88. Doc. of 1610, *MMA²*, vol. 4, 396; doc. of 1621, vol. 4, 662; and doc. of 1671 vol. 6, 310.

89. Doc. of 1554, *MMA¹*, vol. 2, 351; D. Curtin, "Epidemiology and the Slave Trade," *Political Science Quarterly* 83, no. 2 (1968), 190–216, and 203–210. On the African origin of the yellow fever epidemic in Brazil and the Africans' relative immunization, see Gilberto Osório de Andrade and Eustáquio Duarte, *Morão, Rosa & Pimenta* (Recife: [1684–1703] 1957), 176. Data on the first yellow fever epidemic in the Caribbean, recorded in Havana (1649), showed that mortality was much higher among whites than among blacks. See K. F. Kiple, *The Caribbean Slave: A Biological History* (New York: 1984), 162. On yellow fever in West Africa and its transmission to the Americas, see K. F. Kiple and V. Himmelsteib King, *Another Dimension to the Black Diaspora: Diet, Disease and Racism* (London: 1981), 12, and 4–23, 29–49, and 50–56.

90. Despite pressure from the Crown and their own Roman superiors, Portuguese Jesuits refused to establish a college in Cape Verde and in Guinea because of the malignant climes, among other reasons. Doc. of 1596, *MMA²*, vol. 3, 400–403, and vol. 5, 25.

91. Guerreiro, *Relação*, 415.

92. *MMA²*, vol. 4, 552.

93. M. Hubert, *Índios e Jesuítas no tempo das Missões* (São Paulo: 1990), 76. By order of Acquaviva, the Jesuit Province of Paraguay, originally established in 1604, was established in 1607. See *HCJB*, vol. 1, 333–358. J. de Guibert, "Le Généralat de Claude Aquaviva, 1581–1615," *Archivum Historicum Societatis Iesu (AHSI)* 10, no. 1 (1941), 59–93.

94. *MMA²*, V, 456; B. Barry, "L'Impact de la Traite Negrière sur les sociétés sénégambiennes du XVIème au XIXème siècle" (paper presented at the *Congresso Internacional sobre a Escravidão*, Universidade de São Paulo, June 1988).

95. *MMA²*, vol. 4, "Carta do governador de Cabo Verde," 1616, 604.

96. Doc. of January 26, 1582, *MMA²*, vol. 3, 97–107; in 1582 there were ten parishes (*freguesias*) on the island of Santiago, where 1,108 whites, mulattos, and "freed married" blacks lived, all of whom owned 10,700 slaves. The plantations and farmhouses produced sugar, cotton, maize, and cattle. See *MMA²*, vol. 3, 99–100.

97. Decision by the Conselho Ultramarino, August 29, 1687, *MMA¹*, vol. 14, 66–67.

98. W. Hawthorne, *From Africa to Brazil*, 226.

99. *MMA²*, vol. 4, 505, 639–641, and vol. 5, 184 and 192; Vilar, *Hispano-America*, 148–152, 209; A. Carreira, "Tratos e Resgates dos Portugueses nos Rios da Guiné e Ilhas

de C. Verde nos começos do século XVII," *RHES* 2 (1978), 91–103. Carreira's figures do not consider smuggling to Indias de Castela, a fact well demonstrated. See doc. of 1614, *MMA¹*, vol. 6, 171–172, *MMA²*, vol. 4, 697–699, and doc. of 1622, *MMA²*, vol. 4, 698–704. See also, A. de Almeida Mendes, "The Foundations of the System: A Reassessment of the Slave Trade to the Spanish Americas in the Sixteenth and Seventeenth Centuries," in *Extending the Frontiers: Essays on the New Transatlantic Slave Trade Database*, D. Eltis and D. Richardson, eds. (New Haven: 2008), 83–85, table 2.6.

100. On the Portuguese administration in Cape Verde, see Z. Cohen, "O provimento dos oficiais da justiça e da fazenda para as ilhas de Cabo Verde," *Studia* 51 (1992), 145–176.

101. An especially fast voyage was registered by the governor of Pernambuco, Correia de Sá, in 1750. Then, a captain sailed from Lisbon to Rio de Janeiro in thirty-three days. See "O diário do governador Correia de Sá 1749–1756," introduction and notes J. A. Gonsalves de Mello, *RIAHGP* 56 (1983), 9–378, 100.

102. F. de Brito Freyre, *Viagem da Armada da Companhia do Comércio e Frotas do Estado do Brasil* (Lisbon: 1657), 4.

103. "Carta de Álvaro Sanches de Brito para el-rei, expondo os riscos que corriam as frotas do Brasil e da Índia, e apontando os meios de os suprimir," c. 1706. Brito was a pilot boasting thirty years of experience on the sea routes between Portugal and India. See V. Rau and M. F. Gomes da Silva, *Os Manuscritos do Arquivo da Casa de Cadaval respeitantes ao Brasil*, vol. 2 (Coimbra: 1956–1958), 332–334.

104. M. Figueiredo, *Hidrographia, exame de pilotos: no qual se contem as regras que todo piloto deue guardar em suas nauegações: com os roteiros de Portugal pera o Brasil, Rio da Prata, Guinè, S. Thomé, Angolla, & Indias de Portugla* [sic], *& Castella* (Lisbon: 1625); A. Mariz de Carneiro was royal cosmographer in 1631, under the Hapsburg Crown, and again in 1641, under the Braganza, he published *Regimento de pilotos e Roteiro da navegaçam e conquistas do Brasil, Angola, S. Thome, Cabo Verde, Maranhão, Ilhas, & Indias Occidentais* (Lisbon: 1655). Luís Serrão Pimentel, chief cosmographer (*cosmógrafo-mor*) of the kingdom from 1647, had his *Arte Prática de Navegar* published by his son, Manuel Pimentel, in 1681. From this book, M. Pimentel excerpted the *Arte de Navegar, BNL*, res., codice 862 (1712), in 1699; a more complete edition was prepared by the author in 1712. See A. Cortesão, F. Aleixo, and L. Albuquerque, 1969, for the first part of the treaty that does not include the several "itineraries" (*roteiros*) of the 1712 manuscript (*BNL*, res. 862), to which I refer from now on.

105. M. Pimentel, *Arte de Navegar, BNL* (1712), 286. See also R. de Cortez Matos, "O Cosmógrafo-Mor: o ensino náutico em Portugal nos séculos XVI e XVII," *Oceanos* 38 (1999), 55–65.

106. Commanding a fleet of thirty-six carracks in 1656, Brito Freyre sailed from Lisbon in April out of the "ordinary monsoon" to Brazil, and had his vessels dispersed by storms. Some vessels sailed too close to the African coast and were carried along the windless Mina Coast. As Brito Freyre's vessel went northward his pilots warned that "if they do not turn

the Cape Santo Agostinho they will be either pushed towards the (West) Indies or make their way back to the Mainland." See Freyre, *Viagem*, 10.

107. Vieira, *Cartas*, 314.

108. A. Vieira, "Relação da Missão da Serra de Ibiapaba," *Obras Escolhidas*, vol. 5, A. Sérgio and H. Cidade, eds. (Lisbon: [1659] 1951–1954), 86–87.

109. The galleon *São Lucas* that left Lisbon in March 1588, bringing Francisco Geraldes to assume the general government of Brazil in Bahia, wandered for a year and a half between the Guinea Coast and the West Indies without being able to cross the equator. Eventually, the *São Lucas* returned to Lisbon, in September 1589, and Geraldes gave up his position in Brazil. The case illustrates difficulties of the Lisbon-Bahia route during the early decades of Portuguese America. See J. de Mirales, "História militar do Brazil," *ABNRJ* 22 ([1762] 1900), 128.

110. The equatorial countercurrent is known as the Guinea current along the coast of Ghana.

111. M. Justo Guedes, "O Condicionalismo Físico do Atlântico e a Navegação à Vela," *História Naval Brasileira*, vol. 1 (Rio de Janeiro: 1972), 117–134.

112. S. E. da Sylveira, "Relação sumária das cousas do Maranhão dirigida aos pobres deste reyno de Portugal" *ABNRJ* 94 ([1624] 1974), 43.

113. Brandão, *Diálogos*, 70. See also S. B. Schwartz, *Sovereignty and Society in Colonial Brazil: The High Court of Bahia and Its Judges* (Berkeley, CA: 1973), 233.

114. Letters of April 4, 1654, May 14, 1654, and May 1, 1660, Vieira, *Cartas* 1, no. 1, 414 and no. 3, 727–733 and 749–755.

115. Letter of August 25, 1706, *DH*, vol. 83, 58–59.

116. Vieira, "Carta ao provincial do Brasil," in *Cartas*, vol. 1, 369–400, here 393–400.

117. M. Justo Guedes, "Guerra da Independência: as Forças de Mar," in *História da Independência do Brasil*, vol. 2, J. Montello, ed. (Rio de Janeiro: 1972), 167–211.

118. Bettendorf, *Crônica*, 607.

119. *HGB*, vol. 2, book 3, 195.

120. "East Coast of South America," *Sailing Directions*, 56.

121. Caldas, "Notícia Geral de Toda esta Capitania da Bahia Desde o Seu Descobrimento Até o Presente Ano de 1759" *Revista*, 297–301, here 297.

122. M. Pimentel, "Roteiro do Brasil," *BNL*, Res. 862, 276–308.

123. "Parecer ao Conselho Ultramarino," October 13, 1646, *ABNRJ* 39 (1917), 51–53. Underlining the navigation difficulties beetween Salvador de Bahia and South Brazil's coast, Fr. Lourenço de Mendonça suggested in 1631 the establishement of a diocese with its seat in Rio de Janeiro, Diogo Ramada Curto, "O P. Lourenço de Mendoça: entre o Brasil e o Peru (c. 1630–c. 1640)," *Topoi*. 11, 20 (2010), 27–35.

124. Consultation to the Conselho Ultramarino, 10 October 1658, *PLMH*, V. II, 521–524.

125. The steamboat *São Sebastião* left at the same time as the *Beranger* carrying the then-colonel Luiz Alves de Lima, future Duke of Caxias, and his officers. It also experienced difficulties in completing its itinerary, being forced to take shelter in Vitória (Espírito Santo), where it remained for three days, waiting for winds to lessen. See D. J. Gonçalves de Magalhães, "Memória Histórica e Documentada da Revolução da Província do Maranhão desde 1839 até 1840," *Novos Estudos: Cebrap* 23 (1989), 14–66, 37.

126. A. L. Nunes Penha, *Nas águas do Canal: política e poder na contrução do canal Campos-Macaé 1835–1875* (PhD thesis, Universidade Federal Fluminense, Niterói, 2012).

127. J. A. Gonsalves de Mello, *Fontes para a História do Brasil Holandês* (hereafter *FHBH*), vol. 1 (Recife: 1981), 186. D. de Alencar Guzmán and L. A. H. C. Hulsman, *Holandeses na Amazônia (1620–1650): documentos inéditos* (Belém: 2016), 118–119.

128. A. Rodrigues Ferreira, "Diário da viagem filosófica pela capitania de São José do Rio Negro com a informação do estado presente" *RIHGB*, vol. 48 (1885), 1–234, 57. I further discuss the issue of the Indian slave trade and Rodrigues Ferreira's proposal in chapter 4.

129. Otherwise "no Negro would arrive alive" said governor Miguel Antônio de Mello in a document to the commerce board (*Junta de Comércio*), where he criticized the embarkation conditions of slaves. Luanda, March 12, 1799, *AA*, vol. 20 (1963), 78–85.

130. Miller, *Way of Death*, 318.

131. "Southwest Coast of Africa," *Sailing*, 71.

132. St. Helena High is also called Capricorn Anticyclone, South Atlantic Gyre, or South Atlantic High.

133. Vieira, "Sermão XXVII do Rosário," *Sermões*, 1205.

134. Mpinda is present-day Soyo, in Angola, on the southern bank of the Congo River delta. See M. E. Madeira Santos, "Rotas Atlânticas, o caso da Carreira de S. Tomé," in *Actas do II Colóquio Internacional de História da Madeira* (Lisbon: 1989), 649–655.

135. S. B. Alpern, "The European Introduction of Crops into West Africa in Precolonial Times," *History in Africa* 19 (1992), 13–43, 16.

136. But the horses only survived one year in São Tomé. With regards to 2,000 Jewish boys under eight years of age, kidnapped by the Crown and brought over in 1492 by the first captain of the island, Valentim Fernandes said that there were 600 still alive in 1506. See Valentim Fernandes *Códice*, 169–177; C. A. Garcia, "A Ilha de São Tomé como centro experimental do comportamento do Luso nos trópicos," *Studia* 19 (1966), 209–222.

137. "Do not give for each piece (slave) more than 40 tin bracelets, and the least possible under that," "Regimento do Trato de São Tomé," 8 February 1519, *MMA*[1], IV, 124–133.

138. *MMA*[1], vol. 1, 41–45 and 129. Before the introduction of American maize and manioc in the sixteenth and seventeenth centuries, there were three alimentary regimes in tropical Africa: banana and hunting (Central Africa); yam and hunting (from Cameroon to Ghana); and yam, hunting, and rice (to the west of Ghana). See J. Vansina, "l'Homme, les

forêts et le passé en Afrique," *Annales* 40, no. 6 (1985), 1,307–1,334. The malagueta pepper was used in the same manner as garlic in Europe: as seasoning, but also as medicine "for stomach ache and colds." See Almada, "Tratado," 312. "Frialdade" was the advanced phase of the "opilação" disease, a general term referring to "blocking up" (*entupimento*), which resulted from the verminous disease and from malaria, two chronic illnesses in the tropics. On maize in São Tomé and the Gold Coast, see O. Dapper, *Description de l'Afrique contenant les noms, la situation et les confins de toutes ses parties* (Amsterdam: 1686), 291; see also, M. Miracle, "The Introduction and Spread of Maize in Africa," *J. Afr. H.* 6, no. 1 (1965), 39–55.

139. "Foral de São Tomé," March 26, 1500, *MMA*[1], vol. 15, 17–20.

140. Wilks, "Waranga," 333–349; ibid., "Wangara, Akan and Portuguese in the Fifteenth and Sixteenth Centuries. II. The Struggle for Trade," *J. Afr. H.* 23, no. 4 (1982), 463–472.

141. "Foral de São Tomé," *As Gavetas da Torre do Tombo*, vol. 2 (1524), 506–513, here 508.

142. Report by J. Lobato, royal factor in São Tomé to King João III, April 13, 1529, *MMA*[1], vol. 1, 505–518; J. L. Vogt, "The Early Sao Tomé," 453–467.

143. *MMA*[1], vol. 4, 21–22 and 35; Sandoval, *Un tratado*, 139–140; C. Rosselli, "Relaciones de conctato de criollo palenquero de Colômbia," *Forma y Función* 11 (1998), 77–101, and 27 (1987), 140.

144. Doc. of 1506, *MMA*[1], vol. 4, 21–23, 33–45, and 34.

145. "Carta de Privilégios," November 21, 1493, *DP*, vol. 3, 422–424, 423.

146. G. Parker, *The Military Revolution: Military Innovation and the Rise of the West, 1500–1800* (Cambridge, UK: 1988), 82–114; L. A. Clayton, "The Iberian Advantage," in *Technology, Disease, and Colonial Conquests, Sixteenth to Eighteenth Centuries: Essays Reappraising the Guns and Germs Theories*, G. Raudzens, ed. (Leiden: 2003), 211–236; T. Hoffman, "Prices, the Military Revolution, and Western Europe's Comparative Advantage in Violence," *The Economic History Review* 64, no. S1 (2011), 39–59.

147. Felner, *Angola*, 70–71 and 116–117. About the *nzandu*, Congo's trade fairs, see I. do Amaral, "Mbanza Congo, cidade do Congo, ou São Salvador:" Contribuição para o conhecimento geográfico de uma aglomeração urbana africana ao Sul do Equador, nos séculos XVI e XVII," *Garcia de Orta* 12 (1987), 1–40n1-2, 26–28.

148. Doc. of 1548, *MMA*[1], vol. 2, 199–200; J. Vansina, *Kingdoms of the Savannah* (Madison, WI: 1975), 53–54.

149. Doc. of November 11, 1554, *MMA*[1], vol. 15, 204–205. In the beginning of the 1600s the island produced, on average, 60,000 arrobas (one *arroba* = 14.689 kg) of sugar. See doc. of 1607, *MMA*[1], vol. 5, 381.

150. On the first stages of colonization in São Tomé, see A. Massing, "Valentim Fernandes's Five Maps and the Early History and Geography of São Tomé," *History in Africa* 36 (2009), 367–386; T. Madeira da Silva, "*A cidade de São Tomé no Quadro das Cidades Insulares Atlânticas de Origem Portuguesa*" (2012), https://repositorio.iscte-iul.pt/handle/10071/3921, accessed January 2013.

151. L. da Cunha Pinheiro, "A conflitualidade social e institucional em S. Tomé ao longo do século XVI," *Actas do Congresso Internacional Atlântico de Antigo Regime: poderes e sociedades* (Universidade Nova de Lisboa, 2005), 1–17.

152. R. Ramos, "Rebelião e sociedade colonial: 'alvoroços' and 'levantamentos' in São Tomé 1545–1555," *Revista Internacional de Estudos Africanos* 4–5 (1986), 17–24; Fernanda Olival and João de Figuerôa-Rêgo, "Cor da pele, distinções e cargos: Portugal e espaços atlânticos portugueses (séculos XVI a XVIII)," *Tempo* 26 no. 30 (2011), 115–145.

153. Slave escapes have been reported since 1529, and in 1531 the Casa da Mina directors wrote that the whole of São Tomé could fall into the rebelling slaves' hands. The word *mocambo* appeared in 1535, and the expression "to do a mocambo" (*fazer mocambo*), meaning a group of slaves taking refuge in the São Tomé hills is noted in a document by the island's municipal council dated 1554; *MMA*[1], vol. 1, 517, and vol. 2, 331–333.

154. A. M. Caldeira, "Rebelião e outras formas de resistência à escravatura na Ilha de São Tomé," *Africana Studia* 7 (2004), 101–136.

155. The word appeared for the first time in Brazil at the beginning of the seventeenth century, already with interethnic meaning, indicating its wider insurrectional character: "Mocambos and knavery (*ladroeiras*), of bands of Indians and Negros." See D. de Lopes Moreno, *Livro que dá Razão do Estado do Brasil–1612*, introduction and notes by H. Vianna (Recife: 1955), 113. On the definition in Kimbundu, see the glossary by J. M. Delgado, *HGGA*, vol. 1, 618.

156. J. C. Miller, *Kings and Kinsmen: The Imbangala Impact on the Mbundu of Angola* (Madison, WI: U of Wisconsin P, 1972), 151–175; K. Munanga, "Origem e Histórico do Quilombo na África," *Revista da USP* 28 (1995–1996), 1–13.

157. G. Freyre, "Introdução," *Sobrados e Mucambos* (Lisbon: 1936), 23–67; Costa, *Vocabulário*, 492.

158. Raimundo José da Cunha Mattos (Faro, Portugal 1776 to Rio de Janeiro 1839) also had a relevant role in Brazil as a politician, officer, and historian. Acting as governor and representative of the Goiás' province in the general legislative assembly in Rio de Janeiro, he became later the military academy director in 1833. He was also one of the main founders of the Instituto Histórico e Geográfico Brasileiro in 1838. See J. H. Rodrigues, "Nota preliminar" in *Compêndio Histórico das Possessões de Portugal na África*, R. J. Cunha Mattos, ed. (Rio de Janeiro: 1963), 7–21; Bianca Martins de Queiroz, *Raimundo José da Cunha Matos (1776–1839): A pena e a espada a serviço da pátria* (master's thesis, Universidade Federal de Juiz de Fora, Juiz de Fora, 2009).

159. R. J. da Cunha Matos, *Corographia historica das ilhas de S. Thomé, Principe, Anno Bom, e Fernando Po* (Porto: 1842), 12–13; Kaori Kodama, "Itinerários, corografias e escritas da história: as viagens e os registros de Raimundo José da Cunha Matos no Império do Brasil," *Escritos. Revista do Centro de Pesquisa da Casa de Rui Barbosa* 2, no. 2 (2008), 373–395.

160. On slave insurrections between 1593 and 1599, see *MMA¹*, vol. 3, 461–463, 521–523, and 598–602. The most complete report on King Amador's revolt came from an anonymous text that originated in the narration written in 1734 by the dean of São Tomé's cathedral, Manuel do Rosário Pinto, *Relação do Descobrimento da Ilha de São Tomé. Manuel do Rosário Pinto*, A. Caldeira, ed. (Lisbon: 2006), 71–78.

161. The São Tomé bishop denounced in 1798 the presence of blacks "living [. . .] without communication or domestic behavior" in the island's backland. See *IHGB*, DL40, 03.06.

162. TSTD, accessed November 2015.

163. "Resolução que o Bispo e o Ouvidor Geral do Brasil tomaram sobre os injustos cativeiros dos Índios do Brasil e do remédio para o aumento da conversão e da conservação daquele Estado," *Biblioteca Pública de Évora*, cod. 116/1–33, fs. 69–71, here fl. 69. Serrão acted as Bahia's college rector from 1578 until 1584, and the report was written between these dates.

164. *Regimento* of July 26, 1596, *HCJB*, vol. 2, 623–624.

165. Besides Beliarte, a Jesuit provincial in Brazil between 1587 and 1594, the junta was composed of Portuguese America ex-Crown judges. See C. Rangel, A. de Aguiar, and M. Leitão, *Inventário dos Manuscritos da Biblioteca da Ajuda referentes à América do Sul* (Coimbra: 1946), 13–14.

166. Pero Rodrigues writes that the second main colonists' enemies were the Aymoré (*Tapuya*) Indians and the third were the French corsairs. Only the seaside (*Tupy*) Indians were Portuguese allies. See letter to J. Alvarez (Claudio Acquaviva's assistant), Bahia, May 1, 1597, *ABNRJ* 20 (1898), 255–265, here 255.

167. "Carta do pe. Balthazar Afonso ao Geral da Companhia," Luanda, June 28, 1595, *MMA¹*, vol. 15, 348–349.

168. "Informação do reino de Angola" (c. 1600), *MMA¹*, XV, 368–373, here 372.

169. Anchieta's biographer, the Jesuit Pero Rodrigues, was the author of several important texts about Brazil and Angola, as will be seen below. See Pero Rodrigues, "Vida do Padre José de Anchieta," *ABNRJ* 19 (1897), 2–49.

170. V. do Salvador, *História do Brasil 1500–1627* (São Paulo: [1627] 1982), 116–117.

171. The term had a precise meaning in the seventeenth century: "'meek' [*mansos*] we call those [Amerindians] who have some kind of republic, however rudimentary, are easier to deal with and persevere longer amongst the Portuguese, letting themselves to be instructed and cultivated. We call 'wild' [*bravos*], on the contrary, those who live without any kind of republic, are intractable and with difficulty let themselves be taught." S. de Vasconcellos, *Notícias curiosas e necessárias das cousas do Brasil* (Lisbon: 1668), 152.

172. About the difference between the "*aldeia*" (Amerindian traditional villages), sites chosen by the native communities to establish residence, and "*aldeamento*" (Amerindian colonial settlement), compulsory dwelling places fixed by authorities, see chapter 4.

173. About the origins of the Santomese communities that had revolted, see J. Vansina, "Quilombos on Sao Tomé, or in Search of Original Sources," *History in Africa* 23 (1996), 453–459. On the Amador's revolt interpretation written by the Portuguese colonialist geographer Francisco Tenreiro in his monography *A Ilha de São Tomé* (1961), see G. Seibert, "Tenreiro, Amador e os Angolares ou a reinvenção da história da Ilha de São Tomé," *Revista de Estudos Antiutilitaristas e PosColoniais* 2, no. 2 (2013), 21–40 http://www.nucleodecidadania.org/revista/index.php/realis/article/view/32, accessed in January 2014. Concluding an essay on Quilombos and slaves, Florentino and Amantino wrote: "The American continent never felt any impact from [. . .] the actions of rebelled slaves against the slavery plantation system in the São Tomé island." M. Florentino and M. Amantino, "Escapes, Quilombos and Fugitives in the Americas (Sixteenth-Nineteenth Centuries)," *Análise Social* 203 (2012), 236–267, 264.

174. "King Amador" became a Santomese and an African hero. In 2004, Kofi Annan, general secretary of the United Nations, inaugurated his statue in São Tomé. On the insurrection see also I. B. de Sousa, *São Tomé et Principe de 1485 à 1755, une société coloniale: du blanc au noir* (Paris: 2008), 167–174.

175. Commenting on P. C. Emmer's paper in the September 1988 Harvard conference on slavery and the Atlantic system, Philipp Curtin observed that the Caribbean slave system, denominated by Emmer as the second Atlantic system (following a first system created by the Iberian countries in South America) appeared in reality as a third system, since the first had been that of the Atlantic Islands (Canaries, Madeira, Cape Verde, and São Tomé), distinct from the second system, established later in South America. Emmer seemed not to have been convinced by Curtin. See Solow, *Slavery*, 75–96.

176. Royal letter of King João III, July 9, 1526, *MMA¹*, vol. 1, 472. See also J. Scarano, *Devoção e escravidão: A irmandade de Nossa Senhora do Rosário dos Pretos no Distrito Diamantino no século XVIII*, 2nd ed. (São Paulo: 1978); M. de Carvalho Soares, *Devotos da cor: identidade étnica, religiosidade e escravidão no Rio de Janeiro, século XVIII* (Rio de Janeiro: 2000); L. Reginaldo, *Os Rosarios dos Angolas: irmandades negras, experiencias escravas e identidades africanas na Bahia setecentista* (São Paulo: 2011).

177. See chapter 3.

178. D. Pacheco Pereira, *Esmeraldo*, 133–134.

179. F. Leite de Faria, "Uma Relação de Rui de Pina sobre o Congo escrita em 1492," *Studia* 19 (1966), 223–303, here 252–254.

180. Letters by King Afonso to his subjects, 1512, *MMA¹*, vol. 1, 262–268, and vol. 15, 24. See also F. Bontinck, "Du Nouveau sur Dom Afonso, roi de Congo," *African Historical Studies* 3, no. 1 (1970), 151–162.

181. "Carta do Coletor Apostólico em Lisboa sobre uma carta do rei do Congo," Lisbon, March 28, 1587, *MMA¹*, vol. 15, 306–307.

182. Doc. of December 12, 1596, *MMA*[1], vol. 3, 515–516. The Cochin diocese dates from 1558, and Macau's from 1576. Japan's diocese, established in Funai, was created in 1588, when Toyotomi Hideyoshi's anti-Western policy was still unknown in Europe. Macau and Cochin were under partial control of the *Estado da India* vice-kingdom, but Funai and Japan remained completely outside Portuguese dominion. See J. Oliveira e Costa, "Em torno da criação do Bispado do Japão," in *As relações entre a Índia portuguesa, a Ásia do Sueste e o Extremo Oriente*, A. T. de Matos and L. F. F. Reis Thomaz, eds. (Lisbon: 1993), 141–171, 142. The *Mesa da Consciência e Ordens* was a high court created in 1532 by King João III to counsel the monarch with regard to issues relative to the church, to military orders, and to Coimbra University. See J. M. Subtil, "Administração Central da Coroa," in *História de Portugal*, vol. 3, J. Mattoso, ed. (Lisbon: 1994), 78–90, 87.

183. Bull of Clemens VIII, promoting São Salvador to the honor of the city and the parochial church with the honor of the cathedral, May 20, 1596, *BAL*, 46-XI-7, fs. 521–535.

184. F. de Almeida, *História da Igreja em Portugal*, D. Peres, ed. (Porto: Barcelos, 1967–1971), 26–27 and 693; since 1587, Mbanza Congo had gained the name of "Cidade de São Salvador do Congo." See *MMA*[1], vol. 3, 348–355, 350.

185. About the use of Christianity as a source of *ngolo*, or political power in the Congolese monarchy, see A. Brásio, "O problema da eleição e coroação dos reis do Congo," *Revista Portuguesa de História*, vol. 1, book 12 (Coimbra: 1969), 351–381.

186. Letters by the king of Congo, 1526, *MMA*[1], vol. 1, 468–484, 470–471.

187. Letters by the king of Congo, 1517, *MMA*[1], vol. 1, 404. Gregório de Quadra made an accusation, in 1520, that there were Portuguese members of King Afonso's entourage who played a game of their own against Lisbon's policy. Gregorio was sent to the Congo to open the way up to Ethiopia (*Abexi*). See *MMA*[1], vol. 15, 59–60. Such an expedition illustrates the break with Ptolemaic geography, relaunched by Duarte Pacheco Pereira, according to which the Pacific and Atlantic formed a single ocean surrounded by land. Seamen and other cosmographers did not share such ideas and continued to seek straits between the two oceans. In 1539, Fernão de Magalhães set sail in his celebrated voyage that disproved Ptolemy's theory once and for all. See W. G. L. Randles, *Da terra plana ao globo terrestre* (Lisbon: 1990), 98–110.

188. Generally, in the sixteenth to nineteenth centuries Iberia documents the verb and the practice of *resgatar* or its Spanish equivalent *rescatar* to mean, in fact, to ransom a prisoner or a slave (a Moor, Asian, Amerindian, or an African) from his native captors or owners in order to have full possession of him and to own him as slave. Following Bluteau's definition (*resgate: a ação de resgatar ou comutar*), I consider the verb synonymous with *comutar* (barter). See Bluteau, *Vocabulario portuguez e latino* (Coimbra: 1,712–1,728), 280. Hence, I translate *resgate* as "enslavement by barter," instead of *rachat* or "ransoming" as most Francophone and Anglophone authors do.

189. "Letter by D. João III," 1529, *MMA*[1], vol. 1, 525–527.

190. *MMA*¹, vol. 2, 101; A. Hilton, *The Kingdom of Kongo* (Oxford: 1985), 59–60.

191. D. Henrique was a bishop in *partibus infidelium* ("in the region of the infidels"), according to the Pope's practice of attributing the bishopric of ancient or extinct dioceses to the Roman Curia clergy. Such was the case of the Utica diocese in North Africa: it had been dissolved since the Arab invasion. F. Bontinck, "L'ancien Congo et le Concile de Trente," *Antennes* 12, no. 2 (1962–1963), 453–464; C. M. de Witte, "Henri de Congo, évêque titulaire d'Utique d'après les documents romains," *Euntes Docete* 21 ([1531] 1968), 587–599.

192. *MMA¹*, vol. 1, 88–524, and vol. 2, 6, 73.

193. Regimento de Simão da Silva, 1512, *MMA*¹, vol. 1, 228–246, 240. See A. C. Gonçalves, *Congo. Le lignage contre l'État—Dynamique politique au Congo du XVIème au XVIIIème siècle* (Lisbon: 1985), 137.

194. D. Thorner, "Marx et l'Inde: le mode de production asiatique," *Annales* (1969), 337–369. For a remarkable analysis on the European colonial exploitation of the Goan village communities, and on the opinions of Marx, Maine, and the British and Portuguese scholars on these matters, see Axelrod and M. A. Fuerch, "Portuguese Orientalism and the Making of the Village Communities of Goa," *Ethnohistory* 45, no. 3 (1998), 439–476. The authors consider the Portuguese revenue superintendent (*Vedor da Fazenda*) Afonso Mexia, who scrutinized the political and economic structure of the Indian village communities in 1526, as the "first Portuguese Orientalist." For that matter, Mexia should be considered the first European Orientalist.

195. W. C. Neale, "Réciprocité et redistribution dans le village indien: Suite a quelques célèbres discussions," in *Trade and Market in Early Empires: Economies in History and Theory*, K. Polanyi and C. Arensberg, eds. (New York: 1957), 217–231, 218.

196. Doc. of 1512, *MMA¹*, vol. 1, 247–253; "Vestidos enviados ao el-Rei do Congo por el-Rei de Portugal," doc. of 1520, vol. 15, 57–58.

197. "Ordem de Duarte Pacheco Pereira ao feitor da Mina," doc. of 1512, *MMA*¹, vol. 15, 48; A. Teixeira da Mota, "Duarte Pacheco Pereira Capitão e Governador de São Jorge da Mina," *Mare Liberum* 1 (1990), 1–27.

198. S. Halikowski-Smith, " 'The Friendship of Kings Was in the Ambassadors': Portuguese Diplomatic Embassies in Asia and Africa during the Sixteenth and Seventeenth Centuries," *Portuguese Studies* 22, no. 1 (2006), 101–134, here 118–120.

199. M. N. Pearson, *Os Portugueses na Índia* (Lisbon: 1990), 44–46.

200. In 1507, A. da Silva Rego, *DHMPPO*, vol. 1 (Lisbon: 1991), 300–301, 301n1. The book *O Livro dos Pesos, Medidas e Moedas, De Sofala à China*, by A. Nunes and edited by L. Felner, was published in 1554. About the insertion of Portugal in a pre-European economy. See J. Marinho dos Santos, "As economias do Índico aquando da chegada dos portugueses," *RPH* 27 (1992), 203–214.

201. M. Newitt, "Plunder and the Rewards of Office in the Portuguese Empire," in *The Military Revolution and the State, 1500–1800*, M. Duffy, ed. (Exeter: 1980), 10–28.

202. The Bijagos islands, then called Buão, are situated below the river Casamance delta, in Guinea-Bissau. See the royal letter of March 27, 1532, *MMA²*, vol. 2, 227.

203. A. Sérgio, ed., *Antologia dos Economistas Portugueses: século XVII* (Lisbon: 1974), 243, note 2; E. Axelson, *South-East Africa 1488–1530* (London and Toronto: 1969), 6–11.

204. P. Beaujard, and S. Fee, "The Indian Ocean in Eurasian and African World-Systems before the Sixteenth Century," *Journal of World History* 16, no. 4 (2005), 411–465; E. Pollard, "Safeguarding Swahili Trade in the Fourteenth and Fifteenth Centuries: A Unique Navigational Complex in South-East Tanzania," *World Archaeology* 43, no. 3 (2011), 458–477.

205. J. de Barros, *Ásia: Primeira Década*, vol. 2 (Lisbon: [1552] 1920), 373–423, here 380.

206. Sepúlveda to the king, 1542, see L. De Albuquerque, T. W. Baxter, and A. da Silva Rego, *Documentos sobre os portugueses em Moçambique e na África Central 1497–1840*, vol. 7 (Lisbon: 1962–1989), 130–141, 137.

207. Ibid., 168–183; W. G. L. Randles, "La fondation de l'empire du Monomotapa," *CEA* 14-2, no. 54 (1974), 207–236.

208. *MMA¹*, vol. 12, 172–175, 173.

209. S. de Vasconcellos, *Vida do Joam d'Almeida da Companhia de Jesu na Província do Brazil* (Lisbon: 1658), 132.

Chapter 3

1. Lisbon's maritime and geopolitical significance to the Spanish Habsburg empire is underlined by L. Mendes de Vasconcelos's *Diálogos do sítio de Lisboa* (1608), which stated that the Crown should adopt the city as its capital. The same point of view is adopted by D. Gomes Solís in his *Alegación en Fauor de La Compañia de La India Oriental Y Comercios Ultramarinos Que de Nueuo Se Instituyó en El Reyno de Portugal* (1628), edited by M. B. Amzalak, Lisbon: 1955, 64–65. After the Braganza's restoration, a third illustrious Portuguese writer praised Lisbon's geopolitical prominence in Europe. See F. Manuel de Melo, *Epanáforas de vária história portuguesa*, 3rd ed. (Coimbra: [1660] 1931), 126–127.

2. Doc. of 1604, *MMA²*, vol. 4, 4. After the Treaty of Alcaçovas (1479), Spain recognized, albeit reluctantly, the Portuguese monopoly on the slave trade in sub-Saharan Africa. See R. Pike, *Aristocrats and Traders: Sevillian Society in the Sixteenth Century* (Ithaca, NY: Cornell UP, 1972), 174–175.

3. R. Sampaio Garcia, "Contribuição ao estudo do aprovisionamento de escravos negros na América espanhola 1580–1640," *Anais do Museu Paulista* 16 (1962), 8–12; M. da Graça Mateus Ventura, *Negreiros portugueses na rota das Índias de Castela 1541–1556* (Lisbon: 1999), 32–36; Almeida Mendes, "Les réseaux," 739–768.

4. The Spanish slave-trade authorizations took four forms: the *de merced* or *de servicios* license (1492–1510), commercial licenses (1510–1575), contract licenses (1576–1594),

and *Asiento* licenses (1595–1640). See E. G. Peralta Rivera, *Les mécanismes du commerce esclavagiste*, vol. 1 (PhD thesis, École des Hautes Études em Sciences Sociales, Paris: 1977), 7–52; E. Mira Caballos, "Las Licencias de Esclavos Negros a Hispanoamérica (1544–1550)," *Revista de Indias* 54, no. 201 (1994), 273–298.

5. M. M. F. Torrão, "Os portugueses e o trato de escravos de Cabo Verde com a América espanhola no final do século XVI: Os Contratadores do trato de Cabo Verde e a Coroa, uma relação de conveniência numa época de oportunidades 1583–1600," in *Portugal na Monarquia Hispânica: Dinâmicas de integração e de conflito*, Cardim, L. F. Costa, and M. S. da Cunha, eds. (Lisbon: 2013), 93–106.

6. TSTD, accessed September 2015.

7. B. Afonso, Luanda, July 31, 1582, *MMA¹*, vol. 3, 219; D. do Santíssimo Sacramento, Luanda, 14/9/1584, ibid., 304. The narratives of Novais's victories rarely mention the actions of such "*Chombari*" archers. See ibid., 319–321. About horses shipped from Brazil to Angola, see Cardim, *Tratado*, 66.

8. R. Austen," The Mediterranean," 214–248; TSTD, accessed September 2015.

9. J.L. Cortés López, "Felipe II, III y IV, Reyes de Angola y protectores del reino del Congo (1580–1640)," *Studia Histórica* 9 (1991), 223–246.

10. "Escritura da trespassação do trepiche ao governador d'Angola e aforamento dos dízimos," Rio de Janeiro, April 3, 1579, *ABNRJ* 82 (1962), 130–131.

11. "Carta do padre Balthazar Barreira," Massangano, August 27, 1585, *MMA¹*, vol. 3, 323–325.

12. Abreu e Brito, *Sumário*, 34–35.

13. J. L. Cortés López, 230.

14. "Relatorio de Duarte Lopes," Madrid, December 14, 1589, *MMA*¹, vol. 4, 514–518.

15. D. Wheat, "Garcia Mendes Castelo Branco, fidalgo de Angola y mercader de esclavos en Veracruz y el Caribe a principios del siglo XVII," *Centro de estudios mexicanos y centroamericanos* (2011), http://books.openedition.org/cemca/197, accessed in July 2015.

16. Newson and Minchin, *From Capture*, 187–234, 293–296, table 8.6. A century later, in a similar situation, when trade linked the Brazilian inland gold mines to the seaports, the Rio de Janeiro governor stated that most of the enslaved Africans arriving from Angola and the Gulf of Guinea through Bahia and Pernambuco died on the trails before reaching the villages of Minas Gerais. See letter May 27, 1722, *AHU*, Rio de Janeiro, box 13, doc. 88.

17. M. da Graça A. Mateus Ventura, "Os Gramaxo, Um Caso Paradigmático de Redes de Influência em Cartagena das índias," *Cadernos de Estudos Sefarditas* 1 (2001), 65–81; E. Vila Vilar, "Extranjeros en Cartagena (1593–1630)," *Jamrbuch fur Geschichte von Staat, Wietschaft und Gesellschaft Lateinamerikas* 16 (1979), 147–184. On Cartagena and the *Asiento*, see Chaunu and Chaunu, *Séville*, 1,031–1054; D. Wheat, "The First Great Waves: African Provenance Zones for the Transatlantic Slave Trade to Cartagena de Indias, 1570–1640," *J. Afr. H.* 52 (2011), 1–22.

18. See chapter I, note 119.

19. R. Sampaio Garcia, "O português Duarte Lopes e o comércio espanhol de escravos negros," *Revista de História* 7, no. 30 (1957), 375–385, here 379–380.

20. Abreu e Brito, *Sumário*, 30; letter of the governor Fernão de Sousa to the Crown, Luanda, June 12, 1626, "In times of the Antonio Fernandes de Elvas Contract, some ships bound to Brazil [. . .] were diverted to the Río de la Plata," *AHU*, Angola, box 2/98; see also Heintze, *Fontes*, 138n232, 333–334. On the smuggling to Spanish America from Cacheu and Cape Verde, see doc. of 1614, *MMA*[1], vol. 6, 171–172, *MMA*[1], vol. 7, 67–74, here 68–69; *MMA*[2], vol. 4, 697–699 and doc. of 1622, *MMA*[2], vol. 4, 698–704; on slave ships ostensibly bound for Brazil that arrived in the Spanish Caribbean, see Wheat, *The Afro-Portuguese*, 45–46.

21. Doc. of January 22, 1657, *AHU*, Angola, box 6/98.

22. Doc. of February 8, 1676, *AHU*, Angola, box 11/61; doc. of July 20, 1677, *AHU*, Angola, box 11/87.

23. H. Lapeyre, "Le trafic négrier avec l'Amérique espagnole," *Homenaje a Jaime Vicens Vives* (Barcelona: 1967), 285–304.

24. Royal order of May 20, 1578; primeros siete capítulos del Asiento hecho com Pedro Gomez Reynel, Madrid, royal order of January 30, 1595, see Salmoral, *Regulación*, 128 and 114–146, here 145.

25. The *Asiento* contractor (the *asentista*) bought the lot of *licencias*, which could be used by the buyer himself or sold to third parties for the shipping of "pieces." Likewise, the Crown and the Cape Verde and Guinea contractors kept a number of licenses for personal trade or for later sale. See G. Scelle, *Histoire politique de la traite négrière aux Indes de Castille*, vol. 1 (Paris: 1906), 386–389.

26. Magalhães Godinho, *Os Descobrimentos*, 178–181, 196–197. Vila Vilar, *Hispano-America*, 27.

27. Lopo de Sousa Coutinho (the elder), an officer in India at the time of Governor Nuno da Cunha (1528–1538), fought at Diu in 1538 and wrote the *História do cerco de Diu*. Later, as São Jorge da Mina governor, he also did slave trade. João Rodrigues Coutinho was in the India fleet (1581–1584), together with his brothers André and Diogo. João fought alongside his brother Diogo in the Indian Ocean battles, and, like his father, he was nominated governor of Elmina. See royal letter of April 1, 1586, *ANTT*, Felipe I's chancery, book 15, sheet 287. Below, I write about the fourth Sousa Coutinho brother, Manuel de Sousa Coutinho, and about the fifth, Gonçalo Vaz Coutinho. See M. Lopes De Almeida, "Introdução," in *História de São Domingos*, vol. 1, Friar Luís de Sousa, ed. (Porto, 1977), 10–46; J. Leitão Manso de Lima, *Famílias de Portugal*, vol. 9 (Lisbon, 1925), 50–54.

28. R. Ricard, "Los Portugueses en las Indias Españolas," *Revista de Historia de América* 34 (1952), 449–456. Scelle, *Histoire*, 390n2.

29. Given the strong presence of women among the signatories of this *Asiento*'s guarantees (51.5 percent of the total), Peralta Rivera suggests that the true investors were

merchants of Portuguese and Spanish new Christian communities. See Peralta Rivera, "Les mécanismes," 104–112.

30. Vila Vilar, *Hispano-America*, 106–108.

31. B. Heintze, "Historical Notes on the Kisama of Angola," *Journal of African History* 13, no. 3 (1972), 407–418.

32. "História da residência dos padres da Companhia de Jesus em Angola e cousas tocantes ao reino e à conquista," Luanda, May 1, 1594, *MMA¹*, vol. 4, 546–581, here 550.

33. "Informação do reino de Angola e das suas minas de prata e sal" (c. 1600), *MMA¹*, vol. 15, 368–373, here 371.

34. *HGGA*, vol. 1, 67–70.

35. João R. Coutinho's *Asiento*, administered by his brother and partner Gonçalo, was valid up to 1605. From 1605 to 1609, the *Asiento* was in the hands of Gonçalo. The Angola contract also came into his hands from 1603 to 1606. See Peralta Rivera, "Les mécanismes," 118–133; *MMA¹*, vol. 5, 487–488.

36. *MMA¹*, vol. 6, 21n1, and *HGGA*, vol. 1, 63n1, and vol. 3, 564; M. J. da C. Felgueiras Gayo, *Nobiliário de famílias de Portugal*, vol. 4 (Braga: 1992), 21–22; Leitão Manso de Lima, *Famílias*, 52–54.

37. Manuel Cerveira Pereira was the son of Gaspar Cerveira Pereira. See R. Delgado, *O Reino de Benguela: descobrimento à criação do governo subalterno* (Lisbon: 1945), 41–43n1. To distinguish him from the following governor, whose family name was also Pereira, I henceforth name him Manuel Cerveira, as the documents do. See *MMA¹*, vol. 5, 60–62, and 82–83.

38. Following my remarks in chapter 1, "Luso-Brasílico" relates to the Portuguese from Lisbon or newly arrived in Portuguese America and the settler already has rooted interests in the area.

39. The governor took to the field "with many and handsome people, and many and good horses," stated a document of that time. See *MMA¹*, vol. 5, 224.

40. TSDT, accessed September 2015.

41. R. Bonciani, "Os irmãos Coutinho no Atlântico: escravidão, governo e ascensão social no tempo da monarquia hispânica," *5º Encontro Internacional de História Colonial* (Maceió: 2014), 1–11.

42. Vila Vilar, *Hispano-America*, 70.

43. Bonciani, "Os irmãos Coutinho no Atlântico," 7.

44. "Aprovação [. . .] à terceira parte da 'História de s. Domingos' da Província de Portugal, reformada pelo pe. frei Luís de Sousa," Vieira, *Obras*, vol. 7, 158–163.

45. Friar Luís de Sousa died in 1623. M. C. Pereira da Costa, "O cronista frei Luís de Sousa, contribuição para um estudo biográfico e genealógico," *Arquivo Histórico Dominicano Português*, vol. 2 (Lisbon: 1979), 76, 140, 144–145, and vol. 3 (1987), 29–50; Lopes de Almeida, "Introdução," XLI–XLII.

46. E. Prestage, de Azevedo, and M. Laranjo Coelho, eds, *Correspondência Diplomática de Francisco de Sousa Coutinho durante sua embaixada em Holanda 1643–1650* (hereafter *CD*), vol. 1 (Coimbra, Lisbon: 1920), XI–XII.

47. Gonçalo Vaz Coutinho (the younger) and his homonym *asentista* grandfather are mixed up by some authors. See, for instance, R. M. d'A. Fonseca Gadelha, "Judeus e cristãos-novos no Rio da Prata. A ação do governador Hernandarias de Saavedra," in A. Novinsky and M. L. Tucci Carneiro, eds., *Inquisição Ensaios sobre mentalidade, heresias e arte* (São Paulo: 1992), 370; and F. Ribeiro da Silva, "Crossing Empires: Portuguese, Sephardic, and Dutch Business Networks in the Atlantic Slave Trade, 1580–1674," *The A* 68, no. 1 (2011), 7–32, 19.

48. A. C. da Costa, *Corografia portugueza e descripçam topografica do famoso Reyno de Portugal*, vol. 1 (Lisbon: 1706–1712), 490–494. In his comments, this famous genealogist claimed to possess important documents on the Pereira Coutinho family.

49. Henriques's contract covered the years 1607–1615, *AHU*, Angola, box 1/6; J. Gonçalves Salvador, *Os magnatas do tráfico negreiro* (São Paulo: 1988), 43, 131–132, 170. Drago remained involved in the Luanda slave trade until late 1620. See December 17, 1627, *AHU*, Angola, box 2/119.

50. Dias Henriques's agents operated in Olinda, Bahia, Madeira Island, Oporto, Lisbon, Madrid, Seville, Antwerp, Venice, and Hamburg. See J. C. Boyajian, *Portuguese Bankers at the Court of Spain 1626–1640* (New Brunswick, NJ: 1983), 33–34 and A–2.

51. In colonial Brazil, the word was probably used in the original *Kimbundu* meaning: to name the files of recently arrived slaves traveling to the countryside farms and sugar mills.

52. J. C. Miller, *Way of Death*, 322–324; "Southwest Coast of Africa" *Sailing Directions*, 71.

53. F. Damião Cosme, "Tractado das queixas endemicas e mais fataes nesta Conquista," Luanda: [1770], *Studia* 20–22 (1967), 264–267.

54. O. Dapper, *Description de l'Afrique* (Amsterdam: 1686), 368.

55. J. C. Miller, "Overcrowded and Undernourished: Techniques and Consequences of Tight-Packing in the Portuguese Southern Atlantic Slave Trade," in *De la Traite a L'Esclavage*, vol. 2, S. Daget, ed. (Paris, Nantes: 1988), 395–424.

56. Eltis and Richardson, *Atlas of the Transatlantic*, 182, map 125.

57. B. Bailyn, *The Peopling of British America: An Introduction* (New York: 1988), 8–9.

58. Calculated from the TSTD, accessed in December 2015; see also chapter 1, notes 133 and 134.

59. Two hundred and fifty Africans perished in this voyage made between December 1649 and January 1650. The overcrowding of this vessel is atypical, taking place during the Luso-Dutch War, when there were few ships available in the Angola thoroughfare. See *DHCMA*, vol. 1, 379.

60. H. Casado Alonso, "El Comercio de Nueva España con Castilla en la Época de Felipe II: Redes Comerciales Y Seguros Marítimos," *Historia Mexicana* 61, no. 3 (2012), 935–993, here 94n18.

61. M. A. de G. da Regio and D. de C. da Piacenza, *Viaggio nel Regno del Congo* (Bologna: 1674), 182.

62. Vieira, *Cartas*, vol. 1, 398–399.

63. Rodrigues, "Apontamentos sobre a fundação de um Colégio no reino de Angola," June 15, 1593, *MMA¹*, vol. 15, 333–340, here 336.

64. J. O. Beozzo, *Leis e regimentos das Missões* (São Paulo: 1983), 179–187.

65. *HCJB*, vol. 5, 5–24.

66. Letter by d. Diogo de Menezes, Bahia, *ABNRJ*, vol. 57 (1611), 71–75; *HGB*, vol. 1, book 2, 112.

67. Bettendorf, the Jesuit missionary and Amazonian expert, explained in 1698 that the Crown authorized Amerindian's enslavement "because of the *just war*, or because [these Indians] had been tied up in order to be eaten" by their enemies. To him, the Amerindians "preferred to be slaves to the Portuguese rather than be killed"; Bettendorf, *Crônica*, 485.

68. *Ley sobre a liberdade do Gentio da Terra e guerra que se lhe pode fazer* (September 10, 1611), *DI*, vol. 3 (1894), 71–73. Although the *Estado do Pará e Maranhão* was administratively separate from the *Estado do Brasil* in 1621, until 1624 the legislation concerning the Amerindians remained the same in both parts of Portuguese America. See M. C. Kiemen, *The Indian Policy of Portugal in the Amazon Region 1614–1693* (New York: 1973), 3–5.

69. J. Mathiex, "Trafic et prix de l'homme en Méditerranée aux XVIIe et XVIIIe siècles," *Annales E.S.C.* vol. 9, no. 2 (1954), 157–164; F. Braudel, *La Méditerranée*, vol. 2, 353–475; D. Hershenzon, "'[P]ara Que Me Saque Cabesea Por Cabesa': Exchanging Muslim and Christian Slaves across the Western Mediterranean," *African Economic History* 42, no. 1 (2014), 11–36.

70. On corsair activity from 1580 to 1680, during the "Mediterranean crisis," see M. Fontenay, "La Place de la Course dans l'économie portuaire: L'exemple de Malte et des ports barbaresques," *Annales* 43, no. 6 (1988), 1,321–1,347; E. Alberto, "Corsários argelinos na costa atlântica: o resgate de cativos de 1618," *Actas do Congresso Internacional Atlântico de Antigo Regime: poderes e sociedades* (Lisbon: Universidade Nova de Lisboa, 2005), 1–6. The *Mamposteiros* were, in general, revenue and alms collectors for the redemption of Christians captured by the Moors, while the *Alfaqueque* was in charge of rescuing the captives and negotiating the conditions of their liberation. See M. T. Racine, *'A Most Opulent Iliad': The Portuguese Occupation of Southern Morocco (1505–1542): The Fortunes of a Frontier Society* (PhD thesis, University of California, Santa Barbara, 2003), 354 and 357–362.

71. I. M. R. M. D. Braga, *Entre a cristandade e o islão, séculos XV–XVIII Cativos e renegados nas franjas de duas sociedades em confronto* (Ceueta: 1998), 77 and 219–221, table 11;

E. M. C. Martins Alberto, *Um Negócio Piedoso: o Resgate de Cativos em Portugal na Época Moderna* (PhD thesis in history, University of Minho, 2010), 61–120.

72. The Order of the Trinitarian priests, founded in 1198 with the aim of collecting alms for the redemption of captives in the hands of the Muslims, was extinct in 1830, after the conquest of Algiers by the French. See R. Ricard, "Recherches sur les relations des Iles Canaries et de la Berbérie au XVIe siècle," *Hespéris* 21 (1935), 79–129; J. Vidago, "Anda mouro na costa," *Studia* 45 (1981), 295–306; Braga, *Entre a Cristandade*, 145–168.

73. E. Benveniste, *Le Vocabulaire des Institutions Indo-Européennes*, vol. 1 (Paris: 1969), 129–137 and 355–361; Martins Alberto, *Um Negócio Piedoso: o Resgate de Cativos*, 39–42.

74. "Regimento do Trato de São Tomé," February 8, 1519, *MMA*[1], vol. 4, 124–133, here 126.

75. In Mbundu, the language of the Ovimbundu peoples, "captive" or "prisoner" = *ohwate, omandekwa*; "the soba's slave" = *kale, omunu*; and "slave" = *kalenge, kapinji, okalumba, upika, upili*. See G. Le Guennec and J. F. Valente, *Dicionário português-umbundu* (Luanda: 1972). In the Kimbundu and Mbundu dialects, "captive" = *hute, amunguata, amupape* and "slave" = *mumbika, upika*. See A. da Silva Maia, *Dicionário elementar português-omumbuim-mussele* (Cucujães, 1955). In the Chokwe language, of the ethnic group of the same name in Angola's northeast and Congo-Kishasa, "purchased slave" = *mwána wa kupita* and "son-of-the-village slave" = *mwána wa cihúnda*. See A. Barbosa, *Dicionário cokwe-português* (Coimbra: 1989). In Kikongo, spoken in Congo and north of Angola, "captive" = *anfungi* and "slave" = *mubiika*. See R. Butaye, *Dictionnaire kikongo-français, français-kikongo* (Roulers, Belgium: 1910). In Makua, the Mozambique idiom, "captive, prisoner of war" = *nanvariwa, mukhole* and "slave" = *kapuro, kaporo*. See A. Valente de Matos, *Dicionário português-macua* (Lisbon: 1974). In Nagot (Yoruba), spoken in Nigeria, considered by Nina Rodrigues as the main language of the Bahia slaves, "slave" = *erú* and "born-in-the-house slave" = *erú-ibíle*. See E. Fonseca, Jr., *Dicionário yorubá (nagô)-português* (Rio de Janeiro: 1983).

76. Bluteau, *Vocabulário portuguez e latino*, book 2, 202, book 3, 224–225.

77. *AHU*, Angola, box 1, docs. 3 and 4; *MMA*[1], vol. 5, 166–167 and 264–279; A. C. de Sousa, *História genealógica da Casa Real portuguesa*, book 11 (Coimbra: [1740] 1949), 417 and 549.

78. Letter by Father Pero de Sousa, Luanda, May 18, 1604, *MMA*[1], vol. 15, 391–395, 394.

79. "Regimento [. . .] ao capitão-mor e governador do reino de Angola, d. Manuel Pereira Forjaz," *Boletim do Arquivo Histórico Colonial*, vol. 1 ([1607] 1950), 235–243.

80. In Angolistas texts *baqueano* means a "man experienced in the hinterlands," "Angolan hinterlander," *HGGA*, vol. 1, 600. In Brazil, *baqueano* (in the north and nordeast), the noun also means "practical," "knowledgeable about a region," *Dicionário Aurélio* and F. A. de Varnhagen, *HGB*, vol. 1, book 1, 200.

81. *MMA*[1], vol. 5, doc. of 1607, 357–358.

82. *DHCMA*, vol. 2, 157; "Informação do bispo do Congo e Angola em 1619," *MMA*[1], vol. 5, 359–384.

83. *HGGA*, vol. 3, 165.

84. J. C. Miller, "Requiem for the Jaga," *CEA*, 13 (1973), 121–149; J. K. Thornton, "A Resurrection for the Jaga," *CEA* 18, no. 1–2 (1978), 223–228; J. C. Miller, "Thanatopsis," *CEA* 18, no. 1–2 (1978), 229–231; F. Bontinck, "Un mausolée pour les Jaga," *CEA* 20, no. 3 (1980), 387–390. J. de Sousa Pinto, "Em torno de um problema de identidade: os 'Jaga' na Historia do Congo e Angola," *Mare Liberum* 18–19 (1999), 193–243.

85. As early as 1623, Jesuits in Angola had characterized the Jaga as a "profession," *MMA¹*, vol. 15, 517, as did Cadornega, who fought them in 1681. See *HGGA*, vol. 2, 179. Eventually, in the eighteenth century, some Jaga's groups settled. See J. Nepomuceno Correia, "Notícia Geral dos costumes da província de Behe," *IHGB*/Africa [c. 1797]; J.-L. Vellut, "Le royaume de Cassange et les réseaux luso-africains, ca. 1750–1810," *Cahiers d'Études Africaines* 15, no. 57 (1975), 117–136; I. Castro Henriques, *Commerce et changement en Angola au XIXe siècle: Imbangala et Tshokwe face à la modernité*, vol. 1 (Paris: 1995), 184–191. However, in 1782, captain Silva Correa, who also fought the Jaga, still qualifies them as nomadic and multiethnic warriors: "The Jaga are governors of a bellicose and wandering people who admit a variety of nations, and under the same [Jaga] name are included the governors and the governed who make up this band." See E. A. da Silva Correa, *História de Angola*, vol. 2 (Lisbon: [1787–1799] 1937), 50. B. Heintze, "The Extraordinary Journey of the Jaga through the Centuries: Critical Approaches to Precolonial Angolan Historical Sources," *History in Africa*, 34 (2007), 67–101.

86. Heintze, "The Angolan Vassals," 34.

87. "Regimento de Manuel Cerveira," March 23, 1615, *MMA¹*, vol. 15, 455–463.

88. Delgado, *O Reino*, 76.

89. Doc. of 1623, *MMA¹*, vol. 15, 517. Without mentioning the Brazilian synonymy between *desdentado* and *benguela* (both meaning "toothless"), Joseph C. Miller analyzes the relationship between the words *Imbangala* and *Benguela*. See Miller, "The Imbangala and the Chronology of Early Central African History," *J. Afr. H.* 13, no. 4 (1972), 561.

90. In European Portuguese, the noun *banguela* it is not a synonym of toothless, nor in Kimbundu, which uses the word *kuboboka* or *wabo'boka* to say toothless. *Boboca* has two meanings in Portuguese Brazilian: simpleton and toothless. Yet the two definitions could have the same Kimbundu origin, since *boboca* designates a person with the absent-mindedness typical of babies and the elderly, also characteristic of the toothless. For the noun *boboca*, see A. J. de Macedo Soares, *Dicionário brasileiro da língua portuguesa Elucidário, etimológico, crítico*, vol. 1 (Rio de Janeiro: 1954), 47, and *Dicionário Houaiss da Língua Portuguesa* (Rio de Janeiro: 2001).

91. Luís Mendes de Vasconcelos left the manuscript for *História do Cunhale célebre cossário da Índia*. André Furtado de Mendonça executed the famous Malabar captain, Mahomet Kunhali Marakkar, denominated by the Portuguese as *Cunhale Marcá*. Feared from the Indic to the Yellow Sea by the Europeans who sailed those parts, Cunhale Marcá allegedly held the unusual titles of "Expeller of the Portuguese and Spiller of Christian Blood"; see C. R.

Boxer and F. de Vasconcelos, *André Furtado de Mendonça* (Lisbon: 1989), 11–25; I. F. da Silva, *Diccionario bibliographico portuguez*, vol. 5 (Lisbon: 1860), 306–307.

92. See appendix 1.

93. July 9, 1616, *AHU*, Angola, box 1/50; *MMA¹*, vol. 6, 263–270.

94. "Carta a el-rei," November 28, 1617, *MMA¹*, vol. 6, 283–285.

95. "Informação do bispo do Congo e Angola em 1619," *MMA¹*, vol. 6, 368.

96. Heintze, "The Angolan Vassal Tributes," 38.

97. Royal letter, March 20, 1620, *CCLP*, 1620–1627, 7.

98. L. M. de Vasconcelos, *Arte militar* (Lisbon: 1612), 183.

99. On the "ethnic soldiering" and the native military alliances in the European colonization in South America, see N. L. Whitehead, "Ethnic Transformation and Historical Discontinuity in Native Amazonia and Guyana, 1500–1900," *L'Homme* 33, no. 126 (1993), 285–305.

100. *MMA¹*, vol. 9, 82–84.

101. Doc. of August 9, 1616, *AHU*, Angola, box 1/50. Article 28 of Governor Tristão da Cunha's statute [*Regimento*], of April 10, 1666, bears the regal order determining that the ships from Brazil loaded with horses had preference in the shipping of slaves and in leaving Luanda. Horses, but not mares! After the defeats inflicted by the Moroccan cavalry in the sixteenth century, the Portuguese feared that the introduction of mares would lead the Angola natives to raise horses to form a combat cavalry. See *Boletim do Conselho Ultramarino anos 1446–1754*, vol. 1 (Lisbon: 1867), 297–307.

102. After his arrival in Luanda, Vasconcelos wrote the Court to complain about the scarce funds for governing Angola. See September 15, 1617, *AHU*, Angola, box 1/76; see also, *MMA¹*, vol. 6, 366–374. Author of the denunciation against Vasconcelos, Baltasar Rebelo de Aragão had built, in his words, "at my own expense," the Muxima fortress. Experienced in the affairs of Angola, where he had arrived in 1592, he received the nickname of *Bangalambota*, or Ironwood, a name through which the Mbundu wished to define his sturdiness in tackling life in the hinterland. Despite his truculence, Bangalambota thought that Luís Mendes de Vasconcelos went too far in his predatory greed and criticized him in a report to the Crown. See L. Cordeiro, *1593–1631 Terras e minas africanas segundo Balthazar Rebello de Aragão* (Lisbon: 1881), and in *MMA¹*, vol. 6, 332–343, 342; Anonymous, *História do reino do Congo*, A. Brásio, ed. (Lisbon: [1625] 1969), 29–30.

103. Pope Gregory XV proclaimed the five new saints in 1622: Loyola, Francis Xavier, Filippo Néri, Teresa d'Ávila, and Isidoro (the founder of the Jesuit Order, the apostle of the Asian missions, the apostle of Rome, the mystic Sister, and the Madrid patron saint, respectively). See M. Venard, "Les formes personnelles da la vie religieuse," in J. M. Mayeur, C. Pietri, A. Vauchez, and M. Venard, eds., *Histoire du christianisme des origines à nos jours*, vol. 8 (Paris: 1992), 991–1,027.

104. "Com fazenda de lei de Graça e vida/Divino Xavier, a este contrato/vos manda e avisa que vendais barato/a responder no Céu qualquer partida," *Procissam, relação das festas que a residência de Amgolla fez* [1620], A. Parreira, ed. (Lisbon: 1993). On this celebration in honor of Xavier, where Vasconcelos organized what seems be the first known *Congada*, see also, Albuquerque Felner, *Angola, Apontamentos sobre a ocupação e início do estabelecimento dos portugueses no Congo, Angola e Benguela (extraídos de documentos históricos)* (Coimbra: 1933), 311–320.

105. *MMA¹*, vol. 6, 511–513. The scheme, common during the *Asiento* period, consisted of dispatching slave ships to Spanish America, paying dues as if they were bound to Brazil (4,000 *réis*, instead of 7,000 *réis*), doc. of 1622, *MMA¹*, vol. 7, 67–74, 68–69. See also 5.

106. *ANTT*, Tribunal do Santo Ofício, Inquisição de Lisboa, maço 9, doc. no. 8 http://digitarq.arquivos.pt/details?id=2318699, accessed November 2013. About Father J. Vogado, see also L. Jadin, "Pero Tavares, missionnaire jésuite, ses travaux apostoliques au Congo et en Angola 1629–1635," *Bulletin de l'Institut Historique Belge de Rome*, vol. 38 (Brussels: 1967), 272n1.

107. Vasconcelos was in Madrid in January 1614, as member of a royal commission [*Junta*] called by Felipe III to discuss issues related on Portuguese India. At that time, Antonio Fernandes de Elvas was also in Madrid, maneuvering to obtain the *Asiento* that he would operate from in 1615. See G. Scelle, *Histoire politique de la traite négrière aux Indes de Castille: Contrats et traités d'Assiento*, vol. 1 (Paris: 1906), 420–428.

108. Wheat, "The first great waves,"15–16, 19; ibid., *The Afro-Portuguese Maritime World*, 252–256.

109. M.C. Navarrete, *Genesis y Desarrollo de La Esclavitud En Colombia Siglos XVI y XVII* (Cali: 2005), 44–45.

110. Eltis and Richardson, *Atlas of the Transatlantic*, 151, map 105.

111. L. A. Newson and S. Minchin, "Cargazones de negros en Cartagena de Índias en el siglo XVII: nutrición, salud y mortalidad," *Cartagena de Indias en el Siglo XVII*, H. Calvo Stevenson and A. Meisel Roca, eds. (Cartagena: 2007), 207–243.

112. Scelle, *Histoire*, 415. Analyzing 180 complete *Asiento* voyages, Vila Vilar found that 14.7 percent spend less than a year, 33.1 percent from one to two years, 37 percent from two to four years, and 9.7 percent delayed more than four years. See E. Vila Vilar, "Aspectos marítimos del comercio de esclavos con hispanoamerica en el siglo XVII," *Revista de Historia Naval* 19 (1987), 113–131.

113. E. Vila Vilar quotes a 1614 document of the Sevillian *Asiento*'s *Junta de Negros* stating that delay to embark a slave shipment in African ports might take twelve to eighteen months. See Vila Vilar, "Aspectos marítimos," 122.

114. On the allies of Antonio Fernandes de Elvas in Madrid in his maneuver to obtain the *Asiento*, Vila Vilar, *Hispano-America*, 43n76. Albuquerque Felner suspects that Elvas also

manipulated the king's confessor, Fray Luis de Aliga. See A. de Albuquerque Felner, *Angola, Apontamentos sobre a ocupação e início do estabelecimento dos portugueses no Congo, Angola e Benguela* (*extraídos de documentos históricos*) (Lisbon: 1933), 295n1. On Fray Aliga, confessor and state councilor of Felipe III, see I. Poutrin, "L'oeil du souverain: Luis de Aliaga et le métier de confesseur royal sous Felipe III," in *Observation and Communication: The Construction of Realities in the Hispanic World*, J.-M. Scholz and T. Herzog, eds. (Frankfurt: 1997), 253–270.

115. F. Pyrard, *Voyage*, 234–235. Stuart B. Schwartz, "Prata, açúcar e escravos: de como o império restaurou Portugal." *Tempo* 12 no. 24 (2008) 201–223, here 218.

116. Mathias Delgado labels Vasconcelos as "one of the most pernicious governors of Angola," making him responsible for the attacks that have engendered the long "Jinga War" and the slave-trading kingdoms of Matamba and Kasanje. See *HGGA*, vol. 1, 98n1; B. Heintze, "Angola nas garras do tráfico de escravos As guerras do Ndongo, 1611–1630," *Revista Internacional de Estudos Africanos*, vol. 1 (1984), 15–16; Miller, "The Imbangala," 568n73. Curtin notes, however, the increase in the Angolan slave trade as early as the turn of the sixteenth century, Curtin, *The Atlantic*, 108–112. John Thornton dates the Vasconcelos-Jaga alliance as the beginning of the "Imbangala period" (1615–1665) that consolidated the slave trade and the Portuguese presence in Angola. See J. K. Thornton, "The Portuguese in Africa," in *Portuguese Oceanic Expansion 1400–1800*, F. Bethencourt and D. R.Curto, eds. (New York: 2007), 153.

117. Report by Sottomayor, Angola's Chief judge, in 1620, *MMA¹*, vol. 15, 475–780, 478; *HGGA*, vol. 1, 89n1.

118. Almeida Mendes, "The Foundations of the System," 85, table 2.6; TSTD, accessed September 2012.

119. Wheat, "The First Great Waves," 11–16, table 3.

120. Ibid., 20.

121. *HGGA*, vol. 1, 77. Contrary to Thornton's argument, Cardonega stated that the military offensive of that time was essential to activate the slave trade in the Angolan hinterland. J. Thornton, *Africa and Africans in the Making of the Atlantic World, 1400–1680* (New York: 1992), 115.

122. C. Alão de Morais, *Pedatura lusitana-hispanica em quem se contém várias famílias nobres e ilustres*, vol. 2, book 1, A. A. Pereira de Miranda Vasconcellos, A. A. Ferreira da Cruz, and E. E. A. da Cunha e Freitas, eds. (Porto: 1943), 131–134. *MMA¹*, vol. 6, 366–374.

123. Franciscan friar Manuel Baptista Soares, third bishop of Congo and of Angola (1606–1623), officiating at the See in the dioceses and in the capital of São Salvador do Congo, former (and later) Mbanza Congo. See *MMA¹*, ibid.

124. A. R. Disney, *A Decadência do ompério da pimenta* (Lousã: 1981), 115–116. According to Gonçalves Salvador, Elena's father, Jorge Rodrigues Solís, owned, at least since 1600, a sugar plantation in Pernambuco. He seems also to have lived in Luanda, where he traded

slaves. Gonçalves Salvador, *Os Magnatas*, 45, 88, and 206; F. Ribeiro da Silva, *Dutch and Portuguese in Western Africa: Empires, Merchants, and the Atlantic System, 1580–1674* (PhD thesis, Leyde: 2009), 190.

125. J. I. Pulido Serrano, "Las negociaciones con los cristianos nuevos en tiempos de Felipe III a la luz de algunos documentos inéditos (1598–1607)," *Sefarad* 66, no. 2 (2006), 345–376; T. Green, *Masters of Difference: Creolization and the Jewish Presence in Cabo Verde, 1497–1672* (PhD thesis, University of Birmingham, 2007), 185–186.

126. N. Alessandrini, "Vida, história e negócios dos mercadores italianos no Portugal dos Filipes," in *Portugal na Monarquia Hispânica*, Cardim, L. F. Costa, and M. S. da Cunha (Lisbon: 2013), 107–134.

127. Vila Vilar, *Hispano-America*, 111.

128. N. Wachtel, "The '"Marrano"' Mercantilist Theory of Duarte Gomes Solis," *Jewish Quarterly Review* 101, no. 2 (2011), 164–188.

129. J. B. Ruiz Rivera, "Los Portugueses y la trata negrera en Cartagena de Índias," *Temas Americanistas* 15 (2002), 19–41.

130. Boyajian, *Portuguese Bankers at the Court*, 108–109.

131. Magalhães Godinho, *Os Descobrimentos*, 63, and Vila Vilar, *Hispano-America*, 70, 111–113, and 164; Boyajian, *Portuguese Trade*, 125, 132; ibid., *Portuguese Bankers at the Court*, appendix A-4.

132. António Fernandes de Elvas went bankrupt and died in 1622. See doc. of November 24, 1623, *AHU*, Angola, box 2/2. On Elena's businesses, see G. Scelle, who names Elena's brother, Francisco Rodrigues Solís, and not Francisco Gomes Solís, *Histoire politique*, 446–453. On Francisco Rodrigues Solís, see also Newson and Minchin, *From Capture to Sale*, 21 and 149.

133. On the crisis in the *Estado da India* at the beginning of the 1600s, see Disney, *A Decadência*, 67–89; Subrahmanyam, *The Portuguese Empire*, 158–163; H. Kellenbenz, "Autour de 1600: Le commerce du poivre des Fuggers et le marché international du poivre," *Annales E.C.S.* 11 (1956), 1–28; Boyajian, *Portuguese Trade*, 210–215.

134. J. H. Elliot, *The Count-Duke of Olivares: The Statesman in an Age of Decline* (Princeton: 1988), 300–303.

135. Manuel Rodrigues Lamego had a partner in the *Asiento*, Cristóvão Mendes de Barros, about whom little is known. However, Lamego had direct links with Felipe IV's banker, João Nunes Saraiva, of whom his brother Antônio Rodrigues Lamego was an agent in Rouen; Manuel Lamego also appears among the investors in India, by means of the Brandão familiy consortium and the Silveira consortium. See Boyajian, *Portuguese Trade*, 255–256; Gonçalves Salvador, *Os Magnatas*, 138–139. Vila Vilar, *Hispano-America*, 95; Elliot, *The Count-Duke*, 300–305.

136. J. C. Boyajian follows the first phase of the mercantile capital circulation, around 1600, when new Christians made rich in the Brazilian slave and sugar business went on to

invest in Asian markets. Having studied two sides of the triangle in depth (the Portuguese Marranos' Indian business and their role as the Crown's bankers in Madrid after 1626), Boyajian's essential books did not pay due attention to the third side of the new Christian merchant activities. See Boyjian, *Portuguese Bankers at the Court*, 26–37, *Portuguese Trade*, 131–134, 142–143.

137. *BAL*, Cod. 51-8-18, no. 161, fl. 82, doc. of October 14, 1606.

138. About the book and its author, J. Capistrano de Abreu, *Ensaios e estudos* (Rio de Janeiro: 1975), 205–232. About Bento Dias de Santiago's and Ambrósio Fernandes Brandão's links, see Boyajian, *Portuguese Bankers at the Court*, appendix A-2, ibid., *Portuguese Trade*, 34 and 254–255; L. Freire Costa, *O Transporte no Atlântico e a Companhia Geral do Comércio do Brasil 1580–1663* (Lisbon: 2002), v. 1, 189.

139. For a discussion of the role of the merchant-entrepreneur in merchant capitalism, see the dossier on J. L. van Zanden's book, "The Rise and Decline of Holland's Economy: Merchant Capitalism and the Labour Market," with texts by the author and A. Knotter, C. Lis, H. Soly, and I. Wallerstein, "Merchant capitalism," *Review* 2 (1997), 189–271.

140. Fernandes Brandão, *Diálogos*, 63.

141. D. G. Solis, *Alegación En Fauor de La Compañia de La India Oriental Y Comercios Vltramarinos Que de Nueuo Se Instituyó En El Reyno de Portugal* ([1628] Lisbon: 1955), 270–271.

142. N. Wachtel, "The 'Marrano' Mercantilist Theory of Duarte Gomes Solis," *Jewish Quarterly Review* 101, no. 2 (2011), 164–188; A. Borges Coelho provides a more conservative analysis of Solis's economic ideas. See A. B. Coelho, "O mercantilista Duarte Gomes Solis: análises e modelos dirigidos ao governo filipino," *Arquipélago. História* 1, no. 1 (1995), 161–179.

143. The Paz family was a contract holder of the Porto customs and had mercantile activities in Europe before entering the sugar and slave-trade business in the Atlantic Islands and Brazil. See C. M. Valentim, *Uma Família de Cristãos-Novos do Entre Douro e Minho: Os Paz, Reprodução Familiar, Formas de Mobilidade Social, Mercancia e Poder (1495–1598)* (master's thesis, Universidade de Lisboa, 2007), 85.

144. Boyajian, *Portuguese Bankers at the Court*, 26–27, 45, 108–109, 119, 158–159.

145. R. de la Campa Carmona, "Un Ejemplo de Patronazgo Nobiliario en la Catedral de Sevilla: La Capilla de La Concepción Grande y Don Gonzalo Núñez de Sepulveda," in *El comportamiento de las catedrales españolas: del Barroco a los Historicismos: actas del congreso* (Murcia: 2003), 425–448, 428; Boyajian, *Portuguese Bankers at the Court*, 51–52.

146. Heintze, *Fontes*, 94.

147. "Procuraçam de Henrique Gomes da Costa Contratador por el rey em Angola, Congo e Loango, morador na Cordoaria Velha (Porto), a Gonçalo Nunes de Sepulveda e Fernão Vogado Sotomaior e Luiz Gonçalves, moradores em Angola," in *Index das Notas de vários Tabelliães de Lisboa, entre os annos de 1580 e 1747*, vol. 2 (Lisbon: [1624] 1937), 102.

148. J. C. Boyajian, *The Portuguese Bankers and the International Payments Mechanism, 1626–1647* (PhD thesis, University of California, Berkeley, 1978), 117n32.

149. Boyajian, *Portuguese Bankers at the Court*, 143.

150. C. Marsilio, "Lisbon, London, or Genoa? Three Alternative Destinations for the Spanish Silver of Philip IV (1627–1650)," in *Three Conferences on International Monetary History* (Wetteren: 2013), 399–413, here 400–402.

151. Both Gramaxos, uncle and nephew, underwent a trial before the Inquisition Tribunal of Cartagena. See L. C. Restrepo, *Los Portugueses: La trata de negros esclavos y el Tribunal de la Inquisición en la ciudad de Cartagena de Indias, siglos XVI y XVII* (Seville: 2011), 216–233, here 225.

152. J. Aguado de los Reyes, "El Apogeo de los Judíos Portugueses en la Sevilla Americanista," *Cadernos de Estudos Sefarditas* 5 (2005), 135–157, 144 and 154; J. M. D. Blanco, "La Corona y Los Cargadores a Indias Portugueses de Sevilla (1583–1645)," in *Iberismo. Las relaciones entre España y Portugal. Historia y tiempo actual: y otros estudios sobre Extremadura*, F. L. de la Puente and F. J. M. Ascacibar, eds. (Llerena, 2008), 91–104.

153. Elliott, *The Count-Duke of Olivares*, 104.

154. By the royal letter of November 9,1639, the Crown stated that Gonçalo Nunes de Sepúlveda should be knighted "without delay." See J. J. de Andrade e Silva, *Collecção Chronologica da Legislação Portugueza—1634–1640* (Lisbon: 1854–1859), 197; de la Campa Carmona, "Un Ejemplo de Patronazgo Nobiliario," 429.

155. D. O. de Zuñiga, *Annales eclesiásticos y seculares de la muy noble, y muy leal ciudad de Sevilla . . . , Que contienen sus mas principales memorias desde el año de 1246 . . . hasta el de 1671 . . .* (Madrid: 1677), 753.

156. T. Falcón Márquez, "El Arquitecto de Retablos Y Escultor Martín Moreno Y Los Primeros Retablos Con Columnas Salomónicas En Sevilla," *Boletín de Arte* 34 (2013), 69–87; M. A. Ramos Suárez, "Noticias Sobre El Pintor-Restaurador Sevillano Diego Mateo Del Parque," *Laboratorio de Arte: Revista Del Departamento de Historia Del Arte* 22 (2010), 577–587, 580.

157. Sevilla, April 29, 1840, *Semanario pintoresco español*, 2 (1840), 277.

158. Manuel was the son of Diogo Fernandes do Brasil and Ana da Paz, a nephew on his father's side, of Duarte Fernandes do Brasil and Simão Rodrigues do Brasil, who were rich traders in Lisbon. On his mother's side, he descended from the celebrated Branca Dias, and was affiliated with Dias Henriques and Santiago, sugar-mill owners and contract holders in Brasil. His father widowed and married Violante Tinoco, of the powerful Tinoco consortium, which operated in the Asian trade. Manuel da Paz married his cousin Isabel Denis Pacheco, related to important overseas merchants. See Boyajian, *Portuguese Bankers at the Court*, 26–27, 45, 108–109, 119, 158–159. Regarding the concealment of this and other new Christian bloodlines in Pernambuco and Portuguese genealogists, see E. Cabral de Mello, *O nome e o sangue: Uma fraude genealógica no Pernambuco colonial* (São Paulo:

1989), 89–105, which portrays the constant tension created in Portuguese America by inquisitorial snitching.

159. The Portuguese legal system included the *Bem de capela* (church trust), which consisted of properties set up in donation to a Parish church, whose incomes and products, except for the stipend of the manager, were all destined to perpetual ecclesiastical incumbency (prayer of masses, distribution of alms, chapel candles) to the benefit of the donor's soul. See F. J. de Santa Rosa de Viterbo, *Elucidário das palavras, termos e frases*, vol. 2 (Porto-Lisbon: [1798–1799], 1983), 68.

160. Alexandre de Moura e Albuquerque, affiliated with two important Pernambucano families, fought in Pernambuco from 1647 to 1651, having participated in the first Guararapes battle. Transferred to the Alentejo front, he took the post of Portalegre field master (*mestre-de-campo*) in 1662. Owner of the Guararapes sugar plantation, he came to reside in Lisbon. Nominated general captain of Madeira, he bid for the post of governor of Angola, but lost to D. João de Lencastre. See doc. of March 30, 1686, *AHU*, Angola, box 13/20; Cabral de Mello, *O Nome*, 220–223, 315. On Salvador Correia de Sá and Joane Mendes de Vasconcelos, see appendix 3.

161. Salvador Correia Vasqueanes, nephew of Salvador Correia de Sá e Benevides, captain of a Rio de Janeiro cavalry company and officer in the Alentejo, joined the 1648 expedition for the retaking of Angola, where he become sergeant major. Instead of following his influential uncle to Lisbon, he settled in Bahia. Twice widowed, he married rich Bahian spouses in succession, and became a prosperous sugar-mill owner. A. de S. M. Jaboatão, *Catálogo genealógico das principais famílias* (hereafter *CGPF*), vol. 2 edited by P. Calmon (Salvador: 1985), 572, 594–596, and 599; A. A. Vieira Nascimento, *Patriarcado e religião: As enclausuradas clarissas do Convento do Desterro da Bahia 1677–1890* (Bahia: 1994), 74–75 and 429. On João Fernandes Vieira and André Vidal de Negreiros, see chapter 6.

162. Newson and Minchin, *From Capture to Sale*, 25.

163. Vila Vilar, *Hispano-America*, 51, 128, 137, and 143–144.

164. Wheat, *The Afro-Portuguese Maritime World*, 92–93.

165. João Correia de Sousa was captain major of the India ships, where he served for many years. He held the post of captain of Ceuta before becoming governor of Angola. See C. J. de Senna Barcellos, *Subsídios para a História de Cabo Verde e Guiné*, vol. 1, part 1 (Lisbon: 1899–1911), 53.

166. Letter of Joao Correa de Sousa, Luanda, December 24, 1621, *AHU*, Angola, box 2/4.

167. The royal order stated: "[Y]ou shall not force them to pay me tribute unless they voluntarily offer to do so." Statute [*Regimento*] of João Correia de Sousa, 1621, *BNL*, Res. Ms., cod. 7627.

168. Scelle, *Histoire*, 446.

169. B. Heintze, "Das ende des Unabhängigen Staats Ndongo (Angola): Neue Chronologie und Reinterpretation (1617–1630)," *Paideuma* 27 (1981), 197–273. The Bembe copper mines are situated in the Uige province.

170. Doc. of April 12, 1622, *AHU*, Bahia, box 1/7.

171. E. van den Boogaart, "The Trade between Western Africa and the Atlantic World, 1600–1690—Estimates of Trends in Composition and Value," *J. Afr. H.* 33 (1992), 369–385; Malekandathil, *Portuguese Cochin*, 193.

172. April 6, 1623, *AHU*, Angola, box 2/15.

173. See "Relação," October 20, 1623, *MMA¹*, vol. 15, 508–529.

174. Royal letter, August 31, 1623, *AHU*, Angola, box 2/20.

175. From Havana he tried to mediate the split between the viceroy Marquis de Gelves and the archbishop of Mexico during the 1624 rebellion. In a letter to the archbishop, João Correia de Sousa also mentions the plot against him in Angola: "[W]hen the rebels tried to detain or to kill me, I arrested, confiscated and decapitated them and I deported three clergymen as chiefs (of the rebellion)." See *Copia de una carta que el Governador de Angola escribió al Arcobispo de Mexico, a tres dias llegado a esta ciudad de la Habana a veinte de Marco de 1624* (Biblioteca Digital Hispanica, Biblioteca Nacional de España, Madrid); R. Feijoo, "El Tumulto de 1624," *Historia Mexicana* 14, no. 1 (1964), 42–70.

176. On the native porters issue, see the pioneering essay of A. Margarido, "Les porteurs formes de domination et agents du changement en Angola, XVIe–XIXe siècles," *Revue Française d'Histoire d'Outre-Mer* 65, no. 240 (1978), 377–399.

177. Luanda, April 8, 1653, *MMA¹*, vol. 11, 286–287.

178. Fajardo Report [*Relação*], February 24, 1624, *MMA¹*, vol. 7, 205–213, 208; Heintze, *Fontes*, 86–87. Boxer wrote that the royal ban on inland wars only starts in 1669. See Boxer, *Portuguese Society*, 119.

179. The captain-majors nominated by the governors had no pay and lived off the soba's donations and off the prey "who do not come as gifts." Doc. of 1633, Heintze, *Fontes*, 339.

180. Silva Correa, *História*, 15.

181. For the calculations, I made use of the indications recorded by J. M. Delgado, *HGGA*, vol. 2, 547n80–549n2.

182. "Relaçam do Felice Successo que conseguirão as armas do Serenissimo Principe D. Pedro N.S., governadas por Francisco de Távora, governador & capitam general do reyno de Angola contra a rebelião de D. João rey das Pedras & Dongo, no mez de dezembro de 1671," *AHU*, Angola, box 12/126, *MMA¹*, vol. 13, 143–152.

183. *Pombeiro*: a native Angolan peddler, agent, or slave of the Angolistas Luanda merchants, who went up to the inland slave fairs (the *pumbos*).

184. "Relaçam do Felice Successo,"143–152.

185. Doc. of 1618, *MMA¹*, vol. 6, 366–374.

186. The W.I.C. registers from 1637 to 1645 show that children represented 33.2 percent (686) of the deportees from Angola and 12.7 percent (393) of those from the Gulf of Guinea. See E. Van den Boogaart and Emmer, "The Dutch Participation in the Atlantic Slave Trade 1596–1650," in *The Uncommon Market*, J. Hogendorn and H. Gemery, eds. (New York: 1979), 353–375, 366.

187. A. E. Taunay, *História seiscentista da Villa de São Paulo*, vol. 1 (São Paulo: 1926), 15; C. R. Boxer, "Macao as a Religious and Commercial Entrepot in the Sixteenth and Seventeenth Centuries," *Acta Asiatica* 26 (1974), 64–90; E. R. Saguier, "The Social Impact of a Middleman Minority in a Host Society—The Case of the Portuguese in Early Seventeenth-Century Buenos Aires," *HAHR* 65, no. 3 (1985), 467–491; S. Gruzinski, "Les élites de la monarchie catholique au carrefour des empires (fin XVIe-début XVIIe siècle)," in *L'Empire portugais face aux autres empires XVIe–XIXe siècle*, F. Bethencourt and L. F. de Alencastro, eds. (Paris: 2007), 273–288.

188. S. Gorban, "El trafico negrero en el Rio de La Plata," *EH* 10 (1971), 117–139; C. Coelho da Cruz, *O tráfico negreiro da 'Costa de Angola*, 18, 33, and 59.

189. The *asentista* Reynel was authorized to introduce 600 slaves in Buenos Aires yearly between 1594 and 1601. João Rodriguez Coutinho also obtained the same authorization during his *Asiento* between 1601 and 1609. See M. A. Campetella, *At the Periphery of Empire: Indians and Settlers in the Pampas of Buenos Aires, 1580–1776* (PhD thesis, Rutgers, 2008), 108–126.

190. Brandão, *Diálogos*, 96; Pyrard, *Voyage*, 234–235.

191. A. Mariz de Carneiro, "Roteiro de Portugal pera o Brazil, Rio da Prata, Angola e S. Thomé, segundo os pilotos antigos e modernos, agora a quinta vez impresso," *Regimento de pilotos*, 15–19.

192. In the Río de La Plata, Veiga had arrangements with *asentista* Gonçalo Coutinho's factor. Later he became Angola contractor Duarte Dias Henriques's mandatary and *asentista* Antônio Fernandez de Elvas's factor. See Boyajian, *Portuguese Bankers at the Court*, appendix A-6; A. Canabrava, *O comércio português no Rio da Prata 1580–1640* (São Paulo: 1984), 124–130.

193. Newson and Minchin, *From Capture to Sale*, 67.

194. J. Torre Revello, "Un contrabandista del siglo XVII en el Rio de La Plata," *Revista de Historia de America* 45 (1958), 121–130; Z. Moutoukias, "Power, Corruption, and Commerce: The Making of the Local Administrative Structure in Seventeenth-Century Buenos Aires," *HAHR* 68, no. 4 (1988), 771–801. According to the eighteenth Portuguese genealogist, Veiga was from the Algarve and not from the Madeira Island, as stated by Torre Revello. See Leitão Manso de Lima, *Famílias*, 50–54.

195. Doc. of May 25, 1616, in R. Levillier, *Antecedentes de política económica en el Río de La Plata documentos originales de los siglos XVI al XIX seleccionados en al Archivo de Indias de Sevilla*, vol. 1 (Madrid: 1915), 354–355.

196. E. R. Saguier, *The Uneven Incorporation of Buenos Aires into World Trade Early in the Seventeenth Century (1602–42): The Impact of Commercial Capitalism Under the Iberian Mercantilism of the Habsburgs* (PhD thesis, Washington University, Saint Louis, Missouri, 1982), chapter 7.

197. On Forjaz's governorship in Angola, see R. Bonciani, "A disputa por gentios e escravos no Atlântico Sul (1600–1615)," in *Corporaciones religiosas y evangelización em Iberoamérica. Siglos XVI–XVIII*, D. L. Medina and K. M. Estrada, eds. (Lima, Peru: 2011), 23–60, 44–49.

198. High Court judge (*Desembargador*) Francisco Cardoso do Amaral, judge of the *Casa da Mina e Índia* (the royal agency for overseas affairs) established that Argomedo had an association with Governor Forjaz, in order to export wines from the Canaries and Portugal to Angola and to carry slaves from Luanda to Brazil and Spanish America. Their agent in Cartagena was Jorge Fernandez Gramaxo; in Vera Cruz it was Duarte de Leão Marquez and Luis Alvarez Caldeira and others; in Bahia (Brazil) it was Julio de Moura; in Pernambuco it was Manuel Lopes Correa, Francisco de Villas Boas, and others. Following the judge, the Argomedo-Forjaz association bypassed the *Asiento* legislation and Sevillan interests. In fact, they had ordered their agents in Luanda "not to carry slaves for any ship-owner or captain from Seville nor do any selling or business with them." Doc. of September 29, 1611 *AHU*, Angola, box 1, doc. no. 15. I am grateful to Diogo Ramada Curto for offering me information on Argomedo.

199. *Peruleiros*: a Spanish-origin noun used at the beginning of the seventeenth century in Portugal and Brazil to designate Portuguese-American traders who did business with lower Peru Spaniards and, more concretely, those who imported silver from the Río de La Plata. In Spanish America, the noun gained a pejorative meaning, referring to mainland Spanish who came down to exploit Peru and then returned to Spain.

200. Worshipped since the last decades of the sixteenth century at the Isla del Sol, in Lake Tititica, Our Lady of Copacabana reflected the Inca cult of the sun. After miracles were attributed to her, the saint started to be worshiped in the whole of upper Peru. See S. MacCormack, "From the Sun of the Incas to the Virgin of Copacabana," *Representations* 8 (1984), 30–60; M. M. McGlone, "The King's Surprise: The Mission Methodology of Toribio de Mogrovejo." *The A* 50, no. 1 (1993), 65–83.

201. Aracy Amaral, *A Hispano-América na Arte Seiscentista do Brasil* (São Paulo: 1972), 67; Canabrava, *O Comércio Português*, 79–110.

202. Peralta Rivera, *Les mécanismes* 153–157.

203. Scelle, *Histoire*, 403–435.

204. D. Studnicki-Gizbert, "Revisiting 1640; or, How the Party of Commercial Expansion Lost to the Party of Political Conservation in Spain's Atlantic Empire, 1620–1650," in *The Atlantic Economy during the Seventeenth and Eighteenth Centuries: Organization, Operation, Practice, and Personnel*, A. Coclanis, ed. (Columbia, SC: 2005), 152–177.

205. In 1643, Buenos Aires was home to 2,000 residents, including many Portuguese, numbering around 370 and 490 individuals. See Saguier, "The Social Impact," 479–480; de Azevedo, *História dos cristãos novos portugueses*, 233–235; Collado Villalta, "El embargo

de bienes de los portugueses en la flotta de tierra firme de 1641," *Anuario de Estudios Americanos* 36 (1979), 169–207.

206. Peralta Rivera, *Les mécanismes*, 196.

207. Decree [*Alvará*] of February 2, 1641.

208. Discussion held in Lisbon's court in March and April 1647. See M. Laranjo Coelho, *Cartas de el-rei d. João IV ao conde de Vidigueira (marquês de Niza) embaixador em França*, vol. 2 (Lisbon: 1945–1947), 106–107.

209. On Portugal's royal finances in the period 1600–1640, see A. M. Hespanha, "A Fazenda," in Mattoso, *História*, 203–232.

210. In the 1680s, a new inland fortress was erected in Pungo-Andongo, the last capital of the Ndongo kingdom, doc. of January 7, 1681, *AHU*, Angola, box 12/39. On Benguela, see de Albuquerque Felner, *Angola*, 331–350.

211. In 1649, protesting against the new 3,000-*réis* tax imposed by the governor Salvador de Sá on each exported enslaved "piece," the Luanda municipal council still mirrored the slave market segmentation prevailing during the *Asiento* period. Truly, the chamber clearly distinguished the pieces of Indies (*peças de Indias*), worth 22,000 *réis*, from the pieces of Brazil (*peças do Brasil*), of lesser value. See *AA*, vol. 2, no. 13 (1936), 484.

212. TSTD, accessed September 2015.

213. TSTD, accessed September 2015.

214. On recent research related to the Spanish Habsburg administration of Portuguese America, see Cardim, "O governo e a administração do Brasil sob os Habsburgo e os primeiros Bragança," *Hispania* 64, no. 1 (2004), 117–156, and J. M. Santos Pérez, "Brazil and the Politics of Spanish Habsburgs in the South Atlantic 1580–1640," *Portuguese Literary & Cultural Studies* 27 (2015), 104–120.

215. TSTD, accessed September 2015.

216. Regarding Spanish-American ports, Almeida Mendes gives high estimates, concluding that eight or nine out of every ten Africans deported to the area came from Angola between 1576 and 1640. See de Almeida Mendes, "The Foundations of the System," 85. Yet new data analyzed by D. Wheat indicate that ships from Angola represent 54 percent of all known voyages to both ports between 1570 and 1640. From a total of 660 known ships unloading Africans in Cartagena and Vera Cruz, 49 (7.4 percent) are of unknown origin. Still, one central question concerning the Portuguese *Asiento* remains unanswered: the number of ships and of Africans arriving in Buenos Aires. See Wheat, "The First Great Waves,"1–22, here 4n12.

217. C. Richard de Silva, "The Portuguese East India Company 1628–1633," *Luso-Brazilian Review* 11, no. 2 (1974), 152–205, 181–182.

218. van Veen, *Decay or Defeat?*, 254.

219. D. O. Flynn and A. Giráldez, "Born with a 'Silver Spoon': The Origin of World Trade in 1571," *Journal of World History* 6, no. 2 (1995), 201–221, here 209–218.

220. In spite of the war with Spain, Lisbon had already authorized former *asentistas* agents to send enslaved Africans to Spanish America. See Gomes da Silva, "Parecer do marquês de Montalvão . . . ," Lisbon, November 12, 1641, *Os Manuscritos*, 28–29. As the *asentistas* networks in Spanish America were dismantled, the order was not improved.

221. *BNRJ*, "Consultas Mistas do Conselho Ultramarino," cod. 23, 1643–1646, vol. 1; "Consulta sobre o comercio dos negros de Guiné para índias de Castella," Lisbon, January 21, 1646, fs. 282v–283.

222. Scelle, "Introduction," *Histoire*, v. 1.

223. Archeological evidence indicates that manioc was already cultivated in many parts of tropical America during the first millennium BC. See W. R. Deboer, "The Archaeological Evidence for Manioc Cultivation: A Cautionary Note," *American Antiquity* 40, no. 4 (1975), 419–433.

224. *HCJB*, vol. 1, 33.

225. M. da Nóbrega, "Cartas do Brasil," *Cartas jesuíticas*, vol. 1 (São Paulo [1549] 1988), 98; A. G. da Cunha, *Dicionário histórico das palavras portuguesas de origem tupi* (São Paulo: 1998), 197–200.

226. Brandão, *Diálogos*, 118.

227. The edict aimed at masters owning fewer than six slaves. See doc. of 1646, *O Rio de Janeiro no século XVII: Accordãos e vereanças do Senado da Câmara [. . .] relativos aos annos de 1635 até 1650*, 109–110.

228. "Registo da conta do que importam os soldos," Bahia, *DH*, vol. 83 (1684), 7–8.

229. Letter from the Pernambuco governor to the Crown, Recife, July 24, 1725, *AHU*, Pernambuco, box 31, doc. no. 3164.

230. Vicente do Salvador, *História do Brasil* [1627] (São Paulo: 1982) 112; S. de Vasconcelos, *Crônica da Companhia de Jesus*, vol. 1 (Petrópolis: 1977), 83, 123–124; Brandão, *Diálogos*, 194. The banana was introduced from Africa, as clearly noted by G. Soares de Sousa, *Notícia do* Brasil, vol. 2 (São Paulo: n.d.), 6. About the Sumeh myth, see S. Buarque De Holanda, *Visão do Paraíso*, 5th ed. (São Paulo: 1992), 108–129. The Spanish Jesuits in Paraguay also indoctrinated Guarany Indians into the idea that *Sumeh* had taught their ancestors how to use the yerba maté. See B. A. Ganson, *Better Not Take My Manioc: Guarani Religion, Society, and Politics in the Jesuit Missions of Paraguay 1500–180*" (PhD thesis, University of Texas at Austin, 1994), 77.

231. Overlooking the importance of maize and cassava cultivation in pre-Colombian times, contemporary archaeologists have also stated that agriculture had been introduced in America by the Europeans. See G. Martin, *Pré-História do Nordeste do Brasil*, 2nd ed. (Recife: 1997), 183.

232. Jesuit document from the end of the sixteenth century. See *MMA¹*, vol. 15, 372.

233. Petition by Maria de Tavora, the widow of Manoel [Pereira] Forjaz, January 26, 1612, *AHU*, Angola, box 1/17.

234. F. de Oliveira, "Primeira Parte," in *A Arte da Guerra no Mar* (Coimbra: 1555), 27.

235. Vasconcelos, *Arte militar*, 220; da Sylveira, *Relação Sumária*, 26.

236. Wheat, *The Afro-Portuguese Maritime World*, 152, 159.

237. Code Noir, article 22, *Recueils de règlements, édits, déclarations et arrêts, avec le Code noir*, vol. 2, 89.

238. Duarte Lopes, *Relação do Reino do Congo*, 61; M. Miracle, "The Introduction and Spread of Maize in Africa," *J. Afr. H.* 6, no. 1 (1965), 39–55.

239. Maize could have entered sub-Saharan Africa from two origins: from Brazil through São Tomé and Elmina, and from the Caribbean through the Mediterranean, Egypt, and then Nigeria. See M. Keul, J.-J. Hémardinquer, and J. Bertin, "Cartes historiques des cultures vivrières," *Annales* 21, no. 5 (1966), 1,012–1,025.

240. Echoing such information, Antonio José Caldas, a Bahian engineer knowledgeable about the Mina Coast peoples, who sailed across the area around 1750, wrote, with exaggeration, that African peasants obtained as many as four maize harvests yearly. See Caldas, "Notícia Geral," 301. Today, in exceptional conditions, hybrid maize may be planted and harvested three times yearly.

241. *DHCMA*, vol. 1, 56.

242. Anonymous, *História do reino do Congo*, A. Brásio, ed. (Lisbon: 1969), 41.

243. A recollection of narratives on Angola, wrote in Luanda ca. 1700, states that the Brazilian manioc plant was introduced in Angola through São Tomé in 1623. See "Memória intitulada Livro Primeiro da Monarquia Angolana," ca. 1700, *IHGB*, África/Angola, Col. IHGB DL41, 13, fs. 1–9v. The document is mistakenly dated from "before 1600" in the *IHGB* repertory. See *RIHGB*, vol. 427 (2005), 49.

244. Dapper, *Description*, 368.

245. "Regimento do Trato de São Tomé," February 8, 1519, *MMA¹*, vol. 4, 124–133, here 129.

246. José de Pernambuco studied in Salamanca, entered the novitiate, and was ordained a Capuchin in 1634, in Spain. He arrived in Mpinda with fourteen other Capuchin missionaries in March 1648 and died in 1652 in Mpemba, a Congo province. See *DHCMA*, vol. 1, 374, and vol. 2, 443; "Carta de 23.3.1648 ao provincial na Espanha," *MMA¹*, vol. 10, 106–117. Alongside Capuchins Francisco de Veas and Luso-Congolese dean Manoel Roboredo, José de Pernambuco contributed to the writing of "Vocabularium Latinum, Hispanicum et Congoense, ad usum missionariorum transmit orum ad Regni Congo missiones," organized by Capuchin Bonaventura da Sardegna. See T. Filesi and I. Villapardiena, *La "Missio Antiqua" dei Cappuccini nel Congo (1645–1835)* (Rome: 1978), 182–183.

247. "Relação de uma viagem a Angola" (1652), *MMA¹*, vol. 11, 250; Dapper, *Description*, 364–365.

248. Report by Moortamer, Luanda, October 14, 1642; L. Jadin, *L'Ancien Congo et l'Angola 1639–1655, d'après les archives romaines, portugaises, néerlandaises et espagnoles* (hereafter *ACA*), 3 vols. (Brussels: 1975), vol. I, 350–359.

249. *DHCMA*, vol. 1, 37–38. For sweet potato (*Ipomoea batatas*), which the Portuguese introduced in Angola from the end of the sixteenth century, see *MMA¹*, vol. 5, 548. Maize (*Zea mayz*) was introduced in Portugal in the first decades of the sixteenth century and soon spread out, changing the rural landscape, but potato and rice began to be cultivated only in the second half of the eighteenth century. See J. V. Serrão, "O quadro econômico, configurações estruturais e tendências de evolução," in Mattoso, *História*, 71–117, 74–79, and O. Ribeiro, "Milho," *DHP*, vol. 3 (Lisbon), 58–64.

250. "Inventario dos Sobas, Quilambas e Quimbares do Distrito do Golungo," *IHGB*, África/Angola, Col. *IHGB* DL81.02.19, n.d., c. 1800.

251. Letter from the Crown to the governor of Angola, Mafra, April 11, 1799, *IHGB*, África/Angola, Col. *IHGB*, DL 82.1, doc. no. 320, fl. 13.

252. H. B. Ross, *The Diffusion of the Manioc Plant from South America to Africa: An Essay in Ethnobotanical Culture History* (PhD thesis, Columbia University, New York, 1954), 60–117.

253. *The New York Times*, 9.06.1988, C4. In some parts of sub-Saharan Africa, where the cassava's soaking time was reduced from three days to one, due to the high demand for food caused by drought or war, cyanogens intoxication led to a form of tropical myelopathy called the konzo disease. See T. Tylleskär, M. Banea, N. Bikangi, R. D. Cooke, N. H. Poulter, and H. Rosling, "Cassava cyanogens and *konzo*, an upper motoneuron disease found in Africa," *Lancet* 339, no. 8787 (1992), 208–211.

254. Brandão, *Diálogos*, 118–123, compares cassava and maize, noting the former's "twice-yearly *novidades* [harvests]" and cassava's once-yearly harvest. S. Buarque de Holanda analyzes this question in *Caminhos*, 185–186.

255. *HGGA*, vol. 1, 354–355.

256. E. G. Ravenstein, *The Strange Adventures of Andrew Battel of Leigh, in Angola and the Adjoining Regions* (London: 1901), 6.

257. L.-B. Proyart, *Histoire de Loango, Kakongo, et Autres Royaumes d'Afrique: Rédigée d'après Les Mémoires des Préfets Apostoliques de La Mission Françoise, enrichie d'une carte utile aux navigateurs* (Paris: 1776), 15.

258. F. J. de Lacerda e Almeida, *Diários de Viagem*, 258; "Notícia dadas por Manoel Caetano Pereira [. . .] que se entranhou [. . .] até a cidade do rei Cazembe . . . [1798]," *AA*, vol. 3 (1937), 39.

259. *DHCMA*, vol. 1, XXIII–XXIX and 49–53; *HGGA*, vol. 3, 373; Alpern, "The European Introduction of Crops into West Africa," 13–43.

260. *MMA¹*, vol. 5, 109–110.

261. Friar Merolla lived in West Central Africa between 1684 and 1688. See G. Merolla da Sorrento, *Breve Relazione del Viaggio nel Regno di Congo Nell' Africa Meridionale* (Naples: 1692), 120. According to Mestri, the *ncanza* is the *Maesa Welwitschii*. See M. J. Mestri Filho, "A agricultura africana nos séculos XVI e XVII no litoral angolano," *Caderno* 4 (1978).

262. "Moamba" is also a sauce made with *dendê* nut oil; it has nothing to do with *muamba*, another Kimbundo word that means "load" and in Brazil became the synonym for "trunk" and, more recently, of "smuggled goods." Doc. of 1645, *MMA¹*, vol. 9, 363; *DHCMA*, vol. 1, 37–38; *HGGA*, vol. 5, 358.

263. S. Buarque de Holanda, *Monções* (São Paulo: 1990), 100. *Abatiapé* is also known as "red rice of the Pantanal" (*Oryza latifolia*), cultivated by the Guató Indians. Case Watkins, "Dendezeiros: African Oil Palm Agroecologies in Bahia, Brazil, and Implications for Development," *Journal of Latin American Geography* 10, no. 1 (2011), 9–26.

264. "A mode of maize, similar to what is called *naxenim* in India [. . .] that was brought over from Angola, and which the slaves call *masa*," A. F. Brandão, *Diálogo* . . . , 127. In his excellent dictionary, Macedo Soares detected the confusion that emerged in the nineteenth century around the naming of African sorghum in Brazil: "*massambará*, sorgo, introduced by the Blacks; but in Pernambuco, with the same name, it indicates a kind of grass employed as a diuretic. The Rio de Janeiro Blacks give *massarambá* or sorghum the name 'massango,' which is of a different species," A. J. de Macedo Soares, *Dicionário brasileiro da língua portuguesa—Elucidário, etimológico, crítico* (1875–1888), 2 vols, v. 1, *passim*. The Massangano is, indeed, a kind of millet.

265. Doc. of 1623, *MMA¹*, vol. 15, 517.

266. *DHCMA*, vol. 1, XXIII–XXIX and 49–53.

267. S. B. Alpern, "Exotic Plants of Western Africa: Where They Came From and When," *History in Africa* 35, no. 1 (2008), 63–102, here 76n50.

268. Antônio Houaiss analyzes the nouns *ananás* and *abacaxi*, stating that the former was used in the north and the second in the south of Portuguese America. But Pereira da Costa had already demonstrated that the word *abacaxi* had been recorded in Maranhão, by Father Bettendorf, since the seventeenth century. See A. Houaiss, "Prefácio," in A. G. da Cunha, *Dicionário histórico das palavras portuguesas de origem tupi* (São Paulo: 1998), 8–9; "Abacaxi," in Pereira da Costa, *Vocabulário*, 12–13.

269. L. da Câmara Cascudo, *A cozinha africana no Brasil* (Luanda: 1964), 26–27.

270. V. do Salvador, *História do Brasil 1500–1627* (São Paulo: 1982), 289–290. Jaime Welter has demonstrated that the book was still not finished in 1627. See J. Welter, "Estudo," in C. de Lisboa, *História dos animais e árvores do Maranhão* (Lisbon: [1640] 1967), 24.

271. Commissioned by Governor Cerveira in 1612 for the conquest of Benguela, and by Governor Vasconcelos in 1616. See *MMA*, vol. 1, 78 and 267. The São Paulo doublets were exported again to Angola at least twice again, in 1684 and 1688. See *AHU*, Angola, cod. 545, fl. 28, and box 13/84.

272. A. R. de Montoya, "Primeva catechese dos índios selvagens feita pelos padres da Companhia de Jesus," *ABNRJ* 6 (1878–1879), 91–366, here 231–232. The *Primeva catechese* is a Portuguese translation of the 1733 edition of the *Conquista Espiritual* written in the

Guarani language. The passage quoted above is not included in the 1639 original edition of Montoya's book.

273. Letter to the king, Luanda, November 1, 1617, *AHU*, Angola, box 1/50. On the *tipoye*, L. da Câmara Cascudo, *Made in Africa* (Rio de Janeiro: 1965), 69–73. Zana Etambala, "Notes sur le tipoye em Afrique noire," *Ngonge, Carnets de Sciences Humaines*, 6 (2011), 7–15.

274. On the Angola pombeiros, see note 178 above and R. A. Ferreira, *Cross-Cultural Exchange in the Atlantic World: Angola and Brazil during the Era of the Slave Trade* (Cambridge, UK: Cambridge UP, 2012), 59–65.

275. Doc, January 23, 1619, *AHU*, São Paulo, box 1/2; enquiry [*Devassa*] of February 9, 1624, *AHU*, São Paulo, box1/3.

276. Regimento de Cerveira, March 23, 1615, *MMA¹*, vol. 15, 455–463, 457. Cerveira asked for well-acclimatized soldiers. Ibid., vol. 6, 79–80.

277. Doc. from 1694, *MMA¹*, vol. 14, 359–363. See also "Relations Sur Le Congo Du Père Laurent de Lucques (1700–1717)," in *Institut Royal Colonial Belge—Mémoires*, J. Cuvelier, ed. (1953), 194n1. See also N. Papavero and D. Martins Teixeira, "Recife e Salvador na visão dos capuchinhos missionários no Reino do Congo (1667–1703)," in *Cadernos do IEB* (2015), 136–138.

278. "*Quitanda* . . . fairs where one finds everything for sale," *HGGA*, vol. 1, 277.

279. Brandão, *Diálogos*, 82–83.

280. According to Cavazzi, "[I]n times past" [*antigamente*], one *xinga* or *nduro* was worth one slave, and "now" (the 1660s) a slave was worth two *xingas*. See *DHCMA*, vol. 1, 59. In Brazil, *quimbembe* means "straw hut." See Phyllis M. Martin, "Power, Cloth, and Currency on the Loango Coast," *African Economic History* 15 (1986), 1–12.

281. *MMA¹*, vol. 8, 124–125, 134.

282. Silva Correa, *História*, 154–155.

283. *Banzo* derives from the Kimbundo verb *kubanza*, meaning both "to calculate" and "to think." In Brazilian, the term became known only in the second meaning. See J. M. Delgado in *HGGA*, vol. 1, 143n1. See also K. Polanyi, "Sortings and 'Ounce trade'in the West African Slave Trade," in *Primitive, Archaic, and Modern Economies: Essays of Karl Polyani*, G. Dalton, ed. (1971), 261–279, here chapter 1.

284. Silva Correa, *História*, 147.

285. I. Wallerstein, *The Modern World-System I, I* (Berkeley: 2011), 90.

286. F. Braudel, *Civilisation Matérielle, Economie et Capitalisme, XVIe–XVIIIe siècles*, vol. 3 (Paris: 1979), 536–552. Braudel's unreserved statement about the triangular trade as a generalized pattern is surprising. At that time, he had already advised, promoted, and published Verger's doctoral dissertation that, following several Brazilian authors, plainly demonstrates the bilateral slave trade between Bahia and the Bight (or Bay) of Benin. In

fact, in his *Civilisation Matérielle* Braudel does not quote Verger's book. See Verger, *Flux et reflux de la traite des nègres entre le Golfe de Bénin et Bahia de Todos os Santos, XVIe–XIXe siècles* (Paris: 1968).

Chapter 4

1. F. Santos-Granero, *Vital Enemies: Slavery, Predation, and the Amerindian Political Economy of Life* (Austin: U of Texas P, 2009), 48, 123, 219–222, and 226.

2. Clastres, *La société contre l'Etat* (Paris: 1974), 25–42.

3. R. Carneiro, "Slash-and-Burn Cultivation among the Kuikuru and Its Implications for Cultural Development in the Amazon Basin," in *The Evolution of Horticultural Systems in Native South America, Causes and Consequences*, J. Wibert, ed. (Caracas: 1961), 47–67; M. Arroyo-Kalin, "Slash-Burn-and-Churn: Landscape History and Crop Cultivation in Pre-Columbian Amazonia," *Quaternary International* 249 (2012), 4–18.

4. A. Metraux, *Les Indiens de l'Amérique du Sud* (Paris: 1982), 46; J. M. Monteiro, "The Crises and Transformations of Invaded Societies: Coastal Brazil in the Sixteenth Century," in *The Cambridge History of the Natives*, vol. 3, part 1, F. Salomon and S. B. Schwartz eds. (Cambridge, UK: Cambridge UP, 1996), 973–1,023, especially 982–984 and 993–994.

5. G. Wilde, *Religión y Poder en las misiones de Guaraníes* (Buenos Aires: 2009), 125–131, 137–144.

6. J. Daniel, "Tesouro descoberto no rio Amazonas [1757–1776]" *ABNRJ*, vol. 2 (Rio de Janeiro: 1976), 249. Anna Roosevelt highlights *chiefdom*, a hierarchized institution that would have characterized recent prehistoric Amazonian people, distinct from the existing societies at the time of the Europeans' arrival studied here. See A. C. Roosevelt, "Chiefdoms in the Amazon and Orinico," in *Chiefdoms in the Americas*, R. Drennan and C. Uribe, eds. (Laham, MD: 1987), 153–184.

7. J. D. French, "Riqueza, poder e mão-de-obra numa economia de subsistência—São Paulo 1596–1625," *R.A.M.S.* 195 (1987), 79–107; W. Dean, "Indigenous Populations of the São Paulo—Rio de Janeiro Coast: Trade, 'Aldeamento,' Slavery, and Extinction," *Revista de História* 117 (1984), 1–26.

8. J. Eisenberg, "A escravidão voluntária dos índios do Brasil e o pensamento político moderno," *Análise Social* 39, no. 170 (2004), 7–35.

9. M. L. Carneiro da Cunha and E. B. Viveiros de Castro, "Vingança e temporalidade os tupinambás," *Anuário Antropológico* (Brazil: 1985), 57–78. See also Metraux, *Les Indiens de l'Amérique du Sud*, 49; V. Nemésio, *A Companhia de Jesus e o Plano português do Brasil* (Lisbon: 1971), 310–321; F. Fernandes, "A função social da guerra na sociedade tupinambá," *RMP* 6 (1951), 7–426, 48–67, and 264.

10. J. Vansina, "The Foundation of the Kingdom of Kasange," *J. Afr. H.* 4, no. 3 (1963), 355–374; J. C. Miller, "Nzinga of Matamba in a new perspective," *J. Afr. H.* 16, no. 2 (1975), 201–216.

11. R. Arnold, "Séparation du commerce et du marché: le grande marché d'Ouidah," in *Les systemes économiques dans l'histoire et dans la théorie* (French translation), K. Polanyi and C. Arensberg, eds. (Paris: 1975), 187–191; R. Law, "Dahomey and the Slave Trade: Reflections on the Historiography of the Rise of Dahomey," *J. Afr. H.* 27, no. 2 (1986), 237–267.

12. Decree of January 6, 1574; see A. M. Perdigão Malheiro, *A escravidão no Brasil—Ensaio jurídico, histórico, social*, vol. 1 (Petrópolis: [1867]: 1976), 174; G. Thomas, *Política indigenista dos portugueses no Brasil 1500–1640* (Brazilian translation) (São Paulo: 1982), 48–49; J. L. de Azevedo, *Os jesuítas no Grão-Pará* (Coimbra: 1930), 134; B. Perrone-Moisés, "Índios livres e índios escravos: Os princípios da legislação indigenista do período colonial (séculos XVI a XVIII)," in *História dos índios no Brasil*, M. Carneiro da Cunha, ed. (São Paulo: 1992), 115–132, 127–128.

13. Thomas, *Politica indigensista*, 49–54.

14. Bettendorf, *Crônica*, 485; R. Chambouleyron and F. A. Bombardi, "Descimentos privados de índios na Amazônia colonial (séculos XVII e XVIII)." *Varia História* 27, no. 46 (2011), 601–623.

15. J. J. Machado de Oliveira, "Notícia racionada sobre as aldeias de índios da Província de São Paulo," *RIHGB*, vol. 8 (1846), 204–254.

16. The decree of July 30, 1609, affirmed Amerindians' freedom, determining that "fair wages" were to be paid. See F. de Almeida, *História de Portugal*, 6 vols. (Coimbra: 1922–1929) vol. 5, 131–132. The law of April 9, 1655, regarding the Maranhão Amerindians describes the daily wages of an unskilled [*sem ofício*] worker at twice the price of the food taken by the individual. See *ABNRJ* 66 (1948), 25–28. On the difference between Indian tradtional villages and Indian colonial settlements, see A. de Azevedo, "Aldeias e aldeamentos de índios," *Boletim Paulista de Geografia* 33 (1959), 26.

17. L. Palacin, *Sociedade Colonial 1549 a 1599* (Goiânia: 1981), 149–174. J. Monteiro, "O escravo índio, esse desconhecido," in *Índios no Brasil*, L. D. Benzi Grupioni, ed. (São Paulo: 1992), 105–120.

18. Alcântara Machado, J. de *Vida e morte do bandeirante* (São Paulo: 1930), 29–30.

19. French, "Riqueza, poder e mão-de-obra numa economia de subsistência," 87; A. C. Metcalf, *Family and Frontier in Colonial Brazil Santana de Parnaíba, 1580–1822* (Los Angeles: 1992), 38–43.

20. J. R. Russel-Wood, "Iberian Expansion and the Issue of Black Slavery: Changing Portuguese Attitudes 1440–1770," *The American Historical Review* 83, no. 1 (1978), 16–46; R. Blackburn, "The Old World Background to European Colonial Slavery," *The William and Mary Quarterly* 54, no. 1 (1998), 65–102.

21. Provision of May 6, 1672. See *AHU*, Rio de Janeiro, Documentos Avulsos, maço 142 (old cataloging); J. C. Fernandes Pinheiro, "A Carioca—Memória Histórica e Documentada," *RIHGB*, vol. 25 (1862), 565–588.

22. The Overseas Council examined the matter in 1716, but the quoted text dates from a few years before. See *DI*, vol. 49 (1929), 193–195.

23. J. C. Melatti, *Índios do Brasil* (São Paulo: 1989), 12–13; Martin, *Pré-História*, 205–206.

24. On the enslaving raids in Pernambuco and Bahia, where twenty-four entradas were launched between 1572 and 1592, see A. C. Metcalf, "The Entradas of Bahia of the Sixteenth Century," *The A* 61, no. 3 (2005), 373–400, table 1, 383.

25. "Instrumentos dos serviços de Mem de Sá," *ABNRJ*, vol. 27 (1905), 130; Soares de Sousa, *Notícia do Brasil*, 143–146; J. Capistrano de Abreu, *Caminhos antigos e povoamento do Brasil* (Rio de Janeiro: 1930), 27–83.

26. Letter by Luís Dias to Miguel Arruda, Bahia, July 13, 1551, *ABNRJ*, vol. 57 (1935), 27.

27. "Representação do pe. Luís da Fonseca (1585)," *HCJB*, vol. 5, 620–622.

28. A. Marchant, *From Barter to Slavery—The Economic Relations of Portuguese and Indians in the Settlement of Brazil 1500–1580* (Gloucester, MA: 1966), 97–99; Monteiro, "The Crises and Transformations of Invaded Societies," 990–1,014.

29. J. Cortesão, *A Colonização do Brasil* (Lisbon: 1969), 167–200; J. Veríssimo Serrão, *Do Brasil filipino ao Brasil de 1640* (São Paulo: 1968), 72–78 and 101–106. *Aldeamento* was the name given by the Portuguese military to the Mozambican villages they fortified and circled with barbed wire, where civilians, mostly peasants, usually brought over from different locations, were forcibly taken to avoid contact with the Frelimo (Mozambique Liberation Front).

30. "Capítulos de Gabriel Soares de Souza contra os padres da Companhia de Jesus que residem no Brasil," *ABNRJ*, vol. 5 (1943), 43–44.

31. A. M. Pelúcia, *Martim Afonso de Sousa e a sua Linhagem: A Elite Dirigente do Império Português nos Reinados de D. João III e D. Sebastião* (PhD thesis in history, New University of Lisbon, Lisbon, 2007), 277–279.

32. "Regimento de Tomé de Souza," *RIHGB*, vol. 61 (1898), 39–57; M. H. B. Paraiso, *Revoltas indígenas, a criação do governo geral e o regimento de 1548*, *Clio—Revista de pesquisa histórica* 29, no. 1 (2011), 1–21.

33. Doc. of April 20, 1617, *ABNRJ*, vol. 39 (1917), 2–3.

34. A. Vieira, *Cartas*, vol. 1, 38.

35. Petition of November 20, 1630. See B. da Silva Lisboa, *Annaes do Rio de Janeiro*, vol. 1 (Rio de Janeiro: 1834), 356–360.

36. "Processo das despesas feitas por Martim de Sá, no Rio de Janeiro 1628–1638," *ABNRJ*, vol. 59 (1940), 178–179.

37. F. M. Calado, *O Valeroso Lucideno*, vol. 2 (São Paulo: 1987), 161.

38. S. B. Schwartz underscores this mode of control and capture of *quilombolas* in "Rethinking Palmares: Slave Resistance in Colonial Brazil," in *Slaves, Peasants, and Rebels* (Chicago: 1992), 111.

39. Letter by Anrique Gomes of 1614. See S. Leite, *HCJB*, vol. 5, 23.

40. Salvador, *História*, 273, 287–288; *HGB*, vol. 1, 60–63; letter by governor-general Diogo de Menezes, to the king, Bahia, December 4, 1608, *ABNRJ*, vol. 57 (1935), 43.

41. J. M. Monteiro, *Tupis, Tapuias e Historiadores, Estudos de História Indígena e do Indigenismo* ("Livre Docência" thesis in anthropoloy, Universidade Estadual de Campinas, Unicamp, Campinas, 2001), 68–70.

42. J. Nieuhof, *Gedenkweerdige Brasiliaense Zee-en-Lant Reize (1682)* (Brazilian translation) (Sao Paulo: 1981), 125–126.

43. Doc. of January 13, 1645, "Manuscritos—Consultas Mistas do Conselho Ultramarino, 1643-1646," *BNRJ*, vol. 1, fs. 154v–159v.

44. Salvador, *História*, 86, 236, and 275.

45. Daniel, *Tesouro*, 45.

46. Rodrigues Ferreira, "Diário da viagem filosófica," 1–234, 57.

47. F. A. de Varnhagen, *HGB*, vol. 1, book 1, 223, and vol. 2, book 3, 98; Alv. de June 2, 1766, J. Ribeiro, *Índice chronológico remissivo da legislação portuguêza posterior à publicação do Código Filipino*, vol. 3 (Lisbon: 1805–1820).

48. Braudel, *Civilisation matérielle*, 121.

49. O. de Campos Mota, *Do rancho ao palácio: evolução da civilização paulista* (Rio de Janeiro: 1941), 87.

50. I am grateful to geneticist Dr. M. A. Zago, professor at the São Paulo University School of Medicine, for the help given in the preparation of this section of the book.

51. D. Henige, *Numbers from Nowhere: The American Indian Contact Population Debate* (Norman, OK: 1998); M. Livi-Bacci, "The Depopulation of Hispanic America after the Conquest," *Population* and Development Review 32, no. 2 (2006), 199–232; Henige mentions Pierre Chaunu's important contribution on this debate. See Chaunu, Séville, 8, book 2, part 2, 1523–1560.

52. S. B. Schwartz and F. Salomon, "New Peoples and New Kinds of People: Adaptation, Readjustment, and Ethnogenesis in South American Indigenous Societies—Colonial Era," *The Cambridge History of the Native*, vol. 3, part 2 (Cambridge, UK: Cambridge UP, 1999), 443–501. See also G. Boccara, "Mundos nuevos en las fronteras del Nuevo Mundo," *Nuevo Mundo Mundos Nuevos*, February 2005, accessed September 2015.

53. W. Crosby, *Ecological Imperialism—The Biological Expansion of Europe 900–1900* (New York: 1989), 230.

54. Coelho and Mcguire, "African and European Bound Labor," 90–92; L. Black, "Why Did They Die?" *Science* 258, no. 11 (1992), 1,739–1,740.

55. Dean, "Indigenous Populations,"10.

56. D. Henige, "When Did Smallpox Reach the New World, and Why Does It Matter?" in *Africans in Bondage*, E. Lovejoy, ed. (Madison, WI: 1986), 11–26.

57. In the memorial by the Jesuits to King Pedro II, in 1684, they requested the observance of a period of two years before the settled Amerindians could have their services required by settlers and authorities, so that the natives could tend to their crops and get used to the new habitat. See Bettendorf, *Crônica*, 398.

58. L. dos Santos Filho, "Medicina tropical," in *HGCB*, vol. 2, book 1, S. Buarque de Holanda, ed. (São Paulo: 1977), 145–161.

59. The dracunculiasis is also known as "Guinea worm infection," a nematode infection by the guinea worm *Dracunculus medinensi*.

60. Another nematode responsible for the hookworm infection in Brazil is *Ancylostoma stercoralis*.

61. F. D. Ashburn, *Ranks of Death: A Medical History of the Conquest of America* (New York: 1947), 102–104; H. G. Cagle III, *Dead Reckonings: Disease and the Natural Sciences in Portuguese Asia and the Atlantic, 1450–1650* (PhD thesis, Rutgers, 2011), 20–21, 31–32.

62. J. E. Bryant, E. C. Holmes, and A. D. T. Barrett, "Out of Africa: A Molecular Perspective on the Introduction of Yellow Fever Virus into the Americas," *PLoS Pathogens* 3.5 (2007) post.

63. F. Guerra, "Aleixo de Abreu [1568–1630], Author of the earliest book on Tropical Medicine describing Amoebiasis, Malaria, Typhoid Fever, Scurvy, Yellow Fever, Dracontiasis, Trichuriasis and Tungiasis in 1623," *Journal of Tropical Medicine and Hygiene* 71 (1968), 55–69.

64. A. de Abreu, *Tratado de las Siete Enfermedades* (Lisbon: 1623), 12, 153–190, 194–200.

65. C. C. Dennie, *A History of Syphillis* (Springfield, IL: 1962); J.-C. Sournia, *Histoire et médicine* (Paris: 1982), 167–170; F. Guerra, "The Dispute over Syphillis—Europe versus America," *Clio Medica* 13 (1978), 39–61.

66. J. de Léry quotes the *piã* as the "most dangerous malady of Brazil." See *Narrative d'un voyage fait à la Terre du Brésil* (São Paulo: [1578] 1980), 245–246; L. Santos Filho, *História geral da medicina brasileira*, vol. 1 (São Paulo: 1977), 185–188; doc. of 1513 describes the *piã* in Cape Verde, where it even caused lesions in the bones. See *MMA*[2], vol. 2, 59n1. On the Angola coast, the disease became endemic in the seventeenth century.

67. As is known, gonorrhea can cause bilateral fallopian tube sclerosis and sterility.

68. L. Gomes Ferreyra, *Erário mineral dividido em doze tratados* (Lisbon: 1732). Ferreyra called himself a surgeon (*cirurgião*), but he was a "practical" (i.e., without a medical degree) physician. Anyhow, his book is a key text for the understanding of the new epidemiological environment created in Minas Gerais by mining activity.

69. A. Ribeiro Sanches, *Tratado da Conservação da Saúde dos Povos* (Lisbon: 1756), 13.

70. M. X. de Vasconcelos Pedrosa, "O exercício da medicina nos séculos XVI, XVII e a primeira metade do século XVIII no Brasil colonial," *Anais*, vol. 3 (4th Congress of National History, Rio de Janeiro: 1951), 268–274.

71. Vasconcellos, *Crônica*, 257; J. Hemming, *Red Gold: The Conquest of the Brazilian Indians, 1500–1760* (Cambridge, MA: 1978), 139–146.

72. On the flu infection the pigs brought over from Madeira Island with Columbus, see F. Guerra, "The Earliest American Epidemic—The Influenza of 1493," *Social Science History* 12, no. 3 (1988), 305–325.

73. Cardim, *Tratados* 66–67; M. de Heriarte, "Descrição do Estado do Maranhão, Pará, Corupá e rio das Amazonas," [1662] *HGB*, vol. 2, book 3 (1662–1667), 174.

74. Brandão, *Diálogos*, 68; *mordexim* or *mordoxi*, *DHMPPO*, vol. 5, 283n4; G. da Orta, *Colóquios dos simples e drogas da Índia*, vol. 1 (Lisbon: 1987), 272–276.

75. J. de Anchieta, *Poesias* (São Paulo: 1954), 567. "Corruções" also encompassed some forms of diarrhea.

76. P. Puntoni, *A Guerra dos Bárbaros—Povos indígenas e a colonização do sertão nordeste do Brasil 1650–1720* (São Paulo: 2000), 196n14.

77. In Europe, *Variola major*, the most lethal, normally killed 25 percent of its victims. *Variola minor*, which emerged at the end of the nineteenth century, caused 1 percent of deaths among the infected. See D. R. Hopkins, *Princes and Peasants—Smallpox in History* (Chicago: 1983), 3–9.

78. S. Leite, ed., *Monumenta Brasiliae*, vol. 3 (Rome: 1956–1965), 379, 451, 454–455, and vol. 4 (ibid.), 178, 267–269; de Vasconcellos, *Crônica*, 101.

79. L. Fróis, *História de Japam*, vol. 5, J. Wicki, ed. ([1584–1594] Lisbon: 1976), 55.

80. D. Alden and J. C. Miller, "Unwanted Cargoes—The Origins and Dissemination of Smallpox via the Slave Trade from Africa to Brazil, c. 1560–1830," in *The African Exchange—Toward a Biological History of Black People*, K. F. Kiple, ed. (Durham, NC: 1987), 38; A. W. Crosby, "Conquistador y Pestilencia—The first New World Pandemic and the Fall of the Great Indian Empires," *HAHR* 47 (1967), 321–337; N. D. Cook, *Demographic Collapse—Indian Peru 1520–1620* (New York: 1981).

81. R. Chambouleyron, "Escravos do Atlântico equatorial: tráfico negreiro para o Estado do Maranhão e Pará, século XVII e início do século XVIII," *Revista Brasileira de História* 26, no. 52 (2006), 79–114.

82. Heriarte, "Descrição do Estado do Maranhão," 171.

83. *HGGA*, vol. 1, 139–141.

84. M. Meuwese, *'For the Peace and Well-Being of the Country': Intercultural Mediators and Dutch-Indian Relations in New Netherland and Dutch Brazil, 1600–1664* (PhD thesis, University of Notre Dame, 2003), 170–173, 295.

85. Rio de Janeiro Municipal Council Minutes of February 19, 1642, *Accordãos e Vereanças*, 58–59.

86. Bettendorf, *Crônica*, 213.

87. R. Southwell, Lisbon, November 20, 1666; C. R. Boxer and J. C. Aldridge, *Descriptive List of the State Papers "Portugal" 1661–1780 in the Public Record Office*, v. 1 (Lisbon: 1979), 64.

88. A similar measure was taken by the Luanda Municipal Council in 1688. See *MMA¹*, vol. 14, 95–97.

89. V. Coaracy, *O Rio de Janeiro no século dezessete* (Rio de Janeiro), 86–88.

90. R. Mols, "Population in Europe 1500–1700," in *The Fontana Economic History of Europe*, vol. 2, C. M. Cipolla, ed. (Glasgow: 1979), 15–82; D. Alden, J. C. Miller, *Unwanted Cargoes*, 44.

91. J. H. Sweet, *Recreating Africa: Culture, Kinship, and Religion in the African-Portuguese World, 1441–1770* (Chapel Hill, NC: 2003), 61–66.

92. R. McCaa, "Spanish and Nahuatl Views on Smallpox and Demographic Catastrophe in Mexico," *The Journal of Interdisciplinary History* 25, no. 3 (1995), 397–431; Crosby, "Conquistador y pestilencia," 321–337.

93. O. A. Rink, *Holland on the Hudson—An Economic and Social History of Dutch New York* (New York: 1989), 258n2.

94. Salvador, *História* 107, 427.

95. Cardim, *Tratados*, 102–103, 135–136, 145, 152, and 160.

96. Hopkins, *Princes*, 164–171.

97. Brandão, *Diálogos*, 64. Brandão often uses "Guinea" to designate the whole of West Africa, but, as here, he opposes Guinea to Congo and Ardra. He must refer, I believe, to Upper Guinea. There had been a smallpox outbreak in Cape Verde in 1610–1611. See MMA², vol. 4, 460.

98. In 1630–1640, slaves were bought more than 700 miles away from Luanda. See L. Jadin, "Pero Tavares missionnaire jésuite, ses travaux apostoliques au Congo et en Angola 1629–1635," *Bulletin de l'Institut Historique Belge de Rome*, vol. 38 (Brussels: 1967), 388; "Le commissaire Moet au comte de Nassau," Luanda, September 11, 1641, *ACA*, vol. I 95–97.

99. Schwartz, *Sugar Plantations*, 51–52; Scelle, *Histoire*, 455; Royal provision of October 13, 1670, *MMA¹*, vol. 13, 124–125.

100. J. Diamond, *Guns, Germs, and Steel: The Fates of Human Societies* (New York: W. W. Norton & Co., 1999), 214.

101. Although this statement sparked controversy, it is part of the study by Coelho and McGuire, "African and European Bound Labor in the British New World," 83–115. The study examines the effects of diseases on the work of African slaves and British-American servants, with no mention of Amerindian slavery.

102. S. Morão, *Queixas repetidas em ecos nos Arrecifes de Pernambuco contra os abusos médicos que nas suas capitanias se observam tanto em dano das vidas de seus habitadores* (Lisbon: [1677] 1965), 68–70.

103. Regarding the yellow fever, at the time it became an epidemic in nineteenth-century Brazil, see J. Pereira Rêgo, *História e descrição da febre amarela epidêmica que grassou no Rio de Janeiro em 1850* (Rio de Janeiro: 1850).

104. V. Nutton, "The Changing Language of Medicine, 1450–1550," *CIVICIMA—Etudes sur le vocabulaire intellectuel du Moyen Age*, 3 (1995), 184–198.

105. See the pioneering studies by de Andrade and Duarte, *Morão*, 9–34 and 35–72.

106. Morão, *Queixas repetidas*, 5–14.

107. This is Dr. Francisco Marquez Coelho, ship surgeon of the galley *Magdalena*, who settled in Rio de Janeiro. See J. Leite Cordeiro, "Alguns documentos sôbre médicos e medicina do Brasil Seiscentista," *RIHGB*, vol. 216 (1952), 36–41.

108. Cardim, *Tratados*, 42–50.

109. T. D. Walker, "The Medicines Trade in the Portuguese Atlantic World: Acquisition and Dissemination of Healing Knowledge from Brazil (c. 1580–1800)," *Social History of Medicine* 26, no. 3 (2013), 403–431, here 428–430.

110. W. Piso, *História natural e médica da Índia Occidental* (Rio de Janeiro: [1648–1658] 1957); G. Marcgrave, *História natural do Brasil* (São Paulo: [1648] 1942); Guerra, "Medicine in Dutch," 487–488.

111. Vasconcelos, *Crônica*, 163–164; D. J. Struik, "Mauricio de Nassau, Scientific Maecenas in Brazil," *Revista da Sociedade Brasileira de História da Ciência*, vol. 2 (1985), 21–27.

112. I refer to the distinction established by Foster between personalist etiology, grounded on the idea that disease, like all human afflictions, is explained by supernatural reasons, and naturalist etiology, heir to the medic tradition of the classic civilizations of Greece, Rome, India, and China, for which disease originates from an imbalance of natural elements—above all the cold/heat dichotomy—present in the body. Hybrid systems, combining naturalist and personalist etiologies, exist in various parts of the world. See G. M. Foster, "Disease Etiologies in Non-Western Medical Systems," *American Anthropologist* 78, no. 4 (1976), 773–782.

113. Buarque de Holanda, *Caminhos e fronteiras*, 76.

114. Y. David-Peyre, "La peste et le mal vénérien dans la littérature portugaise du xvie et xviie siècles," *Arquivos do Centro Cultural Português*, vol. 1 (Paris: 1969), 196; Drumond Braga, "Dois surtos de peste em Lisboa—1579–1581," *Revista da Biblioteca Nacional* 7, no. 2 (1992), 7–22.

115. S. Leite, *Artes e Ofícios dos Jesuítas no Brasil 1549–1760* (Rio de Janeiro: 1953), 83–100.

116. Walker has analyzed a later copy of the volume written around 1580. See Walker, "The Medicines Trade in the Portuguese Atlantic World," 412–414.

117. Born in Olmütz, Moravia, the Jesuit Valentim Stancel was a math master at the Colégio de Santo Antão, Lisbon, and lived in Brazil in 1663. See C. Ziller Camenietzki, "Esboço biográfico de Valentin Stansel (1621–1705), matemático jesuíta e missionário na Bahia," *Ideação* 3 (1999), 159–182.

118. S. C. da Costa Sacadura, "Profilaxia seiscentistas das pestilências na capitania de Pernambuco," *Primeiro Congresso da História da Expansão Portuguesa no Mundo*, seção Brasil, Lisbon (1938), 379–399.

119. Rocha Pitta, *História da América portuguesa*, 196.

120. N. Hudson-Rodd, "Hygeia or Panacea? Ethnogeography and Health in Canada—Seventeenth to Eighteenth Century," *History of European Ideas* 21, no. 2 (1995), 235–246; Fróis, *História*, 124.

121. M. E. Del Rio Hijas and M. Revuelta Gonzales, "Enfermarías y boticas en las casas de la Compañia en Madrid, siglos XVI–XIX," *AHSI* 64, no. 127 (1995), 39–81.

122. R. Mosia Reinhipo, an anagram of Simão Pinheiro Morão, *Queixas repetidas*, and *Trattado único das bexigas e sarampo* (Lisbon: 1683).

123. J. Ferreira da Rosa, *Trattado único da constituiçam pestilencial de Pernambuco* (Lisbon: 1694); de Andrade, *Morão, Rosa*, 153–156.

124. S. Morão, *Queixas*, 33.

125. F. de Nossa Senhora dos Prazeres Maranhão, *Poranduba maranhense* (São Luís: [c. 1820] 1946), 259.

126. F. Burke, "Malaria in the Greco-Roman World—A Historical and Epidemiological Survey," in *Aufstieg und Niedergang der römischen Welt*, vol. 2, H. Temporini and W. Haase, eds., 2252–2281; F. Braudel, *La Méditerranée*, 69–73.

127. The anemia falciform gene, a genetic disease of the Afro-descendants, is the most resistant to malaria. Thus, this disease carrier is more likely to survive in regions where malaria is an epidemic. Research carried out in Brazil showed the prevalence of a genetic factor specific to individuals hailing from West Central Africa, the Bantu haplotype, in those hit by falciform malaria. Indirectly, the antiquity and persistence of malaria in that African region is thus proved. See M. A. Zago, "Quadro mundial das enfermidades e doenças consideradas genéticas," *Cadernos de Pesquisa—Cebrap* 2 (1994), 3–14; M. A. Zago, S. Figueiredo, and S. H. Ogo, "Bantu ßs cluster hapotype predominates among Brazilian Blacks,"*American Journal of Physical Anthropology* 88 (1985), 295–298.

128. For a more detailed discussion on the hematic characteristics propitious to immunization in populations where malaria *falciparum* is endemic, see K. F. Kiple and V. Himmelsteib King, *Another Dimension to the Black Diaspora: Diet, Disease, and Racism* (London: 1981), 12–23.

129. F. Guerra, "Medicine in Dutch Brazil 1624–1654," in *Johan Maurits van Nassau-Siegen—A Humanist Prince in Europe and Brazil 1604–1679*, E. van den Boogaart, H. R. Hoetink, and J. Whitehead, eds. (The Hague: 1979), 477–478.

130. D. Curtin, *The Rise and Fall of the Plantation Complex* (New York: 1990), 79–81; H.M. Beckles, *White Servitude and Black Slavery in Barbados 1627–1715* (Knoxville, TN: 1989), 115–130; L. Gragg, "'To Procure Negroes'—The English Slave Trade to Barbados, 1627–1660," *Slavery and Abolition* 16, no. 1 (1995), 65–84.

131. Rocha Pitta, *História da América*, 181.

132. Pires de Lima, A."Nota sobre algumas epidemias na cidade da Bahia," *Brasilia*, vol. 5 (1950), 503–518.

133. R. Chambouleyron, "Suspiros por um escravo de Angola. Discursos sobre a mão-de-obra africana na Amazônia seiscentista," *Humanitas* 20, no. 1–2 (2004), 99–111, here 105.

134. Letter of February 12, 1661, Vieira, *Cartas*, 556–560. On his arrival in São Luís, Maranhão's capital, Vieira writes to the governor of the Estado do Maranhão to report his first analysis of the enslavement of the Amazon's Indians.

135. Decision of 1645; see S. A. Zavala, *La Encomienda Indiana* (Mexico: 1973), 974.

136. "Carta de Luís da Grã a S. Inácio, Piratininga," in *Diálogo sobre a conversão do gentio pelo Manuel da Nóbrega*, S. Leite, ed. (Rio de Janeiro), 115, appendix B. On the same issue in Amazonia, see Arenz, *De l'Alzette à l'Amazonie*, 179–182.

137. The only son of Francisco Dias d'Ávila, Garcia d'Ávila Pereira, inherited the properties of his mother's family. In 1654, he joined with his armed Indians and mestizos, the "bandeira" of Gaspar Rodrigues that destroyed the Tapuia's villages in the south of the Bahia's Bay. See A. E. da Silva Pessoa, *As ruínas da tradição: 'A Casa da Torre' de Garcia D' Ávila—família e propriedade no nordeste colonial* (PhD thesis in social history, Universidade de São Paulo, São Paulo, 2003), 162–163, 224–225.

138. Letter by João de Lencastre, Bahia, July 18, 1697. See Rau and Gomes da Silva, *Os Manuscritos*, 305–306.

139. W. T. Easterbrook and H. G. J. Aitken, *Canadian Economic History* (Toronto: 1988), 76–84.

140. Rodrigues Ferreira, "Diário da viagem filosófica," 65–66.

141. Bettendorf, *Crônica*, 665. On Bettendorf and the Amazon economy, see Arenz, *De l'Alzette à l'Amazonie: Jean-Philippe Bettendorf*, 425–429.

142. Hemming, *Red Gold*, 458–460; R. M. Delson, "Inland Navigation in Colonial Brazil: Using Canoes on the Amazon," *International Journal of Maritime History* 7, no. 1 (1995), 1–28.

143. Daniel, "*Tesouro*," 31. A document of the end of the 1700s reports "the extraordinary death toll among the Indians" in the river routes between Pará and Mato Grosso. "Informação sobre o modo porque se efetua a navegação do Pará para o Mato Grosso," Pará, August 4, 1797, *RIHGB*, vol. 25 (1865).

144. Dockès, *L'espace dans la pensée économique du XVIe au XVIIIe siècle*, 176–178.

145. A. Cardoso, *Maranhão na monarquia hispânica: intercâmbios, guerra e navegação nas fronteiras das Índias de Castela (1580–1655)* (PhD thesis, Universidad de Salamanca 2012), 82–85.

146. Doc. of December 19, 1665, *AHU*, Overseas Council, cod. 16, fl. 187.

147. Royal provision of March 18, 1672, *AA*, 1st series, vol. 3 (1937), 15nn16–18. There was a protest from the Angola contractor against the concession of such fiscal sub-

sidy to Maranhão, and the Overseas Council supported his claim. Nevertheless, the Crown maintained the privilege. See doc. of January 17, 1680, *AHU*, Angola, box 12/40.

148. This was governor Pedro César de Meneses (1673–1678). See Bettendorf, *Crônica*, 291–293.

149. L. Ferrand de Almeida, "Aclimatação de plantas do Oriente no Brasil durante os séculos XVII e XVIII," *Revista Portuguesa de História*, vol. 15 (Coimbra: 1975), 339–481.

150. For a study of Portuguese recession between 1670 and 1690, see Mauro, *Le Portugal*, 489.

151. L. Monteiro Baena, *Compendio das eras da Província do Pará* (Rio de Janeiro: [1838] 1969), 111–117; *AHU*, Angola, box 12/44.

152. Royal letter of July 14, 1681, *DH*, vol. 82 (1948), 323–324.

153. After having Beckman hanged, Governor Gomes Freire de Andrade pleaded for the re-enslavement of the Amerindians to appease the local colonists. See M. Liberman, *O Levante do Maranhão "Judeu Cabeça de Motim"—Manoel Beckman* (São Paulo: 1983), 115; Arenz, *De l'Alzette*, 456–486, 564–594.

154. Azevedo, *Os Jesuítas*, 243, 403–409.

155. D. Alden, "Economic Aspects of the Expulsion of the Jesuits from Brazil—A Preliminary Report," in *Conflict and Continuity in Brazilian Society*, H. H. Keith and S. F. Edwards, eds. (Colombia: 1969), 26–41.

156. "Warnings to the governors . . ." Lisbon, March 18, 1755, AHU, ACL, C.U., 035 (Ultramar), cx. 4/317; A. Delgado da Silva, *Colleção da Legislação Portugueza desde a última compilação das Ordenações*, vol. 1 (Lisbon: 1830–1835), 369–376. On the new Directorio (royal directives) edicts in 1758 to organize the administration of the Indian's settlements, see B. A. Sommer, *Negotiated Settlements: Native Amazonians and Portuguese Policy in Para, Brazil, 1758–1798* (PhD thesis, University of New Mexico, 2000), 55–152.

157. A transformation noted in the 1850–1860 reports by the French consulate in São Luís do Maranhão. See *Archives Nationales de France*, Paris, series F[12], 2,699.

158. C. Meillassoux, *Femmes, Greniers & Capitaux* (Paris: 1975), 71–81.

159. F. A. de Varnhagen, *HGB*, vol. 1, book 1 (Rio de Janeiro: 1854–1857), 220–221.

160. Goulart, *A Escravidão*, 54.

161. Magalhães Godinho, *Os Descobrimentos*, 184.

162. Meillassoux, *Anthropologie de l'esclavage* (Paris: 1990), chapter 5, passim.

163. Platon, *La République*, book 5, 469c, Estienne, ed. (Paris: 1966), 225.

164. M. I. Finley, "Slavery," *International Encyclopaedia of the Social Sciences*, vol. 14 (New York: 1968), 307–313; M. I. Finley, *Aspects of Antiquity: Discoveries and Controversies* (New York: Penguin, 1977), 190–191; Y. Garlan, *Les esclaves en Grèce ancienne* (Paris: 1982), 59–62.

165. H. Levy-Bruhl, "Esquisse d'une théorie sociologique de l'esclavage à Rome," *Revue générale du droit, de la législation et de la jurisprudence en France et à l'étranger* 55 (1931), 1–17. See also A. Paturet, "L'individu entre l'homme et la chose. Note sur l'esclave en droit romain," *Droits* 51 (2010), 3–26.

166. Benveniste, *Le Vocabulaire*, 359–361; A. Ernout and A. Meillet, *Dictionnaire etymologique de la langue latine—Histoire des mots* (Paris: 1985), 620; M. I. Finley, *L'economie antique* (Paris: 1975), 77–123; G. Duby, *L'economie rurale et la vie des campagnes dans l'Occident médiéval*, vol. 2 (Paris: 1977), 78–93; Duby, *Guerriers*, 41–60.

167. S. M. Stuard, "Ancillary Evidence for the Decline of Medieval Slavery," *Past & Present* 149 (1995), 3–28; M. Fontenay, "Routes et modalités du commerce des esclaves dans la Méditerranée des Temps modernes (XVIe, XVIIe, et XVIIIe siècles)," *Revue Historique* 640, no. 4 (2006), 813–830.

168. L. F. F. R. Thomaz, "A escravatura em Malaca no século XVI," *Studia* 53 (1994), 253–316, 264–265; J. Machado, *Dicionário etimológico da língua portuguesa*, vol. 2 (Lisbon: 1977), 449.

169. R. McColley, "Slavery in Virginia," in *Dictionary of Afro-American Slavery*, R. M. Miller and J. D. Smith, eds. (Westport, CT: 1988), 779–787, 781.

170. L. Caldas Tibiriçá, *Dicionário tupi-português* (Santos: 1984); A. G. da Cunha, *Dicionário Histórico*; L. do Vale, *Vocabulário na língua brasílica*, vol. 2, C. Drummond, ed. (São Paulo: 1953); C. Tastevin, "Vocabulario Tupy-Portuguez," *Revista do Museu Paulista* 13 (1923), 633, 668; V. C. de Miranda, "Estudos sôbre o Nhêengatú," *ABNRJ* 64 (1942), 112; doc. of 1625, *Inventários e testamentos*, vol. 31 (1940), 166.

171. Mungo Park, *Voyage dans l'intérieur de l'Afrique 1795–1797* (Paris: 1980), 285.

172. Pará, December 1, 1659, Vieira, *Cartas*, 723–728.

173. Ennes, *Os Palmares*, 84–7.

174. Minutes of January 19, 1637, *Rio de Janeiro no século XVII: Accordãos e vereanças do Senado da Câmara [. . .] relativos aos annos de 1635 até 1650* (Rio de Janeiro: 1935), 15.

175. L. A. de Oliveira Mendes, *Memória a respeito dos escravos e tráfico da escravatura entre a Costa d'África e o Brasil* (Porto: [1793] 1977), 43–54.

176. D. Birmingham, *The Portuguese Conquest of Angola* (Oxford, UK: Oxford UP, 1965), 51; J. C. Miller, "A Note on Kasanze and the Portuguese," *Canadian Journal of African Studies* 6 (1972), 43–56.

177. There was the extreme 1614 case of a slaver that waited for a year and a half in the port of trade before it completed its load. See Vila Vilar, *Hispano-America*, 146.

178. Abreu e Brito, *Sumário*, 73; ord. man., de 1514, *MMA²*, vol. 2, 67–68.

179. Silva Correa, *História*, 126n2.

180. Birmingham, *The Portuguese Conquest of Angola*, 51.

181. R. H. Rainero, *Il Congo agli inizi del Settecento nella relazione di Luca da Caltanissetta* (Florence: [1701] 1974), 466.

182. *DHCMA*, vol. 1, 160, and vol. 2, 146 and 171. Slaves boarded in Dahomey also believed that the white men would devour them. See J. Barbot, *A Description of the Coasts of North and South-Guinea, and of Ethiopia Inferior, Vulgarly Angola* (London: 1732), 327.

183. Damião Cosme, "Tractado das queixas endemicas," 264.

184. Doc. of November 20, 1694, *AHU*, Angola, box 15/20.

185. Vila Vilar, "Introducción," in *Um Tratado*, 32.

186. Ribeiro Rocha, *Ethiope resgatado, empenhado, sustentado, corregido, instruído e libertado*, 188–189.

187. A. D'assier, "Le Mato Virgem," *Revue des Deux Mondes* 1 (1864), 561.

188. Meillassoux, *Anthropologie*, 86–98.

189. O. Patterson, *Slavery and Social Death—A Comparative Study* (Cambridge, MA: 1982), 132–135.

190. T. Wiedemann, *Greek and Roman Slavery* (Canberra: 1983), 108–109 and 146–147. In 1643, A. Vieira considered that the Angolan slaves were the most adequate to Brazil. See A. Vieira, *Obras escolhidas*, vol. 5 (Lisbon: 1951), 8.

191. Doc. of 1640, J. A. Gonçalves de Mello, ed., *Fontes para a história do Brasil holandês* (*FHBH*), vol. 1 (Recife: 1981–1985), 186–187.

192. Postma, *The Dutch*, 106–109.

193. Letter from Maranhão, Vieira, *Cartas*, 392–400.

194. *HGGA*, vol. 3, 173 and 283; C. Moseley and R. E. Asher, eds., *Atlas of the World's Languages* (New York: 1994), 293–294.

195. "Of this cast of animals it is said that they do not speak so as not to work [*não falam por não trabalharem*]," *HGGA*, vol. 3, 283.

196. Daniel, "Tesouro," 147.

197. In a process of humanization of the overseas beings, Rousseau, referring to the great apes, wonders if "various animals similar to men . . . are not true savage men." See J.-J. Rousseau, *Discours sur l'origine et les fondements de l'inegalité parmi les hommes* (Geneva: 1755), first part, note 10. An admirable essay of Claude Lévi-Strauss teaches that Rousseau "preferred [to] recognize the great apes of Africa and Asia as men of an unknown race rather than run the risk of denying human nature to creatures who might possess it." See C. Lévi-Strauss, "Rousseau, père de l'Ethnologie," *Le Courrier de l'Unesco* 16 (1963), 10–14, here 14.

198. See, for instance, the assessment of the Franciscan historian Loreto do Couto about the enslavement of Amerindians: "[I]t cannot be denied that it is laudable and charitable" when one intends "to keep a prisoner of a good war and to feed him, dress him and not kill him, as the winner may do, having sustained war with justice." See D. do Loreto Couto, *Desagravos do Brazil e glórias de Pernambuco* (Rio de Janeiro: [1757] 1904), 68.

199. Xenophon, *Économique*, P. Chantraine, ed. and trans. (Paris: 1949), 37 and 89.

200. A. Kojeve, *Introduction à la lecture de Hegel* (Paris: 1947). Vernant recalls that the idea of abstract labor, indispensable for the free man or the slave to apprehend his own activity as worker in general, is not operational in Antiquity. See J.-P. Vernant, "Travail et nature dans la Grèce ancienne" and "Aspects psychologiques du travail dans la Grèce ancienne" in Vernant and Vidal-Naquet, *Travail et esclavage en Grèce ancienne* (Paris: 1988), 1–33.

201. K. Marx, *Le Capital*, vol. 1 (Paris: 1976), 149, 595–596n17.

202. R. Martin, "'Familia rustica'—Les esclaves chez les agronomes latins," *Annales Littéraires de l'Université de Besançon* (Paris: 1974), 267–298. Regarding Roman paternal-

ism, Martin refers, in particular, to Varro (116–127 BC), author of *Rerum rusticarum* and Columela (first century), author of *De re rustica*. Fenoaltea, in his well-known essay on the slavery system, does not pay sufficient attention to the use of positive incentives and rewards in the exploitation of the slave. See S. Fenoaltea, "Slavery and Supervision in Comparative Perspective—A Model," *The Journal of Economic History* 44, no. 3 (1984), 635–668.

203. E. Genovese, *Roll, Jordan, Roll—The World the Slaves Made* (London: 1975), 50.

Chapter 5

1. Part of this chapter has been published as chapter 2, in J. M. Fradera and C. Schmidt-Nowara, eds., *Slavery and Antislavery in Spain's Atlantic Empire* (Oxford: 2013).

2. On the first steps of Xavier in Japan and the "new radicality" of the Jesuit's mission in the country, see N. Kouame, "Quatre règles à suivre pour bien comprendre le 'siècle chrétien' du Japon," *Histoire et missions chrétiennes* 11, no. 3 (2009), 9–38.

3. Letter by Valignano, Japan, August 15, 1580, see D. Pacheco, *A fundação do Porto de Nagasaqui* (Macau: 1989), 16–21, 20. On the duties of a *visitador*, see D. Alden, *The Making of an Enterprise: The Society of Jesus in Portugal, Its Empire, and Beyond, 1540–1750* (Stanford, CA: 1996), 247–254.

4. Response by Hideyoshi to Francisco Garcez, 1588, see L. Fróis, *História de Japam*, vol. 5 (Lisbon: 1976), 25.

5. Ibid., 366–370.

6. H. Vu Thant, *Pastorale et missions au Japon pendant le siècle chrétien (XVIe–XVIIe siècles)* (PhD thesis, Université de Paris-Sorbonne, 2012), 147–172.

7. Although also suffering restrictions, Siamese and Korean merchants carried on some trade with Japan. See R. Toby, "Reopening the Question of Sakoku: Diplomacy in the Legitimation of the Tokugawa Bakufu," *Journal of Japanese Studies* 3, no. 2 (1977), 323–363; E. Kato, "Unification and Adaptation, the Early Shogunate and Dutch Trade Policies," in *Companies and Trade: Essays on Overseas Trading Companies during the Ancient Regime*, L. Blussé and F. Gaastra, eds. (Leiden: 1981), 207–229; C. D. Sheldon, "Merchants and Society in Tokugawa Japan," *Modern Asian Studies* 17, no. 3 (1983), 477–488; A. Curvelo, "Nagasaki/Deshima after the Portuguese in Dutch Accounts of the 17th Century," *Bulletin of Portuguese-Japanese Studies* 6 (2003), 147–157.

8. Other missionaries shared the Jesuits' fascination with China. In his book on China, the first work exclusively dedicated to that country in Europe, Dominican friar Gaspar da Cruz expresses his admiration for the Chinese central power and bureaucracy. See G. da Cruz, *Tratado das coisas da China* (Lisbon: [1570] 1997), 200, 219.

9. Born in 1628 in the island of Itaparica, Bahia, Francisco de Sousa went to Portugal at the age of fourteen. He traveled to India when he was sixteen, where he did missionary work and wrote his book, dying in Goa in 1713. He spent most of life as a theology

teacher at the São Paulo de Goa College. According to specialists, he was knowledgeable in Hindu religion, which few Europeans were familiar with at the time. See F. de Sousa, *Oriente conquistado a Jesus Cristo pelos padres da Companhia de Jesus da Província de Goa* 2 vols. (Porto [1710]: 1978), vol. 1, XIV–XV, 68 and 471.

10. Especially Jesuit Francisco Suárez (1617), who taught at Salamanca and Coimbra. See J. Lafaye, *Quetzalcóatl et Guadalupe—La formation de la conscience nationale au Méxique* (Paris: 1974), 73–74.

11. Goa, December 1, 1560, *Documentos sobre os portugueses em Moçambique e na África Central 1497–1840*, vol. 7 (Lisbon: 1971), 518–555, 532. Jesuit Luís Fróis would later go to Japan, where he would write his monumental *História de Japam* (1584–1594).

12. D. B. Davis, *The Problem of Slavery in Western Culture* (Middlesex, England: 1970), 127.

13. M. Venard, "Les bases de la Réforme catholique," in Venard, *Histoire*, vol. 8, 223–279.

14. *MMA[1]*, vol. 2, 169–173, 179–188, and 209–217.

15. "Do grande fervor que houve no colégio de Coimbra para a missão de Congo." See Telles, *Chronica*, vol. 1, 355.

16. There is no copy left of that book, but its existence is recorded in documents of the time. See V. van Bulck, "Operum Iudicia," *AHSI* 24, no. 48 (1955), 455; F. Bontinck and N. Nsasi, *Le catéchisme kikongo de 1624—Réédition critique* (Brussels: 1978), 17–23. About the Franciscans in the Congo, see J. Cuvilier and L. Jadin, *L'Ancien Congo d'après les archives romaines 1518–1640* (hereafter *AC*) (Brussels: 1954), 62–64.

17. M. L. Carvalhão Buescu, "A gramaticalização das línguas exóticas no quadro cultural da Europa do século XVI," *RHES* 10 (1982), 15–28.

18. Pedro Dias, *Arte da língua de Angola oferecida a Virgem Senhora N. do Rosário, Mãy & Senhora dos mesmos Pretos* (Lisbon: 1697). See also HCJB, vol. 5, 355n4.

19. For the stages on the studies of the Kimbundu language, from the seventeenth to the nineteenth century, see C. E. Vieira-Martinez, *Building Kimbundu: Language Community Reconsidered in West Central Africa, c. 1500–1750* (PhD thesis, University of California, Los Angeles, 2006), 91–143. Unlike E. Bonvini, C. Vieira-Martinez does not assign particular significance to Father Dias's grammar.

20. E. Bonvini, "Repères pour une histoire des connaissances linguistiques des langues africaines," *Histoire Épistémologie Langage* 18, no. 2 (1996), 127–148, here 145–146.

21. I agree here with Alden's opinion. See D. Alden, "Changing Jesuit Perceptions of the Brasis during the Sixteenth Century," *Journal of World History* 3, no. 2 (1992), 212–213.

22. D. Ramada Curto, "A língua e o império," in *História da Expansão*, vol. 1, F. Bethencourt and K. Chaudhuri, eds. (Lisbon: 1998), 413–431.

23. Bahia, August 9, 1549, M. da Nóbrega, "Cartas do Brasil," in *Cartas jesuíticas*, vol. 1(São Paulo: 1988), 79–87.

24. "Carta do pe. Inácio de Azevedo a Inácio de Loyola," December 7, 1553, *MMA¹*, vol. 15, 167–172, and A. A. Banha de Andrade, ed., *Dicionário de história da Igreja em Portugal*, vol. 1 (Lisbon: 1979), 258–260.

25. *MMA¹*, vol. 2, 229, 275, and 377.

26. Having returned to Portugal and ordained as a priest, Diogo de Soveral, member of the disastrous 1548 mission, was rewarded by being sent to India "as pay for the services rendered, in the many labors he had performed in the Congo mission." See Telles, *Chronica*, vol. 1, 362, and vol. 2, 489.

27. *MMA¹*, vol. 15, 221–225.

28. "Apontamentos das cousas de Angola" (1563), *AA*, 2nd series, vol. 17, no. 67–70 (1960), 28–31.

29. "Carta de doação de Paulo Dias ao pe. Balthazar Barreira," Luanda, July 11, 1583, *MMA¹*, vol. 15, 279.

30. See chapter 2 note 33.

31. F. de Oliveira, "Primeira Parte," in *A Arte da Guerra no Mar* (Coimbra: 1555), 15; C. Callier-Boisvert, "Captifs et esclaves au XVIe siècle. Une diatribe contre la traite restée sans écho," *L'Homme* 38, no. 145 (1998), 109–126. On Oliveira and the black antislavery ideas in Ibero-America in the sixteenth and seventeenth centuries, see S. B. Schwartz, *All Can Be Saved: Religious Tolerance and Salvation in the Iberian Atlantic World* (New York: 2008), 160–167.

32. B. de Las Casas, *Brevísima relación de la destrucción de África* [1540–1554] (Salamanca: 1989), 80.

33. Nóbrega, *Cartas*, 103–113.

34. G. Duby, *Le Chevalier, la Femme et le Prêtre* (Paris: 1981), 44–47.

35. Duval, *Des Sacrements au Concile de Trente* (Paris: 1985), 281–326.

36. On the debate in France about the Council of Trent, see A. Tallon, *La France et le Concile de Trente (1518–1563)* (Rome: 1997), passim.

37. Royal ordinance of 1579, R. Mousnier, *Les institutions de la France sous la monarchie absolue*, vol. 1 (Paris: 1974), 56–60.

38. On the Catholic doctrine concerning the relationship between parents and sons, see A. Tallon, "'Père et mère honoreras': quelques commentaires catholiques du quatrième commandement au XVIe siècle," in *Histoire des familles, des démographies et des comportements—Mélanges en hommage à Jean-Pierre Bardet*, J.-P. Poussou and I. Robin-Romero, eds. (Paris: 2007), 699–711.

39. Nóbrega, *Cartas*, 123–127.

40. Ibid., and letter of 1552 to the Lisbon's Jesuits Superior, 128–132.

41. J. Benci, *Economia Cristã dos Senhores no governo dos escravos* (Lisbon: [1700] 1954), 82–85. On the separation of slaves' families, see also J. H. Sweet, *Recreating Africa:* 77–83.

42. *Constituçoens Primeyras do Arcebispado da Bahia, feytas & ordenadas pelo ilustríssimo e reverendissimo Sr. D. Sebastião Monteyro da Vide, arcebispo do dito arcebispado* (Coimbra: [1707] 1720), canon 50 and 57, 20 and 22.

43. *Constituiçoens*, canon 177, 75–76.

44. *Constituiçoens*, canon 303, 125; G. A. Titton, "O Sínodo da Bahia (1707) e a escravatura," in *Anais do VI Simpósio Nacional dos Professores Universitários de História*, vol. 1 (São Paulo: 1973), 285–306.

45. In her professorial thesis, C. de Castelau extensively analyzes the slaves' marriage in the Catholic Church, albeit without taking in account the status of the slaves' children. See C. de Castelnau L'Estoile, *Les Chaînes du Mariage. Catholicisme, colonisation et esclavage au Brésil XVIe–XVIIIe siècles* (PhD thesis, Université de Paris Sorbonne, Paris, 2013), 256–267.

46. *Constituiçoens*, Canons 303 and 989, 125, 340–341.

47. Ibid., Canon 304, 125–126.

48. Ibid., Canon 303, 125.

49. A. M. Perdigão Malheiro, *A escravidão no Brasil, ensaio jurídico, histórico, social*, vol. 2 (Petrópolis: [1867] 1976), 60–61. The law of September 15, 1869. prohibited slave sales separating husband from wife, as well as parent from children less than fourteen years old. The Free Womb law (1871) extended the prohibition to separations and donations derived from inheritance, but lowered the age of the children protected by law: only those younger than twelve years old would be kept together with father *or* mother. Eventually, the parliamentary debate on the project of the 1869 law revealed the frauds that allowed for the sale of family members separately. See *Jornal do Commércio*, Rio de Janeiro, April 4, 1864. Researches demonstrated that in Rio de Janeiro, one-third to one-fifth of the lots of slaves recorded in testamentary divisions of inheritance correspond to groups of first-degree relatives living together after property transmission. See M. Florentino and J. R. Góes, "Parentesco e estabilidade familiar entre os escravos do agro-fluminense, 1790–1830," *Cadernos em História Social* 1 (1995), 13–19. However, the heirs and new owners of a plantation might not be interested in disbanding parental groups adapted to laboring for the same owners and even less in separating slave families. In fact, the threat of a masters' retaliation against their relatives intimidated rebellious slaves or those prone to escaping. The percentage of kindred slaves kept after the *sale* of slave lots could have been much lower.

50. O. Patterson, *Slavery and Social Death* (Cambridge, MA: 1982), 29.

51. For the royal ordinance of March 8, 1546, on the Christianity of India, see *DHMPPO*, vol. 3, 315–317; royal letter of 1557 to Francisco Barreto, governor of India (1555–1558), *MMA¹*, vol. 2, 404. In the same vein, "Carta dos governadores de Portugal sobre a alforria dos gentios," March 1580, *MMA¹*, vol. 3, 84–85. In 1560, Felipe II prohibits the "Moors" still living in Andalusia from owning slaves to prevent the latter from being converted to Muslim customs.

52. Report of 1618, *MMA¹*, vol. 6, 341.

53. C.J. de Senna Barcellos, *Subsídios para a história de Cabo Verde e Guiné*, vol. 1, part 2 (Lisbon: 1899), 173.

54. D. Maurício, "A Universidade de Évora e a escravatura," *Didaskalia* 8 (1977), 153–200, 172, and 185.

55. In 1567, superior general Francisco de Borja spoke out against the Japan contract, in which Portuguese merchants would buy a certain amount of silk in Macau and sell it in Japan, handing over the revenue to the Jesuit mission. See J. Wicki, "Dois compêndios das ordens dos padres gerais e congregações da província dos jesuítas de Goa," *Studia* 43–44 (1980), 400; C. R. Boxer, *O Grande Navio de Amacau* (Portuguese translation) (Macau: 1989), 175–179.

56. F. de Almeida, *HIP*, vol. 2, 169–181, and 297–310. The College of São Paulo de Goa enjoyed revenues from villages and also from the *namoxim*—the land of an agrarian community whose product returns to a religious cult—of Goa and surroundings. See A. de Almeida Calado, "A Companhia de Jesus na Índia em meados do século xvii," *Studia* 40 (1978), 349–366. On the *namoxim*, see also Axelrod and Fuerch, "Portuguese Orientalism and the Making of the Village Communities of Goa," 446–447, 456.

57. On the Jesuits commercial activity in Asia, see C. J. Borges, "How Shall We Manage? Catholic Religious Orders Based in Portuguese India in the 16th–18th Centuries," in *Indo-Portuguese History—Global Trends*, F. da Silva Gracias, C. Pinto, and C. Borges, eds. (Goa: 2005), 233–250.

58. Complying with a charter of July 20, 1611, which ordered Ignatians to list their properties in Angola, the missionaries listed several farms in Luanda, Bengo, and Massangano, but declared that they did not produce anything. See *MMA¹*, vol. 6, 91–102.

59. Arrived in Bahia in 1576 with other Jesuits. See *HCJB*, vol. 2, 567.

60. *HCJB*, vol. 2, 227–228.

61. "Carta ao Geral da Companhia," Lisbon, September 6, 1586, *MMA¹*, vol. 15, 298–299.

62. Remarks on slavery written by theologians L. de Molina, F. Perez, and G. Gonçalves, scholars at Coimbra and the University of Évora. See Telles, *Chronica*, vol. 2, 454–470.

63. Letter from C. de Gouveia, Bahia, July 25, 1583, *MMA¹*, vol. 15, 280–281.

64. G. Jacquemet, G. Mathon, G. H. Baudry, P. Guilluy, and E. Thiery, "Confessionnal," in *Catholicisme—Hier, aujourd'hui, demain*, vol. 2 (Paris: 1954), 1507–1510.

65. L. L. da Gama Lima, *A confissão pelo avesso—O crime de solicitação no Brasil colonial*, vol. 1 (PhD thesis in history, Univeristy of São Paulo, 1990), 184–185; J. Delumeau, *L'aveu et le pardon—Les difficultés de la confession XIIIe–XVIIIe siècle* (Paris: 1995), 46–71. The theologian M. de Bay said Baius (1513–1589) taught at the University of Louvain, which kept close relations with Spanish and Portuguese universities.

66. *MMA¹*, vol. 8, 37–38.

67. Duval, *Des Sacrements*, 153–154.

68. Royal provision of 1556, Telles, *Chronica*, vol. 2, 188–189.

69. Fernão Cardim, "Narrativa epistolar," *Tratado* 171.

70. Letter to the superior general of the S.J., 1586, *HCJB*, vol. 2, 228–229. On the confession and penance, see M.-C. Varachaud, *Le Père Houdry S.J—Prédication et pénitence, 1631–1729* (Paris: 1993), 263–269.

71. "Ao provincial do Brasil, Maranhão May 22, 1653," *Cartas*, vol. 1, 317–318.

72. T. Hall, *The Role of Cape Verde Islanders*, 68.

73. A. Arrais, a theologian from the University of Coimbra, joined the Carmelites as a novice in 1545. In 1581, he was appointed bishop of Portalegre, a position from which he resigned in 1596. A. Arrais was also fanatically anti-Jewish, to the point of accusing the Jews of having founded Islam. For him, the forced conversions of the Jews would not change their "vices" in any way, and, for this reason, he opposed this practice. See A. Arrais, *Diálogos* (Porto: 1974), 112–115, 207, and 285. Here I distinguish anti-Judaism based on religious motives from the contemporary anti-Semitism based on the idea of race.

74. A. Vacant, E. Mangenot, and E. Amman, "Baptême," in *Dictionnaire de Théologie Catholique*, vol. 2, part 1 (Paris: 1908), 167–377.

75. Anon, *Proposta sobre escravaria das terras da conquista de Portugal. Tratando da situação nos cativeiros onde ocorrem injustiças, violência e escândalos contra os escravos e de como remediar a situação fazendo-se cumprir uma lei da época da guerra contra mouros e turcos onde nenhum gentio tornava-se cativo em função da mesma. Pedindo que o mesmo seja aplicado no Brasil, Guiné e Angola*, *IHGB*, manuscripts, col. IHGB DL 45.11. The proposal, drafted after Felipe II's death (1598), was written by someone acquainted with Bishop Brandão's ideas. The author is knowledgeable about canon and royal laws and about discussions to legitimate slavery and the slave trade. He was also aware of Portugal's overseas territories and of the forms of indigenous coerced labor existing in America, Africa, and Asia, although his main concern was the slave trade in upper Guinea and Brazil. These circumstances makes me wonder that the author is perhaps Bishop Brandão himself.

76. The issue of manumitting slaves converted to Judaism was also put before the Jewish hierarchy in Dutch Brazil. The 1648 rulings of the congregation Zur Israel of Recife, the first to be written by a Jewish community in a modern slave society, featured measures to prevent slaves converted to Judaism from being kept in bondage. Trying to hinder masters from selling already-converted slaves, the congregation prohibited the circumcision of slaves before they had been properly manumitted. See A. Wiznitzer, "The Minute Book of Congregations Zur Israel of Recife and Magen Abraham of Mauricia, Brazil," *American Jewish Historical Society* 42, no. 3 (1953), 238.

77. The always reliable notes by A. Brásio guarantee it is a text written by Bishop Brandão and dated from 1606–1608, *MMA²*, vol. 3, 442–445. About the manumission given to captives converted to Islam, a process more complex than suggested here by the Carmelite, see J. R. Willis, "The Ideology of Enslavement in Islam" and "Jihad and the Ideology of Enslavement," *Slaves & Slavery in Muslim Africa* (London: 1985), 1–15 and 16–26.

78. Curiously, Bishop Brandão, retired since 1594 in Lisbon, where he established an entail (*morgado*), was accused of having become rich at the expense of his Cape Verdean diocesans, and also of having trafficked African slaves. See F. de Almeida, *HIP*, vol. 2, 685. Barcellos does not mention it. He says that Brandão was a merchant and that he and his diocesans disagreed, because he wished to impose religious fasting on them and to prohibit concubinage. Was the accusation of slave trading forged by his enemies? It does not matter. Even if written by a bishop who became rich through questionable means, or by a remorseful slave trader, the text by Brandão develops very consistent argumentation. See *MMA²*, vol. 4, 26–27, 28–29, 50–51, 92–95, 178–181, and 299–300; Barcelos, *Subsídios*, vol. 1, part 2, 159–60, 172–175, and 178.

79. Friar Antônio de São Domingos (1531–1596), who taught at the University of Coimbra, states about the Atlantic slave trade: "Either it is acknowledged that the king does not care about this business, or it is not. If it is, nobody can buy these Blacks, except those who want to undertake this diligence; if it is not, then, one should presume that all is being done correctly, for this duty [*munus*] belongs to him only and one should believe he fulfills it perfectly, otherwise a manifest injury is being done to him. Consequently, we can buy Blacks with a safe conscience as long as things stand thus." A. de C. X. Monteiro, "Como se ensinava o Direito das Gentes na Universidade de Coimbra no século XVI," *Anais da Academia Portuguesa da História*, vol. 33, 2nd series (Lisbon: 1993), 9–36, 26. See also *Scholasticon*, http://scholasticon.ish-lyon.cnrs.fr/Database/Scholastiques_php?ID=2120, accessed on December 15, 2015.

80. Hespanha argues that the issue of the African slave trade, compared to early controversies over Amerindian slavery, was discussed with great delay in the Iberian universities. Nevertheless, the papacy endorsed the justification of the slave trade formulated by the Portuguese Crown since 1455, as seen in chapter 1 note 82. Moreover, Molina's reflections were timely, elaborated in 1593–1597, in the wake of the first Portuguese *Asiento*, which provided full royal legitimacy and lawfulness to the massive transatlantic slave trade. See M. Hespanha, "Luís de Molina e a escravização dos negros," *Análise Social* 35, no. 157 (2001), 937–960. See also G. Marcocci, "Escravos ameríndios e negros africanos: uma história conectada. Teorias e modelos de discriminação no império português (ca. 1450–1650)," *Tempo* 16 (2011), 41–70.

81. Volume I, which includes the subjects discussed in this chapter, can be accessed online. See L. de Molina, *De Justitia et Jure* (Geneva: [1593] 1733). The *disputatio* thirty-two to forty studying slavery and, more precisely, the African slave trade (thirty-four to thirty-six), are on pages 86–117 of the edition quoted above. Hespanha believes that this text was discussed by Molina in his lectures at the Coimbra and Évora Universities Hespanha, "Luís de Molina." http://books.google.fr/books?id=5xFGAAAAcAAJ&printsec=frontcover&hl=fr&source=gbs_ge_summary_r&cad=0#v=onepage&q&f=false, accessed on January 10, 2015.

82. See also, J. M. García Añoveros, "Luis de Molina y la esclavitud de los Negros Africanos en el Siglo XVI. Principios Doctrinales y Conclusiones," *Revista de Indias* 60, no. 219 (2000), 307–329.

83. The axiome is repeated several times in the *disputatio* 35 and 36. See de Molina, *De justitia et Jure*, 105–107.

84. The visit to Angola was decided on January 4, 1592, in Lisbon; P. Rodrigues inspected the missions of Luanda and Massangano. See *MMA¹*, vol. 3, 471.

85. P. Rodrigues arrived in Luanda, traveling from Bahia, in March 1593. See *MMA¹*, vol. 3, 471.

86. *MMA¹*, vol. 3, 471–479 and vol. 15, 333–338. S. Leite omits the Jesuits' opposition to royal orders on the control of the natives of Angola expressed by the congregation held in Bahia. See *HCJB*, vol. 2, 502–503.

87. *HCJB*, vol. 2, 496–497.

88. G. M. Correia de Castro, *O percurso geográfico e missionário de Baltasar Barreira em Cabo Verde, Guiné, Serra Leoa* (Lisbon: 2001).

89. Telles, *Chronica*, vol. 2, 192–197, 617–624; M. da Costa Roque, "A 'peste grande' de 1569 em Lisboa," in *Anais*, vol. 28, 2nd series (Lisbon: 1982), 71–90.

90. Nobles who had taken the order's vows continued to use the aristocratic title "dom" before their names up to the second general Jesuit congregation (1558), when Diogo Laínez took up the post of general and this privilege was abrogated.

91. "Carta Ânua da Residência de Angola," 1579, *MMA¹*, vol. 3, 184–186.

92. "Carta do pe. Balthazar Barreira para o pe. Sebastião de Morais," Luanda, January 31, 1582, *MMA¹*, vol. 3, 208–211.

93. Doc. of January 31, 1582, *MMA¹*, vol. 3, 212–213.

94. In 1584, Barreira sent Balthazar Afonso, another bellicist missionary, to the island of São Tomé to bring men and powder to help governor Novais. See *MMA¹*, vol. 3, 265–267. J. Pereira Bayão, *Portugal cuidadoso, e lastimado com a Vida, e Perda do Senhor Rey Dom Sebastião, o desejado de saudosa memoria* (Lisbon: 1737), 386.

95. F. Rodrigues, *História da Companhia de Jesus na Assistência de Portugal*, vol. 2 (Porto: 1931–1950), 473; "Carta do governador de Cabo Verde a el-rei d. Filipe II, July 25, 1613," *MMA²*, vol. 4, 507–541.

96. B. Barreira has now his own online page created by a pious Portuguese Facebooker, https://www.facebook.com/pages/Baltasar-Barreira/164575493581004?rf=138832882812889#.

97. Letter of December 25, 1652, *MMA²*, vol. 4, 24–26; Telles, *Chronica*, vol. 2, 617–652; Rodrigues, *Chiponda*, 471–477. See also D. Barbosa Machado, *Biblioteca Lusitana*, vol. 4 (Lisbon: 1930–1933), 435; C. Sommervogel, ed., *Bibliothèque de la Compagnie de Jesus*, vol. 1 (Brussels, Paris, Louvain: 1890–1960), 918–919. For a more recent and more balanced reference on Barreira, see Banha de Andrade, ed., *Dicionário*, vol. 2, 186–187.

98. Letter from superior general F. de Borja to the provincial J. Henriques, 1566, *MMA¹*, vol. 3, 476–467n1. Another letter in the same vein to G. Alvarez on November 2, 1569, and a letter from Acquaviva to F. Monclaro in 1588. See Wicki, "Dois compêndios," 376–371.

99. "Our people [of the Society of Jesus] shall not possess, nor buy or sell captives suspicious enslaved, nor absolve those who own them, nor follow the opinion of those who say that it is better to hold them in bondage than to have them lost, nor buy or sell them to seculars." Decision of the superior general Cláudio Acquaviva, 1588. See Wicki, "Dois compêndios," 376.

100. "Guinea" here means sub-Saharan Africa. "Informação acerca dos escravos de Angola," 1582–1583, *MMA¹*, vol. 3, 227–231.

101. A. Araújo, *Catecismo na lingoa brasilica, no qual se contem a summa da doctrina christã . . . composto a modo de Dialogos por Padres Doctos, & bons lingoas da Companhia de Jesu* (Lisbon: 1618), 132. The book's first page says: "Printed at the expense of the Fathers [Jesuits] of Brazil."

102. A. Vieira, "Informação sobre o modo com que foram tomados e sentenciados por cativos os índios do ano de 1655," *Obras escolhidas*, vol. 5 (Lisbon: 1951), 51–52.

103. "The main merchandise there (in Upper Guinea) is slaves, bought by the Portuguese, who sell them again and send them to [the] Indies of Castile, and the purchase and sale of these slaves is deemed more dangerous than those from Angola." See F. de Gouveia, "Carta ao geral da Companhia," December 16, 1596, *MMA²*, vol. 3, 402. For ten years, Gouveia had taught moral theology at the college of Évora, before becoming rector of the same college, procurator of the province at the Curia, and, finally, provincial in Portugal. His opinions on the matter carried great authority.

104. For a nonexclusive repertoire of Barreira's letters, see S. R. Streit and J. Dindinger, *Bibliotheca Missionum*, vols. 15 and 16 (Freiburg: 1963–1975). About the meaning of "edifying letters," A. da Silva Rego, "Instruções de Francisco Xavier," *DHMPPO*, vol. 4 ([1549] 1950), 286–300, 292, and vol. 5 (1950), X–XIII.

105. J. Polanco, born in Burgos in 1516 of noble family, studied at the Sorbonne and in Rome. Loyola asked him to organize the order's general secretary. D. Laínez and F. de Borja kept him in the post of general secretary. When Borja died, Polanco was elected general vicar of the S.J. He would have been chosen for the post of general except for the Portuguese veto. "It may well happen that we are satisfied with what a man is but unhappy about what he has inherited from his parents," wrote B. Telles. The stated motive to elect the Belgian Mercurian and to bar Polanco—Pope Clement VII's alleged wish that the company's generals should not be Castilian again—was a pretext. Indeed, Henriques, vice provincial of Portugal and close to cardinal infant D. Henrique, the kingdom's inquisitor major, carried "strong recommendations from Portugal that the Company should not admit those who bear that smear [of being a New Christian]." Telles, *Chronica*, vol. 2, 438–439. A. Sérgio,

this document unbeknownst to him, gave credit to the anti-Spanish argument in the veto to Polanco. See A. Sérgio, *Ensaios*, vol. 5 (Rio de Janeiro: 1975), 153–154.

106. Bertrand, *La Politique*, 275–291; P. Chaunu, *Eglise, culture et société* (Paris: 1981), 397–401.

107. Decision taken after the fifth general congregation held in Rome in 1594. See Wicki, "Dois compêndios," 376 and 431.

108. J. A. Duarte Leitão, "A Missão do Padre Baltasar Barreira no Reino de Angola (1580–1592)," in *Lusitania Sacra* 5, no. 2 (1993), 43–91.

109. Brevis by Urban VIII of March 13, 1625, and other pontifical decrees of June 5, 1631, and June 25, 1634.

110. "Carta do padre Balthazar Barreira," Massangano, August 27, 1585, *MMA¹*, vol. 3, 323–325; Telles, *Chronica*, v. 2, 628.

111. Patterson, *Slavery*, 3.

112. *MMA¹*, vol. 3, 198–207, 199.

113. For a distinction between internal and external heresies fought by the Catholic hierarchy, see L. Link, *The Devil—A Mask without a Face*, Brazilian translation (São Paulo: 1995), 95–130.

114. *MMA¹*, vol. 3, 375–382, 375.

115. *MMA¹*, vol. 3, doc. of April 15, 1594, 471–499, art. 26 of "Instruções," 477.

116. Memorial of June 15, 1593, *MMA¹*, vol. 15, 333–338.

117. The crucial role played by the Jesuits' heads and Fathers P. Rodrigues and B. Barreira in the construction of the South Atlantic slave system has been ignored. D. Alden does not even mention those two Jesuits. See D. Alden, *The Making of an Enterprise—The Society of Jesus in Portugal, Its Empire, and Beyond 1540–1750* (Stanford, CA: Stanford UP, 1996).

118. *História da residência dos padres da Companhia de Jesus em Angola e cousas tocantes ao reino e à conquista*, Luanda, May 1, 1594. Visitador P. Rodrigues wrote the first chapter and B. Afonso chapters 6, 7, 8, and 9. B. Afonso was a missionary in Angola for twenty-eight years and died there in 1603. Barreira's faithful mate, he also championed the military conquest of the territory. See *MMA¹*, vol. 4, 546–581.

119. "Dos escravos que saem de Cabo Verde," 1606, text sent to the provincial of Portugal, *MMA²*, vol. 4, 190–199. E. H. Hair analyzes this and other texts written by Barreira in Cape Verde and Guinea. See P. H. E. Hair, "Heretics, Slaves and Witches—As Seen by Guinea Jesuits c. 1610," *Journal of Religion in Africa* 28, no. 2 (1998), 121–144.

120. On this specific point, see Ribeiro Rocha, *Ethiope Resgatado*, 37–63.

121. Vieira, "Informação sobre o modo com que foram tomados e sentenciados por cativos os índios," *Obras escolhidas*, vol. 5 (Lisbon: 1951), 61.

122. Letter from B. Barreira, Sierra Leone, March 4, 1607, *MMA²*, vol. 4, 220–222.

123. Letter of March 5, 1607, *MMA²*, vol. 4, 223–228, 227.

124. Doc. of August 21, 1611, *MMA¹*, vol. 15, 442–443.

125. Milhou, "L'Afrique," in *Histoire du Christianisme des origins à nos jours*, vol. 8, J. M. Mayeur, C. Pietri, A. Vauchez, and M. Venard, eds. (Paris: 1992–1994), 685–690; de Sandoval, *Un tratado*, 154.

126. L. M. de Vasconcellos wrote about the *jagas*: "[T]here are likely more [slaves] who they eat than who they deliver alive, for this is their most ordinary food." *AHU*, Angola, box 1/74, August 28, 1617.

127. A. Torrent, "Segunda Escolástica Española y renovación de la ciencia del derecho en el siglo XVI: un capítulo de los fundamentos del derecho europeo. I. Francisco de Vitoria, Domingo de Soto," *Teoria e Storia del Diritto Privato* 6 (2013), 1–60.

128. J. Baptista Fragoso (1559–1639) has taught theology at the Jesuit's College of Santo Antão de Lisboa and at the University of Évora. Maurício, "A Universidade de Évora," 153, 191–195.

129. F. Rebelo was L. de Molina's assistant and substitute in the chair of theology at the University of Évora from 1586 to 1596. See Maurício, "A Universidade," 183.

130. I owe Roberto Schwarz the idea of drawing a parallel between Vieira and Pascal's reflections.

131. B. Pascal, "Huitième provinciale," *Oeuvres complètes*, vol. 5, L. Brunschvig, P. Boutroux, and F. Gazier, eds. (Paris: 1914), 148–151. See also M. Le Guern's comments in B. Pascal, *Les provinciales*, M. L. Guern, ed. (Paris: 1987), 135 and 351; J. Schmutz, "La Querelle Des Possibles. Recherches Philosophiques et Textuelles Sur La Métaphysique Jésuite Espagnole (1540–1767)," *École Pratique des Hautes Études, Section des Sciences Religieuses* 115, no. 111 (2002), 405–411.

132. J. L. de Azevedo, *História de Antônio Vieira*, vol. 1 (Lisbon: 1992), 35.

133. Hair, *"Heretics, Slaves and Witches,"* 16.

134. Delumeau, *L'aveu et le pardon*, chapter 12; Hair, *"Heretics, Slaves and Witches,"* 133.

135. *MMA¹*, vol. 5, 134–137.

136. *MMA¹*, vol. 5, 224. In 1631, a man earned 1,000 *cruzados* (1 *cruzado* = 400 *réis*) a year for branding. Branders used to earn 2 *vinténs* (40 *réis*) per brand made. Therefore, their earnings corresponded to 10,000 brands per year in Luanda alone. See L. Cordeiro, *1593–1631 Terras e minas africanas segundo Balthazar Rebello de Aragão* (Lisbon: 1881), 23.

137. From *ka* = diminutive prefix and *rimu* = brand. As early as 1844 the word "carimbo" (stamp) features as an entry in the Morais Dictionary. However, in Portugal, the noun was, and still is, *ferrete* (branding iron).

138. "[O]n arriving at the maritime port whence they will be shipped and transported, they are again branded on the right chest with the king's and the nation's arms, of whom they become vassals; their red hot sign is branded on them with a silver instrument at the moment of paying the rights, and this brand is called *carimbo*." See de Oliveira Mendes, *Memória a respeito dos escravos*, 29.

139. J. Vansina, *Kingdoms of the Savannahs*, 145–146.

140. *MMA¹*, vol. 13, 465–473; BNL, res. 2761 (P), *Ao senhor governador e capitam geral Ayres de Saldanha de Menezes, & Souza, os religiosos da Companhia de Jesu, sobre o Collegio, Missoens, & Seminario de Angola* (Lisbon: 1680), BNL, res. 2761 (P), reproduced in *MMA¹*, vol. 13, 455–464.

141. A recent review on Jesuits mission around the world does not mention the activities of the S.J. missionaries in Angola, were their presence, lasting from 1559 until their expulsion in 1759, was critical to Portugal's and Europe's economic and political domination. See S. Ditchfield, "Of Missions and Models: The Jesuit Enterprise (1540–1773) Reassessed in Recent Literature," *The Catholic Historical Review* 93, no. 2 (2007), 325–343.

142. *HCJB*, vol. 6, 552, and vol. 5, 23 and 165.

143. M. da Nóbrega, "Carta de Luís da Grã a Santo Inácio," *Diálogo sobre a conversão do gentio* (Lisbon: 1954), 115, appendix B.

144. J. de Anchieta, *Poesias* (São Paulo: 1954), 578–580.

145. M. Bataillon, "Le Cosmopolitisme de Damião de Gois," "Études Sur Le Portugal Au Temps de L'humanisme," *Acta Universitatis Conimbrigensis*, 1952, 149–196, 159, and 175–177.

146. S. de Freitas, *De Justo Imperio Lusitanorum Asiatico*, vol. 1 (Lisbon: [1625] 1983), 217, 364, and 367, and vol. 2, 94. Friar Serafim was a religious believer of the Order of Mercy.

147. Vieira, "Sermões XIV," vol. 4, 733–769. In "Sermon XXVII," Vieira contradictorily classifies the slave trade as a "diabolical trade" [mercancia diabólica] and justifies it in "Sermon XIV": "[C]aptivity in the first transmigration (deportation to Brazil) is ordained by her (Our Lady of the Rosary) mercy for the freedom in the second (transmigration to Heaven)." A slave should work diligently for this master, because, after death, he would receive payment for the unpaid labor performed on the plantations and sugar-mills of Brazil directly from God. See ibid., 1,202–1.241. For other comments on this topic, see L. Koshiba, *A Honra e a Cobiça*, vol. 2 (PhD thesis in history, Universidade de São Paulo, 1988), 293–298, and A. Bosi, *Dialética da colonização* (São Paulo: 1992), 143–148.

148. In fact, the saga of the Jesuits of Japan and China—where the situation became unfavorable to them under internal political reversals (in Japan) or changes of the Roman missionary strategy (China)—can be regarded as "glorious failures." But the records of their missions' setbacks in Angola and Congo, at the core of the slave-trade network, appear as "shameful failures" and therefore are hardly mentioned. As noted above, studies on Jesuit missions often neglect their involvement in the West Central African slave trade.

149. J. F. Lisboa, *Vida do padre Antônio Vieira* (Rio de Janeiro: [c. 1840] 1891), 352. Published posthumously, this book was written before the end of the slave trade to Brazil in 1850. More recently, Saraiva insisted on Vieira's support for the introduction of African slavery in Maranhão. Nevertheless, the key point in Vieira's slave theory, emphasized by J. Francisco Lisboa, is his justification for the Atlantic trade in Africans. See A. J. Saraiva, "Le père Antonio Vieira SJ et la liberté des indiens." *T.I.L.A.S.*, 3 (1963) 483–516, idem,

"Le père Antonio Vieira S.J. et la question de l'esclavage des Noirs au XVIIème siècle," *Annales E.S.C.* 22 (1967), 1,289–1,309.

150. Vieira, "Sermão XXVII," *Sermões*, vol. 4, 1205.

151. The wording and chronology of the sermons are the object of an argument among Vieira's scholars. See R. Cantel, *Les Sermons de Vieira—Etude du style* (Paris: 1959); F. Smulders, "Tradições manuscritas na obra de Antônio Vieira," in *Vieira escritor*, M. Vieira Mendes, M. L. Gonçalves Pires, and J. da Costa Miranda, eds. (Lisbon: 1997) 53–66; A. Pinto de Castro, "Os sermões de Vieira—da palavra dita à palavra escrita," ibid., 79–94; J. F. Marques, "A cronologia da pregação de Vieira," ibid., 117–134.

152. N. Marques Pereira, *Compêndio Narrativo do Peregrino da América*, vol. 1 (Rio de Janeiro: [1728] 1988), 148–150. The author has lived in Bahia, where he might have been born, and in Minas Gerais. See ibid., 3–22.

153. Letter to S. de Matos e Sousa, Bahia, July 10, 1697, *Cartas*, vol. 3, 712–714.

154. Contrary to the arguments of A. Pécora, there is no contradiction at all in Vieira's ideas on slavery. Very much to the contrary: Vieira is favorable to the slave trade as an instrument of colonial politics, but at the same time he encourages masters to treat black slaves humanely, and vigorously opposes the enslavement of Amerindians. His statements are complementary, not at all divergent. See A. Pécora, *Teatro do Sacramento* (São Paulo: 1994), 46–54.

155. Benci, *Economia Cristã*, 63–104.

156. Ribeiro Rocha, *Ethiope*, 227, 232–233. I. Francisco da Silva, in his *Diccionário Bibliographico Portuguez*, reports that the edition of Ribeiro Rocha's book has sold out in Brazil.

Chapter 6

1. J. S. Goldstein, *Long Cycles—Prosperity and War in the Modern Age* (London: 1988), 306–313; M. D. D. Newitt, *Charles Ralph Boxer 1904–2000* (London: 2000); L. Bély, "La dimension diplomatique de l'impérialisme européen," in *L'Empire portugais face aux autres empires XVIe–XIXe siècle*, F. Bethencourt and L. F. de Alencastro, eds. (Paris: 2007), 15–40.

2. The treaty between Paris and Lisbon was signed on June 1, 1641, days before the Portuguese Truces Treaty with the states-general. The enthronement of João IV took place during the "French period" (1635–1648) of the Thirty Years' War, encompassing the entry of France in the war, against Spain (1635), until the Westphalia Treaties (1648). See E. Prestage, *As Relações diplomáticas de Portugal com a França, Inglaterra e Holanda de 1640 a 1668* (Coimbra: 1932), 123–147; L. André and E. Bourgeois, "Espagne," in *Recueil des Instructions aux Ambassadeurs et Ministres de France depuis les Traités de Westphalie jusqu'à la Révolution Française* (*RIAMF*), vol. 1 (Paris: 1894), 83–85.

3. "England's friendship interests Portugal more than any other kingdom, due to the great power she wields at sea, which is the one aspect the Dutch fear," wrote ambassador

S. Coutinho to the king João IV, The Hague, August 5, 1647. See E. Prestage, P. de Azevedo, and M. Laranjo Coelho, *Correspondência diplomática de Francisco de Sousa Coutinho durante sua embaixada em Holanda 1643–1650* (hereafter *CD*), vol. 2 (Lisbon: 1920), 161–163.

4. C. R. Boxer, *The Dutch Seaborne Empire 1600–1800* (London: 1965), 96, 113. Contrary to the arguments of Fernand Braudel, J. I. Israel shows the real impact of the 1621 Spanish embargo against Dutch trade, particularly regarding the Setubal salt trade. See J. I. Israel, *Dutch Primacy in World Trade 1585–1740* (Oxford, UK: 1992), 125–140.

5. M. Morineau, "Le siècle," in *Histoire économique et sociale du monde*, vol. 2, P. Leon, ed. (Paris: 1978), 91.

6. F. Manuel de Melo, *Carta de guia de casados*, part 43 (Lisbon: 1650), 146.

7. V. Rau, *Estudos sobre a história do sal português* (Lisbon: 1984), 147–155, 233–296; R. W. Unger, "Dutch Herring, Technology, and International Trade in the Seventeenth Century," *JEH* 11, no. 2(1980), 253–256.

8. Prestage, *As Relações Diplomáticas de Portugal*, 195.

9. M. Kennedy, *The Rise and Fall of British Naval Mastery* (London: 1983), 48–49; Braudel, *Civilisation Matérielle*, v. 3, 177–181.

10. Doc. of the Overseas Council, May 5, 1671, *AHU*, Angola, box 10/37.

11. L. Blusse and G. Winius, "The Origin and Rhythm of Dutch Aggression against the 'Estado da Índia,'" in *Indo-Portuguese History: Old Issue, New Questions*, T. R. de Sousa, ed. (New Dehli: 1985), 73–83; A. M. Awad, "The Gulf in the Seventeenth Century," *Bulletin (British Society for Middle Eastern Studies)* 12, no. 2 (1985), 123–134, especially 124–126; E. Carreira, "Un empire à vendre: stratégies d'appropriation des ports de *l'Estado da Índia* par les compagnies britannique et française (1661–1813)," in *L'Empire portugais*, 79–120.

12. M. A. Meilink-Roelofsz, "Aspects of Dutch colonial development in Asia in the seventeenth century," in *Britain and the Netherlands in Europe and Asia*, J. S. Bromley and E. H. Kossman, eds. (London: 1968), 56–82; A. Botelho de Sousa, *Subsídios para a história militar marítima da Índia, 1585–1669*, vol. 4 (Lisbon: 1930), 196–201.

13. Prestage, *A Embaixada*, 31–32; ibid., *CD*, vol. 1, 1–3.

14. Bahia was occupied (May 1624), restored (April 1625), and again attacked (April 1626); Espírito Santo was assaulted in March 1625, Paraíba in July 1625, Benguela in June 1624, Luanda in June and October 1624, and Elmina in 1625; *MMA¹*, vol. 8, 131–155; C. Barlaeus, *Rerum per octennium* . . . [1647]. Transl. *História dos feitos recentemente praticados durante oito anos no Brasil* (São Paulo: 1974), 56; B. Guerreiro, *Jornada dos Vassalos da Coroa de Portugal* (Rio de Janeiro: [1625] 1966), 66–67.

15. J. Thornton, "The African Experience of the '20 and Odd Negroes' Arriving in Virginia in 1619," *The William and Mary Quarterly* 55, no. 3 (1998), 421–434; Postma, "The Dispersal of African Slaves in the West by Dutch Slave Traders," 284.

16. Postma, *The Dutch in the Atlantic*, 13–14 and 32. On the role of piracy and privateering in the seventeenth century, see A. Pérotin-Dumont, "The Pirate and the Emperor," in *The Political Economy of Merchant Empires* (Cambridge, UK: 1991), 196–227.

17. *MMA¹*, vol. 8, 395; van den Boogaart and Emmer, "The Dutch Participation," 365–366.

18. The Dutch erected Fort Nassau (1612) in the port the Portuguese-denominated Moure, next to Elmina. Another trading port was installed in 1617 in Gouré Island (Bezeguiche), Dakar Cape. Taken by the French in 1677, Gouré became an important slave port. See *MMA²*, vol. 5, 581, and vol. 8, 1st series, 318; N. I. de Moraes, "Sur les prises de Gorée par les Portugais au XVIIème siècle," *Bulletin de l'Institut Fondamental d'Afrique Noire* 21, series B (1969), 989–1,013.

19. *MMA¹*, vol. 8, 328.

20. *MMA¹*, vol. 7, 417–420. São Tomé was attacked frequently. Between October 1641 and July 1642 it was in the hands of the W.I.C. See *MMA¹*, vol. 8, 313–314, 330–331, and 457–459.

21. *MMA¹*, vol. 8, 134, 156–163, and 242.

22. A post-1640 document records the royal treasury's losses resulting from the interruption in trade among Guinea, Peru, and New Spain. According to the text, the slaves exported from Guinea to Brazil were few, because the South American colony received only "Blacks from Angola." See *Os Manuscritos*, v. 1, 329; E. Correia Lopes, *Escravatura—Subsídios para a sua história* (Lisbon: 1944), 59–63.

23. "I do not want doubloons or garments, (I want) Blacks and more Blacks, all in my name, which I will share with the soldiers." Such was the stark order given by Luís Barbalho to his nephew, Captain João Lopes Barbalho, in 1639, on the verge of an attack against the Dutch. See "Documentos pela maior parte em portuguez sobre vários assumptos," *RIAGP* 34 (1887), 33–34; J. Lopes Barbalho was a field master in Olivença during the Alentejo war. See M. Laranjo Coelho, ed., *Cartas dos governadores da Província do Alentejo a el-rei d. João IV*, vol. 1 (Lisbon: 1947), 331–332 and 339, vol. 2, 179.

24. Calado, *O Valeroso Lucideno*, v. 2, 21 and 122.

25. TSTD, accessed November 2015.

26. See chapter 3, 6–7.

27. Salvador, *História*, 408.

28. "Representação da Câmara da Bahia," June 12, 1626, *ABNRJ*, vol. 31 (1909), 1–2; A. E. Taunay, "Notas sobre o imperativo do tráfico," *Revista do Instituto Histórico e Geográfico da Bahia* 67 (1941), 311–315. The "Indians of the fifth" [*índios do quinto*], referred to in the representation, were slaves received by the governor in payment for the royal fith (20 percent) tax charged on the lots of captives brought in by the *bandeiras*. In Angola, the same procedure was followed with the slaves captured in the "backland wars" [*guerras do sertão*].

29. *AMP*, vol. 3, 2nd part, 1929, 125–128; *DH*, vol. 15, 251–256; W. Pinho, *História social da Cidade do Salvador*, vol. 1 (Salvador: 1968) 75–77; G. Thomas, *Politica indigenista*, 176–177, 188–190.

30. J. D. French, "Riqueza, poder e mão-de-obra numa economia de subsistência: São Paulo 1596–1625," *RAMSP* 195 (1987), 79–107, 87n24; Paes Leme, *Nobiliarquia Paulistana Histórica e Genealógica*, v. 1, 76; Gonçalves Salvador, *Os cristãos-novos*, 308–309.

31. Wilde, *Religión y Poder*, 89–92.

32. Paes Leme, *Nobiliarquia*, v. 1, 108; E. Taunay, *História geral das bandeiras paulistas* v. 1 (São Paulo: 1924–1950), 241, vol. 2, passim; Hemming, *Red Gold*, 259–260, 268–271.

33. Taunay, *História geral*, vol. 2, 3–150.

34. J. A. Cardoso and C. M. Westphalen, *Atlas histórico do Paraná* (Curitiba: 1986), 34.

35. J. Cortesão, *Jesuítas e bandeirantes do Itatim 1596–1760* (Rio de Janeiro: 1952), 16–63.

36. M. Livi-Bacci and E. J. Maeder, "The Missions of Paraguay: The Demography of an Experiment," *The Journal of Interdisciplinary History* 35, no. 2 (2004), 185–224, 187.

37. Cortesão, *Jesuítas e bandeirantes*, 319–326.

38. A. Porto, *História das Missões Orientais do Uruguai* (Rio de Janeiro: 1943), 82–120.

39. Doc. of the Overseas Council, March 14, 1658, *ABNRJ*, vol. 39 (1917), 80–82.

40. W. Dean, *A ferro e fogo* (São Paulo: 1996), 81–82.

41. L. Ferrand de Almeida, *A Colônia do Sacramento na época da sucessão de Espanha* (Coimbra: 1973), 96–116, 339.

42. F. Pastells and P. Mateos, *Historia de la Compañia de Jesus en la Província del Paraguay* (Madrid: 1948–1949), vol. 8, 1st part, 1751–1760, doc. of 1748, 15. Spanish American historiography coherently refers to the *bandeirantes* as "Paulista slavers" [*esclavistas paulistas*]. See, for instance, D. A. Esponera Cerdan, "La presencia de los dominicos en Buenos Aires y Asuncion durante el siglo XVII," *Los Dominicos y el Nuevo Mundo: Actas del III Congreso Internacional* (Madrid: 1991), 358n72.

43. Monteiro, *Negros da terra: Indios e bandeirantes nas origens de São Paulo* (São Paulo: 1994) 76–79.

44. P. and B. Correa do Lago, *Frans Post 1612–1680, Catalogue Raisonné*, Paris: 2007 passim.

45. L. Norton, *A dinastia dos Sás no Brasil 1558–1662* (Lisbon: 1943), 179–180; Boxer, *Salvador de Sá e a luta*, 128–130.

46. Paes Leme, *Nobiliarquia*, vol. 1, 76, vol. 2, 226; Norton, *A Dinastia*, 216–225, 221.

47. Monteiro, *Negros*, 80, table 2.

48. Adriaen van der Dussen, "Relatório," of December 10, 1639, *FHBH*, vol. 1, J. A. Gonsalves de Mello, ed. (Recife: 1981) 131–232, 183. Van der Dussen refers to the Amerindians settling in Pernambuco, Paraíba, and Rio Grande do Norte. However, in the salt mines of Ceará and Maranhão, the Dutch submitted the Amerindians to coerced labor. See J. A. Gonsalves de Mello, *Tempo dos flamengos* (Recife: 1987), 208–209.

49. Vieira, *Cartas*, vol. 1, 431–441; J. L. de Azevedo, *Os jesuítas no Grão Pará* (Coimbra: 1930), 71–75.

50. J. M. Monteiro, "500 Years of Native Brazilian History," 2–15.

51. Doc. of the Rio de Janeiro Municipal Council, July 6, 1643, and February 25, 1647, in *Accordãos e Vereanças* (Rio de Janeiro: 1935), 71, 139–140.

52. A. Metcalf, *Family and Frontier*, 51–53.

53. J. Cortesão, "Informe de Manuel Juan de Morales de las cosas de San Pablo," in *Jesuítas e bandeirantes no Guairá 1594–1640* (Rio de Janeiro: 1952), 182–193, here 186.

54. *HCJB*, vol. 6, 239–240; "Parecer ao Conselho Ultramarino," October 13, 1646, *ABNRJ*, vol. 39 (1917), 51–53.

55. On hired Amerindians, see "Testamento de Ana Ribeira (1662)," in *Inventários e testamentos*, vol. 40, 80, and also J. D. French, *Riqueza*, 88.

56. Buarque de Holanda, *Caminhos*, 127–132.

57. *ACA*, vol. 1, 60–73.

58. Despite its size, the ship's mainmast seemed "un peu petit pour une si extraordinaire machine," in the words of a French diplomat who saw it in Lisbon. Perhaps this was the cause of the ship's demise a few years later. The *Padre Eterno* (2,000 tons) was bigger than some of the greatest vessels of the 1600s, such as the English *Sovereign of the Seas* (1,500 tons) or the French *Saint-Philippe* (1,500 tons), but was on par with *La Salvadora* (2,000 tons), a Spanish gallion from Manilla, and was smaller than the *Kronan* (2,200 tons), armed with 128 cannon, belonging to the Swedish navy, or the French *Soleil-Royal* (2,500 tons, 110 cannon). See C. R. Boxer, "English Shipping in the Brazil Trade 1640–1665," *Mariner's Mirror* 37, no. 3 (1951), 197–230; ibid., *Salvador de Sá*, 341–345; Mauro, *Le Portugal*, 35–36; L. Einarsson, "Le vaisseau royal Kronan. Des explorations archéologiques sous-marines d'une épave du XVIIe siècle," in *L'Invention du vaisseau de ligne 1450–1700*, M. Acerra, ed. (Paris: 1997), 135–142 and 143–162.

59. L. Freire Costa, *O Transporte no Atlântico e a Companhia Geral do Comércio do Brasil 1580–1663* (Lisbon: 2002), v. 1,573–580.

60. A. de Souza de Macedo, "*Mercurio Portuguez, com as novas da guerra entre Portugal e Castella,*" *BNL* (Lisbon: 1663), 141, 296–302.

61. "Breve manifesto de nutiçiozas utilidades pertensentes à este Estado do Brasil," in A. de Magalhães Basto, "Alguns documentos de interesse para a história do Brasil," in *Brasilia*, vol. 7 (Coimbra: 1952), 183–185.

62. J. R. Amaral Lapa, *A Bahia e a carreira da Índia* (São Paulo: 1968), 25–138, 307–308.

63. S. Schwartz, *Sugar Plantations*, 190, figure 7–4.

64. J. C. Miller, "Slave Prices in the Portuguese Southern Atlantic, 1600–1830," in *Africans in Bondage: Studies in Slavery and the Slave Trade*, P. E. Lovejoy, ed. (Madison, WI: 1986), 43–77, 47 and 63.

65. Doc. of January 8, 1843, box 4/17; doc. of May 10, 1659, *AHU*, Angola, box 6/149.

66. V. L. Amaral Ferlini, *Terra, trabalho e poder—O mundo dos engenhos no Nordeste colonial* (São Paulo: 1986), 67–70.

67. Doc. of January 8, 1643, *AHU*, Angola, box 4/17.

68. L. Freire Costa, *O Transporte no Atlântico e a Companhia Geral do Comércio do Brasil 1580–1663* (Lisbon: 2002), v. 1, 190–192.

69. Doc. of November 22, 1644, "Manuscritos, Consultas Mistas do Conselho Ultramarino," *BNRJ*, cod. 25, fs. 154v–159v.

70. On March 24, 1699, Secretary of State Mendo de Foyos Pereira sent to the viceroy of India reports on the opening of the trade between Brazil and Mozambique, followed by a series of consultations to Indian Ocean experts. All were against the initiative: for them, Brazilian merchandise did not find acceptance in Mozambique. A Goa merchant explained that the gold, ivory, and amber trade exported from Mozambique was vital for Portuguese traders in the Indian Ocean. Regarding slaves, mortality rates would be too high due to the distances involved in transportation. In view of such difficulties, nothing was implemented. See V. Rodrigues, "Livro das Monções," in *Boletim da Filmoteca Ultramarina Portuguesa* 50 (1993), 173–176. In the middle of the eighteenth century, Portuguese authorities tried unsuccessfully to reorient to Brazil the trafficking of Mozambicain slaves hooking up with the French plantations in the Indian Ocean. See J. Capela, *O tráfico da escravatura nas relações Moçambique-Brasil* (Lisbon: 2002), 1–33, here 2–6.

71. Gaspar Pacheco requested a new authorization in 1645. There is no evidence that it went ahead. Another trade operation took place on a date before 1620, when Manuel Moreno Chaves obtained a license to bring over slaves from Mozambique in two ships. One ship sank, but the other did business. See doc. of February 28, 1620, *AHU*, Moçambique, box 1/31. See also doc. of August 6, 1645, *AHU*, Moçambique, box 1/68, and doc. of February 12, 1656, *MMA[1]*, vol. 12, 5–10, 9; D. G. Smith, "Old Christian Merchants and the Foundation of the Brazil Company, 1649," *HAHR* 54, no. 2 (1974), 233–259, 246–247. The TSTD registers three more voyages in 1664, 1679, and 1690 (voyage IDs 46409, 48931, and 19719, respectively), all three from and to Bahia. Those are the only known slave-trade operations between Mozambique and Brazil in the sixteenth and seventeenth centuries.

72. Salvador de Sá was born in Cadiz. His mother's name was Maria de Benavides (or Benevides in Portuguese). See F. Dutra, "Charles Boxer's Salvador de Sá and the Struggle for Brazil and Angola Revisted 50 Years Later" *Imperial (Re)Visions: Brazil and the Portuguese Seaborne Empire: A Conference in Memory of Charles R. Boxer* (unpublished paper presented at a conference, Yale University, November 1, 2002).

73. R. Sampaio Garcia, "A margem de 'Comércio e contrabando entre a Bahia e Potosí no século XVI,'" *RH* 23 (1955), 169–176, here 170. Salvador Correia de Sá (the elder) was a cousin of Estácio de Sá, founder and first governor of Rio (1565–1567). Both were nephews of the governor-general Mem de Sá (1557–1572). See appendix 3.

74. "Representação da Câmara da vila de Santos," January 23, 1619, *AHU*, ACL, Conselho Ultramarino 023–01, box 1, doc. 2.

75. J. Marchena Fernandez, "Dominicos y encomenderos en el Tucuman del siglo XVII," *Los Dominicos y el Nuevo Mundo: Actas del III Congreso Internacional* (Madrid: 1991), 433–442.

76. Paes Leme, "Notícia histórica da expulsão dos jesuítas do Collégio de São Paulo," *RIHGB*, vol. 12 (1849), 5–40, 12.

77. Juan de Avalos (or Davalos) would have taken advantage, with Salvador de Sá, of the sequestered property of the Rio de Janeiro Spanish in 1640. The confiscation of the Avalos' estate took place in 1643. Decreed by Governor Luís Barbalho (1643–1644) after Duarte Correa Vasqueanes was removed from the post, such an act could have prompted the vendetta between the Sá and Barbalho families that flared some years later. In fact, Agostinho and Jerônimo Barbalho, sons of the former governor, led the Rio de Janeiro riot of 1660 against the Sá oligarchy. Salvador retaliated harshly, confiscating the rebel's property and hanging Jerônimo Barbalho. See Lamego, *A Terra Goyatacá*, v. 1, 53.

78. O. J. Trujillo, "Facciones, parentesco y poder—La élite de Buenos Aires y la rebelión de Portugal de 1640," in *Las redes del imperio. Élites sociales en la articulación de la monarquía hispánica, 1492–1714*, B. Y. Casalilla, ed. (Madrid: 2009), 341–358.

79. "Relacion de los servicios del capitan de Cavallos don Juan Davalos," (Madrid: 1652). Avalos sent the petition from Baeza (Andalusia), where he lived after quitting Buenos Aires and where the Benavides family came from. His petition prudently does not bear the name "Benavides," denouncing his kinship with Salvador de Sá. In a 1659 document, he retook his full family name: Juan de Avalos y Benavides. See E. de Cárdenas Piera, *Expedientes de Militares (siglos XVI al XIX)* (Madrid: 1968), 100; E. Toral, "Cuatro relaciones de méritos y servicios," *Boletín del Instituto de Estudios Giennenses* 3 (1953), 103–122.

80. O. J. Trujillo, "Integración y conflicto en uma elite fronteriza: los Portugueses em Buenos Aires a mediados del siglo XVII," in *Portugal na Monarquia Hispânica*, P. Cardim, L. F. Costa, and M. S. da Cunha, eds. (Lisbon: 2013), 309–329.

81. Boxer, *Salvador de Sá*, 98–99; J. Cortesão, *Raposo Tavares e a formação territorial do Brasil*, v. 2, 216.

82. Will of 1667, Coaracy, *O Rio de Janeiro*, 184; R. T. Rudge, *As sesmarias de Jacarepaguá* (São Paulo: 1983), 11–12.

83. Cortesão, *Raposo Tavares*, vol. 2, 106.

84. On the Portuguese presence in Potosi, see L. Hanke, "The Portuguese in Spanish America with Special Reference to the Villa Imperial de Potosi," *Revista de Historia de America* 51 (1961), 1–48.

85. Doc. of March 8, 1636, *ABNRJ*, vol. 39 (1917), 192–193; Coaracy, *O Rio de Janeiro no século dezessete*, 86–88.

86. E. S. Barros, Negócios de Tanta Importância—O Conselho Ultramarino e a disputa pela condução da guerra no Atlântico e no Índico 1643–1661 (Lisbon: 2008), 279–292.

87. L. Norton, "Carta de Salvador de Sá a el-rei," *A Dinastia* (Rio de Janeiro: 1648), 240–242.

88. "Carta dos oficiais da Câmara do Rio de Janeiro a el-rei," December 31, 1660, *ABNRJ* 39 (1917), 94–95.

89. "Informe JB," *Jornal do Brasil* (1966), 6; F. Fridman, *Donos do Rio em nome do rei—Uma história fundiária da cidade do Rio de Janeiro* (Rio de Janeiro: 1999), passim.

90. "Papel que se deu a S.M. (. . .) sobre o modo que devia dispor a deferência deste reino e suas conquistas e alianças . . . ," *Os Manuscritos*, vol. 2 (c. 1641), 338–339.

91. News of the enthronement of João IV reached Rio on March 19, 1641. In a representation written two years later, Salvador de Sá claimed to have sent word to Bahia and Angola about Rio de Janeiro's support for João IV's throne. But he did not mention the ship he had immediately sent to Buenos Aires. See J. A. Castello, "Relação da Aclamação que se fez na capitania do Rio de Janeiro do Estado do Brasil," in *O movimento academicista no Brasil*, vol. 3, book 1 (Lisbon: 1641), 5–12; doc. of January 10, 1643, *PLMH*, vol. 2, 144.

92. Doc. of September 28, 1644, *ABNRJ*, vol. 39 (1917), 37; Barros, "Negócios de Tanta Importância," 279–280.

93. Doc. of 1648, *Os Manuscritos*, v. 1, 351–354; doc. of December 18, 1648, *Accordãos e Vereanças*, 166–167.

94. Letters of February 26, 1658, to Tomé de Alvarenga, and April 10, 1659, to Salvador de Sá, *DH*, vol. 52, 91–92 and 106–108.

95. Doc. of May 6, 1645, *Accordãos e Vereanças*, 97–98.

96. Royal order of November 22, 1698, subjecting to the Rio government all southern lands until subject to the Bahian government-general; royal order of November 9, 1709, creating the captaincy of São Paulo e Minas do Ouro, royal provision of January 16, 1726, detaching Parati from São Paulo and incorporating it into Rio de Janeiro. See *DI*, vol. 48, 1929, 49–51, 65–68, and 101–102, passim.

97. "Method to be practiced in order to avoid the loss of slaves," in which the count of Rezende proposes strict control measures on the export of slaves from Africa, and their sale and purchase in Brazil, so as to avoid their smuggling to the Río de la Plata, Rio de Janeiro, December 12, 1798, *AHU*, Documentos Avulsos, *maço* 450 (old cataloguing).

98. J. C. Vilardaga, *São Paulo na órbita do império dos Felipes: conexões castelhanas de uma vila da América portuguesa durante a União Ibérica (1580–1640)* (PhD thesis in history, Universidade de São Paulo, 2010), 189–278.

99. Paes Leme, *Nobiliarquia*, v. 4, 77, 268, 269, passim; J. Gonçalves Salvador, *Os Cristãos-Novos—Povoamento*, 306.

100. "Real Cédula al Virrey del Peru . . . ," 16 September 1638, *AMP*, 5, part 2, 1931, 131–138.

101. Gonçalves Salvador, *Os Cristãos-Novos—Povoamento*, 54 and 311.

102. J. C. Boyajian, *Portuguese Trade*, 178.

103. A. R. de Montoya, *Conquista Espiritual hecha por los religiosos de la Compañia de Jesus* [1639] (Bilbao: 1892), 15, 173.

104. "Real Cédula al Virrey del Peru," September 16, 1638, *AMP*, vol. 5, part 2, 1931, 131–138; R. R. Gonzales, *A vila de São Paulo durante a União das Coroas: Estratégias políticas e transformações Jurídicas* (PhD thesis in history, Universidade de São Paulo, 2002), 158–168.

105. H. E. Cross, "Commerce and Orthodoxy: A Spanish Response to Portuguese Commercial Penetration in the Viceroyalty of Peru, 1580–1640," *The A* 35, no. 2 (1978), 151–167; A. E. Schaposchnik, *Under the Eyes of the Inquisition: Crypto-Jews in the Ibero-American World (Peru, 1600s)* (PhD thesis in history, University of Wisconsin–Madison, 2007), 100–141.

106. Salvador de Sá had been received in 1642 as a brother of the Company of Jesus. See *MMA[1]*, vol. 9, 55. A Jesuit brother pronounces the "Simple Vows"—poverty, chastity, and obedience—without ordination to the priesthood.

107. *HCJB*, vol. 3, 32–39, and vol. 6, 572–588; "Escriptura de transação e amigável composição e renunciação que fizeram os padres . . . , 22 de junho de 1640," *RIHGB*, vol. 3 (1841), 113–118.

108. *HCJB*, vol. 6, 253–254 and 416–420.

109. J. H. Bennett, "The English Caribbees in the Period of the Civil War, 1642–1646," *The William and Mary Quarterly* 24, no. 3 (1967), 359–377.

110. Four hundred Irish, among them fifty or sixty couples, requested a licence to dwell in Maranhão (1643). The Overseas Council vetoed the request, underlining the inconvenience of settling foreigners so close to the Antillean thoroughfares. There was a fresh proposal requesting lands in São Paulo (1646), followed by a fresh veto from the council. "It is not convenient to give any motive to the Parliament (of Britain) to displease your Majesty and to accept . . . those who they [from Parliament] understand are their vassals and as such wage them just wars." Decision by the Overseas Council on December 9, 1650, *BNL*, res. cod. 7627, fs. 78 ss., 110–113. J. L. de Azevedo wrote that the Jesuits could have been sponsoring the project to settle the Irish in São Paulo. See A. Vieira, *Cartas*, vol. 1, 214n1. See also M. Gonçalves da Costa, "Orientação da Política Colonial Portuguesa: Colonos Irlandeses no Brasil e Política Colonial Portuguesa (1643–1650)." *Revista Portuguesa de Filosofia* 14, no. 1 (1958) 65—79; and Nini Rodgers *Ireland, Slavery and Anti-Slavery 1612–1865* (New York: 2009), 33–35.

111. Paes Leme, *Nobiliarquia*, v. 1, 269.

112. J. Gonçalves Salvador, *Os Cristãos-Novos*, 52 and 91–100; H. E. Cross, "Commerce and Orthodoxy," 151 and 158.

113. Salvador de Sá confiscated the Spaniards' property in Rio de Janeiro and had his own estates seized by them at Buenos Aires. See Norton, *A Dinastia* . . . 185.

114. Paes Leme, "Notícia Histórica," 5–40, 18; Gonzales, *A vila de São Paulo durante a União das Coroas*, 172–176.

115. Memorandum of October 29, 1643, *PLMH*, v. 2, 463–464.

116. Doc. of 1651, *HCJB*, vol. 6, 265.

117. Doc. of May 16, 1646, *BNRJ, Manuscritos, Consultas Mistas do Conselho Ultramarino*, cod. 25, fs.fs. 341–341v.

118. Doc. of March 10, 1647, *BNRJ, Manuscritos*, ibid., cod. 24, fs. 14–17.

119. Doc. of 1678, *MMA¹*, vol. 13, 465–473, 470.

120. C. R. Boxer, *The Christian Century in Japan: 1549–1650* (Berkeley, CA: 1951), 233–236; A. de Almeida Calado, "A Companhia de Jesus na Índia em meados do século XVII," *Studia* 40 (1978), 349–366; M. Blanco Velez, "Notas sobre o poder temporal da Companhia de Jesus na Índia: século XVII," *Studia* 49 (1989), 195–214.

121. Paes Leme, *Nobiliarquia*, v. 2, 278.

122. J. A. Ossanna, "Las misiones jesuitas en la región del Guayrá en las primeras décadas del siglo XVII," *Mundo Agrario* 8, no. 16 (2008), 1–15.

123. Some *reducciones* had been using firearms against the Paulistas since 1634. See Cortesão, *Raposo*, v. 1, 200–201.

124. For A. R. de Montoya's petition to the viceroy of Peru, 1640, see J. Cortesão, ed., *Jesuítas e bandeirantes no Uruguai* (Rio de Janeiro: 1970), 434–437; A. Alvarez Kern, *Missões—Uma utopia política* (Porto Alegre: 1985), 185–195.

125. Porto, *História das Missões*, 121; A. E. Taunay, *História geral*, vol. 2, 289–355; Kern, *Missões*, 168; A. Ellis, Jr., *O bandeirantismo paulista e o recuo do meridiano* (São Paulo: 1936), 176–182.

126. Wedgwood, *The Thirty Years War*, 272. The "leather cannons" made of light metal reinforced with leather were increasingly abandoned. In China, however, the rope-wrapped bamboo cannons—like the ones at Mbororé—continued to be used until the end of the eighteenth century. See C. M. Cipolla, *Guns, Sails, and Empires* (Lisbon: 1989), 110n314; G. Parker, *The Military Revolution: Military Innovation and the Rise of the West, 1500–1800*, 33–35.

127. About the siting of the Parapuava, or Paraupaba, see B. A. Genofre Prezia, *Os indígenas do Planalto Paulista: Etnôminos e grupos indígenas nos relatos dos viajantes, cronistas e missionários dos séculos XVI e XVII* (PhD thesis in linguistics, Universidade de São Paulo, 1997), 64.

128. Monteiro, *Negros*, 79–85.

129. L. Norton, "Os planos de Salvador Correia de Sá," *Brasília* 2 (1943), 612–613.

130. M. Weber, *General Economic History*, [1927] (New York: 2003), 298; J. de Vries, *The Economy of Europe in an Age of Crisis 1600–1750* (Cambridge: 1976), 129–130; for a point of view expressed in a much more radical and simplistic way, see J. C. Van Leur, *Indonesian Trade and Society: Essays in Asian Social and Economic History* (The Hague: 195). Opposing these approaches, Boyajian points out the many similarities between Portuguese and Dutch activities and methods in Asia at the beginning of the seventeenth century, concluding that the victory of the latter, and of the English, over the former resulted from superiority in their naval powers. See Boyajian, *Portuguese Trade*, 106–127.

131. To lure shareholders, the WIC propagandists claimed that the enterprise constituted a lucrative response to the setback inflicted on the United Provinces after the embargo issued in 1621 by Spain. See Israel, *Dutch Primacy*, 156–158.

132. P. C. Emmer, "The West India Company 1621–1791: Dutch or Atlantic?" in *Companies and Trade*, L. Blusse and F. Gaastra, eds. (Leiden: 1981), 71–95.

133. Unlike the VOC, constituted by various companies, and financed by great maritime markets and by prestigious merchants, the incorporation of the WIC was completed with investments made by inland towns governed, above all, in Zeeland by hard-boiled Calvinists, persons engaged in reducing the Catholic presence in the Americas but little learned in the ways of great oceanic trade. See Barlaeus, *História dos feitos*, 10–12; G. Masselman, "Dutch Colonial Policy in the Seventeenth Century," *JEH* 21, no. 4 (1961), 455–468; O. A. Rink, *Holland on the Hudson: An Economic and Social History of Dutch New York* (New York: 1989), 60–68; Israel, *Dutch Primacy*, 67–73 and 156–159.

134. The Portuguese report mentions as many as 1,950 WIC soldiers beheaded. See *MMA¹*, vol. 7, 389–393.

135. S. Arasaratnam, "Monopoly and Free Trade in Dutch-Asian Commercial Policy: Debate and Controversy within the VOC," *Journal of Southeast Asian Studies* 4, no. 1 (1973), 1–15.

136. On the debate over monopoly and free trade in Dutch Brazil, see "Carta do coronel Artichofsky ao conde Maurício e ao Conselho Supremo do Brasil" (Brazilian translation), *RIAGPE* 35 (1888), 3–27; H. Watjen, *O domínio colonial holandês no Brasil* (São Paulo: 1938), 200, 383, and especially 448–462; Postma, *The Dutch in the Atlantic*, 23. See also C. C. Goslinga, *The Dutch in the Caribbean and on the Wild Coast 1580–1680* (Assen and Maastricht: 1971), 109.

137. Barlaeus, *História dos feitos*, 90–93. E. Cabral de Mello, *O Negócio do Brasil: Portugal, os Países Baixos e o Nordeste, 1641–1669* (Rio de Janeiro: 1998), 57–58.

138. A shorter version of this section was published as L. F. Alencastro, "Johann Moritz und der Sklavenhandel," in *Sein Feld war die Welt—Johann Moritz von Nassau-Siegen 1604–1679*, G. Brunn and C. Neusch, eds. (Münster: 2008), 123–144.

139. Watjen, *O domínio colonial*, 154–155, 422–424.

140. *FHBH*, vol. 1, 102, 104, and 108.

141. Report dated 1640, *FHBH*, vol. 1, 137–232, 18; about Van der Dussen, see Boxer, *The Dutch*, 265–266.

142. *FHBH*, vol. 1, 104.

143. Watjen, *O domínio colonial*, 138–143.

144. On Nassau-Siegen governorship, see E. Cabral De Mello, ed., *O Brasil holandês (1630–1654)* (São Paulo: 2010), chapters 7, 9, 10, and 11. On the debate about primitive accumulation and mercantile capitalism, see the review of Hagen on P. Kriedte's *Spätfeudalismus*

und Handelskapital, see W. W. Hagen, "Capitalism and the countryside in Early Modern Europe: Interpretations, Models, Debates," *Agricultural History* 62, no. 1 (1988), 13–47.

145. See H. R. Hoetink, "Some Remarks on the Modernity of Johan Maurits," M. E. H. N. Mout, "The Youth of Johan Maurits and Aristocratic Culture in the Early 17th Century," and G. Freyre, "Johan Maurits van Nassau-Siegen from a Brazilian Viewpoint," in *Johan Maurits van Nassau-Siegen: A Humanist Prince in Europe and Brazil 1604–1679,* E. van Den Boogaart, H. R. Hoetink, and J. Whitehead, eds. (The Hague: 1979). Thanks to Gerard Brunn; the book published for the fourth centennial of the Nassau-Siegen death (2004) included a chapter on his role in the WIC decision to invade Angola and to undertake the Atlantic slave trade. See note 138.

146. R. V. Welie, "Slave Trading and Slavery in the Dutch Colonial Empire: A Global Comparison," *NWIG: New West Indian Guide/Nieuwe West-Indische Gids* 82, no. 1/2 (2008), 47–96, 57n26.

147. Barlaeus, *História dos feitos,* 192–193 and 355.

148. Postma, *The Dutch,* 12, 21, and 358. See also innovative research on the subject by John Ladhams, "In Search of West African Pidgin Portuguese." *Revista Internacional de Lingüística Iberoamericana* 4, no. 1.7 (2006), 87–105.

149. MMA^1, vol. 8, 124, and 134; director dispatched in 1637. See P. M. Martin, *The External Trade of the Loango Coast 1576–1870—The Effects of Changing Commercial Relations on the Vili Kingdom of Loango* (Oxford, UK: 1972), 55.

150. Aside from the enslaved, there were 35 tons of ivory and 1.5 tons of gold. See MMA^1, vol. 8, 397–398.

151. MMA^1, vol. 8, 125, 133. On the Dutch trade in the slave coast, see R. Law, "The Slave Trade in Seventeenth-Century Allada: A Revision," *African Economic History* 22 (1994), 59–92. For the presence of the Dutch trading in copper and ivory from Mpinda until Beny was reported to Lisbon by the Angolan governor in 1625, see B. Heintze, "Carta de Fernão de Sousa," in *Fontes,* vol. 2, 145.

152. Postma, *The Dutch,* 16. Rik van Welie, "Slave Trading and Slavery in the Dutch Colonial Empire: A Global Comparison," *NWIG: New West Indian Guide* (*Nieuwe West-Indische Gids*), 82, no. 1–2 (2008) 47–96.

153. H. Watjen, *O domínio colonial,* 184–185; Dapper, *Description de l'Afrique,* 370.

154. M. Netscher, *Les Hollandais au Brésil* (The Hague: 1853); E. Cabral de Mello, *Nassau* (São Paulo: 2006), 126.

155. Regarding the blunders of Restoration diplomacy, the count of Ericeira elegantly ponders, "At the time in Portugal there was so little exercise of direction of political and military affairs that one cannot fairly condemn those who did not adjust to all the circumstances of the tasks they were sent to fulfill." See C. de Ericeira, *História de Portugal restaurado,* vol. 5 (Porto: 1945), 155. About the 1641 Luso-Dutch Treaty, see Prestage, *A Embaixada de Tristão,* 10–61 and 69–86.

156. "Instrução de Nassau ao almirante Jol," Recife, May 28, 1641, *ACA*, vol. 1, 34–42. Yet Dapper states that the Portuguese Crown attributed the order to invade Angola to the WIC board in Amsterdam. See Dapper, *Description de l'Afrique*, 371–372.

157. Doc. of February 6, 1642, *ACA*, vol. 1, 200–202 and 237–239; Watjen, *O domínio colonial*, 187–188.

158. Barlaeus, *História dos feitos*, 215; Mpinda copper, West Central African ivory and gold, were reexported to Amsterdam from Recife. See "A Bolsa do Brasil, onde claramente se mostra a aplicação que teve o dinheiro dos accionistas da Companhia das Índias Occidentaes," *RIAGP* 28 ([1647] 1883), 127–201, 156–162.

159. Barlaeus, *História dos feitos*, 327.

160. F. Ribeiro da Silva, "Os Holandeses e a consolidação do sistema económico do Atlântico Sul Seiscentista, c. 1630–1654," *RIAHGP* 67 (2014), 11–38.

161. Recife, May 31, 1641, *ACA*, vol. 1, 44–50.

162. Postma, *The Dutch in the Atlantic*, 18.

163. F. Ribeiro da Silva, "Dutch Labor Migration to West Africa," in *Migration, Trade and Slavery in an Expanding World, Essays in Honor of Pieter Emmer*, W. Klooster, ed. (Leiden: 2009), 73–98, table 5, and 86.

164. Watjen, *O domínio colonial*, 222–223.

165. Letter of May 23, 1689, *Cartas*, vol. 3, 572–588. See note 189 below.

166. Salvador, *História*, 251. On the "Privilégio de senhor de engenho": royal order of February 26, 1681, exempting sugar mills from debt execution; royal decree of March 2, 1756, cancelling the sugar and tobacco contracts established below fair price; royal decree of March 5, 1814, declaring debts and fiscal executions included in the privileges enjoyed by sugar mill owners.

167. Following the specific cycle of merchant capitalism, the Dutch later abandoned their mercantile dynamism to become patrimonialists and rentiers, causing the country's economic decline. See J. Adams, "Trading States, Trading Places—The Role of Patrimonialism in Early Modern Dutch Development," *Comparative Studies in Society and History* 36, no. 2 (1994), 319–355.

168. Regarding the WIC and the VOC, Sombart writes: "[T]he spirit presiding over all of the colonial enterprises, since it was not European colonization proper, was just the spirit of rape and piracy," adding Goethe's epigram in *Wilhelm Meister*: "Krieg, Handel und Piraterie / Dreieinig sind sie; nicht su trennen" ("The War, the Trade and the Piracy form an indivisible trinity"). See W. Sombart, Le *Bourgeois*.(French translation) (Paris: 1926), 95.

169. *FHBH*, vol. 2, 434.

170. About the selling on credit debate, see doc. of February 18, 1642, *ACA*, vol. 1, 266–270, and J. A. Gonsalves de Mello, *Gente da nação*, 234–235 (Recife: 1989).

171. "A Bolsa do Brasil onde claramente se mostra a aplicação que teve o dinheiro dos acionistas da Companhia das Índias Ocidentais," *RIAHGP*, vol. 28 (Recife: 1647), 127–201,

128. See also another celebrated pamphlet issued in the same year of 1647, "O Machadão do Brasil," *RIAGP* 71 (1908), 125–170.

172. van den Boogaart and Emmer, "The Dutch Participation," 370.

173. Regarding the 1668 Dutch *Asiento* contract, Postma writes: "Generally the WIC refused to make deliveries without prompt payments, and that was a perennial problem in the *Asiento* trade." See Postma, *The Dutch in the Atlantic*, 37.

174. J. Nieuhof, *Gedenkweerdige Brasiliaense Zee-en-Lant Reize* (Brazilian translation) (Amsterdam: 1682), 119–121 and 366.

175. Ibid., 391–392.

176. Nieuhof underlines the vain effort of the Compagnie to extend credit to the indebted sugar-mill owners. As the Portuguese colonists were "overwhelmed by debts," they felt in despair. See Ibid., 119–121.

177. J. H. Duarte Pereira, "Relatórios e cartas de Gedeon Morris de Jonge no tempo do domínio holandez no Brazil," *RIHGB*, vol. 58 (1895), 300.

178. "Instruction pour M. de Bellièvre, conseiller du roi," *RIAMF*, vol. 21, book 1, 47.

179. J. Israel attributes the fall in sugar prices in Amsterdam to the fresh exports from southern Brazil's mills, after the retreat of the WIC's war fleet, following the Luso-Dutch Truce Treaty (1641). See Israel, *Dutch Primacy*, 167–168. However, the fall in sugar prices was evident in 1640, predating the Truce. Israel does not mention Nieuhof's book, a key source on New Holland's economic crisis. Mixing skepticism and self-criticism, the book features one of the traits of the great essays of historical reflection. In fact, following Nieuhof's analysis, E. Cabral de Mello elaborates with a deeper explanation, pointing out the factors interacting in the crisis of Dutch Brazil: the inversion in the century's upward tendency of prices for colonial products, conjunctural overproduction of sugar, the relaunch of the southern sugar zones, and the increase in the Compagnie's costs due to Angola. See Cabral de Mello, *Olinda*, 266–274.

180. Nieuhof, *Gedenkweerdige Brasiliaense Zee-en-Lant Reize*, 109; Barlaeus, *História dos feitos*, 337.

181. "Sousa Coutinho ao conde da Vidigueira," November 23, 1643, *CD*, vol. 1, 77–79, 78.

182. Doc. of October 1643, *MMA¹*, vol. 9, 81.

183. The Portuguese rescue expedition was aborted due to the start of the Montijo battle against Spain. See "Sousa Coutinho a El-Rei," April 6, 1644, *CD*, vol. 1, 127–129, 128.

184. M. Calado, *O Valeroso*, vol. 1, 187, 189, and 206.

185. On the issue, see the anthological pages of E. Cabral de Mello, *Olinda*, 260–275.

186. "Cartas nassovianas 1637–1646," *RIAGP* 69 (1906), 532–255; letter of January 10, 1641, 545–547.

187. "Sousa Coutinho a el-rei," set. 1643, *CD*, vol. 1, 53–55.

188. Laranjo Coelho, *Cartas de el-rei d. João IV para diversas autoridades do Reino*, vol. 2 (Lisbon: 1940), 128, 163; Cabral de Mello, ed., *O Brasil holandês*, chapters 17 and 18.

189. Doc. of February 19, 1647, *BNRJ*, Consultas Mistas do Conselho Ultramarino, cod. 24, Livro de Registro, 1647–1652, vol. 2, fls. 13v–14. Full of denunciations against João Fernandes Vieira and "tirany" in Pernambuco, the file contains a note with the advice of Salvador de Sá and of the Marquis of Montalvão, chairman of the Overseas Council, "to keep these documents in a place where it will not be seen."

190. A. Vieira, "Papel Forte," *Obras Escolhidas*, vol. 4, 35. Referring to the testimony in an inquisitorial process by a New Christian who shared this opinion, Lipiner stated that the allegation attributing the mutiny to Brasílico debtors translated to "the subjective view of the Dutch and Jews (about the Portuguese settlers)." As we see, Vieira's judgment on the matter was very objective and realistic. See E. Lipiner, *Izaque de Castro, o mancebo que veio preso do Brasil* (Recife: 1992), 61n1.

191. Doc. of 1591, MMA¹, vol. 3, 429–430. The memorials by Diogo Ferreira (or Diego de Herrera) complete the information about Angola sent around this time to the Madrilian court. See J. L. Cortés López, "Felipe II, III y IV, Reyes de Angola y protectores del reino del Congo (1580–1640)," *Studia Histórica* 9 (1991), 223–246.

192. Angola could be attacked, due to the "need of Blacks for the cultivation of the land and labor in the mills (of Bahia)," September 29, 1624, *MMA¹*, vol. 8, 258–261, and vol. 8, 181.

193. "Memorial de Luís Mendes de Vasconcellos," July 9, 1616, *AHU*, Angola, box 1/50.

194. Two WIC expeditions attacked Luanda: the first, planned since 1622 and commanded by Van Zuylen, cast anchor close to Benguela in September 1623 and laid siege to Luanda in June 1624; the second, sent after the conquest of Bahia and commanded by Piet Heyn, surrounded Luanda in October–November of the same year. *ACA*, vol. 1, XXIV–XXV; Vicente do Salvador, *História* 392.

195. Vieira, *Cartas*, vol. 1, 55.

196. D. Gomes Solís, *Alegación En Fauor de La Compañia de La India Oriental Y Comercios Ultramarinos Que de Nueuo Se Instituyó En El Reyno de Portugal* (1628), edited by M. B. Amzalak (Lisbon: 1955), 40.

197. Doc. of December 26, 1626, *AHU*, Angola, box 2, doc. 114; doc. of 1631, *MMA¹*, vol. 8, 93.

198. Doc. of October 1636, *MMA¹*, vol. 8, 378.

199. In 1645, King João IV summed up Luso-Spanish relations: it had all been a disaster during the last sixty years. In addition, "[I]f Castile sought to help Brazil it was not for the damage inflicted in Portugal, but, instead, for fear of their [West] Indies, with such a powerful enemy as the Dutch for neighbors. And for this reason they did not relive India and let Mina [Coast] go." See Laranjo Coelho, *Cartas de el-rei D. João IV ao conde*, vol. 1, 217–224. An identical argument was written by Manuel de Melo, *Epanáforas*, 378.

200. For an analysis of Portugal's economic and fiscal difficulties in Brazil after 1640, see W. Lenk, *Guerra e Pacto Colonial: Exército, Fiscalidade e Administração Colonial da Bahia (1624–1654)* (PhD thesis in economic history, IE, Unicamp, São Paulo, 2009), 153–183.

201. Prestage, *A Embaixada*, 52–53. More Dutch weapons and ammunition would be sent in 1647 to Bahia with the count of Vila Pouca's fleet. See Cabral de Mello, *O Negócio*, 35n1.

202. "Instruction au Sieur Marquis de Rouillac," ambassador to Portugal, *RIAMF*, vol. 3 (1644), 3–9; "Instructions à M. de Lionne" plenipotentiary in Madrid, *RIAMF*, vol. 11, book 1 (1656), 83–84.

203. Lisbon, August 6, 1645, *MMA¹*, vol. 9, 347–348.

204. The United Provinces' governmental administration was incomprehensible to absolutist monarchies' chanceries. "It is the most extravagant government one [has] ever seen," stated the count Guzman de Peñaranda, Spanish ambassador to Münster. See L. André and E. Bourgeois, "Introduction," *RIAMF*, vol. 21, book 1, XI; Cabral de Mello, *O Negócio*, 46–52.

205. Informed in Lisbon of the taking of Luanda by the WIC, Admiral Gysels, commander of the Dutch task force, vowed to the king that the attack had been the work of the WIC merchants and not by the states-generals. April 16, 1642, *MMA¹*, vol. 8, 579, and M. de Galhegos, *Gazeta, em que relatam as novas todas, que ouve nesta corte, e que vieram de varias partes no mês de novembro de 1641, Lisbon, 1641* (Lisbon: 1641–1644), 6.

206. C. R. Boxer, "Portuguese and Dutch Colonial Rivalry, 1641–1661," *Studia* 2 (1958), 7–42, 20.

207. Sousa Coutinho to the count of Vidigueira, The Hague, April 18, 1644, *CD*, vol. 5, 130.

208. The main palatine councils were the *Desembargo do Paço* (Royal Council of justice), the *Conselho da Fazenda* (Council of Finance), the *Conselho de Estado* (State Council), the *Conselho de Guerra* (War Council), and the *Conselho Ultramarino* (Overseas Council).

209. F. Dores Costa, "As forças sociais perante a guerra: as Cortes de 1645–46 e de 1653–54," *Análise Social* 36, no. 161 (2001), 1,147–1,181; P. Cardim, *Cortes e Cultura Política no Portugal do Antigo Regime* (Lisbon: 1998), 102 passim.

210. A. Manuel Hespanha, *As vésperas do Leviathan: Instituições e poder político: Portugal— séc. XVII*, vol. 1 (Lisbon: 1986), 351–361; for a discussion of the Restoration ideological scenario, see L. R. Torgal, *Ideologia política e teoria do Estado na Restauração* (Coimbra: 1981–1982) passim.

211. Ericeira, *História*, vol. 1, 333.

212. "Parecer do marquês de Montalvão," in *Os Manuscritos*, vol. 1 (Lisbon: 1641), 28–29.

213. Consultation by the Conselho da Fazenda, March 31, 1649, *AHU*, Angola, box 5/13.

214. Heintze, *Fontes*, vol. 1, 81–82.

215. News of the fall of Luanda reached Rio de Janeiro in October 1641. See doc. of November 2, 1641 of the Rio de Janeiro Municipal Council, *Accordãos e Vereanças*, 49–50.

216. K. Ratelband, *Os holandeses no Brasil e na Costa Africana, Angola, Kongo e S. Tomé 1600–1650*, edited and commented by Carlos Pacheco (Lisbon: 2003), 223–234.

217. *MMA¹*, vol. 8, 6–12 and 364–366; vol. 9, 23–27; doc. of March 5, 1643. About Diogo Lopes de Faria, see Heintze, *Fontes*, vol. 1, 87–88.

218. Bahia, August 6, 1643, *MMA¹*, vol. 15, 575–577. Antônio Telles da Silva arrived in Bahia as governor-general in May 1642. At the end of 1647 he was replaced by Antônio Telles de Meneses, Count Villa Pouca d'Aguiar, who was brother to Fernão Telles de Menezes, an influential character in Lisbon. Fernão Telles was one of the actors in the 1640 Restoration, Beira's military commander, and the governor of Oporto. He sent out an infantry, supplies, and arms to his brother in Bahia in 1647. See Laranjo Coehlho, *Cartas de el-rei D. João IV para diversas autoridades*, vol. 2, 128, 163.

219. *AHU*, Angola, box 4/35; doc. of September 1, 1643; about Fernão de Matos de Carvalhosa, see Heintze, *Fontes*, vol. 1, 81–82.

220. "Parecer do Conselho Ultramarino sobre Angola," September 19, 1643. Note that there is an error in the record, because it is a report by the Council of Finance (Conselho da Fazenda). See *MMA¹*, vol. 9, 65–80.

221. Norton, *A dinastia*, 191–192; ibid., "Os planos que Salvador Correia de Sá e Benevides apresentou em 1943 para se abrir o comércio com Buenos Aires e reconquistar o Brasil e Angola," *Brasília* 2 (1943), 594–613, doc. no. 1, 605–606, and doc. no. 3, 608–609. For the Dutch, the aim of shipping Angolan slaves to Buenos Aires was stated in the invasion's preparatory report that Maizeelis Hendrickz Ouman—a Dutch factor in Loango since 1629 and future WIC director—sent to the Recife Council; Loango, February 28, 1641, *ACA*, vol. 1, 21–25.

222. Buenos Aires, March 15, 1638, in J. Cortesão, ed., *Jesuítas E Bandeirantes no Tape, 1615–1641*, vol. 3 (Rio de Janeiro: 1952), 251–252.

223. Duarte Pereira, "Relatórios e Cartas," 295–302.

224. J. T. Polo, "Relacion del Estado del govierno del Peru," in *Memorias de los Virreys del Perú, Marques de Mancera y Conde de Salvatierra* (Lima: [1648] 1899), 62–64. On the concerns raised in Spanish American by the Braganza Restoration, Stuart B. Schwartz, "Pânico nas Índias: a ameaça portuguesa ao império espanhol, 1640–1650," idem ed. *Da América Portuguesa ao Brasil* (Lisboa: 2003), 185–216.

225. "Proposta feita a el-rei d. João iv, em que se lhe representava o miserável estado do reino e necessidade que tinha de admitir os judeus mercadores que andavam por diversas partes da Europa," Lisbon, July 3, 1643; Vieira, *Obras escolhidas*, vol. 4, 1–26, 7–8.

226. Doc. of March 19, 1646, *BNRJ*, Manuscritos, Consultas Mistas do Conselho Ultramarino, cod. 25, fl. 324.

227. Consultation of February 12, 1656, *MMA¹*, vol. 12, 6.

228. In November 1642, governor-general Telles da Silva, announcing the lack of slaves and silver *patacas* in Bahia due to the rupture in the Angolan trade, began to arrange for the reopening of trade with the Río de la Plata. See Luísa da Fonseca, Luísa da Fonseca,

Bahia, Índice dos documentos do século XVII, 2 vols: (Lisbon: n/d) v. I, docs. 975, 995, 1002, and 1003.

229. Nearly 500 men participated in João Correa de Sá's expedition. Salvador de Sá's field-master patent had passed to his son, Captain João Correa de Sá. See Bahia, doc. of October 5, 1659, *PLMH*, vol. 2, 242. For the general picture of this search for precious metals, see C. A. Hanson, "The European 'Renovation' and the Luso-Atlantic Economy, 1560–1715," *Review* 6, no. 4 (1983), 506–509.

230. L. Freire Costa and M. Soares da Cunha, *D. João IV* (Rio de Mouro, Portugal: 2006), 201–202.

231. Norton, "Os planos," 605–609.

232. *MMA¹*, vol. 9, 82–84.

233. J. Veríssimo Serrão, *Do Brasil Filipino ao Brasil de 1640*, 234–235.

234. The royal decree of July 14, 1642, about the Overseas Council explicitly states: "By the state in which the affairs of India, Brazil, Angola and other of the kingdom's conquests find themselves in, due to the need to preserve and increase what I own in them and to recuperate what has been lost (. . .) I resolve to nominate a separate tribunal to particularly deal with those parts' affairs." See M. Caetano, "Governo e administração Central após a Restauração," *História da expansão de Portugal no mundo*, vol. 3 (Lisbon: 1942), 189–198, 196.

235. Norton, "Os planos," doc. of June 10, 1644, 611–613.

236. Doc. October 4, 1642, "Relação do sucesso do Arraial dos nossos em Luanda, dada por dois padres da Companhia que que de là vieram," *BAL*, 49-X-24, fl. 404–404v.

237. Doc. examined at the Overseas Council on July 5, 1646, *MMA¹*, vol. 9, 424–425 and 428.

238. *Os Manuscritos*, vol. 1, 359.

239. Duarte Pereira, "Relatórios e Cartas de Gedeon," 303.

240. Barlaeus, *História dos feitos*, 214.

241. "I am not saying your Majesty should wage open war on them, but instead to resort to the same means they make use of, there will be no lack of opportunity to do so." See "Sousa Coutinho a El-Rei," November 15, 1643, after the arrival of news about the Bengo; "Carta a el-rei," July 8, 1644: "With regards to Angola I am certain we shall have great doubts, and if Your Majesty's arms do not win, I do not know how we over here could manage to do so, because the Compagnie [WIC] is well aware that as soon as it lets that city go they will be forced to leave Brazil." See *CD*, vol. 1, 127–129 and 166–167.

242. Letter from the king to the marquis of Niza, November 29, 1648, "Treslado das capitulações das fortalezas de Luanda, Cuanza e Insandeira," *Cartas de el-rei D. João IV ao conde*, vol. 2, 297–311.

243. *CD*, vol. 3, 226–229, 228. About the Portuguese secret agent network in Europe, see P. Demerson, "Correspondance diplomatique de François Lanier résident de France à Lisbonne 1642–1644," *Arquivos do Centro Cultural Português*, vol. 32 (Paris: 1993), 523.

244. Duarte Nunes da Costa, alias Jacob Curiel, a Lisbon New Christian, was the representative of the Portuguese Crown in Hamburg from 1641 until his death in 1664, and chief financial agent for the insertion of the Braganza monarchy into the European scenario. Jerônimo Nunes da Costa was his eldest son. See J. I. Israel, *Empires and Entrepots: The Dutch, the Spanish Monarchy, and the Jews 1585–1713* (London: 1990), 333–354; ibid., "The Diplomatic Career of Jerônimo Nunes da Costa: An Episode in Dutch-Portuguese Relations of the Seventeenth Century," *Bijdragen en Mededelingen betreffende de Geschiedenis der Nederlanden* 98 (1983), 167–190. Jerônimo was aware of the Dutch slave trade in West Central Africa and informed Lisbon of the contraband between the Luanda traders and the Dutch outpost in the Loango coast. See doc. of April 10, 1670, *AHU*, Angola, box 10/8.

245. *CD*, vol. 1, 203–206, 205.

246. "Sousa Coutinho ao conde da Vidigueira," *CD*, vol. 1 (1644), 168–169.

247. Doc. of April 28, 1645, *AA*, vol. 5, 2nd series (1948), 19–23. The documents refer to the "Black soldiers of Henrique Dias," *MMA¹*, vol. 9, 486.

248. *MMA¹*, vol. 9, 332–344, 480–482; *AHU*, Angola, box 4, docs. 54, 57, 58, 59, 60, 62, 65, and 64.

249. *AA*, vol. 1, 2nd series (1943), 136–137, 193–194.

250. *BNRJ*, Manuscritos, Consultas Mistas do Conselho Ultramarino, cod. 25, fs. 283v–285; doc. of January 17, 1646, *MMA¹*, vol. 10, 66–71; G. de Sousa Dias, "Francisco de Souto Maior, capitão-geral e governador do reino de Angola 1645–1646," *Congresso do Mundo Português* (Lisbon: 1940) vol. 7, 337–356.

251. *CD*, vol. 1, 146.

252. Doc. of September 13, 1645, *MMA¹*, vol. 9, 352–364, 398–411.

253. *MMA¹*, vol. 9, 470–471.

254. An eighteenth-century military writer underlined the ecological context that delivered Pernambucan ambush captains success in Brazil: "As the land (is) covered by a continuous bush, in a few days the manifest utility of this peculiar mode of war was felt, in the damage done to the Dutch and the fear instilled in them." J. de Mirales, "História militar do Brazil" *ABNRJ* 22 ([1762] 1900), 3–238, 36; E. Cabral de Mello, *Olinda*, 204–248.

255. E. Cabral de Mello, *O Negócio*, 62.

256. P. Cardim, "Os 'Rebeldes de Portugal' no Congresso de Münster 1644–1648," *Penélope* 19–20 (1998), 101–128.

257. G. Parker, ed., *The Thirty Years War* (Barcelona: 1988), 268; J. I. Israel, *La Republica Holandesa y el Mundo Hispánico 1606–1661* (Madrid: 1982), 304–305.

258. *Cartas de el-rei D. João IV ao conde*, vol. 1, letter of December 31, 1642, 27–29.

259. J. F. C. Fuller, *A Military History of the Western World*, vol. 2, 73.

260. Prestage, *Relações*, 36–37; Demerson, "Correspondance Diplomatique," 568.

261. I sketch out the military axis of an international picture rich in diplomatic developments, analyzed by Cabral de Mello, *O Negócio*, 65–118.

262. Francisco de Sousa Coutinho was a grandson, son, and nephew of Portuguese *fidalgos* involved in the great slaving business, as stated in chapter 3. See Prestage, *A Embaixada de Tristão*, 28n1; A. Vieira a Sousa Coutinho, November 10, 1648, *CD*, vol. 3, 156–158.

263. Cabral de Mello, *Olinda*, 91–102; ibid., *O Negócio*, chapter 4.

264. "Ao marquês de Nisa," The Hague, August 12, 1648, *Cartas*, vol. 1, 243.

265. Consultation by the Overseas Council, November 27, 1648, *MMA¹*, vol. 10, 268; *AA*, vol. 5, 2nd series (1948), 77–78; Boxer, *The Dutch in Brazil*, 199.

266. "The ease with which the Dutch took this town [Luanda] from us and we fom them, shows how little defensible it is [. . .]." Vieira's "Papel Forte" is usually dated December 1648, but its internal analysis demonstrates that it was concluded in January 1649. See A. Vieira, "Papel a favor da entrega de Pernambuco . . . ," *Obras Escolhidas*, vol. 4 (Lisbon: 1951), 29–106. Gonsalves de Mello thinks that news of the fall of Luanda had only reached Lisbon in December (1648). See Gonsalves de Mello, *João Fernandes*, vol. 1, 258, 265.

267. Zeeland was favorable to the WIC's monopoly and presence in Brazil, as it feared the competition from the ports of Amsterdam and Rotterdam, where the sugar refineries were established. See P. C. Emmer, "The West India Company," 79–81.

268. The Hague, January 4, 1649, *CD*, vol. 3, 226–229, 227.

269. A. Vieira, *Livro anteprimeiro da História do futuro*, J. van den Besselaar, ed. (Lisbon, 1983), 69.

270. Boxer, *Salvador*, 404.

271. In an essay on the WIC in Brazil, P. C. Emmer, a leading scholar of Atlantic history, writes that the episode "has been labeled [as] the worst miscalculation of the Dutch's history in the Atlantic." However, analyzing the reasons for the Dutch's failure in the Atlantic, Emmer does not mention the WIC's invasion and defeat in Angola. See P. C. Emmer, "Los holandeses y el reto atlántico en el siglo XVII," in *El desafío holandés al dominio ibérico en Brasil en el siglo XVII*, J. M. Santos Perez and G. F. Cabral de Souza, eds. (Salamanca: 2006), 17–31.

272. Report by M. de Almeida, H. Correia da Silva, and F. de Carvalho, "Sobre coisas particulares do reino de Angola," *AA*, vol. 1, 2nd series (Lisbon: [1643] 1943), 85–97.

273. Not enough attention has been given to the political cleavage dividing the debates at the 1940 Congresso do Mundo Português promoted by the Salazar regime in Lisbon. There was a faction of Fascist Iberianism, which, in the wake of Franco's victory, minimized the antagonism between the two peninsular countries (notably all kinds of damage that the Habsburg period could have caused to Portugal). From Brazil hailed conferencists defending the Paulistas, Pernambucanos, and Luso-Fluminenses and regional decisional autonomy in the battles that marked the Empire's restoration in the Southern Atlantic. In between both tendencies, Portuguese scholars supported a pure and stiff Lusitanism, which aimed to prove that the initiative in Pernambuco or in the Angola expedition was exclusively the

Portuguese Crown's. See J. Cayola, "A reconquista de Angola por Salvador Correia de Sá," *Congresso do Mundo Português*, vol. 9, book 1 (Lisbon: 1940), 423–435, and also 289–335. For a defense of the Crown's initiative in the Angolan journey, see A. da Silva Rêgo, *A Dupla Restauração de Angola 1641–1648* (Lisbon: 1948), 235–240.

274. J. L. de Azevedo, *História de Antônio Vieira*, [1918], 2 vols. (Lisbon: 1992) vol. 1, 404–409, 408.

275. Royal letter of April 8, 1647, *AA*, vol. 5, 2nd series (1948), 43–44.

276. Carta September 12, 1647, *AA*, vol. 5, 2nd series (1948), 55–58.

277. Doc. of February 4, 1648, *BNRJ*, Manuscritos, Consultas Mistas do Conselho Ultramarino, cod. 24, fl. 106v.

278. Doc. of May 26, 1648, *BNRJ*, Manuscritos, Consultas Mistas do Conselho Ultramarino, cod. 24, fl. 116v.

279. L. Norton, "Carta a el-rei," in *A Dinastia* (Rio de Janeiro: 1648), 240–242.

280. "Livro de Patentes do tempo do Senhor Salvador Correia de Sá e Benevides," *Arquivo Histórico de Angola* (Luanda: 1969), 44.

281. Besides Duarte da Silva, his brothers-in-law Rodrigo Aires Brandão and Jorge Dias Brandão, as well as Jorge Lopes da Gama—all with their capital invested in Rio de Janeiro—had been arrested in Lisbon by the Inquisition at the end of 1647 and beginning of 1648. This was a reaction by Old Christian merchants plotting with Inquisitorial agents against the privilege afforded to New Christians in the planned General Company of Brazil (*Companhia Geral do Brasil*). See Doc. of April 2, 1648, *Accordãos e Vereanças*, 159–160; Lipiner, *Izaque de Castro*, 269–270; F. Mauro, "Mercadores e mercadores-banqueiros portugueses no século XVII," in *Nova história e Novo Mundo* (São Paulo: 1969), 131–133.

282. Conde da Ericeira, *História*, vol. 2, 286–287. There is a similar explanation in A. de Oliveira de Cadornega, *HGGA*, vol. 2, 2, and in the *Catálogo dos governadores de Angola* (1825), *AA*, vol. 3, 1st series (1937), 459–538. For a study of the latter source, see J. C. Miller and J. K. Thornton, "The Chronicle as Source, History, and Hagiography: The Catálogo dos Governadores de Angola," *Paideuma* 33 (1987), 360–388.

283. About Mathias de Albuquerque Maranhão, see Jaboatão and P. Calmon, *CGPF*, vol. 1, 87–88 and 92; Vaz became a municipal councilor in 1649, *Accordãos e Vereanças*, *HGGA*, vol. 2, 2.

284. Doc. of 2 January 1646, *Accordãos e Vereanças*, 109.

285. Doc. of February 6, 1646, *BNRJ*, Manuscritos, Consultas Mistas do Conselho Ultramarino, cod. 25, fls 303–303v.

286. Doc. of May 10, 1647, *BNRJ*, Manuscritos,Consultas Mistas do Conselho Ultramarino, cod. 24, Livro de Registro, 1647–1652, vol. 2, fs. 38–38v.

287. *MMA¹*, vol. 10, 229; A. da Silva Rego, *A Dupla Restauração de Angola 1641–1648*, 245–256.

288. W. J. van Hoboken, *Witte de With in Brazilië 1648–1649* (Amsterdam: 1955), 58–93.

289. H. Watjen, *O domínio colonial holandês no Brasil* (São Paulo: 1938), 260–264; Rio de Janeiro, May 15. 1648; Norton, *A Dinastia*, 252–255, 254.

290. "Carta do Pe. Antônio do Couto, Luanda 5.9.1648," *MMA¹*, vol. 5, 228–242, 229–230. Born in Luanda in 1614 from a Portuguese man and a Mbundu woman Antônio do Couto was skilled in Angola's political affairs and languages, according to a missionary document of the time. See *MMA¹*, vol. 14, 484. He published in 1642 the adapted version of Francisco Pacconio's catechism, *Gentio de Angola sufficientemente instruido nos mysterios de nossa sancta Fé*, the first printed text in the Kimbundu language. See E. Bonvini, "Repères pour une histoire des connaissances linguistiques des langues africaines," *Histoire Épistémologie Langage* 18, no. 2 (1996), 127–148.

291. Martin, *The External Trade*, 67; Boxer, *Salvador de Sá*, 282–283.

292. P. A. I. Magalhães, "A Relação do engenho de Sergipe do Conde em 1625," *Afro-Ásia* 41 (2010), 237–264.

293. *MMA¹*, vol. 9, 341, 373.

294. Setting sail from Guanabara on May 8, 1645, the five ships from Souto Maior's fleet lost contact with each other after a violent storm off the Rio de Janeiro coast two days later. See *MMA¹*, vol. 9, 352–354.

295. Laranjo Coelho, *Cartas de el-rei*, vol. 2, 238–289; minutes of the Rio de Janeiro Municipal Council, April 2, 1648, *Accordãos e Vereanças*, 160.

296. "Carta do pe. Antônio do Couto," Luanda, September 5, 1648, *MMA¹*, vol. 10, 228–242. João de Almeida or, in English, John Meade or May, born in London in 1571. At the age of ten he started as an apprentice as a Portuguese trader at Viana do Castelo's. He traveled to Pernambuco in 1588 and never left Brazil. A missionary to the Amerindians of Espírito Santo, São Paulo, and Patos (Rio Grande do Sul). From 1639 to 1653, the date of his death, he lived in the Rio de Janeiro College, where he was the confessor of many important figures, among them Salvador de Sá. See *HCJB*, vols. 3, 4, 5, and 6 passim.

297. *MMA²*, vol. 4, 103. Cadornega states that the appearance of Saint Michael the Archangel was celebrated on May 7. See *HGGA*, vol. 5, 3. However, the date for this secondary feast, celebrated in some Roman dioceses but not in Portugal, was May 8. See F. Caraffa and G. Morelli, *Bibliotheca Sanctorum*, vol. 9 (Rome: 1961–1970), 410–446. Christian calendars recorded the feast of Saint Michael on September 29, a holy day observed in the Jesuit colleges and rural properties, as was the case with the Engenho Sergipe. See Schwartz, *Sugar Plantations*, 102, tables 5–2.

298. About the seasonal rhythm of the Brazil–Angola route, see Miller, *Way*, 318–324.

299. Very popular during the Middle Ages, the legend, fabricated in the ninth century about Saint Ursula and the 11,000 virgins and her martyrdom in Cologne (Germany), fostered a profitable trade in relics that exhausted the city's cemetery, which sold tibiae, ribs, and heads said to belong to the "saints" all over Europe. See *Vies des saints et des Bienheureux*

selon l'ordre du calendrier avec l'Historique des Fêtes, vol. 10 (Paris: 1952), 674–688. About the export of skulls from the German cemetery to Brazil (three heads arrived in Bahia in 1575 and 1583), see M. L. Carneiro da Cunha, "Da guerra das relíquias ao Quinto Império," *Novos Estudos Cebrap* 44 (1996), 73–87.

300. Vasconcellos, *Vida*, 237–238.

301. *DHCMA*, vol. 2, 13.

302. Vasconcellos, *Vida*, 220–221.

303. Prestage, "As lutas luso-holandesas em Angola de 1641 a 1648," 41–76.

304. F. Manuel de Melo, Letter of March 15, 1649, *Cartas familiares* (Lisbon: [1664] 1981), 240.

305. This was the part regarding J. de Almeida. See J. L. de Azevedo, *História*, vol. 1, 407, appendix 7.

306. Consultation to the Overseas Council, July 2, 1649, *AA*, vol. 2, 2nd series (1944), 175–179.

307. F. de Brito Freyre, *Viagem da Armada*, 37.

308. A. Lamego, *A Terra Goyatacá*, vol. 1 (Brussels: 1913), 88; *HCJB*, vol. 6, 426–428; F. Martins dos Santos, *História de Santos 1532–1936* (São Paulo: 1937), 332–333.

309. *HGGA*, vol. 2, 18–19.

310. Franco died in 1673. See *ACA*, vol. 1, 398n3; *MMA¹*, vol. 9, 369 and 373; Schwartz, *Sugar Plantations*, 328–329 and 489–497.

311. S. de Vasconcellos, preface, *Vida do padre Joam d'Almeida*.

312. The Municipal Council of Rio de Janeiro "voluntarily" donated 60,000 *cruzados* to the task force. See doc. of September 1, 1648, *BNRJ*, Manuscritos, Consultas Mistas do Conselho Ultramarino, cod. 24, fl. 131.

313. *MMA¹*, vol. 5, 228–230, 357. For Salvador de Sá's officers, see the 267 patents in *AA*, vol. 2, 2nd series (1944), up to vol. 8 (1951), and appendix 4.

314. The twenty-one-ship fleet headed by Cornelis C. Jols had left Recife for Luanda in 1641, taking 1,866 soldiers, 240 Potiguar Amerindians, and 851 sailors. However, its origin and aims were exclusively European. See K. Ratelband, *Os holandeses no Brasil e na Costa Africana* (Portugal: 2003), 127–134.

315. Doc. of January 27, 1649, *AA*, vol. 5, 2nd series (1948), 79–80.

316. Petition by the Rio de Janeiro Municipal Council against the *Companhia Geral do Brasil* in 1654. See da Silva Lisboa, *Annaes*, vol. 3, 218.

317. Indeed, Salvador de Sá was linked to the count of Castelo Melhor, strongman of the regime between 1662 and 1666, and was also very close to King Afonso VI, thus disgraced during the regency of Dom Pedro. Given the title "Restorer of Angola," Salvador requested a title of nobility as a reward for the services rendered in the course of the century to the Crown by his grandfather, his father, and himself, on both margins of the Atlantic. His eldest, Martim Correa de Sá, ended up being ennobled by Afonso VI, on the merits

of the Sá family, but also on the ground that Salvador agreed to sell the vessel *Padre Eterno* to the Crown. However, Salvador's satisfaction was short-lived. The coup d'état that opened D. Pedro's regency (1667–1683), the future King Pedro II (1683–1706), took place in the following year. The regent mistrusted him, and Salvador de Sá was expelled from his posts, but managed to commute his banishment sentence to internment in a Lisbon convent, with the help from Jesuits and a few bribes. Four years later, he managed to again take his seat in the Overseas Council. Boxer, *Salvador*, passim. See also appendix 3.

318. "And I say to Your Highness about linking Angola to the Cuama [Zambeze], because he who says it cannot be done, does not speak with the experience I have accumulated in the three years and nine months I have governed those kingdoms, which had been in the hands of the Dutch for 7 years [. . . ;] it is known that in the Monomotapa there are great profits, as it is certain that the French are neighboring the Monomotapa's sandbars, river Cuama's sandbars, and I will not boast if I say that God takes me as an instrument to request [this mission], because He had already taken me so to restore those kingdoms, having first spent five years chasing ministers, until the King d. João IV who is in heaven, Y.H. father, almost on his own accord, ordered me to restore it (the kingdom of Angola) granting in homage in the same day, as can be seen in their Book, one government in Brazil and another in Angola [. . . .]" August 21, 1672, *AHU*, Angola, box 10/71.

319. *DH*, vol. 4 (1928), 421–428 and 432–438. Maybe Raposo Tavares and his column had already left São Paulo at the end of 1647. But his lieutenant-general, Antônio Pereira de Azevedo, in the second column of the leading exposition, with 80 Paulistas and over 800 Amerindians, began to march up the Tietê River in April or May 1648, at the exact time when Salvador de Sá was striving to recruit men for the Luanda expedition, as well as to find personnel to secure the defense of Rio de Janeiro against a possible Dutch attack. See Cortesão, *Raposo Tavares*, vol. 2, 175–176.

320. Royal letter of October 7, 1647; de Andrade, *Colleção Chronológica*, vol. 5, 172, supplement.

321. *MMA¹*, vol. 9, 82–84.

322. Vieira, *Cartas*, vol. 1, 392–400.

323. Cortesão, *Raposo Tavares*, vol. 1, 91–95.

324. Vieira, *Cartas*, vol. 1, 395.

325. de Vasconcellos, *Vida*, 254–255.

326. C. C. Moreira Bento, "Angola—a primeira Força Expedicionária Brasileira," *Leitura* (São Paulo: 1989), 16.

327. "Carta de Brito Freyre a el-rei," November 29, 1657, *MMA¹*, vol. 12, 147–153.

328. "Carta de Paulo Freire de Noronha," *MMA¹*, vol. 13 (1671), 153–159.

329. Vieira, *Cartas*, vol. 2 (1672), 474–475.

330. P. Verger. *Flux et Reflux*, 61–87.

331. "Os negociantes e fabricantes da Praça de Lisboa," December 14, 1825, *AHU*, Angola, box 150/17.

332. E. Cabral de Mello, *Olinda Restaurada*, 2nd ed., 219–220.

333. Boxer, *Salvador*, 171–172.

334. Salvador, *História*, 426–427; Coaracy, *O Rio de Janeiro*, 70, 133; C. Boxer, *Salvador*, 299–300, 390–391.

335. *AUC*, Colecção Conde dos Arcos, Dispozicoens dos Governadores de Pernambuco, vol. 1, fl. 49, doc. 16, March 23, 1661.

336. Ibid., vol. 1, fl. 74, doc. 85, April 18, 1663.

337. M. A. de G. da Reggio and D. de C. da Piacenza, *Viaggio nel regno del Congo* (Bologna: [1671] 1674), 52–53; L. Dantas Silva, ed., "Relação das guerras," in *Alguns documentos* (Recife: 1988), 31.

338. Brito Freyre, *Nova Lusitânia*, 282. In 1640, the Marquis of Montalvão also suggested integrating the Palmaristas into de Henrique Dias's Terço, but the Bahian Municipal Council refused the measure in the name of the safety of the slave system. See S. Schwartz, "Rethinking Palmares: Slave Resistance in Colonial Brazil," *Slaves, Peasants, and Rebels* (Chicago, IL: 1992), 112.

339. *BNL*, Correspondence of the Marquis of Montebelo (1690–1693), Coleção Pombalina, cod. 239, ff. 109, 109v.

340. Bahia, 2 August 2, 1691, Vieira, *Cartas*, vol. 3, 636–640. Later, Bonucci received orders from his superiors to help Vieira in writing his last work *Clavis Prophetarum*. Bonucci would be Vieira's faithful secretary and would handle his manuscripts after his death. See R. Cantel, *Prophétisme et messianisme dans l'oeuvre d'Antonio Vieira* (Paris: 1960), 133, 181–182, and 240.

341. Domingos Jorge Velho and his men did not come directly from São Paulo to Palmares. They went first to the Ceará-Piauí border, where they settled with cattle bought in the area since 1679 or 1680, close to modern Parambú (Ceará) and Teresina (Piauí). See "Carta de sesmaria conferida . . . a D. Jerônima Cardim Próis viúva do mestre-de-campo D. Jorge Velho," Recife, January 3, 1705; F. A. Pereira da Costa, *Anais Pernambucanos*, vol. 5 (Recife: 1951–1966), 75–80.

342. A. Vieira, "Voto sobre as dúvidas dos moradores," in *Obras Escolhidas*, vol. 5 (Lisbon: 1951), 353; ibid., *Cartas*, vol. 3, 677 and 685.

343. "Informação do secretário do Conselho Ultramarino acerca dos moradores da vila de São Paulo," Lisbon, June 6, 1674, *ABNRJ*, vol. 39 (1921), 132–133.

344. On the Temiminos, see B. A. Genofre Prezia, *Os indígenas do Planalto Paulista*, 156, and J. M. Monteiro, *Negros*, 62–63.

345. Ennes, *Os Palmares*, 59–61 and 150–153.

346. Following the contemporary documents, I use the word *Palmarista* to define the Palmares settlers. See L. Dantas Silva, ed., "Relação das guerras feitas aos Palmares de

Pernambuco no tempo do governador D. Pedro de Almeida, de 1675 a 1678," in *Alguns documentos para a história da escravidão*, 31.

347. Bento Sorrel Camiglio had been superintendent of the captaincy of the São Francisco river mines. See doc. of April 6, 1691, *AHU*, Angola, box 14/55.

348. "Carta autografa de d. Jorge Velho escrita do Outeiro da Barriga," July 15, 1694; Ennes, *Os Palmares*, 66–69, 79–80, 123, 135.

349. Ennes, *As guerras nos Palmares* (São Paulo: 1938), 353 and 396. The Brazilian edition of the documents contain texts not published in the Portuguese edition.

350. *Inventário dos Manuscritos da Biblioteca da Ajuda referentes à América do Sul* (Coimbra: 1946), 491. Gregório de Matos wrote a poem on the event, *Obra poética*, vol. 1 (Rio de Janeiro: 1990), 311–318.

351. Documents of 1694 published by Ennes, *Os Palmares*, 61–63 and 80–83. Caetano de Melo e Castro, made governor of Sofala and Moçambique in 1682, was nominated governor of Pernambuco in 1693 and, in 1702, viceroy of India.

352. Doc. quoted by M. Ellis, *O Monopólio do sal no Estado do Brasil 1631–1801* (São Paulo: 1955), 166n655. About the change in French naval strategy at the time, see M. Vergé-Franceschi, "Les compagnons d'armes de Tourville à Barfleur-La Hougue," in *L'Invention du vaisseau de ligne 1450–1700*, M. Acerra, ed. (Paris: 1997), 237–240.

353. "Parecer de Francisco de Brito Freyre sobre os meios da conservação do Brasil," September 2, 1654, *PLMH*, vol. 2 (1961), 45–55, 46; Vieira, *Cartas*, vol. 1, 406; ibid., *Obras escolhidas*, vol. 5, 78; Ennes, *Os Palmares*, 61.

354. V. Coaracy, *O Rio de Janeiro*, 243–244.

355. Royal letter of November 17, 1695 *DH*, vol. 83 (1695), 246–247.

356. Consultation by the Overseas Council, February 3, 1705, L. Ferrand de Almeida, *A Colônia do Sacramento*, 461.

357. In a context similar to the nineteenth century Boers War, the *Emboaba War* featured the Paulistas' armed resistance to control the gold-mining areas, against newcomers from other captaincies and Portugal.

358. José Bonifácio de Andrada e Silva (1763–1838), a Brazilian-born scientist and statesman, considered as the main mentor of Brazilian Independence, Oliveira Martins, *O Brasil e as colônias portuguesas*, 100.

Chapter 7

1. L. de Camões, *Os lusíadas*, cantos VII.14.7 and X.63.3, 178 and 262. On King João IV's phrase, dubbing Brazil the "milch cow" of Portugal, see Visconde de Santarém, *Quadro elementar*, vol. IV, book 2, pp. CXLVIII-CLI and Cabral de Mello, *O Negócio*, 45. On the importance of Brazil in seventeenth-century economy, see J. Pedreira, "Costs and

Financial Trends in the Portuguese Empire, 1415–1822," in *Portuguese Oceanic Expansion 1400–1800*, F. Bethencourt and D. R. Curto, eds. (New York: 2007), 49–87.

2. Conceived in the nationalist context of the Braganza's restoration, Balthazar Telles's work was a response to the pro-Habsburg interpretation of the Ignatian evangelization expounded by Spanish Jesuit Pedro da Ribadeneyra in his *Chronica de las Provincias de España de la Compañia de Jesus*. See Telles, *Chronica*, vol. 1, 438–439.

3. Various texts underline such postulates; see, for instance, Feliciano Dourado in the Overseas Council on June 18, 1671, *AHU*, Angola, box 10/55, and further, among other documents, *AHU*, Angola, box 6/59, document of 1656, 7/9, documents of 1660, 7/97, 11/38, document of 1675, 14/109; documents of 1656 and 1687; in *MMA¹*, vol. 12, 7; vol. 14, 87–88; document of 1797, in *AA*, vol. 16 (1959), 2nd series, 14.

4. Carneiro published in 1641 a book, *Oração apodíxica aos scismaticos da pátria*," with the following authorship "pello Doutor Diogo Gomez Carneiro brasiliense natural do Rio de Janeiro" (Lisbon: 1641). To my knowledge, this is the first printed work by an author underlining his Brazilian origins with the noun from the Latin *Brasiliensis*, then employed in ecclesiastical documents referring to the Amerindians in Portuguese America.

5. Royal provision of June 1, 1661, and consultation to the Overseas Council of November 22, 1662, *ABNRJ*, vol. 39 (1917), 128. What is perhaps more relevant is that another manuscript of a book on Brazil's history, written around 1630, also disappeared. Indeed, the celebrated Portuguese historian and poet Manuel de Faria e Sousa wrote an essay entitled "America Portuguesa." The book should complete Faria e Sousa's oeuvre on the Portuguese domains in Europe and overseas. In the 1630s, Duarte de Albuquerque Coelho (1591–1658), the fourth Pernambuco donatary, presented the Faria e Sousa's manuscript to the royal council of Spain to obtain the required print license. But the manuscript was then stolen and probably destroyed by Diogo Soares, count-duke of Olivares's protégé and Albuquerque Coelho's enemy. See P. de Faria e Sousa, *Asia Portuguesa*, vol. 2 (Lisbon, 1674), III–IV.

6. Varnhagen, and others historians who followed him, mentioned Bahia, Recife, and Rio de Janeiro, but did not cite Luanda among the municipal councils that funded Gomes Carneiro's *História do Brasil*. See F. A. de Varnhagen, *História Geral do Brazil*, book 2 (Rio de Janeiro: 1854, 1857), 53.

7. F. Pyrard, *Voyage de François Pyrard, de Laval. Contenant sa navigation aux Indes orientales, Maldives, Moluques*, Bresil . . . (Paris: 1619), 231–232. Pyrard refers mostly to the first four itineraries. In fact, the route Brazil-Angola-Brazil, corresponding to the two last itineraries, was taken regularly only after Salvador de Sa's fleet retook Angola in 1648.

8. Vessels leaving Lisbon outside the propitious season stayed sometimes "two or three months in the *Palmar*, unable to cross that point, and this is in the mouth of the river Congo." See "Monção da viagem de Angola" (end of the sixteenth century), *MMA¹*, vol. 15, 362. The doldrums are located for most of the year north of the equator, but from

February through March their effects can be felt from five degrees north to five degrees south of the equator. See "Southwest Coast of Africa," *Sailing Directions (En Route)*, 3.

9. "Monção da viagem de Angola," *MMA¹*, vol. 15, 362–363. There are other instances of the tribulations in the Angola-bound voyages from the north. In August 1641, after two months and twenty-five days at sea, now close to Luanda, the Dutch fleet approached the caravel *Jesus, Maria, Joseph*, which had departed from Madeira to Luanda loaded with wine casks, three months and twenty-one days before, one month more than the slow fleet of nineteen warships that had come from Pernambuco. See "Journal de bord du voyage du Brésil à la côte d'Afrique de l'expédition de 1641," May 30–Aug. 26, 1641, *ACA*, vol. 1, 60–73. Sailing direct to Luanda, Governor Tristão da Cunha left Lisbon at the end of March 1666, hit a calm area at the "Palmar,"—the doldrums—and docked in the Angolan capital four and a half months later. See *AHU*, Angola, box 9/62.

10. R. Capeans, "Resumo do estudo arqueológico das viagens de Lisboa a Angola e de Lisboa à ilha de Santa Helena, em navios de vela, baseado na 'Relatione del Reame di Congo et delle circonvicine contrade' de Duarte Lopez & Filippo Pigafetta," in *Primeiro Congresso da História da Expansão Portuguesa no Mundo*, vol. 2 (Lisbon: 1938), 153–175.

11. A. Mariz de Carneiro, "Derrota de Portugal pera Angola," in *Regimento de pilotos*, 26; M. Pimentel, *Roteiro de Portugal para Angola*, BNL, res. 862, 267–270.

12. Abreu e Brito, *Sumário*, 83–84. See Pigafetta, 10.

13. Letter by apostolic collector to cardinal Pavilicino, Lisbon, October 19, 1624, *MMA¹*, vol. 15, 538. "By way of Bahia and of Pernambuco I have reported to Y.M. for everything that happened this year[. . . .]" Thus governor João de Lencastre began his letter to the king, Luanda, October 28, 1690, *AHU*, Angola, box 14/38.

14. Doc. of December 18, 1640, *ACA*, vol. 1, 11.

15. Doc. of June 17, 1799, *AA*, vol. 1, 1st series (1933).

16. Miller, *Way*, 321–322.

17. D. B. Domingues da Silva has show that 65 percent of slaves disembarked in Maranhão and Pará and came on a triangular trade circuit, with vessels leaving Portugal to Africa and then sailing to São Luís or Belém. D. B. Domingues da Silva, "The Atlantic Slave Trade to Maranhão, 1680–1846: Volume, Routes and Organization," *Slavery & Abolition* 29, no. 4 (2008), 477–501.

18. The royal decree of March 18, 1684, on the the slavers' overall tonnage (*arqueação*). See *MMA¹*, vol. 13, 551–558, here 553. TSTD, accessed December 2015.

19. A. de Abreu, *Tratado de las Siete Enfermedades* (Lisbon: 1623), 152.

20. Doc. of 1610, *HCJB*, vol. 8, 398: 40,000 *alqueires* of manioc flour per year. The volume corresponded to 1.45 million liters. As it was roughly grated flour, 1 kg = 2.14 liters. Such was the basis for the calculations I made.

21. Pyrard, *Voyage*, 335–336.

22. Referring to the economic improvements introduced by Diogo Menezes e Siqueira, governor-general of Brazil (1608–1612), V. do Salvador wrote: "[I]n Rio de Janeiro [. . . there are] over forty (sugar-cane) mills." V. do Salvador, *História*, 421.

23. For a discussion on this matter, see J. Daniels and C. Daniels, "The Origin of the Sugarcane Roller Mill," *Technology and Culture* 29, no. 3 (1988), 493–535.

24. Brandão, *Diálogos*, 87 and 95.

25. Barros de Castro, A. "Brasil, 1610—Mudanças técnicas e conflitos sociais," *Pesquisa e Planejamento Econômico* 10, no. 3 (1980), 679–712.

26. Schwartz, *Sugar*, tables 7–1, 127–129, and 165.

27. "Relatório do diretor Moortamer, Luanda 14.10.1642." Moortamer's informant was Luís, Captain Antônio Bruto's former Angolan slave. Luís had traveled the hinterlands in the company of Bruto, as well as having twice done return voyages from Brazil aboard slavers, accompanying the captives by order of his master. See *ACA*, vol. 1, 353–354; *HGGA*, vol. 3, 341, 360. On the *emba*, see G. Merolla, *Breve e succinta relazione*, 97–98.

28. "La situation d'Angola," Recife, 1643; L. Jadin, "Rivalités luso-neerlandaises au Soyo, Congo, 1600–1675," *Bulletin Historique Belge de Rome* 36 (1964), 236.

29. Bettendorf, *Crônica*, 498.

30. "Les XIX aux directeurs de Luanda," June 14, 1642, *ACA*, vol. 1, 296–302, and vol. 2, 711–712. See also F. Guerra, "Medicine in Dutch Brazil 1624–1654," in *Johan Maurits van Nassau Siegen: A Humanist Prince in Europe and Brazil 1604–1679*, E. van den Boogaart, H. R. Hoetink, and P. J. P. Whitehead, eds. (The Hague: 1979), 475.

31. "Petição dos moradores de Luanda," August 12, 1664, *AHU*, Angola, box 8/35. In a voyage between Luanda and Bahia or Recife (the source does not specify the exact destination) lasting only one month, taking place between the end of December and the end of January 1650, a vessel overloaded with 900 slaves recorded an epidemic that caused 250 [27.7 percent] deaths among the deportees. Despairing with the loss, the captain tried a grotesque suicide aboard his slaver. See *DHCMA*, vol. 1, 379.

32. Representation of the Luanda Municipal Council in 1664 relates the costs of the "old right" (4,000 *réis*) of the "new right" (3,000 *réis*) created in 1649 by Salvador de Sá, and the 4,000 *réis* tax on slaves; at the time, one "piece" was worth around 25,000 *réis*. See *HGGA*, vol. 2, 199. Thus, export taxes corresponded to 28 percent around that time, instead of the 20 percent recorded forty years earlier. See note 102 of chapter 1.

33. Each hundred slaves were allocated twenty-five casks of water. For the calculation of the daily volume of water per individual I considered the period of six weeks, the average duration of the Luanda–Rio de Janeiro trip. See Royal Order September 23, 1664, *AHU*, Angola, box 8/46. The ration for the Iberian infantry in Pernambuco included, in 1637, 1.6 liters, but also 0.7 liters of wine per day and per man. See Norton, *A Dinastia dos Sás*, 163–164.

34. Consultation to the Overseas Council, May 15, 1694, *AHU*, Angola, box 15/14.

35. K. F. Kiple and B. T. Higgins, "Mortality Caused by Dehydration during the Middle Passage," in *The Atlantic Slave Trade: Effects on Economies, Societies, and Peoples in Africa, the Americas, and Europe*, J. E. Inikor and S. L. Engerman, eds. (London: 1992), 320–338, here 325–328.

36. R. L. Cohn, "Deaths of Slaves in the Middle Passage," *JEH* 45 (1985), 685–692; R. L. Stein, *The French Slave Trade in the Eighteenth Century: An Old Regime Business* (Madison, WI: 1979); H. S. Klein, *The Atlantic Slave Trade*, 138–139; H. S. Klein, S. L. Engerman, R. Haines, and R. Shlomowitz, "Transoceanic Mortality: The Slave Trade in Comparative Perspective," *The William and Mary Quarterly* 58, no. 1 (2001), 93–118; D. Eltis, F. D. Lewis, and K. McIntyre, "Accounting for the Traffic in Africans: Transport Costs on Slaving Voyages," *The Journal of Economic History* 70, no. 4 (2010), 940–963.

37. Eltis and Richardson, *Atlas*, 160, 167–187.

38. The version of the Portuguese slaver traders' "generosity" was diffused by the Dutch themselves, grounded on the reports of Moortamer, WIC's director in Luanda. The document related the hygienic and feeding practices of the Lusitanian slave traders aiming to decrease mortality during the crossing at the beginning of the 1640s. See *ACA*, vol. 1, 350–359. At the end of the seventeenth century, these documents were published all over Europe by Dapper. See Dapper, *Description de l'Afrique*, 368.

39. Abreu, *Tratado de las siete enfermedades*; Guerra, "Aleixo de Abreu 1568–1630," *Journal of Tropical Medicine and Hygiene* 71 (1968), 55–69.

40. K. F. Kiple and B. T. Higgins, "Mortality Caused by Dehydration," 329–330; A. de Abreu, *Tratado de las Siete Enfermedades*, BNL, res. no. 558.

41. *ACA*, vol. 1, 350–359; Dapper, *Description de l'Afrique*, 368.

42. Based on a few series on maritime mortality and on statistical projections, Miller calculates mortality in the Rio de Janeiro–Angola axis at the end of the eighteenth century and beginning of the nineteenth in the following way: 40 percent of the slaves purchased in the backland fairs of Angola died before arriving at the seashore ports, 10 to 12 percent passed away during the month-long wait at the port, and 9 percent during the Atlantic crossing. The lot of survivors (40 percent of those who had left the Angolan fairs) was reduced to half in the course of the first four years in Brazil. Of the total contingent of Africans culled from inland Angola, only one in five individuals was able to survive the fourth year of slavery in Portuguese America. See J. C. Miller, "Mortality in the Atlantic Slave Trade: Statistical Evidence on Casualty," *Journal of Interdisciplinary History* 11, no. 3 (1981), 385–423.

43. Doc. of November 7, 1576, *MMA¹*, vol. 3, 145–147; A. Carreira, *Os portugueses nos rios de Guiné 1500–1900* (Lisbon: 1984), 66.

44. The flour measure in Angola was the *enseque* or *exeque*, holding two *alqueires*, that is, approximately seventy liters. Following the calculation exposed in note 15, the enseque must

have weighed thirty-two kg, close to the *alqueire do Pará*'s thirty kg, holding two *paneiros*, the standard measure for manioc flour in Amazônia. One concludes that the calculated figure of 540 tons/year consumption in Luanda in the 1660s can be related to the total of 680 tons/year exported from Rio into Angola around 1610, when trade was more intense and when the cultivation of manioc in Africa was not yet carried out. See *DHCMA*, vol. 1, 31–32.

45. There were manioc fields along the trade route between Luanda and the Katanga Lunda empire. See J. Vansina, "Finding Food and History of Precolonial Equatorial Africa—A Plea," *African Economic History* 7 (1979), 9–20. I owe Alfredo Margarido for first indicating this issue.

46. Klein, "The Impact of the Atlantic Slave Trade on the Societies of the Western Sudan," 30.

47. *MMA¹*, vol. 8, 79 passim.

48. For the value of manioc and maize production, see doc. of 1633, *MMA¹*, vol. 8, 244; for the price of slaves, see Heintze, "The Angolan," 62.

49. Rio de Janeiro traders who exported flour to Angola also protested against the requisitions, for feeding the troops, carried out by local authorities. See, for instance, the petition by Domingos Soares Guedes, dated December 1630, from Rio de Janeiro, "Processo das despesas feitas por Martim de Sá, no Rio de Janeiro 1628-1638," *ABNRJ*, LIX (1940), 101–103.

50. Consultation to the Overseas Council, February 19, 1688, *AHU*, Angola, box 13/56; letter by governor F. I. Sousa Coutinho, March 4, 1766, *Livros de Ofícios para o Reino 1726–1801*, Luanda, 1959, 80; Luís Lobo, nominated governor of Angola in May 1682, arrived in Luanda in September 1684, *MMA¹*, vol. 14, 10n1.

51. Royal order of April 20, 1740, *ABNRJ*, vol. 28 (1906), 212–213; doc. of August 8, 1817, *AA*, vol. 18, 2nd series (1961), 131–132.

52. Braudel, *Civilisation Matérielle*, vol. 1, 131.

53. Couto, *O zimbo na historiografia angolana*.

54. Brazil zimbos' exports to Africa are barely mentioned in the most complete study on the matter. See J. Hogendorn and M. Johnson, *The Shell Money of the Slave Trade* (Cambridge, MA: 1986), 12, 166n91.

55. Although the Manueline Ordinations (book 5) had considered the *caurim* trade between Upper Guinea and the Mina Coast as a royal monopoly since 1514, no similar measure regarding the *zimbo* trade between Bahia and Congo-Angola is known.

56. Doc. of 1612, *MMA¹*, vol. 6, 108; doc. of 1618, vol. 6, 342–343.

57. Salvador, *História*, 110. *Búzio* is the general Brazilian term for concave seashells, be it the *Cyprea moneta* or the *Cyprea annulus*. The "zimbo" is the *Ollinvancillaria nana*. For western Africa, see the synthesis by A. F. Iroko, "Cauris et esclaves en Afrique Occidentale entre le XVIe. et le XIXe s.," *Actes du Colloque International sur la Traite des Noirs (CITN)*, vol. 1 (Paris: 1988), 193–204.

58. Vieira, "Papel Forte" *Obras Escolhidas*, vol. 4, 45.

59. J. B. Nardi, *O fumo brasileiro no período colonial* (São Paulo: 1996), 276–280.

60. A *cofo* contained 10,000 small *zimbos*. See Heintze, *Fontes*, vol. 1, 116; Parreira, *Documento*, 22.

61. "Relação do bispo frei Manuel Baptista, Lisboa, 7.9.1619," written after ten years of episcopal activity in São Salvador. See *MMA[1]*, vol. 6, 375–384, 383. See A. Parreira, *Documento n 105 da caixa n. 1, Angola, manuscrito avulso depositado no Arquivo Histórico Ultramarino, "Procissam, relação das festas que a residência de Amgolla fez na beatificação do beato pe. Fco. Xavier (1620),"* (Lisbon: 1993).

62. Provision of January 20, 1658, *AHU*, Angola, box 8/64.

63. *AC*, 34–35 and 545–546.

64. Director Moortamer to the Recife Council, Luanda, January 24, 1642, *ACA*, vol. 1, 196.

65. P. M. Martin, *The External Trade*, 62. The Dutch purchased from the Angolistas most of the slaves sent to Pernambuco between 1637 and 1645. Later, they set up their own trade networks in the ports to the north of Congo and in the Gulf of Guinea. See E. van den Boogaart and P. C. Emmer, "The Dutch Participation in the Atlantic Slave Trade 1596–1650," in *The Uncommon*, J. Hogendron and H. Gemery, 353–375.

66. "Condições de paz do reino do Congo," February 19, 1649, *MMA[1]*, vol. 10, 326–328. For a requisition already formulated in 1627, see Heintze, *Fontes*, vol. 1, 261. J. Thornton seems not to have taken into account the protests by Bishop Soares and by the kings of Congo against the import of *zimbos*, as he states that such imported money did not have an impact on Congolese monetary circulation, J. K. Thornton, *The Kingdom* . . . , 33.

67. Vieira, "Papel Forte," *Obras Escolhidas*, vol. 4, 45.

68. Silva Correa, *História*, vol. 1, 136–137.

69. M. Florentino, "The Slave Trade, Colonial Markets, and Slave Families in Rio de Janeiro, Brazil, ca. 1790–ca. 1830," in *Extending the Frontiers: Essays on the New Transatlantic Slave Trade Database* (New Haven: 2008), 275–312, 286.

70. J. S. Hogendorn and H. A. Gemery, "Abolition and Its Impact on Monies Imported to West Africa," in *The Abolition of the Atlantic Slave Trade*, D. Eltis and J. Walvin, eds. (Madison, WI: 1981), 99–116, 101. A study on the *samoos* (Burkina-Fasso) comes to analogous conclusions in F. Heritier, "Des cauris et des hommes—Production d'esclaves et accumulation de caurís chez les Samoo," in *L'esclavage en Afrique précoloniale*, C. Meillassoux, ed. (Paris: 1975), 477–508. For a study on the *caurim* emphasizing the role played by political power in the establishment of a monetary standard, against an interpretation by Hogendorn and Johnson (*The Shell Money*), based on Gresham's Law and on the quantitative Theory of Money, see C. A. Gregory, "Cowries and Conquest: Towards a Subaltern Quality Theory of Money," *Comparative Studies in Society and History* 38, no. 2 (1996), 195–217.

71. "Informação dada ao Conselho Ultramarino (. . .) pelo sr. Jacinto Pereira Carneiro,"

in *Annaes do Conselho Ultramarino*, 1st series (Lisbon: 1854–1858), 17–21. For a study on a similar reaction, taken pace in the Congolese watershed, see J. Vansina, "Trade and Markets among the Kuba," in *Markets in Africa*, P. Bohannan and G. Dalton, eds. (New York: 1965), 190–210.

72. They relayed information from Luandans who had escaped from Recife, where they had been sent as prisoners. See the letter of November 27, 1646, *Cartas . . . ao conde da Vidigueira*, vol. 2, 88–89. In another occasion, Fernandes Vieira alerted Lisbon that three Spanish ships from the Canary Islands smuggled wine into Luanda, June 6, 1653, *AHU*, C.U., Consultas Mistas, cod. 15, fs. 44.

73. M. L. Esteves, "Para o estudo das relações comerciais de Angola com as Índias de Castela e Gênova no período da Restauração 1640–1668," *Studia* 51 (1992), 34–35.

74. Letter of June 26, 1653, *AHU*, C.U., Consultas Mistas, cod. 15, fl. 44.

75. April 17, 1654, *AHU*, C.U., Consultas Mistas, cod. 15, fs. 94, 94v.

76. Decision by the Overseas Council, made after the blockage of the Tagus by Parliament's fleet, commanded by Blake, in the wake of the shelter given by Portugal to Prince Ruppert's monarchist fleet, cousin of Charles II. See letter of December 9, 1650, *BNL*, res., cod. 7627; E. Prestage, *D. Francisco Manuel de Melo—Esboço biographico* (Coimbra: 1914), 241–247.

77. Brito Freyre, *Viagem da Armada da Companhia do Commércio e frotas do Estado do Brasil*, 4–6 and 43–44; "Carta do conde de Atouguia para D. Luís de Almeida," Bahia, July 27, 1655, *DH*, vol. 48 (1928), 61–62.

78. "Carta de Pedro Vieira da Silva, 31.12.1655," *AHU*, Angola, box 6/35. Letter by Francisco Ferreira Rabelo to the king (D. João IV), September 24, 1655, London, about preparations by the Dutch to defend trade in the Baltic Sea, and the opinion of the general-at-sea of the states preferring to launch a fresh attack on Portuguese colonies, believing that this attack was aimed at Angola, due to the lack of defensive capacity in that coast and the interest in the trading in slaves, *AHU*, Rio de Janeiro, box 3, doc. 79.

79. Decision by the Overseas Council, December 1655, *AHU*, Angola, box 6/35.

80. Mauro, *Portugal*, 516–517; Schwartz, *Sugar Plantations*, 163–166.

81. Consultation of February 12, 1656, *MMA¹*, vol. 12, 7. Shortly before, Brito Freyre stated that the surge in sugar prices could relaunch a Dutch foray in Brazil, "Parecer de Francisco de Brito Freyre sobre os meios da conservação do Brasil," September 2, 1654, *PLMH*, v. 2, 52.

82. G. Scelle, *La Traite Negrière*, vol. 1 (Paris: 1906), 483–493.

83. F. Leite de Faria, "A situação de Angola e Congo apreciada em Madrid em 1643," *Portugal em África* 52 (1952), 235–248; Madrid, February 8, 1644, *MMA¹*, vol. 15, 578.

84. Doc. of February 17, 1645, *MMA¹*, vol. 15, 586. On Portuguese spying methods of the period, see F. Cortés Cortés, *Espionagem e contra-espionagem numa guerra peninsular 1640–1668* (Lisbon: 1989).

85. L. de Aspurz, *Redin, soldado y misionero 1597–1651* (Madrid: 1951); *DHCMA*, vol. 1, 290, and vol. 2, 407–408; F. Leite de Faria, "Frei João de Santiago and his 'Relação' on the Capuchins in the Congo," *Portugal em África* 59 (1953), 316–333.

86. "Sobre as novas que há de ir hua não fretada pela contratação de Sevilha aos portos de Angola a resgatar escravos para as índias," doc. of September 11, 1647, *BNRJ*, Manuscritos—Consultas Mistas do Conselho Ultramarino, cod. 24, livro de registro, 1647–1652, vol. 2, fl. 81.

87. July 1666, *BNL*, res., 111–112, 261–266, and 261. To understand Portuguese paranoia, consider that some Italian missionaries were indeed subjects of the king of Spain. Lord of the duchy of Milan and of the kingdom of Naples and of Sicily, dominating the Pontifical States, threatening Genoa and Venice, Felipe IV held sovereignty over a good part of Italy. Only the duchies of Parma, Mantua, and Savoy were free from his rule. But he subjugated the pope, stopping the Holy See from recognizing the Portuguese government. Thus the suspicions of the Capuchin mission to the Congo, organized by Propaganda Fide and by the Order's Spanish province. D. Alden seems not to have taken this fact into consideration when he examined the nationality of the Ignatians recruited for the Portuguese missions. See Alden, "The Making of an Elite Enterprise," 16–17.

88. Doc. of October 15, 1681, *MMA¹*, vol. 13, 523.

89. At practically the same time that Luanda was retaken, Sousa Coutinho wrote to the king: "Consider Y.M. an article of faith that if we do not give negroes to the Company (WIC), (that) there is no agreement with them [the Dutch], and if Salvador Correa had expelled the Dutch from Angola, we shall have no peace but by the means we offer [negroes] to them." The Hague, August 24, 1648, *CD*, vol. 3, 77–81, 80.

90. "Representação do Conselho da Fazenda," May 23, 1656, *ANTT*, manuscripts of the Livraria, book 1146, 63.

91. Vieira, "Papel Forte," *Obras Escolhidas*, vol. 4, 90.

92. Silva Rêgo, *A Dupla Restauração*, 235.

93. D. Birmingham, *Trade and Conflict in Angola: The Mbundu and Their Neighbours Under the Influence of the Portuguese 1483–1790* (London: 1966), 111–132; Thornton, *The Kingdom of Congo*, 73–75; Miller, *Way of Death*, 315–378; van den Boogaart, "The Trade Between Western Africa," 382.

94. Royal letter of April 26, 1649, *MMA¹*, vol. 10, 344.

95. *HGGA*, vol. 2, 369n5.

96. The expedition's contingent was composed, officially, of 1,200 men, comprised of 400 sailors and crew plus 300 soldiers. But A. Vieira gives a bigger figure, accusing Salvador de Sá of leaving Rio unguarded as he took away 1,000 men, who were added to a further 1,000 coming from Lisbon, *Cartas*, vol. 1, 223. Finally, expeditionary Luis Felix Cruz, witness to the events, wrote that 750 new soldiers were recruited in Rio. See E. Prestage, "As lutas luso-holandesas em Angola de 1641 a 1648 contadas por Luis Felis Crus, testemunha

ocular," *Academia de Sciencias de Lisboa, Boletim da Classe das Letras*, vol. 13 (1918–1919), 41–76. Written in Luanda in 1649, in the heat of the hour, and published in Lisbon in 1651, very likely on the pay of Salvador de Sá, Luís Felix Cruz's report is dedicated to Salvador's wife, Catarina de Velasco. See F. Topa, "Entre a *Terra de gente oprimida* e a *Terra de gente tostada:* Luís Félix da Cruz e o primeiro poema *angolano*," *Literatura em Debate* 7, no. 13 (2013), 122–147.

97. Consultation to the Overseas Council, July 8, 1649, *MMA¹*, vol. 10, 357.

98. Letter by Bonaventura da Sorrento to the Propaganda Fide, Luanda, April 21, 1650, *ACA*, vol. 3, 1221–1223.

99. Letter by Njinga to Governor Chichorro, Matamba, December 13, 1655, *DHCMA*, vol. 2, 330–332.

100. To the old right of 4,000 *réis* per "piece," a "new right" of 3,000 *réis* was added, *MMA¹*, vol. 10, 360. See note 32.

101. Patent granted to Manuel de Almeida Falcão, a captain of the vessel *Santo Milagre*, bound to Buenos Aires, Luanda, January 4, 1649, *Livro de Patentes*, 105.

102. *AHU*, Angola, box 5/157. See also appendix 4.

103. Esteves, "Para o estudo das relações comerciais," 41; R. Valladares Ramirez, "El Brasil y las Indias españolas durante la sublevación de Portugal 1640–1668," *Cuadernos de Historia Moderna* 14 (1993), 151–172, here 161–162.

104. Docs. of October 5, 1659 and April 14, 1660, *PLMH*, vol. 2, 242 and 246–247.

105. Royal orders of April 23 and 26, 1649, *AHU*, cod. 275, sheets 147 and 147v.

106. On the relay trade (*échanges par relais*) and the trade expedition (*négoce par expédition*) in West Africa, see Meillassoux, *The Development of Indigenous Trade*, 3–86. On Angola's context, see Miller, *Way of Death*, 189–192.

107. Consultation to the Overseas Council, August 14, 1661, *AHU*, Angola, 7/14.

108. Document of May 8, 1650, *AA*, vol. 2 (1936), 7–8.

109. Doc. of October 3, 1657, *AHU*, Angola, box 6/133.

110. *AHU*, Angola, cod. 15, fl. 81v, 6/133; *HGGA*, vol. 2, 69–72, 497.

111. R. Boxer, "Subsídios para a história dos capitães-gerais e governadores de Macau 1557–1770," *Estudos para a história de Macau*, vol. 1 (Lisbon: 1991), 227.

112. *AHU*, Angola, 6/165. A new church under the same patron was built in 1748 and still exists in Benguela.

113. Vidal received the *São Pedro do Sul* decorations and the mayorship (*alcaidaria*) of Marialva and Moreira. His natural son, Francisco Vidal de Negreiros, obtained an annual pension and the habit of the Order of Christ. His nephew, Antônio Curado Vidal, also obtained the same privileges. João Fernandes Vieira, a mulatto, despite "vicious remarks by a number of contemporaries regarding the color of his skin," writes Francis Dutra, received the Order of Christ (1652), the commandery of Santa Eugenia de Ala (1653), and the commandery of São Pedro de Torrados (1655). See *HGB*, vol. 2, book 3, 93n50;

A. Machado de Faria, *O mestre de campo João Fernandes Vieira, herói da Restauração de Pernambuco* (Lisbon: 1955), 243–248; F. A. Dutra, *Military Orders in the Early Modern Portuguese World* (Aldershot, UK: 2006), 31.

114. João Fernandes Vieira received a patent on July 8, 1654, and took office on April 18, 1658. André Vidal de Negreiros received a patent on November 2, 1654, and took office on May 10, 1661. See "Catálogo dos Governadores do reino de Angola," *AA*, vol. 3 (1937), 450–549, 545.

115. Since 1650, Francisco Barreto had requested this post for the friar. See *MMA¹*, vol. 10, 622–623; royal letter of May 16, 1655, *MMA¹*, vol. 11, 482–483, Cabral de Mello, *Olinda Restaurada*, 186. He did not take office in the end, however, because the post was not confirmed by the pope. About his presence in Luanda in 1636, see *MMA¹*, vol. 14, 488.

116. *AHU*, Overseas Council, cod. 14, sheet 145v; Barcellos, *Subsídios*, vol. 1, part 2, 12–13; Figueroa had been nominated on April 27, 1654. See J. A. Gonsalves de Mello, *Francisco de Figueroa—Mestre de campo do Terço das Ilhas em Pernambuco* (Recife: 1954), 33. Roque de Barros Rego is probably one of the four combatant brothers of Cristóvão de Barros Rego, although genealogist Borges de Macedo does not mention that fact. See A. J. V. Borges da Fonseca, "Nobiliarchia pernambucana," *ABNRJ*, vol. 47, part 1 ([1748] 1925), 468. See also *Listas cronológicas dos governadores do Ultramar português* (Lisbon: n.d.), deposited in the *AHU*.

117. Editor and commentator of the first two volumes of Cadornega's work, dean J. Mathias Delgado (d. 1932) left an important contribution to the history of the Southern Atlantic, highlighting the role played by the Angolista colonists. See *HGGA*, vol. 2, 515 and 520.

118. *Cartas de el-rei . . . ao conde de Vidigueira . . .* , vol. 2, 7–9.

119. J. Nieuhof, *Gedenkweerdige Brasiliaense Zee-en-Lant Reize*, Brazilian transl., 160.

120. Letters by Francisco Barreto to the court, December 9, 1649, and December 14, 1649, *AHU*, Overseas Council, cod. 14, fs. 203 and 204.

121. Cabral de Mello, *Olinda*, 249–293.

122. Mazarin thus increased the price to eventually recognize Spanish rights on the Portuguese Crown in the Treaty of the Pyrenees (1659). See "Instruction donnée à M. De Lionne s'en allant en Espagne," June 1, 1656, *RIAMF*, vol. 11, and "Espagne," vol. 1, 85.

123. Doc. of November 23, 1656, *MMA¹*, vol. 12, 83–84.

124. João Fernandes resquested authorization by the Overaseas Council to take 400 soldiers and 3,000 muskets. See docs. of 1656, *AHU*, Angola, box 6, nos. 83, 84, 86, and 141.

125. April 2, 1657, *AHU*, Angola, box 6/121. Francisco de Faro e Noronha, count of Odemira, president of the Overseas Council from 1651 to 1659, and member of the government junta during the regency of the Queen Luísa (1656–1666).

126. *HGGA*, vol. 2, 139.

127. Gonsalves de Mello, *João Fernandes*, vol. 2, 165–167.

128. Boxer and Aldridge, *Descriptive List of the State Papers*, vol. 1 (1661–1723), 62.

129. December 20, 1657, *AHU*, Angola, box 6/141. Manuel Berenguer would be murdered in Luanda by Captain Álvaro de Aguilar Osório, a 1648 expeditionary. Agostinho César de Andrade was nominated to and then demoted from the post of captain-major of the Itamaracá captaincy in 1674, sparking a quarrel between João Fernandes and Governor Pedro de Almeida. See Gonsalves de Mello, *João Fernandes*, vol. 2, 295–302, Cabral de Mello, *A Fronda*, 72.

130. G. Sousa Dias, *A Batalha de Ambuíla* (Lisbon: 1942), 114.

131. Doc of August 11, 1664, *AHU*, Angola, box 8/34.

132. Between 1661 and 1664, doc. of December 15, 1660, *AHU*, Angola, box 7/18 and doc. of May 7, 1661, box 7/28.

133. Gonsalves de Mello, *João Fernandes*, vol. 2, 170; "friar Dust" was later leader of a dissidence to emancipate the Benedictins of Brazil from the Portuguese hierarchy. See E. Cabral de Mello, *Rubro Veio: O imaginario da Restauração pernambucana* (Rio de Janeiro: 1997), 237–238.

134. May 20, 1659, *AHU*, Angola, box 6/156, and February 13, 1662, box 7/63.

135. R. Delgado, *História de Angola*, vol. 3 (Luanda: n.d.), 191.

136. Consultation to the Overseas Council, June 22, 1664, *AHU*, Angola, box 8/40.

137. E. van Veen, "Les interactions luso-néerlandaises en Europe et en Asie (1580–1663)," in *L'Empire portugais*, 41–68.

138. February 15, 1659, *AHU*, Angola, box 6/159, and box 9/73–75. Boxer writes that it was the *unedifying* pigs' incident that caused the attack by João Fernandes on the Jesuits. I think the opposite took place: in the face of the animosity of the governor, the priests made use of this pretext to excommunicate him. Actually, the governor continued the anti-Jesuit offensive put in motion by Chichorro, his predecessor. See C. R. Boxer, *The Dutch in Brazil 1624–1654* (Oxford, UK: 1957), 275.

139. Luís Martins de Sousa Chichorro to the Overseas Council, Luanda, September 17, 1655, *AHU*, Angola, box 6, docs. 23 and 62.

140. Doc. of July 5, 1658, *MMA[1]*, vol. 12, 167.

141. In the decade of 1680, Afro-Brazilian Capuchin Lourenço da Silva de Mendonça, supported by the *Propaganda Fide*, militated in Rome against the slave trade. See R. Gray, "The Papacy and the Atlantic Slave Trade: Lourenço da Silva, the Capuchins, and the Decisions of the Holly Office," *Past & Present* 115 (1987), 52–68.

142. Propaganda Fide was created by Pope Gregory XV in 1622. Monsigneur Francesco Ingoli, secretary-general of the institution between 1622 and 1649, supported a missionary policy contrary to the exclusivism of the Portuguese *Padroado* (Patronage), whose statute was not recognized by Rome between 1640 and 1668. See R. Hoffman, "Propagation of the Faith," *New Catholic Encyclopaedia*, vol. 11 (London: 1967), 840–844. In an audience with King João IV's envoy, Pope Innocent X underlined Portugal's incapacity to carry out

the missionary task in the Lusitanian overseas: "His Sanctity [. . .] adding that Portugal's Conquests laid unaided, and that [. . .] even if Y.M. sent out all clergy there was in Portugal, it would not be enough to perform the least [of tasks], and for me to contradict this would amount to denying something evident and showing that I did not care for the main [motive] due to which the Conquests were granted [to the king of Portugal], which is the salvation of souls." Letter by Nuno da Cunha to the king, August 24, 1648, *MMA¹*, vol. 10, 212.

143. Letter by Capuchin Serafino de Cortona, then prefect of the Matamba mission, who had done missionary work since 1649. He had been confessor of many Luandan colonists and of Dona Bárbara, Queen Njinga's sister, who was held prisoner in the capital. See Luanda, February 10, 1655, *ACA*, vol. 3, 1,530–1,534.

144. Letter by G.-M. da Busseto, who had been living in Angola for twenty-two years, to the Propaganda Fide, Luanda, March 8, 1687, *MMA¹*, vol. 14, 47–48.

145. The conversion of Queen Njinga took place in 1656. See F. M. Gioia da Napoli, *La maravigliosa conversione alla Santa Fede di Cristo della Regina Singa e del suo regno di Matamba* (Nápoles: 1669) and *DHCMA*, vol. 2, 97–112.

146. *HGGA*, vol. 1, 416. Indeed, the precious commentaries and annotations that the learned Graciano Maria de Leguzzano wrote in his edition of the work by Cavazzi, constitute, as Adriano Carreira observed, a decisive contribution to the study of Central Africa. See *DHCMA*, vol. 2, 424–428; J. Thornton, "Legitimacy and Political Power: Queen Njinga, 1624–1663," *Journal of African History* 32, no. 1 (1991), 25–40; about Njinga see J. C. Miller, "Nzinga of Matamba in a new perspective," *J. Afr. H.* 16, no. 2 (1975), 201–216.

147. *Nganga*: a word in Kimbundu used for both native shamans and European Catholic priests, perpetuating the magical character of the clergy's intervention.

148. Doc. of April 7, 1657, *AHU*, Angola, box 6/110. About the peception of anthropophagy in Portuguese America, see L. de Mello e Souza, *Inferno Atlântico: Demonologia e colonização, séculos XVI–XVIII* (São Paulo: 1993), 58–88.

149. In its essence, the book by Gioia reproduces the report written by Gaeta himself and published in Naples in 1669. See Gioia da Napoli, *La Maravigliosa Conversione*, 119–120, 187, 199, and 406.

150. The queen died after receiving the last rites from Cavazzi. Bearing the golden crown studded with jewels, dressed in the Capuchin habit, and escorted by twelve brothers of the Rosary, two Jaga squadrons, 100 musicians, and thousands of subjects, Njinga was buried in the church of Saint Ana of Matamba. See *DHCMA*, vol. 2, 153–156.

151. Cavazzi's book was issued in Bologna in 1687. According to Leite Faria, in the same year, a review of the work appeared in the *Giornale de' Letterati* of Parma, and in the *Acta Eruditorum* of Leipzig. In the following year, the Dutch protestant publication, *Bibliothèque Universelle et Historique*, dedicated thirty-eight pages to the book. Other summaries were edited in several idioms. In 1680 there was a French edition in Lyon, in 1694 a German edition in Munich, and in 1732 the most celebrated French version, that by Dominican

Jean-Baptiste Labat, *Relation historique de l'Ethiopie occidentale* was published in Paris in five volumes, with previously unpublished complements. See F. Leite de Faria, "João Antônio Cavazzi: A sua obra e a sua vida," *DHCMA*, vol. 1, XI–LVIII.

152. Marquis de Sade, *La philosophie dans le boudoir* (Paris: [1795] 1976), 131–133. de Sade quotes as a reference one of the reeditions of the book by L. Castilhon, *Zingha, Reine d'Angola*, based on Cavazzi, reedited in 1770 in Paris, and in 1775 in Rotterdam.

153. G. W. Hegel, *Die Vernunft in der Geschichte* (*La raison dans l'histoire*) (Paris: 1965), 267–269. As is known, Hegel did not write this text: it resulted from the transcription of his lectures by his students. We do not know where the philosopher received his information on Njinga. But, as stated above, there was a German translation of Cavazzi's work from 1694. On Hegel and Africa, see O. Taiwo, "Exorcising Hegel's Ghost: Africa's Challenge to Philosophy," *African Studies Quarterly* 1, no. 4 (1998), 1–16.

154. M. M. du Bocage, *Poesias* (Lisbon: 1966), 102–103.

155. L. da Câmara Cascudo, "A rainha Jinga no Brasil," in *Made in Africa* (Rio de Janeiro: 1965), 25–32.

156. I owe this piece of information to ethnomusicologist Paulo Dias. The conversion of King Afonso I, *Njinga Muemba* (1506–1543), was staged in the Jesuit European colleges for the benefit of the seminarians, aiming to encourage missionary vocation. Thus, in the Jesuit college of Dinant (present Belgium), plays [*autos*] of such content were staged in the course of the seventeenth and eighteenth centuries. See L. Jadin, "Les Flamands au Congo et en Angola au XVIIème siècle," in *Revista Portuguesa de História*, vol. 1, book 6 (1955), 383. In Recife, in the Rosário dos Homens Pretos church, there is, since 1675, a record of the election of two slaves, one to be "Queen of the Angolas" and another to be "Queen of the crioulas," who might have taken the title of "Queen Njinga." See R. C. Smith, "Décadas do Rosário dos Pretos, documentos da irmandade," in *Alguns documentos para a história da escravidão*, L. Dantas Silva, ed. (Recife: 1988), 126. See also Marina de Mello e Souza, *Reis Negros no Brasil Escravista: História da festa de coroação do rei do Congo* (Belo Horizonte: 2002). After the death of the queen of Matamba (1663), one of her generals, Antônio Carrasco, whose native name was Njinga-Amona, launched the Jaga once again in combat against the Portuguese; then the Matamba region began to be called Jinga. In 1682, the captain of the slaver *Santo Antônio e Almas* transported seventy-four soldiers and fifteen horses from Bahia to Luanda, in aid of local authorities fighting the "Jinga war." See *AHU*, Angola, box 15/19. In this way, the name Njinga was perpetuated as if she were an immortal female warrior.

157. On Queen Njinga in today's Angolan literature, see I. Mata, "Representações da rainha Njinga/Nzinga na literatura angolana," in idem, ed., *A Rainha Nzinga Mbandi— História, Memória e Mito* (Lisbon: 2014), 23–46.

158. See comments in the "Feminist Majority Newsletter," fall of 1997, on the book by E. DeLamotte, N. Meeker, and J. O'Barr, eds., *Women Imagine Change: A Global Anthology of Women's Resistance from 600 B.C.E. to Present* (New York: 1997). For the UNESCO

celebration of anniversaries in 2013, see "350th Anniversary of the Death of Queen Nzinga Mbande Ngola Kiluanji (Kingdom of Matamba-Ndongo), Emblematic Figure of the Struggle against Slavery and for Women's Empowerment in Africa (1583–1663)," http://www.unesco.org/new/en/unesco/events/prizes-and-celebrations/celebrations/anniversaries-celebrated-by-member-states/2013/, accessed in April 2015. See also the book (which I have not yet read) by a leading historian of Angola, Linda M. Heywood, *Njinga of Angola: Africa's Warrior Queen* (Cambridge, MA: Harvard UP, 2017).

159. Salvador, through his father, Martim de Sá, and his aunt, countess of Linhares, founder of the college of Santo Antão in Lisbon, had strong links with the Jesuits. See "Carta de Salvador de Sá ao geral dos jesuítas," May 10, 1648, *MMA¹*, vol. 10, 147–148.

160. Consultation of the Overseas Council August 3, 1656, *AHU*, Angola, box 6/62, and *MMA¹*, vol. 12, 44–46.

161. Doc. of 1632, *MMA¹*, vol. 8, 171. This stipend of 2,000 *cruzados*, or 80,000 *reis*, established in 1615, would be paid continuously up to 1760, the year of the expulsion of the Jesuits. See *AA*, vol. 2 (1936), 541. Reference to Chichorro's initiative is in *AHU*, Angola, box 6/62.

162. G. da Reggio and C. da Piacenza, *Viaggio*, 94.

163. November 5, 1658, *AHU*, Angola, box 6/150.

164. February 15, 1659, *AHU*, Angola, box 6/159, and November 8, 1661, box 7/51.

165. V. Magalhães Godinho, "Restauração," in *DHP*, vol. 3, 618.

166. Consultation of the Overseas Council about Governor João Fernandes Vieira's residence/residência do governo, May 27, 1665, *AHU*, Angola, box 8/110, and May 27, 1665, *AHU*, Angola, box 8/110.

167. *AHU*, Angola, box 9/72–74 and doc. of November 9, 1666, *MMA¹*, vol. 13, 50–51.

168. *DHCMA*, vol. 2, 322–323, and *ACA*, vol. 2, 1,111–1,115, 1,118–1,126.

169. On the king of Congo's diplomatic maneuvers to remove the São Salvador bishopric from the Portuguese Padroado and, with the help of Italian Capuchins, transform the country into a papal protectorate, see *MMA¹*, vol. 11, 216–226.

170. Hailing from the kingdom of Loango, the Vili had formed a mercantile community covering the Congo and Matamba areas since the mid-seventeenth century. See Thornton, *The Kingdom of Congo*, 26.

171. According to Italian Capuchin Guattini da Reggio, he saw, in 1667, an expedition of 1,400 "caboclo" soldiers departed from Recife against Palmares. See da Reggio and da Piacenza, *Viaggio*, 52.

172. Doc. of April 9, 1659, *AHU*, Angola, box 6/154, doc. of May 7, 1659, box 7/55, and doc. of May 7, 1659, *MMA¹*, vol. 12, 234–236; B. Heintze, *Asilo ameaçado: Oportunidades e conseqüências da fuga de escravos em Angola no século XVII* (Luanda: 1995).

173. Boxer, *Race Relations* (Portuguese translation), 125.

174. J. Fernandes to the Municipal Council on March 12, 1659; Municipal Council to the Overseas Council on April 29, 1659, *AHU*, Angola, box 6/154; Negreiros to the Court on December 20, 1661, *AHU*, Angola, box 7/55; declaration of war by the king of Congo signed by J. Fernandes Vieira on March 11, 1659, *MMA¹*, vo. 12, 223–230.

175. January 25, 1658, *AHU*, Angola, box 6/124, and February 12, 1661, box 7/21.

176. Letter by João Fernandes, October 6, 1660, *AHU*, Angola, 7/11. The Jesuits later alleged that the Kisama would have been pacific, thanks to their own talent as missionaries. See doc. of November 2, 1678, *MMA¹*, vol. 13, 461; Heintze, "Historical notes on the Kisama of Angola," *J. Afr. H.* 13, no. 3 (1972), 407–418.

177. Cavazzi, in his book previously censored by Capuchin superiors and by the Propaganda Fide, always speaks well of Salvador de Sá, João Fernandes, and Negreiros. As is known, Roman missionary authorities sought to keep good relations with Portuguese royal officers so as to avoid the suspicion of sympathies toward Spain or toward Congolese autonomism that weighed on the Capuchins in São Salvador do Congo. This explains why the constant references to the Portuguese and the Brasílico are always full of praise in the book. See *DHCMA*, vol. 2, 250–261.

178. October 6, 1660, *AHU*, Angola, box 7/11.

179. See, for instance, the "[c]eremonial that the viceroys of India use when they write to the kings of Asia and other potentates." See *BNL*, res., cod. 257, fl. 150.

180. Letters to the war council, doc. of September 9, 1658, *MMA¹*, vol. 12, 173.

181. May 7, 1661, *AHU*, Angola, box 7/28.

182. December 15, 1661, *AHU*, Angola, box 7/54.

183. Translation by Richard Burton, 1880 edition.

184. Petition of September 27, 1660, *AHU*, Angola, box 7/9.

185. Consultation of the Overseas Council of June 8, 1703, examining a letter by the governor of Angola, *AHU*, Angola, box 17/20.

186. Francisco de Távora, nominated governor in May 1668, would remain in office until 1676, serving, therefore, a longer term than Negreiros. But the lengthening of his term was due to the death of Pedro César de Menezes, who disappeared in a shipwreck in 1673, on his way to take office as governor of Angola.

187. Consultation of the Overseas Council, Lisbon, October 1, 1663, *AHU*, Angola, box 7/97; "Carta do vice-rei, Conde de Óbidos, para S. M. sobre o socorro de gente que há de enviar do Brasil a Angola por causa da notícia da armada com que Castela intenta invadir esta conquista," Bahia, January 31, 1664, da Fonseca, *HCJB*, vol. 1, doc. no. 1,992. The second Anglo-Dutch war (1665–1667) led London to pull back the naval cover until then given to Lisbon. Next, France entered the conflict on the side of the Low Countries. Portugal, devoid of external help, was for the first time vulnerable to a Spanish offensive. In the summer of 1665, an armada from Cadiz was expected against Lisbon, and, further,

a raid against Angola. The expedition never happened, and Schomberg's victory at Montes Claros (June 1665) put an end to the Spanish threat. See Boxer, *Salvador*, 350–352.

188. August 8, 1664, *AHU*, Angola, box 8/28; *ABNRJ*, Carta de S.M. ao Conde de Obidos, vol. 4, 1877–1878.

189. C. Selvagem, *Portugal militar* (Lisbon: 1991), 447–452; L. White, "Estrategia Geográfica y Fracaso en La Reconquista de Portugal Por La Monarquía Hispánica, 1640–1668," *Studia Historica. Historia Moderna* 25 (2003), 59–91.

190. October 29, 1665, "Relação da Batalha de Mbwila," *MMA¹*, vol. 12, 582–591, 582; Consultation of the Overseas Council of September 7, 1665, R. Delgado, *História*, vol. 3, 268n1.

191. Report by the provisor R. B. Paes Bulhões, doc. of May 16, 1664, *AHU*, Angola, box 8/8.

192. Consultation of the Overseas Council of September 27, 1660, and of May 1664, *AHU*, Angola, box 7/8 and box 8/8. After the enquiry, the royal provider [*provedor*], Bartolomeu Paes Bulhões, was persecuted and illegally removed from his post by Negreiros. But the Crown reestablished his seat and later made him a member of the Overseas Council.

193. Consultations of the Overseas Council of October 1665, *AHU*, Angola, box 8/8.

194. *MMA¹*, vol. 12, 551–552.

195. G. Saccardo, *Congo e Angola con la storia dell'antica missione dei capuccini*, vol. 1 (Venezia-Mestre: 1982–1983), 122–125.

196. Letter by A. do Couto to D. João IV, S. Salvador, October 14, 1651, *AA*, vol. 7, 2nd series (1950), 31.

197. Consultation of the Overseas Council of September 15, 1651, *MMA¹*, vol. 11, 64.

198. *MMA¹*, vol. 9 passim.

199. Letter from dean Manoel Fernandes Curado to the king, July 29, 1665, *AHU*, Angola 8/115; consultation of August 17, 1665, *MMA¹*, vol. 12, 563–564.

200. About the change in São Salvador Capuchin's policy, see the acurate analysis by Hilton, *The Kingdom of Congo*, 184–198, and further *DHCMA*, vol. 2, 415, and *ACA*, vol. 5, 1,482n5.

201. Only the version published in the *Mercúrio Portuguez* of the proclamation is known. Excepting the part analyzed above and in the arbitrary use of capital letters, the text accords with other proclamations written by the king of Congo's secretaries.

202. Until 1636 the kings of Congo belonged to the *kimpanzu* clan. With D. Álvaro VI (1636–1641), the *kimulaza* clan ascended to the throne. Álvaro VI and Garcia II (1641–1661) tried to obtain Rome's support to transform the elective monarchy into a hereditary monarchy. With the death of Mani Mulaza at Mbwila, the rival clan tried once again to take power. The Capuchin tried reunification of the kingdom. See F. Bontinck, *Diaire congolais 1690–1701 de fra Luca da Caltanisetta* (Louvain: 1970), XLVI–LI. On the Capuchin relations with king Garcia II, see Saccardo, *Congo e Angola*, vol. 1, 463–469, 475–487.

203. See A. Hilton's analysis, inspired by the remarks by S. da Leguzanno, Cavazzi's commentator: Hilton, *The Kingdom*, 198; A. Hilton, "Family and Kinship among the Congo South of the Zaïre River from the Sixteenth to the Nineteenth Centuries," *J. Afr. H.* 24, no. 2 (1983), 189–206. Francisco Bethencourt, "Creolization of the Atlantic World: The Portuguese and the Kongolese." *Portuguese Studies*, 27, no. 1 (2011) 56–69. Regarding *kimpasi* or *kimpaxi* and the *Matambula*, or *Matambola* title, see *DHCMA*, vol. 1, 99–100, and vol. 2, 469; on the *kimpaxi*, see also A. C. Gonçalves, *La symbolisation politique—Le "prophétisme" au Congo au XVIIIème siècle* (Munique: 1980), 31–34; Thornton, *The Kingdom*, 61, and G. Balandier, *La vie quotidienne au royaume de Kongo. Du XVIe au XVIIIe siècle* (Paris: 1965), 215.

204. *Mercúrio Portuguez*, 1663–1667, *BNL*, res., 111–112 (V), 261–266.

205. A. Suassuana (1927–2014) is a Brazilian playwright and author, born in João Pessoa (Paraíba), whose plays deal with the traditional popular culture of Brazil's northeast region.

206. H. de Oliveira Marques, *História de Portugal*, vol. 2 (Lisbon: 1963), 184; A. C. de Sousa, *História genealógica da Casa Real Portuguesa*, vol. 8 (Coimbra: 1949), 212.

207. M. Guattini and D. Carli, *Viaggio nel Regno del Congo* (French translation, *La Mission au Congo*) (Bologna: 1674), 129. Friar Piacenza, who wrote this section of the book, pretended he had talked with the Portuguese soldier who beheaded *Vita-a-Nkanga* at the battle of Mbwila.

208. *MMA¹*, vol. 12, 584.

209. *DHCMA*, vol. 2, 410; *MMA¹*, vol. 14, 482.

210. Delgado, *História*, vol. 3, 249–268.

211. Manoel Soares was perhaps related to field-master Jorge Luís Soares, soldier in the Brasílico war and third successor of Henrique Dias at the head of the Henriques in Pernambuco. See Loreto Couto, *Desagravos*, 457; J. A. Gonsalves de Mello, *Henrique Dias* (Recife: 1954), 71; *MMA¹*, vol. 12, 582–591, 584. On the "guerra preta," see H. Matos, "Black Troops and Hierarchies of Color in the Portuguese Atlantic World: The Case of Henrique Dias and his Black Regiment," *Luso-Brazilian Review* 45, no. 1 (2008), 6–29.

212. According to the rules laid down in 1600s military manuals, a company should hold 300 men, and ten companies formed the *terço* with 3,000 men. In practice, the companies had a fixed contingent of thirty-eight men and were completed with native warriors. See L. M. de Vasconcellos, *A arte militar* (Lisbon: 1612) 128–135.

213. Consultation of the Overseas Council of February 27, 1657, *AHU*, Angola, box 6/104; D. Albuquerque Coelho, *Memórias diárias da Guerra do Brasil* (Recife [1630–1638]: 1981), 169, 203–204.

214. Cabral de Mello, *Olinda*, 229–230. In the equipment allocated to the 1645 expedition leaving from Bahia to Angola, which included thirty-two privates from Henrique Dias' *terço*, there is reference to "geared muskets" (*mosquetes aparelhados*), but no mention of fuses or matchlocks. See *MMA¹*, vol. 9, 489.

215. Gonsalves de Mello, *Gente da nação*, 346. On the use of native fibers for producing fuses to matchlocks and guns in the Brasilico war, see J. de Laet, *Historie ofte Iaerlyck Verhael de verrichtinghen der Geoctroyeerde West-Indische Compagnie* (Brazilian translation "Historia ou Annaes dos feitos da Companhia privilegiada das Indias occidentaes desde o seu começa até ao fim do anno de 1636 [1644]," *ABNRJ* 41–42 (1919–1920), 98.

216. "(The Amerindians) smell the fire half a league away, even though there is no visible smoke." See V. do Salvador, *História*, 85 and 89. See also Calado, *O Valeroso*, vol. 5, 71–72.

217. Richshoffer, *Diário de um soldado*, 52–53.

218. P. Olinto, "Uma jóia da armaria," *Anais do Museu Histórico Nacional* 2 (1941), 129–137.

219. J. de Laet, *História ou Anais dos feitos da Companhia Privilegiada das Índias Ocidentais*), vol. 1 (Rio de Janeiro: 1916), 243, 245, 251.

220. S. Marks, "Khoisan Resistance to the Dutch in the Seventeenth and Eighteenth Centuries," *J. Afr. H.* 12, no. 2 (1971), 55–80.

221. R. A. Kea, "Firearms and Warfare on the Gold and Slave Coast from the Sixteenth to the Nineteenth Centuries," *J. Afr. H.* 12, no. 2 (1971), 209.

222. Doc. of 1665, *MMA¹*, vol. 12, 587.

223. Letter of November 6, 1666, *AHU*, Angola, box 9/71.

224. *MMA¹*, vol. 12, 587.

225. *BNL*, res., 111–112 (V), 266; *MMA¹*, vol. 12, 589; *HGGA*, vol. 2, 213; D. M. Nunes Gabriel, *Padrões da fé—Igrejas antigas de Angola* (Luanda: 1981), 67–79.

226. November 6, 1666, *AHU*, Angola, box 9/71, 9/75. About Curado Vidal, see A. J. V. Borges da Fonseca, "Nobiliarchia pernambucana" part 1, and Cabral de Mello, *A Fronda*, 89.

227. Doc. of November 2, 1687, *MMA¹*, vol. 14, 76–78.

228. "Relations Sur Le Congo du Père Laurent de Lucques (1700–1717)," 71.

229. *AHU*, Angola, box 9/71; *MMA¹*, vol. 14, 47–48; Delgado, *História*, vol. 3, 276.

230. December 7, 1665, "Carta da Câmara de Luanda," *AHU*, Angola, box 8/128.

231. Of course, at Mbwila Vita-a-Nkanga's army did not have any artillery, which was the main weapon of the Muslim victory at Ksar el-Kebir. Military historians of Colonial Africa generally ignore the Battle of Mbwila. See, for instance, D. Trim, "Early-Modern Colonial Warfare and the Campaign of Alcazarquivir, 1578," *Small Wars & Insurgencies* 8, no. 1 (1997), 1–34.

232. *MMA¹*, vol. 12, 587.

233. July 1666, *BNL*, res., 111–112 (V), 261–266.

234. *AA*, vol. 3, 1st series (1937), 500.

235. Doc. published by J. M. Delgado, *HGGA* 2, no. 69 (n.d.), 532–523.

236. Letter by André Duarte de Vasconcellos to the king, Luanda, April 15, 1667, *BNL*, res., 206, no. 137.

237. During the Angolan civil war (1975–2002) the offensives of the FAPLA, the government army, against the UNITA combatants in central Angola followed the same seasonal pattern as the colonial wars: the hostilities were usually interrupted in the rainy season.

238. In the offensive launched by Luís Mendes de Vasconcellos in 1617–1618 against Ngola Bandi, king of Ndongo, Portuguese troops also got stuck in the hinterland from the months of November to May due to the rains and floodings. Noted by J. M. Delgado, *HGGA*, vol. 1, 155.

239. Doc. of October 20, 1666, *AHU*, Angola, box 9/62; Consultation of the Overseas Council, May 24, 1667, *AHU*, Angola, box 9/93.

240. In his article on the 1667 revolt, Alves Ferronha does not mention the André Vidal de Negreiros and Brasílico role in the overthrowing and expulsion of Governor Tristão da Cunha. See A. L. Alves Ferronha, "A revolta de Luanda de 1667 e a expulsão do governador geral Tristão da Cunha," in *Diálogos Oceânicos: Minas Gerais e as novas abordagens para uma história do império ultramarino português*, J. Furtado, ed. (Belo Horizonte: 2001), 255–279.

241. "Parecer de Salvador de Sá sobre el-rei do Congo," August 21, 1672. In his report on the Kitombo battle at the Overseas Council, Salvador de Sá states, "[T]he ambitious Corporals of our army, not content with over 2,000 black prisoners, wished to acquire more, entering their lands [. . .] then the Soyo army went out to meet them and devoured our army[. . . .]" August 21, 1672, *AHU*, Angola, box 10/71; *MMA¹*, vol. 13, 113–114.

242. "Carta de Fco. de Távora a el-rei," Luanda, July 27, 1671, *AHU*, Angola, box 10/43; Gonsalves de Mello, *João Fernandes*, vol. 2, 226; S. B. Schwartz, *A Governor and His Image in Baroque Brazil: The Funereal Eulogy of Afonso Furtado de Castro do Rio de Mendonça by Juan Lopes Sierra* (Minneapolis, MN: [1676] 1979), 44.

243. June 18, 6171, *AHU*, Angola, box 10/55.

244. "Relaçam do Felice Sucesso que conseguiram [. . .] contra a rebelião de d. João rei das Pedras & Dongo," *MMA¹*, vol. 13, 143–152. See also R. Ferreira, "O Brasil e a arte da guerra em Angola (sécs. XVII e XVIII)," *Estudos Históricos* 39 (2007), 3–23.

245. *HGGA*, vol. 2, 299.

246. Doc. of May 12, 1670, *AHU*, Angola, box 10/8; *HGGA*, vol. 2, 545. In 1689, João de Lencastre, governor of Angola and later general governor of Brazil, writes to Bahia's authorities seeking with "earnest solicitation" 200 soldiers and fifty horses. See Doc. of July 28, 1689, *AHU*, ACL, Bahia, doc. 35531.

247. Regarding the recession of Brazilian colonial economy of the last quarter of the 1600s, a phenomenon in the wider picture of the general crisis of the seventeenth century, see C. A. Hanson, *Economia e sociedade no Portugal barroco 1668–1703* (Lisbon: 1986), 231–260.

248. The *Regimento de Fronteiras* of August 29, 1645, regulated the promotions, leaves of absence, pay, supplies, and general accounts of the troops in Portuguese America. The provision of October 16, 1659, confirmed the enforcement of this regiment, giving it an

effectiveness that began to be discussed in service records. See G. Salgado, ed., *Fiscais e meirinhos: A administração no Brasil colonial* (Rio de Janeiro: 1985), 102–103.

249. Thus, for instance, João de Lencastre, the prestigious cavalry captain in the battles of Montes Claros and Ameixal, obtained the post of governor of Angola (1686), to the detriment of another candidate who had fought in Brazil and in the Alentejo: Alexandre de Moura e Albuquerque, veteran of the Brasílico war, infantry captain in the first battle of Guararapes, and combatant in a minor post in the Alentejo, doc. of March 30, 1686, *AHU*, Angola, box 13/20.

250. F. Manuel de Melo, *Tácito português* (Lisbon: [1650] 1995), 151; see A. de Almeida, "D. Francisco Manuel de Melo, historiador," *Península—Revista de Estudos Ibéricos* 6 (2009), 17–60, here 36n143.

251. Doc. of April 29, 1662, *DH*, vol. 5, 1928, 146–148.

252. Regarding the fidalgos' bastards "who for the lack of estate, and burdened with the obligations of their names, find themselves in countless afflictions [. . .] India (royal service), and religion, usually welcome this kind of people." See de Melo, *Carta de Guia*, 124–125.

253. E. L. Myrup, *To Rule from Afar: The Overseas Council and the Making of the Brazilian West 1642–1807* (PhD thesis, Yale University, 2006), 115–119.

254. For a study of the post of sergeant-major in the southern Atlantic, see D. Tengwall, "A Study in Military Leadership: The *Sargento Mor* in the Portuguese South Atlantic Empire," *The A* 11, no. 1 (1983), 73–94. Although the author defines *guerra viva* merely as "combat experience," as we will see below, there were several ways to reward and evaluate the combat experience.

255. Overseas Council, September 5, 1656, *PLMH*, vol. 2, 520–521.

256. Coata-coata = *kuata-kuata* means "catch-catch" from the Kimbundu verb *kikuata* = to catch; *HGGA*, vol. 2, 105–106n2; *MMA¹*, vol. 13, 44–45; doc. of October 10, 1666, *AHU*, Angola, box 9/55.

257. Loreto Couto, *Desagravos do Brazil*, 421, 437–438. Gonsalves de Mello, "Brito Freyre e a sua História de Pernambuco," in *Nova Lusitânia*; Cabral de Mello, *O Nome e o sangue*, 223, and ibid., *A Fronda*, 87–88.

258. *AHU*, Angola, box 8/132.

259. João da Silva e Sousa (1680–1684), former governor of Rio; João de Lencastre (1688–1691), later governor-general of Brazil; Luís Cesar de Menezes (1697–1701), former governor of Rio and later governor-general of Brazil; Lourenço de Almeida (1705–1709), later governor-general of Brazil; Antônio de Albuquerque Coelho de Carvalho (1722–1725), former governor of Maranhão, of Rio de Janeiro, of São Paulo e Minas Gerais; Rodrigo César de Menezes (1733–1738), son of Luís Cesar de Menezes, quoted above, former governor of São Paulo; Antônio Álvares da Cunha (1753–1758), the count of Cunha, later first viceroy of Brazil in Rio de Janeiro; the baron of Moçamedes (1784–1790), former governor of Goiás; Fernando Antônio Soares de Noronha (1807–1810), former governor of Maranhão; Antônio de Saldanha da Gama (1807–1810), former governor of Maranhão

(1807–1810). See A. W. Pardo, *A Comparative Study of the Portuguese Colonies of Angola and Brasil and Their Interdependence from 1648 until 1825* (PhD thesis, Boston University, Boston, Massachussets, 1977), 192–194.

260. *Cachaça* is not the only instance of Portuguese intercolonial trade of manufactured products: Cape Verde sugar-cane distillate was also exported to Guinea, whence came the "fabrics of the land" [*panos da terra*] that were used in the purchase of 23 percent of the 20,000 slaves deported to Pará and Maranhão between 1756 and 1777. See Carreira, *Os Portugueses*, 65–66.

261. Braudel, *Civilisation*, vol. 1, 194–213; "Eau-de-vie," in *Dictionnaire Universel du Commerce, d'Histoire Naturelle et des Arts et Métiers*, vol. 2, J. Savary des Bruslons, ed. (Copenhague: 1759–1762), 206–216; J. J. McCusker, *Rum and the American Revolution: The Rum Trade and the Balance of Payments of the Thirteen Continental Colonies 1650–1775* (New York: 1989), 55–60.

262. For a general view of the issue, see G. Parker and L. M. Smith, eds., *The General Crisis of the Seventeenth Century*, 2nd ed. (New York: 1997).

263. W. Abel, *Agrarkrisen und Agrarkonjunktur* (French translation, *Crises agraires en Europe XIIIe–XXe siècle*) (Paris: 1973), 206–267, 432–436; F. Braudel and F. Spooner, "Prices in Europe from 1450 to 1750," *Cambridge Economic History of Europe* 4 (1967), 378–486; for the specificity of the French situation, which featured two downturn cycles (1661–1684 and 1692–1715), with a high turn cycle in between (1685–1691), see also J. Meuvret, *Études d'Histoire Économique* (Paris: 1971), 84–111.

264. Wallerstein, *The Modern World-System II*, 140–141.

265. W. Minchinton, "Patterns and Structure of Demand 1500–1750," in *The Fontana Economic History of Europe*, vol. 2 (Glasgow: 1979), 123–130.

266. Data on the correlation between the increase in *cachaça* consumption and the increase in unemployment levels were published under the title "A Dram to Forget" ("Un trago para esquecer"), *Folha de S.Paulo*, March 30, 1999. More thorough research, in the context of the new Brazilian economic crisis, reaches the same conclusions. See "Quando expectativa econômica cai, venda de cachaça dispara," *Exame*, August 12, 2016. Accessed August 2016: http://exame. abril.com.br/economia/noticias/quando-expectativa-economica-cai-venda-de-cachaca-dispara.

267. S. W. Mintz, *Sweetness and Power: The Place of Sugar in Modern History* (New York: 1986), 137–138; G. Mezza Cuadra, "Le Pisco, eau de vie du Pérou," in *Premier Symposium International sur les eaux-de-vie traditionnelles d'origine viticole* (Paris: 1991), 28–31.

268. W. V. Pokhlióbkin, *Istória vódki* (Brazilian translation, *Uma história da vodca*) (São Paulo: 1995), 61–64.

269. H. Levine, "Gentry, Jews, and Serfs: The Rise of Polish Vodka," *Review* 4, no. 2 (1980), 223–250; W. V. Pokhlióbkin, *Uma história*, 122–182.

270. In New Granada, Madrid established a monopoly in the regional production of sugar-cane distillate, sparking uprisings and conflicts among the colonists. See G. Mora de Tovar, *Aguardiente y conflictos sociales en la Nueva Granada durante el siglo XVIII* (Bogotá:

1988); M. Moreno, "Aguardientes y alcoholismo en el Mexico colonial," *Cuadernos hispanoamericanos*, vol. 42 (Madrid: 1985), 81–96; T. Lozano Armendares, *El chinguirito vindicado: El contrabando de aguardiente de caña y la política colonial* (Mexico: 1995); P. M. Rice, "Wine and Brandy Production in Colonial Peru: A Historical and Archaelogical Investigation," *Journal of Interdisciplinary History* 27 (1997), 455–479.

271. Contrary to G. Ostrander, who underplayed the rum exports and the slave trade in Massachusetts and Rhode Island, J. Coughtry demonstrated the significance of the triangular trade to Rhode Island's economy. See G. M. Ostrander, "The Colonial Molasses Trade," *Agricultural History* 30, no. 2 (1956), 77–84; ibid., "The Making of the Triangular Trade Myth," *The William and Mary Quarterly* 30, no. 4 (1973), 635–644; J. Coughtry, *The Notorious Triangle: Rhode Island and the African Slave Trade, 1700–1807* (Philadelphia: 1981), 6, 15, 110. The TSTD shows that Rhode Island figures amount to almost the half of all the US slave trade. See D. Eltis and D. Richardson, "A New Assessment of the Transatlantic Slave Trade," *Extending the Frontiers*, 28–31.

272. Stein, *The French Slave Trade in the Eighteenth Century*, 7; D. Richardson, "Slavery, Trade, and Economic Growth in Eighteenth-Century New England," in *Slavery and the Rise of the Atlantic System*, B. L. Solow, ed. (New York: 1991), 237–264; D. Mannix and M. Cowley, *Black Cargoes* (Ontario: 1976), 160–161; McCusker, *Rum and the American Revolution*, 396–401, 417–448, and 492–95. A history reader narrates the travels of American schooner *Sukey*, leaving from Bristol (Rhode Island) in 1802 laden with local distilleries' rum, sailing to Grand Popo (the Bight of Benin) to purchase slaves later sold in Havana, where it was then loaded with molasses for the making of rum in New England. See C. L. Alderman, *Rum, Slaves and Molasses: The Story of New England's Triangular Trade* (Folkstone: 1972).

273. Mauro, *Le Portugal*, graphs 512–526; Schwartz, *Sugar Plantations*, 190; V. Magalhães Godinho, *Introdução à história econômica* (Lisbon: n.d.), 173–174.

274. "Cachaça não é água," special issue on *cachaça*, and "Agrofolha," *Folha de S.Paulo*, February 18, 1993, and September 9, 1997, respectively.

275. On the *lavradores* relationship with the sugar-mill owners, see S. B. Schwartz, ed., "A Commonwealth within Itself, the Early Brazilian Sugar Industry 1550–1670," in *Tropical Babylons: Sugar and the Making of the Atlantic World, 1450–1680* (Chapel Hill: University of North Carolina Press, 2004), 158–200, here 182–198.

276. Schwartz, *Sugar Plantations*, 163–166 and 213–214, and 190, figure 7–4.

277. In Vili, the Bantu language of the Loango kingdom (south of modern Gabon), *malafú* designates any alcoholic beverage. See J. P. Rékanga, *Presénce de cognats de Bantouismes Cubains dans le Vili parlé au Gabon* (unpublished paper, Porto Velho, Brazil: 2008), 1–7.

278. Merolla, *Breve e succinta relazioneo*, 462.

279. Heintze, *Fontes*, vol. 1, 121.

280. Miller, "The Imbangala," 572.

281. Ravenstein, *The Strange Adventures*, 30.

282. *Malafo* or *malavo*, from Kikong *ma-lávu* meaning "palm wine." Extracted chiefly from the *Raphia gentili* palm tree; from *Raphia laurenti* are extracted the fiber used in the manufacture of fabrics, and it is also used to make wine. *Malafo* is also extracted from the *Elaeis guineensis*, the *dendê* palm tree, which was later transplanted from Africa into Brazil. See Anonymous, *História do reino do Congo* [1625], edited by A. Brásio (Lisbon: 1969) 40n2. Cadornega distinguishes the *malafo*, palm wine from the land, from the *malufo*, imported Portuguese wine. See *HGGA*, vol. 3, 357–359. The coconut tree itself (*Cocos nucifera*), successfully transplanted from Oceania into Brasil, does not exist on a large scale in Angola.

283. Letter by B. Afonso, January 19, 1585, *MMA*[1], vol. 3, 311–313. On the palm tree as valuble inheritable property, see P. M. Martin, "Power, Cloth and Currency on the Loango Coast," *African Economic History* 15 (1986), 1–12.

284. "Such trees [*palmeiras*] are of great use: when in waging war on the *sobas*, [who are] the king's vassals of Angola, there is nothing they more deeply feel than the cutting down of such trees, for they esteem them as we do our vines and olive groves in Europe." See Anonymous, *História*, 40; "[T]hey arrived in the king's city of Angola, who had left it unaided so [as a result] many souls were made captive, eaten and killed [also] felling the palm tree groves from which those people extract wine and oil, which is why today the village suffers great lack of everything there was before," about a Jaga raid, circa 1620, *MMA*[1], vol. 15, 476; "[T]hey abandoned their villages, which were burnt and the palm tree groves cut down, which they feel more deeply than the loss of their own sons," about the Portuguese assault on Kisama, consultation of the Overaseas Council, September 4, 1655, *AHU*, Angola, box 6/25 and box 6/27.

285. "Diário da viagem do capitão João Blaer aos Palmares em 1645," and "Relação das guerras feitas aos Palmares de Pernambuco," in *Alguns documentos*, L. Dantes Silva, ed. (Recife: 1988), 23 and 28.

286. Inventory of Governor Forjaz, doc. of 1612, *AHU*, Angola, box 1/17; *MMA*[1], vol. 6, 105.

287. July 29, 1611, *AHU*, Angola, box 1/15. J. de Laet, *Historie ofte Iaerlyck*, vol. 1, 244.

288. "Memoriais de Pedro Sardinha," 1612, *MMA*[1], vol. 6, 105, and vol. 8, 116–117.

289. *HGGA*, vol. 2, 79–80.

290. January 14, 1655, *AHU*, Angola, box 6/20.

291. *HGGA*, vol. 2, 544–545.

292. *Gerebita*: a "word from Brazil, [meaning] distillate that is made with the sugar cane sludge [borra]." See Bluteau, *Vocabulário*, vol. 4; Lopes Gama, *O Carapuceiro* (São Paulo: [1832–1842] 1996), 249.

293. Brandão, *Diálogos das Grandezas*, 129.

294. In the *candomblé de caboclo* of Bahia, the alcoholic beverage distributed among the assistants is called *malafa*.

295. M. Souto Maior, *Dicionário folclórico da cachaça* (Recife: 1973).

296. R. W. Slenes, "'Malungu, ngoma vem!': África coberta e descoberta do Brasil," *Revista USP* 12 (1992), 48–67.

297. Also called Santo Benedetto da San Fratello, the name of the town near Messina where he was born. Worshipped in Portugal since 1600, he was beatified in 1743 and canonized in 1807. His feast is celebrated on April 4, the date of his death. See *Bibliotheca Sanctorum*, vol. 2 (Roma: 1961–1970), 1,103–1,104; S. Bono, "Un saint africain pour Palerme!" *L'Histoire* 222 (1998), 16–17.

298. *HGGA*, vol. 3, 27. In 1667 the Confraria de São Benedito and the Nossa Senhora do Rosário brotherhood, both dedicated to the slaves, merged in Rio de Janeiro. See Fridman, *Donos do Rio*, 25. On the dissemination of the cult in Brazil, see chapter 2, 48n176.

299. L. Reginaldo, *Os Rosarios dos Angolas: irmandades negras, experiencias escravas e identidades africanas na Bahia setecentista* (São Paulo: 2011), chapter 2 passim; J. H. Sweet, *Recreating Africa*, 205–206.

300. Souto Maior, *Cachaça*, 123.

301. Doc. of February 17, 1647, *BNRJ*, Manuscritos, Consultas Mistas do Conselho Ultramarino, cod. 24, Livro de Registro, 1647–1652, vol. 2, fs. 12v–13.

302. G. de Freitas, *A Companhia Geral do Comércio do Brasil 1649–1720* (São Paulo: 1951), 43; about the participation of New Christians in the C.G.C., see J. I. Israel, *European Jewry in the Age of Mercantilism 1550–1750* (New York: 1991), 109–110, 119, and 139.

303. Royal provision of September 13, 1649, *ABNRJ*, vol. 39 (1917), 79.

304. A. F. P. Caetano, "*Entre a Sombra e o Sol—A Revolta Da Cachaça, A Freguesia de São Gonçalo de Amarante e a crise política fluminense, Rio de Janeiro, 1640–1667*" (master's thesis in history, Universidade Federal Fluminense, Niterói, 2003), 104–120.

305. Letter of 1655 to Salvador de Sá. See da Silva Lisboa, *Annaes*, vol. 3, 242–252; Vieira, *Cartas*, vol. 1, 240.

306. His nephew, Martim Correia Vasques, was sergeant-major of the CGC's armada, where more of his relatives were also employed. The career of Salvador de Sá's nephew shows that the Sás changed their approach in the captaincy after the head of the oligarchy came to see himself as an "overseas man" in the kingdom and not as a "colonial man," but continued to be influential. Thus, Martim Correa Vasques, sergeant-major of Rio at the time of the *cachaça* uprising, continued in his post until his death in 1699, forty-three long years. See *AHU*, Angola, box 10/84, and Tengwall, "A Study in Military Leadership," 93.

307. Silva Lisboa, *Annaes*, vol. 3, 211–212, 302–303, and 365–369.

308. The 1663 Crown inquiry on the government of Salvador de Sá states that he extorted *cachaça* makers and monopolized the sales of empty casks to such manufacturers. See A. Lamego, *A Terra Goytacá*, vol. 2 (Paris, Brussels, Niterói: 1913), 486.

309. For a study on the issue, see the clarifying thesis by L. Figueiredo, *Revoltas, fiscalidade e identidade colonial na América portuguesa: Rio de Janeiro, Bahia e Minas Gerais, 1640–1761* (PhD thesis in history, Universidade de São Paulo, 1997), chapter 1.

310. "Notícia de um motim no Rio de Janeiro," representation by Tomé Correa de Alvarenga addressed to King D. Afonso VI as he arrived from Rio deported by the rebels, Lisbon, April 8, 1661, *BNL*, res., mss., box 199, doc. 47.

311. Coaracy, *O Rio*, 164–173. About the Fluminense context at the time of the revolt, see M. F. Bicalho, *A cidade e o Império—O Rio de Janeiro na dinâmica colonial portuguesa, séculos XVII e XVIII* (Rio de Janeiro: 2003), 152–154.

312. Luísa da Fonseca, *Bahia, Índice dos documentos do século XVII*, 2 vols. (Lisbon: n/d) vol. 1, doc. 1811, Bahia, June 4, 1661.

313. Vieira, *Obras*, vol. 5, 295.

314. Boxer, *The Portuguese Seaborne Empire*, 183–188.

315. A. Alves Carrara, *Receitas e despesas da Real Fazenda do Brasil, século XVII* (M. G.: 2009), 70.

316. Following an order issued by Vidal de Negreiros in 1664, "aguardente e farinha," most likely *cachaça* and manioc flour were furnished to some *sobas* and the Jaga troops sent to Luanda to protect the town against the threat of a Spanish invasion. See doc. of October 6, 1664, *AHU*, box 8/84.

317. Letter of January 31, 1679, from governor Aires de Saldanha, *AHU*, codice 554, sheets 21 and 21v.

318. Simão Vandernez was the name of the royal treasury (*Fazenda Real*) factor. He helped to foment the mutiny using his friend, a soldier of captain Luis Ferreira de Macedo's company who was "not used to drink." See doc. of April 2, 1667, *AHU*, Angola, box 9/90.

319. Provision of April 8, 1679, *AHU*, códice 545, sheets 20 and 20v.

320. November 25, 1684, *AHU*, Angola, box 13/9, and January 13, 1687, box 13/36.

321. On the Angolista lobby favoring the *cachaça* imports in Luanda, see F. N. de Carvalho, "Aspectos do tráfico de escravos de Angola para o Brasil no século XVII: prolegómenos do inferno," in *Carlos Alberto Ferreira de Almeida: In Memoriam*, vol. 1, M. J. Barroca, ed. (Porto: 1999), 231–243, here 238.

322. J. C. Curto, "Vinho verso *cachaça*: A luta luso-brasileira pelo comércio do álcool e de escravos em Luanda, c. 1648–1703," in *Angola e Brasil nas rotas do Atlântico Sul*, S. Pantoja and J. F. Sombra Saraiva, eds. (Rio de Janeiro: 1998), 78–97.

323. João de Lencastre (1646–1707) married Maria Teresa Antônia de Portugal, daughter and heiress of Pedro de Almeida, governor of Pernambuco (1674–1678). Lencastre served in the Alentejo war and was cavalry captain in the Battle of Montes Claros. He held the post of governor in Angola in 1688 and in 1694 was the governor-general of Brazil. In 1704, in beginning of the succession war with Spain, he was nominated governor of Algarve and a member of the war council. His cousin Antônio Gonçalves da Câmara Coutinho was governor of Mozambique (1682–1686), governor of Pernambuco (1689–1690), governor-general of Brazil (1690–1694) and viceroy of India (1702–1707). At that time the Crown, using the experience of Câmara Coutinho and his officers, sought to open the slave trade

between Brazil and Mozambique. The initiative failed because, contrary to the Brazil-Angola connection, there were no mercantile exchanges between Portuguese America and East Africa. See *AHU*, Angola, box 13/20.

324. "Traslado da proposta feita ao gov. João de Alemcastro pellos oficiais da Câmara sobre a entrada das aguardentes e da resposta do dito governador," Luanda, February 9, 1689, *AHU*, Angola, box 13/97.

325. "Tomo que mandaram fazer os officiais do Sennado da Câmara," June 22, 1689, *AHU*, Angola, box 13/97.

326. Cosme, "Tractado das queixas endêmicas," 266. Angola historian A. Parreira does not consider the commercial rivalry between Brasílicos and mainlanders, accepting the official explanation of the time, in which the *jeribita* was banned to protect the Angolans' health. In fact, Parreira unknowingly endorses the false protectionist argument of the mainland spirits traders. A. Parreira, *Dicionário glossográfico e toponímico da documentação sobre Angola, séculos XV–XVII* (Lisbon: 1990), 48–49; ibid., *Economia e sociedade em Angola na época da rainha Jinga* (Lisbon: 1990), 125.

327. Testimony by Antônio Pacheco de Almeida, Crown judge of the kingdom of Angola, Luanda, February 23, 1689, *AHU*, Angola, box 13/97.

328. "Representação da Câmara da Bahia, de 18.VI.1690," *Cartas do Senado da Bahia, 1638–1698*, vol. 3 (Salvador: 1951), 94–96.

329. Royal letter of November 1, 1690, demanding the prohibition to be "inviolately" (*inviolavelmente*) enforced. See a letter by the marquis of Montebelo, Pernambuco, December 4, 1690, *BNL*, res., Col. Pombalina, cod. 239, fl. 100b.

330. Antônio Paes de Sande, a noble of the royal household and secretary of the *Estado da India*, member of the Overseas Council and governor of Rio de Janeiro, was one of A. Vieira's correspondents; about the transfer of the cultivations of pepper and cinnamon, and also of jackfruit and Asian mango, into Brazil, see Ferrand de Almeida, "Aclimatação de plantas," in particular, 432–433.

331. Consultation of the Overseas Council of October 20, 1689, *AHU*, Angola, box 13/97.

332. See also the to and fro of the measures recorded in the royal letters of February 28, 1688, February 14, 1689, and February 15, 1689. On interests in *cachaça* production and trade in Bahia, Thiago Nascimento Krause, *A formação de uma nobreza ultramarina: Coroa e elites locais na Bahia seiscentista* (PhD thesis, Universidade Federal do Rio de Janeiro, 2015), 35–36, 212–249.

333. Wallerstein, *The Modern*, vol. 2, 186–187.

334. The global export of Portuguese wine into Britain took off around 1685 and sharply increased from the five years between 1715 and 1720 and later. See J. Veríssimo Serrão, "O quadro econômico, configurações estruturais e tendências de evolução," in *História*, vol. 4, J. Mattoso, ed., 80–81 and table 1.

335. J. C. Miller, "Capitalism and Slaving: The Financial and Commercial Organization of the Angolan Slave Trade According to the Accounts of Antônio Coelho

Guerreiro, 1684–1892," *International Journal of African Historical Studies* 17, no. 1 (1984), 1–56.

336. Rocha Pitta, *História*, 26, 71–72.

337. February 23, 1689, *AHU*, Angola, box 13/97.

338. Like José Curto, I suppose that the "distillates" (*aguardentes*) mentioned in the documents referred always to the distillates produced in the ports whence the ships left from.

339. José Curto, *Alcohol and Slaves*, table 5, 85.

340. Silva Correa, *História*, vol. 1, 39–42.

341. "Ofício de 16.8.1800, do gov. Miguel Antônio de Mello" and "ofício 30.7.1803 do gov. Fernando Antônio de Noronha," *AA*, vol. 19, 2nd series (1962), 53.

342. The rights charged on distillates were created in 1818, but apparently did not yet apply to *cachaça*, consulta de January 21, 1829. See M. dos A. da Silva Rebelo, *Relações entre Angola e Brasil 1808–1830* (Lisbon: 1970), 437–440.

343. V. Ferreira Pires, *Viagem de África em o Reino de Dahomé* (São Paulo: [1800] 1957), 15, 20, and 112; Verger, *Flux et Reflux*, 122, 232, 259, and 460–467; K. Polanyi, *Dahomey and the Slave Trade: An Analysis of an Archaic Economy* (London: 1966), 136; R. J. Barman, "Business and Government in Imperial Brazil: The Experience of Viscount Maua," *Journal of Latin American Studies* 13, no. 2 (1981), 239–264.

344. D. Domingues da Silva, "The Atlantic Slave Trade to Maranhão"; Hawthorne, *From Africa to Brazil*, chapter 3.

345. Curto, *Alcohol and Slaves*, 179–263; ibid., "Luso-Brazilian Alcohol and the Legal Slave Trade at Benguela and its Hinterland, c. 1617–1830," in *Négoce Blanc en Afrique Noire: L'évolution du commerce à longue distance en Afrique noire du 18e au 20e siècles*, H. Bonin and M. Cahen, eds. (Paris: 2001), 351–369.

346. Verger, *Flux et Reflux*, passim.

347. Nardi, *O Fumo Brasileiro*, 115, 125, 150, 163, appendix 1.1, and 366–369, TSTD.

348. Ribeiro Júnior, *Colonização e monopólio no Nordeste brasileiro*, 130–131; Verger, *Flux et Reflux*, 651–654; Manning, "The Slave Trade in the Bight of Benin 1640–1890," in *The Uncommon*, 138, table 4.5; D. Eltis, "Geographic Data," TSTD, accessed in 2010. See also on bilateral trade between Brazil and Angola, Medeiros Dos Santos, "Relações de Angola com o Rio de Janeiro," 19, table 1; Curto, *Alcohol and Slaves*, 109, table 9.

349. TSTD, accessed in December 2015.

350. Alpers, *Ivory and Slaves in East Central Africa*, 127, 210–218; M. Newitt, *História de Moçambique* (Lisbon: 1997), 227–234.

Conclusion

1. Mauro, *Portugal*, 516–517.

2. The *Asiento* was contracted with Grillo and Lomelin. With the death of the latter, Grillo became the chief contractor. See G. Scelle, *Histoire de la traite Négrière*, vol. 1, 506–574. About the Bravos, who hailed from Oporto but had relatives in Rio, Bahia, and Luanda, see Gonçalves Salvador, *Os Magnatas*, 139; ibid., *Os cristãos-novos e o comércio*, 309–311; ibid., *Os cristãos-novos, povoamento*, 169–177; Jaboatão-Calmon, *CGPF*, vol. 2, 566, 701, and 767; L. Gonçalves Bravo, resident in Luanda and nicknamed "the Sun" because of his fame as a great merchant in West Central Africa, engaged in the slave trade and acted as agent of Luís Mendes de Vasconcellos. See Heintze, *Fontes*, vol. 1, 76. There is at least one Bravo who followed a rather different path: Manoel Jácome Bravo, high court magistrate of Bahia, rigorous royal agent, and author of judicial enquiries in Rio de Janeiro (1612) and in São Paulo (1614). See S. B. Schwartz, *Sovereignty and Society*, 164–166.

3. Goslinga, *The Dutch in the Caribbean*, 360.

4. M. Vega Franco, *El tráfico de Esclavos con America—asientos de Grillo y Lomelin 1663–1674* (Seville: 1984); E. Vila Vilar, "La sublevación de Portugal y la trata de negros," *Ibero-Amerikanisches Archiv* 2 (1976), 171–192. Angola's traders transported slaves to the Loango Dutch port of trade in order to sell them to Grillo's agents, who then shipped them to Curaçao, informed Jerônimo Nunes da Costa, Portuguese agent in Amsterdam. See doc. of October 4, 1670, *AHU*, Angola, box 10/8.

5. D. Ribeiro de Macedo, "Discurso sobre a introdução das artes no reino," in *Antologia dos economistas*, A. Sérgio, ed. (Lisbon: [1675] 1974), 167–230. The protection to the national factories proposed by Macedo would be applied in the regency (1667–1683) and the reign (1683–1706) of Pedro II by the count of Ericeira and the marquis of Fronteira. See Hanson, *Economia*, 179–200; J. Pedreira, "Industrialização e flutuações econômicas, preços, mercados e inovação tecnológica 1670–1890," in *Estudos e Ensaios em homenagem a Vitorino Magalhães Godinho* (Lisbon: 1988), 277–292; A. M. H. L. de Faria, "Duarte Ribeiro De Macedo A Modern Diplomat (1618–1680)," *e-JPH* 4, no. 1 (2006), 1–14.

6. Letter of April 7, 1678 sent to the Overseas Council, *AHU*, Angola, box 11/103.

7. About the first Companhia de Cacheu (1676), see C. da Silva Teixeira, "Companhia de Cacheu, Rios e Guiné," *Boletim do Arquivo Histórico Colonial* 1 (1950), 85–132; the second Companhia de Cacheu, the C.C.C.V., secured the *Asiento* in 1696 and delivered close to five thousand Africans to Spanish América. See C. J. de Senna Barcellos, *Subsídios para a História de Cabo Verde e Guiné*, vol. 2 (Lisbon: 1899), 84–95. The C.C.C.V. introduced less than a thousand enslaved to Pará and Maranhão colonists, under complains that its prices were too high. See W. Hawthorne, *From Africa to Brazil*, 42–43.

8. Doc. of January 29, 1693, *AHU*, Angola, box 14/109.

9. With the death of Marin, the *Asiento* came directly under the C.C.C.V. In the years 1696–1701, incidents between the Spanish and Portuguese damaged the C.C.C.V.'s transactions, until the Compagnie de Guinée, a French enterprise partially funded by Louis XIV, secured the *Asiento* (1701–1707), after negotiations conducted in Madrid by direct

representatives of the French Crown; Scelle, *Traite Negrière*, vol. 2, 3–270. In spite of the documents studied more than a century ago by G. Scelle, the direct involvement of Louis XIV in the slave trade is generally overlooked by the biographers of the Roi-Soleil.

10. D. do Couto, *O Soldado Prático* (Lisbon: 1980), 201–202.

11. Four hundred infantry aided by the "Black war" (*guerra preta*) (i.e., native irregular forces) would compose the Angola to Mozambique expedition. Simultaneously, the plan included the settling of 600 mainland colonist couples in Angola to consolidate populating the area. Consultation of February 12, 1656, *MMA¹*, vol. 12, 9–10.

12. The commander indicated by Salvador was Bartolomeu Vasconcellos da Cunha, nephew of former governor of Rio de Janeiro and governor of Angola Francisco Vasconcellos da Cunha. Bartolomeu had arrived in Luanda along with his uncle in 1635. See doc. of February 27, 1657, *AHU*, Angola, box 6/104.

13. *HGGA*, vol. 3, 173 and 283.

14. G. J. Ames, "An African Eldorado? The Portuguese Quest for Wealth and Power in Mozambique and the Rios de Cuama, C. 1661–1683," *The International Journal of African Historical Studies* 31, no. 1 (1998), 91–110, here 93–96.

15. G. Ames states that the third Anglo-Dutch war (1672–1674) would save the Estado da Índia from ruin, just as the first Anglo-Dutch (1652–1654) had saved Portuguese America. See G.J. Ames, "The Estado da Índia 1663–1677: Priorities and Strategies in Europe and the East," *Revista Portuguesa de História* 22 (1985), 31–46.

16. On Dourado, see do Loreto Couto, *Desagravos do Brazil*, 401–405.

17. Doc. of May 5, 1671, *AHU*, Angola, box 10/37, and doc. of June 18, 1671, box 10/55.

18. J. H. Elliot, *Richelieu y Olivares* (Barcelona: 1984), 202–205.

19. Doc. of May 5, 1671, *AHU*, Angola, box 10/37. Salvador and Feliciano would further elaborate the issue, especially in the document quoted in chapter 6 in which Salvador claims to have been the only one responsible for the recapture of Angola. See doc. of August 21, 1672, *AHU*, Angola box 10/71.

20. There would be fresh discussions of the issue in the eighteenth century, but I think that the crucial moment of the debate is to be found in the conjuncture that I analyze here. Regarding the geopolitical aspects of the Portuguese territorial claims over a corridor connecting Angola an Mozambique at the end of the nineteenth century, see C. E. Nowell, *The Rose-Colored Map* (Lisbon: 1982).

21. Consultation of March 9, 1696, *AHU*, Angola, box 15/57; *MMA¹*, vol. 14, 426–427. The opinion was signed jointly by the Count of Alvor, José de Freitas Serrão, former magistrate of the high court of Bahia, and João Sepúlveda de Matos.

22. In a 1672 session of the Overseas Council, Salvador de Sá declared: "[W]hoever tells Your Majesty that it [the Angola-Mozambique expedition] cannot be carried out, does not speak with the experience I have after the three years and 9 months that I governed those

kingdoms." The authority stating that the enterprise was difficult was precisely Francisco de Távora, then governor de Angola. See *AHU*, Angola, box 10/71.

23. J. Cortesão, *O Ultramar português depois da Restauração* (Lisbon: 1971), 16 and 294. The imperialist scramble into Africa in the second half of the nineteenth century, based on another conception of territory and of colonial occupation, opened the discussion about the precedence of the Portuguese in the discoveries of Africa. See A. A. Banha de Andrade, "Antecedentes da travessia de África," *Anais*, vol. 27, series 2 (1981), 321–354.

24. Consultation of the Overseas Council in which the counselors follow the advice by the Treasury procurator (*Procurador da Fazenda*), March 27, 1688, MMA^1, vol. 14, 51–52, 102–103, and 113–114.

25. L. Mendes de Vasconcellos, *Diálogos do Sítio de Lisboa* (Lisbon: 1608), 76.

26. Boxer, a former British officer and war prisoner in Japan, protested against Cortesão's attempt to present the destruction of the Guairá missions by Rapôso Tavares (1629) as the "liberation" of the region. See Cortesão, *Rapôso Tavares*, vol. 2, 144, 240–241; Boxer, *Salvador de Sá*, 133, 151. S. Buarque convincingly refuted Cortesão's point of view, grounded in the myth of the "Brazil island," which would have prefigured the borders of national territory. But, as demonstrated by F. de Almeida, Sérgio also incurred an anachronism as he extended the 1700s idea of "natural frontiers" to Portuguese America of the sixteenth and seventeenth centuries. See S. Buarque de Holanda, *Tentativas de Mitologia* (São Paulo: 1979), 71–84; Ferrand de Almeida, *A Colônia do Sacramento*, 313–319.

27. Bahia, September 21, 1695, *Cartas*, vol. 3, 689; de Montoya, *Conquista Espiritual*, 78.

28. Bettendorf, *Crônica*, 91.

29. "Cartas de S. Magestade escriptas ao Senhor Conde de Obidos," May 11, 1668, *AUC*, Colecção Conde dos Arcos, vol. 5, fl. 201, doc. no. 457.

30. L. F. de Alencastro, "História geral das guerras sul-atlânticas: o episódio de Palmares," in *Mocambos de Palmares. Histórias e fontes (séculos XVI–XIX)*, F. Gomes dos Santos, ed., 61–99, translated into a shorter version as "South Atlantic Wars: The Episode of Palmares," *Portuguese Studies Review* 19, no. 1 and 2 (2012), 35–58.

31. The "Barbarians War" did not constitute "a general uprising of the Tapuya," as stated by Wright and Carneiro da Cunha. It was rather a general offensive of colonists, militiamen, and authorities against most of the northeast's indigenous communities and the nomadic Tapuya as well as the settled Tupi and other *língua geral*–speaking Indians. In fact, it was a war of extermination waged against the north and northeast Indians. See R. M. Wright and M. Carneiro da Cunha, "Destruction, Resistance, and Transformation—Southern Coastal and Northern Brazil 1580–1890," in *The Cambridge History of the Natives*, vol. 3, part 2, F. Salomon and S. B. Schwartz, eds. (Cambridge, UK: 1999), 287–381, specifically 336–339.

32. P. Puntoni, *A guerra dos bárbaros—povos indígenas e a colonização do sertão nordeste do Brasil 1650–1720* (São Paulo: 2000), 136–137.

33. Royal letter of December 3, 1692, *DH*, vol. 83 (1949), 243–244.

34. "Exposição do padre Antônio de Sousa Leal," in *Os Manuscritos*, vol. 2, 384–393, 388.

35. A. Vieira noted in 1648: "Sergipe" named a much bigger area—the whole of the Bahian northern hinterland plus the Sergipe captaincy itself. See Vieira, *Obras Escolhidas*, vol. 3, 48.

36. J. Antonil, *Cultura e opulência do Brasil* (São Paulo: 1711), 199–201; da Rocha Pitta, *História*, 180–181.

37. A. Sepp, *Viagem às missões jesuítas e trabalhos apostólicos* (São Paulo: [1691] 1980), 143.

38. Nardi, *O Fumo*, 92, 109.

39. L. R. B. Mott, "Estrutura demográfica das fazendas de gado do Piauí colonial: um caso de povoamento rural centrífugo," *Ciência e Cultura* 30 (1978), 1,196–1,210.

40. In April 1645, troops embarked from Bahia to Angola. The troops included 200 Portuguese and some Angolistas, who were refugees in Bahia, and Brasílicos, among them 32 musketeers from Henrique Dias's famous regiment of mulattos and blacks in Brazil. Three hundred soldiers and some dozens of Indians embarked to Angola from Rio de Janeiro in May 1645; in 1648, 1,000 soldiers from Portugal and another 750 from Rio de Janeiro embarked from there with Salvador de Sá; in 1657, 200 veterans of the Dutch wars in Pernambuco embarked from Recife for Angola with Fernandes Vieira; in 1660, 200 veterans left with Vidal de Negreiros from Recife; in 1664 and 1665, rescue troops were sent from Bahia and Pernambuco; in 1667, an unknown number of soldiers embarked in Rio; in 1671, 400 soldiers left Bahia and Pernambuco; troops were sent again from Pernambuco in 1674; in 1681, two vessels with soldiers left from Bahia and Pernambuco; in 1690, fifty soldiers from Bahia took to the sea en route to Angola; in 1703, 100 soldiers from Pernambuco; in 1704, 195 privates from Pernambuco embarked as well. Dispatches of smaller contingents continued in the first decades of the eighteenth century, when a royal order determined the embarkation of eight to ten recruits in each ship leaving Pernambuco for Angola; see chapter 6 and appendix 4; see also R. Ferreira, "O Brasil e a arte da guerra em Angola (sécs. XVII e XVIII)," *Estudos Históricos* 39 (2007), 1–24.

41. Doc. of March 28, 1678, *AHU*, Angola, box 11/101.

42. Although most soldiers who settled in Luanda could ride a horse, not all of them adapted to Brazil's horses, which were accustomed to being mounted without saddles or horseshoes (as in Brazil, horseshoes started being employed only in the eighteenth century). After that, the knights of Pernambuco and Bahia gained importance in Angola. The regular trade of horses in exchange for slaves never worked because only the colonial government military forces in Angola bought horses. With so few buyers, demand was not comparable to the demand for slaves in Brazil. See also Ferreira, "O Brasil e a arte da guerra," 7.

43. Royal decrees of June 21, 1675; July 10, 1675; March 10, 1680; March 16, 1680; February 2, 1684; February 26, 1684; March 22, 1688; March 7, 1691; January 26, 1694; J. J. de Andrade e Silva, *Collecção chronologica da legislação portugueza* (Lisbon: 1854–1859).

44. The ship diverted to Itamaracá Island, north of Recife, abandoning the mission. See June 26, 1664, *AUC*, Colecção Conde dos Arcos, vol. 5, Despozições de Jerónimo de Mendonça Furado, fl. 111v, doc. 4.

45. Born and raised in Luanda, Fernao Velho de Araujo fled to Bahia when the WIC invaded Luanda and fought against the Dutch in the Brasílico War. See doc. of March 15, 1656, *AHU*, Angola, box 15/47.

46. Doc. of December 20, 1685, *AHU*, Angola, box 13/12; *DH*, vol. 7, 293–294; Jaboatão and P. Calmon, *CGPF*, vol. 1, 483.

47. Doc. of April 28, 1673, *AHU*, Angola, box 10/101.

48. Doc. of December 12, 1698, *AHU*, Angola, box 15/89, box 15/92.

49. Doc. of February 15, 1682, *AHU*, Angola, box 12/65. About the jurisdiction conflict, see Cabral de Mello, *A Fronda*, 71–72.

50. Consultation of the Overseas Council, April 6, 1691; *AHU*, Angola, box 14/55.

51. *MMA*, vol. 9, 335–337 and vol. 15, 517.

52. *AA*, vol. 1, 2nd series (1943–1944), 136–137, 193–194; and C. Dias Coimbra, *Livro de patentes do tempo do senhor Salvador Correia de Sá e Benevides* (Luanda: 1969), 95.

53. B. Studart, "Documentos para a história do Brasil e especialmente a do Ceará," in *Revista Trimensal do Instituto do Ceará*, vol. 42 (1928), 103–105.

54. Studart, "Documentos," *RTIC*, vol. 37 (1923), 134–136.

55. S. N. A. dos Santos, *Conquista e resistência dos Payayá no sertão das Jacobinas: Tapuias, Tupi, colonos e missionários 1651–1706* (master's thesis in history, Universidade Federal da Bahia, 2011), 173–182.

56. September 18, 1677, "Consulta do Conselho Ultramarino"; November 17, 1677, *AHU*, ACL, Bahia, doc. 34576, Conselho Ultramarino, cod. 245 (1675–1695), doc. 52.

57. November 17, 1677, *AHU*, ACL, Bahia, doc. 34576, Conselho Ultramarino, cod. 245, doc. 52, and September 7, 1684, *AHU*, ACL, CU, 015, box 13, doc. 1312; doc. of June 28, 1677, *BNL*, manuscritos, cod. 2–33, 4, and 32. The genealogist Borges da Fonseca mistakenly wrote that Manoel Inojosa was the great-grandson of Sargento-Mor Jerônimo de Inojosa. See A. J. V. Borges da Fonseca, "Nobiliarchia Pernambucana (1748)," 80. In fact, M. Inojosa stated he was a "poor soldier" and never mentioned any illustrious ancestry in his requests.

58. In 1681, Inojosa might have killed a chief thought to be Zumbi. Indeed, Loreto do Couto mentions the death of Zumbi on three different dates—the first in 1680 and the second in 1681. The third date is not precise, but the facts coincide with the death of Zumbi in 1695. See Couto, "Desagravos do Brazil," 98–99, 106, and 108. These claims contributed the idea that Zumbi had several lives or was indeed immortal. For a discussion about the name Zumbí, see R. N. Anderson, "The Quilombo of Palmares: A New Overview of a Maroon State in Seventeenth-Century Brazil," *Journal of Latin American Studies* 28, no. 3 (1996), 545–566, especially pages 560–562.

59. Studart, "Documentos," *RTIC*, vol. 36 (1922), 112–113.

60. Docs. of January 26, 1685, and July 18, 1690, *AHU*, Angola, box 13/3 and box 14/27.

61. The Inojosa report of 1677 was quoted among others by J. K. Thornton, "Les États de l'Angola et la formation de Palmares (Brésil)," *Annales: Histoire, Sciences Sociales* 63, no. 4 (2008), 776–778.

62. Consulta do Conselho Ultramarino, March 22, 1688, *AHU*, cod. 18, fs. 135–135v. I am grateful to Roquinaldo Ferreira for this reference.

63. Angelo Cruz arrived in Luanda with the troops brought from Rio de Janeiro by Antônio Juzarte de Almeida. He participated in the battles in the Angolan backlands with Luís Lopes Siqueira and was captain-major of Pungo Andongo. See doc. of May 13, 1672, *AHU*, Angola, box 10/67and doc. of July 1690, box 14/27.

64. See J. C. Curto, "Luso-Brazilian Alcohol and the Legal Slave Trade at Benguela and its Hinterland, c. 1617–1830," in *Négoce Blanc en Afrique Noire: L'évolution du 18e au 20e siècles*, H. Bonin and M. Cahen, eds. (Paris: 2001), 351–369; M. Cândido, *Enslaving Frontiers: Slavery, Trade and Identity in Benguela, 1780–1850* (PhD thesis, York University, 2006), passim; ibid., "Merchants and the Business of the Slave Trade at Benguela, 1750–1850," *African Economic History* 35 (2007), 1–30; Ferreira, *Transforming Atlantic*, 70–143.

65. F. A. Varnhagen, *HGB*, vol. 2, book 3, 227–229.

66. *MMA¹*, vol. 13, 435–457. In 1716 the diocese of Angola and Congo was again submitted to the Lisbon archbishopric but that of São Tomé remained under Bahia's archbishop jurisdiction until 1844. See F. de Almeida, *HIP*, vol. 2, 26. Illustrating the territorial bias of Portuguese America's historiography, a textbook on the chronology of colonial Brazil, edited in 1994 by the Department of History of the University of São Paulo, records the creation of Bahia's archdiocese in 1676, with its suffragan dioceses in Brazil, but fails to report its African diocesis in Congo, Angola, and São Tomé; István Jancso, ed., *Cronologia de História do Brasil Colonial 1500–1831* (São Paulo: 1994), 112–114. See also chapter 7, note 6.

67. T. R. de Souza, *Goa Medieval—A cidade e o interior no século XVII* (Lisbon: 1993), 110–120; S. Subrahmanyam, *The Portuguese Empire in Asia 1500–1700: A Political and Economic History* (London: 1993), 261–269. G. V. Scammell, "The Pillars of Empire: Indigenous Assistance and the Survival of the 'Estado da India' c. 1600–1700." *Modern Asian Studies*, 22, no. 3 (1988) 473–489. For a balance of the economic situation of 1600s Portuguese Ásia, see K. Chaudhuri, "O Comércio Asiático," in *História da Expansão Portuguesa*, vol. 2, F. Bethencourt and K. Chaudhuri, eds. (Lisbon: 1998), 194–212.

68. Although the Palmares maroons' villages had been attacked by colonists since their early development in the beginning of the seventeenth century, the "Palmares War" commonly refers to the last decades of the century, when the expeditions against the *quilombolas* became more frequent. During the 1694 attack, led by the Paulista troops of Domingos Jorge Velho, the quilombos of Palmares were destroyed. Their leader, Zumbí, escaped but was killed a year later. A small group of warriors pursued the fight until their defeat in 1700.

For new research and historiographical debates on Palmares, see F. Gomes, ed., *Mocambos de Palmares. História, historiografia e fontes* (Rio de Janeiro: 2009).

69. Letters of March 23, 1688, and February 23, 1689, *AUC*, Colecção Conde dos Arcos, vol. 5, fl. 464, doc. 880 and fl. 472, doc. 893.

70. Schwartz, "Rethinking Palmares," 109; P. Malheiro, *A escravidão no Brasil—Ensaio jurídico, histórico, social*, vol. 1, 50–1.

71. Since the pioneering book of F. Teixeira Salles, *Associações religiosas no ciclo do ouro: Introdução ao estudo do comportamento social das irmandades de Minas no século XVIII* (Belo Horizonte, Brazil: 1963), the connections between catholic broterhoods [*irmandades*] and slavery and Afro-Brazilian culture have been extensively studied. See, for instance, M. de Carvalho Soares, *Devotos da cor: Identidade étnica, religiosidade e escravidão no Rio de Janeiro, século XVIII* (Rio de Janeiro: 2000); M. Karash, "Construindo comunidades: As irmandades de Pretos e Pardos no Brasil colonial e Goiás" (paper presented at the Conference on American Counterpoint: New Approaches to Slavery and Abolition in Brazil, Yale University, October 2010); L. Reginaldo, *Os Rosários dos Angolas: irmandades negras, experiências escravas e identidades africanas na Bahia setecentista* (São Paulo: 2011).

72. Schwartz, *Sugar Plantation*, 137, 278.

73. H. S. Klein and F. V. Luna, *Slavery and the Economy of São Paulo, 1750–1850* (Stanford, CA: Stanford University Press, 2003), 165–167.

74. Ibid., *Slavery in Brazil*, 263, 276.

75. Francisco Manuel de Melo was deported to Salvador in 1657–1658; E. Prestage, *D. Francisco Manuel de Melo: esboço biographico* (Coimbra: 1914), 291.

76. B. des Periers, "Paris c'est le paradis des femmes, l'enfer des mules, et le purgatoire des solliciteurs," in *Nouvelles Recréations* (1558); J. Florio, *Second Fruits* (1591): "England is the paradise of women, the purgatory of men, and the hell of horses"; *Oxford Dictionary of Proverbs*, accessed October 2015, http://www.answers.com/topic/england-is-the-paradise-of-women-the-hell-of-horses-and-the-purgatory-of-servants.

77. A. J. Antonil, *Cultura e opulência do Brasil* (São Paulo: [1711] 1982), 90.

78. See, for instance, the G. de Matos poem "Mulatinhas da Bahia." Several other of de Matos's poems offer degrading descriptions of *mulatas*. His writings thus portray the misogyny common to other contemporary poets. See J. Adolfo Hansen, *A sátira e o engenho, Gregório de Matos e a Bahia do século XVII* (São Paulo: 2004), 65, 198, 221, 348, 411–422, and 499.

79. On the mestizos soldiers in Portuguese America, see S. B. Schwartz, "Tapanhuns, Negros da Terra e Curibocas: Causas Comuns e Confrontos entre Negros e Indígenas," *Afro-Ásia* 29/30 (2003), 13–40.

80. Loreto Couto, *Desagravos do Brasil*, 457–458.

81. L. dos Santos Vilhena, *Notícias Soteropolitanas e Brasílicas*, vol. 1 (Bahia: [1802] 1921), 267.

82. *Quilambas* (*Kilamba*): Indigenous captains commanding native troops under colonial authorities, *HGGA*, vol. 2, 237; Heintze, *Fontes*, vol. 1, 126; Silva Correa, *História*, vol. 2, 50; "*quimbares*": native men bound by the vassalage of their *sobas* to join colonial troops. See Heintze, *Fontes*, vol. 1, 126; *empacasseiros*: native hunters of buffalos (*mpacassa*), also incorporated in colonial troops, *HGGA*, vol. 3, 345; Silva Correa, *História*, vol. 2, 50. Yet a document dated from 1643 explains that those men should serve the Portuguese authorities, "but they only perform this duty when it seems convenient to them." See *MMA¹*, vol. 9, 29. See also J. Vansina, "Ambaca Society and the Slave Trade c. 1760–1845," *J. Afr. H.* 46 (2005), 1–27.

83. D. Miguel Antônio de Mello Luanda, October 30, 1798, *AA*, vol. 20, 2nd series (1963), 54–59.

84. Realizing that the Portuguese bishops banned "ordaining mulattos," the Overseas Council recommended that the Crown ask the papacy to "moderate" such interdict "because of the lack of white clergy [in Angola]." See consultation of April 24, 1693, *MMA¹*, vol. 14, 296–303, and *AHU*, Angola, box 13/28, box 13/79; *MMA¹*, vol. 8, 176.

85. *HGGA*, vol. 3, 327–329; vol. 1, 259.

86. "Aqui onde o meu desejo / não chega ao seu fim / porque me acho sem mim / quando me busco / Aqui onde o filho é fusco / e quase negro o neto, / e todo negro o bisneto, / e tudo escuro." With forty-eight strophes, the poem describes the evils of Angola and the sufferings of Europeans there, written before 1680. There is one version of the poem in the manuscript titled "Descrição da cidade de Loanda, reino de Angola," *BNL*, reservados, fs. 317ss, cod. 905 of Carvalho, *História de Coimbra* (1795), vol. 1. Another version is included in the *História Geral das Guerras Angolas*, with commentaries by Cadornega, *HGGA*, vol. 3, 382–383n80. The commentator of the third volume of Cadornega's work, M. Alves da Cunha, writes that the poem is the same as in the *BNL* manuscript quoted above. But it is not quite like that: in Cadornega's book 5, strophes criticizing Angolistas priests have been deleted. More recently, Francisco Topa convincingly demonstrated that Luis Félix da Cruz authored this poem. Interesting enough, Cruz, a veteran Angola officer who witnessed the Dutch occupation and the retaking of Luanda by Salvador de Sá, was a brother-in-law of the mulatto captain Luis Lopes, the winner at the Battle of Mbwila and an Angolista hero, as mentioned in chapter 7. See F. Topa, "Entre a *Terra de gente oprimida* e a *Terra de gente tostada*."

87. Francisco Inocêncio de Sousa Coutinho, Luanda, September 13, 1769, *IHGB*, manuscritos, DL81, 02.14, fols. 46–47. The letter is surely addressed to Francisco Xavier de Mendonça Furtado, the overseas minister.

88. I discussed this issue more extensively in "Mulattos in Brazil and Angola: A Comparative Approach, Seventeenth to Twenty-First Centuries," in *Racism and Ethnic Relations in the Portuguese-Speaking World*, F. Bethencourt and A. Pearce, eds. (London: 2012), 71–96.

89. Felner, "Carta de D. Francisco Inocêncio de Sousa Coutinho," in *Angola—Apontamentos sôbre a colonização dos planaltos e litoral do Sul de Angola*, vol. 1, 160–162, Luanda, November 24, 1768, doc. 3.

90. I. Kantor, "Representação da Mesa do Bem Comum de Lisboa contra a Pragmática de 1749," in *Pacto festivo em Minas colonial: A entrada triunfal do primeiro bispo na Sé de Mariana, 1748* (master's thesis, Universidade de São Paulo, 1996), 113.

91. "Alvará porque V. M. ha por bem . . . ordenar que por hora não tenha efeito o cap⁰ 9 da Pramatica de 24 de Mayo a respeito dos negros, e mulatos das Conquistas," Lisbon, September 20, 1749, *AUC*, Colecção Conde dos Arcos, vol. 9, 420.

92. L. Heywood, "Portuguese into African: The Eighteenth-Century Central African Background to Atlantic Creole Cultures," in *Central Africans and Cultural Transformations in the American Diaspora*, L. Heywood, ed. (Cambridge, UK: 2002), 91–114, see 92–96; R. Ferreira, *Transforming Atlantic Slaving: Trade, Warfare and Territorial Control in Angola, 1650–1800* (PhD thesis, University of California, Los Angeles, 2003), 159–171.

93. A. Vieira, "A Voz de Deus à Bahia," *Sermões*, vol. 12.

94. L. F. de Alencastro, "Continental Drift—The Independence of Brazil, Portugal and Africa," in *From Slave Trade to Empire*, O.-P. Grenouilleau, ed. (London: 2004), 98–109; TSTD, accessed in May 2015.

Appendix 1

1. C. Alão de Morais, *Pedatura lusitana-hispanica em quem se contém várias famílias nobres e ilustres*, 131–134; J. Salgado de Araújo, *Sumario de la familia ilustrissima de Vasconcelos, historiada y con elogios* (Madrid: 1638), 40–43; M. Laranjo Coelho, ed., *Cartas dos governadores da província do Alentejo a el-rei d. João IV*, vol. 2 (Lisbon: 1945–1947), 243; Heintze, *Fontes*, vol. 1, 111; J. de Mirales, "História militar do Brazil" *ABNRJ* 22 ([1762] 1900), 143–144; F. A. das Chagas, member of the Academia dos Generosos and author of "Spiritual Letters" (*Cartas espirituais*) composed a sonnet praising Joane's fighting in the Alentejo war. See das Chagas, "Colleção de sonetos sérios," *BNL*, res., cod. 8610, fs. 85, 1786.

2. Doc. of November 6, 1635, *AHU*, Angola, box 3/20.

3. Calado, *O Valeroso*, vol. 1, 166.

4. C. Alão de Morais, *Pedatura lusitana-hispanica em quem se contém várias famílias nobres e ilustres*, vol. 2, book 1, 131–134; Esteves Pereira and Guilherme Rodrigues, *Portugal—Dicionário Histórico, Corográfico, Heráldico, Biográfico, Bibliográfico, Numismático e Artístico* (Lisbon: 1904), vol. 7, 322–324.

Appendix 2

1. F. Mauro, "Discripcion de la Provincia del Brasil," in *Le Brésil au XVIIème siècle: Documents inédits relatifs à l'Atlantique portugais* (Coimbra: 1963), 167–182.

2. The regular measure was of one alqueire (around 13 liters) of flour per month per individual. See "Processo das despesas feitas por Martim de Sá, no Rio de Janeiro 1628–1638," *ABNRJ* 59 (1940), 76.

3. The enterprise may have aborted after the Restoration but the amounts planned are considerable, revealing the alimentary production that could have been extracted from Amerindian labor concentrated in Rio, in São Vicente, and in São Paulo: around 300 tonnes of wheat flour, 37 tonnes of manioc flour, 29 tonnes of beef and pork meat, 58 tonnes of fish, 14 tonnes of vegetables, quince preserve, and hens, "as many as necessary for the sick." See provision and royal letter of August 10, 1639, and royal decree of April 17, 1640, *PLMH*, vol. 2 (Lisbon: 1961), 27–35.

4. L. Norton, "Consulta do Co. da Fazenda," in A. Dinastia, 181–187, 188–189, Lisbon, March 16, 1640, and ibid., "Carta de Salvador de Sá," Rio de Janeiro, May 30, 1642.

5. Laranjo Coelho, "Carta do conde de Villa Pouca a el-rei, Bahia 9.1.1648," in *Cartas de el-rei D. João IV ao conde de Vidigueira (marquês de Niza) embaixador em França*, vol. 2 (Lisbon: 1945–1947), 238–289.

6. Minutes of the town council in the years of 1648 and 1649, *Accordãos e Vereanças*, 159–179. Cananéia, with its 100 dwellers, exported wheat flour to Rio de Janeiro and to Angola, "Parecer de Salvador de Sá ao Co.Uo. 13.10.1646," ABNRJ 39 (1917), 51.

7. Service record of Pedro Gomes de Brito, captain in Angola in 1649, who had served from 1640 to 1648 in Rio. See *AA*, vol. 7, 2nd series (1950), 127–128.

8. D. Alden, "Price Movements in Brazil Before, During, and After the Gold Boom, with Special Reference to the Salvador Market, 1670–1769," in *Eighteenth-Century Price Movements in Latin America*, L. Johnson and E. Tandeter, eds. (Albuquerque, NM: 1989) 353.

9. *DH*, vol. 5, 74–76 and 224–226.

10. Minutes of the Rio de Janeiro town council, January 22, 1646, *Accordãos e Vereanças*, 109–110.

Appendix 3

1. Alão de Morais, *Pedatura*, vol. 2, book 3, 372–377; J. Leitão Manso de Lima, *Famílias de Portugal*, vol. 8 (Braga: 1992), 532–539.

2. Royal letter of July 10, 1647, de Andrade e Silva, *Collecção*, vol. 5, 172.

3. *CGPF*, vol. 1, 287–288, and vol. 2, 595 and 599. Both Jaboatão and Calmon mix up Joane Mendes de Vasconcelos, son of Luís Mendes de Vasconcellos, with a homonym; on the Mendes de Vasconcellos, see appendix 1.

4. In his fine essay on Salvador de Sá, F. Dutra questions the Alão de Morais affirmations. See Dutra, *"Charles Boxer's Salvador de Sá and the Struggle for Brazil and Angola Revisted: 50 Years Later,"* 10.

Appendix 4

1. Bultão was later named general trustee (Provedor-Mor) of Angola by the governor André Vidal de Negreiros, a commander of the war against the Dutch in Pernambuco, doc. of November 21, 1664, *AHU*, Angola, box 8/73.

2. Salvador de Sá created a post of field-master of Angola for his nephew, son of interim governor of Rio de Janeiro, Duarte Correia Vasqueanes. The Overseas Council vetoed the act, considering that it amounted to a royal prerogative unduly appropriated by the governor. See *HGGA*, vol. 2, 588, note by J. M. Delgado; see further Jaboatão-Calmon, *CGPF*, vol. 2, 572 and 599, notes by Calmon.

3. The *Livro de Patentes do tempo do sr. Salvador Correia de Sá e Benevides* includes 438 patent letters and provisions related to the nomination of military personnel and agents in Angola and in Rio de Janeiro. See further *ACA*, vol. 2, 1040–1041 and documents of boxes 5 to 15 of the Angola series of the *AHU*. Antônio Lito, nominated in 1688 captain of the Santo Amaro fortress in Luanda, claimed his services rendered in the 1648 expedition. See *AHU*, Angola, 13/70. Pascoal Rodrigues obtained the post of captain in Angola in 1698, claiming further participation in the two Guararapes battles that had taken place half a century before, as well as in aid sent in 1674 from Pernambuco to Luanda. See *AHU*, Angola, 15/89; B. Bandeira de Mello, in B. da Fonseca, *"Nobiliarchia Pernambucana* (1748)," part 1, 191; D. de Albuquerque Coelho, *Memórias diárias da guerra no Brasil: 1630–1638* (Recife: 1981) 120; S. de Vasconcellos, *Vida*, 223–225; about the two expeditionary physicians, see *AA*, vol. 9, 2nd series (1952), 9–12; about J. Antônio Correia, *AA*, vol. 16, 2nd series (1959), 25; about M. de Souza da Silva, *PLMH*, vol. 2, 410–411; on J. Correia Ximenes, J. Gonçalves Salvador, *Os cristãos-novos e o comércio no Atlântico Meridional*, 157 and 351; about F. Gonçalves Ferraz, *AHU*, box 5/74.

Appendix 5

1. Larry H. Addington, *The Patterns of War Since the Eighteenth Century*, 2nd ed. (Indiana University P, 1994), 84–93.

2. Fróis, *História de Japam*, vol. 1, 39.

3. "Espingarda," *Enciclopédia luso-brasileira de cultura*, vol. 7, 1215.

4. W. Di Lichii, *Kriegsbüch darin die Alte ünd Newe Militia* (Frankfurt: 1689), 107–113, 126–131.

5. D. B. Ralston, *Importing the European Army: The Introduction of European Military Techniques and Institutions into the Extra-European World* (London: 1990), 7.

6. J. F. C. Fuller, *A Military History of the Western World* (New York: 1955), vol. 2, 129–130.

7. A. Corvisier, "Louis XIV, la guerre et la naissance de l'armée moderne," *Histoire militaire de la France*, vol. 1 (Paris: 1992), 408–411.

8. Royal decree of November 6, 1613, *BNL*, res., 1203A.

9. Braga, *Entre a Cristandade e o Islão*, 24.

10. Royal decree of July 24, 1626, de Andrade e Silva, *Collecção*, vol. 2, part 1, 162.

11. A. T. de Matos, ed., *Diário do conde Sarzedas—Vice-rei do Estado da Índia 1655–1656* (Lisbon: 2001), 125.

12. H. Peckham, *The Colonial Wars 1689–1762* (Chicago: 1964), 26.

13. *MMA¹*, vol. 2, 340, and vol. 3, 312; *Diogo Cão*, 2nd series (Luanda: 1933), 24.

14. R. Gray, "Portuguese Musketeers on the Zambezi," *J. Afr. H.* 12, no. 2 (1971), 531–533; R. A. Kea, "Firearms and Warfare on the Gold and Slave Coast from the 16th to the 19th Centuries," *J. Afr. H.* 12, no. 2 (1971), 185–213.

15. K. Mellander and E. Prestage, *The Diplomatic and Commercial Relations of Sweden and Portugal from 1641 to 1670* (Watford: 1930), 71.

16. M. Calado, *O Valeroso*, vol. 2, 20 and 171; E. Cabral de Mello, *Olinda*, 2nd ed., 231–232.

17. Royal letter of May 9, 1675, *AHU*, Angola, cod. 545, fl. 11; doc. of April 23, 1675, *AHU*, Angola, box 11/38.

18. Provision of November 22, 1679, de Andrade e Silva, *Collecção*, vol. 5, 348.

19. Royal decree of December 20, 1696, *BNL*, res., 1875/23V.

20. Cardini, *La culture de la guerre*, 87–88, G. White, "Firearms in Africa: An Introduction," *J. Afr. H.* 12, no. 2 (1971), 173–184.

21. C. Coquery-Vidrovitch and H. Moniot, *L'Afrique Noire de 1800 à nos jours* (Paris: 1974), 298–299.

22. Buarque de Holanda, *O Extremo*, 50–53; Parker, *The Military Revolution*, 120–121.

23. *MMA¹*, vol. 9, 335–337, and vol. 15, 517.

24. Dantas Silva, *Alguns documentos*, 29; "Carta do cap mor Domingos Jorge Velho sobre o levantamento do Tapuya q' estava em sua companhia," August 7, 1691; B. Studart, "Dezenove documentos sobre os Palmares pertencentes à Colleção Studart," *RTIC* 20 (1906), 254–289; Ennes, *Os Palmares*, doc. of 1693, 115.

25. Richards, "The Import of Firearms into West Africa in the Eighteenth Century," *J. Afr. H.* 11 (1980), 43–59; Inikori, "The Import of Firearms into West Africa, 1750 to 1807: A Quantitative Analysis," 126–253.

BIBLIOGRAPHY

Abbreviations and Special Terms

AA: Arquivos de Angola
ABNRJ: Anais da Biblioteca Nacional do Rio de Janeiro
ACA: L'Ancien Congo et l'Angola 1639–1655, d'après les archives romaines, portugaises, néerlandaises, et espagnoles
AHU: Arquivo Histórico Ultramarino
ANTT: Arquivo Nacional da Torre do Tombo
AUC: Arquivo da Universidade de Coimbra
BAL: Manuscripts of the Biblioteca da Ajuda, Lisbon
BNL: Biblioteca Nacional de Lisboa
BNRJ: Biblioteca Nacional do Rio de Janeiro
CCLP: Collecção chronologica da legislação portuguesa
CD: Correspondência Diplomática
CEA: Cahiers d'Etudes Africaines
CHLA: The Cambridge History of Latin America
cx: caixa (box with documents in Portuguese archives)
cod. cods.: codex, codices
Col: Collection
DH: Documentos Históricos da Biblioteca Nacional do Rio de Janeiro
DHCMA: Istorica Descrizione de' Tre Regni, Congo, Matamba et Angola, "Descrição Histórica dos Três Reinos do Congo, Matamba e Angola"
DHMPPO: Documentação para a História das Missões do Padroado Português do Oriente
DHP: Dicionário de História de Portugal
DI: Documentos Interessantes para a história e costumes de São Paulo
DP: Descobrimentos Portugueses, documentos para a sua história
EH: Estudos Históricos
f., fs.: folio, folios
FHBH: Fontes para a História do Brasil holandês
HAHR: Hispanic America Historical Review
HCJB: História da Companhia de Jesus no Brasil
HGGA: História Geral das Guerras Angolanas

IHGB: Instituto Histórico e Geográfico Brasileiro
J. Afr. H.: The Journal of African History
maço: bundle (with documents in Portuguese archives)
mss.: manuscripts
MMA: Monumenta Missionaria Africana
PLMH: Pauliceae lusitana Monumenta historica
R.A.M.SP.: Revista do Arquivo Municipal de São Paulo
res.: reserved section
RHES: Revista de História Econômica e Social
RIAHGP: Revista do Instituto Arqueológico, Histórico e Geográfico Pernambucano
RIAMF: Recueil des Instructions aux Ambassadeurs et Ministres de France depuis les Traités de Westphalie jusqu'à la Révolution Française
RIHGB: Revista do Instituto Histórico e Geográfico Brasileiro
RTIC: Revista Trimensal do Instituto do Ceará
The A: The Americas
TSTD: Trans-Atlantic Slave Trade Database
v. (verso): obverse

Written Sources

AHU, Angola, boxes 1–18 (1602–1709)
AHU, Angola, cód. 544 (1594–1759); cód. 545 (1673–1725)
AHU, Consultas mistas do Conselho Ultramarino, códs. 14, 15, 16
AHU, Moçambique, box 1
AHU, Rio de Janeiro, Documentos Avulsos, maço 142; maço 450
Arquivo Histórico Ultramarino (*AHU*), Lisbon
Arquivo Nacional da Torre do Tombo (*ANTT*), Lisbon
Biblioteca Nacional do Rio de Janeiro (*BNRJ*) "Manuscritos, Consultas Mistas do Conselho Ultramarino"
Chancelaria de Filipe I, liv. 15
Chancelaria de Filipe III, liv. 37
Colecção Conde dos Arcos, 39 vols., 1578–1823, Arquivo da Universidade de Coimbra, vols, 4, 5, and 9
Coleção Resgate
Correspondência do marquês de Montebelo (1690–1693), col. Pombalina, *BNL*, res., mss., códice 239
Instituto Histórico e Geográfico Brasileiro (*IHGB*), Manuscritos, África
"Irlandeses." *BNL*, res., cod. 7627, fls. 78 ss

Manuscritos da Livraria, liv. 1,146

Pimentel, M. *Arte de Navegar, BNL*, res., cod. 862 (1712)

"Resolução que o Bispo e o Ouvidor Geral do Brasil tomaram sobre os injustos cativeiros dos Índios do Brasil e do remédio para o aumento da conversão e da conservação daquele Estado," Biblioteca Pública de Évora, cod. 116/1–33

Published Documents, Classical Texts, and Contemporary Works from the Period of Brazilian Slavery

"A Bolsa do Brazil, onde claramente se mostra a aplicação que teve o dinheiro dos acionistas da Companhia das Índias Ocidentais" [1647], *RIAHGP*, 28 (1883): 127–201.

Abreu, Aleixo de *Tratado de las siete enfermedades*. Lisbon: 1623.

Abreu e Brito, D. de. *Sumário e descripção do reino de Angola e do descobrimento da ilha de Loanda e da grãdeza das capitanias do Estado do Brasil*, edited by A. de Albuquerque Felner. Coimbra [1592]: 1931.

Acuña, Cristóbal de. *Novo descobrimento do grande rio das Amazonas*. Rio de Janeiro [1641]: 1994.

Alão de Morais, C. *Pedatura lusitana-hispanica em quem se contém várias famílias nobres e ilustres*, A. A. Pereira de Miranda Vasconcellos, A. A. Ferreira da Cruz, and E. E. A. da Cunha e Freitas, eds. 6 vols., Porto [1667]: 1943.

Albuquerque, L. de, T. W. Baxter, and António da Silva Rego. *Documentos sobre os portugueses em Moçambique e na Africa Central 1497–1840/Documents on the portuguese in Mozambique and Central Africa*, 9 vols., Lisbon: 1962–1989.

———, ed. *Dicionário de História dos Descobrimentos Portugueses*. 2 vols. Lisbon: 1994.

Albuquerque Coelho, Duarte de. *Memórias diárias da guerra do Brasil*. Preface by J. A. Gonsalves de Mello. Recife [1630–1638]: 1981.

Alvarez Manuel, *Ethiopia Menor e descripção geografica da Província da Serra Leoa* [c. 1615], An interim translation and introduction by P. E. H. Hair. Part two, chap. 1, p. 9, accessed at: http://digicoll.library.wisc.edu/cgi-bin/AfricanStudies/AfricanStudies-idx?type=div&did=AfricanStudies.Alvares01.i0002&isize=text.

Alvise Cà da Mosto and Luís de Cadamosto e Pedro de Sintra. *Viagens de Luís de Cadamosto e de Pedro de Sintra* (notes of Damião Peres). Academia Portuguesa de História. Lisbon [1455–1462]: 1948.

Amado, J., ed. *Obras completas de Gregório de Matos*. 2 vols. Rio de Janeiro [17th Century]: 1990.

Anchieta, José de. *Poesias*. São Paulo [16th Century]: 1954.

Andrade e Silva, J. J. de. *Collecção chronologica da legislação portuguesa, 1603–1701*. 11 vols. Lisbon, 1854–1859.

Andre, L., and E. Bourgeois. *Recueil des Instructions aux Ambassadeurs et Ministres de France depuis les Traités de Westphalie jusqu'à la Révolution Française (RIAMF)*. Vol. III, "Portugal," Paris: 1886; vol. XXI, "Hollande," book 1, Paris, 1892; vol. XI, "Espagne," book 1, Paris, 1894.

Anonymous. *História do reino do Congo*, edited by A. Brásio. Lisbon [1625]: 1969.

Antonil, A. J. *Cultura e opulência do Brasil*. 3rd ed. São Paulo [1711]: 1982.

Araújo, Antonio, S.J., *Catecismo na lingoa brasilica, no qual se contem a summa da doctrina christã . . . composto a modo de Dialogos por Padres Doctos, & bons lingoas da Companhia de Jesu*. Lisbon: 1618.

Arrais, Amador. *Diálogos*. Porto [1589]: 1974.

Barbosa Machado, D. *Biblioteca Lusitana*. 4 vols. Lisbon [1741–1759]: 1930–1933.

Barbot, J. *A description of the coasts of north and south-Guinea, and of Ethiopia inferior, vulgarly Angola. . . .* London: 1732.

Barlaeus, Caspar. *Rerum per octennium. . . .* Brazilian transl. *História dos feitos recentemente praticados durante oito anos no Brasil*. São Paulo [1647]: 1974.

Barros, João de. "Ásia, Primeira Década," in *Da Ásia de João de Barros e de Diogo do Couto*. Lisbon [1552]: 1777–1788.

Pereira Bayão, J. *Portugal cuidadoso, e lastimado com a a Vida, e Perda do Senhor Rey Dom Sebastião, o desejado de saudosa memoria*, Lisbon: 1737.

Benci, J. *Economia Cristã dos Senhores no governo dos escravos*. Lisbon [1700]: 1954.

Beozzo, J. O. *Leis e regimentos das missões*. São Paulo: 1983.

Bettendorf, J. F. *Crônica dos padres da Companhia de Jesus no Estado do Maranhão*. Belém, Pará [1698], 1990.

Biker, J. F. Judice, ed. *Memória sobre o estabelecimento de Macau, pelo visconde de Santarem. Abreviada relação da embaixada que el-rei João v mandou ao imperador da China e Tartaria. Relatorio de Francisco de Assis Pacheco de Sampaio a el-rei José I dando conta dos successos da embaixada a que fôra mandado á côrte de Pekim, 1752*. Lisbon: 1879.

Bluteau, R. *Vocabulario portuguez e latino*. 10 vols. Coimbra: 1712–1728.

Bocage, M. M. du *Poesias*. Lisbon [c. 1790]: 1966.

Bontinck, F. *Diaire congolais 1690–1701 de fra Luca da Caltanisetta*. Louvain: 1970.

Borges da Fonseca, A. J. V. "Nobiliarchia pernambucana" [1748]. *ABNRJ*, 47 no. 1, Rio de Janeiro: 1925, 5–488.

Botelho, S. X. *Memórias estatísticas sobre os domínios portuguezes na África Oriental*. Lisbon, 1835.

Boxer, C. R., and J. C. Aldridge. *Descriptive List of the State Papers "Portugal" 1661–1780 in the Public Record Office*, v. 1. Lisbon: 1979.

Brandão, A. F. *Diálogos das grandezas do Brasil*. Recife [1618]: 1962.

Brásio, Antônio. *Monumenta Missionária Africana*. Series 1 (West Central Africa). 15 vols. Lisbon, 1952–1988, *MMA¹*; series 2 (West Africa), 7 vols. Lisbon, 1958–2004; hereafter *MMA²*.

"Breve manifesto de nutiçiozas utilidades pertensentes à este Estado do Brasil," in A. de Magalhães Basto, "Alguns documentos de interesse para a história do Brasil," in *Brasilia*, vol. 7. Coimbra: 1952, 183–185.

Brito Freyre, F. de *Viagem da Armada da Companhia do Comércio e Frotas do Estado do Brasil.* Lisbon: 1657.

———. *Nova Lusitânia—História da Guerra Brasílica.* Recife [1675]: 1977.

Cadornega, Antônio de Oliveira de. *História Geral das Guerras Angolanas (HGGA).* 3 vols. Edited by José Mathias Delgado (vols. 1 e 2) and Manuel Alves da Cunha (vol. 3). Lisbon [1681]: 1972.

Calado, Manuel. *O Valeroso Lucideno.* 2 vols. São Paulo [1648]: 1987.

Caldas, José Antônio. "Notícia Geral de Toda Esta Capitania da Bahia desde o Seu Descobrimento até o Presente Anno de 1759," *Revista do Instituto Geográphico e Histórico da Bahia* 57 (1931).

Caraffa, F., and G. Morelli. *Bibliotheca sanctorum.* 12 vols. Roma: 1961–1970.

Cardim, Fernão. *Tratado da terra e gente do Brasil.* São Paulo [1585]: 1978.

Carneiro de Mendonça, Marcos. *O marquez de Pombal e o Brasil.* São Paulo: 1960.

Cartas do Senado da Bahia, 1638–1698. 5 vols. Salvador, 1951.

Cavazzi Da Montecuccolo, G. A. *Istorica Descrizione de' Tre Regni, Congo, Matamba et Angola* (Portuguese translation, *Descrição Histórica dos Três reinos do Congo, Matamba e Angola* [*DHCMA*]), 2 vols. Lisbon [1687]: 1965.

Colleção das Leis do Brazil de 1809. Rio de Janeiro: 1891.

Conceição, A. da "Tratado dos Rios de Cuama." *O Chronista de Tissuary* 2, no. 15 ([1696] 1867), 39–45, 43, 63–69, 84–92, and 105–111.

Constituçoens Primeyras do Arcebispado da Bahia, feytas & ordenadas pelo ilustríssimo e reverendissimo Sr. D. Sebastião Monteyro da Vide, arcebispo do dito arcebispado Coimbra [1707]: 1720.

Cordeiro, Luciano. *1593–1631 Terras e minas africanas segundo Balthazar Rebello de Aragão.* Lisbon: 1881.

Cortesão, Jaime, *Jesuítas e bandeirantes do Itatim 1596–1760.* Rio de Janeiro: 1952.

———. *Jesuítas e Bandeirantes no Tape, 1615–1641.* Rio de Janeiro: 1969.

———. *Jesuítas e bandeirantes no Guairá 1594–1640.* Rio de Janeiro: 1951.

———. *Pauliceae lusitana Monumenta historica 1494–1600.* 3 vols. Lisbon–Rio de Janeiro: 1956–1961.

———. *Jesuítas e bandeirantes no Uruguai, 1611–1758.* Rio de Janeiro: 1970.

Correia, Gaspar. *Lendas da Índia.* 4 vols. Introduction by M. Lopes de Almeida. Porto [1563]: 1975.

Costa, A. C. da. *Corografia portugueza e descripçam topografica do famoso Reyno de Portugal.* 3 vols. Lisbon: 1706–1712.

Couto, Carlos. "Documentos para a história da sucessão de Paulo Dias Novais na doação da capitania de Angola." *Estudos Históricos* 15 (1976): 133–185.

Couto, Diogo do. *O soldado prático* [1593–1610]. Lisbon: 1980, preface and notes by M. Rodrigues Lapa.

Cruz, Gaspar da. *Tratado das coisas da China*, edited by Rui Manuel Moreno. Lisbon [1570]: 1997.

Cunha Matos, R. J. da *Corographia historica das ilhas de S. Thomé, Principe, Anno Bom, e Fernando Po.* Porto: 1842.

———. *Compêndio Histórico das Possessões de Portugal na África*, edited by J. H. Rodrigues. Rio de Janeiro [c. 1820]: 1963.

Cuvelier, J., and L. Jadin. *L'Ancien Congo d'après les archives romaines 1518–1640*. Brussels: 1954.

Damião Cosme, F. "Tractado das queixas endemicas e mais fataes nesta Conquista." Luanda [1770] *Studia* 20–22 (1967): 119–268.

Daniel, João. "Tesouro descoberto no rio Amazonas [1757–1776]." *ABNRJ*. 2 vols. Rio de Janeiro: 1976.

Dantas Silva, L., ed. *Alguns documentos para a história da escravidão*. Recife: 1988.

Dapper, O. *Description de l'Afrique contenant les noms, la situation et les confins de toutes ses parties*. Amsterdam: 1686.

D'Assier, A. "Le Mato Virgem." *Revue des Deux Mondes* 1: 1864.

De Backer, Augustin, E. Aloys, and A. Carayon, A. *Bibliothèque de la Compagnie de Jesus*, edited by C. Sommervogel. 12 vols. Brussels, Paris, Louvain: 1890–1960.

Degranpré, L. *Voyage à la côte occidentale d'Afrique: fait dans les années 1786 et 1787, contenant la description des mœurs, usages, lois, gouvernement et commerce des états du Congo*. 2 vols. Paris: 1800–1801.

Delgado da Silva, A. *Colleção da Legislação Portugueza desde a última compilação das Ordenações*. 6 vols. Lisbon: 1830–1835.

Demerson, P. "Correspondance diplomatique de François Lanier résident de France à Lisbonne 1642–1644.," *Arquivos do Centro Cultural Português*. Vol. 32. Paris: 1993, 509–570.

de Sade, Marquis. *La philosophie dans le boudoir*. Paris [1795]: 1976.

Dias Coimbra. C. *Livro de patentes do tempo do senhor Salvador Correia de Sá e Benevides*. Luanda [1648–1652]: 1969.

Dias, Pedro. *Arte da língua de Angola oferecida a Virgem Senhora N. do Rosário, Mãy & Senhora dos mesmos Pretos*. Lisbon: 1697.

Di Lichii, W. *Kriegsbüch darin die Alte ünd Newe Militia*. Frankfurt: 1689.

Documentos Interessantes para a história e costumes de São Paulo (DI). 22 vols. São Paulo: 1895–1968.

Ericeira, Conde da. *História de Portugal restaurado*. 4 vols. Porto [1679–1698]: 1945.

Faria e Sousa, P. de. *Asia Portuguesa*. Vol. 2. Lisbon: 1674.

Felgueiras Gayo, M. J. da C. *Nobiliário de famílias de Portugal*. 12 vols. Braga [1830]: 1992.

Fernandes, Valentim. *Códice Valentim Fernandes*. Academia Portuguesa da História. Lisbon: 1997.

Fernandes Pinheiro, J. C. "A Carioca—Memória Histórica e Documentada." *RIHGB*, vol. 25 (1862): 565–588 [1507]: 1997.

Ferrand de Almeida, L. *A Colônia do Sacramento na época da sucessão de Espanha*. Coimbra: 1973.

Ferreira Pires, V. *Viagem de África em o Reino de Dahomé*. São Paulo [1800]: 1957.

Figueiredo, M. *Hidrographia, exame de pilotos: no qual se contem as regras que todo piloto deue guardar em suas nauegações: com os roteiros de Portugal pera o Brasil, Rio da Prata, Guinè, S. Thomé, Angolla, & Indias de Portugla* [sic], *& Castella*. Lisbon: 1625.

Findlay, A. G. *A sailing directory for the Ethiopic or South Atlantic Ocean, Including the Coasts of South America and Africa*. London: 1867.

Fonseca, Luísa da. *Bahia, Índice dos documentos do século XVII*. 2 vols. Lisbon: n/d.

Freitas, Serafim, *De Iusto Imperio Lusitanorum Asiatico*, Portuguese translation. Lisbon [1625]: 1983.

Fróis, Luís. *História de Japam*. Vol. 5. Edited by J. Wicki. Lisbon [1584–1594]: 1976.

Galhegos, M. de. *Gazeta, em que relatam as novas todas, que ouve nesta corte, e que vieram de varias partes no mês de novembro de 1641*, Lisbon: 1641–1644.

Garlan, Y., *L'Esclavage dans le monde grec*. Paris: 1984.

Gioia da Napoli, F. M. *La maravigliosa conversione alla Santa Fede di Cristo della Regina Singa e del suo regno di Matamba*. Napoli: 1669.

Gomez Carneiro, D. *Oração apodíxica aos scismaticos da pátria*. Lisbon: 1641.

Gomes Ferreyra, L. *Erário mineral dividida em doze tratados*. Lisbon: 1732.

Gonçalves de Magalhães, D. J. "Memória Histórica e Documentada da Revolução da Província do Maranhão desde 1839 até 1840." *Novos Estudos: Cebrap* 23 (1989): 14–66:

Gonsalves de Mello, J. A. *Fontes para a História do Brasil Holandês*. 2 vols. Recife: 1981–1985.

Guerreiro, B. *Jornada dos Vassalos da Coroa de Portugal*. Rio de Janeiro [1625]: 1966.

Guerreiro, F. *Relação anual das coisas que fizeram os padres da Companhia de Jesus nas suas missões*. 3 vols. Coimbra: 1930–1942.

Guzmán, D. de Alencar, and L. A. H. C. Hulsman. *Holandeses na Amazônia (1620–1650): documentos inéditos*. Belém: 2016.

Hegel, G. W. *Die Vernunft in der Geschichte (La raison dans l'histoire)*. Paris [1822–1823]: 1965.

Heintze, B. *Fontes para a história de Angola do século XVII: Cartas e documentos oficiais da colectânea documental de Fernão de Sousa, 1624–1635*. 2 vols. Stuttgart: 1985–1988.

Herbert, William. *A New Map, or Chart in Mercator's Projection of the Ethiopic Ocean with Part of Africa and South America*. London: 1763.

Index das Notas de vários Tabelliães de Lisboa, entre os annos de 1580 e 1747. Vol. 2. Lisbon [1624]: 1937.

Inventários e testamentos (século XVII). São Paulo 31, 1940; 34, 1951; 37, 1953; 40, 1955.

Jaboatão, A. de S. M. *Catálogo genealógico das principais famílias* (hereafter *CGPF*). 2 vols. edited by P. Calmon. Salvador [1768]: 1985.

Jadin, L. *L'Ancien Congo et l'Angola 1639–1655, d'après les archives romaines, portugaises, néerlandaises et espagnoles.* 3 vols. Brussels: 1975.

Jornal do Commercio. Rio de Janeiro: 1850–1860.

Lacerda e Almeida, F. J. de. "Diário da viagem de Moçambique para os rios de Sena, 1797–1798." *Diários de viagem.* Rio de Janeiro: 1944.

Laet, Johannes de. *Historie ofte Iaerlyck Verhael de verrichtinghen der Geoctroyeerde West–Indische Compagnie* [1644] (Brazilian translation, *História ou Annaes dos feitos da Companhia Privilegiada das Índias Ocidentais*). 2 vols. Rio de Janeiro: 1916 and 1925. The last part of the text can be found in J. de Laet, "Historia ou Annaes dos feitos da Companhia privilegiada das Indias occidentaes desde o seu começa até ao fim do anno de 1636," *ABNRJ* 41–42 (1919-1920): 1–222.

L'Africain, Léon. *Description de l'Afrique.* 2 vols. Paris [1550]: 1956.

Laranjo Coelho, P. M., ed. *Cartas de el-rei d. João IV ao conde de Vidigueira (marquês de Niza) embaixador em França.* 2 vols. Lisbon: 1945–1947.

———. *Cartas de el-rei d. João IV para diversas autoridades do Reino.* 2 vols. Lisbon: 1940.

———. *Cartas dos governadores da província do Alentejo a el-rei d. João IV.* 2 vols. Lisbon: 1947.

Las Casas, Bartolomé de. *Brevísima relación de la destrucción de África: Preludio de la destrucción de Indias* [1540–1554], edition and notes by Isacio Pérez Fernández. Salamanca: 1989.

Leite, Serafim. *História da Companhia de Jesus no Brasil, 1549–1760.* 10 vols. Lisbon and Rio de Janeiro: 1938–1950.

———. *Monumenta Brasiliae.* 5 vols. Rome: 1956–1968.

Lemos Coelho, Francisco de. *Duas Descrições Seiscentistas da Guiné,* Lisbon [1669 and 1684]: 1953.

Léry, Jean de. *Narrative d'un voyage fait à la terre du Brésil.* Brazilian trans., "Viagem à terra do Brasil." São Paulo [1578]: 1980.

Levillier, R. *Antecedentes de política económica en el Río de La Plata documentos originales de los siglos XVI al XIX seleccionados en al Archivo de Indias de Sevilla.* Vol. 1. Madrid: 1915.

Lisboa, Cristovão de. *História dos animais e árvores do Maranhão.* Lisbon [1640]: 1967.

Lisboa, João Francisco. *Obras.* 4 vols. São Luís: 1865–1866.

———. *Vida do padre Antônio Vieira.* Rio de Janeiro [c. 1840]: 1891.

"Livro das monções," n. 63, 1692–1699, summarized by Vítor Rodrigues. *Boletim da Filmoteca Ultramarina Portuguesa,* no. 50. Lisbon: 1993.

Livros de oficios para o Reino 1726–1801. Luanda, 1959.

Livro de rezão de Antônio Coelho Guerreiro, preface by V. Rau. Lisbon [1684–1692]: 1956.

"Livro de Tombo do Colégio de Jesus do Rio de Janeiro," *ABNRJ,* vol. 82, 1962.

Lopes de Lima, J. J., and F. Bordalo. *Ensaios sobre a statística das possessões portuguezas*. 5 vols. Lisbon: 1844–1862.

Lopes Moreno, D. *Livro que dá Razão do Estado do Brasil–1612*. Introduction and notes by H. Vianna. Recife: 1955.

Loreto Couto, Domingos do. *Desagravos do Brazil e glórias de Pernambuco*. Rio de Janeiro [1757]: 1904.

Macedo Soares, A. J. de *Dicionário brasileiro da língua portuguesa Elucidário, etimológico, crítico*. 2 vols. Rio de Janeiro [1875–1888]: 1954.

Machado de Oliveira, J. J. "Notícia racionada sobre as aldeias de índios da Província de São Paulo." *RIHGB*, vol. 8 (1846): 204–254.

Madre de Deus, Gaspar da. *Memórias para a história da capitania de São Vicente*. São Paulo [1797]: 1975.

Magalhães Gandavo, Pero de. *Tratado da Terra do Brasil* e *História da Província de Santa Cruz*. Rio de Janeiro [1576]: 1911.

Manso de Lima, J. Leitão. *Famílias de Portugal*. 15 vols. Lisbon [1730]: 1925.

Maranhão, F. de Nossa Senhora dos Prazeres *Poranduba maranhense*. São Luís [c. 1820]: 1946.

Marcgrave, Geed. *História natural do Brasil*. Brazilian translation. São Paulo [1648]: 1942.

Mariz de Carneiro, A. *Regimento de pilotos e Roteiro da navegaçam e conquistas do Brasil, Angola, S. Thome, Cabo Verde, Maranhão, Ilhas, & Indias Occidentais*. Lisbon: 1655.

Marques Pereira, Nuno. *Compêndio Narrativo do Peregrino da América*. 2 vols. Rio de Janeiro [1728]: 1988.

Martins Penna. "Os dois ou o inglês maquinista." *Comédias*, scene 9. Rio de Janeiro [1842]: n.d.

Marx, K. *Le Capital*, French translation. 3 vols. Paris [1867–1894]: 1976.

Matos, A. T. de, ed., *Diário do conde Sarzedas—Vice-rei do Estado da Índia 1655–1656*. Lisbon: 2001.

Mauro, Frédéric, ed. *Le Brésil au XVIIème siècle: Documents inédits relatifs à l'Atlantique portugais*. Coimbra: 1963.

Melo, Francisco Manuel de. *Politica militar en avisos de generales*. Madrid: 1638.

———. *Carta de guia de casados*. Lisbon: 1650.

———. *Tácito português*. Lisbon [1650]: 1995.

———. *Epanáforas de vária história portuguesa*. 3rd ed. Coimbra [1660]: 1931.

———. *Cartas familiares*. Lisbon [1664]: 1981.

Mendes Pinto, Fernão. *Peregrinação*, 5 vols. Lisbon [1614]: 1967.

Mercado, Thomas de. *Suma de tratos y contratos* [1571], 2 vols. (Madrid: 1977).

Merolla da Sorrento, G. *Breve Relazione del Viaggio nel Regno di Congo Nell' Africa Meridionale*. Naples: 1692.

Mirales, J. de. "História militar do Brazil." *ABNRJ* 22 [1762]: 1900.

Molina, Luís de. *De Justitia et Jure*. Geneva [1593]: 1733.

Monteiro, J. J. "On the Quissama Tribe of Angola." *The Journal of the Anthropological Institute of Great Britain and Ireland* 5 (1876): 198–201.

Monteiro Baena, A. L. *Compêndio das eras da província do Pará*. Rio de Janeiro [1838]: 1969.

Montoya, Antonio. Ruiz de. *Conquista Espiritual hecha por los religiosos de la Compañia de Jesus*. Bilbao [1639]: 1892.

———. "Primeva catechese dos índios selvagens feita pelos padres da Companhia de Jesus." *ABNRJ*, v. 6 ([1733] 1878–1879): 91–366.

Morão, S. *Queixas repetidas em ecos nos Arrecifes de Pernambuco contra os abusos médicos que nas suas capitanias se observam tanto em dano das vidas de seus habitadores*. (Lisbon [1677]: 1965.

Mousse, Jean de la, S.J. *Les Indiens de la Sinnamary 1684–1691*, introduction, édition et notes de Gérard Collomb. Paris: 2006.

Netscher, M. *Les Hollandais au Brésil*. The Hague: 1853.

Nieuhof, J. *Gedenkweerdige Brasiliaense Zee-en-Lant Reize*. Amsterdam: 1682; (Brazilian translation, *Memorável viagem marítima e terrestre ao Brasil*), São Paulo: 1981.

Nóbrega, Manuel da *Cartas Jesuiticas*. 2 vols. São Paulo [1549–1560]: 1988.

———. *Diálogo sobre a conversão do gentio*, notes by Serafim Leite. Lisbon [1557]: 1954.

Norton, Luís. "Os planos que Salvador Correia de Sá e Benevides apresentou em 1643 para se abrir o comércio com Buenos Aires e reconquistar o Brasil e Angola." *Brasília*, vol. II, 1943, 594–613.

O Compilador Paulistano. São Paulo: 1852.

"O diário do governador Correia de Sá 1749–1756. "Introduction and notes, J. A. Gonsalves de Mello. *RIAHGP* 56 (1983): 9–378.

Oliveira, Fernão de. *A Arte da Guerra no Mar*. Coimbra: 1555.

Oliveira Mendes, L. A. de. *Memória a respeito dos escravos e tráfico da escravatura entre a Costa d'África e o Brasil*. Porto [1793]: 1977.

Orta, Garcia de. *Colóquios dos simples e drogas da Índia*. 2 vols. Lisbon [1563]: 1987.

Osório de Andrade, Gilberto, and Eustáquio Duarte. *Morão, Rosa & Pimenta*. Recife [1684–1703]: 1957.

Pacheco Pereira, Duarte. *Esmeraldo de situ orbis*. Lisbon [1505–1508]: 1975.

Paes Leme, Pedro Taques de Almeida. *Nobiliarquia paulistana histórica e genealógica*. 3 vols. 5th ed. São Paulo [1763–1773]: 1980.

———. "Notícia histórica da expulsão dos jesuítas do Collégio de São Paulo." *RIHGB*, vol. 12. (1849): 5–40.

Park, Mungo. *Voyage dans l'intérieur de l'Afrique* 1795–1797. French translation, Paris [1799]: 1980.

Pascal, Blaise. "Huitième provinciale." *Oeuvres complètes*. Eds. L. Brunschvig, P. Boutroux e F. Gazier. Paris, 1914, vol. v, pp. 148–151.

Pastells F. and P. Mateos, *Historia de la Compañia de Jesus en la Província del Paraguay* Madrid: 1948–1949, vol. 8, 1st part, 1751–1760.

Penn, J. *The South American Pilot*. Part 1. *The East Coast of South America from Cape St. Roque to Cape San Antonio, Rio de la Plata; and the North Coast from Cape St. Roque to the Rio Maroni in French Guyana*. London: 1864.

Perdigão Malheiro, Agostinho M. *A escravidão no Brasil, ensaio jurídico, histórico, social* 2 vols. Petrópolis [1867]: 1976.

Pereira Rêgo, J. *História e descrição da febre amarela epidêmica que grassou no Rio de Janeiro em 1850*. Rio de Janeiro: 1850.

Peres, Damião. *Regimento das Cazas das Índias e Mina* Coimbra: [1509] 1947.

Pigafetta, F. *Relação do Reino do Congo e das terras circunvizinhas*, edited by A. L. Alves Ferronha. Lisbon [1591]: 1989.

Piso, W. *História natural e médica da Índia Occidental*. Brazilian translation. Rio de Janeiro [1648–1658]: 1957.

Platon. *La République*, translated and commented on by R. Baccou. Paris: 1966.

Polo, J. T. "Relacion del Estado del govierno del Peru." In *Memorias de los Virreys del Perú, Marques de Mancera y Conde de Salvatierra*. Lima [1648]: 1899.

Prestage, Edgar. "As lutas luso-holandesas em Angola de 1641 a 1648 contadas por Luis Felis Crus, testemunha ocular." Academia de Sciencias de Lisboa, *Boletim da Classe das Letras* 13 (1918–1919): 41–76.

Prestage, Edgar, Azevedo P. de, and P. M. Laranjo Coelho, eds. *Correspondência Diplomática de Francisco de Sousa Coutinho durante sua embaixada em Holanda 1643–1650*. 3 vols. Coimbra-Lisbon: 1920–1955.

Procissam, relação das festas que a residência de Amgolla fez, edited by A. Parreira. Lisbon [1620]: 1993.

Proyart, L.-B. *Histoire de Loango, Kakongo, et Autres Royaumes d'Afrique: Rédigée d'après Les Mémoires des Préfets Apostoliques de La Mission Françoise, enrichie d'une carte utile aux navigateurs*. Paris: 1776.

Pyrard, François. *Voyage de François Pyrard, de Laval, Contenant sa navigation aux Indes orientales, Maldives, Molugues, Bresil* . . . Paris, Samuel Thiboust, 1619.

Rainero, R. H. *Il Congo agli inizi del Settecento nella relazione di Luca da Caltanissetta*. Florence [1701]: 1974.

Rangel, C. A. de Aguiar, and M. Leitão. *Inventário dos Manuscritos da Biblioteca da Ajuda referentes à América do Sul*. Coimbra: 1946.

Rau, V., and M. F. Gomes da Silva. *Os Manuscritos do Arquivo da Casa de Cadaval respeitantes ao Brasil*. 2 vols. Coimbra: 1956–1958.

Ravenstein, E. G. *The Strange Adventures of Andrew Battel of Leigh, in Angola and the Adjoining Regions*. London [1598]: 1901.

Rebello da Silva, L. A. *História de Portugal: Séculos XVI e XVII*. 5 vols. Lisbon: 1860–1871.
"Regimento [. . .] ao capitão-mor e governador do reino de Angola d. Tristão da Cunha" [1666]. *Boletim do Conselho Ultramarino*, Legislação Antiga. Lisbon 1 (1867): 297–307.
"Regimento [. . .] ao capitão-mor e governador do reino de Angola, d. Manuel Pereira Forjaz" [1607]. *Boletim do Arquivo Histórico Colonial* 1 (1950): 235–243.
Regio, M. A. de G. da, and D. de C. da Piacenza. *Viaggio nel Regno del Congo*. Bologna: 1674.
"Relação da Aclamação que se fez na capitania do Rio de Janeiro do Estado do Brasil . . ." In José A. Castello. *O movimento academicista no Brasil*. Vol. III, Book 1. São Paulo [1641] 1969: 5–12.
Relacion de los servicios del capitan de Cavallos don Juan Davalos. Madrid: 1652.
"Relations Sur Le Congo du Père Laurent de Lucques (1700–1717)." In *Institut Royal Colonial Belge—Mémoires*, edited by J. Cuvelier. (Brussels: 1953).
Ribeiro, Francisco de Paula. "Memória sobre as nações gentias que presentemente habitam o continente do Maranhão." *RIHGB* 3 ([1819] 1842).
Ribeiro, J. *Índice chronológico remissivo da legislação portuguêza posterior à publicação do Código Filipino*. 6 vols. Lisbon: 1805–1820.
Ribeiro Rocha, M. *Ethiope resgatado, empenhado, sustentado, corregido, instruído e libertado: Discurso theologico-juridico em que se propõem o modo de comerciar, haver, e possuir validamente, quanto a hum e outro foro, os pretos cativos africanos, e as principais obrigações que correm a quem delles se servir*. Lisbon: 1758.
Ribeiro Sanches, A. *Tratado da Conservação da Saúde dos Povos*. Lisbon: 1756.
Richshoffer, Ambrósio. *Diário de um soldado* [1677]. Ed. conjunta com a crônica do padre J. Baers, *Olinda conquistada* [1630]. Recife: 1977.
Rio de Janeiro no século XVII: Accordãos e vereanças do Senado da Câmara [. . .] relativos aos annos de 1635 até 1650. Rio de Janeiro: 1935.
Ripley, G., and Charles A. Dana. *The American Cyclopaedia: A Popular Dictionary of General Knowledge* 2. New York: 1873.
Rocha Pitta, Sebastião da. *História da América portuguesa* [1730]. São Paulo: 1976.
Rodrigues Ferreira, A. "Diário da viagem filosófica pela capitania de São José do Rio Negro com a informação do estado presente." *RIHGB*, vol. 48 (1885): 1–234.
Rodrigues Lobo, Francisco. *Corte na aldeia*. Lisbon [1618]: 1997.
Rodrigues, Pero. "Vida do Padre José de Anchieta." *ABNRJ* 19 ([1607] 1897): 2–49.
Rosário Pinto, Manuel do. *Relação do Descobrimento da Ilha de São Tomé. Manuel do Rosário Pinto*, edited by A. Caldeira. Lisbon [1734]: 2006.
Rousseau, J.-J. *Discours sur l'origine et les fondements de l'inegalité parmi les hommes*. Geneva: 1755.
Salmoral, Manuel Lucena. *Regulación de la esclavitut negra en las colonias de América Española (1503–1886): documentos para su studio*. Espinardo, Murcia: 2005.
Salvador, Vicente do *História do Brasil 1500–1627*. São Paulo [c. 1627]: 1982.

Salgado de Araújo, João. *Sumario de la familia ilustrissima de Vasconcelos, historiada y con elogios*. Madrid: 1638.

Sandoval, Alonso, *Naturaleza, policía sagrada y profana, costumbres y ritos, disciplina y catecismo evangelico de todos los etíopes* (Sevilla: 1627), reedited by E. Vila Vilar, *Un tratado sobre la esclavitud*. Madrid: 1987.

Santa Rosa de Viterbo, F. J. de. *Elucidário das palavras, termos e frases [1798–1799]*. 2 vols. Porto-Lisbon: 1983.

Santarém, visconde de. *Quadro elementar das relações políticas e diplomáticas de Portugal com as diversas potências do mundo*. 18 vols. Paris, Lisbon, 1842–1860.

Santa Teresa, Giovanni Giuseppi di. *Istoria delle guerre del regno del Brasile accadute tra la corona di Portogallo e la repubblica di Olanda*. Roma: 1698.

Santos, Frei João dos. *Ethiopia Oriental e Vária história de cousas notáveis do Oriente*. Évora: 1609.

Savary des Bruslons, J., ed. *Dictionnaire Universel du Commerce, d'Histoire Naturelle et des Arts et Métiers*. 4 vols. Copenhague: 1759–1762.

Schwartz, Stuart B. *A Governor and His Image in Baroque Brazil: The Funereal Eulogy of Afonso Furtado de Castro do Rio de Mendonça by Juan Lopes Sierra* (Minneapolis, MN [1676]: 1979).

Sepp, A. *Viagem às missões jesuítas e trabalhos apostólicos*. São Paulo [1691]: 1980.

Sérgio, A., ed. *Antologia dos Economistas Portugueses: século XVII*. Lisbon: 1974.

Serrão Pimentel, L. *Arte Prática de Navegar*. Lisbon: 1681.

Silva, I. F. da. *Diccionario bibliographico portuguez*. Vol. 5. Lisbon: 1860.

Silva Correa, E. A. da. *História de Angola*. 2 vols. Lisbon [1787–1799]: 1937.

Silva Lisboa, Balthazar da. *Annaes do Rio de Janeiro*. 7 vols. Rio de Janeiro: 1834–1835.

Silva Marques, J. M. da. *Descobrimentos Portugueses, documentos para a sua história*. 3 vols. Lisbon: 1971.

Silva Rego, Antonio da. *Documentação Para a História das Missões do Padroado Português do Oriente: Índia, 1548–1550*. 10 vols. Lisbon, 1947–1958.

———. *As Gavetas da Torre do Tombo*. 12 vols. Lisbon: 1960–1977.

Solís, Duarte Gomes, *Alegación en Fauor de la Compañia de La India Oriental Y Comercios Vltramarinos Que de Nueuo Se Instituyó en El Reyno de Portugal*, edited by M. B. Amzalak. Lisbon [1628]: 1955.

Sousa, A. Caetano. de *História genealógica da Casa Real portuguesa*. 12 vols. Coimbra [1740]: 1949.

Sousa, Francisco de. *Oriente conquistado a Jesus Cristo pelos padres da Companhia de Jesus da província de Goa*. 2 vols. Porto [1710]: 1978.

Sousa, Luís de. *História de são Domingos*. 2 vols. 4th ed. Porto [1623]: 1977.

Souza de Macedo, Antonio de. *Mercurio Portuguez, com as novas da guerra entre Portugal e Castella*. BNL, Res. Lisbon: 1663–1667.

Souza Silva, Joaquim Norberto de. "Memória histórica e documentada das aldeias de índios da província do Rio de Janeiro." *RIHGB* 17 (1854): 110–344.

Studart, Barão. "Dezenove documentos sobre os Palmares pertencentes à Colleção Studart." *Revista Trimensal do Instituto do Ceará* (hereafter *RTIC*) 20 (1906): 254–289.

———. "Documentos para a história do Brasil e especialmente a do Ceará." In *Revista Trimensal do Instituto do Ceará*. Vol. 42 (1928): 103–105.

Sylveira, S. E. da. "Relação sumária das cousas do Maranhão dirigida aos pobres deste reyno de Portugal." *ABNRJ* 94 ([1624] 1974): 1–43.

Tavares de Macedo, J. "Do que eram os tangomãoes de que se fala na Ordenação do Reino," *Annaes do Conselho Ultramarino, parte não oficial*. Lisbon [1854–1858]: 1867: 313–315.

Teixeira Albernas, João. *Atlas do Estado do Brasil, coligido das mais sertas notícias que pode ajuntar d. Jerônimo de Ataide*. Rio de Janeiro [1631]: 1997.

Teixeira Coelho, J. J. "Instrucção para o governo de capitania de Minas Geraes." *Revista do Instituto Histórico e Geográphico do Brazil (RIHGB)*. Vol. 7. Rio de Janeiro [1780]: Nacional, 1852: 255–481.

Telles, Balthazar. *Chronica da Companhia de Jesu nos reinos de Portugal*. 2 vols. Lisbon: 1645–1647.

Toledo Rendon, J. A. de. "Memória sobre as aldeias de índios da província de São Paulo, segundo observações feitas em 1798." *Revista do Instituto Histórico e Geográfico Brasileiro (RIHGB)* 4, 1842: 295–317.

Vale, Leonardo do. "Vocabulário na língua brasílica [1621]." 2 vols. Edited by C. Drumond. *Boletim da Fac. de Filosofia, Ciências e Letras da USP*, 137 (1952) and 164 (1953).

Vasconcellos S. de. *Vida do Joam d'Almeida da Companhia de Jesu na Província do Brazil* Lisbon: 1658.

———. *Notícias curiosas e necessárias das cousas do Brasil*. Lisbon: 1668.

Vasconcelos, Luís Mendes. *Diálogos do sítio de Lisboa*. Lisbon [1608]: 1990.

———. *A Arte militar*. Lisbon: 1612.

"Viagem que fez o Pe. Ant. Gomes, da Companhia de Jesus, ao império de Manomotapa [1648]." *Studia* 3 (1959): 155–242.

Vies des saints et des bienheureux selon l'ordre du calendrier avec l'historique des fêtes. 13 vols. Paris: 1952.

Vieira, Antonio [1608–1697]. *Cartas do Pe Antônio Vieira*, prefaced and reviewed by J. L. de Azevedo. 3 vols. Lisbon: 1997.

———. *História do Futuro*, edited by Maria Leonor Carvalhão Buescu. Lisbon, 1992.

———. *Livro anteprimeiro da História do Futuro*, edited by J. van den Besselaar. Lisbon, 1983.

———. *Obras escolhidas*, prefaced and reviewed by A. Sérgio and H. Cidade. 12 vols. Lisbon: 1951–1954.

———. *Sermões*, prefaced and reviewed by Gonçalo Alves. 5 vols. Porto: 1993.

Wiedemann, Thomas. *Greek and Roman Slavery*. Canberra: 1983.

Xenophon. *Économique*, edited and translated by P. Chantraine. Paris: 1949.
Zuñiga, D. O. de *Annales eclesiásticos y seculares de la muy noble, y muy leal ciudad de Sevilla . . . , Que contienen sus mas principales memorias desde el año de 1246 . . . hasta el de 1671 . . .* Madrid: 1677.
Zurara, G. E. de. *Crônica de Guiné* [1453–1460]. Introduction by J. de Bragança. Barcelos: 1973.

Books and Articles

Abel, W. *Agrarkrisen und Agrarkonjunktur* (French translation, *Crises agraires en Europe XIIIe–XXe siècle*. Paris: 1973.
Addington, Harry H. *The Patterns of War Since the Eighteenth Century*. 2nd ed. Indiana U P, 1994.
Aguado de los Reyes, J. "El Apogeo de los Judios Portugueses en la Sevilla Americanista." *Cadernos de Estudos Sefarditas* 5 (2005): 135–157.
Akinjogbin, I. A. *Dahomey and Its Neighbours, 1708–1818*. Cambridge: 1967.
Albuquerque Felner, A. de. *Angola, Apontamentos sobre a ocupação e início do estabelecimento dos portugueses no Congo, Angola e Benguela (extraídos de documentos históricos)*. Coimbra: 1933.
———. *Apontamentos sobre a ocupação e início do estabelecimento dos portugueses no Congo, Angola e Benguela (extraídos de documentos históricos)*. 3 vols. Lisbon: 1940.
Alcântara Machado, J. de *Vida e morte do bandeirante*. São Paulo: 1930.
Alden, Dauril. "Black Robes versus White Settlers: The Struggle for Freedom of the Indians in Colonial Brazil." In *Attitudes of Colonial Powers toward the American Indian*, edited by H. Peckham and C. Gibson, 19–46. Salt Lake City: 1969.
———. "Economic Aspects of the Expulsion of the Jesuits from Brazil—A Preliminary Report." In *Conflict and Continuity in Brazilian Society*, edited by H. H. Keith and S. F. Edwards. Columbia: U of South Carolina P, 1969: 25–65.
———. "Price Movements in Brazil Before, During, and After the Gold Boom, with Special Reference to the Salvador Market, 1670–1769." In *Eighteenth-Century Price Movements in Latin America*, edited by L. Johnson and E. Tandeter, 335–371. Albuquerque, NM: 1989.
———. "Changing Jesuit Perceptions of the Brasis during the Sixteenth Century." *Journal of World History* 3, no. 2 (1992): 212–213.
———. *The Making of an Enterprise: The Society of Jesus in Portugal, Its Empire, and Beyond, 1540–1750*. Palo Alto, CA: Stanford UP, 1996.
Alden, Dauril, and J. C. Miller. "Unwanted Cargoes—The Origins and Dissemination of Smallpox via the Slave Trade from Africa to Brazil, c. 1560–1830." In *The African*

Exchange—Toward a Biological History of Black People, edited by K. F. Kiple. Durham, NC: 1987, 35–109.

Alden, Dauril, and Joseph C. Miller. "Out of Africa: The Slave Trade and the Transmission of Smallpox to Brazil, 1560–1831." *The Journal of Interdisciplinary History* 18, no. 2 (1987): 195–224.

Alderman, C. L. *Rum, Slaves and Molasses: The Story of New England's Triangular Trade*. Folkstone: 1972.

Alencastro, Luiz Felipe de. "La traite négrière et l'unité nationale brésilienne." *Revue française d'histoire d'outre-mer* 66, no. 244–245 (1979): 395–414.

———. "Rio de Janeiro, Bahia et le Nouvel Ordre Colonial 1808–1860." In *Géographie du Capital Marchand aux Amériques*, edited by Jane Chase, 131–151. Paris: 1987.

———. "A Interação européia com as sociedades brasileiras entre os séculos XVI e XVIII." In *Brasil, nas vésperas do mundo moderno*, edited by Francisco Faria Paulino, 97–120. Lisbon: 1992.

———. "L'Atlantique de Bahia: rivalités portugaises et luso-brésiliennes dans l'Atlantique Sud à l'époque du marquis de Pombal." In *Pour l'histoire du Brésil: Mélanges en l'honneur de Katia Mattoso*, edited by Françios Crouzet, Denis Rolland, and Philippe Bonnichon, 331–341. Paris: 2000.

———. "La puissance maritime portugaise du XVIe siècle au XIXe siècle." In *La Puissance Maritime*, edited by Christian Buchet, Jean Meyer, and Jean Pierre Poussou, 395–412. Paris: 2004.

———. "Continental drift—The Independence of Brazil, Portugal and Africa." In *From Slave Trade to Empire*, edited by Olivier Pétré-Grenouilleau, 98–109. London: 2004.

———."Le versant brésilien de l'Atlantique Sud: 1550–1850," *Annales, Histoire, Sciences Sociales* 61, no. 2 (2006), 339–382.

———. "The Economic Network of Portugal's Atlantic World." In *The Portuguese Oceanic Expansion 1400–1800*, edited by Francisco Bethencourt and Diogo Ramada Curto, 109–136. Cambridge, UK: 2007.

———. "Johann Moritz und der Sklavenhandel." In *Sein Feld war die Welt—Johann Moritz von Nassau-Siegen 1604–1679*, edited by G. Brunn and C. Neusch, 123–144. Münster: 2008.

———. "História geral das guerras sul-atlânticas: o episódio de Palmares." In *Mocambos de Palmares. Histórias e fontes (séculos XVI–XIX)*, edited by Flávio dos Santos Gomes, 61–99. Rio de Janeiro: 2010. Translated in a shorter version, "South Atlantic Wars: The Episode of Palmares," *Portuguese Studies Review* 19, nos. 1–2 (2012): 35–58.

———. "Mulattos in Brazil and Angola: A Comparative Approach, Seventeenth to Twenty-First Centuries." In *Racism and Ethnic Relations in the Portuguese-Speaking World*, edited by Francisco Bethencourt and Adrian Pearce, 71–96. London: 2012.

———. "The Ethiopic Ocean—History and Historiography 1600–1975." *Portuguese Literary & Cultural Studies* 27 (2015): 1–79.

———. "The African Slave Trade and the Construction of the Iberian Atlantic." In *The Global South Atlantic*, edited by K. Bystrom and Joseph R. Slaughter, 192–209. New York: 2017.

Alessandrini, N. "Vida, história e negócios dos mercadores italianos no Portugal dos Filipes." In *Portugal na Monarquia Hispânica*, edited by P. Cardim, L. F. Costa, and M. S. da Cunha, 107–134. Lisbon: 2013.

Almeida, Antônio de. "D. Francisco Manuel de Melo, historiador." *Península—Revista de Estudos Ibéricos* 6 (2009): 17–60.

Almeida, Fortunato de. *História da Igreja em Portugal* [1910–28]. 4 vols. Edited by Damião Peres. Porto: 1967–1971.

Almeida Calado, A. de. "A Companhia de Jesus na Índia em meados do século XVII." *Studia* 40 (1978): 349–366.

Almeida Mendes, António de. "Les réseaux de la traite ibérique dans l'Atlantique nord (1440–1640)." *Annales* 63 no. 4 (2008): 739–768.

———. "The Foundations of the System: A Reassessment of the Slave Trade to the Spanish Americas in the Sixteenth and Seventeenth Centuries." In *Extending the Frontiers: Essays on the New Transatlantic Slave Trade Database*, edited by D. Eltis and D. Richardson, 83–85. New Haven, CT: 2008.

Almeida Prado, J. F. de. "Les relations de Bahia (Brésil) avec le Dahomey." *Revue d'Histoire des Colonies* 41, no. 143 (1954): 167–226.

Alpern, Stanley B. "The European Introduction of Crops into West Africa in Precolonial Times." *History in Africa* 19 (1992): 13–43.

———. "Exotic Plants of Western Africa: Where They Came From and When," *History in Africa* 35, no. 1 (2008): 63–102.

Alpers, Edward A. *Ivory and Slaves in East Central Africa*. London: 1975.

———. *História de Moçambique*. Lisbon: 1997.

Alvarez Kern, A. *Missões: Uma utopia política*. Porto Alegre, RS: 1985.

Alves Carrara, A. *Receitas e despesas da Real Fazenda do Brasil, século XVII*. Juiz de Fora: 2009.

Amado J., and E. Jackson. "Mythic Origins: Caramuru and the Founding of Brazil." *HAHR* 80, no. 4 (2000): 783–811.

Amaral, A. *A Hispano-América na arte seiscentista do Brasil*. São Paulo: 1972.

Amaral, Ilidio do. "Mbanza Kongo, Cidade do Congo, ou São Salvador: Contribuição para o conhecimento geográfico de uma aglomeração urbana africana ao sul do Equador, nos séculos XVI e XVII." *Garcia de Orta* 12, no. 1–2 (1987): 1–40.

Amaral Ferlini, V. L. *Terra, trabalho e poder: O mundo dos engenhos no Nordeste colonial*. São Paulo: 1986.

Amaral Lapa, José Roberto de A. *Bahia e a Carreira da Índia.* São Paulo: 1968.
——— et al. *Modos de produção e realidade brasileira.* Rio de Janeiro: 1980.
Ames, G. J. "The *Estado da Índia* 1663–1677: Priorities and Strategies in Europe and the East," *Revista Portuguesa de História* 22 (1985): 31–46.
———. "An African Eldorado? The Portuguese Quest for Wealth and Power in Mozambique and the Rios de Cuama, c. 1661–1683." *The International Journal of African Historical Studies* 31, no. 1 (1998): 91–110.
Anan, M. R. *Marx and Engels on India.* Allahabad, India: 1933.
Andaya, L. Y. The "Informal Portuguese Empire and the Topasses in the Solor Archipelago and Timor in the Seventeenth and Eighteenth Centuries." *Journal of Southeast Asian Studies* 41, no. 3 (2010): 391–420.
Anderson, Robert N. "The Quilombo of Palmares: A New Overview of a Maroon State in Seventeenth-Century Brazil." *Journal of Latin American Studies* 28, no. 3 (1996): 545–566.
Arasaratnam, S. "Monopoly and Free Trade in Dutch-Asian Commercial Policy: Debate and Controversy within the VOC." *Journal of Southeast Asian Studies* 4, no. 1 (1973): 1–15.
Arenz, Karl-Heinz. *De l'Alzette à l'Amazonie: Jean-Philippe Bettendorf et les jésuites en Amérique portugaise 1661–1693.* Luxemburg: 2008.
Armitage, David. "The Elizabethan Idea of Empire." *Transactions of the Royal Historical Society* 14 (2004): 269–277.
Arnaux, Expedito. *Aspectos da legislação sobre os índios do Brasil.* Belém: 1973.
Arnold, R. "Séparation du commerce et du marché: le grande marché d'Ouidah," in *Les systemes économiques dans l'histoire et dans la théorie* (French translation), K. Polanyi and C. Arensberg, eds. (Paris: 1975), 187–191;
Assadourian, C. S. "Fray Bartolomé de Las Casas obispo: la naturaleza miserable de las naciones indianas y el derecho de la Iglesia. Un escrito de 1545." *Historia Mexicana* 40, no. 3 (1991): 387–451.
Aubin, Jean. "Albuquerque et les négociations de Cambaye." In *Mare Luso-Indicum*, vol. 1, 3–63. Geneva: 1971–1973.
Aucante, Vicente. "Os médicos e a medicina." *Cadernos de História e Filosofia da Ciência* 8, no. 1 (1998): 59–78.
Austen, Ralph A. "From the Atlantic to the Indian Ocean: European Abolition, the African Slave Trade, and Asian Economic Structures." In *The Abolition of the Atlantic Slave Trade*, edited by D. Eltis and J. Walvin, 117–140. Madison, WI: 1981.
———. "The Trans-Saharan Slave Trade: A Tentative Census." In *The Uncommon Market, Essays in the Economic History of the Atlantic Slave Trade*, edited by H. A. Gemery and J. S. Hogendorn, 23–72. New York: 1979.
———. "The Mediterranean Islamic Slave Trade Out of Africa: A Tentative Census." *Slavery and Abolition* 13, no. 1 (1992): 214–248.

———. "Marginalization, Stagnation, and Growth: The Trans-Saharan Caravan Trade in the Era of European Expansion, 1500–1900." In *The Rise of Merchant Empires: Long Distance Trade in the Early Modern World, 1350–1750*, edited by J. D. Tracy. Cambridge: 1993.

———. *Trans-Saharan Africa in World History*. New York: 2010.

Awad, A. M. "The Gulf in the Seventeenth Century." *Bulletin (British Society for Middle Eastern Studies)* 12, no. 2 (1985): 123–134.

Axelrod, Paul, and M. A. Fuerch. "Portuguese Orientalism and the Making of the Village Communities of Goa." *Ethnohistory* 45, no. 3 (1998): 439–476.

Axelson, E. *South-East Africa 1488–1530*. London: 1969, 6–11.

Azevedo, A. de "Aldeias e aldeamentos de índios." *Boletim Paulista de Geografia* 33 (1959): 23–40.

Azevedo, João Lúcio de Os. *Jesuítas no Grão-Pará*. Coimbra: 1930.

———. *História dos cristãos novos portugueses*. Lisbon: 1975.

———. *Épocas de Portugal econômico*. Porto: 1978.

———. *História de Antônio Vieira*. 2 vols. Lisbon: 1992.

Baghdiantz-McCabe, I. "Trading Diaspora, State Building, and the Idea of National Interest." In *Views from the Edge: Essays in Honor of Richard W. Bulliet*, edited by Neguin Yavari, L. G. Potter, and J.-M. Ran Oppenheim, 3–18. New York: Columbia UP, 2005.

Bailyn, Bernard. *The Peopling of British America: An Introduction*. New York: 1988.

———. *Atlantic History: Concept and Contours*. Cambridge, MA: 2005.

Balandier, G. *La vie quotidienne au royaume de Kongo. Du XVIe au XVIIIe siècle*. Paris: 1965.

Ballong-Wen-Mewuda, J. B. *São Jorge da Mina, 1482–1637*. 2 vols. Paris: 1993.

Banha de Andrade, A. A. "Antecedentes da travessia de África." *Anais* 27, series 2 (1981): 321–354.

———, ed. *Dicionário de história da Igreja em Portugal*. Vol. 1. Lisbon: 1979.

Barbosa, A. *Dicionário cokwe-português*. Coimbra: 1989.

Barendse, R. J. "Trade and State in the Arabian Seas: A Survey from the Fifteenth to the Eighteenth Century," *Journal of World History* 11, no 2 (2000), 173–225.

———, *The Arabian Seas: The Indian Ocean World of the Seventeenth Century (Asia and the Pacific)*. London: 2002.

Barman, R. J. "Business and Government in Imperial Brazil: The Experience of Viscount Maua." *Journal of Latin American Studies* 13, no. 2 (1981): 239–264.

Barradas de Carvalho, J. "As edições e as traduções da 'Crônica dos feitos da Guiné.'" *Revista de História* 61 (1965): 181–190.

Barros, E. S. *Negócios de Tanta Importância—O Conselho Ultramarino e a disputa pela condução da guerra no Atlântico e no Índico 1643–1661*. Lisbon: 2008.

Barros de Castro, A. "Brasil, 1610—Mudanças técnicas e conflitos sociais." *Pesquisa e Planejamento Econômico* 10, no. 3 (1980): 679–712.

Barry, B. *La Sénégambie du XVe au XIXe siècle: Traite Negrière, Islam et Conquête Coloniale*. Paris: 1988.

Bartlett, R. J. "Technique militaire et pouvoir politiquen 900–1300." *Annales* 41, no. 5 (1986): 1,135–1,159.

Bastide, Roger. *As religiões africanas no Brasil*. 2 vols. São Paulo: 1971.

Bataillon, Marcel. "Le Cosmopolitisme de Damião de Gois," "Études Sur Le Portugal Au Temps de L'humanisme." *Acta Universitatis Conimbrigensis* (1952): 149–196.

———. "La rébellion pizarriste, enfantement de l'Amérique espagnole." *Diogène* 43 (1963).

———. *Études sur Bartolomé de Las Casas*. Paris: 1965.

Bean, R. "A Note on the Relative Importance of Slaves and Gold in West African Exports." *J. Afr. H*. 15 (1974): 351–366.

Beaujard, Ph., and S. Fee, "The Indian Ocean in Eurasian and African World-Systems before the Sixteenth Century." *Journal of World History* 16, no. 4 (2005): 411–465.

Beckles, H. M. *White Servitude and Black Slavery in Barbados 1627–1715*. Knoxville, TN: 1989.

Bély, Lucien. "La dimension diplomatique de l'impérialisme européen." In *L'Empire portugais face aux autres empires XVIe XIXe siècle*, edited by F. Bethencourt and L. F. de Alencastro, 15–40. Paris: 2007.

Bennassar, Bartolomé e L. *Les chrétiens d'Allah: L'histoire extraordinaire des renégats*. Paris: 1989.

Bennett, J. H. "The English Caribbees in the Period of the Civil War, 1642–1646." *The William and Mary Quarterly* 24, no. 3 (1967): 359–377.

Benveniste, E. "Civilisation: Contribution à l'histoire du mot." In *Problèmes de linguistique générale*. Vol. 1. Edited by E. Benveniste et al., 336–345. Paris: 1966.

———. *Le vocabulaire des institutions indo-européennes*. 2 vols. Paris: 1969.

Bertrand, D. *La Politique de saint Ignace de Loyola*. Paris: 1985.

Bethencourt, Francisco. *História das Inquisições, Portugal Espanha e Itália*. Lisbon: 1994.

———. "Political Configurations and Local Powers." In *Oceanic Expansion, 1400–1800*, edited by F. Bethencourt and D. Ramada Curto, 197–254. Portuguese. Cambridge, UK: Cambridge UP, 2007.

———. "Creolization of the Atlantic World: The Portuguese and the Kongolese." *Portuguese Studies* 27, no. 1 (2011): 56–69.

———. "Iberian Atlantic: Ties, Networks, and Boundaries." In *Theorising the Iberian Atlantic*, edited by Harald E. Braun and Lisa Vollendorf, 15–36. Leiden: 2013.

Bicalho, M. F. *A cidade e o Império—O Rio de Janeiro na dinâmica colonial portuguesa, séculos XVII E XVIII*. Rio de Janeiro: 2003, 152–154.

Birmingham, David. *The Portuguese Conquest of Angola*. Oxford, UK: Oxford UP, 1965.

———. *Trade and Conflict in Angola: The Mbundu and Their Neighbours Under the Influence of the Portuguese 1483–1790*. London: 1966.

———. "Central Africa from Cameroon to the Zambezi." In *The Cambridge History of Africa c. 1050–c. 1600*. Vol. 3. Edited by J. D. Fage and R. Oliver, 519–566. London: 1977.

———. *Trade and Empire in the Atlantic, 1400–1600*. London: 2000.

Bischof, Barbie Elizabeth Rowe, Arthur J. Mariano, and Edward H. Ryan. "The Brazil Current." *Ocean Surface Currents* (2004). http://oceancurrents.rsmas.miami.edu/atlantic/brazil.html.

Bisson, M. S. "Trade and Tribute: Archeological Evidence for the Origin of States in South Central Africa," *CEA* 22, nos. 3–4 (1982): 343–362.

Black, L. "Why Did They Die?" *Science* 258, no. 11 (1992): 1,739–1,740.

Blackburn, R. "The Old World Background to European Colonial Slavery," *The William and Mary Quarterly* 54, no. 1 (1998), 65–102.

Blanco, J. M. D. "La Corona y Los Cargadores a Indias Portugueses de Sevilla (1583–1645)." In *Iberismo. Las relaciones entre España y Portugal. Historia y tiempo actual: y otros estudios sobre Extremadura*, edited by F. L. de la Puente and F. J. M. Ascacibar, 91–104. Llerena, 2008.

Blasco Martinez, A. "Razones y consecuencias de una decisión controvertida la expulsión de los judíos de España en 1492." *Kalakorikos* 10 (2005): 9–36.

Blusse, L., and G. Winius. "The Origin and Rhythm of Dutch Aggression against the 'Estado da Índia.' " In *Indo-Portuguese History: Old Issue, New Questions*, edited by T. R. de Sousa. New Dehli: 1985, 73–83.

Boccara, G. "Mundos nuevos en las fronteras del Nuevo Mundo." *Nuevo Mundo Mundos Nuevos*. February 2005, accessed September 2015.

Boncioni, Rodrigo. "A disputa por gentios e escravos no Atlântico Sul (1600–1615)." In *Corporaciones religiosas y evangelización em Iberoamérica. Siglos XVI–XVIII*, edited by D. L. Medina and K. M. Estrada, 23–60. Lima, Peru: 2011.

———. "A emergência de uma sociedade nova em São Tomé 1485–1535." In *Estudos Africanos: múltiplas abordagens*, edited by A. Vieira Ribeiro and A. L. de Almeida Gebara, 171–201. Niterói, Rio de Janeiro: 2013.

———. "Os irmãos Coutinho no Atlântico: escravidão, governo e ascensão social no tempo da monarquia hispânica." *5º Encontro Internacional de História Colonial*. Maceió: 2014: 1–11.

Bonifácio, Monique da Silva, and Vanice Siqueira de Melo. "Pelos sertões 'estão todas as utilidades.' Trocas e conflitos no sertão amazônico (século XVII)," *Revista de História* 162 (2010): 13–49.

Bono, S. "Un saint africain pour Palerme!" *L'Histoire* 222 (1998): 16–17.

Bonvini, E. "Repères pour une histoire des connaissances linguistiques des langues africaines," *Histoire Épistémologie Langage* 18, no. 2 (1996): 127–148.

Bontinck, F. "L'ancien Congo et le Concile de Trente." *Antennes* 12, no. 2 (1962–1963): 453–464.

———. "Du Nouveau sur Dom Afonso, roi de Congo." *African Historical Studies* 3, no. 1 (1970): 151–162.

———. "Un mausolée pour les Jaga." *CEA* 20, no. 3 (1980): 387–390.

Bontinck, F. and N. Nsasi. *Le catéchisme kikongo de 1624—Réédition critique*. Brussels: 1978.

Boogaart, E. van den, and P. Emmer. "The Dutch Participation in the Atlantic Slave Trade 1596–1650." In *The Uncommon Market*, edited by J. Hogendorn and H. Gemery, 353–375. New York: 1979.

———. "The Trade between Western Africa and the Atlantic World, 1600–1690—Estimates of Trends in Composition and Value." *J. Afr. H.* 33 (1992): 369–385.

Boogaart, E. van den, H. R. Hoetink, and J. Whitehead, eds. *Johan Maurits van Nassau-Siegen—A Humanist Prince in Europe and Brazil 1604–1679*. The Hague: 1979.

Borges, Graça Almeida. "¿Un Império Ibérico integrado? El Arbitrismo y el imperio ultramarino portugués (1580–1640)." *Obradoiro de Historia Moderna* 23 (2014): 71–102.

Borges, C. J. "How Shall We Manage? Catholic Religious Orders Based in Portuguese India in the 16th–18th Centuries." In *Indo-Portuguese History—Global Trends*, edited by F. da Silva Gracias, C. Pinto, and C. Borges, 233–250. Goa: 2005.

Bosi, A. *Dialética da colonização*. São Paulo: 1992.

Boston, T. D. "On the Transition to Feudalism in Mozambique," *Journal of African Society* 8, no. 4 (1981): 182–187.

Botelho de Sousa, A. *Subsídios para a história militar marítima da Índia, 1585–1669*. Vol. 4. Lisbon: 1930, 196–201.

Botte, Roger. "Les réseaux transsahariens de la traite de l'or et des esclaves au haut Moyen Âge: VIIIe–XIe siècle." *L'Année du Maghreb* 6 (2011): 27–59.

Boulègue, Jean. *Les luso-africains de Sénégambie XVIe–XIXe siècles*. Lisbon: 1989.

———. *Les royaumes wolofs dans l'espace sénégambien (XIIIe–XVIIIe siècles)*. Paris: 2013.

Boutry, Philippe. "Assurances et errances de la raison historienne." In *Autrement*, edited by Jean Boutier and Dominique Julia, 56–68. Paris: 1995.

Boxer, Charles R. *Portuguese Society in the Tropics: The Municipal Councils of Goa, Macao, Bahia and Luanda 1510–1800*. Madison, WI: 1950.

———. *The Christian Century in Japan 1549–1650*. London: 1951.

———. "English Shipping in the Brazil Trade 1640–1665." *Mariner's Mirror* 37, no. 3 (1951): 197–230.

———. *Salvador de Sá and the Struggle for Brazil and Angola 1602–1686* (Portuguese translation, *Salvador de Sá e a luta pelo Brasil e Angola 1602–1686*). London: 1952.

———. *The Dutch in Brazil 1624–1654*. Oxford: 1957.

———. "Portuguese and Dutch Colonial Rivalry, 1641–1661." *Studia* 2 (1958): 7–42.

———. "A 'História' de Cadornega no Museu Britânico." *Boletim Cultural* 1 (1960): 73–80.

———. *Race Relations in the Portuguese Colonial Empire* (Portuguese translation, *Relações raciais no Império colonial português 1415–1825*). London: 1963.

———. *The Dutch Seaborne Empire, 1600–1800*. London: 1965.

———. *The Portuguese Seaborne Empire 1415–1825* (Portuguese translation, *O Império colonial português*). New York: 1969.

———. "Macao as a Religious and Commercial Entrepot in the 16th and 17th Centuries." *Acta Asiatica, Bulletin of the Institute of Eastern Culture*, Tokyo 26 (1974): 64–90.

———. *Mary and Misogyny, Women in Iberian Expansion. Overseas, 1415–1815, Facts, Fancies and Personalities*, London: 1975.

———. "Sailing Orders for the Portuguese East-Indiamen of 1640 and 1646." *Terrae Incognitae* 12 (1980): 37–48.

———. *A India portuguesa em meados do século XVII*. Lisbon: 1982.

———. *O grande navio de Amacau*. Macao: 1989.

———. "Subsídios para a história dos capitães-gerais e governadores de Macau 1557–1770." *Estudos para a história de Macau* 1, Lisbon: 1991.

———. *The Church Militant and Iberian Expansion, 1440–1770*. Baltimore: Johns Hopkins UP, 2001.

Boxer, Charles R. and J. Frazão de Vasconcelos. *André Furtado de Mendonça*. Lisbon: 1989.

Bowser, F. *The African Slave in Colonial Peru, 1524–1650*. Palo Alto, CA: Stanford UP, 1974.

Boyajian, J. C. *Portuguese Bankers at the Court of Spain 1626–1640*. New Brunswick, NJ: 1983.

———. *Portuguese Trade in Asia under the Habsburgs 1580–1640*. Baltimore, MD: 1993.

Bradley, Peter T. "The Portuguese Peril in Peru." *Bulletin of Spanish Studies: Hispanic Studies and Researches on Spain, Portugal and Latin America* 79 no. 5 (2002): 591–613.

Braga, I. M. R. M. D. *Entre a cristandade e o islão, séculos XV–XVIII: Cativos e renegados nas franjas de duas sociedades em confronto*. Ceuta: 1998.

Brásio, A. "Do último cruzado ao Padroado Régio." *Studia* 3 (1959): 125–153.

———. "O problema da eleição e coroação dos reis do Congo." *Revista Portuguesa de História*, 12, no. 1 (1969): 351–381.

Braudel, Fernand, and F. Spooner. "Prices in Europe from 1450 to 1750." In *Cambridge Economic History of Europe* 4 (1967): 378–486.

———. *Civilisation matérielle, économie et capitalisme XVème–XVIIIè siècles*. 3 vols. Paris: 1979.

———. *La Méditerranée et le monde méditerranéen à l'époque de Philippe II*. 3 vols. 9th edition. Paris: 1990.

Brenner, Robert. "The Civil War Politics of London's Merchant community." *Past & Present* 58 (1973): 53–107.

Britto, R. G. *A saga de Pero do Campo Tourinho: o primeiro processo da Inquisição do Brasil*. Petrópolis, R.J.: 2000.

Bromley, J. S., and E. H. Kossman, eds. *Britain and the Netherlands in Europe and Asia*. London: 1968.

Brooks, G. E. *Kola Trade and State-Building: Upper Guinea Coast and Senegambia, 15th–17th Centuries.* Boston: 1980.
Brunn, Gerhard, and Neusch, Cornelius (eds.), *Sein Feld war die Welt—Johann Moritz von Nassau-Siegen 1604–1679.* Waxmann Verlag, Münster: 2008.
Brustein, William, and Margaret Levi. "The Geography of Rebellion: Rulers, Rebels and Regions, 1500 to 1700." *Theory and Society* 16, no. 4 (1987): 467–495.
Bryant, J. E., E. C. Holmes, and A. D. T. Barrett, "Out of Africa: A Molecular Perspective on the Introduction of Yellow Fever Virus into the Americas." *PLoS Pathogens* (2007) 3.5. https://doi.org/10.1371/journal.ppat.0030075.
Buarque de Holanda, S. *Tentativas de mitologia.* São Paulo: 1979.
———. *O Extremo Oeste.* São Paulo: 1986.
———. *Monções.* São Paulo: 1990.
———. *Visão do Paraíso.* 5th ed. São Paulo: 1992.
———. *Caminhos e fronteiras.* 3rd. ed. São Paulo: 1994.
Bulck, V. Van. "Operum Iudicia." *Archivum Historicum Societatis Iesu* 24 no. 48 (1955): 429–477.
Burke, P. F. "Malaria in the Greco-Roman World: A Historical and Epidemiological Survey." *Aufstieg und Niedergang der römischen Welt.* Vol. 2. Edited by H. Temporini and W. Haase, 2,252–2,281. Berlin: (1996).
Butaye, R. *Dictionnaire kikongo-français, français-kikongo.* Roulers, Belgium: 1910.
Cabral de Mello, Evaldo. *Olinda restaurada: Guerra e açúcar no Nordeste 1630–1654.* São Paulo: 1976.
———. *Rubro veio: O imaginario da Restauração pernambucana.* Rio de Janeiro: 1987.
———. *O nome e o sangue—Uma fraude genealógica no Pernambuco colonial.* São Paulo: 1989.
———. *A Fronda dos Mazombos: Nobres contra mascates, Pernambuco 1666–1716.* São Paulo: 1995.
———. *O negócio do Brasil—Portugal, os Países Baixos e o Nordeste, 1641–1669.* Rio de Janeiro: 1998.
———. *Nassau.* São Paulo: 2006.
———. *O Brasil holandês (1630–1654).* São Paulo: 2010.
Caetano, Marcelo. "Governo e administração central após a Restauração." *História da expansão de Portugal no mundo.* Vol. 3, 189–198. Lisbon: 1942.
Caldas Tibiriçá, L. *Dicionário tupi-português.* Santos, SP: 1984.
Caldeira, Arlindo Manuel. "A terra que seus pais povoaram e defenderam . . . A questão do protonacionalismo em São Tomé e Príncipe nos séculos XVII e XVIII." *Anais de História de Além-Mar.* Vol. 2, 299–326. Lisbon: 2001.
———. "Rebelião e outras formas de resistência à escravatura na Ilha de São Tomé." *Africana Studia* 7 (2004): 101–136.
Callier-Boisvert, C. "Captifs et esclaves au XVIe siècle. Une diatribe contre la traite restée sans écho." *L'Homme* 38, no. 145 (1998): 109–126.

Calvo Stevenson, H., and Adolfo Meisel Roca. *Cartagena de Indias en el Siglo XVII*. Cartagena: 2007.
Câmara Cascudo, Luís da. *A cozinha africana no Brasil*. Luanda: 1964.
———. *Made in Africa*. Rio de Janeiro: 1965.
Campa Carmona, R. de la. "Un Ejemplo de Patronazgo Nobiliario en la Catedral de Sevilla: La Capilla de La Concepción Grande y Don Gonzalo Núñez de Sepulveda." In *El comportamiento de las catedrales españolas: del Barroco a los Historicismos: actas del congresso*, 425–448. Murcia: 2003.
Canabrava, Alice P. *O comércio português no Rio da Prata 1580–1640* [1943]. São Paulo: 1984.
Candido, Mariana I. "Merchants and the Business of the Slave Trade at Benguela, 1750–1850." *African Economic History* 35 (2007): 1–30.
Cantel, Raymond. *Les Sermons de Vieira—Etude du style*. Paris: 1959.
———. *Prophétisme et messianisme dans l'oeuvre d'Antonio Vieira*. Paris: 1960.
Capeans, Rosa. "Resumo do estudo arqueológico das viagens de Lisbon a Angola e de Lisbon à ilha de Santa Helena, em navios de vela, baseado na 'Relatione del reame di Congo et delle circonvicine contrade' de Duarte Lopez & Filippo Pigafetta." In *Primeiro Congresso da História da Expansão Portuguesa no Mundo*. Vol. 2, 153–175. Lisbon: 1938.
Capela, José. *O Tráfico de Escravos nos Portos de Moçambique, 1733–1904*. Lisbon: 2002.
———. *O tráfico da escravatura nas relações Moçambique-Brasil*. Lisbon: 2002.
Capistrano de Abreu, J. *Caminhos antigos e povoamento do Brasil*. Rio de Janeiro [1853–1927]: 1930.
———. *O descobrimento do Brasil*. Rio de Janeiro: 1976.
———. *Ensaios e estudos*. Rio de Janeiro: 1975.
Cárdenas Piera, Emilio de. *Expedientes de Militares (siglos XVI al XIX)*. Madrid: 1968.
Cardim, Pedro. *Cortes e Cultura Política no Portugal do Antigo Regime*. Lisbon: 1998.
———. "Os 'Rebeldes de Portugal' no Congresso de Münster 1644–48." *Penélope* nos. 19–20 (1998): 101–128.
———. "O governo e a administração do Brasil sob os Habsburgo e os primeiros Bragança." *Hispania* 64 no. 1 (2004): 117–156.
Cardini, Franco. *La culture de la guerre*. Paris: 1992.
Cardoso, Jayme A., and C. M. Westphalen. *Atlas histórico do Paraná*. Curitiba: 1986.
Cardoso Naud, L. M. "Documentos sobre o índio brasileiro." *Revista de Informação Legislativa* 8, no. 71 (1971): 297–335.
Carneiro, Edison. *O Quilombo de Palmares*. 3rd ed. Rio de Janeiro [1946]: 1966.
Carneiro, Robert. "Slash-and-Burn Cultivation among the Kuikuru and Its Implications for Cultural Development in the Amazon Basin." In *The Evolution of Horticultural Systems in Native South America—Causes and Consequences*, edited by J. Wilbert, 47–67. Caracas, Venezuela: 1961.

Carneiro da Cunha, Manuela L. "Da guerra das relíquias ao Quinto Império." *Novos Estudos Cebrap* 44 (1996): 73–87.

Carneiro da Cunha, Manuela L., and E. B. Viveiros de Castro. "Vingança e temporalidade—Os tupinambás." *Anuário Antropológico* 57–78. Brasília: 1985.

Carreira, Antonio. "Tratos e resgates dos portugueses nos rios da Guiné e ilhas de Cabo Verde nos começos do século XVII." *RHES* 2 (1978): 91–103.

———. *Os portugueses nos rios de Guiné 1500–1900*. Lisbon, 1984.

———. "A capitania das ilhas de Cabo Verde." *RHES* 19 (1987): 33–76.

Carreira, Ernestine. "Un empire à vendre: stratégies d'appropriation des ports de *l'Estado da Índia* par les compagnies britannique et française (1661–1813)." In *L'Empire portugais face aux autres empires XVIe XIXe siècle*, edited by F. Bethencourt and L. F. de Alencastro, 79–120. Paris: 2007.

Carvalhão Buescu, Maria L. "A gramaticalização das línguas exóticas no quadro cultural da Europa do século XVI." *RHES* 10 (1982): 15–28.

Carvalho, Filipe Nunes de. "Aspectos do tráfico de escravos de Angola para o Brasil no século XVII: prolegómenos do inferno." Vol. 1 of 2 vols. In *Carlos Alberto Ferreira de Almeida: In Memoriam*, edited by Mário Jorge Barroca, 231–243. Porto: 1999.

Carvalho Soares, Mariza de. "*Devotos da cor: identidade étnica, religiosidade e escravidão no Rio de Janeiro, século XVIII.*" Rio de Janeiro: 2000.

Casado Alonso, H. "El Comercio de Nueva España con Castilla en la Época de Felipe II: Redes Comerciales Y Seguros Marítimos." *Historia Mexicana* 61, no. 3 (2012): 935–993.

Castello, J. A. "Relação da Aclamação que se fez na capitania do Rio de Janeiro do Estado do Brasil." In *O movimento academicista no Brasil*, 5–12. Vol. 3, book 1 (Lisbon: 1641).

Castro, Armando. *Doutrinas econômicas em Portugal, séculos XVI a XVIII*. Lisbon: 1978.

Castro Henriques, Isabel. *Commerce et changement en Angola au XIXe siècle: Imbangala et Tshokwe face à la modernité*. 2 vols. Paris: 1995.

Cayola, Júlio. "A reconquista de Angola por Salvador Correia de Sá." *Congresso do Mundo Português*. Vol. 9, no. 1 (1939): 423–435.

Chambouleyron, R. "Suspiros por um escravo de Angola. Discursos sobre a mão-de-obra africana na Amazônia seiscentista." *Humanitas* 20, no. 1–2 (2004): 99–111.

———. "Escravos do Atlântico equatorial: tráfico negreiro para o Estado do Maranhão e Pará, século XVII e início do século XVIII." *Revista Brasileira de História* 26, no. 52 (2006): 79–114.

Chambouleyron, R., and Fernanda Aires Bombardi. "Descimentos privados de índios na Amazônia colonial (séculos XVII e XVIII)." *Varia história* 27, no. 46 (2011): 601–623.

Chanaiwa, David. "Politics and Long-Distance Trade in the Mwene Mutapa Empire During the Sixteenth Century," *International Journal of African Historical Studies*, 5 no. 3 (1972): 424–435.

Chaudhuri, Kirti. "A concorrência holandesa e inglesa." In *História da expansão portuguesa*, edited by F. Bethencourt and Kirti Chaudhuri, 82–111. Vol. 2. Lisbon: 1998.

———. "O Comércio Asiático." In *História da Expansão Portuguesa*. Vol. 2, 194–212.
Chaunu, Pierre. and Huguette Chaunu *Séville et l'Atlantique, 1504–1650*. 12 vols. Paris: 1955–1959.
———. *L'Espagne de Charles Quint*. 2 vols. Paris: 1973.
———. *Histoire, science sociale: la durée, l'espace et l'homme à l'époque moderne*. Paris: 1974.
———. *Eglise, culture et société*. Paris: 1981.
Chittenden, Hiran M. *A History of the American Fur Trade of the Far West*. 2 vols. Stanford, CA: 1954.
Cipolla, C. M. *Guns, Sails, and Empires*. New York: 1966.
Clastres, P. *La société contre l'Etat*. Paris: 1974.
Clayton, L. A. "The Iberian Advantage." In *Technology, Disease, and Colonial Conquests, Sixteenth to Eighteenth Centuries: Essays Reappraising the Guns and Germs Theories*, edited by G. Raudzens, 211–236. Leiden: 2003.
Coaracy, V. *O Rio de Janeiro no século dezessete*. Rio de Janeiro: 1965.
Coelho, A. Borges "O mercantilista Duarte Gomes Solis: análises e modelos dirigidos ao governo filipino" *Arquipélago. História* 1, no. 1 (1995): 161–179.
Coelho, Philip R., and R. A. Mcguire. "African and European Bound Labor in the British New World: The Biological Consequences of Economic Choices." *The Journal of Economic History* 57, no. 1 (1997): 83–115.
———. "African and European Bound Labor in the British New World: The Biological Consequences of Economic Choices." *The Journal of Economic History* 57, no. 1 (1997): 83–115.
Campos Mota, O. de. *Do rancho ao palácio: evolução da civilização paulista*. Rio de Janeiro: 1941.
Cohen, Zelinda, "O provimento dos oficiais da justiça e da fazenda para as ilhas de Cabo Verde." *Studia* 51 (1992): 145–176.
Cohn, R. L. "Deaths of Slaves in the Middle Passage." *JEH* 45 (1985): 685–692.
Collado Villalta, Pedro. "El embargo de bienes de los portugueses en la flotta de tierra firme de 1641." *Anuario de Estudios Americanos* 36 (1979): 169–207.
Cook, N. D. *Demographic collapse—Indian Peru 1520–1620*. New York: 1981.
Cooper, F. *Plantation Slavery on the East Coast of Africa*. New Haven, CT: 1977.
Coquery-Vidrovitch, Catherine. "Recherches sur un mode de production africain." In *Sur le Mode de production asiatique*, 345–368. Paris: 1974.
Coquery-Vidrovitch, Catherine, and H. Moniot. *L'Afrique Noire de 1800 à nos jours*. Paris: 1974.
Cornell, V. J. "Socioeconomic Dimensions of Reconquista and Jihad in Morocco: Portuguese Dukkala and the Sadid Sus, 1450–1557." *International Journal of Middle East Studies* 22, no. 4 (1990): 379–418.
Correa do Lago, P., and B. Correa do Lago. *Frans Post 1612–1680, Catalogue Raisonné*. Paris: 2007.

Correia de Castro, Graça M. *O percurso geográfico e missionário de Baltasar Barreira em Cabo Verde, Guiné, Serra Leoa*. Lisbon: 2001.
Correia Lopes, E. *Escravatura—Subsídios para a sua história*. Lisbon: 1944.
Cortés, Fernando C. *Espionagem e contra-espionagem numa guerra peninsular 1640–1668*. Lisbon: 1989.
Cortés López, J. L. "Felipe II, III y IV, Reyes de Angola y protectores del reino del Congo (1580–1640)." *Studia Histórica* 9 (1991): 223–246.
Cortesão, Jaime. *Raposo Tavares e a formação territorial do Brasil*. 2 vols. Lisbon: 1966.
———. *A Colonização do Brasil*. Lisbon: 1969.
———. *O Ultramar português depois da Restauração*. Lisbon: 1971.
Cortez Matos, Rita de. "O Cosmógrafo-Mor: o ensino náutico em Portugal nos séculos XVI e XVII." *Oceanos* 38 (1999): 55–65.
Corvisier, A. "Louis XIV, la guerre et la naissance de l'armée moderne." In *Histoire militaire de la France*. Vol. 1 of 2 vols., edited by A. Covisier, 408–411. Paris: 1992.
Costa, Leonor Freire, and Mafalda Soares da Cunha. *Portugal na Monarquia Hispânica— Dinâmicas de integração e de conflito*. Lisbon: 2013.
Costa Roque, Mario da. "A 'peste grande' de 1569 em Lisboa." *Anais* 28, 2nd series. Lisbon: 1982, 71–90.
Costa Sacadura, S. C. da. "Profilaxia seiscentistas das pestilências na capitania de Pernambuco." *Primeiro Congresso da História da Expansão Portuguesa no Mundo*, seção Brasil. Lisbon: 1938, 379–399.
Coughtry, Jay. *The Notorious Triangle: Rhode Island and the African Slave Trade, 1700–1807*. Philadelphia: 1981.
Couto, Carlos. *O zimbo na historiografia angolana*. Luanda: 1973.
Couto, Djanira. "Algumas notas sobre a questão dos colaboradores dos Portugueses no Estado da Índia (séculos XVI e XVII)." In *Contrabandista entre mundos fronterizos*, edited by Nicolas Balutet, 265–284. Paris: 2010.
Crosby, Alfred W., Jr. "Conquistador y Pestilencia—The First New World Pandemic and the Fall of the Great Indian Empires." *HAHR* 47 (1967): 321–337.
———. *The Columbian Exchange: Biological and Cultural Consequences of 1492*. Westport, CT: Greenwood Publishing Group, 1972.
———. *Ecological Imperialism—The Biological Expansion of Europe 900–1900* (New York: 1989.
Cross, H. E. "Commerce and orthodoxy: A Spanish Response to Portuguese Commercial Penetration in the Ciceroyalty of Peru, 1580–1640." *The Americas* 35, no. 2 (1978): 151–167.
Cruz e Silva, Rosa da "As feiras do Ndongo: a outra vertente do comercio no século XVII." *Actas do seminario: Encontro de povos e culturas em Angola*, 405–422. Lisbon: 1997.
Cunha, A. G. da. *Dicionário histórico das palavras portuguesas de origem tupi*. São Paulo: 1998.

Cunha Pinheiro, L. da. "A conflitualidade social e institucional em S. Tomé ao longo do século XVI." *Actas do Congresso Internacional Atlântico de Antigo Regime: poderes e sociedades*, 1–17 (Universidade Nova de Lisboa, 2005).

Curtin, Philipp D. "Epidemiology and the Slave Trade." *The Political Science Quarterly* 83 no. 2 (1968): 190–216.

———. *The Atlantic Slave Trade: A Census*. Madison, WI: 1969.

———. *Economic Change in Precolonial Africa—Senegambia in the Era of Slave Trade*. 2 vols. Madison, WI: 1975.

———. "The Abolition of the Slave Trade from Senegambia." In *The Abolition of the Atlantic Slave Trade*, edited by D. Eltis and J. Walvin, 83–99. Madison, WI: 1981.

———. "Africa and the Wider Monetary World 1250–1850." In *Precious Metals in the Later Medieval and Early Modern Worlds*, edited by J. F. Richards. Durham: Carolina Academic P, 1983, 238–239.

———. *The Rise and Fall of the Plantation Complex*. New York: 1990.

Curto, José C. "The Legal Portuguese Slave Trade from Benguela, Angola, 1730–1828: A Quantitative Reappraisal." *Africa* 16–17 (1993): 101–116.

———. "Vinho verso cachaça: A luta luso-brasileira pelo comércio do álcool e de escravos em Luanda, c. 1648–1703." In *Angola e Brasil nas rotas do Atlântico Sul*, edited by S. Pantoja and J. F. Sombra Saraiva, 78–97 (Rio de Janeiro: 1998).

———. "Luso-Brazilian Alcohol and the Legal Slave Trade at Benguela and its Hinterland, c. 1617–1830." In *Négoce Blanc en Afrique Noire: L'évolution du 18e au 20e siècles*, edited by H. Bonin and M. Cahen, 351–369. Paris: 2001.

———. *Enslaving Spirits: The Portuguese-Brazilian Alcohol Trade at Luanda and Its Hinterland, c. 1550–1830*. Leiden: 2004.

Curvelo, Alexandra. "Nagasaki/Deshima after the Portuguese in Dutch Accounts of the 17th Century." *Bulletin of Portuguese-Japanese Studies* 6 (2003): 147–157.

Darricau, C. "La course basque et bayonnaise au XVIIe siècle (1663–1698) d'après les registres de l'amirauté de Bayonne." *Revue Historique*, vol. 588 (1993): 401–419.

David-Peyre, Y. "La peste et le mal vénérien dans la littérature portugaise du XVIe et XVIIe siècles." *Arquivos do Centro Cultural Português*. Vol. 1. Paris: 1969, 195–207.

Davis, David B. *The Problem of Slavery in Western Culture*. Middlesex, England: 1970.

Dean, W. "Indigenous Populations of the São Paulo—Rio de Janeiro Coast: Trade, 'Aldeamento,' Slavery, and Extinction." *Revista de História* 117 (1984): 1–26.

———. *A ferro e fogo*. São Paulo: 1996.

Deboer, W. R. "The Archaeological Evidence for Manioc Cultivation: A Cautionary Note," *American Antiquity* 40, no. 4 (1975): 419–433.

Del Rio Hijas, M. E., and M. Revuelta Gonzales. "Enfermarías y boticas en las casas de la Compañia en Madrid, siglos XVI–XIX." *Archivum Historicum Societatis Iesu* 64, no. 127 (1995): 39–81.

Delgado, Ralph. *A Famosa e Histórica Benguela—Catálogo dos Governadores 1779–1940.* Lisbon: 1940.

———. *O Reino de Benguela: Do descobrimento à criação do governo subalterno.* Lisbon: 1945.

———. *História de Angola.* 4 vols. Luanda-Lisbon: 1948–1978.

Delson, Roberta M. "Inland Navigation in Colonial Brazil: Using Canoes on the Amazon," *International Journal of Maritime History* 7, no. 1 (1995): 1–28.

Delumeau, Jean. *L'aveu et le pardon—Les difficultés de la confession XIIIe–XVIIIe siècle* Paris: 1995.

Dennie, C. C. *A History of Syphillis.* Springfield, IL: 1962.

De Vertot, Abbot. *Histoire des Chevaliers hospitaliers de Saint Jean de Jérusalem, appellez depuis les Chevaliers de Rhodes, et aujourd'hui les Chevaliers de Malte.* 4 vols. Paris: 1726.

Devisse, Jean. "L'Apport de l'Archéologie à l'Histoire de l'Afrique occidentale entre le Ve et le XIIe siècle." *Académie des Inscriptions et Belles-Lettres—Comptes Rendus des séances de l'année* no. 3 (1982): 156–177.

———. "Routes de commerce et échanges en Afrique Occidentale en relation avec la Méditerranée: Un essai sur le commerce médiéval du xie au xvie siècle." *Revue d'Histoire Economique et Sociale* 50, no. 1 (1972): 43–73, and no. 3 (1972): 357–397.

de Witte, C.-M. "Les Bulles pontificales et l'expansion portugaise au XVe siècle." *Revue d'Histoire Ecclesiastique* 48 (1953): 683–718; 49 (1954): 438–461; 51 (1956): 413–453, and 809–836; and 53 (1958): 5–46 and 443–471.

———. "Henri de Congo, évêque titulaire d'Utique (décedé c. 1531) d'après les documents romains." *Euntes Docete* 21 (1968): 587–599.

Diamond, J. *Guns, Germs, and Steel: The Fates of Human Societies.* New York: 1999.

Dias Antunes, L. F. "O comércio com o Brasil e a comunidade mercantil em Moçambique (séc. XVIII)." *Actas do Congresso Internacional Atlântico de Antigo Regime: poderes e sociedades*, 1–9. Lisbon: Universidade Nova de Lisboa, 2005.

Dias Farinha, A. *Os Portugueses em Marrocos.* Lisbon, 2002.

Diffie, B. W. "The Legal Privileges of the Foreigners in Portugal and Sixteenth-Century Brazil." In *Conflict and Continuity in Brazilian Society*, edited by H. H. Keith and S. F. Edwards, 1–19. Columbia: U of South Carolina P, 1969.

Disney, A. R. *A Decadência do império da pimenta.* Lousã, Portugal: 1981.

———. "Getting to the China Mission in the Early Seventeenth Century." In *As Relações entre a Índia Portuguesa, a Ásia do Sueste e o Extremo Oriente*, edited by A. T. de Matos and L. F. F. Reis Thomaz, 95–109. Macau-Lisbon, 1993.

Ditchfield, Simon. "Of Missions and Models: The Jesuit Enterprise (1540–1773) Reassessed in Recent Literature." *The Catholic Historical Review* 93, no. 2 (2007): 325–343.

Dockès, Pierre. *L'espace dans la pensée économique du XVIe au XVIIIe siècle.* Paris: 1969.

Dolhnikoff, Miriam, ed. *José Bonifácio de Andrada e Silva: Projetos para o Brasil.* São Paulo: 1998.

Domingues da Silva, Daniel B. "The Atlantic Slave Trade to Maranhão, 1680–1846: Volume, Routes and Organization." *Slavery & Abolition* 29, no. 4 (2008): 477–501.
Domínguez Ortiz, A. *Los judeos conversos en España y América.* Madrid, 1971.
Dores Costa, F. "As forças sociais perante a guerra: as Cortes de 1645–46 e de 1653–54." *Análise Social* 36, no. 161 (2001): 1,147–1,181.
Drumond Braga, Paulo. "Dois surtos de peste em Lisboa—1579–1581." *Revista da Biblioteca Nacional* 7, no. 2 (1992): 7–22.
Duarte Leitão, J. A. "A Missão do Padre Baltasar Barreira no Reino de Angola (1580–1592)." *Lusitania Sacra* 5, no. 2 (1993): 43–91.
Duby, Georges. *L'economie rurale et la vie des campagnes dans l'Occident médieval.* 2 vols. Paris: 1977.
———. *Guerriers et Paysans.* Paris: 1978.
———. *Le Chevalier, la Femme et le Prêtre.* Paris: 1981.
Dumont, Louis. *Introduction à deux théories d'anthropologie sociale: Groupes de filiation et alliance de mariage.* Paris: 1971.
Dunn, Richard. *Sugar and Slaves: The Rise of the Planter Class in the English West Indies, 1623–1713.* London: 1972.
Dupré, G., and P. Ph. Rey. "Réflexions sur la pertinence d'une théorie de l'histoire des échanges." *Cahiers Internationaux de Sociologie* 46 (1969): 133–162.
Durães, M. "Herdeiros e não herdeiros: Nupcialidade e celibato no contexto da propriedade enfiteuta," *Revista de História Econômica e Social (RHES)* 2 (1987): 47–56.
Dutra, Francis A. "Centralization vs. Donatorial Privilege: Pernambuco, 1602–1630." In *Colonial Roots of Modern Brazil: Papers of the Newberry Library Conference*, edited by D. Alden, 19–60. Berkeley: U of California P, 1973.
———. *Military Orders in the Early Modern Portuguese World.* Aldershot, UK: 2006.
Duval, A. *Des Sacrements au Concile de Trente.* Paris: 1985.
Easterbrook, W. T., and H. G. J. Aitken. *Canadian Economic History.* Toronto: 1988.
Ebert, Christopher. *Between Empires: Brazilian Sugar in the Early Atlantic Economy, 1550–1630.* Leiden: 2008.
———. "European Competition and Cooperation in Pre-Modern Globalization: 'Portuguese' West and Central Africa, 1500–1600." *African Economic History* 36 (2008): 53–78.
Edmundson, George. "The Dutch Power in Brazil I: The Struggle for Bahia 1624–1627"; "The Dutch Power in Brazil II: The First Conquests." *The English Historical Review* 11 (1896): 231–259; 14 (1899): 676–699; and 15 (1900): 38–57.
Einarsson, L. "Le vaisseau royal Kronan. Des explorations archéologiques sous-marines d'une épave du XVIIe siècle," In *L'Invention du vaisseau de ligne 1450–1700,* M. Acerra, ed. (Paris: 1997): 135–142 and 143–162.
Eisenberg, J. "A escravidão voluntária dos índios do Brasil e o pensamento político moderno." *Análise Social* 39, no. 170 (2004): 7–35.

Elbl, Ivana. "The Horse in Fifteenth-Century Senegambia." *The International Journal of African Historical Studies* 24, no. 1 (1991): 85–110.

———. "The Volume of the Early Atlantic Slave Trade, 1450–1521." *J. Afr. H* 38 (1997): 31–75.

Elliot, J. H. *Richelieu y Olivares*. Barcelona: 1984.

———. *The Count-Duke of Olivares: The Statesman in an Age of Decline*, Princeton: 1988.

Ellis, Alfredo, Jr. *O bandeirantismo paulista e o recuo do meridiano*. São Paulo: 1936.

———. "Capítulos da história psicológica de São Paulo." *Boletim da Fac. de Filosofia, Ciências e Letra* 53 (1945): 70–75.

Ellis, M. *O Monopólio do sal no Estado do Brasil 1631–1801*. São Paulo: 1955.

Eltis, David. *Economic Growth and the Ending of the Transatlantic Slave Trade*. New York: 1987.

———. "Trade Between West Africa and the Atlantic World Before 1870: Estimates of Trends in Value, Composition, and Direction." *Research in Economic History* 12 (1989): 197–239.

———. "The Relative Importance of Slaves and Commodities in the Atlantic Trade of Seventeenth-Century Africa." *J. Afr. H.* 35, no. 2 (1994): 237–249.

———. *The Rise of African Slavery in the Americas*. New York: 2000.

Eltis, David, and L. C. Jennings. "Trade between West Africa and the Atlantic World in the Pre-Colonial Era." *American Historical Review* 93 (1988): 936–959.

Eltis, David, F. D. Lewis, and K. McIntyre., "Accounting for the Traffic in Africans: Transport Costs on Slaving Voyages." *The Journal of Economic History* 70, no. 4 (2010): 940–963.

Eltis, David, and D. Richardson. "A New Assessment of the Transatlantic Slave Trade." In *Extending the Frontiers: Essays on the New Transatlantic Slave Trade Database*, edited by David Eltis and D. Richardson, 28–31. New Haven: 2008.

———. *Atlas of the Transatlantic Slave Trade*. New Haven, CT: Yale UP, 2010.

Emmer, P. C. "The West India Company 1621–1791: Dutch or Atlantic?" In *Companies and Trade*, edited by L. Blusse and F. Gaastra, 71–95. Leiden: 1981.

———. "The Dutch and the Making of the Second Atlantic System." In *Slavery and the Rise of the Atlantic System*, edited by B. L. Solow, 75–96. New York: Cambridge UP, 1991.

———. "Los holandeses y el reto atlántico en el siglo XVII." In *El desafío holandés al dominio ibérico en Brasil en el siglo XVII*, edited by J. M. Santos Perez and G. F. Cabral de Souza, 17–31. Salamanca: 2006.

———. "The First Global War: The Dutch versus Iberia in Asia, Africa, and the New World, 1590–1609" *E-Journal of Portuguese History* 1, no. 1 (2003).

Ennes, Ernesto. *Os Palmares—Subsídios para a sua História* Lisbon: 1938.

———. *As guerras nos Palmares*. São Paulo: 1938.

Ernout, A., and A. Meillet. *Dictionnaire etymologique de la langue latine—Histoire des mots* Paris: 1985.

Esponera Cerdan, A. D. "La presencia de los dominicos en Buenos Aires y Asuncion durante el siglo XVII." *Los Dominicos y el Nuevo Mundo: Actas del III Congreso Internacional.* Madrid: 1991, 358–372.

———. "Bartolomé de las Casas y la esclavización de los negros, según las aportaciones de I. Pérez Fernández O." *Studium* 43 (2003): 87–100.

Esteves, M. L. "Para o estudo das relações comerciais de Angola com as Índias de Castela e Gênova no período da Restauração 1640–1668." *Studia* 51 (1992): 34–35.

Etambala, Zana. "Notes sur le tipoye em Afrique noire." *Ngonge, Carnets de Sciences Humaines* 6 (2011): 7–15.

Fage, J. D. *A History of West Africa.* Cambridge: 1969.

———. *An Atlas of African History.* London: 1975.

———. "African Societies and the Atlantic Slave Trade." *Past & Present*, no. 125 (1989): 97–115.

Falcon, F. C., and F. A. Novais. "A extinção da escravatura africana e Portugal no quadro da política econômica pombalina." *Anais do VI Simpósio Nacional dos Professores Universitários de História.* Vol. 1. São Paulo: 1973: 405–432.

Falcón Márquez, T. "El Arquitecto de Retablos Y Escultor Martín Moreno Y Los Primeros Retablos Con Columnas Salomónicas En Sevilla.," *Boletín de Arte* 34 (2013): 69–87.

Faria, A. M. H. L. de. "Duarte Ribeiro De Macedo A Modern Diplomat (1618–1680)." *e-JPH* 4, no. 1 (2006): 1–14.

Faria, Júlio C. de. "Apontamentos sobre a condição social dos índios nos primeiros tempos da colonização ibero-americana." In *IV Congresso de História Nacional*, vol. 5, 441–516. Rio de Janeiro: 1950.

Farinha de Carvalho, A. *Diogo do Couto, O soldado prático* Lisbon: 1979.

Feijoo, Rosa. "El Tumulto de 1624." *Historia Mexicana* 14, no. 1 (1964): 42–70.

Fenoaltea, S. "Slavery and Supervision in Comparative Perspective—A Model." *The Journal of Economic History* 44, no. 3 (1984): 635–668.

Fernandes, Florestan. "A função social da guerra na sociedade tupinambá." *RMP* 6 (1951): 7–426.

Ferrand de Almeida, L. "Aclimatação de plantas do Oriente no Brasil durante os séculos XVII e XVIII." *Revista Portuguesa de História*, vol. 15. Coimbra: 1975, 339–481.

Ferreira, Roquinaldo. "O Brasil e a arte da guerra em Angola (sécs. XVII e XVIII)." *Estudos Históricos* 39 (2007): 3–23.

———. "Supply and Deployment of Horses in Angolan Warfare (17th–18th centuries)." In *Angola on the Move: Transport Routes, Communications, and History*, edited by Beatrix Heintze and Achim von Oppen, 41–51. Frankfurt am Main: 2008.

———. *Cross-Cultural Exchange in the Atlantic World: Angola and Brazil During the Era of the Slave Trade.* Cambridge, UK: Cambridge UP, 2012.

Ferreira Reis, A. C. "O comércio colonial e as companhias privilegiadas." *História geral da civilização brasileira* 1, vol. 2. São Paulo: 1960: 316–318.

Ferronha, A. L. Alves. "A revolta de Luanda de 1667 e a expulsão do governador geral Tristão da Cunha." In *Diálogos Oceânicos: Minas Gerais e as novas abordagens para uma história do império ultramarino português*, edited by J. Furtado, 255–279. Belo Horizonte: 2001.

Ferry, R. J. "Encomienda, African Slavery and Agriculture in Seventeenth-century Caracas." *HAHR* 61, no. 4 (1981): 609–636.

Filesi, T., and I. Villapardiena. *La "Missio Antiqua" dei Capuccini nel Congo (1645–1835)*. Rome: 1978.

Finley, Moses I. *International Encyclopaedia of the Social Sciences*, vol. 14. New York: 1968, 307–313.

———. *Aspects of Antiquity: Discoveries and Controversies*. New York: Penguin, 1977.

———. *L'economie antique*. Paris: 1975.

———. *Esclavage antique et idéologie moderne*. Paris: 1979.

Fisher, H. J. "He Swallowed the Ground with Fierceness and Rage: The Horse in the Central Sudan." *J. Afr. H* 13, no. 3 (1972): 367–388.

Fisher, H. J., and V. Rowland. "Firearms in the Central Sudan." *J. Afr. H.* 12, no. 2 (1971): 215–239.

Florentino, Manolo, and J. R. Góes. "Parentesco e estabilidade familiar entre os escravos do agro-fluminense, 1790–1830." *Cadernos em História Social* 1 (1995): 13–19.

———. "The Slave Trade, Colonial Markets, and Slave Families in Rio de Janeiro, Brazil, ca. 1790–ca. 1830." In *Extending the Frontiers: Essays on the New Transatlantic Slave Trade Database*. New Haven: 2008: 275–312.

———. and M. Amantino. "Escapes, Quilombos and Fugitives in the Americas (sixteenth-Nineteenth Centuries)." *Análise Social* 203 (2012): 236–267.

Flynn, D. O., and A. Giráldez. "Born with a 'Silver Spoon': The Origin of World Trade in 1571." *Journal of World History* 6, no. 2 (1995): 201–221.

Fonseca, E., Jr. *Dicionário yorubá (nagô)-português*. Rio de Janeiro: 1983.

Fonseca, Jorge. *Escravos e senhores na Lisboa Quinhentista*. Lisbon: 2010.

Fonseca Gadelha, R. M. d'A. "Judeus e cristãos-novos no Rio da Prata. A ação do governador Hernandarias de Saavedra." In *Inquisição Ensaios sobre mentalidade, heresias e arte*, edited by A. Novinsky and M. L. Tucci Carneiro. São Paulo: 1992: 355–373.

Fontenay, M. "La Place de la Course dans l'économie portuaire: L'exemple de Malte et des ports barbaresques." *Annales* 43, no. 6 (1988): 1,321–1,347.

———. "Routes et modalités du commerce des esclaves dans la Méditerranée des Temps modernes (XVIe, XVIIe, et XVIIIe siècles)." *Revue Historique* 640, no. 4 (2006): 813–830.

Ford, J. *The Role of the Trypanosomiases in African Ecology: A Study of the Tsetse Fly Problem.* Oxford: 1971.

Foster, G. M. "Disease Etiologies in Non-Western Medical Systems." *American Anthropologist* 78, no. 4 (1976): 773–782.

Fradera, J. M., and C. Schmidt-Nowara, eds. *Slavery and Antislavery in Spain's Atlantic Empire.* Oxford: 2013.

———. *La nación imperial (1750–1918).* 2 vols. Barcelona: 2015.

Franco, A. "Vida do padre Manuel da Nóbrega." In Manoel da Nóbrega, *Cartas Jesuiticas 1: Cartas Do Brasil (1549–1560),* Rio de Janeiro: 1931, 21–69.

Franco, J. E. "A Companhia de Jesus e a Inquisição: afectos e desafectos entre duas instituições influentes (Séculos XVI–XVII)." *Actas do Congresso Internacional Atlântico de Antigo Regime: poderes e sociedades.* Universidade Nova de Lisboa, 2005, 1–23.

Frazão de Vasconcelos, J. "A Marinha da Coroa de Portugal no tempo dos Felipes." In *Congresso do mundo português,* vol. 6, 25–64. Lisbon: 1940.

Freire Costa, L. *O Transporte no Atlântico e a Companhia Geral do Comércio do Brasil 1580–1663.* 2 vols. Lisbon: 2002.

———. "Merchant Groups in the 17th-Century Brazilian Sugar Trade: Reappraising Old Topics with New Research Insights." *e-Journal of Portuguese History* 2, no. 1 (2004).

Freire Costa, L., and M. Soares da Cunha. *D. João IV.* Rio de Mouro, Portugal: 2006.

Freitas, Décio. *República de Palmares: Pesquisa e comentários em documentos históricos do século XVI.* Maceió, Alagoas: 2004.

Freitas, G. de. *A Companhia Geral do Comércio do Brasil 1649–1720.* São Paulo: 1951.

French, J. D. "Riqueza, poder e mão-de-obra numa economia de subsistência—São Paulo 1596–1625." *R.A.M.S.* 195 (1987): 79–107.

Freyre, Gilberto. *Casa grande e senzala.* 25th ed. Rio de Janeiro [1936]: 1987.

———. *Sobrados e Mucambos.* 2 vols. Lisbon [1936]: n.d.

Fridman, Fania. *Donos do Rio em nome do rei—Uma história fundiária da cidade do Rio de Janeiro.* Rio de Janeiro: 1999.

Fuller, J. F. C. *A Military History of the Western World.* 4 vols. New York: 1955.

Furtado, C. *L'Amérique Latine* Paris: 1970.

Gabriel, D. M. Nunes. *Padrões da fé—Igrejas antigas de Angola.* Luanda: 1981.

Garcia, C. A. "A Ilha de São Tomé como centro experimental do comportamento do Luso nos trópicos." *Studia* 19 (1966): 209–222.

García Añoveros, J. M. "Luis de Molina y la esclavitud de los Negros Africanos en el Siglo XVI. Principios Doctrinales y Conclusiones." *Revista de Indias* 60, no. 219 (2000): 307–329.

Garcia Nolasco da Silva, Maria da Graça. "Subsídios para o estudo dos 'Lançados' na Guiné." *Boletim Cultural da Guiné Portuguesa* 25, no. 100 (1970): 513–560.

Garlan, Y. *Les esclaves en Grèce ancienne.* Paris: 1982.
Geffray, C. "Nobles, Bourgeois, Inquisition: Les Prémisses de L'expansion Coloniale Portugaise Au XVIe Siècle." *Cahiers d'études Africaines* 21, no. 84 (1981): 523–546.
Genovese, E. *Roll, Jordan, Roll—The World the Slaves Made.* London: 1975.
Gerbeau, H. "La traite esclavagiste dans l'Océan Indien." *La traite négrière du XVe au XIXe siècle.* Paris: 1979: 194–217.
Gerbi, Antonello. *La disputa del Nuovo Mundo.* Milão: 1955.
Geyl, P. *The Netherlands in the Seventeenth Century.* 2 vols. London: 1961–1964.
Giblin, J. "Trypanosomiasis Control in African History: An Evaded Issue?" *J. Afr. H.* 31, no. 1 (1990): 59–80.
Goertz, R. O. W. "The Portuguese in Cochin in the Mid-Sixteenth Century." *Studia* 49 (1989): 5–38.
Goldstein, J. S. *Long Cycles—Prosperity and War in the Modern Age.* London: 1988.
Gomes, F. ed. *Mocambos de Palmares. História, historiografia e fontes.* Rio de Janeiro: 2010.
Gomez, M. A. "Timbuktu under Imperial Songhay: A Reconsideration of Autonomy." *J. Afr. H.* 31, no. 1 (1990): 5–24.
Gonçalves, A. C. *La symbolisation politique—Le "prophétisme" au Congo au XVIIIème siècle.* Munich: 1980.
———. *Congo. Le lignage contre l'État—Dynamique politique au Congo du XVIème au XVIIIème siècle.* Lisbon: 1985.
Gonçalves da Costa, M. "Orientação da Política Colonial Portuguesa: Colonos Irlandeses no Brasil e Política Colonial Portuguesa (1643–1650)." *Revista Portuguesa de Filosofia* 14 no. 1 (1958): 65—79.
Gonsalves de Mello, J. A. *Tempo dos flamengos.* 3rd ed. Recife [1947]: 1987.
———. *Henrique Dias* Recife: 1954.
———. *João Fernandes Vieira, mestre de campo do terço de infantaria de Pernambuco,* Recife: 1956, 2 vols.
———. *Francisco de Figueroa—Mestre de campo do Terço das Ilhas em Pernambuco.* Recife: 1954.
———. *Gente da nação.* Recife: 1989.
———. "Brito Freyre e a sua História de Pernambuco." In F. de Brito Freyre, *Nova Lusitânia—História da Guerra Brasílica* ([1675] Recife: 1977), postscript (not paginated).
Gonçalves Salvador, J. *Os Cristãos-Novos—Povoamento e conquista do solo brasileiro 1530–1680.* São Paulo: 1976.
———. *Os cristãos-novos e o comércio no Atlântico Meridional.* São Paulo: 1978.
———. *Os magnatas do tráfico negreiro.* São Paulo: 1988.
Good, C. M. "Markets in Africa: A Review of Research Themes and the Question of Market Origins." *CEA* 13, no. 4 (1972): 769–780.
Goody, J. *Technology, Tradition and the State in Africa.* New York: Cambridge UP, 1971.
Gorban, S. "El trafico negrero en el Rio de La Plata," *EH* 10 (1971): 117–139.

Goslinga, C. C. *The Dutch in the Caribbean and on the Wild Coast 1580–1680*. Assen and Maastricht: 1971.

Goulart, M. *A escravidão africana no Brasil: Das origens à extinção do tráfico*. 3rd ed. São Paulo: 1975.

Grace, John J. "Slavery and Emancipation among the Mende in Sierra Leone." In *Slavery in Africa: Historical and Anthropological Perspectives*, edited by Suzanne Miers and Igor Kopytoff, 416–417. Madison: U of Wisconsin P, 1979.

Gragg, L. " 'To Procure Negroes'—The English Slave Trade to Barbados, 1627–1660." *Slavery and Abolition* 16, no. 1 (1995): 65–84.

Grant Smith, D. "Old Christian merchants and the foundation of the Brazil Company, 1649." *HAHR* 54 (1974): 233–259.

Graslin, Laetitia, and Jérôme Maucourant. "Le port de commerce: un concept en débat." *Topoi Orient—Occident* (2005): 216–257.

Gray, Richard. "Portuguese Musketeers on the Zambezi." *J. Afr. H.* 12, no. 2 (1971): 531–533.

———. "The Papacy and the Atlantic Slave Trade: Lourenço da Silva, the Capuchins, and the Decisions of the Holly Office." *Past & Present* 115 (1987): 52–68.

Green, Tobias. "Further Considerations on the Sephardim of the Petite Côte." *History in Africa* 32, no. 1 (2005): 165–183.

———. "Silent Trade," *History in Africa* 1 (2013): 3–6.

Gregory, C. A. "Cowries and Conquest: Towards a Subaltern Quality Theory of Money." *Comparative Studies in Society and History* 38, no. 2 (1996): 195–217.

Grove, A. T. *The Changing Geography of Africa*. Oxford: Oxford UP, 1969.

Gruzinski, Serge. "Les élites de la monarchie catholique au carrefour des empires (fin XVIe–début XVIIe siècle)." In *L'Empire portugais*, 273–288.

———. *Les quatre parties du monde—Histoire d'une mondialisation*. Paris: 2004.

Guerra, F. "Aleixo de Abreu [1568–1630], Author of the earliest book on Tropical Medicine describing Amoebiasis, Malaria, Typhoid Fever, Scurvy, Yellow Fever, Dracontiasis, Trichuriasis and Tungiasis in 1623." *Journal of Tropical Medicine and Hygiene* 71 (1968): 55–69.

———. "Abreu, Aleixo de." *Dictionary of Scientific Biography*. New York: 1970: 25–26.

———. "The Dispute over Syphillis—Europe versus America." *Clio Medica* 13 (1978): 39–61.

———. "Medicine in Dutch Brazil 1624–1654." In *Johan Maurits van Nassau-Siegen—A Humanist Prince in Europe and Brazil 1604–1679*, edited by E. van den Boogaart, H. R. Hoetink, and J. Whitehead, 477–478. The Hague: 1979.

———. "The Earliest American Epidemic—The Influenza of 1493." *Social Science History* 12, no. 3 (1988): 305–325.

Guerreiro, A. "Inquérito em Moçambique no ano de 1573." *Studia* 6 (1960): 7–18.

Guibert, J. de. "Le Généralat de Claude Aquaviva, 1581–1615." *Archivum Historicum Societatis Iesu* 10, no. 1 (1941): 59–93.

Gutmann, Myron P. "The Origins of the Thirty Years' War." *Journal of Interdisciplinary History* 18, no. 4 (1988): 749–770.

Hagen, W. W. "Capitalism and the countryside in Early Modern Europe: Interpretations, Models, Debates." *Agricultural History* 62, no. 1 (1988): 13–47.

Hair, P. H. E. "Heretics, Slaves and Witches—As Seen by Guinea Jesuits c. 1610," *Journal of Religion in Africa* 28, no. 2 (1998): 121–144.

Halikowski-Smith, Stefan. " 'The Friendship of Kings Was in the Ambassadors': Portuguese Diplomatic Embassies in Asia and Africa during the Sixteenth and Seventeenth Centuries." *Portuguese Studies* 22, no. 1 (2006): 101–134.

Hanke, L. "The Portuguese in Spanish America with Special Reference to the Villa Imperial de Potosi." *Revista de Historia de America* 51 (1961): 1–48.

Hansen, J. Adolfo, *A sátira e o engenho, Gregório de Matos e a Bahia do século XVII.* São Paulo: 2004.

Hanson, Carl A. "The European 'Renovation' and the Luso-Atlantic Economy, 1560–1715." *Review* 6, no. 4 (1983): 506–509.

———. *Economia e sociedade no Portugal barroco 1668–1703.* Lisbon: 1986.

Harvey, L. P. *Muslims in Spain, 1500 to 1614.* Chicago: U of Chicago P, 2005.

Havik, Philip J. "A Dinâmica das relações de gênero e parentesco num contexto comercial: um balanço comparativo da produção histórica sobre a região da Guiné-Bissau, Séculos XVII e XIX." *Afro-Ásia* 27 (2002): 79–120.

Hawthorne, W. "The Production of Slaves Where There Was No State: The Guinea-Bissau Region, 1450–1815." *Slavery & Abolition* 20, no. 2 (1999): 97–124.

———. "Nourishing a Stateless Society during the Slave Trade: The Rise of Balanta Paddy-Rice Production in Guinea-Bissau." *J. Afr. H.* 42, no. 1 (2001): 1–24.

———. *From Africa to Brazil: Culture, Identity, and an Atlantic Slave Trade, 1600–1830.* New York: 2010.

Heckscher, E. F. *La época mercantilista* (Spanish translation). México: 1983.

Heers, Jacques. *Esclaves et doméstiques au Moyen-Age dans le monde méditerranéen.* Paris, 1981: 89–93.

Heintze, Beatrix. "Historical notes on the Kisama of Angola." *J. Afr. H.* 13, no. 3 (1972): 407–418.

———. "Die portugiesische Besiedlungs-und Wirtschaftspolitik in Angola 1570–1607." *Aufsitze zur portugiesischen Kulturgeschichte* 17 (1979): 200–219.

———. "Luso-African Feudalism in Angola? The Vassal Treaties of the 16th to the 18th Century." *Revista Portuguesa de História* (*RPH*) 18 (1980): 111–131.

———. "The Angolan Vassal Tributes of the 17th Century." *Revista de História Económica e Social* (*RHES*) 6 (1980): 57–78.

———. "Angola nas garras do tráfico de escravos As guerras do Ndongo, 1611–1630." *RIEA*, vol. 1 (1984).

———. "Traite de 'pièces' en Angola—ce que nos sources passent sous silence." In *Actes du Colloque International sur la Traite des Noirs* (*CITN*), vol. 1, edited by S. Daget, 147–172. Paris: 1988.

———. *Asilo ameaçado—Oportunidades e conseqüências da fuga de escravos em Angola no século XVII*. Luanda: 1995.

———. "Antônio de Oliveira de Cadornegas Geschichtswerk: Eine außergewöhnliche Quelle des 17 Jahrhunders." In *Studien Zur Geschichte Angolas im 16. und 17. Jahrhundert—Ein Lesebuch*, edited by B. Heintze, 48–58. Koln: 1996.

———. "The Extraordinary Journey of the Jaga Through the Centuries: Critical Approaches to Precolonial Angolan Historical Sources." *History in Africa* 34 (2007): 67–101.

Hemming, John. *Red Gold: The Conquest of the Brazilian Indians, 1500–1760*. Cambridge, MA: 1978.

———. "The Indians of Brazil in 1500." In *The Cambridge History of Latin America* (*CHLA*), vol. 1, edited by L. Bethell, 119–143. Cambridge: Cambridge UP, 1984.

Henders, S. J. "So What If It's Not a Gamble? Post-Westphalian Politics in Macau." *Pacific Affairs* 74, no. 3 (2001): 342–360.

Henige, D. "When Did Smallpox Reach the New World, and Why Does It Matter?" In *Africans in Bondage*, edited by E. Lovejoy, 11–26. Madison, WI: 1986.

———. *Numbers from Nowhere: The American Indian Contact Population Debate*. Norman, OK: 1998.

Heritier, F. "Des cauris et des hommes—Production d'esclaves et accumulation de cauris chez les Samoo." In *L'esclavage en Afrique précoloniale*, edited by C. Meillassoux, 477–508. Paris: 1975.

Hershenzon, D. "'[P]ara Que Me Saque Cabesea Por Cabesa': Exchanging Muslim and Christian Slaves across the Western Mediterranean." *African Economic History* 42, no. 1 (2014): 11–36.

Hespanha, A. M. *As vésperas do Leviathan: Instituições e poder político—Portugal—séc. XVII*. Lisbon: 1986.

———. "A Fazenda." In J. Mattoso, *História de Portugal*. Vol. 4 of 8 vols. Lisbon: 1994, 203–232.

———. "Luís de Molina e a escravização dos negros." *Análise Social* 35, no. 157 (2001): 937–960.

Heywood, Linda. "Portuguese into African: The Eighteenth-Century Central African Background to Atlantic Creole Cultures." In *Central Africans and Cultural Transformations in the American Diaspora*, edited by L. Heywood, 91–114. Cambridge, UK: 2002.

———. *Njinga of Angola—Africa's Warrior Queen* (Cambridge, MA: 2017).

Hilton, Anne. "The Jaga Reconsidered." *J. Afr. H.* 22 (1981): 191–202.

———. "Family and Kinship among the Congo South of the Zaïre River from the Sixteenth to the Nineteenth Centuries." *J. Afr. H.* 24, no. 2 (1983): 189–206.

———. *The Kingdom of Kongo*. Oxford: 1985.

Hoboken, W. J. van *Witte de With in Brazilië 1648–1649*. Amsterdam: 1955.

Hoffman, R. "Propagation of the Faith." *New Catholic Encyclopaedia*, vol. 11. London: 1967: 840–844.

Hoffman, T. "Prices, the Military Revolution, and Western Europe's Comparative Advantage in Violence." *The Economic History Review* 64, no. S1 (2011): 39–59.

Hogendorn, J. S., and H. A. Gemery. "Abolition and Its Impact on Monies Imported to West Africa." In *The Abolition of the Atlantic Slave Trade*, edited by D. Eltis and J. Walvin, 99–116. Madison, WI: 1981.

Hogendorn, J. S., and M. Johnson. *The Shell Money of the Slave Trade*. Cambridge, MA: 1986.

Hopkins, D. R. *Princes and Peasants—Smallpox in History*. Chicago: 1983.

Hoppe, F. *A África Oriental portuguesa no tempo do marquês de Pombal*. Lisbon: 1970.

Houaiss, A. "Prefácio." In A. G. da Cunha, *Dicionário histórico das palavras portuguesas de origem tupi*. São Paulo: 1998.

Hromnik, C. A. "Canarins in the Rios de Cuama, 1501–1576." *Journal of African Society* 6, no. 1 (1979): 27–37.

Hubert, M. *Índios e Jesuítas no tempo das Missões*. São Paulo: 1990.

Hudson-Rodd, N. "Hygeia or Panacea? Ethnogeography and Health in Canada—Seventeenth to Eighteenth Century." *History of European Ideas* 21, no. 2 (1995): 235–246.

Hunwick, J. O. "Songhay, Borno and Hausaland in the 16th Century." In *History of West Africa*, 2nd ed., edited by J. F. Ade Ajayi and Michael Crowder, 264–301. London: 1976.

Imperial Y Gomez, Claudio Miralles de, ed. *Angola en tempos de Felipe II y de Felipe III: Los memoriales de Diego de Herrera y de Jeronimo de Castaño*. Madrid: 1951.

Inikori, J. E. "Introduction." In *Forced Migration: The Impact of the Export Slave Trade on African Societies*, edited by J. E. Inikori, 45–51. New York: 1982.

———. "The Import of Firearms into West Africa, 1750 to 1807: A Quantitative Analysis." In *Forced Migration: The Impact of the Export Slave Trade on African Societies*, edited by J. E. Inikori, 126–253. New York: 1982.

Iria, Alberto. "Da fundação e governo do Castelo ou Fortaleza de São Jorge da Mina pelos Portugueses e da sua acção missionária após o descobrimento desta costa." *Studia* 1 (1958): 25–69.

Iroko, A. F. "Cauris et esclaves en Afrique Occidentale entre le XVIe. et le XIXe s." *Actes du Colloque International sur la Traite des Noirs*. Vol. 1, edited by S. Daget, 193–204. Paris: 1988.

Isaacman, A. F. *Mozambique: The Africanization of a European Institution: The Zambezi Prazos, 1750–1902*. Madison: University of Wisconsin P, 1972.

Isaacman, A. F., and B. Isaacman. "The Prazeros as Transfrontiersman: A Study in Social and Cultural Change." *International Journal of African Historical Studies* 8, no. 1 (1975): 1–39.

Israel, Jonathan I. "A Conflict of Empires: Spain and the Netherlands 1618–1648." *Past and Present* 76 (1977): 48–54.

———. *La Republica Holandesa y el Mundo Hispánico 1606–1661.* Madrid: 1982.

———. "The Diplomatic Career of Jerônimo Nunes da Costa: An Episode in Dutch-Portuguese Relations of the Seventeenth Century." *Bijdragen en Mededelingen betreffende de Geschiedenis der Nederlanden* 98 (1983): 167–190.

———. *Empires and Entrepots: The Dutch, the Spanish Monarchy and the Jews 1585–1713.* London: 1990.

———, ed. *The Anglo-Dutch Moment—Essays on the Glorius Revolution and Its World Impact.* Cambridge: 1991.

———. *European Jewry in the Age of Mercantilism 1550–1750.* New York: 1991.

———. *Dutch Primacy in World Trade 1585–1740.* Oxford: 1992.

———. *Diasporas within a Diaspora: Jews, Crypto-Jews, and the World of Maritime Empires (1540–1740).* Leiden, The Netherlands: Brill, 2002.

Jacquemet, G., G. Mathon, G. H. Baudry, P. Guilluy, and E. Thiery. "Confessionnal." In *Catholicisme—Hier, aujourd'hui, demain*, 1,507–1,510. Vol. 2. Paris: 1954.

Jadin, Louis. "Les flamands au Congo et en Angola au XVIIème siècle." In *Revista Portuguesa de História*, 6 no. 1 (1955): 383–452.

———. "Rivalités luso-néerlandaises au Sohio, Congo 1600–1675." *Bulletin de l'Institut Historique Belge de Rome* 37 (1966): 137–360.

———. "Pero Tavares, missionnaire jésuite, ses travaux apostoliques au Congo et en Angola, 1629–1635." *Bulletin de l'Institut Historique Belge de Rome* 38 (1967): 271–402.

Jancso, István, ed. *Cronologia de História do Brasil Colonial 1500–1831.* São Paulo: 1994.

Jeannin, Pierre. *Les marchands au XVIe siècle.* Paris: 1957.

Johnson, H. B. "The Donatary Captaincy in Historical Perspective: Portuguese Backgrounds to the Settlement of Brazil." *HAHR* 52 (1972): 203–214.

———. "*The Portuguese Settlement of Brazil, 1500–1580.*" In *The Cambridge History of Latin America*, vol. 1, edited by L. Bethell, 258–259. Cambridge, UK: Cambridge UP, 1995.

Justo Guedes, Max. "O Condicionalismo Físico do Atlântico e a Navegação à Vela." *História Naval Brasileira.* Vol. 1. Rio de Janeiro: 1972: 117–134.

———. "Guerra da Independência: as Forças de Mar." In *História da Independência do Brasil.* Vol. 2, edited by J. Montello, 167–211. Rio de Janeiro: 1972.

Kaba, L. "Background to the Change in West African Economic History: Songhay, 1492–1750." *Journal of African Society* 4, no. 3 (1977): 344–356.

———. "Les archers, les mousquetaires et les moustiques: une interprétation de l'invasion marrocaine du Soudan et la résistance Songhay, 1591–1612." *Bulletin de l'Institut Fondamental d'Afrique Noire* 42 (1980): 1–36.

Kato, E. "Unification and Adaptation, the Early Shogunate and Dutch Trade Policies." In *Companies and Trade: Essays on Overseas Trading Companies during the Ancient Regime*, edited by L. Blussé and F. Gaastra, 207–229. Leiden: 1981.

Kea, R. A. "Firearms and Warfare on the Gold and Slave Coast from the Sixteenth to the Nineteenth Centuries." *J. Afr. H.* 12, no. 2 (1971): 185–213.

Kellenbenz, Hermann. "Autour de 1600: Le commerce du poivre des Fuggers et le marché international du poivre." *Annales E.C.S.* 11 (1956): 1–28.

———. *Sephardin auf der unteren Elbe*. Wiesbaden: 1958.

Kennedy, Paul M. *The Rise and Fall of British Naval Mastery.* London: 1983.

Keul, M., J.-J. Hémardinquer, and J. Bertin, "Cartes historiques des cultures vivrières." *Annales* 21, no. 5 (1966): 1,012–1,025.

Kiemen, M. C. *The Indian Policy of Portugal in the Amazon Region 1614–1693.* New York: 1973.

Kiple, K. F., and B. T. Higgins. "Mortality Caused by Dehydration during the Middle Passage." In *The Atlantic Slave Trade: Effects on Economies, Societies, and Peoples in Africa, the Americas, and Europe*, edited by J. E. Inikori and S. L. Engerman, 320–338. London: 1992.

Kiple, K. F., and V. Himmelsteib King. *Another Dimension to the Black Diaspora: Diet, Disease and Racism.* London: 1981.

———. *The Caribbean Slave: A Biological History.* New York: 1984.

Klein, A. Norman. "Toward a New Understanding of Akan Origins, "*Africa: Journal of the International African Institute* 66, no. 2 (1996): 248–273.

Klein, Herbert S., and Stanley L Engerman. "Shipping Patterns and Mortality in the African Slave Trade to Rio de Janeiro, 1825–1830." *CEA* 15 (1975): 381–398.

———. "Recent Trends in the Study of Atlantic Slave Trade." *História y Sociedad* 1, no. 1. Puerto Rico: 1988.

———. *The Atlantic Slave Trade: New Approaches to the Americas.* Cambridge, UK: Cambridge UP, 1999.

Klein, Herbert S., S. L. Engerman, R. Haines, and R. Shlomowitz. "Transoceanic Mortality: The Slave Trade in Comparative Perspective." *The William and Mary Quarterly* 58, no. 1 (2001): 93–118.

Klein, Martin A. "The Impact of the Atlantic Slave Trade on the Societies of the Western Sudan." *Social Science History* 14, no. 2 (1990): 231–253.

———. "The Slave Trade and Decentralized Societies." *J. Afr. H.* 42, no. 1 (2001): 49–65.

Knight, Franklin W. "The Atlantic Slave Trade and the Development of an Afro-American Culture." In *The Abolition of the Atlantic Slave Trade*, edited by D. Eltis and J. Walvin, 287–302. Madison, WI: 1981.

Knotter, A., C. Lis, H. Soly, and I. Wallerstein. "Merchant Capitalism." *Review* 2 (1997): 189–271.

Kodama, Kaori. "Itinerários, corografias e escritas da história: as viagens e os registros de Raimundo José da Cunha Matos no Império do Brasil," *Escritos. Revista do Centro de Pesquisa da Casa de Rui Barbosa* 2, no. 2 (2008): 373–395.

Kojeve, A. *Introduction à la lecture de Hegel.* Paris: 1947.

Koshiba, Luiz. "Conservadorismo e radicalidade na poesia de Gregório de Matos." *Revista de História* 116 (1984): 3–24.

Kossmann, E. H. "Freedom in Seventeenth-Century Dutch Thought and Practice." In *The Anglo-Dutch Moment: Essays on the Glorius Revolution and Its World Impact*, edited by J. I. Israel, 281–298. Cambridge, UK: 1991.

Kouame, Nathalie. "Quatre règles à suivre pour bien comprendre le 'siècle chrétien' du Japon." *Histoire et missions chrétiennes* 11, no. 3 (2009): 9–38.

Kriger, Colleen E. "Mapping the History of Cotton Textile Production in Precolonial West Africa." *African Economic History* 33, no. 1 (2005): 87–116.

Kusimba, C. M. "Archaeology of Slavery in East Africa." *The African Archaeological Review* 21, no. 2 (2004): 59–88.

Ladhams, John. "In Search of West African Pidgin Portuguese." *Revista Internacional de Lingüística Iberoamericana*, 4, no. 1.7 (2006): 87–105.

Lafaye, J. *Quetzalcóatl et Guadalupe—La formation de la conscience nationale au Méxique* Paris: 1974.

Lamego, Alberto. *A terra goyatacá.* 5 vols. Paris: Brussels: Niterói, 1913–1942.

Lang, J. *Portuguese Brazil: The King's Plantation.* Cambridge: Academic Press, 2013.

Lapeyre, H. "Le trafic négrier avec l'Amérique espagnole." *Homenaje a Jaime Vicens Vives.* Barcelona: 1967, 285–304.

Lara Ribeiro, Silvia. "Do mouro cativo ao escravo negro: Continuidade ou ruptura?" *Anais do Museu Paulista* 30 (1980–1981): 375–398.

Law, Robin. "A West African Cavalry State: The Kingdom of Oyo." *J. Afr. H.* 16, no. 1 (1975): 1–15.

———. "Horses, Firearms, and Political Power in Pre-Colonial West Africa." *Past & Present* 72 (1976): 112–132.

———. *The Horse in West African History: The Role of the Horse in the Societies of Pre-Colonial West Africa.* Ann Arbor: U of Michigan P, 1980.

———. "Trade and Politics Behind the Slave Coast: The Lagoon Traffic and the Rise of Lagos, 1500–1800." *J. Afr. H.* 24 (1983): 321–348.

———. "Dahomey and the Slave Trade: Reflections on the Historiography of the Rise of Dahomey." *J. Afr. H.* 27, no. 2 (1986): 237–267.

———. "The Slave Trade in Seventeenth-Century Allada: A Revision." *African Economic History* 22 (1994): 59–92.

Le Guern, M. "Comments." B. Pascal, *Les provinciales*, edited by M. L, 135 and 351. Guern. Paris: 1987.

Leite, Aureliano. "Amador Bueno, sua vida e em especial o seu papel dentro da capitania de S. Vicente do Estado do Brasil nos acontecimentos da restauração da Monarquia Portuguesa." In *Congresso do mundo português.* Vol. 7. (Lisbon: 1940) 547–568.

Leite, Serafim. *Artes e Ofícios dos Jesuítas no Brasil 1549–1760*. Rio de Janeiro: 1953.
Leite Cordeiro, J. P. *São Paulo e a invasão holandesa no Brasil*. São Paulo: 1949.
———. "Alguns documentos sôbre médicos e medicina do Brasil Seiscentista." *RIHGB*, vol. 216 (1952): 36–41.
Leite de Faria, F. "A situação de Angola e Congo apreciada em Madrid em 1643." *Portugal em África* 52 (1952): 235–248.
———. "Frei João de Santiago e sua 'Relação' sobre os capuchinhos no Congo." *Portugal em África* 59 (1953): 316–333.
———. "Uma Relação de Rui de Pina sobre o Congo escrita em 1492." *Studia* 19 (1966): 223–303.
———. "João Antônio Cavazzi: A sua obra e a sua vida." *DHCMA*, vol. 1, XI–LVIII.
———. "A difusão extraordinária do relato de Duarte Lopes sobre o Congo." *Revista da Biblioteca Nacional* 7, no. 2 (1992): 103–128.
Le Guennec, G., and J. F. Valente. *Dicionário português-umbundu*. Luanda: 1972.
Le Roy Ladurie, Emmanuel, J. N. Barrandon, B. Collin, M. Guerra, and C. Morrisson. "Sur les traces de l'argent du Potosí." *Annales E.S.C.* 45, no. 2 (1990): 483–505.
Le Tourneau, R. "North Africa to the Sixteenth Century." In *The Cambridge History of Islam (CHI)*, Vol. 2, edited by P. M. Holt, A. K. S. Lambton, and Bernard Lewis, 211–237. Cambridge, UK: 1970.
Leur, J. C. Van. *Indonesian Trade and Society: Essays in Asian Social and Economic History*. The Hague: 1955.
Levine, H. "Gentry, Jews, and Serfs: The Rise of Polish Vodka." *Review* 4, no. 2 (1980): 223–250.
Lévi-Strauss, C. "Rousseau, père de l'Ethnologie." *Le Courrier de l'Unesco* 16 (1963): 10–14.
Levtzion, N. "The Western Maghrib and Sudan." *Cambridge History of Africa* 3 (1977): 331–462.
Levy-Bruhl, H. "Esquisse d'une théorie sociologique de l'esclavage à Rome." *Revue générale du droit, de la législation et de la jurisprudence en France et à l'étranger* 55 (1931): 1–17.
———. "Slavery and Islamization in Africa." *Slaves & Slavery in Muslim Africa*, vol. 1, edited by J. R. Willis, 182–198. London: 1985.
Lewis, Bernard. *Race and Slavery in the Middle East: An Historical Enquiry*. New York: 1990.
Liberman, M. *O Levante do Maranhão "Judeu Cabeça de Motim"—Manoel Beckman*. São Paulo: 1983.
Link, L. *The Devil—A Mask Without a Face*. Brazilian translation. São Paulo: 1995.
Livi-Bacci, M. "The Depopulation of Hispanic America after the Conquest." *Population and Development Review* 32, no. 2 (2006): 199–232.
Lipiner, E. *Izaque de Castro, o mancebo que veio preso do Brasil*. Recife: 1992.
Lobato, A. *Evolução administrativa e econômica de Moçambique 1752–1763*. Lisbon: 1957.
———. *Colonização senhorial da Zambézia e outros estudos*. Lisbon: 1962.

Lobato, Manuel. "Relações comerciais entre a Índia e a costa africana nos séculos XVI e XVII—O papel do guzerate no comércio de Moçambique." *Mare Liberum* 9 (1995): 157–173.

Lobo Cabrera, M. *La Esclavitud En Las Canarias Orientales En El Siglo XVI: Negros, Moros Y Moriscos*. Santa Cruz de Tenerife: 1982.

———. "El comercio entre Portugal y Canarias en el Quinientos." *RHES* 19 (1987): 1–16.

Lopes Moreno, D. *Livro que dá Razão do Estado do Brasil–1612*, introduction and notes by H. Vianna. Recife: 1955.

Loureiro, Rui Manuel. "Portuguese Involvement in Sixteenth Century Horse Trade through the Arabian Sea." In *Pferde in Asien: Geschichte, Handel Und Kultur (Horses in Asia: History, Trade and Culture)*, edited by Bert G. Franger, 139–145. Wien: 2009.

———. "Chinese Commodities on the India Route in the Late 16th–Early 17th Centuries." *Bulletin of Portuguese-Japanese Studies* 20 (2010): 81–94:

Lovejoy, Paul E. "The Volume of the Atlantic Slave Trade: A Synthesis." *J. Afr. H.* 23 (1982): 473–501.

———. *Transformations in Slavery*. New York: 1983.

———. "Kola in the History of West Africa [La Kola Dans L'histoire de l'Afrique Occidentale]." *Cahiers d'Etudes Africaines* 20, no. 77/78 (1980): 97–134.

Lozano Armendares, T. *El chinguirito vindicado: El contrabando de aguardiente de caña y la política colonial*. Mexico: 1995.

Luna, F. V., and Herbert S. Klein. *Slavery and the Economy of São Paulo, 1750–1850*. Stanford, CA: Stanford University Press, 2003.

MacCormack, S. "From the Sun of the Incas to the Virgin of Copacabana." *Representations* 8 (1984): 30–60.

Machado de Faria, A. *O mestre de campo João Fernandes Vieira, herói da Restauração de Pernambuco*. Lisbon: 1955.

MacLachlan, C. M. "The Indian Labor Structure in the Portuguese Amazon 1700–1800." In *Colonial Roots of Modern Brazil*, edited by D. Alden, 199–230. London: 1973.

Madeira da Silva, T. "A cidade de São Tomé no Quadro das Cidades Insulares Atlânticas de Origem Portuguesa." (2012): https://repositorio.iscte-iul.pt/handle/10071/3921, accessed January 2013.

Madeira Santos, Maria E. "Rotas Atlânticas, o caso da Carreira de S. Tomé," in *Actas do II Colóquio Internacional de História da Madeira*, 649–655. Lisbon: 1989.

———. "Mulatos: sua legitimação pela Chancelaria Régia no século xvi." *Studia* 53 (1994): 237–246.

Magalhães, Basílio de. *Expansão geográfica do Brasil colonial*. 3rd ed. Rio de Janeiro: 1944.

Magalhães, P. A. I. "A Relação do engenho de Sergipe do Conde em 1625." *Afro-Ásia* 41 (2010): 237–264.

Magalhães Godinho, V. "Problèmes d'économie atlantique: Le Portugal, flottes du sucre et flottes de l'or, 1670–1770." *Annales ECS* 5, no 2 (1950): 184–197.

———. "Restauração." In *Dicionário de história de Portugal*. Vol. 3, 618.

———. "1580 e a Restauração." *Ensaios*. Vol 2: *Sobre historia de Portugal*. 2nd ed. Lisbon: 1978.

———. *Os descobrimentos e a economia mundial*. 4 vols. Lisbon: 1981–1983.

———. *Introdução à história econômica*, Lisbon: n.d.

Maia, José Antonio. *Memoria sobre a franquia do porto de Macáo*. Lisbon: 1849.

Malekandathil, P. *Maritime India: Trade, Religion, and Polity in the Indian Ocean*. Delhi: 2010.

Mann, Kristin. *Slavery and the Birth of an African City: Lagos, 1760–1900*. Bloomington: Indiana UP, 2008.

Manning, Patrick. "The Slave Trade in the Bight of Benin 1640–1890." In *The uncommon market, essays in the economic history of the Atlantic slave trade*, edited by H. A. Gemery and J. S. Hogendorn, 107–140. New York, N.Y.: 1979.

———. *Slavery, Colonialism and Economic Growth in Dahomey, 1640–1960*. Cambridge, UK: 1982.

———. "The Impact of Slave Trade Exports on the Population of the Western Coast of Africa 1700–1850." *Actas du Colloque International sur la Traite des Noirs (CITN)*. Vol. 2. Nantes: 1988.

———. *Slavery and African Life—Occidental, Oriental and African Slave Trades*. Cambridge, UK: 1990.

———. *Slave Trades 1500–1800: Globalization of Forced Labor*. Farnham: 1996.

———. *Navigating World History: Historians Create a Global Past*. Basingstoke: 2003.

Mannix, D., and M. Cowley. *Black Cargoes*. Ontario: 1976.

Mantran, Roger. "North Africa in the Sixteenth and Seventeenth Centuries." In *The Cambridge History of Islam (CHI)*. Vol. 2, 211–237. Cambridge, UK: 1970.

Marchant, Alexander. "Feudal and Capitalistic Elements in the Portuguese Settlement of Brazil." *Hispanic America Historical Review* 22 (1942): 493–512.

———. *From Barter to Slavery—The Economic Relations of Portuguese and Indians in the Settlement of Brazil 1500–1580*. Gloucester, MA: 1966.

Marchena Fernandez, J. "Dominicos y encomenderos en el Tucuman del siglo XVII." *Los Dominicos y el Nuevo Mundo: Actas del III Congreso Internacional*. Madrid: 1991, 433–442.

Marcílio, Maria Luiza. "The Population of Colonial Brazil." *CHLA* 2 (n.d.): 37–63.

Marcocci, G. "Escravos ameríndios e negros africanos: uma história conectada. Teorias e modelos de discriminação no império português (ca. 1450–1650)." *Tempo* 16 (2011): 41–70.

Margarido, A. "Les porteurs formes de domination et agents du changement en Angola, XVIe–XIXe siècles." *Revue Française d'Histoire d'Outre-Mer* 65, no. 240 (1978): 377–399.

Marinho dos Santos, J. "As economias do Índico aquando da chegada dos portugueses." *RPH* 27 (1992): 203–214.

Mark, P. "The Evolution of 'Portuguese' Identity: Luso-Africans on the Upper Guinea Coast from the Sixteenth to the Early Nineteenth Century." *J. Afr. H.* 40, no. 2 (1999): 173–191.

Mark, P., and J. da Silva Horta. "Two Early Seventeenth-Century Sephardic Communities on Senegal's Petite Côte." *History in Africa* 31, no. 1 (2004): 231–256.

Marks, S. "Khoisan Resistance to the Dutch in the Seventeenth and Eighteenth Centuries." *J. Afr. H.* 12, no. 2 (1971): 55–80.

Marques, J. F. "A cronologia da pregação de Vieira." In *Vieira escritor*, edited by M. Vieira Mendes, M. L. Gonçalves Pires, and J. da Costa Miranda. Lisbon: 1997, 117–134.

Marquez Villanueva, F. "El problema historio-gráfico de los moriscos." *Bulletin Hispanique* 86, no. 1–2 (1984): 61–135.

Marsilio, C. "Lisbon, London, or Genoa? Three Alternative Destinations for the Spanish Silver of Philip IV (1627–1650)." In *Three Conferences on International Monetary History*. 399–413. Wetteren: 2013.

Martin, Phyllis M. *The External Trade of the Loango Coast 1576–1870—The Effects of Changing Commercial Relations on the Vili Kingdom of Loango*. Oxford, UK: 1972.

———. "Power, Cloth, and Currency on the Loango Coast." *African Economic History* 15 (1986): 1–12.

Martin, R. "'Familia rustica'—Les esclaves chez les agronomes latins." *Annales Littéraires de l'Université de Besançon*. Paris: 1974: 267–298.

Martins Alberto, E. M. C. "Corsários argelinos na costa atlântica: o resgate de cativos de 1618." *Actas do Congresso Internacional Atlântico de Antigo Regime: poderes e sociedades*. Lisbon: Universidade Nova de Lisboa, 2005: 1–6.

Martins dos Santos, F. *História de Santos 1532–1936*. São Paulo: 1937.

Masselman, G. "Dutch Colonial Policy in the Seventeenth Century." *JEH* 21, no. 4 (1961): 455–468.

Massing, Andreas W. "The Mane: The Decline of Mali and Mandinka Expansion towards the South Windward Coast." *CEA* 97, nos. 25–26 (1985): 21–55.

———. "Mapping the Malagueta Coast: A History of the Lower Guinea Coast, 1460–1510, through Portuguese Maps and Accounts." *History in Africa* 36 (2009): 331–365.

———. "Valentim Fernandes' Five Maps and the Early History and Geography of São Tomé." *History in Africa* 36 (2009): 367–386.

Mathew, K. S. "India Merchants and the Portuguese Trade on the Malabar Coast during the Sixteenth Century," *Indo-Portuguese History—Old Issues, New Questions*, edited by T. R. de Souza, 1–12. New Delhi: 1985.

———. *Indo-Portuguese Trade and the Fuggers of Germany*. New Delhi: Manohar, 1997.

Mathiex, J. "Trafic et prix de l'homme en Méditerranée aux XVIIe et XVIIIe siècles." *Annales E.S.C.* 9, no. 2 (1954): 157–164.

Mata, I. "Representações da rainha Njinga/Nzinga na literatura angolana." In *A Rainha Nzinga Mbandi—História, Memória e Mito*, edited by I. Mata. Lisbon: 2014, 23–46.
Matos, A. Teodoro de. *O Orçamento do Estado da India, 1571*. Lisbon: 1999.
Matos, H. "Black Troops and Hierarchies of Color in the Portuguese Atlantic World: The Case of Henrique Dias and his Black Regiment." *Luso-Brazilian Review* 45, no. 1 (2008): 6–29.
Maurício, D. "A Universidade de Évora e a escravatura." *Didaskalia* 8 (1977): 153–200.
Mauro, Frédéric. "De Madère à Mazagan: une Méditerranée atlantique." *Hesperis* (1953): 250–254.
———. *Le Portugal et l'Atlantique au XVIIe siècle, 1570–1670*. Paris, 1960.
———. *Nova história e Novo Mundo*. São Paulo: 1969.
———. *Etudes economiques sur l'expansion portugaise*. Paris: 1970.
———. *Des produits et des hommes: Essais historiques latino-américains XVIe–XXe siècles*. Berlin: 1973.
———. *Le Brésil du XVe à la fin du XVIIIe s*. Paris: 1977.
———. *Le XVIe s. Européen: Aspects économiques*. 3rd ed. Paris: 1981.
McCaa, R. "Spanish and Nahuatl Views on Smallpox and Demographic Catastrophe in Mexico." *The Journal of Interdisciplinary History* 25, no. 3 (1995): 397–431.
McColley, R. "Slavery in Virginia." In *Dictionary of Afro-American Slavery*, edited by R. M. Miller and J. D. Smith, 779–787. Westport, CT: 1988.
McCusker, J. J. *Rum and the American Revolution: The Rum Trade and the Balance of Payments of the Thirteen Continental Colonies 1650–1775*. New York: 1989.
McGlone, M. M. "The King's Surprise: The Mission Methodology of Toribio de Mogrovejo." *The Americas* 50, no. 1 (1993): 65–83.
Medeiros, F. de. *L'Occident et l'Afrique XIIIe–XVIe siècles*. Paris: 1985.
Medeiros dos Santos, Corcino. "Relações de Angola com o Rio de Janeiro 1736–1808." *Estudos Históricos* 12 (1973): 7–68.
Meilink-Roelofsz, M. A. "Aspects of Dutch Colonial Development in Asia in the Seventeenth Century." In *Britain and the Netherlands in Europe and Asia*, edited by J. S. Bromley and E. H. Kossman, 56–82. London: 1968.
Meillassoux, Claude. "L'évolution du commerce en Afrique de l'Ouest." In *The Development of Indigenous Trade and Markets in West Africa*, edited by C. Meillassoux, 7–16. London: 1971.
———. *Femmes, greniers & capitaux*. Paris: 1975.
———. *Anthropologie de l'esclavage—Le ventre de fer et d'argent*. Paris: 1990.
Mellander, K., and E. Prestage. *The Diplomatic and Commercial Relations of Sweden and Portugal from 1641 to 1670*. Watford: 1930.
Mello e Souza, L. *Inferno Atlântico: Demonologia e colonização, séculos XVI–XVIII*. São Paulo: 1993.

Mello e Souza, Marina de. *Reis Negros no Brasil Escravista: História da festa de coroação do rei do Congo.* Belo Horizonte: 2002.

Mello Pereira, Magnus Roberto de. "Brasileiros a serviço do Império; a África vista por naturais do Brasil, no século XVIII." *Revista Portuguesa de História* 33 (1999): 153–190.

Metcalf, A. C. *Family and Frontier in Colonial Brazil Santana de Parnaíba, 1580–1822.* Los Angeles: 1992.

———. *Go-Betweens and the Colonization of Brazil, 1500–1600.* Austin: U of Texas P: 2005.

———. "The Entradas of Bahia of the Sixteenth Century." *The Americas* 61, no. 3 (2005): 373–400.

Metraux, Alfred. *La civilization matérielle des tupí-guaraní.* Paris: 1928.

Meuvret, J. *Études d'Histoire Économique.* Paris: 1971.

Mezza Cuadra, G. "Le Pisco, eau de vie du Pérou." In *Premier Symposium International sur les eaux-de-vie traditionnelles d'origine viticole.* (Paris: 1991): 28–31.

Milhou, Alain. "Los intentos de repoblación de la isla Hispaniola por colonias de labradores (1518–1603): Razones de un fracaso." *Actas del Quinto Congreso Internacional de Hispanistas.* Vol. 2, 643–654. Bordeaux: 1977:

———. "Sufficientia, les notions d'autosuffisance e de dépendance dans la pensée politique espagnole au XVIe siècle: De la Castille des comuneros au Pérou colonial." In *Mélanges de la Casa de Velazquez.* Vol. 17, 106–145. Paris: 1981.

———. "L'Afrique." In *Histoire du Christianisme des origins à nos jours.* Vol. 8, edited by J. M. Mayeur, C. Pietri, A. Vauchez, and M. Venard, 685–690. Paris: 1992–1994.

Miller, Joseph C. "A note on Kasanze and the Portuguese." *Canadian Journal of African Society* 6 (1972): 43–56.

———. "The Imbangala and the chronology of Early Central African History." *J. Afr. H.* 12, no. 4 (1972): 549–574.

———. "Requiem for the Jaga." *CEA* 13 nos. 49–52 (1973): 121–149.

———. "Nzinga of Matamba in a New Perspective." *J. Afr. H.* 16 no. 2 (1975): 201–216.

———. *Kings and Kingsmen—The Imbangala Impact on the Mbundu of Angola.* Oxford, UK: 1976.

———. "Thanatopsis." *CEA* 18 no. 69–70 (1978): 229–231.

———. "Mortality in the Atlantic Slave Trade—Statistical Evidence on Causality." *Journal of International History* 11 no. 3 (1981): 385–423.

———. "Capitalism and Slaving—The Financial and Commercial Organization of the Angolan Slave Trade, According to the Accounts of Antônio Coelho Guerreiro, 1684–1892." *International Journal of African Historical Studies* 17 no. 1 (1984): 1–56.

———. "Slave Prices in the Portuguese Southern Atlantic 1600–1830." In *Africans in Bondage,* edited by Paul E. Lovejoy, 43–77. Madison, WI: 1986.

———. "Overcrowded and Undernourished: Techniques and Consequences of Tight-Packing in the Portuguese Southern Atlantic Slave Trade." In *De la traite à l'esclavage: Actes* du Colloque international sur la traite des noirs, edited by Serge Daget. Vol. 2, 395–424. Nantes: 1985.

——. *Way of Death—Merchant Capitalism and the Angolan Slave Trade 1730–1830*. Madison: U Wisconsin P, 1988.

Miller, Joseph C., and J. K. Thornton. "The Chronicle as Source, History, and Hagiography—The Catálogo dos governadores de Angola." *Paideuma* 33 (1987): 360–388.

Mintz, S. W. *Sweetness and Power: The Place of Sugar in Modern History*. New York: 1986.

Mira Caballos, E. "Las Licencias de Esclavos Negros a Hispanoamérica (1544–1550)." *Revista de Indias* 54, no. 201 (1994): 273–298.

Miracle, M. "The Introduction and Spread of Maize in Africa." *J. Afr. H.* 6, no. 1 (1965): 39–55.

Miranda, Nicanor. "Vocabulário do padre Manuel Bernardes." In *Revista do Arquivo Municipal*, vol. 168. São Paulo: 1962.

Miranda, V. C. de "Estudos sôbre o Nhêengatú." *ABNRJ* 64 (1942): 5–127.

Mitchell, Peter, and Gavin Whitelaw. "The Archaeology of Southernmost Africa from c. 2000 BP to the Early 1800s: A Review of Recent Research." *J. Afr. H.* 46, no. 2 (2005): 209–241.

Mogo Demaret, Mathieu. "Portugueses e Africanos em Angola no século XVII: Problemas de representação e de comunicação a partir da História Geral das Guerras Angolanas." In *Representações de África e dos Africanos na História e Cultura Séculos XV a XXI*, edited by J. D. Rodrigues and Casimiro Rodrigues, 107–130. Linda-a-Velha: 2011.

Moisés, M. *Pequeno dicionário de literatura portuguesa*. São Paulo: 1981.

Molho, A., and D. Ramada Curto. "Les réseaux marchands à l'époque moderne." *Annales* 58, no. 3 (2003): 569–579.

Mols, R. "Population in Europe 1500–1700," in *The Fontana Economic History of Europe*. Vol. 2, edited by C. M. Cipolla. Glasgow: 1979, 15–82.

Monteiro, A. de C. X. "Como se ensinava o Direito das Gentes na Universidade de Coimbra no século XVI." *Anais da Academia Portuguesa da História*. Vol. 33, 2nd series (Lisbon: 1993): 9–36.

Monteiro, John M. "O escravo índio, esse desconhecido." In *Índios no Brasil*, edited by L. D. Benzi Grupioni. São Paulo: 1992, 105–120.

——. *Negros da terra—Índios e bandeirantes nas origens de São Paulo*. São Paulo: 1994.

——. "The Crises and Transformations of Invaded Societies: Coastal Brazil in the Sixteenth Century." In *CHNPA*, vol. 3, part 1, edited by F. Salomon and S.B. Schwartz, 973–1023. Cambridge, UK: Cambridge UP, 1996.

——. "500 Years of Native Brazilian History." *Diálogos Latinoamericanos* 2 (2000): 2–15.

Mora de Tovar, G. *Aguardiente y conflictos sociales en la Nueva Granada durante el siglo XVIII*. Bogotá: 1988.

Moraes, N. I. de "Sur les prises de Gorée par les Portugais au XVIIème siècle." *Bulletin de l'Institut Fondamental d'Afrique Noire* 21, series B (1969): 989–1,013.
Moreno, M. "Aguardientes y alcoholismo en el Mexico colonial." *Cuadernos hispanoamericanos.* Vol. 42 (1985): 81–96.
Moore, J. W. "Madeira, Sugar, and the Conquest of Nature in the 'First' Sixteenth Century: Part I: From 'Island of Timber' to Sugar Revolution, 1420–1506." *Review* 32, no. 4 (2009): 1–24.
———. "Madeira, Sugar, and the Conquest of Nature in the 'First' Sixteenth Century, Part II: From Regional Crisis to Commodity Frontier, 1506–1530." *Review* 33, no. 1 (2010): 9–13.
Moraes Farias, P. F. de. "Silent Trade: Myth and Historical Evidence." *History in Africa* 1 (1974): 9–24.
Moreira Bento, C. C. "Angola—a primeira Força Expedicionária Brasileira." *Leitura.* São Paulo: 1989.
Moreira de Azevedo, M. D. "Amador Bueno: Memória lida em sessão do Instituto Histórico." *RIHGB* 75, 2nd part (1887): 1–10.
Morineau, M. "Le siècle." In Histoire *économique et sociale du monde.* Vol. 2, edited by P. Leon, 63–106. Paris: 1978.
Moseley, K. "Caravel and Caravan, West Africa and the World-Economies, ca. 900–1900 AD." *Review* 15, no. 3 (1992): 523–555.
Mousnier, Roland. *Les institutions de la France sous la monarchie absolue.* 2 vols. Paris: 1974.
Mott, L. R. B. "Estrutura demográfica das fazendas de gado do Piauí colonial: um caso de povoamento rural centrífugo." *Ciência e Cultura* 30 (1978): 1,196–1,210.
Moutoukias, Zacarías. "Power, Corruption, and Commerce: The Making of the Local Administrative Structure in Seventeenth-Century Buenos Aires." *HAHR* 68, no. 4 (1988): 771–801.
———. "Comércio y Producción." In *Nueva Historia de la Nación Argentina,* vol. 3, 2nd part, 51–103. Buenos Aires: 1999–2003.
Muhana, Adma. "Quando não se escreve o que se fala." In *Vieira escritor,* edited by Margarida Vieira Mendes, M. L. Gonçalves Pires, and José da Costa Miranda, 107–116. Lisbon: 1997.
Munanga, K. "Origem e Histórico do Quilombo na África." *Revista da USP* 28 (1995–1996): 1–13.
Nardi, Jean-Baptiste. *O fumo brasileiro no período colonial.* São Paulo, 1996.
Navarrete, M. C. *Genesis y Desarrollo de La Esclavitud En Colombia Siglos XVI y XVII.* Cali: 2005.
Ndaywel E Nziem, Isidore. "L'historiographie congolaise—Un essai de bilan." *Civilisations* 54 (2006): 237–254.

Neale, W. C. de. "Réciprocité et redistribution dans le village indien: Suite a quelques célèbres discussions." In *Trade and Market in Early Empires: Economies in History and Theory*, edited by K. Polanyi and C. Arensberg. New York: 1957, 217–231.

Nemésio, Vitorino. *A Companhia de Jesus e o plano português do Brasil*. Lisbon: 1971.

Newitt, Malyn D. D. "The Portuguese on the Zambezi: An Historical Interpretation of the Prazo." *J. Afr. H.* 10 (1969): 67–85.

———. *Portuguese Settlement on the Zambezi: Exploration, Land Tenure, and Colonial Rule in East Africa*. London: 1973.

———. "Plunder and the Rewards of Office in the Portuguese Empire." In *The Military Revolution and the State, 1500–1800*, edited by M. Duffy. Exeter: 1980.

———. "The Early History of the Marawi." *J. Afr. H.* 23 (1982): 145–162.

———. *Charles Ralph Boxer 1904–2000*. London: 2000.

Newson, Linda A. "Africans and Luso-Africans in the Portuguese Slave Trade on the Upper Guinea Coast in the Early Seventeenth Century." *J. Afr. H.* 53, no 1 (2012): 1–24.

———. "Cargazones de negros en Cartagena de Índias en el siglo XVII: nutrición, salud y mortalidad." In *Cartagena de Indias en el Siglo XVII*, edited by Haroldo Calvo Stenvenson and Adolfo Meisel Roca, 207–243. Cartagena, 2007.

Newson, Linda A., and Susie Minchin. *From Capture to Sale: The Portuguese Slave Trade to Spanish South America in the Early Seventeenth Century*. Leiden, 2007.

Norton, Luís. *A dinastia dos Sás no Brasil 1558–1662*. Lisbon: 1943.

Novais, F. A. *Portugal e Brasil na crise do antigo sistema colonial, 1777–1808*. São Paulo: 1979.

———. "Caio Prado Jr. na historiografia brasileira." In *Inteligência brasileira*, edited by R. Moraes et al., 68–69. São Paulo: 1986.

Novinsky, Anita. *Cristãos novos na Bahia*. São Paulo: 1967.

Noya Pinto, V. *O ouro brasileiro e o comércio anglo-português*. São Paulo: 1979.

Nowell, C. E. *The Rose-Colored Map*. Lisbon: 1982.

Nutton, V. "The Changing Language of Medicine, 1450–1550." *CIVICIMA—Etudes sur le vocabulaire intellectuel du Moyen Age*. Vol. 3 (1995): 184–198.

Ogundiran, Akinwumi. "Material Life and Domestic Economy in a Frontier of the Oyo Empire During the Mid-Atlantic Age." *The International Journal of African Historical Studies*, 42, no. 3 (2009): 351–385.

Olinto, Paulo. "Uma jóia da armaria." *Anais do Museu Histórico Nacional*, vol. 2, 129–137. Rio de Janeiro, 1941.

Olival, Fernanda, and João de Figuerôa-Rêgo. "Cor da pele, distinções e cargos: Portugal e espaços atlânticos portugueses (séculos XVI a XVIII)." *Tempo* 26 no. 30 (2011): 115–145.

Oliveira Boleo, J. de. "Vicissitudes históricas da política de exploração mineira no império de Muenemutapa." *Studia* 32 (1971): 167–209.

Oliveira e Costa, J. "Em torno da criação do Bispado do Japão." In *As relações entre a Índia portuguesa, a Ásia do Sueste e o Extremo Oriente*, edited by A. T. de Matos and L. F. F. Reis Thomaz, 141–171. Lisbon: 1993.

Oliveira Marques, A. H. de. *História de Portugal*. 3 vols. Lisbon: 1984.

Oliver, R., and A. Atmore. *The African Middle Ages 1400–1800*. Cambridge: 1989.

Orta, J. A. "L'empire Monomotapa, Etat et Pouvoir dans une société étatique traditionnelle africaine." *Africana* 23 (2001): 32–63.

Ossanna, J. A. "Las misiones jesuitas en la región del Guayrá en las primeras décadas del siglo XVII." *Mundo Agrario* 8, no. 16 (2008): 1–15.

Ostrander, Gilman M. "The Colonial Molasses Trade," *Agricultural History* 30, no. 2 (1956): 77–84.

———. "The Making of the Triangular Trade Myth." *The William and Mary Quarterly* 30, no. 4 (1973): 635–644.

Pacheco, Diego. "The Founding of the Port of Nagasaki and Its Cession to the Society of Jesus." *Monumenta Nipponica* 25, no. 3–4 (1970): 303–323.

Pagden, A. *The Fall of Natural Man: The American Indian and the Origins of Comparative Ethnology*, 2nd ed. New York: Cambridge UP, 1986.

Palacin, L. *Sociedade Colonial 1549 a 1599*. Goiânia: 1981.

Papagno, G. *Colonialismo e feudalesimo: La questione dei prazos da Coroa nel Mozambico alla fine del secolo XIX*. Torino: 1972.

Papavero, N., and D. Martins Teixeira. "Recife e Salvador na visão dos capuchinhos missionários no Reino do Congo (1667–1703)." In *Cadernos do IEB* (2015): 136–138.

Paquette, Gabriel. "After Brazil: Portuguese Debates on Empire, c. 1820–1850." *Journal of Colonialism and Colonial History* 11, no. 2 (2010), https://muse.jhu.edu/, accessed December 2015.

Paraiso, M. H. B. "Revoltas indígenas, a criação do governo geral e o regimento de 1548," *Clio—Revista de pesquisa histórica* 29, no. 1 (2011): 1–21.

Parker, G. *The Military Revolution: Military Innovation and the Rise of the West, 1500–1800*. Cambridge: 1988.

———, ed. *The Thirty Years War*. Barcelona: 1988.

Parker, G., and L. M. Smith, eds. *The General Crisis of the Seventeenth Century*. 2nd ed. New York: 1997.

Parreira, A. *Dicionário glossográfico e toponímico da documentação sobre Angola, séculos XV–XVII*. Lisbon: 1990.

———. *Economia e sociedade em Angola na época da rainha Jinga*. Lisbon: 1990.

Patterson, O. *Slavery and Social Death*. Cambridge, MA: 1982.

Paturet, A. "L'individu entre l'homme et la chose. Note sur l'esclave en droit romain." *Droits* 51 (2010): 3–26.

Pearson, M. N. "The People and Politics of Portuguese India during the Sixteenth and Early Seventeenth Centuries." In *Essays Concerning the Socioeconomic History of Brazil and Portuguese India*, edited by D. Alden and W. Dean, 1–25. Gainesville: The University Presses of Florida, 1977.

———. *Os Portugueses na Índia*. Lisbon: 1990.

Peckham, H. *The Colonial Wars 1689–1762*. Chicago: 1964.

Pécora, A. *Teatro do Sacramento*. São Paulo: 1994.

Pedreira, J. "Industrialização e flutuações econômicas, preços, mercados e inovação tecnológica 1670–1890." In *Estudos e Ensaios em homenagem a Vitorino Magalhães Godinho*, 277–292. Lisbon: 1988.

———. "Costs and Financial Trends in the Portuguese Empire, 1415–1822." In *Portuguese Oceanic Expansion 1400–1800*, edited by F. Bethencourt and D. R. Curto, 49–87. New York: 2007.

Pereira, E., and Guilherme Rodrigues. *Portugal—Dicionário Histórico, Corográfico, Heráldico, Biográfico, Bibliográfico, numismático e Artístico*. Vol. 7. Lisbon: 1904.

Pereira da Costa, F. A. "Vocabulário Pernambucano" (1916), *Revista do Instituto Arqueológico Histórico e Geográfico Pernambucano*, 34, no. 159–162 (1936).

———. *Anais Pernambucanos*. 10 vols. Recife: 1951–1966.

Pereira da Costa, M. C. "O cronista frei Luís de Sousa, contribuição para um estudo biográfico e genealógico." *Arquivo Histórico Dominicano Português*. Vol. 2 (1979): 76–145, and Vol. 3 (1987): 29–50.

Pereira do Nascimento, J. *Diccionario portuguez-kimbundu*. Huíla: 1903.

Pérotin-Dumont, A. "The Pirate and the Emperor." In *The Political Economy of Merchant Empires*, 196–227. Cambridge: 1991.

Peterson, R. G., L. Stramma, and G. Kortum. "Early Concepts and Charts of Ocean Circulation." *Progress in Oceanography* 37, no. 1 (1996): 1–115.

Petrone, Pasquale. *Aldeamentos Paulistas*. São Paulo: 1995.

Pike, R. *Aristocrats and Traders: Sevillian Society in the Sixteenth Century*. Ithaca, NY: Cornell UP, 1972.

Pikirayi, Innocent. "Palaces, Feiras, and Prazos: An Historical Archaeological Perspective of African-Portuguese Contact in Northern Zimbabwe." *The African Archaeological Review* 26, no. 3 (2009): 163–185.

Pinho, W. *História social da Cidade do Salvador*. 2 vols. Salvador: 1968.

Pinto de Castro, A. "Os sermões de Vieira—da palavra dita à palavra escrita." In *Vieira escritor*, edited by M. Vieira Mendes, M. L. Gonçalves Pires, and J. da Costa Miranda, 79–94. Lisbon: 1997.

Pires de Lima, A. "Nota sobre algumas epidemias na cidade da Bahia." *Brasília*. Vol. 5 (1950): 503–518.

Pokhlióbkin, W. V. *Istória vódki* (Brazilian translation, *Uma história da vodca*). São Paulo: 1995.
Polanyi, Karl. *Dahomey and the Slave Trade: An Analysis of an Archaic Economy.* London: 1966.
———. "Ports of Trade in Early Societies." In *Primitive, Archaic, and Modern Economies—Essays of Karl Polanyi*, edited by G. Dalton, 238–260. New York: 1971.
———. "Sortings and 'Ounce trade' in the West African Slave Trade." In *"Primitive, Archaic, and Modern Economies,"* 261–279.
Pollard, E. "Safeguarding Swahili Trade in the Fourteenth and Fifteenth Centuries: A Unique Navigational Complex in South-East Tanzania." *World Archaeology* 43, no. 3 (2011): 458–477.
Polónia, Amélia. "Mestres e pilotos das carreiras ultramarinas, 1596–1648: subsídios para o seu estudo." *Revista da Faculdade de Letras—História.* Vol. 12, 271–354. Porto: 1995.
Porto, A. *História das Missões Orientais do Uruguai.* Rio de Janeiro: 1943.
Postma, J. M. *The Dutch in the Atlantic Slave Trade 1600–1815.* New York: 1990.
———. "The Dispersal of African Slaves in the West by Dutch Slave Traders." In *The Atlantic Slave Trade: Effects on Economies, Societies, and Peoples in Africa, the Americas, and Europe*, edited by J. E. Inikori and S. L. Engerman. Chapter 10.
Poutrin, I. "L'oeil du souverain: Luis de Aliaga et le métier de confesseur royal sous Felipe II." In *Observation and Communication: The Construction of Realities in the Hispanic World*, edited by J.-M. Scholz and T. Herzog, 253–270. Frankfurt: 1997.
Prado, Caio, Jr. "O fator geográfico na formação e desenvolvimento da cidade de São Paulo." *Geografia* 1, no. 3 (1935): 239–262.
———. *Formação do Brasil Contemporâneo.* São Paulo: 1971.
Prakash, O. *European Commercial Enterprise in Pre-Colonial India.* London: 1998.
Prestage, E. *D. Francisco Manuel de Melo—Esboço biographico.* Coimbra: 1914.
———. *A embaixada de Tristão de Mendonça Furtado à Holanda em 1641.* Coimbra: 1920.
———. *The Diplomatic Relations of Portugal with France, England and Holland from 1640 to 1668.* Portuguese translation. Coimbra: 1932.
Ptak, R. "Macao entre la Chine et l'Asie Maritime: cycles d'économie." In *L'Empire portugais*: 137–165.
Pulido Serrano, J. I. "Las negociaciones con los cristianos nuevos en tiempos de Felipe III a la luz de algunos documentos inéditos (1598–1607)." *Sefarad* 66, no. 2 (2006): 345–376.
Puntoni, P. *A guerra dos bárbaros—povos indígenas e a colonização do sertão nordeste do Brasil 1650–1720.* São Paulo: 2000.
Qichen, Huang. "O exercício da Soberania e da Administração por parte do governo chinês em Macau entre o século XVI e meados do século XIX." *Administração* 48, no. 10 (2000): 657–675.

Quiroz Norris, Alfonso W. "La Expropiacion Inquisitorial De Cristianos Nuevos Portugueses en Los Reyes, Cartagena y Mexico, 1635–1649." *Historica* 10, no. 2 (1986): 237–303.

Rainero, R. H. "La bataille de Tondibi (1591) et la conquête marocaine de l'Empire Songhay." *Genève-Afrique* 5, no. 2 (1966), 217–247.

Ralston, D. B. *Importing the European Army: The Introduction of European Military Techniques and Institutions into the Extra-European World.* London: 1990.

Ramada Curto, D. "A língua e o império." In *História da Expansão.* Vol. 1, edited by F. Bethencourt and K. Chaudhuri, 413–431. Lisbon: 1998.

———. "Idéologies impériales dans l'Afrique occidentale au début du dix-septième siècle." *L'Empire Portugais*: 203–247.

———. "Early Modern European Empires and Networks." *International Journal of Maritime History* 21 (2009): 318–325.

———. "O P. Lourenço de Mendoça: entre o Brasil e o Peru (c. 1630–c. 1640)." *Topoi* 11, no. 20 (2010): 27–35.

Ramos, R. "Rebelião e sociedade colonial: "alvoroços" e "levantamentos" in São Tomé 1545–1555." *RIEA* 4–5 (1986): 17–24.

Ramos Suárez, M. A. "Noticias Sobre El Pintor-Restaurador Sevillano Diego Mateo Del Parque." *Laboratorio de Arte: Revista Del Departamento de Historia Del Arte* 22 (2010): 577–587.

Randles, W. G. L. "La fondation de l'Empire du Monomotapa." *CEA*, vol. XIV-2, no. 54 (1974): 207–236.

———. *L'Empire du Muenemutapa du XVe au XIXe siècle.* Paris, La Haye: 1975.

———. *L'Ancien royaume du Congo, des origines à la fin du XIXe siècle.* Paris, La Haye: 1978.

———. *Da terra plana ao globo terrestre.* Lisbon: 1990.

Ratelband, K. *Os holandeses no Brasil e na Costa Africana, Angola, Kongo e S. Tomé 1600–1650*, edited and commented on by Carlos Pacheco. Lisbon: 2003.

Rau, Virgínia, and Jorge de Macedo, eds. *O açúcar da madeira nos fins do século XV.* Funchal: 1962.

———. *Estudos sobre a história do sal português.* Lisbon: 1984.

Ravichander, Annapoorna. "Coastal Society of Gujarat in the Sixteenth Century." *Studia* 49 (1989): 161–180.

Reginaldo, L. *Os Rosarios dos Angolas: irmandades negras, experiencias escravas e identidades africanas na Bahia setecentista.* São Paulo: 2011.

Restrepo, L. C. *Los Portugueses: La trata de negros esclavos y el Tribunal de la Inquisición en la ciudad de Cartagena de Indias, siglos XVI y XVII.* Seville: 2011.

Ribeiro, O. "Milho." *DHP.* Vol. 3, 58–64. Lisbon.

Ribeiro da Silva, F. "Dutch Labor Migration to West Africa." In *Migration, Trade and Slavery in an Expanding World, Essays in Honor of Pieter Emmer*, edited by W. Klooster, 73–98. Leiden: 2009.

———. "Crossing Empires: Portuguese, Sephardic, and Dutch Business Networks in the Atlantic Slave Trade, 1580–1674." *The Americas* 68, no. 1 (2011): 7–32.

———. "Os Holandeses e a consolidação do sistema económico do Atlântico Sul Seiscentista, c. 1630–1654." *RIAHGP* 67 (2014): 11–38.

Ricard, Robert. "A propos de rebato. Note sur la tactique militaire dans les places portugaises du Maroc." *Bulletin Hispanique* 35, no. 4 (1933): 448–453.

———. "Recherches sur les relations des Iles Canaries et de la Berbérie au XVIe siècle." *Hespéris* 21 (1935): 79–129.

———. "Le problème de l'occupation restreinte dans l'Afrique du Nord (XVe–XVIIIe siècles)." *Annales* 8, no. 41 (1936): 426–437.

———. "Los Portugueses en las Indias Españolas." *Revista de Historia de América* 34 (1952): 449–456.

Rice, P. M. "Wine and Brandy Production in Colonial Peru: A Historical and Archaelogical Investigation." *Journal of Interdisciplinary History* 27 (1997): 455–479.

Richard de Silva, C. "The Portuguese East India Company 1628–1633." *Luso-Brazilian Review* 11, no. 2 (1974): 152–205.

Richards, W. A. "The Import of Firearms into West Africa in the Eighteenth Century." *J. Afr. H.* 11 (1980): 43–59.

Richardson, D. "Slavery, Trade, and Economic Growth in Eighteenth-Century New England." In *Slavery and the Rise of the Atlantic System*, edited by B. L. Solow, 237–264. New York: 1991.

Righetti, Mário. *História de la liturgia*. 2 vols. Madrid: 1956.

Rink, O. A. *Holland on the Hudson—An Economic and Social History of Dutch New York*. New York: 1989.

Rodgers, Nini. *Ireland, Slavery and Anti-Slavery 1612–1865*. New York: 2009.

Rodney, W. *A History of the Upper Guinea Coast: 1545–1800*. New York: New York UP, 1970.

Rodrigues, E. "Chiponda, a 'senhora que tudo pisa com os pés': estratégias de poder das donas dos prazos do Zambeze no século XVIII." *Anais de História de Além-Mar* 1 (2000): 101–131.

———. " 'Em Nome do Rei': O levantamento dos Rios de Sena de 1763." *Anais de História de Além-Mar* 4 (2003): 335–380.

Rodrigues, F. *História da Companhia de Jesus na Assistência de Portugal*. 7 vols. Porto: 1931–1950.

Rodrigues Cavalheiro, R. "A colaboração da Metrópole na reconquista do Brasil." In *Congresso do Mundo Português*, vol. 9, 289–335. Lisbon: 1940.

Romero Magalhães, Joaquim. *O Algarve Económico, 1600–1773*. Lisbon: 1988.

———. "Os limites da expansão asiática." In *História da expansão portuguesa*, vol. 2, edited by F. Bethencourt and Kirti Chaudhuri, 8–27. Lisbon: 1998.

———. "Articulações inter-regionais e economias-mundo." In *História da expansão portuguesa*, vol. I, 308–337.

Rooney, T. "Habsburg Fiscal Policies in Portugal, 1580–1640." *The Journal of European Economic History* 23, no. 3 (1994): 545–562.

Roosevelt, A. C. "Chiefdoms in the Amazon and Orinoco." In *Chiefdoms in the Americas*, edited by R. Drennan and C. Uribe, 153–184. Laham, MD: 1987.

Rosselli, C. "Relaciones de conctato de criollo palenquero de Colômbia." *Forma y Función* 11 (1998): 77–101.

Rudge, R. T. *As sesmarias de Jacarepaguá*. São Paulo: 1983.

Ruiz Rivera, J. B. "Los Portugueses y la trata negrera en Cartagena de Índias." *Temas Americanistas* 15 (2002): 19–41.

Russel Wood, A. J. R. "Políticas de fixação e integração," "Comunidades Étnicas," and "Grupos Sociais." In *História da expansão portuguesa*, vol. 2, edited by F. Bethencourt and Kirti Chaudhuri, 126–191. Lisbon: 1998.

Saccardo, G. *Congo e Angola con la storia dell'antica missione dei capuccini*. 3 vols. Venezia-Mestre: 1982–1983.

Scammell, G. V. "The Pillars of Empire: Indigenous Assistance and the Survival of the 'Estado da India' c. 1600–1700." *Modern Asian Studies* 22, no. 3 (1988): 473–489.

Saguier, E. R. "The Social Impact of a Middleman Minority in a Host Society—The Case of the Portuguese in Early Seventeenth-Century Buenos Aires." *HAHR* 65, no. 3 (1985): 467–491.

Saint-Lu, André. *La Vera Paz: Esprit évangélique et colonisation*. Paris: 1968.

Sala-Molins, L. *Le Code Noir ou le calvaire de Canaan*. Paris: 2012.

Salgado, G., ed. *Fiscais e meirinhos: A administração no Brasil colonial* Rio de Janeiro: 1985.

Salles, Pedro. *História da medicina no Brasil*. Belo Horizonte: 1971.

Sampaio Garcia, R. "A margem de 'Comércio e contrabando entre a Bahia e Potosí no século XVI,'" *RH* 23 (1955): 169–176.

———. "O português Duarte Lopes e o comércio espanhol de escravos negros." *Revista de História* 7, no. 30 (1957): 375–385.

———. "Contribuição ao estudo do aprovisionamento de escravos negros na América espanhola 1580–1640." *Anais do Museu Paulista* 16 (1962): 8–12.

Santos Filho, L. *História geral da medicina brasileira*. 2 vols. São Paulo: 1977.

Santos-Granero F. *Vital Enemies: Slavery, Predation, and the Amerindian Political Economy of Life*. Austin: U of Texas P, 2009.

Saraiva, Antonio José, and Oscar Lopes. *História da literatura portuguesa*. Porto: 1955.

———. "Le père Antonio Vieira SJ et la liberté des indiens." *T.I.L.A.S.* 3 (1963): 483–516.

———. "Le padre Antônio Vieira, S.J. et la question de l'esclavage des Noirs au XVIIe siècle." *Annales E.C.S.* 22 (1967): 1,289–1,309.

———. *Inquisição e cristãos-novos*. 5th ed. Lisbon: 1985.

Saunders, A. C. de C. M. *A Social History of Black Slaves and Freedmen in Portugal, 1441–1555*. Cambridge: Cambridge UP, 1982.

Savage, E. "Berbers and Blacks: Ibādī Slave Traffic in Eighth-Century North Africa." *J. Afr. H.* 33, no. 3 (1992): 351–368.

Senna Barcellos, C. J. de. *Subsídios para a História de Cabo Verde e Guiné*. 3 vols. Lisbon: 1899–1911.

Serrão, Joel. "Le blé des îles atlantiques—Madère et Açores aux XVe et XVIe siècles." *Annales E.S.C.* 9, no. 3 (1954): 336–341.

Serrão, Joel, et al. *Dicionário de história de Portugal* (DHP). 4 vols. Lisbon: 1963–1971.

Scarano, J. *Devoção e escravidão: A irmandade de Nossa Senhora do Rosário dos Pretos no Distrito Diamantino no século XVIII*. 2nd ed. São Paulo: 1978.

Scelle, G., *Histoire politique de la traite négrière aux Indes de Castille—Contrats et traités d'Assiento*. 2 vols. Paris: 1906.

Schaub, Jean-Frédéric. *Le Portugal au temps du comte-duc d'Olivares, 1621–1640*. Madrid: 2001.

Schmutz, J. "La Querelle Des Possibles. Recherches Philosophiques et Textuelles Sur La Métaphysique Jésuite Espagnole (1540–1767)." *École Pratique des Hautes Études, Section des Sciences Religieuses* 115, no. 111 (2002): 405–411.

Schneider, Susan C. "Commentary." In *Conflict and Continuity in Brazilian Society*, edited by H. H. Keith and S. F. Edwards, 20–23. Columbia: U of South Carolina P, 1969.

Schoenbrun, D. L. "We Are What We Eat: Ancient Agriculture between the Great Lakes." *J. Afr. H.* 34, no. 1 (1993): 1–32.

Schwartz, Stuart B. "Luso-Spanish Relations in Hapsburg Brazil, 1580–1640." *The Americas* 25, no. 1 (1968): 33–48.

———. *Sovereignty and Society in Colonial Brazil: The High Court of Bahia and Its Judges*. Berkeley, CA: 1973.

———. "Indian Labor and New World Plantations: European Demands and Indian Response in the Northeastern Brazil." *American Historical Review (AHR)* 1 (1983): 43–79.

———. *Sugar Plantations in the Formation of Brazilian Society: Bahia, 1550–1835*. London: 1985.

———. "The Voyage of the Vassals: Royal Power, Noble Obligations, and Merchant Capital before the Portuguese Restoration of Independence, 1624–1640." *American Historical Review* (June 1991).

———. *Slaves, Peasants, and Rebels*. Chicago: 1992.

———. "Tapanhuns, Negros da Terra e Curibocas: Causas Comuns e Confrontos entre Negros e Indígenas." *Afro-Ásia* 29/30 (2003): 13–40.

———. "Pânico nas Índias: a ameaça portuguesa ao império espanhol, 1640–1650." In *Da América Portuguesa ao Brasil*, edited by Stuart B. Schwartz, 185–216. Lisboa: 2003.

———. "A Commonwealth within Itself, the Early Brazilian Sugar Industry 1550–1670." In *Tropical Babylons: Sugar and the Making of the Atlantic World, 1450–1680*, edited by Stuart B. Schwartz, 158–200. Chapel Hill: U North Carolina P, 2004.

———. *All Can Be Saved: Religious Tolerance and Salvation in the Iberian Atlantic World*. New York: 2008.

———. "Prata, açúcar e escravos: de como o império restaurou Portugal." *Tempo* 12, no. 24 (2008): 201–223.

Schwartz, Stuart B., and F. Salomon. "New Peoples and New Kinds of People: Adaptation, Readjustment, and Ethnogenesis in South American Indigenous Societies—Colonial Era." *The Cambridge History of the Native Peoples of the Americas*, edited by F. Salomon and S. B. Schwartz, 443–501. Vol. 3, part 2. Cambridge: Cambridge UP, 1999.

Seibert, G. "Tenreiro, Amador e os Angolares ou a reinvenção da história da Ilha de São Tomé." *Revista de Estudos AntiUtilitaristas e PosColoniais* 2, no. 2 (2013): 21–40.

Selvagem, C. *Portugal militar*. Lisbon: 1991.

Semedo de Matos, L. J. "A navegação: Os caminhos de uma ciência indispensável." In *História da expansão portuguesa*, vol. 1, edited by F. Bethencourt and Kirti Chaudhuri, 72–87. Lisbon: 1998.

Sérgio, A. *Ensaios*. Vol. 5. Rio de Janeiro: 1975.

Sheldon, C. D. "Merchants and Society in Tokugawa Japan." *Modern Asian Studies* 17, no. 3 (1983): 477–488.

Sheriff, Abdul. *Slaves, Spices, and Ivory in Zanzibar: Integration of An East African Commercial Empire into the World Economy, 1770–1873*. Athens, OH: Ohio UP, 1987.

Silva Horta, J. da. "A representação do africano na literatura de viagens do Senegal à Serra Leoa 1453–1508." *Mare Liberum* 2 (1991): 209–327.

———. "Evidence for a Luso-African Identity in 'Portuguese' Accounts on 'Guinea of Cape Verde' (Sixteenth–Seventeenth Centuries)." *History in Africa* 27 (2000): 101–107.

Silva Maia, A. da *Dicionário elementar português-omumbuim-mussele*. Cucujães, 1955.

Silva Rebelo, M. dos A. da *Relações entre Angola e Brasil 1808–1830*. Lisbon: 1970.

Silva Rego, Antonio da. *A Dupla Restauração de Angola 1641–1648*. Lisbon: 1948.

———. *Portuguese Colonization in the Sixteenth Century: A Study of the Royal Ordinances*. Johannesburg: 1965.

———. "Instruções de Francisco Xavier." *DHMPPO*, vol. 4 ([1549] 1950): 286–300, 292, and vol. 5 (1951): X–XIII.

Silva Teixeira, C. da. "Companhia de Cacheu, Rios e Guiné." *Boletim do Arquivo Histórico Colonial* 1 (1950): 85–132.

Sinclar, Paul J. J. "Archaeology in Eastern Africa: An Overview of Current Chronological Issues." *J. Afr. H.* 32, no. 2 (1991): 179–220.

Slenes, R. W. "'Malungu, ngoma vem!': África coberta e descoberta do Brasil." *Revista USP* 12 (1992): 48–67.

Smaldone, J. "Firearms in the Central Sudan: A Revaluation." *J. Afr. H.* 13, no. 4 (1972): 591–607.

Smith, R. C. "Décadas do Rosário dos Pretos, documentos da irmandade." In *Alguns documentos para a história da escravidão*, edited by L. Dantas Silva, 93–122. Recife: 1988.
Smulders, F. "Tradições manuscritas na obra de Antônio Vieira." In *Vieira escritor*, edited by M. Vieira Mendes, M. L. Gonçalves Pires, and J. da Costa Miranda, 53–66. Lisbon: 1997.
Soares de Azevedo, M. A. "Armadas do Brasil." *DHP*, vol. 1, 186–188.
Solow, Barbara L., ed. *Slavery and the Rise of the Atlantic System*. Cambridge, UK: Cambridge UP, 1993.
Sombart, W. *Le Bourgeois. Contribution à l'histoire morale et intellectuelle de l'homme économique moderne*. (French translation), Paris [1913]: 1926.
Sousa, I. B. de. *São Tomé et Principe de 1485 à 1755, une société coloniale: du blanc au noir*. Paris: 2008.
Sousa Dias, G. de. "Francisco de Souto Maior, capitão-geral e governador do reino de Angola 1645–1646." *Congresso do Mundo Português*. Vol. 7, 337–356. Lisbon: 1940.
Sousa Pinto, J. de. "Em torno de um problema de identidade: os 'Jaga' na Historia do Congo e Angola." *Mare Liberum* 18–19 (1999): 193–243.
———. *A Batalha de Ambuíla*. Lisbon: 1942.
Souto Maior, M. *Dicionário folclórico da cachaça*. Recife: 1973.
Souza, T. R. de. *Goa Medieval—A cidade e o interior no século XVII*. Lisbon: 1993.
Spence, Jonathan D. *O Palácio da Memória de Matteo Ricci* (Brazilian translation). São Paulo: 1986.
Stein, R. L. *The French Slave Trade in the Eighteenth Century: An Old Regime Business*. Madison, WI: 1979.
Stella, A. "L'esclavage en Andalousie à l'époque moderne." *Annales E.S.C.* 47, no. 1 (1992): 35–64.
Stevens-Arroyo, A. M. "The Inter-Atlantic Paradigm: The Failure of Spanish Medieval Colonization of the Canary and Caribbean Islands." *Comparative Studies in Society and History* 35, no. 3 (1993): 515–543.
Strandes, Justus. *The Portuguese Period in East Africa*. 3rd ed. Nairobi: 1968.
Streit, S. R., and J. Dindinger, *Bibliotheca Missionum*, vols. 15 and 16 Freiburg: 1963–1975.
Struik, D. J. "Mauricio de Nassau, Scientific Maecenas in Brazil." *Revista da Sociedade Brasileira de História da Ciência*. Vol. 2 (1985): 21–27.
Stuard, S. M. "Ancillary Evidence for the Decline of Medieval Slavery." *Past & Present* 149 (1995): 3–28.
Studnicki-Gizbert, D. "Revisiting 1640; or, How the Party of Commercial Expansion Lost to the Party of Political Conservation in Spain's Atlantic Empire, 1620–1650." In *The Atlantic Economy during the Seventeenth and Eighteenth Centuries: Organization, Operation, Practice, and Personnel*, 152–177, edited by A. Coclanis. Columbia, SC: 2005.

———. *A Nation Upon the Ocean Sea—Portugal's Atlantic Diaspora and the Crisis of the Spanish Empire, 1492–1640.* New York: 2007.

Subrahmanyan, Sanjay. "Staying On: The Portuguese of Southern Coromandel in the Late Seventeenth Century." *Indian Economic and Social History Review* 22, no. 4 (1985): 445–463.

———. *The Political Economy of Commerce: Southern India 1500–1650.* Cambridge: 1990.

———. *The Portuguese Empire in Asia, 1500–1700, A Political and Economic History.* London: 1993.

Subtil, J. M. "Administração Central da Coroa." In *História de Portugal*, vol. 3, edited by J. Mattoso, 78–90. Lisbon: 1994.

Sundiata, I. "Capitalism and Slavery: 'The Commercial Part of the Nation.'" In *Capitalism and Slavery Fifty Years Later: Eric Eustace Williams—A Reassessment of the Man and His Work*, edited by H. Cateau and S. H. H. Carrington, 121–136. New York: Peter Land, 2010.

Sweet, J. H. *Recreating Africa: Culture, Kinship, and Religion in the African-Portuguese World*, Chapel Hill, NC: 2003: 1,441–1,770.

Szaszdi, A., and D. L. Borja Szaszdi. "El comercio de cacao de Guayaquil." *Revista de Historia de America* 57–58 (1964): 1–50.

Taiwo, O. "Exorcising Hegel's Ghost: Africa's Challenge to Philosophy." *African Studies Quarterly* 1, no. 4 (1998): 1–16.

Tallon, Alain. *La France et le Concile de Trente (1518–1563).* Rome: 1997.

———. "'Père et mère honoreras': quelques commentaires catholiques du quatrième commandement au XVIe siècle." In *Histoire des familles, des démographies et des comportements—Mélanges en hommage à Jean-Pierre Bardet*, edited by J.-P. Poussou and I. Robin-Romero, 699–711. Paris: 2007.

Tardieu, J.-P. "Du bon usage de la monstruosité: la vision de l'Afrique chez Alonso de Sandoval (1627)." *Bulletin Hispanique* 86, no. 1–2 (1984): 164–178.

Tastevin, C. "Vocabulario Tupy-Portuguez." *Revista do Museu Paulista* 13 (1923): 599–686.

Taunay, Alfredo E. "Na era das bandeiras." *RIHGB* 84 (1918): 449–478.

———. *História seiscentista da Villa de São Paulo.* Vol. 1. São Paulo: 1926.

———. *História geral das bandeiras paulistas (HGBP).* 11 vols. São Paulo: 1924–1950.

———. "Notas sobre o imperativo do tráfico." *Revista do Instituto Histórico e Geográfico da Bahia* 67 (1941): 311–315.

Teixeira da Mota, A. "Duarte Pacheco Pereira Capitão e Governador de São Jorge da Mina." *Mare Liberum* 1 (1990): 1–27.

Teixeira Pinto, Maria do Carmo, and L. M. L. Ferreira Runa. "Inquisição de Évora: Dez anos de funcionamento 1541–1550." *RHES* 22 (1988): 51–76.

Tenenti, Alberto. "O mercador e o banqueiro." In *O homem renascentista* (Portuguese translation), edited by E. Garin. Lisbon: 1991.

Tengwall, David. "A Study in Military Leadership: The Sargento Mor in the Portuguese South Atlantic Empire." *The Americas* 11, no. 1 (1983): 73–94.

———. "The Portuguese Revolution of 1 December 1640: A Reappraisal." *eHumanista: Journal of Iberian Studies* 17 (2011): 448–459.

Tepaske, John J., and H. S. Klein. "The Seventeenth-Century Crisis in New Spain: Myth or Reality?" *Past & Present* 90 (1981): 116–135.

Thomas, G. *Política indigenista dos portugueses no Brasil 1500–1640* (Brazilian translation). São Paulo: 1982.

Thomaz, L. F. F. R. "A escravatura em Malaca no século XVI." *Studia* 53 (1994): 253–316.

Thorner, D. "Marx et l'Inde: le mode de production asiatique." *Annales* (1969): 337–369.

Thornton, John K. "A Resurrection for the Jaga." *CEA* 18, no. 1–2 (1978): 223–228.

———. *The Kingdom of Congo: Civil War and Transition, 1641–1718*. Madison: U of Wisconsin P, 1983.

———. "The Art of War in Angola 1575–1680." *Comparative Studies in Society and History* 30, no. 2 (1988): 360–378.

———. "Legitimacy and Political Power: Queen Njinga, 1624–1663." *Journal of African History* 32, no. 1(1991): 25–40.

———. *Africa and Africans in the Making of the Atlantic World, 1400–1680*. New York, 1992.

———. "The African Experience of the '20 and Odd Negroes' Arriving in Virginia in 1619." *The William and Mary Quarterly* 55, no. 3 (1998): 421–434.

———. "The Portuguese in Africa." In *Portuguese Oceanic Expansion 1400–1800*, edited by F. Bethencourt and D. R. Curto, 138–160. New York: 2007.

———. "Les États de l'Angola et la formation de Palmares (Brésil)." *Annales: Histoire, Sciences Sociales* 63, no. 4 (2008): 776–778.

Titton, G. A. "O Sínodo da Bahia (1707) e a escravatura." In *Anais do VI Simpósio Nacional dos Professores Universitários de História*. Vol. 1, 285–306. São Paulo: 1973.

Toby, R. "Reopening the Question of Sakoku: Diplomacy in the Legitimation of the Tokugawa Bakufu." *Journal of Japanese Studies* 3, no. 2 (1977): 323–363.

Tomich, Dale. "The 'Second Slavery': Bonded Labor and the Transformations of the Nineteenth-Century World Economy." In *Rethinking the Nineteenth Century: Contradictions and Movement*, edited by Francisco O. Ramírez, 103–117. New York: 1988.

———. *Through the Prism of Slavery: Labor, Capital, and World Economy*. Lanham, MD: 2004.

———. "Vitorino Magalhaes Godinho: Atlantic History, World History." *Review* 28, no. 4 (2005): 305–312.

———. "Econocide? From Abolition to Emancipation in the British and French Caribbean." In *The Caribbean: An Illustrated History*, edited by Stephan Palmié and Francisco Scarano, 303–316. Chicago: 2011.

Topa, F. "Entre a *Terra de gente oprimida* e a *Terra de gente tostada*: Luís Félix da Cruz e o primeiro poema *angolano*." *Literatura em Debate* 7, no. 13 (2013): 122–147.

Toral, E. "Cuatro relaciones de méritos y servicios." *Boletín del Instituto de Estudios Giennenses* 3 (1953): 103–122.

Torgal, L. R. *Ideologia política e teoria do Estado na Restauração*. 2 vols. Coimbra: 1981–1982.

Torrão, M. M. F. "Os portugueses e o trato de escravos de Cabo Verde com a América espanhola no final do século XVI: Os Contratadores do trato de Cabo Verde e a Coroa, uma relação de conveniência numa época de oportunidades 1583–1600." In *Portugal na Monarquia Hispânica: Dinâmicas de integração e de conflito*, edited by P. Cardim, L. F. Costa, and M. S. da Cunha, 93–106. Lisbon: 2013.

Torre Revello, J. "Un contrabandista del siglo XVII en el Rio de La Plata." *Revista de Historia de America* 45 (1958): 121–130.

Torrent, A. "Segunda Escolástica Española y renovación de la ciencia del derecho en el siglo XVI: un capítulo de los fundamentos del derecho europeo. I. Francisco de Vitoria, Domingo de Soto." *Teoria e Storia del Diritto Privato* 6 (2013): 1–60.

Toso, Carlo. "Relazioni inedite di Cherubino Cassinis da Savona sul 'Regno del Congo e sue Missioni.'" *L'Italia Francescana* 45 (1974): 135–214.

Tracy, James, ed. *The Rise of Merchant Empires: Long-Distance Trade in the Early Modern World 1350–1750*. Cambridge: 1990.

Trim, D. "Early-Modern Colonial Warfare and the Campaign of Alcazarquivir, 1578." *Small Wars & Insurgencies* 8, no. 1 (1997): 1–34.

Trivellato F. "Juifs de Livourne, Italiens de Lisbonne, hindous de Goa." *Annales: Histoire, Sciences, Sociales* 58, no. 3 (2003): 581–603.

Trujillo, O. J. "Facciones, parentesco y poder—La élite de Buenos Aires y la rebelión de Portugal de 1640." In *Las redes del imperio. Élites sociales en la articulación de la monarquía hispánica, 1492–1714*, edited by B.Y. Casalilla, 341–358. Madrid: 2009.

———. "Integración y conflicto en uma elite fronteriza: los Portugueses em Buenos Aires a mediados del siglo XVII." In *Portugal na Monarquia Hispânica*, edited by P. Cardim, L. F. Costa, and M. S. da Cunha, 309–329. Lisbon: 2013.

Tucci Carneiro, Maria Luiza. *Preconceito racial no Brasil Colônia: Os cristãos novos*. São Paulo: 1983.

Tylleskär, T. M. Banea, N. Bikangi, R. D. Cooke, N. H. Poulter, and H. Rosling. "Cassava cyanogens and *konzo*, an upper motoneuron disease found in Africa." *Lancet* 339, no. 8787 (1992): 208–211.

Tymowski, M. "Le Niger, voie de communication des grands Etats du Soudan Occidental jusqu'à la fin du XVIème siècle." *Africana Bulletin* 6 (1967): 73–98.

Unger, R. W. "Dutch Herring, Technology, and International Trade in the Seventeenth Century." *JEH* 11, no. 2 (1980): 253–256.

Vacant, E., E. Mangenot, and E. Amman., "Baptême." Kn *Dictionnaire de Théologie Catholique*, vol. 2, part 1, 167–377. Paris: 1908.

Vainfas, Ronaldo. *A heresia dos índios: Catolicismo e rebeldia no Brasil colonial*. São Paulo: 1995.

Valensi, Lucette. "Silence, dénégation, affabulation: Le souvenir d'une grande défaite dans la culture portugaise." *Annales E.S.C.* 46, no. 1 (1991): 3–44.

Valente de Matos, A. *Dicionário português-macua.* Lisbon: 1974.

Valladares Ramirez, Rafael, "El Brasil y las Indias españolas durante la sublevación de Portugal 1640–1668." *Cuadernos de Historia Moderna* 14 (1993): 151–172.

———. "Las dos guerras de Pernambuco. La armada del conde da Torre y la crisis del Portugal hispánico, 1638–1641." In *El desafío holandés al dominio ibérico en Brasil en el siglo XVII,* edited by J. M. Santos Perez and G. F. Cabral de Souza, 33–66. Salamanca: 2006.

Vansina, Jan. "Long Distance Trade Routes in Central Africa." *J. Afr. H.* 3, no. 3 (1962): 375–390.

———. "The Foundation of the Kingdom of Kasange." *J. Afr. H.* 4, no. 3 (1963).

———. "Trade and Markets among the Kuba." In *Markets in Africa,* edited by P. Bohannan and G. Dalton, 190–210. (New York: 1965).

———. *Kingdoms of the Savannah.* Madison, WI: 1975.

———. "Finding Food and History of Precolonial Equatorial Africa—A Plea." *African Economic History* 7 (1979): 9–20.

———. "L'homme, les forêts et le passé en Afrique." *Annales* 40, no. 6 (1985): 1,307–1,334.

———. "Quilombos on Sao Tomé, or in Search of Original Sources." *History in Africa* 23 (1996): 453–459.

———. *How Societies Are Born: Governance in West Central Africa Before 1600.* Charllottesville, VA: 2004.

———. "Ambaca Society and the Slave Trade c. 1760–1845." *J. Afr. H.* 46 (2005): 1–27.

Varachaud, M.-C. *Le Père Houdry S.J.—Prédication et pénitence, 1631–1729.* Paris: 1993.

Vargas Arana, Paola. "Pedro Claver y la labor de evangelización en Cartagena de Indias (siglo XVII). Fuentes claves para analizar a los africanos en el Nuevo Mundo." *Revista de História* 155, no. 2 (2006): 43–79.

Varnhagen, F. A. de. *História Geral do Brazil,* 2 vols. Rio de Janeiro: 1854, 1857.

———. *História Geral do Brasil (HGB),* 3 vols., 10th edition, SãoPaulo: 1978.

Vasconcelos Pedrosa, M. X. de. "O exercício da medicina nos séculos xvi, xvii e a primeira metade do século XVIII no Brasil colonial." *Anais* 3, 4th Congress of National History, Rio de Janeiro: 1951: 268–274.

Veen, E. van. *Decay or Defeat? An Inquiry into the Portuguese Decline in Asia, 1580–1645.* Leiden, 2000.

Vega Franco, M. *El tráfico de Esclavos con America—Asientos de Grillo y Lomelin 1663–1674.* Seville: 1984.

Vellut, J.-L. "Le royaume de Cassange et les réseaux luso-africains, ca. 1750–1810." *Cahiers d'Études Africaines* 15, no. 57 (1975): 117–136.

Venard, M. "Les formes personnelles da la vie religieuse." In *Histoire du christianisme des origines à nos jours*. Vol. 8, edited by J. M. Mayeur, C. Pietri, A. Vauchez, and M. Venard, 991–1027. Paris: 1992.

———. "Les bases de la Réforme catholique." In Venard, *Histoire*, vol. 8: 223–279.

Ventura, Maria da Graça Mateus. *Negreiros portugueses na rota das Índias de Castela 1541–1556*. Lisbon: 1999.

———. "Os Gramaxo, Um Caso Paradigmático de Redes de Influência em Cartagena das Índias." *Cadernos de Estudos Sefarditas* 1 (2001): 65–81.

———. "A participação dos portugueses no comércio regional e inter-regional hispano-americano, a partir do Rio da Prata (1580–1640)." *Actas do Colóquio internacional Território e Povoamento—A presença portuguesa na região platina*, 1–25. Colonia del Sacramento, Uruguai, 2004.

———. "Jorge Fernandes Gramaxo, um mercador algarvio em Cartagena das Índias (1590–1626)." *Revista Atlântica de Cultura Ibero-americana* 3 (2006): 14–17.

Vergé-Franceschi, M. "Les compagnons d'armes de Tourville à Barfleur-La Hougue." In *L'Invention du vaisseau de ligne 1450–1700*, edited by M. Acerra (Paris: 1997): 237–240.

Verger, Pierre. *Flux et reflux de la traite des nègres entre le Golfe de Bénin et Bahia de Todos os Santos, XVIe–XIXe siècles*. Paris: 1968.

Verissimo Serrão, Joaquim, *Do Brasil filipino ao Brasil de 1640*. São Paulo: 1968.

———. "O quadro econômico, configurações estruturais e tendências de evolução." In *História*, vol. 4, edited by J. Mattoso, 80–81 and table 1.

Verlinden, Charles. "Péninsule Ibérique-France." *L'esclavage dans l'Europe médiévale*. Vol. 1. Bruges: 1955.

Vernant, J.-P. "Travail et nature dans la Grèce ancienne" and "Aspects psychologiques du travail dans la Grèce ancienne." In *Travail et esclavage en Grèce ancienne*, edited by J.-P. Vernant and P. Vidal-Naquet. Paris: 1988, 1–33.

Vianna Filho, Luiz. "O trabalho do engenho e a reação do índio: Estabelecimento da escravatura africana." In *Congresso do Mundo Português*, vol. 10, 11–29. Lisbon: 1940.

———. *O Negro na Bahia*. Rio de Janeiro, 1946.

Vieira, Alberto. *O Escravo no Arquipélago da Madeira, séculos XV a XVII*. Funchal: 1991.

———. *A Escravatura na Madeira nos séculos XVI a XVII: o ponto da situação*. Funchal: 1996.

———. *Escravos com ou sem açúcar: O caso da Madeira*. Funchal: 1997.

Vieira Nascimento, A. A. *Patriarcado e religião: As enclausuradas clarissas do Convento do Desterro da Bahia 1677–1890*. Bahia: 1994.

Vidago, J. "Anda mouro na costa." *Studia* 45 (1981): 295–306.

Vila Vilar, Enriqueta. "Los Asientos Portugueses y el contrabando de negros." *Anuario de estudios americanos* 30 (1975): 557–609.

———. "La sublevación de Portugal y la trata de negros." *Ibero-Amerikanisches Archiv* 2 (1976): 171–192.

———. *Hispano-America y el Comercio de esclavos: Los Asientos Portugueses*. Sevilha: 1977.

———. "Extranjeros en Cartagena (1593–1630)." *Jamrbuch fur Geschichte von Staat, Wietschaft und Gesellschaft Lateinamerikas* 16 (1979): 147–184.

———. "El consulado de Sevilla, asentista de esclavos: una nueva tentativa para el mantenimiento del monopolio comercial." *Primeras Jornadas de Andalucía y América* 1 (1981): 181–196.

———. "Aspectos marítimos del comercio de esclavos con hispanoamerica en el siglo XVII." *Revista de Historia Naval* 19 (1987): 113–131.

Villiers, J. "Albuquerque and the Imperial Strategy of King Manuel the Fortunate." In *Albuquerque, Caesar of the East: Selected Texts by Afonso de Albuquerque and His Son*. Warminster: 1990.

Vink, M. "'The World's Oldest Trade': Dutch Slavery and Slave Trade in the Indian Ocean in the Seventeenth Century." *Journal of World History* 14, no. 2 (2003): 131–177.

Vogt, John. "The Early São Tomé–Principe Slave Trade with Mina, 1500–1540." *The International Journal of African Historical Studies* 6, no. 3 (1973): 453–467.

———. "Notes on the Portuguese Cloth Trade in West Africa, 1480–1540." *The International Journal of African Historical Studies* 8, no. 4 (1975): 623–651.

Vries, J. de. *The Economy of Europe in an Age of Crisis 1600–1750*. Cambridge, UK: 1976.

Wachtel, N. "The '"Marrano"' Mercantilist Theory of Duarte Gomes Solis." *Jewish Quarterly Review* 101, no. 2 (2011): 164–188.

Walker, T. D "The Medicines Trade in the Portuguese Atlantic World: Acquisition and Dissemination of Healing Knowledge from Brazil (c. 1580–1800)." *Social History of Medicine* 26, no. 3 (2013) (3): 403–431.

Wallerstein, Immanuel. "Y a-t-il une crise au XVIIe. siècle?" *Annales E.S.C.* 34, no. 1 (1979): 126–144.

———. *The Modern World-System II—Mercantilism and the Consolidation of the European World-Economy, 1600–1750*. Berkeley: U of California P, 2011.

Walvin, J. "Why Did the British Abolish the Slave Trade? Econocide Revisited." *Slavery & Abolition* 32, no. 4 (2011): 583–588.

Watjen, H. *O domínio colonial holandês no Brasil*. São Paulo: 1938.

Watkins, Case "Dendezeiros: African Oil Palm Agroecologies in Bahia, Brazil, and Implications for Development." *Journal of Latin American Geography* 10, no. 1 (2011): 9–26:

Watson, I. Bruce. "Fortifications and the 'Idea' of Force in Early English East India Company Relations with India." *Past & Present* 88 (1980): 70–87.

Webb, J. L. A. "The Horse and Slave Trade between the Western Sahara and Senegambia." *J. Afr. H.* 34, no. 2 (1993): 221–246.

Weber, Max. *General Economic History*. Mineola, NY [1927]: 2003.
Welie, Rik van. "Slave Trading and Slavery in the Dutch Colonial Empire: A Global Comparison." *NWIG: New West Indian Guide / Nieuwe West-Indische Gids* 82, nos. 1–2 (2008): 47–96.
Wheat, David. "Garcia Mendes Castelo Branco, fidalgo de Angola y mercader de esclavos en Veracruz y el Caribe a principios del siglo XVII." *Centro de estudios mexicanos y centroamericanos* (2011). http://books.openedition.org/cemca/197, accessed July 2015.
———. "The First Great Waves: African Provenance Zones for the Transatlantic Slave Trade to Cartagena de Indias, 1570–1640." *J. Afr. H* 52 (2011): 1–22.
White, L. "Estrategia Geográfica y Fracaso en La Reconquista de Portugal Por La Monarquía Hispánica, 1640–1668." *Studia Historica. Historia Moderna* 25 (2003): 59–91.
Whitehead, N. L. "Ethnic Transformation and Historical Discontinuity in Native Amazonia and Guyana, 1500–1900." *L'Homme* 33, no. 126 (1993): 285–305.
Wicki, J. "Dois compêndios das ordens dos padres gerais e congregações da província dos jesuítas de Goa." *Studia* 43–44 (1980): 343–532.
Wilde, G. *Religión y Poder en las misiones de Guaraníes*. Buenos Aires: 2009.
Wilks, Ivor. "The State of the Akan and the Akan States: A Discursion." *CEA* 22, no. 3–4 (1982): 231–249.
———. "Wangara, Akan and Portuguese in the Fifteenth and Sixteenth Centuries: 1. The Matter of Bitu." *J. Afr. H.* 23, no. 3 (1982): 333–349.
Willis, J. R. "The Ideology of Enslavement in Islam" and "Jihad and the Ideology of Enslavement." *Slaves & Slavery in Muslim Africa*. London: 1985, 1–15 and 16–26.
Wiznitzer, A. "The Minute Book of Congregations Zur Israel of Recife and Magen Abraham of Mauricia, Brazil." *American Jewish Historical Society* 42, no. 3 (1953): 217–302.
———. *Jews in Colonial Brazil*. New York: 1960.
Wright, R. M., and M. Carneiro da Cunha, "Destruction, Resistance, and Transformation—Southern Coastal and Northern Brazil 1580–1890." In *The Cambridge History of the Native Peoples of the Americas*, vol. 3, part 2, edited by F. Salomon and S. B. Schwartz, 287–381. Cambridge, UK: 1999.
Zago, M. A. S. Figueiredo, and S. H. Ogo. "Bantu ßs Cluster Hapotype Predominates among Brazilian Blacks." *American Journal of Physical Anthropology* 88 (1985): 295–298.
———. "Quadro mundial das enfermidades e doenças consideradas genéticas." *Cadernos de Pesquisa—Cebrap* 2 (1994): 3–14.
Zanden, Jan Luiten van. *The Rise and Decline of Holland's Economy: Merchant Capitalism and the Labour Market*. Manchester: 1993.
Zavala, S. A. *La Encomienda Indiana*. Mexico: 1973.
Zeron, Carlos Alberto. "Les jésuites et le commerce d'esclaves entre le Brésil et l'Angola à la fin du XVIe. Siècle: Contribution à un débat." *Traverse* 1 (1986): 34–50.
Ziller Camenietzki, C. "Esboço biográfico de Valentin Stansel (1621–1705), matemático jesuíta e missionário na Bahia." *Ideação* 3 (1999): 159–182.

Theses and Unpublished Works

Acioli Lopes, Gustavo. *Negócio da Costa da Mina e comércio atlântico: tabaco, açúcar, ouro e tráfico de escravos, Pernambuco (1654–1760)*. PhD thesis in history, Universidade de São Paulo, 2008.

Alves Ferronha, Antônio Luís. *Angola: 10 anos de história 1666–1676*. 2 vols. Master's thesis in history, Universidade Clássica de Lisbon, Lisbon, 1988.

Barry, B. *L'Impact de la Traite Negrière sur les sociétés sénégambiennes du XVIème au XIXème siècle*. Paper presented at the Congresso Internacional sobre a Escravidão, Universidade de São Paulo, June 1988.

Bentes Monteiro, Rodrigo N. *O rei no espelho: A monarquia portuguesa e a colonização da América 1640–1720*. PhD thesis in history, Universidade de São Paulo, 1998.

Boyajian, J. C. *The Portuguese Bankers and the International Payments Mechanism, 1626–1647*. PhD thesis, University of California, Berkeley, 1978.

Caetano, A. F. P. *Entre a Sombra e o Sol—A Revolta Da Cachaça, A Freguesia de São Gonçalo de Amarante e a crise política fluminense, Rio de Janeiro, 1640–1667*. Master's thesis in history, Universidade Federal Fluminense, Niterói, 2003.

Cagle, H. G., III. *Dead Reckonings: Disease and the Natural Sciences in Portuguese Asia and the Atlantic, 1450–1650*. PhD thesis, Rutgers, State University of New Jersey, 2011.

Campetella, M. A. *At the Periphery of Empire: Indians and Settlers in the Pampas of Buenos Aires, 1580–1776*. PhD thesis, Rutgers, State University of New Jersey, 2008.

Candido, Mariana. *Enslaving Frontiers: Slavery, Trade, and Identity in Benguela*. PhD thesis, York University, Toronto, 2006.

Cardoso, A. *Maranhão na monarquia hispânica Maranhão na monarquia hispânica: intercâmbios, guerra e navegação nas fronteiras das Índias de Castela (1580–1655)*. PhD thesis, Universidad de Salamanca, 2012.

Coelho da Cruz, Celme. *O tráfico negreiro da 'Costa de Angola*. Dissertação de licenciatura, Faculdade de Letras da Universidade de Lisbon, 1966.

de Castelnau L'Estoile, C. *Les Chaînes du Mariage. Catholicisme, colonisation et esclavage au Brésil XVIe–XVIIIe siècles*. PhD thesis, Université de Paris Sorbonne, Paris, 2013.

Dominguez, Rodrigo da Costa. *O Financiamento da coroa portuguesa nos finais da Idade Média: entre o 'Africano' e o 'Venturoso*. PhD thesis in history, Universidade do Porto, 2013.

Dutra, Francis A. *Charles Boxer's Salvador de Sá and the Struggle for Brazil and Angola Revisted 50 Years Later*. Unpublished paper presented at Imperial (Re)Visions: Brazil and the Portuguese Seaborne Empire: A Conference in Memory of Charles R. BoxerYale University, November 1, 2002.

Eltis, David. S. D. Behrendt, and D. Richardson. *The Volume of the Transatlantic Slave Trade: A Reassessment with Particular Reference to the Portuguese Contribution*. Unpublished paper, 1998.

Ferreira, Roquinaldo. *Transforming Atlantic Slaving: Trade, Warfare and Territorial Control in Angola, 1650–1800*. PhD thesis, University of California, Los Angeles, 2003.

Figueiredo, L. *Revoltas, fiscalidade e identidade colonial na América portuguesa: Rio de Janeiro, Bahia e Minas Gerais, 1640–1761*. PhD thesis in history, Universidade de São Paulo, 1997.

Gama Lima, L. L. da *A confissão pelo avesso—O crime de solicitação no Brasil colonial*. 2 vols. PhD thesis in history, University of São Paulo, 1990.

Ganson, B. A. *Better Not Take My Manioc: Guarani Religion, Society, and Politics in the Jesuit Missions of Paraguay 1500–1800*. PhD thesis, University of Texas at Austin, 1994.

Genofre Prezia, B. A. *Os indígenas do Planalto Paulista: Etnôminos e grupos indígenas nos relatos dos viajantes, cronistas e missionários dos séculos XVI e XVII*. PhD thesis in linguistics, Universidade de São Paulo, 1997.

Gonzales, R. R. *A vila de São Paulo durante a União das Coroas: Estratégias políticas e transformações Jurídicas*. PhD thesis in history, Universidade de São Paulo, 2002.

Green, Tobias. *Masters of Difference: Creolization and the Jewish Presence in Cabo Verde, 1497–1672*. PhD thesis, University of Birmingham, 2007.

Hall, Trevor P. *The Role of the Cape Verde Islanders in Organizing and Operating Maritime Trade between West Africa and Iberian Territories 1441–1616*. PhD thesis, Dept. of History, Johns Hopkins University, Baltimore, MD, 1993.

Kantor, I. *Pacto festivo em Minas colonial: A entrada triunfal do primeiro bispo na Sé de Mariana, 1748,* Master's thesis, Universidade de São Paulo, 1996.

Karash, M. *Construindo comunidades: As irmandades de Pretos e Pardos no Brasil colonial e Goiás*. Paper presented at the Conference on American Counterpoint: New Approaches to Slavery and Abolition in Brazil, Yale University, October 2010.

Koshiba, Luiz. *A honra e a cobiça*. 2 vols. PhD thesis in history, Universidade de São Paulo, 1988.

Krause, Thiago N. *A formação de uma nobreza ultramarina: Coroa e elites locais na Bahia seiscentista*. PhD thesis, Universidade Federal do Rio de Janeiro, 2015.

Lenk, W. *Guerra e Pacto Colonial: Exército, Fiscalidade e Administração Colonial da Bahia (1624–1654)*. PhD thesis in economic history, Unicamp, São Paulo, 2009.

Malekandathil, Pius. *Portuguese Cochin and the Maritime Trade of India, 1500–1663*. PhD thesis, Pondicherry University, 1998.

Martins Alberto, E. M. C. *Um Negócio Piedoso: o Resgate de Cativos em Portugal na Época Moderna*. PhD thesis in history, University of Minho, 2010.

Martins de Queiroz, B. *Raimundo José da Cunha Matos (1776–1839): A pena e a espada a serviço da pátria*. Master's thesis, Universidade Federal de Juiz de Fora, Juiz de Fora, 2009.

Meuwese, M. *'For the Peace and Well-Being of the Country': Intercultural Mediators and Dutch-Indian Relations in New Netherland and Dutch Brazil, 1600–1664*. PhD thesis, University of Notre Dame, 2003.

Monteiro, J. M. *Tupis, Tapuias e Historiadores, Estudos de História Indígena e do Indigenismo*. Livre Docência thesis in anthropology, Universidade Estadual de Campinas, Unicamp, Campinas, 2001.

Myrup, E. L. *To Rule from Afar: The Overseas Council and the Making of the Brazilian West 1642–1807*. PhD thesis, Yale University, 2006.

Nunes Penha, A. L. *Nas águas do Canal: política e poder na contrução do canal Campos-Macaé 1835–1875*. PhD thesis, Universidade Federal Fluminense, Niterói, 2012.

Pardo, A.W. *A Comparative Study of the Portuguese Colonies of Angola and Brasil and Their Interdependence from 1648 until 1825*. PhD thesis, Boston University, Boston, Massachussets, 1977.

Pelúcia, A. M. *Martim Afonso de Sousa e a sua Linhagem: A Elite Dirigente do Império Português nos Reinados de D. João III e D. Sebastião*. PhD thesis in history, New University of Lisbon, Lisbon, 2007.

Peralta Rivera, E. G. *Les mécanismes du commerce esclavagiste*. Thèse de doctorat en Histoire EHESS. 2 vols. Paris: 1977.

Racine, M. T. *'A Most Opulent Iliad': The Portuguese Occupation of Southern Morocco (1505–1542): The Fortunes of a Frontier Society*. PhD thesis, University of California, Santa Barbara, 2003.

Rékanga, J. P. *Presénce de cognats de Bantouismes Cubains dans le Vili parlé au Gabon*. Unpublished paper, Porto Velho, Brazil: 2008.

Ribeiro da Silva, Filipa. *Dutch and Portuguese in Western Africa: Empires, Merchants, and the Atlantic System, 1580–1674*. PhD thesis, Leyde: 2009.

Ribeiro Thomaz, Omar. *Ecos do Atlântico Sul: Representações sobre o Terceiro Império Português*. PhD thesis in anthropology, Tese de doutorado em antropologia. Universidade de São Paulo, 1997.

Ross, H. B. *The Diffusion of the Manioc Plant from South America to Africa: An Essay in Ethnobotanical Culture History*. PhD thesis, Columbia University, New York, 1954.

Saguier, E. R. *The Uneven Incorporation of Buenos Aires Into World Trade Early in the Seventeenth Century (1602–42): The Impact of Commercial Capitalism Under the Iberian Mercantilism of the Habsburgs*. PhD thesis, Washington University, Saint Louis, MO, 1982.

Santos, S. N. A. dos. *Conquista e resistência dos Payayá no sertão das Jacobinas: Tapuias, Tupi, colonos e missionários 1651–1706*. Master's thesis in history, Universidade Federal da Bahia, 2011.

Schaposchnik, A. E. *Under the Eyes of the Inquisition: Crypto-Jews in the Ibero-American World (Peru, 1600s)*. PhD thesis in history, University of Wisconsin Madison, 2007.

Silva Pessoa, A. E. da. *As ruínas da tradição: 'A Casa da Torre' de Garcia D' Ávila—família e propriedade no nordeste colonial*. PhD thesis in social history, Universidade de São Paulo, São Paulo, 2003.

Sommer, B. A. *Negotiated Settlements: Native Amazonians and Portuguese Policy in Para, Brazil, 1758–1798*. PhD thesis, University of New Mexico, 2000.

Traoré, Makhroufi Ousmane. *Marge de manoeuvre, négociations et pouvoir de décision: les souverains de la Sénégambie dans le système des relations internationales transatlantiques et dans l'évolution du capitalisme moderne du XVe au XVIIIe siècle.* PhD thesis in history, Université de Paris Sorbonne, 2009.

Valentim, C. M. *Uma Família de Cristãos-Novos do Entre Douro e Minho: Os Paz, Reprodução Familiar, Formas de Mobilidade Social, Mercancia e Poder (1495–1598).* Master's thesis, Universidade de Lisboa, 2007.

Vieira-Martinez, C. E. *Building Kimbundu: Language Community Reconsidered in West Central Africa, c. 1500–1750.* PhD thesis, University of California, Los Angeles, 2006.

Vilardaga, J.C. *São Paulo na órbita do império dos Felipes: conexões castelhanas de uma vila da América portuguesa durante a União Ibérica (1580–1640).* PhD thesis in history, Universidade de São Paulo, 2010.

Vilela Fernandes, Guilherme. *Tributação e escravidão: o imposto da meia siza sobre o comercio de escravos (1809–1850).* Monografia apresentado ao Curso de Ciências Econômicas, Universidade Estadual de Campinas [UNICAMP], 2006.

Vu Thant, H. *Pastorale et missions au Japon pendant le siècle chrétien (XVIe–XVIIe siècles).* PhD thesis, Université de Paris—Sorbonne, 2012.

Wheat, David. *The Afro-Portuguese Maritime World and the Foundations of Spanish Caribbean Society, 1570–1640.* PhD thesis, Vanderbilt University, 2009.

INDEX

Abreu, Aleixo de, physician, practiced in Lisbon, Luanda and Bahia, authored the first book on tropical medicine, 128, 292, 428n63

Abreu e Brito, Domingos de, promoted slave trade in Angola, 72, 517

Abreu Soares, Manuel de, militia captain, fought Rio Grande Indians and Palmares, 325

Acquaviva, Claudio, Superior General of the S.J., 368n118; condemned Jesuits' slave ownership, later accept it, 168, 445n99; missionaries' mortality in Guinea, 50

Afonso, Estevão, first known European enslaver in sub-Saharan Africa, 40

Afonso V, King of Portugal, 14; inspired bull *Romanus Pontifex*, 47, 365n82; re-export of enslaved, 25. See *Romanus Pontifex*

Afonso VI, King of Portugal, 287, 291; and Angola's Jesuits, 278, 287. *See also* Salvador de Sá

African Slave Trade, voyages Brazil-West Africa shorter than the Caribbean-West Africa, 37; benefits to Portugal during *Asientos*, 51, 105, 106; colonists dependence, 250, 251; and evangelization in the Americas, 48, 49; taxes, 376n186, 477n32. *See* Bilateral Trade

Alcântara Machado, Antônio de, Paulista historian, 120

Almada, André Álvares de Almada, 45, 375n175; Guinea better than Brazil, 29; Jola did not trade slaves, 41; Luso-African author, 29, 375n175

Almeida, Francisco de, Angola's governor, expelled from Luanda by Jesuits and colonists, 4, 80, 166, 167, 173, 278

Almeida, Francisco de, Viceroy of Portuguese India, matched Indian and Portuguese weighing scales, 68, 339n200

Almeida, Jerônimo de, 4

Almeida, Joam de, Jesuit missionary, 236, 470n296; and the reconquest of Angola, 229, 233, 234

Almeida, Lourenço de, governor of Angola and governor-general of Brazil, 494n259

Almeida, Luís de, Rio de Janeiro's governor, backed *cachaça* makers, 306. *See also Jeribita*

Almeida, Pedro de, Pernambuco's governor, 309; attacked Palmares, 303. *See also* Palmares

Álvarez, Gaspar, Luanda slave trader, Jesuits benefactor, 96, 278

Alvarez, Manuel, Jesuit missionary and author, knowledgeable about West Africa trades, 44, 45, 385n44

Amador, King of Santomese rebels, 61, 63; historians' debate, 397n173; new African hero, 397n174; revolt, 396n160. *See also* São Tomé enslaved revolt; Cunha Matos

Amaral, Paulo do, Bandeirante, ransacked Guayrá missions, 188, 263. *See also* Bandeirantes

Anchieta, José de, Jesuits' superior in Brazil, 72, 123, 129, 155, 166, 168, 179; informed on battles of Angola, 72, 170–171; sought to control Angola's Jesuits, 3

Andrada e Silva, José Bonifácio, 252, 474n358

Andrade, Agostinho César de, veteran of Pernambuco and Angola's Wars, 272, 485n129

Andrade, Antônio de, veteran of Pernambuco and Angola's Wars, 294

Angolistas, ix, xiv, xv, 64, 105, 110, 112, 149, 170, 195, 218, 219, 223–226, 234, 240, 263, 270, 273, 280–282, 288, 290, 292–295, 309, 311, 319, 320, 329, 331, 336, 355; Brasílico-Angolista alliance against *Asiento* business, 318–319; and Brasílicos, 105, 268, 273, 279; characterization and historiography, 29, 48, 375n178; favored relay trade over enslavement raids, 95–98, 261, 266, 267; favored the *cachaça* trade, 499n321; traded slaves with the WIC, 480n65. *See also* Brasílicos

Angel, Melchior Gomes, *asentista*, 90; and Spanish Inquisition, 101

Anjos, Gregório dos, first bishop of Maranhão, 333

Ansures, Pedro, Luanda lawyer, witnessed mutiny against governor Tristão da Cunha, 329

Antonil, A. J., Jesuit missionary and author, cattle expansion and ranchers in the Northeast, 227, 228; on Mulattos, 335

Argomedo, João de, slave trader, 100, 453n198

Arrais, Amador, Carmelite bishop of Portalegre, reactionary critic of the Slave Trade and slavery, 163, 164, 442n73

Arzão, Braz, Bandeirante, raided Indian villages in Bahia, 245

Arte da língua de Angola (1696), first grammar on an African-American language, 155, 438n19

Aruan, Aymoré, Guarani, Kaingang, Temimino and Potiguar Indians enslaved due to Trans-Atlantic slave trade decline, 195

Asiento de Negros, xii, xiv, 4, 17, 19, 26, 34, 35, 46, 51, 63, 71, 78, 86, 89–91, 94, 95, 105–107, 120, 163, 165, 174, 177, 218, 264, 317–318, 322; Angolan slave trade to Brazil, 102, 104; Angolan's enslaved deported to Cartagena and Vera Cruz, 418n216; benefited Portuguese Crown and merchants, 51; developments in Angola, 102; excluded Mulattos and Mestizos slaves 74; Fernandes de Elvas, 101; France and Louis XIV, 502n9; Genoese 32, 317, 318; impact on inland trade in Angola, 98; and Peruleiros, 100 (*see also* Peruleiros); prompted new critics on the slave trade 164–165; Rio de Janeiro-Buenos Aires connection, 99; Sousa Coutinho family, 76–77

Avalos y Benavides, Juan de, Spanish captain, cousin and lieutenant of Salvador de Sá in Rio de Janeiro, fled to Buenos Aires after the Restoration, 196, 197, 350, 455n77, 455n79

Azevedo, João Lúcio de, 176

Bagnuolo, count of, Dutch War, 344, 345

Bailyn, Bernard, x, 78
Bandeirantes, Bandeiras, Paulistas, Indians enslavement raids, 188–191; and Braganza authorities, 249, 250; differences with the Peruleiros, 195, 197, 200; feared by the Spanish, 200, 201; fighting Indians, quilombos and Palmares at service of Northeast authorities, ranchers and planters, 205 (*see also* Domingos Jorge Velho); hated by Antônio Vieira, Guarani Indians and Paraguayans, 189, 323 (*see also* Raposo Tavares); Indians as slave soldiers, 245 (*see also* Temimino; Potiguar); mutiny in Bahia, 249; self-sufficiency reined by Atlantic slave trade and Crown, 121, 199, 200 (*see also* Amador Bueno); turned ranchers, 251, 252
Banha, Bento, Angola's governor, allied with Jagas, 82, 83, 88
Barbalho, Agostinho, Cachaça Riot leader, 307; hanged by Salvador de Sá's order, 455n77
Barbalho, Jeronimo, 307
Barbalho, Luis, 351; feud with Salvador de Sá Family, 455n77; seized Dutch's slaves, 451n23
"Barbarians War," extermination attacks waged against Northeast Indians, 298, 299, 504n31; beheading, instead of enslaving prisoners, 325; perceptions on enslaved Blacks and hostile Indians, 326; and Ethiopic Ocean Wars, 324
Barzan, Álvaro de, marquis of Santa Cruz, 343
Barreira, Balthazar, Jesuit missionary, 167; expelled from Angola 3, 4, 358n16; main auxiliary of Dias Novais in the Angola's invasion, 168; most experienced missionary of sub-Saharan Africa, 169;
 in Sierra Leone, 173–174; staunch promoter of Angola's slave trade, 169–172, 173–178, 183
Barreto, Francisco, governor-general of Brazil, 119, 270, 297, 307
Barros, João de, sixteenth century historian, 359n20; caravels versus camels, 42; conquest of Sofala, 69; rivalry between Venice and Lisbon, 4
Barros Rego, Cristovão de, veteran Brasílico, governor of São Tomé, 270
Barros Rego, Roque de, veteran Brasílico, governor of Cape Verde, 270
Bassano, Giuseppe de, Italian Capuchin missionary in Mbanza Congo, cosigner of Mani-Mulaza's call to arms before the Battle of Mbwila, 284
Bataillon, Marcel, 180
Battel, Andrew, 111, 303
Battle of Kitombo, Soyo County army led by count Estevão da Silva, defeated Portuguese troops, 294, 324, 493n241
Battle of Ksar El Kebir, Morocco, defeat of the Portuguese army and king, 3, 81, 164, 266, 343; and Mbwila, 292
Battle of Luanda, retook Luanda from the WIC, 218–228, 236, 237, 482n96; slave trade to Buenos Aires and Potosí fostered Angola's reconquest, 241, 263. *See also* Salvador de Sá
Battle of Mbororé, defeat of Bandeirantes by Guarani warriors commanded by Spanish Jesuit Domingos de Torres, former military, 204, 205, 458n126
Battle of Mbwila, ruined the Congo kingdom, won by Portuguese, Brasílico, Angolista and Jagas, 67, 76, 284, 287, 288, 290–294, 298, 324, 329, 335, 336, 355

589

Battle of Pungo-Andongo, ended Ndongo kingdom sovereignty; and Ethiopic Ocean wars, 324; expenses and benefits, 98; Ngola a Kiluanuje resistance, 329

Beckman, Manoel, Maranhão settler, rebellion and Amazon's Indians enslavement, 15, 141, 434n153

Beliarte, Marçal, Jesuit missionary in Brazil, 62, 166

Benci, Jorge, Italian Jesuit missionary, 158, 183

Benveniste, Emile, 143

Bettendorf, João Felipe, Jesuit missionary and Amazonian expert, 55, 518; forest exploitation 139; Ethiopic Ocean Wars, 324

Bilateral trade, x, xii, xiii, 20–22, 56, 255, 263, 315; accounts, 313–316; with Angola, 17, 22; to the detriment of Lisbon, 241; *jeribita* and tobacco, 314; and manioc flour, 259; with Mozambique, 8, 314, 315, 339, 454n70, 499n322; shell-money, 260 (see also *zimbo*); Verger and Braudel analyses, 423n286; with West Africa, 37; WIC, 210; winds and currents, 51–58, 255, 314, 368n112 (see also Ethiopic Ocean)

Bluteau, Raphel, 82, 304

Bocage, M. M., derogatory poem on Queen Njinga, 276, 277

Bonucci, Antonio Maria, Italian Jesuit missionary in Brazil, 243, 244

Boyajian, James C., 91

Borja, Francisco de Borja, Superior General of the S.J., restricted Jesuits' commercial activity, 160, 441n55; blamed Jesuits' slave ownership, 160, 168

Boxer, Charles R., 14, 66, 185, 232, 504n26

Braganza dynasty, xiv, 26, 35, 51, 76, 77, 80, 81, 93, 101, 105, 197, 198, 201, 202, 216, 221, 253, 265, 283, 292, 304, 344, 355; aided by Portuguese Jesuits, 15, 16; not recognized by Popes, 185, 285, 366n89; sovereignty in Europe and overseas, 271, 295, 296, 344, 467n244; Westphalia Treaty, 226, 227

Brandão, Luís, Jesuit chief in Angola, justified slave trade, 174

Brandão, Pedro, Carmelite bishop of Cape Verde, reactionary critic of the slave trade, 163, 164, 165, 173, 177, 442n75, 442n77, 443n78

Brasílico, vi, vii, ix, xii–xv, 35, 58, 64, 76, 79, 80, 91, 100, 104, 105, 113–115, 117, 126, 132, 137, 143, 146, 147, 158, 179, 184, 186, 187, 195, 209, 218, 224, 225, 227, 235, 238, 257, 278, 287, 288, 293, 294, 299, 302, 305, 314, 315, 319, 320, 324, 330–332, 334, 351, 355, 489n177; advancements in royal positions, 295–298; Afro-brasílicos, defending Palmares, 245; aid to Angola 505n40; allies in Overseas Council, 272, 463n189; in Amazon basin, 250 (see also Beckman; in Angola, Angolistas); Angola's expedition, 236, 237, 240; attacking Palmares, 330, 335; in Bahia and Pernambuco, 212–214, 231, 246, 270, 271; against Braganza Crown, 270; in Brazil, Angola and Congo, 240, 260, 271–273; and *cachaça*'s market, 307–312; characterization, 20, 370n127, 403n38; comanagement in Ethiopic Ocean, 220, 340; control of enslaved, 146, 158; cotton armors, 113; interests and self-perceptions, in São Paulo, 80, 238, 239, 246, 250, 251 (*see also* Bandeirantes); against Jagas and Queen Njinga, 255, 266; against kingdom of Congo, 280–283; main battles in Angola, 296; at Mbwila, 288, 491n211 (*see also* Domingos Jorge Velho); militiamen in Angola, 42, 351–352; mutiny in Angola, 292, 493n240; rewards by the Crown, 270, 272, 483n113; in Rio de Janeiro, 263, 270 (*see also* Peruleiros); trade and war in West Central Africa, 260–269, 279, 463n190; weapons, 289, 290, 492n215; against the WIC in Pernambuco, 212–215, 231, 463n190

Brasio, Antonio, Spiritan missionary and historian, 47, 274

Braudel, Fernand, xvi, 116, 126, 186, 248, 259

Bravo Family and slave trade, 317, 502n2

Brito Freyre, Francisco, skilled Portuguese admiral, 52, 299; failed plan to reconquer Elmina, 240, 241; governor of Pernambuco and appeasement policy with Palmares, 242–243; Lisbon-Bahia route, 391n106; against Paulistas, 250; sugar-mill owner in Bahia, 240

Buarque de Holanda, Sérgio, Jesuits' medicine, 134; about the Sumeh myth, 419n230; "Brazil island," 504n26; firearms and Indian wars, 355; Guaicuru Indians horsemen, 387n63; horse-raising in São Paulo, 192; on Vicente do Salvador's *História*, 364n73

Bueno, Amador, allegedly "King of São Paulo," 201, 203; enslaving raids, 188; justification of Indians slavery, 202

Buíça, Antônio de, in Pernambuco and Angola, 272

Cá Da Mosto, Luigi da, 40, 45, 517

Cabrada, Pedro de, commander of a company of Portuguese, Angolistas and Congolese who fought alongside King of Congo's army in Mbwila, 287

Cabral de Mello, Evaldo, 226, 227, 270; on WIC crisis in Brazil, 462n179

Cadornega, Antônio de Oliveira de, 88, 112, 231, 235, 272; African wizards and magics to tame wild beasts and unchain enslaved, 336; authored *História Geral das Guerras Angolanas* (1681), first book on settlers' viewpoint in sub-Saharan Africa, 48, plate 9, 298; dendê palm tree, 303; enslavement raids in Angola during *Asientos*, 88; on the Jaga, 407n85; Khoisan speakers, 149; life, 388n76; Njinga transsexualism, 275; palm wine malafo, 497n282; praised Angola's colonial wars, 298, 494n256

Calado, Manuel, Franciscan historian on the Dutch War in Brazil, 124, 187, 214, 355

Caldas Barbosa, Domingos, 276

Caldas, José Antônio, Luso-Brazilian cartographer, 21, 56, 371, 519

Caldeira, Beatriz, daughter of Manuel Caldeira, wife of Luís Mendes de Vasconcelos, 343

Caldeira, Manuel, slave trader with business in Indian, 343

Câmara Cascudo, L., 113

Câmara Coutinho, Antônio Gonçalves da, governor of Pernambuco, 309

Camoanga, Zumbi's brother and successor, 335

Camões, Luís de, *The Lusiads*, 1, 253, 282
Campo Tourinho, Pero do, donatary of Porto Seguro captaincy, 11, 31, 377n191
Cão, Diogo, 64
Cápac, Manco, 43
Caraibebê-guaçu, Carijó shaman, envisioned the Ethiopic Ocean space, 70
Caramuru, 43, 188, 384n37
Carneiro, Antonio Mariz de, royal cosmographer, 52, 99, 254, 391n104
Castanho, Jerônimo, promoted slave trade in Angola, 72, 215
Castelhano, Alonso, veteran of Pernambuco and mainland Wars, expeditionary in the 1648 Task-Force, 351
Cavazzi Da Montecuccolo, Capuchin missionary in Angola and author, 112, 234, 287, plates 7, 8, 10–12; colonial slavery in Angola and Brazil, 145; relations with governors in Angola, 281, 489n177; on Njinga 274–276 (*see also* Queen Njinga); slaves' prices, 423n280
Celestino, Paulo de Tarso, xix
Cerveira, Manuel, Angola's governor, 76, 83
Chombari Angolan native troops, 71, 85
Cochrane, Thomas, British admiral, 55
Code Noir, 49, on manioc flour to Caribbean enslaved, 109
Colbert, J.-B., 109, 318, 320
Coelho, Duarte, donatary of Pernambuco, 11
Coelho de Albuquerque, Diogo, Brasílico veteran, expeditionary at the Battle of Luanda, 351
Colonial Men and *Overseas men*, characterization, 93, 94, 494n249
Columbus, C., 27, 126, 151, 321

Conceição, Antônio da, Dominican missionary and author on East Africa, 8, 362n53
Cordeiro, Domingos, Bandeirante defeated by Jesuits led Guarani warriors, 204
Cortesão, Jaime, 191, 322, 323
Correia de Sousa, João, Angola's governor, 95, 96, 278
Correia Ximenes, José, expeditionary of the 1648 Task-Force, 352
Costa de Almeida, Rodrigo da, wealth slave trader in Luanda, moved to Bahia, 312
Coutinho, Gonçalo Vaz, *asentista*, 75–77; Sousa Coutinho's Family, 402n27
Coutinho, Gonçalo Vaz (the younger), 77
Couto, Diogo do, 6
Couto, Antônio, Luso-African Jesuit, expeditionary in the 1648 Task-Force, 231, 232, 234; Portuguese representative in Mbanza Congo, 279; resisted Capuchin influence in Congo, 235
Couto, Loreto, Franciscan historian, praised Pernambucans fights in Angola, 298; on the Indian enslavements, 436n198
Crasto, Miguel de, Congolese dean of the Congo diocese, backer of Mani Mulaza, 285
Cruz, Luis Felix, expeditionary of the 1648 Task-Force, 234, 482n96
Cunha, Matias da, governor-general of Brazil, ordered beheading of all male Indians prisoners during the Barbarians War, 325
Cunha Matos, Raimundo da, 395n158, 520; on São Tomé revolt, 61. *See also* São Tomé enslaved revolt
Cunha, Tristão da Cunha, governor of Angola, expelled by a mutiny fomented

by Angolistas and Brasílico militiamen, 292–294, 308
Curado, Manoel, dean of the Congo and Angola dioceses, attacked Mani Mulaza, 285
Curado Vidal, Antonio, 291
Curibocas and Mamelucos, Luso-Indian mestizos, 117; with Bandeirantes militias against Indians, 245
Curto, José, 314, 501n338
Curraleiros, ranch's cowboys in the São Francisco valley, breached the slave system, 328
Curtin, Philip D., 63, 87
Cuvelier, J., Belgian missionary and historian of West Central Africa, 262

Daniel, João, Jesuit missionary and author, very knowledgeable about Amazonia, 177; canoe transportation in the Amazon basin, 139; on human-like apes, 149
Davis, David Brion, 154
Dean, Warren, 127, 189
Delgado, José Mathias, Cardonega's editor and commentator, 87, 270
Delgado, Ralph, Angolista historian, 273
Delumeau, Jean, 177
Dias, Bartolomeu, 3
Dias, Duarte (Abraão Aboab), 77
Dias, Henrique, Afro-Brasílico commander and his regiment, 240, 243; in Angola, 225, 263, 329, 336; in the Battle of Mbwila, 288; against Palmares, 330, 335; regiment against the Dutch in Pernambuco, 335. *See also* Brasílicos
Dias Brandão, Jorge, 469n281
Dias Henriques, Duarte, from Pernambuco, 416n192; family and business connections, 413n158,
416n192; later Spanish Crown banker, 77; tax-collector in Angola (*Contratador*), 90, 404n49, 404n50
Dias Novais, Paulo, first Angola's governor, 3, 71; business with Brazil's Jesuits, 72, 85, 167, 170, 171, 215, 292, 303; representatives in Madrid, 72
Donelha, André, report on Portuguese trade in Upper Guinea, 382n24; Mandinka, greatest traders in Guinea, 42; Serer and Fulani cavalry, 45; on Susu blacksmiths, 46
Dourado, Feliciano, born in Paraíba, later diplomat and overseas councilor, 186; backed Brasílico commanders, 284, 295, 320, 322
Drago, Manuel, *asentistas*' agent in Luanda, 77, 404n10

Eltis, David, x, 22, 78, 242, 258
Elvas, Antônio Fernandes de, *asentista* and tax-collector in Angola, 73, 77, 86, 411n132; contraband in the Río de la Plata, 402n20; essential role in the expansion of Angolan slave trade, 87; influential in Madrid, 101, 409n107, 409n114; kinship and alliances with the Solís family, 89; transition from the Asian spices trade to slave trade in Angola, 89, 90, 94, 95, 389n85. *See* Portuguese *asentistas*
Elvas, Jorge Fernandes de, son and factor of Antônio Fernandes de Elvas in Cartagena, 73, 89
Ericeira, conde de, Portuguese historian, 211, 218, 231; on the Braganza's diplomacy, 460n155
Escobar, Antônio de, Spanish Jesuit, one of the formulators of the Catholic

593

Escobar, Antônio de *(continued)*
  probabilism, criticized by Blaise Pascal, 176
Estado da Índia, embraced Portuguese territories east of the Cape of Good Hope, 6; differences with sixteenth century Brazil, 364n73
Estado do Maranhão, isolation and sailing obstacles, 54, 55
Ethiopic Ocean, geohistorical entity characterized by direct exchanges between Africa and South America, formed by the South Atlantic gyre and overreaching mathematical equator, so called until the end of the Sailing Age, xviii, xix, 12, 357n1 (*see also* Bilateral Trade); alimentary transfers, 107–113; Brasílico military, 263, 265–266, 328–331 (*see also* Brasílico); Cape Santo Agostinho, 52; colonial spatial matrix, 62, 339, 340; firearms, 353–356; food and diet, 109, 113, 115; geopolitics, 21, 298, 323, 324; main routes, 53; microbial and viral shock, 128–133; networks in the eighteen century, 86; and Portuguese Jesuits, 182–183, 232 (*see also* Jesuits); seventeenth century dioceses, 332, 333; wars, 324 (*see also* Battle of Mbwila; Battle of Pungo Andongo; Palmares; Barbarians War); and the WIC, 207, 210 (*see also* Battle of Luanda)

Faria, Severim de, Portuguese priest and author, condemned Angola's plundering by Luís Mendes de Vasconcelos, 87
Felipe II, King of Spain and Portugal, 4, 13, 26; declared the freedom of Portuguese American Indians, 80; 87, 134, 165, 168, 172, 173, 343; established the Asiento de Negros system, 71, 73 (see also *Asiento de Negros*)
Felipe III, King of Spain and Portugal, 343
Felipe IV, King of Spain and Portugal, 26, 35, 89–92, 101, 200, 204, 210, 216, 226, 227, 265, 271
Fernandes Brandão, Ambrósio, Portuguese planter in Brazil, global trader and sixteenth century historian, 21, 34, 54, 90, 91, 99, 114, 131, 132, 256, 412n138, 430n97
Fernandes de Aguiar, Francisco, Brasílico expeditionary in 1648, captain-major of Angola, member of Rio de Janeiro's municipal council, 351
Fernandes de Mesquita, Tomás, participant in the 1648 expeditionary fleet, Angola's captain of infantry, 351
Fernandes Furnas, Francisco, slave trade in Mozambique, founder of the Companhia Geral do Comércio do Brasil, 194; captain of his own ship in the 1648 expedition, 352
Fernandes Vieira, João, commander of the Colonist revolt against the WIC, governor of Angola, 69, 94, 215, 263, 266, 269–271; conflict with Angolan Jesuits, 278–280, 283, 294–296; on the Ethiopic Ocean, 480n72. See also Brasílicos; colonial men
Fernandes, Valentim, 59
Ferreira de Vasconcellos, Francisco, 276; Veteran of the Pernambuco and Angola Wars, 273
Ferreira, Diogo, promoted slave trade in Angola, 72, 463n191
Ferreira da Rosa, João Francisco, physician in Pernambuco, 134

Ferreira, João (Gana-Goga), 43
Ferreira, Roquinaldo, 329, 338, 382, 507n62
Fiering, Norman, xix
Figueiredo, Manoel de, royal cosmographer, 52; sailing between Rio de Janeiro and Buenos Aires, 99
Figueroa, Francisco de, commander in the Guararapes Battle and governor in Cape Verde, 270
Filgueira Bultão, veteran of Pernambuco, treasurer of the 1648 expeditionary fleet, 352; General trustee (*Provedor-Mor*) of Angola, 512n1; Salvador de Sa's front man in Luanda, tax-collector in Angola, 267
Finley, Moses, 143
Flanders War, 13, 73, 83, 84, 108, 297, 344
Forjaz, Manuel, Angola's governor, 77, 82, 100, 376n181; Iberian wine and slave trade to Cartagena, 304, 417n198
Fragoso, João Baptista, Jesuit theologian at Evora University, slavery as an act of generosity, 176
Franco, Felipe, Jesuit missionary, rector of Luanda College, fled to Bahia at the Dutch invasion, manager of a Jesuit's sugar-mill in Bahia, participant in the 1648 expeditionary fleet in retaking Angola, 235, 236
Freitas, Serafim, Portuguese Friar and Jurist, 180, 251
Fróis, Luís, Jesuit author and missionary in India and Japan, 129, 154, 175
Fuggers, bankers, 6

Galen, 133, 134
Gama, Vasco da, xiii, 1
Gandavo, Pero de Magalhães, 34
Garcia Florentino, Manolo, 262
Genovese, Eugene, 151
Góes, Antonio Jorge de, veteran of Brazil and Angola Wars, captain-major of Benguela, 273
Gomes, Cornélio, Portuguese Jesuit born in Mbanza Congo, wrote the first book in a Bantu (Kikongo) language, 155
Gomes Carneiro, Diogo, 253
Gomes da Costa, Henrique, tax-collector of Angola, 92, 412n147
Gomes Solís, Duarte, economic writer, 91, 216
Gonçalo, João, Jesuit very knowledgeable about Angola, reports on Angola during the WIC occupation, 223, 227, 235
Gonsalves de Mello, José A., 90
Goulart, Maurício, 30, 142
Grã, Luís da, Jesuit missionary, 41, 123, 166, 179
Gramaxo, Antônio Nunes, Jorge Fernandes Gramaxo heir in Cartagena, 92, 413n151. See also Portuguese *asentistas*
Gramaxo, Jorge Fernandes, *asentistas'* factor in Cartagena, 73, 92, 413n151, 417n198. See also Portuguese *asentistas*
Grillo, Domingo, Genoese *asentista*, 317, 502n2
Guariba, Heleny, xix
Guerra preta, native irregular forces in Angola, 288, 503n11
Guerreiro, Fernam, Jesuit chronicler, 50, 173
Guimarães, Honestino, xix

Habsburg dynasty, 71–74, 76, 80, 81, 89, 123, 196, 216, 221, 287, 292, 297, 318, 323, 330

595

Hari A Ngola, Felipe, King of Ndongo, 97
Hawthorne, Walter, 367
Hegel, G. W., 150, 151; information on Queen Njinga, 487n153
Heintze, Beatrix, 87, 95, 358
Henrique, Cardinal, regent of Portugal, 162
Henrique, Infant, Prince of Portugal, 14
Henrique, bishop of Utica, son of Nzinga Muemba (Afonso I), King of Congo, 66, 399n191
Henriques, Afonso, Afonso I, first King of Portugal, 235
Henriques, Henrique, Jesuit missionary and grammarian in Ceylon, 155
Henriques, Leão, vice-provincial of Portugal's Jesuits, 445n105
Heriarte, Maurício de, Crown Judge in Maranhão, 130
Hernandéz Girón, Francisco, rebelled captain in Peru, 3, 10
Hespanha, Antônio Manuel, 165, 218, 443n80, 443n81
Heywood, Linda, 338, 487n158
Hilton, Anne, 286, 491n203
Hippocrates, 133, 134
Hoppe, Fritz, 8
Horse trade in Africa, 44, 72; to Angola, from Buenos Aires, 75, 76, 85, 196; from Brazil, 85, 113, 273, 291, 294, 401n7, 408n101, 487n156, 505n42; exchanged for enslaved, 45, 47, 48, 386n52, 387n66; parity, 45

Indians, "natural freedom," 81; coerced labor in São Paulo, 120, 192, 511n3; Habsburg and Braganza legislation, 80. *See also* Bandeirantes, Barbarians War, Just War, Vieira
Innocent X, Pope, 284

Innocent XI, Pope, 332
Inojosa, Manuel de (Hinojosa, Nojoza), Brasílico captain, fought marron villages and Palmares, fought together with Bandeirantes against Bahia's Indians, 330; captain-major of Benguela, travel to Lisbon, 331, 506n57, 506n58, 507n61; fought in Angola (*see also* Bandeirantes; Palmares). *See also* Brasílicos
Irish request to migrate to Brazil, 201, 457n110
Israel, Jonathan I., 17, 462n179
Ita, Pieter, Dutch admiral, invaded Pernambuco, 289

Jagas, 14, 42, 60, 84, 85–89, 111, 118, 150, 226, 274, 287, 302, 303, 330, 356, 497n284, 499n316, plate 8, 11; allied with Portuguese at Mbwila, 287, 288, 290; and the Battle of Bambi, 355, 447n126; historians' debate on, 83–85, 366n84, 407n84, 410n116; imported *Jeribita*, 304; and Kasanje, 95; most feared in West Central Africa, 82–83; and Queen Njinga, 224, 275, 280, plate 7; sobas deported to Pernambuco, 96
Jadin, Louis, Belgian missionary and historian of West Central Africa, 262
James, C. L. R., xi
Jeribita, *cachaça*, Brazilian sugar-cane rum, 22; and Amerindians trade, 308; Brasílico and Angolistas' lobby against Iberian alcoholic beverages in Angola, 308–313; Brasílico economic gains, 257, 301, 302, 313, 314, 319; the "Cachaça Riot" in Rio de Janeiro, 198, 199, 306–307, 498n308, 500n332; and

Caribbean rum, 301; consumption in today's Brazil, 300, 495n266, 496n274; intercolonial trade, 115, 147, 299, 300, 304, 305, 314, 332, 495n260; market Angola, 312, 499n316; as medicine, 500n326

Jesuits, Society of Jesus, S.J., Company of Jesus, Ignatians, translators and grammarians of overseas languages, 143, 146, 153, 155, 156, 179, 422n272, 470n290; legitimated African slave trade in the Ethiopic Ocean, 182; medicine and pharmacology, 134; transplanted Asian spices into Brazil, 111, 310, 500n330

João III, King of Portugal, 66, 343

João IV, King of Portugal, xix, 16, 18, 26, 101, 203–204, 201; reliance on palatine councils, 217, 218, 221, 222, 224, 226–227, 229–230, 234, 237, 253, 263–266, 270–271, 344–345

Jorge Velho, Domingos, and Paulistas against Palmares, 144, 244, 245; fought fire-armed Tapuia warriors in Bahia, 356; justification of Indian slavery, 246; lack of land in São Paulo, 247, 248

José I, King of Portugal, 141

Just War, Indians' enslavement in Brazil, 119; against Amazonian Indians, 405n67; considered illegal against the Angolans and the Congo Kingdom, 284; against the Monomotapa, 7; against the Ndongo, 169, 173; against Potiguar Indians, 188

Kasanje, 14, 60, 95, 118, 287; origin of most of the deported after 1648, imported *Jeribita*, 304; sobas deported to Pernambuco, 96

Kilombo, Quilombo, Mukambo, Mocambo, Mucambo, 60; Jaga's kilombo, 366n84

Kisama, 281, 289, 305; and quiçamã, 113; stronghold of Angolan sobas holding rock-salt mines, 39, 75, 76

Kímpako, Garcia II Afonso, King of Congo, 266, 291, 490n202

Klein, Herbert S., 256, 334, 372n141

Kojève, Alexandre, 150

KPengla, King of Dahomey, 112

Lacerda e Almeida, Francisco José de, Luso-Brazilian cartographer, in Mozambique, 10

Lamego, Alberto, 326

Lamego, Manuel Rodrigues, *asentista*, 90; associates and businesses in Europe, Africa and India, 411n135; close to Manuel da Paz, 91

Language barrier and enslavement in Brazil and Angola, 148–150

Las Casas, Bartolomé, Dominican missionary and author, inspirer of the *Leyes Nuevas*, 2; favored and later condemned the African slave trade, 32, 34, 157, 377n192

Laudati, Emílio, duke of Marzano, better known under the name of Antonio de Gaeta, Neapolitan Capuchin, converted Queen Njinga, 274

Leguzzano, frei Graciano Maria de, or Saccardo da Leguzzano, Italian Capuchin, editor and commentator of Cavazzi's book, 275, 486n146

Leitão, Catarina de, prazo holder in Mozambique, 9

Leite, Gonçalo, Jesuit missionary, condemned unjust enslavements in Bahia, 160, 161, 163; banished to Lisbon, 162

Leite Pais, Pedro, Paulista commander defeated by Jesuit-led Guarani warriors, 204

Lencastre, João de, governor of Angola and governor-general of Brazil, 49, 138, 499n323; backed *jeribita*'s import in Angola, 309; mistrusted Paulistas, 249, 250

Leo Africanus, 40

Leo X, Pope, 66

Leys Nuevas, 2, 80

Lichthardt, Dutch Admiral, battled in Brazil, 223

Lisboa, João Francisco, nineteenth century Brazilian historian, criticized Fr. Vieira on slave trade, 448n149

Lito, Antônio, participant in the 1648 expeditionary fleet, later commander of a Luanda fortress, 352

Lobato, Alexandre, 7, 363n56

Lomelin, Ambrosio, Genoese *asentista*, 317

Lopes Gama, Miguel, Pernambucan priest and author, 304

Lopes de Faria, Diogo, Angola's veteran, 219

Lopes de Figueiredo, Gaspar, wealthy Rio de Janeiro's settler, participant in the 1648 expeditionary fleet, 352

Lopes Sequeira, Domingos, Angolista captain killed by Jagas who bore firearms, 225, 226, 356

Lopes Sequeira, Luís, Angolista captain, son of Domingos and of a Mbundu woman, commander of the Portuguese army at Mbwila Battle, 287, 288, 294

Loyola, Ignatius, Jesuit, 85, 135, 168, 170, 179

Luísa de Guzman, Queen of Portugal, 76

Machado, Antônio, participant in the 1648 expeditionary fleet, veteran of Angola, Pernambuco, later sergeant-major of Benguela, 351

Magalhães Godinho, Vitorino, 6, 74, 142, 278

Maine, Henry, 67

Manasseri, Benedetto (Saint Benedict), protector of Black persons in Portuguese America, associated with *cachaça*, 305

Mani Mulaza (Antônio I, Vita-a-Nkanga), King of Congo, and Bakongo clergy, 285; call to arms manifesto against Portuguese invasion, 286; Mbwila combat and death, 287, 290, 291, 294, 355, 490n202. *See also* Battle of Mbwila

Manning, Patrick, ix

Manuel, King of Portugal, 1, 5, 59, 66–67, 145, 157

Marcgrave, Georg, Dutch physician arrived in Pernambuco with Nassau-Siegen, studied Brazilian plants and Indians pharmacology, 133, 134

Marin, Bernardo, Spanish *asentista* and front man for the Portuguese, 318

Martin, René, on Roman and Greek slavery, 151

Martins Pena, Luís Carlos, Brazilian play-writer, 33

Marx, Karl, 67, 151

Matos, Gregório de, Brasílico Barocco poet, 304, 335

Matos, Simão de, *Guerra preta* captain, fought alongside the Luanda army in Mbwila, 20

Matos, Teodoro de, 6

Mattos de Carvalhosa, Fernão, 218; High Court magistrate knowledgeable about Angola, 218, 219

Mauro, Frédéric, xvi
Mazarin, 226, 253; recognized Braganza's sovereignty in mainland and overseas, 271
Mbiki-a-Mpanzu (Álvaro III), King of Congo, banned the import of Brazil's *zimbo*, 261
Medeiros, Simão de, Bakongo dean of the Congo diocese, backer of Mani Mulaza, 285
Meillassoux, Claude, 32, 141
Mello, Miguel Antônio de, governor of Angola, 336
Mello, Pedro de, governor of Rio de Janeiro, 297, 350
Melo e Castro, Caetano de, governor de Mozambique, governor of Pernambuco, 249
Melo, Francisco Manuel de, military and writer, 234, 297, 334
Mendes de Brito, Heitor, 77
Mendes de Vasconcelos, Francisco, 97, 358
Mendes de Vasconcelos, Joane, 85, 88, 94, 225, 343, 344
Mendes de Vasconcelos, Luís, 83–89, 108, 113, 215, 320, 323, 343, 344, 512n3
Menezes e Siqueira, Diogo de, governor-general of Brazil, 81
Menezes, Pedro Cesar de, governor of Angola, defeated by the WIC expeditionary fleet, 206
Mendonça Furtado, Diogo de, governor-general of Brazil, 95
Mercado, Thomas de, Spanish Dominican jurist, 523; first generation of slave trade critics, 164, 165; on the slave trade legislation 29
mercadores de portada (established merchants) in Luanda, 96

Mercurian, Everard, Superior General of the Jesuits, 168; relations with Inquisition, 368n118
Merolla da Sorrento, Girolamo, Capuchin missionary in Congo, 112, 421n261
Miller, Joseph C., xi, 53, 57, 78, 87, 193
Minchin, Susie, 566
Miranda Henriques, Bernardo de, Angola's captain and Pernambuco's governor, 268; attacked Palmares, 243
Miranda Henriques, Henriques, Brasílico veteran, captain and slave trader in Angola, 268. *See also* Brasílicos
Miranda Henriques, Rodrigo de, Angola's governor, 352; slave trade to Río de la Plata, 268; associated to Salvador de Sá, 195–197. *See also* Peruleiros
Molina, Luís de, Jesuit theologian, wrote methodically on the slave trade, condemned slavery, and yet recognized the legitimacy slaves' property if the purchaser was in good faith, 165, 443n80, 443n81
Moniz Barreto, Antônio, sugar-mill owner in Bahia, served under Salvador de Sá in Rio de Janeiro, participant 1648 in the expeditionary fleet, captain of Massangano, 351
Monomotapa (*Mwenemutapa*), 7, 9, 10, 69, 84, 321
Montalvão, marquês de, viceroy of Brazil, 101, 230; on appeasement policy in Palmares, 473n338
Montebelo, marquês de, governor of Pernambuco, 244; favored *Jeribita* exports to Angola, 310
Monteiro da Fonseca, Diogo, 351
Monteiro Paim, Roque, 243
Monteiro, John M., 120, 190, 191

Moraes, Alão, 344
Moura e Albuquerque, Alexandre de, 94
Moura Meneses, Francisca Josefa de (*Chiponda*) prazo holder, 9
Mulattos in Brazil and Angola, 333–338
Muniz da Câmara, Sebastião da, expeditionary in João Fernandes Vieira fleet to Luanda, 272

Nassau-Siegen, governor of the Dutch possessions in Brazil, xiv, 133; aroused the WIC slave trade 206–211, 213–214, 224
Native sovereignty and trade in India, Brazil and Angola, 280, 281, 322
Newson, Linda, 44, 566
Nicholas V, Pope, 14, 47–49
Nieuhof, J., served the WIC in Pernambuco and the VOC in Asia, critical report on WIC in Brazil, 212, 213, 462n179
Njinga, Queen of Matamba, 187, 224, 226, plates 7, 8; conversion by the Capuchin and rivalry with Jesuits 273–276; as an immortal female warrior, 487n156; perceptions in Brazil and abroad, 277; truces with Salvador de Sá, 266, 267, 279, 280, 324. *See also* Cadornega; Cavazzi
Nkumbi a Nzinga, Diogo, 66, 67
Nóbrega, Manoel da, Jesuit missionary, in Bahia 107; appalled by Indians' enslavement in Bahia, 157; monitored missions in Congo, 156; requested African slaves, 158, 159
Nunes da Costa, Antônio, slave trader and *asentista* agent in Upper Guinea, 44
Nunes da Costa, Jerônimo, as known as Moseh Curiel, WIC shareholder and Portugal's representative in Amsterdam, 224, 467n244
Nunes Collares, Manuel, 55
Nzinga Muemba (Afonso I, King of Congo), 65, 66
Nzinga Nkuwu (João I, King of Congo), 65, plate 5

Odemira, count of, 272, 320, 484n125
Olivares, count-duke of, 91, 92, 101, 321
Oliveira Martins, J. P. de, 252, 322, 474n358
Oliveira, Diogo Luís de, governor-general of Brazil, backed Indians' enslavement, 188
Oliveira, Fernão de, Dominican Friar, 108, strongly criticized the African slave trade, 157
"onboard trade" and "inland trade," 218

Pacheco Pereira, Duarte, Renaissance geographer, 24, 48, 65
Pacheco, Gaspar, Mozambique-Brazil slave trade, 194, 454n71
Paiva Severim, participant in the 1648 expeditionary fleet, 351
Palmares, xiii, xv, 61, 125, 144; consequences of the Dutch War, 241–244; Paulistas attack, 224–250; resistance and freedom, 303
Parente, Bayão, Bandeirante, raided Indian villages in Bahia, 245
Parker, Geoffrey, 355
Pascal, Blaise, criticized Jesuits' probabilism, 163, 176, 177
Patterson, Orlando, 159, 171
Paul III, Pope, 67
Paul V, Pope, recognize Congo as a Christian and sovereign kingdom, 284

Paz, Manuel da, born in Olinda, Pernambuco, sugar-mill owner, invested in Asia, Felipe IV's banker in Madrid, 91, 92
Pearson, Michael, 6
peças, 42, 48, 159, 169, 188, 383n28, 418n211; and *piezas de Indias*, 71, 85, 383n28
Pedroso de Almeida, Francisco, Bandeirante turned rancher 251
Perdigão Malheiro, Agostinho M., Brazilian jurist, 159
Pereira Coutinho, Manuel, governor of Angola, 77
Pereira da Gama, Domingos, physician in Pernambuco, 134, 135
Pereira de Azevedo, Antônio, Bandeirante, lieutenant of Raposo Tavares, 297, 298
Pereira, Paulo, afro-brasílico captain of Henrique Dias' regiment, 225; fought against the Dutch in Pernambuco, against Palmares, against the Jaga, sergeant-major of African trops in Benguela, 330
Peres, Manuel Batista, one of the most important slave trader in Peru, 44
Pernambuco, José de, Afro-Brasílico Capuchin missionary and linguist in Congo, 110
Peruleiros, definition, 100, 417n199; and Angola's expedition, 238; and Peruvian silver, 100, 197; and Salvador de Sá, 263
Piacenza, Diogini de Carli da, Capuchin missionary, 79, 278, 287, 526
Pigafetta, Antonio, 48
Pimentel, Manuel, royal cosmographer, 52, 55, 254, 391n104

Pinheiro Morão, Simão, physician in Pernambuco, 133, 135, 136
Pinto de Barros, João, physician, experienced in the Pernambuco War against the Dutch, surgeon-major of the 1648 Expedition, 352
Pinto, Bernardo, physician, participant in the 1648 expeditionary fleet, later established in Benguela, 353
Piso, Willem, German physician and naturalist arrived with Nassau-Siegen in Pernambuco, 134
Plato, Hellenic slavery, 143
Polanco, João, 172, high-ranked Jesuit targeted by Anti-judaism, 445n105
Polanyi, Karl, 40, 153, 313, 323
Pombal, Marquis of, 9, 141, 325
pombeiro, 98, 113, 268, 279
Portuguese *asentistas*, 92, 97, 117, 169, 187, 256, 272, 279, 281; acting as tax-collectors, 4, 74, 75, 86; illicit trade, 73–74; kinship and business connections, 77; partnership with Angola's governors, 87–89; persecuted by Spanish Inquisition, 101
Postma, Johannes M., 211
Potiguar Indians, first hostile to the colonists, 122, 124, 188; joined Luso-Brasílico troops attacking Palmares, 125; later colonists' slaves' soldier, 85, 124; participants in the WIC's Angola's expedition, 125, 471n314
Potosí, Upper Peru's town and silver mine, 3, 35; direct trade with Angola, 260; fostered the global scheme of Rio de Janeiro's trade and oligarchies, 22, 100, 102, 105, 106, 195, 196, 197, 263; key role of Buenos Aires' trade to connect the Atlantic to the Pacific, the Potosí's

Potosí *(continued)*
    silver to the Macao silk, 105, 106; and the retaking of Angola, 231, 241, 267, 268, 270; Sacramento Colony foundation, 199. *See also* Peruleiros
Preto, Manuel, Bandeirante, plundered Spanish Jesuits missions in the South, 188
Preto, Sebastião, Bandeirante, attacked Spanish Jesuits missions in the South, 188
pumbos (inland fairs) in West Central Africa, 97, 98, 295
Pyrard, François, 21, 256; on silver imports in Brazil and Angola from Río de la Plata, 99

Ramalho, João, Indian slave trader in São Paulo, 41
Raposo Tavares, Antônio, 55, 148, 188, 197, 200, 203, 297, 323; and the "Borders Bandeira," 55, 238, 239; contrast with Angola's expedition, 472n319
Rebelo, Fernão, Jesuit theologian at the University of Evora, 164; against unjust enslavements, 176
Rediker, Marcus, xi
Ressurreição, João da, Benedictine friar, chaplain-major of João Fernandes Vieira troops in Pernambuco and Angola, 273
Reynel, Pedro Gomes, first Portuguese *asentista*, 73, 74
Rezende, Garcia de, 43
Ribeiro de Macedo, Duarte, Crown counselor, diplomat and economic writer, 317, 318
Ribeiro Rocha, M., priest and jurist, wrote on colonial slavery, 146, 184, 378n204

Ricard, Robert, 19
Richardson, David, 22, 78, 242, 258
Richelieu, Cardinal de, 185, 250, 321
Roboredo, Manuel, Luso-Congolese Capuchin, marched with Mani Mulaza's army in the Battle of Mbwila, 287
Rocha Pitta, Sebastião, Luso-Brasílico historian, 21, 134, 135, 312, 327
Rodrigues Adorno, Afonso, Indians enslavement raids, 188
Rodrigues Carneiro, Domingos, Luso-African militian, killed Camoanga, Zumbi's brother and successor, 335
Rodrigues Coutinho, João, Portuguese *asentista*, 75–77, 85, 87, 91, 281
Rodrigues Ferreira, Alexandre, Luso-Brazilian naturalista and explorer, 57, 125, 138, 329, 392n128
Rodrigues Lamego, Manuel, *asentista*, 90, 91
Rodrigues Solís, Elena, Antonio Fernandes de Elvas wife and slave trader, 89, 92, 410n124
Rodrigues Solís, Jorge, 89
Rodrigues, Pascoal, veteran of Pernambuco War, lieutenant of Angola, 329
Rodrigues, Pero, Jesuit missionary, knowledgeable about enslavements in Angola and Brazil, 62, 63, 123, 166, 172, 173
Romanus Pontifex bull, 14, 47, 49, 156, 175, 180
Rosa, Valentim da, expeditionary of the 1648 Task Force that recaptured Angola, 351
Rubim, Gaspar, bought two ships for 1648 Task Force, 352

Sá e Benevides, Salvador de, xv, 35, 56, 147, 225, 227, plate 6, 270, 273, 281, 284, 296, 326–327, 329–330, 346,

352; ally of Jesuits (*see also* Jesuits), 277, 457n106; Angola's expedition 1648, 229–239, 482n96; the "Cachaça riot" and loss of power in Rio de Janeiro, 306, 307, 498n308; disapproved Bandeirantes, 298 (*see also* Bandeirantes); enslavement raids in Angola, 266–268; his family, 349–350, 454n72; King Afonso VI, 471n317; kinship and alliance with platense families, 196–199, 455n77, 455n79, 456n91; as overseas man, 94, 498n306; *Padre Eterno* galleon, 192–193, 307, 453n58; Paulista rebellion, 201, 203–204; prized Jagas' alliance, 85; plan to occupy territory between Angola and Mozambique, 320–322, 503n22; planned to attack Buenos Aires and Luanda, 215, 220–222

Sá, Martim de, Rio de Janeiro's governor, 123; slave trade in Angola and horse trade in Buenos Aires, 196, 197, 345, 349, 350. *See also* Salvador de Sá

Sá, Victória de, Luis Céspedes Xeri'a wife and Jesuits' benefactor, 197

Saavedra, Hernandarías, governor of Buenos Aires, opposed to Portuguese illegal slave trade, 100

Sade, Marquis de, comments on Queen Njinga, plate 8, 276, 277

Saint-Domingue (Haiti) Revolution, 61

Saldanha, Aires de, governor of Angola, 355; criticized Jesuits' abandon of inland missions in Angola, 178

Salgado de Araújo, João, Deacon of Congo and Luís Mendes de Vasconcelos biographer, 343

Salvador, Vicente do, Franciscan missionary and historian, 21, 125, 188, 212, 216, 256, 260

Sande, Antônio Paes, Crown officer in India, governor of Rio de Janeiro, backed the *jeribita* producers, 310, 311, 500n330

Sandoval, Alonso de, Jesuit missionary and author, inquire on slavery and slave trade, 48, 59, 146, 174, 175; accepted African's enslavement

Santiago, Bento Dias de, Pernambuco and Bahia's tax-collector, 90, 413n158

Santiago, Manoel Justo, fought the São Francisco valley Indians and Palmares, later captain of Massangano in Angola, 329, 330

Santos Vilhena, Luís dos, 335

Santos-Granero, Fernando, 117

Santos, João dos, Dominican missionary in East Africa and author, 7, 361n43

São Domingos, frei Antônio de, Dominican theologian at the University of Coimbra, taught the legality and legitimacy of the African slave trade submitted to royal contracts, 165

São Tomé enslaved revolt, impact in Brazil slave laws, Impact on the Asiento, 4, 7, 123, 124; first Atlantic Revolution 60–63; parallel with the Saint-Domingue (Haiti) Revolution, 61. *See also* Amador

Scelle, Georges, 106

Schwartz, Stuart B., 33, 87, 193, 302, 304

Sebastião, King of Portugal, 13, 164, 292

Sepp, Anton, Jesuit missionary in South Brazil, on the cattle expansion, 327

Sepúlveda, Gonçalo Nunes de, Slave trade and enrichment in Luanda, 91; social ascension and patronage in Seville, 92–93

Serrão, Gregório, Jesuit missionary, 62

Silva Correa, Elias Alexandre da, Luso-Brasílico captain in Angola, trade-war-trade cycle in Angola, 97; on the Jagas, 407n85; on *Jeribita* market, 312; on *zimbo* market, 262

Silva Telles, Luís da, 349

Silva e Sousa, João da, governor of Rio de Janeiro, later governor of Angola and *Jeribita* smuggler in Luanda, 308, 309

Silveira e Albuquerque, Alvaro da, governor of Rio de Janeiro, 121

Simões Madeira, Diogo, captain in Zambezia, 354

Simões, Antônio, veteran of the Pernambuco War, later captain of Massangano, 329

Sixtius IV, Pope, 24

Soares, Cristóvão, heir of bishop Manuel Baptista Soares, 262

Soares, Manoel, captain of the Afro-Brasílico Henrique's platoon in Mbwila, 288, 290, 491n211. *See also* Brasílicos

Soares, Manuel Baptista, bishop of the Congo and Angola dioceses, resident at the Mbanza Congo See, blamed zimbo money imports from Brazil, 261, 410n123; slave trader, 262

Soares de Sousa, Gabriel, sugar-mill owner and author, 122; favored Indians enslavement, 122

Soares Moreno, Martim, commander of the Pernambuco uprising against the Dutch, 263, 270

Sorrel Camiglio, Bento, representative of Raposo Tavares and his fellow Bandeirantes, 245

Sorrento, Bonaventura da, Capuchin missionary in West Central Africa, 79

Soto, Domingo de, Dominican theologist, 164, 165

Sousa Chichorro, Luís Martins, surrendered to the Dutch in Malacca, later Angola's governor, 269; conflict with the Angola's Jesuits, 273, 277–279, 485n138, 488n161

Sousa de Macedo, Antônio de, Crown officer and publisher of the monthly gazette *Mercúrio Portuguez*, Portugal's first printed periodical of political propaganda, 192, 292

Sousa, Fernão de, governor of Angola, 29, 110; alliances with sobas and the King of Ndongo, 96, 97; against the WIC, 115, 216

Sousa, Luís de (Manoel de Sousa Coutinho) Dominican friar and historian, 76

Sousa Coutinho, Fernão de, governor of Pernambuco, 294

Sousa Coutinho, Francisco de, main Portuguese Ambassador, *asentista* family and interests in Angola, 76, 77, 224, 214; on the reconquest of Angola, 225, 227, 228

Sousa Coutinho, Lopo (the elder), 75

Sousa Coutinho, Manuel de, 76. *See also* Luís de Sousa

Sousa Coutinho, Lopo de, 77

South Atlantic. *See* Ethiopic Ocean

South Atlantic captains and militiamen, 330, 331, 506n45

Souto Maior, Francisco, veteran of Pernambuco War, governor of Rio de Janeiro, 198, 199; Rio de Janeiro's 1645 expedition to retake Angola, 225, 226, 231, 232, 240

Soyo, Count of (sometimes kingdom), controlled Mpinda port, 49, 114, 115, 209, 291. *See also* Battle of Kitombo
Souza Pereira, Pero de, Crown officer in Rio de Janeiro, Salvador de Sá's cousin, 198
Souza, Francisco Felix de (Xaxá), Brazilian slave trader at Whydah, 313
Souza, Francisco de, Jesuit author and missionary in Goa, 153
Souza, Teotônio de, 333
Souza, Tomé de, first governor-general of Brazil, experienced in Africa and India, 123
Spice Wars vs. Sugar and Slaves Wars, 324
St Helena high, 56, 57, 233, 393n132
Suassuna, Ariano, Brazilian play-writer, 286
Subrahmanyam, Sanjay, 322
Sylveira, Simão Estácio da, 11, 108

Taques, Pedro, Paulista genealogist and historian, 202
Tavares, Pero, Jesuit missionary, 17, 18
Távora, Francisco, count of Alvor, governor of Angola, viceroy of India, 294, 295, 322, 489n186, 503n22
Taunay, Alfredo E., Paulista historian, 190
Telles (or Tellez), Balthazar, Jesuit, author of a global history of the Portuguese Jesuits on Braganza's viewpoint, 168, 171, 253, 475n2
Telles Barreto, Manoel, governor-general of Brazil, 212
Telles da Silva, Antonio, governor-general of Brazil, 219, 221
Temimino Indians, Bandeirantes slaves' soldiers, 124, 245, 473n344

Thornton, John K., 87, 89, 275
Toyotomi, Hideyoshi, Regent of Japan, expelled the Jesuits, 153, 398n82
Traoré, Makhroufi, 41
Trouillot, Michel-Rolph, xi

Urban VII, Pope, 135
Urban VIII, Pope, 142, 201

Valignano, Alessandro, Jesuit itinerant inspector in Asia, 153
Varnhagen, Francisco Adolfo de, Brazilian historian, 126; approved Indians' enslavement, 142; on cattle expansion in Maranhão, 332; on the donataries' prerogatives, 12
Vasconcelos da Cunha, Bartolomeu, Angola's governor, 284, 503n12; fought against the Dutch in Brazil, 289, 379n215
Vauban, Marquis de, French economist and strategist, 139
Vaz Aranha, Francisco, 276; former captain in Pernambuco, active in Angola, 272
Vaz, Cristóvão, Rio de Janeiro planter, sponsored the 1648 Expeditionary Task-Force, 231
Vega, Lope de, Spanish play-writer, 305
Veiga Cabral, Jerônimo da, 329; captain in Bahia, Crown officer in Angola, 329
Veiga, Barbara da, 77
Veiga, Diogo da, 77, wealthy Portuguese slave trader in Buenos Aires, 99, 100
Velasco, Catalina de, landowner in the Río de la Plata, Salvador de Sá's wife, 196
Velasco, Luís de, viceroy of Peru, relative of Catalina de Velasco, 196

Vidal de Negreiros, André, sugar-mill owner, 266; as colonial man, 94; commander of the Brasílico uprising against the Dutch, 263, 269, 296; governor of Angola, 270, 320, 329–331; governor of Maranhão, 55; *jeribita* consumption in Angola, 308; wage war against Congo kingdom, 64, 67, 279, 281–285, 287, 290–294, 298

Vieira, Antônio, Jesuit missionary and Statesman, 168; and Africans' evangelization 48, 58, 180–183, 338, 448n147; on allied Indians, 123; and in Angola, 221, 227–229, 235, 265, 468n266; on Black slaves dissocialization, 144; condemned mistreatment of enslaved Africans and Blacks, 183; cultivation of Asian spices in Brazil, 500n330; on Dutch conquest in Brazil, 211, 216; on Elmina, 240; on enslaved Angolans, 436n190; favored Marranos merchants 18, 465n225; and hostile Indians, 250; against Palmares, 243, 244; probabilism and enslaved freedom, 162, 163, 169, 174, 177, 191, 244; proposed African slave trade to ensure Indians freedom 32, 137, 140, 377n192, 449n154; on Rio de Janeiro's sugar-canne, 307

Vila Vilar, Enriqueta, 74
Victorian England, 2
Vitoriano, Friar, bishop of Cape Verde, 159, 160
Vogado, Jerônimo, Jesuit missionary, 86

Wachtel, Nathan, 91
Wallerstein, Immanuel, 116, 300
With, Witte de, Dutch admiral, 231, 232
Wheat, David, 88, 109
Wolfers, Michael, xix

Xavier, Francis (Francisco), Jesuit missionary in Asie, 85, 86, 153, 168, 353
Xenophon, on Greek slavery, 150, 151, 176
Xeri'a, Luis Céspedes, alliance with Salvador de Sá, 196, 197, 204, 349

Zimbo, Brazil's exports and the Angolan slave trade, 261, 301, 302, 304, 310, 314
Zurara, Gomes Eanes de, 40, 47, 68

www.ingramcontent.com/pod-product-compliance
Lightning Source LLC
Chambersburg PA
CBHW021845300426
44115CB00005B/18